1 MONTH OF
FREE
READING

at

www.ForgottenBooks.com

By purchasing this book you are eligible for one month membership to ForgottenBooks.com, giving you unlimited access to our entire collection of over 1,000,000 titles via our web site and mobile apps.

To claim your free month visit: www.forgottenbooks.com/free913228

ISBN 978-0-265-94203-1
PIBN 10913228

This book is a reproduction of an important historical work. Forgotten Books uses
state-of-the-art technology to digitally reconstruct the work, preserving the original format
whilst repairing imperfections present in the aged copy. In rare cases, an imperfection in
the original, such as a blemish or missing page, may be replicated in our edition. We do,
however, repair the vast majority of imperfections successfully; any imperfections that
remain are intentionally left to preserve the state of such historical works.

BILL.

An Act respecting certain lands mortgaged by John D. Ronald to the Corporation of the Village of Brussels.

WHEREAS the Corporation of the Village of Brussels have, Preamble.
by their petition, represented that in the month of September, 1878, they did, for the purpose of promoting manufactures in the said village, pass a by-law granting a bonus of
5 $20,000 to one John D. Ronald, to aid him in establishing, at
that place, a manufactory of steam fire engines and agricultural implements, and providing for the issue of debentures
therefor, subject to the conditions, *inter alia*, that the said
John D. Ronald should, before receiving any part of said
10 debentures, execute and deliver to the reeve of the said municipality a mortgage upon certain premises, securing the due
performance on his part of the conditions of the said by-law,
and a bond of himself personally for the further sum of $10,000,
conditioned to be void on performance of the said conditions,
15 and it further appearing by the said petition that the said
John D. Ronald, in pursuance of the conditions of the said
by-law, executed an indenture of mortgage, dated the twenty-
seventh day of January, 1879, in favour of the said corporation
of the said Village of Brussels, upon certain lands and premises
20 therein described as being composed of park lot lettered " C "
in the Village of Brussels, containing by admeasurement one
acre and fifty-nine one-hundredths of an acre, more or less, and
also lot number four hundred and seventeen, on Queen Street,
in the said village, containing by admeasurement one quarter
25 of an acre of land, more or less, and did on said date, execute
and deliver his bond to the said corporation for the penal sum
of $10,000, conditioned to be void on the same terms as the said
mortgage, and it also appearing that the said corporation,
charging and alleging that the said John D. Ronald had not
30 complied with the terms and conditions of the said mortgage
and bond, but had made default therein, filed their bill of complaint against the said John D. Ronald in Her Majesty's then
Court of Chancery for Ontario, praying to have the equity of
redemption of the said John D. Ronald and his wife one Laura
35 G. Ronald in the said lands foreclosed, and the sum of $10,000,
mentioned in said bond, paid, by reason of such alleged default,
and that such proceedings were had in the said suit as resulted
in a judgment by the Honourable Mr. Justice Proudfoot, dated
the eighteenth day of May, 1882, which judgment was affirmed
40 by the Court of Appeal for Ontario; and it further appearing
by said petition that the said corporation of the Village of
Brussels and the said John D. Ronald have mutually agreed to
a settlement of the said suit, the said corporation agreeing to
release and reconvey the said lands and premises to the said

John D. Ronald, freed and discharged from the said mortgage, and to release and discharge him from the said bond, and from all claims and demands thereon, and the said John D. Ronald agreeing to pay to the said corporation the sum of $1,100, and release and discharge them from all claims and demands for 5 costs in said suit or otherwise howsoever ; and it further appearing that a deed dated the eleventh day of October, 1886, made between the said corporation of the first part and the said John D. Ronald of the second part, has been executed, and doubts have been expressed as to the validity of such settle- 10 ment and deed ; and it further appearing that the municipal council of the said village unanimously approved of such settlement, and of the execution of such deed, and have prayed that the said settlement and deed may be confirmed and declared legal and valid, and it is expedient to grant the prayer of said 15 petition ;

Therefore Her Majesty, by and with the advice and consent of the Legislative Assembly of the Province of Ontario, enacts as follows :—

Deed of Oct. 11th, 1886, confirmed.

1. The said deed dated the eleventh day of October, 1886, 20 whereby the said parties thereto purported to settle such litigation ; and whereby the said corporation purported to grant, release and reconvey to the said John D. Ronald, his heirs and assigns, the said lands and premises freed and discharged from all claims under and in respect of the said mortgage, is hereby 25 ratified and confirmed, and declared to be legal and valid to all intents and purposes.

1st Session, 6th Legislature, 50 Vic, 1887.

BILL.

An Act respecting certain lands mortgaged by John D. Ronald to the Corporation of the Village of Brussels.

First Reading,   1887.

(Private Bill.)

An Act to incorporate the Town of Thornbury.

WHEREAS the unincorporated Village of Thornbury, in the Preamble.
Township of Collingwood, in the County of Grey, has
a population of one thousand souls, or thereabouts; and
whereas the population of the said village is increasing, and
5 will continue to increase in consequence of being on the line
of the North Grey Railway, and from other causes; and
whereas the inhabitants of the said village have, by their
petition represented that they are desirous of having the said
village incorporated as a town, in order the better to enable
10 them to carry out certain necessary improvements, which can
be more readily effected under the powers granted to towns;
and whereas it is expedient to grant the prayer of said
petition;
   Therefore Her Majesty, by and with the advice and consent
15 of the Legislative Assembly of the Province of Ontario, enacts
as follows :—

   1. From and after the holding of the first election under Town incor-
this Act, the inhabitants of the said Village of Thornbury shall porated.
be and they are hereby constituted a corporation or body
20 politic, under the name of " The Corporation of the Town of
Thornbury," apart from the Township of Collingwood, in which
the said village is situate, and shall enjoy and have all the
rights, powers and privileges which could have been enjoyed
and exercised by the said Town of Thornbury if the same had
25 been incorporated as a town under *The Consolidated Municipal Act, 1883*, except where otherwise provided by this
Act.

   2. The said Town of Thornbury shall comprise and consist Limits of
of all that part of the said Township of Collingwood, described town.
30 as follows :—Starting at a point on the lake shore, at a depth
of sixteen feet of water, in a line with the centre of Russell
Street, thence westerly along the centre line of said Russell
Street, to the intersection of the line between the tenth and
eleventh concessions of the said township; thence northerly
35 following the said line between the tenth and eleventh concessions to the intersection of the centre line of Peel Street;
thence easterly along the centre line of said Peel Street to the
lake shore, and continuing on the same course till a depth of
sixteen feet of water is found; thence following the lake
40 shore (but at such a distance therefrom as to include within
the limits of said incorporation a depth of sixteen feet of
water) to the intersection with the centre line of the said
Russell Street at the place of beginning, and comprising within
the said limits the town plot of Thornbury, all the land lying

between Bay Street in the said town plot and the lake, and the Mill Reserve within the said town plot.

Wards.   **3.** The said Town of Thornbury shall be divided into three wards, to be called respectively, East Ward, North Ward, and South Ward;   5

1. East Ward shall be composed of that part of the said town described as follows:—Commencing at the lake shore and continuing westerly along the centre line of the said Russell Street to the centre of the Beaver River; thence following the centre of said Beaver River to the lake; thence 10 easterly along the lake shore to the place of beginning.

2. North Ward shall be composed of that part of the said town described as follows:—Commencing at a point on the lake shore on a line with the centre of the said Beaver River; thence south-westerly along the centre of the said Beaver 15 River to the intersection of the centre line of Alice Street; thence north-westerly along the centre line of said Alice Street to the intersection of the centre line of Peel Street; thence easterly along the centre line of said Peel Street to the lake shore; thence south-westerly along the lake shore to the place 20 of beginning.

3. South Ward shall be composed of that part of the said town described as follows:—Commencing at a point in the centre of the said Beaver River at the intersection of the centre line of the said Alice Street; thence south-westerly 25 along the centre of the said Beaver River to the intersection of the centre line of the said Russell Street; thence westerly along the centre line of the said Russell Street to the intersection of the line between the tenth and eleventh concessions of the said township; thence northerly along the line between 30 the said tenth and eleventh concessions to the intersection of the centre line of said Peel Street; thence easterly along the centre line of the said Peel Street to the intersection of the centre line of the said Alice Street; thence south-easterly along the centre line of the said Alice Street to the place of 35 beginning.

Nomination for first election of Mayor and Councillors.   **4.** After the passing of this Act it shall be lawful for   who is hereby appointed the returning officer, to hold the nomination for the first election of mayor, reeve, and councillors, at the Music Hall in the said Town of Thornbury, at the hour of 40 noon, on the   day of   next, of which he shall give at least one week's notice, in the two newspapers published in the said town, and by a like notice, in writing, posted up in at least two of the most public places in each of wards of the said town; and the said   shall preside 45 at the said nomination, or in case of his absence the electors present shall choose from among themselves a chairman to preside at the said nomination, and such chairman shall have all the powers of a returning officer; and the polling for the said election, if necessary, shall be held on the same day of the 50 week next following; and the returning officer or chairman shall, at the close of the nomination, publicly announce the place in each ward at which the polling is to take place.

Deputy returning officers.   **5.** The said returning officer shall, by his warrant, appoint a deputy returning officer for each of the wards into which the 55 said town is divided; and such returning officer and each of such deputy returning officers shall, before holding the said election, take the oath or affirmation required by law, and shall respectively be subject to all the provisions of the municipal laws of Ontario, applicable to returning officers at elec- 5 tions in towns, in so far as the same do not conflict with this Act; and the said returning officer shall have all the powers and perform the several duties devolving on town clerks with respect to municipal elections in towns.

Clerk of township of Collingwood to furnish copy of assessment roll. **6.** The clerk of the said Township of Collingwood and any 10 other officer thereof shall, upon demand made upon him by the said returning officer, or any other officer of the said town, or by the chairman hereinbefore mentioned, at once furnish such returning officer, officers or chairman, with a certified copy of so much of the last revised assessment roll for the said village 15 and township as may be required to ascertain the names of the persons entitled to vote in each of the said wards at the said first election, or with the collector's roll, document, statement, writing or deed that may be required for that purpose; and the said returning officer shall furnish each of the said 20 deputies with a true copy of so much of the said roll as relates to the names of the electors entitled to vote in each of the said wards respectively, and each such copy shall be verified on oath.

Council. **7.** The council of the said town, to be elected in manner 25 aforesaid, shall consist of a mayor, who shall be the head thereof, a reeve and nine councillors, three councillors being elected for each ward; and they shall be organized as a council on the same day of the week next following the week of the polling; or, if there be no polling, on the same day of the next 30 week following the week of nomination; and subsequent elections shall be held in the same manner as in towns incorporated under the provisions of the municipal laws of Ontario; and the said council and their successors in office shall have, use, exercise and enjoy all the powers and privileges vested by 35 the said municipal laws in town councils, and shall be subject to all the liabilities and duties imposed by the said municipal laws on such councils.

Oaths of office and qualification. **8.** The several persons who shall be elected or appointed under this Act shall take the declarations of office and qualifi- 40 cations now required by the municipal laws of Ontario, to be taken by persons elected or appointed to like office in towns

Qualification at first election. **9.** At the first election of mayor, reeve and councillors for the said Town of Thornbury, the qualifications of electors and that of the officers required to qualify, shall be the same as 45 that required in townships by the municipal laws of Ontario; and the qualification of mayor shall be the same as that of a reeve in a township.

Assets and liabilities. **10.** The council of the said Town of Thornbury shall be entitled to recover from the said Township of Collingwood 50 such share of all moneys on hand, due, owing and of right collectable by and belonging to the said township at and prior to the said time of incorporation, or thereafter, if entitled thereto, as shall bear such proportion to the whole as the

amount of the assessed property within the limits of the said
town, as shown by the collector's roll of the year 1886, bears
to the whole amount of the assessed property of the said
Township of Collingwood, each to each, and the said town
5 shall be liable to pay to the said township a share, in the same
proportion, of all debts and liabilities existing against the said
township at the time this Act shall come into force, as the
same shall become due, and which are fairly and equitably
chargeable against the said town ; and in case of dispute the
10 share to be borne by each respectively, shall be ascertained
and settled under the provisions of the municipal laws of
Ontario.

11. The expenses incurred in obtaining this Act, and those Expenses of
of furnishing any documents, copies of papers, writings, deeds, Act.
15 or any matters whatsoever required by the clerk or other officer
of the said town or otherwise, shall be borne by the said town,
and paid by it to any party that may be entitled thereto.

1st Session, 6th Legislature, 50 Vic., 1887.

O. 2.

BILL.

An Act to incorporate the Town of Thornbury.

First Reading, 1887.

(Private Bill.)

Mr. RORKE.

TORONTO:
PRINTED BY WARWICK & SONS, 26 AND 28 FRONT ST. W.

BILL.

An Act to authorize the Roman Catholic Episcopal Corporation of the Diocese of London to sell certain lands.

WHEREAS by an Act passed in the eighth year of the Reign of Her Majesty Queen Victoria, chaptered eighty-two, intituled *An Act to incorporate the Roman Catholic Bishops of Toronto and Kingston, in Canada, in each*
5 *diocese*, it was enacted amongst other things that each of the Bishops of Toronto and Kingston, in Canada (thereby declared to be bodies corporate respectively), and his successors should, by his separate name, from time to time, and at all times thereafter, be able and capable to have, hold, purchase, acquire,
10 possess and enjoy for the general use or uses eleemosynary, ecclesiastical or educational, of the said church, or of the religions community, or of any portion of the said community within his diocese, any lands, tenements or hereditaments, within the Province of Canada, and the same real estate, or
15 any part thereof, from time to time (by and with the advice and consent in said Act mentioned), to sell or exchange alienate, let, demise, lease or otherwise dispose of, but in case of sale, to purchase other real estate in lieu of that sold, with the proceeds or purchase money arising from such sale,
20 and to hold and enjoy such newly purchased or exchanged estate for the purposes therein mentioned ; and whereas by the said Act it was further enacted that whenever it might be deemed necessary to erect any new diocese in that part of the province formerly called Upper Canada, the bishop or bishops
25 of such new diocese, or dioceses, and his or their successor, or successors, for the time being, should have the same powers as are by the said Act conferred upon the said bishops of Kingston and Toronto respectively ; and whereas in pursuance of the authority conferred by the said Act, and by an Act
30 amending the same, passed in the thirty-sixth year of Her Majesty's Reign, intituled *An Act to amend the Act of the Parliament of the late Province of Canada, passed in the eighth year of the Reign of Her Majesty Queen Victoria, chaptered eighty-two, and to incorporate the Roman Catholic Episcopal*
35 *Corporation of the Diocese of London, in Ontario*, the Right Reverend John Walsh, Doctor of Divinity, and his successors, being Bishops of the Diocese of London, in communion with the Church of Rome, were declared to be a body corporate by the name of " The Roman Catholic Episcopal Corporation of
40 the Diocese of London in Ontario," enjoying all the powers and privileges. and also subject to the provisions contained in the said Act passed in the eighth year of Her Majesty's reign, and chaptered eighty-two ; and whereas the said the Roman Catholic Corporation of the Diocese of London in Ontario,

BILL.

An Act to authorize the Roman Catholic Episcopal Corporation of the Diocese of London to sell certain lands.

First Reading,   1887.

(Private Bill.)

BILL.

An Act to authorize the Directors of the Royal College of Dental Surgeons of Ontario, to grant a Certificate of License to Marshall Bidwell Mallory to practise Dental Surgery in the Province of Ontario.

WHEREAS Marshall Bidwell Mallory has by his petition Preamble. set forth that, for five years previous to the fourth day of March, in the the year 1868, he had been constantly engaged in the practice of dentistry, and that he was then and now is a 5 British subject; and whereas, *The Act respecting Dentistry* as assented to on the said fourth day of March, in the year 1868, provided that dentists being British subjects and having been engaged for five years in an established office practice of dentistry and furnishing proof of the same, upon payment of 10 the prescribed fees, should be entitled to a certificate of license to practise dentistry in Ontario without passing any examination; and whereas, by amendments to the said Act passed in the year 1872, it was required that the said practice should be carried on in the Province of Ontario; and whereas, the said 15 Marshall Bidwell Mallory returned to the Province of Ontario in the year 1873; and whereas, it is expedient to revive the rights of the said Marshall Bidwell Mallory under the said Act of 1868; and whereas, the petition of the said Marshall Bidwell Mallory has been submitted to the directors of the Royal 20 College of Dental Surgeons of Ontario and the said Board, assuming that the facts are as stated in the said petition, offer no opposition to the rights of the said Marshall Bidwell Mallory being revived; and whereas, the said Marshall Bidwell Mallory has prayed that an Act may be passed to autho- 25 rize him to practise dental surgery in Ontario; and whereas, it is expedient to grant the prayer of the said petition;

Therefore Her Majesty by and with the advice and consent of the Legislative Assembly of the Province of Ontario enacts as follows:—

30 **1.** It shall and may be lawful for the Board of Directors of Authority to the Royal College of Dental Surgeons of Ontario, and they are admit M. B. Mallory hereby directed to grant to the said Marshall Bidwell Mallory, to practise on payment of the prescribed fees, a certificate of license to Surgery. practise dentistry in the Province of Ontario.

BILL.

An Act to authorize the Directors of the Royal College of Dental Surgeons of Ontario to grant a certificate of license to Marshall Bidwell Mallory to practise dental surgery in the Province of Ontario.

First Reading,   1887.

(Private Bill.)

BILL.

An Act respecting the Debt of the City of Kingston.

WHEREAS the Corporation of the City of Kingston, by Preamble.
their petition, shew that by an Act of the Legislature
of the Province of Ontario passed on the 2nd day of March,
1872, the debt of the said Corporation was consolidated at the
5 sum of $470,000, of which sum $300,000 was a bonus granted
by the said Corporation to the Kingston and Pembroke Railway Company, to assist in the building of the Kingston and
Pembroke Railway, a work which will continue to confer
advantages upon the ratepayers of the said city permanently;
10 and whereas by the said Act the said debt was made payable
in annual instalments during a period of thirty years, debentures therefor being issued accordingly, the last of said instalments falling due in the year 1901 ; and whereas since the said
Act was passed the said Corporation has raised a loan on the
15 credit of the debentures of the said Corporation of $25,000, also
payable by annual instalments during a period of twenty years,
the last of said instalments falling due in the year 1896 ; and
whereas there has been paid on account of the principal of the
said debenture debt besides the interest the sum of $147,300,
20 leaving unpaid of the principal on the 31st day of December,
1886, the sum of $347,700 ; and whereas the said Corporation
has also incurred since the passing of the said Act a floating debt
amounting to the sum of $24,000 ; and whereas the said Cor-
poration has petitioned to be authorized to consolidate the
25 said floating debt, and to issue debentures for a loan for the
payment of the same, bearing interest and payable as set
forth in Schedule " A " to this Act, without providing a
sinking fund or making other provision for the payment
of the principal than as hereinafter provided, the interest
30 to be levied by an annual special rate, over and above all
other rates, on the ratable property of the said municipality, and the principal of the said debt to be similarly
levied for, in the years in which the said debentures therefor
shall fall due respectively, as set forth in Schedule " A " to this
35 Act, and also to be authorized to relieve the ratepayers of the
of the said city by effecting an extension of the time for the final
payment of a portion, amounting to the sum of $305,600, of
the said debenture debt remaining unpaid, by issuing and
negotiating a loan or loans upon the credit of new debentures
40 for the sums, and to be issued and payable as set forth in
Schedule " B " to this Act, and without providing a sinking
fund or making other provision for the payment of the
principal than as hereinafter provided, the interest and the
principal to be levied for as aforesaid, and to pass without the
45 formalities required by law in such cases, all necessary by-laws
for the issue of the debentures aforesaid and for the levying of

SCHEDULE A.

Amount of the Debentures to be issued for the floating debt.	Date of the Debentures.	Period for which the Debentures are to run.	Time when the Debentures fall due.
$6,900 00	Dec. 31, 1886	16 years.	Dec. 31, 1902
7,400 00	" "	17 "	" 1903
7,800 00	" "	18 "	" 1904
1,900 00	" "	19 "	" 1905
$24,000 00			

SCHEDULE B.

Amounts for which new Debentures for the present Debenture debt are to be issued.		Date of the issue as per Act.	Period for which the Debentures are to run.	Time when the Debentures fall due.
$6,200		Dec. 31, 1887	18 years.	Dec. 31, 1905
8,000		" "	19 "	" 1906
	$14,200			
1,800		" 1888	18 "	" 1906
10,300		" "	19 "	" 1907
2,800		" "	20 "	" 1908
	14,900			
8,000		" 1889	19 "	" 1908
7,600		" "	20 "	" 1909
	15,600			
3,800		" 1890	19 "	" 1909
11,800		" "	20 "	" 1910
800		" "	21 "	" 1911
	16,400			
11,700		" 1891	20 "	" 1911
5,500		" "	21 "	" 1912
	17,200			
7,700		" 1892	20 "	" 1912
10,400		" "	21 "	" 1913
	18,100			
3,400		" 1893	20 "	" 1913
14,500		" "	21 "	" 1914
1,100		" "	22 "	" 1915
	19,000			
14,100		" 1894	21 "	" 1915
5,800		" "	22 "	" 1916
	19,900			
10,200		" 1895	21 "	" 1916
10,700		" "	22 "	" 1917
	20,900			
6,100		" 1896	21 "	" 1917
15,900		" "	22 "	" 1918
	22,000			
1,700		" 1897	21 "	" 1918
18,500		" "	22 "	" 1919
2,900		" "	23 "	" 1920
	23,100			
16,600		" 1898	22 "	" 1920
7,600		" "	23 "	" 1921
	24,200			
12,800		" 1899	22 "	" 1921
12,600		" "	23 "	" 1922
	25,400			
8,800		" 1900	22 "	" 1922
17,900		" "	23 "	" 1923
	26,700			
4,600		" 1901	22 "	" 1923
23,400		" "	23 "	" 1924
	28,000			

SCHEDULE C.

Column 2 shows amount of the debenture debt falling due in the following years.

Column 3 shows amount of the said debt in respect of which new debentures are to be issued in each of the said years, the balances to be paid in the said years.

Year.	No. 1.	No. 2.	No. 3.
1887		$15,500	$14,200
1888		16,400	14,900
1889		17,300	15,600
1890		18,500	16,400
1891		19,500	17,200
1892		20,800	18,100
1893		21,900	19,000
1894		23,200	19,900
1895		24,700	20,900
1896		26,100	22,000
1897		25,500	23,100
1898		27,100	24,200
1899		28,700	25,400
1900		30,400	26,700
1901		32,100	28,000
		$347,700	$305,600

1st Session, 6th Legislature, 50 Vic., 1887.

BILL.

An Act respecting the Debt of the City of Kingston.

First Reading, 1887.

(Private Bill.)

BILL.

An Act respecting the Debt of the City of Kingston.

WHEREAS the corporation of the city of Kingston, by Preamble.
their petition, shew that by an Act of the Legislature
of the Province of Ontario passed on the 2nd day of March,
1872, the debt of the said corporation was consolidated at the
5 sum of $470,000, of which sum $300,000 was a bonus granted
by the said corporation to the Kingston and Pembroke Railway Company, to assist in the building of the Kingston and
Pembroke Railway, a work which will continue to confer
advantages upon the ratepayers of the said city permanently;
10 and whereas by the said Act the said debt was made payable
in annual instalments during a period of thirty years, debentures therefor being issued accordingly, the last of said instalments falling due in the year 1901 ; and whereas since the said
Act was passed the said corporation has raised a loan on the
15 credit of the debentures of the said corporation of $25,000, also
payable by annual instalments during a period of twenty years,
the last of said instalments falling due in the year 1896 ; and
whereas there has been paid on account of the principal of the
said debenture debt besides the interest the sum of $147,300,
20 leaving unpaid of the principal on the 31st day of December,
1886, the sum of $347,700 ; and whereas the said corporation
has also incurred since the passing of the said Act a floating debt
amounting to the sum of $24,000; and whereas the said cor-
poration has petitioned to be authorized to consolidate the
25 said floating debt, and to issue debentures for a loan for the
payment of the same, bearing interest and payable as set
forth in schedule " A " to this Act, without providing a
sinking fund or making other provision for the payment
of the principal than as hereinafter provided, the interest
30 to be levied by an annual special rate, over and above all
other rates, on the ratable property of the said municipality, and the principal of the said debt to be similarly
levied for, in the years in which the said debentures therefor
shall fall due respectively, as set forth in schedule " A " to this
35 Act, and also to be authorized to relieve the ratepayers of the
of the said city by effecting an extension of the time for the final
payment of a portion, amounting to the sum of $305,600, of
the said debenture debt remaining unpaid, by issuing and
negotiating a loan or loans upon the credit of new debentures
40 for the sums, and to be issued and payable as set forth in
schedule " B " to this Act, and without providing a sinking
fund or making other provision for the payment of the
principal than as hereinafter provided, the interest and the
principal to be levied for as aforesaid, and to pass without the
45 formalities required by law in such cases, all necessary by-laws
for the issue of the debentures aforesaid and for the levying of
the special rates thereunder required for the payment of the
interest and principal of the said debts as aforesaid ; ☞ and
whereas the council of the said corporation have also asked for
50 special powers in the matter of certain proposed debentures

for a loan to purchase and improve the waterworks of the said city, or to pay a bonus to the Napanee and Tamworth Railway Company ; and it is expedient to grant the prayer of the said petition :

Therefore Her Majesty, by and with the advice and consent 5 of the Legislative Assembly of the Province of Ontario, enacts as follows :—

Mode of citation.

1. This Act may be cited as " *The City of Kingston Debt Arrangement Act, 1887."*

Floating debt consolidated at $24,000.

2. The said floating debt of the said corporation is hereby 10 consolidated at the sum of $24,000, and the said corporation is hereby authorized to issue debentures therefor, as set out in schedule " A " to this Act, in sums not less than $100, and not exceeding in the whole the sum of $24,000, bearing interest from the date at a rate not exceeding six per centum per 15 annum, and to be issued as of the date and payable as set forth in schedule " A," and to raise thereon a loan for the purpose of paying off the said debt of $24,000.

Issue of new debentures in payment of old debt authorized.

3. The said corporation is hereby authorized to liquidate each year from the passing of this Act, inclusive, the portions 20 of the said debenture debt yearly falling due, amounting together to the sum of $305,600, as aforesaid, as set forth in column three of schedule " C " to this Act, by issuing new debentures for such portions as set forth in said column three of schedule " C," in sums not less than $100, and not exceed- 25 ing in the whole in any year the proportion of the said debt to be so liquidated in that year, as set forth in said column three of schedule " C," and raising a loan thereon for the said purpose, which said debentures shall be issued as of the dates, and be payable as set forth in schedule " B " to this Act, and 30 shall bear interest from such dates at a rate not exceeding six per centum per annum.

By-law for issue of debentures.

4. The said corporation is hereby authorized to pass a by-law, or by-laws, for the issue of the said debentures and the levying on the ratable property of the municipality of 35 an annual special rate in each year until the said debentures shall all be paid, over and above all other rates, sufficient for the purpose of paying the interest on the said debentures, in each year while the same are running, and in the years in which the said debentures shall respectively become due, sufficient 40 also to pay the principal of the debentures so becoming due, and it shall not be necessary to provide for the payment of such principal by a sinking fund or otherwise, until the years respectively in which the debentures for the respective portions of the same become due as aforesaid, in which years respectively 45 the respective portions of the said principal due therein shall be levied for and paid as aforesaid, and the said by-laws may be passed without obtaining the assent of the electors of the said municipality to the same, and without observing any of the other formalities required by law in such cases, and the 50 interest on the said debentures may be made payable yearly or half-yearly, as the council of the said corporation may provide in the said by-law or by-laws.

Levy of rates.

5. So much of the special rates provided to be levied by the by-laws under which the outstanding debentures for the said

debenture debt were issued as would be required to provide
the portion of the said debt to be liquidated in each year by
means of a new issue of debentures as aforesaid, shall not be
levied after the issue of the new debentures for or in respect
5 of the same, and nothing in this Act contained shall authorize
the statutory limit of two cents in the dollar on the whole
ratable property of the said municipality for the general and
special rates of the same, over and above school rates, to be
exceeded in any year.

10 **6.** The series of the said debentures to be issued for the Date of debentures.
said floating debt may be issued and dated as of the 31st day
of December, 1886, and shall bear interest from that date.

7. No irregularity or informality in the form of the said Irregularities not to affect debentures.
debentures or of the by-law or by-laws authorizing their
15 issue, or in the passing of said by-law or by-laws, or in the
special rates to be levied under the same, shall render the said
debentures, by-laws or rates, or any or either of them, invalid
or illegal, or be allowed as a defence to any action or proceeding brought or taken to recover or enforce the same, or either
20 of them.

8. Every special rate to be levied under the authority of Name of rate.
this Act may be levied under the name of " Debt arrangement
loan rate," and when more than one such rate is to be levied in
the same year they shall be levied together as one rate under
25 the said name.

9. It shall not be necessary in the by-law or by-laws to Recitals in by-law.
be passed under this Act to recite any of the matters required
to be recited in by-laws creating debts not payable within the
year, but it shall be sufficient to state instead that such by-law
30 or by-laws is or are passed in pursuance of this Act, citing it.

10. The debentures for the said loans may be, principal Debentures may be payable in sterling money.
and interest, made payable in the sterling money of the United
Kingdom of Great Britain and Ireland, not exceeding in value
the sums hereby authorized, and may be negotiated there.

35 **11.** The council of the said corporation, in the case of the Extension of time of payment of debentures.
issue of debentures for a loan to purchase and improve the
water works of the said city, or to pay a bonus to the Napanee
and Tamworth Railway Company, should such issue be first
duly authorized for both or either of the said objects by
40 by-laws or a by-law duly assented to by the electors of the
said municipality and passed as required by law, may extend
the period within which such debentures shall be payable to
thirty years from the date of issue.

12. Nothing in this Act contained shall affect the debt Debt for school purposes not affected.
45 incurred or to be incurred by the said corporation on account
of the public schools of the said municipality, or the debentures
issued, or to be issued, for or on account of the same.

13. Nothing in this Act contained shall be held or taken to Liability not affected.
discharge the said corporation from any indebtedness or liability
50 not included in the said debts dealt with hereby.

SCHEDULE A.

Amount of the debentures to be issued for the floating debt	Date of the debentures.	Period for which the debentures are to run.	Time when the debentures fall due.
$6,900 00	Dec. 31, 1886	16 years.	Dec. 31, 1902
7,400 00	" "	17 "	" 1903
7,800 00	" "	18 "	" 1904
1,900 00	" "	19 "	" 1905
$24,000 00			

SCHEDULE B.

Amounts for which new debentures for the present debenture debt are to be issued.		Date of the issue as per Act.	Period for which the debentures are to run.	Time when the debentures fall due.
$6,200		Dec. 31, 1887	18 years.	Dec. 31, 1905
8,000		" "	19 "	" 1906
	$14,200			
1,800		" 1888	18 "	" 1906
10,300		" "	19 "	" 1907
2,800		" "	20 "	" 1908
	14,900			
8,000		" 1889	19 "	" 1908
7,600		" "	20 "	" 1909
	15,600			
3,800		" 1890	19 "	" 1909
11,800		" "	20 "	" 1910
800		" "	21 "	" 1911
	16,400			
11,700		" 1891	20 "	" 1911
5,500		" "	21 "	" 1912
	17,200			
7,700		" 1892	20 "	" 1912
10,400		" "	21 "	" 1913
	18,100			
3,400		" 1893	20 "	" 1913
14,500		" "	21 "	" 1914
1,100		" "	22 "	" 1915
	19,000			
14,100		" 1894	21 "	" 1915
5,800		" "	22 "	" 1916
	19,900			
10,200		" 1895	21 "	" 1916
10,700		" "	22 "	" 1917
	20,900			
6,100		" 1896	21 "	" 1917
15,900		" "	22 "	" 1918
	22,000			
1,700		" 1897	21 "	" 1918
18,500		" "	22 "	" 1919
2,900		" "	23 "	" 1920
	23,100			
16,600		" 1898	22 "	" 1920
7,600		" "	23 "	" 1921
	24,200			
12,800		" 1899	22 "	" 1921
12,600		" "	23 "	" 1922
	25,400			
8,800		" 1900	22 "	" 1922
17,900		" "	23 "	" 1923
	26,700			
4,600		" 1901	22 "	" 1923
23,400		" "	23 "	" 1924
	28,000			

SCHEDULE C.

Column 2 shows amount of the debenture debt falling due in the following years.

Column 3 shows amount of the said debt in respect of which new debentures are to be issued in each of the said years, the balance to be paid in the said years.

Year.	No. 1.	No. 2.	No. 3.
1887		$15,500	$14,200
1888		16,400	14,900
1889		17,300	15,600
1890		18,500	16,400
1891		19,500	17,200
1892		20,800	18,100
1893		21,900	19,000
1894		23,200	19,900
1895		24,700	20,900
1896		26,100	22,000
1897		25,500	23,100
1898		27,100	24,200
1899		28,700	25,400
1900		30,400	26,700
1901		32,100	28,000
		$347,700	$305,600

No. 5.

1st Session, 6th Legislature, 50 Vic., 1887.

BILL.

An Act respecting the Debt of the City of Kingston.

(*Reprinted as amended by Private Bills Committee*).

First Reading, 9th March, 1887.

(Private Bill.)

BILL.

An Act to declare and define the correct boundary between the Township of Smith and the Town of Peterborough.

WHEREAS the Lieutenant-Governor of the Province of Ontario,on the application of the Town of Peterborough, by his proclamation dated the 27th day of April, 1872, duly published in the *Ontario Gazette*, added to the Town of Peter-
5 borough a portion of the Township of Smith, in the County of Peterborough, described in the said proclamation as follows :— Commencing at the northern extremity of Reid Street in the Town of Peterborough, thence in a north-easterly direction and along the newly opened road (leading from the said
10 northern extremity of Reid Street to the communication road in the said Township of Smith) to the said communication road, thence northerly along the said communication road to the northern limit of the south half of Township lot number three east of the said communication road ; thence easterly
15 along the said northern limit of the said south half of the said Township lot number three, to the road or road allowance in the rear of the range of lots on the east of the communication road ; thence in a north-westerly direction along such road, or road allowance, to the concession line between the first and
20 second concessions of the said Township of Smith ; thence easterly along the said concession line to where the same will strike the waters of the River Otonabee ; and whereas such description is erroneous and impossible, and it was intended by the said Town of Peterborough to extend their limits only
25 to the northern limit of the south half of lot number one east of the said communication road, and the said Town of Peterborough and the said Township of Smith have always treated the said intended limit as the true and correct limit ; and whereas it is expedient to correct such erroneous description
30 and correctly define the limit between the said Town and Township ;

Therefore Her Majesty, by and with the advice and consent of the Legislative Assembly of the Province of Ontario, enacts as follows :—

35 **1.** The true and correct boundary between the Town of Peterborough and the Township of Smith is declared to be as follows : Commencing at the northern extremity of Reid Street in the Town of Peterborough, thence in a north-easterly direc- tion and along the newly opened road (leading from the said
40 northern extremity of Reid Street to the communication road in the said Township of Smith) to the said communication road, thence northerly along the said communication road to

Preamble.

True boundary between Town of Peterborough and Township of Smith defined.

the northern limit of the south half of Township lot number
one east of the said communication road, thence easterly along
the said northern limit of the said south half of the said
Township lot number one, to the road or road allowance in
the rear of the range of lots on the east of the communication 5
road; thence in a north-westerly direction along such road or
road allowance to the concession line between the first and
second concessions of the said Township of Smith; thence
easterly along the said concession line to where the same will
strike the waters of the River Otonabee, and the same is 10
hereby declared to be the limit intended by the said Proclamation, which shall be read and construed as if the same were
contained therein.

No. 6.

1st Session, 6th Legislature, 50 Vic, 1887.

An Act to declare and define the correct
boundary between the Township of
Smith and the Town of Peterborough.

First Reading,   1887.

(Private Bill.)

Mr. STRATTON.

TORONTO:
PRINTED BY WARWICK & SONS, 26 AND 28 FRONT ST. W.

BILL.

An Act to incorporate the Thames Valley Tramway Company.

WHEREAS Thomas H. Smallman, V. Cronyn, William Preamble.
Bowman, Samuel Crawford and William Saunders, have
petitioned that an Act may be passed incorporating them
under the name of the Thames Valley Tramway Company, and
5 authorizing the construction, operation and maintenance of a
tramway from a point in or near the City of London, along or
near the valley of the River Thames, to a point on the river at
or near Springbank, where the works which supply the said
city with water are situated ; and whereas it is expedient to
10 grant the prayer of the said petition ;

Therefore Her Majesty, by and with the advice and consent
of the Legislative Assembly of the Province of Ontario, enacts
as follows :—

1. The said Thomas H. Smallman, V. Cronyn, William Incorporation.
15 Bowman, Samuel Crawford and Willinm Saunders, and such
other persons and corporations as shall, in pursuance of this
Act, become shareholders, are hereby constituted a body corporate and politic by the name of "The Thames Valley
Tramway Company."

20 **2.** *The Railway Act of Ontario*, chapter one hundred and R. S. O. c.
sixty- five of the Revised Statutes of Ontario, and the several 165, incorpor-
clauses thereof respecting "interpretation," "incorporation," with. ated here-
"powers," "plans and surveys," "lands and their valuation,"
"highways and bridges," "fences," "tolls," general meetings,"
25 "president and directors," "calls," "dividends," "shares and
their transfer," "shareholders," "municipalities taking stock,"
"by-laws, notices, etc.," "actions for indemnity, and fines and
penalties, and their prosecution," are incorporated with and
form part of this Act, and shall apply to the said company and
30 the tramway to be constructed by them, except only in so far
as they are inconsistent with the express enactments hereof, and
the expression "this Act" when used herein shall include the
clauses of the said *Railway Act of Ontario*, so incorporated
with this Act.

35 **3.** The said company shall have full power, under this Act, Powers of
to construct, maintain and operate a tramway from a point in company.
or near the City of London, along or near the valley of the
River Thames to a point on the river near Springbank, aforesaid, and to construct and maintain at Springbank, aforesaid,
40 a bridge over the said river for the use of passengers by the
said tramway.

Gauge.   **4**. The said tramway may be of any gauge.

Provisional directors.   **5**. The persons named in section 1 shall be provisional directors of the said company to organize the same, three to form a quorum, and shall hold office until the election of directors as hereinafter provided for.   5

Number of directors.   **6**. The number of directors of the said company shall be five, who shall be elected annually at a general meeting of the shareholders, to be held wherever the said provisional directors shall locate the office of the company, on the first Monday in the month of March, in each year, three of whom shall form a 10 **First annual meeting.** quorum for the transaction of business. The first annual meeting of the shareholders of the company shall be held on the first Monday of March, after the organization of the company has taken place. The method of calling general meetings, or any other meeting of the shareholders of the company, 15 shall be determined and settled by by-law of the directors.

Powers as to lands.   **7**. The company may construct their tramway upon and along the margin of the River Thames, and upon and along any land adjacent thereto, the use of which to the public, has been reserved by the Crown ; and upon and over any private 20 property in the Village of London West, and in the Townships of London and Westminster ; and upon and along such portions of the streets and highways of the said Village of London West, and of the said townships under and subject, as to such streets and highways, to any agreement or agreements here- 25 after to be made between the company and the municipalities of London West, the Township of London and the Township of Westminster, or any or either of them, and under and subject to any by-law or by-laws of the council or councils of the said municipalities passed in pursuance thereof.   30

Acquiring land for purposes of recreation.   **8**. In addition to the lands required for the use of the said tramway, the company may purchase, take on lease, or otherwise acquire along the route, or at the terminus of said tramway, such lands, buildings and personal property, as may be deemed sufficient by the directors of the company, for the 35 purposes of recreation and the entertainment of the patrons of the said tramway.

Amalgamation with London Street Railway authorized.   **9**. The said company may amalgamate with the London Street Railway Company upon such terms as shall be agreed upon by the directors of both companies, provided such 40 amalgamation is approved of and confirmed by a vote of at least two-thirds of the shareholders of each company present at special meetings of the shareholders of each company, respectively, called for the purpose of considering the same.

Capital.   **10**. The capital of the company hereby incorporated shall 45 be $100,000 in five thousand shares of $20 each ; and so soon as $20,000 worth of stock is subscribed, and ten per cent. paid thereon, the company may commence operations, and exercise **Time of commencement.** the powers hereby granted ; but the company shall commence operations within two years from the passing of this Act.   50

No. 7.

1st Session, 6th Legislature, 50 Vic., 1887.

BILL.

An Act to incorporate the Thames Valley Tramway Company.

First Reading,   1887.

(Private Bill.)

BILL.

An Act to incorporate the Thames Valley Tramway Company.

WHEREAS Thomas H. Smallman, V. Cronyn, William Bowman, Samuel Crawford and William Saunders, have petitioned that an Act may be passed incorporating them under the name of the Thames Valley Tramway Company, and 5 authorizing the construction, operation and maintenance of a tramway from a point in or near the city of London, along or near the valley of the River Thames, to a point on the river at or near Springbank, where the works which supply the said city with water are situated ; and whereas it is expedient to 10 grant the prayer of the said petition ; *Preamble.*

Therefore Her Majesty, by and with the advice and consent of the Legislative Assembly of the Province of. Ontario, enacts as follows :—

1. The said Thomas H. Smallman, V. Cronyn, William 15 Bowman, Samuel Crawford and William Saunders, and such other persons and corporations as shall, in pursuance of this Act, become shareholders, are hereby constituted a body corporate and politic by the name of "The Thames Valley Tramway Company." *Incorporation.*

20 **2.** *The Railway Act of Ontario*, chapter 165 of the Revised Statutes of Ontario, and the several clauses thereof respecting "interpretation," "incorporation," "powers," "plans and surveys," "lands and their valuation," "highways and bridges," "fences." "tolls," general meetings," "president and directors," 25 "calls," "dividends," "shares and their transfer," "shareholders," "municipalities taking stock," "by-laws, notices, etc.," "actions for indemnity, and fines and penalties, and their prosecution," *and section 92 of the "general provisions" of the said Act*, are incorporated with and form part of this Act, 30 and shall apply to the said company and the tramway to be constructed by them, except only in so far as they are inconsistent with the express enactments hereof, and the expression "this Act" when used herein shall include the clauses of· the said *Railway Act of Ontario*, so incorporated with this Act, 35 *but in case the motive power used be a steam locomotive it shall only be such as is known as the " dummy engine."* *R. S. O. c. 165, incorporated herewith.*

3. The said company shall have full power, under this Act, to construct, maintain and operate a tramway from a point in or near the city of London, along *at* or near the valley of the 35 River Thames to a point on the river near Springbank, afore- *Powers of company.*

said, and *having obtained the consent of the corporation of the city of London* to construct and maintain at Springbank, aforesaid, a bridge over the said river for the use of passengers by the said tramway.

Gauge.

4. The said tramway may be of any gauge. 5

Provisional directors.

5. The persons named in section 1 shall be provisional directors of the said company to organize the same, three to form a quorum, and shall hold office until the election of directors as hereinafter provided for.

Number of directors.

6. The number of directors of the said company shall be 10 five, who shall be elected annually at a general meeting of the shareholders, to be held wherever the said provisional directors shall locate the office of the company, on the first Monday in the month of March, in each year, three of whom shall form a

First annual meeting.

quorum for the transaction of business. The first annual 15 meeting of the shareholders of the company shall be held on the first Monday of March, after the organization of the company has taken place. The method of calling general meetings, or any other meeting of the shareholders of the company, shall be determined and settled by by-law of the directors. 20

Powers as to lands.

7. The company may construct their tramway upon and along the margin of the River Thames ; and upon and over any private property in the village of London West, and in the townships of London and Westminster ; and upon and along such portions of the streets and highways of the said village of London 25 West, and of the said townships under and subject, as to such streets and highways, *to the use of a rail similar to the tram-rail at present in use by the London Street Railway Company in the city of London, laid flush with the surface of such streets and highways and* to any agreement or agreements hereafter 30 after to be made between the company and the municipalities of London West, the township of London and the township of Westminster, or any or either of them, and under and subject to any by-law or by-laws of the council or councils of the said municipalities passed in pursuance thereof, *but the company* 35 *shall not have power to expropriate any property of the corporation of the city of London, except with their consent in writing first had.*

Acquiring land for purposes of recreation.

8. In addition to the lands required for the use of the said tramway, the company may purchase, take on lease, or other- 40 wise acquire along the route, or at the terminus of said tramway, such lands, buildings and personal property, as may be deemed sufficient by the directors of the company, for the purposes of recreation and the entertainment of the patrons of the said tramway, *but the expropriation clauses of The Rail-* 45 *way Act of Ontario shall not apply to this section.*

Amalgamation with London Street Railway authorized.

9. The said company may amalgamate with the London Street Railway Company upon such terms as shall be agreed upon by the directors of both companies, provided such amalgamation is approved of and confirmed by a vote of at 50 least two-thirds of the shareholders of each company present at special meetings of the shareholders of each company, respectively called for the purpose of considering the same.

10. Tne capital of the company hereby incorporated shall Capital.
be $100,000 in five thousand shares of $20 each ; and so soon
as $20,000 worth of stock is subscribed, and ten per cent. paid
thereon, the company may commence operations, and exercise
5 the powers hereby granted ; but the company shall commence Time of
operations within two years *and shall complete their tramway* commence-
within three years from the passing of this Act. ment.

BILL.

An Act to incorporate the Thames Valley
Tramway Company.

*(Reprinted as amended by Railway Com-
mittee.)*

First Reading, 9th March, 1887.

(Private Bill.)

Mr. Tooley.

No. 8.]   **BILL.**   [1887.

An Act to incorporate the Town of Sault Ste. Marie.

WHEREAS it is expected that the lands hereinafter Preamble.
described will rapidly increase in population upon the
construction of a line of railway to them, and that such line
of railway will shortly be completed, and that various manu-
5 factories will utilize the unimproved water power included in
their limits ; and whereas the residents and ratepayers of the
said lands have petitioned to be separated from the municipality of Sault Ste. Marie and formed into a corporate town,
and the council of the municipality of Sault Ste. Marie have
10 by their petition set forth that the incorporation of the said
lands as a town would tend to its advancement and empower
its ratepayers to make the most desirable regulations for the
protection and improvement of property and have prayed for
its incorporation accordingly ; and whereas it is expedient to
15 grant the prayers of the said petitions ;
Therefore Her Majesty by and with the advice and consent
of the Legislative Assembly of the Province of Ontario enacts
as follows :—

1. On and after the passing of this Act the lands herein- Town of Sault
20 after described shall be separated from the municipality of Ste. Marie,
Sault Ste. Marie, and the residents and ratepayers thereof shall incorporated.
be, and they hereby are, constituted a corporation or body
politic under the name of "The Corporation of the Town of
Sault Ste. Marie" and shall have all the rights, powers and
25 privileges enjoyed and exercised by incorporated towns
separated from counties in the Province of Ontario under the
existing municipal laws cf the said province, except where
otherwise provided by this Act.

2. The said town of Sault Ste. Marie shall comprise and Limits of
30 consist of the following lands that is to say :—The town plot Town.
of Sault Ste. Marie and the broken front lying south and in
front of Portage Street in the said town plot according to
survey of A. Vidal, P. L. S.; the park lots adjoining the said
town plot also according to survey of A. Vidal, P. L. S.; the
35 broken Township of St. Mary ; broken section number one in
the Township of Awenge ; lots one, two, three, four, five and
six, in the Stewart Survey of portion of the Township of
Korah ; and all the islands and waters, or land covered with
water, in the River St. Mary, lying to the south and west and
40 south and east in front of or immediately adjacent to the above
described lands and north of the International Boundary
between Canada and the United States of America.

Wards. **3.** The said town shall be divided into two wards to be called respectively the first and second wards. The first ward shall comprise and consist of all the land within the said Town of Sault Ste. Marie lying west of the following described line:—Commencing at the intersection of the northern 5 boundary of the park lots adjoining the town plot of Sault Ste. Marie, with the division line between lots five and six in the fourth concession of said park lots, thence south and along said division line to the intersection of the centre line of the road between the third and fourth concessions, thence west and 10 along said centre line to the intersection of the division line between park lots ten and eleven in the third concession produced; thence south and along the division line between said lots ten and eleven in the third concession and lots ten and eleven in the second concession, to the intersection of the 15 centre line of Wellington Street; thence west and along said centre line to the intersection of the centre line of East Street produced; thence south-westerly and following the said centre line of East Street and the production thereof, to the intersection of the International Boundary line between Canada 20 and the United States of America. The second ward shall comprise and consist of all the land within the said Town of Sault St. Marie lying east of the said above described line

Acts respecting municipal institutions to apply. **4.** Except where otherwise provided by this Act the provisions of *The Consolidated Municipal Act, 1883*, and of any 25 Act amending the same, with regard to matters consequent upon the formation of new corporations, shall apply to the said Town of Sault Ste. Marie in the same manner as if the said lands had been an incorporated village and had been erected into a town under the provisions of the said Acts. 30

Nomination for first election. **5.** On the ninth day of May, 1887, it shall be lawful for the Sheriff of the District of Algoma, who is hereby appointed the Returning Officer, to hold the nomination for the first election of Mayor and Councillors at Dawson's Hall in the said Town of Sault Ste. Marie; and he shall preside at the said nomina- 35 tion, or in case of his absence the electors present shall choose from among themselves a chairman to preside at the said nomination, and such chairman shall have all the powers of a returning officer; and the polling for the said election, if necessary, shall be held on the same day of the week in the week follow- 40 ing the nomination; and the returning officer or chairman shall at the close of the nomination publicly announce the place in each ward at which the polling shall take place.

Oaths of returning officer and deputy returning officers. **6.** The said returning officer shall by his warrant appoint a deputy-returning officer for each of the wards into which the 45 said town is divided; and such returning officer and each of such deputy-returning officers shall, before holding the said election, take the oath or affirmation required by law and shall respectively be subject to all the provisions of the municipal laws of Ontario applicable to returning officers and deputy- 50 returning officers at elections in towns, in so far as the same do not conflict with this Act; and the said returning officer shall have all the powers and perform the several duties devolving on town clerks with respect to municipal elections in towns.

7. The clerk of the said Municipality of Sault Ste. Marie and any other officer thereof shall, upon demand made upon him by the said returning officer or any officer of the said town, or by the chairman hereinbefore men-
5 tioned, at once furnish such returning officer, officer or chairman with a certified copy of so much of the last revised assessment roll for the said Municipality of Sault Ste. Marie, as may be required to ascertain the names of the persons entitled to vote in each of the said wards at the
10 said first election, or with the collector's roll, document, state-ment, writing or deed that may be required for that purpose, and the said returning officer shall furnish each of the said deputies with a true copy of so much of the said roll as relates to the names of electors entitled to vote in each of the said
15 wards respectively, and each such copy shall be verified on oath.

Copy of assessment roll to be furnished on demand of returning or other officer.

8. The council of said town, to be elected in manner afore-said, shall consist of the mayor who shall be the head thereof, and six councillors, three councillors being elected for each
20 ward; and they shall be organized as a council on the same day of the week next following the week of the polling, or if there be no polling, on the same day of the week next follow-ing the week of the said nomination; and subsequent elections shall be held in the same manner; and the qualification of
25 mayor and councillors and for electors at such subsequent elections shall be the same as in towns incorporated under the provisions of *The Consolidated Municipal Act, 1883*, and any Act amending the same; and the said council and their successors in office shall have, use, exercise and enjoy all the
30 powers and privileges vested by the said municipal laws in councils of towns separated from counties, and shall be subject to all the liabilities and duties imposed by the said municipal laws on such councils.

Council.

9. The several persons who shall be elected or appointed
35 under this Act shall take declarations of office and qualifi-cation now required by the municipal laws of the Province of Ontario to be taken by persons elected or appointed to like offices in towns.

Oaths of office and qualifica-tion.

10. At the first election of mayor and councillors for the
40 said Town of Sault Ste. Marie the qualification of mayor and councillors, of officers required to qualify and of electors, shall be the same as that required in the municipality of Sault Ste. Marie.

Qualification at first elec-tion.

11. The expenses incurred to obtain this Act and of furnish-
45 ing any documents, copies of papers, writings, deeds or any matters whatsoever required by the clerk or other officer of the said town, or otherwise, shall be borne by the said town and paid by it to any party that may be entitled thereto.

Expenses of Act.

12. All by-laws which are in force in the municipality of
50 Sault Ste. Marie shall continue to be in force as if they had been passed by the corporation of the Town of Sault Ste. Marie, and shall extend and have full effect within the limits of the town hereby incorporated until repealed by the new corporation.

By-laws con-tinued.

Property and.
obligations.

13. Except as otherwise provided by this Act the property, assets, debts, liabilities, and obligations of the municipality of Sault Ste. Marie shall be apportioned between the said municipality of Sault Ste. Marie and the said Town of Sault Ste. Marie as may be agreed upon; and in case of no agreement 5 then by the award of three arbitrators or a majority of them, one of such arbitrators being appointed by each of the said Municipalities of Sault Ste. Marie and the Town of Sault Ste. Marie, and the third being chosen by the said two; and if from any cause whatever either of the said municipalities shall 10 not have appointed an arbitrator within three months after the other of them has appointed an arbitrator, then the Lieutenant-Governor in Council shall appoint an arbitrator on behalf of the municipality so making default, and the two so appointed shall choose a third; and if they shall not agree upon such 15 third arbitrator, then the Lieutenant-Governor in Council shall appoint such third arbitrator, and the award of the said arbitrators, or a majority of them, shall be as valid and binding in all respects as if the said arbitrators had been regularly appointed by the said respective municipalities. 20

Collection of
arrears of
taxes.

14. Arrears of taxes due to the said corporation of the Town of Sault Ste. Marie shall be collected and managed in the same way as the arrears due to towns separated from counties, and the mayor and treasurer of the said town shall perform the like duties in the collection and management of 25 arrears of taxes as are performed by the said officer in other towns in Ontario separated from counties, and the various provisions of law relating to sales of land for arrears of taxes, or to deeds given therefor, shall apply to the said corporation of the Town of Sault Ste. Marie and to sales of land therein for arrears of taxes due thereon and to deeds given therefor. 30

Assessment
for 1887.

15. The council of the said town may pass a by-law for taking the assessment of the said town for the year from the first of January to the thirty-first of December, 1887, between the first day of April and the first day of August, 1887; and if any such by-law extends the time for making and com- 35 pleting the assessment rolls beyond the first day of June, 1887, then the time for closing the Court of Revision shall be six weeks from the day to which such time is extended, and the final return by the Judge twelve weeks from that day.

Existing
liabilities
not affected.

16. Nothing contained in this Act shall free the townships 40 or wards comprising the municipality of the Town of Sault Ste. Marie hereby formed from any liability now existing against the Municipality of Sault Ste. Marie, and the creditors of the said Municipality of Sault Ste. Marie shall continue to have all the rights and remedies which they had previous to 45 the passing of this Act, for the enforcement of their claims against the townships and wards heretofore comprising the said municipality of Sault Ste. Marie.

Provisions of
law relating
to the munici-
pality of Sault
Ste Marie
not to affect
town so far as
inconsistent
herewith.

17. All provisions of law relating to the municipality of Sault Ste. Marie, and inconsistent with this Act shall not 50 apply to the Town of Sault Ste. Marie, or the lands within the limits of the said town.

No. 8.

1st Session, 6th Legislature, 50 Vic., 1887.

BILL.

An Act to incorporate the Town of Sault Ste. Marie.

First Reading,   1887.

(Private Bill.)

No. 8.] **BILL.** [1887.

An Act to incorporate the Town of Sault Ste. Marie.

WHEREAS it is expected that the lands hereinafter Preamble.
described will rapidly increase in population upon the
construction of a line of railway to them, and that such line
of railway will shortly be completed, and that various manu-
5 factories will utilize the unimproved water power included in
their limits ; and whereas the residents and ratepayers of the
said lands have petitioned to be separated from the municipality of Sault Ste. Marie and formed into a corporate town,
and the council of the municipality of Sault Ste. Marie have
10 by their petition set forth that the incorporation of the said
lands as a town would tend to its advancement and empower
its ratepayers to make the most desirable regulations for the
protection and improvement of property and have prayed for
its incorporation accordingly ; and whereas it is expedient to
15 grant the prayers of the said petitions ;

Therefore Her Majesty by and with the advice and consent
of the Legislative Assembly of the Province of Ontario enacts
as follows :—

   1. On and after the passing of this Act the lands herein- Town of Sault
20 after described shall be separated from the municipality of Ste. Marie,
Sault Ste. Marie, and the residents and ratepayers thereof shall incorporated.
be, and they hereby are, constituted a corporation or body
politic under the name of "The Corporation of the Town of
Sault Ste. Marie" and shall have all the rights, powers and
25 privileges enjoyed and exercised by incorporated towns
separated from counties in the Province of Ontario under the
existing municipal laws of the said province, except where
otherwise provided by this Act.

   2. The said town of Sault Ste. Marie shall comprise and Limits of
30 consist of the following lands that is to say :—The town plot Town.
of Sault Ste. Marie and the broken front lying south and in
front of Portage Street in the said town plot according to
survey of A. Vidal, P. L. S.; the park lots adjoining the said
town plot also according to survey of A. Vidal, P. L. S.; the
35 broken Township of St. Mary ; broken section number one in
the Township of Awenge ; and all the islands and waters, or
land covered with water, in the River St. Mary, lying to the
south and west and south and east in front of or immediately
adjacent to the above described lands and north of the Inter-
40 national Boundary between Canada and the United States of
America.

   3. The said town shall be divided into two wards to be Wards.
called respectively the first and second wards. The first ward

shall comprise and consist of all the land within the said Town
of Sault Ste. Marie lying west of the following described
line:—Commencing at the intersection of the northern
boundary of the park lots *ten and eleven in the third conces-*
sion of said park lots adjoining the town plot of Sault Ste. 5
Marie, with the division line between said lots *ten and eleven,*
thence south and along said division line to the intersection of
the centre line of the road between the third and fourth concessions; thence south and along the division line between
said lots ten and eleven in the third concession and lots ten 10
and eleven in the second concession, to the intersection of the
centre line of Wellington Street; thence west and along said
centre line to the intersection of the centre line of East Street
produced; thence south-westerly and following the said centre
line of East Street and the production thereof, to the inter- 15
section of the International Boundary line between Canada
and the United States of America. The second ward shall
comprise and consist of all the land within the said Town of
Sault St. Marie lying east of the said above described line.

Acts respect-
ing municipal
institutions
to apply.

4. Except where otherwise provided by this Act the pro- 20
visions of *The Consolidated Municipal Act, 1883,* and of any
Act amending the same, with regard to matters consequent
upon the formation of new corporations, shall apply to the
said Town of Sault Ste. Marie in the same manner as if the 25
said lands had been an incorporated village and had been
erected into a town under the provisions of the said Acts.

Nomination
for first elec-
tion.

5. On the ninth day of May, 1887, it shall be lawful for the
Sheriff of the District of Algoma, who is hereby appointed the
Returning Officer, to hold the nomination for the first election 30
of Mayor and Councillors at Dawson's Hall in the said Town
of Sault Ste. Marie, *having first caused one week's notice there-*
of to be posted up in three conspicuous places in each of
said wards; and he shall preside at the said nomination,
or in case of his absence the electors present shall choose 35
from among themselves a chairman to preside at the said
nomination, and such chairman shall have all the powers of a
returning officer; and the polling for the said election, if necessary,
shall be held on the same day of the week in the week following the nomination; and the returning officer or chairman 40
shall at the close of the nomination publicly announce the
place in each ward at which the polling shall take place.

Oaths of
returning
officer and
deputy return-
ing officers.

6. The said returning officer shall by his warrant appoint a
deputy-returning officer for each of the wards into which the
said town is divided; and such returning officer and each of 45
such deputy-returning officers shall, before holding the said
election, take the oath or affirmation required by law and shall
respectively be subject to all the provisions of the municipal
laws of Ontario applicable to returning officers and deputy-
returning officers at elections in towns, in so far as the same do 50
not conflict with this Act; and the said returning officer shall
have all the powers and perform the several duties devolving
on town clerks with respect to municipal elections in towns.

Copy of assess-
ment roll to
be furnished
on demand of

7. The clerk of the said Municipality of Sault Ste. Marie
and any other officer thereof shall, upon demand made upon 55
him by the said returning officer or any officer of

the said town, or by the chairman hereinbefore men- tioned, at once furnish such returning officer, officer or chairman with a certified copy of so much of the last revised assessment roll for the said Municipality 5 of Sault Ste. Marie, as may be required to ascertain the names of the persons entitled to vote in each of the said wards at the said first election, or with the collector's roll, document, state-ment, writing or deed that may be required for that purpose, and the said returning officer shall furnish each of the said 10 deputies with a true copy of so much of the said roll as relates to the names of electors entitled to vote in each of the said wards respectively, and each such copy shall be verified on oath.

8. The council of said town, to be elected in manner afore- said, shall consist of the mayor who shall be the head thereof, 15 and six councillors, three councillors being elected for each ward ; and they shall be organized as a council on the same day of the week next following the week of the polling, or if there be no polling, on the same day of the week next follow-ing the week of the said nomination ; and subsequent elections 20 shall be held in the same manner ; and the qualification of mayor and councillors and for electors at such subsequent elections shall be the same as in towns incorporated under the provisions of *The Consolidated Municipal Act, 1883*, and any Act amending the same ; and the said council and their 25 successors in office shall have, use, exercise and enjoy all the powers and privileges vested by the said municipal laws in councils of towns separated from counties, and shall be subject to all the liabilities and duties imposed by the said municipal laws on such councils.

30 9. The several persons who shall be elected or appointed under this Act shall take declarations of office and qualifi-cation now required by the municipal laws of the Province of Ontario to be taken by persons elected or appointed to like offices in towns.

35 10. At the first election of mayor and councillors for the said Town of Sault Ste. Marie the qualification of mayor and councillors, of officers required to qualify and of electors, shall be the same as that required in the municipality of Sault Ste. Marie.

40 11. The expenses incurred to obtain this Act and of furnish- ing any documents, copies of papers, writings, deeds or any matters whatsoever required by the clerk or other officer of the said town, or otherwise, shall be borne by the said town and paid by it to any party that may be entitled thereto.

45 12. All by-laws which are in force in the municipality of Sault Ste. Marie shall continue to be in force as if they had been passed by the corporation of the Town of Sault Ste. Marie, and shall extend and have full effect within the limits of the town hereby incorporated until repealed by the new 50 corporation.

13. Except as otherwise provided by this Act the property, assets, debts, liabilities, and obligations of the municipality of Sault Ste. Marie shall be apportioned between the said munici-pality of Sault Ste. Marie and the said Town of Sault Ste.

Marie as may be agreed upon; and in case of no agreement then by the award of three arbitrators or a majority of them, one of such arbitrators being appointed by each of the said Municipalities of Sault Ste. Marie and the Town of Sault Ste. Marie, and the third being chosen by the said two; and if 5 from any cause whatever either of the said municipalities shall not have appointed an arbitrator within three months after the other of them has appointed an arbitrator, then the Lieutenant-Governor in Council shall appoint an arbitrator on behalf of the municipality so making default, and the two so appointed 10 shall choose a third; and if they shall not agree upon such third arbitrator, then the Lieutenant-Governor in Council shall appoint such third arbitrator, and the award of the said arbitrators, or a majority of them, shall be as valid and binding in all respects as if the said arbitrators had been regularly 15 appointed by the said respective municipalities.

Collection of arrears of taxes.

14. Arrears of taxes due to the said corporation of the Town of Sault Ste. Marie shall be collected and managed in the same way as the arrears due to towns separated from counties, and the mayor and treasurer of the said town shall 20 perform the like duties in the collection and management of arrears of taxes as are performed by the said officer in other towns in Ontario separated from counties, and the various provisions of law relating to sales of land for arrears of taxes, or to deeds given therefor, shall apply to the said corporation of 25 the Town of Sault Ste. Marie and to sales of land therein for arrears of taxes due thereon and to deeds given therefor.

Assessment for 1887.

15. The council of the said town may pass a by-law for taking the assessment of the said town for the year from the first of January to the thirty-first of December, 1887, between 30 the first day of April and the first day of August, 1887; and if any such by-law extends the time for making and completing the assessment rolls beyond the first day of June, 1887, then the time for closing the Court of Revision shall be six weeks from the day to which such time is extended, and the 35 final return by the Judge twelve weeks from that day.

Existing liabilities not affected.

16. Nothing contained in this Act shall free the townships or wards comprising the municipality of the Town of Sault Ste. Marie hereby formed from any liability now existing against the Municipality of Sault Ste. Marie, and the creditors 40 of the said Municipality of Sault Ste. Marie shall continue to have all the rights and remedies which they had previous to the passing of this Act, for the enforcement of their claims against the townships and wards heretofore comprising the said municipality of Sault Ste. Marie.   45

Inconsistent provisions of law relating to the municipality of Sault Ste Marie not to affect town.

17. All provisions of law relating to the municipality of Sault Ste. Marie, and inconsistent with this Act shall not apply to the Town of Sault Ste. Marie, or the lands within the limits of the said town.

Local improvements.

18. All expenditure in the Municipality for the improve- 50 ments and services for any class or classes of improvement, or service for which special provisions are made in sections 612 and 624 of *The Consolidated Municipal Act, 1883*, and amendments thereto, shall be by special assessment on the property benefited and not exempt by law from assessment.   55

1st Session, 6th Legislature, 50 Vic., 1887.

BILL.

An Act to incorporate the Town of Sault Ste. Marie.

(*Re-printed as amended by Private Bills Committee.*)

First Reading, 11th March, 1887.

(Private Bill.)

An Act to incorporate the Village of Tilbury Centre.

WHEREAS the inhabitants of the Village of Tilbury Preamble.
Centre have by their petition represented that the said
village has a population of over eight hundred and fifty souls,
and by reason of the rapid increase of the population of said
5 village, and owing to its situation and location, which will
likely cause it to attract the trade of a large, populous and
wealthy section of country, and in compliance with a resolution passed at a public meeting duly convened to consider the
matter of incorporation, and numerously attended, have prayed
10 for its incorporation accordingly; and whereas it is expedient
to grant the prayer of the said petition;

Therefore Her Majesty, by and with the advice and consent
of the Legislative Assembly of the Province of Ontario, enacts
as follows :—

15   **1.** On and after the passing of this Act the inhabitants of Village of Til-
the said Village of Tilbury Centre, comprised within the bury Centre,
boundaries in section two of this Act mentioned, shall be, and incorporated.
they are hereby constituted a body corporate, separate and
apart from the Townships of Tilbury East and Tilbury West,
20 in which the said village is now situate, under the name of
" The Corporation of the Village of Tilbury Centre," and shall
enjoy all such rights, powers, and privileges as are now, or
shall hereafter, be conferred upon incorporated villages in the
Province of Ontario.

25   **2.** The said Village of Tilbury Centre shall be contained Boundaries.
within the following limits, namely :—Commencing at the
north-east angle of lot number twenty-two, in the third concession of the Township of Tilbury West ; thence west, following the northerly limit of said lot twenty-two, seven chains,
30 fifty links ; thence south, parallel with the road allowance
between said townships, fifty chains, more or less, to the centre
line of the south half of lot twenty-two ; thence west twenty-
two chains, fifty links, more or less, to the limit between lots
numbered twenty-one and twenty-two ; thence south, following
35 said limit, sixteen chains, sixty-seven links, more or less, to the
north side of the fourth concession road ; thence south, following said limit produced, and the limit between lots twenty-one
and twenty-two in the fourth concession, thirty-six chains,
eighty-nine links, more or less, to the north side of the road in
40 rear of the middle road lots ; thence south, following said
limit produced and the limit between lots twenty-one and
twenty-two north of the middle road, seventeen chains, sixty-
seven links, more or less, to the centre line of the north half of
lot twenty-two ; thence easterly, parallel with the said rear

road, twenty-five chains, eighty-seven links, more or less, to the centre line of the east half of lot twenty-two ; thence south, parallel with the town line, fifty chains, more or less, to the northerly limit of the middle road ; thence easterly, following said northerly limit, eight chains, sixty-two links, more or less, 5 to the west limit of the town line ; thence easterly, following said northerly limit of the middle road, ten chains, eighty links, more or less, to the limit between lots twenty-seven and twenty-eight, north of the middle road, in the Township of Tilbury East ; thence north, following the limit 10 between lots twenty-seven and twenty-eight, thirty-three chains, thirty-four links, more or less, to the centre line between the middle road and the road in the rear of the middle road lots ; thence easterly, following said centre line, thirty-four chains, sixty links, more or less, to the limit 15 between lots twenty-six and twenty-seven ; thence north, following the limit between said lots and said limit produced, thirty-four chains, thirty-four links, more or less, to the northerly limit of the road in rear of the middle road lots ; thence easterly, following said northerly limit, fifteen chains, 20 eight links, more or less, to the limit between lots sixteen and seventeen in the fifth concession ; thence north, forty-five degrees west, following the limit between lots sixteen and seventeen and said limit produced, seven chains, more or less, to the northerly limit of the fifth concession road ; thence 25 northerly, following the limit between lots sixteen and seventeen in the fourth concession, sixteen chains, sixty-seven links ; thence south, forty-five degrees west, parallel with the fifth concession road, fifteen chains ; thence north, forty-five degrees west, sixteen chains, sixty-seven links, more or less, to the 30 centre line of the fourth concession ; thence south, forty-five degrees west, parallel with the fifth concession road, seven chains, more or less, to a point seven chains and fifty links from the east side of the town line, and measured on a course at right angles to said town line ; thence north, parallel with 35 the aforesaid town line, forty-four chains, more or less, to the southerly limit of the fourth concession road ; thence westerly, following said limit and said limit produced, twelve chains, more or less, to the west limit of the town line ; thence north, following said west limit, seven chains, seven links, more or less, 40 to the place of beginning ; containing by admeasurement five hundred and seventy-seven acres, more or less.

First election of council. **3.** Immediately after the passing of this Act it shall be lawful for Frederic Ernest Nelles, of the said Village of Tilbury Centre, who is hereby appointed the returning officer, to hold 45 the nomination for the first election of reeve and four councillors at Victoria Hall, or some other prominent place in the said village, at the hour of noon, and he shall give at least one week's notice thereof, by causing at least ten notices to be posted up in conspicuous places in said village, and one inser- 50 tion in a newspaper published in the village ; and he shall preside at such nomination, or in case of his absence the electors present shall choose from among themselves a chairman, who shall officiate and shall have all powers of a returning officer ; and the polling for the said election, in the event of there being a 55 poll required, shall be held on the same day of the week in the week next following the said nomination, and at the same

place, and the duties of the returning officer shall be those prescribed by law with respect to incorporated villages.

4. At the first election the qualification of the electors, and Qualification of electors, etc.
of the reeve and councillors for the said village, shall be the
5 same as that required in townships, and at all subsequent
elections the qualification of the reeve, councillors, and other
officers, shall be the same as that required in incorporated
villages.

5. The township clerks of the Township of Tilbury East, Copies of as-sessment rolls
10 and the Township of Tilbury West, shall furnish the return- to be furnished
ing officer, upon demand being made upon them for the same, on demand of
with certified copies of so much of the last revised assessment the returning
rolls of the said townships as may be required to ascertain the officer.
names of persons entitled to vote at such first election, or with
15 the collector's roll, or any other writing or statement that may
be necessary for that purpose.

6. The reeve and councillors, so to be elected, shall hold their First meeting
first meeting at Victoria Hall, in the said village, at the hour of council.
of noon, on the same day of the week in the week next follow-
20 ing the polling, or if there be no polling on the same day of the
week, in the week next following the nomination.

7. Except, as otherwise provided by this Act, the provisions Acts respect-ing municipal
of *The Consolidated Municipal Act, 1883*, and of all other institutions to
general Acts respecting municipal institutions, with regard to apply unless
25 matters consequent on the formation of new corporations and otherwise pro-
other provisions of the said Acts applicable to incorporated vided.
villages, shall apply to the Village of Tilbury Centre, in the
same manner as they would have been applicable, had the said
Village of Tilbury Centre been incorporated under the pro-
30 visions of the said Act.

8. The said Village of Tilbury Centre shall be liable to pay Payment of
to the treasurer of each of the Townships of Tilbury East and existing liabili-ties.
Tilbury West, in each and every year, such and the same pro-
portion of any debts contracted by the said townships, or either
35 of them, prior to the present year, as the amount of the
assessed property for each township within the limits of the
said village, as shown by the assessment rolls of the said Townships of Tilbury East and Tilbury West, for the year of Our
Lord, 1886, bears to the whole amount of the assessed property,
40 of the said townships respectively. until such debts shall be
fully satisfied, and the parts of the said village situated in the
Townships of Tilbury East and Tilbury West, respectively,
shall contribute towards the payment of the said debts, in the
same proportion as if this Act had not been passed, and for
45 that purpose special rates shall be levied ; and the council of
the said Village of Tilbury Centre shall be entitled to recover
from the said Townships of Tilbury East and Tilbury West
respectively, such shares of all money on hand, due, or owing,
or of right collectable by, and belonging to the said townships
50 respectively, at and prior to the said time of incorporation, or
thereafter, if entitled thereto, as shall bear such proportions to
the whole, as the amounts of the assessed property within the
limits of the said village, as shown by the said assessment rolls

of the year 1886 bears to the whole amount of the assessed property of the said townships respectively.

Village separated from Townships of Tilbury East and Tilbury West. **9.** From and after the passing of this Act the said village shall cease to form part of the Townships of Tilbury East and Tilbury West, and shall, to all intents and purposes, form a 5 separate and independent municipality in the County of Kent and said Province of Ontario, with all the rights, privileges, and jurisdiction of an incorporated village in Ontario.

Expenses of Act. **10.** The expenses of obtaining this Act, and of furnishing any documents, copies of papers, writings, deeds, or any matter 10 whatsoever required by the clerk of the said village, or otherwise, shall be borne by the said village, and paid by it to any party, or parties, that may be entitled thereto.

Qualification of members of councils of Tilbury East and Tilbury West for 1887, not affected. **11.** Nothing in this Act contained shall have the effect of disqualifying any member of the municipal councils of the said 15 Townships of Tilbury East and Tilbury West, or either of them, from holding office in said councils during the current year.

Liquor licenses. **12.** Notwithstanding the provisions of *The Liquor License Act*, the License Commissioners may, subject to the provisions 20 of any by-law of the municipality, grant as many tavern licenses in the said corporation as there are in the said village, at the time of the passing of this Act, namely, four, subject to the statutory conditions as to accommodation.

No. 9.

1st Session, 6th Legislature, 50 Vic., 1886.

BILL.

An Act to incorporate the Village of Tilbury Centre.

First Reading,   , 1887.

(Private Bill.)

Mr. BALFOUR.

TORONTO:
PRINTED BY WARWICK & SONS, 26 AND 28 FRONT ST. W.

BILL.

An Act to incorporate the Village of Tilbury Centre.

WHEREAS the inhabitants of the village of Tilbury Preamble. Centre have by their petition represented that the said village has a population of over eight hundred and fifty souls, and by reason of the rapid increase of the population of said 5 village, and owing to its situation and location, which will likely cause it to attract the trade of a large, populous and wealthy section of country, and in compliance with a resolution passed at a public meeting duly convened to consider the matter of incorporation, and numerously attended, have prayed 10 for its incorporation accordingly ; and whereas it is expedient to grant the prayer of the said petition ;

Therefore Her Majesty, by and with the advice and consent of the Legislative Assembly of the Province of Ontario, enacts as follows :—

15 **1.** On and after the passing of this Act the inhabitants of Village of Til-the said village of Tilbury Centre, comprised within the bury Centre, incorporated. boundaries in section 2 of this Act mentioned, shall be, and they are hereby constituted a *corporation and* body corporate, separate and apart from the townships of Tilbury East and 20 Tilbury West, in which the said village is now situate, under the name of "The Corporation of the Village of Tilbury Centre," and shall enjoy all such rights, powers, and privileges as are now, or shall hereafter, be conferred upon incorporated villages in the Province of Ontario.

25 **2.** The said village of Tilbury Centre shall be contained Boundaries. within the following limits, namely :—Commencing at the north-east angle of lot number twenty-two, in the third concession of the township of Tilbury West ; thence west, following the northerly limit of said lot twenty-two, seven chains, 30 fifty links ; thence south, parallel with the road allowance between said townships, fifty chains, more or less, to the centre line of the south half of lot twenty-two ; thence west twenty-two chains, fifty links, more or less, to the limit between lots numbered twenty-one and twenty-two ; thence south, following 35 said limit, sixteen chains, sixty-seven links, more or less, to the north side of the fourth concession road ; thence south, following said limit produced, and the limit between lots twenty-one and twenty-two in the fourth concession, thirty-six chains, eighty-nine links, more or less, to the north side of the road in 40 rear of the middle road lots ; thence south, following said limit produced and the limit between lots twenty-one and twenty-two north of the middle road, seventeen chains, sixty-seven links, more or less, to the centre line of the north half of lot twenty-two ; thence easterly, parallel with the said rear

road, twenty-five chains, eighty-seven links, more or less, to the centre line of the east half of lot twenty-two ; thence south, parallel with the town line, fifty chains, more or less, to the northerly limit of the middle road ; thence easterly, following said northerly limit, eight chains, sixty-two links, more or less, 5 to the west limit of the town line ; thence easterly, following said northerly limit of the middle road, ten chains, eighty links, more or less, to the limit between lots twenty-seven and twenty-eight, north of the middle road, in the township of Tilbury East ; thence north, following the limit 10 between lots twenty-seven and twenty-eight, thirty-three chains, thirty-four links, more or less, to the centre line between the middle road and the road in the rear of the middle road lots ; thence easterly, following said centre line, thirty-four chains, sixty links, more or less, to the limit 15 between lots twenty-six and twenty-seven ; thence north, following the limit between said lots and said limit produced, thirty-four chains, thirty-four links, more or less, to the northerly limit of the road in rear of the middle road lots ; thence easterly, following said northerly limit, fifteen chains, 20 eight links, more or less, to the limit between lots sixteen and seventeen in the fifth concession ; thence north, forty-five degrees west, following the limit between lots sixteen and seventeen and said limit produced, seven chains, more or less, to the northerly limit of the fifth concession road ; thence 25 northerly, following the limit between lots sixteen and seventeen in the fourth concession, sixteen chains, sixty-seven links ; thence south, forty-five degrees west, parallel with the fifth concession road, fifteen chains ; thence north, forty-five degrees west, sixteen chains, sixty-seven links, more or less, to the 30 centre line of the fourth concession ; thence south, forty-five degrees west, parallel with the fifth concession road, seven chains, more or less, to a point seven chains and fifty links from the east side of the town line, and measured on a course at right angles to said town line ; thence north, parallel with 35 the aforesaid town line, forty-four chains, more or less, to the southerly limit of the fourth concession road ; thence westerly, following said limit and said limit produced, twelve chains, more or less, to the west limit of the town line ; thence north, following said west limit, seven chains, seven links, more or less, 40 to the place of beginning ; containing by admeasurement five hundred and seventy-seven acres, more or less.

First election
of council.

3. Immediately after the passing of this Act it shall be lawful for Frederic Ernest Nelles, of the said village of Tilbury Centre, who is hereby appointed the returning officer, to hold 45 the nomination for the first election of reeve and four councillors at Victoria Hall, or some other prominent place in the said village, at the hour of noon, and he shall give at least one week's notice thereof, by causing at least ten notices to be posted up in conspicuous places in said village, and one inser- 50 tion in a newspaper published in the village ; and he shall preside at such nomination, or in case of his absence the electors present shall choose from among themselves a chairman, who shall officiate and shall have all powers of a returning officer; and the polling for the said election, in the event of there being a 55 poll required, shall be held on the same day of the week in the week next following the said nomination, and at the same place, and the duties of the returning officer shall be those prescribed by law with respect to incorporated villages.

4. At the first election the qualification of the electors, and Qualification of the reeve and councillors for the said village, shall be the of electors, etc.
5 same as that required in townships, and at all subsequent
elections the qualification of the *electors*, reeve, councillors, and
other officers, shall be the same as that required in incorporated villages.

5. The township clerks of the township of Tilbury East, Copies of as-
10 and the township of Tilbury West, shall furnish the return- sessment rolls to be furnished
ing officer, upon demand being made upon them for the same, on demand of
with certified copies of so much of the last revised assessment the returning
rolls of the said townships as may be required to ascertain the officer.
names of persons entitled to vote at such first election, or with
15 the collector's roll, or any other writing or statement that may
be necessary for that purpose.

6. The reeve and councillors, so to be elected, shall hold their First meeting
first meeting at Victoria Hall, in the said village, at the hour of council.
of noon, on the same day of the week in the week next follow-
20 ing the polling, or if there be no polling on the same day of the
week, in the week next following the nomination.

7. Except, as otherwise provided by this Act, the provisions Acts respect-
of *The Consolidated Municipal Act, 1883*, and of all other ing municipal institutions to
general Acts respecting municipal institutions, with regard to apply unless
25 matters consequent on the formation of new corporations and otherwise pro-
other provisions of the said Acts applicable to incorporated vided.
villages, shall apply to the village of Tilbury Centre, in the
same manner as they would have been applicable, had the said
village of Tilbury Centre been incorporated under the pro-
30 visions of the said Act.

8. The said village of Tilbury Centre shall be liable to pay Payment of
to the treasurer of each of the townships of Tilbury East and existing liabili ties.
Tilbury West, in each and every year, such and the same pro-
portion of any debts contracted by the said townships, or either
35 of them, prior to the present year, as the amount of the
assessed property for each township within the limits of the
said village, as shown by the assessment rolls of the said townships of Tilbury East and Tilbury West, for the year of Our
Lord, 1886, bears to the whole amount of the assessed property,
40 of the said townships respectively, until such debts shall be
fully satisfied, and the parts of the said village situated in the
townships of Tilbury East and Tilbury West, respectively,
shall contribute towards the payment of the said debts, in the
same proportion as if this Act had not been passed, and for
45 that purpose special rates shall be levied; and the council of
the said village of Tilbury Centre shall be entitled to recover
from the said townships of Tilbury East and Tilbury West
respectively, such shares of all money on hand, due, or owing,
or of right collectable by, and belonging to the said townships
50 respectively, at and prior to the said time of incorporation, or
thereafter, if entitled thereto, as shall bear such proportions to
the whole, as the amounts of the assessed property within the
limits of the said village, as shown by the said assessment rolls

of the year 1886 bear to the whole amount of the assessed
property of the said townships respectively.

Village sepa-
rated from
townships of
Tilbury East
and Tilbury
West.

9. From and after the passing of this Act the said village
shall cease to form part of the townships of Tilbury East and
Tilbury West, and shall, to all intents and purposes, form a 5
separate and independent municipality in the county of Kent
and said Province of Ontario, with all the rights, privileges,
and jurisdiction of an incorporated village in Ontario, ☞and
shall for the purpose of elections to the Legislative Assembly
of Ontario form part of the Electoral District of the West 10
Riding of the County of Kent.☜

Expenses of
Act.

10. The expenses of obtaining this Act, and of furnishing
any documents, copies of papers, writings, deeds, or any matter
whatsoever required by the clerk of the said village, or otherwise, shall be borne by the said village, and paid by it to any 15
party, or parties, that may be entitled thereto.

Qualification
of members of
councils of
Tilbury East
and Tilbury
West for 1887,
not affected.

11. Nothing in this Act contained shall have the effect of
disqualifying any member of the municipal councils of the said
townships of Tilbury East and Tilbury West, or either of
them, from holding office in said councils during the current 20
year.

BILL.

An Act to incorporate the Village of
Tilbury Centre.

*(Reprinted as amended by Private Bills
Committee).*

First Reading, 9th March, 1887.

(Private Bill.)

BILL.

An Act to incorporate the Village of Tilbury Centre.

WHEREAS the inhabitants of the village of Tilbury Preamble.
Centre have by their petition represented that the said
village has a population of over eight hundred and fifty souls,
and by reason of the rapid increase of the population of said
5 village, and owing to its situation and location, which will
likely cause it to attract the trade of a large, populous and
wealthy section of country, and in compliance with a resolution passed at a public meeting duly convened to consider the
matter of incorporation, and numerously attended, have prayed
10 for its incorporation accordingly ; and whereas it is expedient
to grant the prayer of the said petition ;

Therefore Her Majesty, by and with the advice and consent
of the Legislative Assembly of the Province of Ontario, enacts
as follows :—

15 **1.** On and after the passing of this Act the inhabitants of Village of Til-
the said village of Tilbury Centre, comprised within the bury Centre,
boundaries in section 2 of this Act mentioned, shall be, and incorporated.
they are hereby constituted a *corporation and* body corporate,
separate and apart from the townships of Tilbury East and
20 Tilbury West, in which the said village is now situate, under
the name of "The Corporation of the Village of Tilbury
Centre," and shall enjoy all such rights, powers, and privileges as are now, or shall hereafter, be conferred upon incorporated villages in the Province of Ontario.

25 **2.** The said village of Tilbury Centre shall be contained Boundaries.
within the following limits, namely :—Commencing at the
north-east angle of lot number twenty-two, in the third concession of the township of Tilbury West ; thence west, following the northerly limit of said lot twenty-two, seven chains,
30 fifty links ; thence south, parallel with the road allowance
between said townships, fifty chains, more or less, to the centre
line of the south half of lot twenty-two ; thence west twenty-
two chains, fifty links, more or less, to the limit between lots
numbered twenty-one and twenty-two ; thence south, following
35 said limit, sixteen chains, sixty-seven links, more or less, to the
north side of the fourth concession road ; thence south, following said limit produced, and the limit between lots twenty-one
and twenty-two in the fourth concession, thirty-six chains,
eighty-nine links, more or less, to the north side of the road in
40 rear of the middle road lots ; thence south, following said
limit produced and the limit between lots twenty-one and
twenty-two north of the middle road, seventeen chains, sixty-
seven links, more or less, to the centre line of the north half of
lot twenty-two ; thence easterly, parallel with the said rear

road, twenty-five chains, eighty-seven links, more or less, to
the centre line of the east half of lot twenty-two ; thence south,
parallel with the town line, fifty chains, more or less, to the
northerly limit of the middle road ; thence easterly, following
said northerly limit, eight chains, sixty-two links, more or less, 5
to the west limit of the town line ; thence easterly, following
said northerly limit of the middle road, ten chains, eighty
links, more or less, to the limit between lots twenty-seven
and twenty-eight, north of the middle road, in the township of Tilbury East; thence north, following the limit 10
between lots twenty-seven and twenty-eight, thirty-three
chains, thirty-four links, more or less, to the centre line
between the middle road and the road in the rear of the
middle road lots ; thence easterly, following said centre
line, thirty-four chains, sixty links, more or less, to the limit 15
between lots twenty-six and twenty-seven ; thence north, following the limit between said lots and said limit produced,
thirty-four chains, thirty-four links, more or less, to the
northerly limit of the road in rear of the middle road lots ;
thence easterly, following said northerly limit, fifteen chains, 20
eight links, more or less, to the limit between lots sixteen and
seventeen in the fifth concession ; thence north, forty-five
degrees west, following the limit between lots sixteen and
seventeen and said limit produced, seven chains, more or less,
to the northerly limit of the fifth concession road ; thence 25
northerly, following the limit between lots sixteen and seventeen in the fourth concession, sixteen chains, sixty-seven links ;
thence south, forty-five degrees west, parallel with the fifth
concession road, fifteen chains ; thence north, forty-five degrees
west, sixteen chains, sixty-seven links, more or less, to the 30
centre line of the fourth concession ; thence south, forty-five
degrees west, parallel with the fifth concession road, seven
chains, more or less, to a point seven chains and fifty links
from the east side of the town line, and measured on a course
at right angles to said town line ; thence north, parallel with 35
the aforesaid town line, forty-four chains, more or less, to the
southerly limit of the fourth concession road ; thence westerly,
following said limit and said limit produced, twelve chains,
more or less, to the west limit of the town line ; thence north,
following said west limit, seven chains, seven links, more or less, 40
to the place of beginning; containing by admeasurement five
hundred and seventy-seven acres, more or less.

First election of council.

3. Immediately after the passing of this Act it shall be lawful for Frederic Ernest Nelles, of the said village of Tilbury
Centre, who is hereby appointed the returning officer, to hold 45
the nomination for the first election of reeve and four councillors at Victoria Hall, or some other prominent place in the
said village, at the hour of noon, and he shall give at least one
week's notice thereof, by causing at least ten notices to be
posted up in conspicuous places in said village, and one inser- 50
tion in a newspaper published in the village ; and he shall
preside at such nomination, or in case of his absence the electors
present shall choose from among themselves a chairman, who
shall officiate and shall have all powers of a returning officer; and
the polling for the said election, in the event of there being a 55
poll required, shall be held on the same day of the week in the
week next following the said nomination, and at the same

place, and the duties of the returning officer shall be those prescribed by law with respect to incorporated villages.

4. At the first election the qualification of the electors, and Qualification
of the reeve and councillors for the said village, shall be the of electors,
5 same as that required in townships, and at all subsequent etc.
elections the qualification of the *electors*, reeve, councillors, and
other officers, shall be the same as that required in incorporated villages.

5. The township clerks of the township of Tilbury East, Copies of as-
10 and the township of Tilbury West, shall furnish the return- sessment rolls
ing officer, upon demand being made upon them for the same, to be furnished
with certified copies of so much of the last revised assessment the returning
rolls of the said townships as may be required to ascertain the officer.
names of persons entitled to vote at such first election, or with
15 the collector's roll, or any other writing or statement that may
be necessary for that purpose.

6. The reeve and councillors, so to be elected, shall hold their First meeting
first meeting at Victoria Hall, in the said village, at the hour of council.
of noon, on the same day of the week in the week next follow-
20 ing the polling, or if there be no polling on the same day of the
week, in the week next following the nomination.

7. Except, as otherwise provided by this Act, the provisions Acts respect-
of *The Consolidated Municipal Act 1883*, and of all other ing municipal
institutions to
general Acts respecting municipal institutions, with regard to apply unless
25 matters consequent on the formation of new corporations and otherwise pro-
other provisions of the said Acts applicable to incorporated vided.
villages, shall apply to the village of Tilbury Centre, in the
same manner as they would have been applicable, had the said
village of Tilbury Centre been incorporated under the pro-
30 visions of the said Act.

8. The said village of Tilbury Centre shall be liable to pay Payment of
to the treasurer of each of the townships of Tilbury East and existing liabili
ties.
Tilbury West, in each and every year, such and the same proportion of any debts contracted by the said townships, or either
35 of them, prior to the present year, as the amount of the
assessed property for each township within the limits of the
said village, as shown by the assessment rolls of the said townships of Tilbury East and Tilbury West, for the year of Our
Lord, 1886, bears to the whole amount of the assessed property,
40 of the said townships respectively until such debts shall be
fully satisfied, and the parts of the said village situated in the
townships of Tilbury East and Tilbury West, respectively,
shall contribute towards the payment of the said debts, in the
same proportion as if this Act had not been passed, and for
45 that purpose special rates shall be levied ; and the council of
the said village of Tilbury Centre shall be entitled to recover
from the said townships of Tilbury East and Tilbury West
respectively, such shares of all money on hand, due, or owing,
or of right collectable by, and belonging to the said townships
50 respectively, at and prior to the said time of incorporation, or
thereafter, if entitled thereto, as shall bear such proportions to
the whole, as the amounts of the assessed property within the
limits of the said village, as shown by the said assessment rolls

of the year 1886 bear to the whole amount of the assessed property of the said townships respectively.

Village separated from townships of Tilbury East and Tilbury West.

9. From and after the passing of this Act, the said village shall cease to form part of the townships of Tilbury East and Tilbury West, and shall, to all intents and purposes, form a 5 separate and independent municipality in the county of *Essex* and said Province of Ontario, with all the rights, privileges, and jurisdiction of an incorporated village in Ontario, ☞and shall for the purpose of elections to the Legislative Assembly of Ontario form part of the Electoral District of the South 10 Riding of the County of Essex.

Agricultural Society.

☞**10.** Notwithstanding any of the provisions of *The Agriculture and Arts Act,* the Agricultural Society of the Township of Tilbury East may hold their meetings, or exhibitions, or such of them as they may desire, in the said village of Til- 15 bury Centre, and may purchase such lands and erect such buildings thereon within the said village as are authorized to be purchased and held by any Township Agricultural Society.

Expenses of Act.

11. The expenses of obtaining this Act, and of furnishing 20 any documents, copies of papers, writings, deeds, or any matter whatsoever required by the clerk of the said village, or otherwise, shall be borne by the said village, and paid by it to any party, or parties, that may be entitled thereto.

Qualification of members of councils of Tilbury East and Tilbury West for 1887, not affected.

12. Nothing in this Act contained shall have the effect of 25 disqualifying any member of the municipal councils of the said townships of Tilbury East and Tilbury West, or either of them, from holding office in said councils during the current year.

Liquor licenses.

☞**13.** Notwithstanding the provisions of *The Liquor License* 30 *Act,* the License Commissioners may, subject to the provisions of any by-law of the Municipality, grant as many tavern licenses in the said corporation for the ensuing license year as there are in the said village, at the time of the passing of this Act, namely, four, subject to the statutory conditions as to 35 accommodation.

1st Session, 6th Legislature, 50 Vic., 1887.

BILL.

An Act to incorporate the Village of Tilbury Centre.

(Reprinted as referred back to and again amended by Private Bills Committee).

First Reading, 9th March, 1887.

(Private Bill.)

BILL.

An Act to incorporate the Village of Tilbury Centre.

WHEREAS the inhabitants of the village of Tilbury Preamble. Centre have by their petition represented that the said village has a population of over eight hundred and fifty souls, and by reason of the rapid increase of the population of said 5 village, and owing to its situation and location, which will likely cause it to attract the trade of a large, populous and wealthy section of country, and in compliance with a resolution passed at a public meeting duly convened to consider the matter of incorporation, and numerously attended, have prayed 10 for its incorporation accordingly ; and whereas it is expedient to grant the prayer of the said petition ;

Therefore Her Majesty, by and with the advice and consent of the Legislative Assembly of the Province of Ontario, enacts as follows :—

15 **1.** On and after the passing of this Act the inhabitants of Village of Tilbury Centre, incorporated. the said village of Tilbury Centre, comprised within the boundaries in section 2 of this Act mentioned, shall be, and they are hereby constituted a *corporation and* body corporate, separate and apart from the townships of Tilbury East and 20 Tilbury West, in which the said village is now situate, under the name of " The Corporation of the Village of Tilbury Centre," and shall enjoy all such rights, powers, and privileges as are now, or shall hereafter, be conferred upon incorporated villages in the Province of Ontario.

25 **2.** The said village of Tilbury Centre shall be contained Boundaries. within the following limits, namely :—Commencing at the north-east angle of lot number twenty-two, in the third concession of the township of Tilbury West ; thence west, following the northerly limit of said lot twenty-two, seven chains, 30 fifty links ; thence south, parallel with the road allowance between said townships, fifty chains, more or less, to the centre line of the south half of lot twenty-two ; thence west twenty-two chains, fifty links, more or less, to the limit between lots numbered twenty-one and twenty-two ; thence south, following 35 said limit, sixteen chains, sixty-seven links, more or less, to the north side of the fourth concession road ; thence south, following said limit produced, and the limit between lots twenty-one and twenty-two in the fourth concession, thirty-six chains, eighty-nine links, more or less, to the north side of the road in 40 rear of the middle road lots ; thence south, following said limit produced and the limit between lots twenty-one and twenty-two north of the middle road, seventeen chains, sixty-seven links, more or less, to the centre line of the north half of lot twenty-two ; thence easterly, parallel with the said rear

road, twenty-five chains, eighty-seven links, more or less, to
the centre line of the east half of lot twenty-two ; thence south,
parallel with the town line, fifty chains, more or less, to the
northerly limit of the middle road ; thence easterly, following
said northerly limit, eight chains, sixty-two links, more or less, 5
to the west limit of the town line ; thence easterly, following
said northerly limit of the middle road, ten chains, eighty
links, more or less, to the limit between lots twenty-seven
and twenty-eight, north of the middle road, in the township of Tilbury East ; thence north, following the limit 10
between lots twenty-seven and twenty-eight, thirty-three
chains, thirty-four links, more or less, to the centre line
between the middle road and the road in the rear of the
middle road lots ; thence easterly, following said centre
line, thirty-four chains, sixty links, more or less, to the limit 15
between lots twenty-six and twenty-seven ; thence north, following the limit between said lots and said limit produced,
thirty-four chains, thirty-four links, more or less, to the
northerly limit of the road in rear of the middle road lots ;
thence easterly, following said northerly limit, fifteen chains, 20
eight links, more or less, to the limit between lots sixteen and
seventeen in the fifth concession ; thence north, forty-five
degrees west, following the limit between lots sixteen and
seventeen and said limit produced, seven chains, more or less,
to the northerly limit of the fifth concession road ; thence 25
northerly, following the limit between lots sixteen and seventeen in the fourth concession, sixteen chains, sixty-seven links ;
thence south, forty-five degrees west, parallel with the fifth
concession road, fifteen chains ; thence north, forty-five degrees
west, sixteen chains, sixty-seven links, more or less, to the 30
centre line of the fourth concession ; thence south, forty-five
degrees west, parallel with the fifth concession road, seven
chains, more or less, to a point seven chains and fifty links
from the east side of the town line, and measured on a course
at right angles to said town line ; thence north, parallel with 35
the aforesaid town line, forty-four chains, more or less, to the
southerly limit of the fourth concession road ; thence westerly,
following said limit and said limit produced, twelve chains,
more or less, to the west limit of the town line ; thence north,
following said west limit, seven chains, seven links, more or less, 40
to the place of beginning ; containing by admeasurement five
hundred and seventy-seven acres, more or less.

First election of council. **3.** Immediately after the passing of this Act it shall be lawful for Frederic Ernest Nelles, of the said village of Tilbury
Centre, who is hereby appointed the returning officer, to hold 45
the nomination for the first election of reeve and four councillors at Victoria Hall, or some other prominent place in the
said village, at the hour of noon, and he shall give at least one
week's notice thereof, by causing at least ten notices to be
posted up in conspicuous places in said village, and one inser- 50
tion in a newspaper published in the village ; and he shall
preside at such nomination, or in case of his absence the electors
present shall choose from among themselves a chairman, who
shall officiate and shall have all powers of a returning officer ; and
the polling for the said election, in the event of there being a 55
poll required, shall be held on the same day of the week in the
week next following the said nomination, and at the same

place, and the duties of the returning officer shall be those prescribed by law with respect to incorporated villages.

4. At the first election the qualification of the electors, and of the reeve and councillors for the said village, shall be the 5 same as that required in townships, and at all subsequent elections the qualification of the *electors*, reeve, councillors, and other officers, shall be the same as that required in incorporated villages. Qualification of electors, etc.

5. The township clerks of the township of Tilbury East, 10 and the township of Tilbury West, shall furnish the returning officer, upon demand being made upon them for the same, with certified copies of so much of the last revised assessment rolls of the said townships as may be required to ascertain the names of persons entitled to vote at such first election, or with 15 the collector's roll, or any other writing or statement that may be necessary for that purpose. Copies of assessment rolls to be furnished on demand of the returning officer.

6. The reeve and councillors, so to be elected, shall hold their first meeting at Victoria Hall, in the said village, at the hour of noon, on the same day of the week in the week next follow- 20 ing the polling, or if there be no polling on the same day of the week, in the week next following the nomination. First meeting of council.

7. Except, as otherwise provided by this Act, the provisions of *The Consolidated Municipal Act, 1883*, and of all other general Acts respecting municipal institutions, with regard to 25 matters consequent on the formation of new corporations and other provisions of the said Acts applicable to incorporated villages, shall apply to the village of Tilbury Centre, in the same manner as they would have been applicable, had the said village of Tilbury Centre been incorporated under the pro- 30 visions of the said Act. Acts respecting municipal institutions to apply unless otherwise provided.

8. The said village of Tilbury Centre shall be liable to pay to the treasurer of each of the townships of Tilbury East and Tilbury West, in each and every year, such and the same proportion of any debts contracted by the said townships, or either 35 of them, prior to the present year, as the amount of the assessed property for each township within the limits of the said village, as shewn by the assessment rolls of the said townships of Tilbury East and Tilbury West, for the year of Our Lord, 1886, bears to the whole amount of the assessed property, 40 of the said townships respectively. until such debts shall be fully satisfied, and the parts of the said village situated in the townships of Tilbury East and Tilbury West, respectively, shall contribute towards the payment of the said debts, in the same proportion as if this Act had not been passed, and for 45 that purpose special rates shall be levied ; and the council of the said village of Tilbury Centre shall be entitled to recover from the said townships of Tilbury East and Tilbury West respectively, such shares of all money on hand, due, or owing, or of right collectable by, and belonging to the said townships 50 respectively, at and prior to the said time of incorporation, or thereafter, if entitled thereto, as shall bear such proportions to the whole, as the amounts of the assessed property within the limits of the said village, as shewn by the said assessment rolls Payment of existing liabilities.

of the year 1886 bear to the whole amount of the assessed property of the said townships respectively.

Village separated from townships of Tilbury East and Tilbury West.

9. From and after the passing of this Act, the said village shall cease to form part of the townships of Tilbury East and Tilbury West, and shall, to all intents and purposes, form a 5 separate and independent municipality in the county of *Kent* and said Province of Ontario, with all the rights, privileges, and jurisdiction of an incorporated village in Ontario, ☞ and shall for the purpose of elections to the Legislative Assembly of Ontario form part of the Electoral District of the *West* 10 Riding of the County of *Kent.*☞

Assessment for year 1887.

☞ **10.** The time for taking the assessment in the said village of Tilbury Centre for the year 1887, and for the return of the assessment roll to the clerk of the municipality is hereby extended to the first day of July, and the time for revision shall 15 be the same as in cases provided for by sub-section 2 of section 46 of *The Assessment Act;* and the property within the limits of the said village shall not be liable for any rates levied by the corporations of the townships of Tilbury East and Tilbury West on the assessments made by the said townships for the 20 year 1887.☞

Expenses of Act.

11. The expenses of obtaining this Act, and of furnishing any documents, copies of papers, writings, deeds, or any matter whatsoever required by the clerk of the said village, or otherwise, shall be borne by the said village, and paid by it to any 25 party, or parties, that may be entitled thereto.

Qualification of members of councils of Tilbury East and Tilbury West for 1887, not affected.

12. Nothing in this Act contained shall have the effect of disqualifying any member of the municipal councils of the said townships of Tilbury East and Tilbury West, or either of them, from holding office in said councils during the current 30 year.

Liquor licenses.

☞ **13.** For the purposes of *The Liquor License Acts* and *The Canada Temperance Act* that part of the village hereby incorporated which lies in the township of Tilbury West shall continue to be part of the said township, and shall not be part 35 of the county of Kent; subject to any by-law of the Village Council, the License Commissioners may grant licenses to as many taverns in that part of the village so now lying in the township of Tilbury West as have licenses now, but the said village shall be entitled to the share of license fees payable to 40 the municipality on account of licenses issued within the limits thereof.☞

1st Session, 6th Legislature, 50 Vic., 1887.

BILL.

An Act to incorporate the Village of Tilbury Centre.

(*Reprinted as amended by Committee of the Whole House.*)

First Reading, 9th March, 1887.
Second " 6th April, 1887.

(Private Bill.)

BILL.

An Act to further extend the powers of the Consumers' Gas Company of Toronto.

WHEREAS the Consumers' Gas Company of Toronto have Preamble.
petitioned for authority to increase the capital stock of
the said Company and the amount of their real estate, to meet
the requirements of the rapidly increasing population of the
5 City of Toronto, and it is expedient to grant the prayer of the
said petition ;
Therefore Her Majesty, by and with the advice and consent
of the Legislative Assembly of the Province of Ontario, enacts
as follows :—

10 **1**. It shall be lawful for the said Company to add to their Increase of
present capital stock such an amount as shall increase the capital stock
same to a sum not exceeding $2,000,000, divided into shares authorized.
of $50 each, provided that such increase of capital stock shall
be first agreed upon by a majority of the votes of the share-
15 holders present at any annual general meeting or meetings or
at any special meeting or meetings called from time to time
for that purpose, and any new stock forming part of any
increase of capital stock made under the authority of this Act
shall be dealt with in all respects as if the same formed part
20 of the last increase of capital stock of said Company made
under the authority of this Legislature prior to the passing of
this Act.

2. All the provisions of the Act incorporating the Company Former Acts
and the Acts amending the same applicable to the present to apply to
25 stock of the Company, not inconsistent with the provisions of new stock.
this Act, shall apply to the new stock authorized to be issued
under this Act.

3. Notwithstanding anything contained in former Acts Power to hold
affecting the Company, it shall be lawful for the Company to real estate of
30 hold real estate, of which the total yearly value shall not value.
exceed $20,000 over and above the yearly value of any build-
ings and works now or hereafter erected thereon.

1st Session, 6th Legislature, 50 Vic., 1887

BILL.

An Act to further extend the powers of the Consumers' Gas Company of Toronto.

First Reading. 1887.

(Private Bill.)

No. 10.] **BILL.** [1887.

An Act to further extend the powers of the Consumers' Gas Company of Toronto.

WHEREAS the Consumers' Gas Company of Toronto have Preamble.
petitioned for authority to increase the capital stock of
the said company and the amount of their real estate, to meet
the requirements of the rapidly increasing population of the
5 City of Toronto, and it is expedient to grant the prayer of the
said petition ;
   Therefore Her Majesty, by and with the advice and consent
of the Legislative Assembly of the Province of Ontario, enacts
as follows :—

10 ☞ **1.** It shall be lawful for the company to add to their Increase of capital stock authorized.
present capital stock such an amount as shall increase the
same to a sum not exceeding $2,000,000, divided into shares
of $50 each, provided that such increase of capital stock shall
be first agreed upon by a majority of the votes of the share-
15 holders present at any annual general meeting or meetings, or
at any special meeting or meetings called from time to time
for that purpose.

☞ **2.** It shall not be obligatory upon the company to sell, at Stock may be issued in parcels.
one time, the whole amount of stock authorized by this Act,
20 but the company may, from time to time, limit the number of
shares to be offered for sale to such an amount as may be from
time to time agreed and decided upon by a majority of the
votes of shareholders present at any general or special meetings of the shareholders as aforesaid called for that purpose.

25 ☞ **3.** The notice of any special meeting or meetings of the Notice of meetings.
stockholders of the company called by the directors of the
company in pursuance of this Act, may be given by inserting
a notice specifying the time, place and object of such meeting
in at least two daily newspapers published in the City of
30 Toronto in each issue thereof during the three weeks next
preceding the day fixed for such meeting.

☞ **4.** All shares to be issued under the provisions of this Stock to be sold by auction and surplus over par value added to reserve.
Act shall be sold by public auction after three weeks' notice
in two of the daily newspapers published in the City of
35 Toronto, such shares to be put up in lots of ten shares each,
and all surplus realized over the par value of the shares so
sold shall be added to the rest or reserve fund of the
company, until the same shall be equal to one-half of the
paid up capital stock of the company, the true intent and
40 meaning being that the company may at all times have and
maintain a rest or reserve fund, equal to, but not exceeding,

one-half of the then paid up capital of the company, and which rest or reserve fund may be invested in Dominion or Provincial stock, municipal debentures, school debentures, drainage debentures, debentures of loan companies, and mortgages on real estate.   5

Payments on new stock.
5. The shares of such increased stock shall be paid in, together with the premiums (if any) thereon, by such instalments and at such times and places and under such regulations as the directors may from time to time appoint.

Renewal fund.
6. There shall be created and maintained by the company, 10 out of the earnings of the company, another fund, to be called the plant and buildings renewal fund, to which fund shall be placed each year the sum of five per cent. on the value at which the plant and buildings in use by the company, stand in the books of the company, at the end of the then fiscal 15 year of the company, and all usual and ordinary renewals and repairs shall be charged against this fund.

Special surplus account.
7. Any surplus of net profit, from any source whatever, including premiums on sales of stock, after the rest or reserve fund shall have been established and maintained as aforesaid, 20 remaining at the close of any fiscal year of the company after payment of fees to the president, vice-president, and directors of the company, (not exceeding in all the sum of $9,000 per annum), after payment of dividend at the rate of ten per cent. per annum on the paid up capital stock of the company, and 25 the establishment and maintenance of the said rest or reserve fund, and providing for said plant and buildings renewal fund, shall be carried to a special account, to be known as the special surplus account, and whenever the amount of such surplus is equal to five cents per thousand cubic feet on the quantity of 30 gas sold during the preceding year, the price of gas shall be reduced for. the then current year, at least five cents per thousand cubic feet to all consumers.

Application of reserve fund.
8. If in any year, the net profits of the company, from all sources, are not sufficient to meet the require- 35 ments of the company for the payment of fees to the president, vice president and directors (limited as aforesaid), the payment of dividends at said rate of ten per cent. per annum, as aforesaid, and to provide for the plant and buildings renewal fund, it shall and may be lawful for the direc- 40 tors of the company in their discretion, to draw upon the said rest or reserve fund to the extent of any such deficiency, and to restore any amount so drawn from time to time from said rest or reserve fund, out of the earnings of the company, but the said rest or reserve fund shall not be other- 45 wise drawn upon.

Audit of Company's accounts.
9. The company shall give not less than two weeks written notice by registered letter, to the mayor of the city of Toronto for the time being of the time of commencing the annual audit of the books and accounts of the company, and it shall 50 and may be lawful for an auditor to be appointed by the mayor of the corporation of the city of Toronto, should he deem

it advisable to make such appointment to be present at such annual audit, and for the purpose of verifying the company's annual statement, to have access at the company's office to all books, accounts and papers necessary for such purpose.

5 ☞ **10.** Notwithstanding anything contained in former Acts affecting the company, it shall be lawful for the company to acquire and hold real estate, of which the total yearly value shall not exceed $25,000, over and above the yearly value of any buildings and works now, or which may be hereafter 10 erected thereon.

Power to hold real estate of $25,000 yearly value.

1st Session, 6th Legislature, 50 Vic, 1887.

BILL.

An Act to further amend the powers of the Consumers' Gas Company of Toronto.

(*Reprinted as amended by Private Bills Committee.*)

First Reading, 15th March, 1887.

(Private Bill.)

An Act respecting the City of Stratford.

WHEREAS the City of Stratford, by a by-law No. 410, Preamble.
dated the sixth day of September, in the year of our
Lord 1886, granted a bonus of $120,000 to aid and assist the
Grand Trunk Railway Company of Canada, which said bonus
5·was to be raised by issuing, as required in accordance with the
terms of their agreement with the said the Grand Trunk
Railway Company of Canada, debentures payable in twenty
years from the first day of January, in the year of our Lord
1887 ; and whereas the said City of Stratford, by virtue of
10 their Act of incorporation, entitled *An Act to incorporate the
City of Stratford and for other purposes*, being chapter
seventy-two of the Acts passed by the Legislative Assembly of
the Province of Ontario, in the forty-eighth year of Her
Majesty's Reign, obtained the power of consolidating the
15 greater part of their municipal debt, and issuing therefor
debentures to the amount of $215,000, payable in thirty years
from the sixteenth day of November, in the year of our Lord
1885 ; and whereas the said by-law was duly voted on and
approved by the electors of the said city, and it is desirable
20 that the same should be confirmed with the amendment
hereinafter expressed ; and whereas the municipal council of
the said City of Stratford has petitioned that an Act be passed
extending the time of payment of the debentures to be issued
in pursuance of the said bonus by-law to forty years from the
25 issue thereof, or a period of thirty years from said sixteenth
day of November, 1885, instead of as expressed in said by-law,
and that said by-law be amended in that respect, and also by
providing a sinking fund of one per centum per annum, to
be raised to meet the payment of the said debentures instead
30 of as therein expressed ; and whereas it is expedient to grant
the prayer of the said petition ;

Therefore Her Majesty, by and with the advice and consent
of the Legislative Assembly of the Province of Ontario, enacts
as follows :—

·35   **1.** The said by-law of the City of Stratford is hereby By-law 410.
amended by substituting in clause three thereof the word clause 1, amended.
" forty" for the word " twenty."

2. The said by-law is hereby further amended by the sub- By-law 410,
stitution for clause five thereof of the following :—" That the clause 5, amended.
40 said annual sum of $6,000 for the payment of the interest
upon said sum of $120,000, shall be raised and levied
in each year by special rate sufficient therefor on all the
ratable property in the said municipality, in addition to all
other rates during the continuance of the said debentures, or

any of them, and a further special rate per annum over and above all other rates, shall be raised and levied on all said ratable property which shall be sufficient to form a sinking fund of one per centum per annum, to meet the payment of the principal of said debentures." 5

48 V. c. 72. s. 14, amended. **3.** Section 14 of the said Act entitled *An Act to incorporate the City of Stratford and for other purposes*, passed in the forty-eighth year of the Reign of Her Majesty, chapter seventy-two, is hereby amended by substituting the words "three-hundred and thirty-five thousand dollars" in lieu and stead of 10 the words " two hundred and fifteen thousand dollars."

Application of additional sum of $120,000. **4.** The additional sum of $120,000, authorized by the last preceding section hereof, shall only be raised, and debentures be issued therefor by said City of Stratford in the event of the same being required, and so far only as the same may be 15 required to carry out from time to time the provisions of the said by-law No. 410, as amended, and no further, and the proceeds thereof shall be applied only as required by said by-law and in no other manner and for no other purpose whatsoever

By-law 410 confirmed. **5.** The said by-law No. 410 of the City of Stratford is 20 hereby, as amended, declared to be valid and binding in every respect.

PRINTED BY WARWICK & SONS, 26 AND 26 FRONT ST. W.

TORONTO

(Private Bill)

First Reading,

1887.

BILL.

An Act respecting the City of Stratford.

1st Session, 6th Legislature, 50 Vic., 1887.

11.

MR. HESS.

BILL.

An Act to incorporate the International Ferry Railway Company.

WHEREAS Benjamin Baxter, Edwy Baxter, and W. B. Preamble.
Pierce, have petitioned for an act to incorporate a
company to construct a railway from some point at or near
the western boundary of the Garrison Reserve, in the Town-
5 ship of Bertie, to some point in the Corporation of the Village
of Fort Erie, with power to acquire and own pleasure grounds
at the western terminus of the said railway, and to acquire
water lots and docks, and to acquire, own, equip and operate·
steam vessels and boats in connection therewith, and for other
10 purposes ; and whereas it is expedient to grant the prayer of
the said petition ;   ·
Therefore Her Majesty, by and with the advice and consent of the Legislative Assembly of the Province of Ontario,
enacts as follows :—

15 **1.** Benjamin Baxter, Edwy Baxter, and W. B. Pierce, Incorpora-
together with such other persons and corporations as shall, in tion.
pursuance of this Act, become shareholders of the company
hereby incorporated, are hereby constituted and declared to
be a body corporate and politic by the name of " The Inter-
20 national Ferry Railway Company."

2. The said company shall have full power and authority Location of
under this Act to construct a railway from some point in or line.
near the western boundary of the Garrison Reserve in the
Township of Bertie, to some point in the corporation of the
25 Village of Fort Erie.

3. The gauge of the said railway shall be four feet and Gauge.
eight and one-half inches.

4. It shall and may be lawful for the said company at any Power to pur-
points where the railway approaches any navigable waters, to chase and
30 purchase and hold wharves, piers, docks, water lots, and hold wharves,
lands, and upon the said water lots and lands, and in and etc.
over the waters adjoining the same, to build sheds, wharves,
docks, piers, offices, and other erections, for the use of the
company, and the steam vessels owned, worked, or controlled
35 by the company.

5. It shall and may be lawful for the company to purchase, Power to pur-
build, complete, fit out, and charter, sell, and dispose of, work, chase and
and control, and keep in repair steam vessels from time to in connection
time, to ply on the lakes, rivers, and canals of this Province in with the rail-
40 connection with the said railway, and to make arrangements way.

and agreements with steamboat and vessel proprietors, by
chartering or otherwise, to ply on the said lakes, rivers, and
canals in connection with the said railway.

Power to
acquire whole
lots.

6. It shall and may be lawful for the said company to purchase, hold, use, and enjoy at or near the western terminus of 5
the said railway, sufficient lands for their stations, buildings,
and erections, and for a summer resort and pleasure grounds,
and to erect and maintain thereon suitable buildings and
erections for that purpose, and in case by purchasing the
whole of any lot or parcel of land over or near which the rail- 10
way is to run the company can obtain the same at a more
reasonable price, or to greater advantage than by purchasing
the railway line only, the company may purchase, hold, use
or enjoy such lands, and may sell and convey the same or any
part or parts thereof from time to time as they may deem ex- 15
pedient, but the compulsory clauses of *The Railway Act of
Ontario* shall not apply to this section.

Form of Con-
veyance.

7. Conveyances of land to the said company for the purposes
of and under the powers given by this Act made in the form
set out in schedule A, hereunder written, or to the like effect, 20
shall be sufficient conveyances to the said company, their successors and assigns, of the estate or interest, and sufficient bar
of dower, respectively, of all persons executing the same; and
such conveyances shall be registered in such manner and upon
such proof of execution as is required under the Registry 25
Laws of Ontario, and no registrar shall be entitled to demand
more than seventy-five cents. for registering the same, including
all entries and certificates thereof, and certificates endorsed on
the duplicates thereof.

Provisional
directors and
their powers.

8. From and after the passing of this Act, the said Ben- 30
jamin Baxter, Edwy Baxter, and W. B. Pierce, until others
shall be chosen as hereinafter provided, shall be and are
hereby constituted the board of provisional directors of the
said company, three of whom shall be a quorum, with power
to any two in case of vacancies occuring thereon to fill such 35
vacancies; to associate with themselves thereon not more than
two others, who, upon being so named, shall also become and
be provisional directors, equally with themselves; and they
shall have power and authority immediately after the passing
of this Act to open stock books and receive subscriptions of 40
stock for the undertaking, and may allot and apportion the
stock amongst the subscribers as to them may seem meet, and
may cause surveys and plans to be made and executed, and
may enter into a contract or contracts for building and
equipping the said railway and carrying out the other pur- 45
poses of the said company, and may exercise all such other
powers as under *The Railway Act*, or any other law in force in
Ontario, are vested in such boards.

Capital.

9. The capital stock of the company shall be $50,000,
to be divided into five hundred shares of $100 each, with 50
power to increase the same in the manner provided
in *The Railway Act of Ontario*, and all moneys paid
to the company in respect of such shares shall be applied, in
the first place, to the payment of all costs, charges, and expenses of and incidental to the obtaining of this Act, and of all 55

expenses of making the surveys, plans, and estimates connected with the works hereby authorized, and all the remainder of such money shall be applied to the making, equipment and completion of the said railway, and the other pur-
5 poses of the company.

10. It shall be competent for the directors of the said company to issue as paid up stock any ordinary stock of the company, and allot and pay the same for right of way or other real estate which the company is authorized by this Act to 10 acquire, and for plant, vessels, rolling stock, or material, or erections of any kind.

Certain payments allowed to be made in stock.

11. When and so soon as shares to the amount of $25,000 in the capital stock of the said company shall have been subscribed and allotted, and the sum of $2,500 paid thereon, the provisional 15 directors shall call a meeting of the shareholders of the said capital stock at the Village of Fort Erie, for the purpose of electing directors of the said company, giving at least two weeks notice by advertisement in the *Ontario Gazette*, and in one of the papers published in the County of Welland, of the 20 time, place and purpose of said meeting.

First general meeting.

12. At such general meeting the shareholders assembled in person or by proxy, who shall have paid up ten per cent. on their shares, shall choose not more than nine persons to be directors of said company (of whom three shall be a quorum) 25 and may also pass such rules, regulations and by-laws as may be deemed expedient, provided they be not inconsistent with this Act and *The Railway Act of Ontario*.

First election of directors.

13. Thereafter a general annual meeting of the share-holders of the said company shall be held at their head office, 30 on such days and at such hours as may be directed by the by-laws of the company, and public notice thereof shall be given at least fourteen days previously in the *Ontario Gazette*, and in at least one newspaper published in the County of Welland, and special general meetings of the shareholders of the said com-35 pany may be held at such places in Ontario, and at such times, and in such manner as may be provided by the by-laws of the company.

Annual meeting.

14. Every shareholder of one or more shares of the capital stock shall at any general meeting of such shareholders, be 40 entitled to one vote for every share held by him, and no share-holder shall be entitled to vote on any matter whatever unless all calls due on the stock upon which such shareholder seeks to vote shall have been paid up at least one week before the day appointed for such meeting.

Votes.

45 **15**. No person shall be qualified to be elected as such director by the shareholders unless he be a shareholder holding at least ten shares of stock in the company, and unless he has paid up all calls thereon.

Qualification of directors.

16. Calls on the subscribed capital of the company may be 50 made by the directors for the time being as they shall see fit: provided that no calls shall be made at any one time of more

Calls.

than ten per centum of the amount subscribed by each subscriber, and at intervals of not less than one month, and notice
of each call shall be given as provided for calling general
meetings of the shareholders.

Rights of
aliens.

17. Aliens as well as British subjects, and whether resident 5
in this Province or elsewhere, may be shareholders,in the said
company, and all such shareholders shall be entitled to vote on
their shares equally with British subjects, and shall also be
eligible to office as directors of the said company.

Issue of bonds
authorized.

18. For the purposes of the company, the directors from 10
time to time may issue bonds, and to secure the same, and the
interest thereon, they may mortgage the undertaking, or part
thereof, in the manner provided in *The Railway Act of
Ontario*, and in this respect the provisions of the said Railway
Act shall apply.   15

Company may
become parties
to notes.

19. The said company shall have power and authority to
become parties to promissory notes and bills of exchange for
sums of not less than $100, and any such promissory notes
or bills made, accepted, or indorsed by the president or
vice-president of the company, and countersigned by the 20
secretary and treasurer of the said company, and under
the general or special authority of a majority of a quorum of
the directors, shall be binding on the said company, and every
such promissory note or bill of exchange so made shall be presumed to have been made with proper authority until the 25
contrary be shewn, and in no case shall it be necessary to have
the seal of the said company affixed to such promissory note
or bill of exchange; nor shall the said president, or vice-
president, or the secretary and treasurer, be individually
responsible on any bill or note made, accepted, or indorsed by 30
him or them on behalf of the company, provided the consideration for the said bill or note was received by the company,
unless the said promissory notes or bills of exchange have
been issued without the sanction and authority, either general
or special of the board of directors, as herein provided and 35
enacted: provided, however, that nothing in this section shall
be construed to authorize the said company to issue notes or
bills of exchange payable to bearer, or intended to be circulated as money, or as the notes or bills of a bank.

Exemption
from taxes.

20. It shall further be lawful for the corporation of 40
any municipality, in or through any part of which the
railway of the said company passes, or is situate, by
by-law specially passed for that purpose, to exempt the
company and its property within such municipality, either
in whole or in part, from municipal assessment or taxa- 45
tion, or by fixing the assessable value of such property,
or to agree to a certain sum per annum, or otherwise,
in gross, or by way of commutation, or composition for payment, or in lieu of all or any municipal rates or assessments to
be imposed by such municipal corporation, and for such term 50
of years as such municipal corporation may deem expedient,
not exceeding twenty-one years; and any such by-law shall
not be repealed unless in conformity with any condition contained in such by-law.

21. It shall and may be lawful for any municipality *Municipalities* through which the said railway passes, and having juris- *may allow company to* diction in the premises, to pass a by-law, or by laws, em- *lay its tracks* powering the company to work their road, and lay their rails *on highways.*
5 along any of the highways within such municipality, without liability to fence the same, and whether or not the same be in the possession, or under the control of any joint stock company, and if such highway be either in the possession, or under the control of any joint stock company, then with the
10 assent of such company; and it shall be lawful for the company to enter into and perform any such agreements as they may from time to time deem expedient, with any municipality, corporation, or person for the construction, or for the maintenance and repair of gravel or other public roads leading to
15 the said company.

22. All the provisions of *The Railway Act of Ontario*, ex- *Railway Act* cept as varied by this Act, shall apply to the said company. *to apply.*

23. The railway shall be commenced within one year, and *Time for con-* completed within two years after the passing of this Act. *struction.*

20 **24.** The said company shall not be compelled to run or *Time for* operate in any way the said railway at any time during the *running road.* year, excepting in the summer or excursion season.

SHEDULE A.

(Section 7.)

Know all men by these presents that I (or we) [*insert the* *Schedule A.* *name or names of the vendors*] in consideration of .
dollars, paid to me (or us) by the International Ferry Railway Company, the receipt, whereof is hereby acknowledged, do grant and convey to the said company, and I (or we) [*insert name of any other party or parties*] in consideration of
dollars, paid to me (or us) by the said company, the receipt whereof is hereby acknowledged, do grant and release to the said company, all that certain parcel (*or* those certain parcels, *as the case may be*) of land [*describe the land*], the same having been selected and laid out by the said company for the purposes of their railway, to hold, with the appurtenances, unto the said The International Ferry Railway Company, their successors and assigns (*here insert any other clauses, conditions and covenants required*), and I (*or* we), wife (*or* wives) of the said do hereby bar my (*or* our) dower in the said lands. As witness, my (*or* our) hand and seal (*or* hands and seals) this day of one thousand eight hundred and

Signed, sealed and
delivered in the
presence of

No 12.

1st Session, 6th Legislature, 50 Vic., 1887.

BILL.

An Act to incorporate the International Ferry Railway Company.

First Reading, 1887.

(Private Bill.)

An Act to incorporate the International Ferry Railway Company.

WHEREAS Benjamin Baxter, Edwy Baxter, and W. B. Preamble.
Pierce, have petitioned for an act to incorporate a
company to construct a railway from some point at or near
the western boundary of the Garrison Reserve, in the town-
5 ship of Bertie, to some point in the corporation of the village
of Fort Erie, with power to acquire and own pleasure grounds
at the western terminus of the said railway, and to acquire
water lots and docks, and to acquire, own, equip and operate
steam vessels and boats in connection therewith, and for other
10 purposes ; and whereas it is expedient to grant the prayer of
the said petition ;
　　Therefore Her Majesty, by and with the advice and consent of the Legislative Assembly of the Province of Ontario,
enacts as follows :—

15 **1.** Benjamin Baxter, Edwy Baxter, and W. B. Pierce, Incorpora-
together with such other persons and corporations as shall, in tion.
pursuance of this Act, become shareholders of the company
hereby incorporated, are hereby constituted and declared to
be a body corporate and politic by the name of " The Inter-
20 national Ferry Railway Company."

　　2. The said company shall have full power and authority Location of
under this Act to construct a railway from some point in or line.
near the western boundary of the Garrison Reserve in the
township of Bertie, to some point in the corporation of the
25 village of Fort Erie.

　　3. The gauge of the said railway shall be four feet and Gauge.
eight and one-half inches.

　　4. It shall and may be lawful for the said company at any Power to pur-
points where the railway approaches any navigable waters, to chase and
30 purchase and hold wharves, piers, docks, water lots, and hold wharves,
lands, and upon the said water lots and lands, and in and etc.
over the waters adjoining the same, to build sheds, wharves,
docks, piers, offices, and other erections, for the use of the
company, and the steam vessels owned, worked, or controlled
35 by the company.

　　5. It shall and may be lawful for the company to purchase, Power to pur-
build, complete, fit out, and charter, sell, and dispose of, work, chase and
and control, and keep in repair steam vessels from time to work vessels
time, to ply on the lakes, rivers, and canals of this Province in with the rail-
40 connection with the said railway, and to make arrangements way.

and agreements with steamboat and vessel proprietors, by
chartering or otherwise, to ply on the said lakes, rivers, and
canals in connection with the said railway.

Power to acquire whole lots.   **6.** .It shall and may be lawful for the said company to purchase, hold, use, and enjoy at or near the western terminus of 5
the said railway, sufficient lands for their stations, buildings,
and erections, and for a summer resort and pleasure grounds,
and to erect and maintain thereon suitable buildings and
erections for that purpose, and in case by purchasing the
whole of any lot or parcel of land over or near which the rail- 10
way is to run the company can obtain the same at a more
reasonable price, or to greater advantage than by purchasing
the railway line only, the company may purchase, hold, use
or enjoy such lands, and may sell and convey the same or any
part or parts thereof from time to time as they may deem ex- 15
pedient, but the compulsory clauses of *The Railway Act of
Ontario* shall not apply to this section.

Form of Conveyance.   **7.** Conveyances of land to the said company for the purposes
of and under the powers given by this Act made in the form
set out in schedule A, hereunder written, or to the like effect, 20
shall be sufficient conveyances to the said company, their successors and assigns, of the estate or interest, and sufficient bar
of dower, respectively, of all persons executing the same; and
such conveyances shall be registered in such manner and upon
such proof of execution as is required under the Registry 25
Laws of Ontario, and no registrar shall be entitled to demand
more than seventy-five cents for registering the same, including
all entries and certificates thereof, and certificates endorsed on
the duplicates thereof.

Provisional directors and their powers.   **8.** From and after the passing of this Act, the said Ben- 30
jamin Baxter, Edwy Baxter, and W. B. Pierce, until others
shall be chosen as hereinafter provided, shall be and are
hereby constituted the board of provisional directors of the
said company, three of whom shall be a quorum, with power
to any two in case of vacancies occurring thereon to fill such 35
vacancies; to associate with themselves thereon not more than
two others, who, upon being so named, shall also become and
be provisional directors, equally with themselves; and they
shall have power and authority immediately after the passing
of this Act to open stock books and receive subscriptions of 40
stock for the undertaking, and may allot and apportion the
stock amongst the subscribers as to them may seem meet, and
may cause surveys and plans to be made and executed, and
may enter into a contract or contracts for building and
equipping the said railway and carrying out the other pur- 45
poses of the said company, and may exercise all such other.
powers as under *The Railway Act*, or any other law in force in
Ontario, are vested in such boards.

Capital.   **9.** The capital stock of the company shall be $50,000,
to be divided into five hundred shares of $100 each, with 50
power to increase the same in the manner provided
in *The Railway Act of Ontario*, and all moneys paid
to the company in respect of such shares shall be applied, in
the first place, to the payment of all costs, charges, and expenses of and incidental to the obtaining of this Act, and of all 55

expenses of making the surveys, plans, and estimates connected with the works hereby authorized, and all the remainder of such money shall be applied to the making, equipment and completion of the said railway, and the other pur-
5 poses of the company.

10. It shall be competent for the directors of the said company to issue as paid up stock any ordinary stock of the company, and allot and pay the same for right of way or other real estate which the company is authorized by this Act to
10 acquire, and for plant, vessels, rolling stock, or material, or erections of any kind. *Certain payments allowed to be made in stock.*

11. When and so soon as shares to the amount of $25,000 in the capital stock of the said company shall have been subscribed and allotted, and the sum of $2,500 paid thereon, the provisional
15 directors *or a majority of them* shall call a *general* meeting of the *subscribers to* the said capital stock, at the village of Fort Erie, for the purpose of electing directors of the said company, giving at least *four* weeks notice by advertisement in the *Ontario Gazette*, and in one of the *news*papers published in the
20 county of Welland, of the time, place and purpose of said meeting. *First general meeting.*

12. At such general meeting the shareholders assembled in person or by proxy, who shall have paid up ten per cent. on their shares, shall choose not more than nine persons to be directors of said company (of whom three shall be a quorum)
25 and may also pass such rules, regulations and by-laws as may be deemed expedient, provided they be not inconsistent with this Act and *The Railway Act of Ontario*. *First election of directors.*

13. Thereafter a general annual meeting of the shareholders of the said company shall be held at their head office,
30 *in the said village of Fort Erie, or in such other place, and* on such days and at such hours as may be directed by the by-laws of the company, and public notice thereof shall be given at least *four weeks* previously in the *Ontario Gazette*, and in at least one newspaper published in the county of Welland, *during the four*
35 *weeks preceding the week in which such meeting is to be held*, and special general meetings of the shareholders of the said company may be held at such places in Ontario, and at such times, and in such manner as may be provided by the by-laws of the company, *upon such notice as is provided by this section.* *Annual meeting.*

40 **14**. Every shareholder of one or more shares of the capital stock shall at any general meeting of such shareholders, be entitled to one vote for every share held by him, and no shareholder shall be entitled to vote on any matter whatever unless all calls due on the stock upon which such shareholder
45 seeks to vote shall have been paid up at least one week before the day appointed for such meeting. *Votes.*

15. No person shall be qualified to be elected as such director by the shareholders unless he be a shareholder holding at least ten shares of stock in the company, and unless he has
50 paid up all calls thereon. *Qualification of directors.*

16. Calls on the subscribed capital of the company may be made by the directors for the time being as they shall see fit: *Calls.*

provided that no calls shall be made at any one time of more than ten per centum of the amount subscribed by each subscriber, and at intervals of not less than one month, and notice of each call shall be given as provided for calling general meetings of the shareholders.   5

Rights of aliens.

17. Aliens as well as British subjects, and whether resident in this Province or elsewhere, may be shareholders in the said company, and all such shareholders shall be entitled to vote on their shares equally with British subjects, and shall also be eligible to office as directors of the said company.   10

Issue of bonds authorized.

18. For the purposes of the company, the directors from time to time may issue bonds, and to secure the same, and the interest thereon, they may mortgage the undertaking, or part thereof, in the manner provided in *The Railway Act of Ontario*, and in this respect the provisions of the said Railway 15 Act shall apply.

Company may become parties to notes.

19. The said company shall have power and authority to become parties to promissory notes and bills of exchange for sums of not less than $100, and any such promissory note or bill *of exchange* made, accepted, or indorsed by the president or 20 vice-president of the company, and countersigned by the secretary and treasurer of the said company, and under the general or special authority of a quorum of the directors, shall be binding on the said company, and every such promissory note or bill of exchange so made shall be pre- 25 sumed to have been made with proper authority until the contrary be shewn, and in no case shall it be necessary to have the seal of the said company affixed to such promissory note or bill of exchange; nor shall the said president, or vice-president, or the secretary and treasurer, be individually 30 responsible on any bill or note made, accepted, or indorsed by him or them on behalf of the company, provided the consideration for the said bill or note was received by the company, unless the said promissory notes or bills of exchange have been issued without the sanction and authority, either general 35 or special of the board of directors, as herein provided and enacted: provided, however, that nothing in this section shall be construed to authorize the said company to issue notes or bills of exchange payable to bearer, or intended to be circulated as money, or as the notes or bills of a bank.   40

Exemption from taxes.

20. It shall further be lawful for the corporation of any municipality, in or through any part of which the railway of the said company passes, or is situate, by by-law specially passed for that purpose, to exempt the company and its property within such municipality, either 45 in whole or in part, from municipal assessment or taxation, or by fixing the assessable value of such property, or to agree to a certain sum per annum, or otherwise, in gross, or by way of commutation, or composition for payment, or in lieu of all or any municipal rates or assessments to 50 be imposed by such municipal corporation, and for such term of years as such municipal corporation may deem expedient, not exceeding twenty-one years; and any such by-law shall not be repealed unless in conformity with any condition contained in such by-law.   55

21. It shall and may be lawful for any municipality through which the said railway passes, and having jurisdiction in the premises, to pass a by-law, or by-laws, empowering the company to *make* their road, and lay their rails
5 along any of the highways within such municipality, and whether or not the same be in the possession, or under the control of any joint stock company, and if such highway be either in the possession, or under the control of any joint stock company, then with the assent of such company; and it shall
10 be lawful for the company to enter into and perform any such agreements as they may from time to time deem expedient, with any municipality, corporation, or person for the construction, or for the maintenance and repair of gravel or other public roads leading to the said *railway*. Municipalities may allow company to lay its tracks on highways.

15 **22.** The said company shall have power to make traffic and running arrangements, either or both, with the Erie and Niagara Railway Company and the Canada Southern Railway Company, if lawfully empowered to enter into such arrangements, or for connecting with the said railways, or with either
20 or both, upon such terms as may be agreed upon. Traffic and running arrangements with the other companies.

23. The said company may also construct a telephone line and an electric telegraph line in connection with their railway, and for the purpose of constructing, working and protecting the said telephone and telegraph lines, the powers conferred
25 upon telegraph companies by *The Act respecting Electric Telegraph Companies* (chapter 151 of the Revised Statutes of Ontario), are hereby conferred upon the said company. Telephone and telegraph lines.

24. The head offices and repair shops shall be located in the said village of Fort Erie at or near the eastern terminus
30 of the company's railway. Site of head office and work shops.

25. All persons owning or residing upon any lands adjoining and fronting upon the Lake Shore Road, where the same passes through the said village of Fort Erie, may at any time cross and take their boats and nets across the track and
35 lands of the c mpany, where the same lie between the lands of the persons aforesaid and the water's edge, without doing unnecessary damage or interfering with the company's rights; and all persons travelling upon the roads or streets in the township of Bertie, where the said roads and streets intersect
40 the said railroad, may in like manner, with their boats and nets, cross the said railroad. Right of certain persons to cross railway.

26. All the provisions of *The Railway Act of Ontario*, except as varied by this Act, shall apply to the said company. Railway Act to apply.

27. The railway shall be commenced within one year, and
45 completed within two years after the passing of this Act. Time for construction.

28. The said company shall not be compelled to run or operate in any way the said railway at any time during the year, excepting in the summer or excursion season. Time for running road.

6

SHEDULE A.

(Section 7.)

Schedule A.   Know all men by these presents that I (or we) [*insert the name or names of the vendors*] in consideration of
dollars, paid to me (*or* us) by the International Ferry Railway Company, the receipt, whereof is hereby acknowledged, do grant and convey to the said company, and I (*or* we) [*insert name of any other party or parties*] in consideration of
dollars, paid to me (or us) by the said company, the receipt whereof is hereby acknowledged, do grant and release to the said company, all that certain parcel (*or* those certain parcels, *as the case may be*) of land [*describe the land*], the same having been selected and laid out by the said company for the purposes of their railway, to hold, with the appurtenances, unto the said the International Ferry Railway Company, their successors and assigns (*here insert any other clauses, conditions and covenants required*), and I (*or* we), wife (*or* wives) of the said   do hereby bar my (*or* our) dower in the said lands. As witness, my (or our) hand and seal (*or* hands and seals) this   day of   one thousand eight hundred and

Signed, sealed and
delivered in the
presence of

1st Session, 6th Legislature, 50 Vic., 1887.

BILL.

An Act to incorporate the International Ferry Railway Company.

(Reprinted as amended by Railway Committee.)

First Reading, 9th March, 1887.

(Private Bill.)

No. 13.]　　　**BILL.**　　　[1887.

An Act to authorize the Trustees of the Warwick Congregation of the Methodist Church at Warwick Village to sell certain lands.

WHEREAS the congregation of the Methodist Church at Warwick Village, in the Township of Warwick, in the County of Lambton, known as the Warwick congregation of the Methodist Church, at Warwick Village, do hold in fee 5 simple, all and singular, that parcel or tract of land situate in the Town of Warwick (now known as Warwick Village), in the County of Lambton, and Province of Ontario, containing seven acres, be the same more or less, and being composed of "The Park Lot," bounded by Manchester, William, Park, and 10 George Streets, in the aforesaid Town of Warwick, which said lands were granted by the Crown by a Crown grant, bearing date the seventeenth day of August, 1858, to the trustees of the said congregation (then known as the congregation of the Wesleyan Methodist Church in Canada, at Warwick Village 15 aforesaid); and whereas the above mentioned congregation have, according to the rules of said Church, determined to sell and convey said lands, the same having become wholly unnecessary for the purposes of said Church, and apply the proceeds of such sale for such purposes as the rules and regulations of such 20 Church may warrant; and whereas said lands were granted to the trustees of said Church in trust, to hold as a site for a church and parsonage, only without power to said trustees to sell or convey said lands; and whereas the said congregation have by their petition represented that the said lands are no 25 longer requisite for such purpose, and have prayed for power to sell the same; and whereas it is expedient to grant the prayer of the said petition;

Therefore Her Majesty, by and with the advice and consent of the Legislative Assembly of the Province of Ontario, enacts 30 as follows :—

1. The trustees of the congregation of the Methodist Church at Warwick Village, in the said Township of Warwick, for the time being, and their successors in office, are hereby empowered to grant, bargain, sell, and convey the lands and 35 premises in the preamble to this Act mentioned, and they are hereby empowered to sell and convey absolutely, and freed from all trusts of whatsoever nature or kind, created by or under said Crown Grant mentioned in the preamble to this Act, or otherwise howsoever, and in such quantity or quantities as 40 they see fit, and for such price or prices as to them may seem reasonable.

Purchaser not responsible for application of purchase money.

2. The purchaser, or purchasers of the said lands, or any part thereof, shall not be in any way bound to see to the application, or be answerable for the non-application of the purchase money, or any part thereof.

Application of proceeds.

3. After payment of the expenses of obtaining this Act, and all proper and reasonable charges and expenses of effecting and carrying out such sale, or sales, the said trustees, the survivor or survivors of them, and any succeeding trustees of said congregation of said church, shall hold and apply the proceeds of such sale, or sales, as the case may be, for such purposes as the laws, rules, and regulations of said church shall warrant their expenditure upon.

5

10

No. 13.

1st Session, 6th Legislature, 50 Vic., 1887.

BILL.

An Act to authorize the Trustees of the Warwick Congregation of the Methodist Church at Warwick village to sell certain lands.

First Reading.

1887.

(Rrivate Bill)

Mr. GRAHAM.

TORONTO:

PRINTED BY WARWICK & SONS, 26 AND 28 FRONT ST. W.

No. 14.] **BILL.** [1887.

An Act respecting the City of Ottawa.

WHEREAS the Municipal Councils of the village of New Edinburgh and of the city of Ottawa did on or about the 6th day of August, A. D. 1886, petition the Lieutenant-Governor in Council, praying that a proclamation be issued to
5 give effect to an agreement previously entered into by the said municipalities, providing for the annexation of the village of New Edinburgh to the city of Ottawa pursuant to the provisions of *The Consolidated Municipal Act, 1883;* and whereas on the 5th day of November, 1886, a proclamation
10 was issued giving effect to the said annexation; and whereas the said municipalities have acted upon the said proclamation and have held their municipal and school trustee elections as if the said annexation became effective on the 1st day of January, 1887; and whereas the corporation of the city of
15 Ottawa have by their petition prayed for legislation to remove any doubts that may exist in reference to the legality of the said elections and to provide for the assessment of the said village of New Edinburgh as a ward of the city of Ottawa for the year 1887, and for the other matters and things herein-
20 after set forth; and whereas it is expedient to grant the prayer of the said petition;

Therefore Her Majesty, by and with the advice and consent of the Legislative Assembly of the Province of Ontario, enacts as follows:—

25 **1.** All that part of the township of Gloucester, in the county of Carleton, formerly comprised within the limits of the village of New Edinburgh, is hereby annexed to and shall be henceforth included within the limits of the city of Ottawa (which limits are hereby extended so as to include the same),
30 and shall constitute a ward of the city of Ottawa to be known as New Edinburgh ward, subject to the same provisions of law as if such annexation had been made and the proclamation giving effect to the same had been issued before the first day of October, 1886.

35 **2.** The municipal elections held in the said New Edinburgh ward for the year 1887 are hereby ratified and confirmed and declared to be valid and effectual, and John Henderson, John Askwith and John Charles Roger are hereby declared to be the three aldermen and members of the council of the corpora-
40 tion of the city of Ottawa for the said New Edinburgh ward for the year 1887.

3. The elections held in the said New Edinburgh ward for public and separate school trustees for the year 1887 are

2

hereby ratified and confirmed and declared to be valid and
effectual.

Assessment rolls and voters' lists confirmed.
    4. The assessment rolls and voters' lists of the village of
New Edinburgh for the year 1886, as finally revised for that   5
year are hereby confirmed, and the said assessment rolls and
voters' lists are hereby constituted the assessment rolls and
voters' lists for New Edinburgh ward of the city of Ottawa
for the year 1887, and the council of the corporation of the
city of Ottawa are hereby authorized to levy and collect the 10
rates and taxes of the said New Edinburgh ward for the
year 1887 on the basis of said assessment rolls. And no
further or other assessment of New Edinburgh ward for the
year 1887 need be made by the said council.

Mode of determining cost of drainage works.
    5. In ascertaining and determining the cost of draining any
locality, or making and laying or prolonging any common 15
sewer, the council of the corporation of the city of Ottawa
may estimate the cost of the construction of branch drains to
the line of street, and include the cost of such branch drains
in making the assessment for such drains or common sewer as a
local improvement pursuant to section 612 of *The Consolidated* 20
Municipal Act, 1883, as amended by subsequent Acts of the
Legislature of Ontario.

Local improvement by-laws for raising money by special assessment confirmed.
    6. All by-laws heretofore passed by the council of the
corporation of the city of Ottawa for borrowing money by the
issue of debentures secured by special assessment on the real 25
property benefited by local improvements, works and services,
the debentures issued thereunder and the special assessment
made to provide for the cost of such local improvements,
works or services, are hereby confirmed and declared valid
and effectual.   **30**

By-laws for providing for the city's share of cost of local improvements confirmed.
    7. All by-laws heretofore passed by the council of the
corporation of the city of Ottawa for borrowing money on the
general credit of the city to provide for the payment of the
city's share of local improvements, works and services, and the
debentures issued thereunder, are hereby declared valid and 35
effectual, notwithstanding that such by-laws have not been
submitted for the assent of the electors of the said city
of Ottawa.

Water works debentures.
    8. To enable the corporation of Ottawa to enlarge the
capacity of the water works, the council of the corporation of 40
the city of Ottawa shall have power to pass a by-law to authorize the issue of debentures of the said corporation for a sum
not exceeding $100,000, in such sums—of not less than $100—
as the said corporation may deem expedient, which said debentures shall be made payable not more than twenty years from 45
the day on which they respectively bear date, and may be in
the form A in the schedule to this Act set forth ; which said
debentures shall bear interest at the rate of five per cent. per
annum, payable half-yearly, and such debentures shall be signed
by the mayor and the treasurer of the said city for the time 50
being, and may be made payable, either in sterling or currency,
in Great Britain, in this Province, or elsewhere, as to the
council of the corporation of the city of Ottawa shall seem
expedient.

9. For the purpose of providing a sinking fund for the pay- ment of the said debentures, and the interest on the same, semi-annually, the council of the corporation of the city of Ottawa shall raise, annually, from the water rates, and with the
5 authority conferred upon them in and by the Act of the Legislature of this Province, intituled, *An Act for the Construction of Water Works for the City of Ottawa*, and the Acts amending the same, a sum of money sufficient to pay the interest, semi-annually, on the days appointed for the payment thereof,
10 upon the principal money of the said debentures; and shall also raise, annually, a further sum sufficient to form a sinking fund to pay off the principal money when the same shall become payable, such sums to be in addition to the moneys required to be raised, to meet the charges for maintenance, the
15 cost of renewals, and the amounts required to pay off the water works debentures already issued by the corporation of the city of Ottawa, and the said corporation shall pay the principal moneys and interest on the said debentures herein authorized to be issued, as the same shall from time to time fall due.

20 **10.** If, from any cause, the moneys annually accruing under the water rates, after deducting the present charges thereon, shall be less than the sums of money from time to time necessary for the payment of the interest and of the sinking fund to pay off the debentures herein authorized to be issued, it shall
25 be the duty of the corporation of the city of Ottawa, and they are hereby authorized and required, when and as often as the same may occur, forthwith to settle, impose, levy and collect an equal special rate upon all the assessable property of the city of Ottawa, in the manner and with the like powers as shall exist
30 in respect to municipal assessments, rates and taxes, and out of the proceeds thereof to pay and discharge all sums of money for interest or principal, which shall or may be due, or accruing due, to meet the interest and sinking fund to pay the debentures herein authorized to be issued.

35 **11.** The by-law or by-laws of the said corporation, passed under the authority of this Act, shall not require to be submitted to or to have the assent of the electors of the said city before the final passing thereof.

12. No irregularity in the form of the said debentures, or
40 of the by-laws authorizing the issue thereof, shall render the same invalid or illegal, or be allowed as a defence to any action brought against the said corporation for the recovery of the amount of the said debentures and interest, or any or either of them or any part thereof.

45 **13.** The surplus revenues arising from the supply of water by the water works of the said city, after providing for maintenance and renewals, for the payment of the interest on the water works debentures already issued, for the payment of the sinking fund, amounting annually to $11,700, as required by
50 section 14 of *The Act to Consolidate the Debenture Debt of the City of Ottawa*, passed in the 41st year of Her Majesty's reign, and chaptered 37, and also after providing for the moneys required to pay the interest and the sinking fund for the debentures herein authorized to be issued, may, in any year, if the
55 city council so direct, be used and applied in the enlargement,

construction and improvement of the water works, notwithstanding the provision contained in the said section, but if such surplus revenue, or some portion thereof, be not so used in the improvement of the water works, then the said surplus revenue, or the portions thereof not so used, shall be immediately placed 5 at the credit of and become a part of the general sinking fund as required by the said section.

Power to agree with Government of Canada as to control of police.

14. Notwithstanding anything in *The Consolidated Municipal Act, 1883*, contained, it shall and may be lawful for the council of the city of Ottawa to enter into an agreement 10 with the Government of the Dominion of Canada, whereby the said Government of the Dominion of Canada may assume the appointment and control of the city police force and may make all regulations in reference to the same, and in the event of such agreement being entered into the enactments of 15 sections 433 to 450, inclusive, of *The Consolidated Municipal Act, 1883*, shall not be applicable to the said city of Ottawa.

Powers of constables.

15. All peace officers and police constables, appointed by the Government of the Dominion of Canada, pursuant to any such agreement, shall have the same power and authority in the 20 said city of Ottawa as is conferred on peace officers and police constables in the Province of Ontario under any law in force in the said Province of Ontario.

SCHEDULE.

(*Form A.*)   25

WATER WORKS DEBENTURE.

No. $

Province of Ontario,

City of Ottawa.

Under and by virtue of the Act passed in the fiftieth 30 year of the Reign of Her Majesty, Queen Victoria, and Chaptered   , and by virtue of By-law No.   , of the Corporation of the City of Ottawa, passed under the powers contained in the said Act.

The Corporation of the City of Ottawa promise to pay the 35 bearer, at   , in the sum of
on the day of   A.D.   and the half-yearly coupons hereto attached as the same shall severally become due.   40

L.S.

Mayor.
Treasurer.

1st Session, 6th Legislature, 50 Vic., 1887.

BILL.

An Act respecting the City of Ottawa.

First Reading,

1887.

(Rrivate Bill.)

BILL.

An Act respecting the City of Ottawa.

WHEREAS the municipal councils of the village of New Preamble. Edinburgh and of the city of Ottawa did on or about the 6th day of August, A. D. 1886, petition the Lieutenant-Governor in Council, praying that a proclamation be issued to ·
5 give effect to an agreement previously entered into by the said municipalities, providing for the annexation of the village of New Edinburgh to the city of Ottawa pursuant to the provisions of *The Consolidated Municipal Act, 1883;* and whereas on the 5th day of November, 1886, a proclamation
10 was issued giving effect to the said annexation ; and whereas the said municipalities have acted upon the said proclamation and have held their municipal and school trustee elections as if the said annexation became effective on the 1st day of January, 1887 ; and whereas the corporation of the city of
15 Ottawa have by their petition prayed for legislation to remove any doubts that may exist in reference to the legality of the said elections and to provide for the assessment of the said village of New Edinburgh as a ward of the city of Ottawa for the year 1887, and for the other matters and things herein-
20 after set forth ; and whereas it is expedient to grant the prayer of the said petition ;

Therefore Her Majesty, by and with the advice and consent of the Legislative Assembly of the Province of Ontario, enacts as follows :—

25 **1.** All that part of the township of Gloucester, in the county New Edin-of Carleton, formerly comprised within the limits of the burgh annexed village of New Edinburgh, is hereby annexed to and shall be to Ottawa. henceforth included within the limits of the city of Ottawa (which limits are hereby extended so as to include the same),
30 and shall constitute a ward of the city of Ottawa to be known as New Edinburgh ward, subject to the same provisions of law as if such annexation had been made and the proclamation giving effect to the same had been issued before the first day of October, 1886.

35 **2.** The municipal elections held in the said New Edinburgh Municipal ward for the year 1887 are hereby ratified and confirmed and elections declared to be valid and effectual, and John Henderson, John confirmed. Askwith and John Charles Roger are hereby declared to be the three aldermen and members of the council of the corpora-
40 tion of the city of Ottawa for the said New Edinburgh ward for the year 1887.

3. The elections held in the said New Edinburgh ward for School trustee public and separate school trustees for the year 1887 are elections confirmed.

hereby ratified and confirmed and declared to be valid and effectual.

Assessment rolls and voters' lists confirmed.

4. The assessment rolls and voters' lists of the village of New Edinburgh for the year 1886, as finally revised for that year are hereby confirmed, and the said assessment rolls and 5 voters' lists are hereby constituted the assessment rolls and voters' lists for New Edinburgh ward of the city of Ottawa for the year 1887, and the council of the corporation of the city of Ottawa are hereby authorized to levy and collect the rates and taxes of the said New Edinburgh ward for the 10 year 1887 on the basis of said assessment rolls; and no further or other assessment of New Edinburgh ward for the year 1887 need be made by the said council.

Allowance to county of Carleton in respect of the New Edinburgh iron bridge.

5. The arbitrators in determining the amount to be paid by the corporation of the city of Ottawa to the corporation 15 of the county of Carleton, or by the latter corporation to the former corporation, consequent on the addition to the limits of the said city of Ottawa hereinbefore mentioned, may take into consideration, and allow to the corporation of the county of Carleton such part (if any) of the cost of construction of 20 the iron bridge over the river Rideau, known as the New Edinburgh iron bridge, as they may deem just.

Local improvement by-laws for raising money by special assessment confirmed.

6. All by-laws heretofore passed by the council of the corporation of the city of Ottawa for borrowing money by the issue of debentures secured by special assessment on the real 25 property benefited by local improvements, works and services, the debentures issued thereunder and the special assessment made to provide for the cost of such local improvements, works or services, are hereby confirmed and declared valid and effectual. 30

By-laws for providing for the city's share of cost of local improvements confirmed.

7. All by-laws heretofore passed by the council of the corporation of the city of Ottawa for borrowing money on the general credit of the city to provide for the payment of the city's share of local improvements, works and services, and the debentures issued thereunder, are hereby declared valid and 35 effectual, notwithstanding that such by-laws have not been submitted for the assent of the electors of the said city of Ottawa.

Water works debentures.

8. To enable the corporation of Ottawa to enlarge the capacity of the water works, the council of the corporation of the city of 40 Ottawa shall have power to pass a by-law *or by-laws* to authorize the issue of debentures of the said corporation for a sum not exceeding $100,000, in such sums—of not less than $100— as the said corporation may deem expedient, which said debentures shall be made payable not more than *thirty* years from 45 the day on which they respectively bear date, and may be in the form A in the schedule to this Act set forth ; which said debentures shall bear interest at *a* rate *not exceeding* five per cent. per annum, payable half-yearly, and such debentures shall be signed by the mayor and the treasurer of the said city for the time 50 being, and may be made payable, either in sterling or currency, in Great Britain, in this Province, or elsewhere, as to the council of the corporation of the city of Ottawa shall seem expedient.

9. For the purpose of providing a sinking fund for the payment of the said debentures, and the interest on the same, semi-annually, the council of the corporation of the city of Ottawa shall raise, annually, from the water rates, and with the
5 authority conferred upon them in and by the Act of the Legislature of this Province, intituled, *An Act for the Construction of Water Works for the City of Ottawa,* and the Acts amending the same, a sum of money sufficient to pay the interest, semi-annually, on the days appointed for the payment thereof,
10 upon the principal money of the said debentures ; and shall also raise, annually, a further sum *not less than one and one-half per cent. on the principal of the said debentures* sufficient to form a sinking fund to pay off the principal money when the same shall become payable, such sums to be in addition
15 to the moneys required to be raised, to meet the charges for maintenance, the cost of renewals, and the amounts required ☞for the payment of the interest on the water works debentures already issued for the payment of the sinking fund, amounting annually to $11,700, as required by section 14 of
20 the Act to consolidate the debenture debt of the city of Ottawa, passed in the 41st year of Her Majesty's reign, and chaptered 37☞and the said corporation shall pay the principal moneys and interest on the said debentures herein authorized to be issued, as the same shall from time to time fall due.

(margin: Corporation to provide annually by the water rates the amount required for sinking fund and interest.)

25 **10**. If, from any cause, the moneys annually accruing under the water rates, after deducting the present charges thereon, shall be less than the sums of money from time to time necessary for the payment of the interest and of the sinking fund to pay off the debentures herein authorized to be issued, it shall
30 be the duty of the corporation of the city of Ottawa,and they are hereby authorized and required, when and as often as the same may occur, forthwith to settle, impose, levy and collect an equal special rate upon all the assessable property of the city of Ottawa, in the manner and with the like powers as shall exist
35 in respect to municipal assessments, rates and taxes, and out of the proceeds thereof to pay and discharge all sums of money for interest or principal, which shall or may be due, or accruing due, to meet the interest and sinking fund to pay the debentures herein authorized to be issued.

(margin: Special rate if water rates prove insufficient.)

40 **11**. The by-law or by-laws of the said corporation, passed under the authority of this Act, shall not require to be submitted to or to have the assent of the electors of the said city before the final passing thereof;☞nor shall it be necessary that any of the provisions of the Consolidated Municipal Act, 1883,
45 relating to by-laws for creating debts be complied with.☞

(margin: Assent of electors to by-laws not required.)

12. No irregularity in the form of the said debentures, or of the by-laws authorizing the issue thereof, shall render the same invalid or illegal, or be allowed as a defence to any action brought against the said corporation for the recovery of the
50 amount of the said debentures and interest, or any or either of them or any part thereof.

(margin: Irregularities not to render debentures void.)

13. *Any* surplus revenues arising from the supply of water by the water works of the said city, after providing for maintenance and renewals, for the payment of the interest on the
55 water works debentures already issued, for the payment of the

(margin: Application of surplus revenue from water works.)

sinking fund, amounting annually to $11,700, as required by
section 14 of *The Act to Consolidate the Debenture Debt of the
City of Ottawa*, passed in the 41st year of Her Majesty's reign,
and chaptered 37, and also after providing for the moneys
required to pay the interest and the sinking fund for the deben- 5
tures herein authorized to be issued, may, in any year, if the
city council so direct, be used and applied in the enlargement,
construction and improvement of the water works, notwithstanding the provision contained in the said section, or in
section 32 of " *The Act for the construction of Water Works* 10
for the city of Ottawa," passed in the 35th year of Her
Majesty's reign, and chaptered 80, but if such surplus revenue,
or some portion thereof, be not so used in the improvement of
the water works, then the said surplus revenue, or the portions
thereof not so used, shall be immediately placed at the credit of 15
and become a part of the general sinking fund as required by
the said section.

SCHEDULE.

(*Form A.*)

WATER WORKS DEBENTURE.   20

No. $

Province of Ontario,

City of Ottawa.

Under and by virtue of the Act passed in the fiftieth
year of the Reign of Her Majesty, Queen Victoria, and Chap- 25
tered   , and by virtue of By-law No.   , of the
Corporation of the City of Ottawa, passed under the powers
contained in the said Act.

The Corporation of the City of Ottawa promise to pay the
bearer, at   , in   30
the sum of
on the day of   A.D.   and the
half-yearly coupons hereto attached as the same shall severally
become due.

L.S.   35

Mayor.
Treasurer.

No. 14.

1st Session, 6th Legislature, 50 Vic., 1887.

BILL.

An Act respecting the City of Ottawa.

(*Reprinted as amended by Private Bills
Committee.*)

First Reading, 15th March, 1887.

No. 14.]   **BILL.**   [1887.

An Act respecting the City of Ottawa.

WHEREAS the municipal councils of the village of New Preamble.
Edinburgh and of the city of Ottawa did on or about
the 6th day of August, A. D. 1886, petition the Lieutenant-
Governor in Council, praying that a proclamation be issued to
5 give effect to an agreement previously entered into by the
said municipalities, providing for the annexation of the village
of New Edinburgh to the city of Ottawa pursuant to the provisions of *The Consolidated Municipal Act, 1883;* and
whereas on the 5th day of November, 1886, a proclamation
10 was issued giving effect to the said annexation; and whereas
the said municipalities have acted upon the said proclamation
and have held their municipal and school trustee elections as
if the said annexation became effective on the 1st day of
January, 1887; and whereas the corporation of the city of
15 Ottawa have by their petition prayed for legislation to remove
any doubts that may exist in reference to the legality of the
said elections and to provide for the assessment of the said
village of New Edinburgh as a ward of the city of Ottawa for
the year 1887, and for the other matters and things herein-
20 after set forth; and whereas it is expedient to grant the
prayer of the said petition;
Therefore Her Majesty, by and with the advice and consent
of the Legislative Assembly of the Province of Ontario, enacts
as follows:—

25   **1.** All that part of the township of Gloucester, in the county New Edin-
of Carleton, formerly comprised within the limits of the burgh annexed to Ottawa.
village of New Edinburgh, is hereby annexed to and shall be
henceforth included within the limits of the city of Ottawa
(which limits are hereby extended so as to include the same),
30 and shall constitute a ward of the city of Ottawa to be known
as New Edinburgh ward, subject to the same provisions of law
as if such annexation had been made and the proclamation
giving effect to the same had been issued before the first day
of October, 1886.

35   **2.** The municipal elections held in the said New Edinburgh Municipal elections confirmed.
ward for the year 1887 are hereby ratified and confirmed and
declared to be valid and effectual, and John Henderson, John
Askwith and John Charles Roger are hereby declared to be
the three aldermen and members of the council of the corpora-
40 tion of the city of Ottawa for the said New Edinburgh ward
for the year 1887.

3. The elections held in the said New Edinburgh ward for School trustee elections confirmed.
public and separate school trustees for the year 1887 are

hereby ratified and confirmed and declared to be valid and
effectual.

Assessment rolls and voters' lists confirmed.
4. The assessment rolls and voters' lists of the village of
New Edinburgh for the year 1886, as finally revised for that
year are hereby confirmed, and the said assessment rolls and 5
voters' lists are hereby constituted the assessment rolls and
voters' lists for New Edinburgh ward of the city of Ottawa
for the year 1887, and the council of the corporation of the
city of Ottawa are hereby authorized to levy and collect the
rates and taxes of the said New Edinburgh ward for the 10
year 1887 on the basis of said assessment rolls; and no
further or other assessment of New Edinburgh ward for the
year 1887 need be made by the said council.

Allowance to county of Carleton in respect of the New Edinburgh iron ridge.
5. If the corporation of the county of Carleton shall
within six months elect to require an arbitration thereon 15
arbitrators shall be appointed as provided by *The Consolidated
Municipal Act, 1883*, to determine whether anything and
what shall be paid by the corporation of the city of Ottawa
to the corporation of the county of Carleton, or by the latter
corporation to the former corporation, consequent on the 20
addition to the limits of the said city of Ottawa hereinbefore
mentioned, and the said arbitrators, if they see fit, may take
into consideration, and allow to the corporation of the county
of Carleton such part (if any) of the cost of construction of
the iron bridge over the river Rideau, known as the New 25
Edinburgh iron bridge, as they may deem just, having regard,
if they see fit, to the value of the same bridge either as an
asset of the county or otherwise at the time of the proclamation, and having regard also, if they see fit, to the interest, if
any, of New Edinburgh in the other bridges of the county. 30

Local improvement by-laws for raising money by special assessment confirmed.
6. All by-laws heretofore passed by the council of the
corporation of the city of Ottawa for borrowing money by the
issue of debentures secured by special assessment on the real
property benefited by local improvements, works and services,
the debentures issued thereunder and the special assessment 35
made to provide for the cost of such local improvements,
works or services, are hereby confirmed and declared valid
and effectual.

By-laws for providing for the city's share of cost of local improvements confirmed.
7. All by-laws heretofore passed by the council of the
corporation of the city of Ottawa for borrowing money on the 40
general credit of the city to provide for the payment of the
city's share of local improvements, works and services, and the
debentures issued thereunder, are hereby declared valid and
effectual, notwithstanding that such by-laws have not been
submitted for the assent of the electors of the said city 45
of Ottawa.

Water works debentures.
8. To enable the corporation of Ottawa to enlarge the capacity
of the water works, the council of the corporation of the city of
Ottawa shall have power to pass a by-law *or by-laws* to authorize the issue of debentures of the said corporation for a sum 50
not exceeding $100,000, in such sums—of not less than $100—
as the said corporation may deem expedient, which said debentures shall be made payable not more than *thirty* years from
the day on which they respectively bear date, and may be in the

form A in the schedule to this Act set forth ; which said debentures shall bear interest at *a rate not exceeding* five per cent. per annum, payable half-yearly, and such debentures shall be signed by the mayor and the treasurer of the said city for the time 5 being, and may be made payable, either in sterling or currency, in Great Britain, in this Province, or elsewhere, as to the council of the corporation of the city of Ottawa shall seem expedient.

9. For the purpose of providing a sinking fund for the pay- Corporation to 10 ment of the said debentures, and the interest on the same, provide annually by the semi-annually, the council of the corporation of the city of water rates the Ottawa shall raise, annually, from the water rates, and with the amount required for authority conferred upon them in and by the Act of the Legis- sinking fund ture of this Province, intituled, *An Act for the Construction* and interest. 15 *of Water Works for the City of Ottawa*, and the Acts amending the same, a sum of money sufficient to pay the interest, semi-annually, on the days appointed for the payment thereof, upon the principal money of the said debentures ; and shall also raise, annually, a further sum *not less than one and one-half* 20 *per cent. on the principal of the said debentures* sufficient to form a sinking fund to pay off the principal money when the same shall become payable, such sums to be in addition to the moneys required to be raised, to meet the charges for maintenance, the cost of renewals, and the amounts required 25 ☞ for the payment of the interest on the water works debentures already issued for the payment of the sinking fund, amounting annually to $11,700, as required by section 14 of the Act to consolidate the debenture debt of the city of Ottawa, passed in the 41st year of Her Majesty's reign, and 30 chaptered 37 ◁ and the said corporation shall pay the principal moneys and interest on the said debentures herein authorized to be issued, as the same shall from time to time fall due.

10. If, from any cause, the moneys annually accruing under Special rate if the water rates, after deducting the present charges thereon, water rates prove insuf- 35 shall be less than the sums of money from time to time neces- ficient. sary for the payment of the interest and of the sinking fund to pay off the debentures herein authorized to be issued, it shall be the duty of the corporation of the city of Ottawa, and they are hereby authorized and required, when and as often as the same 40 may occur, forthwith to settle, impose, levy and collect an equal special rate upon all the assessable property of the city of Ottawa, in the manner and with the like powers as shall exist in respect to municipal assessments, rates and taxes, and out of the proceeds thereof to pay and discharge all sums of money 45 for interest or principal, which shall or may be due, or accruing due, to meet the interest and sinking fund to pay the debentures herein authorized to be issued.

11. The by-law or by-laws of the said corporation, passed Assent of electors to by-laws under the authority of this Act, shall not require to be sub- not required. 50 mitted to or to have the assent of the electors of the said city before the final passing thereof; ☞ nor shall it be necessary that any of the provisions of the Consolidated Municipal Act, 1883, relating to by-laws for creating debts be complied with. ◁

12. No irregularity in the form of the said debentures, or Irregularities not to render 55 of the by-laws authorizing the issue thereof, shall render the debentures void.

same invalid or illegal, or be allowed as a defence to any action brought against the said corporation for the recovery of the amount of the said debentures and interest, or any or either of them or any part thereof.

Application of surplus revenue from water works.

13. *Any* surplus revenues arising from the supply of water 5 by the water works of the said city, after providing for maintenance and renewals, for the payment of the interest on the water works debentures already issued, for the payment of the sinking fund, amounting annually to $11,700, as required by section 14 of *The Act to Consolidate the Debenture Debt of the* 10 *City of Ottawa,* passed in the 41st year of Her Majesty's reign, and chaptered 37, and also after providing for the moneys required to pay the interest and the sinking fund for the debentures herein authorized to be issued, may, in any year, if the city council so direct, be used and applied in the enlargement, 15 construction and improvement of the water works, notwithstanding the provision contained in the said section, or in section 32 of *The Act for the construction of Water Works for the city of Ottawa,* passed in the 35th year of Her Majesty's reign, and chaptered 80, but if such surplus revenue, 20 or some portion thereof, be not so used in the improvement of the water works, then the said surplus revenue, or the portions thereof not so used, shall be immediately placed at the credit of and become a part of the general sinking fund as required by the said section. 25

SCHEDULE.

(Form A.)

WATER WORKS DEBENTURE.

No. $

Province of Ontario,   30

City of Ottawa.

Under and by virtue of the Act passed in the fiftieth year of the Reign of Her Majesty, Queen Victoria, and Chaptered   , and by virtue of By-law No.   , of the Corporation of the City of Ottawa, passed under the powers 35 contained in the said Act.

The Corporation of the City of Ottawa promise to pay the bearer, at   , in the sum of
on the   day of   A.D.   and the 40 half-yearly coupons hereto attached as the same shall severally become due.

L.S.

Mayor.

Treasurer. 45

1st Session, 6th Legislature, 50 Vic., 1887.

BILL.

An Act respecting Knox Church Cemetery and Knox Church lot in the Village of Ayr.

(Reprinted as amended by Private Bills Committee.)

First Reading, 9th March, 1887.

(Private Bill.)

No. 16.]　　　　**BILL.**　　　　[1887.

An Act to authorize William Charles Kaake to
practise Dental Surgery in the Province of
Ontario.

WHEREAS William Charles Kaake has by his petition set Preamble.
forth that for some years previous to the year 1879 he had
been constantly engaged in the practice of dentistry, in the office
of a licentiate practitioner in this Province, and that since the
5 said year he has been constantly engaged in the practice of
the profession of dentistry until a very recent period, and that
he is now, and has been during all the time of such practice a British subject, and that in the said year 1879 he was
about to present himself to the board of examiners of the
10 Royal College of Dental Surgery of Ontario to be examined,
concerning his fitness to enter upon the course prescribed by
the Board of Directors of the said Royal College of Dental
Surgery of Ontario, before becoming a properly qualified
dental surgeon, but he was informed by the said Board of
15 Directors that he might delay until the year 1880, and not
lose any time thereby, and that, acting upon such information
he did not present himself to the said Board of Examiners to
be examined as aforesaid, and that at the commencement of
the year 1880, the standard for matriculation into the said col-
20 lege was raised, and the said William Charles Kaake was unable
to pass the examination then prescribed without considerable
study and loss of time, and that he has since requested the
said Board of Directors to be allowed to pass the matriculation examination required previous to the year 1880, and also
25 the final examination prescribed by the said Board of Directors
required to be passed previous to their granting a certificate
to permit practice as a dental surgeon, and to pay the required
fees, which request was refused, and the said William Charles
Kaake was consequently unable to obtain such certificate, and
30 that he is thoroughly competent to practise dental surgery ;
and whereas the said William Charles Kaake has prayed that
an Act be passed to authorize him to practise dental surgery
in Ontario, and whereas it is expedient to grant the prayer of
the said petition ;
35　　Therefore Her Majesty, by and with the advice and consent
of the Legislative Assembly of the Province of Ontario, enacts
as follows:—

1. It shall and may be lawful for the said William Charles W. C. Kaake,
Kaake to practise dental surgery in all its departments, within practise
40 the Province of Ontario, and to charge regular fees therefor, dentistry.
and to collect the same in as full and ample a manner as if he
had taken out, obtained and held a certificate of license to practise dentistry under the Act respecting dentistry, or under any
Act now in force in this Province respecting dentistry.

1st Session, 6th Legislature, 50 Vic., 1887.

BILL.

An Act to authorize William Charles Kaake to practise Dental Surgery in the Province of Ontario.

First Reading.   1887.

(Private Bill.)

No. 17.] **BILL.** [1887.

An Act to amend the Act incorporating the Toronto
School of Medicine.

WHEREAS by an Act of the Parliament of Canada, passed Preamble.
in the fourteenth and fifteenth years of the reign of
Her Majesty Queen Victoria, chapter one hundred and fifty-
five, John Rolph, Joseph Workman, William Thomas Aikins,
5 James Langstaff, Gavin Russell, and Thomas David Morrison,
and their successors, were constituted a body politic and corporate by the name of the Toronto School of Medicine, and provisions were made for the election of new members on the
death or resignation of any member or members, or in case it
10 should be desired to increase the number ; and whereas the
present members of the said Corporation are Joseph Workman, James Langstaff, William Thomas Aikins, Henry Hoover
Wright, James Henry Richardson, Uzziel Ogden, James Thor-
burn, Michael Barrett, William Winslow Ogden, Moses Henry
15 Aikins, William Oldright, Lachlan McFarlane, George Wright,
James Elliott Graham, and Richard Andrews Reeve ; and
whereas the said corporation by its petition has represented
that it would increase the efficiency and the operations of the
said corporation if power were granted thereto to confer
20 degrees in the faculty of mĕdicine upon those who shall seek
the same at the hands of the said corporation, and if increased
powers were given to take, receive, purchase, hold and convey,
real estate and to regulate the membership of the said corporation ; and whereas it is expedient to grant the prayer of the
25 said petition ;
Therefore Her Majesty, by and with the advice and consent
of the Legislative Assembly of the Province of Ontario, enacts
as follows :—

1. Section 1 of the Act of the Parliament of Canada passed 14 & 15 V. c.
30 in the fourteenth and fifteenth years of the reign of Her 155, s. 1,
Majesty, chapter one hundred and fifty-five, is hereby amended amended.
by inserting the words " forty thousand dollars" in lieu of
the words " five thousand pounds."

2. Section 2 of the said Act is hereby repealed, and in lieu 14 & 15 V. c.
35 thereof be it enacted, That whenever any of the members of 155, s. 2,
the said Corporation shall die, resign, be removed, or cease to repealed.
be a member, or it shall be deemed advisable by the corpora- Election of
tion to increase the number of members thereof, then the said members.
Corporation shall proceed, according to their by-laws for that
40 purpose made and enacted, to elect members in the place and
stead of those so dying, resigning, removed or ceasing to be
members or a member, or needed to be elected as the case may
be : Provided that no member shall be removed unless by the

vote of at least two-thirds of the members present at a meeting called for such purpose, nor until a by-law or by-laws shall be passed providing the procedure for the removal or expulsion of a member or members.

Power to confer degrees. **3.** The said corporation, by or through such member or 5 members as they may from time to time elect or appoint for such purpose, shall have power to confer the degrees of Master of Surgery and Doctor of Medicine upon graduates in medicine of such universities or colleges as the said corporation shall recognize for that purpose, as well as upon such students or 10 candidates of the said corporation as are now taking, or shall hereafter take, the regular course of study therein, or have before the passing of this Act completed their course of study, subject however in any case to such regulations as to examination or otherwise, as may from time to time be prescribed by 15 by-law of the said corporation.

No. 17.

1st Session, 6th Legislature, 50 Vic., 1887.

BILL.

An Act to amend the Act incorporating the Toronto School of Medicine.

First Reading, 1887.

(Private Bill.)

Mr. LEYS.

TORONTO:
PRINTED BY WARWICK & SONS, 26 AND 28 FRONT ST. W.

An Act to amend the Act incorporating the Brockville Gas Light Campany.

WHEREAS the Brockville Gas Light Company have, by *Preamble.* their petition, prayed that an Act may be passed authorizing the said company to increase the amount of the capital stock thereof, as fixed by the Act incorporating the 5 said company, passed in the sixteenth year of Her Majesty's reign, and chaptered one hundred and eight, extending the powers of the said company, and enabling the said company to borrow money on mortgage, and otherwise ; and whereas it is expedient to grant the prayer of the said petition ;

10 Therefore Her Majesty, by and with the advice and consent of the Legislative Assembly of the Province of Ontario, enacts as follows :—

1. It shall be lawful for the said company to add to their *Increase of* present capital stock such sums that the said capital stock may *capital stock* 15 equal, but not exceed the sum of $80,000, and to raise such *authorized.* additional capital stock either by subscription among the. present shareholders, or by the admission of new shareholders, or partly in one way, and partly in the other way.

2. Every person subscribing for, or taking any share, or *Rights and* 20 shares, in such additional capital stock, shall have the same *liabilities of* rights, and be subject to the same provisions, rules, and *subscribers for new stock.* liabilities, as the original subscribers and shareholders of the said company, and the various clauses of the said Act of incorporation, applicable to the shares and shareholders of the said 25 company, shall apply to the shares hereby authorized to be issued, or subscribed for, except so far as the same may be inconsistent with the provisions hereof.

3. The said company may, from time to time, borrow money, *Power to bor-* and as security for the money so borrowed, may give its *row on mort-* 30 promissory note, or notes signed by the president, or vice- *gage, etc.* president, and manager, or secretary thereof, or may mortgage the whole, or any part of the real and personal estate, plant, buildings and machinery of said company, and may insert in the instrument or instruments of mortgage all such powers of 35 sale, and other powers and covenants as are usual and proper in a mortgage from a private individual.

4. Chapter 157 of the Revised Statutes of Ontario, and *R. S. O. c.* amendments thereto, respecting joint stock companies, for *157, to apply* supplying cities, towns and villages, with gas and water, shall *to company.* 40 apply to the said company.

1st Session, 6th Legislature, 50 Vic., 1887.

BILL.

An Act to amend the Act incorporating the
Brockville Gas Light Company.

First Reading,   1887.

(Private Bill.)

BILL.

An Act to amend the Act incorporating the Brockville, Westport, and Sault Ste. Marie Railway
Company.

WHEREAS it is expedient to amend the Act passed in the Preamble.
forty-seventh year of Her Majesty's reign, chaptered
63, incorporating the Brockville, Westport and Sault Ste.
Marie Railway Company;
5   Therefore Her Majesty, by and with the advice and consent
of the Legislative Assembly of the Province of Ontario, enacts
as follows :—

1. Section 50 of the said Act, passed in the forty-seventh 47 V. c. 63, s.
year of Her Majesty's reign, and chaptered 63, is hereby 50, amended.
10 amended by striking out the words "and treasurer" in the
eighth line thereof, and by altering the first proviso in said section contained so as to read as follows : " Provided, however,
that the issue of bonds and debenture stock shall not exceed
$25,000 per mile of said railway and branches;", in all other
15 respects the said section shall remain unaltered.

2. Section 47 of the said Act is amended by striking out 47 V. c. 63, s.
the word "six," in the third line thereof, and by substituting 47, amended.
the word " one " in lieu thereof.

3. Section 20 of said Act is amended by striking out all of 47 V. c. 63, s.
20 said section after the word " and," in the fifth line thereof, and 20, amended.
substituting the following : " public notice thereof shall be
given by advertisement in the *Ontario Gazette*, and in one
newspaper published in the Town of Brockville at least one
week before the time of such meeting."

25   4. The said company is hereby authorized and empowered Power to
to make necessary arrangements to contract and agree with amalgamate
any railway company now incorporated, or hereafter incor- companies.
porated by Act of this Legislature, or of the Parliament of
Canada, if lawfully authorized to enter into such arrangements,
30 for amalgamation with any such company, or companies, provided that the terms of amalgamation are approved of by two-
thirds of the shareholders voting, either in person or represented by proxy at a special general meeting to be held for
that purpose.

35   5. The said company shall have power to enter into and Power to lease
conclude any agreement with any such company, or companies, or acquire
as are mentioned in the preceding section, if lawfully au- powers.
thorized to enter into such agreement, to lease the said Brockville, Westport and Sault Ste. Marie Railway, or any part

thereof, or to lease or acquire running powers over the lines of
such other railway companies, or any or either of them, or any
part or parts thereof, or where any other railway built, or proposed to be built, is parallel with said Brockville, Westport
and Sault Ste. Marie Railway, or any portion thereof, or nearly 5
so, to build one joint line of railway, or to acquire or give
joint running powers, or for leasing or hiring any locomotives,
tenders, plant, rolling stock, or other property, or touching any
service to be rendered by the one company to the other, and
the compensation therefor; provided that the agreements shall 10
be approved of by two-thirds of the shareholders voting either
in person or by proxy at any special general meeting called
for that purpose, but nothing in this or the preceding section
shall be construed as purporting, or intending to confer rights
or powers upon any company which is not within the legis- 15
lative authority of this Province.

**Time limited
in by-laws
granting aid
extended
where munici-
pality in de-
fault.**
    6. Where any municipality, or municipalities, has, or have
passed, or shall hereafter pass, any by-law, or by-laws, granting
any aid by way of bonus or gift, or otherwise, to said company,
and in and by any such by-law, or by-laws, any time is fixed 20
or limited for the commencement or completion of the said
railway, or any portion thereof, and any such municipality, or
municipalities has not, or have not complied with the Act hereby amended, by depositing the debentures, or money, or other
securities authorized by such by-law, or by-laws, with the 25
trustees in manner, and at the time in said Act specified, then
the time or period for the completion of said railway, or the
particular portion thereof specified in said by-law, or by-laws,
shall not be deemed, or taken to have commenced to run until
from and after the date of the deposit of such debentures, money, 30
or other securities in the hands of said trustees.

**User of bridge
on St. Law-
rence and St.
Mary rivers.**
    7. The said company shall have full power to acquire the
right to use, or running powers over any bridges that may be
built across the St. Lawrence river and across the St. Mary
river, so as to connect its railway with other railways on such 35
terms as may be agreed upon, provided that the contracts or
agreements in respect thereof shall be approved of by two-
thirds of the shareholders voting either in person, or by proxy,
at any special general meeting called for that purpose.

**Time for com-
pletion ex-
tended.**
    8. The time for completion of said railway is hereby ex- 40
tended until the termination of eight years from the passing
of the said Act hereby amended.

1st Session, 6th Legislature, 50 Vic., 1887.

BILL.

An Act to amend the Act incorporating the Brockville, Westport and Sault Ste. Marie Railway Company.

First Reading,   1887.

(Private Bill.)

BILL.

An Act to amend the Act incorporating the Brockville, Westport, and Sault Ste. Marie Railway Company.

W HEREAS it is expedient to amend the Act passed in the Preamble.
forty-seventh year of Her Majesty's reign, chaptered
63, incorporating the Brockville, Westport and Sault Ste.
Marie Railway Company;
5   Therefore Her Majesty, by and with the advice and consent
of the Legislative Assembly of the Province of Ontario, enacts
as follows :—

1. Section 50 of the said Act, passed in the forty-seventh 47 V. c. 63, s.
year of Her Majesty's reign, and chaptered 63, is hereby 50, amended.
10 amended by striking out the words " and treasurer " in the
eighth line thereof, and by altering the first proviso in said section contained so as to read as follows.: " Provided, however,
that the issue of bonds and debenture stock shall not exceed
$25,000 per mile of said railway and branches;" in all other
15 respects the said section shall remain unaltered.

2. The said company is authorized and empowered to make Amalgama-
necessary arrangements to contract and agree with the Iron- tion with other
dale, Bancroft and Ottawa Railway Company, the Kingston companies
and Pembroke Railway Company, the Ottawa and Thousand authorized.
20 Island Railway Company, the Northern Pacific Junction Railway Company, or the Gananoque, Perth and James' Bay Railway Company, if lawfully empowered to enter into such
arrangement, for amalgamation with the said companies, or
either of them : provided that the terms of such amalgamation
25 are approved of by two-thirds of the shareholders present in
person or represented by proxy at a special general meeting to
be held for that purpose.

3. The said company is also authorized to enter into any Agreements
agreement with the Canadian Pacific Railway Company, the for running
30 Grand Trunk Railway Company of Canada or any of the com- authorized.
panies mentioned in the preceding section or either of them, if
lawfully empowered to enter into such agreement for running
powers over the said railways or either of them, on such terms
and conditions as the directors of the several contracting com-
35 panies may agree on; the said company shall also have the
power to enter into agreements with any railway company
owning or controlling or in possession of a railway in the State
of New York connecting directly, or by bridge or ferry, with
its road, for the use by either of the road of the other : provided
40 that every such agreement shall first be sanctioned by two-
thirds of the shareholders present in person or represented by
proxy at a special general meeting called for the purpose of

considering the same ; but nothing in this or the preceding
section shall be construed as purporting or intending to confer
rights or powers upon any company which is not within the
legislative authority of this Province.

Time limited
in by-laws
granting aid
extended
where munici-
pality in de-
fault.

4. Where any municipality, or municipalities, has, or have 5
passed, or shall hereafter pass, any by-law, or by-laws, granting
any aid by way of bonus or gift, or otherwise, to said company,
and in and by any such by-law, or by-laws, any time is fixed
or limited for the commencement or completion of the said
railway, or any portion thereof, and any such municipality, or 10
municipalities has not, or have not complied with the Act hereby. amended, by depositing the debentures, or money, or other
securities authorized by such by-law, or by-laws, with the
trustees in manner, and at the time in said Act specified, then
the time or period for the completion of said railway, or the 15
particular portion thereof specified in said by-law, or by-laws,
shall not be deemed, or taken to have commenced to run until
from and after the date of the deposit of such debentures, money,
or other securities in the hands of said trustees ; Provided
that the agreement dated March 31st, 1887, made between the 20
Railway Company and the municipality of Bastard and Burgess
South, shall be legal and binding upon the company and their
assignees and upon the said municipality.

User of bridge
on St. Law-
rence and St.
Mary rivers.

5. The said company shall have full power to acquire the
right to use, or running powers over any bridges that may be 25
built across the St. Lawrence river and across the St. Mary
river, so as to connect its railway with other railways on such
terms as may be agreed upon, provided that the contracts or
agreements in respect thereof shall be approved of by two-
thirds of the shareholders voting either in person, or by proxy, 30
at any special general meeting called for that purpose.

Time for com-
pletion ex-
tended.

6. The time for completion of said railway is hereby extended until the termination of eight years from the passing
of the said Act.

1st Session, 6th Legislature, 50 Vic., 1887.

BILL.

An Act to amend the Act incorporating the Brockville, Westport and Sault Ste. Marie Railway Company.

(Reprinted as amended by Railway Committee.)

First Reading, 9th March, 1887.

(Private Bill.)

Mr. FRASER.

BILL.

An Act to amend the Acts relating to the Long
Point Company.

WHEREAS the Long Point Company were incorporated Preamble.
under an Act of incorporation, passed in the twenty-
ninth and thirtieth years of Her Majesty's reign, which Act of
incorporation was amended by an Act of the Legislative
5 Assembly of the Province of Ontario, passed in the forty-
ninth year of Her Majesty's reign and chaptered eighty-
three; and whereas the said company have expended large
sums of money in carrying on the purposes and business for
which they were incorporated, and have no power to mortgage
10 or bond the lands and property of the company, for the purpose of borrowing money ; and whereas it will benefit and
advance the purposes and business of the company to grant
such power to the extent hereafter set forth ; and whereas
they have prayed for the passing of an Act to that end, and it
15 is expedient to grant the prayer of the said petition ;

Therefore Her Majesty, by and with the advice and consent
of the Legislative Assembly of the Province of Ontario, enacts
as follows—

1. In this Act, and the by-laws of said company heretofore Interpretation
20 or hereafter made, the expression " the company," shall mean
the Long Point Company, the word "shareholders" shall mean
every subscriber to, or holder of, stock in the company, and
shall extend to, and include, the personal representatives of the
shareholders, and the words "life right member" shall mean
25 the holder of any right to hunt, shoot, or fish, upon any part
of the company's property, for life, or any less term.

2. The directors of the company, after the sanction of the Power to
shareholders shall have been first obtained, at any special issue bonds.
general meeting, to be called from time to time for such pur-
30 pose, shall have power to issue bonds, made and signed by the
president, and two of the directors of the company, and countersigned by the secretary, and under the seal of the company, to
the extent of not more than $25,000, and such bonds shall,
without registration, or formal conveyance, be taken, and con-
35 sidered to be the first, and preferential claims, and charges
upon the franchises, and real and personal property of the company, then, and at any time thereafter acquired, and each
holder of the said bonds shall be deemed to be a mortgagee and
incumbrancer, *pro rata*, with all the other holders thereof upon
40 the franchises, and real and personal property of the company
then, and at any time thereafter acquired, and the directors
may, after such sanction as aforesaid, from time to time, to the
extent aforesaid, renew, or re-issue, such bonds as aforesaid,
upon the surrender, or expiration, of any issue, or issues
45 thereof.

Coupons or interest warrants.

3. All such bonds may have coupons, or interest warrants thereon, or attached thereto, for payment of interest half-yearly, at a rate not to exceed six per centum per annum, and such bonds and coupons may be made payable to bearer, and transferable by delivery, and any holder of any such bond, 5 coupon, or interest warrant, so made payable to bearer, may sue at law thereon, in his own name.

Power to mortgage bonds.

4. The company may, from time to time, for advances of money to be made thereon, mortgage, or pledge any of said bonds, and they may, from time to time, sell them for such 10 price as they may see fit, and the money so procured may not only be applied and used for the general purposes of the company, but also wholly, or in part, in purchasing capital stock of the company from the holders thereof, from time to time, as the directors may deem expedient.   15

Calls.

5. The directors may, from time to time, make calls or assessments upon the shareholders for a sufficient amount per share upon all outstanding stock not held by the company, to pay the interest accruing due upon all sold or mortgaged bonds, and also, from time to time, make calls, or assessments, 20 upon the shareholders and life right members, for the general purposes of the company, and to pay the current expenses of the company, and the cost of the management, operation, and control of its business and affairs, and the protection, preservation, maintenance, repair, improvement, and enlargement of its 25 property and franchises; provided, however, that such last mentioned calls and assessments shall not exceed in all, in any one year, upon shareholders, $150, for every five shares of stock, and upon a life right member, one-half the amount assessed upon five shares of stock, and no life right member 30 shall be liable to be assessed for any year in which he does not shoot upon the company's property.

Proviso.

Enforcing payment of calls.

6. All such calls and assessments shall be paid when, and as the directors of the company shall require, or as the by-laws may provide, and if not paid at the day required, interest at 35 the rate of seven per cent per annum shall be payable after the said day upon the amount due and unpaid, and in case any such call or assessment shall not be paid, as required by the directors, with interest thereon, after such demand or notice, as the by-laws may prescribe, and within the time 40 limited by such notice, the company may collect the amount of such call or assessment, by action in any Court of competent jurisdiction, in the name of the company, with interest at seven per centum per annum, and all such calls and assessments shall be a first lien and charge upon the stock in 45 whosesoever hands the same may be, and the company may, by by-law, debar any shareholder or life right member from any of the privileges of the company and from coming upon its property, so long as he shall be in default in the payment of any such call or assessment.   50

1st Session, 6th Legislature, 50 Vic., 1887.

BILL.

An Act to amend the Acts relating to the
Long Point Company.

First Reading,   1887

(Private Bill)

BILL.

An Act to amend the Acts relating to the Long Point Company.

WHEREAS the Long Point Company were incorporated Preamble. under an Act of incorporation, passed in the twenty-ninth and thirtieth years of Her Majesty's reign, which Act of incorporation was amended by an Act of the Legislative
5 Assembly of the Province of Ontario, passed in the forty-ninth year of Her Majesty's reign and chaptered eighty-three; and whereas the said company have expended large sums of money in carrying on the purposes and business for which they were incorporated, and have no power to mortgage
10 or bond the lands and property of the company, for the purpose of borrowing money; and whereas it will benefit and advance the purposes and business of the company to grant such power to the extent hereinafter set forth; and whereas they have prayed for the passing of an Act to that end, and it
15 is expedient to grant the prayer of the said petition;

Therefore Her Majesty, by and with the advice and consent of the Legislative Assembly of the Province of Ontario, enacts as follows—

1. In this Act, and the by-laws of said company heretofore Interpretation
20 or hereafter made, the expression "the company," shall mean the Long Point Company, the word "shareholders" shall mean every subscriber to, or holder of, stock in the company, and shall extend to, and include, the personal representatives of the shareholders, and the words "life right member" shall mean
25 the holder of any right to hunt, shoot, or fish, upon any part of the company's property, for life, or any less term.

2. The directors of the company, after the sanction of *a* Power to *majority of* the shareholders shall have been first obtained, issue bonds.
30 at any special general meeting, to be called from time to time for such purpose, shall have power to issue bonds, *of not less than $100 each,* made and signed by the president, and two of the directors of the company, and countersigned by the secretary, and under the seal of the company, to the extent of not more than $25,000, and such bonds shall, without registra-
35 tion, or formal conveyance, be taken, and considered to be the first, and preferential claims, and charges upon the franchises, and real and personal property of the company, then, and at any time thereafter acquired, and each holder of the said bonds shall be deemed to be a mortgagee and incumbrancer, *pro*
40 *rata,* with all the other holders thereof upon the franchises, and real and personal property of the company then, and at any time thereafter acquired, and the directors may, after such sanction as aforesaid, from time to time, to the extent aforesaid, renew, or re-issue, such bonds as aforesaid, upon the sur-
45 render, or expiration, of any issue, or issues thereof.

Coupons or i nterest warrants.

3. All such bonds may have coupons thereon, or attached thereto, for payment of interest half-yearly, at a rate not to exceed six per centum per annum, and such bonds and coupons may be made payable to bearer, and transferable by delivery, and any holder of any such bond, or coupon, so made payable 5 to bearer, may sue at law thereon, in his own name.

Power to mortgage bonds.

4. The company may, from time to time, for advances of money to be made thereon, mortgage, or pledge any of said bonds, and they may, from time to time, sell them for such 10 price as they may see fit, and the money so procured may not only be applied and used for the general purposes of the company, but also wholly, or in part, in purchasing capital stock of the company from the holders thereof, from time to time, as the directors may deem expedient.   15

Calls.

5. The directors may, from time to time, make calls or assessments upon the shareholders for a sufficient amount per share upon all outstanding stock not held by the company, to pay the interest accruing due upon all sold or mortgaged bonds, and also, from time to time, make calls, or assessments, 20 upon the shareholders and life right members, for the general purposes of the company, and to pay the current expenses of the company, and the cost of the management, operation, and control of its business and affairs, and the protection, preservation, maintenance, repair, improvement, and enlargement of its 25 property and franchises ; provided, however, that such last **Proviso.** mentioned calls and assessments shall not exceed in all, in any one year, upon shareholders, $150, for every five shares of stock, and upon a life right member, one-half the amount assessed upon five shares of stock, and no life right member 30 shall be liable to *pay the assessment* for any year in which he does not shoot upon the company's property.

Enforcing payment of calls.

6. All such calls and assessments shall be paid when, and as the directors of the company shall require, or as the by-laws may provide, and if not paid at the day required, interest at 35 the rate of seven per cent per annum shall be payable after the said day upon the amount due and unpaid, and in case any such call or assessment shall not be paid, as required by the directors, with interest thereon, after such demand or notice, as the by-laws may prescribe, and within the time 40 limited by such notice, the company may collect the amount of such call or assessment, by action in any Court of competent jurisdiction, in the name of the company, with interest at seven per centum per annum ; *Provided always*, that all such calls and assessments shall be a first lien and charge upon 45 the stock in whosesoever hands the same may be, and the holders of such stock, and the life right members, shall be debarred from entry upon the company's property while in default for any assessment so made, and no share shall be transferred while in default for, or charged with any assess- 50 ment or other liability to the company.

☞ **7.** Nothing hereinbefore contained shall be construed to interfere with or prejudice the rights and privileges vested in and acquired by James M. Salmon, of the town of Simcoe, in the county of Norfolk, physician, under and by virtue of a 5 license granted to him by said company, bearing date the fourth day of March, 1871, and registered in the registry office in the said county on the 25th day of July, 1874, in Book No. 36,523, or to render him liable as a life right member or otherwise, on account of having said license to any such calls 10 or assessments aforesaid, or shall empower the company to assess or impose the same against or upon him. ☜

Rights of J. M. Salmon not affected.

1st Session, 6th Legislature, 50 Vic., 1887.

BILL.

An Act to amend the Acts relating to the Long Point Company.

(*Re-printed as amended by Private Bills Committee.*)

First Reading, 11th March, 1887.

(Private Bill.)

An Act to authorize the Corporation of the City of
London to borrow certain moneys for Public School
purposes.

WHEREAS the municipal council of the Corporation of the Preamble.
city of London and the board of education of the city of
London have, by their petition, represented that the said corporation are the owners of lots numbers six, seven, eight, nine
5 and ten, on the south side of East King Street, and of lots
numbers six, seven, eight, nine and ten, on the north side of
East York Street, in the said city of London, and that it is
desired by the said corporation and the said board to sell the
said lands and acquire other lands in lieu thereof, and to erect
10 buildings thereon for public school purposes ; and that to carry
out the said object it will be necessary for the said corporation
to be authorized to borrow money, and have prayed for the
passing of an Act to enable them to carry out the said object,
and whereas it is expedient to grant the prayer of the said
15 petition ;
Therefore Her Majesty, by and with the advice and consent
of the Legislative Assembly of the Province of Ontario, enacts
as follows :—

1. The said municipal council may from time to time pass Power to pass
20 by-laws for acquiring such lands as they may deem necessary by-laws for
for providing additional public school accommodation for the for school pur-
said city, and for erecting buildings thereon and otherwise poses.
improving the same for the said purposes.

2. The said municipal council may pass a by-law or by-laws Power to
25 for borrowing such sum or sums of money as they may deem borrow.
necessary for the purposes mentioned in section 1, and issue
debentures therefor which may be payable at any time within
such period not exceeding twenty years, and with such rate of
interest not exceeding six per centum per annum, payable
30 yearly, half-yearly or otherwise as the said council may direct
or think fit.

3. The amount to be borrowed, under the authority of this Limit of
Act, shall not exceed the value of so much of the lands herein- borrowing
after and in the preamble to this Act mentioned as the said powers.
35 council shall, within three years after the passing of this Act,
declare it to be expedient to dispose of.

4. The value of the said lands shall be ascertained and How value of
determined by the estimate of the city assessors or such other lands is to be
person as the said municipal council may by by-law appoint for determined.
40 that purpose, and such estimate shall, when filed with the clerk

of the said municipality, be conclusive evidence for the purposes of this Act of the value of the said lands.

Power to sell lands.

5. The said municipal council may sell and dispose of lots numbers six, seven, eight, nine and ten, on the south side of East King Street, and lots numbers six, seven, eight, nine and 5 ten, on the north side of East York Street, in the said city of London, being the lands mentioned in the preamble to this Act, either together or in parcels, and for cash or on credit, and either by public auction or private sale, and may convey the same to the purchasers thereof and may take mortgages or other secur- 10 ities thereon for the unpaid purchase money, and may sell, dispose of and assign such mortgages or other securities.

Purchasers not responsible for application of purchase money.

6. The purchasers of the said lands shall not be bound to see to the application of their purchase money or to inquire whether any of the conditions of this Act have been complied 15 with.

Application of proceeds of sale.

7. The whole of the proceeds of the sale of the said lands shall form a fund for the payment of the principal and interest of the debentures by this Act authorized to be issued and shall, until the same shall be fully paid and satisfied, be applied 20 for no other purpose.

Council to raise balance needed.

8. If the produce of the sale of the said lands shall not be sufficient to pay off the moneys borrowed under the authority of this Act and the interest thereof within five years from the passing of this Act, it shall be the duty of the said municipal 25 council, upon the expiration of the said period of five years, to raise by special rate upon all the ratable property within the said city yearly during the currency of the said debentures, a sum sufficient to pay the annual interest of the then outstanding debentures, and a sum sufficient with the estimated interest 30 on the investments thereof, the rate of such interest not to exceed five per centum per annum capitalized annually, to discharge the debt when payable.

Assent of of electors to by-laws not required.

9. It shall not be necessary that any by-law passed under the authority of this Act shall receive the assent of the elec- 35 tors, or that any of the provisions of *The Consolidated Municipal Act, 1883*, relating to by-laws for creating debts shall be complied with.

Form of debentures.

10. Every debenture issued under the authority of this Act shall have upon the face of it written or printed the words 40 "Public School Debenture, 1887," and it shall be conclusively presumed in favour of the holder of every such debenture, that the same was lawfully issued under the authority of this Act,

No. 21.

1st Session, 6th Legislature, 50 Vic., 1887.

BILL.

An Act to authorize the corporation of the City of London to borrow certain moneys for public school purposes.

First Reading,   1887.

(Private Bill.)

BILL.

An Act to authorize the Corporation of the City of London to borrow certain moneys for Public School purposes.

WHEREAS the municipal council of the corporation of the Preamble. city of London and the board of education of the city of London have, by their petition, represented that the said corporation are the owners of lots numbers six, seven, eight, nine 5 and ten, on the south side of East King Street, and of lots numbers six, seven, eight, nine and ten, on the north side of East York Street, in the said city of London, and that it is desired by the said corporation and the said board to sell the said lands and acquire other lands in lieu thereof, and to erect 10 buildings thereon for public school purposes ; and that to carry out the said object it will be necessary for the said corporation to be authorized to borrow money, and have prayed for the passing of an Act to enable them to carry out the said object ; and whereas it is expedient to grant the prayer of the said 15 petition ;

Therefore Her Majesty, by and with the advice and consent of the Legislative Assembly of the Province of Ontario, enacts as follows :—

1. The said municipal council may from time to time pass Power to pass 20 by-laws for acquiring such lands as they may deem necessary by-laws for for providing additional public school accommodation for the for school pur- said city, and for erecting buildings thereon and otherwise poses. improving the same for the said purposes.

2. The said municipal council may pass a by-law or by-laws Power to 25 for borrowing such sum or sums of money as they may deem borrow. necessary for the purposes mentioned in section 1, and issue debentures therefor which may be payable at any time within such period not exceeding twenty years, and with such rate of interest not exceeding six per centum per annum, payable 30 yearly, half-yearly or otherwise as the said council may direct or think fit.

3. The amount to be borrowed, under the authority of this Limit of Act, shall not exceed the value of so much of the lands herein- borrowing after and in the preamble to this Act mentioned as the said powers. 35 council shall, within three years after the passing of this Act, declare it to be expedient to dispose of.

4. The value of the said lands shall be ascertained and How value of determined by the estimate of the city assessors or such other lands is to be person as the said municipal council may by by-law appoint for determined. 40 that purpose, and such estimate shall, when filed with the clerk

of the said municipality, be conclusive evidence for the purposes of this Act of the value of the said lands.

Power to sell lands.

5. The said municipal council may sell and dispose of lots numbers six, seven, eight, nine and ten, on the south side of East King Street, and lots numbers six, seven, eight, nine and 5 ten, on the north side of East York Street, in the said city of London, being the lands mentioned in the preamble to this Act, either together or in parcels, and for cash or on credit, and either by public auction or private sale, and may convey the same to the purchasers thereof and may take mortgages or other secur- 10 ities thereon for the unpaid purchase money, and may sell, dispose of and assign such mortgages or other securities.

Purchasers not responsible for application of purchase money.

6. The purchasers of the said lands shall not be bound to see to the application of their purchase money or to inquire whether any of the conditions of this Act have been complied 15 with.

Application of proceeds of sale.

7. The whole of the proceeds of the sale of the said lands shall form a fund for the payment of the principal and interest of the debentures by this Act authorized to be issued and shall, until the same shall be fully paid and satisfied, be applied 20 for no other purpose.

Council to raise balance needed.

8. If the produce of the sale of the said lands shall not be sufficient to pay off the moneys borrowed under the authority of this Act and the interest thereof within five years from the passing of this Act, it shall be the duty of the said municipal 25 council, upon the expiration of the said period of five years, to raise by special rate upon all the ratable property within the said city, *except the property of the supporters of separate schools*, yearly during the currency of the said debentures, a sum sufficient to pay the annual interest of the then outstanding 30 debentures, and a sum sufficient with the estimated interest on the investments thereof, the rate of such interest not to exceed five per centum per annum capitalized annually, to discharge the debt when payable.

Assent of of electors to by-laws not required.

9. It shall not be necessary that any by-law passed under 35 the authority of this Act shall receive the assent of the electors, or that any of the provisions of *The Consolidated Municipal Act, 1883*, relating to by-laws for creating debts shall be complied with.

Form of debentures.

10. Every debenture issued under the authority of this Act 40 shall have upon the face of it written or printed the words " Public School Debenture, 1887," and it shall be conclusively presumed in favour of the holder of every such debenture, that the same was lawfully issued under the authority of this Act.

Exemption of property of separate school supporters.

11. Notwithstanding anything herein contained, this 45 Act shall be taken and construed as enacting and intending that all persons who are supporters of separate schools within the said city of London, and the property of every such person, shall be exempted from, and shall not be liable for, the payment of the debentures hereby authorized to be issued, or for 50 any part thereof, or for any rate or assessment made, levied, or authorized in respect of said debentures or any of them, or of the payment thereof.

BILL.

An Act to authorize the corporation of the City of London to borrow certain moneys for public school purposes.

(Re-printed as amended by Committee of the Whole House.)

First Reading 9th March, 1887.
Second   "   24th   "   1887.

Mr. MEREDITH.

An Act to legalize and confirm an agreement entered
into by and between the Municipality of Dysart
and the Canadian Land and Emigration Company
(Limited).

WHEREAS for some time past differences and disagree- Preamble.
ments have existed between the Municipality of Dysart
and The Canadian Land and Emigration Company (Limited),
regarding the assessment of the real and personal property of
5 the said company in the townships of Dysart, Dudley, Harcourt, Guilford, Harburn, Havelock, Bruton, Eyre, and Clyde,
forming the united Municipality of Dysart ; and whereas both
the said municipality and the said company became involved
in heavy and costly litigation arising out of the differences
10 between them in connection with the said assessment of the
said company's aforesaid property ; and whereas, after much
cost and expense had been incurred by both parties, in connection with the said litigation, the assessed value of the
company's property was, after a protracted trial before the
15 Judge of the County Court of the County of Victoria, on an
appeal to him from the Court of Revision of the Municipality
of Dysart, fixed on the thirty-first day of July, A. D., 1885,
at the sum of $73,920, and thereupon the municipality and the
company entered into an agreement for the settlement of the
20 said litigation, and to regulate the assessment of the company's
property for the future, with the view of avoiding further
litigation and expense ; and whereas it was agreed between
the company and the said municipality that the said agreement of the thirty-first day of July, A. D., 1885, a copy of
25 which is set out in the schedule hereto, should be confirmed
by an Act of this Legislature ; and whereas the said company
and the said municipality have bound themselves to seek confirmation of the said agreement from this Legislature, and
it is in the interest of both parties that further litigation
30 should cease, and whereas the said parties have, by their petition, prayed for an Act accordingly, and it is expedient to
grant the prayer of the said petition ;

Therefore Her Majesty, by and with the advice and consent
of the Legislative Assembly of the Province of Ontario, enacts
35 as follows :—

1. The said agreement entered into by and between the Agreement
Municipality of Dysart and the Canadian Land and Emigra- confirmed.
tion Company (Limited), and which is set out in the schedule
to this Act, is hereby legalized and confirmed.

SCHEDULE.

The Municipality of Dysart and The Canadian Land and Emigration Company agree as follows:—

That the suit now pending in the Chancery Division of the High Court of Justice of the Province of Ontario, between the Canadian Land and Emigration Company and the Municipality of Dysart, James Dover, *et al*, be settled on the following terms:

The assessment of the property, real and personal, of the company and its lessees, other than those of property now assessed to lessees for the next ten years to be fixed at fifteen twenty-ninths of the total assessment of the real and personal property in the Townships of Dysart, Dudley, Harcourt, Guilford, Harburn, Bruton, Havelock, Eyre, and Clyde; the real and personal property of the settlers in the said townships, during the next ten years, to be assessed at fourteen twenty-ninths of the total assessment of all the real and personal property in the said townships; upon the sale or leasing by the company of any of its property the amount of the company's assessment to be reduced by the assessable value of the property so sold or leased.

The costs of the company and the municipality and the members of the Court of Revision, as between solicitor and client, of the action and appeals, and of these proceedings and appeal to Judge Dean, to be paid by the municipality, such costs, however, not to exceed three thousand dollars in all.

The company to pay to the Municipality of Dysart two thousand dollars, by way of bonus, to help the municipality to meet the moneys due by the municipality on the railway bonus for the year 1884.

The company to take out of court the moneys now lying in the Chancery Division of the High Court of Justice for the Province of Ontario, in the said suit of the Canadian Land and Emigration Company *v.* Dysart, James Dover, *et al*; the municipality and the other defendants in the said suit to give all necessary consents, to enable the plaintiffs to get out of court all moneys paid in by them to the credit of the cause, whether the same be on account of taxes alleged to have been due to the municipality for the year 1884, or for costs awarded to defendants, or as security for the plaintiffs' appeal to the Court of Appeal for Ontario, or as security for the plaintiffs' appeal to the Supreme Court of Canada; and on such moneys being paid out to the plaintiffs, the plaintiffs forthwith to pay over to the Municipality of Dysart the said bonus of $2,000, and also a sufficient amount to make up, with the moneys already paid by the plaintiffs on their assessment for the year 1884, fifteen twenty-ninths of all the taxation levied by the municipality in that year; it being understood and agreed that the assessment of the company and the settlers, for the year 1884, shall be considered to have been on the same proportions as it is hereby agreed for the subsequent ten years; and upon payment by the company to the municipality of the said bonus of $2,000 the said municipality to give to the company a receipt in full for their taxes for the year 1884; the municipality to include in their levy for the year 1885 a sufficient sum to meet the liabilities of the municipality for the year 1884, which will still be outstanding after the municipality has applied the sum of $2,000, given them by the company, towards liquidating the railway bonus debt; the municipality to strike a sufficient rate to raise the same in the present year; the moneys paid over by the municipality to the company, to make up fifteen twenty-ninths of the taxation of the year 1884, to be considered an advance by the company to the municipality on their taxes for the year 1885, including the taxes levied to pay the balance of liabilities due by the municipality for the year 1884; and the company to get credit from the municipality and its collectors on the taxes for the year 1885, for such advances.

In the event of this agreement not being carried out in its integrity by the municipality, and the company's assessment not being retained at fifteen twenty-ninths of the whole of the assessable property in the said townships, in manner aforesaid, then the municipality to repay to the company the said bonus of $2,000, together with interest thereon at the rate of six per cent. per annum from the date of its payment to the municipality.

It is further agreed that this agreement is to be confirmed, if possible, by an Act of the Legislature of the Province of Ontario, the costs of obtaining such Act to be paid by the municipality.

In witness whereof the said Municipal Corporation of Dysart have hereunto set their corporate seal, and the said Canadian Land and Emigration Company, the hands of their commissioners, and their corporate seal, this thirty-first day of July, one thousand eight hundred and eighty-five.

In the presence of
F. D. MOORE.

JAMES DOVER, [L.S.]
Reeve.

JAMES M. IRWIN
W. H. LOCKHART GORDON, [L.S.]
Commissioners.

BILL.

An Act to legalize and confirm an agreement entered into between the Municipality of Dysart and the Canadian Land and Emigration Company (Limited.)

First Reading,   1887.

(Private Bill.)

No. 23.]   **BILL.**   [1887.

An Act to unite Toronto Baptist College and
Woodstock College under the name of McMaster
University.

WHEREAS it has been represented by petition of the Preamble.
Toronto Baptist College and Woodstock College, two
institutions of learning, carried on in connection with
the denomination of Christians called Regular Baptists,
5 that the Toronto Baptist College was incorporated by
an Act passed in the forty-fourth year of the reign
of Her Majesty Queen Victoria, for the training of students preparing for the ministry of the Regular Baptist
denomination, with power to confer degrees in Divinity, and
10 has, since its incorporation, been in operation in the City of
Toronto; that Woodstock College was incorporated under the
name of the Canadian Literary Institute in the twentieth
year of the same reign; that by an Act passed in the fortieth
year of the same reign, the name thereof was changed to
15 Woodstock College, and that the work of education has been
carried on in such institution at the Town of Woodstock for
the last twenty-eight years; that it would conduce to the success of the educational work of the said denomination to have
the property and control of the said colleges vested in a board
20 of governors, subject to the powers and rights of a senate as
herinafter provided, and to have the usual powers and privileges of a university conferred upon such board and senate,
and whereas it is expedient to grant the prayer of the said
petition;
25   Therefore Her Majesty, by and with the advice and consent of the Legislative Assembly of the Province of Ontario,
enacts as follows :—

1. From and after the date hereinafter fixed for the coming McMaster
into effect of this Act, the Toronto Baptist College and Wood- University
30 stock College shall be united and form one corporation under constituted.
the name of McMaster University, and shall be under the
management and administration of a Board of Governors,
which, until the appointment of a chancellor as hereinafter
provided, shall consist of sixteen members, who shall be elected
35 as follows : twelve members by the Regular Baptist Missionary Society of Ontario, and four members by the Regular
Baptist Missionary Convention, East, which said sixteen
members shall hold office for four years, except that of those
first elected by the Regular Baptist Missionary Society of
40 Ontario, three shall retire at the expiration of one year, three
at the expiration of two years, and three at the expiration of
three years, from the date of their appointment; and of
those elected by the Regular Baptist Missionary Convention

East, one shall retire at the expiration of one year, one at the
expiration of two years, and one at the expiration of three years.
And upon the appointment of a chancellor, as hereinafter provided, such chancellor shall be ex-officio a member of the said
board, which will then consist of seventeen members.   5

Board of
governors to
be a body
corporate.

2. Such appointments may be made by such society and
convention before the coming into effect of this Act, and the
persons so appointed, and their successors in office, are hereby
constituted a body corporate and politic under the name of
the McMaster University, with perpetual sucession and a 10
common seal, with power to break, alter, and change the same
at pleasure, and by that name may sue and be sued, and be
able and capable in law to take, purchase, and hold any personal property whatsoever ; and shall also be able and capable,
notwithstanding the Statues of Mortmain, to take, purchase, 15
and hold to them and their successors, not only all such lands,
buildings, hereditaments, and possessions as may from time to
time be used or occupied for the purposes of the said university,
including any preparatory or academical department, and for
residences of the chancellor, principals, professors, tutors, stu- 20
dents, and officers, with gardens and lawns attached thereto, but
also any other lands, buildings, hereditaments, and premises not
exceeding the annual value of $10,000, such annual value to
be calculated and ascertained with reference to the period of
taking, purchasing, or acquiring the same ; and to accept on 25
behalf of the said university, or any department thereof, including any preparatory or academical department, any gifts,
devises, or bequests of any property, real or personal, and they
and their successors shall be able and capable in law to grant,
demise, alien, lease, or otherwise dispose of all or any of the 30
property, real or personal, at any time belonging to the said
university, or to any department thereof, including any preparatory or academical department, and to invest the proceeds
thereof upon such securities, or in such way as to the said
board of governors shall seem best, and also to do all other 35
matters and things incidental or appertaining to such body
corporate.

Power to
accept gifts
and bequests.

3. The said university shall be entitled to receive and hold
gifts, devises, and bequests already made, or hereafter coming
into effect, by any person or persons, to or for the benefit of 45
Toronto Baptist College and Woodstock College, or either of
them, as fully and effectually as if the said university was
named in such gifts, devises, or bequests, instead of Toronto
Baptist College and Woodstock College, or either of them,
subject, however, to all the trusts in such gifts, devises, and 50
bequests provided. And all persons shall have the power, notwithstanding the Statutes of Mortmain, at any time to grant,
devise, bequeath, or convey by deed, will, or otherwise, any
real or personal property to the said university, either for its
purposes generally, or for any department thereof, or other- 55
wise, as may be provided by such grant, devise, bequest, or
conveyance, and no gift to the said university shall be void by
reason of the grantor having reserved any interest therein, or
the income thereof, for the term of his life, or any part thereof.
And it is hereby declared that section 2 of the Act, passed in 60
the forty-fourth year of Her Majesty's reign, chapter 87, being
the Act incorporating the said Toronto Baptist College, shall

be construed to have conferred the power and right upon all
persons, notwithstanding the Statutes of Mortmain, to grant,
devise, bequeath, or convey to or for the benefit of the said
Toronto Baptist College, any real or personal property in the
5 terms in said section provided, as well as the power to said
college to receive such grants, devises, bequests and conveyances.

4. McMaster University shall be a Christian school of Religious
learning, and the study of the Bible, or sacred scriptures, shall tests.
10 form a part of the course of study taught by the professors,
tutors, or masters appointed by the board of governors. And
no person shall be eligible to the position of chancellor, principal, professor, tutor, or master, who is not a member in good
standing of an Evangelical Christian church; and no person
15 shall be eligible for the position of principal, professor, tutor,
or master who is not a member in good standing of a Regular
Baptist church, and the said board of governors shall have
the right to require such further or other test as to religious
belief, as a qualification for any such position in the faculty
20 of theology, as to the said board of governors may seem
proper; but no compulsory religions qualification, or examination of a denominational character shall be required from, or
imposed upon any student whatever, other than in the faculty
of theology.

25   **5.** The board of governors shall have full power and au- Powers of
thority to fix the number, residence, duties, salary, provision, board of gover-
and emolument of the chancellor, principals, professors, tutors, nors.
masters, officers, agents, and servants of the said university,
including any preparatory or academical department, and may
30 from time to time remove the chancellor, principals, professors,
tutors, masters, and all other officers, agents, and servants of the
university, and of all departments thereof, including any preparatory or academical department. and may also appoint the
chancellor, principals, professors, tutors, masters., and all other
35 officers, agents, and servants, provided that such power of appointment as to the chancellor, principals, professors, tutors,
and masters shall be exercised only upon the recommendation
of the senate, as hereinafter provided. And the said board
shall have the control and management of the property and
40 funds of the said university, and shall have power to adopt
by-laws and regulations touching and concerning all or any of
the matters aforesaid, as well as concerning the time and place
of meetings of the said board and notices thereof, the officers
of the said board, and their election and duties, and all other
45 matters and things which to them may seem good, fit and useful for the well ordering and advancement of the said university, including any preparatory or academical department, not
repugnant to the provisions of this Act, or any public law in
force in this Province, and the same to alter or vary from
50 time to time in accordance with any provision for that purpose contained in such by-laws and regulations, and after the
common seal of the university has been affixed thereto such
by-laws and regulations shall be binding upon all parties,
members thereof, and upon all others whom the same may
55 concern.

Duties of board of governors.

6. It shall be the duty of the said board of governors to keep proper records and minutes of all and every their proceedings, and to keep proper books of account of the financial affairs of the said university, including any preparatory or academical department, and to present a report of the work of 5 the said university, accompanied by a duly audited financial statement, to each annual meeting of the said the Regular Baptist Missionary Society of Ontario, and the Regular Baptist Missionary Convention, East, respectively. Should the said society and convention unite, such report and financial 10 statement shall be presented to such united society, and such united society shall thereafter have the right to elect the aforesaid sixteen members of the said board of governors.

Chairman of board.

7. The board of governors shall elect one of their number to preside at their meetings, and to affix the university seal; and 15 to sign all its papers and instruments in writing, for or on behalf of such body corporate, as may be necessary.

Property and franchises of Toronto Baptist College and of Woodstock College vested in new corporation.

8. All real and personal property, rights, franchises, and privileges of Toronto Baptist College, and Woodstock College shall, from the coming into effect of this Act, be held and 20 vested in the corporation hereby constituted, subject to all trusts attaching thereto respectively, and the said board of governors shall thereupon continue to exercise all the rights, powers, franchises and privileges not inconsistent with the provisions of this Act, that prior to that time shall have been 25 exercised or enjoyed by the said Toronto Baptist College and Woodstock College, or either of them, in as full and ample a manner as the same shall theretofore have been exercised by the said Toronto Baptist College and Woodstock College, or either of them, subject, however, to the powers and rights of 30 the senate of the said university, as hereinafter provided; but all legal or other proceedings, prior to the coming into effect of this Act, taken by or against the Toronto Baptist College, or Woodstock College, may be continued under the same name or style of cause in which they have been instituted. 35

Trusts of Toronto Baptist College not affected.

9. Nothing in this Act contained shall be deemed to authorize the use of the lands and premises conveyed to the trustees of the Toronto Baptist College by the Honourable William McMaster, by deed bearing date the first day of December, one thousand eight hundred and eighty, for any 40 other purposes than those set out in said deed, nor to otherwise alter or affect the trusts in said deed contained, otherwise than by vesting the rights and powers of the said trustees in the university hereby created.

48 V. c. 96, ss. 2-10 and 12, repealed from commencement of this Act.

10. Sections 2 to 10, inclusive, and section 12 of the Act 45 passed in the forty-eighth year of Her Majesty's reign, chapter 96, being an Act to amend the said Act incorporating the Toronto Baptist College, shall from the coming into effect of this Act be deemed to be repealed, saving all acts, matters and things lawfully done thereunder up to the time of such 50 repeal.

Senate.

11. The senate of the said university shall be constituted as follows : (a) The members of the board of governors ; (b) the principal for the time being of the faculty of Toronto Bap-

tist College, and two of the professors thereof, to be elected
by the said faculty annually ; (c) the principal for the time
being of the faculty of arts, and two of the professors thereof,
to be elected by the said faculty annually ; (d) five represen-
5 tatives of the graduates in theology, to be elected by the
Alumni Association of such graduates in theology for a term of
five years, except that of those first appointed, one shall retire
at the expiration of one year, one at the expiration of two
years, one at the expiration of three years, and one at the ex-
10 piration of four years; (e) five representatives of the graduates
in arts, to be elected by the Alumni Association of such
graduates in arts for a term of five. years, subject to the like
exception as to those first appointed ; (f) two representatives
of the teachers of the preparatory or academical department
15 of Woodstock College, to be elected by such teachers annually.
In addition to the senate, as above constituted, for the general
purposes of the university, the following shall be members of
the senate, so far as the work of the senate concerns Toronto
Baptist College, with the same powers and rights as other
20 members of the senate as to all matters pertaining to the
said Toronto Baptist College ; (g) eight members to be elected
by the Baptist Convention of the maritime provinces, to serve
for such terms as the said convention may decide ; (h) the
president of Acadia College. and two of the professors of said
25 college, to be elected by the faculty thereof annually ; (i) two
members to be elected by the Baptist Convention of Manitoba
and the North-West. to serve for such term as the said convention may decide.

12. The senate shall have the control of the system and Powers of
30 course of education pursued in the said university, and of all Senate.
matters pertaining to the management and discipline thereof,
and of the examinations of all departments thereof; and shall
have the power to confer degrees in theology now vested in
the Toronto Baptist College, together with the power to con-
35 fer the degrees of Bachelor, Master, and Doctor, in the several
arts, sciences, and faculties, and any and all other degrees
which may properly be conferred by a university ; and shall
have the right to determine the courses of study and the qualification for degrees, and the granting of the same; and shall
40 make recommendations from time to time to the board of
governors for the appointment of chancellor, principals, professors, tutors, teachers, and masters, and no such appointment shall
be made by the board of governors except upon the recommendation of the senate. And the senate shall have the
45 power to settle, subject to ratification by the board, the terms
upon which other colleges and schools may become affiliated
with the said university ; Provided, however, that the said
university shall not have the power or right to establish,
maintain, or be connected with any school or college in
50 theology other than Toronto Baptist College, nor the right to
affiliate under any conditions with any other school or college
in theology; and may from time to time make by-laws,
statutes or regulations affecting any of the matters aforesaid, as well as regulating the holding of meetings of the
55 said senate, and the conduct generally of its business, and defining the respective duties, rights, and powers of the chancellor, principals, professors, tutors, and teachers of the said

university, and the same from time to time to alter or amend, as may be provided by such by-laws, statutes or regulations.

Certain persons not to be members of board of governors. **13.** Save as to the chancellor of the university, who shall, as aforesaid, be ex-officio, a member of the board of governors, no member of any of the faculties of the said university, or of 5 the faculties of any school or college being entitled to representation upon the said senate, and no member of the faculty of any affiliated school or college shall be eligible for election to a position on the said board of governors. And no person shall at any time be eligible for election to a position on 10 either the said board of governors, or said senate, who is not then a member in good standing of some Regular Baptist church in Canada; and in case any member of said board, or any senator ceases at any time during his term of office to be a member in good standing of a Regular Baptist church in 15 Canada, or removes from the Dominion of Canada, or in the case of a representative of the said missionary society, or any of said conventions, removing beyond the bounds of the society or convention which appointed him, or in case a representative of any of the said colleges or faculties severs his connection with the college or faculty from which he is a representative, he shall thereupon cease to be a member of said board or senate, as the case may be, and the vacancy caused thereby, or caused by the death or resignation of any member of the said board or of the said senate, shall be filled by the 25 body which appointed such member or such senator.

Quorum. **14.** Five members, or such larger number as the board may fix, shall constitute a quorum of the board; and nine members, or such larger number as the senate may fix, shall constitute a quorum of the senate. 30

Majority to decide. **15.** All questions shall be decided by the majority of the members present at the meeting of the board of senate.

Chairman of Senate. **16.** The chancellor of the university shall be ex-officio a member of and the chairman of the senate. In the absence of the chancellor, or at his request, a chairman shall be chosen by 35 the senate from among its members.

Seal to be affixed to diplomas. **17.** The seal of the university shall be affixed to all diplomas whenever directed by the senate.

When degrees in arts may be conferred. **18.** The senate shall not confer any degrees in the faculty of arts until five professorships, at least, have been established 40 in the faculty of arts, and five professors appointed to discharge the respective duties thereof, nor until this has been made to appear to the satisfaction of the Lieutenant-Governor in Council: nor until it shall have been made to appear to the satisfaction of the Lieutenant-Governor in Council that the sum 45 of $250,000, at least, in property, securities, or money, is held for the purposes of the arts department of the said university, including any preparatory or academical department.

Degrees in arts. **19.** The said university shall not have the power to confer any degrees in arts except after examination, duly had in pur- 50 suance of the by-laws and regulations of the senate respecting **Ad eundem degrees.** such degrees; but degrees, *ad eundem statum*, may be conferred by the said senate upon the graduates of any university approved of for that purpose by the senate, and such graduates shall have, after the granting of such degrees *ad eundem*, the same privileges as graduates of the university.

5   **20.** No person shall be admitted as a candidate for any Degrees in medicine. degree in medicine or surgery unless such person shall have completed the course of instruction which the senate, by by-law or regulation in that behalf, may determine, in such one or more medical schools, as shall also be mentioned in said 10 by-law or regulation.

  21. The treasurer, or bursar of said university, shall be Treasurer to give security. bound, before assuming office, to furnish security for the faithful discharge of his duties by good and sufficient sureties, to be approved of by the board of governors, to the amount of 15 $10,000, or such larger sum as the board of governors may by by-law or regulation fix.

  22. This Act shall come into effect on the first day of Commencement of Act. November, one thousand eight hundred and eighty-seven, and the first meeting of the board of governors shall be held on the 20   day of   at two o'clock in the afternoon, in McMaster Hall, Toronto, and notice thereof shall be published in the newspaper called *The Canadian Baptist* for two weeks prior thereto; and the first meeting of the senate shall be held at such time and place as the said board of governors may at 25 such meeting appoint, and thereafter all meetings of the board and senate shall be held at such time and place as may be determined on by the said board and senate respectively.

1st Session, 6th Legislature, 50 Vic., 1887.

BILL.

An Act to unite Toronto Baptist College and Woodstock College under the name of McMaster University.

First Reading,   1887.

(Private Bill.)

BILL.

An Act to unite Toronto Baptist College and Woodstock College under the name of McMaster University.

W HEREAS it has been represented by petition of the Preamble.
Toronto Baptist College and Woodstock College, two
institutions of learning, carried on in connection with
the denomination of Christians called Regular Baptists,
5 that the Toronto Baptist College was incorporated by
an Act passed in the forty-fourth year of the reign
of Her Majesty Queen Victoria, for the training of students preparing for the ministry of the Regular Baptist
denomination, with power to confer degrees in Divinity, and
10 has, since its incorporation, been in operation in the city of
Toronto ; that Woodstock College was incorporated under the
name of the Canadian Literary Institute in the twentieth
year of the same reign ; that by an Act passed in the fortieth
year of the same reign, the name thereof was changed to
15 Woodstock College, and that the work of education has been
carried on in such institution at the town of Woodstock for
the last twenty-eight years ; that it would conduce to the success of the educational work of the said denomination to have
the property and control of the said colleges vested in a board
20 of governors, subject to the powers and rights of a senate as
hereinafter provided, and to have the usual powers and privileges of a university conferred upon such board and senate,
and whereas it is expedient to grant the prayer of the said
petition ;
25 Therefore Her Majesty, by and with the advice and consent of the Legislative Assembly of the Province of Ontario,
enacts as follows :—

1. From and after the date hereinafter fixed for the coming McMaster
into effect of this Act, the Toronto Baptist College and Wood- University
30 stock College shall be united and form one corporation under constituted.
the name of McMaster University, and shall be under the
management and administration of a Board of Governors,
which, until the appointment of a chancellor as hereinafter
provided, shall consist of sixteen members, who shall be elected
35 as follows : twelve members by the Regular Baptist Missionary Society of Ontario, and four members by the Regular
Baptist Missionary Convention, East, which said sixteen
members shall hold office for four years, except that of those
first elected by the Regular Baptist Missionary Society of
40 Ontario, three shall retire at the expiration of one year, three
at the expiration of two years, and three at the expiration of
three years, from the date of their appointment ; and of
those elected by the Regular Baptist Missionary Convention

East, one shall retire at the expiration of one year, one at the
expiration of two years, and one at the expiration of three years.
And upon the appointment of a chancellor, as hereinafter provided, such chancellor shall be ex-officio a member of the said
board, which will then consist of seventeen members. 5

**Board of
governors to
be a body
corporate.**

2. Such appointments may be made by such society and
convention before the coming into effect of this Act, and the
persons so appointed, and their successors in office, are hereby
constituted a body corporate and politic under the name of
the McMaster University, with perpetual succession and a 10
common seal, with power to break, alter, and change the same
at pleasure, and by that name may sue and be sued, and be
able and capable in law to take, purchase, and hold any personal property whatsoever; and shall also be able and capable,
notwithstanding the Statutes of Mortmain, to take, purchase, 15
and hold to them and their successors, not only all such lands,
buildings, hereditaments, and possessions as may from time to
time be used or occupied for the purposes of the said university,
including any preparatory or academical department, and for
residences of the chancellor, principals, professors, tutors, stu- 20
dents, and officers, with gardens and lawns attached thereto, but
also any other lands, buildings, hereditaments, and premises not
exceeding the annual value of $10,000, such annual value to
be calculated and ascertained with reference to the period of
taking, purchasing, or acquiring the same; and to accept on 25
behalf of the said university, or any department thereof, including any preparatory or academical department, any gifts,
devises, or bequests of any property, real or personal, and they
and their successors shall be able and capable in law to grant,
demise, alien, lease, or otherwise dispose of all or any of the 30
property, real or personal, at any time belonging to the said
university, or to any department thereof, including any preparatory or academical department, and to invest the proceeds
thereof upon such securities, or in such way as to the said
board of governors shall seem best, and also to do all other 35
matters and things incidental or appertaining to such body corporate; 🖙 provided always that the real estate not required
for use and occupation or for the residences of the chancellor, principals, professors, tutors and students as aforesaid shall not at
any time be held by the said university for a longer period 40
than seven years, and that any such real estate not sold and
alienated within seven years of the time when the same is received by the said corporation shall revert to the party from
whom it came to the corporation or to his or her heirs or
devisees. 🖙 45

**Power to
accept gifts
and bequests.**

3. The said university shall be entitled to receive and hold
gifts, devises, and bequests already made, or hereafter coming
into effect, by any person or persons, to or for the benefit of
Toronto Baptist College and Woodstock College, or either of
them, as fully and effectually as if the said university was 50
named in such gifts, devises, or bequests, instead of Toronto
Baptist College and Woodstock College, or either of them,
subject, however, to all the trusts in such gifts, devises, and
bequests provided. And all persons shall have the power, notwithstanding the Statutes of Mortmain, at any time to grant, 55
devise, bequeath, or convey by deed, will, or otherwise, any
real or personal property to the said university, either for its

purposes generally, or for any department thereof, or otherwise, as may be provided by such grant, devise, bequest, or
conveyance, and no gift to the said university shall be void by
reason of the grantor having reserved any interest therein, or
5 the income thereof, for the term of his life, or any part thereof;
☞ Provided that no gift or devise of any real estate or of any
interest therein in favour of the said corporation, shall be valid
unless made by deed or will executed by the donor or testator, or
at least six months before his death. ☞ And it is hereby de-
10 clared that section 2 of the Act, passed in the forty-fourth year
of Her Majesty's reign, chapter 87, being the Act incorporating
the said Toronto Baptist College, shall be construed to have
conferred the power and right upon all persons, notwithstanding the Statutes of Mortmain, to grant, devise, be-
15 queath, or convey to or for the benefit of the said Toronto
Baptist College, any real or personal property in the terms in
said section provided, as well as the power to said college to
receive such grants, devises, bequests and conveyances.

4. McMaster University shall be a Christian school of Religious
20 learning, and the study of the Bible, or sacred scriptures, shall tests.
form a part of the course of study taught by the professors,
tutors, or masters appointed by the board of governors. And
no person shall be eligible to the position of chancellor, principal, professor, tutor, or master, who is not a member in good
25 standing of an Evangelical Christian church; and no person
shall be eligible for the position of principal, professor, tutor,
or master *in the faculty of theology* who is not a member in
good standing of a Regular Baptist church, and the said
board of governors shall have the right to require such
30 further or other test as to religious belief, as a qualification
for any such position in the faculty of theology, as to the
said board of governors may seem proper ; but no compulsory
religious qualification, or examination of a denominational
character shall be required from, or imposed upon any student
35 whatever, other than in the faculty of theology.

5. The board of governors shall have full power and au- Powers of
thority to fix the number, residence, duties, salary, provision, board of gover-
and emolument of the chancellor, principals, professors, tutors, nors.
masters, officers, agents, and servants of the said university,
40 including any preparatory or academical department, and may
from time to time remove the chancellor, principals, professors,
tutors, masters, and all other officers, agents, and servants of the
university, and of all departments thereof, including any preparatory or academical department. and may also appoint the
45 chancellor, principals, professors, tutors, masters., and all other
officers, agents, and servants, provided that such power of appointment as to the chancellor, principals, professors, tutors,
and masters shall be exercised only upon the recommendation
of the senate, as hereinafter provided. And the said board
50 shall have the control and management of the property and
funds of the said university, and shall have power to adopt
by-laws and regulations touching and concerning all or any of
the matters aforesaid, as well as concerning the time and place
of meetings of the said board and notices thereof, the officers
55 of the said board, and their election and duties, and all other
matters and things which to them may seem good, fit and useful for the well ordering and advancement of the said univer-

sity, including any preparatory or academical department, not
repugnant to the provisions of this Act, or any public law in
force in this Province, and the same to alter or vary from
time to time in accordance with any provision for that purpose contained in such by-laws and regulations, and after the 5
common seal of the university has been affixed thereto such
by-laws and regulations shall be binding upon all parties,
members thereof, and upon all others whom the same may
concern.

Duties of board of governors.

6. It shall be the duty of the said board of governors to 10
keep proper records and minutes of all and every their proceedings, and to keep proper books of account of the financial
affairs of the said university, including any preparatory or
academical department, and to present a report of the work of
the said university, accompanied by a duly audited financial 15
statement, to each annual meeting of the said the Regular
Baptist Missionary Society of Ontario, and the Regular Baptist Missionary Convention, East, respectively.   Should the
said society and convention unite, such report and financial
statement shall be presented to such united society, and such 20
united society shall thereafter have the right to elect the aforesaid sixteen members of the said board of governors.

Chairman of board.

7. The board of governors shall elect one of their number to
preside at their meetings, and to affix the university seal, and
to sign all its papers and instruments in writing, for or on 25
behalf of such body corporate, as may be necessary.

Property and franchises of Toronto Baptist College and of Woodstock College vested in new corporation.

8. All real and personal property, rights, franchises, and
privileges of Toronto Baptist College, and Woodstock College
shall, from the coming into effect of this Act, be held and
vested in the corporation hereby constituted, subject to all 30
trusts attaching thereto respectively, and the said board of
governors shall thereupon continue to exercise all the rights,
powers, franchises and privileges not inconsistent with the
provisions of this Act, that prior to that time shall have been
exercised or enjoyed by the said Toronto Baptist College and 35
Woodstock College, or either of them, in as full and ample a
manner as the same shall theretofore have been exercised by
the said Toronto Baptist College and Woodstock College, or
either of them, subject, however, to the powers and rights of
the senate of the said university, as hereinafter provided ; but 40
all legal or other proceedings, prior to the coming into effect of
this Act, taken by or against the Toronto Baptist College, or
Woodstock College, may be continued under the same name or
style of cause in which they have been instituted.

Trusts of Toronto Baptist College not affected.

9. Nothing in this Act contained shall be deemed to au- 45
thorize the use of the lands and premises conveyed to the
trustees of the Toronto Baptist College by the Honourable
William McMaster, by deed bearing date the first day of
December, one thousand eight hundred and eighty, for any
other purposes than those set out in said deed, nor to otherwise 50
alter or affect the trusts in said deed contained, otherwise than
by vesting the rights and powers of the said trustees in the
university hereby created.

10. Sections 2 to 10, inclusive, and section 12 of the Act 48 V. c. 96, ss. passed in the forty-eighth year of Her Majesty's reign, chapter 2-10 and 12, repealed from 96, being an Act to amend the said Act incorporating the commence-Toronto Baptist College, shall from the coming into effect of ment of this Act. 5 this Act be deemed to be repealed, saving all acts, matters and things lawfully done thereunder up to the time of such repeal.

11. The senate of the said university shall be constituted Senate. as follows : (a) The members of the board of governors; (b) 10 the principal for the time being of the faculty of Toronto Baptist College, and two of the professors thereof, to be elected by the said faculty annually; (c) the principal for the time being of the faculty of arts, and two of the professors thereof, to be elected by the said faculty annually ; (d) five represen-15 tatives of the graduates in theology, to be elected by the Alumni Association of such graduates in theology for a term of five years, except that of those first appointed, one shall retire at the expiration of one year, one at the expiration of two years, one at the expiration of three years, and one at the ex-20 piration of four years; (e) five representatives of the graduates in arts, to be elected by the Alumni Association of such graduates in arts for a term of five years, subject to the like exception as to those first appointed; (f) two representatives of the teachers of the preparatory or academical department 25 of Woodstock College, to be elected by such teachers annually. In addition to the senate, as above constituted, for the general purposes of the university, the following shall be members of the senate, so far as the work of the senate concerns Toronto Baptist College, with the same powers and rights as other 30 members of the senate as to all matters pertaining to the said Toronto Baptist College; (g) eight members to be elected by the Baptist Convention of the maritime provinces, to serve for such *term or* terms as the said convention may decide; (h) the president of Acadia College. and two of the professors of said 35 college, to be elected by the faculty thereof annually ; (i) two members to be elected by the Baptist Convention of Manitoba and the North-West *Territories.* to serve for such term *or terms* as the said convention may decide.

12. The senate shall have the control of the system and Powers of 40 course of education pursued in the said university, and of all Senate. matters pertaining to the management and discipline thereof, and of the examinations of all departments thereof; and shall have the power to confer degrees in theology now vested in the Toronto Baptist College, together with the power to con-45 fer the degrees of Bachelor, Master, and Doctor, in the several arts, sciences, and faculties, and any and all other degrees which may properly be conferred by a university ; and shall have the right to determine the courses of study and the qualification for degrees, and the granting of the same; and shall 50 make recommendations from time to time to the board of governors for the appointment of chancellor, principals, professors, tutors, teachers, and masters, and no such appointment shall be made by the board of governors except upon the recommendation of the senate. And the senate –shall have the 55 power to settle, subject to ratification by the board, the terms upon which other colleges and schools may become affiliated with the said university, ☞ but no such affiliation shall

take effect unless and until the same shall have been approved
by the Lieutenant-Governor in Council ; Provided, however,
that the said university shall not have the power or right to establish, maintain, or be connected with any school or college in
theology other than Toronto Baptist College, nor the right to 5
affiliate under any conditions with any other school or college
in theology; and may from time to time make by-laws,
statutes or regulations affecting any of the matters aforesaid, as well as regulating the holding of meetings of the
said senate, and the conduct generally of its business, and de- 10
fining the respective duties, rights, and powers of the chancellor, principals, professors, tutors, and teachers of the said
university, and the same from time to time to alter or amend,
as may be provided by such by-laws, statutes or regulations.

Certain persons not to be members of board of governors. **13**. Save as to the chancellor of the university, who shall, 15
as aforesaid, be ex-officio a member of the board of governors,
no member of any of the faculties of the said university, or of
the faculties of any school or college being entitled to representation upon the said senate, and no member of the faculty
of any affiliated school or college shall be eligible for election 20
to a position on the said board of governors. And no person
shall at any time be eligible for election to a position on
either the said board of governors, or said senate, who is not
then a member in good standing of some Regular Baptist
church in Canada ; and in case any member of said board, or 25
any senator ceases at any time during his term of office to be
a member in good standing of a Regular Baptist church in
Canada, or removes from the Dominion of Canada, or in the
case of a representative of the said missionary society, or
any of said conventions, removing beyond the bounds of the 30
society or convention which appointed him, or in case a representative of any of the said colleges or faculties severs his connection with the college or faculty from which he is a representative, he shall thereupon cease to be a member of said
board or senate, as the case may be, and the vacancy caused 35
thereby, or caused by the death or resignation of any member
of the said board or of the said senate, shall be filled by the
body which appointed such member or such senator. .

Quorum. **14**. Five members, or such larger number as the board may
fix, shall constitute a quorum of the board ; and nine members, 40
or such larger number as the senate may fix, shall constitute a
quorum of the senate.

Majority to decide. **15**. All questions shall be decided by the majority of the
members present at the meeting of the board or senate.

Chairman of Senate. **16**. The chancellor of the university shall be ex-officio a
member of and the chairman of the senate. In the absence of 45
the chancellor, or at his request, a chairman shall be chosen by
the senate from among its members.

Seal to be affixed to diplomas. **17**. The seal of the university shall be affixed to all
diplomas whenever directed by the senate.

When degrees in arts may be conferred. **18**. The senate shall not confer any degrees in the faculty 50
of arts until five professorships, at least, have been *permanently*
established *and adequately provided for* in the faculty of arts,

and five professors appointed to discharge the respective duties
thereof, nor until this has been made to appear to the satisfaction of the Lieutenant-Governor in Council, nor until it shall
have been made to appear to the satisfaction of the Lieutenant-
5 Governor in Council that the sum of $600,000, at least, in
property, securities, or money, is held for the purposes of the
said university, *including any preparatory or academic
department.*

19. ☞ It shall be the duty of the board of governors Returns.
10 wherever called upon to do so to furnish full and accurate
accounts in writing of the property of the university and the
income derived therefrom in order that the same may be laid
before the Provincial Legislature at any session thereof.☜

20. The said university shall not have the power to confer Degrees in
15 any degrees in arts except after examination, duly had in pur- arts.
suance of the by-laws and regulations of the senate respecting
such degrees; but *ad eundem* degrees may be conferred *Ad eundem*
by the said senate upon the graduates of any university ap- degrees.
proved of for that purpose by the senate, and such graduates
20 shall have, after the granting of such degrees *ad eundem,* the
same privileges as graduates of the university.

21. No person shall be admitted as a candidate for any Degrees in
degree in medicine or surgery unless such person shall have medicine.
completed the course of instruction which the senate, by by-
25 law or regulation in that behalf, may determine, in such one
or more medical schools, as shall also be mentioned in said
by-law or regulation.

22. The treasurer, or bursar of said university, shall be Treasurer to
bound, before assuming office, to furnish security for the faith- give security.
30 ful discharge of his duties by good and sufficient sureties, to
be approved of by the board of governors, to the amount of
$10,000, or such larger sum as the board of governors may by
by-law or regulation fix.

23. This Act shall come into effect on the first day of Commence-
35 November, one thousand eight hundred and eighty-seven, and ment of Act.
the first meeting of the board of governors shall be held on the
eighth day of *the said month of November* at two o'clock in
the afternoon, in McMaster Hall, Toronto, and notice thereof
shall be published in the newspaper called *The Canadian
40 Baptist* for two weeks prior thereto; and the first meeting of
the senate shall be held at such time and place as the said
board of governors may at such meeting appoint, and thereafter all meetings of the board and senate shall be held at
such time and place as may be determined on by the said board
45 and senate respectively.

BILL.

An Act to unite Toronto Baptist College
and Woodstock College under the name
of McMaster University.

(*Reprinted as amended by Private Bills
Committee.*)

First Reading, 15th March, 1887.

(Private Bill.)

No. 23.]   **BILL.**   [1887.

An Act to unite Toronto Baptist College and
Woodstock College under the name of McMaster
University.

WHEREAS it has been represented by petition of the ^{Preamble.}
Toronto Baptist College and Woodstock College, two
institutions of learning, carried on in connection with
the denomination of Christians called Regular Baptists,
5 that the Toronto Baptist College was incorporated by
an Act passed in the forty-fourth year of the reign
of Her Majesty Queen Victoria, for the training of students preparing for the ministry of the Regular Baptist
denomination, with power to confer degrees in Divinity, and
10 has, since its incorporation, been in operation in the city of
Toronto; that Woodstock College was incorporated under the
name of the Canadian Literary Institute in the twentieth
year of the same reign; that by an Act passed in the forty-sixth
year of the same reign, the name thereof was changed to
15 Woodstock College, and that the work of education has been
carried on in such institution at the town of Woodstock for
the last twenty-eight years; that it would conduce to the success of the educational work of the said denomination to have
the property and control of the said colleges vested in a board
20 of governors, subject to the powers and rights of a senate as
hereinafter provided, and to have the usual powers and privileges of a university conferred upon such board and senate,
and whereas it is expedient to grant the prayer of the said
petition;
25 Therefore Her Majesty, by and with the advice and consent of the Legislative Assembly of the Province of Ontario,
enacts as follows :—

1. From and after the date hereinafter fixed for the coming ^{McMaster}
into effect of this Act, the Toronto Baptist College and Wood- ^{University constituted.}
30 stock College shall be united and form one corporation under
the name of McMaster University, and shall be under the
management and administration of a Board of Governors,
which, until the appointment of a chancellor as hereinafter
provided, shall consist of sixteen members, who shall be elected
35 as follows: twelve members by the Regular Baptist Missionary Society of Ontario, and four members by the Regular
Baptist Missionary Convention, East, which said sixteen
members shall hold office for four years, except that of those
first elected by the Regular Baptist Missionary Society of
40 Ontario, three shall retire at the expiration of one year, three
at the expiration of two years, and three at the expiration of
three years, from the date of their appointment; and of
those elected by the Regular Baptist Missionary Convention

East, one shall retire at the expiration of one year, one at the
expiration of two years, and one at the expiration of three years.
And upon the appointment of a chancellor, as hereinafter provided, such chancellor shall be ex-officio a member of the said
board, which will then consist of seventeen members.   5

Board of governors to be a body corporate. 2. Such appointments may be made by such society and
convention before the coming into effect of this Act, and the
persons so appointed, and their successors in office, are hereby
constituted a body corporate and politic under the name of
the McMaster University, with perpetual succession and a 10
common seal, with power to break, alter, and change the same
at pleasure, and by that name may sue and be sued, and be
able and capable in law to take, purchase, and hold any personal property whatsoever; and shall also be able and capable,
notwithstanding the Statutes of Mortmain, to take, purchase, 15
and hold to them and their successors, not only all such lands,
buildings, hereditaments, and possessions as may from time to
time be used or occupied for the purposes of the said university,
including any preparatory or academical department, and for
residences of the chancellor, principals, professors, tutors, stu- 20
dents, and officers, with gardens and lawns attached thereto, but
also any other lands, buildings, hereditaments, and premises not
exceeding the annual value of $10,000, such annual value to
be calculated and ascertained with reference to the period of
taking, purchasing, or acquiring the same; and to accept on 25
behalf of the said university, or any department thereof, including any preparatory or academical department, any gifts,
devises, or bequests of any property, real or personal, and they
and their successors shall be able and capable in law to grant,
demise, alien, lease, or otherwise dispose of all or any of the 30
property, real or personal, at any time belonging to the said
university, or to any department thereof, including any preparatory or academical department, and to invest the proceeds
thereof upon such securities, or in such way as to the said
board of governors shall seem best, and also to do all other 35
matters and things incidental or appertaining to such body corporate; ☞ provided always that the real estate not required
for use and occupation or for the residences of the chancellor, principals, professors, tutors and students as aforesaid shall not at
any time be held by the said university for a longer period 40
than seven years, and that any such real estate not sold and
alienated within seven years of the time when the same is received by the said corporation shall revert to the party from
whom it came to the corporation or to his or her heirs or
devisees.   45

Power to accept gifts and bequests. 3. The said university shall be entitled to receive and hold
gifts, devises, and bequests already made, or hereafter coming
into effect, by any person or persons, to or for the benefit of
Toronto Baptist College and Woodstock College, or either of
them, as fully and effectually as if the said university was 50
named in such gifts, devises, or bequests, instead of Toronto
Baptist College and Woodstock College, or either of them,
subject, however, to all the trusts in such gifts, devises, and
bequests provided. And all persons shall have the power, notwithstanding the Statutes of Mortmain, at any time to grant, 55
devise, bequeath, or convey by deed, will, or otherwise, any
real or personal property to the said university, either for its

purposes generally, or for any department thereof, or otherwise, as may be provided by such grant, devise, bequest, or conveyance, and no gift to the said university shall be void by reason of the grantor having reserved any interest therein, or
5 the income thereof, for the term of his life, or any part thereof; ☞ Provided that no gift or devise of any real estate or of any interest therein in favour of the said corporation, shall be valid unless made by deed or will executed by the donor or testator, or at least six months before his death. ☞ And it is hereby de-
10 clared that section 2 of the Act, passed in the forty-fourth year of Her Majesty's reign, chapter 87, being the Act incorporating the said Toronto Baptist College, shall be construed to have conferred the power and right upon all persons, notwithstanding the Statutes of Mortmain, to grant, devise, be-
15 queath, or convey to or for the benefit of the said Toronto Baptist College, any real or personal property in the terms in said section provided, as well as the power to said college to receive such grants, devises, bequests and conveyances.

4. McMaster University shall be a Christian school of Religious tests.
20 learning, and the study of the Bible, or sacred scriptures, shall form a part of the course of study taught by the professors, tutors, or masters appointed by the board of governors. And no person shall be eligible to the position of chancellor, principal, professor, tutor, or master, who is not a member in good
25 standing of an Evangelical Christian church ; and no person shall be eligible for the position of principal, professor, tutor, or master *in the faculty of theology* who is not a member in good standing of a Regular Baptist church, and the said board of governors shall have the right to require such
30 further or other test as to religious belief, as a qualification for any such position in the faculty of theology, as to the said board of governors may seem proper ; but no compulsory religious qualification, or examination of a denominational character shall be required from, or imposed upon any student
35 whatever, other than in the faculty of theology.

5. The board of governors shall have full power and au- Powers of board of governors.
thority to fix the number, residence, duties, salary, provision, nors.
and emolument of the chancellor, principals, professors, tutors, masters, officers, agents, and servants of the said university,
40 including any preparatory or academical department, and may from time to time remove the chancellor, principals, professors, tutors, masters, and all other officers, agents, and servants of the university, and of all departments thereof, including any preparatory or academical department. and may also appoint the
45 chancellor, principals, professors, tutors, masters, and all other officers, agents, and servants, provided that such power of appointment as to the chancellor, principals, professors, tutors, and masters shall be exercised only upon the recommendation of the senate, as hereinafter provided. And the said board
50 shall have the control and management of the property and funds of the said university, and shall have power to adopt by-laws and regulations touching and concerning all or any of the matters aforesaid, as well as concerning the time and place of meetings of the said board and notices thereof, the officers
55 of the said board, and their election and duties, and all other matters and things which to them may seem good, fit and useful for the well ordering and advancement of the said univer-

sity, including any preparatory or academical department, not
repugnant to the provisions of this Act, or any public law in
force in this Province, and the same to alter or vary from
time to time in accordance with any provision for that purpose contained in such by-laws and regulations, and after the 5
common seal of the university has been affixed thereto such
by-laws and regulations shall be binding upon all parties,
members thereof, and upon all others whom the same may
concern.

Duties of board of governors.

6. It shall be the duty of the said board of governors to 10
keep proper records and minutes of all and every their proceedings, and to keep proper books of account of the financial
affairs of the said university, including any preparatory or
academical department, and to present a report of the work of
the said university, accompanied by a duly audited financial 15
statement, to each annual meeting of the said the Regular
Baptist Missionary Society of Ontario, and the Regular Baptist Missionary Convention, East, respectively. Should the
said society and convention unite, such report and financial
statement shall be presented to such united society, and such 20
united society shall thereafter have the right to elect the aforesaid sixteen members of the said board of governors.

Chairman of board.

7. The board of governors shall elect one of their number to
preside at their meetings, and to affix the university seal, and
to sign all its papers and instruments in writing, for or on 25
behalf of such body corporate, as may be necessary.

Property and franchises of Toronto Bap-tist College and of Wood-stock College vested in new corporation.

8. All real and personal property, rights, franchises, and
privileges of Toronto Baptist College, and Woodstock College
shall, from the coming into effect of this Act, be held and
vested in the corporation hereby constituted, subject to all 30
trusts attaching thereto respectively, and the said board of
governors shall thereupon continue to exercise all the rights,
powers, franchises and privileges not inconsistent with the
provisions of this Act, that prior to that time shall have been
exercised or enjoyed by the said Toronto Baptist College and 35
Woodstock College, or either of them, in as full and ample a
manner as the same shall theretofore have been exercised by
the said Toronto Baptist College and Woodstock College, or
either of them, subject, however, to the powers and rights of
the senate of the said university, as hereinafter provided; but 40
all legal or other proceedings, prior to the coming into effect of
this Act, taken by or against the Toronto Baptist College, or
Woodstock College, may be continued under the same name or
style of cause in which they have been instituted.

Trusts of Toronto Bap-tist College not affected.

9. Nothing in this Act contained shall be deemed to au- 45
thorize the use of the lands and premises conveyed to the
trustees of the Toronto Baptist College by the Honourable
William McMaster, by deed bearing date the first day of
December, one thousand eight hundred and eighty, for any
other purposes than those set out in said deed, nor to otherwise 50
alter or affect the trusts in said deed contained, otherwise than
by vesting the rights and powers of the said trustees in the
university hereby created.

10. Sections 2 to 10, inclusive, and section 12 of the Act 48 V. c. 96, ss.
passed in the forty-eighth year of Her Majesty's reign, chapter 2-10 and 12, repealed from
96, being an Act to amend the said Act incorporating the commence-
Toronto Baptist College, shall from the coming into effect of ment of this Act.
5 this Act be deemed to be repealed, saving all acts, matters
and things lawfully done thereunder up to the time of such
repeal.

11. The senate of the said university shall be constituted Senate.
as follows : (a) The members of the board of governors ; (b)
10 the principal for the time being of the faculty of Toronto Baptist College, and two of the professors thereof, to be elected
by the said faculty annually ; (c) the principal for the time
being of the faculty of arts, and two of the professors thereof,
to be elected by the said faculty annually ; (d) five represen-
15 tatives of the graduates in theology, to be elected by the
Alumni Association of such graduates in theology for a term of
five years, except that of those first appointed, one shall retire
at the expiration of one year, one at the expiration of two
years, one at the expiration of three years, and one at the ex-
20 piration of four years; (e) five representatives of the graduates
in arts, to be elected by the Alumni Association of such
graduates in arts for a term of five years, subject to the like
exception as to those first appointed ; (f) two representatives
of the teachers of the preparatory or academical department
25 of Woodstock College, to be elected by such teachers annually.
In addition to the senate, as above constituted, for the general
purposes of the university, the following shall be members of
the senate, so far as the work of the senate concerns Toronto
Baptist College, with the same powers and rights as other
30 members of the senate as to all matters pertaining to the
said Toronto Baptist College; (g) eight members to be elected
by the Baptist Convention of the maritime provinces, to serve
for such term or terms as the said convention may decide; (h) the
president of Acadia College, and two of the professors of said
35 college, to be elected by the faculty thereof annually ; (i) two
members to be elected by the Baptist Convention of Manitoba
and the North-West *Territories* to serve for such term or
terms as the said convention may decide.

12. The senate shall have the control of the system and Powers of
40 course of education pursued in the said university, and of all Senate.
matters pertaining to the management and discipline thereof,
and of the examinations of all departments thereof; and shall
have the power to confer degrees in theology now vested in
the Toronto Baptist College, together with the power to con-
45 fer the degrees of Bachelor, Master, and Doctor, in the several
arts, sciences, and faculties, and any and all other degrees
which may properly be conferred by a university ; and shall
have the right to determine the courses of study and the qualification for degrees, and the granting of the same ; provided
50 the course of study prescribed for matriculation into the said
university shall in no essential sense differ or vary from that
prescribed for matriculation into the University of Toronto,
and in respect to any degree which the said senate has power
to confer, the course of instruction and the scope of the exami-
55 nation for such degree shall be as thorough and comprehensive
as the courses and examinations for corresponding degrees in
the University of Toronto; and the senate shall make

recommendations from time to time to the board of governors for
the appointment of chancellor, principals, professors, tutors,
teachers, and masters, and no such appointment shall be
made by the board of governors except upon the recommendation of the senate. And the senate shall have the 5
power to settle, subject to ratification by the board, the terms
upon which other colleges and schools may become affiliated
with the said university, &c. but no such affiliation shall
take effect unless and until the same shall have been approved
by the Lieutenant-Governor in Council ; Provided, however, 10
that the said university shall not have the power or right to establish, maintain, or be connected with any school or college in
theology other than Toronto Baptist College, nor the right to
affiliate under any conditions with any other school or college
in theology; and may from time to time make by-laws, 15
statutes or regulations affecting any of the matters aforesaid, as well as regulating the holding of meetings of the
said senate, and the conduct generally of its business, and defining the respective duties, rights, and powers of the chancellor, principals, professors, tutors, and teachers of the said 20
university, and the same from time to time to alter or amend,
as may be provided by such by-laws, statutes or regulations.

Certain persons not to be members of board of governors. **13.** Save as to the chancellor of the university, who shall,
as aforesaid, be ex-officio a member of the board of governors,
no member of any of the faculties of the said university, or of 25
the faculties of any school or college being entitled to representation upon the said senate, and no member of the faculty
of any affiliated school or college shall be eligible for election
to a position on the said board of governors. And no person
shall at any time be eligible for election to a position on 30
either the said board of governors, or said senate, who is not
then a member in good standing of some Regular Baptist
church in Canada; and in case any member of said board, or
any senator ceases at any time during his term of office to be
a member in good standing of a Regular Baptist church in 35
Canada, or removes from the Dominion of Canada, or in the
case of a representative of the said missionary society, or
any of said conventions, removing beyond the bounds of the
society or convention which appointed him, or in case a representative of any of the said colleges or faculties severs his con- 40
nection with the college or faculty from which he is a representative, he shall thereupon cease to be a member of said
board or senate, as the case may be, and the vacancy caused
thereby, or caused by the death or resignation of any member
of the said board or of the said senate, shall be filled by the 45
body which appointed such member or such senator.

Quorum. **14.** Five members, or such larger number as the board may
fix, shall constitute a quorum of the board; and nine members,
or such larger number as the senate may fix, shall constitute a
quorum of the senate. 50

Majority to decide. **15.** All questions shall be decided by the majority of the
members present at the meeting of the board or senate.

Chairman of Senate. **16.** The chancellor of the university shall be ex-officio a
member of and the chairman of the senate. In the absence of
the chancellor, or at his request, a chairman shall be chosen by 55
the senate from among its members.

17. The seal of the university shall be affixed to all Seal to be affixed to diplomas.diplomas whenever directed by the senate.

18. The senate shall not confer any degrees in the faculty When degrees in arts may be conferred.of arts until five professorships, at least, have been *permanently*
5 established *and adequately provided for* in the faculty of arts,
and five professors appointed to discharge the respective duties
thereof, nor until this has been made to appear to the satisfaction of the Lieutenant-Governor in Council, nor until it shall
have been made to appear to the satisfaction of the Lieutenant-
10 Governor in Council that the sum of $700,000, at least, in
property, securities, or money, is held for the purposes of the
said university, *including any preparatory or academic
department.*

19. It shall be the duty of the board of governors Returns.
15 ☞to furnish from time to time, or when called upon, to the
Provincial Secretary full and accurate information as to the
curriculum of study in every faculty of the said University
(excepting Divinity) the number of professors, lecturers or
other teachers in every faculty, and the subject of instruction
20 assigned to each of such professors, lecturers or teachers; the
subjects in which examinations are held for degrees in arts
or medicine, and on which such degrees are granted, and
wherever called upon to do so to furnish full and accurate
accounts in writing of the property of the university and the
25 income derived therefrom in order that the same may be laid
before the Provincial Legislature at any session thereof.

20. The said university shall not have the power to confer Degrees in arts.any degrees in arts except after examination, duly had in pursuance of the by-laws and regulations of the senate respecting
30 such degrees; but *ad eundem* degrees may be conferred Ad eundem degrees.by the said senate upon the graduates of any university approved of for that purpose by the senate, and such graduates
shall have, after the granting of such degrees *ad eundem*, the
same privileges as graduates of the university.

35 **21.** No person shall be admitted as a candidate for any Degrees in medicine.degree in medicine or surgery unless such person shall have
completed the course of instruction which the senate, by by-
law or regulation in that behalf, may determine, in such one
or more medical schools, as shall also be mentioned in said
40 by-law or regulation.

22. The treasurer, or bursar of said university, shall be Treasurer to give security.bound, before assuming office, to furnish security for the faithful discharge of his duties by good and sufficient sureties, to
be approved of by the board of governors, to the amount of
45 $10,000, or such larger sum as the board of governors may by
by-law or regulation fix.

Commence-
ment of Act.

23. This Act shall come into effect on the first day of
November, 1887, and the first meeting of the board of governors shall be held on the *eighth* day of *the said month of
November* at two o'clock in the afternoon, in McMaster Hall,
Toronto, and notice thereof shall be published in the news- 5
paper called *The Canadian Baptist* for two weeks prior
thereto ; and the first meeting of the senate shall be held at
such time and place as the said board of governors may at
such meeting appoint, and thereafter all meetings of the
board and senate shall be held at such time and place as may 10
be determined on by the said board and senate respectively.

1st Session, 6th Legislature, 50 Vic., 1887.

No. 23.

BILL.

An Act to unite Toronto Baptist College
and Woodstock College under the name
of McMaster University.

*(Reprinted as amended by Committee of the
Whole House.)*

First Reading, 15th March, 1887.
Second   " 15th April, 1887.

(Private Bill.)

Mr. HARCOURT.

TORONTO.
PRINTED BY WARWICK & SONS, 26 AND 28 FRONT ST. W.

BILL.

An Act respecting the Gore District Mutual Fire Insurance Company.

WHEREAS the Gore District Mutual Fire Insurance Preamble. Company have petitioned for certain amendments to the Act entitled, *An Act to extend the powers of the Gore District Mutual Fire Insurance Company*, passed in the 5 thirty-first year of Her Majesty's reign and chaptered 56, and it is expedient to grant the prayer of the said petition;

Therefore Her Majesty, by and with the advice and consent of the Legislative Assembly of the province of Ontario, enacts as follows:—

10 **1.** Sections three, nine, ten, eleven, fourteen and fifteen of 31 V. c. 5, 6, the said Act are hereby repealed and the following section is ss. 3, 9-11, 14 and 15, re-substituted therefor:— pealed.

"After the reserve fund of the company has reached the Bonus to sum of $100,000, all liabilities being deducted, it shall be law- members. 15 ful for the directors to declare from time time, by by-law passed in that behalf, a bonus out of the net profits after the sum aforesaid has been reserved; and, subject to the terms of said by-law, to issue the said bonus to the then members of the company either by way of cash refund, or of bonus scrip, 20 to be applied towards the payment of future premiums or assessments; it shall also be lawful for the directors, pursuant to by-law passed in that behalf, to allow interest on cash payments made in advance of premiums or assessments thereafter due, or to become due."

BILL.

An Act respecting the Gore District Mutual
Fire Insurance Company.

First Reading, 1887.

(Private Bill.)

BILL.

An Act respecting the Ontario and Sault Ste. Marie Railway Company.

WHEREAS the Ontario Sault Ste. Marie Railway Company *Preamble.* have by their petition prayed that the time for the completion of their Railway should be extended; and whereas it is expedient to grant the prayer of the said petition;

5   Therefore Her Majesty by and with the advice and consent of the Legislative Assembly of the Province of Ontario, enacts as follows :—

Section 23 of the Act of the Province of Ontario passed in *44 V. c. 68. s.* the forty-fourth year of Her Majesty's reign, Chapter 68, is *23 amended.*
10 hereby amended, and the time for the completion of the said Railway is extended to six years from the passing of this Act. And this amendment shall have the same effect as if the time so extended was the period fixed in the said section for the completion of the said Railway.

1st Session, 6th Legislature, 50 Vic., 1887.

BILL.

An Act Respecting the Ontario and Sault
Ste. Marie Railway Company.

First Reading,   1887.

(Private Bill.)

BILL.

An Act respecting the Ontario Sault Ste. Marie Railway Company.

WHEREAS the Ontario Sault Ste. Marie Railway Com- Preamble.
pany have by their petition prayed that the time for the
completion of their Railway should be extended; and whereas
the Ontario Sault Ste. Marie Railway Company in the years 1881
and 1882 surveyed and located their line of railway between
5 the Ste. Marie River and Spanish River, and expended on the
said surveys, and otherwise, large sums of money; and whereas,
owing to the depression which intervened, and the fact that
the lines west of the Sault Ste. Marie were not proceeded with,
the work of the said company's line was not in the meantime
completed; and whereas the Canadian Pacific Railway Com-
10 pany have located their line between the above points and
commenced work thereon; and whereas their said line between
the above points crosses, re-crosses and interferes with the said
location of the Ontario Sault Ste. Marie Railway Company
between the said points, so as to render it impossible to use
15 their said line so located as aforesaid, and proceedings were
taken by the said company to prevent such or any interference
with their said line; and whereas to end all litigation and
disputes the said companies have agreed that the Canadian
Pacific Railway Company shall not cross or interfere with the
line of the Ontario Sault Ste. Marie Railway Company as now
20 located between the points aforesaid save as is hereinafter
indicated and in the manner hereby defined; and whereas it
is alleged that at certain points, owing to the formation of the
ground, it is difficult to give each company their full location-
width, and the Canadian Pacific Railway Company would be
25 put to great expense if compelled to avoid the whole right of
way of the Ontario Sault Ste. Marie Railway Company as
located at these points, or were prevented from crossing it;
and whereas it is alleged that the lines of both companies may
be so arranged as to avoid crossings and interference; it is
hereby referred to Walter Shanly, of the City of Montreal,
30 Esquire, to locate the two lines so that each of them shall have
sufficient space without injury to the line of the other. The
said Walter Shanly to have power to direct the removal of
tracks, the change of alignment and otherwise, as he shall
think right, so as to secure the best practicable lines in all
35 respects for both companies between the said points. In the
adjustment of such alignments the said Shanly, where, from
the formation of the country, it is necessary to do so, is to have
liberty to narrow the right of way of either or both of the said
companies, but at the same time he is to give to each an
independent track; and he shall also have the right to direct
and order how and in what portions the companies respectively

shall bear any extra expense which may be caused by his
decision or orders. In all matters referred to him the finding
of the said Shanly is to be final; and in case the said Shanly
shall fail or refuse to act, then the matters hereby referred to
him shall be referred to a competent disinterested engineer, to 5
be named by the said Shanly, who shall have all the powers
hereby conferred upon the said Shanly;
☞Therefore Her Majesty, by and with the advice and consent
of the Legislative Assembly of the Province of Ontario, enacts
as follows :— 10

44 V. c. 68. s.
ed.
☞1. Section 23 of the Act of the Province of Ontario passed in
the forty-fourth year of Her Majesty's reign, Chapter 68, is
hereby amended, and the time for the completion of the said
Railway is extended to six years from the third day of March,
1887. This amendment shall have the same effect as if the 15
time so extended was the period originally fixed in the said
section for the completion of the said railway, and as if this
had been enacted on the said third day of March.

Agreement
confirmed.
☞2. It is hereby further enacted that so far as this Legislature
has the power and to the extent that this Legislature has such 20
power the above agreement is hereby confirmed.☜

No. 25.

1st Session 6th Legislature, 50 Vic., 1887.

BILL.

An Act Respecting the Ontario Sault Ste. Marie Railway Company.

(*Reprinted as Amended by Railway Committee.*)

First Reading, 9th March, 1887.

(Private Bill)

BILL.

An Act to amend the Act to incorporate the Eastern Ontario Railway Company.

WHEREAS it has been found impracticable to build the Preamble.
line of railway authorized to be constructed under and
by virtue of an Act passed by the Legislative Assembly of the
Province of Ontario in the 46th year of Her Majesty's reign,
5 chaptered 51, and intituled "An Act to incorporate the Eastern
Ontario Railway Company" within the time limited for that
purpose ; and whereas Alexander MacLean and other shareholders and provisional Directors of the said Eastern Ontario
Railway Company have, by their petition, represented that
10 since the passing of the said Act no work has been done
towards the commencement and completion of the said Railway, and have prayed that the said Act may be revived
and amended, and also that the time fixed for the commencement and completion of the said Railway may be extended,
15 and it is expedient to grant the prayer of the said petition ;
Therefore Her Majesty, by and with the advice and consent
of the Legislative Assembly of the Province of Ontario, enacts
as follows :—

1. The Act hereinbefore recited is hereby revived and Time for com-
20 declared to be in full force and effect, and the time limited for mencement
and comple-
the commencement of the said Railway is extended for three tion extended.
years from the passing of this Act, and the time for the completion thereof is extended to eight years from the passing of
this Act.

25 2. Section 1 of the said Act is hereby amended by adding 46 V. c. 51, s. 1
the names of Francis H. Chrysler, Donald P. Mackinnon, John amended.
G. Snetsinger, Donald B. Maclennan and John Bennett, after
the name John Sweetland in the said section.

3. Section 6 of the said Act is hereby amended by substi- 46 V. c. 51, s. 6
30 tuting the following persons as the provisional Board of amended.
Directors of the Company instead of those named in the said
section, namely, Alexander MacLean, Donald B. Maclennan, J.
G. Snetsinger, Francis H. Chrysler and James W. Russell.

1st Session, 6th Legislature, 50 Vic., 1887.

BILL.

An Act to amend the Act to incorporate the Eastern Ontario Railway Company.

First Reading,   1887.

(Private Bill.)

BILL.

An Act to change the name of the Thunder Bay Colonization Railway Company.

WHEREAS the Thunder Bay Colonization Railway Com- Preamble.
pany was duly incorporated under the provisions of an
Act of the Legislature of Ontario passed in the 46th year of
Her Majesty's reign, chaptered 56 ; and whereas certain
5 further powers were given and amendments made by an Act
of the Legislature of Ontario passed in the 49th year of Her
Majesty's reign, chaptered 79 ; and whereas the said Thunder
Bay Colonization Railway Company has by its petition prayed
that its corporate name may be changed ; and whereas it is
10 expedient to grant the prayer of such petition;

Therefore Her Majesty, by and with the advice and consent
of the Legislative Assembly of the Province of Ontario, enacts
as follows :—

1. The corporate name of the said company shall be changed Name
15 to that of "The Port Arthur, Duluth and Western Railway changed.
Company," by which name instead of "The Thunder Bay
Colonization Railway Company" the said company shall have
and exercise all the powers and privileges granted by the said
Acts or any other Acts relating to the said company.

20 2. Notwithstanding the said change of name it shall be Right to cer-
lawful for the said company to apply for and receive in the tain subsidies
name of the Thunder Bay Colonization Railway Company all not affected.
subsidies or aid granted to the Thunder Bay Colonization
Railway Company under or by virtue of any Act of the Par-
25 liament or Order in Council of the Dominion of Canada in the
same manner as if this Act had not been passed.

BILL.

An Act to change the name of the Thunder Bay Colonization Railway Company.

First Reading,   ·   1887.

(Private Bill.)

BILL.

An Act to change the name of the Thunder Bay Colonization Railway Company.

WHEREAS the Thunder Bay Colonization Railway Com- Preamble. pany was duly incorporated under the provisions of an Act of the Legislature of Ontario passed in the 46th year of Her Majesty's reign, chaptered 56; and whereas certain 5 further powers were given and amendments made by an Act of the Legislature of Ontario passed in the 49th year of Her Majesty's reign, chaptered 79; and whereas the said Thunder Bay Colonization Railway Company has by its petition prayed that its corporate name may be changed; and whereas it is 10 expedient to grant the prayer of such petition;

Therefore Her Majesty, by and with the advice and consent of the Legislative Assembly of the Province of Ontario, enacts as follows :—

1. The corporate name of the said company shall be changed Name 15 to that of "The Port Arthur, Duluth and Western Railway changed. Company," by which name instead of "The Thunder Bay Colonization Railway Company," the said company shall have and exercise all the powers and privileges granted by the said Acts or any other Acts relating to the said company.

20 **2.** Notwithstanding the said change of name it shall be Right to cer- lawful for the said company to apply for and receive in the tain subsidies name of the Thunder Bay Colonization Railway Company all not affected. subsidies or aid granted to the Thunder Bay Colonization Railway Company under or by virtue of any Act of the Par- 25 liament or Order in Council of the Dominion of Canada in the same manner as if this Act had not been passed.

☞**3.** Section 30 of the Act passed in the 46th year of Her 46 V. c. 56, s. Majesty's reign, chaptered 56, as amended by section 3 of the 30 & 49 V. c. Act passed in the 49th year of Her Majesty's reign, chaptered 79, s. 3, re- 79, is hereby repealed, and the following section is substituted pealed. 30 therefor :

The directors of the company, after the sanction of the Issue ☐ bonds shareholders shall have been first obtained at any annual general meeting, or any special general meeting, to be called from time to time for such purpose, shall have power to issue 35 bonds of the company for the purpose of raising money for prosecuting the said undertaking, and such bonds shall, without registration or formal conveyance, be taken and considered to be the first and preferential claim and charge upon the under- taking and real property of the company, including its roll- 40 ing stock and equipments, then existing and at any time thereafter acquired; and each holder of the said bonds shall be

deemed a mortgagee and incumbrancer *pro rata* with all the 5
other holders thereof upon the undertaking and the property
of the company as aforesaid; and the company may by by-law
before issue, fix and define the amount or denomination of such
bonds, the time or times and the place or places for payment of
the principal moneys thereof, and the interest thereon; and 10

Proviso. other particulars in reference thereto : Provided, however, that
the whole amount of such issue of bonds shall not exceed
$20,000 per mile of the said railway, and that the rate of
interest thereon shall not exceed six per centum per annum ;

Proviso. and provided, also further, that in the event at any time of the 15
interest of the said bonds remaining unpaid and owing, then at
the next ensuing general meeting of the company and at all
subsequent general meetings, so long as such interest or any part
thereof shall remain unpaid and in arrear, all holders of bonds
shall have and possess the same rights and privileges and quali- 20
fications for directors, and for voting, and for all purposes as

Proviso. are attached to shareholders : Provided that the holder of any
bond or bonds shall have at least three days before any
such meeting produced the bond or bonds held by him to
the secretary for registration in his name, or that in the 25
case of the holder of any bond or bonds residing in Great
Britain and Ireland, and having such bond or bonds in
his custody or under his control, then such holder shall
have, at least three days before any such meeting produced
to the secretary, a certificate under the hand and official seal of 30
a notary public stating the number of such bond or bonds,
and that they had been produced before him by such holder,
and in either of such cases it shall be the duty of the secretary
to register the name of such holder and the numbers of the
· bonds held by him, but the failure or neglect of the secretary 40
in that respect shall not affect the rights, privileges and qualifications of such holder or holders ; any such bondholder shall
be entitled to five votes for every bond of the amount of one
hundred pounds sterling held by him, or in that proportion.

BILL.

An Act to change the name of the Thunder Bay Colonization Railway Company.

(Reprinted as amended by Railway Committee.)

First Reading, 11th March, 1887.

(Private Bill.)

No. 28.] **BILL.** [1887.

An Act to amend the Act Incorporating the Queen City Fire Insurance Company.

WHEREAS The Queen City Fire Insurance Company have Preamble.
by their petition prayed for an Act to amend their Act of
Incorporation passed in the 34th year of Her Majesty's reign,
chaptered 73; and whereas it is expedient to grant the prayer
5 of the said petition ;
Therefore Her Majesty, by and with the advice and consent
of the Legislative Assembly of the Province of Ontario, enacts
as follows :—

Section 6 of the Act passed in the 34th year of Her 34 V. c. 73, s.
10 Majesty's reign, chaptered 73, and intituled "*An Act to Incor-* 6 amended.
porate the Queen City Fire Insurance Company" is hereby
amended by striking out the words " provided always that all
risks insured against shall be within the County of York in
the Province of Ontario" which occur in the said section.

No. 28.

1st Session, 6th Legislature, 50 Vic., 1887.

BILL.

An Act to amend the Act Incorporating
the Queen City Fire Insurance Company.

First Reading,   1887.

(Private Bill.)

No. 29.] **BILL.** [1887.

An Act respecting a certain Railway Debenture Debt of the Township of Eldon.

WHEREAS the corporation of the township of Eldon, under Preamble. their by-law passed on the thirty-first day of December, 1869, incurred a debenture debt of $44,000 in aid of the Toronto and Nipissing Railway Company, maturing on the 5 first day of July, 1889, and by reason of the financial condition of the said corporation, the sum of $13,000 only has been provided in the meantime to meet the said debt, which said sum, together with the further sum of $11,000, to be levied on account of said debt before the said first day of July, 1889, will still leave 10 a deficiency of $20,000 ; and whereas the said corporation by their petition have prayed that an Act may be passed to empower them to pass a by-law to borrow on new debentures of the said corporation the said sum of $20,000, payable with interest thereon in twenty years at furthest from the said first 15 day of July, 1889, in manner hereinafter provided ; and whereas it is expedient to grant the prayer of the said petition ;

Therefore Her Majesty, by and with the advice and consent of the Legislative Assembly of the Province of Ontario, enacts as follows :—

20 **1.** The corporation of the township of Eldon for the pur- Issue of new pose of retiring and paying off the $20,000 mentioned in the debentures for preamble to this Act, may pass a by-law authorizing the issue $20,000 authorized. of new debentures of the said corporation for the said sum of $20,000, and for the payment of interest thereon, payable in 25 twenty year at furthest from the said first day of July, 1889, in equal annual payments, in such way that the aggregate amount payable for principal and interest in any year shall be equal, as nearly as may be to what is payable for principal and interest, during each of the other years of such period as pro- 30 vided by section 344 of *The Consolidated Municipal Act, 1883:* Proviso. Provided always that such by-law shall in all respects conform to and comply with the provisions of the said *Consolidated Municipal Act,* and the general municipal law in force in this Province, except that it shall not be necessary to obtain 35 the assent of the electors of the said township of Eldon to the passing of such by-law ; and provided further that the said Proviso. new debentures and all moneys arising therefrom shall, to the full extent thereof, be applied only to paying off the said sum of $20,000 required for the above recited purpose.

No. 29.

1st Session, 6th Legislature, 50 Vic., 1887.

BILL.

An Act respecting a certain Railway Debenture Debt of the Township of Eldon.

First Reading,   1887.

(Private Bill.)

No. 29.] **BILL.** [1887.

An Act respecting a certain Railway Debenture Debt of the Township of Eldon.

WHEREAS the corporation of the township of Eldon, under Preamble.
their by-law passed on the thirty-first day of December, 1869, incurred a debenture debt of $44,000 in aid of the
Toronto and Nipissing Railway Company, maturing on the
5 first day of July, 1889, and by reason of the financial condition
of the said corporation, the sum of $13,000 only has been pro-
vided in the meantime to meet the said debt, which said sum, together with the further sum of $11,000, to be *provided* on account
of said debt before the said first day of July, 1889, will still leave
10 a deficiency of $20,000 ; and whereas the said corporation by
their petition have prayed that an Act may be passed to empower them to pass a by-law to borrow on new debentures of
the said corporation the said sum of $20,000, payable with in-
terest thereon in twenty years at furthest from the said first
15 day of July, 1889, in manner hereinafter provided ; and whereas it is expedient to grant the prayer of the said petition ;

Therefore Her Majesty, by and with the advice and consent
of the Legislative Assembly of the Province of Ontario, enacts
as follows :—

20 **1.** The corporation of the township of Eldon for the pur- Issue of new
pose of retiring and paying off the $20,000 mentioned in the debentures for
preamble to this Act, may pass a by-law authorizing the issue ized.
of new debentures of the said corporation for the said sum of
$20,000, and for the payment of interest thereon, payable in
25 twenty years at furthest from the said first day of July, 1889,
either in equal annual payments, in such way that the aggregate
amount payable for principal and interest in any year shall be
equal, as nearly as may be to what is payable for principal and
interest, during each of the other years of such period as pro-
30 vided by section 344 of *The Consolidated Municipal Act, 1883:* Proviso.
or by special rate providing for the annual interest and a
further sum annually as a sinking fund, according to the
provisions of section 342 of the said Act. Provided always
that such by-law shall in all respects conform to and comply
35 with the provisions of the said *Consolidated Municipal Act,*
and the general municipal law in force in this Province, except
that it shall not be necessary to obtain the assent of the electors
of the said township of Eldon to the passing of such by-law ;
and provided further that the said new debentures and all Proviso.
40 moneys arising therefrom shall, to the full extent thereof, be
applied only to paying off the said sum of $20,000 *and interest*
required for the above recited purpose.

No. 29.

1st Session, 6th Legislature, 50 Vic., 1887.

BILL.

An Act respecting a certain Railway Debenture Debt of the Township of Eldon.

(Reprinted as amended by the Private Bills Committee.)

First Reading, 23rd March, 1887.

(Private Bill)

BILL.

An Act to incorporate the Ottawa and Thousand Island Railway Company.

WHEREAS Robert G. Hervey, and others, have by their Preamble.
petition represented that it is desirable that a railway
should be constructed from the City of Ottawa, in the County
of Carleton, to the Town of Brockville, or some other point on
5 the Brockville, Westport and Sault Ste. Marie Railway, in the
County of Leeds, and have prayed for an Act accordingly;
and whereas it is expedient to grant the prayer of the said
petition;

Therefore Her Majesty, by and with the advice and consent of
10 the Legislative Assembly of the Province of Ontario, enacts
as follows :—

1. Robert G. Hervey, William B. Smellie, Hugh T. Fitz- Incorpora-
simmons, and William H. Jones, all of the Town of Brockville, tion.
in the County of Leeds, and Province of Ontario, and Clark-
15 son Jones, of the City of Toronto, in the Province of Ontario,
with such other persons and corporations as shall, in pursuance of this Act, become shareholders of the said company
hereby incorporated, are hereby constituted and declared a
body corporate and politic by the name of " The Ottawa and
20 Thousand Island Railway Company," hereinafter called the
company.

2. The several clauses of *The Railway Act of Ontario* shall R. S. O. c.
be incorporated with and be deemed to be a part of this Act, 165, incorpor-
and shall apply to the said company and to the railway to be ated.
25 constructed by them, except only so far as they may be inconsistent with the express enactments hereof; and the expression " this Act," when used herein, shall be understood to include the clauses of the said *Railway Act* so incorporated with
this Act.

30 3. The said company, their agents and servants shall have Location of
full power and authority to survey, lay out, construct, com- line.
plete, lease, purchase and operate a single or double line of
railway from a point in or near the City of Ottawa, in the
County of Carleton, through the County of Carleton and the
35 County of Grenville, and the County of Leeds, to a point on
the line of the Brockville, Westport, and Sault Ste. Marie
Railway, either in or near the Town of Brockville, or at some
other point in the County of Leeds.

4. The gauge of the said railway shall be four feet eight Gauge.
40 and one-half inches.

Power to purchase and work vessels.   **5.** The company shall have power to construct, purchase, sell, charter, own and use scows, boats and steam or other vessels on the lakes, rivers and canals of this Province in connection with their railway.

Power to acquire wharves, etc.   **6.** The company shall have power to purchase, lease, or ac- 5 quire, at any point where their railway or any branch thereof touches or approaches within two miles of any navigable waters, sufficient land for the uses of the company, their railway, and vessels, run or navigated in connection with said railway, and the company may erect warehouses, elevators, 10 docks, wharves, stations, workshops and such other buildings as may be necessary for the purposes of the company, and may sell and convey such lands as may be found superfluous for any such purposes ; and shall also have full power to connect any of the works herein mentioned with any point on the 15 railway, or its branches, by means of any line or lines of railway for such purposes.

Amalgamation with other companies authorized.   **7.** The company is authorized and empowered to make necessary arrangements to contract and agree with any other company, or companies, incorporated or to be incorporated by 20 this Legislature, or the Parliament of Canada, or any or either of them, if lawfully authorized to enter into such arrangements, for amalgamation with any or either of them, provided that the terms of such amalgamation are approved of by two-thirds of the shareholders, voting either in person or re- 25 presented by proxy at a special general meeting to be held for that purpose, in accordance with this Act.

Proviso.

Agreements with other companies.   **8.** The company shall have power to enter into and conclude any agreement with any such other company or companies, or any or either of them, if lawfully authorized to enter into 30 such agreement, to lease the railway herein authorized, or any part thereof, or to lease or acquire running powers over the lines of such other railway companies, or any or either of them, or any part or parts thereof, or for leasing or hiring any locomotives, tenders, plant, rolling stock, or other property, or 35 touching any service to be rendered by the one company to the other, and the compensation therefor ; provided that the agreement shall be approved of by two-thirds of the shareholders, voting either in person, or by proxy, at any special general meeting called for that purpose ; but nothing in this 40 or the preceding section shall be construed as purporting or intending to confer rights or powers upon any company which is not within the legislative authority of this Province.

Telegraph and telephone lines.   **9.** For the purpose of constructing, working, and protecting the telegraph and telephone lines to be constructed by the 45 company on their line of railway, the powers conferred upon telegraph and telephone companies by *The Act respecting Electric Telegraph Companies* are hereby conferred upon the company, and the other provisions of the said Act for the working and protection of telegraph and telephone lines shall 50 apply to any such telegraph or telephone lines constructed by the company.

Snow fences.   **10.** The company shall have the right, on and after the first day of November in each year, to enter into and upon any

lands of Her Majesty, or into or upon any lands of any corporation or person whatsoever lying along the route or line of the said railway, and to erect and maintain snow fences thereon, subject to the payment of such damages (if any) as
5 may be thereafter established in the manner provided by law in respect of such railway to have been actually suffered; provided always that any such snow fences so erected shall be removed on or before the first day of April following.

11. Robert G. Hervey, William B. Smellie, Hugh T. Fitz- Provisional
10 simmons, Clarkson Jones, and John Chapman, with power to directors. add to their numbers, are hereby constituted a board of provisional directors of the company, and shall hold office as such until other directors shall be elected under the provisions of this Act by the shareholders, and shall have power to fill the
15 place or places of any of their number which may become vacant, and to open stock books, and to procure subscriptions for the undertaking, to make calls upon the subscribers, to cause surveys and plans to be executed, and to call a general meeting of the shareholders for the election of directors, as
20 hereinafter provided; and with all such other powers as under *The Railway Act of Ontario* are vested in ordinary directors; and such provisional directors may appoint a committee from their number to open such stock books and to receive such subscriptions; and the said committee, or a majority
25 of them may, in their discretion, exclude any person from subscribing.

12. The capital stock of the company hereby incorporated Capital stock. shall be $1,250,000 (with power to increase the same in the manner provided by *The Railway Act of Ontario*), to be
30 divided into twelve thousand five hundred shares of $100 each, and shall be raised by the persons and corporations who may become shareholders in such company; and the money so raised shall be applied, in the first place, to the payment of all fees expenses, and disbursements of and incidental to the
35 passing of this Act, and for making the surveys, plans, and estimates connected with the works hereby authorized, and the remainder of said money shall be applied to the making, equipping, completing and maintaining of the said railway and to the other purposes of this Act.

40 **13.** When and so soon as shares to the amount of $50,000, First election in the capital stock of the company shall have been subscribed, of directors. and ten per cent. thereof shall have been paid into one of the chartered banks of the Dominion, having an office in the Province of Ontario.(which shall on no account be withdrawn
45 therefrom unless for the service of the company), the provisional directors, or a majority of them present at a meeting duly called for the purpose, shall call a meeting of the subscribers for the purpose of electing directors, giving at least two weeks' notice in a paper published in the Town of
50 Brockville, and in the *Ontario Gazette*, of the time, place, and object of such meeting; and at such general meeting the shareholders present, either in person or by proxy, and who shall at the opening of such meeting have paid ten per centum on the stock subscribed by them, shall elect not less than five nor
55 more than thirteen persons to be directors of the company in

4

manner and qualified as hereinafter directed, which said
directors shall constitute a board of directors, and shall hold
office until the next general annual meeting.

How first meeting may be called if provisional directors neglect to call same. **14.** In case the provisional directors neglect to call such
meeting, to be held on some day within the space of three 5
months after such amount of the capital stock shall have been
subscribed and ten per centum thereof so paid up, the same
may be called by any five of the subscribers who shall have so
paid up ten per centum, and who are subscribers among them
for not less than $25,000 of the said capital stock, and who 10
have paid up all calls thereon.

Allotment of stock. **15.** It shall be lawful for the directors, in procuring subscriptions for stock, to allot such stock in such amounts, and
subject to the payment of such calls of such amount, and at
such times, and at such discount as they may think fit, or they 15
may agree for the sale of such stock or any part thereof at
such price as they may think fit, and may stipulate for the
payment of the purchase money at the time of subscription or
by instalments, and the amount of every such instalment
as and when payable shall be deemed to be money 20
due in respect of a call duly made in accordance with
the provisions contained in Section 27 of the *Railway Act of
Ontario*, and non-payment of any such instalment shall carry
with it all the rights, incidents and consequences as mentioned
in the said Act, as in the case of a call due by a shareholder on 25
a share.

Certain payments may be made in stock or bonds. **16.** The said provisional directors or the elected directors
may pay, or agree to pay, in paid up stock, or in the bonds of
the said company, such sums as they may deem expedient to
engineers or contractors, or for right of way or material, 30
plant or rolling stock, and also when sanctioned by a vote of
the shareholders at any general meeting, for the services of promoters or other persons who may be employed by the directors,
for the purpose of assisting the directors in the furtherance
of the undertaking, or purchase of right of way, material, 35
plant or rolling stock, whether such promoters or other persons,
be provisional or elected directors or not, and any agreements
so made shall be binding on the company.

Annual meeting. **17.** The general annual meeting of the shareholders of the
company shall be held in such place, in the Town of 40
Brockville, or at such other place, and on such days, and at
such hours, as may be directed by the by-laws of the company,
and public notice thereof shall be given at least two weeks
previously in the *Ontario Gazette*, and once a week in one
newspaper published in the Town of Brockville, during the 45
two weeks preceding the week in which such meeting is to be
held.

Special meetings. **18.** Special general meetings of the shareholders of the company may be held at such place in the Town of Brockville, or
at such other place, and at such times, and in such manner, 50
and for such purposes, as may be provided by the by-laws of
the company, upon such notice as is provided in the last preceding section.

19. In the election of directors under this Act no person shall be elected a director unless he shall be the holder and owner of at least ten shares of the stock of the company, upon which all calls have been paid up. Qualification of directors.

5 **20.** Aliens and companies incorporated abroad as well as British subjects and corporations, and whether resident in this Province or elsewhere, may be shareholders in the company, and all such shareholders shall be entitled to vote on their shares equally with British subjects, and shall also be eligible 10 to office as directors in the company. Rights of aliens.

21. Every holder of one or more shares of the said capital stock shall, at any general meeting of the shareholders, be entitled to one vote for every share held by him ; and no shareholder shall be entitled to vote on any matter whatever unless 15 all calls due on the stock upon which such shareholder seeks to vote shall have been paid up at least one week before the day appointed for such meeting. Votes.

22. At all meetings of the company the stock held by municipal and other corporations may be represented by such 20 person as they shall respectively have appointed in that behalf by by-law ; and such person shall, at such meeting, be entitled equally with other shareholders to vote by proxy. Representation of stock held by corporations.

23. At all meetings of the board of directors, whether of provisional directors or of those elected by the shareholders, 25 four directors shall form a quorum for the transaction of business, and the said board of directors may employ and pay one of their number as managing director. Quorum of directors.

24. Should the shareholders of the company resolve that the interests of the company would be best promoted by 30 enabling one or more of the directors to act for the company in any particular matter or matters, it shall be lawful for the directors, after each resolution, to confer such power upon one or more of their number. Delegation of powers to directors in special cases.

25. It shall be lawful for the directors to enter into any 35 contract or contracts with any individual or association of individuals for the construction or equipment of the line or any portion thereof, including or excluding the purchase of the right of way, and to pay therefor, either in the whole or in part, either in cash or bonds, or in paid-up stock ; provided that 40 no such contract shall be of any force or validity till approved of by two-thirds of the shareholders present, in person or by proxy, at a meeting specially convened for considering the same. Power to make contracts for construction of the railway.
Proviso.

26. The said company may receive from any government 45 or from any persons or bodies corporate, municipal or politic, who may have power to make or grant the same, aid towards the construction, equipment or maintenance of the said railway by way of bonus, gift or loan, in money or debentures, or other securities for money, or by way of guarantee, upon such 50 terms and conditions as may be agreed upon. Aid to company.

Aid from municipalities.

27. Any municipality through which the said railway may pass is empowered to grant, by way of gift, to the company, any lands belonging to such municipality or over which it may have control, which may be required for right of way, station grounds or other purposes connected with the running or 5 traffic of the said railway, and the company shall have power to accept gifts of land from any government, or any person, or any body politic or corporate. and shall have power to sell or otherwise dispose of the same for the benefit of the company.

Power to hold additional property at extremities of railway.

28. The company shall have power to purchase and hold 10 such land as may be required at each extremity of the said railway for the purpose of building thereon storehouses, warehouses, engine houses and other erections for the uses of the said company, and the same, or portions thereof, in their discretion to sell or convey, and also to make use for the purpose 15 of the said railway of any stream or water-course at or near which the said railway passes, doing, however, no unnecessary damage thereto, and not impairing the usefulness of such stream or water-course.

Right to use highways.

29. It shall and may be lawful for any municipality through 20 which the said railway passes, and having jurisdiction in the premises, to pass a by-law or by-laws empowering the company to make their road and lay their rails along any of the highways within such municipality, and whether or not the same be in possession or control of any joint-stock companies, and if 25 such highway be either in the possession of or under the control of any joint stock company, then also with the assent of such company, and it shall and may be lawful for the company to enter into and perform any such agreement as they may from time to time deem expedient, with any municipality, 30 corporation or person, for the construction or for the maintenance and repair of gravel or other public roads leading to the said railway.

Exemption from taxation.

30. It shall further be lawful for the council of any municipality through which any part of the said railway passes or 35 is situate, by by-law specially passed for that purpose, to exempt the company and its property within such municipality, either wholly or in part, from municipal assessment and taxation, or agree to a certain sum per annum or otherwise, in gross, by way of commutation or composition for payment, or 40 in lieu of all or of any municipal rates or assessments to be imposed by such municipal corporation, and for such term of years as such municipal corporation may deem expedient, not exceeding twenty-one years; and any such by-law shall not be repealed unless in conformity with a condition contained 45 therein.

Aid from municipalities.

31. Any municipality or any portion of a township municipality which may be interested in securing the construction of the said railway, or through any part of which or near which the railway or works of the said company shall pass or 50 be situate, may aid the said company by giving money or debentures by way of bonus or gift, or may aid the said company by way of loan or by guarantee of the municipal corporation under and subject to the provisions hereinafter contained; provided always that such aid shall not be given except after 55

the passing of a by-law for the purpose, and the adoption of
such by-law by the qualified ratepayers of the municipality or
portion of municipality (as the case may be), in accordance
with and as provided by law in respect to granting aid by
5 way of bonuses to railways.

32. Such by-law shall be submitted by the municipal Provisions as
council to the vote of the ratepayers in manner following, to bonus by-
namely :— laws.

1. The proper petition shall first be presented to the coun-
10 cil, expressing the desire to aid the railway, and stating in
what way and for what amount, and the council shall, within
six weeks after the receipt of such petition by the clerk of
the municipality, introduce a by-law to the effect petitioned
for, and submit the same for the approval of the qualified
15 voters.

2. In the case of a county municipality the petition shall
be that of a majority of the reeves and deputy reeves, or of
fifty resident freeholders in each of the minor municipalities
of the county who are qualified voters under *The Municipal*
20 *Act.*

3. In the case of other municipalities the petition shall be
that of a majority of the council thereof, or of fifty resident
freeholders, being duly qualified voters under *The Municipal
Act* as aforesaid.

. 25 4. In the case of a section of a township municipality the
petition is to be presented to the council, defining the section
by metes and bounds or lots and concessions, and shall be that
of a majority of the council of such township municipality, or
of fifty resident freeholders in such section of the munici-
30 pality being duly qualified voters as aforesaid.

33. In case of aid from a county municipality fifty resi- Provisions
dent freeholders of the county may petition the county coun- for referring to
cil against submitting the said by-law, upon the ground that disputes as to
certain minor municipalities or portions thereof comprised in bonus by-laws.
35 the said by-law would be injuriously affected thereby, or upon
any other ground, ought not to be included therein ; and upon
deposit by the petitioners with the treasurer of the county of
a sum sufficient to defray the expenses of such reference the
said council shall forthwith refer the said petition to three
40 arbitrators, one being the Judge of the County Court, one
being the Registrar of the county or of the riding in which the
county town is situate, and one being an engineer appointed
by the Commissioner of Public Works for Ontario, who shall
have power to confirm or amend the said by-law by excluding
45 any minor municipality or any section thereof therefrom, and
the decision of any two of them shall be final, and the by-law
so confirmed or amended shall thereupon, at the option of the
company, be submitted by the council to the duly qualified
voters ; and in case the by-law is confirmed by the arbitrators
50 the expense of the reference shall be borne by the petitioners
against the same, but if amended then by the company or the
county, as the arbitrators may order.

Deposit for expenses.

34. Before any such by-law is submitted the railway company shall, if required, deposit with the treasurer of the municipality a sum sufficient to pay the expenses to be incurred in submitting said by-law.

Rate not exceeding three cents in the dollar valid.

35. Any municipality or portion of a township munici- 5 pality interested in the construction of the road of the said company may grant aid by way of bonus to the said company towards the construction of such road, notwithstanding that such aid may increase the municipal taxation of such municipality or portion thereof beyond what is allowed by law, pro- 10 vided that such aid shall not require the levying of a greater aggregate annual rate for all purposes, exclusive of school rates, than three cents in the dollar upon the value of the ratable property therein.

By-law, what to contain.

36. Such by-law shall in each case provide :— 15

1. For raising the amount petitioned for in the municipality or portion of the township municipality (as the case may be) mentioned in the petition, by the issue of debentures of the county or minor municipality respectively, and shall also provide for the delivery of the said debentures or the 20 application of the amount to be raised thereby, as may be expressed in the said by-law.

2. For assessing any levying upon all ratable property lying within the municipality or portion of the township municipality defined in said by-law (as the case may be) an 25 annual special rate sufficient to include a sinking fund for the repayment of the said debentures within twenty years, with interest thereon, payable yearly or half-yearly, which debentures the respective municipal councils, wardens, mayors, reeves and other officers thereof, are hereby authorized to 30 execute and issue in such cases respectively.

"Minor municipality," meaning of.

37. Ths term "minor municipality" shall be construed to mean any town not separated from the municipal county, township or incorporated village situate in the county municipality. 35

If by-law carried council to pass same.

38. In case the by-law submitted be approved of and carried in accordance with the provisions of the law in that behalf, then within four weeks after the date of such voting the municipal council shall read the said by-law a third time and pass the same. 40

And issue debentures.

39. Within one month after the passing of such by-law the said council and the mayor, warden, reeve or other officers thereof, shall issue the debentures provided for by the by-law and deliver the same duly executed to the trustees appointed or to be appointed under this Act. 45

Levying rate on portion of a municipality.

40. In case any such loan, guarantee or bonus be so granted by a portion of the township municipality, the rate to be levied for payment of the debentures issued therefor and the interest thereon shall be assessed and levied upon such portion only of such municipality. 50

41. The provisions of *The Consolidated Municipal Act,* Application of *1883,* and the amendments thereto, so far as the same are not municipal inconsistent with this Act, shall apply to any by-law so passed Acts as to by-law so passed by or for a portion of a township municipality to the same
5 extent as if the same had been passed by or for the whole municipality.

42. It shall and may be lawful for the council of any muni- Extension of cipality that may grant aid by way of bonus to the said com- time for pany, by resolution or by-law, to extend the time for the com- commencement.
10 pletion of the works (on the completion of which the said company would be entitled to such bonus), from time to time, provided that no such extension shall be for a longer period than one year at a time.

43. The councils for all corporations that may grant aid Extension of
15 by way of bonus to the said company may, by resolution or time for completion. by-law, extend the time for the commencement of the work beyond that stipulated for in the by-law or by-laws granting such aid from time to time, provided that no such extension shall be for a longer period than one year.

20 **44.** Whenever any municipality or portion of a township Trustees of municipality shall grant aid by way of bonus or gift to the debentures. railway company, the debentures therefor shall, within one month after the passing of the by-law authorizing the same, be delivered to three trustees, to be named, one by the
25 Lieutenant-Governor in Council, one by the said company, and one by the majority of the heads of the municipalities which have granted bonuses, all of the trustees to be residents of the Province of Ontario; provided that if the said heads of the Proviso. municipalities shall refuse or neglect to name such trustees
30 within one month after notice in writing of the appointment of the company's trustee, or if the Lieutenant-Governor in Council shall omit to name such trustee within one month after notice in writing to him of the appointment of the other trustees, then, in either case the company shall be at liberty to
35 name such other trustee or trustees; any of the said trustees may be removed and a new trustee appointed in his stead at any time by the Lieutenant-Governor in Council, and in case any trustee dies, or resigns his trust, or goes to live out of the Province of Ontario, or otherwise become incapable to act, his
40 trusteeship shall become vacant and a new trustee may be appointed by the Lieutenant-Governor in Council.

45.—(1) The said trustees shall receive the said debentures Trusts of or bonds in trust, firstly, under the directions of the company, proceeds of debentures. but subject to the conditions of the by-law in relation thereto,
45 as to time or manner to convert the same into money or otherwise dispose of them; secondly, to deposit the debentures or amount realized from the sale in some chartered bank having an office in the Province of Ontario in the name of "Ottawa and Thousand Island Railway Trust Account," and to
50 pay the same out to the said company, from time to time, as the said company becomes entitled thereto, under the conditions of the by-law granting the said bonus and on the certificate of the chief engineer of the said railway for the time being in the form set out in schedule B hereto, or to the
55 like effect, which certificate shall set forth that the conditions

2—30

of the by-law have been complied with, and is to be attached
to the cheque or order drawn by the said trustees for such
payment or delivery of debentures, and such engineer shall
not wrongfully grant any such certificate under a penalty of
$500 recoverable in any court of competent jurisdiction by 5
any person who may sue therefor.

(2) Whenever any municipality or municipalities or·portion
thereof shall pass a by-law or by-laws granting any aid by
way of bonus or otherwise to said company, and in and by
any such by-law or by-laws any time shall be fixed or limited 10
for the commencement or completion of the said railway or
any portion thereof, and any such municipality or municipalities or portion thereof shall not comply with this Act by
depositing the debentures or money or other securities
authorized by such by-law or by-laws with the trustees in 15
manner and at the time in this Act specified, then the time
or period for the commencement or the completion of said
railway or the particular portion thereof specified in said
by-law or by-laws, shall not be deemed or taken to have commenced to run until from and after the date of the deposit of 20
such debentures, money or other securities in the hands of
said trustees.

Fees to
trustees.

46. The trustees shall be entitled to their reasonable fees
and charges from said trust fund, and the act of any two of
such trustees shall be as valid and binding as if the three had 25
agreed.

Acquiring
lands for
stations, grav-
el pits, etc.

47. Whenever it shall be necessary for the purpose of procuring sufficient land for stations, or gravel pits, or for constructing, maintaining and using the said railway, and in case
by purchasing the whole of any lot, or parcel of land over 30
which the railway is to run, the company can obtain the same
at a more reasonable price, or to greater advantage than by
purchasing the railway line only, the company may purchase,
hold, use, and enjoy such lands, and also the right of way
thereto if the same be separated from their railway, and may 35
sell and convey the same, or part thereof, from time to time as
they may deem expedient, but the compulsory clauses of *The
Railway Act of Ontario* shall not apply to this section.

Acquiring
gravel, etc.,
for construc-
tion and main-
tenance of rail-
way.

48. When stone, gravel, earth, or sand is or are required
for the construction or maintenance of said railway, or any 40
part thereof, the company may, in case they cannot agree with
the owner of the lands on which the same is situate for the
purchase thereof, cause a provincial land surveyor to make a
map and description of the property so required, and they
shall serve a copy thereof, with their notice of arbitration as 45
in case of acquiring the roadway, and the notice of the arbitration, the award, and the tender of the compensation shall
have the same effect as in the case of arbitration for the roadway; and all the provisions of *The Railway Act of Ontario*,
and of this Act, as to the service of the said notice, arbitra- 50
tion, compensation, deeds, payment of money into court, the
right to sell, the right to convey, and the parties from whom
lands may be taken, or who may sell, shall apply to the subject matter of this section as to the obtaining materials as
aforesaid, and such proceedings may be had by the company, 55

either for the right to the fee simple in the land from which
said material shall be taken, or for the right to take material
for any time they shall think necessary; the notice of arbitration, in case arbitration is resorted to, to state the interest re-
5 quired.

49.—(1) When said gravel, stone, or other material shall be Sidings to
taken under the preceding section of this Act, at a distance gravel pits,
from the line of the railway, the company may lay down the etc.
necessary sidings and tracks over any lands which may inter-
10 vene between the railway and the lands on which said material shall be found, whatever the distance may be, and all
the provisions of *The Railway Act of Ontario*, and of this Act,
except such as relate to filing plans and publication of notice
shall apply, and may be used and exercised to obtain the right
15 of way from the railway to the land on which such materials
are situated, and such right may be so acquired for a term of
years or permanently, as the company may think proper ; and
the powers in this and the preceding section may at all times
be exercised and used in all respects after the railway is con-
20 structed, for the purpose of repairing and maintaining the said
railway.

(2) When estimating the damages for the taking of gravel,
' stone, earth, or sand, sub-section 8 of section 20 of *The Railway Act of Ontario* shall not apply.

25 **50.** The company shall have power and authority to be- Bills and
come parties to promissory notes and bills of exchange for notes.
sums not less than $100, and any such promissory note or bill
of exchange made, accepted, or endorsed by the president of
the company, and countersigned by the secretary of the said
30 company, and under the authority of a quorum of the directors,
shall be binding on the company, and every such promissory note
or bill of exchange so made shall be presumed to have been made
with proper authority until the contrary be shewn, and in no
case shall it be necessary to have the seal of the company
35 affixed to such promissory note or bill of exchange, nor shall
the persons signing the same be individually responsible for
the same, unless the said promissory notes or bills of exchange
have been issued without the sanction and authority of the
directors as herein provided and enacted, provided, however,
40 that nothing in this section shall be construed to authorize the
said company to issue any promissory note or bill of exchange,
payable to bearer, or intended to be circulated as money, or as
the notes or bills of a bank.

51. The company shall have power and authority, upon the Bonds.
45 approval of a majority of the shareholders voting in person or
by proxy, at any regular annual meeting or special general
meeting called for that purpose, to issue mortgage bonds, not
to exceed $25,000 per mile for each and every mile of railway
herein authorized to be built for the purposes of the under-
50 taking authorized by this Act, which shall constitute a first
mortgage and lien upon the undertaking and the real property
of the company, including its rolling stock and equipments
then existing, and at any time thereafter acquired, and each
holder of the said bonds shall be deemed to be a mortgagee
55 and incumbrancer *pro rata* with all the other holders thereof

upon the undertaking and property of the company as aforesaid, and such mortgage shall be evidenced by a deed or deeds of trust, executed by the company, which deed or deeds shall contain such conditions respecting the payment of the said bonds and of the interest thereon, and respecting the remedies which shall be enjoyed by the holders thereof, or by any trustee or trustees for them in default of such payment, and for enforcing such remedies thereof, and of the interest or coupons thereon as are approved by a majority of the board of directors of the said company at any regular meeting, or a 10 special meeting called for that purpose, and as are not contrary to law or the provisions of this Act.

Mortgaging bonds for advances.
52. The said company may from time to time, for advances of money to be made thereon, mortgage or pledge any stock, bonds or debenture stock, which they can under the powers 15 of this Act issue for the construction of the railway or otherwise.

Regulations as to transfers of stock.
53. The directors may from time to time make such regulations as they may think fit for facilitating the transfer and registration of shares of the capital stock, and the forms in 20 respect thereof, as well in this Province as elsewhere, and as to the closing of the registers and transfer books for the pur-, pose of dividends as they may find expedient, and all such regulations not being inconsistent with this Act and with *The Railway Act of Ontario* as altered and modified by this Act, 25 shall be valid and binding.

Power to collect back charges on goods.
54. The company shall have power to collect and receive all charges, subject to which goods or commodities may come into their possession, and on payment of such back charges, and without any formal transfer, shall have the same lien for 30 the amount thereof, upon such goods or commodities as the persons to whom such charges were originally due had upon such goods or commodities while in their possession, and shall be subrogated by such payment in all the rights and remedies of such persons for such charges.   35

Form of conveyances.
55. Conveyances of lands to the said company for the purposes of and powers given by this Act, made in the form set forth in schedule A, hereto, or to the like effect, shall be sufficient conveyance to the said company, their successors and assigns of the estate, or interest therein mentioned, 40 and sufficient bar of dower, respectively of all persons executing the same ; and such conveyances shall be registered in such manner and upon such proof of execution as is required under the registry laws of Ontario, and no registrar shall be entitled to demand more than seventy-five cents for 45 registering the same, including all entries and certificates thereof, and certificates indorsed on the duplicate thereof.

Power to construct railway in sections.
56. The company is hereby authorized and empowered to take and make the surveys and levels of the land through which the railway of the company is to pass, together with 50 the map or plan thereof, and of its course and direction, and of the lands intended to be passed over and taken therefor as far as then ascertained, and also the book of reference for the railway, and to deposit the same as required by the

clauses of *The Railway Act of Ontario* and amendments
thereto, with respect to "plans and surveys" by sections, or
portions less than the whole length of the said railway authorized, of such length as the company may from time to
5 time see fit, so that no one of such sections or portions shall
be less than ten miles in length, and upon such deposit as
aforesaid of the map or plan, and book of reference of any and
each of such sections, or portions of the said railway, all and
every one of the clauses of the said Railway Act and the
10 amendments thereto applied to, included in or incorporated
with this Act, shall apply and extend to any and each of such
sections or portions of the said railway, as fully and
effecctually as if the surveys and levels had been taken and
made of the lands through which the whole of the said rail-
15 way is to pass, together with the map or plan of the whole
thereof, and of its whole course and direction, and of the lands
intended to be passed over and taken, and the book of
reference for the whole of the said railway had been taken,
made, examined, certified and deposited, according to the said
20 clauses of the said Railway Act and the amendments thereof,
with respect to "plans and surveys."

57. The railway shall be commenced within three years, and completed within seven years after the passing of this Act. *Commence-ment and completion of railway.*

SCHEDULE "A."

(SECTION 55.)

KNOW all men by these presents that I (*or* we) (*insert the name or names of the vendor or vendors*), in consideration of   dollars paid to me (*or* us)
by the Ottawa and Thousand Island Railway Company, the
receipt whereof is hereby acknowledged, do grant and convey
unto the said company, and I (*or* we) (*insert the name or names of any other party or parties*), in consideration of   dollars, paid to me (*or* us)
by the said company, the receipt whereof is hereby acknow-
ledged, do grant and release to the said company all that certain parcel (*or* those certain parcels, *as the case may be*) of
land (*describe the land*), the same having been selected and
laid out by the said company for the purposes of its railway,
to hold with the appurtenances unto the said Ottawa and
Thousand Island Railway Company, its successors and assigns
(*here insert any other clauses, conditions and covenants re-quired*), and I (*or* we) wife (*or* wives) of the said
           do hereby bar
my (*or* our) dower in the said lands. As witness my (*or* our)
hand and seal (*or* hands and seals) this   day of
188   .
Signed, sealed and delivered   [L.S.]
   in presence of

3—30

SCHEDULE " B."

(Section 45.)

Chief Engineer's Certificate.

Ottawa and Thousand Island Railway
Company's Office.

No.   Engineer's Department,   A.D., 188

Certificate to be attached to cheques drawn on the Ottawa
and Thousand Island Railway Company Municipal Trust
Account, given under section   chapter
of the Acts of the Legislature of Ontario, passed in the
year of Her Majesty's reign.

I, *A.B.*, Chief Engineer for the Ottawa and Thousand Islan-
Railway Company, do certify that the said company has fuld
filled the terms and conditions necesssary to be fulfilled under
the by-law No.   of the township of
(*or* under the agreement dated the   day of
          between the corporation of
and the said company) to entitle the said company to receive
from the said trust the sum of
*(here set out the terms and conditions, if any, which have been
fulfilled.)*

No 30.

1st Session, 6th Legislature, 50 Vic., 1887.

BILL.

An Act to incorporate the Ottawa and
Thousand Island Railway Company.

First Reading,   1887.

(Private Bill.)

Mr. Fraser.

TORONTO.

No. 30.] **BILL.** [1887.

An Act to incorporate the Ottawa and Thousand
Island Railway Company.

WHEREAS Robert G. Hervey, and others, have by their
petition represented that it is desirable that a railway
should be constructed from the city of Ottawa, in the county
of Carleton, to the Town of Brockville, or some other point on
5 the Brockville, Westport and Sault Ste. Marie Railway, in the
County of Leeds, and have prayed for an Act accordingly;
and whereas it is expedient to grant the prayer of the said
petition ;
Therefore Her Majesty, by and with the advice and consent of
10 the Legislative Assembly of the Province of Ontario, enacts
as follows :—

1. Robert G. Hervey, William B. Smellie, Hugh T. Fitzsimmons, and William H. Jones, all of the town of Brockville,
in the county of Leeds, and Province of Ontario, and Clark-
15 son Jones, of the city of Toronto, in the Province of Ontario,
with such other persons and corporations as shall, in pursuance of this Act, become shareholders of the said company
hereby incorporated, are hereby constituted and declared a
body corporate and politic by the name of " The Ottawa and
20 Thousand Island Railway Company," hereinafter called the
company.

2. The several clauses of *The Railway Act of Ontario* shall
be incorporated with and be deemed to be a part of this Act,
and shall apply to the said company and to the railway to be
25 constructed by them, except only so far as they may be inconsistent with the express enactments hereof ; and the expression " this Act," when used herein, shall be understood to include the clauses of the said Railway Act, so incorporated with
this Act.

30 3. The said company, their agents and servants shall have
full power and authority to survey, lay out, construct, complete, lease, purchase and operate a single or double line of
railway from a point in or near the city of Ottawa, in the
county of Carleton, through the county of Carleton and the
35 county of Grenville, and the county of Leeds, to a point on
the line of the Brockville, Westport, and Sault Ste. Marie
Railway, either in or near the town of Brockville, or at some
other point in the county of Leeds.

4. The gauge of the said railway shall be four feet eight
40 and one-half inches.

Power to purchase and work vessels.

5. The company shall have power to construct, purchase, sell, charter, own and use scows, boats and steam or other vessels on the lakes, rivers and canals of this Province in connection with their railway.

Power to acquire wharves, etc.

6. The company shall have power to purchase, lease, or acquire, at any point where their railway or any branch thereof touches or approaches within two miles of any navigable waters, sufficient land for the uses of the company, their railway, and vessels, run or navigated in connection with said railway, and the company may erect warehouses, elevators, docks, wharves, stations, workshops and such other buildings as may be necessary for the purposes of the company, and may sell and convey such lands as may be found superfluous for any such purposes ; and shall also have full power to connect any of the works herein mentioned with any point on the railway, or its branches, by means of any line or lines of railway for such purposes.

Agreements with other companies.

7. The company shall have power to enter into and conclude any agreement with *the Brockville, Westport and Sault Ste. Marie Railway Company* if lawfully authorized to enter into such agreement, to lease the railway herein authorized, or any part thereof, or to lease or acquire running powers over the line of *the said company*, or any part or parts thereof, or for leasing or hiring any locomotives, tenders, plant, rolling stock, or other property, or touching any service to be rendered by the one company to the other, and the compensation therefor ; provided that the agreement shall be approved of by two-thirds of the shareholders, voting either in person, or by proxy, at any special general meeting called for that purpose ; but nothing in this section shall be construed as purporting or intending to confer rights or powers upon any company which is not within the legislative authority of this Province.

Telegraph and telephone lines.

8. For the purpose of constructing, working,.and protecting the telegraph and telephone lines to be constructed by the company on their line of railway, the powers conferred upon telegraph and telephone companies by *The Act respecting Electric Telegraph Companie*s are hereby conferred upon the company, and the other provisions of the said Act for the working and protection of telegraph and telephone lines shall apply to any such telegraph or telephone lines constructed by the company.

Snow fences.

9. The company shall have the right, on and after the first day of November in each year, to enter into and upon any lands of Her Majesty, or into or upon any lands of any corporation or person whatsoever lying along the route or line of the said railway, and to erect and maintain snow fences thereon, subject to the payment of such damages (if any) as may be thereafter established in the manner provided by law in respect of such railway to have been actually suffered; provided always that any such snow fences so erected shall be removed on or before the first day of April following.

Provisional directors.

10. Robert G. Hervey, William B. Smellie, Hugh T. Fitzsimmons, Clarkson Jones, and John Chapman, with power to add to their number, are hereby constituted a board of provisional directors of the company, and shall hold office as such until other directors shall be elected under the provisions of this Act by the shareholders, and shall have power to fill the place or places of any of their number which may become 5 vacant, and to open stock books, and to procure subscriptions for the undertaking, to make calls upon the subscribers, to cause surveys and plans to be executed, and to call a general meeting of the shareholders for the election of directors, as hereinafter provided; and with all such other powers as 10 under *The Railway Act of Ontario* are vested in ordinary directors; and such provisional directors may appoint a committee from their number to open such stock books and to receive such subscriptions; and the said committee, or a majority of them may, in their discretion, exclude any person from sub- 15 scribing.

11. The capital stock of the company hereby incorporated Capital stock. shall be $1,250,000 (with power to increase the same in the manner provided by *The Railway Act of Ontario*), to be divided into twelve thousand five hundred shares of $100 20 each, and shall be raised by the persons and corporations who may become shareholders in such company; and the money so raised shall be applied, in the first place, to the payment of all fees, expenses, and disbursements of and incidental to the passing of this Act, and for making the surveys, plans, and es- 25 timates connected with the works hereby authorized, and the remainder of said money shall be applied to the making, equipping, completing and maintaining of the said railway and to the other purposes of this Act.

12. When and so soon as shares to the amount of $50,000, First election 30 in the capital stock of the company shall have been subscribed, of directors. and ten per cent. thereof shall have been paid into one of the chartered banks of the Dominion, having an office in the Province of Ontario (which shall on no account be withdrawn therefrom unless for the service of the company), the pro- 35 visional directors, or a majority of them present at a meeting duly called for the purpose, shall call a *general* meeting of the subscribers for the purpose of electing directors, giving at least *four* weeks' notice in a paper published in the town of Brockville, and in the *Ontario Gazette*, of the time, place, and 40 object of such meeting; and at such general meeting the shareholders present, either in person or by proxy, and who shall at the opening of such meeting have paid ten per centum on the stock subscribed by them, shall elect not less than five nor more than thirteen persons to be directors of the company in 45 manner and qualified as hereinafter directed, which said directors shall constitute a board of directors, and shall hold office until the next general annual meeting.

13. In case the provisional directors neglect to call such How first meeting, to be held on some day within the space of three meeting may 50 months after such amount of the capital stock shall have been provisional subscribed and ten per centum thereof so paid up, the same directors neg- may be called by any five of the subscribers who shall have so lect to call same. paid up ten per centum, and who are subscribers among them for not less than $25,000 of the said capital stock, and who 55 have paid up all calls thereon.

Allotment of stock.

14. It shall be lawful for the directors, in procuring subscriptions for stock, to allot such stock in such amounts, and subject to the payment of such calls of such amount, and at such times, and at such discount as they may think fit, or they may agree for the sale of such stock or any part thereof at 5 such price as they may think fit, and may stipulate for the payment of the purchase money at the time of subscription or by instalments, and the amount of every such instalment as and when payable shall be deemed to be money due in respect of a call duly made in accordance with 10 the provisions contained in section 27 of the *Railway Act of Ontario*, and non-payment of any such instalment shall carry with it all the rights, incidents and consequences as mentioned in the said Act, as in the case of a call due by a shareholder on a share. 15

Certain payments may be made in stock or bonds.

15. The said provisional directors or the elected directors may pay, or agree to pay, in paid up stock, or in the bonds of the said company, such sums as they may deem expedient to engineers or contractors, or for right of way or material, 20 plant or rolling stock, and also when sanctioned by a vote of the shareholders at any general meeting, for the services of promoters or other persons who may be employed by the directors, for the purpose of assisting the directors in the furtherance of the undertaking, or purchase of right of way, material, 25 plant or rolling stock, whether such promoters or other persons, be provisional or elected directors or not, and any agreements so made shall be binding on the company.

Annual meeting.

16. The general annual meeting of the shareholders of the company shall be held in such place, in the town of 30 Brockville, or at such other place, and on such days, and at such hours, as may be directed by the by-laws of the company, and public notice thereof shall be given at least *four* weeks previously in the *Ontario Gazette*, and once a week in one newspaper published in the town of Brockville, during the 35 *four* weeks preceding the week in which such meeting is to be held.

Special meetings.

17. Special general meetings of the shareholders of the company may be held at such place in the town of Brockville, or at such other place, and at such times, and in such manner, 40 and for such purposes, as may be provided by the by-laws of the company, upon such notice as is provided in the last preceding section.

Qualification of directors.

18. In the election of directors under this Act no person 45 shall be elected a director unless he shall be the holder and owner of at least ten shares of the stock of the company, upon which all calls have been paid up.

Rights of aliens.

19. Aliens and companies incorporated abroad as well as British subjects and corporations, and whether resident in this Province or elsewhere, may be shareholders in the company, 50 and all such shareholders shall be entitled to vote on their shares equally with British subjects, and shall also be eligible to office as directors in the company.

20. Every holder of one or more shares of the said capital stock shall, at any general meeting of the shareholders, be entitled to one vote for every share held by him ; and no shareholder shall be entitled to vote on any matter whatever unless
5 all calls due on the stock upon which such shareholder seeks to vote shall have been paid up at least one week before the day appointed for such meeting. Votes.

21. At all meetings of the company the stock held by municipal and other corporations may be represented by such
10 person as they shall respectively have appointed in that behalf by *resolution under the seal of the corporation ;* and such person shall, at such meeting, be entitled equally with other shareholders to vote by proxy. Representation of stock held by corporations.

22. At all meetings of the board of directors, whether of
15 provisional directors or of those elected by the shareholders, four directors shall form a quorum for the transaction of business, and the said board of directors may employ and pay one of their number as managing director. Quorum of directors.

23. Should the shareholders of the company resolve that
20 the interests of the company would be best promoted by enabling one or more of the directors to act for the company in any particular matter or matters, it shall be lawful for the directors, after such resolution, to confer such power upon one or more of their number. Delegation of powers to directors in special cases.

25 **24.** It shall be lawful for the directors to enter into any contract or contracts with any individual or association of individuals for the construction or equipment of the line or any portion thereof, including or excluding the purchase of the right of way, and to pay therefor, either in the whole or in
30 part, either in cash or bonds, or in paid-up stock ; provided that no such contract shall be of any force or validity till approved of by two-thirds of the shareholders present, in person or by proxy, at a meeting specially convened for considering the same. Power to make contracts for construction of railway. Proviso.

35 **25.** The said company may receive from any government or from any persons or bodies corporate, municipal or politic, who may have power to make or grant the same, aid towards the construction, equipment or maintenance of the said railway by way of bonus, gift or loan, in money or debentures, or
40 other securities for money, or by way of guarantee, upon such terms and conditions as may be agreed upon. Aid to company.

26. Any municipality through which the said railway may pass *or is situate,* is empowered to grant, by way of gift, to the company, any lands belonging to such municipality or over
45 which it may have control, which may be required for right of way, station grounds or other purposes connected with the running or traffic of the said railway, and the company shall have power to accept gifts of land from any government, or any person, or any body politic or corporate, and shall have
50 power to sell or otherwise dispose of the same for the benefit of the company. Aid from municipalities.

vided that such aid shall not require the levying of a greater aggregate annual rate for all purposes, exclusive of school rates, than three cents in the dollar upon the value of the ratable property therein.

By-law, what to contain.

35. Such by-law shall in each case provide :— 5

1. For raising the amount petitioned for in the municipality or portion of the township municipality (as the case may be) mentioned in the petition, by the issue of debentures of the county or minor municipality respectively, and shall also provide for the delivery of the said debentures or the 10 application of the amount to be raised thereby, as may be expressed in the said by-law.

2. For assessing and levying upon all ratable property lying within the municipality or portion of the township municipality defined in said by-law (as the case may be) an annual special rate sufficient to include a sinking fund for the 15 repayment of the said debentures within twenty years, with interest thereon, payable yearly or half-yearly, which debentures the respective municipal councils, wardens, mayors, reeves and other officers thereof, are hereby authorized to execute and issue in such cases respectively. 20

"Minor municipality," meaning of.

36. The term "minor municipality" shall be construed to mean any town not separated from the municipal county, township or incorporated village situate in the county municipality.

If by-law carried council to pass same.

37. In case the by-law submitted be approved of and 25 carried in accordance with the provisions of the law in that behalf, then within four weeks after the date of such voting, the municipal council *which submitted the same*, shall read the said by-law a third time and pass the same.

And issue debentures.

38. Within one month after the passing of such by-law 30 the said council and the mayor, warden, reeve *or other head* or other officers thereof, shall issue the debentures provided for by the by-law and deliver the same duly executed to the trustees appointed or to be appointed under this Act.

Levying rate on portion of a municipality.

39. In case any such loan, guarantee or bonus be so granted 35 by a portion of a township municipality, the rate to be levied for payment of the debentures issued therefor and the interest thereon shall be assessed and levied upon such portion only of such municipality.

Application of municipal Acts as to by-laws.

40. The provisions of *The Consolidated Municipal Act*, 40 *1883*, and the amendments thereto, so far as the same are not inconsistent with this Act, shall apply to any by-law so passed by or for a portion of a township municipality to the same extent as if the same had been passed by or for the whole municipality. 45

Extension of time for commencement.

41. It shall and may be lawful for the council of any municipality that may grant aid by way of bonus to the said company, by resolution or by-law, to extend the time for the completion of the works (on the completion of which the said com-

pany would be entitled to such bonus), from time to time, provided that no such extension shall be for a longer period than
one year at a time.

42. The councils for all corporations that may grant aid Extension of time for completion.
5 by way of bonus to the said company may, by resolution or
by-law, extend the time for the commencement of the work
beyond that stipulated for in the by-law or by-laws granting
such aid from time to time, provided that no such extension
shall be for a longer period than one year.

10 **43.** Whenever any municipality or portion of a township Trustees of debentures.
municipality shall grant aid by way of bonus or gift to the
railway company, the debentures therefor shall, within *six*
months after the passing of the by-law authorizing the same,
be delivered to three trustees, to be named, one by the
15 Lieutenant-Governor in Council, one by the said company, and
one by the majority of the heads of the municipalities which
have granted bonuses, all of the trustees to be residents of the
Province of Ontario; provided that if the said heads of the Proviso.
municipalities shall refuse or neglect to name such trustees
20 within one month after notice in writing of the appointment
of the company's trustee, or if the Lieutenant-Governor in
Council shall omit to name such trustee within one month
after notice in writing to him of the appointment of the other
trustees, then, in either case the company shall be at liberty to
25 name such other trustee or trustees ; any of the said trustees
may be removed and a new trustee appointed in his stead at
any time by the Lieutenant-Governor in Council, and in case
any trustee dies, or resigns his trust, or goes to live out of the
Province of Ontario, or otherwise becomes incapable to act, his
30 trusteeship shall become vacant and a new trustee may be
appointed by the Lieutenant-Governor in Council.

44. The said trustees shall receive the said debentures Trusts of proceeds of debentures.
or bonds in trust, firstly, under the directions of the company,
but subject to the conditions of the by-law in relation thereto,
35 as to time or manner to convert the same into money or otherwise dispose of them ; secondly, to deposit the debentures or
amount realized from the sale in some chartered bank having
an office in the Province of Ontario in the name of " Ottawa
and Thousand Island Railway *Municipal* Trust Account," and
40 to pay the same out to the said company, from time to
time, as the said company becomes entitled thereto, under the
conditions of the by-law granting the said bonus and on the
certificate of the chief engineer of the said railway for the
time being in the form set out in schedule B hereto, or to the
45 like effect, which certificate shall set forth that the conditions
of the by-law have been complied with, and is to be attached
to the cheque or order drawn by the said trustees for such
payment or delivery of debentures, and such engineer shall
not wrongfully grant any such certificate under a penalty of
50 $500 recoverable in any Court of competent jurisdiction by
any person who may sue therefor.

45. The trustees shall be entitled to their reasonable fees Fees to trustees.
and charges from said trust fund, and the act of any two of
such trustees shall be as valid and binding as if the three had
55 agreed.

2—30

46. Whenever it shall be necessary for the purpose of pro-curing sufficient land for stations, or gravel pits, or for con-structing, maintaining and using the said railway, and in case by purchasing the whole of any lot, or parcel of land over which the railway is to run, the company can obtain the same 5 at a more reasonable price, or to greater advantage than by purchasing the railway line only, the company may purchase, hold, use, and enjoy such lands, and also the right of way thereto if the same be separated from their railway, and may sell and convey the same, or part thereof, from time to time as 10 they may deem expedient, but the compulsory clauses of *The Railway Act of Ontario* shall not apply to this section.

47. When stone, gravel, earth, or sand is or are required for the construction or maintenance of said railway, or any part thereof, the company may, in case they cannot agree with 15 the owners of the lands on which the same is situate for the purchase thereof, cause a provincial land surveyor to make a map and description of the property so required, and they shall serve a copy thereof, with their notice of arbitration as in case of acquiring the roadway, and the notice of the arbi- 20 tration, the award, and the tender of the compensation shall have the same effect as in the case of arbitration for the road-way; and all the provisions of *The Railway Act of Ontario,* and of this Act, as to the service of the said notice, arbitra-tion, compensation, deeds, payment of money into court, the 25 right to sell, the right to convey, and the parties from whom lands may be taken, or who may sell, shall apply to the sub-ject matter of this section as to the obtaining materials as aforesaid, and such proceedings may be had by the company, either for the right to the fee simple in the land from which 30 said material shall be taken, or for the right to take material for any time they shall think necessary; the notice of arbitra-tion, in case arbitration is resorted to, to state the interest re-quired.

48.—(1) When said gravel, stone, or other material shall be 35 taken under the preceding section of this Act, at a distance from the line of the railway, the company may lay down the necessary sidings and tracks over any lands which may inter-vene between the railway and the lands on which said ma-terial shall be found, whatever the distance may be, and all 40 the provisions of *The Railway Act of Ontario,* and of this Act, except such as relate to filing plans and publication of notice shall apply, and may be used and exercised to obtain the right of way from the railway to the land on which such materials are situated, and such right may be so acquired for a term of 45 years or permanently, as the company may think proper; and the powers in this and the preceding section may at all times be exercised and used in all respects after the railway is con-structed, for the purpose of repairing and maintaining the said railway. 50

(2), When estimating the damages for the taking of gravel, stone, earth, or sand, sub-section 8, of section 20 of *The Rail-way Act of Ontario* shall not apply.

49. The company shall have power and authority to be-come parties to promissory notes and bills of exchange for 55 sums not less than $100, and any such promissory note or bill

Marginal notes:
- Acquiring lands for stations, gravel pits, etc.
- Acquiring gravel, etc., for construction and main-tenance of rail-way.
- Sidings to gravel pits, etc.
- Bills and notes.

of exchange made, accepted, or endorsed by the president of
the company, and countersigned by the secretary of the said
company, and under the authority of a quorum of the directors,
shall be binding on the company, and every such promissory note
5 or bill of exchange so made shall be presumed to have been made
with proper authority until the contrary be shewn, and in no
case shall it be necessary to have the seal of the company
affixed to such promissory note or bill of exchange, nor shall
the persons signing the same be individually responsible for
10 the same, unless the said promissory notes or bills of exchange
have been issued without the sanction and authority of the
directors as herein provided and enacted, provided, however,
that nothing in this section shall be construed to authorize the
said company to issue any promissory note or bill of exchange,
15 payable to bearer, or intended to be circulated as money, or as
the notes or bills of a bank.

50. The company shall have power and authority, upon the Bonds.
approval of a majority of the shareholders voting in person or
by proxy, at any regular annual meeting or special general
20 meeting called for that purpose, to issue mortgage bonds, not
to exceed $25,000 per mile for each and every mile of railway
herein authorized to be built for the purposes of the undertaking authorized by this Act, which shall constitute a first
mortgage and lien upon the undertaking and the real property
25 of the company, including its rolling stock and equipments
then existing, and at any time thereafter acquired, and each
holder of the said bonds shall be deemed to be a mortgagee
and incumbrancer *pro rata* with all the other holders thereof
upon the undertaking and property of the company as afore-
30 said, and such mortgage shall be evidenced by a deed or deeds
of trust, executed by the company, which deed or deeds shall
contain such conditions respecting the payment of the said
bonds and of the interest thereon, and respecting the remedies
which shall be enjoyed by the holders thereof, or by any
35 trustee or trustees for them in default of such payment, and
for enforcing such remedies thereof, and of the interest or
coupons thereon as are approved by a majority of the board of
directors of the said company at any regular meeting, or a
special meeting called for that purpose, and as are not contrary
40 to law or the provisions of this Act.

51. The said company may from time to time, for advances Mortgaging
of money to be made thereon, mortgage or pledge any stock, bonds for advances.
bonds or debenture stock, which they can under the powers
of this Act issue for the construction of the railway or other-
45 wise.

52. The directors may from time to time make such regula- Regulations as
tions as they may think fit for facilitating the transfer and to transfers of stock.
registration of shares of the capital stock, and the forms in
respect thereof, as well in this Province as elsewhere, and
50 as to the closing of the registers and transfer books for the purpose of dividends as they may find expedient, and all such
regulations not being inconsistent with this Act and with *The
Railway Act of Ontario* as altered and modified by this Act,
shall be valid and binding.

Power to collect back charges on goods.

53. The company shall have power to collect and receive all charges, subject to which goods or commodities may come into their possession, and on payment of such back charges, and without any formal transfer, shall have the same lien for the amount thereof, upon such goods or commodities as the 5 persons to whom such charges were originally due had upon such goods or commodities while in their possession, and shall be subrogated by such payment in all the rights and remedies of such persons for such charges.

Form of conveyances.

54. Conveyances of lands to the said company for the pur- 10 poses of and powers given by this Act, made in the form set forth in schedule A, hereto, or to the like effect, shall be sufficient conveyance to the said company, their successors and assigns of the estate, or interest therein mentioned, and sufficient bar of dower, respectively of all persons exe- 15 cuting the same ; and such conveyances shall be registered in such manner and upon such proof of execution as is required under the registry laws of Ontario, and no registrar shall be entitled to demand more than seventy-five cents for registering the same, including all entries and certificates 20 thereof, and certificates indorsed on the duplicate thereof.

Power to construct railway in sections.

55. The company is hereby authorized and empowered to take and make the surveys and levels of the land through which the railway of the company is to pass, together with the map or plan thereof, and of its course and direction, and 25 of the lands intended to be passed over and taken therefor as far as then ascertained, and also the book of reference for the railway, and to deposit the same as required by the clauses of *The Railway Act of Ontario* and amendments thereto, with respect to "plans and surveys" by sections, or 30 portions less than the whole length of the said railway authorized, of such length as the company may from time to time see fit, so that no one of such sections or portions shall be less than ten miles in length, and upon such deposit as aforesaid of the map or plan, and book of reference of any and 35 each of such sections, or portions of the said railway, all and every one of the clauses of the said Railway Act and the amendments thereto applied to, included in or incorporated with this Act, shall apply and extend to any and each of such sections or portions of the said railway, as fully and 40 effectually as if the surveys and levels had been taken and made of the lands through which the whole of the said railway is to pass, together with the map or plan of the whole thereof, and of its whole course and direction, and of the lands intended to be passed over and taken, and the book of 45 reference for the whole of the said railway had been taken, made, examined, certified and deposited, according to the said clauses of the said Railway Act and the amendments thereof with respect to "plans and surveys."

Commencement and completion of railway.

56. The railway shall be commenced within three years, 50 and completed within seven years after the passing of this Act.

SCHEDULE A.

(Section 54.)

Know all men by these presents that I (or we) (*insert the name or names of the vendor or vendors*), in consideration of dollars paid to me (or us) by the Ottawa and Thousand Island Railway Company, the receipt whereof is hereby acknowledged, do grant and convey unto the said company, and I (or we) (*insert the name or names of any other party or parties*), in consideration of dollars, paid to me (or us) by the said company, the receipt whereof is hereby acknowledged, do grant and release to the said company all that certain parcel (or those certain parcels, *as the case may be*) of land (*describe the land*), the same having been selected and laid out by the said company for the purposes of its railway, to hold with the appurtenances unto the said Ottawa and Thousand Island Railway Company, its successors and assigns (*here insert any other clauses, conditions and covenants required*), and I (or we) wife (or wives) of the said

do hereby bar my (or our) dower in the said lands. As witness my (or our) hand and seal (or hands and seals) this   day of
188 .

Signed, sealed and delivered   [L.S.]
  in presence of

SCHEDULE B.

(Section 44.)

Chief Engineer's Certificate.

OTTAWA AND THOUSAND ISLAND RAILWAY COMPANY'S OFFICE.

No.   Engineer's Department, A.D., 188

Certificate to be attached to cheques drawn on the Ottawa and Thousand Island Railway Company Municipal Trust Account, given under section   chapter of the Acts of the Legislature of Ontario, passed in the year of Her Majesty's reign.

I, *A.B.*, Chief Engineer for the Ottawa and Thousand Island Railway Company, do certify that the said company has fulfilled the terms and conditions necesssary to be fulfilled under the by-law No.   of the township of
(*or* under the agreement dated the   day of between the corporation of and the said company) to entitle the said company to receive from the said trust the sum of
(*here set out the terms and conditions, if any, which have been fulfilled.*)

3—30

BILL.

An Act to incorporate the Ottawa and Thousand Island Railway Company.

(Reprinted as amended by Railway Committee.)

First Reading, 22nd March, 1887.

(Private Bill.)

BILL.

An Act to incorporate the Town of Parry Sound.

WHEREAS the district hereinafter described,—comprising Preamble.
portions of the municipalities of McDougall and Foley,
in which are situate the villages of Parry Sound and Carington—is rapidly increasing in population, and is now a manu-
5 facturing and shipping centre of considerable importance, and
is about to become the terminus of the proposed Parry Sound
Colonization Railway; and whereas the inhabitants of the
said district have petitioned to be separated from the municipalities of McDougall and Foley and formed into a corporate
10 town, and have by their petition represented that the incorporation of the said district as a town would promote its
future progress and prosperity, and enable its inhabitants to
make suitable regulations for the protection and improvement of property, and have prayed for its incorporation
15 accordingly ; and whereas it is expedient to grant the prayer
of the said petition ;

Therefore Her Majesty, by and with the advice and consent
of the Legislative Assembly of the Province of Ontario, enacts
as follows :—

20   **1.** On and after the passing of this Act, the district herein- Town incorafter described shall be separated from the municipalities of porated.
McDougall and Foley, and the inhabitants thereof shall be,
and they hereby are, constituted a corporation or body
politic, under the name of " The Corporation of the Town of
25 Parry Sound " ; and shall enjoy and have all the rights,
powers and privileges enjoyed and exercised by incorporated
towns in the Province of Ontario, under the existing municipal laws of the said Province, except where otherwise provided by this Act.

30   **2.** The said town of Parry Sound, shall comprise, and Limits of
consist, of lots numbers twenty-eight, twenty-nine, and thirty, town.
in the first concession of the township of McDougall; all
those portions of lots numbers twenty-six and twenty-seven
lying north and west of the River Seguin, and lots numbers
35 twenty-eight, twenty-nine, thirty and thirty-one in the
second concession of said township; lot number twenty-six
in the third concession of said township; and lots numbers
one hundred and forty-nine and one hundred and fifty in
concession "A" of the township of Foley ; also Bob's Island,
40 adjoining lot number thirty in the first concession of the
township of McDougall, and the water lots on Parry Sound
Harbor in front of the lots,

Wards.

3. The said town shall be divided into three wards, to be called respectively the "West," "Centre" and "East" wards, which said several wards shall be respectively composed and bounded as follows:—The West Ward shall be composed of that portion of the said town bounded as follows: On the east 5 by Bay Street, James Street, William Street and the Great Northern Road to its intersection with the concession line between the second and third concessions of the township of McDougall; on the north by the said concession line till it intersects the waters of Parry Sound; and on the west and 10 south by the waters of Parry Sound; also including the Conger Lumber Company's mill property and Bob's Island; the Centre Ward shall be composed of that portion of the said town bounded and described as follows: First, commencing at the south-westerly limit of Bay Street, thence 15 northerly along said Bay Street, James Street, William Street and the Great Northern Road to its intersection with the concession line between the second and third concessions of the township of McDougall, thence easterly along said concession allowance till it intersects the River Seguin, thence 20 southerly along the western bank of said river to the limits of the Conger Lumber Company's mill property, thence westerly to the place of beginning, together with lot number twenty-six in the third concession of the township of McDougall; and secondly—that portion of the said town 25 lying east of the River Seguin described as follows:—Commencing at a point on the eastern bank of the River Seguin, at the bridge which crosses the River Seguin at the foot of Seguin Street, thence northerly along said eastern bank of said river to the easterly limit of said town, thence southerly 30 along the easterly limit of said town to the intersection of Bowes Street produced, thence westerly along said Bowes Street to River Street, thence southerly along said River Street to the place of beginning; and the East Ward shall be composed of that portion of the said town lying east of the 35 River Seguin described and bounded as follows:—On the west and south by the River Seguin and the waters of Parry Sound Harbor; on the north by Bowes Street, till said street produced intersects the easterly limit of said town; thence southerly along the easterly limit of said town to the road 40 allowance between the townships of McDougall and Foley; thence westerly along said road allowance to the waters of Parry Sound Harbor; including also lots numbers one hundred and forty-nine and one hundred and fifty in concession "A" of the township of Foley. **45**

Acts respecting municipal institutions to apply.

4. Except as otherwise provided by this Act, the provisions of *The Consolidated Municipal Act, 1883,* and of any Act amending the same, with regard to matters consequent upon the formation of new corporations, shall apply to the said Town of Parry Sound, in the same manner as if the said 50 district had been an incorporated village and had been erected into a town under the provisions of the said Acts.

Ward improvements.

5. The annual appropriations for ward improvements in each ward, after paying the usual and necessary expenses of the said municipality, shall be not less than the *pro rata* share of 55 each of said wards as shown by the assessment roll, unless the councillors for all the wards agree to a larger outlay in one or more wards; and no special rate for which the vote of the ratepayers is by law necessary, shall be imposed in any one ward for debentures or otherwise, without the assent of the majority of the electors of said ward expressed by said vote.

5   **6.** On the third Wednesday after the passing of this Act it Nomination shall be lawful for the Stipendiary Magistrate for the time for first election. being of the District of Parry Sound, who is hereby appointed the returning officer, to hold the nomination for the first election of mayor and councillors, at the Court House in the
10 said Town of Parry Sound; and he shall preside at the said nomination, or in case of his absence the electors present shall choose from among themselves a chairman to preside at the said nomination, and such chairman shall have all the powers of a returning officer, and the polling for the said
15 election, if necessary, shall be held on the same day of the week in the week following the said nomination; and the returning officer or chairman shall at the close of the nomination, publicly announce the place in each ward at which the polling shall take place.

20   **7.** The said returning officer shall by his warrant appoint a Deputy deputy-returning officer for each of the wards into which the returning said town is divided; and such returning officer and each of officers. such deputy-returning officers shall, before holding the said election take the oath or affirmation required by law, and
25 shall respectively be subject to all the provisions of the municipal laws of Ontario, applicable to returning officers at elections in towns, in so far as the same do not conflict with this Act; and the said returning officer shall have all the powers and perform the several duties devolving on town
30 clerks with respect to municipal elections in towns.

  8. The clerks of the municipalities of McDougall and Foley Copies of and any other officer thereof shall, upon demand made upon assessment him by the said returning officer, or any other officer of the furnished. said town, or by the chairman hereinbefore mentioned, at once
35 furnish such returning officer, or chairman with a certified copy of so much of the last revised assessment roll for the said municipality as may be required to ascertain the names of the persons entitled to vote in each of the said wards at the said first election, or with the collector's roll, document,
40 statement, writing or deed, that may be required for that purpose; and the said returning officer shall furnish each of the said deputies with a true copy of so much of the said roll as relates to the names of electors entitled to vote in each of the said wards respectively, and each such copy shall be
45 verified on oath.

  9. The council of said town, to be elected in manner afore- Council. said, shall consist of the mayor, who shall be the head thereof, and six councillors, two councillors being elected for each ward; and they shall be organized as a council on the same
50 day of the week next following the week of the polling, or if there be no polling, on the same day of the week next following the week of the said nomination; and subsequent elections shall be held in the same manner, and the qualification of mayor and councillors and for electors at such subsequent
55 elections shall be the same as in towns incorporated under the

provisions of *The Consolidated Municipal Act, 1883,* and any
Act amending the same ; and the said council and their successors in office shall have, use, exercise and enjoy all the
powers and privileges vested by the said municipal laws in
town councils, and shall be subject to all the liabilities and 5
duties imposed by the said municipal laws on such councils.

Oaths of office
and qualifica-
tion.

10. The said several persons who shall be elected or
appointed under this Act shall take declarations of office and
qualification now required by the municipal laws of Ontario
to be taken by persons elected or appointed to like offices 10
in towns.

Qualification
at first elec-
tion.

11. At the first election of mayor and councillors for the
said town of Parry Sound, the qualification of electors, and
that of officers required to qualify, shall be the same as that
required in the case of incorporated villages.   15

Expenses of
Act.

12. The expenses incurred to obtain this Act, and of furnishing any documents, copies of papers, writings, deeds, or any
matters whatsoever required by the clerk or other officer of
the said town, or otherwise, shall be borne by the said town
and paid by it to any party entitled thereto.   20

By-laws con-
tinued.

13. All by-laws which are in force in the municipalities of
McDougall and Foley shall continue and be in force as if they
had been passed by the corporation of the town of Parry
Sound, and shall extend and have full effect within the limits
of the town hereby incorporated until repealed by the new 25
corporation.

Apportion-
ment of pro-
perty and
liabilities.

14. Except as otherwise provided by this Act, the property
assets, debts, liabilities and obligations of the municipalities of
McDougall and Foley, shall be apportioned between the said
municipalities of McDougall and Foley and the said town of 30
Parry Sound, as may be agreed upon ; and in case of no agreement, then by the award of three arbitrators, or a majority of
them, one of such arbitrators being appointed by the said
municipalities of McDougall and Foley, conjointly, and one by
the town of Parry Sound, and the third being chosen by the 35
said two ; and if from any cause whatever either the said
municipalities of McDougall and Foley or the said town of
Parry Sound shall not have appointed an arbitrator within
two months after the other of them has appointed an arbitrator, then the Lieutenant-Governor in Council shall appoint 40
an arbitrator on behalf of the municipality or municipalities
so making default, and the two so appointed shall choose a
third ; and if they shall not agree upon such third arbitrator,
then the Lieutenant-Governor in Council shall appoint such
third arbitrator, and the award of the said arbitrators, or of a 45
majority of them, shall be as valid and binding in all respects
as if the said arbitrators had been regularly appointed by the
said municipalities.

Collection of
arrears of
taxes.

15. Arrears of taxes due to the said corporation of the
town of Parry Sound shall be collected and managed in the 50
same way as the arrears due to towns separated from counties,
and the mayor and treasurer of the said town shall perform
the like duties in the collection and management of arrears of

taxes as are performed by the said officers in other towns in
Ontario separated from counties, and the various provisions of
law relating to sales of land for arrears of taxes, or to deeds
given therefor, shall apply to the said corporation of the town
5 of Parry Sound, and to sales of land therein for arrears of
taxes due thereon and to deeds given therefor, subject to the
provisions of section 31 of chapter 175 of the Revised Statutes
of Ontario.

16. The council of the said town may pass a by-law for Assessmen
10 taking the assessment of the said town for the year from first for 1887.
January to thirty-first December, 1887, between the first day
of April and the first day of August, 1887. If any such
by-law extends the time for making and completing the
assessment rolls beyond the first day of June next, then the
15 time for closing the Court of Revision shall be six weeks from
the day to which such time is extended, and the final return
by the Stipendiary Magistrate twelve weeks from that day.

17. Until there shall be a resident Judge at Parry Sound Powers of
for the District of Parry Sound, the Stipendiary Magistrate of Stipendiary
20 the said District for the time being shall have and exercise all Magistrate.
the powers of the Judge of the County Court under the exist-
ing municipal laws of the Province of Ontario.

18. Nothing contained in this Act shall free the portions Liabilities not
of the townships or wards comprising the municipality of the affected.
25 town of Parry Sound hereby formed, from their proportion of
any liability now existing against the municipalities of
McDougall and Foley, and the creditors of the said municipalities of McDougall and Foley shall continue to have all the
rights and remedies which they had previous to the passing
30 of this Act for the enforcement of their claims against the
townships and wards heretofore composing the said municipalities of McDougall and Foley.

No. 31.

1st Session, 6th Legislature, 50 Vic, 1887.

BILL.

An Act to incorporate the Town of Parry Sound.

First Reading, 1887.

(Private Bill.)

BILL.

An Act to incorporate the Town of Parry Sound.

WHEREAS the district hereinafter described,—comprising Preamble. portions of the municipalities of McDougall and Foley, in which are situate the *unincorporated* villages of Parry Sound and Carington—is rapidly increasing in population, and is now
5 a manufacturing and shipping centre of considerable importance, and is about to become the terminus of the proposed Parry Sound Colonization Railway; and whereas the inhabitants of the said district have petitioned to be separated from the municipalities of McDougall and Foley and formed into a corporate
10 town, and have by their petition represented that the incorporation of the said district as a town would promote its future progress and prosperity, and enable its inhabitants to make suitable regulations for the protection and improvement of property, and have prayed for its incorporation
15 accordingly; and whereas it is expedient to grant the prayer of the said petition;

Therefore Her Majesty, by and with the advice and consent of the Legislative Assembly of the Province of Ontario, enacts as follows :—

20 **1.** On and after the passing of this Act, the district herein- Town incorafter described shall be separated from the municipalities of porated. McDougall and Foley, and the inhabitants thereof shall be, and they hereby are, constituted a corporation or body politic, under the name of " The Corporation of the Town of
25 Parry Sound"; and shall enjoy and have all the rights, powers and privileges enjoyed and exercised by incorporated towns in the Province of Ontario, under the existing municipal laws of the said Province, except where otherwise provided by this Act.

30 **2.** The said town of Parry Sound, shall comprise, and Limits of consist, of lots numbers twenty-eight, twenty-nine, and thirty, town. in the first concession of the township of McDougall; all those portions of lots numbers twenty-six and twenty-seven lying north and west of the River Seguin, and lots numbers
35 twenty-eight, twenty-nine, thirty and thirty-one in the second concession of said township; lot number twenty-six in the third concession of said township; and lots numbers one hundred and forty-nine and one hundred and fifty in concession "A" of the township of Foley; also Bob's Island,
40 adjoining lot number thirty in the first concession of the township of McDougall, and the water lots on Parry Sound Harbor in front of the lots.

Wards.

3. The said town shall be divided into three wards, to be called respectively the "West," "Centre" and "East" wards, which said several wards shall be respectively composed and bounded as follows:—The West Ward shall be composed of that portion of the said town bounded as follows: On the east 5 by Bay Street, James Street, William Street and the Great Northern Road to its intersection with the concession line between the second and third concessions of the township of McDougall; on the north by the said concession line till it intersects the waters of Parry Sound; and on the west and 10 south by the waters of Parry Sound; also including the Conger Lumber Company's mill property and Bob's Island; the Centre Ward shall be composed of that portion of the said town bounded and described as follows: First, commencing at the south-westerly limit of Bay Street, thence 15 northerly along said Bay Street, James Street, William Street and the Great Northern Road to its intersection with the concession line between the second and third concessions of the township of McDougall, thence easterly along said concession allowance till it intersects the River Seguin, thence 20 southerly along the western bank of said river to the limits of the Conger Lumber Company's mill property, thence westerly to the place of beginning, together with lot number twenty-six in the third concession of the township of McDougall; and secondly—that portion of the said town 25 lying east of the River Seguin described as follows:—Commencing at a point on the eastern bank of the River Seguin, at the bridge which crosses the River Seguin at the foot of Seguin Street, thence northerly along said eastern bank of said river to the easterly limit of said town, thence southerly 30 along the easterly limit of said town to the intersection of Bowes Street produced, thence westerly along said Bowes Street to River Street, thence southerly along said River Street to the place of beginning; and the East Ward shall be composed of that portion of the said town lying east of the 35 River Seguin described and bounded as follows:—On the west and south by the River Seguin and the waters of Parry Sound Harbor; on the north by Bowes Street, till said street produced intersects the easterly limit of said town; thence southerly along the easterly limit of said town to the road 40 allowance between the townships of McDougall and Foley; thence westerly along said road allowance to the waters of Parry Sound Harbor; including also lots numbers one hundred and forty-nine and one hundred and fifty in concession "A" of the township of Foley. 45

Acts respecting municipal institutions to apply.

4. Except as otherwise provided by this Act, the provisions of *The Consolidated Municipal Act, 1883*, and of any Act amending the same, with regard to matters consequent upon the formation of new corporations, shall apply to the said Town of Parry Sound, in the same manner as if the said 50 district had been an incorporated village and had been erected into a town under the provisions of the said Acts.

Ward improvements.

5. The annual appropriations for ward improvements in each ward, after paying the usual and necessary expenses of the said municipality, shall be not less than the *pro rata* share of 55 each of said wards as shown by the assessment roll, unless the councillors for all the wards agree to a larger outlay in one or

more wards; and no special rate for which the vote of the
ratepayers is by law necessary, shall be imposed in any one
ward for debentures or otherwise, without the assent of the
majority of the electors of said ward expressed by said vote.

5   **6.** On the third Wednesday after the passing of this Act it Nomination
shall be lawful for the Stipendiary Magistrate for the time for first election.
being of the District of Parry Sound, who is hereby appointed
the returning officer, to hold the nomination for the first
election of mayor and councillors, at the Court House in the
10 said Town of Parry Sound; *and he shall give at least one
week's notice thereof, by causing at least three notices to be
posted up in conspicuous places in each of the said wards,*
and he shall preside at the said nomination, or in case of his
absence the electors present shall choose from among them-
15 selves a chairman to preside at the said nomination, and
such chairman shall have all the powers of a returning officer,
and the polling for the said election, if necessary, shall be
held on the same day of the week in the week following
the said nomination; and the returning officer or chairman
20 shall at the close of the nomination, publicly announce the
place in each ward at which the polling shall take place.

  7. The said returning officer shall by his warrant appoint a Deputy
deputy-returning officer for each of the wards into which the returning officers.
said town is divided ; and such returning officer and each of
25 such deputy-returning officers shall, before holding the said
election take the oath or affirmation required by law, and
shall respectively be subject to all the provisions of the municipal laws of Ontario, applicable to returning officers at
elections in towns, in so far as the same do not conflict with
30 this Act; and the said returning officer shall have all the
powers and perform the several duties devolving on town
clerks with respect to municipal elections in towns.

  8. The clerks of the municipalities of McDougall and Foley Copies of
and any other officer thereof shall, upon demand made upon rolls to be
35 him by the said returning officer, or any other officer of the furnished.
said town, or by the chairman hereinbefore mentioned, at once
furnish such returning officer, or chairman with a certified
copy of so much of the last revised assessment roll for the
said municipality as may be required to ascertain the names
40 of the persons entitled to vote in each of the said wards at
the said first election, or with the collector's roll, document,
statement, writing or deed, that may be required for that
purpose; and the said returning officer shall furnish each of
the said deputies with a true copy of so much of the said roll
45 as relates to the names of electors entitled to vote in each of
the said wards respectively, and each such copy shall be
verified on oath.

  9. The council of said town, to be elected in manner afore- Council.
said, shall consist of the mayor, who shall be the head thereof,
50 and six councillors, two councillors being elected for each
ward ; and they shall be organized as a council on the same
day of the week next following the week of the polling, or if
there be no polling, on the same day of the week next following the week of the said nomination ; and subsequent elections
55 shall be held in the same manner, and the qualification of
mayor and councillors and for electors at such subsequent

elections shall be the same as in towns incorporated under the provisions of *The Consolidated Municipal Act, 1883,* and any Act amending the same ; and the said council and their successors in office shall have, use, exercise and enjoy all the powers and privileges vested by the said municipal laws in 5 town councils, and shall be subject to all the liabilities and duties imposed by the said municipal laws on such councils.

Oaths of office and qualification. **10.** The said several persons who shall be elected or appointed under this Act shall take declarations of office and qualification now required by the municipal laws of Ontario 10 to be taken by persons elected or appointed to like offices in towns.

Qualification at first election. **11.** At the first election of mayor and councillors for the said town of Parry Sound, the qualification of electors, and that of officers required to qualify, shall be the same as that 15 required in the case of incorporated villages.

Expenses of Act. **12.** The expenses incurred to obtain this Act, and of furnishing any documents, copies of papers, writings, deeds, or any matters whatsoever required by the clerk or other officer of the said town, or otherwise, shall be borne by the said town 20 and paid by it to any party entitled thereto.

By-laws continued. **13.** All by-laws which are in force in the municipalities of McDougall and Foley shall continue and be in force as if they had been passed by the corporation of the town of Parry Sound, and shall extend and have full effect within the limits 25 of the town hereby incorporated until repealed by the new corporation.

Apportionment of property and liabilities. **14.** Except as otherwise provided by this Act, the property assets, debts, liabilities and obligations of the municipalities of McDougall and Foley, shall be apportioned between the said 30 municipalities of McDougall and Foley and the said town of Parry Sound, as may be agreed upon ; and in case of no agreement, then by the award of three arbitrators, or a majority of them, one of such arbitrators being appointed by the said municipalities of McDougall and Foley, conjointly, and one by 35 the town of Parry Sound, and the third being chosen by the said two ; and if from any cause whatever either the said municipalities of McDougall and Foley or the said town of Parry Sound shall not have appointed an arbitrator within two months after the other of them has appointed an arbi- 40 trator, then the Lieutenant-Governor in Council shall appoint an arbitrator on behalf of the municipality or municipalities so making default, and the two so appointed shall choose a third ; and if they shall not agree upon such third arbitrator, then the Lieutenant-Governor in Council shall appoint such 45 third arbitrator, and the award of the said arbitrators, or of a majority of them, shall be as valid and binding in all respects as if the said arbitrators had been regularly appointed by the said municipalities.

Collection of arrears of taxes. **15.** Arrears of taxes due to the said corporation of the 50 town of Parry Sound shall be collected and managed in the same way as the arrears due to towns separated from counties, and the mayor and treasurer of the said town shall perform the like duties in the collection and management of arrears of taxes as are performed by the said officers in other towns in Ontario separated from counties, and the various provisions of law relating to sales of land for arrears of taxes, or to deeds given therefor, shall apply to the said corporation of the town 5 of Parry Sound, and to sales of land therein for arrears of taxes due thereon and to deeds given therefor, subject to the provisions of section 31 of chapter 175 of the Revised Statutes of Ontario.

16. The council of the said town may pass a by-law for **Assessment** 10 taking the assessment of the said town for the year from first **for 1887.** January to thirty-first December, 1887, between the first day of April and the first day of August, 1887. If any such by-law extends the time for making and completing the assessment rolls beyond the first day of June next, then the 15 time for closing the Court of Revision shall be six weeks from the day to which such time is extended, and the final return by the Stipendiary Magistrate twelve weeks from that day.

17. Nothing contained in this Act shall free the portions **Liabilities not** of the townships or wards comprising the municipality of the **affected.** 20 town of Parry Sound hereby formed, from their proportion of any liability now existing against the municipalities of McDougall and Foley, and the creditors of the said municipalities of McDougall and Foley shall continue to have all the rights and remedies which they had previous to the passing 25 of this Act for the enforcement of their claims against the townships and wards heretofore composing the said municipalities of McDougall and Foley.

No. 31.

1st Session, 6th Legislature, 50 Vic., 1887.

BILL.

An Act to incorporate the Town of Parry Sound.

(Reprinted as amended by Private Bills Committee).

First Reading, 11th March, 1887.

(Private Bill.)

BILL.

An Act to Incorporate the Southern Central Railway Company.

W̲HEREAS the persons hereinafter named and others have Preamble. petitioned for incorporation as a company to construct, equip, and operate a railway from a point at or near Port Burwell to Stratford, passing through or near Ingersoll, with a
5 branch to Brantford and Paris ; and whereas it is expedient to grant the prayer of the said petition :
Therefore Her Majesty, by and with the advice and consent of the Legislative Assembly of the Province of Ontario, enacts as follows :—

10 **1.** William Watterworth, of Ingersoll, banker ; James Trow, Incorporation. of Stratford, M.P.; Frank Turner, of Bracondale, C. E.; Joseph Gibson, of Ingersoll, postmaster ; Nicol Kingsmill, of Toronto, barrister ; W. R. Marshall, of Stratford, merchant ; R. T. Sutton, of Toronto, Esquire ; Thomas William Dobbie, of Tilsonburg,
15 lumber manufacturer, and Harry Symons, of Toronto, barrister, and such other persons and corporations as shall hereafter become shareholders of the said company, are hereby constituted a body corporate and politic under the name of the "Southern Central Railway Company " (hereinafter called the
20 company).

2. The several clauses of *The Railway Act of Ontario*, shall Railway Act be incorporated with, and be deemed to be part of this Act, incorporated and shall apply to the said company, and to the railway to be constructed by them, except only so far as they may be incon-
25 sistent with the express enactments hereof ; and the expression " this Act," when used herein, shall be understood to include the clauses of the said Railway Act so incorporated with this Act.

3. The said company hereby incorporated, and their servants Location of
30 and agents, shall have full power under this Act to construct, line. equip and operate a railway, with all its stations, sidings, telegraph and accessories, from any point at or near Port Burwell to Stratford, passing through or near Ingersoll, with a branch to Brantford and Paris.

35 **4.** The gauge of the said railway shall be four feet eight Gauge. and one-half inches.

5. From and after the passing of the Act, the said William Provisiona Watterworth, James Trow, Frank Turner, Joseph Gibson, Nicol directors. Kingsmill, W. R. Marshall, R. T. Sutton, Thomas William
40 Dobbie, and Harry Symons, with power to add to their

number, shall be and are hereby constituted a board of provisional directors of the said company, and shall hold office as such until the first election of directors under this Act.

Powers of provisional directors.

6. The said board of provisional directors shall have power forthwith to open stock books and procure subscriptions 5 of stock for the undertaking, and to allot the stock, and to receive payments on account of stock subscribed, and to make calls upon subscribers in respect to their stock, and to sue for and recover the same; and to cause plans and surveys to be made, and to receive for the company any grant, loan, bonus 10 or gift made to it, or in aid of the undertaking, and to enter into any agreement respecting the conditions or disposition of any gift or bonus in aid of the railway, and with all such other powers as under *The Railway Act of Ontario*, are vested in ordinary directors; the said directors, or a majority of them, 15 or the board of directors to be elected as hereinafter mentioned may, in their discretion, exclude any one from subscribing for stock who, in their judgment, would hinder, delay or prevent the company from proceeding with and completing their undertaking under the provisions of this Act; and if at any 20 time a portion or more than the whole stock shall have been subscribed, the said provisional directors or board of directors, shall allocate and apportion it amongst the subscribers, as they shall deem most advantageous and conducive to the furtherance of the undertaking; and in such allocation, the said direc- 25 tors may, in their discretion, exclude any one or more of the said subscribers, if, in their judgment, such exclusion will best secure the building of the said railway; and all meetings of the provisional board of directors shall be held at the city of Toronto, or at such other place as may best suit the interests 30 of the said company.

Capital stock.

7. The capital of the company hereby incorporated shall be $500,000, with power to increase the same in manner provided by *The Railway Act of Ontario*, to be divided into ten thousand shares of $50 each, and shall be raised by the persons and 35 corporations who may become shareholders in such company; and the money so raised and paid into the company shall be applied in the first place to the payment of all costs, charges and expenses of and incidental to the obtaining of this Act, or in promoting the undertaking, and of all expenses for making 40 the surveys, plans and estimates connected with the works hereby authorized; and all the remainder of such money shall be applied to the making, equipment, completion and the operating of the said railway, and the other purposes of this Act, and to no other purpose whatever; and until such prelim- 45

Municipal aid for preliminary expenses.

inary expenses shall be paid out of such capital stock, the municipal corporation of any municipality on or near the line of such works may, by resolution, of which seven days' previous notice shall have been given, and passed by a majority of the said municipal corporation, authorize the treasurer of such 50 municipality to pay out of the general funds of such municipality its fair proportion of such preliminary expenses, which shall thereafter, if such municipality shall so require, be refunded to such municipality from the capital stock of the said company, or be allowed to it in payment of stock. 55

8. When and so soon as shares to the amount of $50,000 of the capital stock of the said company shall have been sub-scribed, and ten per centum thereon paid into some chartered bank of the Dominion having an office in the Province of
5 Ontario, to the credit of the company, and which shall on no account be withdrawn therefrom unless for the services of the company, the provisional directors shall call a general meeting of the subscribers to the said capital stock, who shall have so paid up ten per centum upon the amounts subscribed by them,
10 for the purpose of electing directors of the said company. *First meeting for election of directors.*

9. In case the provisional directors neglect to call a meeting for the space of three months after $50,000 of the capital stock shall have been subscribed, and ten per centum thereof
15 so paid up, the same may be called by any five of the sub-scribers who shall have so paid up ten per centum, and who are subscribers collectively for not less than $5,000 of the capital stock, and who have paid up all calls thereon. *Provision in case directors neglect to call meeting.*

10. In either of the cases last mentioned, notice of the time
20 and place of holding such general meeting shall be given by publication in at least one of the daily newspapers in the city of Toronto, once in each week for the space of at least one month, and in the *Ontario Gazette;* and such meeting shall be held in the said city of Toronto, at such place therein, and on such day, and at such hour as may be named and set forth in
25 such notice. *Notice and place of meeting.*

11. At such general meeting the subscribers to the capital stock, present in person or by proxy, who shall have so paid up ten per centum in respect to their subscriptions, shall choose not less than five nor more than eight persons to be directors
30 of the said company, which said directors shall constitute a board of directors, and shall hold office until the next annual general meeting, or until other directors be elected in their stead ; and may also make and pass such rules, regulations and by-laws as may be deemed expedient, provided they be not
35 inconsistent with this Act. *Election of directors.*

12. No person shall be qualified to be a director unless he be a shareholder holding at least twenty-five shares of stock in the said company, and unless he has paid up all calls thereon. *Qualification of directors.*

13. Aliens as well as British subjects, and whether resident
40 within this Province or elsewhere, may be shareholders in the said company ; and all such shareholders shall be entitled to vote on their shares equally with British subjects, and shall also be eligible to hold office as directors in the said company. *Rights of aliens.*

14. Thereafter the annual general meeting of the share-
45 holders of the said company shall be held at such place in the city of Toronto, and on such days, and at such hours as may be directed by the by-laws of the said company ; and public notice thereof shall be given at least thirty days previously in the *Ontario Gazette,* and once in each week, during the four
50 weeks preceding the week in which such meeting is to be held, in at least one of the daily newspapers published in the city of Toronto. *Annual meetings.*

Special meetings.

15. Special general meetings of the shareholders of the said company may be held at such places in the city of Toronto, and at such times and in such manner and for such purposes as may be provided by the by-laws of the said company, and after due notice shall be given as provided in the last preceding 5 section.

Scale of votes.

16. Every shareholder of one or more shares of the said capital stock shall at any general meeting of the shareholders be entitled to one vote for every share so held.

Corporations, how represented.

17. At all meetings of the shareholders of the company, 10 the stock held by municipal and other corporations may be represented by such persons as they shall respectively have appointed in that behalf by resolution under the seal of the corporation, and such persons shall at such meeting be entitled equally with other shareholders to vote by proxy; and no 15 shareholder shall be entitled to vote on any matter whatever, unless all calls due on the stock held by such shareholder shall have been paid up at least one week before the day appointed for such meeting.

Quorum of directors.

18. Any meeting of the directors of the said company 20 regularly summoned, at which at least three of the provisional directors or of those elected by the shareholders are present, shall be competent and entitled to exercise and use all and every of the powers hereby vested in the said directors, and the said board may employ one of their number as paid 25 director.

Calls.

19. Calls on the subscribed capital of the said company may be made by the directors for the time being, as they shall see fit: Provided that no calls shall be made at any one time of more than ten per centum of the amount subscribed by 30 each subscriber, and at not less intervals than one month, and notice of each call shall be given as provided in section 11 of this Act.

Transfer of shares.

20. Shares in the capital stock of the said company may be transferred by any form of instrument in writing, but no 35 transfer shall become effectual unless the stock or scrip certificates issued in respect of shares intended to be transferred are surrendered to the company, or the surrender thereof dispensed with by the company.

Appointment of director as special agent.

21. Should the shareholders of the company resolve that 40 the interests of the company would be best promoted by enabling one or more of the directors to act for the company in any particular matter or matters, it shall be lawful for the directors, after such resolution, to confer such power upon one or more of their number. 45

Form of conveyances.

22. Conveyances of land to the said company for the purposes of and powers given by this Act, made in the form set forth in schedule A hereunder written, or to the like effect, shall be sufficient conveyance to the said company, their successors and assigns, of the estate or interest therein mentioned, 50 and sufficient bar of dower, respectively, of all persons executing the same; and such conveyances shall be registered in such

manner and upon such proof of execution as is required under
the Registry Laws of Ontario; and no registrar shall be
entitled to demand more than seventy-five cents for registering
the same, including all entries and certificates thereof, and
5 certificates indorsed on the duplicates thereof.

23. The said company may receive from any Government, Aid to
or municipal council, or from any person or bodies corporate or company.
politic, who may have power to make or grant the same, aid
towards the construction, equipment or maintenance of the
10 said railway, or of any of the works authorized under this Act
to be undertaken, by way of gift, bonus, or loan of money or
debentures, or other securities for money, or by way of guarantee, or any benefit of any sort and with or without terms or
conditions.

15 **24.** Any municipality, or any portion of any township Aid from
municipality, which may be interested in securing the con- municipali-
struction of the said railway, or through any part of which, or ties.
near which, the railway or works of the said company shall
pass or be situate, may aid the said company by giving money
20 or debentures, by way of bonus, gift, or loan, or by the guarantee of the municipal corporation, under and subject to the
provisions hereinafter contained: Provided always that such Proviso.
aid shall not be given except after the passing of a by-law for
the purpose, and the adoption of such by-law by the qualified
25 ratepayers of the municipality or portion of the municipality,
as the case may be, in accordance with and as provided by law
in respect to granting aid by way of bonuses to railways.

25. Such by-law shall be submitted by the municipal Provisions as
council to the vote of the ratepayers, in manner following, to bonus by-
30 namely: laws.

1. The proper petition shall first be presented to the council
expressing the desire to aid the railway, and stating in what
way and for what amount, and the council shall within six
weeks after the receipt of such petition by the clerk of the
35 municipality, introduce a by-law to the effect petitioned
for, and submit the same for the approval of the qualified
voters;

2. In the case of a county municipality, the petition shall
be that of a majority of the reeves and deputy-reeves, or of
40 fifty resident freeholders in each of the minor municipalities
of the county, who are qualified voters under *The Consolidated
Municipal Act, 1883;*

3. In the case of other municipalities the petition shall be
that of a majority of the council thereof, or of fifty resident
45 freeholders, being duly qualified voters under *The Consolidated
Municipal Act, 1883,* as aforesaid;

4. In the case of a section of a township municipality, the
petition is to be presented to the council, defining the section
by metes and bounds, or lots and concessions, and shall be
50 that of a majority of the council of such township municipality,
or of fifty resident freeholders in such section of the municipality, being duly qualified voters as aforesaid.

Provisions of by-law.

26. Such by-law shall in each instance provide:

1. For raising the amount petitioned for in the municipality or portion of the township municipality, (as the case may be,) mentioned in the petition, by the issue of debentures of the county or minor municipality respectively, and shall also 5 provide for the delivery of the said debentures, or the application of the amount to be raised thereby, as may be expressed in the said by-law;

2. For assessing and levying upon all ratable property lying within the municipality or portion of the township 10 municipality defined in said by-law, (as the case may be,) an annual special rate sufficient to include a sinking fund for the repayment of the said debentures within twenty years, with interest thereon, payable yearly or half-yearly, which debentures the respective municipal councils, wardens, mayors, 15 reeves, and other officers thereof, are hereby authorized to execute and issue in such cases respectively.

3. In the case of guarantee, the by-law shall provide for the due application of the amount to be raised for the purpose thereof, and for assessing and levying upon all ratable 20 property lying within the municipality, minor municipality, or portion of the township municipality defined by the said by-law (as the case may be), an annual special rate sufficient to pay from time to time the sum guaranteed, and to include a sinking fund in the case of the principal of the debentures of 25 the company being guaranteed for a period not exceeding twenty years, which guarantee, the respective municipal councils, wardens, mayors, reeves, or other officers, are hereby authorized to execute.

Provisions for referring to arbitration disputes as to bonus by-law.

27. In case of aid from a county municipality, fifty resident 30 freeholders of the county may petition the county council against submitting the said by-law, upon the ground that certain minor municipalities or portions thereof comprised in the said by-law, would be injuriously affected thereby, or upon any other ground ought not to be included therein, and upon 35 deposit by the petitioners with the treasurer of the county, of a sum sufficient to defray the expense of such reference, the said council shall forthwith refer the said petition to three arbitrators, one being the Judge of the County Court, one being the Registrar of the county or of the riding in which 40 the county town is situate, and one being an engineer appointed by the Commissioner of Public Works for Ontario, who shall have power to confirm or amend the said by-law by excluding any minor municipality or any section thereof therefrom, and the decision of any two of them shall be final, 45 and the by-law so confirmed or amended shall thereupon, at the option of the railway company, be submitted by the council to the duly qualified voters, and in case the by-law is confirmed by the arbitrators, the expense shall be borne by the petitioners against the same; but if amended, then by the 50 railway company or the county, as the arbitrators may order.

Minor municipality, meaning of.

28. The term "minor municipality" shall be construed to mean any town not separated from the municipal county, township, or incorporated village situate in the county municipality. 55

29. Before any such by-law is submitted, the railway com- Deposit for expenses. pany shall, if required, deposit with the treasurer of the municipality, a sum sufficient to pay the expenses to be incurred in submitting said by-law.

5   **30**. In case the by-law submitted be approved of and car- If by-law carried, council to pass same. ried in accordance with the provisions of the law in that behalf, then within four weeks after the date of such voting, the municipal council which submitted the same shall read the said by-law a third time, and pass the same.

10   **31**. Within one month after the passing of such by-law, the And issue debentures. said conneil and the mayor, warden, reeve, or other head, or other officers thereof, shall issue or dispose of the debentures provided for by the by-law, and deliver the same duly executed to the trustees appointed, or to be appointed under this Act.

15   **32**. In case any such loan, guarantee or bonus be so granted Levying rate on portions of municipality. by a portion of a township municipality, the rate to be levied for payment of the debentures issued therefor, and the interest thereon, shall be assessed and levied upon such portion only of such municipality.

20   **33**. The provisions of *The Consolidated Municipal Act, 1883* Application of Municipal Act as to by-law. and the amendments thereto, so far as the same are not incon- sistent with this Act, shall apply to any by-law so passed by or for a portion of a township municipality, to the same extent as if the same had been passed by or for the whole 25 municipality.

34. The councils for all corporations that may grant aid by Extension of time for com- mencement. way of bonus to the said company may, by resolution or by-law, extend the time for the commencement of the work beyond that stipulated for in the by-law or by-laws granting 30 such aid from time to time : Provided that no such extension shall be for a longer period than one year.

35. It shall and may be lawful for the council of any muni- Extension of time for com- pletion. cipality that may grant aid by way of bonus to the said com- pany, by resolution or by-law, to extend the time for the com- 35 pletion of the works, on the completion of which the said com- pany would be entitled to such bonus, from time to time : Pro- vided that no such extension shall be for a longer period than one year at a time.

36. Any municipality or portion of a township municipality Rate not exceeding three cents in the dollar valid. 40 interested in the construction of the road of the said company, may grant aid by way of bonus to the said company towards the construction of such road, notwithstanding that such aid may increase the municipal taxation of such municipality or portion thereof, beyond what is allowed by law : Provided that Proviso. 45 such aid shall not require the levying of a greater aggregate annual rate for all purposes, exclusive of school rates, than three cents in the dollar upon the value of the ratable property therein.

37. It shall be lawful for the corporation of any munici- Exemption from taxation. pality, through any part of which the railway of the said 50 company passes or is situated, by by-law expressly passed for that purpose, to exempt the company and its property within such municipality, either in whole or in part, from municipal assessment or taxation, or to agree to a certain sum per annum or otherwise in gross, or by way of commutation or composition for payment, or in lieu of all or any municipal rates or assessments to be imposed by such municipal corporation, and 5 for such term of years as such municipal corporation may deem expedient, not exceeding twenty-one years, and no such by-law shall be repealed unless in conformity with a condition contained therein.

Grants of land.

38. Any municipality through which the said railway may 10 pass or is situate, is empowered to grant by way of gift to the said company, any lands belonging to such municipality or over which it may have control, which may be required for right of way, station grounds or other purposes connected with the running or traffic of the said railway ; and the said 15 railway company shall have power to accept gifts of land from any government, or any person or body politic or corporate, and shall have power to sell or otherwise dispose of the same for the benefit of the said company.

Trustees of debentures.

39. Whenever any municipality or portion of a township 20 municipality shall grant aid by way of bonus or gift to the railway company, the debentures therefor, shall within six months after the passing of the by-law authorizing the same, be delivered to three trustees to be named, one by the Lieut.-Governor in Council, one by the said company, and one by the 25 majority of the heads of the municipalities which have granted bonuses, or in case of only one municipality granting a bonus, then by the head of such municipality, all the trustees to be residents of the province of Ontario : Provided that if the said **Proviso.** heads of the municipalities, or head of the said municipality, 30 shall refuse or neglect to name such trustee within one month after notice in writing of the appointment of the company's trustee, or if the Lieutenant-Governor in Council shall omit to name such trustee within one month after notice in writing to him of the appointment of the other trustees, then in either case 35 the company shall be at liberty to name such other trustee or trustees. Any of the said trustees may be removed and a new trustee appointed in his place at any time by the Lieutenant-Governor in Council, and in case any trustee dies or resigns his trust, or goes to live out of the province of Ontario, or other- 40 wise becomes incapable to act, his trusteeship shall become vacant and a new trustee may be appointed by the Lieutenant-Governor in Council.

Trusts of proceeds of debentures.

40. The said trustees shall receive the said debentures or bonds in trust, (firstly) under the directions of the company, 45 but subject to the conditions of the by-law in relation thereto, as to time or manner to convert the same into money or otherwise dispose of them ; secondly, to deposit the debentures or amount realized from the sale in some chartered bank having an office in the city of Toronto, in the name of " The Southern 50 Central Railway Company Municipal Trust Account," and to pay the same out to the said company from time to time as the said company becomes entitled thereto, under the conditions of the by-law granting the said bonus, and on the certificate of the chief engineer of the said railway for the time being, in 55 the form set out in schedule B, hereto, or to the like effect,

which certificate shall set forth that the conditions of the by-
law have been complied with, and is to be attached to the
cheque or order drawn by the said trustees for such payment
or delivery of debentures, and such engineer shall not wrong-
5 fully grant any such certificate, under a penalty of $500,
recoverable in any court of competent jurisdiction, by any
person who may sue therefor.

41. The trustees shall be entitled to their reasonable fees Fees to
and charges from said trust fund, and the act of any two of Trustees.
10 such trustees shall be as valid and binding as if the three had
agreed.

42. It shall and may be lawful for any municipality through Right to use
which the said railway passes, and having jurisdiction in the highways.
premises, to pass a by-law or by-laws empowering the company
15 to make their road and lay their rails along any of the highways within such municipality, and whether or not the same
be in the possession of or under the control of any joint stock
company; and if such highway be either in the possession of
or under the control of any joint stock company, then also with
20 the assent of such company; and it shall and may be lawful
for the company to enter into and perform any such agreement
as they may from time to time deem expedient, with any
municipality, corporation or person, for the construction or for
the maintenance and repair of gravel or other public roads
25 leading to the said railway.

43. The said company shall have the power of closing up Closing roads.
any road or highway crossing through any of their station
grounds, provided the said company shall have the consent of
the municipality in which the road is situated, by a by-law
30 passed for that purpose, and provided a road adjacent thereto
and convenient for the public, be provided in lieu of any such
closed road.

44. The company shall have the right, on and after the 15th Power to erect
day of November in each year, to enter into and upon any snow-fences.
35 lands of Her Majesty, or into or upon any lands of any corporation or person whatsoever, lying along the route or line of
said railway, and to erect and maintain snow fences thereon,
subject to the payment of such damages (if any) as may be
hereafter established in the manner provided by law, in respect
40 of such railway, to have been actually suffered: Provided Proviso.
always that any such snow fences so erected shall be removed
on or before the 1st day of April following.

45. The directors of the said company, elected by the Branches may
shareholders in accordance with the provisions of this Act, be made to
45 shall have power and authority to enter into and conclude other com-
any arrangements with any other railway company lawfully panies.
authorized to enter into such arrangement, for the purpose of
making any branch to facilitate a connection between this
company and such other chartered railway company.

50 **46.** The said company may also construct a telephone line Telephone and
and an electric telegraph line in connection with their railway, telegraph
and for the purpose of constructing, working and protecting lines.
the said telephone and telegraph lines, the powers conferred

upon telegraph companies by *The Act respecting Electric Telegraph Companies* (chapter 151 of The Revised Statutes of Ontario), are hereby conferred upon the said company.

Power to contract for construction and equipment of railway.

47. It shall be lawful for the directors to enter into a contract or contracts with any individual or association of individuals for the construction or equipment of the line or any portion thereof, including or excluding the purchase of the right of way, and to pay therefor either in cash or bonds, or in paid up stock or otherwise, as may be deemed expedient, notwithstanding that one or more of such contractors may be shareholders or directors in the company : Provided that no such contract in which a shareholder or director of the company shall be a contractor, shall be of any force or validity till approved of by two-thirds of the shareholders present, in person or by proxy, at a meeting specially called for considering the same. 5 10 15

Proviso.

Agreements for use of rolling stock, etc.

48. It shall be lawful for the directors of the company to enter into agreement with any company or companies (if lawfully authorized to enter into such an agreement), person or persons, for the leasing, hiring or use of any locomotives, carriages, rolling stock and other movable property from such companies or persons, for such time or times, and on such terms as may be agreed on, and also to enter into agreement with any railway company or companies (if so lawfully authorized), for the use by one or more of such contracting companies of the locomotives, carriages, rolling stock and other movable property of the other or others of them, on such terms as to compensation and otherwise as may be agreed upon. 20 25

Power to collect backcharges on goods.

49. The said company shall have power to collect and receive all charges subject to which goods or commodities may come into their possession, and on payment of such backcharges, and without any formal transfer, shall have the same lien for the amount thereof upon such goods or commodities, as the persons to whom such charges were originally due, had upon such goods or commodities while in their possession, and shall be subrogated by such payment in all the rights and remedies of such persons for such charges. 30 35

Power to make and endorse notes and bills without affixing seal.

50. The said company shall have power and authority to become parties to promissory notes and bills of exchange for sums not less than $100, and any such promissory note made or endorsed, or any such bill of exchange drawn, accepted or endorsed by the president or vice-president of the company, and countersigned by the secretary, treasurer, or other proper officer of the said company, and under the authority of a quorum of the directors, shall be binding on the said company; and every such promissory note or bill of exchange so made, accepted or endorsed, shall be presumed to have been made, accepted or endorsed with proper authority, until the contrary be shewn ; and in no case shall it be necessary to have the seal of the company affixed to such promissory note or bill of exchange, nor shall the president or vice-president, or the secretary or treasurer, or other officer aforesaid, be individually responsible for the same, unless the said promissory notes or bills of exchange have been issued without the sanction and authority of the board of directors, as herein provided and 40 45 50 55

enacted : Provided, however, that nothing in this section shall Proviso.
be construed to authorize the said company to issue any note
or bill of exchange payable to bearer or intended to be circulated as money, or as the notes or bills of a bank.

5   **51.** The directors of the said company, after the sanction of Issue of bonds.
the shareholders shall have first been obtained at any special
general meeting to be called from time to time for such purpose, shall have power to issue bonds, made and signed by the
president of the said company, and countersigned by the
10 secretary, and under the seal of the said company, for the
purpose of raising money for prosecuting the said undertaking ; and such bonds shall, without registration or formal conveyance, be taken and considered to be the first and preferential claims and charges upon the undertaking and the
15 real property of the company, including its rolling stock and
equipments then existing, and at any time thereafter acquired;
and each holder of the said bonds shall be deemed to be a
mortgagee and incumbrancer, *pro rata*, with all the other
holders thereof, upon the undertaking and property of the
20 company as aforesaid: Provided, however, that the whole
amount of such issue of bonds shall not exceed in all the sum Proviso.
of $20,000 per mile ; and provided that in the event at any
time of the interest upon the said bonds remaining unpaid Proviso.
and owing, then, at the next ensuing general annual meeting
25 of the said company, all holders of bonds shall have and
possess the same rights, privileges and qualifications for
directors and for voting as are attached to shareholders: Pro- Proviso.
vided further, that the bonds and any transfers thereof shall
have been first registered in the same manner as is provided
30 for the registration of shares, and it shall be the duty of the
secretary of the company to register the same on being
required to do so by any-holder thereof.

52. All such bonds, debentures and other securities and Form of bonds.
coupons and interest warrants thereon respectively may be
35 made payable to bearer and transferable by delivery, and any
holder of any such securities so made payable to bearer, may
sue at law thereon in his own name, and all such bonds,
debentures and other securities and coupons and interest
warrants thereon respectively may be made payable in lawful
40 money of Canada, or in sterling money of Great Britain, at
some place in Canada or London, England, or in the city of
New York, in the state of New York, or at all or any of such
places.

53. It shall be lawful for the said company to have and Power to keep duplicate seal.
45 keep a duplicate seal for the transaction of such of their busi-
ness in the United Kingdom of Great Britain and Ireland, or
in the United States of America, as the board of directors of
the said company may from time to time designate, and the
said seal may be used and affixed in all such cases by such
50 officer or officers, agent or agents, as the said directors may by
by-law from time to time direct, and any instrument to which
the said duplicate seal shall be so affixed, shall be valid and
binding upon the said company.

54. The company hereby incorporated may, from time to Power to mortgage bonds.
55 time, for advances of money to be made thereon, mortgage or

pledge any bonds or debentures which, under the powers of this Act can be issued for the construction of the railway or otherwise.

Payments in bonds or stock authorized in certain cases.

55. The said provisional directors, or the elected directors, may pay or agree to pay, in paid up stock or in the bonds of 5 the said company, such sums as they may deem expedient, to engineers or contractors, or for right of way or material, plant or rolling stock, and also, when sanctioned by a vote of the majority of shareholders present at any general meeting, for the services of promoters or other persons who may be 10 employed by the directors for the purpose of assisting the directors in the furtherance of the undertaking or purchase of right of way, material, plant or rolling stock, whether such promoters or other persons be provisional directors or not, and any such agreements so made shall be binding on the 15 company.

Power to purchase, etc., wharves, etc.

56. It shall and may be lawful for the company at any point where the railway, or any branch thereof, approaches within two miles of any navigable waters, to purchase and hold as its own absolute property, and for the use of the company, 20 wharves, piers, docks, water lots, water frontages, and lands; and upon the said water lots, water frontages and lands, and in and over the waters adjoining the same, to build and erect elevators, storehouses, warehouses and engine houses, sheds, wharves, docks, piers and other erections for the use of the 25 company, and the steam and other vessels owned, worked or controlled by the company, or any other steam or other vessels; and to collect wharfage, storage, and other charges for the use of the same; and also to erect, build, repair, and maintain all moles, piers, wharves and docks necessary and proper 30 for the protection of such works, and for the accomodation and convenience of vessels entering. leaving, lying, loading and unloading within the same, and to dredge, deepen, and enlarge such works; and the said wharves, piers, and docks, water lots, water frontages, lands, elevators, storehouses, ware- 35 houses, engine houses, sheds and other erections, or any thereof, or any portions thereof, in its discretion to sell, lease, or convey.

Power to purchase and work vessels in connection with the railway.

57. It shall and may be lawful for the company to purchase, build, complete, fit out and charter, sell and dispose of, 40 work and control, and keep in repair, steam or other vessels, from time to time to ply on the lakes, rivers and canals of this Province, in connection with the said railway; and also to make arrangements and agreements with steamboat and vessel proprietors, by chartering or otherwise, to ply on the said 45 lakes, rivers and canals, in connection with the said railway.

Power to construct railway in sections.

58. The said company is hereby authorized and empowered to take and make the surveys and levels of the land through · which the said railway is to pass, together with the map or plan thereof, and of its course and direction, and of the lands 50 intended to be passed over and taken therefor, so far as then ascertained, and also the book of reference for the railway, and to deposit the same as required by the clauses of *The Railway Act of Ontario*, and amendments thereto, with respect to "plans and surveys," by sections or portions less than the 55

length of the whole railway authorized, of such length as the
said company may from time to time see fit, so that no one of
such sections or portions shall be less than ten miles in length,
and upon such deposit as aforesaid, of the map or plan and
5 book of reference of any and each of such sections or portions
of the said railway, all and every of the clauses of *The Railway Act of Ontario*, and the amendments thereof applied to,
included in, or incorporated with this Act, shall apply and
extend to any and each of such sections or portions of the
10 said railway as fully and effectually as if the surveys and
levels had been taken and made of the lands through which
the whole of the said railway is to pass, together with the
map or plan of the whole thereof, and of its whole course and
direction, and of the lands intended to be passed over and
15 taken, and the book of reference for the whole of the said
railway had been taken, made, examined, certified and
deposited according to the said clauses of the said *Railway
Act of Ontario*, and the amendments thereof, with respect to
" plans and surveys."

20 **59**. Whenever it shall be necessary for the purpose of Power to pur-
procuring sufficient land for stations or gravel pits, or for con- chase whole
structing, maintaining, and using the said railway, and in case lots.
by purchasing the whole of any parcel or lot of land over
which the railway is to run, the company can obtain the same
25 at a more reasonable price or to greater advantage than by
purchasing the railway line only, the company may purchase,
hold, use, or enjoy such lands, and also the right of way thereto
if the same be separate from their railway, and may sell and
convey the same or part thereof, from time to time, as they
30 may deem expedient, but the compulsory clauses of *The Railway Act of Ontario* shall not apply to this section.

60. When stone, gravel, earth, or sand is or are required Acquiring
for the construction or maintenance of said railway, or any gravel, etc ,
for construc-
part thereof, the company may, in case they cannot agree with tion and main-
35 the owner of the lands on which the same is situated for the tenance of
railway.
purchase thereof, cause a provincial surveyor to make a map
and description of the property so required, and they shall
serve a copy thereof, with their notice of arbitration, as in the
case of acquiring the roadway, and the notice of arbitration, the
40 award and the tender of compensation shall have the same effect
as in case of arbitration for the roadway; and all the provisions
of *The Railway Act of Ontario* and of this Act, as to the service of the said notice, arbitration, compensation, deeds, payment of money into Court, the right to sell, the right to con-
45 vey, and the parties from whom lands may be taken, or who
may sell, shall apply to the subject matter of this section as to
the obtaining of materials as aforesaid, and such proceedings
may be had by the said company either for the right to the fee
simple in the land from which said material shall be taken, or
50 for the right to take materials for any time they shall think
necessary, the notice of arbitration, in case arbitration is resorted
to, to state the interest required.

61—(1) When said gravel, sand, stone, or other material Sidings to
shall be taken under the preceding section of this Act at a gravel pits.
55 distance from the line of the railway, the company may lay

down the necessary sidings and tracks over any land which
may intervene between the railway and the lands on which
said material shall be found, whatever the distance may be;
and all the provisions of *The Railway Act of Ontario* and of
this Act, except such as relate to filing plans and publication 5
of notice, shall apply and may be used and exercised to obtain
the right of way from the railway to the land on which such
materials are situated ; and such right may be so acquired for
a term of years, or permanently, as the company may think
proper, and the powers in this and the preceding section may 10
at all times be exercised and used in all respects after the rail-
is constructed for the purpose of repairing and maintaining
the said railway ;

(2) When estimating the damages for the taking of gravel,
stone, or sand, sub-section 8 of section 20 of *The Railway Act* 15
of Ontario shall not apply.

Commence-
ment and
completion of
railway.

62. The construction of the said railway shall be commenced within three years, and the same shall be completed
within five years, after the passing of this Act.

SCHEDULE A.

(*Section* 22.)

Know all men by these presents that I (*or* we) [*insert the
name of the vendors*], in consideration of   dollars paid to
me (*or* us) by the Southern Central Railway Company, the receipt whereof is hereby acknowledged, do grant and convey
unto the said company, and I (*or* we) [*insert the name of any
other party or parties*]   in consideration of   dollars
paid to me (*or* us) by the said company, the receipt whereof is
hereby acknowledged, do grant or release all that certain parcel (*or* those certain parcels *as the case may be*) of land (*describe
the land*) the same having been selected and laid out by the
company for the purposes of their railway, to hold with the
appurtenances unto the said Southern Central Railway Company, their successors and assigns (*here insert any other clauses,
covevants or conditions required*) and I (*or* we) the wife (*or
wives*) of the said   , do hereby bar my (*or* our)
dower in the said lands.

As witness my (*or* our) hand and seal (*or* hands and seals)
this   day of   A.D. 18

Signed, sealed and delivered }
in the presence of   }   [L.S.]

SCHEDULE B.

(Section 40.)

CHIEF ENGINEER'S CERTIFICATE.

THE SOUTHERN CENTRAL RAILWAY COMPANY'S OFFICE,

Engineer's Department,   A.D. 188

No.

Certificate to be attached to cheques drawn on " The Southern Central Railway Company Municipal Trust Account," given under section   , chapter   of the Acts of the Legislature of Ontario, passed in the year of Her Majesty's reign.

I, A.B , Chief Engineer of the Southern Central Railway Company, do hereby certify that the said company has fulfilled the terms and conditions necessary to be fulfilled under the by-law No.   of the township of   (*or* under the agreement dated the   day of   between . the corporation of   and the said company) to entitle the said company to receive from the said trust the sum of   (*here set out the terms and conditions, if any, which have been fulfilled.*)

1st Session, 6th Legislature, 50 Vic., 1887

BILL.

An Act to incorporate the Southern Central Railway Company.

First Reading,   1887.

(Private Bill.)

BILL.

An Act to incorporate the Southern Central Railway Company.

WHEREAS the persons hereinafter named and others have *Preamble.*
petitioned for incorporation as a company to construct,
equip, and operate a railway from *Stratford to a point on
Lake Erie in the township of Bayham,* passing through or near
5 Ingersoll, with a branch to Brantford and Paris ; and whereas
it is expedient to grant the prayer of the said petition :

Therefore Her Majesty, by and with the advice and consent
of the Legislative Assembly of the Province of Ontario, enacts
as follows :—

10 **1.** William Watterworth, of Ingersoll, banker ; *Andrew* *Incorporation.*
Monteith, of Stratford; Frank Turner, of Bracondale, C. E.;
Joseph Gibson, of Ingersoll, postmaster ; Nicol Kingsmill, of
Toronto, barrister ; W. R. Marshall, of Stratford, merchant;
R. T. Sutton, of Toronto, Esquire ; Thomas William Dobbie, of
15 Tilsonburg, lumber manufacturer, and Harry Symons, of
Toronto, barrister, and such other persons and corporations as
shall hereafter become shareholders of the said company, are
hereby constituted a body corporate and politic under the
name of the "Southern Central Railway Company" (herein-
20 after called the company).

2. The several clauses of *The Railway Act of Ontario,* shall *Railway Act*
be incorporated with, and be deemed to be part of this Act, *incorporated.*
and shall apply to the said company, and to the railway to be
constructed by them, except only so far as they may be incon-
25 sistent with the express enactments hereof ; and the expression
"this Act," when used herein, shall be understood to include
the clauses of the said Railway Act so incorporated with
this Act.

3. The said company hereby incorporated, and their servants *Location of*
30 and agents, shall have full power under this Act to construct, *line.*
equip and operate a railway, with all its stations, sidings, telegraph and accessories, from Stratford *to a point on Lake Erie
in the township of Bayham,* passing through or near Ingersoll,
with a branch to Brantford and Paris.

35 **4.** The gauge of the said railway shall be four feet eight *Gauge.*
and one-half inches.

5. From and after the passing of the Act, the said William *Provisions*
Watterworth, *Andrew Monteith,* Frank Turner, Joseph Gibson, *directors.*
Nicol Kingsmill, W. R. Marshall, R. T. Sutton, Thomas William
40 Dobbie, and Harry Symons, with power to add to their

number, shall be and are hereby constituted a board of provisional directors of the said company, and shall hold office as such until the first election of directors under this Act.

Powers of provisional directors. **6.** The said board of provisional directors shall have power forthwith to open stock books and procure subscriptions 5 of stock for the undertaking, and to allot the stock, and to receive payments on account of stock subscribed, and to make calls upon subscribers in respect to their stock, and to sue for and recover the same; and to cause plans and surveys to be made, and to receive for the company any grant, loan, bonus 10 or gift made to it, or in aid of the undertaking, and to enter into any agreement respecting the conditions or disposition of any gift or bonus in aid of the railway, and with all such other powers as under *The Railway Act of Ontario*, are vested in ordinary directors; the said directors, or a majority of them, 15 or the board of directors to be elected as hereinafter mentioned may, in their discretion, exclude any one from subscribing for stock who, in their judgment, would hinder, delay or prevent the company from proceeding with and completing their undertaking under the provisions of this Act; and if at any 20 time a portion or more than the whole stock shall have been subscribed, the said provisional directors or board of directors, shall allocate and apportion it amongst the subscribers, as they shall deem most advantageous and conducive to the furtherance of the undertaking; and in such allocation, the said dirce- 25 tors may, in their discretion, exclude any one or more of the said subscribers, if, in their judgment, such exclusion will best secure the building of the said railway; and all meetings of the provisional board of directors shall be held at the city of Toronto, or at such other place as may best suit the interests 30 of the said company.

Capital stock. **7.** The capital of the company hereby incorporated shall be $500,000, with power to increase the same in manner provided by *The Railway Act of Ontario*, to be divided into ten thousand shares of $50 each, and shall be raised by the persons and 35 corporations who may become shareholders in such company; and the money so raised and paid into the company shall be applied in the first place to the payment of all costs, charges and expenses of and incidental to the obtaining of this Act, or in promoting the undertaking, and of all expenses for making 40 the surveys, plans and estimates connected with the works hereby authorized; and all the remainder of such money shall be applied to the making, equipment, completion and the operating of the said railway, and the other purposes of this Act, and to no other purpose whatever; and until such prelim- 45 **Municipal aid for preliminary expenses.** inary expenses shall be paid out of such capital stock, the municipal corporation of any municipality on or near the line of such works may, by resolution, of which seven days' previous notice shall have been given, and passed by a majority of the said municipal corporation, authorize the treasurer of such 50 municipality to pay out of the general funds of such municipality its fair proportion of such preliminary expenses, which shall thereafter, if such municipality shall so require, be refunded to such municipality from the capital stock of the said company, or be allowed to it in payment of stock. 55

8. When and so soon as shares to the amount of $50,000 of First meeting for election of directors. the capital stock of the said company shall have been subscribed, and ten per centum thereon paid into some chartered bank of the Dominion having an office in the Province of
5 Ontario, to the credit of the company, and which shall on no account be withdrawn therefrom unless for the services of the company, the provisional directors shall call a general meeting of the subscribers to the said capital stock, who shall have so paid up ten per centum upon the amounts subscribed by them,
10 for the purpose of electing directors of the said company.

9. In case the provisional directors neglect to call a meeting Provision in case directors neglect to call meeting. for the space of three months after $50,000 of the capital stock shall have been subscribed, and ten per centum thereof so paid up, the same may be called by any five of the sub-
15 scribers who shall have so paid up ten per centum, and who are subscribers collectively for not less than $5,000 of the capital stock, and who have paid up all calls thereon.

10. In either of the cases last mentioned, notice of the time Notice and place of meeting. and place of holding such general meeting shall be given by
20 publication in at least one of the daily newspapers in the city of Toronto, once in each week for the space of at least one month, and in the *Ontario Gazette ;* and such meeting shall be held in the said city of Toronto, at such place therein, and on such day, and at such hour as may be named and set forth in
25 such notice.

11. At such general meeting the subscribers to the capital Election of directors. stock, present in person or by proxy, who shall have so paid up ten per centum in respect to their subscriptions, shall choose not less than five nor more than eight persons to be directors
30 of the said company, which said directors shall constitute a board of directors, and shall hold office until the next annual general meeting, or until other directors be elected in their stead ; and may also make and pass such rules, regulations and by-laws as may be deemed expedient, provided they be not
35 inconsistent with this Act.

12. No person shall be qualified to be a director unless he be Qualification of directors. a shareholder holding at least twenty-five shares of stock in the said company, and unless he has paid up all calls thereon.

13. Aliens as well as British subjects, and whether resident Rights of aliens.
40 within this Province or elsewhere, may be shareholders in the said company ; and all such shareholders shall be entitled to vote on their shares equally with British subjects, and shall also be eligible to hold office as directors in the said company.

14. Thereafter the annual general meeting of the share- Annual meetings.
45 holders of the said company shall be held at such place in the city of Toronto, and on such days, and at such hours as may be directed by the by-laws of the said company ; and public notice thereof shall be given at least thirty days previously in the *Ontario Gazette,* and once in each week, during the four
50 weeks preceding the week in which such meeting is to be held, in at least one of the daily newspapers published in the city of Toronto.

Special meetings.

15. Special general meetings of the shareholders of the said company may be held at such places in the city of Toronto, and at such times and in such manner and for such purposes as may be provided by the by-laws of the said company, and after due notice shall be given as provided in the last preceding 5 section.

Scale of votes.

16. Every shareholder of one or more shares of the said capital stock shall at any general meeting of the shareholders be entitled to one vote for every share so held.

Corporations, how represented.

17. At all meetings of the shareholders of the company, 10 the stock held by municipal and other corporations may be represented by such persons as they shall respectively have appointed in that behalf by resolution under the seal of the corporation, and such persons shall at such meeting be entitled equally with other shareholders to vote by proxy; and no 15 shareholder shall be entitled to vote on any matter whatever, unless all calls due on the stock held by such shareholder shall have been paid up at least one week before the day appointed for such meeting.

Quorum of directors.

18. Any meeting of the directors of the said company 20 regularly summoned, at which at least three of the provisional directors or of those elected by the shareholders are present, shall be competent and entitled to exercise and use all and every of the powers hereby vested in the said directors, and the said board may employ one of their number as paid 25 director.

Calls.

19. Calls on the subscribed capital of the said company may be made by the directors for the time being, as they shall see fit: Provided that no calls shall be made at any one time of more than ten per centum of the amount subscribed by 30 each subscriber, and at not less intervals than one month, and notice of each call shall be given as provided in section 14 of this Act.

Transfer of shares.

20. Shares in the capital stock of the said company may be transferred by any form of instrument in writing, but no 35 transfer shall become effectual unless the stock or scrip certificates issued in respect of shares intended to be transferred are surrendered to the company, or the surrender thereof dispensed with by the company.

Appointment of director as special agent.

21. Should the shareholders of the company resolve that 40 the interests of the company would be best promoted by enabling one or more of the directors to act for the company in any particular matter or matters, it shall be lawful for the directors, after such resolution, to confer such power upon one or more of their number. 45

Form of conveyances.

22. Conveyances of land to the said company for the purposes of and powers given by this Act, made in the form set forth in schedule A hereunder written, or to the like effect, shall be sufficient conveyance to the said company, their successors and assigns, of the estate or interest therein mentioned, 50 and sufficient bar of dower, respectively, of all persons executing the same; and such conveyances shall be registered in such

manner and upon such proof of execution as is required under
the registry laws of Ontario; and no registrar shall be
entitled to demand more than seventy-five cents for registering
the same, including all entries and certificates thereof, and
5 certificates indorsed on the duplicates thereof.

23. The said company may receive from any Government, Aid to
or from any person or bodies corporate or politic, who may have company.
power to make or grant the same, aid towards the construction,
equipment or maintenance of the said railway, or of any of the
10 works authorized under this Act to be undertaken, by way of
gift, bonus, or loan of money or debentures, or other securities
for money, or by way of guarantee, *upon such terms and conditions as may be agreed upon.*

24. Any municipality, or any portion of any township Aid from
15 municipality, which may be interested in securing the con- municipali-
struction of the said railway, or through any part of which, or ties.
near which, the railway or works of the said company shall
pass or be situate, may aid the said company by giving money
or debentures, by way of bonus, gift, or loan, or by the guar-
20 antee of the municipal corporation, under and subject to the
provisions hereinafter contained : Provided always that such Proviso.
aid shall not be given except after the passing of a by-law for
the purpose, and the adoption of such by-law by the qualified
ratepayers of the municipality or portion of the municipality,
25 as the case may be, in accordance with and as provided by law
in respect to granting aid by way of bonuses to railways.

25. Such by-law shall be submitted by the municipal Provisions as
council to the vote of the ratepayers, in manner following, laws.
namely :

30 1. The proper petition shall first be presented to the council
expressing the desire to aid the railway, and stating in what
way and for what amount, and the council shall within six
weeks after the receipt of such petition by the clerk of the
municipality, introduce a by-law to the effect petitioned
35 for, and submit the same for the approval of the qualified
voters ;

2. In the case of a county municipality, the petition shall
be that of a majority of the reeves and deputy-reeves, or of
fifty resident freeholders in each of the minor municipalities
40 of the county, who are qualified voters under *The Consolidated
Municipal Act, 1883 ;*

3. In the case of other municipalities the petition shall be
that of a majority of the council thereof, or of fifty resident
freeholders, being duly qualified voters under *The Consolidated
45 Municipal Act, 1883,* as aforesaid ;

4. In the case of a section of a township municipality, the
petition is to be presented to the council, defining the section
by metes and bounds, or lots and concessions, and shall be
that of a majority of the council of such township municipality,
50 or of fifty resident freeholders in such section of the municipality, being duly qualified voters as aforesaid.

Provisions of by-law.

26. Such by-law shall in each instance provide :

1. For raising the amount petitioned for in the municipality or portion of the township municipality, (as the case may be,) mentioned in the petition, by the issue of debentures of the county or minor municipality respectively, and shall also 5 provide for the delivery of the said debentures, or the application of the amount to be raised thereby, as may be expressed in the said by-law ;

2. For assessing and levying upon all ratable property lying within the municipality or portion of the township 10 municipality defined in said by-law, (as the case may be,) an annual special rate sufficient to include a sinking fund for the repayment of the said debentures within twenty years, with interest thereon, payable yearly or half-yearly, which debentures the respective municipal councils, wardens, mayors, 15 reeves, and other officers thereof, are hereby authorized to execute and issue in such cases respectively.

3. In the case of guarantee, the by-law shall provide for the due application of the amount to be raised for the purpose thereof, and for assessing, and levying upon all ratable 20 property lying within the municipality, minor municipality, or portion of the township municipality defined by the said by-law (as the case may be), an annual special rate sufficient to pay from time to time the sum guaranteed, and to include a sinking fund in the case of the principal of the debentures of 25 the company being guaranteed for a period not exceeding twenty years, which guarantee, the respective municipal councils, wardens, mayors, reeves, or other officers, are hereby authorized to execute.

Provisions for referring to arbitration disputes as to bonus by-law.

27. In case of aid from a county municipality, fifty resident 30 freeholders of the county may petition the county council against submitting the said by-law, upon the ground that certain minor municipalities or portions thereof comprised in the said by-law, would be injuriously affected thereby, or upon any other ground ought not to be included therein, and upon 35 deposit by the petitioners with the treasurer of the county, of a sum sufficient to defray the expense of such reference, the said council shall forthwith refer the said petition to three arbitrators, one being the Judge of the County Court, one being the Registrar of the county or of the riding in which 40 the county town is situate, and one being an engineer appointed by the Commissioner of Public Works for Ontario, who shall have power to confirm or amend the said by-law by excluding any minor municipality or any section thereof therefrom, and the decision of any two of them shall be final, 45 and the by-law so confirmed or amended shall thereupon, at the option of the railway company, be submitted by the council to the duly qualified voters, and in case the by-law is confirmed by the arbitrators, the expense *of the reference* shall be borne by the petitioners against the same ; but if amended, 50 then by the railway company or the county, as the arbitrators may order.

Minor municipality, meaning of.

28. The term "minor municipality" shall be construed to mean any town not separated from the municipal county, township, or incorporated village situate in the county muni- 55 cipality.

29. Before any such by-law is submitted, the railway company shall, if required, deposit with the treasurer of the municipality, a sum sufficient to pay the expenses to be incurred in submitting said by-law. Deposit for expenses.

5   **30.** In case the by-law submitted be approved of and carried in accordance with the provisions of the law in that behalf, then within four weeks after the date of such voting, the municipal council which submitted the same shall read the said by-law a third time, and pass the same. If by-law carried, council to pass same.

10   **31.** Within one month after the passing of such by-law, the said council and the mayor, warden, reeve, or other head, or other officers thereof, shall issue or dispose of the debentures provided for by the by-law, and deliver the same duly executed to the trustees appointed, or to be appointed under this Act. And issue debentures

15   **32.** In case any such loan, guarantee or bonus be so granted by a portion of a township municipality, the rate to be levied for payment of the debentures issued therefor, and the interest thereon, shall be assessed and levied upon such portion only of such municipality. Levying rate on portions of municipality.

20   **33.** The provisions of *The Consolidated Municipal Act, 1883*, and the amendments thereto, so far as the same are not inconsistent with this Act, shall apply to any by-law so passed by or for a portion of a township municipality, to the same extent as if the same had been passed by or for the whole 25 municipality. Application of Municipal Act as to by-law.

34. The councils for all corporations that may grant aid by way of bonus to the said company may, by resolution or by-law, extend the time for the commencement of the work beyond that stipulated for in the by-law or by-laws granting 30 such aid from time to time: Provided that no such extension shall be for a longer period than one year. Extension of time for commencement.

35. It shall and may be lawful for the council of any municipality that may grant aid by way of bonus to the said company, by resolution or by-law, to extend the time for the com-35 pletion of the works, on the completion of which the said company would be entitled to such bonus, from time to time : Provided that no such extension shall be for a longer period than one year at a time. Extension of time for completion.

36. Any municipality or portion of a township municipality 40 interested in the construction of the road of the said company, may grant aid by way of bonus to the said company towards the construction of such road, notwithstanding that such aid may increase the municipal taxation of such municipality or portion thereof, beyond what is allowed by law : Provided that 45 such aid shall not require the levying of a greater aggregate annual rate for all purposes, exclusive of school rates, than three cents in the dollar upon the value of the ratable property therein. Rate not exceeding three cents in the dollar valid.
Proviso.

37. It shall be lawful for the corporation of any municipality, through any part of which the railway of the said 50 company passes or is situated, by by-law expressly passed for that purpose, to exempt the company and its property within Exemption from taxation.

such municipality, either in whole or in part, from municipal assessment or taxation, or to agree to a certain sum per annum or otherwise in gross, or by way of commutation or composition for payment, or in lieu of all or any municipal rates or assessments to be imposed by such municipal corporation, and 5 for such term of years as such municipal corporation may deem expedient, not exceeding twenty-one years, and no such by-law shall be repealed unless in conformity with a condition contained therein.

Grants of land.

38. Any municipality through which the said railway may 10 pass or is situate, is empowered to grant by way of gift to the said company, any lands belonging to such municipality or over which it may have control, which may be required for right of way, station grounds or other purposes connected with the running or traffic of the said railway ; and the said 15 railway company shall have power to accept gifts of land from any government, or any person or body politic or corporate, and shall have power to sell or otherwise dispose of the same for the benefit of the said company.

Trustees of debentures.

39. Whenever any municipality or portion of a township 20 municipality shall grant aid by way of bonus or gift to the railway company, the debentures therefor, shall within six months after the passing of the by-law authorizing the same, be delivered to three trustees to be named, one by the Lieut.-Governor in Council, one by the said company, and one by the 25 majority of the heads of the municipalities which have granted bonuses, or in case of only one municipality granting a bonus, then by the head of such municipality, all the trustees to be residents of the province of Ontario : Provided that if the said

Proviso.

heads of the municipalities, or head of the said municipality, 30 shall refuse or neglect to name such trustee within one month after notice in writing of the appointment of the company's trustee, or if the Lieutenant-Governor in Council shall omit to name such trustee within one month after notice in writing to him of the appointment of the other trustees, then in either case 35 the company shall be at liberty to name such other trustee or trustees. Any of the said trustees may be removed and a new trustee appointed in his place at any time by the Lieutenant-Governor in Council, and in case any trustee dies or resigns his trust, or goes to live out of the province of Ontario, or other- 40 wise becomes incapable to act, his trusteeship shall become vacant and a new trustee may be appointed by the Lieutenant-Governor in Council.

Trusts of proceeds of debentures.

40. The said trustees shall receive the said debentures or bonds in trust, (firstly) under the directions of the company, 45 but subject to the conditions of the by-law in relation thereto, as to time or manner to convert the same into money or otherwise dispose of them ; secondly, to deposit the debentures or amount realized from the sale in some chartered bank having an office in the city of Toronto, in the name of "The Southern 50 Central Railway Company Municipal Trust Account," and to pay the same out to the said company from time to time as the said company becomes entitled thereto, under the conditions of the by-law granting the said bonus, and on the certificate of

the chief engineer of the said railway for the time being, in
the form set out in schedule B, hereto, or to the like effect,
which certificate shall set forth that the conditions of the by-
law have been complied with, and is to be attached to the
5 cheque or order drawn by the said trustees for such payment
or delivery of debentures, and such engineer shall not wrongfully grant any such certificate, under a penalty of $500,
recoverable in any court of competent jurisdiction, by any
person who may sue therefor.

10 **41.** The trustees shall be entitled to their reasonable fees Fees to
.and charges from said trust fund, and the act of any two of Trustees.
such trustees shall be as valid and binding as if the three had
agreed.

42. It shall and may be lawful for any municipality through Right to use
15 which the said railway passes, and having jurisdiction in the highways.
premises, to pass a by-law or by-laws empowering the company
to make their road and lay their rails along any of the highways within such municipality, and whether or not the same
be in the possession of or under the control of any joint stock
20 company; and if such highway be either in the possession of
or under the control of any joint stock company, then also with
the assent of such company; and it shall and may be lawful
for the company to enter into and perform any such agreement
as they may from time to time deem expedient, with any
25 municipality, corporation or person, for the construction or for
the maintenance and repair of gravel or other public roads
leading to the said railway.

43. The said company shall have the power of closing up Closing roads
any road or highway crossing through any of their station
30 grounds, provided the said company shall have the consent of
the municipality in which the road is situated, by a by-law
passed for that purpose, and provided a road adjacent thereto
and convenient for the public, be provided in lieu of any such
closed road.

35 **44.** The company shall have the right, on and after the 15th Power to erect
day of November in each year, to enter into and upon any snow-fences.
lands of Her Majesty, or into or upon any lands of any corporation or person whatsoever, lying along the route or line of
said railway, and to erect and maintain snow fences thereon,
40 subject to the payment of such damages (if any) as may be
hereafter established in the manner provided by law, in respect
of such railway, to have been actually suffered: Provided Proviso.
always that any such snow fences so erected shall be removed
on or before the 1st day of April following.

45 **45.** The said company may also construct a telephone line Telephone and
and an electric telegraph line in connection with their railway, telegraph
and for the purpose of constructing, working and protecting lines.
the said telephone and telegraph lines. the powers conferred
.upon telegraph companies by *The Act respecting Electric*
50 *Telegraph Companies* (chapter 151 of The Revised Statutes of
Ontario), are hereby conferred upon the said company.

Power to contract for construction and equipment of railway. **46.** It shall be lawful for the directors to enter into a contract or contracts with any individual or association of individuals for the construction or equipment of the line or any portion thereof, including or excluding the purchase of the right of way, and to pay therefor either in cash or bonds, or in 5 paid up stock or otherwise, as may be deemed expedient: Provided that no such contract shall be of any force or validity **Proviso.** till approved of by two-thirds of the shareholders present, in person or by proxy, at a meeting specially called for considering the same.

Agreements for use of rolling stock, etc. **47.** It shall be lawful for the directors of the company to 10 enter into agreement with any company or companies (if lawfully authorized to enter into such an agreement), person or persons, for the leasing, hiring or use of any locomotives, carriages, rolling stock and other movable property from such companies or persons, for such time or times, and on such 15 terms as may be agreed on, and also to enter into agreement with any railway company or companies (if so lawfully authorized), for the use by one or more of such contracting companies of the locomotives, carriages, rolling stock and other movable property of the other or others of them, on such terms 20 as to compensation and otherwise as may be agreed upon.

Power to collect back-charges on goods. **48.** The said company shall have power to collect and receive all charges subject to which goods or commodities may come into their possession, and on payment of such back-charges, and without any formal transfer, shall have the same 25 lien for the amount thereof upon such goods or commodities, as the persons to whom such charges were originally due, had upon such goods or commodities while in their possession, and shall be subrogated by such payment in all the rights and remedies of such persons for such charges. 30

Power to make and endorse notes and bills without affixing seal. **49.** The said company shall have power and authority to become parties to promissory notes and bills of exchange for sums not less than $100, and any such promissory note made or endorsed, or any such bill of exchange drawn, accepted or endorsed by the president or vice-president of the company, 35 and countersigned by the secretary, treasurer, or other proper officer of the said company, and under the authority of a quorum of the directors, shall be binding on the said company; and every such promissory note or bill of exchange so made, accepted or endorsed, shall be presumed to have been made, 40 accepted or endorsed with proper authority, until the contrary be shewn; and in no case shall it be necessary to have the seal of the company affixed to such promissory note or bill of exchange, nor shall the president or vice-president, or the secretary or treasurer, or other officer aforesaid, be individually 45 responsible for the same, unless the said promissory notes or bills of exchange have been issued without the sanction and authority of the board of directors, as herein provided and **Proviso.** enacted: Provided, however, that nothing in this section shall be construed to authorize the said company to issue any note 50 or bill of exchange payable to bearer or intended to be circulated as money, or as the notes or bills of a bank.

50. The directors of the said company, after the sanction of the shareholders shall have first been obtained at any special general meeting to be called from time to time for such purpose, shall have power to issue bonds, made and signed by the
5 president of the said company, and countersigned by the secretary, and under the seal of the said company, for the purpose of raising money for prosecuting the said undertaking ; and such bonds shall, without registration or formal conveyance, be taken and considered to be the first and pre-
10 ferential claims and charges upon the undertaking and the real property of the company, including its rolling stock and equipments then existing, and at any time thereafter acquired; and each holder of the said bonds shall be deemed to be a mortgagee and incumbrancer, *pro rata*, with all the other
15 holders thereof, upon the undertaking and property of the company as aforesaid : Provided, however, that the whole amount of such issue of bonds shall not exceed in all the sum of $20,000 per mile ; and provided that in the event at any time of the interest upon the said bonds remaining unpaid
20 and owing, then, at the next ensuing general annual meeting of the said company, all holders of bonds shall have and possess the same rights, privileges and qualifications for directors and for voting as are attached to shareholders : Provided further, that the bonds and any transfers thereof shall
25 have been first registered in the same manner as is provided for the registration of shares, and it shall be the duty of the secretary of the company to register the same on being required to do so by any holder thereof.

Issue of bonds.

Proviso.

Proviso.

Proviso.

51. All such bonds, debentures and other securities and
30 coupons and interest warrants thereon respectively may be made payable to bearer and transferable by delivery, and any holder of any such securities so made payable to bearer, may sue at law thereon in his own name, and all such bonds, debentures and other securities and coupons and interest
35 warrants thereon respectively may be made payable in lawful money of Canada, or in sterling money of Great Britain, at some place in Canada or London, England, or in the city of New York, in the state of New York, or at all or any of such places.

Form of bonds.

40 **52.** It shall be lawful for the said company to have and keep a duplicate seal for the transaction of such of their business in the United Kingdom of Great Britain and Ireland, or in the United States of America, as the board of directors of the said company may from time to time designate, and the
45 said seal may be used and affixed in all such cases by such officer or officers, agent or agents, as the said directors may by by-law from time to time direct, and any instrument to which the said duplicate seal shall be so affixed, shall be valid and binding upon the said company.

Power to keep duplicate seal.

50 **53.** The company hereby incorporated may, from time to time, for advances of money to be made thereon, mortgage or pledge any bonds or debentures which, under the powers of this Act can be issued for the construction of the railway or otherwise.

Power to mortgage bonds.

Payments in bonds or stock authorized in certain cases.

54. The said provisional directors, or the elected directors, may pay or agree to pay, in paid up stock or in the bonds of the said company, such sums as they may deem expedient, to engineers or contractors, or for right of way or material, plant or rolling stock, and also, when sanctioned by a vote of the 5 majority of shareholders present at any general meeting, for the services of promoters or other persons who may be employed by the directors for the purpose of assisting the directors in the furtherance of the undertaking or purchase of right of way, material, plant or rolling stock, whether such 10 promoters or other persons be provisional directors or not, and any such agreements so made shall be binding on the company.

Power to purchase, etc., wharves, etc.

55. It shall and may be lawful for the company at any point where the railway, or any branch thereof, approaches 15 within two miles of any navigable waters, to purchase and hold as its own absolute property, and for the use of the company, wharves, piers, docks, water lots, water frontages, and lands ; and upon the said water lots, water frontages and lands, and in and over the waters adjoining the same, to build and erect 20 elevators, storehouses, warehouses and engine houses, sheds, wharves, docks, piers and other erections for the use of the company, and the steam and other vessels owned, worked or controlled by the company, or any other steam or other vessels ; and to collect wharfage, storage, and other charges for 25 the use of the same ; and also to erect, build, repair, and maintain all moles, piers, wharves and docks necessary and proper for the protection of such works, and for the accomodation and convenience of vessels entering, leaving, lying, loading and unloading within the same, and to dredge, deepen, and 30 enlarge such works ; and the said wharves, piers, and docks, water lots, water frontages, lands, elevators, storehouses, warehouses, engine houses, sheds and other erections, or any thereof, or any portions thereof, in its discretion to sell, lease, or convey. 35

Power to purchase and work vessels in connection with the railway.

56. It shall and may be lawful for the company to purchase, build, complete, fit out and charter, sell and dispose of, work and control, and keep in repair, steam or other vessels, from time to time to ply on the lakes, rivers and canals of this Province, in connection with the said railway ; and also to 40 make arrangements and agreements with steamboat and vessel proprietors, by chartering or otherwise, to ply on the said lakes, rivers and canals, in connection with the said railway.

Power to construct railway in sections.

57. The said company is hereby authorized and empowered to take and make the surveys and levels of the land through 45 which the said railway is to pass, together with the map or plan thereof, and of its course and direction, and of the lands intended to be passed over and taken therefor, so far as then ascertained. and also the book of reference for the railway, and to deposit the same as required by the clauses of *The Railway* 50 *Act of Ontario*, and amendments thereto, with respect to "plans and surveys," by sections or portions less than the length of the whole railway authorized, of such length as the said company may from time to time see fit, so that no one of such sections or portions shall be less than ten miles in length, 55

and upon such deposit as aforesaid, of the map or plan and
book of reference of any and each of such sections or portions
of the said railway, all and every of the clauses of *The Railway Act of Ontario*, and the amendments thereof applied to,
5 included in, or incorporated with this Act, shall apply and
extend to any and each of such sections or portions of the
said railway as fully and effectually as if the surveys and
levels had been taken and made of the lands through which
the whole of the said railway is to pass, together with the
10 map or plan of the whole thereof, and of its whole course and
direction, and of the lands intended to be passed over and
taken, and the book of reference for the whole of the said
railway had been taken, made, examined, certified and
deposited according to the said clauses of the said *Railway
15 Act of Ontario*, and the amendments thereof, with respect to
" plans and surveys."

58. Whenever it shall be necessary for the purpose of
procuring sufficient land for stations or gravel pits, or for constructing, maintaining, and using the said railway, and in case
20 by purchasing the whole of any parcel or lot of land over
which the railway is to run, the company can obtain the same
at a more reasonable price or to greater advantage than by
purchasing the railway line only, the company may purchase,
hold, use, or enjoy such lands, and also the right of way thereto
25 if the same be separate from their railway, and may sell and
convey the same or part thereof, from time to time, as they
may deem expedient, but the compulsory clauses of *The Railway Act of Ontario* shall not apply to this section.

Power to pur-
chase whole
lots.

59. When stone, gravel, earth, or sand is or are required
30 for the construction or maintenance of said railway, or any
part thereof, the company may, in case they cannot agree with
the owner of the lands on which the same is situated for the
purchase thereof, cause a provincial surveyor to make a map
and description of the property so required, and they shall
35 serve a copy thereof, with their notice of arbitration, as in the
case of acquiring the roadway, and the notice of arbitration, the
award and the tender of compensation shall have the same effect
as in case of arbitration for the roadway; and all the provisions
of *The Railway Act of Ontario* and of this Act, as to the ser-
40 vice of the said notice, arbitration, compensation, deeds, payment of money into Court, the right to sell, the right to convey, and the parties from whom lands may be taken, or who
may sell, shall apply to the subject matter of this section as to
the obtaining of materials as aforesaid, and such proceedings
45 may be had by the said company either for the right to the fee
simple in the land from which said material shall be taken, or
for the right to take materials for any time they shall think
necessary, the notice of arbitration, in case arbitration is resorted
to, to state the interest required.

Acquiring
gravel, etc.,
for construc-
tion and main-
tenance of
railway.

50 **60—(1)** When said gravel, sand, stone, or other material
shall be taken under the preceding section of this Act at a
distance from the line of the railway, the company may lay
down the necessary sidings and tracks over any land which
may intervene between the railway and the lands on which
55 said material shall be found, whatever the distance may be;

Sidings to
gravel pits.

and all the provisions of *The Railway Act of Ontario* and of
this Act, except such as relate to filing plans and publication
of notice, shall apply and may be used and exercised to obtain
the right of way from the railway to the land on which such
materials are situated ; and such right may be so acquired for 5
a term of years, or permanently, as the company may think
proper, and the powers in this and the preceding section may
at all times be exercised and used in all respects after the rail-
is constructed for the purpose of repairing and maintaining
the said railway ;   10

(2) When estimating the damages for the taking of gravel,
stone, or sand, sub-section 8 of section 20 of *The Railway Act
of Ontario* shall not apply.

61. The construction of the said railway shall be com- 15
menced within three years, and the same shall be completed
within five years, after the passing of this Act.

Commence-
ment and
completion of
railway.

SCHEDULE A.

(Section 22.)

Know all men by these presents that 1 (*or* we) [*insert the
name of the vendors*], in consideration of   dollars paid to
me (*or* us) by the Southern Central Railway Company, the receipt whereof is hereby acknowledged, do grant and convey
unto the said company, and I (*or* we) [*insert the name of any
other party or parties*]   in consideration of   dollars
paid to me (or us) by the said company, the receipt whereof is
hereby acknowledged, do grant or release all that certain parcel (*or* those certain parcels *as the case may be*) of land (*describe
the land*) the same having been selected and laid out by the said
company for the purposes of their railway, to hold with the
appurtenances unto the said Southern Central Railway Company, their successors and assigns (*here insert any other clauses,
covenants or conditions required*) and I (*or* we) the wife (*or*
wives) of the said   , do hereby bar my (*or* our)
dower in the said lands.

As witness my (*or* our) hand and seal (*or* hands and seals)
this   day of   A.D. 18

Signed, sealed and delivered }
in the presence of   }   [L.S.]

SCHEDULE B.

(Section 40.)

CHIEF ENGINEER'S CERTIFICATE.

THE SOUTHERN CENTRAL RAILWAY COMPANY'S OFFICE,

Engineer's Department,   A.D. 188

No.

Certificate to be attached to cheques drawn on " The Southern Central Railway Company Municipal Trust Account," given under section   , chapter   of the Acts of the Legislature of Ontario, passed in the year of Her Majesty's reign.

I, *A.B*, Chief Engineer of the Southern Central Railway Company, do hereby certify that the said company has fulfilled the terms and conditions necessary to be fulfilled under the by-law No.   of the township of   (*or* under the agreement dated the   day of   between the corporation of   and the said company) to entitle the said company to receive from the said trust the sum of   (*here set out the terms and conditions, if any, which have been fulfilled.*)

No. 32.

1st Session, 6th Legislature, 50 Vic., 1887.

BILL.

An Act to incorporate the Southern Central Railway Company.

(Re-printed as amended by Railway Committee.)

First Reading, 9th March, 1887.

(Private Bill.)

An Act to authorize the Law Society of Ontario to
admit Eugene Hutchinson Long as a Barrister at
Law.

WHEREAS Eugene Hutchinson Long, of the Village of Preamble.
Waterford, in the County of Norfolk, has by his petition
set forth, that he has for a period of eight years last past been
engaged as a clerk in the office of the clerk of the Second
5 Division Court for said county, and had been for six years
previously in the office of the clerk of the Third Division
Court for the County of Haldimand ; that for the last eight
years he has pursued a course of reading and study in law, but
has been prevented from entering an office and pursuing such
10 a course of study as is usually required of a student at law ;
that for a period of about two years and a half he has read
law under the supervision of a Barrister ; that on the 9th day
of March, 1882, he was duly appointed a Notary Public for the
Province of Ontario, and has for several years devoted himself
15 to the study of the law, and to the practice thereof, so far as
the same could legally be done by one who has not been
admitted as a Solicitor or called to the Bar ; and whereas, in
and by his said petition, the said Eugene Hutchinson Long has
prayed that an Act be passed authorizing the Law Society of
20 Ontario, to call and admit him to the degree of Barrister at
Law, and whereas it is expedient to grant the prayer of said
petitioner ;

Therefore Her Majesty, by and with the advice and consent
of the Legislative Assembly of the Province of Ontario, enacts
25 as follows :—

1. It shall and may be lawful for the Law Society of E. H. Long
Ontario, upon payment of the usual fees chargeable to students may be
at law on final examination, to call and admit the said Eugene barrister
Hutchinson Long to the degree of Barrister at Law, on his under certain
30 passing at any time or times, the usual final examination pre- conditions.
scribed by the rules of the said Law Society, without passing
the primary examination for such degree, or complying with any
other rules and regulations of said Society in that behalf, any
law, usage or custom to the contrary notwithstanding.

BILL.

An Act to authorize the Law Society of
Ontario to admit Eugene Hutchinson
Long as a Barrister at Law.

First Reading,   , 1887.

(Private Bill.)

No. 34.]   **BILL.**   [1887.

An Act to authorize the Township of Howick to
issue debentures.

WHEREAS the corporation of the township of Howick, in
the county of Huron, have by their petition represented
that on the twenty-first day of November, 1887, there will
mature debentures of said corporation to the amount of
5 $8,200 issued under a certain by-law numbered five and
passed on the twentieth · day of November, 1867, for the
purpose of granting a bonus to the Wellington, Grey and
Bruce Railway Company, and that on the thirtieth day of
December, 1891, there will also mature certain other deben-
10 tures of the said corporation to the amount of $11,000 issued
under a certain by-law numbered four, and passed on the
second day of February, 1872, for the purpose of granting a
bonus to the Toronto, Grey and Bruce Railway Company ;
and whereas the said corporation have further represented
15 that funds have not been provided for redeeming the said
debentures and that it would be in their interest to obtain an
Act authorizing the issue of debentures in order to retire the
same ; and whereas it is expedient to grant the prayer of the
said petition ;
20   Therefore Her Majesty, by and with the advice and consent
of the Legislative Assembly of the Province of Ontario, enacts
as follows :—

1. The corporation of the township of Howick, in the Authority to
county of Huron, may pass a by-law or by-laws authorizing pass by-laws
for new deben-
25 the issue of debentures of the said township for a sum not tures.
exceeding in the whole $19,200 to redeem the said outstanding
debentures issued under the aforesaid by-laws; and the corporation may after the redemption of the original debentures Repeal of old
repeal the said by-laws so far as regards the levying of rates by-laws.
·30 imposed by the same for the redemption · of such original
debentures and the payment of the interest of the same.

2. The debentures to be issued under the preceding section New deben-
of this Act shall be made payable at such time or times not tures when and
where payable.
exceeding twenty years after the date thereof, and at such
35 place or places either within or without this province and shall
be for such sums either in sterling or currency not less than
$100 each as the corporation of the said township may by
such by-law or by-laws direct, and the said debentures shall
bear interest at a rate not exceeding six per cent. per annum
40 payable yearly or half-yearly, as by such by-law or by-laws
may be provided.

Power to raise money on new debentures or exchange for old.

3. The corporation of the said township may raise by way of loan upon the credit of the said debentures to be issued under section 1 of this Act a sum of money not exceeding in the whole the sum of $19,200 ; and the treasurer of the said township shall on receiving instructions so to do from the 5 council call in and discharge with the funds raised upon the said debentures, the outstanding debentures mentioned in the preamble to this Act, or may substitute for the said outstanding debentures or any of them, the debentures authorized to be issued under any by-law passed under the provisions of 10 this Act upon such terms as may be agreed on between the corporation and the holders of such outstanding debentures.

Special rate to be levied.

4. The by-law, or by-laws, authorizing the issue of such debentures shall impose a special rate per annum (over and above all other rates to be levied each year) which shall be 15 sufficient to pay the interest on said debentures and to provide a sinking fund for the due payment of the principal of the same when the same shall fall due.

Investment of sinking fund.

5. It shall be the duty of the treasurer of the said corporation by and with the consent and approbation of the council 20 from time to time to invest all moneys raised by special rate, or the sinking fund provided by this Act, or by the by-law, or by-laws, either in the debentures to be issued under this Act or in government securities, municipal debentures or in first mortgages on real estate held and used for farming pur- 25 poses and being the first lien on such real estate, but not to a greater extent than two-thirds of the assessed value of such real estate, or in such manner as the Lieutenant-Governor in council may by general or special order direct, or he may deposit the same in any chartered bank of the Dominion of 30 Canada, or other banking institution that the council may from time to time approve ; and all dividends and interest received on such investments shall be applied to the extinction of the loan authorized to be raised under this Act.

Formalities prescribed by Municipal Acts not required.

6. It shall not be necessary to obtain the assent of the 35 electors of the said township to the passing of any by-law which shall be passed under the provisions of this Act, or to observe the formalities in relation thereto prescribed by *The Consolidated Municipal Act, 1883,* or amendments thereto, and any provisions in the Acts respecting municipal institu- 40 tions in the province of Ontario, which are or may be inconsistent with the provisions of this Act, or any of them, shall not apply to the by-law, or by-laws, to be passed by the said corporation under the provisions of this Act.

Application of proceeds of new debentures.

7. The proceeds of the debentures authorized to be issued 45 by this Act shall be applied to the redemption of the aforesaid outstanding debentures of the said township and for no other purpose whatever.

1st Session, 6th Legislature, 50 Vic, 1887.

BILL.

An Act to authorize the Township of Howick to issue debentures.

First Reading,　　　　　　1887.

(Private Bill.)

Mr. GIBSON.

No. 35.]   **BILL.**   [1887.

An Act to Consolidate the Debt of the City of Guelph and for other purposes.

WHEREAS the corporation of the city of Guelph has Preamble.
incurred debts secured by its debentures amounting to
the sum of $178,000, exclusive of the indebtedness of the city
for public school debentures, and the said corporation has
5 further incurred debts for municipal purposes unsecured by
debentures, and unprovided for, amounting to the sum of
$32,000; and whereas the aggregate rate of two cents in the
dollar on the whole ratable property of the city, will not during the next twenty years, be sufficient to meet the current
10 annual expenses of the city, and such portions of the said
debts as will become due in such years, and the additional rate
·required by By-law 170 hereinafter mentioned; and whereas
the said corporation has by its petition prayed that the said
secured and unsecured debts may be consolidated, and that
15 the corporation may be authorized to issue debentures for that
purpose; and whereas the said corporation did on the thir-
teenth day of December, 1886, pass a by-law after the same
was duly approved of by the ratepayers of the city, entitled
"A By-law to authorize the issue of debentures to the amount
20 of $175,000 for the purpose of paying for shares in the capital
stock and for lending money to the Guelph Junction Railway
Company and to authorize the said subscription of stock and
the said loan," and which said by-law is numbered 170 and no
application has been made to quash the same, but doubts may
25 be raised as to its validity; and whereas the said corporation
has petitioned that for the purpose of removing all doubts as
to the validity of the said by-law the same may be confirmed
and legalized and the debentures and the principal and
interest secured thereby, may be made payable within thirty
30 years instead of twenty years, as in the said by-law provided,
and be made payable either in this province or in Great
Britain, or elsewhere, and may be expressed in sterling money
of Great Britain or currency of Canada as the corporation may
deem expedient; and whereas it is expedient to grant the
35 prayers of the said petition;

Therefore Her Majesty, by and with the advice and consent
of the Legislative Assembly of the Province of Ontario, enacts
as follows :—

1. It shall be lawful for the said corporation of the city of Issue of
40 Guelph from time to time to pass by-laws providing for the debentures for
$210,000
issue of debentures, under their corporate seal, signed by the authorized.
mayor and countersigned by the treasurer for the time being,
in such sums not exceeding $210,000 in the whole, as the said
corporation may from time to time direct, and the principal

sum secured by the said debentures, and the interest accruing thereon, may be payable either in this province or in Great Britain or elsewhere, and may be expressed in sterling money of Great Britain or currency of Canada as the corporation may deem expedient. 5

Power to borrow on or sell debentures. **2.** The corporation of the said city may, for the purpose in section 4 hereof mentioned, raise money by way of loan on the said debentures in this province or in Great Britain or elsewhere, or sell and dispose of said debentures from time to time as they may deem expedient. 10

Payment of debentures and interest. **3.** The said debentures shall be payable in not less than twenty nor more than thirty years from the date thereof, as the said corporation may direct ; coupons shall be attached to the said debentures for the payment of the interest thereon, and such interest shall be payable half-yearly on the first day 15 of the months of January and July in each and every year, at the places mentioned therein and in the coupons attached thereto, and such debentures may bear interest at any rate not exceeding five per cent. per annum.

Application of debentures. **4.** The said debentures and all moneys arising therefrom 20 shall be applied by the said corporation in the redemption of the now outstanding debentures of the city of Guelph, and in the payment of the said unsecured debt of the city, and in no other manner, and for no other purpose whatsoever, and such debentures may be known as the " Consolidated Debt Deben- 25 tures."

Outstandi debentures may be called in. **5.** The treasurer of the said city shall, on receiving instructions from the council so to do, from time to time, but only with the consent of the holders thereof, call in any of the outstanding debentures, and shall discharge the same with the 30 funds raised under the preceding sections of this Act, or may, with the like consent, substitute therefor the said debentures or any of them hereinbefore authorized to be issued, upon such terms as may be agreed upon between the said council and the 35 said holders of the said outstanding debentures.

By laws not to be repealed until debt satisfied. **6.** Any by-law to be passed under the provisions of this Act authorizing the said loan shall not be repealed until the debt created under such by-law and the interest thereon shall be paid and satisfied. 40

7. For payment of the principal of the said debentures to be issued under the preceding sections of this Act, the council shall impose a special rate per annum (over and above and in addition to all other rates to be levied in each year, and over and above all interest to be paid on such debentures) which 45 shall be sufficient to form a sinking fund of one per cent. per annum for that purpose and hereafter it shall not be necessary for the council to enforce the collection of the sinking fund or amounts required to be levied for principal money to pay the said outstanding debentures. 50

Investment of sinking fund. **8.** The said corporation shall have power at any time to invest any moneys standing at the credit of the sinking fund created under this Act in the redemption of the said outstand-

ing debentures of the said city, or in the redemption of the debentures issued under the authority of the preceding sections of this Act, or in government securities, municipal debentures, or in first mortgages on real estate held and used
5 for farming purposes and being the first lien on such real estate, but not to any greater extent than two-thirds of the assessed value of such real estate, or in any other securities authorized by an Act or Acts now or hereafter to be in force in regard to the same, or that may be sanctioned by the
10 Lieutenant-Governor in Council, or may deposit the same in any chartered bank or banks of the Dominion of Canada that the council may from time to time approve.

9. The special rate for the interest and sinking fund for Special rate. payment of the debentures to be issued under the authority
15 of the preceding sections of this Act, shall in each and every year during the continuance of said debentures be inserted in a separate and distinct column on the collectors's roll of the said city, and shall not be included with any other rate or rates.

20 **10.** The debentures issued under the preceding sections of Form of this Act may be in the form contained in the schedule A to debentures and by-laws. this Act, and the by-law or by-laws for the special rate for payment of the interest, and to form a sinking fund for the payment of the said debentures, may be in the form of
25 schedule B to this Act.

11. No irregularity in the form either of the said Irregulations debentures to be issued under the preceding sections of this not to invali date deben-Act or of the by-law authorizing the issuing thereof shall tures. render the same invalid or illegal or be allowed as a defence
30 to any action brought against the said corporation, for the recovery of the amount of said debentures and interest, or any or either of them, or any part thereof.

12. It shall not be necessary to obtain the assent of the Assent of electors of said city to the passing of any by-law under this electors not required.
35 Act, or to observe the formalities in relation thereto prescribed by *The Consolidated Municipal Act, 1883.*

13. Nothing in this Act contained shall be held or taken Indebtedness to discharge the corporation of the city of Guelph from any not discharg-indebtedness or liability which may not be included in the ed. said debt of $210,000.

14. Notwithstanding anything in this Act contained all of Provision as the said now outstanding debentures which are public school to public school deben-debentures, or which have been issued for public school tures. purposes, or which are debentures, for or towards the payment
45 of which the supporters of separate schools or their property in the said city of Guelph are not liable or compellable to be rated or assessed, shall be provided for, retired and paid in all respects, as if this Act had not been passed.

15. The said by-law of the said corporation of the city of By-law 170
50 Guelph numbered 170 and intituled "A By-law to authorize confirmed. the issue of Debentures to the amount of $175,000 for the purpose of paying for shares in the capital stock of and for lending

money to the Guelph Junction Railway Company, and to authorize the said subscriptions of stock and the said loan," is hereby
confirmed and declared to be legal and valid to all intents and
purposes and the debentures to be issued under the said by-
law shall be and the same are hereby declared to be valid, 5
legal and binding upon the corporation of the city of Guelph
and the ratepayers thereof, notwithstanding anything in any
Act or law to the contrary, and such debentures so to be
issued and the principal money secured thereby and the
interest accruing thereon may be made payable either in this 10
province or in Great Britain, or elsewhere, and may be expressed
in sterling money of Great Britain or currency of Canada ;
and the said debentures may be made payable at any time
not more than thirty years from their issue, and the council of
the city of Guelph may pass a by-law, or by-laws, to authorize 15
debentures to be made payable and to amend the said by-law
170 accordingly, and may in such amending by-law or by-laws
settle the specific sum to be raised, levied and collected in each
year during the continuance of the said debentures to be issued
under by-law 170, and any amending by-law by a special rate 20
sufficient therefor on all the ratable property in the said
municipality for the purpose of forming a sinking fund for the
payment of such d;bentures and for the purpose of paying the
interest thereon, the same to be substituted for the specific
annual sums appointed to be raised under the said by- 25
law 170.

Form of debentures issued under by-law 170. **16.** The debentures issued under the said by-law 170, and
any by-law passed in amendment thereof under this Act, may
be in the form contained in schedule C to this Act, and the
by-law or by-laws in amendment of the said by-law 170 to be 30
passed under the authority of this Act may be in the form of
schedule D to this Act.

Irregularities not to invalidate debentures. **17.** No irregularity in the form of the said debentures to
be issued under the said by-law 170 or any by-law
amending the same, or in the form of any such by-law, 35
shall render the same invalid or illegal, or be allowed as a
defence to any action brought against the said corporation for
the recovery of the amount of such debentures and interest, or
any or either of them or any part thereof.

Assent of electors not required. **18.** It shall not be necessary to obtain the assent of the 40
electors of said city to the passing of any by-law amending
the said by-law 170 to be passed under the authority of this
Act, or to observe the formalities in relation thereto prescribed
by *The Consolidated Municipal Act, 1883.*

By-laws not to be repealed. **19.** The said by-law 170 and any by-law to be passed 45
amending the same shall not be repealed until the debt
created in and by such by-laws and the interest thereon shall
be paid and satisfied.

Sec. 8 to apply to sinking fund created under by-law 170. **20.** The provisions of section 8 of this Act shall apply to
the investment of any moneys standing at the credit of the 50
sinking fund created under the said by-law 170 and any
by-law amending the same.

SCHEDULE A.

Province of Ontario, City of Guelph Consolidated Debt Debentures.

Under and by virtue of an Act entitled "An Act to consolidate the debt of the city of Guelph and for other purposes" passed in the fiftieth year of Her Majesty's reign and chaptered   the corporation of the city of Guelph promise to pay the bearer   at   the sum of
            on the   day of   one thousand eight hundred and   and the half-yearly coupons for interest thereon hereto attached, as the same shall severally become due.
Dated at Guelph, Ontario, this   day of A.D. 18

SCHEDULE B.

By-law number   to authorize the issue of debentures under the authority of " An Act to consolidate the debt of the city of Guelph and for other purposes," passed in the fiftieth year of Her Majesty's reign and chaptered and to impose a special rate for the payment of the said debentures.
Whereas the said Act authorizes the issue of debentures for the purpose therein mentioned not exceeding the sum of   dollars in the whole, as the corporation of the city of Guelph may direct;
And whereas for the purposes mentioned in the said Act it is necessary and expedient to issue debentures to the extent of   dollars, payable on the day of   with interest thereon at the rate of   per cent. per annum, payable half-yearly according to the coupons to the said debentures attached;
And whereas the said Act requires for payment of the debentures to be issued thereunder that the council shall impose a special rate which shall be sufficient to form a sinking fund of one per cent. over and above all interest to be paid on said debentures, and it will require the sum of   to be raised annually for the said interest and sinking fund;
And whereas the amount of the whole ratable property of the city of Guelph, according to the last revised assessment roll of the said city, being for the year one thousand eight hundred and   was
Therefore the municipal corporation of the city of Guelph hereby enacts as follows :—

1. That debentures under the said Act, and for the purpose therein mentioned, to the extent of the sum of   are hereby authorized and directed to be issued.

2. The said debentures shall have coupons thereto attached for the payment of the interest at the rate of   per cent. per annum, payable half-yearly on the first days of January and July in each year.

3. That for the purpose of forming a sinking fund of one per cent. for the payment of the said debentures and for the interest at the rate aforesaid to become due thereon, the sum of   shall, over and above and in addition to all other sums or rates be raised, levied and collected in each year, upon all ratable property in the said city of Guelph, during the continuance of the debentures or any of them.

This by-law passed in open council this day of   in the year of our Lord one thousand eight hundred and

---

SCHEDULE C.

PROVINCE OF ONTARIO, CITY OF GUELPH RAILWAY DEBENTURE.

Under and by virtue of by-law 170 of the corporation of the city of Guelph and of by-law No.   of the said city passed to amend the said by-law 170 under the authority of "An Act to consolidate the debt of the city of Guelph and for other purposes," passed in the fiftieth year of Her Majesty's reign, chaptered   the corporation of the city of Guelph promise to pay the bearer at   the sum of   on the   day of   one thousand   hundred and   and the half-yearly coupons thereon hereto attached, as the same shall severally become due.

Dated at Guelph, Ontario, this   day of A.D. 18

SCHEDULE D.

BY-LAW No.   TO AMEND BY-LAW 170 OF THE CITY OF GUELPH.

Under and by virtue of "An Act to consolidate the debt of the city of Guelph and other purposes," passed in the fiftieth year of Her Majesty's reign chaptered

The municipal corporation of the city of Guelph hereby enacts as follows :—

1. The debentures to be issued under by-law 170 of the city of Guelph, entitled "A by-law to authorize the issue of debentures to the amount $175,000 for the purpose of paying for shares in the capital stock of and for lending money to the Guelph Junction Railway Company and to authorize the said subscription of stock," and the said loan shall be made payable not more than thirty years from the issue of such debentures and may be made payable in Great Britain or elsewhere, and may be expressed in sterling money of Great Britain or currency of Canada, and section 4 of the said by-law 170 is hereby declared to be amended accordingly.

2. The following is substituted for section No. 6 of the said by-law No. 170 :—

" 6. That for the purpose of forming a sinking fund for the payment of the said debentures the certain specific sum of $.   and for the purpose of paying interest upon the said debt of $175,000, the certain specific sum of $8,750, making together the sum of $, shall be raised, levied and collected in each year during the continuance of the said debentures or any of them by a special rate sufficient therefor on all the ratable property in the said municipality."

This by-law passed in open council this day of   in the year of our Lord one thousand eight hundred and eighty

BILL.

An Act to consolidate the debt of the City of Guelph and for other purposes.

First Reading,　　　　1887.

(Private Bill.)

Mr. GUTHRIE.

TORONTO.
PRINTED BY WARWICK & SONS, 26 AND 28 FRONT ST. W.

No. 36.] **BILL.** [1887.

An Act to amend the Act to incorporate Trinity
Medical School.

WHEREAS by an Act of the Legislature of the Province Preamble.
of Ontario, passed in the fortieth year of Her Majesty's
reign and chaptered 65, certain persons therein named, together
with such other persons as might thereafter become members
5 of the said corporation, were constituted a body corporate and
politic, under the name of "Trinity Medical School," with the
rights, powers and obligations in and by the said Act conferred
and imposed upon the said corporation ; and whereas the said
corporation has by its petition prayed for an Act changing the
10 name of the said corporation, and conferring upon the said
corporation power to purchase, take and hold real and personal
property to a larger amount than the amount limited by the
said Act, and for other purposes ; and whereas it is expedient
to grant the prayer of the said petition ;
15   Therefore Her Majesty, by and with the advice and consent
of the Legislative Assembly of the Province of Ontario, enacts
as follows :—

1. Sections 2, 4, 6, 11, 12 and 13 of the said Act are hereby 40 V. c. 65, ss.
amended by striking out the word "School" wherever the 2, 4, 6, 11-13
20 same occurs therein and inserting instead thereof the word amended.
"College."

2. Section 1 of the said Act is hereby further amended by 40 V. c. 65, s.
striking out the word "twenty," where the same occurs in the 1, further
last line thereof and inserting instead thereof the words "two amended.
25 hundred."

3. Section 4 of the said Act is hereby amended by striking 40 V. c. 65, s.
out of the fourth line from the end of the said section the 4, amended.
words "not including mortgages."

4. The said corporation shall, in addition to the powers con- Power to con-
30 ferred by the said Act have power to pass by-laws from time fer degrees:
to time prescribing regulations and conditions, including the
completion of such courses of study, the passing of such examinations, and the payment of such fees as the said corporation
may deem proper for the admission to degrees in medicine,
35 surgery, and midwifery of, and to admit to the said degrees
such persons, whether graduates or not, as shall have fully
completed the Curriculum of the said Trinity Medical College,
or of any other university, college, or medical school, which
may from time to time be designated in a by-law of the said
40 corporation to be passed for that purpose, and shall have complied with the said by-laws, regulations and conditions.

No. 36.

1st Session, 6th Legislature, 50 Vic., 1887.

BILL.

An Act to amend the Act to incorporate Trinity Medical School.

First Reading, _____ 1887.

(Private Bill.)

BILL.

An Act vesting certain lands in the Corporation of
the Town of Thorold for the purposes of a Cemetery.

WHEREAS on the 18th day of March, 1802, Jacob Ball, the Preamble.
younger, of the township of Thorold, then in the county
of Lincoln and district of Niagara, did grant unto Peter Lampman, Adam Hutt and George Miller, and to their successors in
5 office, for and on behalf of the whole inhabitants of said county,
the lands and premises therein described for the use of said
inhabitants as a burying ground, and for the purpose of having
a church or chapel for the use of the Lutheran and Presbyter-
ian persuasion, a school house, parsonage and burying ground
10 on said land, and for no other purpose or use whatsoever,
reserving to the said Jacob Ball and his heirs the free liberty
of burying any of their family in said tract of land for ever ;
and whereas the said Peter Lampman and George Miller,
trustees as aforesaid, departed this life, leaving the said Adam
15 Hutt the sole surviving trustee ; and whereas the said Adam
Hutt, on the 6th day of October, 1836, did grant and convey
unto Peter Lampman, George Hutt and Robert E. Burns, in
said instrument named as trustees in the place and stead of the
said Peter Lampman and George Miller, deceased, and of the
20 said Adam Hutt, the lands and premises in said first referred
to deed, save and except one acre thereof in said last mentioned
deed described, to have and to hold the same upon the trusts
set forth in said first referred to deed, and also set forth in last
mentioned conveyance ; and whereas on the 11th day of May,
25 1864, George Hutt, the sole surviving trustee appointed in and
by the last hereinbefore referred to deed, by indenture bearing
that date, duly nominated, constituted and appointed George
Keefer and Frederick Lampman to hold said lands in common
with him as joint trustees for the purpose of fulfilling the trusts
30 in said before referred to deeds particularly set forth ; and
whereas on the 9th day of May, 1873, Thomas Brock Fuller, of
the city of Toronto, by deed, in which Cynthia Fuller, his
wife, joined for the purpose of barring her dower, granted and
conveyed unto George Keefer and Frederick Lampman, two of
35 the trustees in the lastly hereinbefore referred to deed mentioned, their co-trustee, George Hutt, having some time before
that departed this life without having appointed any other
person as his successor in office, the lands and premises therein
described, to hold the said lands as trustees of the German
40 church burial ground ; and whereas on the 6th day of January,
1880, the said George Keefer and Frederick Lampman, the
trustees in the conveyance from the said Thomas Brock Fuller, lastly before referred to, and the sole surviving trustees in
the conveyance from George Hutt hereinbefore referred to, by
45 indenture, granted and conveyed the lands and premises

described as follows :—All and singular those certain parcels
or tracts of land and premises situate, lying and being in the
town of Thorold, in the county of Welland, described as follows : Firstly, commencing at the south-east corner of lot number six of the township of Thorold; thence west four chains and   5
seventeen links ; thence north twelve chains ; thence east four
chains and seventeen links ; and thence south twelve chains to
the place of beginning. Secondly, commencing in the eastern
limit of said lot at a point twelve chains north from the south-
east corner of said lot; thence north forty links along the eastern   10
limit of said lot ; thence west four chains and seventeen links ;
thence south parallel with the eastern limit of said lot forty
links ; thence east four chains and seventeen links to the place
of beginning. Thirdly, commencing at a stone planted at the
south-east corner of said lot; thence east one chain ; thence   15
north twelve chains and fifty links ; thence west one chain ; and
thence south twelve chains and fifty links to the place of
beginning ; said lands being composed of part of said lot number six and of part of the original allowance for road lying on
the east side of said lot, excepting from said lands that portion   20
thereof heretofore conveyed to the Minister of Public Works of
Canada ; unto the corporation of the town of Thorold their
successors and assigns, to hold the same subject to the reservations and trusts upon which the said lands were held by the
said Frederick Lampman and George Keefer ; and whereas the   25
said lands have been for many years used by the citizens of the
town of Thorold exclusively as a public burying ground ; and
whereas the corporation of said town of Thorold, have by their
petition, set forth that the lands hereinbefore particularly
described, were conveyed to them upon the trusts hereinbefore   30
set forth, and that said lands are now held by said corporation
under the conveyances hereinbefore referred to, and have been
used as a burying ground for all classes of citizens of said town,
and that doubt has been cast upon the title to said lands of
said corporation, and upon the right of said corporation to use   35
said lands for the purposes of a general burying ground or
cemetery in said town, and the said corporation has prayed
that its title to said lands under such conveyances may be confirmed and made valid, and that the said corporation may be
empowered to use said lands as a general burying ground or   40
cemetery for the sole benefit of the inhabitants of the said
town of Thorold, and that the said corporation may be author-
izud and empowered to pass all such by-laws and regulations
as may be found necessary ; and whereas it is expedient to
grant the prayer of the said petition ;   45
 Therefore Her Majesty, by and with the advice and consent
of the Legislative Assembly of the Province of Ontario, enacts
as follows :—

Title to lands   **1.** The title of the said corporation of the town of Thorold
confirmed.   to the lands and premises hereinbefore particularly set forth   50
and described, is hereby confirmed and made valid, and the
said lands are hereby vested in the said corporation of said
town of Thorold and its successors, and assigns, to be held by
the said corporation, in trust for the inhabitants of said town,
for their sole and exclusive use as a cemetery or burying   55
ground,

2. The said corporation of said town of Thorold, are hereby **Power to pass** empowered from time to time to pass all by-laws and regula- **by-laws.** tions which may be found necessary and proper for the carrying out of the purposes of this Act, and for the successful
5 government of said cemetery or burying ground: Provided always that such by-laws shall not be inconsistent with law, or contrary to the spirit of this Act.

BILL.

An Act vesting certain lands in the corporation of the Town of Thorold for the purposes of a Cemetery.

First Reading,   1887.

(Private Bill.)

BILL.

An Act to extend the limits of the Town of Waterloo.

WHEREAS the council of the town of Waterloo, in the county of Waterloo and nearly all of the owners of the adjacent territory forming part of the town of Berlin within the boundaries hereinafter mentioned, have by their petitions
5 represented that the extension of the present limits of the said town of Waterloo by setting off and attaching to the said town of Waterloo that portion of the adjacent town of Berlin as hereinafter in this Act more particularly described, would promote its future progress and prosperity, and overcome certain
10 inconveniences in connection with assessments and the registration of title deeds, and enable its inhabitants to carry out improvements they are desirous of making on said territory; and whereas it is expedient to grant the prayer of the said petition;
15   Therefore Her Majesty, by and with the advice and consent of the Legislative Assembly of the Province of Ontario, enacts as follows:— *Preamble.*

1. That portion of the town of Berlin in the county of Waterloo, that is to say all that portion of the survey of John
20 Hoffman, as laid down on the registered plan of Berlin lying on the south side of King Street, excepting lot number two hundred and eighty-six (286) of said survey, and also that part of the south half of township lot fifteen (15) of the German Company Tract, which lies to the south of Park Street on said
25 survey, and which is not included in said survey, and being coloured orange on said registered plan, and thereon said to contain thirty-eight acres, three roods and thirty-six perches, and also the several parcels of land and lots on the north side of said King Street, Berlin, lying west of a line to be made by pro-
30 ducing in a direct line to King Street and northerly to the division line between the said towns, the division line between the Berlin and Waterloo cemeteries shall, notwithstanding anything contained in the proclamation of May the twentieth, one thousand eight hundred and seventy, under which
35 the said town of Berlin was incorporated, from and after the passing of this Act be added to the limits and form part of the said town of Waterloo, subject to the same provisions of law as if such addition had been made under *The Consolidated Municipal Act, 1883,* and amendments thereto, except so far
40 as the same are inconsistent with the provisions of this Act. *Part of town of Berlin added to town of Waterloo.*

2. That portion of the said hereinbefore described territory lying on the south side of King Sreet shall form a part of the south ward of the said town of Waterloo, and that portion of such territory on the north side of said King Street shall form
45 a part of the east ward of the said town of Waterloo, and the *Wards.*

limits of the said wards, as defined and set forth in the Act of incorporation of the said town, passed in the thirty-ninth year of Her Majesty's reign, and chaptered 45, are hereby changed accordingly.

Liability for debts of town of Berlin.

3. Nothing in this Act contained shall exempt any part of 5 the lands so detached as aforesaid from liability for the debts and obligations contracted before the passing of this Act by the said town of Berlin.

Adjustment of liabilities.

4. The said debts and liabilities shall be adjusted between the said towns of Waterloo and Berlin in manner and form as 10 provided in such cases in *The Consolidated Municipal Act, 1883,* and amendments thereto: Provided, however, that the said territory so detached and added as aforesaid, and that portion of the town of Berlin lying north of the Grand Trunk Railway, and west of the Waterloo branch of the said railway, 15 shall constitute a school district for the present ward school in the west ward of Berlin, and there shall be levied and collected upon the taxable property in the said detached territory in Waterloo, and in the aforesaid portion of Berlin lying north of the Grand Trunk Railway and west of the Waterloo branch of 20 the said railway, the moneys required from time to time for the support and maintenence of the said ward school, in the proportion which the assessment of the part of such district within the said respective municipalties, bears to the whole assessment of such district as equalized under section 91 of 25 *The Public Schools Act, 1885.*

BILL.

An Act to extend the limits of the Town of
Waterloo.

First Reading,   1887.

(Private Bill.)

BILL.

An Act to Incorporate the Town of Gravenhurst.

WHEREAS the village of Gravenhurst in the District of Preamble.
Muskoka is rapidly increasing in population and is
likely to become an important business centre; and whereas
the council of the said village have by their petition repre-
5 sented that the incorporation of the said village as a town
would promote its future progress and prosperity and enable
its inhabitants to make suitable regulations for the protection
and improvement of property, and that a portion of the township of Muskoka should be included in the said town; and
10 whereas it is expedient to grant the prayer of the said
petition;

Therefore Her Majesty, by and with the advice and consent
of the Legislative Assembly of the Province of Ontario, enacts
as follows :—

15 **1.** On and after the passing of this Act, the said village of Town incor-
Gravenhurst shall be and is hereby constituted a corporation, porated.
or body politic, under the name of the Corporation of the
Town of Gravenhurst, and shall enjoy and have all the rights,
powers and privileges enjoyed and exercised by incorporated
20 towns in the Province of Ontario under the existing municipal
laws of the said Province.

2. The said town of Gravenhurst shall comprise and consist Limits of
of the lands lying within the limits described as follows, that town.
is to say :—Commencing at the centre of Brock street, at the
25 water's edge of Gull Lake, now in the village of Gravenhurst;
thence south-easterly following the edge of Gull Lake until
the line between lots 6 and 7, on the east side of the Muskoka
road, crosses the said edge; thence westerly along the said line
between lots 6 and 7, east of the Muskoka road, to a point
30 thereon twelve chains east of the east limit of the said Muskoka
road; thence on a line produced southerly averaging twelve
chains east of the said Muskoka road to the blind line between
lots 4 and 5 on the east of the Muskoka road; thence westerly
along the same blind line between four and five to a point
35 eighteen chains west of the west limit of the Muskoka road;
thence northerly in a line produced eighteen chains west of
the said road, until such line crosses the western limit of the
Northern Railway Company's lands on lot 7 west of the road;
thence north-westerly along the said western limit of the
40 Railway Company's lands to the blind line between lots 7 and 8
(originally called Victoria street now Sharpe street west);
thence westerly along the said blind line between lots 7 and 8
to the western limit thereof; thence to a point to where the
south limit of lot 23, in the fourth concession, crosses the said

Musquash road to the blind line between lot 27 on the fifth concession and lot 27 on the sixth concession, township of Muskoka; thence easterly along said blind line, between lots 27 on the fifth and sixth concessions to a point 10 chains and 50 links south of the water edge; thence in a line north forty- 5 four degrees thirty minutes east to the water's edge of South Bay, Lake Muskoka; thence following the said water's edge easterly and southerly as the same doth wind unto the place of beginning.

Acts respect-ing municipal institutions to apply.

4. Except as otherwise provided by this Act the provisions 10 of *The Consolidated Municipal Act, 1883,* and any Act amending the same, with regard to matters consequent upon the formation of new corporations, shall apply to the said town of Gravenhurst in the same manner as they would have been applicable had the said village of Gravenhurst been 15 erected into a town under the provisions of the said Acts.

Nomination for first elec-tion.

5. On the second Monday after the passing of this Act it shall be lawful for Thomas Johnson, or the village clerk for the time being, who is hereby appointed the returning officer, to hold the nomination for the first election of mayor, reeve 20 and councillors at the Town Hall, in the said town of Graven-hurst, at the hour of noon, and he shall preside at the said nomination, or in case of his absence the electors present shall choose from among themselves a chairman to preside at the said nomination, and such chairman shall have all the powers 25 of returning officer, and the polling for the said election (if necessary) shall be held on the same day of the week in the week next following the said nomination, and the returning officer or chairman shall at the said nomination publicly announce the place in each ward at which the polling shall 30 take place.

Deputy re-turning officers.

6. The said returning officer shall by his warrant appoint a deputy-returning officer for each of the wards into which the town is divided and such returning officer, and each deputy-returning officer shall, before holding the said election, 35 take the oath or affirmation required by law and shall respectively be subject to all the provisions of the municipal laws of Ontario, applicable to returning officers at elections in towns, in so far as the same do not conflict with this Act, and the said returning officer shall have all the powers and per- 40 form all the duties devolving on town clerks with respect to municipal elections in towns.

Clerk of town-ship of Muskoka to furnish copy of assessment roll.

7. The clerk of the said township of Muskoka shall upon demand made upon him by the said returning officer, or by the chairman hereinbefore mentioned, at once furnish such 45 returning officer or chairman with a certified copy of so much of the last revised assessment roll for the said township as may be required to ascertain the names of the persons entitled to vote in each of the said wards at the first election, and the said returning officer shall furnish each of the said deputies 50 with a true copy of so much of the said roll as relates to the names of electors entitled to vote in each of the said wards' respectively and each such copy shall be verified on oath.

8. The council of the said town to be elected in manner Council.
aforesaid shall consist of the mayor, who shall be the head
thereof, a reeve and six councillors, two councillors being
elected for each ward ; and they shall be organized as a council
5 on the same day of the week next following the week of the
polling, or if there be no polling on the same day of the week
next following the week of the nomination ; and subsequent
elections, shall be held in the same manner as in towns incorporated under the provisions of *The Consolidated Municipal*
10 *Act, 1883,* and any Act amending the same, and the said
council and their successors in office shall have, use, exercise
and enjoy all the powers and privileges vested by the said
municipal laws in town councils and shall be subject to all the
liabilities and duties imposed by the said municipal laws on
15 such councils.

9. The several persons who shall be elected or appointed Oaths of office
under this Act shall take the declarations of office and qualifi- tion.
cation now required by the municipal laws of Ontario to be
taken by persons elected or appointed to like offices in towns.

20 **10.** At the first election of mayor, reeve and councillors for Qualification
the said town of Gravenhurst the qualification of electors and tion.
that of officers required to qualify shall be the same as that
required in villages by the municipal law of Ontario.

11. The expenses of obtaining this Act and of furnishing Expenses of
25 any documents, copies of papers, writings, deeds, or any matter Act.
whatsoever required by the clerk or other officer of the said
town, or otherwise, shall be borne by the said town and paid
by it to any party that may be entitled thereto.

12. All by-laws and municipal regulations which are in By-laws
30 force in the village of Gravenhurst shall continue and be in continued.
force as if they had been passed by the corporation of the
town of Gravenhurst, and shall extend to and have full effect
within the limits of the town hereby incorporated.

13. The property, assets, debts, liabilities and obligations Property and
35 of the village of Gravenhurst shall belong to and be assumed obligations.
and paid by the corporation of the town of Gravenhurst.

No 39.

1st Session, 6th Legislature, 50 Vic., 1887.

BILL.

An Act to incorporate the Town of Gravenhurst.

First Reading, 1887.

(Private Bill.)

An Act to Incorporate the Town of Gravenhurst.

WHEREAS the village of Gravenhurst in the District of Preamble.
Muskoka is rapidly increasing in population and is
likely to become an important business centre; and whereas
the council of the said village have by their petition repre-
5 sented that the incorporation of the said village as a town
would promote its future progress and prosperity and enable
its inhabitants to make suitable regulations for the protection
and improvement of property, and that a portion of the township of Muskoka should be included in the said town; and
10 whereas it is expedient to grant the prayer of the said
petition;

Therefore Her Majesty, by and with the advice and consent
of the Legislative Assembly of the Province of Ontario, enacts
as follows :—

15 **1.** On and after the passing of this Act, the said village of Town incor-
Gravenhurst shall be and is hereby constituted a corporation, porated.
or body politic, under the name of the Corporation of the
Town of Gravenhurst, and shall enjoy and have all the rights,
powers and privileges enjoyed and exercised by incorporated
20 towns in the Province of Ontario under the existing municipal
laws of the said Province.

2. The said town of Gravenhurst shall comprise and consist Limits of
of the lands lying within the limits described as follows, that town.
is to say :—Commencing at the centre of Brock street, at the
25 water's edge of Gull Lake, now in the village of Gravenhurst;
thence south-easterly following the edge of Gull Lake until
the line between lots 6 and 7, on the east side of the Muskoka
road, crosses the said edge; thence westerly along the said line
between lots 6 and 7, east of the Muskoka road, to a point
30 thereon twelve chains east of the east limit of the said Muskoka
road; thence on a line produced southerly averaging twelve
chains east of the said Muskoka road to the blind line between
lots 4 and 5 on the east of the Muskoka road; thence westerly
along the same blind line between four and five to a point
35 eighteen chains west of the west limit of the Muskoka road;
thence northerly in a line produced eighteen chains west of
the said road, until such line crosses the western limit of the
Northern Railway Company's lands on lot 7 west of the road;
thence north-westerly along the said western limit of the
40 Railway Company's lands to the blind line between lots 7 and 8
(originally called Victoria street now Sharpe street west);
thence westerly along the said blind line between lots 7 and 8
to the western limit thereof; thence to a point where the
south limit of lot 23, in the fourth concession, crosses the said

line; thence westerly on the blind line between concessions
3 and 4, until the same crosses the old concession road between
lots 25 and 26 on the fourth concession; thence along the
centre of the old concession road between lots 25 and 26 on
the fourth concession, to a point about six chains south of the 5
water's edge of the South Bay of Lake Muskoka; thence north
sixty-three degrees west for the distance of two hundred and
sixty-five feet; thence north fifty-three degrees thirty minutes
west to the centre of the road between concessions 4 and 5 in
the township of Muskoka; thence westerly along the centre 10
of the said road between *concessions* four and five to the centre
of the Musquash road; thence along the said centre of the
said Musquash road to the blind line between lot 27, on the
fifth concession, and lot 27, on the sixth concession, of the
township of Muskoka; then easterly along the said blind line 15
between the lots 27, on the fifth and sixth concessions, to a
point ten chains and fifty links *west* of the water's edge;
thence in a line north forty-four degrees thirty minutes east
to the water's edge of South Bay, Lake Muskoka; thence
following the said water's edge easterly and southerly, as 20
the same doth wind, to the centre of the concession line
between lot 10, west of the Muskoka road, and lot 23, on the
fifth concession of the township of Muskoka; then easterly
along the said centre of road between lot 10, west of Muskoka
road, and lots 23, 22 and 21, on the fifth concession of the 25
township of Muskoka, to the centre of the road between said
lot 10 west of the road and lot 10 east of the road; thence
southerly along the said centre of the road between lots 10,
west and east of the road, for a distance of eighteen chains;
thence north forty-two degrees thirty-two minutes east being 30
the centre of the old Bracebridge or Muskoka road for the
distance of about thirteen chains; thence southerly south
thirteen degrees thirty minutes east to the centre of the
new Bracebridge road; then easterly along said centre of the
new Bracebridge road to a point eighteen chains east of the 35
centre stake 🖝 east of the stake at the north-west corner
of 🖝 lot 9, on the east side of the Muskoka road; thence
south in a line eighteen chains east of the said road to the
waters of Gull Lake; thence along the westerly shores of Gull
Lake to the place of beginning, 🖝 and also th highway con- 40
necting the west and south wards which shall be maintained
and kept in repair by the town. 🖝

Wards.   3. The said town shall be divided into three wards, to be
called respectively the "South," "North" and "West" wards
which said several wards shall be respectively composed and 45
bounded as follows:—

The "South Ward" shall comprise all that part of the said
town which is bounded as follows:—Commencing at the
centre of Brock street at the water's edge of Gull Lake in the
village of Gravenhurst, thence south-easterly following the
edge of Gull Lake until the line between lots 6 and 7, east 50
side of Muskoka road crosses the said edge; thence westerly
along the said line between lots 6 and 7 east of Muskoka road
to a point thereon twelve chains east of the east limit of the
said Muskoka road; thence in a line produced southerly
averaging twelve chains east of the said Muskoka road to the 55
blind line between lots 4 and 5 on the east of Muskoka road;

thence westerly along the said blind line between lots 4 and 5 to a point eighteen chains west of the west limit of the said Muskoka road; thence northerly in a line eighteen chains west of said road until such line crosses the western limit of the 5 Northern Railway Company's lands on lot 7 west of the road; thence north-westerly along the said western limit of Railway Company's lands to the blind line between lots 7 and 8 (originally called Victoria street); thence westerly along the said blind line between lots 7 and 8 to the western limit 10 thereof; thence along the western limit or blind line of lot 8 to a point about ten chains north of the south-west corner of said lot 8, being where a line produced westerly *south* seventy-six degrees thirty minutes west from the centre of Brock street at Gull Lake would cross said westerly limit of lot 8 west of 15 Muskoka road: thence easterly on the said line produced north seventy-six degrees thirty minutes east being the centre of Bay street east extended, and of Brock street, to the place of beginning.

The "North Ward" shall comprise all that part of the said 20 town which is bounded as follows:—Commencing at the same point in the centre of Brock street on Gull Lake as the South Ward; thence westerly south seventy-six degrees thirty minutes west through the centre of Brock and Bay streets east extended to the blind line or west limit of lot 8 west of Mus- 25 koka road; thence along the said west limit of lot 8 to the water's edge; thence north-easterly and north-westerly following the said water's edge of South Bay, Lake Mus- koka, to the centre of the concession line between lot 10 west of Muskoka road and lots 21, 22, and 23, on concession 30 V of the township of Muskoka; thence easterly along said centre of road to the centre of the road between the said lot 10 west of road and lot 10 east of road, thence southerly for the distance of about eighteen chains, thence north forty-two degrees thirty minutes east, being the centre of the old Brace- 35 bridge or Muskoka road for the distance of about thirteen chains; thence southerly south thirteen degrees thirty minutes east to the centre of the new Bracebridge road; thence easterly along said centre of the new Bracebridge road to a point eighteen chains east of the corner stake on lot 9 on the 40 east of Muskoka road; thence south in a line eighteen chains east of the said Muskoka road to the waters of Gull Lake; thence along the westerly shore of Gull Lake to the place of beginning.

The "West Ward" shall comprise all that part of the said town 45 which is bounded as follows:—Commencing at the water's edge of the South Bay, Lake Muskoka, at the line between lot 8 west of Muskoka road and lot 23 in the fourth concession of the township of Muskoka, as originally surveyed; thence south along the westerly limit of lot 8 west of road to the blind·line 50 between concessions 3 and 4; thence west along the said blind line between concessions 3 and 4 until the same strikes the centre of the old concession road between lots 25 and 26 on the fourth concession; thence along the centre of the old road between lots 25 and 26 on the fourth concession to a point 55 about six chains south of the water's edge of said South Bay; thence north sixty-three degrees west for the distance of 265 feet, thence north fifty-three degrees thirty minutes west to the centre of the road between concessions 4 and 5 in

School
trustees.

☞ **15.**—(1) The said returning officer shall at the nomination, provided for in section 5 of this Act, receive nominations for two school trustees for each of said wards, and the elections for such school trustees shall, except so far as is otherwise provided by this Act, be held and conducted in conformity to the 5 provisions of *The Public Schools Act, 1885.*

☞ (2) The first meeting of the board of public school trustees shall be held on the Wednesday of the week next following the week of the polling, or if there be no polling, on the Wednesday of the week next following the week of the nomina- 10 tion at noon, when the board of school trustees for the village of Gravenhurst, and also for school section number seven of the township of Muskoka shall cease to exist, and the said new board shall from the said date have control of school section 15 number seven in the township of Muskoka, and the trustees of the late school board and section shall hand over unto the new board of trustees all moneys and properties belonging to the said schools and section; and the municipal councils and officers shall pay over all moneys that may be due or may be- 20 come payable to the old school board and school section seven unto the new board of trustees.

☞ (3) One of said school trustees for each ward shall remain in office only for the unexpired part of the year 1887, and the other one for each ward until the end of the year 1888, and 25 the length of term for each trustee shall be determined by lot at the first meeting of the new board of trustees.

1st Session, 6th Legislature, 50 Vic, 1887.

BILL.

An Act to incorporate the Town of Gravenhurst.

(*Re-printed as amended by Committee of the Whole House.*)

First Reading, 22nd March, 1887.
Second   "   4th April, 1887.

(Private Bill.)

Mr. MARTER.

TORONTO:
PRINTED BY WARWICK & SONS, 26 AND 28 FRONT ST. W.

BILL.

An Act to Incorporate the Township of Keewatin.

WHEREAS the inhabitants, owners and tenants, in that part Preamble. of the District of Rainy River lying to the west of the second outlet of the Lake of the Woods, have by their petition represented that that part of the said district has a population 5 of upwards of four hundred souls, and that the formation of a new municipality in the said District of Rainy River, by dividing the present municipality of the Township of Rat Portage, in the said district of Rainy River, by setting apart from said municipality all that portion of territory lying to the west 10 of the second outlet of the Lake of the Woods, together with sufficient territory to the westward thereof, for the formation of such municipality to be known as " The Municipality of the Township of Keewatin," would promote the progress and prosperity of the said locality, and is essential for the proper 15 government of said inhabitants, and have prayed for such division and incorporation accordingly, and it is expedient to grant the prayer of such petition;

Therefore Her Majesty, by and with the advice and consent of the Legislative Assembly of the Province of Ontario, 20 enacts as follows :—

1. On and after the passing of this Act the present munici- Incorpora- pality of the township of Rat Portage shall be and is hereby tion. divided by setting apart from the said municipality all that portion of territory lying to the west of the second outlet of 25 the Lake of the Woods, said second outlet being between Tunnel Island and the property of Henry Bulmer, Jr., Esquire, and that out of the territory so set apart, together with two miles of territory immediately to the westward thereof, a new municipality shall be and is hereby formed under the name of the 30 " Township of Keewatin "; and the inhabitants of the said township of Keewatin confined within the boundary aforesaid, shall be and are hereby constituted a body corporate, separate and apart from the township of Rat Portage, in which part of the said property was situate, under the name of " The corpora- 35 tion of the Township of Keewatin," and shall enjoy all such rights, powers and privileges as are now or shall be hereafter conferred upon municipal corporations in the Province of Ontario.

2. The said municipality of the township of Keewatin shall Limits of 40 be contained within the same limits from north to south as is township. the present township of Rat Portage, and shall have as its easterly limit the second outlet of the Lake of the Woods, and as its westerly limit a line drawn north and south two miles west from the former western limit of the township of Rat 45 Portage before its separation, made herein.

Nomination for first election. **3.** Immediately after the passing of this Act it shall be lawful for W. J. MacAulay, Esquire, of the said municipality, who is hereby appointed returning officer, to hold the nomination for the first election of Reeve and four Councillors, and he shall give at least eight days' notice thereof by causing at least ten 5 notices to be posted up in conspicuous places, and one insertion in a newspaper, if any, published in the district of Rainy River, and he shall proceed at such nomination, or in case of his absence, the electors present shall choose from among themselves a chairman, who shall officiate and shall have all the 10 powers of the Returning Officer, and the polling for the said election, in the event of a poll being required, shall be held on the same day of the week in the week next following the said nomination, and the duties of the said Returning Officer shall be the same as those required by law in respect of incorporated 15 townships.

Qualification at first election. **4.** At the first election the qualification of the electors and of the Reeve and Councillors for the said municipality shall be the same as that provided by Sections 6 and 7 of *the Act respecting the Establishment of Municipal Institutions in the 20 Districts of Algoma, Muskoka, Parry Sound, Nipissing and Thunder Bay,* as contained in Chapter 175, of the Revised Statutes of Ontario, and amending Acts.

R. S. O. c. 175, to apply. **5.** The provisions contained in the said *Act respecting the Establishment of Municipal Institutions in the Districts of 25 Algoma, Muskoka, Parry Sound, Nipissing and Thunder Bay,* being Chapter 175, of the Revised Statutes of Ontario, with the amending Acts, are hereby incorporated with this Act, in so far as the same are applicable to the management and government of said municipality, and all provisions in the said 30 Act and amending Acts contained applicable to said municipality are hereby incorporated with this Act, except as herein otherwise provided.

First meeting of council. **6.** The Reeve and Council so to be elected shall hold their first meeting within one month after the date of the election, 35 at a place to be fixed by the Reeve so to be elected.

Application of Acts respecting municipal institutions. **7.** Except as otherwise provided by this Act the provisions of *The Consolidated Municipal Act 1883,* and of all other general Acts respecting municipal institutions with regard to matters consequent on the formation of new corporations and 40 other provisions of the said Acts applicable to incorporated municipalities, shall apply to the municipality of Keewatin, in the same manner as they would have been applicable had the said municipality of Keewatin been incorporated under the provisions of the said Act. 45

Expenses of Act. **8.** The expenses of obtaining this Act and of furnishing any copies of documents, writings, papers, or any matter whatever required in the formation of said municipality or otherwise, shall be borne by the said corporation of Keewatin and paid to any party entitled thereto. 50

1st Session, 6th Legislature, 50 Vic., 1887.

BILL.

An Act to incorporate the Township of Keewatin.

First Reading, 11th March, 1887.

(Private Bill.)

BILL.

An Act relating to the Municipality of Rat Portage.

WHEREAS the Minnesota and Ontario Lumber Com- Preamble.
pany, Messrs. Cameron and Kennedy, and F. T. Bulmer
and Company, mill proprietors, in the Municipality of Rat Portage, in the District of Rainy River, have represented to the Coun-
5 cil of the Municipality of Rat Portage, that the taxation under
the municipal law bears inequitably upon them in view of the
value of their property, and the distance thereof from the
Village of Rat Portage, and an agreement has been arrived at
between the said proprietors and the said municipality,
10 and the said proprietors have prayed that the same may be
given effect to, and it is expedient to grant such relief ;
Therefore Her Majesty, by and with the advice and consent
of the Legislative Assembly of the Province of Ontario, enacts
as follows :—

15 1. The Municipality of Rat Portage, shall for the year Remission of
1887, and for the nine succeeding years thereafter, allow and buildings, etc.,
remit to the Minnesota and Ontario Lumber Company, Messrs. of Minnesota
Cameron and Kennedy, and F. T. Bulmer and Company, their Lumber Com-
respective legal representatives and assigns, in respect of the pany.
20 mill-buildings, machinery and plant belonging to the said
parties respectively, within the said Municipality of Rat Portage,
west of the second outlet of the Lake of the Woods, known as
the Winnipeg River, after the rate of taxation for the year 1887,
and each such succeeding year, from time to time, shall have
25 been settled one-half of the amount of the taxes assessed upon
and leviable against their said property, inclusive of the rate
for debenture debt existing at the time of the passing of this
Act, but exclusive of the taxes for school purposes, which shall
be collected as heretofore.

30 2. During the years aforesaid the logs brought and to be Exemption of
hereafter brought to the said mills of the parties aforesaid, and logs.
the stock manufactured, or which shall be hereafter from time to
time manufactured, from logs to be brought to the said mills
respectively, shall be totally exempted from taxation.

35 3. The said, the Minnesota and Ontario Lumber Com- Exemption
pany, Messrs. Cameron and Kennedy and F. T. Bulmer and from rate for
Company, mill proprietors, aforesaid, shall not be liable to debentures.
assessment in respect of the logs and lumber, and the mill-
buildings, machinery and plant aforesaid, for any rate to be
40 hereafter struck for the purpose of raising money for the payment of debentures, which may hereafter be issued by the
Municipality of Rat Portage, unless the by-law under which
such debentures shall be issued shall have been voted on and

supported by a majority of the ratepayers of the said Municipality of Rat Portage assessed in respect of property west of the said second outlet of the Lake of the Woods, or unless such debentures are for the purpose of paying for local improvements, made or to be made, in the said Municipality of 5 Rat Portage, west of the said second outlet of the Lake of the Woods.

Company not entitled to any interests in improvements to which they have not contributed.

☞ **4.** The said, the Minnesota and Ontario Lumber Company, Messrs. Cameron and Kennedy and F. T. Bulmer and Company, their legal representatives or assigns of their said pro- 10 perties, shall not hereafter be entitled to any interest or share in any improvements or property of or in the said Municipality, to the expenditure for making or acquiring whereof they shall not have contributed through the rates.

Adjustment of rates by municipality.

☞ **5.** The said Municipality of Rat Portage, in fixing the 15 annual rates of taxation, shall take into consideration the right of the proprietors aforesaid, to the remission and exemption from taxation hereinbefore mentioned, and may adjust the said rates accordingly.

Rights of debenture-holders not affected.

☞ **6.** Nothing in this Act shall affect the rights of the holders 20 of debentures now in existence. ☞

PRINTED BY WARWICK & SONS, 26 AND 28 FRONT ST. W.

TORONTO:

Mr. GIBSON.
(Hamilton.)

First Reading, 11th March, 1887.
Second " 3 0th " 1887.

(Reprinted as amended by Private Bills Committee.)

BILL.

An Act relating to the Municipality of Rat Portage.

No. 40.

1st Session, 6th Legislature, 50 Vic., 1887.

BILL. .

An Act to separate certain Municipalities from the
Counties of Wellington, Perth and Huron, and to
erect the same into the County of Lansdowne.

WHEREAS the population of the townships of Minto, Preamble.
Arthur, Maryborough and West Luther, in the county of
Wellington, the township of Wallace, in the county of Perth,
5 the township of Howick, in the county of Huron, and of the
towns of Palmerston and Harriston and the villages of Arthur,
Clifford and Drayton, in the said county of Wellington, and of
the village of Wroxeter, in the said county of Huron, is about
twenty-six thousand eight hundred and ninety-two, and the
10 assessed value of the property comprised therein is about
$8,679,914 ; and whereas many of the said municipalties are
inconveniently distant from the county towns of the counties
of which they form part, and the said counties are of unwieldy
size ; and whereas the said municipalties are of such size and
15 wealth, and their relative situation and trade relations are
such as to render it fitting that they should, with the approval
of the people, be formed into a new county ; and whereas
divers petitions have been presented praying for the passing
of this Act, and it is expedient to grant the prayer of the said
20 petitions ;
Therefore Her Majesty, by and with the advice and consent
of the Legislative Assembly of the Province of Ontario, enacts
as follows :—

1. The reeves and deputy-reeves of the townships of Minto, The provi-
25 Arthur, Maryborough and West Luther in the county of Wel- sional council.
lington, of the township of Wallace, in the county of Perth, of
the township of Howick in the county of Huron, and the mayors,
reeves and deputy-reeves of the towns of Palmerston and
Harriston, and the reeves and deputy-reeves of the villages of
30 Arthur, Clifford and Drayton, in the said county of Wellington, and of the village of Wroxeter, in the said county of
Huron, shall form a provisional municipal council, under the
style and name of the county of Lansdowne, for the purposes
of this Act.

35 2. It shall, upon the written request of a majority of the First meeting
mayors, reeves and deputy-reeves of the said towns, villages of mayors
and townships aforesaid, be the duty of the mayor of Palmers- and reeves.
ston to call a meeting of the mayors, reeves and deputy-reeves
of the said towns, villages and townships, at such place and
40 hour within the town of Palmerston as he shall appoint, and a
notice of such meeting shall be inserted in at least one newspaper published within the said counties of Wellington, Perth
and Huron respectively, and a copy of such notice sent by

mail or otherwise to each of such mayors, reeves and deputy-reeves, at least ten days before the day appointed for such meeting and the said provisional council shall at the first meeting thereof to be held under this Act, proceed to elect a provisional warden ; after which, at the same meeting, or some 5 adjournment thereof, they shall proceed to pass a by-law for the purpose of taking a vote of the qualified municipal electors of the said towns, villages and townships aforesaid, on the question of the separation and erection into a new county, by vote to be specially taken for that purpose, each qualified elector 10 having one vote, and voting " yea " or " nay," after at least ten days' notice shall have been given in the manner to be provided by such by-law of the time and places when and where the said vote is to be taken.

Election of warden

Vote for question of separation and erection of new county.

Ascertaining the result of the poll.

3. The provisional council shall meet on the requisition of 15 the warden on some day after the day or days appointed for taking such vote, and proceed in open council to ascertain the number of votes recorded " yea " and " nay," and if the result shall show that a majority of the votes recorded are " nay," then after making a record of the same in the minutes of the 20 said provisional council, the said council shall adjourn *sine die*, and be called together again only on the written request of a majority of the mayors, reeves and deputy-reeves of the said towns, villages and townships in manner as aforesaid.

If the result be " nay."

4. If the results shall show that a majority of the votes 25 recorded are " yea," the said provisional council shall make a record thereof in their minutes, and in that event the county town of the new county shall be Palmerston.

If the result be " yea."

County town.

5. The said provisional council shall and may hereafter pass a by-law for providing means for purchasing and acquiring 30 lands, and erecting the necessary county buildings thereon at Palmerston ; but before its final passing, such by-law shall be submitted to the municipal electors of the said new county, and a vote shall be taken on the same in like manner as provided by *The Consolidated Municipal Act, 1883*, and after 35 passing such by-law the said provisional council shall proceed to erect the necessary county buildings.

Erection of county buildings.

6. After the necessary buildings shall have been erected as aforesaid, it shall be lawful for the Lieutenant-Governor in Council, by proclamation, to declare the said towns, villages 40 and townships separated from the said counties to which they now respectively belong. and declare them to be formed into a new county under the name of the county of Lansdowne, for all judicial and municipal purposes, and also for registry purposes, unless proclamation in that behalf has previously issued 45 under the provisions of this Act, but until the issue of such proclamation, the said towns, villages and townships shall remain, as at present, connected with the counties of which they respectively form a part for all such purposes.

Proclamation of Lieutenant-Governor of the erection of new county,

7. The provisional council aforesaid shall, prior to such proclamation, have only the powers specially given to it by the preceding sections of this Act.

Powers of provisional council prior to proclamation.

8. After such proclamation the provisional council shall and Powers after proclamation. may have and exercise all the rights, powers, privileges and duties conferred on provisional municipal councils by law; and the provisions of any law in force in this Province in any wise
5 affecting or relating to the proceedings consequent upon the dissolution of the union of counties shall apply, so far as applicable, to the separation of the towns, villages and townships aforesaid from the respective counties of which they have heretofore formed part, and the erection thereof into a new
10 county.

9. After such proclamation, the law in force respecting Law respecting municipal institutions municipal institutions of this Province, shall, as far as applicable and not inconsistent with this Act, apply to the county to apply. of Lansdowne.

15 **10.** After such proclamation, the corporations of Minto, Apportionment of existing debt. Arthur township, Maryborough, West Luther, Palmerston, Arthur village, Clifford and Drayton, shall respectively pay to the county of Wellington, and the corporation of Wallace shall pay to the county of Perth, and the corporations of Howick and
20 Wroxeter shall, respectively, pay to the county of Huron such proportion of the then outstanding debt of the counties of Wellngton, Perth and Huron respectively, and in such manner as may be determined under the said *Consolidated Municipal Act, 1883;* and the respective corporations of the said towns, villages
25 and townships shall, respectively receive from the county corporations from which they are respectively separated, a just proportion of the assets of said counties.

11. In case a majority of the votes cast at the polling pro‾ Registry vided for in section 3 of this Act are recorded in favour of the Office.
30 formation of such new county, the Lieutenant-Governor in Council may, by an Order in Council, cause to be issued a proclamation, and thereby set apart and establish a registry office for the said county so to be erected as aforesaid.

1st Session, 6th Legislature, 50 Vic, 1887.

BILL.

An Act to separate certain Municipalities from the Counties of Wellington, Perth and Huron, and to erect the same into the County of Lansdowne.

First Reading,   1887.

(Private Bill.)

No. 42.] **BILL.** [1887.

An Act to amend the Act incorporating the Trustees of
the Toronto House of Industry.

WHEREAS the trustees of the Toronto House of Industry Preamble.
were incorporated by the statute of the Province of
Canada passed in the 14th and 15th years of the
reign of Her Majesty, chapter 35, and intituled *An Act to*
5 *incorporate the House of Industry of Toronto,* and have by
their petition shown that it is desirable for the proper conduct
of the institution that certain amendments be made to the
said Act of incorporation; and whereas it is expedient to
grant the prayer of the petition;
10   Therefore Her Majesty, by and with the advice and consent
of the Legislative Assembly of the Province of Ontario, enacts
as follows :—

1. Section 2 of the said Act is amended by striking out the 14·15 V. c. 35,
words "Provided that the annual income to be derived from s. 2, amended.
15 such property shall not exceed the sum of three thousand
pounds."

2. Section 3 of the said Act is amended by substituting for 14·15 V. c. 35,
the words "on the second Wednesday in the month of s. 3, amended.
January" the words "in the month of April," and for the
20 words "ten shillings" the words "two dollars and fifty cents,"
and for the words "twelve pounds, ten shillings" the words
"fifty dollars," and for the words "twenty-five pounds" "one
hundred dollars."

3. Section 5 of the said Act is amended by inserting after 14·15 V. c. 35,
25 the word "young" the words "and for the establishment and s. 5, amended.
maintenance of an Infirmary and Dispensary and for granting
assistance to the casual poor."

4. The persons now acting on the committee, or board of Acting mana-
management of the said institution, shall be considered as gers continu-
30 managers of the corporation for and until the annual meeting ed.
to be held in April, 1888.

No. 42.

1st Session, 6th Legislature, 50 Vic., 1887.

BILL.

An Act to amend the Act incorporating the Trustees of the Toronto House of Industry.

First Reading,   1887.

(Private Bill.)

No. 42.]   **BILL.**   [1887.

An Act to amend the Act incorporating the Trustees of
the Toronto House of Industry.

WHEREAS the trustees of the Toronto House of Industry *Preamble.*
were incorporated by the statute of the Province of
Canada passed in the 14th and 15th years of the
reign of Her Majesty, chapter 35, and intituled *An Act to*
5 *incorporate the House of Industry of Toronto,* and have by
their petition shown that it is desirable for the proper conduct
of the institution that certain amendments be made to the
said Act of incorporation; and whereas it is expedient to
grant the prayer of the petition;
10   Therefore Her Majesty, by and with the advice and consent
of the Legislative Assembly of the Province of Ontario, enacts
as follows :—

1. Section 2 of the said Act is amended by striking out the *14-15 V. c. 35,*
words " Provided that the annual income to be derived from *s. 2, amended.*
15 such property shall not exceed the sum of three thousand
pounds," and substituting therefor the following : "provided
that the annual income to be derived from any such lands
and tenements other than the lands in the actual use and
occupation of the said corporation shall not exceed the sum
20 of twelve thousand dollars, and no such lands or tenements
not required for the actual use and occupation of the said corporation shall be held for a longer period than seven years
after the acquisition thereof, and within such period the same
shall be absolutely disposed of by the corporation, and the said
25 corporation shall have power within such period to grant and
convey said lands or tenements to any purchasers so that the
corporation no longer retains any interest therein ; and the
proceeds on such disposition shall be invested in public securities, municipal debentures, or other approved securities, includ-
30 ing mortgages on lands, for the use of the corporation ; and any
lands, tenements, or interests therein, required by this Act to
be sold and disposed of, which have not within the said period
been so disposed of, shall revert to the person from whom the
same were acquired, his heirs, executors, administrators, or
35 assigns."

2. Section 3 of the said Act is amended by substituting for *14-15 V. c. 35,*
the words " on the second Wednesday in the month of *s. 3, amended.*
January" the words "in the month of April," and for the
words " ten shillings" the words "two dollars and fifty cents,"
40 and for the words " twelve pounds, ten shillings" the words
"fifty dollars," and for the words "twenty-five pounds" the
words " one hundred dollars."

·15 V. c. 35, **3.** Section 5 of the said Act is amended by inserting after
5, amended. the word " young " the words "and for the establishment and
maintenance of an Infirmary and Dispensary and for granting
assistance to the casual poor."

cting mana- **4.** The persons now acting on the committee, or board of 5
rs continu- management of the said institution, shall be considered as
managers of the corporation for and until the annual meeting
to be held in April, 1888.

No. 42.

1st Session, 6th Legislature, 50 Vic, 1887.

BILL.

An Act to amend the Act incorporating the
Trustees of the Toronto House of Industry.

(*Reprinted as amended by Private
Bills Committee*).

First Reading, 11th March, 1887.

(Private Bill.)

Mr. LEYS.

BILL.

An Act to remove doubts as to the location of certain Park Lots adjoining the Township of Derby and the Town of Owen Sound.

WHEREAS the corporations of the town of Owen Sound Preamble. and of the townships of Derby and Keppel, respectively, in the county of Grey, have by their petition represented that doubts have arisen and now exist as to whether park lots
5 numbers 1 to 10, both inclusive, in or lying east of the half-mile strip in the said township of Derby, form part of the township of Derby or of the township of Keppel, and as to whether park lots lettered B, M, A and K, in or lying east of the said half-mile strip, form part of the town of Owen Sound,
10 or of the township of Keppel; and whereas the proclamation of His Honour the then Lieutenant-Governor of this Province, dated 14th July, 1869, published in the *Gazette* of the 17th July, 1869, purported to annex the said park lots numbers 1 to 10 inclusive, therein described as—" All that block or parcel of
15 land situate in the county of Grey, and lying within the following limits, that is to say, commencing at the north-east angle ot lot number eighteen in the third concession of the township of Derby ; thence on a course north nine degrees west forty chains more or less to the southern limit of the allowance
20 for road running along the southern boundary of the town plot of Brooke, and of. the townships of Sarawak and Keppel ; thence south seventy-six degrees fifteen minutes west, along the southern limit of the said allowance for road to a point where the said southern limit of said allowance for road would be
25 intersected by the easterly limit of the allowance for road between the fourth and fifth concessions of Derby, produced northerly ; thence south nine degrees east along the eastern limit of said last mentioned allowance for road, produced northerly forty chains more or less to the north-west angle of lot
30 number seventeen in the fourth concession of the said township of Derby ; thence easterly along the northerly limits of lots seventeen in the fourth concession, and eighteen in the third concession, to the place of beginning "; and the same have always been considered and treated as part of the township of
35 Derby, and the said park lots lettered B, M, A and K have always been considered and treated as part of the town of Owen Sound, as having been included within the limits thereof as defined in the Act of Incorporation thereof, passed in the 19th year of Her Majesty's reign, chapter 18: and where-
45 as the said corporation have, by their said petition, prayed that such doubts may be removed, and that the said park lots 1 to 10 inclusive, may be annexed to the township of Derby, and that the said park lots lettered B, M, A and K may be annexed

to the town of Owen Sound ; and whereas it is expedient to grant the prayer of the said petition ;

Therefore Her Majesty, by and with the advice and consent of the Legislative Assembly of the Province of Ontario, enacts as follows :— 5

Park lots 1 to 10 annexed to township of Derby. **1.** Park lots numbers 1 to 10, both inclusive, in or lying east of the half-mile strip in the township of Derby, in the county of Grey, shall be annexed to and form part of the said township of Derby, and be considered for all purposes as having been annexed to and as having formed part of the said town- 10 ship of Derby, on and since the 14th day of July, 1869.

Park lots B, M, A and K annexed to town of Owen Sound. **2.** Park lots lettered B, M, A and K in or lying east of the said half-mile strip, shall be annexed to and form part of the town of Owen Sound, and be considered for all purposes as having been annexed to and as having formed part of the said 15 town from the incorporation thereof.

Pending proceedings not affected. **3.** Nothing in this Act contained shall affect any action or other proceeding at law now pending.

1st Session, 6th Legislature, 50 Vic, 1887.

BILL.

An Act to remove doubts as to the location of certain Park Lots adjoining the Township of Derby and the Town of Owen Sound.

First Reading, 9th March, 1887.

(Private Bill.)

Mr CREIGHTON.

BILL.

An Act respecting the Fort George Assembly to be henceforth known as " The Niagara Assembly."

WHEREAS the Fort George Assembly incorporated under *The* *Ontario Joint Stock Companies' Letters Patent Act,* with a capital of $50,000 for the establishment and maintenance of a summer resort under religious, temperance and educational aus-
5 pices, near the town of Niagara, with power to hold real estate, to erect buildings on its grounds, to lease or sell the same, to erect wharves or piers and to supply water and light, has by its petition represented that it has selected for its operations a site adjoining the town of Niagara, but not near Fort George,
10 and that it desires in consequence to have its name changed, and in order better to carry out the objects of its incorporation to have its capital increased ; to have the right to issue publications ; to construct and operate a tramway to its grounds ; to acquire and operate steamers ; to supply the town of Niagara
15 with water and light ; and to have the by-law No. 299 of said town granting it aid to the extent of $5,000 ratified ; and whereas more than four-fifths of the qualified ratepayers of said town have petitioned for an Act ratifying the said by-law and it is expedient to grant the prayer of the said petition ;
20 Therefore Her Majesty, by and with the advice and consent of the Legislative Assembly of the Province of Ontario, enacts as follows :—

Preamble.

1. The corporate name of the Fort George Assembly is hereby changed to the Niagara Assembly.

Name changed.

25 **2.** The capital stock of the said company is hereby increased to $150,000 in one thousand five hundred shares of $100 each.

Capital increased.

3. In addition to the powers conferred by the Letters Patent the said company shall have the right to issue publications ; to acquire and operate steamers ; and may enter into a contract or
30 contracts with the corporation of the town of Niagara to lay down, construct and operate a tramway upon the streets of said town and may also enter into a contract or contracts with the corporation of said town for the supply of water and light to said town and the inhabitants thereof. Such contract or contracts
35 may confer exclusive rights upon said company for said objects or any of them but not for a period exceeding twenty years.

Additional powers.

4. By-law No. 299 of the corporation of the town of Niagara, set out in the Schedule to this Act, is hereby ratified and declared valid and binding to all intents and for all purposes as
40 fully as if the said by-law had been within the competency of the council of said town.

By-law 299 of Niagara confirmed.

SCHEDULE.

By-law to grant five thousand dollars in aid of the Fort George Assembly, and to raise to the same by way of loan.

Whereas the company called the Fort George Assembly propose to acquire the property known as the Crooks Farm containg about ninety acres, in and adjacent to the town of Niagara, in the County of Lincoln, for the purpose of establishing and maintaining a summer resort for literary, social and scientific purposes, as a Canadian Chautauqua, provided they receive aid from said town, to the extent hereinafter set forth;

And whereas it would be for the interest of said town to aid the said enterprise, to the extent of five thousand dollars on the terms and conditions hereinafter mentioned;

And whereas it is necessary to issue debentures for said sum and to provide for the payment of the same in principal and interest;

And whereas the whole ratable property of the municipality of the town of Niagara, according to the last revised assessment roll, amounts to the sum of three hundred and twenty-six thousand seven hundred and seventy-five dollars;

And whereas the existing debenture debt of the said municipality amounts to three thousand five hundred dollars of which no portion of either principal or interest is in arrear;

And whereas the council of said municipality has been advised that *The Municipal Act* does not make provision for granting aid for such a purpose, but it is in the interest of the said town that the same should be granted, and the assent of the Provincial Legislature obtained therefor, provided the same be approved by a majority of the qualified electors of said town, by petition or otherwise;

Be it therefore enacted by the corporation of the town of Niagara:

1. It shall be lawful for the corporation of the town of Niagara to grant to the said Fort George Assembly the sum of five thousand dollars on the terms and conditions hereinafter set forth, subject to ratification by the Legislature of the Province of Ontario, provided the same be approved by a majority of the qualified electors of said town by petition or otherwise.

2. The mayor of the said town may cause debentures of the said corporation to be made and issued, to the amount of five thousand dollars, in sums of five hundred dollars each, signed by the mayor, countersigned by the treasurer and sealed with the corporate seal of the said town.

3. The said debentures shall be payable in sixteen years at the office of the Canadian Bank of Commerce in St. Catharines, and shall have interest coupons attached thereto payable at the same place, as is hereinafter set forth, and the said debentures shall bear date on the day the same are issued.

4. The said debentures shall bear interest at the rate of five per cent. per annum payable yearly on the 31st day of December in each year during the currency thereof.

5. For the purpose of paying the said debentures and coupons there shall be levied and collected a special rate in the dollar, upon all ratable property of the said municipality, in addition to all other rates yearly, until the said debentures and interest thereon shall be fully paid and satisfied.

6· That the sums to be raised in each year, during the curreney of said debentures shall be for principal and interest as follows :

1887			Interest	$250	00
1888			"	250	00
1889			"	250	00
1890			"	250	00
1891			"	250	00
1892			"	250	00
1893	Principal	$500	"	250	00
1894	"	500	"	225	00
1895	"	500	"	£00	00
1896	"	500	"	175	00
1897	"	500	"	150	00
1898	"	500	"	125	00
1899	"	500	"	100	00
1900	"	500	"	75	00
1901	"	500		50	00
1902	"	500		25	00

7. The said debentures shall be delivered to the said Fort George Assembly as follows:—One thousand dollars when the sum of five thousand dollars shall have been expended on said grounds so to be acquired by them, in buildings and improvements in connection with the objects of said company, and shall have given evidence thereof to the said corporation, and the further sum of one thousand dollars for each subsequent sum of five thousand dollars so expended, until the sum of twenty-five thousand dollars shall have been so expended, when the full amount of five thousand dollars shall be paid as aforesaid. The said debentures so delivered shall bear interest only from the date when they should respectively be delivered as aforesaid, and not from the date of the same.

8. The corporation of said town of Niagara shall be represented on the Board of Directors of said company by one of the members of its council who shall be elected thereto by said council from year to year.

9. This by-law shall take effect and come in operation on on the 31st day of December, A.D. 1886, if ratified as aforesaid.

Passed and adopted in open council on the tenth day of December, A.D. 1886, and given under the corporate seal of the said municipality.

DAN. SERVOS,
Town Clerk.

(L. S.) W. A. MILLOY,
Mayor.

1st Session, 6th Legislature, 50 Vic., 1887.

BILL.

An Act respecting the Fort George Assembly to be henceforth known as "The Niagara Assembly."

First Reading,   1887.

(Private Bill)

No. 44.]　　　　　**BILL.**　　　　　[1887.

An Act respecting the Fort George Assembly to be henceforth known as " The Niagara Assembly."

W HEREAS the Fort George Assembly incorporated under *The* Preamble.
　　Ontario Joint Stock Companies' Letters Patent Act, with
a capital of $50,000 for the establishment and maintenance of a
summer resort under religious, temperance and educational aus-
5 pices, near the town of Niagara, with power to hold real estate,
to erect buildings on its grounds, to lease or sell the same, to
erect wharves or piers and to supply water and light, has by its
petition represented that it has selected for its operations a
site adjoining the town of Niagara, but not near Fort George,
10 and that it desires in consequence to have its name changed,
and in order better to carry out the objects of its incorporation
to have its capital. increased ; to have the right to issue publications ; to construct and operate a tramway to its grounds ; to
acquire and operate steamers ; to supply the town of Niagara
15 with water and light ; and to have the by-law No. 299 of said
town granting it aid to the extent of $5,000 ratified ; and
whereas more than four-fifths of the qualified ratepayers of
said town have petitioned for an Act ratifying the said by-law
and it is expedient to grant the prayer of the said petition ;
20 · Therefore Her Majesty, by and with the advice and consent
of the Legislative Assembly of the Province of Ontario, enacts
as follows :—

1. The corporate name of the Fort George Assembly is here- Name
by changed to the Niagara Assembly.　　　　　changed.

25 **2.** The capital stock of the said company is hereby increased Capital
to $150,000 in one thousand five hundred shares of $100 each. increased.

3. In addition to the powers conferred by the Letters Patent Additional
the said company shall have the right to issue publications ; to powers.
30 *contract for,* acquire and operate steamers ☞ to run between
the grounds of the company, or the town of Niagara, and other
places in the Province, for the conveyance of passengers going
to or returning from the grounds of the company ; ☜ and may
enter into a contract or contracts with the corporation of the
town of Niagara to lay down, construct and operate a tramway
upon the streets of said town, ☞ provided a charter be first obtained in accordance with the provisions of *The Street Railway
Act, 1883,* ☜ and may also enter into a contract or contracts
with the corporation of said town for the supply of water and
35 light to said town and the inhabitants thereof. Such contract or
contracts may confer exclusive rights upon said company for
said objects or any of them but not for a period exceeding
twenty years.

4. By-law No. 299 of the corporation of the town of Niagara, By-law 299 of
set out. in the Schedule to this Act, is hereby ratified and Niagara con-
declared valid and binding to all intents and for all purposes as firmed.
40 fully as if the said by-law had been within the competency of
the council of said town.

SCHEDULE.

By-law No. 299, of the Corporation of the Town of Niagara.

By-law to grant five thousand dollars in aid of the Fort George Assembly, and to raise the same by way of loan.

Whereas the company called the Fort George Assembly propose to acquire the property known as the Crooks Farm containing about ninety acres, in and adjacent to the town of Niagara, in the County of Lincoln, for the purpose of establishing and maintaining a summer resort for literary, social and scientific purposes, as a Canadian Chautauqua, provided they receive aid from said town, to the extent hereinafter set forth;

And whereas it would be for the interest of said town to aid the said enterprise, to the extent of five thousand dollars on the terms and conditions hereinafter mentioned;

And whereas it is necessary to issue debentures for said sum and to provide for the payment of the same in principal and interest;

And whereas the whole ratable property of the municipality of the town of Niagara, according to the last revised assessment roll, amounts to the sum of three hundred and twenty-six thousand seven hundred and seventy-five dollars;

And whereas the existing debenture debt of the said municipality amounts to three thousand five hundred dollars of which no portion of either principal or interest is in arrear;

And whereas the council of said municipality has been advised that *The Municipal Act* does not make provision for granting aid for such a purpose, but it is in the interest of the said town that the same should be granted, and the assent of the Provincial Legislature obtained therefor, provided the same be approved by a majority of the qualified electors of said town, by petition or otherwise;

Be it therefore enacted by the corporation of the town of Niagara :

1. It shall be lawful for the corporation of the town of Niagara to grant to the said Fort George Assembly the sum of five thousand dollars on the terms and conditions hereinafter set forth, subject to ratification by the Legislature of the Province of Ontario, provided the same be approved by a majority of the qualified electors of said town by petition or otherwise.

2. The mayor of the said town may cause debentures of the said corporation to be made and issued, to the amount of five thousand dollars, in sums of five hundred dollars each, signed by the mayor, countersigned by the treasurer and sealed with the corporate seal of the said town.

3. The said debentures shall be payable in sixteen years at the office of the Canadian Bank of Commerce in St. Catharines, and shall have interest coupons attached thereto payable at the same place, as is hereinafter set forth, and the said debentures shall bear date on the day the same are issued.

4. The said debentures shall bear interest at the rate of five per cent. per annum payable yearly on the 31st day of December in each year during the currency thereof.

5. For the purpose of paying the said debentures and coupons there shall be levied and collected a special rate in the dollar, upon all ratable property of the said municipality, in addition to all other rates yearly, until the said debentures and interest thereon shall be fully paid and satisfied.

6. That the sums to be raised in each year, during the currency of said debentures shall be for principal and interest as follows :

1887		Interest	$250	00
1888		"	250	00
1889		"	250	00
1890		"	250	00
1891		"	250	00
1892		"	250	00
1893	Principal $500	"	250	00
1894	" 500	"	225	00
1895	" 500	"	200	00
1896	500	"	175	00
1897	" 500	"	150	00
1898	500	"	125	00
1899	500	"	100	00
1900	500		75	00
1901	" 500		50	00
1902	500		25	00

7. The said debentures shall be delivered to the said Fort George Assembly as follows:—One thousand dollars when the sum of five thousand dollars shall have been expended on said grounds so to be acquired by them, in buildings and improvements in connection with the objects of said company, and shall have given evidence thereof to the said corporation, and the further sum of one thousand dollars for each subsequent sum of five thousand dollars so expended, until the *said* sum of twenty-five thousand dollars shall have been so expended, when the full amount of five thousand dollars shall be paid as aforesaid. The said debentures so delivered shall bear interest only from the date when they should respectively be delivered as aforesaid, and not from the date of the same.

8. The corporation of said town of Niagara shall be represented on the Board of Directors of said company by one of the members of its council who shall be elected thereto by said council from year to year.

9. This by-law shall take effect and come in operation on the 31st day of December, A.D. 1886, if ratified as aforesaid.

Passed and adopted in open council on the tenth day of December, A.D. 1886, and given under the corporate seal of the said municipality.

DAN. SERVOS,
Town Clerk.

(L. S.)   W. A. MILLOY,
Mayor.

BILL.

An Act respecting the Fort George Assembly to be henceforth known as "The Niagara Assembly."

Re-printed as amended by Private Bills Committee

First Reading, 9th March, 1887.

(Private Bill.)

Mr. GARSON.

TORONTO:
PRINTED BY WARWICK & SONS, 26 AND 28 FRONT ST. W.

BILL.

An Act to amend the Act respecting the Incorporation of the Village of Huntsville.

WHEREAS by an Act of the Legislature of Ontario passed in the forty-ninth year of Her Majesty's reign, and chaptered 55, the village of Huntsville was constituted a body corporate, separate and apart from the township of Chaffey, in
5 which the said village is situate, under the name of the corporation of the village of Huntsville; and whereas after the passing of said Act it appeared that a clerical error was made in describing the boundaries of the said village of Huntsville, as defined by section 2 of the said Act; and whereas it is
10 expedient to correct the said error;

Therefore Her Majesty, by and with the advice and consent of the Legislative Assembly of the province of Ontario, enacts as follows:—

1. Section 2 of the said Act to incorporate the village of 49 V. c. 55,
15 Huntsville is amended by adding after the word " Brunel " in s. 2, amended. the fourteenth line of said section 2 the words following " thence easterly parallel with the boundary line between the townships of Chaffey and Brunel across lot number ten to a point on the easterly side of the side road between lots
20 numbers ten and eleven, thence southerly along the east side of the said side road to a point distant twenty chains and fifty links from the boundary line between the townships of Chaffey and Brunel."

1st Session, 6th Legislature, 50 Vic., 1887.

BILL.

An Act to amend the Act respecting the
Incorporation of the Village of Huntsville.

First Reading,   1887.

(Private Bill).

BILL.

An Act to incorporate the Western Fair Association.

WHEREAS James Cowan and others, hereinafter named, Preamble.
have by their petition prayed that an association may
be incorporated for the purpose of promoting industries, arts
and sciences generally, and of establishing and holding agri-
5 cultural, industrial, art and other exhibitions at the city of
London; and whereas it is expedient to grant the prayer of
the said petition;

Therefore Her Majesty, by and with the advice and consent
of the Legislative Assembly of the province of Ontario, enacts
10 as follows:—

1. James Cowan, Andrew William Porte, John William Incorporation.
Little, Richard Whetter, Lawrence Cleverdon, Donald Mac-
Kenzie, Geo. Douglass, John Walker, Thomas Green, William
Y. Brunton, T. Herbert Marsh, John Green, Robt. C. Struthers,
15 John Wolfe, William John Reid, A. M. Smart, W. M. Gartshore,
W. R. Hobbs, Thomas R. Parker, Robert Lewis, Moses Masuret,
and others, the several representatives of the several societies,
corporations and associations hereinafter named, together with
all such other persons and representatives of other corpora-
20 tions, societies and associations as shall under the authority of
this Act, be associated with them, in, and become members of, the
corporation hereby created, shall be a body politic and corporate, by the name of the Western Fair Association and by
that name shall and may have perpetual succession, and a
25 common seal, with the power to break and alter the same, and
by that name shall and may sue and be sued in all courts in
this Province; and the said corporation shall have their
principal place of business at London, but may open such
office or offices at such places as may be found necessary or
30 convenient for the purposes of their business.

2. The said association is hereby authorized and empowered Exhibitions
either permanently or periodically in structures, buildings, authorized.
enclosures, and places located in the city of London, or the
township of London or Westminster, suitable for exhibition
35 purposes and for the promotion of industries, arts and sciences
generally, to exhibit any and every variety of thing and
being, found in animal and vegetable life, and every kind and
variety of mineral; to exhibit products, wares, goods, merchandise, machinery, mechanical inventions and improvements of
40 every nature, name and kind, and such as are generally
exhibited at fairs, including the various processes of manufacture; to exhibit paintings and statuary of any and every
nature and kind; to exhibit and develop the points and
qualities of the several breeds of horses and other animals, by

such competitive tests as may be humane and proper, and as may be deemed expedient and to make such other exhibitions as will be in conformity with the purposes and objects of this Act; and the said association is hereby further authorized, but **Authority to acquire and dispose of property.** only for carrying on and maintaining the business aforesaid, 5 and such other business as may be hereafter mentioned, to hold, own, and acquire, by lease, purchase, gift or otherwise, property, real and personal, at such prices and on such terms and conditions as may be agreed upon, and may improve and use the same, by the construction of such building, houses, 10 works, and improvements as are necessary, and as may be deemed proper; and the said association is hereby further authorized to cultivate such portions of their grounds as they may deem proper for the propagation of plants, trees, shrubs or other things of a vegetable nature, and also to manufacture 15 and raise articles and things required in the various exhibitions contemplated; and to sell, mortgage, lease, or otherwise dispose of any property at any time held by the said association; **Proviso.** provided always, and it is enacted, that the said association shall at no time acquire or hold, any lands or tenements 20 or interests therein, exceeding in the whole, at any one time the annual value of $10,000, nor otherwise than for actual use or occupation for the purposes of the said corporation.

Entrance fee, prizes, etc. 3. The said association is hereby authorized to charge such admission fees as may be deemed proper to receive for exhibit- 25 ing every thing contemplated by this Act; to charge such entrance fees and to award, give and pay to exhibitors such prizes, medals and honorary distinctions as they may deem proper, and to let or lease stalls, stands, rooms and places in any of their buildings or structures, or in any part of their 30 grounds or property, upon such terms and conditions and for such purposes, as the board of directors may deem best for the interests of the said association.

Members of association. 4. The mayor of the city of London, the treasurer of the city of London, the chairman of the finance committee of the 35 council of the corporation of the city of London, and the standing committee thereof, known as the exhibition committee (five members); the president, vice-presidents and six members of the electoral division of the city of London Horticultural and Agricultural Society, the warden of the county of 40 Middlesex and two representatives, being members of the county council of the county of Middlesex, to be named and appointed by the said council at the time of the appointment of the several standing committees thereof for the year; the president, vice-president and six members of the electoral 45 division of East Middlesex Agricultural Society; two representatives from the electoral division of North Middlesex Agricultural Society; two representatives from the electoral division of West Middlesex Agricultural Society; the president and six members of the London Board of Trade; two members 50 each from all the electoral district agricultural societies in the western peninsula; two representatives from the board of education of the city of London, viz.: the chairman and one member; two representatives from each of the several corporations, associations, organizations, societies and public bodies 55 following, that is to say: the Ontario Society of Artists, the London Mechanics Institute, the Stock Breeders' Association of

Ontario, the Fruit Growers' Association of Ontario, the Ontario
Veterinary Association, the Ontario College of Pharmacy, the
Poultry Association of Ontario, the Toronto Poultry Association, the London Poultry Association, the Dairymen's Associa-
5 tion of Western Ontario, the Millers' Association, the Photographers' Association, the Entomological Society, the Western
Beekeepers' Association, the Western Ontario Commercial
Travellers' Association, such representatives to be named and
appointed by the said several corporations, associations, organi-
10 zations and societies at their annual meeting for the election
of officers ; such number of representatives of such other corporations, associations, organizations or societies not named
above as may from time to time, upon applications to be made
by such corporations, associations, organizations or societies, be
15 admitted to the said Western Fair Association, by vote thereof,
at the annual meeting thereof, upon such terms and conditions,
and under such regulations and restrictions as may be made
and determined by the board of directors and sanctioned by
the association at its annual meeting, and all such other
20 persons as the board 'of directors may by by-law admit to
membership, as hereinafter provided, shall constitute the said
Western Fair Association, and the said several persons and
representatives named, or hereafter to be admitted under the
provisions of this Act, and the by-laws of the said last men-
25 tioned association, shall be the members of the said Western
Fair Association.

5. James Cowan, Andrew William Porte, John William Provisional
Little, Richard Whetter, Lawrence Cleverdon, Donald Mac- directors.
Kenzie, George Douglass, John Walker, Thomas Green, William
30 Y. Brunton, T. Herbert Marsh, John Green, Robert C. Struthers,
John Wolfe, William John Reid, A. M. Smart, W. M. Gartshore,
Thomas R. Parker, Robert Lewis, William McDonough, John
Labatt, John R. Minhinnick, A. J. B. McDonald, Richard
Denning and John Kennedy, shall be provisional directors of the
35 said Western Fair Association, to organize said association, and
shall hold office until the election of directors, as hereinafter
provided.

6. Forthwith after the passing of this Act, the said provi- Meeting for
sional directors, or a majority of them, shall notify, in writing, first election
of directors.
40 the several corporations, organizations, persons, associations
and societies, specially mentioned in section 4 of this Act,
of the provisions of this Act, and shall at the same time
request each of them to name and appoint representatives
(where the same are provided for in this Act) to the said the
45 Western Fair Association, pursuant to the provisions of this
Act, which appointment shall be evidenced by the corporate
seal of each of the said several societies, organizations, associations or corporations or by a certificate, signed by the presiding officer and secretary or clerk of such organization, society,
50 corporation or association, as the case may be, and such notice
shall likewise contain a statement of the time and place of
holding the first meeting of the members of the association for
the election of directors, and such other business as may
require to be done at such meeting, a copy of which notice
55 shall also be published once in each week for two weeks
before the time appointed for such meeting in one of the
newspapers published in the city of London.

Qualification of directors and voters.

7. At the first meeting of the members of the association, hereby incorporated for the election of directors, each member of the association, being a representative, shall produce to the said provisional directors a certificate, under the seal of the corporation, association, society or organization which he 5 represents or under the hand of the presiding officer and secretary, of his due and proper appointment, and the said provisional directors, or a majority of them, shall, at the time of such election, cause a list of all duly qualified members of the association hereby incorporated to be made out and placed 10 upon the table, and only the persons whose names shall appear upon such list shall be eligible as directors, or entitled to vote for directors, and upon such other matters, questions and things as may be presented for the consideration of the meeting. 15

Representation of societies which have not made any election.

8. In the event of no appointment of representatives under the provisions of this Act having been made, from any cause, by any of the societies, corporations, organizations, or associations specially named in section 4 thereof, before the time fixed by the provisional directors for the holding of the 20 meeting for the election of the directors of the said association hereby incorporated, then and in every such case, the president, vice-president, chairman, or other presiding officer, and the secretary of the association, organization, corporation, or society so having failed to make such appointment, shall be the 25 representatives of such association, organization, corporation, or society, and shall be *ex officio* members of the corporation hereby created, until the appointment contemplated by this Act shall have been made, and shall be entitled to vote at all meetings of members of the said association. 30

Number of directors, etc.

9. The board of directors shall consist of not less than fifteen nor more than twenty-four members (a majority of whom shall be residents of the City of London), to be determined at the meeting to be held as provided for in the seventh section of this Act, save and except that the East Middlesex 35 Agricultural Society shall be entitled to a representation on said board of six members, all of whom shall be residents of the County of Middlesex, and shall be chosen by said society in such a manner as said society may decide, and not more than six directors shall be elected from the representatives 40 sent as members of the Western Fair Association from the Horticultural Society of the Electoral Division of the City of London under section four of this Act. The election of directors (except as to the directors appointed by the East Middlesex Agricultural Society as aforesaid) and every question 45 voted on at said meeting shall, if demanded by two members, be decided by ballot by a majority of votes of the members of the association hereby incorporated, present in person and voting at the meeting; the directors so chosen shall immediately elect one of their own number to be president, and 50 two others of them to be vice-presidents, which president, vice-presidents and directors shall continue in office for one year and until others shall be chosen to fill their places as may be provided for by the by-laws of said association, and if any vacancy shall at any time happen by death, resignation or 55 otherwise in the office of president, vice-president or directors the remaining directors shall supply such vacancy by the appointment of some member of the association for the remainder of the year; and the election of the directors shall take place, annually, either on the anniversary of the day of the first election of directors or such other day as may be fixed by by-law as hereinafter provided and mentioned.

5   **10.** The directors shall have full power to make all by-laws, rules and regulations not inconsistent with the provisions of this Act, for the management of the association hereby incorporated, the securing of the cash fund hereinafter mentioned, and the collection thereof, as also hereinafter men-
10 tioned; the acquisition of exhibition grounds and buildings, by purchase, lease, agreement or otherwise, and the selling, leasing and mortgaging, or otherwise disposing of the same, as occasion may require; the acquisition and management of all property, whether real or personal, which may be required for the
15 purposes of, or in connection with, the exhibition or other business and operations of the said association, and the sale or other disposal thereof, when no longer required for such purposes; the entering into any and all arrangements, agreements and contracts with any person, or corporation, society,
20 or association, as the same may become necessary to carry out the objects of the said association; the admission of other persons as members and of other corporations, societies, associations, or organizations than those named in this Act; to be represented in the said association hereby incorporated and
25 the terms and conditions of such admission, the fees (if any) to be paid by members of the association, the holding of exhibitions, annual or periodical; fixing the time for the annual meeting and the calling of general, special and other meetings of the association; the appointment, removal and remuneration of
30 all officers, agents, clerks, workmen and servants of the association; the admission fees to be received from persons visiting their exhibitions; the entrance fees to be charged exhibitors; the general management of all exhibitions, and in general to do all things and make all contracts and agreements that may
35 be necessary to carry out the objects and exercise the powers incident to the association.

Powers of directors.

    11. Before the directors of said association shall undertake the holding of any exhibition or commence the business and operations contemplated by this Act; they shall secure or have
40 on hand a cash fund of not less than $5,000.

When association may commence operations.

    12. Notwithstanding anything contained in *The Agriculture and Arts Act*, it shall and may be lawful for all or any of the several societies, corporations, organizations, and associations named in section 4 of this Act, and for any of the
45 corporations, associations, organizations or societies formed, or hereafter to be formed, under the provisions of the said Act, and they, and all and every of them are hereby authorized and empowered, through their several and respective councils or boards of directors, or committees of management, and officers,
50 to enter into any arrangements and to make any agreements, and contracts with the board of directors of the said association hereby incorporated for the holding of exhibitions, and taking part in the exhibitions to be holden by the said association, and otherwise promoting the objects contemplated by
55 this Act, and may aid the same with any funds and moneys belonging to any such association or society not otherwise specially appropriated by any statute of this Province.

Certain societies authorized to make agreements with and aid association.

6

Aid from municipalities. **13.** The municipal council of any city, town, village, county or township, in this Province, may grant money or land in aid of the said association, or may lend or grant aid by way of bonus to the said association out of any moneys belonging to the municipality, and may effect such loan, or grant such aid, 5 upon such terms and conditions as may be agreed upon between said association and the council of the municipality making such loan or granting such aid, and may recover the money so lent and may appropriate the moneys so recovered

Proviso. to the purposes of such municipality; provided always that no 10 municipal council shall in any one year grant any such money or bonus to any greater extent than $5,000, nor shall any land be so granted or given under the provisions of *The Consolidated Municipal Act, 1883*, as to by-laws for raising, on the credit of the municipality, money not required for its ordi- 15 nary expenditure and not payable within the same municipal year; such provisions being those which require and relate to the assent of electors and otherwise.

Agreement with municipalities. **14.** The council of any municipality and the association hereby incorporated and the directors thereof, are hereby 20 respectively authorized to make and enter into any agreements or covenants relating to the holding of any exhibition, and granting and accepting aid for the same, and for the furnishing and providing exhibition grounds and buildings suitable for the purposes of the said association and for the representa- 25 tion of such municipality in the said association, by the appointment of members of the council thereof as representatives to such association, and all the representatives so appointed in pursuance of any such agreement shall become members of the said association and entitled to vote upon all 30 matters and questions submitted or voted upon at all meetings of the association, and every such council may pass by-laws for all and every of the purposes aforesaid and in furtherance of the objects contemplated by this Act as occasion may require, but subject to the special provisions contained in 35 section 13 of this Act.

Certain sections of 49 V. s. 11, incorporated. **15.** Sections 5, 6, 15, 16, 17, 30, 31, 38, 41, 42, 72, 73 (1), 74, 75, 78, 81 (1), 82, 83 and 84 of *The Agriculture and Arts Act* are hereby incorporated with, and are to be taken and deemed as part of this Act and shall apply to 40 the said association, and to the exhibitions to be held by them as fully as such sections apply to the Agricultural and Arts Association and to exhibitions held by such association, except in so far as they may be inconsistent with the enactments hereof, and the expression "this Act" when used 45 herein, shall be understood to include the sections of the said last mentioned Act so incorporated with this Act as aforesaid.

Power to expropriate lands for purposes of association. **16.** It shall be lawful for the corporation of the city of London at the request of the Western Fair Association to acquire by expropriation from time to time such lands in the 50 city of London or vicinity as may be required for the purposes of said Western Fair Association and such power of expropriation shall be exercised subject to the provisions of sections 486, 487, 488 and 489 of *The Consolidated Municipal Act, 1883* which sections are hereby declared applicable. 55

BILL.

An Act to incorporate the Western Fair
Association.

First Reading,   1887.

(Private Bill.)

BILL.

An Act to incorporate the Western Fair Association.

WHEREAS James Cowan and others, hereinafter named, Preamble.
have by their petition prayed that an association may
be incorporated for the purpose of promoting industries, arts
. and sciences generally, and of establishing and holding agri-
5 cultural, industrial, art and other exhibitions at the city of
London; and whereas it is expedient to grant the prayer of
the said petition;

Therefore Her Majesty, by and with the advice and consent
of the Legislative Assembly of the Province of Ontario, enacts
10 as follows:—

1. James Cowan, Andrew William Porte, John William Incorporation.
Little, Richard Whetter, Lawrence Cleverdon, Donald Mac-
Kenzie, Geo. Douglass, John Walker, Thomas Green, William
Y. Brunton, T. Herbert Marsh, John Green, Robt. C. Struthers,
15 John Wolfe, William John Reid, A. M. Smart, W. M. Gartshore,
W. R. Hobbs, Thomas R. Parker, Robert Lewis, Moses Masuret,
and others, the several representatives of the several societies,
corporations and associations hereinafter named, together with
all such other persons and representatives of other corpora-
20 tions, societies and associations as shall under the authority of
this Act, be associated with them, in, and become members of, the
corporation hereby created, shall be a body politic and corporate, by the name of the Western Fair Association and by
that name shall and may have perpetual succession, and a
25 common seal, with the power to break and alter the same, and
by that name shall and may sue and be sued in all courts in
this Province; and the said corporation shall have their
principal place of business at London, but may open such
office or offices at such places as may be found necessary or
30 convenient for the purposes of their business.

2. The said association is hereby authorized and empowered Exhibitions
either permanently or periodically in structures, buildings, authorized.
enclosures, and places located in the city of London, or the
township of London or Westminster, suitable for exhibition
35 purposes and for the promotion of industries, arts and sciences
generally, to exhibit any and every variety of thing and
being, found in animal and vegetable life, and every kind and
variety of mineral; to exhibit products, wares, goods, merchandise, machinery, mechanical inventions and improvements of
40 every nature, name and kind, and such as are generally
exhibited at fairs, including the various processes of manufacture; to exhibit paintings and statuary of any and every
nature and kind; to exhibit and develop the points and
qualities of the several breeds of horses and other animals, by

such competitive tests as may be humane and pro er, and as
may be deemed expedient and to make such other exhibitions
as will be in conformity with the purposes and objects of this
Act; and the said association is hereby further authorized,but

Authority to
acquire and
dispose of
property.

only for carrying on and maintaining the business aforesaid, 5
and such other business as may be hereafter mentioned, to
hold, own, and acquire, by lease, purchase, gift or otherwise,
property, real and personal, at such prices and on such terms
and conditions as may be agreed upon, and may improve and
use the same, by the construction of such building, houses, 10
works, and improvements as are necessary, and as may be
deemed proper; and the said association is hereby further
authorized to cultivate such portions of their grounds as they
may deem proper for the propagation of plants, trees, shrubs
or other things of a vegetable nature, and also to manufacture 15
and raise articles and things required in the various exhibitions contemplated; and to sell, mortgage, lease, or otherwise
dispose of any property at any time held by the said associa-

Proviso.

tion; provided always, and it is enacted, that the said association shall at no time acquire or hold, any lands or tenements 20
or interests therein, exceeding in the whole, at any one time
the annual value of $10,000, nor otherwise than for actual use
or occupation for the purposes of the said corporation.

Entrance fee,
prizes, etc.

3. The said association is hereby authorized to charge such
admission fees as may be deemed proper to receive for exhibit- 25
ing every thing contemplated by this Act; to charge such
entrance fees and to award, give and pay to exhibitors such
prizes, medals and honorary distinctions as they may deem
proper, and to let or lease stalls, stands, rooms and places in
any of their buildings or structures, or in any part of their 30
grounds or property, upon such terms and conditions and for
such purposes, as the board of directors may deem best for the
interests of the said association.

Members of
association.

4. *The President of the Agricultural and Arts Association
of Ontario,* the mayor of the city of London, the treasurer 35
of the city of London, *five members of the* council of the corporation of the city of London, *to be appointed by by-law of the
said council at the time when the standing committees thereof
for the year are appointed (but a failure to appoint them
shall not prevent the appointment being made afterwards)* 40
the president, vice-presidents and six members of the
electoral division of the city of London Horticultural
and Agricultural Society, the warden of the county of
Middlesex and two representatives, being members of the
county council of the county of Middlesex, to be named and 45
appointed by the said council at the time of the appointment
of the several standing committees thereof for the year, the
president, two vice-presidents and six members of the electoral
division of East Middlesex Agricultural Society; two representatives from the electoral division of North Middlesex 50
Agricultural Society, two representatives from the electoral
division of West Middlesex Agricultural Society, the president
and six members of the London Board of Trade, two members
each from all the electoral district agricultural societies in the
western peninsula, two representatives from the board of 55
education of the city of London, viz.: the chairman and one

member, two representatives from each of the several corporations, associations, organizations, societies and public bodies following, that is to say: the Ontario Society of Artists, *the Western Ontario School of Art and Design*, the London
5 Mechanics Institute, the Stock Breeders' Association of Ontario, the Fruit Growers' Association of Ontario, the Ontario Veterinary Association, the Ontario College of Pharmacy, the Poultry Association of Ontario, the Toronto Poultry Association, the London Poultry Association, the Dairymen's Associa-
10 tion of Western Ontario, *the Ontario Creameries Association*, the Millers' Association, the Photographers' Association, the Entomological Society, the Western Beekeepers' Association, the Western Ontario Commercial Travellers' Association, *the Trades and Labour Council of London*, such representatives to be named
15 and appointed by the said several corporations, associations, organizations and societies at their annual meeting for the election of officers, such number of representatives of such other corporations, associations, organizations or societies not named above as may from time to time, upon applications to be made
20 by such corporations, associations, organizations or societies, be admitted to the said Western Fair Association, by vote thereof, at the annual meeting thereof, upon such terms and conditions, and under such regulations and restrictions as may be made and determined by the board of directors and sanctioned by
25 the association at its annual meeting, and all such other persons as the board of directors may by by-law admit to membership, as hereinafter provided, shall constitute the said Western Fair Association, and the said several persons and representatives named, or hereafter to be admitted under the
30 provisions of this Act, and the by-laws of the said last mentioned association, shall be the members of the said Western Fair Association.

5. James Cowan, Andrew William Porte, John William **Provisional** Little, Richard Whetter, Lawrence Cleverdon, Donald Mac- **directors.**
35 Kenzie, George Douglass, John Walker, Thomas Green, William Y. Brunton, T. Herbert Marsh, John Green, Robert C. Struthers, John Wolfe, William John Reid, A. M. Smart, W. M. Gartshore, Thomas R. Parker, Robert Lewis, William McDonough, John Labatt, John R. Minhinnick, A. J. B. McDonald, Richard
40 Venning and John Kennedy, shall be provisional directors of the said Western Fair Association, to organize said association, and shall hold office until the election of directors, as hereinafter provided.

6. Forthwith after the passing of this Act, the said provi- **Meeting for**
45 sioual directors, or a majority of them, shall notify, in writing, **first election of directors.** the several corporations, organizations, persons, associations and societies, specially mentioned in section 4 of this Act, of the provisions of this Act, and shall at the same time request each of them to name and appoint representatives
50 (where the same are provided for in this Act) to the said the Western Fair Association, pursuant to the provisions of this Act, which appointment shall be evidenced by the corporate seal of each of the said several societies, organizations, associations or corporations or by a certificate, signed by the presid-
55 ing officer and secretary or clerk of such organization, society, corporation or association, as the case may be, and such notice shall likewise contain a statement of the time and place of

4

Qualification of directors and voters.

holding the first meeting of the members of the association for the election of directors, and such other business as may require to be done at such meeting, a copy of which notice shall also be published once in each week for two weeks before the time appointed for such meeting in one of the 5 newspapers published in the city of London.

Certificates of appointments of members.

7. At the first meeting of the members of the association, hereby incorporated for the election of directors, each member of the association, being a representative, shall produce to the said provisional directors a certificate, under the seal of the 10 corporation, association, society or organization which he represents or under the hand of the presiding officer and secretary, of his due and proper appointment, and the said provisional directors, or a majority of them, shall, at the time of such election, cause a list of all duly qualified members of 15 the association hereby incorporated to be made out and placed upon the table, and only the persons whose names shall appear upon such list shall be eligible as directors, or entitled to vote for directors, and upon such other matters, questions and things as may be presented for the consideration of the 20 meeting.

Representation of societies which have not made any election.

8. In the event of no appointment of representatives under the provisions of this Act having been made, from any cause, by any of the societies, corporations, organizations, or associations specially named in section 4 hereof, before the 25 time fixed by the provisional directors for the holding of the meeting for the election of the directors of the said association hereby incorporated, then and in every such case, the president, vice-president, chairman, or other presiding officer, and the secretary of the association, organization, corporation, or 30 society so having failed to make such appointment, shall be the representatives of such association, organization, corporation, or society, and shall be *ex officio* members of the corporation hereby created, until the appointment contemplated by this Act shall have been made, and shall be entitled to vote at all 35 meetings of members of the said association.

Number of directors, etc.

9. The board of directors shall consist of not less than fifteen nor more than twenty-four members (a majority of whom shall be residents of the City of London), *as shall* be determined at the meeting to be held as provided for in 40 section 7 of this Act. *The mayor of the city of London and the five members of the municipal council thereof, appointed under the provisions of section 4 hereof, shall be members of the said board.* The East Middlesex Agricultural Society shall be entitled to a representation on said board of 45 six members, all of whom shall be residents of the County of Middlesex, *but none of whom shall be residents of the city of London,* and shall be chosen by said society in such a manner as said society may decide, and not more than six *of the* directors shall be elected from the representatives sent as mem- 50 bers of the Western Fair Association from the Horticultural Society of the Electoral Division of the City of London under section 4 of this Act, *and the remainder of the directors shall be chosen from among the members of the said association.* The election of directors (except as to the directors appointed 55

by the *council of the city of London and the* East Middlesex Agricultural Society as aforesaid) and every question
voted on at said meeting shall, if demanded by two members,
be decided by ballot by a majority of votes of the members of
5 the association hereby incorporated, present in person and
voting at the meeting; the directors so chosen · shall immediately elect one of their own number to be president, and
two others of them to be vice-presidents, which president,
vice-presidents and directors shall continue in office for one
10 year and until others shall be chosen to fill their places as may
be provided for by the by-laws of said association, and if any
vacancy shall at any time happen by death, resignation or
otherwise in the office of president, vice-president or directors
the remaining · directors shall supply such vacancy by the
15 appointment of some member of the association for the
remainder of the year; and the election of the directors shall
take place, annually, either on the anniversary of the day of
the first election of directors or such other day as may be fixed
by by-law as hereinafter provided and mentioned.

20 **10.** The directors shall have full power to make all by- Powers of
laws, rules and regulations not inconsistent with the pro- directors.
visions of this Act, for the management of the association
hereby incorporated, the securing of the cash fund hereinafter
mentioned, and the collection thereof, as also hereinafter men-
25 tioned, the acquisition of exhibition grounds and buildings, by
purchase, lease, agreement or otherwise, and the selling, leasing
and mortgaging, or otherwise disposing of the same, as occasion
may require, the acquisition and management of all property,
whether real or personal, which may be required for the
30 purposes of, or in connection with, the exhibition or other
business and operations of the said association, and the sale or
other disposal thereof, when no longer required for such
purposes, the entering into any and all arrangements, agreements and contracts with any person, or corporation, society,
35 or association, as the same may become necessary to carry out
the objects of the said · association, the admission of other
persons as members and of other corporations, societies, associations, or organizations than those named in this Act, to be
represented in the said association hereby incorporated and
40 the terms and conditions of such admission, the fees (if any) to be
paid by members of the association, the holding of exhibitions,
annual or periodical, fixing the time for the annual meeting
and the calling of general, special and other meetings of the
association, the appointment, removal and remuneration of
45 all officers, agents, clerks, workmen and servants of the association, the admission fees to be received from · persons visiting
their exhibitions, the entrance fees to be charged exhibitors;
the general management of all exhibitions, and in general to
do all things and make all contracts and agreements that may
50 be necessary to carry out the objects and exercise the powers
incident to the association.

11. Before the directors of said association shall undertake When associa-
the holding of any exhibition or commence the business and tion may
operations contemplated by this Act, they shall secure or have commence
operations.
55 on hand a cash fund of not less than $5,000.

Certain societies authorized to make agreements with and aid association.

12. Notwithstanding anything contained in *The Agricul-*
ture and Arts Act, it shall and may be lawful for all or any
of the several societies, corporations, organizations, and associations named in section 4 of this Act, and for any of the
corporations, associations, organizations or societies formed, or 5
hereafter to be formed, under the provisions of the said Act,
and they, and all and every of them are hereby authorized and
empowered, through their several and respective councils or
boards of directors, or committees of management, and officers,
to enter into any arrangements and to make any agreements, 10
and contracts with the board of directors of the said association hereby incorporated for the holding of exhibitions, and
taking part in the exhibitions to be holden by the said association, and otherwise promoting the objects contemplated by
this Act, and may aid the same with any funds and moneys 15
belonging to any such association or society not otherwise
specially appropriated by any statute of this Province.

Aid from municipalities.

13. The municipal council of any city, town, village, county
or township, in this Province, may grant money or land in aid
of the said association, or may lend or grant aid by way of 20
bonus to the said association out of any moneys belonging to
the municipality, and may effect such loan, or grant such aid,
upon such terms and conditions as may be agreed upon
between said association and the council of the municipality
making such loan or granting such aid, and may recover the 25
money so lent and may appropriate the moneys so recovered

Proviso.

to the purposes of such municipality; provided always that no
municipal council shall in any one year grant any such money
or bonus to any greater extent than $5,000, nor shall any *money*
or land be so granted or given under the provisions of *The Con-* 30
solidated Municipal Act, 1883, as to by-laws for raising, on
the credit of the municipality, money not required for its ordinary expenditure and not payable within the same municipal
year; such provisions being those which require and relate to
the assent of electors and otherwise. 35

Agreements with munici- palities.

14. The council of any municipality and the association
hereby incorporated and the directors thereof, are hereby
respectively authorized to make and enter into any agreements
or covenants relating to the holding of any exhibition, and
granting and accepting aid for the same, and for the furnish- 4(?)
ing and providing exhibition grounds and buildings suitable
for the purposes of the said association and for the representation of such municipality in the said association, by the
appointment of members of the council thereof as representatives to such association, and all the representatives so 45
appointed in pursuance of any such agreement shall become
members of the said association and entitled to vote upon all
matters and questions submitted or voted upon at all meetings
of the association, and every such council may pass by-laws
for all and every of the purposes aforesaid and in furtherance 50
of the objects contemplated by this Act as occasion may
require, but subject to the special provisions contained in
section 13 of this Act.

Guarantee by city of London of money con- tributed by Agricultural

15. The corporation of the city of London may enter into
any agreement with the East Middlesex Agricultural Society 50

or the Horticultural Society of the city of London, guaranteeing and Horticultural societies to Western Fair Association.
the repayment of any moneys contributed by either of the said
societies to the Western Fair Association. ⨳

16. Sections 5, 6, 15, 16, 17, 30, 31, 38, 41, 42, 72, 73 (1), Certain sections of 49 V. s. 11, incorporated.
5 74, 75, 78, 81 (1), 82, 83 and 84 of *The Agriculture and*
Arts Act are hereby incorporated with, and are to be
taken and deemed as part of this Act and shall apply to
the said association, and to the exhibitions to be held
by them as fully as such sections apply to the Agricultural
10 and Arts Association and to exhibitions held by such association, except in so far as they may be inconsistent with the
enactments hereof, and the expression "this Act" when used
herein, shall be understood to include the sections of the said
last mentioned Act so incorporated with this Act as aforesaid.

15 **17**. It shall be lawful for the corporation of the city of Power to expropriate lands for purposes of association.
London at the request of the Western Fair Association to
acquire by expropriation from time to time such lands in the
city of London or vicinity as may be required for the purposes
. of said Western Fair Association and such power of expropria-
20 tion shall be exercised subject to the provisions of sections 486,
487, 488 and 489 of *The Consolidated Municipal Act, 1883,*
which sections are hereby declared applicable.

⨳**18**. The said association shall not hold their annual Time of exhibition restricted.
exhibition during the week in which the Provincial Fair is
.25 held when the said last mentioned fair is held west of ·
Toronto. ⨳

1st Session, 6th Legislature, 50 Vic., 1887.

BILL.

An Act to incorporate the Western Fair Association.

(Reprinted as amended by Private Bills Committee.)

First Reading, 17th March, 1887.

BILL.

An Act to incorporate the Western Fair Association.

WHEREAS James Cowan and others, hereinafter named, Preamble. have by their petition prayed that an association may be incorporated for the purpose of promoting industries, arts and sciences generally, and of establishing and holding agri-
5 cultural, industrial, art and other exhibitions at the city of London; and whereas it is expedient to grant the prayer of the said petition;

Therefore Her Majesty, by and with the advice and consent of the Legislative Assembly of the Province of Ontario, enacts
10 as follows:—

1. James Cowan, Andrew William Porte, John William Incorporation. Little, Richard Whetter, Lawrence Cleverdon, Donald Mac-Kenzie, Geo. Douglass, John Walker, Thomas Green, William Y. Brunton, T. Herbert Marsh, John Green, Robt. C. Struthers,
15 John Wolfe, William John Reid, A. M. Smart, W. R. Hobbs, Thomas R. Parker, Robert Lewis, Moses Masuret, and others, the several representatives of the several societies, corporations and associations hereinafter named, together with all such other persons and representatives of other corpora-
20 tions, societies and associations as shall under the authority of this Act, be associated with them, in, and become members of, the corporation hereby created, shall be a body politic and cor-porate, by the name of the Western Fair Association and by that name shall and may have perpetual succession, and a
25 common seal, with the power to break and alter the same, and by that name shall and may sue and be sued in all Courts in this Province; and the said corporation shall have their principal place of business at London, but may open such office or offices at such places as may be found necessary or
30 convenient for the purposes of their business.

2. The said association is hereby authorized and empowered Exhibitions either permanently or periodically in structures, buildings, authorized. enclosures, and places located in the city of London, or the township of London or Westminster, suitable for exhibition
35 purposes and for the promotion of industries, arts and sciences generally, to exhibit any and every variety of thing and being, found in animal and vegetable life, and every kind and variety of mineral; to exhibit products, wares, goods, merchan-dise, machinery, mechanical inventions and improvements of
40 every nature, name and kind, and such as are generally exhibited at fairs, including the various processes of manu-facture; to exhibit paintings and statuary of any and every nature and kind; to exhibit and develop the points and qualities of the several breeds of horses and other animals, by

such competitive tests as may be humane and pro er, and as
may be deemed expedient and to make such other exhibitions
as will be in conformity with the purposes and objects of this
Act; and the said association is hereby further authorized, but
Authority to
acquire and
dispose of
property. only for carrying on and maintaining the business aforesaid, 5
and such other business as may be hereafter mentioned, to
hold, own, and acquire, by lease, purchase, gift or otherwise,
property, real and personal, at such prices and on such terms
and conditions as may be agreed upon, and may improve and
use the same, by the construction of such building, houses, 10
works, and improvements as are necessary, and as may be
deemed proper; and the said association is hereby further
authorized to cultivate such portions of their grounds as they
may deem proper for the propagation of plants, trees, shrubs
or other things of a vegetable nature, and also to manufacture 15
and raise articles and things required in the various exhibitions contemplated; and to sell, mortgage, lease, or otherwise
dispose of any property at any time held by the said associa-
Proviso. tion; provided always, and it is enacted, that the said association shall at no time acquire or hold, any lands or tenements 20
or interests therein, exceeding in the whole, at any one time
the annual value of $10,000, nor otherwise than for actual use
or occupation for the purposes of the said corporation.

Entrance fees,
prizes, etc. **3.** The said association is hereby authorized to charge such
admission fees as may be deemed proper to receive for exhibit- 25
ing every thing contemplated by this Act; to charge such
entrance fees and to award, give and pay to exhibitors such
prizes, medals and honorary distinctions as they may deem
proper, and to let or lease stalls, stands, rooms and places in
any of their buildings or structures, or in any part of their 30
grounds or property, upon such terms and conditions and for
such purposes, as the board of directors may deem best for the
interests of the said association.

Members of
association. **4.** *The President of the Agricultural and Arts Association
of Ontario,* the mayor of the city of London, the treasurer 35
of the city of London, *five members of the* council of the corporation of the city of London, *to be appointed by by-law of the
said council at the time when the standing committees thereof
for the year are appointed (but a failure to appoint them
shall not prevent the appointment being made afterwards),* 40
the president, vice-presidents and six members of the
electoral division of the city of London Horticultural
and Agricultural Society, the warden of the county of
Middlesex and two representatives, being members of the
county council of the county of Middlesex, to be named and 45
appointed by the said council at the time of the appointment
of the several standing committees thereof for the year, the
president, two vice-presidents and six members of the electoral
division of East Middlesex Agricultural Society; two representatives from the electoral division of North Middlesex 50
Agricultural Society, two representatives from the electoral
division of West Middlesex Agricultural Society, the president
and six members of the London Board of Trade, two members
each from all the electoral district agricultural societies in the
western peninsula, two representatives from the board of 55
education of the city of London, viz.: the chairman and one

member, two representatives from each of the several corporations, associations, organizations, societies and public bodies following, that is to say: the Ontario Society of Artists, *the Western Ontario School of Art and Design,* the Ontario
5 *Music Teachers' Association,* the London Mechanics Institute, the Stock Breeders' Association of Ontario, the Fruit Growers' Association of Ontario, the Ontario Veterinary Association, the Ontario College of Pharmacy, the Poultry Association of Ontario, the Toronto Poultry Association, the Lon-
10 don Poultry Association, the Dairymen's Association of Western Ontario, *the Ontario Creameries Association,* the Millers' Association, the Photographers' Association, the Entomological Society, the Western Beekeepers' Association, the Western Ontario Commercial Travellers' Association, *the Trades and*
15 *Labour Council of London,* such representatives to be named and appointed by the said several corporations, associations, organizations and societies at their annual .meeting for the election of officers, such number of representatives of such other corporations, associations, organizations or societies not named
20 above as may from time to time, upon applications to be made by such corporations, associations, organizations or societies, be admitted to the said Western Fair Association, by vote thereof, at the annual meeting thereof, upon such terms and conditions, and under such regulations and restrictions as may be made
25 and determined by the board of directors and sanctioned by the association at its annual meeting, and all such other persons as the board of directors may by by-law admit to membership, as hereinafter provided, shall constitute the said Western Fair Association, and the said several persons and
30 representatives named, or hereafter to be admitted under the provisions of this Act, and the by-laws of the said last mentioned association, shall be the members of the said Western Fair Association.

5. James Cowan, Andrew William Porte, John William Provisional
35 Little, Richard Whetter, Lawrence Cleverdon, Donald Mac- directors. Kenzie, George Douglass, John Walker, Thomas Green, William Y. Brunton, T. Herbert Marsh, John Green, Robert C. Struthers, John Wolfe, William John Reid, A. M. Smart, Thomas R. Parker, Robert Lewis, William McDonough, John Labatt,
40 John R. Minhinnick, A. J. B. McDonald, Richard Venning and John Kennedy, shall be provisional directors of the said Western Fair Association, to organize said association, and shall hold office until the election of directors, as hereinafter provided.

45 **6**. Forthwith after the passing of this Act, the said provi- Meeting for sional directors, or a majority of them, shall notify, in writing, first election the several corporations, organizations, persons, associations- of directors. and societies, specially mentioned in section 4 of this Act, of the provisions of this Act, and shall at the same time
50 request each of them to name and appoint representatives (where the same are provided for in this Act) to the said the Western Fair Association, pursuant to the provisions of this Act, which appointment shall be evidenced by the corporate seal of each of the said several societies, organizations, associa-
55 tions or corporations or by a certificate, signed by the presiding officer and secretary or clerk of such organization, society, corporation or association, as the case may be, and such notice

shall likewise contain a statement of the time and place of
holding the first meeting of the members of the association for
the election of directors, and such other business as may
require to be done at such meeting, a copy of which notice
shall also be published once in each week for two weeks 5
before the time appointed for such meeting in one of the
newspapers published in the city of London.

Certificates of
appointments
of members.

7. At the first meeting of the members of the association,
hereby incorporated for the election of directors, each member
of the association, being a representative, shall produce to the 10
said provisional directors a certificate, under the seal of the
corporation, association, society or organization which he
represents or under the hand of the presiding officer and
secretary, of his due and proper appointment, and the said
provisional directors, or a majority of them, shall, at the time 15
of such election, cause a list of all duly qualified members of
the association hereby incorporated to be made out and placed
upon the table, and only the persons whose names shall
appear upon such list shall be eligible as directors, or entitled
to vote for directors, and upon such other matters, questions 20
and things as may be presented for the consideration of the
meeting.

Representa-
tion of
societies which
have not made
any election.

8. In the event of no appointment of representatives under
the provisions of this Act having been made, from any cause,
by any of the societies, corporations, organizations, or associa- 25
tions specially named in section 4 hereof, before the
time fixed by the provisional directors for the holding of the
meeting for the election of the directors of the said association
hereby incorporated, then and in every such case, the president, vice-president, chairman, or other presiding officer, and 30
the secretary of the association, organization, corporation, or
society so having failed to make such appointment, shall be the
representatives of such association, organization, corporation, or
society, and shall be *ex officio* members of the corporation
hereby created, until the appointment contemplated by this 35
Act shall have been made, and shall be entitled to vote at all
meetings of members of the said association.

Number of
directors, etc.

9. The board of directors shall consist of not less than
fifteen nor more than twenty-four members (a majority of
whom shall be residents of the city of London), *as shall* be 40
determined as the meeting to be held as provided for in
section 7 of this Act. *The mayor of the city of London
and the five members of the municipal council thereof,
appointed under the provisions of section 4 hereof, shall be
members of the said board.* The East Middlesex Agricultural 45
Society shall be entitled to a representation on said board of
six members, all of whom shall be residents of the county of
Middlesex, *but none of whom shall be residents of the city of
London*, and shall be chosen by said society in such a manner
as said society may decide, and not more than six *of the* 50
directors shall be elected from the representatives sent as members of the Western Fair Association from the Horticultural
Society of the Electoral Division of the city of London under
section 4 of this Act, *and the remainder of the directors shall
be chosen from among the members of the said association.* 55
The election of directors (except as to the directors appointed

by the *council of the city of London and the* East Middlesex Agricultural Society as aforesaid) and every question voted on at said meeting shall, if demanded by two members, be decided by ballot by a majority of votes of the members of
5 the association hereby incorporated, present in person and voting at the meeting; the directors so chosen shall immediately elect one of their own number to be president, and two others of them to be vice-presidents, which president, vice-presidents and directors shall continue in office for one
10 year and until others shall be chosen to fill their places as may be provided for by the by-laws of said association, and if any vacancy shall at any time happen by death, resignation or otherwise in the office of president, vice-president or directors the remaining directors shall supply such vacancy by the
15 appointment of some member of the association for the remainder of the year; and the election of the directors shall take place, annually, either on the anniversary of the day of the first election of directors or such other day as may be fixed by by-law as hereinafter provided and mentioned.

20 **10.** The directors shall have full power to make all by-laws, rules and regulations not inconsistent with the provisions of this Act, for the management of the association hereby incorporated, the securing of the cash fund hereinafter mentioned, and the collection thereof, as also hereinafter men-
25 tioned, the acquisition of exhibition grounds and buildings, by purchase, lease, agreement or otherwise, and the selling, leasing and mortgaging, or otherwise disposing of the same, as occasion may require, the acquisition and management of all property, whether real or personal, which may be required for the
30 purposes of, or in connection with, the exhibition or other business and operations of the said association, and the sale or other disposal thereof, when no longer required for such purposes, the entering into any and all arrangements, agreements and contracts with any person, or corporation, society,
35 or association, as the same may become necessary to carry out the objects of the said association, the admission of other persons as members and of other corporations, societies, associations, or organizations than those named in this Act, to be represented in the said association hereby incorporated and
40 the terms and conditions of such admission, the fees (if any) to be paid by members of the association, the holding of exhibitions, annual or periodical, fixing the time for the annual meeting and the calling of general, special and other meetings of the association, the appointment, removal and remuneration of
45 all officers, agents, clerks, workmen and servants of the association, the admission fees to be received from persons visiting their exhibitions, the entrance fees to be charged exhibitors; the general management of all exhibitions, and in general to do all things and make all contracts and agreements that may
50 be necessary to carry out the objects and exercise the powers incident to the association.

Powers of directors.

11. Before the directors of said association shall undertake the holding of any exhibition or commence the business and operations contemplated by this Act, they shall secure or have
55 on hand a cash fund of not less than $5,000.

When association may commence operations.

Certain
societies
authorized to
make agree-
ments with
and aid
association.

12. Notwithstanding anything contained in *The Agriculture and Arts Act*, it shall and may be lawful for all or any
of the several societies, corporations, organizations, and associations named in section 4 of this Act, and for any of the
corporations, associations, organizations or societies formed, or 5
hereafter to be formed, under the provisions of the said Act,
and they, and all and every of them are hereby authorized and
empowered, through their several and respective councils or
boards of directors, or committees of management, and officers,
to enter into any arrangements and to make any agreements, 10
and contracts with the board of directors of the said association hereby incorporated for the holding of exhibitions, and
taking part in the exhibitions to be holden by the said association, and otherwise promoting the objects contemplated by
this Act, and may aid the same with any funds and moneys 15
belonging to any such association or society not otherwise
specially appropriated by any statute of this Province.

Aid from
municipalities.

13. The municipal council of any city, town, village, county
or township, in this Province, may grant money or land in aid
of the said association, or may lend or grant aid by way of 20
bonus to the said association out of any moneys belonging to
the municipality, and may effect such loan, or grant such aid,
upon such terms and conditions as may be agreed upon
between said association and the council of the municipality
making such loan or granting such aid, and may recover the 25
money so lent and may appropriate the moneys so recovered

Proviso.

to the purposes of such municipality; provided always that no
municipal council shall in any one year grant any such money
or bonus to any greater extent than $5,000, nor shall any *money
or* land be so granted or given under the provisions of *The Con-* 30
solidated Municipal Act, 1883, as to by-laws for raising, on
the credit of the municipality, money not required for its ordinary expenditure and not payable within the same municipal
year; such provisions being those which require and relate to
the assent of electors and otherwise. 35

Agreements
with munici-
palities.

14. The council of any municipality and the association
hereby incorporated and the directors thereof, are hereby
respectively authorized to make and enter into any agreements
or covenants relating to the holding of any exhibition, and
granting and accepting aid for the same, and for the furnish- 40
ing and providing exhibition grounds and buildings suitable
for the purposes of the said association and for the representation of such municipality in the said association, by the
appointment of members of the council thereof as representatives to such association, and all the representatives so 45
appointed in pursuance of any such agreement shall become
members of the said association and entitled to vote upon all
matters and questions submitted or voted upon at all meetings
of the association, and every such council may pass by-laws
for all and every of the purposes aforesaid and in furtherance 50
of the objects contemplated by this Act as occasion may
require, but subject to the special provisions contained in
section 13 of this Act.

Guarantee by
city of London
of money con-
tributed by
Agricultural

15. The corporation of the city of London may enter into
any agreement with the East Middlesex Agricultural Society 55

or the Horticultural Society of the city of London, guaranteeing the repayment of any moneys contributed by either of the said societies to the Western Fair Association. and Horticultural societies to Western Fair Association.

16. Sections 5, 6, 15, 16, 17, 30, 31, 38, 41, 42, 72, 73 (1),
5 74, 75, 78, 81 (1), 82, 83 and 84 of *The Agriculture and Arts Act* are hereby incorporated with, and are to be taken and deemed as part of this Act and shall apply to the said association, and to the exhibitions to be held by them as fully as such sections apply to the Agricultural
10 and Arts Association and to exhibitions held by such association, except in so far as they may be inconsistent with the enactments hereof, and the expression "this Act" when used herein, shall be understood to include the sections of the said last mentioned Act so incorporated with this Act as aforesaid. Certain sections of 49 V. s. 11, incorporated.

15 **17.** It shall be lawful for the corporation of the city of London at the request of the Western Fair Association to acquire by expropriation from time to time such lands in the city of London or vicinity as may be required for the purposes
20 of said Western Fair Association and such power of expropriation shall be exercised subject to the provisions of sections 486, 487, 488 and 489 of *The Consolidated Municipal Act, 1883,* which sections are hereby declared applicable. Power to expropriate lands for purposes of association.

18. The said association shall not hold their annual exhibition during the week in which the Provincial Fair is
25 held when the said last mentioned fair is held at or west of Toronto: provided that notice of the time and place of holding the Provincial Fair shall have been given to the said association before the first day of April, in the year in which it is proposed to hold such fair, at or west of Toronto. Time of exhibition restricted.

30 **19.**—(1) Section 2 of the Act passed in the 48th year of Her Majesty's reign, chapter 62, intituled "*An Act to authorize the Corporation of the City of London to borrow certain moneys,*" is hereby amended by adding after the word "aforesaid" in the fourth line thereof the words "or for build-
35 ing upon and improving the said lands known as Salter's Grove, for the purposes of a public park and exhibition grounds. 48 V. c. 62, s. 2, amended.

(2) The amount to be borrowed under the authority of the said in part recited Act, shall not exceed the sum of $60,-
40 000 in addition to the sum of $40,000, for which debentures have already been issued.

20. The corporation of the city of London may give to the said association a license to use the said Salter's Grove, and any addition which shall be made thereto, together with
45 the buildings and improvements thereon, for the purposes of holding their exhibitions there for such period not exceeding twenty years, and on such terms and conditions as to the council thereof may seem meet, but no such license shall be granted unless or until the said association shall have procured
50 a release from all corporations having the right to use the lands mentioned in the said in part recited Act as being then used for exhibition purposes, for holding exhibitions or fairs thereon, of their rights in respect of the said last mentioned lands. License to use Salter's Grove

1st Session, 6th Legislature, 50 Vic., 1887.

BILL.

An Act to incorporate the Western Fair
Association.

(*Re-printed as again Amended by Private
Bills Committee.*)

First Reading, 17th March, 1887.
Second   "   28th   "   1887.

(Private Bill.)

Mr Meredith

No. 47.]　　　　　**BILL.**　　　　[1887.

An Act to separate certain Municipalties from the Counties of Perth, Huron, and Wellington, and to erect the same into the County of Maitland.

WHEREAS the population of the town of Listowel, in the Preamble.
county of Perth, and the townships of Wallace, Elma,
and Mornington, in the county of Perth, and the village of
Milverton, also in the county of Perth, the town of Palmerston
5 in the county of Wellington, and the township of Maryborough, also in the county of Wellington, the townships of
Grey and Howick, in the county of Huron, and the villages of
Brussels and Wroxeter, also in the county of Huron, is about
thirty-two thousand five hundred souls, and the assessed value
10 of the property comprised therein is upwards of $5,000,000 ;
and whereas many of the said municipalities are inconveniently
distant from the county towns of the counties of which they
form a part, and the said counties are of an unwieldy size; and
whereas the said municipalities are of such size and wealth,
15 and their relative situation and trade relations are such as to
render it fitting that they should, with the approval of the
people, be formed into a new county ; and whereas divers petitions have been presented praying for the passing of this Act,
and it is expedient to grant the prayer of the said petitions ;
20　Therefore Her Majesty, by and with the advice and consent
of the Legislative Assembly of the Province of Ontario, enacts
as follows :—

1. The reeves and deputy-reeves of the town of Listowel, in The pro-
the county of Perth, and the townships of Wallace, Elma and visional council.
25 Mornington, also in the county of Perth, and the village of
Milverton, also in the county of Perth, and the town of Palmerston, in the county of Wellington, the township of Maryborough, in the said county of Wellington, the townships of
Grey and Howick, in the county of Huron, and the villages of
30 Brussels and Wroxeter, also in the county of Huron, shall form
a provisional municipal council under the style and name of
the " Provisional Council of the County of Maitland," for the
purposes of this Act.

2. It shall, upon the written request of any four of the First meeting of reeves.
35 reeves and deputy-reeves of the said municipalities, be the duty
of the reeve of Listowel to call a meeting of the said reeves
and deputy-reeves of the said towns, townships and villages
aforesaid, at such place and at such hour within the said town
of Listowel as he shall appoint, and a notice of such meeting
40 shall be inserted in at least one newspaper published within
each of the said counties of Perth, Wellington and Huron
respectively, and a copy of such notice sent by mail or other

2

wise to each of such reeves and deputy-reeves at least ten days
before the day appointed for such meeting ; and the said provisional council shall, at the first meeting thereof, to be held
under this Act, proceed to elect a provisional warden; after
which, at the same meeting, or some adjournment thereof, they 5
shall proceed to pass a by-law for the purpose of taking a vote
of the qualified municipal electors of the said towns of Listowel
and Palmerston, and of the townships and villages aforesaid,
on the question of the separation and erection into a new
county by vote to be specially taken for that purpose, each 10
qualified elector having one vote, and voting " yea," or " nay,"
after at least ten days' notice shall have been given in the manner to be provided by such by-law, of the time and places,
when and where the said vote is to be taken.

3. The provisional council shall meet on the requisition of 15
the warden on some day after the day or days appointed for
taking such vote, and shall proceed in open council to ascertain
the number of votes recorded, " yea " and " nay," and if the
result shall show that a majority of the votes recorded are
" nay," then after making a record of the same in the minutes 20
of the said provisional council, the said council shall adjourn
sine die, and be called together again only on the written
request of a majority of the reeves and deputy-reeves of the
said towns, townships and villages in manner as aforesaid.

4. If the result shall show that a majority of the votes 25
recorded are " yea," the said provisional council shall make a
record thereof in their minutes, and in that event the county
town of the new county shall be Listowel.

5. The said provisional council shall and may thereafter pass
a by-law for providing means for purchasing and acquiring 30
lands and erecting the necessary county buildings thereon at
Listowel, but before its final passing such by-law shall be submitted to the municipal electors of the said new county, and a
vote shall be taken on the same in like manner as provided by
The Consolidated Municipal Act, 1883, and any amendment 35
affecting the same, and after passing such by-law the said provisional council shall proceed to erect the necessary county
buildings.

6. After the necessary buildings have been erected as aforesaid, it shall be lawful for the Lieutenant-Governor in Council, 40
by proclamation to declare the said towns, townships and villages separated from the said counties to which they now belong respectively, and declare them to be formed into a new
county under the name of the county of Maitland for all judicial and municipal purposes, and also for registry purposes, 45
unless proclamation in that behalf has previously issued under
the provisions of this Act, but until the issue of such proclamation the said towns and townships shall remain, as at present,
connected with the counties of which they respectively form a
part for all such purposes. 50

7. The provisional council aforesaid shall, prior to such proclamation, have only the powers specially given to it by the
preceding sections of this Act.

3

8. After such proclamation the provisional council shall and Power after may have and exercise all the rights, powers, privileges, and proclamation. duties conferred on municipal councils by law; and the provisions of any law in force in this Province in any wise affect-
5 ing or relating to the proceedings consequent upon the dissolution of the union of counties shall apply so far as applicable to the separation of the towns, townships and villages aforesaid from the respective counties of which they have heretofore formed part, and the erection thereof into a new county.

10 **9.** After such proclamation the law in force respecting Law respect. municipal institutions of this Province shall, as far as applicable ing municipal and not inconsistent with this Act, apply to the county of apply. Maitland. institutions to

10. After such proclamation the corporations of Listowel, Apportion-Wallace, Elma, Mornington and Milverton shall respectively ment of exist-
15 pay to the corporation of the county of Perth, and the corpor-ing debt. ations of Palmerston and Maryborough shall respectively pay to the corporation of the county of Wellington, and the corporations of Grey, Howick, Brussels, and Wroxeter shall respectively pay to the corporation of the county of Huron
20 such proportion of the then outstanding debt of the counties of Perth, Wellington and Huron respectively, and in such manner as may be determined under the said Act respecting municipal institutions of Ontario; and the respective corporations of the said towns, townships and villages shall respectively receive
25 from the county corporations from which they are respectively separated, a just proportion of the assets of said counties.

11. In case a majority of the votes cast at the polling pro- Registry vided for in section 3 of this Act are recorded in favour of the Office. formation of such new county, the Lieutenant-Governor in
30 Council may by order in council cause to be issued a proclamation, and thereby set apart and establish a registry office for the said county so to be erected as aforesaid.

1st Session, 6th Legislature, 50 Vic., 1887

BILL.

An Act to separate certain municipalities from the Counties of Perth, Huron and Wellington, and to erect the same into the County of Maitland.

First Reading,   , 1887.

(Private Bill)

BILL.

An Act to consolidate the Floating Debt of the Township of Colchester North.

WHEREAS the corporation of the township of Colchester North by their petition have represented that they have incurred debts and liabilities to a larger extent than has been provided for by the annual rates levied from year to year, by 5 reason of a large amount of unforeseen expenditure, required to defray the expenses of drainage and other public works in the said township, and costs and expenses incidental to and caused by such drainage and other works, and the said debts and liabilities amount to $8,500, and the annual revenue to be raised 10 by taxation in order to meet the accruing debentures and payment of the current expenses, and the said debt of $8,500 will be insufficient without exceeding the limit authorized by law, and will be oppressive to the ratepayers, and have prayed that the floating debt of the said township amounting to $8,500 as 15 aforesaid may be consolidated, and that they may be authorized to issue debentures for that purpose ; and whereas it is expedient to grant the prayer of said petition ; *Preamble.*

Therefore Her Majesty, by and with the advice and consent of the Legislative Assembly of the Province of Ontario, enacts 20 as follows :—

1. The said floating debt of the corporation of the township of Colchester North, is hereby consolidated at the sum of $8,500 and it shall and may be lawful to and for the said corporation of the township of Colchester North, to raise by way of loan 25 upon the credit of the debentures hereinafter mentioned and by this Act authorized to be issued from any person or persons body or bodies corporate either in this Province, in Great Britain, or elsewhere, who may be willing to lend the same, a sum of money not exceeding $8,500 of lawful money of Canada, 30 and the principal sum secured by the said debentures and the interest accruing thereon may be made payable, either in this Province or in Great Britain, or elsewhere, as the said council shall deem expedient, and may be either in currency or sterling money. *Issue of debentures for $8,500 authorized.*

35 2. The said corporation may pass a by-law authorizing the issue of debentures under the corporate seal signed by the reeve and countersigned by the treasurer of the said corporation for the time being, for such sums not exceeding $8,500 in the whole, as the council of the said township may direct, bear- 40 ing interest at a rate not to exceed five per centum per annum payable yearly. *Authority to pass by-law for issue of debentures.*

3. The funds derived from the negotiation of the said debentures shall be applied by the said council to the payment of the *Application of funds.*

said outstanding floating debts and liabilities, and to and for no other purpose whatever.

Form of debentures. **4.** The debentures to be issued as aforesaid, shall be payable within twenty years from the date thereof, the principal of such debt shall be repayable by annual instalments, such 5 instalments to be of such amounts that the aggregate amount payable for principal and interest in any year shall be equal, as nearly as may be, to what is payable for principal and interest during each of the other years of the period within which the debt is to be discharged. 10

Special rate. **5.** For payment of the debentures to be issued under this Act the municipal council of the said corporation shall impose a special rate per annum, which shall be sufficient to pay the interest on the said debentures and the instalment of principal payable from year to year. 15

Irregularities in debentures or by-law not to render them invalid. **6.** No irregularity in the form of the said debentures or of the by-law authorizing the issuing thereof shall render the same invalid or illegal, or be allowed as a defence to any action brought against the corporation for the recovery of the amount of the said debentures and interest or any or either of them or 20 any part thereof.

Assent of electors not required. **7.** It shall not be necessary to obtain the assent of the electors of the said township to the passing of the said by-law under this Act, or to observe the formalities in relation thereto prescribed by *The Consolidated Municipal Act, 1883*, or amend- 25 ing Acts.

Form of debentures. **8.** The said debentures may be in the form contained in the schedule to this Act, or as near thereto as the corporation may find convenient, according to the places where and the money in which the same are made payable. 30

SCHEDULE.

CONSOLIDATED LOAN DEBENTURE, No.　　　　$

PROVINCE OF ONTARIO, TOWNSHIP OF COLCHESTER NORTH.

Under and by virtue of the Act passed in the fiftieth year of the reign of Her Majesty Queen Victoria and chaptered and by virtue of by-law No.　　　　of the corporation of the township of Colchester North, passed under the powers contained in the said Act,

The corporation of the township of Colchester North promises to pay the bearer at　　　　in the sum of　　　　on the day of　　　　A.D.,　　and the yearly coupons hereto attached, as the same shall severally become due.

Dated at Gesto, in the township of Colchester North, in the county of Essex, this　　　　day of　　　　A.D., 188 .

[L. S.]　　　　　　　　　　　　　Reeve.

　　　　　　　　　　　　　　　　　Treasurer.

1st Session, 6th Legislature, 50 Vic., 1887.

BILL.

.

An Act to consolidate the floating debt of the Township of Colchester North.

First Reading,

1887.

(Private Bill.)

BILL.

An Act to empower Adelia Gould the trustee under a
Deed executed by Daniel Tierney, Jason Gould and
Adelia Gould to sell certain lands.

W HEREAS by indenture bearing date the 15th day of **Preamble.**
October, in the year of our Lord 1878, and made
between Daniel Tierney, of the village of Smiths Falls, in the
county of Lanark, gentleman, (a widower), of the first part,
5 Jason Gould, of the same place, mill owner, of the second part,
and Adelia Gould, wife of the said Jason Gould, and also of
the said village of Smiths Falls, of the third part, the lands
and premises following, that is to say:—All and singular the
west half of lot number thirty in the fifth concession of the
10 township of Montague, in the county of Lanark, in the province of Ontario, and that part of lot number one in the fifth
concession, in the township of North Elmsley, in the said
county of Lanark, known as park lot number two, according
to a plan or map drawn by Josias Richey, P.L.S., containing
15 twenty-four acres more or less, and also that parcel of land
being part of the original allowance for road between lot
number thirty, in the fifth concession of the township of
Montague, and part of lot number one, in the fifth concession
of the said township of North Elmslie, sold and conveyed by
20 the corporation of the then united counties of Lanark and
Renfrew to one Patrick Tierney by deed dated 22nd June,
1860, and also the east half of park lot number three, of said
lot number one, in the fifth concession of Elmsley aforesaid,
which park lot is shewn on the said plan above referred to,
25 and containing six acres more or less, were conveyed by the
said Daniel Tierney with the consent and at the request of the
said Jason Gould to the said Adelia Gould: To have and to
hold unto the said party of the third part (Adelia Gould) her
heirs and assigns upon the trust following, that is to say :—
30 To hold the same in trust for the sole use, benefit and behoof
of the children that are now born, or may be hereafter born,
issue of the marriage of the party of the second part (Jason
Gould) and of Adelia Gould his wife (the party of the third
part) upon trust to apply the use, issues and profits thereof
35 for the support, maintenance and education of such children
until they respectively attain the age of twenty-one years,
then upon trust to convey the said lands in equal shares to
and among the said children their heirs and assigns forever ;
and whereas the said Jason Gould departed this life on or
40 about the 24th day of October, A.D. 1882, intestate, leaving
him surviving his wife, the said Adelia Gould, and four
children, Anna Adelia Clara Gould, Jason Gould, Carrie May
Gould and Harry Johnson Gould, all infants under the age of
twenty-one years ; and whereas the said Jason Gould at the

time of his death was the owner of certain houses and lots, in
the said town of Smiths Falls, and also certain vacant lots in
said town, but was not possessed of personal estate sufficient
for the payment of the debts due and owing by him at the
time of his death; and whereas the income derived from the 5
said lands and premises belonging to the said Jason Gould,
and from the lands and premises hereinbefore described, is
insufficient for the support of the infant children of the said
Jason Gould; and whereas an application was made to the
High Court of Justice, Chancery Division, as appears by 10
petition filed with the proper officer, on the fourteenth day of
February, A.D. 1887, petitioning said Court for the sale of such
portions of the lands belonging to the said Jason Gould, as to
the said Court might seem meet, and also petitioning for the
sale of the lands and premises hereinbefore described, for the 15
purpose of paying the debts of the said Jason Gould and providing means for the support, maintenance and education of
the said infants; and whereas the Act passed in the twelfth
year of Her Majesty's reign empowering the Court to order a
sale of the estates of infants, provided that no sale shall be 20
made against the provisions of any conveyance by which an
estate has been granted to an infant or for his use; and
whereas the official guardian of infant estates for the Province
of Ontario, to whom was submitted the petition and evidence
used on the application to the Court for the sale of said lands, 25
has written to the solicitors for your petitioner in the following terms, that is to say:—"*Re* Gould infants; touching the
application you made for a sale of the farm lands under 12th
Victoria, I beg to say that I am of opinion that the land in
question could not be sold under the provisions of that statute. 30
Should it be in the interests of the infants to sell the property
in question I think you had better apply at once for an Act of
Parliament"; and whereas the portion of the lands and
premises, hereinbefore described, have recently been taken
into the corporation of the said town of Smiths Falls, and 35
taxes will in future have to be paid thereon at the rate levied
in said town; and whereas the said infants will suffer great
loss unless the power to sell said lands is at once conferred
upon your petitioner, so as to enable her to offer said land for
sale during the present year; and whereas it is manifestly to 40
the advantage of the infants that that portion of the said
lands now within the limits of the said town of Smiths Falls
should be subdivided into town lots and sold for the best price
obtainable therefor, and the annual income to be derived from
the proceeds thereof applied towards the support, main- 45
tenance, education and advancement in life of the said children;
and whereas it is expedient to grant the prayer of such
petition;

Therefore Her Majesty, by and with the advice and consent
of the Legislative Assembly of the Province of Ontario, enacts 50
as follows:—

Sale by trus-
tees authoriz-
ed.

1. The said trustee, or the trustees or trustee for the time
being, shall have full power and authority to subdivide into
town lots and sell, convey and absolutely dispose of all and
every or any part of the lands hereinbefore described, situate 55
within the limits of the said town of Smiths Falls, as she or
they in their discretion see fit, to any person or persons, whomsoever, either together or in parcels, and either by public

auction or by private contract, and for such price or prices in money, payable by instalments and to be secured by mortgages, or otherwise, as to the trustee or trustees for the time being shall seem reasonable, and any deed executed by said trustee 5 or trustees, as aforesaid, shall vest in the purchaser a full, clear and absolute title to the said lands, subject only to any rights therein now existing or granted by competent authority prior to such sale, and freed from all trusts whatsoever contained in said deed hereinbefore recited and from all estates, rights and 10 interests whatsoever of the children of the said Jason Gould.

2. The proceeds of such sale after payment of the expenses of obtaining this Act, and all proper and reasonable costs, charges and expenses of effecting and carrying out said sales, as the same may be from time to time paid, shall be paid into 15 the Supreme Court of Judicature for Ontario to the credit of the said infant children of the said Jason Gould in that matter now pending in the High Court of Justice, Chancery Division, entitled :—" In the matter of Anna Adelia Clara Gould, Jason Gould, Carrie May Gould and Harry Johnson Gould, infants 20 under the age of twenty-one years." The proceeds of such sales when so paid, in as aforesaid, shall be held upon the trusts and for the same end, intents and purposes expressed in the said deed with respect to the said lands and subject to the same rules and incidents, with respect to the devolution 22 thereof and otherwise, as if the lands still remained realty. *Application of proceeds of sale.*

3. No purchaser or alienee shall be required to see to the application of the purchase money or other consideration in respect of any disposition made under this Act. *Purchaser not responsible for application of purchase mo*

1st Session, 6th Legislature, 50 Vic., 1887.

BILL.

An Act to empower Adelia Gould the trustee under a Deed executed by Daniel Tierney, Jason Gould and Adelia Gould, to sell certain lands.

First Reading,   1887.

(Private Bill.)

BILL.

An Act Respecting the City of Toronto.

WHEREAS the corporation of the City of Toronto have, *Preamble.*
by their petition prayed for special legislation relating to
the several matters and things hereinafter set forth, and whereas it is expedient to grant the prayers of the said petition :
5   Therefore Her Majesty by and with the advice and consent
of the Legislative Assembly of the Province of Ontario enacts
as follows :—

1. The council of the corporation of the City of Toronto *Powers.*
may pass by-laws for the following amongst other purposes
10 notwithstanding anything, in *The Consolidated Municipal Act,
1883*, or any amending Act or in any special or private Act
relating to the said City of Toronto contained to the contrary :

(1) For entering upon, taking, using and acquiring so much *Acquiring
land in the City of Toronto as may be required for the pur-* land for
drill shed.
15 poses of a new drill-shed for the volunteer force of the City
of Toronto without the consent of the owners of such lands
making due compensation therefore to the parties entitled
thereto under the provisions of *The Consolidated Municipal
Act, 1883*, and amending Acts in that behalf.

20   (2) For entering upon, taking, using and acquiring such land *Acquiring
and lands covered by water as the City may from time to time* land for
parks, etc.
require for public parks, squares, pleasure grounds, boulevards
and drives in the City of Toronto and adjoining municipalities
without the consent of the owners of such lands and lands
25 covered by water making due compensation therefore to the
parties entitled thereto under the provisions of *The Consolidated
Municipal Act, 1883*, and amending Acts in that behalf.

(3) For selling, leasing, or otherwise disposing of such *Selling lands.*
portions of the lands now held or which may be hereafter
30 acquired by the City of Toronto for park purposes and are
found to be unfit for such purposes and applying the proceeds
of such sales, leases or other dispositions to the purchase of
other lands for park purposes : Provided that this power shall
not extend to any lands which shall have been heretofore, or
35 may be hereafter, dedicated by private persons for public uses
except with the consent of the persons who shall have made
such dedication, or with the consent of their heirs or assigns.

(4) For specially assessing and levying upon and collecting *Assessment
from lands and premises adjoining public parks, squares, drives,* of lands
adjoining
40 and boulevards a portion of the cost of the improvements parks, etc.
made upon or in such parks, squares, drives, and boulevards as
for local improvements when any such improvement confers a
special benefit upon such adjoining lands and premises such
assessments, levies and collections to be made under and

subject to the provisions of *The Consolidated Municipal Act 1883*, and amending Acts relating to local improvements and assessments therefor, and no petition against any such assessment shall avail to prevent the same being made.

Borrowing money for park purposes. (5) For borrowing moneys not to exceed the sum of $100,- 5 000 for improving the City parks and for park purposes by the issue and sale of debentures upon the credit of the City at large and also for charging the usual interest and sinking fund required for moneys so borrowed as a first lien upon the income belonging to the " Walks and Garden Fund." But any by-law 10 passed for this purpose shall require the assent of the electors entitled to vote on money by-laws before the final passing thereof.

Defraying part of costs of bridges, streets, etc. (6) For borrowing money by the issue and sale of debentures upon the credit of the City at large to provide as the 15 City's share thereof not more than one-half of the cost of constructing, erecting or building any bridge, culvert or embankment, or opening up or extending any street, lane or alley when the assessment commissioner certifies that such work or improvement benefits the city at large, and that it would be 20 inequitable to raise the whole cost of any such improvement or work by local special assessments.

Authorizing Horticultural Society to issue debentures. (7) For authorizing, in so far as the city has any interest therein, the Horticultural Society of Toronto to create a debt, and to borrow money by the issue and sale of debentures or 25 upon mortgage of the lands and premises occupied by the society to an amount not exceeding in all the sum of $90,000 for the purpose of paying off existing mortgages, debts and liabilities, and improving their property by the erection of a new pavilion or the enlargement and improvement of 30 their present buildings and otherwise.

Preventing cruelty to children. (8) For licensing and regulating persons keeping infant children not their own for hire or gain, and for preventing cruelty to children by their parents, guardians, or other persons having charge of or control over them. 35

Aiding jubilee celebration. (9) For aiding the coming celebration of the Jubilee of Her Majesty to an amount not exceeding $10,000 ; such by-law to be approved of by the electors before the final passing thereof.

By-laws confirmed. 2. All by-laws heretofore passed by the said council of the 35 corporation of the City of Toronto for borrowing money on the general credit of the City to provide for the payment of the City's share of local improvements and works for borrowing moneys by the issue of debentures secured by special assessments on the Toronto Street Railway Company to provide 40 for the payment of their share of local improvements and works, and for borrowing money by the issue of debentures secured by special assessments on the real property benefited by such improvements and works, and all special assessments made and rates imposed for under such by-laws for such 45 purposes are hereby declared valid and effectual.

Appointment of deputy returning officers. 3. In any case where a deputy returning officer appointed by by-law of the city of Toronto refuses and neglects to attend at the time and place, he is required by the returning officer or 50 city clerk to receive his voters' lists and the electors' papers,

etc., the returning officer or city clerk shall have the power and he is hereby authorized to appoint another person to act in his place and stead, and the person so appointed shall have all the powers and authority that he would have had if he had been
5 appointed by by-law.

4. When any polling place in the city of Toronto has been *Change of* fixed by by-law for the holding of any election or the taking *polling place.* of any vote, and it is afterwards found that the building named as such polling place cannot be obtained or is unsuitable for
10 the purpose, the returning officer or city clerk shall have the power and is hereby authorized to choose in lieu thereof as a polling place the nearest available building suitable for the purpose.

5. While the county of York uses the gaol belonging to the *Payment by*
15 city of Toronto, the county shall pay to the city such proper *County of* *York for share* compensation therefor, and for the care and maintenance of the *of gaol ex-* prisoners, as may be mutually agreed upon or settled by arbi- *penses.* tration under *The Consolidated Municipal Act, 1883* and amending Acts in that behalf. In case of arbitration under the
20 preceding provisions of this section, the arbitrators, in determin- ing the compensation to be paid for the care and maintenance of prisoners confined in the gaol, shall take into consideration the original cost of the site and erection of the gaol buildings, and of repairs and insurance, and shall also take into consider-
25 ation the cost of clothing, maintaining and supporting the prisoners, as well as the salaries of all officers and servants con- nected therewith, and the provisions of this section shall apply to determining the compensation to be paid for the care and maintenance of all prisoners maintained in said gaol by the
30 city for the county since the 31st day of December, 1883, the day of the expiration of the last agreement between the city and county in that behalf.

6. A copy of any assessment roll or portion of any assess- *Certified copy* ment roll of the city of Toronto written or printed without *of assessment* *role to be*
35 erasure or interlineation and under the seal of the corporation *evidence.* and certified to be a true copy by the city clerk, or (in his absence) by the assistant city clerk, shall be deemed authentic and be received in evidence in any court of justice, without proof of the seal or signature, or production of the original
40 assessment roll, of which such certified copy purports to be a copy or of part thereof.

7. Notwithstanding anything in *The Consolidated Municipal* *Property* *Act, 1883,* or any amending Act, and notwithstanding anything *assessable for* *local improve-* in *The Assessment Act,* or any amending Act contained, all *ments.*
45 property, except real property exempt from taxation under the provisions of the Act known as *The British North America* *Act, 1867,* situate within the limits of the City of Toronto, is hereby declared to be and shall hereafter be specially assess- able for local improvements when immediately benefited
50 thereby, although such real property may be exempt from taxa- tion for generally City purposes.

8. *The Assessment Act* is hereby amended in so far as the *Assessment* same relates to the City of Toronto by repealing sub-sections *of personal* *property.* eleven (11), twelve (12), thirteen (13), twenty-two (22) and

4

twenty-three (23), and it is hereby declared that all income derived or received by any person in the City of Toronto, from whatever source the same may be derived, shall be liable to assessment as personal property.

Assessment of gas and street railway companies.   **9.** The Act passed by the Legislative Assembly of the 5 Province of Ontario in the 43rd year of the reign of Her Majesty and chaptered 27, is hereby amended, in so far as the same relates to the City of Toronto, by repealing sub-section two (2) of section one; sub-section three (3) of section three; section four and section five thereof, and it is hereby declared 10 that all gas companies, plank or gravel road companies, and street railway companies, are assessable upon and in respect of all personal property owned by them, situate within the limits of the City of Toronto, and all pipes and other fixtures of every such gas company laid in the streets, and the railway 15 tracks and other superstructure of such street railway companies laid in the streets, are hereby declared to be personal property and liable to assessment.

Authority to borrow money for construction of sewers.   **10.** In view of the unsanitary condition of the Rosedale Creek and the Garrison Creek, and the necessity which exists 20 for constructing a sewer on the line of the Rosedale Creek and of completing the Garrison Creek sewers, it shall and may be lawful for the council of the Corporation of the City of Toronto to pass by-laws from time to time, as occasion may require, without obtaining the assent of the electors thereto, 25 before the final passing thereof, for borrowing money by the issue of debentures or city stock on the credit of the city at large a sum not exceeding $175,000.

Police commissioners.   **11.** Section 435 of *The Consolidated Municipal Act, 1883* is hereby repealed in so far as the same relates to the City of 30 Toronto, and the following enacted in lieu thereof: The Board of Police Commissioners for the City of Toronto, shall consist of the Mayor, the Judge of the County Court of the County of York, the Police Magistrate of the City of Toronto, and two Elective Commissioners, the latter to be elected annually by 35 the vote of the electors qualified to vote at Municipal Elections, such election to be held by the same Returning Officer and Deputy Returning Officers who may be appointed to hold the Municipal elections, and at the same times and places, and in the same manner as the Municipal elections are held.   40

Horticultural Society authorized to borrow.   **12.** The Horticultural Society of Toronto is hereby authorized and empowered, subject to the consent of the Honourable George William Allan, his heirs, executors or administrators, and the consent of the corporation of the city of Toronto, to create a debt and to borrow money by the issue and sale of 45 debentures, or upon mortgage of the lands and premises occupied by the Society, to an amount not exceeding in all the sum of $90,000, for the purpose of paying off existing mortgages, debts and liabilities, and improving their property by the erection of a new pavilion or the enlargement and improve- 50 ment of their present buildings, and otherwise.

Rights of ferriage.   **13.** The exclusive right of ferriage between the main land and the island in front of the city of Toronto and the parks,

and also between different points within the city limits on the
main land and on the island, is hereby vested in the corporation of the city of Toronto, and the council of the city of
Toronto is hereby authorized and empowered to pass by-laws
5 for leasing the exclusive right of such ferriage and the
carriage of goods and passengers for hire by water between the
main lands and the island, and also between different points
within the city limits on the main land and on the island, from
time to time, and upon such terms and for such periods (no one
10 period exceeding ten years), and either by public auction or
tender, as the council may think fit.

No. 50.

1st Session, 6th Legislature, 50 Vic., 1887.

BILL.

An Act respecting the City of Toronto.

First Reading, 15th March, 1887.

(Private Bill.)

No. 50.]　　　　　　**BILL.**　　　　　[1887.

An Act respecting the City of Toronto.

WHEREAS the corporation of the city of Toronto have, Preamble.
by their petition prayed for special legislation relating to
the several matters and things hereinafter set forth, and whereas it is expedient to grant the prayer of the said petition :

5　Therefore Her Majesty by and with the advice and consent
of the Legislative Assembly of the Province of Ontario enacts
as follows :—

1. The council of the corporation of the city of Toronto Powers.
may pass by-laws for the following amongst other purposes
10 notwithstanding anything, in *The Consolidated Municipal Act,
1883*, or any amending Act or in any special or private Act
relating to the said city of Toronto contained to the contrary :

1. For entering upon, taking, and acquiring so much Acquiring
land in the City of Toronto as may be required for the pur- land for
drill shed.
15. poses of a new drill-shed for the volunteer force of the City
of Toronto, without the consent of the owners of such lands,
making due compensation therefor to the parties entitled
thereto under the provisions of *The Consolidated Municipal
Act, 1883*, and amending Acts in that behalf.

20　2. For borrowing moneys not to exceed the sum of $100,- Borrowing
000 for improving the City parks and for park purposes by money for
park purposes.
the issue and sale of debentures upon the credit of the city at large
and also for charging the usual interest and sinking fund required for moneys so borrowed as a first lien upon the income
25 belonging to the " Walks and Garden Fund."　But any by-law
passed for this purpose shall require the assent of the electors
entitled to vote on money by-laws before the final passing
thereof.

3. For authorizing, in so far as the city has any interest Authorizing
30 therein, the Horticultural Society of Toronto to create a debt, Society to issue
and to borrow money by the issue and sale of debentures or debentures.
upon mortgage of the lands and premises occupied by the
society to an amount not exceeding in all the sum of $90,000
for. the purpose of paying off existing mortgages, debts
35 and liabilities, and improving their property by the erection
of a new pavilion or the enlargement and improvement of
their present buildings and otherwise.

4. For aiding the coming celebration of the Jubilee of Aiding jubilee
Her Majesty to an amount not exceeding $10,000 ; such by- celebration.
40 law to be approved of by the electors before the final passing
thereof.

2. All by-laws heretofore passed by the said council of the By-laws
corporation of the city of Toronto for borrowing money on confirmed.

the general credit of the city to provide for the payment of
the city's share of local improvements and works, for borrowing moneys by the issue of debentures secured by special
assessments on the Toronto Street Railway Company to provide
for the payment of their share of local improvements and 5
works, and for borrowing money by the issue of debentures
secured by special assessments on the real property benefited
by such improvements and works, and all special assessments
made and rates imposed under such by-laws for such purposes are hereby declared valid and effectual. 10

Authority to borrow money for construction of sewers. **3.** In view of the unsanitary condition of the Rosedale
Creek and the Garrison Creek, and the necessity which exists
for constructing a sewer on the line of the Rosedale Creek and
of completing the Garrison Creek sewers, it shall and may be
lawful for the council of the Corporation of the City of 15
Toronto to pass by-laws from time to time, as occasion may
require, without obtaining the assent of the electors thereto,
before the final passing thereof, for borrowing money by the
issue of debentures or city stock on the credit of the city at
large a sum not exceeding $175,000. 20

1st Session, 6th Legislature, 50 Vic, 1887.

No. 50.

BILL.

An Act respecting the City of Toronto.

(*Re-printed as amended by Private Bills Committee.*)

First Reading, 15th March, 1887.

(Private Bill.)

Mr. LEYS.

TORONTO.
PRINTED BY WARWICK & SONS 26 AND 28 FRONT ST. W.

BILL.

An Act to amend the Act incorporating the Sandwich and Windsor Passenger Railway Company.

WHEREAS the Sandwich and Windsor Passenger Railway Preamble.
Company, by indenture bearing date the 18th day of
November, 1874, mortgaged to George Campbell and Robert
McGregor all and singular the Sandwich and Windsor
5 Passenger Railway, the right of way, ties and rails, and all
other the privileges and appurtenances connected therewith
and thereto belonging, and all tolls and income arising therefrom, also lot number nine in the town of Sandwich containing
one hundred and four thousand, three hundred square feet
10 and being a part of lot number fifty-nine, in the first concession, formerly in the township of Sandwich, but now in the
town of Sandwich, according to the plan and survey of Alexander Wilkinson, Esquire, P.L.S., also that certain other parcel
or tract of land and premises, situate in the said town of
15 Sandwich, containing three-quarters of an acre more or less,
being composed of the south-westerly three-quarters of lot
number nineteen, on the west side of Bedford street, in the
said town of Sandwich, for the purpose of securing the sum
of twenty thousand dollars, with interest thereon, at the rate
20 therein mentioned, payable at the expiration of one year from
the date of the said indenture, and as a further and additional
security for the money so lent and advanced by the said
mortgagees the said company by an indenture by way of
chattel mortgage, also bearing date the 18th day of November,
25 1874, mortgaged to the said Campbell and McGregor all and
singular the horses, harness, passenger and truck cars, with all
the appurtenances and all other the personal property and
effects of the said company; and whereas the said Campbell
and McGregor, by indenture bearing date the 11th day of
30 November, 1876, granted, conveyed and assigned the above
mentioned mortgaged property to one Francis C. Fulmer, who
by indenture bearing date the 15th day of March, 1876,
granted, conveyed and assigned the same to Alfred J. Kennedy;
and whereas the said company having made default the said
35 Alfred J. Kennedy instituted proceedings in the Court of
Chancery for Ontario upon the said mortgages and for divers
other claims and by the decree of the said court dated the 7th
day of May, 1879, the said company was ordered to pay the sum
of $35,018.94 into the Bank of Commerce, at its branch or agency
40 office at the town of Windsor, on the 7th day of November,
then next, and in default of such payment, the said Alfred J.
Kennedy, on the 3rd day of March, 1880, obtained a final order
of foreclosure and having prior thereto under execution issued
upon the said decree acquired all the personal property and
effects above mentioned of the said company, the said Kennedy

became and is the owner of all the real and other property of the said company ; and whereas the said Alfred J. Kennedy hath ever since operated the said railway in accordance with the provisions of the said Act of incorporation of the said company, but is now desirous of reorganizing and extending 5 the said railway to some point within the town of Amherstburg and for other purposes, and hath petitioned that an Act may be passed authorizing the same ; and whereas it is expedient to grant the prayer of the said petition ;

Therefore Her Majesty, by and with the advice and consent 10 of the Legislative Assembly of the Province of Ontario, enacts as follows :—

35 V. c. 64, s. 1, repealed. **1.** Section 1 of chapter 64 of the Acts passed in the thirty-fifth year of Her Majesty's reign is hereby repealed and the following substituted in lieu thereof :— 15

Incorporation and corporate name. Alfred J. Kennedy, and such other persons as shall hereafter become shareholders of the said company, are hereby constituted a body corporate and politic under the name of " The Sandwich, Windsor and Amherstburg Railway.

35 V. c. 64, s. 2, amended. **2.** Section 2 of the said Act is hereby amended by striking 20 out the word " fifty " and substituting in lieu thereof the word " eighty."

Time for commencement and completion. **3.** The company may commence operations and exercise the powers hereby granted as soon as one-third of the capital stock shall be subscribed and twenty per centum thereon paid 25 up, but the said company shall commence the construction of the extensions of the said railway within two years and complete the same within four years from the passing of this Act.

Extension of railway authorized. **4.** The company is hereby authorized and empowered to extend, construct, maintain and complete and operate its rail- 30 way and the extensions, pursuant to the provisions and powers contained in section 4 of the said Act, from the present terminus thereof in the town of Sandwich to any part of the town of Amherstburg and to continue the same from the town of Windsor to any part of the village of Walkerville. 35

35 V. c. 64, s. 6, amended. **5.** Section 6 of the said Act is hereby amended by striking out the word " seven " in the third line of the said section and substituting in lieu thereof the word " three."

35 V. c. 64, s. 7, repealed. **6.** Section 7 of the said Act is hereby repealed.

No. 51.

1st Session, 6th Legislature, 50 Vic., 1887.

BILL.

An Act to amend the Act incorporating the Sandwich and Windsor Passenger Railway Company.

First Reading, 9th March, 1887.

(Private Bill)

BILL.

An Act to amend the Act incorporating the Sandwich and Windsor Passenger Railway Company.

WHEREAS the Sandwich and Windsor Passenger Railway Preamble. Company, by indenture bearing date the 18th day of November, 1874, mortgaged to George Campbell and Robert McGregor all and singular the Sandwich and Windsor
5 Passenger Railway, the right of way, ties and rails, and all other the privileges and appurtenances connected therewith and thereto belonging, and all tolls and income arising therefrom, also lot number nine in the town of Sandwich containing one hundred and four thousand, three hundred square feet
10 and being a part of lot number fifty-nine, in the first concession, formerly in the township of Sandwich, but now in the town of Sandwich, according to the plan and survey of Alexander Wilkinson, Esquire, P.L.S., also that certain other parcel or tract of land and premises, situate in the said town of
15 Sandwich, containing three-quarters of an acre more or less, being composed of the south-westerly three-quarters of lot number nineteen, on the west side of Bedford street, in the said town of Sandwich, for the purpose of securing the sum of twenty thousand dollars, with interest thereon, at the rate
20 therein mentioned, payable at the expiration of one year from the date of the said indenture, and as a further and additional security for the money so lent and advanced by the said mortgagees the said company by an indenture by way of chattel mortgage, also bearing date the 18th day of November,
25 1874, mortgaged to the said Campbell and McGregor all and singular the horses, harness, passenger and truck cars, with all the appurtenances and all other the personal property and effects of the said company; and whereas the said Campbell and McGregor, by indenture bearing date the 11th day of
30 November, 1876, granted, conveyed and assigned the above mentioned mortgaged property to one Francis C. Fulmer, who by indenture bearing date the 15th day of March, 1876, granted, conveyed and assigned the same to Alfred J. Kennedy; and whereas the said company having made default the said
35 Alfred J. Kennedy instituted proceedings in the Court of Chancery for Ontario upon the said mortgages and for divers other claims and by the decree of the said court dated the 7th day of May, 1879, the said company was ordered to pay the sum of $35,018.94 into the Bank of Commerce, at its branch or agency
40 office at the town of Windsor, on the 7th day of November, then next, and in default of such payment, the said Alfred J. Kennedy, on the 3rd day of March, 1880, obtained a final order of foreclosure and having prior thereto under execution issued upon the said decree acquired all the personal property and
45 effects above mentioned of the said company, the said Kennedy

became and is the owner of all the real and other property of the said company; and whereas the said Alfred J. Kennedy hath ever since operated the said railway in accordance with the provisions of the said Act of incorporation of the said company, but is now desirous of reorganizing and extending 5 the said railway to some point within the town of Amherstburg and for other purposes, and hath petitioned that an Act may be passed authorizing the same; and whereas it is expedient to grant the prayer of the said petition;

Therefore Her Majesty, by and with the advice and consent 10 of the Legislative Assembly of the Province of Ontario, enacts as follows:—

35 V. c. 64, s. 1, repealed.

1. Section 1 of chapter 64 of the Acts passed in the thirty-fifth year of Her Majesty's reign is hereby repealed and the following substituted in lieu thereof:— 15

Incorporation and corporate name.

Alfred J. Kennedy, and such other persons as shall hereafter become shareholders of the said company, are hereby constituted a body corporate and politic under the name of " The Sandwich, Windsor and Amherstburg Railway.

35 V. c. 64, s. 2, amended.

2. Section 2 of the said Act is hereby amended by striking 20 out the word " fifty " and substituting in lieu thereof the word " eighty."

Time for commencement and completion.

3. The company may commence operations and exercise the powers hereby granted as soon as one-third of the capital stock shall be subscribed and twenty per centum thereon paid 25 up, but the said company shall commence the construction of the extensions of the said railway within two years and complete the same within four years from the passing of this Act.

Extension of railway authorized.

4. The company is hereby authorized and empowered to extend, construct, maintain and complete and operate its rail- 30 way and the extensions, pursuant to the provisions and powers contained in section 4 of the said Act, from the present terminus thereof in the town of Sandwich to any part of the town of Amherstburg and to continue the same from the town of Windsor to any part of the village of Walkerville, subject, 35 however, to the provisions contained in a certain agreement, in writing, entered into between the said A. J. Kennedy and the corporation of the town of Windsor, respecting the construction and operation of the said railway within the said town of Windsor, as set forth in schedule A to this Act: provided that 40 the streets of the said towns, or the highways of any municipality, shall not be occupied or used by the said company for such extension unless by the permission heretofore or hereafter given by the municipal councils of the towns and municipalities expressed by by-law regulating the same. 45

35 V. c. 64, s. 6, amended.

5. Section 6 of the said Act is hereby amended by striking out the word "seven" in the third line of the said section and substituting in lieu thereof the word "three."

35 V. c. 64, s. 7, repealed.

6. Section 7 of the said Act is hereby repealed.

☞ SCHEDULE "A."

MEMORANDUM OF AGREEMENT, made this twenty-sixth day of March, 1887, between the Corporation of the Town of Windsor, of the first part, and Alfred J. Kennedy, of the township of Sandwich West, Superintendent, of the second part:—

WITNESSETH, that for divers considerations and the sum of one dollar, mutually paid each to the other of the parties hereto, whereof the receipt is hereby acknowledged, they the said parties hereto mutually agree each with the other as follows, that is to say :—

1st. That in the event of the municipal council of the corporation of the town of Windsor deeming it necessary or desirable to pave with wood or stone, or partly wood and partly stone, or with any other material, any street or part of any street occupied or traversed by the track of the Sandwich and Windsor Passenger Railway, it shall be obligatory for the said railway company, within thirty days from the day upon which written notice thereof shall by the said council be given in writing to the superintendent or acting superintendent of the said railway, to take up and remove the rails, ties and all other materials whereof the said track may be composed, from the said street or portion of street so occupied as aforesaid ; and when the work of laying such pavement shall have progressed sufficiently for that purpose, shall replace the said track, including ties, stringers and rails, at the expense of the said company, and the said company shall make no claim against the said town for loss of time or business by reason of any interruption of the traffic upon or over the said railway during the necessary period required for such work, nor for the removal and re-laying of the said track.

2nd. That in the event of the said council deeming it necessary to regrade or alter the grade of any street or portion of street occupied or traversed by the track of the said railway, and it be found necessary to raise, lower or remove the said track, the said company shall, within thirty days after notice (given in the manner hereinbefore provided) requiring the said company so to do, raise, lower or remove the said track or the materials constituting the same, and shall, so soon as the said work of re-grading or of altering the grade is completed or sufficiently advanced, replace or relay the said track at the expense of the said company, and the said company shall make no claim against the said town for loss of time or business by reason of any interruption of the traffic upon or over the said railway during the necessary period required for such work, nor for the removal and relaying of the said track.

3rd. That in the event of the said council deeming it necessary to make or cause to be made along or under any street or portion of street occupied or traversed as aforesaid, any sewer or drain, or to open a trench or trenches in which to lay water-pipes, and it be found necessary to remove the said track, the said company shall within thirty days after notice (given in the manner hereinbefore provided) requiring the said company so to do, remove the said track or materials thereof, and shall, so soon as the said work is completed or sufficiently advanced, replace or relay the said track at the expense of the said company, and the said company shall make no claim against the said town for loss of time or business by reason of any interruption of the traffic upon or over the said railway during the necessary period required for such work or removal and relaying of the said track.

4th. That in the event of the said council authorizing any gas, water or oil company, or companies, to operate such works within the said corporation, the said railway company shall permit such company or companies to open a trench or trenches for the purpose of placing mains or pipes necessary for such works under or along the said railway track without compensation for loss of traffic or business during the necessary period required for such work, upon thirty days' notice (given in the manner hereinbefore provided), and if necessary the said railway company shall take up, remove and relay its track for such purposes, but the same shall be done by the said railway company at the expense of the said company or companies requiring the same.

5th. The said railway company shall keep their track, whether the same traverses or follows a paved street or otherwise, in a thorough state of repair at its own expense, with materials of a like character and kind employed in the other portions of the street between the space of the rails, but in the case of streets repaved or to be paved, the space or spaces between the rails of the said track shall be paved by the town at its expense, free of cost to the said company.

IN WITNESS WHEREOF, the parties hereto have hereunto set their hands and seals, and have affixed the corporate seal of the said town, signed by the mayor and clerk thereof, the day and year first above written.

Signed, sealed and delivered in the presence of,

As to the signatures of J. H. Beattie and Stephen Lusted,

(Signed), GEO. CHEYNE.

As to the signature of Alfred J. Kennedy,

(Signed), J. F. EGAN.

(Signed),
ALFRED J. KENNEDY, (SEAL)
Superintendent of the Sandwich and Windsor Passenger Railway.

(Signed), J. H. BEATTIE, (SEAL)
Mayor, Town of Windsor.

(Signed),
STEPHEN LUSTED, (SEAL)
Clerk, Town of Windsor.

No 51.

1st Session, 6th Legislature, 50 Vic., 1887.

BILL.

An Act to amend the Act incorporating the Sandwich and Windsor Passenger Railway Company.

(*Reprinted as amended by Railway Committee*).

First Reading, 9th March, 1887.

(Private Bill.)

No. 52.]   **BILL.**   [1887.

An Act to amend the Act incorporating the London and South-Eastern Railway Company.

WHEREAS the London and South-Eastern Railway Com- Preamble.
pany have by their petition prayed that the Act passed
in the 49th year of Her Majesty's reign, chapter 72, incorporating the said company, may be amended as hereinafter set forth,
5 and it is expedient to grant the prayer of the said petition ;
    Therefore Her Majesty, by and with the advice and consent
of the Legislative Assembly of the Province of Ontario, enacts
as follows :—

1. It shall be lawful for the said company to enter into an Agreement
10 agreement with the Canada Southern Railway Company for with Canada
the leasing to them of the said the London and South-Eastern Railway
Railway, or any part thereof, and such agreement shall be authorized.
valid and binding on the said the London and South-Eastern
Railway Company and shall be enforced by Courts of Law,
15 according to the terms and tenor thereof.

2. Section 56 of the said Act is hereby amended by striking 49 V. c. 72, s.
out of the first line of the said section the words " three months " 56, amended.
and substituting therefor the words " two years."

3. The mayor of the city of London for the time being shall Mayor of
20 *ex officio* be a member of the board of directors of the London London to be
and South-Eastern Railway Company. director.

4. Section 57 of the said Act is hereby repealed. 49 V. c. 72, s.
 57, repealed.

5. The said the London and South-Eastern Railway Com- Extension of
pany may also construct and continue their line of railway railway
25 easterly from the point where it intersects the line of the authorized.
London and Port Stanley Railway to some other point or
points where it will connect with the oil works in East London
and the line of the West Ontario Pacific Railway.

No. 52.

1st Session, 6th Legislature, 50 Vic., 1887.

BILL.

An Act to amend the Act incorporating the London and South-Eastern Railway Company.

First Reading, 1887.

(Private Bill.)

No. 52.]　　　**BILL.**　　　[1887.

An Act to amend the Act incorporating the London and South-Eastern Railway Company.

WHEREAS the London and South-Eastern Railway Com- Preamble.
pany have by their petition prayed that the Act passed
in the 49th year of Her Majesty's reign, chapter 72, incorporating the said company, may be amended as hereinafter set forth,
5 and it is expedient to grant the prayer of the said petition ;
　　Therefore Her Majesty, by and with the advice and consent
of the Legislative Assembly of the Province of Ontario, enacts
as follows :—

　　1. It shall be lawful for the said company *having first ob-* Agreement
10 *tained the consent of the Corporation of the City of London to* with Canada
enter into an agreement with the Canada Southern Railway Railway
Company, *the Grand Trunk Railway Company of Canada,* authorized.
or the London and Port Stanley Railway Company, for
the leasing to them of the said the London and South-Eastern
15 Railway, or any part thereof, and such agreement shall be
valid and binding on the said the London and South-Eastern
Railway Company and shall be enforced by Courts of Law,
according to the terms and tenor thereof.

　　2. Section 56 of the said Act is hereby amended by striking 49 V. c. 72, s.
20 out of the first line of the said section the words " three months " 56, amended.
and substituting therefor the words " two years."

　　3. The mayor of the city of London for the time being shall Mayor of
ex officio be a member of the board of directors of the London an *ex officio*
and South-Eastern Railway Company. director.

25　　**4.** The said the London and South-Eastern Railway Com- Extension of
pany may also construct and continue their line of railway railway
easterly from the point where it intersects the line of the authorized.
London and Port Stanley Railway to some other point or
points where it will connect with the oil works in East London
30 and the line of the West Ontario Pacific Railway *Company.*

　　5. Sub-section 5 of section 36 of *The Railway Act of* R.S. O. c. 165,
Ontario shall not apply to the said the London and South- s. 36 (5) not to
Eastern Railway Company. apply to Com-
pany.

No. 52.

1st Session, 6th Legislature, 50 Vic., 1887.

BILL.

An Act to amend the Act incorporating the London and South-Eastern Railway Company.

(*Reprinted as amended by Railway Committee.*)

First Reading, 15th March, 1887.

(Private Bill.)

No. 53.]　　　　　　　**BILL.**　　　　　[1887.

An Act to consolidate the Floating Debt of the Town of Trenton.

WHEREAS the corporation of the town of Trenton by their Preamble.
petition have represented that they have incurred debts
and liabilities for the repairing of the bridge across the river
Trent in said town, and for other permanent improvements
5 therein, to an amount of $20,000 or thereabouts, which have not
been secured by debentures, and have prayed that the said
debt may be consolidated and that they may be authorized to
issue debentures for that purpose; and whereas it is expedient
to grant the prayer of the said petition ;
10　Therefore Her Majesty, by and with the advice and consent
of the Legislative Assembly of the Province of Ontario, enacts
as follows :—

1. The corporation of the town of Trenton may pass a by- Issue of
law authorizing the issue of debentures under the corporate debentures for
15 seal, signed by the mayor and countersigned by the treasurer, $20,000. authorized.
for such sums not exceeding in the whole the sum of $20,000, as
the council of the said town may direct, and the principal sum
secured by the said debentures, and the interest accruing
thereon, may be made payable either in this Province or in
20 Great Britain, or elsewhere, as the said council may deem expedient, and may be either in currency or sterling money.

2 The said corporation may raise by way of loan upon the Power to
credit of the said debentures from any person or persons, body borrow on
or bodies corporate either in this Province or in Great Britain debentures.
25 or elsewhere, who may be willing to lend the same a sum not
exceeding in the whole the sum of $20,000 of lawful money of
Canada.

3. The funds derived from the negotiation of the said deben- Application of
tures shall be applied by the said council to the payment of funds.
30 the said outstanding floating liabilities and to and for no other
purpose whatever.

4. For payment of the debentures to be issued under this Special rate
Act, the municipal council shall impose a special rate per for payment of
annum (over and above and in addition to all other rates to debentures.
35 be levied in each year) which shall be sufficient to pay the
interest on the said debentures and to form a sinking fund of
four per centum per annum, for the purpose of paying the
principal thereof.

5. The said council shall, and it shall be the duty of the Investment
40 treasurer, to invest from time to time all moneys raised by of sinking fund.

special rate for the sinking fund provided in this Act, either
in redemption of any of the debentures hereby authorized to
be issued or in Government securities, or in such other manner
as the Lieutenant-Governor in Council may by general or
special order direct, or may deposit the sum in any chartered 5
bank of the Dominion of Canada, that the council may from
time to time approve.

Payment of debentures and interest.

6. The debentures to be issued as aforesaid, shall be payable
in not more than twenty years from the date thereof, as the
said council may direct; and the interest thereon at such rate 10
not exceeding six per centum per annum as the said council
shall determine, shall be payable half-yearly according to the
coupons attached thereto.

Irregularities not to render debentures invalid.

7. No irregularity in the form of the said debentures, or of
the by-law authorizing the issuing thereof, shall render the same 15
invalid or illegal, or be allowed as a defence to any action
brought against the corporation for the recovery of the said
debentures and interest or any or either of them or any part
thereof.

Assent of electors not required.

8. It shall not be necessary to obtain the assent of the elec- 20
tors of the said town to the passing of the said by-law under
this Act, or to observe the formalities in relation thereto, prescribed by *The Consolidated Municipal Act, 1883.*

Form of debentures.

9. The said debentures may be in the form " A " in the
schedule to this Act, or as near thereto as the said corporation 25
may find convenient, according to the places where, and the
money in which the same are made payable.

SCHEDULE.

(*Form " A."*)

CONSOLIDATED LOAN DEBENTURE.

No. $

PROVINCE OF ONTARIO, TOWN OF TRENTON.

Under and by virtue of the Act passed in the fiftieth year
of the reign of Her Majesty Queen Victoria, and chaptered
            and by virtue of By-law No.   of the cor-
poration of the town of Trenton, passed under the provisions
contained in the said Act.

The corporation of the town of Trenton promises to pay
the bearer at   in   the sum of
on   day   A.D.   and the half-yearly
coupons hereto attached as the same shall severally become due.

Dated at Trenton, in the county of Hastings, this
day of   A.D.

[L.S.]

                                        A. B.,
                                            Mayor.
                                        C. D.,
                                            Treasurer.

No. 53.

1st Session, 6th Legislature, 50 Vic., 1887.

BILL.

An Act to consolidate the Floating Debt of
the Town of Trenton.

First Reading, 15th March, 1887.

(Private Bill.)

No. 54.]   **BILL.**   [1887.

An Act to amend the Act incorporating the Girls' Home and Public Nursery of Toronto.

WHEREAS "The Girls' Home and Public Nursery" of the city of Toronto, was incorporated by an Act of the late Province of Canada, passed in the 26th year of Her Majesty's reign, chaptered 63, and has by petition prayed that an Act
5 may be passed changing the name of the said corporation, authorizing the election of four directresses, extending the authority of the directresses and managers to bind or apprentice children and further amending the said Act of incorporation, and it is expedient to grant the prayer of the said
10 petition;
Therefore Her Majesty, by and with the advice and consent of the Legislative Assembly of the Province of Ontario, enacts as follows :—

1. The name of the said corporation is hereby changed to Name chang-
15 " The Girls' Home," of Toronto and the said Act of incorporation ed.
shall be amended accordingly.

2. The said corporation under its new name shall not be Corporation deemed to be a new corporation, but it shall continue to exer- continued. cise all the rights, powers and privileges, which, prior to the
20 passing of this Act, have been held, exercised and enjoyed by the said corporation, subject only after the passing of this Act to the amendments in this Act contained.

3. Section 3 of the said Act is hereby amended by inserting 26 v. c. 63, after the word "ensuing" in the seventh line of the said sec- amended.
25 tion the words "or the said meeting shall be held on such other day as may be named by the directresses and managers," and by striking out the words "and third directress" in the twenty-seventh line of the said section, and by inserting in lieu thereof the words " third and fourth directresses," and by
30 striking out the words "at a special meeting of the subscribers called for the purpose by a notice given in a similar manner to that required to be given for the annual meeting," in the thirty-second and two following lines of the said section, and by inserting in lieu thereof the words "by the remaining
35 directresses and managers, either at any regular meeting, or at a special meeting called for that purpose."

4. Section 4 of the said Act is hereby amended by striking 26 v. c. 63, s. out the words "to any healthy trade or business until the age 4, amended. of sixteen," in the second and third lines of the said section,
40 and by inserting in lieu thereof the words " to any mechanic, farmer, or other person carrying on a trade or calling, until the age of eighteen."

1st Session, 6th Legislature, 50 Vic, 1887.

BILL.

An Act to amend the Act incorporating the Girls' Home and Public Nursery of Toronto."

First Reading,   ·   1887.

(Private Bill.)

An Act to amend the Act incorporating the Home of the Friendless, of Hamilton.

WHEREAS the Home of the Friendless have, by their peti- Preamble.
tion, prayed that their name should be changed to "The
Home of the Friendless and Infants' Home," and that in addition to the present objects and purposes of the institution, they
5 may be authorized and empowered to receive and take into
the Home infant children who are homeless, or whose homes
are scenes of vice, and to provide for nursing such children,
with further powers for the due care, maintenance and protection of such children ; and whereas it is expedient to grant
10 the prayer of the said petition ;
Therefore Her Majesty, by and with the advice and consent
of the Legislative Assembly of the Province of Ontario, enacts
as follows :—

1. The name of the said corporation of "The Home of the Name
15 Friendless," at Hamilton, is hereby changed to "The Home of changed.
the Friendless and Infants' Home."

2. It shall be lawful for the said corporation to receive Powers as to
and take into the said Home, infant children who are home- receiving and
less, or whose homes are scenes of vice, or who are being un- children.
20 cared for, and to keep such children and provide for their
nursing, care, maintenance and protection; and the said corporation shall have and may exercise over and in respect to
such children the same powers as their parents, if living, would
have and might exercise.

No. 55.

1st Session, 6th Legislature, 50 Vic., 1887.

BILL.

An Act to Amend the Act incorporating the Home of the Friendless, of Hamilton.

First Reading, 11th March, 1887.

(Private Bill)

No. 56.]　　　　**BILL.**　　　[1887.

An Act to Provide for the Division of the Township of Gosfield.

WHEREAS certain inhabitants and ratepayers of the town- Preamble.
　　ship of Gosfield, in the county of Essex, have, by their
petition, represented that it is expedient to separate the said
township of Gosfield, into two distinct municipalities, inasmuch
5 as such division of the said township will greatly promote the
welfare and convenience of its inhabitants ; and whereas it is
expedient to grant the prayer of the said petition;
　　Therefore Her Majesty, by and with the advice and consent
of the Legislative Assembly of the Province of Ontario, enacts
10 as follows :—

　　1. Upon, from and after the last Monday in December, Township of
1887, the inhabitants of all that portion of the said township South Gos-
of Gosfield, which lies south of the centre of the allowance for field.
road between the fifth and sixth concessions, including also
15 lots numbers two hundred and sixty-one, two hundred and
sixty-two and two hundred and sixty-three, south of Talbot
Road, and lots numbers two hundred and sixty-one, two hundred and sixty-two and two hundred and sixty-three, north of
the said Talbot Road, in the said township of Gosfield shall
20 constitute a separate township or corporation, under the name
of the corporation of the township of South Gosfield, and the
said territory shall thereafter be deemed to be such separate
municipality for all municipal, school and other purposes
whatsoever, in the same manner to all intents and purposes as,
25 and such municipality and township corporation hereby created
shall enjoy all the rights and privileges and be subject to all
the liabilities appertaining to, other townships in the Province
of Ontario.

　　2. Upon, from and after the said last Monday in December, Township of
30 1887, the inhabitants of all that portion of the said township North Gos-
of Gosfield, which lies north of the centre of the allowance for field.
road between the fifth and sixth concessions, excluding there-
out and therefrom lots numbers two hundred and sixty-one,
two hundred and sixty-two and two hundred and sixty-three,
35 south of said Talbot Road, and lots numbers two hundred and
sixty-one, two hundred and sixty-two and two hundred and
sixty-three, north of the said Talbot Road, in the said township of Gosfield, shall constitute a separate township or corporation under the name of the corporation of the township of
45 North Gosfield, and the said territory shall thereafter be deemed
to be such separate municipality for all municipal, school and
other purposes whatsoever, in the same manner to all intents
and purposes as, and such municipality and township corpor-

ation hereby created shall enjoy all the rights and privileges
and be subject to all the liabilities appertaining to, other townships in the Province of Ontario.

Division of
assets.

3. All and every the assets and debts of the present municipality of Gosfield shall be divided between the said respec- 5
tive municipalities of South Gosfield, on the one hand, and
North Gosfield, on the other, in the same manner and by the
same proceedings as nearly as may be as in the case of a separation of a junior township from a senior township, and so
soon as the said debts shall have been divided as aforesaid, 10
each of the said municipalities shall be bound to the re-payment of the share of the said debts which shall have been so
assigned to it as aforesaid, as though such share of the said
debts had been incurred by such municipalities respectively;
each of the townships hereby created remaining, however, 15
liable as surety in respect of the share (if any) of the said
debts which it is not its duty primarily to pay.

Election of
council.

4. The first nomination for the election of municipal councillors for the said townships shall take place on the said last
Monday of December, in the year 1887, and the polling (if any) 20
at such election shall take place on the first Monday in January next thereafter; and the place for holding such election
for the township of North Gosfield shall be where the last
annual election of councillors for the township of Gosfield was
holden, and the returning officer at such election shall be the 25
township clerk of the present township of Gosfield; and the
place for holding the election for the township of South Gosfield shall be at the Town Hall in the village of Kingsville,
and the sheriff, for the time being, of the county of Essex,
shall be the returning officer for the said last mentioned elec- 30
tion; and the provisions of *The Consolidated Municipal Act,
1883*, and amendments thereto, having reference to the case of
the separation of a junior from a senior township, shall apply
to the townships hereby formed; as if such townships had
been a union of townships, except where it is otherwise herein 35
specifically provided; and for the purpose of applying such
provisions, the said township of South Gosfield shall be deemed
to have been the senior township, and the said township of
North Gosfield shall be deemed to have been the junior township; and the corporation of the township of South Gosfield 40
shall be deemed to be a continuation of the said corporation of
the township of Gosfield.

Township
clerk to
furnish return-
ing officer
of South Gos-
field with
copy of assess-
ment roll.

5. The clerk of the said township of Gosfield shall furnish
to the returning officer of the township of South Gosfield before
the said election, a copy of the assessment roll of the township 45
of Gosfield for the year 1887, so far as the same contains the
ratable property assessed and the names of the owners, tenants
and occupants thereof within that part of the said township
which is hereby constituted the township of South Gosfield.

By-law to aid
the Lake Erie,
Essex and
Detroit River
R'y Co'y., to
be submitted
to electors in

6. Immediately after the final passage of this Act it shall 50
be the duty of the municipal council of the present township
of Gosfield to submit to the duly qualified electors of that portion of the present township which is hereafter to be known
as South Gosfield, a by-law granting a bonus to the Lake Erie,
Essex and Detroit River Railway Company, in accordance with 55

the terms of any petition presented to the said municipal part of town-ship constitut-ing South Gos-field.
council, by the ratepayers and freeholders of that portion of
the said township of Gosfield hereafter to be known as South
Gosfield ; and, provided the said by-law receives the assent of
5 the electors of South Gosfield, in accordance with the provisions of *The Consolidated Municipal Act, 1883*, and amendments thereto, it shall be the duty of the municipal council of
the township of Gosfield to finally pass the said by-law, and
of the reeve and council and the township clerk of the present
10 township of Gosfield to carry out all the provisions of *The
Consolidated Municipal Act, 1883*, and amendments thereto,
relating to the publication and promulgation of the said by-
law, and the registration of the same, if carried, and the publication of all notices relating to the said by-law ; and the said
15 *Consolidated Municipal Act, 1883*, and amendments thereto,
shall apply to the said by-law in a like manner as to all other
by-laws of a similar character ; and the reeve and council and
the township clerk of the present township of Gosfield are
hereby empowered and required to carry out all the provisions
20 of the said by-law just as if the same were submitted to the
said township of Gosfield, but the debenture debt hereby
created shall not affect the township hereafter to be known as
North Gosfield, but shall be binding only upon the township
hereafter to be known as South Gosfield ; and for the purpose
25 of submitting and carrying out the provisions of the said by-
law and enabling the reeve and municipal council and clerk of
the said township of Gosfield to comply with the requirements
of the law relating to the same, this Act shall take effect and
come into full force from and after the day upon which it
30 receives the assent of His Honour, the Lieutenant-Governor of
Ontario.

No. 56.

1st Session, 6th Legislature, 50 Vic., 1887

BILL.

An Act to provide for the division of the Township of Gosfield.

First Reading, 17th March, 1887.

(Private Bill.)

No. 56.]   **BILL.**   [1887.

An Act to Provide for the Division of the Township of
Gosfield.

Preamble. WHEREAS certain inhabitants and ratepayers of the township of Gosfield, in the county of Essex, have, by their
petition, represented that it is expedient to separate the said
township of Gosfield, into two distinct municipalities, inasmuch
5 as such division of the said township will greatly promote the
welfare and convenience of its inhabitants ; and whereas it is
expedient to grant the prayer of the said petition ;

Therefore Her Majesty, by and with the advice and consent
of the Legislative Assembly of the Province of Ontario, enacts
10 as follows :—

1. Upon, from and after the said last Monday in December, Township of North Gos-field.
1887, the inhabitants of all that portion of the said township
of Gosfield, which lies north of the centre of the allowance for
road between the fifth and sixth concessions, ☞and north-
15 westerly of the centre of the allowance for road between lots
numbers two hundred and sixty-three and two hundred and
sixty-four north *and south* of the Talbot Road, in the said
township of Gosfield, shall constitute a separate township or corporation under the name of the corporation of the township of
20 Gosfield North, and the said territory shall thereafter be deemed
to be such separate municipality for all municipal, school and
other purposes whatsoever, in the same manner to all intents
and purposes as, and such municipality and township corporation hereby created shall enjoy all the rights and privileges
25 and be subject to all the liabilities appertaining to, other townships in the Province of Ontario.

2. Upon, from and after the last Monday in December, Township of South Gos-field.
1887, the inhabitants of all that portion of the said township
of Gosfield, which lies south of the centre of the allowance for
30 road between the fifth and sixth concessions, ☞and south-
easterly of the centre of the allowance for road between lots
numbers two hundred and sixty-three and two hundred and
sixty four, north and south of the Talbot Road, ☞ in the
said township of Gosfield shall constitute a separate township
35 or corporation, under the name of the corporation of the township of Gosfield South, and the said territory shall thereafter
be deemed to be such separate municipality for all municipal,
school and other purposes whatsoever, in the same manner to
all intents and purposes as, and such municipality and town-
40 ship corporation hereby created shall enjoy all the rights and
privileges and be subject to all the liabilities appertaining to,
other townships in the Province of Ontario.

Division of assets.

3. All and every the assets and debts of the present municipality of Gosfield shall be divided between the said respective municipalities of Gosfield North, on the one hand, and Gosfield South, on the other, in the same manner and by the same proceedings as nearly as may be as in the case of a separation of a junior township from a senior township, and so soon as the said debts shall have been divided as aforesaid, each of the said municipalities shall be bound to the re-payment of the share of the said debts which shall have been so assigned to it as aforesaid, as though such share of the said debts had been incurred by such municipalities respectively; each of the townships hereby created remaining, however, liable as surety in respect of the share (if any) of the said debts which it is not its duty primarily to pay.

Election of council.

4. The first nomination for the election of municipal councillors for the said townships shall take place on the said last Monday of December, in the year 1887, and the polling (if any) at such election shall take place on the first Monday in January next thereafter; and the place for holding such election for the township of Gosfield North shall be where the last annual election of councillors for the township of Gosfield was holden, and the returning officer at such election shall be the township clerk of the present township of Gosfield; and the place for holding the election for the township of Gosfield South shall be at the Town Hall in the village of Kingsville, and the clerk, for the time being, of the Third Division Court of the county of Essex, shall be the returning officer for the said last mentioned election; and the provisions of *The Consolidated Municipal Act, 1883,* and amendments thereto, having reference to the case of the separation of a junior from a senior township, shall apply to the townships hereby formed, as if such townships had been a union of townships, except where it is otherwise herein specifically provided; and for the purpose of applying such provisions, the said township of Gosfield North shall be deemed to have been the senior township, and the said township of Gosfield South shall be deemed to have been the junior township; and the corporation of the township of Gosfield North shall be deemed to be a continuation of the said corporation of the township of Gosfield.

Township clerk to furnish returning officer of Gosfield South with copy of assessment roll.

5. The clerk of the said township of Gosfield shall furnish to the returning officer of the township of Gosfield South before the said election, a copy of the assessment roll of the township of Gosfield for the year 1887, so far as the same contains the ratable property assessed and the names of the owners, tenants and occupants thereof within that part of the said township which is hereby constituted the township of Gosfield South.

By-law to aid the Lake Erie, Essex and Detroit River R'y Co'y., to be submitted to electors in part of township constituting Gosfield South.

6. Immediately after the final passage of this Act it shall be the duty of the municipal council of the present township of Gosfield to submit to the duly qualified electors of that portion of the present township which is hereafter to be known as Gosfield South, a by-law granting a bonus to the Lake Erie, Essex and Detroit River Railway Company, in accordance with the terms of any petition presented to the said municipal council, by the ratepayers and freeholders of that portion of the said township of Gosfield hereafter to be known as Gosfield South; and, provided the said by-law receives the assent of the electors of Gosfield South, in accordance with the provisions of *The Consolidated Municipal Act, 1883*, and amendments thereto, it shall be the duty of the municipal council of the township of Gosfield to finally pass the said by-law, and

5 of the reeve and council and the township clerk of the present township of Gosfield to carry out all the provisions of *The Consolidated Municipal Act, 1883*, and amendments thereto, relating to the publication and promulgation of the said by-law, and the registration of the same, if carried, and the publi-

10 cation of all notices relating to the said by-law ; and the said *Consolidated Municipal Act, 1883*, and amendments thereto, shall apply to the said by-law in a like manner as to all other by-laws of a similar character ; and the reeve and council and the township clerk of the present township of Gosfield are

15 hereby empowered and required to carry out all the provisions of the said by-law just as if the same were submitted to the said township of Gosfield, but the debenture debt hereby created shall not affect the township hereafter to be known as Gosfield North, but shall be binding only upon the township

20 hereafter to be known as Gosfield South ; and for the purpose of submitting and carrying out the provisions of the said by-law and enabling the reeve and municipal council and clerk of the said township of Gosfield to comply with the requirements of the law relating to the same, this Act shall take effect and

25 come into full force from and after the day upon which it receives the assent of His Honour, the Lieutenant-Governor of Ontario.

☞ **7.** All expenses of obtaining this Act and of furnishing Expenses of Act.
30 any documents, copies of papers, writings, deeds or any matter whatsoever required by the township of Gosfield South, as well as all expenses connected with the giving effect to the provisions of the preceding section of this Act, shall be paid by the said township of Gosfield South to any party or parties
35 that may be entitled thereto. ☜

1st Session, 6th Legislature, 50 Vic, 1887.

BILL.

An Act to provide for the division of the Township of Gosfield.

(*Re-printed as amended by Private Bills Committee.*)

First Reading, 17th March, 1887.

(Private Bill)

No. 57.]   **BILL.**   [1887.

An Act to Legalize certain By-Laws of the Town of Sarnia.

WHEREAS the corporation of the town of Sarnia by Preamble.
their petition have represented that on the third day
of May, 1886, they did pass certain by-laws, numbered 279
and 281, after the said by-laws had been duly approved by
5 the ratepayers, that by-law number 279 was passed to raise
the sum of $20,000 for the construction of a main sewer in
the said town, and by-law number 281 to raise the sum of
$3,800 to purchase certain shares of the capital stock of the
Sarnia and Florence Road Company, and that they have
10 issued debentures under the aforesaid by-laws, and whereas
doubts have arisen as to the validity of the said by-laws,
and they have prayed that an Act may be passed to render
the said by-laws valid and legal, and whereas it is expedient
to grant the prayer of the said petition ;
15   Therefore Her Majesty, by and with the advice and consent of the Legislative Assembly of the Province of Ontario,
enacts as follows:—

1. The aforesaid by-laws, numbers 279 and 281 of the By-laws 279
municipal council of the corporation of the town of Sarnia, and 281 con-
20 are hereby confirmed and declared legal and valid to all firmed.
intents and purposes, and the debentures issued under the
said by-laws declared valid and binding upon the said corporation of the town of Sarnia and the ratepayers thereof.

1st Session, 6th Legislature, 50 Vic., 1887.

BILL.

An Act to legalize certain by-laws of the Town of Sarnia.

First Reading, 17th March, 1887.

(Private Bill.)

No. 58.] **BILL.** [1887.

An Act respecting the Agricultural Society of the
North Riding of the County of Oxford.

WHEREAS at the annual meeting of the Electoral District Preamble.
Society of the Electoral District of the North Riding
of the County of Oxford, duly held on the eighteenth day of
January, 1887, in pursuance of the provisions of *The Agriculture*
5 *and Arts Act,* Joseph L. Peers was duly elected president of
the said society for the year ending on the third Wednesday
of January, 1888; and whereas, also, at the said meeting
Valentine Ficht and J. F. Wilson were duly elected vice-
presidents of the said society, and William Donaldson, John
10 M. Grant, George R. Pattullo, John Peers, Hugh McDonald,
F. Green, R. Moysey, Thomas Lockhart, and Angus Rose, were
elected directors of the said society, and the said William
Donaldson was duly elected representative of the said Division
in the council of the Agriculture and Arts Association, and
15 John Craig was duly elected secretary-treasurer, and Roland
W. Sawtell and Richard W. Knight were elected auditors,
and doubts have arisen as to the regularity of their election
and it is expedient to remove such doubts and to confirm such
election; and whereas in consequence of the taking by the
20 Western Ontario Pacific Railway Company of a portion of
the present site for fairs and exhibitions of the said society it
has been necessary to sell the said site and to acquire a new
one in the said district, and by resolution of the members of
the said society called for that purpose the then board of
25 directors were authorized to sell the said lands; and whereas
it is necessary for the said society to acquire and hold land as
a new site for its fairs and exhibitions, and to mortgage the
same for the purpose of paying the whole or a portion of the
said purchase money, and it is expedient to give such power to
30 the said board of directors without the approval of a meeting
of the society for that purpose;
Therefore Her Majesty, by and with the advice and consent
of the Legislative Assembly of the Province of Ontario, enacts as
follows :—

35 **1.** The election of the said president, vice-presidents, directors, Election of
secretary-treasurer, and auditors and representative, is hereby officers con-
declared valid, and they are hereby declared to have been, and firmed.
to be, and to continue to be, the officers of the said society until
the next annual election.

40 **2.** It shall be lawful for the said board of directors during Sale of lands
their said term of office to sell the said site now owned by the authorized.
said society to such person or persons and in such manner as

they shall determine, without any further approval of a meeting of the said society.

Power to purchase and mortgage land.

3. It shall be lawful for the said board of directors to acquire and hold within the said district land sufficient for a site for the fairs and exhibitions of the said society, and to mortgage the same to secure the payment of the whole or any part of the purchase money without the approval of a meeting of the said society called for that purpose.

5

1st Session, 6th Legislature, 50 Vic., 1887.

BILL.

An Act respecting the Agricultural Society of the North Riding of the County of Oxford.

First Reading, March, 1887.

(Private Bill.)

Mr.

No. 59.]　　　　　　**BILL.**　　　　　[1887.

An Act to incorporate the Niagara Tunnel and Water
Power Company of Ontario.

WHEREAS the municipal corporation of the town of Preamble.
Niagara Falls, R. F. Carter, Alex. Logan, merchant,
M. M. Buckley, R. P. Skinner, Wm. McHattie, H. C. Symmes,
contractor, John Bender, mayor, William Cole, Wm. Nichols,
5 J. L. Macartney, J. T. Brundage, merchant, Thos. Reade,
Thomas Wilson, E. E. Buckley, W. L. Lundy, G. W.
Ellis, Wm. Lacey, C. W. Tossell, W. H. Wishart, A. Dennis, W.
G. Webster, W. E. Riggs, T. F. Ellis, Frank Kenney, J. W.
Monro, John Murray, George Coulson, S. K. Binkley, E. Moire,
10 A. Duncan, Charles Miller, Anson Garner, J. S. Rogger, Jas.
Pope, J. H. Hazlewood, Frank Minzie, John Ganzan, Edward
Cooney, Geo. Applegate, Frank Thomas, J. M. Douglas, Jas.
Parker, M. H. Buckley, Henry Powell, A. F. Preuter, Henry
Quill, John McGeorge, Jacob Heximer, James Brown, J. Butters,
15 H. J. Gasson, W. T. Ross, Wm. McMurray, A. Glover, P. Eagan,
D. Morice, C. Cornel, E. Titthitt, Robert Acheson, J. J. Flynn,
John Fahey, Donald McLean, J. Robertson, Wm. C. Bennett,
Chas. Bampfield, John G. Bampfield, Wm. L. Doran, J. Zybach,
Garrett O'Connor, W. P. Lym, Donald Morrison, W. M. Parker,
20 H. Preston, H. McMurray, John R. Price, James Quillinan,
Charles C. Cole, H. W. Hagin, P. A. Skinner, James Johnson,
G. T. Putman, W. P. Buckley, Hope McIntyre, A. Sayers, H.
W. Skinner, Robert Gibson, C. Lymon, P. M. Buckley, Samuel
Patten, Martin L. Miller, R. Baird, John Harrington, Godfrey
25 Watson, John Hawley, C. E Lacey, Wm. Burke, H. Phipps, E.
Dell, J. Lovell, R. Coulson, Lymen D. Groom, S. D. Smythe,
Frank Anderson, John Lowe, John Shaw, Thos. Hutchinson,
A. Mowrings, W. H. Parmilie, Geo. W. Vanclerk, R. Sprong,
J. H. Flynn, John E. Moye, Wm. Commarford, Harry Hawkins,
30 Wm. H. House, R. Stark, Geo. Pirie, G. H. Clark, J. T. Hen-
derson, J. H. Wily, Wm. H. Campbell, J. H. Buckley, M. S.
Bradt, W. A. Pew, David Latter, A. Moore, J. F. Tait, P. Cul-
hane, John Bell, D. O. Leary, Chas. Newman, James Donald, J.
McNevin, all of the town of Niagara Falls ; James Ross, of
35 Sherbrooke, Quebec, C. E. ; Charles Patrick, of Cloughford,
Manchester, England, Esquire : Frank Turner, of Bracondale,
C.E. ;　Harry　Symons,　of　Toronto,　Barrister ;　R. T.
Sutton, of Toronto, Contractor, and others have, by
their petitions, represented that the incorporation of the
40 company hereinafter mentioned for the purpose of utilizing the
waters and falls of the Niagara and Chippawa Rivers and the
natural power thereby afforded with the object of promoting
manufactures, electric supply and other businesses, will materi-
ally advance the interests and welfare of the town of Niagara

Falls and vicinity, and have prayed for the incorporation of such a company ; and, whereas, it is expedient to grant the prayer of the said petitions;

Therefore Her Majesty, by and with the advice and consent of the Legislative Assembly of the Province of Ontario, enacts 5 as follows :—

Incorporation. **1.** The said persons named in the foregoing preamble, and such other persons and corporations as shall hereafter become shareholders of the said company, are hereby constituted a body corporate and politic under the name of the "Niagara Tunnel 10 and Water Power Company of Ontario" (hereinafter called the company), with full power to construct, equip, maintain, and operate, a hydraulic tunnel or covered water way from some point on the west bank of Niagara river, above the falls of Niagara, or from the Chippawa river, in the county of 15 Welland, to some other point or points on the said west bank of the Niagara river, with all works, buildings and other accessories necessary to give effect to the intent of this Act.

Authority to supply power for manufacturing purposes. **2.** The said company are hereby empowered by means of and through the works aforesaid to supply manufacturers, 20 corporations and persons, along the route of the said tunnel, with water, hydraulic, electric or other power, for use in manufacturing or any other business or purpose and by means of cables, machinery or other appliances ; and at such rates and upon such conditions as may be agreed upon between the said 25 company and such manufacturers, corporations or persons.

Provisional directors. **3.** From and after the passing of this Act, the said James Ross, H. C. Symmes, John Bender, Charles Patrick, Frank Turner, J. T. Brundage, Harry Symons, Alex. Logan, and R. T. Sutton, with power to add to their number, shall be and are here- 30 by constituted a board of provisional directors of the said company, and shall hold office as such until the first election of directors under the provisions hereinafter contained.

Powers of provisional directors. **4.** The said board of provisional directors shall have power forthwith to open stock books and procure subscriptions of 35 stock for the undertaking, and to allot the stock, and to receive payments on account of stock subscribed, and to make calls upon subscribers in respect to their stock, and to sue for and recover the same ; and to cause plans and surveys to be made, and to receive for the company any grant, loan, bonus or gift 40 made to it, or in aid of the undertaking, and to enter into any agreement respecting the conditions or disposition of any gift or bonus in aid of the railway, and with all such other powers as under *The Railway Act of Ontario*, are vested in ordinary directors ; the said directors, or a majority of them, or the 45 board of directors to be elected as hereinafter mentioned may, in their discretion, exclude any one from subscribing for stock who, in their judgment, would hinder, delay or prevent the company from proceeding with and completing their undertaking under the provisions of this Act; and if at any time a 50 portion or more than the whole stock shall have been subscribed, the said provisional directors or board of directors, shall allocate and apportion it amongst the subscribers, as they hall deem most advantageous and conducive to the further-

ance of the undertaking; and in such allocation, the said directors may, in their discretion, exclude any one or more of the said subscribers, if, in their judgment, such exclusion will best secure the building of the said railway; and all meetings of
5 the provisional board of directors shall be held at the city of Toronto, or at such other place as may best suit the interests of the said company.

5. The capital of the company hereby incorporated shall be Capital stock.
10 $500,000, with power to increase the same in manner provided by *The Railway Act of Ontario*, to be divided into ten thousand shares of $50 each, and shall be raised by the persons and corporations who may become shareholders in such company; and the money so raised and paid into the company shall be
15 applied in the first place to the payment of all costs, charges and expenses of and incidental to the obtaining of this Act, or in promoting the undertaking, and of all expenses for making the surveys, plans and estimates connected with the works hereby authorized; and all the remainder of such money shall
20 be applied to the making, equipment, completion and the operating of the said railway, and the other purposes of this Act, and to no other purpose whatever.

6. When and so soon as shares to the amount of $50,000 of First meeting for election of
25 the capital stock of the said company shall have been sub- directors. scribed, and ten per centum thereon paid into some chartered bank of the Dominion having an office in the Province of Ontario, to the credit of the company, and which shall on no account be withdrawn therefrom unless for the services of the company, the provisional directors shall call a general meeting
30 of the subscribers to the said capital stock, who shall have so paid up ten per centum upon the amounts subscribed by them, for the purpose of electing directors of the said company.

7. In case the provisional directors neglect to call a meeting Provision in case
35 for the space of three months after $50,000 of the capital stock directors shall have been subscribed, and ten per centum thereof so paid neglect to up, the same may be called by any five of the subscribers who call meeting. shall have so paid up ten per centum, and who are subscribers collectively for not less than $5,000 of the capital stock, and
40 who have paid up all calls thereon.

8. In either of the cases last mentioned, notice of the time Notice and place of and place of holding such general meeting shall be given by meeting. publication in at least one of the daily newspapers in the city of Toronto, and in a weekly newspaper published in the county
45 of Welland, once in each week for the space of at least one month, and in the *Ontario Gazette;* and such meeting shall be held in the said city of Toronto, at such place therein, and on such day, and at such hour as may be named and set forth in such notice.

50 **9.** At such general meeting the subscribers to the capital Election of stock, present in person or by proxy, who shall have so paid directors. up ten per centum in respect to their subscriptions, shall choose not less than seven nor more than eleven persons to be directors of the said company, which said directors shall constitute
55 a board of directors, and shall hold office until the next annual

general meeting, or until other directors be elected in their stead; and may also make and pass such rules, regulations and by-laws as may be deemed expedient, provided they be not inconsistent with this Act.

Qualification of directors.

10. No person shall be qualified to be a director unless he 5 be a shareholder holding at least twenty-five shares of stock in the said company, and unless he has paid up all calls thereon.

Rights of aliens.

11. Aliens, as well as British subjects, and whether resident within this Province or elsewhere, may be shareholders in the said company; and all such shareholders shall be entitled to 10 vote on their shares equally with British subjects, and shall also be eligible to hold office as directors in the said company.

Annual meetings.

12. Thereafter the annual general meeting of the shareholders of the said company shall be held at such place in the city of Toronto, and on such days, and at such hours as may 15 be directed by the by-laws of the said company; and public notice thereof shall be given at least thirty days previously in the *Ontario Gazette*, and once in each week, during the four weeks preceding the week in which such meeting is to be held, in at least one of the daily newspapers published in the city of 20 Toronto, and in a weekly newspaper published in the county of Welland.

Special meetings.

13. Special general meetings of the shareholders of the said company may be held at such places in the city of Toronto, and at such times and in such manner and for such purposes as 25 may be provided by the by-laws of the said company, and after due notice shall be given as provided in the last preceding section.

Scale of votes.

14. Every shareholder of one or more shares of the said capital stock shall at any general meeting of the shareholders 30 be entitled to one vote for every share so held.

Corporations, how represented.

15. At all meetings of the shareholders of the company the stock held by municipal and other corporations may be represented by such persons as they shall respectively have appointed in that behalf by resolution under the seal of the 35 corporation, and such persons shall at such meeting be entitled equally with other shareholders to vote by proxy; and no shareholder shall be entitled to vote on any matter whatever, unless all calls due on the stock held by such shareholder shall have been paid up at least one week before the day appointed 40 for such meeting.

Quorum of directors.

16. Any meeting of the directors of the said company regularly summoned, at which at least three of the provisional directors or of those elected by the shareholders are present, shall be competent and entitled to exercise and use all and 45 every of the powers hereby vested in the said directors, and the said board may employ one of their number as paid director.

Calls.

17. Calls on the subscribed capital of the said company may be made by the directors for the time being, as they shall 50 see fit: Provided that no calls shall be made at any one time

of more than ten per centum of the amount subscribed by each
subscriber, and at not less intervals than one month, and notice
of each call shall be given as provided in section 12 of this Act.

18. Shares in the capital stock of the said company may be Transfer of
5 transferred by any form of instrument in writing, but no trans- shares.
fer shall become effectual unless the stock or scrip certificates
issued in respect of shares intended to be transferred are surrendered to the company, or the surrender thereof dispensed
with by the company.

10 **19.** Should the shareholders of the company resolve that the Appointment
interests of the company would be best promoted by enabling of director as
one or more of the directors to act for the company in any special agent.
particular matter or matters, it shall be lawful for the directors,
after such resolution, to confer such power upon one or more
15 of their number.

20. Conveyances of land to the said company for the pur- Form of
poses of and powers given by this Act, made in the form set conveyances.
forth in schedule A hereunder written, or to the like effect,
shall be sufficient conveyance to the said company, their suc-
20 cessors and assigns, of the estate or interest therein mentioned,
and sufficient bar of dower, respectively, of all persons executing the same ; and such conveyances shall be registered in such
manner and upon such proof of execution as is required under
the Registry Laws of Ontario ; and no registrar shall be entitled
25 to demand more than seventy-five cents for registering the
same, including all entries and certificates thereof, and certificates indorsed on the duplicates thereof.

21. The said company may receive from any Government. Aid to
or municipal council, or from any person or bodies corporate or company.
30 politic, aid towards the construction, equipment or maintenance
of the works authorized under this Act to be undertaken, by
way of gift, bonus, or loan of money or debentures, or other
securities for money, or by way of guarantee.

22. Any municipality, or any portion of any township muni- Aid from
35 cipality, which may be interested in securing the construction or municipali-
operation of the said works or through any part of which, or ties.
near which, the works of the said company shall pass or be
situate, may aid the said company by giving money or debentures, by way of bonus, gift, or loan, or by the guarantee of the
40 municipal corporation, under and subject to the provisions here- Proviso.
inafter contained : Provided always that such aid shall not be
given except after the passing of a by-law for the purpose, and
the adoption of such by-law by the qualified ratepayers of the
municipality or portion of the municipality, as the case may be,
45 in accordance with and as provided by law in respect to granting aid by way of bonuses to railways.

23. Such by-law shall be submitted by the municipal Provisions as
council to the vote of the ratepayers, in manner following, to bonus
namely : by-laws.

50 1. The proper petition shall first be presented to the council,
expressing the desire to aid the said works and stating in what
way and for what amount, and the council shall, within six
weeks after the receipt of such petition by the clerk of the

municipality, introduce a by-law to the effect petitioned
for, and submit the same for the approval of the qualified
voters ;

2. In the case of a county municipality, the petition shall be
that of a majority of the reeves and deputy-reeves, or of fifty
resident freeholders in each of the minor municipalities of the 5
county, who are qualified voters under *The Consolidated
Municipal Act, 1883;*

3. In the case of other municipalities the petition shall be
that of a majority of the council thereof, or of fifty resident
freeholders, being duly qualified voters under *The Consolidated* 10
Municipal Act, 1883, as aforesaid ;

4. In the case of a section of a township municipality, the
petition is to be presented to the council, defining the section by
metes and bounds, or lots and concessions, and shall be that of
a majority of the council of such township municipality, or of 15
fifty resident freeholders in such section of the municipality
being duly qualified voters as aforesaid.

Provisions of
by-law.

24. Such by-law shall in each instance provide :

1. For raising the amount petitioned for in the municipality or portion of the township municipality, (as the case may 20
be,) mentioned in the petition, by the issue of debentures of
the county or minor municipality respectively, and shall also
provide for the delivery of the said debentures, or the application of the amount to be raised thereby, as may be expressed
in the said by-law.   25

2. For assessing and levying upon all ratable property
lying within the municipality or portion of the township
municipality defined in said by-law, (as the case may be,) an
annual special rate sufficient to include a sinking fund for the
repayment of the said debentures within twenty years, with 30
interest thereon, payable yearly or half-yearly, which debentures the respective municipal councils, wardens, mayors,
reeves, and other officers thereof, are hereby authorized to
execute and issue in such cases respectively.

3. In the case of guarantee, the by-law shall provide for 35
the due application of the amount to be raised for the purpose thereof, and for assessing, and levying upon all ratable
property lying within the municipality, minor municipality,
or portion of the township municipality defined by the said
by-law (as the case may be,) an annual special rate sufficient 40
to pay from time to time the sum guaranteed, and to include a
sinking fund in the case of the principal of the debentures of
the company being guaranteed for a period not exceeding
twenty years, which guarantee the respective municipal councils, wardens, mayors, reeves, or other officers, are hereby 45
authorized to execute.

Provisions for
referring to
arbitration
disputes as to
bonus by-laws.

25. In case of aid from a county municipality, fifty resident
freeholders of the county may petition the county council
against submitting the said by-law, upon the ground that
certain minor municipalities or portions thereof comprised in 50
the said by-law, would be injuriously affected thereby, or upon
any other ground ought not to be included therein, and upon

deposit by the petitioners with the treasurer of the county, of
a sum sufficient to defray the expense of such reference, the
said council shall forthwith refer the said petition to three
arbitrators, one being the judge of the County Court, one
5 being the Registrar of the county or of the riding in which
the county town is situate, and one being an engineer
appointed by the Commissioner of Public Works for Ontario,
who shall have power to confirm or amend the said by-law by
excluding any minor municipality or any section. thereof
10 therefrom, and the decision of any two of them shall be final,
and the by-law so confirmed or amended shall thereupon, at
the option of the company, be submitted by the council to the
duly qualified voters; and in case the by-law is confirmed by
the arbitrators, the expense shall be borne by the petitioners
15 against the same, but if amended, then by the company or the
county, as the arbitrators may order.

26. The term " minor municipality " shall be construed to Minor munici-
mean any town not separated from the municipal county, ing of.
ownship, or incorporated village situate in the county muni-
20 ᵗipality.
c

27. Before any such by-law is submitted, the company Deposit for
shall, if required, deposit with the treasurer of the municipality, expenses.
a sum sufficient to pay the expenses to be incurred in submitting said by-law.

25 **28.** In case the by-law submitted be approved of and car- If by-law
ried in accordance with the provisions of the law in that council to pass
behalf, then within four weeks after the date of such voting, same,
the municipal council which submitted the same shall read the
said by-law a third time, and pass the same.

30 **29.** Within one month after the passing of such by-law, the And issue
said council and the mayor, warden, reeve, or other head, or debentures.
other officers thereof, shall issue or dispose of the debentures
provided for by the by-law, and deliver the same duly executed
to the trustees appointed, or to be appointed under this Act.

35 **30.** In case any such loan, guarantee or bonus be so granted Levying rate
by a portion of a township municipality, the rate to be levied on portions of
for payment of the debentures issued therefor, and the interest
thereon, shall be assessed and levied upon such portion only of
such municipality.

40 **31.** The provisions of *The Consolidated Municipal Act,1883,* Application of
and the amendments thereto, so far as the same are not incon- as to by-law.
sistent with this Act, shall apply to any by-law so passed by
or for a portion of a township municipality, to the same
extent as if the same had been passed by or for the whole
45 municipality.

32. The councils for all corporations that may grant aid by Extension of
way of bonus to the said company may, by resolution or mencement.
by-law, extend the time for the commencement of the work
beyond that stipulated for in the by-law or by-laws granting
50 such aid from time to time : Provided that no such extension
shall be for a longer period than one year.

Extension of time for completion.

33. It shall and may be lawful for the council of any municipality that may grant aid by way of bonus to the said company, by resolution or by-law, to extend the time for the completion of the works, on the completion of which the said company would be entitled to such bonus, from time to time : Provided that no such extension shall be for a longer period than one year at a time.

Rate not exceeding three cents in the dollar valid.

34. Any municipality or portion of a township municipality interested in the construction of the works of the said company, may grant aid by way of bonus to the said company towards the construction of such works, notwithstanding that such aid may increase the municipal taxation of such municipality or **Proviso.** portion thereof, beyond what is allowed by law : Provided that such aid shall not require the levying of a greater aggregate annual rate for all purposes, exclusive of school rates, than three cents in the dollar upon the value of the ratable property therein.

Exemption from taxation.

35. It shall be lawful for the corporation of any municipality, in which the works of the said company, or any part thereof are situate, by by-law expressly passed for that purpose, to exempt the company and its property within such municipality, either in whole or in part, from municipal assessment or taxation, or to agree to a certain sum per annum or otherwise in gross, or by way of commutation or composition for payment, or in lieu of all or any municipal rates or assessments to be imposed by such municipal corporation, and for such term of years as such municipal corporation may deem expedient, not exceeding twenty-one years, and no such by-law shall be repealed unless in conformity with a condition contained therein.

Grants of land.

36. Any municipality in which the said works or any part thereof are situate, is empowered to grant by way of gift to the said company, any lands belonging to such municipality or or over which it may have control, which may be required for any purpose connected with the said company, and the said company shall have power to accept gifts of land from any government, or any person or body politic or corporate, and shall have power to sell or otherwise dispose of the same for the benefit of the said company.

Trustees of debentures.

37. Whenever any municipality or portion of a township municipality shall grant aid by way of bonus or gift to the said company, the debentures therefor shall, within six months after the passing of the by-law authorizing the same, be delivered to three trustees to be named, one by the Lieutenant-Governor in Council, one by the said company, and one by the majority of the heads of the municipalities which have granted bonuses, or in case of only one municipality granting a bonus, then by the head of such municipality, all the trustees to be **Proviso.** residents of the Province of Ontario : Provided that if the said heads of the municipalities, or head of the said municipality, shall refuse or neglect to name such trustee within one month after notice in writing of the appointment of the company's trustee, or if the Lieutenant-Governor in Council shall omit to name such trustee within one month after notice in writing to him of the appointment of the other trustees, then in either case the company shall be at liberty to name such other trustee or

trustees. Any of the said trustees may be removed and a new
trustee appointed in his place at any time by the Lieutenant-
Governor in Council, and in case any trustee dies or resigns his
trust, or goes to live out of the Province of Ontario, or other-
5 wise becomes incapable to act, his trusteeship shall become
vacant and a new trustee may be appointed by the Lieutenant-
Governor in Council.

38. The said trustees shall receive the said debentures or
bonds in trust, (firstly) under the directions of the company,
10 but subject to the conditions of the by-law in relation thereto,
as to time or manner to convert the same into money or otherwise dispose of them; secondly, to deposit the debentures or
amount realized from the sale in some chartered bank having
an office in the city of Toronto, in the name of "The Niagara
15 Tunnel and Water Power Company Municipal Trust Account,"
and to pay the same out to the said company from time to time
as the said company becomes entitled thereto, under the conditions of the by-law granting the said bonus, and on the certificate of the chief engineer of the said company for the time
20 being, in the form set out in schedule B, hereto, or to the like
effect, which certificate shall set forth that the conditions of
the by-law have been complied with, and is to be attached to
the cheque or order drawn by the said trustees for such payment
or delivery of debentures, and such engineer shall not wrong-
25 fully grant any such certificate, under a penalty of $500,
recoverable in any Court of competent jurisdiction, by any
person who may sue therefor.

Trusts of proceeds of debentures.

39. The trustees shall be entitled to their reasonable fees
and charges from said trust fund, and the act of any two of
30 such trustees shall be as valid and binding as if the three had
agreed.

Fees to trustees.

40. It shall and may be lawful for any municipality having
jurisdiction in the premises, to pass a by-law or by-laws
empowering the company to construct and operate their works
35 under or along any of the highways within such municipality,
and whether or not the same be in the possession of or under
the control of any joint stock company; and if such highway
be either in the possession of or under the control of any joint
stock company, then also with the assent of such company.

Right to use highways.

40 **41.** It shall be lawful for the directors to enter into a contract or contracts with any individual or association of individuals for the construction or equipment of the works authorized by this Act, or any portion thereof, and to pay therefor
either in cash or bonds, or in paid up stock or otherwise, as
45 may be deemed expedient.

*Power to con-
tract for con-
struction and
equipment of
works.*

42. The said company shall have power and authority to
become parties to promissory notes and bills of exchange for
sums not less than $100, and any such promissory note made
or endorsed, or any such bill of exchange drawn, accepted or
50 endorsed by the president or vice-president of the company,
and countersigned by the secretary or treasurer, or other proper
officer of the said company, and under the authority of a
quorum of the directors, shall be binding on the said company;
and every such promissory note or bill of exchange so made,

*Power to make
and endorse
notes and bills
without
affixing seal.*

2—59

accepted or endorsed, shall be presumed to have been made, accepted or endorsed with proper authority, until the contrary be shewn; and in no case shall it be necessary to have the seal of the company affixed to such promissory note or bill of exchange, nor shall the president or vice-president, or the 5 secretary or treasurer, or other officer aforesaid, be individually responsible for the same, unless the said promissory notes or bills of exchange have been issued without the sanction and authority of the board of directors, as herein provided and enacted: Provided, however, that nothing in this section shall 10 be construed to authorize the said company to issue any note or bill of exchange payable to bearer or intended to be circulated as money, or as the notes and bills of a bank.

Proviso

Issue of bonds.

43. The directors of the said company, after the sanction of the shareholders shall have first been obtained at any special 15 general meeting to be called from time to time for such purpose, shall have power to issue bonds, made and signed by the president of the said company, and countersigned by the secretary, and under the seal of the said company, for the purpose of raising money for prosecuting and operating the 20 said works ; and such bonds shall, without registration or formal conveyance, be taken and considered to be the first and preferential claims and charges upon the said works and the real property of the company, including all equipments and attachments then existing, and at any time thereafter acquired 25 and necessary for the operation of the said works; and each holder of the said bonds shall be deemed to be a mortgagee and incumbrancer, *pro rata*, with all the other holders thereof, upon the undertaking and property of the company as aforesaid : Provided, however, that the whole amount of such issue 30 of bonds shall not exceed in all the amount of the subscribed capital stock of the said company from time to time ; and and provided that in the event at any time of the interest upon the said bonds remaining unpaid and owing, then, at the next ensuing general annual meeting of 35 the said company, all holders of bonds shall have and possess the same rights, privileges and qualifications for directors and for voting as are attached to shareholders : Provided further, that the bonds and any transfers thereof shall have been first registered in the same manner as is provided 40 for the registration of shares, and it shall be the duty of the secretary of the company to register the same on being required to do so by any holder thereof.

Proviso.

Proviso.

Proviso.

Form of bonds.

44. All such bonds, debentures and other securities and coupons and interest warrants thereon respectively may be made payable to bearer and tranferable by delivery, and any 45 holder of any such securities so made payable to bearer, may sue at law thereon in his own name, and all such bonds, debentures and other securities and coupons and interest warrants thereon respectively may be made payable in lawful money of Canada, or in sterling money of Great Britain, at 50 some place in Canada, or London, England, or in the city of New York, in the state of New York, or at all or any of such places.

45. The company hereby incorporated may, from time to time, for advances of money to be made thereon, mortgage or pledge any bonds or debentures which, under the powers of this Act can be issued for the construction of the said works,
5 or otherwise.

46. The said provisional directors, or the elected directors, may pay or agree to pay, in paid up stock or in the bonds of the said company, such sums as they may deem expedient, to
10 engineers or contractors, or for right of way, privileges or material, plant or equipment, and also, when sanctioned by a vote of the majority of shareholders present at any general meeting, for the services of promoters or other persons who may be employed by the directors for the purpose of assisting
15 the directors in the furtherance of the said works or purchase of right of way, privileges, material, or plant whether such promoters or other persons be provisional directors or not, and any such agreements so made shall be binding on the company.

20 **47.** The said company is hereby authorized and empowered to take and make the surveys and levels of the land upon, through, or under which, the said works are to pass or be operated together with the map or plan thereof, and of the course and direction of the said tunnel and waterway, and of
25 the other works and of the lands intended to be passed through or under so far as then ascertained, and also the book of reference for the works, and to deposit the same as required by the clauses of *The Railway Act of Ontario* and amendments thereto, with respect to plans and surveys by sections
30 or portions less than the whole length of the said tunnel or covered waterway authorized, and of such length as the said company may from time to time see fit, and upon such deposit as aforesaid of the map or plan and book of reference, and any and each of such sections or portions of the said tunnel or
35 covered waterway all and every of the clauses of *The Railway Act of Ontario* and the amendments thereof applied to, included in or incorporated with this Act, shall apply and extend to any and each of such sections or portions of said tunnel or covered waterway or other work authorized, as fully and
40 effectually as if the said surveys and levels had been taken and made of the lands through or under which the whole of the said tunnel or covered waterway is to pass, together with the map or plan of the whole thereof, and of its whole course and direction and of the lands intended to be passed through or
45 under and taken or affected and the book of reference for the whole of the said tunnel or covered waterway had been taken, made, examined, certified and deposited according to the said clauses of the said Railway Act of Ontario and the amendments thereof, with respect to plans and surveys.

50 **48.** The construction of the said works shall be commenced within three years, and the same shall be completed within ten years from the passing of this Act.

49. Sections 9, 10, 11, 12, 13, 14, 15, 16, 17, 18, 19 and 20 of *The Railway Act of Ontario* shall, so far as applicable,
55 apply to the company hereby incorporated as if the said sec-

tions had been specially set out in this Act, and as if the said company had been specially named in the said sections ; and it is hereby declared that the word "lands" mentioned in the said sections shall include any privilege required by the said company of constructing or operating its works or any portion 5 thereof, under or through any land without the necessity of acquiring a title in fee simple thereto.

Restriction as to exercise of powers.

50. None of the works hereby authorized shall be constructed or the powers given by this Act exercised within the Niagara Falls Park reservation until the works that may be 10 proposed to be exercised in regard thereto, shall have been sanctioned by the Commissioner of Public Works, and upon such terms and conditions as may be required by him, but this section shall not apply to surveys.

By-laws.

51. The said company may pass by-laws regulating its 15 business and affairs, and may repeal or amend the same in the mode provided by *The Ontario Joint Stock Companies' Letters Patent Act.*

Powers contained in R. S. O. c. 157 and in 45 V. c.19, conferred on company.

52. The powers of companies incorporated under the provisions and for the purposes mentioned in chapter 157 of the Revised Statutes and in the Act of the Legislative 20 Assembly of the Province of Ontario, passed in the forty-fifth year of Her Majesty's reign and chaptered 19, are hereby conferred upon the said company so far as the same are not inconsistent with the provisions of this Act.

SCHEDULE A.

(*Section 20.*)

Know all men by these presents that I (*or* we) [*insert the name of the vendors*] in consideration of   dollars paid to me (*or* us) by the Niagara Tunnel and Water Power Company of Ontario, the receipt whereof is hereby acknowledged, do grant and convey unto the said company, and I (*or* we) [*insert the names of any other party or parties*]   in consideration of   dollars paid to me (*or* us) by the said company, the receipt whereof is hereby acknowledged, do grant or release all that certain parcel (*or* those certain parcels *as the case may be*) of land (*describe the land*) the same having been selected and laid out by the company for the purposes of their works, to hold with the appurtenances unto the said company, their successors and assigns (*here insert any other clauses, covenants or conditions required*) and I (*or* we) the wife (*or* wives) of the said   , do hereby bar my (*or* our) dower in the said lands.

As witness my (*or* our) hand and seal (*or* hands and seals) this   day of   ¹A.D. 18

Signed, sealed and delivered ⎫
in the presence of   ⎬   [L.S.]

SCHEDULE B.

(*Section* 38.)

CHIEF ENGINEER'S CERTIFICATE.

THE NIAGARA TUNNEL AND WATER POWER COMPANY OF ONTARIO,

Engineer's Department, A.D. 188

No.

Certificate to be attached to cheques drawn on " The Niagara Tunnel and Water Power Company Municipal Trust Account," given under section , chapter of the Acts of the Legislature of Ontario, passed in the year of Her Majesty's reign.

I, A.B., Chief Engineer of the Niagara Tunnel and Water Power Company of Ontario, do hereby certify that the said company has fulfilled the terms and conditions necessary to be fulfilled under the by-law No. of the of (*or* under the agreement dated the day of between the corporation of and the said company) to entitle the said company to receive from the said trust the sum of (*here set out the terms and conditions, if any, which have been fulfilled.*)

BILL.

An Act to incorporate the Niagara Tunnel and Water Power Company of Ontario.

First Reading, 17th March 1887.

(Private Bill.)

Mr. MORIN.

TORONTO:

Printed by Warwick & Sons, 26 and 28 Front St. W.

No. 60.]　　　　　**BILL.**　　　　[1887.

An Act respecting the Revised Statutes of Ontario, 1887.

WHEREAS it has been found expedient to revise, classify, _{Preamble.} and consolidate the Public General Statutes, which apply to the Province of Ontario and are within the legislative authority of the Legislature of Ontario; and whereas such
5 revision, classification, and consolidation, have been made accordingly; and whereas it is expedient to provide for the incorporation therewith of the Public General Statutes, passed during the present session, and for giving the force of law to the body of revised statutes to result from such incorporation :
10 Therefore Her Majesty, by and with the advice and consent of the Legislative Assembly of the Province of Ontario, enacts as follows :—

1. The printed roll, attested as that of the said statutes re- Original Roll
vised, classified, and consolidated as aforesaid, under the signa- of Statutes re-
15 ture of His Honour the Lieutenant-Governor, and that of the vised, etc., to
Clerk of the Legislative Assembly, and deposited in the office and deposited.
of the Clerk of the Legislative Assembly, shall be held to be the
original thereof, and to embody the several Acts and parts of
Acts mentioned as to be repealed in the schedule A thereto
20 annexed ; but the marginal notes thereon, and the headings in As to marginal
the body of the Act, and the references to former enactments at notes, mis-
the foot of the several sections thereof, and the sections printed prints, etc.
in bourgeois type, form no part of the said statutes, and shall be
held to have been inserted for convenience of reference only,
25 and may be omitted or corrected, and any misprint or error,
whether of commission or omission, or any contradiction or
ambiguity in the said roll may also be corrected, but without
changing the legal effect, and such alterations in the language
of said statutes as are requisite, in order to preserve a uniform
30 mode of expression, and do not alter the legal effect may be
made, and any of the enacting clauses in said statutes may be
printed in bourgeois type, and any of the sections in bourgeois
type may be printed among the enacting clauses where proper
—in the roll hereinafter mentioned.

35 **2.** The Lieutenant-Governor may select such Acts and parts Lieutenant-
of Acts, passed during the present Session, as he may deem it Governor may
advisable to incorporate with the said statutes contained in lation of the
the said first mentioned roll, and may cause them to be so in- present
corporated therewith, adapting their form and language to incorporated
45 those of the said statutes (but without changing their effect), in the said
inserting them in their proper places in the said statutes, Roll
striking out of the latter any enactments repealed by or inconsistent with those so incorporated, altering the numbering of

the chapters and sections, if need be, and adding to the said
schedule A a list of the Acts and parts of Acts of the present
session so incorporated as aforesaid.

Certified Roll including the legislation of the present Session to be deposited and serve as the original thereof. **3.** So soon as the said incorporation of such Acts, and parts
of Acts, with the said statutes, and the said addition to the said 5
schedule A has been completed, the Lieutenant-Governor may
cause a correct printed roll thereof, attested under his signature
and countersigned by the Provincial Secretary, to be deposited
in the office of the Clerk of the Legislative Assembly, which
roll shall be held to be the original thereof, and to embody the 10
several Acts, and parts of Acts, mentioned as repealed in the
amended schedule A thereto annexed; any marginal notes,
however, and headings in the body of the Act and references
to former enactments, and sections printed in bourgeois type
which may appear thereon, being held to form no part of the 15
said statutes, but to be inserted for convenience of reference
only.

Proclamation for bringing the Revised Statutes into force. **4.** The Lieutenant-Governor in Council, after such deposit
of the said last mentioned roll, may by proclamation declare
the day on, from and after which the same shall come into 20
force and have effect as law, by the designation of "The Revised Statutes of Ontario."

On and after day named in Proclamation Statutes to be in force and the enactments embodied in them repealed. Exception. **5.** On, from and after such day, the same shall accordingly
come into force and effect as and by the designation of "The
Revised Statutes of Ontario," to all intents as though the same 25
were expressly embodied in and enacted by this Act, to come
into force and have effect on, from and after such day; and on,
from and after the same day, all the enactments in the several
Acts and parts of Acts in such amended schedule A mentioned,
so far as they relate to this Province, shall stand and be re- 30
pealed to the extent mentioned in the third column of said
schedule A, save only as hereinafter is provided.

Repeal not to extend to Acts over which the Dominion Parliament has jurisdiction. **6.** Such repeal shall not be construed as intended to extend to such of the provisions of said Acts and parts of Acts as
relate to subjects in regard to which the Parliament of Canada 35
has exclusive powers of legislation; but the said Acts and parts
of Acts (in so far only as is necessary to give effect to every
such provision) shall remain in full force and effect, subject
however, to section 9 of this Act.

Saving as to transactions, etc., anterior to the repeal. **7.** The repeal of the said Acts and parts of Acts shall not 40
revive any Act or provision of law repealed by them; nor shall
the said repeal prevent the effect of any saving clause in the
said Acts and parts of Acts, or the application of any of the
said Acts or parts of Acts or of any Act or provision of law
formerly in force, to any transaction, matter or thing anterior 45
to the said repeal, to which they would otherwise apply.

Certain matters anterior to the repeal not to be affected by it. Penalties, etc. **8.** (1) The repeal of the said Acts and parts of Acts shall not
affect—

(a.) Any penalty, forfeiture or liability incurred before
the time of such repeal, or any proceedings for en- 50
forcing the same, had, done, completed or pending
at the time of such repeal,—

(b.) Nor any action, suit, judgment, decree, certificate, ex- Actions, etc., ecution, process, order, rule, or any proceeding, matter or thing whatever respecting the same, had, done, made, entered, granted, completed, pending, 5   existing, or in force at the time of such repeal,—

(c.) Nor any act, deed, right, title, interest, grant, assur- Acts, deeds, ance, descent, will, registry, by-law, rule, regula- rights, etc. tion, contract, lien, charge, matter or thing, had, done, made, acquired, established or existing at the 10   time of such repeal,—

(d.) Nor any office, appointment, commission, salary, Offices, etc. allowance, security, duty, or any matter or thing appertaining thereto, at the time of such repeal,—

(e.) Nor any marriage, certificate or registry thereof, law- Marriages, etc. 15   fully had, made, granted or existing before or at the time of such repeal,—

(f.) Nor shall such repeal defeat, disturb, invalidate or pre- And other judicially affect any other matter or thing what- matters, etc. soever, had, done, completed, existing or pending 20   at the time of such repeal ;

(2.) But every such   But the same shall remain valid, etc.

Penalty, forfeiture and liability, and every such

Action, suit, judgment, decree, certificate, execution, pro- secution, order, rule, proceeding, matter or thing, and every 25 such

Act, deed, right, title, interest, grant, assurance, descent, will, registry, by-law, rule, regulation, contract, lien, charge, matter or thing, and every such

Office, appointment, commission, salary, allowance, security 30 and duty, and every such

Marriage, certificate and registry thereof, and every such other matter and thing, and the force and effect thereof, respectively.

may and shall, remain and continue as if no such repeal had And may be 35 taken place, and so far as necessary, may and shall be con- enforced, etc., and under tinued, prosecuted, enforced and proceeded with under the said what laws. Revised Statutes and other the statutes and laws having force in this Province, so far as applicable thereto, and subject to the provisions of the said several statutes and laws.

40   **9.**—(1.) The said Revised Statutes shall not be held to oper- Revised ate as new laws, but shall be construed and have effect as a Statutes not to be deemed consolidation of the law as contained in the said Acts and new laws. parts of Acts so repealed, and for which the said Revised Stat- utes are substituted, and the Legislature is not to be deemed to 45 have adopted the construction which may by judicial decision, or otherwise, have been placed upon the language of any of the statutes included amongst the said Revised Statutes.

(2.) The various provisions in the Revised Statutes corres- How constru- ed where the ponding to and substituted for the provisions of the Acts and same in effect 50 parts of Acts so repealed, shall, where they are the same in as the repealed Acts.

effect as those of the Acts and parts of Acts so repealed, be held
to operate retrospectively as well as prospectively, and to have
been passed upon the days respectively upon which the Acts
and parts of Acts so repealed came into effect.

How construed
if in any case
they differ
from the re-
pealed Acts
    (3.) If upon any point the provisions of the said Revised 5
Statutes are not in effect the same as those of the repealed Acts
and parts of Acts for which they are substituted, then as respects all transactions, matters and things, subsequent to the
time when the said Revised Statutes take effect, the provisions contained in them shall prevail, but as respects all trans- 10
actions, matters and things anterior to the said time, the
provisions of the said repealed Acts and parts of Acts shall
prevail.

As to refer-
ences to re-
pealed Acts
in former Acts,
etc.
    10. Any reference in any former Act remaining in force, or
in any instrument or document, to any Act or enactment so 15
repealed, shall, after the Revised Statutes take effect, be held,
as regards any subsequent transaction, matter or thing, to be
a reference to the enactments in the Revised Statutes having
the same effect as such repealed Act or enactment.

As to effect of
insertion of an
Act in sche-
dule A.
    11. The insertion of any Act in the said schedule A shall 20
not be construed as a declaration that such Act or any part of
it was or was not in force immediately before the coming into
force of the said Revised Statutes.

Copies printed
by Queen's
Printer to be
evidence.
    12. Copies of the said Revised Statutes, printed by the
Queen's Printer from the amended roll so deposited, shall be 25
received as evidence of the said Revised Statutes in all Courts
and places whatsoever.

As to distribu-
tion of copies.
    13. The laws relating to the distribution of the printed
copies of the Statutes shall not apply to the said Revised
Statutes, but the same shall be distributed in such numbers 30
and to such persons only as the Lieutenant-Governor in Council may direct.

This Act to be
printed with
Revised
Statutes.
    14. This Act shall be printed with the said Revised
Statutes, and shall be subject to the same rules of construction
as the said Revised Statutes.   35

How they may
be cited.
    15. Any chapter of the said Revised Statutes may be cited
and referred to in any Act or proceeding whatever, either by
its title as an Act, or by its short title, or by using the expression " The Revised Statute respecting—" (adding the remainder
of the title given at the beginning of the particular chapter), 40
or by using the expression " The Revised Statutes of Ontario
1887,, chapter   " (adding the number of the particular
chapter in the copies printed by the Queen's Printer.)

No. 60.

1st Session 6th Legislature, 50 Vic., 1887.

BILL.

An Act respecting the Revised Statutes of Ontario, 1887.

First Reading, 3rd March, 1887.

No. 61.]　　　　　　　**BILL.**　　　　　[1887.

An Act to enable Married Women to Vote for Members of Municipal Councils.

HER MAJESTY, by and with the advice and consent of the Legislative Assembly of the Province of Ontario, enacts as follows:—

    1. Section 3 of *The Municipal Amendment Act, 1884*, is 5 hereby repealed and the following substituted therefor:— 47 V. c. 32, s. 3, repealed.

    3. In order that widows, and unmarried or married women, who are in their own right rated for a property or income qualification sufficient to qualify male voters, shall hereafter have the right to vote at municipal elections, it is enacted that 10 section 79 of *The Consolidated Municipal Act, 1883*, is hereby amended, by inserting after the word "being" in the third line thereof, the words "widows and unmarried or married women or." Female franchise.

    2. Section 4 of the said Act is hereby repealed and the 15 following substituted therefor:— 47 V. c. 32, s. 4, repealed.

    4. In addition to any other oath or affirmation which now may be required of any person claiming to vote at a municipal election the following oath or affirmation may also be required of any widow, and unmarried or married women, so claiming 20 to vote:— Oath to be taken by women.

    "You swear (*or* solemnly affirm) that you are the person named or purporting to be named in the list (*or* supplementary list) of voters now shewn to you."

    "That you are unmarried (*or* married, *or* a widow, *as the case may be*)."

25   **3.** Sub-section 3 of section 2 of *The Voters' Lists Amendment Act, 1885*, is hereby amended by inserting the words "or married" between the words "unmarried" and "women," in the third line thereof. 48 V. c. 3, s. 2, (3) amended.

No. 61.

1st Session, 6th Legislature, 50 Vic., 1887.

BILL.

An Act to enable Married Women to vote for Members of Municipal Councils.

First Reading, 4th March, 1887.

No. 62.]   **BILL.**   [1887.

An Act to Abolish Distress for Rent.

HER MAJESTY by and with the advice and consent of
the Legislative Assembly of the Province of Ontario
enacts as follows:—

1. Distress for rent is hereby abolished.   Distress for
                                                                rent abolished.

No. 62.

1st Session, 6th Legislature, 50 Vic., 1887.

BILL.

An Act to Abolish Distress for Rent.

First Reading, 7th March, 1887.

BILL.

An Act to amend "The Consolidated Municipal Act, 1883."

HER MAJESTY by and with the advice and consent of the Legislative Assembly of the Province of Ontario, enacts as follows :—

1. Section 416 of *The Consolidated Municipal Act, 1883,* 46 V. c. 18, s. 416, repealed.
5 is hereby repealed and the following substituted in lieu thereof —:

416. The head of every council and the reeve, of every town, Certain township, and incorporated village, and each deputy-reeve and persons to be councillor of every township council shall *ex-officio* be Justices *ex-officio* justices of the
10 of the Peace for the whole county or union of counties in which peace. their respective municipalities lie, and aldermen in cities shall be Justices of the Peace for such cities.

2. Section 418 of the said Act is hereby repealed and the 46 V. c. 18, s. following substituted in lieu thereof :—. 418, repealed.

15   418. No warden, mayor, reeve, deputy-reeve, or councillor of Qualification any township council, or alderman, after taking the oaths or of certain making the declarations as such, shall be required to have any justices. property qualification, or to take any further oath to enable him to act as a Justice of the Peace.

BILL.

An Act to amend "The Consolidated Municipal Act, 1883."

First Reading, 7th March, 1887.

BILL.

An Act to amend the Ditches and Water-courses Act, 1883.

HER MAJESTY, by and with the advice and consent of the Legislative Assembly of the Province of Ontario, enacts as follows :—

1. Every railway company shall be considered as an owner
5 of lands under the provisions of *The Ditches and Water-courses Act, 1883.* Owners of lands to include Railway Companies.

2. Every existing ditch, drain, creek, or water-course, running along or under any railway, may be used when it is found and reported upon in an award made by the engineer of the
10 municipality under the provisions of the said Act, that such ditch, drain, creek or water-course, is necessary as an outlet for any ditch, or drain that has been, or may be constructed under the provisions of the said Act, and any such existing ditch, drain, creek or water-course, running along or under such rail-
15 way may be deepened or widened so as to meet the requirements of the ditch, or drain heretofore, or hereafter constructed, (or of the deepening or widening of any water-course) under the provisions of the said Act; such work shall be done in such a manner as not to injure the bridges, culverts or road bed of
20 the railway, or in any way to interfere with traffic. *Ditches, drains, creeks or water-courses, along and under railways, to be used as outlets for draining. Work not to injure railway or impede traffic.*

3. The engineer in every case when he awards that the ditch, drain, creek or water-course, running along or under any railway is to be used for the purposes aforesaid, shall file with such award a plan or profile of the position of the ditch, drain,
25 creek or water-course, running along or under such railway. *Engineer to file with award a profile of drains, etc.*

4.—(1) When so found and awarded, the clerk of the municipality shall within six days after the filing of the award, send by registered letter to the engineer of the railway, a copy of the award with a copy of the plan or profile of the proposed
30 work. *Copy of award to be sent to railway engineer.*

(2) The said clerk shall within four days after the expiration of the time for appeal, or if an appeal has been made, after such appeal has been decided, send to the railway engineer by registered letter, a notice stating the time and day upon which
35 the work will be commenced and proceeded with, said day not to be sooner than ten days from the day of mailing the notice. *Clerk to notify railway engineer when work is to begin.*

5. The engineer of the railway (or some one on his behalf) may, if he sees fit, inspect the work as it is being proceeded with, but such inspection shall not interfere with the engineer work. *Railway engineer may inspect the work.*

No charge for inspection. of the municipality as regards his duties of inspection under the provisions of said Act. The railway engineer, or any one acting on his behalf, shall have no claim for any remuneration, for the inspection or supervision of the work.

Company not liable for work. **6.** The railway company shall not be liable for any por- 5 tion of the work, or for the cost thereof.

Company's right of appeal confined. **7.** The railway company shall have the same right of appeal as any owner has under the said Act; but the appeal of the railway company shall be confined to the right to use the ditch, drain, creek or water-course, running along or 10 under the railway.

No. 64.

1st Session, 6th Legislature, 50 Vic., 1887.

BILL.

An Act to amend the Ditches and Water-courses Act, 1883.

First Reading, 7th March, 1887.

Mr. WATERS.

TORONTO:
PRINTED BY WARWICK & SONS, 26 AND 28 FRONT ST. W

No. 65.]　　　　　　　**BILL.**　　　　　[1887.

An Act to amend the Municipal Act.

Preamble.

WHEREAS it is expedient to define more clearly the bridges that have to be erected and maintained by the council of a county, or by the council of two or more counties, or by the council of a county and city, and also to define the 5 bridges that the councils of minor municipalities have to erect and maintain upon boundary lines, and the opening up and keeping in repair of such lines, and also the mode of procedure if arbitration takes place and other matters ;

Therefore Her Majesty, by and with the advice and consent 10 of the Legislative Assembly of the Province of Ontario, enacts as follows :—

1. Section 532 of *The Consolidated Municipal Act, 1883,* is hereby repealed and the following substituted therefor:—

46 V. c. 18, s. 532, (amended by 49 V. c. 37, s. 16), repealed.

532. The county council shall have exclusive jurisdiction over 15 all roads lying within any township, town or village of the county, and which the council by by-law assumes with the assent of such township, town or village municipality, as a county road or bridge, until the by-law has been repealed by the council, and over all bridges across rivers or streams separ- 20 ating two townships in the county, and over all bridges crossing rivers or streams over 100 feet in width within the limits of any town, township or incorporated village in the county, and connecting any highway leading through the county, and over all bridges, over rivers or streams forming boundary lines, and 25 over all bridges of 100 feet in length or more, over rivers or streams crossing boundary lines, or crossing any deviated roads used in lieu of any such boundary line, between two or more municipalities within the county.

Jurisdiction of County Council over roads and bridges.

2. Section 535 of the said Act as amended by section 22 of 30 *The Municipal Amendment Act, 1885,* is hereby repealed, and the following substituted therefor :—

46 V. c. 18, s. 535, (amended by 48 V. c. 39. s. 22), repealed.

535.—(1) The council of each county shall erect, maintain and keep in repair all bridges over rivers or streams forming boundary lines between two municipalities within the county, 35 other than in the case of a separated town, and all bridges of 100 feet in length, or more, over rivers or streams crossing boundary lines between two municipalities within the county, or crossing a deviated road used in lieu of any such boundary line, and shall also erect, maintain and keep in repair all bridges 40 over rivers or streams over 100 feet in width, within the limits of any town, township, or incorporated village in the county, and connecting any highway leading through the county.

Bridges which the county has to erect and maintain.

Bridges which two or more counties have to erect and maintain. (2) The councils of counties shall join in erecting, maintaining and keeping in repair, all bridges over rivers or streams forming boundary lines between two or more counties, and all bridges of 100 feet in length, or more, over rivers or streams crossing boundary lines between two counties, or crossing a 5 deviated road used in lieu of any such boundary line.

Bridges which a county and city or separated town has to erect. (3) The councils of a county and city, or of a separated town as the case may be, shall join in erecting and keeping in repair all bridges over rivers or streams forming boundary lines between a county and city, as well as all bridges of 100 feet in 10 length, or more, over rivers or streams crossing boundary lines between a county and city, or crossing a deviated road used in lieu of any such boundary line.

A deviated road shall be regarded as a boundary line. Bridges on deviated roads are bridges on boundary lines. (4) A road which lies wholly or partly between two municipalities, shall be regarded as a boundary line, within the 15 meaning of this section, although such road may deviate, so that it is in some place or places wholly within one of such municipalities, and a bridge of 100 feet in length, or more, built over a river or stream crossing such road where it deviates as aforesaid, shall be held to be a bridge over a river or stream 20 crossing a boundary line, within the meaning of this section.

Any of the councils may pass a by-law. (5) In the case of a bridge coming within the meaning of sub-sections 1 and 2 of this section, the council of any one of the counties, or the council of the city, or the council of the separated town, as the case may be, may pass a by-law pro- 25 viding for the erection of any such bridge, setting forth in the by-law, first, the public necessity that exists for the erection of the bridge ; second, the place or site where the bridge is to be erected ; third, the kind of bridge and material to be used in the construction ; fourth, the proportion of the cost of construc- 30 tion and maintenance to be borne by the municipality passing the by-law ; fifth, the time within which the bridge is to be completed.

By law if not agreed upon, to be referred to arbitration. (6) In case the other council or councils, as the case may be, for six months after receiving the copy of the by-law, omits or 35 refuses to pass a similar, or any by-law, or passes a by-law agreeing to one or more of the provisions of the first-mentioned by-law, then in either of such cases the matters in dispute shall be referred to arbitration, under the provisions of this Act, respecting arbitrations, and the arbitration shall proceed 40 as hereinafter provided :

Arbitrators to decide upon the whole by-law or so much as is not agreed upon. (a) In case the council which receives a copy of the first-mentioned by-law omits or refuses to pass a similar or any by-law, then in such case the arbitrators shall decide and determine upon all the provisions 45 of the first-mentioned by-law, or in case the council pass a by-law agreeing to one or more of the provisions of the first-mentioned by-law, then in such case the by-law shall be binding upon the municipality to the extent of the provisions agreed upon, 50 and the arbitrators shall only decide and determine upon the provisions not agreed upon, and the award so made shall be final.

If arbitrators decide against erection, no (b) If the arbitrators decide against the erection of the bridge, no further proceedings shall be taken by 55

any of the councils having jurisdiction in the premises for the period of two years, or such further time as the arbitrators may determine upon, but not exceeding four years in all, but at the expiration of
5 such time, any one of the councils interested may again take proceedings for the erection of such bridge, as if no award had been made.

proceedings to be taken for two or four years.

3. Section 536 of the said Act is hereby repealed, and the following substituted therefor :—

46 V. c. 18, s. 536, repealed.

10 536. All township boundary lines, not forming county boundary lines, and all deviated roads used in lieu of such boundary lines, and all bridges of less than 100 feet in length over rivers or streams crossing such boundary lines, or crossing any deviated road used in lieu of such boundary line, and not
15 assumed by the county council, shall be opened, maintained and improved, including the erecting and maintaining of all such bridges, by the township council.

Boundary lines and bridges less than 100 feet not assumed by County Council, to be maintained by Township.

4. Section 537 of the said Act is hereby repealed, and the following substituted therefor :—

46 V. c. 18, s. 537, repealed.

20 537. Township boundary lines, forming also the county boundary lines, and all deviated roads used in lieu of such boundary lines, and all bridges of less than 100 feet in length, over rivers or streams crossing such boundary lines, or crossing any deviated road used in lieu of such boundary line between
25 two municipalities, and not assumed by the respective counties interested, shall be opened, maintained and improved, including the erecting and maintaining of all such bridges, by the councils of the townships bordering on the same.

Township boundary lines being also county boundary lines if not assumed by county, to be maintained by township.

30 **5.** Section 538 of the said Act is hereby repealed, and the following substituted therefor :—

46 V. c. 18, s. 538, repealed.

538. In case a road lies wholly or partly between a county, city, town, township, or incorporated village, and an adjoining county or counties, city, town, township, or incorporated vil-
35 lage, the councils of the municipalities between which the road lies, shall have joint jurisdiction over the same, although the road may so deviate as in some places to be wholly or in part within one or either of them ; and such councils shall have jurisdiction over all bridges of less than 100 feet in length over
40 all rivers or streams crossing such boundary lines, or crossing any deviated road in lieu of such boundary line between two or more municipalities.

Joint jurisdiction over roads.

6. Section 539 of the said Act, is hereby repealed, and the following substituted in lieu thereof :—

46 V. c. 18, s. 539, repealed.

45 539.—(1) No by-law of the council of any one of such municipalities, shall have any force respecting any such road or bridge mentioned in sections 536, 537 and 538 of this Act, until a by-law has been passed in similar terms as nearly as may be by the other council or councils having jurisdiction in the pre-
50 mises.

Both councils must concur in by-laws.

What the
by-law is to
set forth.

(2) The by-law shall set forth firstly, the kind of work that is to be performed upon the road; secondly, the extent of the work; thirdly, the kind of material that is to be used in the construction of the road; fourthly, the proportion of the cost that the municipality is willing to assume; and fifthly, the 5 time within which the work is to be completed; and in the case of a bridge the by-law shall set forth firstly, the necessity for the bridge; secondly, the site where the bridge is to be built; thirdly, the kind of bridge to be built; fourthly, the material to be used in the construction; fifthly, the time when 10 the bridge is to be completed.

46 V. c. 18, s.
540, repealed.

7. Section 540 of the said Act is hereby repealed, and the following snbstituted therefor :—

Proceedings
under by-law.

540.—(1) In case the other council or councils, as the case may be, for six months after receiving a copy of the first-men- 15 tioned by-law omits or refuses to pass a similar or any by-law or passes a by-law agreeing to one or more of the provisions of the first-mentioned by-law, then, in either of such cases, the mat-

Arbitration if
by-law not
agreed upon.

ters in dispute shall be referred to arbitration under the provisions of this Act, respecting arbitration, and the arbitrators 20 shall proceed, as in the next sub-section directed.

Arbitrators to
decide upon
the unaccepted
provisions of
the by-law.

(2) In case the council which receives the copy of the first-mentioned by-law omits or refuses to pass a similar or any by-law, then in such case the arbitrators shall decide and determine 25 upon all the provisions of the first-mentioned by-law; or in case the council pass a by-law agreeing to one or more of the provisions of the first-mentioned by-law, then in such case, the by-law shall be binding upon the municipality to the extent of the provisions agreed upon, and the arbitrators shall only decide 30 and determine upon the provisions of the by-law not agreed upon, and the award so made shall be final.

46 V. c. 18, ss.
556-564, re-
pealed.

8. Sections 556, 557, 558, 559, 560, 561, 562, 563 and 564 of the said Act, are hereby repealed.

1st Session, 6th Legislature, 50 Vic., 1887.

BILL.

An Act to amend the Municipal Act.

First Reading, 7th March, 1887.

BILL.

An Act consolidating and amending the Acts respecting Insurance Companies.

SUMMARY OF PROVISIONS.—

Title XV.—Premium Notes and Assessments (*Mutual and Cash-Mutual Fire Insurance Companies*), ss. 121-136.

Title XVI.—Inspection of Companies (*all Companies*), ss. 137-149.

Title XVII.—Liquidation and Winding-up of Companies (*all Companies*), ss. 150-153. (*See also as to Joint Stock Companies, s. 7.*)

Short Title.

1. This Act may be cited as *The Ontario Insurance Act, 1887*, and shall go into effect on the 31st day of December next after the passing hereof. R. S. O. 1877, c. 160, s. 1.

Interpretation. 5

[New except as to sub-section 13.]

2. In this Act, unless the context otherwise requires :—

"Province."
"Legislature." (1) " Province " and " Legislature " mean respectively the Province and the Legislature of Ontario.

"Treasurer." (2) " Treasurer," means the Treasurer of the Province ; or 10 any member of the Executive Council to whom from time to time may be transferred, either for a limited period, or otherwise, the powers and duties which are by this Act assigned to the Treasurer. R. S. O. c. 14, s. 3.

"Inspector." (3) " Inspector " means the Inspector of Insurance for the 15 Province.

"Company." (4) " Company " means and includes any corporation, or any society or association, incorporated or unincorporated, or any partnership, or any underwriter, not being within the intent of the *Ontario Friendly Societies Act, 1887*, that under- 20 takes or effects for valuable consideration, or agrees or offers so to undertake or effect, in the Province, any contract of indemnity, guarantee, suretyship, insurance, endowment, tontine, or annuity on life, or any like contract which accrues payable on or after the occurrence of some contingent event. 25

(5) The expression "offer to undertake contracts" shall include the setting up of a sign or inscription containing the name of the company or the distribution or publication of any proposal, circular, card ,advertisement, printed form, or like document in 30 the name of the company, or any written or oral solicitation in the company's behalf. [*cf.* Laws of New York (1886), chap. 488, s. 3 ; Dominion Insurance Act, 49 V. c. 45, s. 2 ; and R. S. O. 1877, c. 160, s. 19.]

"Contract." (6) " Contract " means and includes any contract or agree- 35 ment, sealed, written or oral, the subject matter of which is within the intent of the 4th sub-section.

"Written." (7) " Written," as applied to any instrument, includes written or printed, or partly written and partly printed.

"Provincial. Company." (8) " Provincial Company " means a company which has its head office in Ontario. 40

"Canadian Company." (9) " Canadian Company " means a company incorporated or legally constituted in the Dominion of Canada, but which has its head office in some Province of Canada other than Ontario,

(10) "Municipality" has the same meaning as in the Municipal Act. "Municipality."

(11) "Mutual Insurance" means insurance given in consideration of a premium note, with or without an immediate cash "Mutual Insurance."
5 payment thereon ; and "Mutual Company" means a Company "Mutual Company."
empowered solely to transact such insurance.

(12) "Cash-Mutual Company" means a company organized "Cash Mutual Company."
to transact mutual insurance, but empowered to undertake
contracts of insurance on both the cash plan and the premium
10 note or mutual plan.

(13) "Inland-Marine Insurance" means marine insurance "Inland Marine Insurance."
in respect of subjects of insurance at risk above the harbour of
Montreal. Dom. Act, 49 Vic. c. 45, s. 1 (g); cf. R. S. O c. 160, s. 6.

(14) "Member" means a policy-holder on the premium note "Member."
15 plan ; but as to those mutual, or cash-mutual companies which,
in terms of this Act have guarantee or joint stock capital,
"Member" includes, where the context so requires, any holder
of one or more shares of the capital. 46 V. c. 15, s. 15 ; 44 V.
c. 20, ss. 7, 12.

20 (15) "Registry Office" means the registry office of the Reg- "Registry Office."
istry Division within which the head office of the company is
situate ; and "Registrar" includes the Registrar and Deputy "Registrar."
Registrar of such registry office.

APPLICATION OF ACT.

25 **3.** The provisions of this Act shall not apply :—

(1) To a company licensed by the Dominion of Canada, Dominion licenses ex-
except as to sections 114 to 120 inclusive, which shall apply empted,
to all Fire Insurance companies transacting business in Ontario. except as to
R. S. O. 1877, c. 162, ss. 2, 3 ; c. 161, s. 79 ; c. 160, s. 2. sections 114-120 and

30 [(2) To any society or association within the intent of the statutory conditions.
Ontario Friendly Societies Act, 1887.]

———

(NEW.)

[TITLE I.—JOINT STOCK COMPANIES : Formation and general
provisions governing, s. 4 ; Directors, s. 5, (*see also* ss.
35 89-98) · Capital Stock, s. 6 (for share or stock capital
in Mutual or Cash-Mutual Fire Insurance companies,
see under Title VI.) ; Forfeiture of corporate powers,
s. 7 ; Liquidation, s. 7 (*see also* under TITLE XVII.)].

INCORPORATION OF JOINT STOCK COMPANIES.

40 **4.** (1)—Notwithstanding the 4th section of the Ontario Formation of Insurance.
Joint Stock Companies' Letters Patent Act, the Lieutenant-
Governor in Council may, on the written recommendation
of the Inspector, approved by the Treasurer, or some other
member of the Executive Council, grant by letters patent,

under the Great Seal, a charter to any number of persons
not less than five, who shall petition therefor, constituting
such persons and others who may become. shareholders
in the company thereby created a body corporate and politic
for any purpose or object within the intent of this Act; but 5
such incorporated company, before undertaking, effecting.
or offering to undertake or effect, or soliciting any
contract within this Act, shall file in the office of the
Inspector satisfactory evidence that this Act has been complied with in respect of stock subscribed and of calls thereon 10
paid, and further shall make the necessary deposit with,
and be licensed as hereinafter provided. [*cf.* 44 V. c. 20, s. 19,
which extends the application of J. S. Cos. Letters Patent
Act, to Mutual Companies desirous of conversion into Joint
Stock companies; also s. 38 of this Act.] 15

Acts applying to Joint Stock Fire Insurance companies.   (2) To every company so incorporated *The Ontario Joint
Stock Companies' Letters Patent Act* and *The Ontario Joint
Stock Companies' General Clauses Act*, shall apply in all unprovided cases so far as not repugnant to the express provisions of this Act. 20

(3) To every company heretofore incorporated and acting
under license of the Province the Acts cited in the
last sub-section shall also apply, except where repugnant to the express provisions of this Act, or to the special Act
of the Province incorporating the company, or to any Act of 25
the Province amending the special Act of incorporation.

Directors.   **5**. (1)—The affairs of every company incorporated under the
4th section shall be managed by a board of not less than [five]
nor more than nine directors.   (*cf.* R. S. O. 1877, c. 149, s. 8.)

(2) The first five of the persons named in the charter of 30
incorporation shall be directors of the company until replaced
by others duly named in their stead.   (*cf.* R. S. O. 1877, c. 149,
s. 9.)

(3) The after directors of the company shall be elected by
the shareholders in general meeting of the company, assembled 35
at such times, in such wise, and for such term, not exceeding
two years, as the by-laws of the company may prescribe.
R. S. O. 1877, c. 149, s. 11.

6. The capital stock of a company incorporated under the
4th section shall be as follows :— 40

1. If a Fire, or Fire and Inland Marine, or Accident, or Life
Accident, or Guarantee, or Surety company, the capital stock
shall be not less than $500,000, with liberty to increase the
same to $1,000,000 with the assent of the Lieutenant-Governor
in Council; and before applying for license the company 45
shall furnish to the Inspector satisfactory evidence that
of the said capital stock at least $300,000 has been sub-
scribed for and taken up *bona fide*, and that $30,000
of the said subscribed stock has been paid into some chartered
bank.   (*cf.* 49 Vic. c. 86.) 50

(2.) If a live stock insurance company, the capital stock shall
be at the least $300,000, with liberty to increase the same as
in the first sub-section to $500,000, of which, as in said sub-

section, $150,000 shall be shewn to have been subscribed, and
$15,000 to have been paid into some chartered bank. (*cf.*
37 V. c. 88.)

(3.) If a plate glass insurance company, or a company insuring
5 against the explosion of steam boilers, the capital stock shall
be at the least $100,000, with liberty to increase the same as
in the first sub-section to $250,000, of which as in said sub-
section $60 000 shall be shewn to have been subscribed, and
$6,000 to have been paid into some chartered bank. (*cf.* Dom.
10 Act, 38 V. c. 95.)

7. The corporate powers of any company whether incor- Corporate
porated under this Act or under any special Act shall be for- power forfeited by non-user during three years after the date of its in- non-user,
corporation; or if, after a company has undertaken contracts or discontinu-
15 within the intent of this Act, such company discontinues business;
business for one year; or if its license remains suspended for or suspension
one year; or if its license is cancelled otherwise than by mere of license;
effluxion of time and is not renewed within the period limited
in the 46th section; and thereupon the company's corporate
20 powers shall *ipso facto* cease and determine, except for the
sole purpose of winding up its affairs; and the High Court, except for
upon the petition of the Attorney-General, or of any person winding-up;
interested, may by decree limit the time within which the which may be
company shall settle and close its accounts, and may for this limited by
25 specific purpose, or for the purpose of liquidation generally,
appoint a receiver. R.S.O. 1887, c. 150, s, 63, and Public Receiver.
Statutes of Mass., 119, ss. 24, 37, 50.

TITLE II.—FORMATION AND INCORPORATION OF MUTUAL AND CASH-MUTUAL FIRE INSURANCE COMPANIES.

30 **8.** Ten freeholders in any municipality or association of Meetings to
municipalities may call a meeting of the freeholders thereof to establish Com-
consult whether it be expedient to establish therein a Fire panies, how
Insurance company upon the mutual or cash-mutual principle. called.
R. S, O. 1877, c. 161, s. 1.

35 **9.** The meeting shall be called by advertisement, mentioning Advertise-
the time and place and object of the meeting; and the adver- ment calling
tisement shall be published [once in the *Ontario Gazette* and] such meeting.
for three weeks in one or more of the newspapers published in
the County. *cf.* R. S. O. 1877, c. 161, s. 2.

40 **10.** If thirty freeholders of the municipality are present at Subscription
the meeting, and a majority of them determine that it is ex- books.
pedient to establish a Mutual [or Cash-Mutual Fire Insurance]
company, they may elect three persons from among them to
open and keep a subscription book, in which owners of
45 property, moveable or immovable, within the Province of
Ontario, may sign their names, and enter the sums for which
they shall respectively bind themselves to effect insurances
with the company. R. S. O. 1877, c. 161, s. 3.

11. Where fifty or more persons, being owners of mov- When meeting
50 able or immovable property in the Province of Ontario, have may be called.
signed their names in the subscription book, and bound themselves to effect insurances in the company, which in the aggre-

gate shall amount to \$100,000 at least, a meeting shall be called, as hereinafter provided. R. S. O. 1877, c. 161, ss. 4, 33.

How meeting to be called.

12.—(1) As soon as convenient after the subscription book has been completed in manner aforesaid, any ten of the subscribers thereto may call the first meeting of the Company, at 5 such time and place within the municipality as they may determine; such meeting shall be called by sending a printed notice by mail, addressed to every subscriber at his post office address, at least ten days before the day of the meeting, and by advertisement in one or more papers published in the county 10 in which the municipality is situated.

(2) The said notice and advertisement shall contain the object of the meeting, and the time and place at which it is to be held. R. S. O. 1877, c. 161, s. 5.

Election of directors.

13.—(1) At such meeting the name and style of the com- 15 pany, including the appellations " Fire " and " Mutual," shall be adopted, and a Secretary *ad interim* appointed, and a Board of Directors elected as hereinafter provided (*post* s. 74 *et seq.*) and the place named at which the head office of the company shall be located. R. S. O. 1877, c. 161, s. 6 ; 48 Vic. c. 36. s. 1. 20

(2) To constitute a valid meeting for the purposes of the first subsection, at least twenty-five of the aforesaid subscribers must be present.

(3) In case of a county or township the head office may be in any city, town, or village within the boundaries of the county 25 or township or adjacent thereto.

Names of directors to be filed in registry office.

14. Copies of the resolutions adopting the name or style and the place of the head office of the company, and of the subscription book, and the names of the directors elected shall thereupon be made ; and all such documents certified as 30 correct under the hands of the chairman and secretary, shall be filed in the Registry Office. R. S. O. 1877, c. 161, s. 7.

Thereon the corporation formed.

15.—(1) Upon the filing of said documents, with the certificate, the subscribers above mentioned, and all other persons thereafter effecting insurances in the company, shall become 35 members of the company and shall be a body corporate by and under the name so adopted. R.S.O. 1877, c. 161, s. 8 ; 44 V. c. 20, s. 26.

Forfeiture of corporate powers.

[(2) But the corporate powers of the company shall be forfeited by non-user, or by discontinuance of business, or by 40 suspension or cancellation of license as is provided in section 7, which section shall in all respects apply as well to Mutual and Cash-Mutual companies as to joint stock companies. *cf.* R. S. O. 1877, c. 150, s. 63 ; and Public Statutes of Mass., 119, ss. 24, 37, 50.] 45

Meeting of directors to elect president and officers.

16. As soon after the aforesaid meeting as convenient, the Secretary *ad interim* shall call a meeting of the Board of directors, for the election of a President and Vice-President from amongst themselves, for the appointment of a Secretary, Treasurer, or Manager, and the transaction of such other busi- 50 ness as may be brought before them. R. S. O. 1877, c. 161, s. 9.

Copies of resolutions, subscription

17. After the company has filed in the registry office, the documents mentioned in section 14, and before the com-

pany shall transact or be entitled to transact any insurance books, and statements of proposed business to be transmitted to Insurance Inspector.
business, the chairman and secretary shall transmit or deliver
like copies duly certified by them to be true copies [and endorsed
by the Registrar as having been duly filed] to the
5 Inspector at his office in Toronto, accompanied by a statement
signed by the chairman and secretary, stating the kind and
character of the risks intended to be taken by the company,
that is to say, whether the business to be transacted is the
insurance of farm and isolated buildings and property, or of
10 mercantile manufacturing and other hazardous and extra
hazardous properties, or of both; [also whether the company
has been organized and incorporated as a Mutual or as a Cash-
Mutual company.] 44 V. c. 20, s. 1.

18. Upon receipt of such certified copies and of the afore- Inquiries to be made by Inspector after receiving statement.
15 said statement by the Inspector, he shall proceed to ascertain
whether the proceedings for the incorporation of the company
·have been taken in accordance with the law in that behalf,
and whether the subscriptions are *bona fide*, and by persons
possessing property to insure, and whether the proposed name
20 is the same as that of any existing company, or may be easily
confounded therewith, and he may require the declaration of
any person or persons upon oath to be filed with him, touching any matters concerning which he is called upon to make
inquiry. 44 V. c. 20, s. 2.

25 **19.** If, upon examination, the Inspector shall find that the On report of Inspector Treasurer may issue license.
said subscriptions have been made in good faith by persons
entitled to make the same, and that the proposed name is satisfactory, and that the company has complied with this Act in
respect of deposit, and in all other respects, the Treasurer may
30 thereupon issue a license under his hand and seal setting forth
that it has been made to appear to him that the company has
complied with the requirements of the law ; and that the company is accordingly licensed to transact the kind of business
specified in the license, for a term therein also specified, but
35 not exceeding twelve months from the date of issue; but such
license may from time to time be renewed as hereinafter provided. [*cf.* 44 V. c. 20, s. 3 ; but annual license substituted for
certificate of authority to transact business.]

TITLE III.—CHANGE OF NAME OR OF HEAD OFFICE.—(*All*
40 *Companies.*)

20. Where any company is desirous of adopting a name Change of name.
differing from that by which it was incorporated ; or where in
the opinion of the Lieutenant-Governor in Council the name
by which such company within the legislative authority of this
45 province was incorporated, may be easily confounded with
that of any other existing company, the Lieutenant-Governor
in Council, upon being satisfied that a change of name will not
work or effect any improper purpose, may by Order in Council
change the name of the company to some other name to be set
50 forth in the Order in Council; but no such change of name
shall affect the rights or obligations of the company ; and all
proceedings which might have been continued or commenced
by or against the company by its former name may be con-

tinned and commenced by or against the company by its new
name. 44 V. c. 20, s. 24; 46 V. c. 15, s. 4, *part.*

Change of name, or of head office.

21. The name of any insurance company may be changed
by authority of the Lieutenant-Governor in Council upon
application of the company; and the head office of any company 5
may be removed from one municpality to another by the like
authority. Where any company is entitled to remove its head
office from one place to another, without the consent of the
Lieutenant-Governor in Council, notice of any such change
and of any resolution or by-law authorizing the same, shall be 10
forthwith given by the secretary of the company to the Inspector of Insurance. 46 V. c. 15, s. 4; R. S. O. 1877, c. 161, s. 70.

Notice of application for change of name.

22. The Lieutenant-Governor in Council may require the
same notice to be given upon any application for such change
of name [or of head office] as is required upon an application for 15
Letters Patent by the Act entitled "*An Act respecting the
Incorporation of Joint Stock Companies by Letters Patent.*"
44 V. c. 20, s. 25.

[**23.** Notice of any change of name or of head office shall
be forthwith inserted by the company in the *Ontario Gazette.*] 20

TITLE IV.—BRANCHES AND DEPARTMENTS IN MUTUAL AND
CASH-MUTUAL FIRE INSURANCE COMPANIES.

Establishment of branches.

24. Any Mutual [or Cash-Mutual] Company may, [with the
previous assent of the Lieutenant-Governor in Council,] separate its business into branches or departments, with reference 25
to the nature or classification of the risks, or of the localities in
which insurances may be effected. R. S. O. 1877, c. 161, s. 64.

Scale of risks to be made for each branch.

25. The Directors of every such company so separating its
business shall make a scale of risks and tariff of rates for each
branch, and direct that the accounts of each shall be kept sepa- 30
rate and distinct the one from the other. R. S. O. 1877, c. 161,
s. 65.

Expenses to be divided between branch-es propor-tionately.

26. All necessary expenses incurred in the conducting and
management of such companies shall be assessed upon and
divided between the several branches in such proportion as the 35
directors determine. R. S. O. 1877, c. 161, s. 67.

TITLE V.—GUARANTEE CAPITAL IN MUTUAL OR CASH-MUTUAL
FIRE INSURANCE COMPANIES.

Power to raise a guarantee capital.

27. Any Mutual or Cash-Mutual Fire Insurance Company,
incorporated under this Act or any former Act, may raise by
subscription of its members, or some of them, or by the admis- 40

ERRATUM.

Section 21 should read as follows :—

21.—(1) The head office of any company may be removed Change of from one municipality to another by authority of the head office. Lieutenant-Governor in Council. 46 V. c. 15, s. 4 *part.*

(2) In other cases the present location of head offices of companies in existence, and the original location of head offices of companies hereafter to be formed, shall only be changed by a two-thirds vote of the members [or shareholders] of the company at a special meeting called for that purpose. R. S. O. 1877, c. 161, s. 70; 46 V. c. 15, s. 4 *part.*

(3) Where any company is entitled to remove its head office from one place to another, without the consent of the Lieutenant-Governor in Council, notice of any such change and of any resolution or by-law authorizing the same, shall be forthwith given by the secretary of the company to the Inspector of Insurance. 46 V. c. 15; s. 4.

sion of new members not being persons insured in the company, or by loan or otherwise, a guarantee capital of any sum not less than $20,000, nor exceeding $200,000, which guarantee capital shall belong to the company and be liable for all the
5 losses, debts and expenses of the company ; and subscribers of such capital shall, in respect thereof, have such rights as the directors of the company declare and fix by a by-law to be passed before the capital is subscribed, and unless the capital is paid off or discharged, the by-law shall not be repealed or
10 altered [without the prior assent of the Lieutenant-Governor in Council] nor without the consent of the majority of votes of the shareholders or subscribers of such capital who represent a majority of the shares subscribed, either personally or by proxy, at a meeting held for that purpose of the holders of such
15 capital, each shareholder or subscriber being entitled to a vote for every share of $50 held by him.   44 V. c. 20, s. 7.

28.—(1) The capital shall be subscribed by not less than Limitations as ten persons, and no one person shall subscribe, or hold, or receive to guarantee dividends, interest or commissions upon, more than twenty per capital.
20 centum of the guaranteed capital of the stock ; the original list of the subscribers to the guarantee capital shall be transferred to and be deposited with the Treasurer of this Province, and shall be held as security for the payment of all losses and other policy liabilities of such companies.

25   (2) The company may from time to time, in accordance with Calls upon the provisions of any by-law in that behalf [approved by the guarantee Lieutenant-Governor in Council,] require any portion of the capital. subscribed guarantee capital to be paid over to the company for the purpose of settling any losses of the company. 'Any
30 sums so advanced shall be repaid by the company within one year thereafter from the proceeds of assessments upon the premium notes liable to assessment for the purpose, and assessments may be made from time to time by the company for the purpose of repaying the advances.   44 V. c. 20, s. 8.

35   [**29.** In substitution for the subscription list of guarantee Substitution capital deposited as security with the Treasurer, the company of other may, with the Treasurer's consent, deposit cash or unconditional securities. securities for cash of the kind and to the amount prescribed in the 40th section of this Act ; and the Treasurer shall thereupon
40 release and discharge the said subscription list.]

TITLE VI.—SHARE OR STOCK CAPITAL IN MUTUAL OR CASH-
   MUTUAL FIRE INSURANCE COMPANIES.

30. Any Mutual [or Cash-Mutual] Fire Insurance Company, Power to raise incorporated under this or any former Act, may [with the prior share capital.
45 assent of the Lieutenant-Governor in Council] raise a share or stock capital of not less than $100,000, and may [with the like assent] increase the same from time to time to a sum not exceeding $500,000 : [Provided that the same public notice as that prescribed by the 9th section has been given by the
50 company of its intention to raise, or to increase such capital.]
44 V. c. 20, s 11.

31. Every subscriber shall, on allotment of one or more Subscribers to shares to him, become a member of the company ; with all become members of comincidental rights, privileges and liabilities. 44 V. c. 20, s. 12. pany.
66—2

Transfer of shares.

32. The shares shall be personal estate, and shall be transferable, but no transfer shall be valid unless made on the books of the company; and, until fully paid up, no share shall be transferable without the consent of the board of directors, nor shall any transfer be valid while any call previously 5 made remains unpaid; and the company shall have a lien on the shares of any shareholder for unpaid calls or other debts due by him to the company, and for any obligation held by the company against him; and after any call, debt or obligation becomes due, the company may, upon one month's notice to the 10 shareholder, his executors, or administrators, sell his shares or a sufficient portion thereof to pay the call, debt or obligation, and transfer the shares so sold to the purchaser. 44 V. c. 20, s. 13.

Forfeiture of shares.

33. The company may, also, after default made in the pay- 15 ment of any call upon any share for one month, and after notice having been first given as in the next preceding section mentioned, declare the share and all sums previously paid theron, forfeited to the company, and the company may sell or re-issue forfeited shares on such terms as they think fit for 20 the benefit of the company. 44 V. c. 20, s. 14.

When company may make insurances for premiums payable wholly in cash.

34. After the sum of $100,000 of the stock or share capital has been *bona fide* subscribed, and twenty per centum paid thereon into the funds of the company, the company may make insurances for premiums payable wholly in cash; 25 but no insurance on the wholly cash principle shall make the insured a member of the company, or make him liable to contribute or pay any sum to the company, or to its funds, or to any other member thereof, beyond the cash premium agreed upon, or give him any right to a participation in the profits 30 or surplus funds of the company, but the company shall not transact any business wholly on the cash principle without first procuring a license from the Treasurer, pursuant to this Act. 44 V. c. 20, s. 15.

Dividends.

35. The net annual profits and gains of the company 35 not including therein any premium notes or undertakings shall be applied, in the first place, to pay a dividend on the share capital, not exceeding the rate of ten per centum per annum, and the surplus, if any, shall be applied in the manner provided by the by-laws of the company. 44 V. c. 20, s. 16. 40

Qualification of directors.

36. After the share capital has been subscribed as aforesaid, at least two-thirds of the persons to be elected directors of the company in addition to the qualifications required by section 74 of this Act, shall be holders of shares of the capital stock to the amount of $3,000, on which all calls have been 45 fully paid; the other one-third of the directors to be elected shall possess at least the qualifications required by section 74. 44 V. c. 20 s. 17.

By-laws.

37. The board of directors of any company which shall raise a share or stock capital under this Act, may make such 50 by-laws, subject to the provisions of this Act and not inconsistent with or contrary to law, as may be necessary to carry out the objects and intentions of this Act, and to give effect to the provisions thereof; and may rescind, alter, vary, or add to the same from time to time. 44 V. c. 20, s. 18.

38. Any Mutual or [Cash-Mutual Fire] Insurance Company How a mutual company may become a stock company. heretofore incorporated or organized, or which may be hereafter incorporated or organized under any of the laws of this Province, having surplus assets, aside from premium notes or
5 undertakings, sufficient to reinsure all its outstanding risks, after having given notice once a week for four weeks of their intention, and of the meeting hereinafter provided for, in the *Ontario Gazette* and in a newspaper published in the the County where the company is located, may, with the
10 consent of two-thirds of the members present at any regular annual meeting, and of two-thirds of the subscribers of guarantee capital or share or stock capital, or at any special meeting duly called for the purpose, or with the consent, in writing, of two-thirds of the members of the company, and
15 the consent, also, of three-fourths of the directors, and of two-thirds of the subscribers to the guarantee capital and share or stock capital, may, as provided in 4th section of this Act, be formed into a joint stock company under *The Ontario Joint Stock Companies Letters Patent Act*, application hav-
20 ing been made in terms of that Act; and every member of such company, on the day of said annual or special meeting, or the date of the written consent, shall be entitled to priority in subscribing to the capital stock of the company, for one month after the opening of the books of subscription
25 to the capital stock, in proportion to the amount of insurance held by such members on unexpired risks in force on the day of the annual or special meeting, or the date of the written consent; and every company so changed or organized shall come under and be subject to the provisions of the said last
30 mentioned Act as provided in the 4th section of this Act.
44 V: c. 20, s. 19.

39. Any company which may be formed under the provi- New company to be answerable for all liabilities of former company. sions of the last preceding section shall be answerable for all the liabilities of the company from which it has been formed,
35 and may be sued therefor by or under its new corporate name, and the assets, real and personal, of the old company shall pass to and become vested in the new company. 44 V. c. 20, s. 20.

TITLE VI.—GOVERNMENT DEPOSITS. (ALL COMPANIES.)

[**40**.—(1) Except Mutual Fire Insurance companies licensed
40 only for the insurance of farm buildings and isolated risks, every company shall, before the original issue or renewal of the license, lodge with the Treasurer either in cash, or in any stock, debentures, or other securities in which trustees may invest trust money, the initial or renewal deposits respectively below
45 stated : Provided that this section, in so far as it amends the statutes heretofore in force shall not apply to such companies as have heretofore reported to the Department of the Treasurer ; Application of section. but shall, from the passing of this Act, apply to all other companies thereafter licensed. 49 V. c. 16, s. 24 ; 42 V. c. 21, s. 1 ;
50 R.S.O. c. 107, s. 28.

(2) The initial deposit to be made by any company before Initial deposits. the original issue of the license shall be the sum appointed for such company in the 4th sub-section of this section. R. S. O. c. 160, s. 6 (1).

Renewal deposits.

(3) Before the annual renewal of licenses the amount of deposit required of any company shall on or before the first day of July in each year be readjusted in terms of the next following two sub-sections. R. S. O. c. 160, s. 6 (1).

Deposits for contingent liability of $2,000,000 and under.

(4) If on the preceding 31st day of December in any year 5 the company's total contingent liability or amount at risk does not exceed two millions of dollars ;

Then every Joint Stock Fire, or Fire and Inland-Marine Insurance company, and every Life, or Life and Accident company, and every Guarantee and Surety company shall keep 10 on deposit with the Provincial Treasurer, if a Provincial or Canadian company, $25,000 [and if a foreign company $50,000]. R. S. O. c. 169, s. 6 (1);

Every Accident company, if Provincial or Canadian, shall keep on deposit with the Provincial Treasurer, $20,000 [and if a 15 Joint Stock foreign company, $40,000]. R. S. O. 1877, c. 160, s. 6 (1);

Every Provincial Mutual Fire, or Fire and Inland-Marine company, insuring mercantile and manufacturing risks shall keep on deposit with the Provincial Treasurer, $5,000 ; and 20 every Provincial Cash-Mutual Fire, or Fire and Inland-Marine company insuring mercantile and manufacturing risks, $10,000.

Every Live Stock Insurance company shall keep on deposit as aforesaid, if Provincial or Canadian, $10,000 ; and if foreign Joint Stock, $25,000 ; 25

Every Plate Glass Insurance company, and every company insuring against the explosion of steam boilers shall keep on deposit, as aforesaid, if Provincial or Canadian, $5,000 ; and if foreign Joint Stock, $10,000.

Additional deposit for each additional million or fraction thereof.

(5) If on the preceding 31st day of December in any year, 30 the company's total contingent liability, or the amount at risk, exceeds two millions of dollars, then for each additional million, or fraction thereof, the companies enumerated in the sub-section next preceding shall respectively keep on deposit, with the Provincial Treasurer, by way of additional security, a sum 35 equal to one-fifth of the initial deposit ; and the additional deposit shall be either in cash or securities as aforesaid. R.S.O. c. 160, s. 6 (1).]

Deposits, in what securities.

41.—(1) Securities of the Dominion of Canada, or securities issued by any of the Provinces of Canada, shall be accepted at their market value at the time when they are deposited. 40

(2) The other securities above specified shall be accepted at such valuation and on such conditions as the Treasurer may direct.

If market value declines company to make further deposit.

(3) If the market value of any of the securities which have been deposited by any company declines below the value at 45 which they were deposited, the Treasurer may, from time to time, call upon the company to make a further deposit, so that the market value of all the securities deposited by any com-

pany shall be equal to the amount which they are required to deposit by this Act. R. S. O. 1877, c. 160, s. 7.

(4) Where any security, obligation or covenant, or any interest in any real or personal estate, effects, or property is given, or transferred to, made with, or vested in the Treasurer of Ontario, by virtue of his office of Treasurer, such security, obligation or covenant, and any right of action in respect thereto, and all the estate, right or interest of the said Treasurer in respect of such real or personal estate, effects or property upon 10 the death, resignation or removal from office of the Treasurer, from time to time, and as often as the case happens and the appointment of a successor takes place, shall, subject to the same trusts as the same were respectively subject to, vest in the succeeding Treasurer by virtue of this Act, and shall 15 and may be proceeded on by any action or in any other manner, or may be assigned, transferred or discharged, in the name of such succeeding Treasurer as the same might have been proceeded on, assigned, transferred or discharged by the Treasurer to, with or in whom they were first given, transferred, 20 made, or vested if he had continued to hold office. 47 V. c. 6. s. 1.

Securities, etc., vested in Treasurer of Ontario by virtue of his office, to vest in his successor.

(5) Every such security, obligation, covenant or interest in real or personal estate, effects and property may in like manner as in the last section mentioned be proceeded on, assigned, 25 transferred or discharged by and in the name of any member of the Executive Council of Ontario, acting under the authority of section 3 of the *Revised Statute respecting the Executive Council.* 47 V. c. 6, s. 2.

Assignment, etc., of securities.

(6) The fourth sub-section shall apply to every security, obligation or covenant, and every interest in real or personal estate, 30 effects or property given or transferred to, made with, or vested in any former Treasurer of Ontario, by virtue or on account of his office, and shall transfer all the interest, rights and estate of the former Treasurer to the present Treasurer of Ontario, to be vested in him by virtue of his office and subject 35 to the provisions of this Act. 47 V. c. 6, s. 3.

Application of sub-sect. 4.

(7) Where any company desires to substitute other securities within the 40th section for securities deposited with the Treasurer, the Treasurer, if he thinks fit, may permit the substitution to be made. 47 V. c. 6, s. 4.

Treasurer may allow companies to change securities deposited with him.

42. A company may deposit in the hands of the Treasurer any sums of money or securities of the kind prescribed by the 40th section, beyond the sum by the said section required; and such further sums of money or securities shall be dealt 45 with as if the same had been part of the original deposit; and no part of the additional deposit shall be withdrawn except with the sanction of the Lieutenant-Governor in Council. R. S. O. 1877, c. 160, s. 11.

Company may deposit beyond the amount absolutely required.

As to withdrawal of surplus.

43. A company having made a deposit under this Act shall 50 be entitled to withdraw the deposit, with the sanction of the Lieutenant-Governor in Council, whenever it is made to appear to the satisfaction of the Lieutenant-Governor in Council that the company is carrying on its business of insurance under license from the Dominion of Canada. R. S. O. 1877, c. 160, 55 s. 12.

Withdrawal of deposit where company licensed by Dominion.

Any deficiency of security to be made good or license forfeited.

44. If from the annual statements, or after examination of the affairs and condition of any company, it appears that the re-insurance value of all its risks outstanding in Ontario, together with any other liabilities in Ontario, exceeds its assets in Ontario, including the deposit in the hands of the Treasurer, 5 then the company shall be called upon by the Treasurer to make good the deficiency at once, and on failure so to do, its license shall be cancelled, [and its corporate powers shall thereupon cease and determine, except for the purpose of winding up its affairs as provided in section 7.] R. S. O. 1877, c. 160, 10 ss. 13, 3.

As to interest on securities.

45. Except in cases with respect to which it may be otherwise provided by the Lieutenant-Governor in Council, so long as any company's deposit is unimpaired and no notice of any final judgment or order to the contrary is served upon the 20 Provincial Treasurer, the interest upon the securities forming the deposit shall be handed over to the company. R. S. O. 1877, c. 160, s. 14.

Licenses forfeited by failure to deposit, non-payment of claims and consequent deficiency of security.

46. Where a company fails to make the deposits under this Act at the time required, or where written notice has been 25 served on the Provincial Treasurer of an undisputed claim arising from loss insured against in Ontario remaining unpaid for the space of sixty days after being due, or of a disputed claim after final judgment in a regular course of law and tender of a legal valid discharge being unpaid, so that the amount 25 of securities representing the deposit of the company is liable to be reduced by sale of any portion thereof, the license of the company shall *ipso. facto* be null and void, and shall be deemed to be cancelled as in the 44th section; but the license may in the two last mentioned cases be 30

Renewal on certain conditions.

renewed, and the company may again transact business, if within sixty days after notice to the Provincial Treasurer of the company's failure to pay any undisputed claim, or the amount of any final judgment as provided in this section, such undisputed claims or final judgments upon or 35 against the company in Ontario are paid and satisfied, and the company's deposit is no longer liable to be reduced below the amount required by this Act. R. S. O. 1877, c. 160, s. 20.

Government deposit security for certain contracts only.

47. The securities deposited with the Treasurer shall be subject to administration only in respect of any contract which 40 falls within the 2nd section, and which further has for its subject some property in the province, or property in transit to or from the province, or the life, safety, health, fidelity, or insurable interest of some resident of the province, or where the contract itself makes the payment thereunder primarily pay- 45 able to some resident of the province. 46 V. c. 15, s. 14.

When a company shall be liable to have deposits administered.

48.—(1) Any company shall be liable to have its deposits in the hands of the Treasurer administered in manner hereinafter mentioned upon the failure of the company to pay any undisputed claim arising under any contract within the 47th section 50 for the space of sixty days after being due, or, if disputed, after final judgment and tender of a legal valid discharge, and (in either case) after notice thereof to the Provincial Treasurer, [and to the Inspector of Insurance.] In case of such administration, all deposits of the company, held by the Treasurer, shall be Provisions for application of deposits in such case. applied *pro rata* towards the payment of all claims duly au-thenticated against the company, as well as in respect of unearned premiums, [such being claims and premiums under the 5 contracts aforesaid,] and the distribution of the proceeds of such deposits may be made by order of the High Court.

(2) In any case where a claim [accruing on the occurrence of Proviso, if delay was given for the payment of any loss. any event] is by the terms of the contract payable on proof of such occurrence, without any stipulated delay, the notice 10 required under this section shall not be given until after the lapse of sixty days from the time when the claim becomes due. R. S. O. 1877, c. 160, s. 21.

49. Before an application is made to a court for the sur- Surrender of deposit. render of a company's deposit with the Government at least ten 15 days' notice of such intended application shall be served on the Treasurer or his deputy, and also upon the Inspector of Insur-ance; and the notice shall designate the Court to which appli-cation is proposed to be made, and shall state the day named for the hearing of the same. 46 V. c. 15, s. 12.

20 **50.**—(1) Upon granting an order for administration as afore- Appointment of receiver; his duty. said, the Court shall appoint a receiver, who may be an officer of the Court, who shall forthwith call upon the company to furnish a statement of all its outstanding [contracts, being within the 2nd and 47th sections,] and upon all [claimants under such 25 contracts] to file their claims; and upon the filing of the claims Proceedings in case of admin-istration. before the receiver, the parties interested shall have the right of contestation thereof, and the right of appeal from the deci-sion of the receiver to the court as aforesaid, according to the practice of the Court; and in case of any such administration, What may be claimed by parties insured in Ontario. 30 the claimants aforesaid shall be entitled to claim for a part of the premiums paid proportionate to the unexpired period of their [contracts] respectively, and such [unearned] premiums shall rank with judgments obtained and claims accrued, in the dis-tribution of the assets; and upon the completion of the schedule 35 to be prepared by the receiver of all judgments against the Sale of securi-ties deposited. company upon the said outstanding [contracts,] and of all claims for unearned premiums or for surrender of policies, the Court shall cause the securities held by the Treasurer for the company, or any part of them, to be sold in such manner and after such 40 notice and formalities as the Court appoints; and the proceeds thereof, after paying expenses incurred, shall be distributed *pro rata* amongst the claimants according to the schedule, and the balance, if any, shall be surrendered to the company. But, if any claim arises within the 47th section after the state- If further loss occurs and deposits do not cover claims. 45 ment of the said outstanding contracts has been obtained from the company, as hereinbefore provided, and before the final order of the Court for the distribution of the proceeds of the securities, or if the proceeds of the securities are not sufficient to cover in full all claims recorded in the schedule, such addi-50 tional claimants shall not be barred from any recourse they may have against the company in respect of such defi-ciency.

(2) The Court, by the order appointing a receiver, or by any Court may confer upon receiver the power of a Master. subsequent order, may authorize the receiver to exercise in 55 respect of the accounts of the company all or any of the pow-ers which the Master in Ordinary would have if he were tak-

ing an account of the claims against the said deposit, and every receiver so authorized shall possess the said powers as well as the powers usually enjoyed by a receiver appointed under an order of the said Court. R. S. O. 1877, c. 160, s. 22.

Duty of Company ceasing busil'es'. **51.** Where a company has ceased to transact business in Ontario, and has given written notice to that effect to the Treasurer, [and to the Inspector,] it shall re-insure [all such outstanding contracts as are within the 47th section] in some company or companies licensed to do business in Ontario, or obtain a discharge of such contracts, and its securities shall not be delivered to the company until the same is done, to the satisfaction of the Treasurer. R. S. O. 1877, c. 160, s. 23.

Conditions on which deposits may be released. **52.** Upon making application for its securities, the company shall file with the [Inspector] a list of [all contracts within the 47th section] which have not been so re-insured or have not been [discharged]; and it shall at the same time publish in the *Ontario Gazette* a notice that it has applied to Government for the release of its securities on a certain day, not less than three months after the date of the notice, and calling upon [all claimants, contingent or actual,] opposing the release to file their opposition with the [Inspector] on or before the day so named; and after that day, if the Treasurer is satisfied that the company has ample assets to meet its liabilities [under the 47th section,] all the securities may be released to the Company by an order of the Lieutenant-Governor in Council, or a sufficient amount of them may be retained to cover the [claims filed]; and the remainder may be released, and thereafter from time to time as such opposing [claims] lapse, or proof is adduced that they have been satisfied, further releases may be made on the authority aforesaid. R. S. O. 1877, c. 160, s. 24.

5

10

15

20

25

30

TITLE VIII.—LICENSE—(*All Companies.*)

Certain documents to be filed before license is granted; what they must show. **53.** (1) Before the issue of a license to a company [not incorporated by Provincial authority,] the company shall file in the office of the [Inspector,] a certified copy of the Act of incorporation, or other instrument of association of the company, and also a power of attorney from the company to its [chief] officer or agent in the Province, under the seal of the company, and signed by the president and secretary or other proper officer thereof, containing the matters hereinafter mentioned, verified by their oath, and further corroborated on oath by the said chief officer or agent in the Province, or by some person cognizant of the facts necessary to its verification, and also a statement of the condition and affairs of the company on the 31st day of December then next preceding. or up to the usual balancing day of the company (but such day shall not be more than twelve months before the filing of the statement), in such form as may be required by the Treasurer of Ontario.

35

40

45

Contents of power of attorney. (2) The power of attorney shall declare at what place in the Province the chief agency of the company is, or is to be established, and shall expressly authorize the attorney to receive process in all actions and proceedings against the company in the Province for any liabilities incurred by the company

50

therein, and shall declare that service of process for or in respect of such liabilities at chief agency, or personally on the attorney, at the place where such chief agency is established, shall be legal and binding on the company to all intents and purposes.

5   (3) Whenever a company licensed under this Act changes its chief agent or chief agency in Ontario, the company shall file a power of attorney as hereinbefore mentioned, specifying the change, and containing a similar declaration as to service of process as hereinbefore mentioned. *If changes are made in chief agency, document to be filed.*

10   (4) Duplicates of all such documents duly verified as aforesaid shall be filed at Toronto, in the office of the Clerk of the Process. R. S. O. 1877, c. 160, s. 15. *Such documents to be filed in Court.*

  (5) There shall be kept in the office of the [Inspector] a record of the several documents filed by every 15 company under this section, and under the heading of the company shall be entered the securities deposited on its account with the Provincial Treasurer, naming in detail the several securities, their par value, and value at which they are received as deposit; and before the 20 issue of a new license, or the renewal of a license to a company, the requirements of the law shall be complied with by the company, and the statement of its affairs must show that it is in a condition to meet its liabilities ; and a record of the licenses as they are issued or renewed shall also be kept 25 in the office of the [Inspector]. R. S. O. 1877, c. 160, s. 29. *Certain records to be kept in the Treasury Department.* *Terms whereon license may be renewed.*

  54. (1) After the certified copies referred to in the last preceding section and the power of attorney are filed as aforesaid, any process in any action or proceeding against the company, for liabilities incurred in the Province, may be served on 30 the company at its chief agency, and all proceedings may be had thereupon to judgment and execution in the same manner and with the same force and effect as in the proceedings in civil action in the Province. *Process and actions.*

  (2) Nothing herein contained shall render invalid service in 35 any other mode in which the company may be lawfully served. R. S. O. 1877, c. 160, s. 16. *Service otherwise than as above.*

  55. Except companies licensed by the Treasurer, and, companies specified in the 3rd section, it shall not be lawful for a company to undertake or effect or solicit, 40 or to agree or offer to undertake or effect, any contract within the intent of the 2nd section, whether the contract be original or renewed ; or to accept, or agree or negotiate for any premium or other consideration for the contract; or to prosecute or maintain any action or proceeding 45 in respect of the contract, except such actions or proceedings as arise in winding up the affairs of the company under the 7th section. R. S. O. 1877, c. 160, s. 3. *Companies required to be licensed.*

  56. Any director, officer, agent, employee, or other person who, in contravention of the 55th section undertakes or effects, or 50 agrees or offers to undertake or effect, or solicits, any contract or collects any premium in behalf of any company, without the company being licensed under this Act, or if such license has been withdrawn, without the renewal thereof, or *Penalty for transacting business in contravention of this Act.*

    3—In.

without filing the copy of the Act of incorporation, or other instrument of association of the company, and the power of attorney or any renewal thereof in the event of any change as hereinbefore provided, shall be liable to a penalty of $200 for **How enforced** every such contravention of this Act, which penalty may be 5 **and applied.** sued for and recovered on information filed in the name of the Attorney-General of Ontario ; and one-half of the penalty, when recovered, shall be paid for the use of the Province, and the other half of the penalty to the informer ; and in case of non-payment of the penalty and costs within one month after judg- 10 ment, the person so offending shall be liable to imprisonment in any gaol or prison for a period not exceeding three months, in the discretion of the Court wherein he is convicted. R.S.O. 1877, c. 160, s. 19; 44 V. c. 20, s. 23.

Form of license. **57.** The license shall be in such form as may be from time 15 to time determined by the Treasurer, and shall specify the business to be carried on by the company ; and shall expire on the thirtieth day of June in each year, but shall be renewable from year to year. R. S. O. 1877, c. 160, s. 4.

When license shall issue. **58.** As soon as the company applying for a license has 20 deposited with the Treasurer the securities hereinbefore mentioned, and has otherwise conformed to the requirements of this Act, the Treasurer [may] issue the license. R. S. O. 1877, c. 160 s. 5.

Companies to give notice of license. **59.** Every company obtaining a license shall forth- 25 with give due notice thereof in the *Ontario Gazette*, and in at least one newspaper in the county, city, or place where the head office or chief agency is established, and shall continue the publication thereof once each week for the space **and of ceasing business.** of four weeks : and the like notice shall be given for the same 30 period when the company ceases, or notifies that it intends to cease, to carry on business in Ontario. R. S. O. 1877, c. 160, s. 17.

60.—(1) Where a company desires to extend its business to some other branch within the intent of this Act, and has 35 complied with the law in respect of additional deposit and otherwise, the Treasurer may on the report of the Inspector issue to the company a supplementary license authorizing it to undertake such other branch of business.

(2) When a supplementary license is granted. it shall be 40 recorded in the books of the Inspector and filed in the same registry office as the original or prior license.

(3) The provisions herein enacted as to the continuance, renewal, suspension, and cancellation of licenses, shall equally apply to supplementary licenses. 44. V. c. 20, s. 6; 47 V. c. 45 28, s. 1.

Company ceasing business in certain cases to pay losses. **61.** After a company has ceased to transact business in Ontario after the notice hereby required, and its license has in consequence been withdrawn, the company shall nevertheless pay the losses arising from policies not re-insured or surren- 50 dered, as if the license had not been withdrawn. R. S. O. 1877, c. 160, s. 25.

62. The Provincial Treasurer shall cause to be published
half-yearly in the *Ontario Gazette*, a list of companies licensed
under this Act, with the amount of the deposit made by each
company ; and upon a new company being licensed, or upon
5 the license of a company being withdrawn in the interval
between two such half-yearly statements, he shall publish a
a notice thereof in the *Ontario Gazette* for the space of two
weeks. R. S. O. 1877, c. 160, s. 18.

Statement to be published by Provincial Treasurer.

10 ——>—

TITLE IX.—FEES.—(*All Companies.*)

63.—Each company respectively shall pay to the treasurer the following
fees :—

(1) For recording and filing in the office of the inspector the
documents required by sections 4, 17, 53. [New as to
ss. 4, 17 .... $ 10 00
(2) For change of attorney under section 53 .... 5 00
Application for change of name or of head office [new].... 10 00

(3) For initial license to do business :—

Joint stock company 100 00
Cash-Mutual company 50 00
Mutual 25 00

(4) For each annual renewal of license :—

Joint stock company 50 00
Cash-Mutual company 25 00
Mutual (new) 5 00

(5) For each Supplementary License :—

Initial 20 00
Renewal 10 00

(6) For filing annual statements :—

Joint stock company 5 00
Cash-Mutual company 5 00

R. S. O. 1877, c. 160, s. 35 ; *cf.* 44 V. c. 20 s. 5 ; 47 V. c. 28, s. 2.

———

TITLE X.—INTERNAL MANAGEMENT OF MUTUAL AND CASH-MUTUAL FIRE INSURANCE COMPANIES.

15 **64**. Sections 65 to 87 inclusive, shall apply only to Mutual
and Cash-Mutual Fire Insurance companies.

Restricted application.

1.—Admission and withdrawal of members.

65. The company may admit, as a member thereof, the
owner of any property, movable or immovable, and may insure
20 the same, whether the owner thereof is or is not a freeholder ;
and every person admitted a member of the company by the
insurance shall be entitled to the like rights, and be subjected
to the like liabilities as other members of the company. R.
S. O. 1877, c. 161, s. 30.

Power to admit members and insure.

25 **66**. Members of any such company insuring in one Mutual
branch shall not be liable for claims on any other Mutual
branch ; but this limitation of liability shall not apply as
between the Cash branch of a Cash-Mutual company and any
other branch thereof. R. S. O. 1877, c. 161, ss. 66, 29.

Members to be liable to one branch only.

Liability of members.

67.—No member of any Mutual Insurance company to which this Act may apply shall be liable in respect of any loss or other claim or demand against the company, otherwise than upon and to the extent of the amount unpaid upon his premium note or undertaking. R. S. O. 1877, c. 161, s. 68.   5

Members withdrawing.

68. Any member of the company may, with the consent of the directors, withdraw therefrom upon such terms as the directors may [lawfully] require. R. S. O. 1877, c.161, s. 31.

2.—General Meetings.

Annual meeting for election of Directors.

69. A meeting of the members for the election of directors 10 shall be held in every year, within two months after the thirty-first day of December in each year, at the time and place as may be prescribed by the by-laws of the company. R. S. O. 1877, c. 161, s. 10.

Annual report and statement.

70. At annual meetings, in addition to the election of direce- 15 tors, a report of the transactions of the company for the year ending on the previous thirty-first day of December, shall be presented and read, together with a full and unreserved statement of its affairs, exhibiting receipts and expenditures, assets and liabilities. R. S. O. 1877, c. 161, s. 11.   20

Notice of annual or special meetings.

71. Notice of any annual or special meeting of the members of the company shall be published in one or more newspapers for at least two weeks previous to the day of the meeting ; and the board of directors may convene at any time a general meeting of the company upon any urgent occasion, giving 25 notice thereof as herein provided. R. S. O. 1877, c. 161, s. 12.

Members to have votes proportionate to the amount of their insurance.

72. Each member of the company shall be entitled, at all meetings of the company, to the number of votes proportioned to the amount by him insured, according to the following rates, that is to say : For any sum under $1,500, one vote ; from 30 $1,500 to $3,000, two votes ; from $3,000 to $6,000, three votes ; and one vote for every additional $3,000 ; but no member shall be entitled to vote while in arrear for any assessment or premium due by him to the company. R. S. O. 1877, c. 161, s. 13.   35

Right of applicants to vote.

73. No applicant for insurance shall be competent to vote or otherwise take part in the company's proceedings until his application has been accepted by the board of directors. 48 V. c. 36, s.6.

3.—Directors.—Qualification, Election, etc.   40

Qualification of Directors.

74. The Directors shall be members of the company, and insured therein, for the time they hold office, to the amount of $800 at least. R. S. O. 1877, c. 161, s. 14.

Number of directors to be determined by resolution.

75.—(1) The Board of Directors shall consist of six, nine, twelve or fifteen directors, as shall be determined by resolu- 45 tion passed at the meeting held under the 13th section or at an annual meeting of the company, or at a special general meeting called for the purpose of such determination and election.

(2) The number of directors constituting such board may from time to time be increased or decreased, if so decided at a special general meeting of the company called for the purpose, or at an annual meeting, if notice in writing of the 5 intention to move a resolution for that purpose at such annual meeting is given to the secretary of the company at least one month before the holding of the meeting: but the increased or decreased number of directors shall in any such case be six, nine, twelve or fifteen as aforesaid. 48 V. c. 36, s. 1.

10 **76.** A copy of the resolution specified in the last preceding section, together with a list of the directors elected there- under, both documents being duly certified under the hands of the chairman and secretary of the annual meeting or special general meeting aforesaid, shall be filed in the office of the 15 Inspector and also in the Registry Office. 48 V. c. 36, s. 2. *Copy of reso- lution and list of directors to be filed.*

77. Of the directors elected, as hereinbefore provided, one- third shall retire annually in rotation, and at the first meeting of the directors, or as soon thereafter as possible, it shall be determined by lot which of them shall hold office for one, 20 two or three years respectively, and the determination shall be entered of record as part of the minutes of said first meet- ing. 48 V. c. 36, s. 3. *Retirement of directors in rotation.*

78. At every annual meeting of the company thereafter, one- third of the total number of directors shall be elected for a 25 period of three years, to fill the places of the retiring members, who shall be eligible for re-election. 48 V. c. 36, s. 4. *Annual elec- tion to fill vacancies.*

79. The Manager of a Mutual Insurance Company may be a director of the company, and may be paid an annual sal- ary, but only under a by-law of the company. R. S. O. 1877, 30 c. 161, s. 15. *Manager may be a Director. His salary.*

80. No agent or paid officer, or person in the employment of the company, other than the manager, shall be eligible to be elected a director. or shall be allowed to interfere in the election of directors for the company. R. S. O. 1877, c. 161, 35 s. 16. *Certain per- sons not eligible to be elected Direc- tors.*

81. The election of directors shall be held and made by such members of the company as attend for that purpose in their own proper persons. R. S. O. 1877, c. 161, s. 17. *Election of Directors.*

82. The election of directors shall be by ballot. R. S. O. 40 1877, c. 161, s. 18. *Mode of election.*

83. If at any such election two or more members have an equal number of votes, in such manner that a less number of persons than the whole number to be elected appear to have been chosen directors by a majority of votes, then the said 45 members of the company shall proceed to elect by ballot. until it is determined which of the persons so having an equal num- ber of votes shall be the director or directors, so as to complete the whole number of directors to be elected; and the directors shall at their first meeting after any such election, proceed to 50 elect by ballot among themselves, a president and vice-presi- *Case of a tie at an election.*

Election of a President and Vice- President.

dent, and at such election the secretary shall preside. R. S. O. 1877, c. 161, s. 19..

Vacancies in office of Director, how filled up.

84. If a vacancy happens among the directors during the term for which they have been elected, by death, resignation, ceasing to have the necessary qualification under section 74 of 5 this Act, insolvency, or by being absent, without previous leave of the board, from the board for three regular meetings in succession, which shall *ipso facto* create such vacancy, the vacancy shall be filled up, until the next annual meeting, by any person duly qualified, to be nominated by a majority of the remaining 10 directors, and as soon as may be after the vacancy occurs ; and at the next annual meeting the vacancy shall be filled for the portion of the term still unexpired R. S. O. 1877, c. 161, s. 20 ; 48 V. c. 36, s. 5.

Provision in case of failure to elect Directors on proper day.

85. In case an election of directors is not made on the day 15 on which it ought to have been made, the company shall not for that cause be dissolved, but the election may be held on a subsequent day, at a meeting to be called by the directors, or as otherwise provided by the by-laws of the company, and in such case the directors shall continue to hold office till their 20 successors are elected. R. S. O. 1877, c. 161, s. 21.

Quorum of Directors.

86. Three directors shall constitute a quorum for the transaction of business ; [and in any case of an equality of votes the chairman shall have the casting vote in addition to his own.] R. S. O. 1877, c. 161, s. 22 ; c. 204, s. 98.   **25**

Directors disagreeing may record their dissent.

87. A director disagreeing with the majority of the board at a meeting, may have his dissent recorded, with his reasons therefor. R. S. O. 1877, c. 161, s. 23.

———

TITLE XI.—POWERS OF DIRECTORS—GENERAL PROVISIONS— 30
(*All Companies.*)

88. Sections 89 to 98 inclusive shall apply to all companies transacting business under license of the Provincial Treasurer. [New as to Joint Stock Companies, except ss. 90 (3), 96, 98.]   **35**

Appointment of Manager and other officers.

89. The board of directors may from time to time appoint a manager, secretary, treasurer, and such other officers, agents, or assistants, as to them seem necessary ; prescribe their duties, fix their compensations or allowances ; take such security from

Board may adopt a tariff of rates.

them as is required by this Act for the faithful performance of 40 their respective duties, and remove them and appoint others instead ; the board may also adopt a table of rates, [premiums, or premium notes, as the case may be,] and vary such table from time to time, and determine the amount of the contract

Meetings of the board.

to be undertaken ; they may hold their meetings monthly, or 45 oftener if necessary, for transacting the business of the company ; and they shall keep a record of their proceedings. R. S. O. 1877, c. 161, s. 24.

90.—(1) The board may from time to time make and pre- The Board
scribe such by-laws as to them appear needful and proper, may pass
respecting the funds and property of the company, the duty by-laws.
of the officers, agents and assistants thereof, the effectual car-
5 rying out of the objects contemplated by this Act, the holding
of the annual meeting, and all such other matters as appertain
to the business of the company, and are not contrary to law,
and may from time to time alter and amend the said by-laws,
except in cases with regard to which it is provided that any
10 such by-laws shall not be repealed, or where the repeal would When by-laws
affect the rights of others than the members of the company, are not repeal-
in any of which cases such by-law shall not be repealed. able.

(2) Every by-law of the board shall be duly entered in the When resolu-
minutes, and when confirmed at any subsequent meeting of tion to have
the effect of
15 the members, shall be held to be and have the same force and a by-law.
effect as a by-law of the company. R. S. O. 1877, c. 161, s. 25.

(3) There shall be filed with the Inspector copies of all by-
laws that may from time to time be passed by the company or
the board. 46 V. c. 15, s. 2, *part.*

20 **91.** The board shall superintend and have the management The Board to
of the funds and property of the company, and of all matters manage the
property, etc.,
relating thereto, and not otherwise provided for. R. S. O. of the Com-
1877, c. 161, s. 26. pany.

92. The board may make arrangements with any other Re-insurance
25 company [licensed to transact business in the Province] for the of risks.
re-insurance, on such conditions with respect to the payment
of premiums thereon as may be agreed between them. R. S. O.
1877, c. 161, s. 27.

93. The board may, [in the name of the company], invest Investment of
30 the capital and funds of the company in any stock, debentures, capital and
funds of the
or other securities in which trustees may invest trust money, Company.
—49 V. c 16, s. 24; 42 V. c. 21, s. 1; R. S. O. c. 107, s. 28; and
may, [if a Mutual or Cash-Mutual Company,] in the name
of the company, recover from any member of such company,
35 in any Court of competent jurisdiction, any premium or assess- Recovery of
ment upon his premium note payable by him. R. S. O. 1877, assessments.
c. 161, s. 28.

94.—(1) The board may issue debentures or promissory
notes in favour of any person, firm, building society, banking Directors may
40 or other company, for the loan of money, and may borrow issue debentures and
money therefrom on such debentures or promissory notes for promissory no-
any term not exceeding twelve months, and on such conditions for loans; tes
as they think proper, and may renew the same from time to
time for any such term, the whole of the assets, including
45 premium notes of the company, being held liable to pay the assets of the
Company to
same at maturity, but no such debenture or promissory note be liable for
shall be for a less sum than $100. the same.

(2) All the debentures and promissory notes at any one time
outstanding shall not exceed one-fourth of the amount remain- Amount of
debentures,
50 ing unpaid upon the same premium notes. R. S. O. 1877, etc., limited.
c. 161, s. 29.

Land that may be held by the Company. **95.** Every company may hold such lands only as are requisite for the accommodation of the company, in relation to the transaction of their business, or such lands as have been *bona fide* mortgaged to them by way of security, or conveyed to them in satisfaction of debts contracted in the course of their dealings previously to such conveyance, or purchased at sales upon judgments obtained for such debts, and may from time to time sell and convey or lease any such lands. R. S. O. 1877, c. 161, s. 72.

Loans to or from Directors, etc., forbidden. **96.** No company shall contract with any director or officer thereof for any loan or credit, or borrowing of money, and every such attempted loan or borrowing is hereby prohibited; and any contract in violation of this section shall be void. R. S. O. 1877, c. 161, s. 74; 46 V. c. 15, s. 3.

Treasurer of Company to give security. **97.** The treasurer of the Company or other officer having charge of the money of the company shall give security to the satisfaction of the board of directors in a sum of not less than $2,000 for the faithful discharge of his duties. R. S. O. 1877, c. 161, s. 69.

Remuneration of directors. **98.** At any annual meeting of the members or stockholders of a company, or at any special general meeting thereof, if such purpose was clearly expressed in the notice of the special general meeting, it shall be lawful to enact by-laws or pass resolutions for the remuneration of the directors of the company, and copies of such by-laws or resolutions shall, within one week after their passing, be filed with the Inspector of Insurance, with whom also shall be filed copies of all other by-laws that may from time to time be enacted by the company or by the board of directors. 46 V. c. 15, s. 2.

TITLE. XII.—BOOKS, ACCOUNTS AND RETURNS,—(*All Companies.*)

99. Sections 100 to 105 shall apply to all companies within the intent of this Act.

Company to keep such books as may be directed by Treasurer. **100.** Every company shall keep such a classification of its contracts, and such registers and books of account as may from time to time be directed or authorized by the Provincial Treasurer; and if it appears at any time to the Inspector that such books are not kept in such business-like way as to make at any time a proper showing of the affairs and standing of the company, he shall report the same to the Provincial Treasurer who shall thereupon nominate a competent accountant to proceed, under the directions of the Inspector, to audit such books and to give such instructions as will enable the officers of the company to keep them correctly thereafter, the expense of the accountant to be borne by the company to which he is sent, and shall not exceed $5 per day and necessary travelling expenses; the account for such audit and instructions shall be certified and approved as provided in 148th section and thereupon shall be payable by the company forthwith. 44 V. c. 20, s. 21; 43 V. c. 20, s. 1; 42 V. c. 25, s. 5 *part.*

101. Where the company has a share or stock capital, the *Transfer register.* company shall keep a stock register, in which a register of the transfers of stock shall be accurately kept, and it shall at all reasonable times be open to the examination of any share-
5 holder and the Inspector. The entries in such register shall include the following particulars : the register numbers of the shares transferred ; the amount of subscribed stock transferred ; the amount heretofore paid up on such stock ; the names and addresses of the transferor and the transferee ; the date of the
10 transfer and the date of confirmation or disallowance by the board. 46 V. c, 15, s. 13.

102. The books and records required to be kept by section *Separate record of* 100 and 101, shall include only contracts within the 47th sec- *Provincial* tion. 46 V. c. 15, s. 14. *business.*

15 **103**.—(1) It shall be the duty of the president, vice-presi- *Yearly statement to* dent, or managing director, secretary, or manager, and treasurer, *Treasurer of* when the secretary is not also treasurer of the company, to *Ontario, what it must show,* prepare annually under their oath, on the first day of January, *and how it* or within one month thereafter, a statement of the condition *must be verified.*
20 and affairs of the company on the 31st of December then next preceding, exhibiting assets, liabilities, receipts and expenditure, in such form and with such items and detail as shall be required by the Provincial Treasurer, and to cause such statement to be deposited in the office of the [Inspector], such state-
25 ment to be accompanied by a declaration to the effect shown in the form to this sub-section annexed, sworn to before some person duly authorized to administer oaths in any legal proceeding, and every such person is hereby authorized to administer any oath required under this Act. R. S. O. 1877, c. 160,
30 s. 26 ; c. 161, s. 76.

Form of Declaration to accompany the Statement.

Province of Ontario, ⎱ We,
County of ⎰

                 President, and
       Secretary and   Treasurer
of   company, severally made oath and say, and each for himself says, that we are the above described officers of the said company, [and that we have, each of us individually, the means of verifying the correctness of the statement within contained of the affairs of the said company,] and that on the   . day of   last, all the above described assets were the absolute property of the said company, free and clear from any liens or claims thereon, except as above stated, and that the foregoing statement, with the schedules and explanations hereunto annexed, and by us subscribed, are a full and correct exhibit of all the liabilities, and of the income and expenditure, and of the general condition and affairs of the said company, on the said   day of   last, and for the year ending on that day.

                 Signatures.

Sworn before me, at the   ⎫
in the county of   , this ⎬
  day of   , A.D. 18 ⎭

      R. S. O. 1877, c. 160, *Sched.* B.

(2) The Provincial Treasurer may, from time to time make *Form of statement may be* such changes in the form of the statements as seem to him best *changed by* adapted to elicit from the companies a true exhibit of their *Provincial Treasurer.*
   4—IN.

condition in respect to the several points hereinbefore enumerated. R. S. O. 1877, c. 160, s. 26.

Companies to reply to inquiries of Lt.-Governor in Council.

(3) Any company shall further, when required, make prompt and explicit answer in reply to any inquiries in relation to its transactions which may be required by the Lieutenant-Governor in Council. R. S. O. 1877, c. 161, s. 76 (2). 5

Penalty for contravention of above section.

104. Any violation of the next preceding section shall subject the company violating the same to a penalty of $200 for every violation, and of the additional sum of $100 for every month during which the company neglects to file such 10 affidavits and statements as are therein required ; if such penalties are not paid, the Lieutenant-Governor in Council may order such company's license to be suspended or cancelled, as may be deemed expedient. R. S. O. 1877, c. 160, s. 27. *See* c. 161, s. 76. 15

Report of Provincial Treasurer to be laid before the Legislature.

105. The Provincial Treasurer from the yearly statements required to be made, shall prepare an annual report, showing the results of every company's business together with an analysis of every branch of insurance, with the company's name, classified from the statements made by the respective companies; 20 and the Treasurer shall lay such annual report before the Legislative Assembly at each session thereof. R. S. O. 1877, c. 160, s. 30.

TITLE XIII.—CONTRACTS OF FIRE INSURANCE—GENERAL PROVISIONS.—(*All Companies.*) 25

[S. 106 NEW AS TO MUTUAL COMPANIES ; s.s. 108, 110, 111, 112 NEW AS TO JOINT STOCK COMPANIES.]

Term of contracts.

106. Contracts of fire insurance shall not in any case exceed the term of three years ; and the insurance of mercantile and manufacturing risks shall be for terms not exceeding one year. 30 R. S. O. 1877, c. 161, s. 75 ; 41 V. c. 8, s. 17 ; *cf.* Statutes of Canada 49 V. c. 45, s. 48 : and *see* R. S. O. c. 161, s. 32.

Renewing policies.

107. Any [contract] that may be made for one year or any shorter period, may be renewed at the discretion of the board of directors by renewal receipts instead of policy, on the 35 insured paying the required premiums, or giving his premium note or undertaking : and any cash payments for renewal must be made at the end of the year, or other period for which the the policy was granted, otherwise the policy shall be null and void. R. S. O. 1877, c. 161, s. 34. 40

Property which may be insured.

108. The company may, [within the limits prescribed by the license,] insure dwelling houses, stores, shops and other buildings, household furniture, merchandize, machinery, live stock, farm produce and other commodities, against damage or loss by fire or lightning, whether the same happens by 45 accident or any other means, except that of design on the part of the insured, or by the invasion of an enemy, or by insurrection. R. S. O. 1877, c. 161, s. 36.

Minimum rates.

109. The minimum rate to be charged or taken by way of premium note for insuring first-class isolated non-hazardous 50 property shall be not less than [one dollar] per one hundred dollars per annum; and the minimum rate of insurance upon other property shall be increased relatively with the increased risk, according to the nature of such property. R. S. O. 1877, c. 161, s. 37.

5 **110.** All contracts of fire insurance issued by the Board of Directors, sealed with the seal of the company, signed by the President or Vice-President, and countersigned by the secretary or acting secretary, shall be binding on the company. R. S. O. 1877, c. 161, s. 38.

Policies to be binding on the Company.

10 **111.** Whenever notification in writing has been received by a company from an applicant for insurance, or from a person already insured, of his intention to insure, or of his having insured an additional sum on the same property in some other company, the said additional insurance shall be deemed to 15 be assented to unless the company so notified, within two weeks after the receipt of such notice, signify to the party, in writing, their dissent; and, in case of dissent, the liability of the insured on the premium note or undertaking, if any, shall cease from the date of such dissent, on account of any loss that 20 may occur to such company thereafter, and the policy of the assured shall be void, at the option of the directors of the company. R. S. O. 1877, c. 161, s. 40.

Notification of insurance in another Company.

Dissent of the Company to the additional insurance.

112. It shall be optional with the directors to pay or allow claims which are void under the 3rd, the 4th, or the 8th Statu-25 tory Condition, or the 111th section of this Act, in case the said directors think fit to waive the objections mentioned in the said sections. R. S. O. 1877, c. 161, s. 43.

Optional with Directors to pay claims void under ss. 51-54.

113. The party insured shall if insured against fire on the Mutual plan be liable to pay his proportion of the losses and 30 expenses of the company to the time of cancelling the policy, and on payment of his proportion of all assessments then payable and to become payable in respect of losses and expenses sustained up to such period, shall be entitled to a return of his premium note or undertaking. R. S. O. 1877, 35 c. 161, s. 44.

Cancellation of policies.

TITLE XIV.—STATUTORY CONDITIONS AND PROVISIONS RELATING THERETO *(Binding all Fire Insurance Contracts whatsoever in Ontario. See Section 3).*

114. The conditions set forth in this section shall, as 40 against the insurers, be deemed to be part of every contract, whether sealed, written or oral, of fire insurance hereafter entered into or renewed or otherwise in force in Ontario with respect to any property therein [or in transit therefrom or thereto], and shall be printed on every such policy with the 45 heading *Statutory Conditions;* and no stipulation to the contrary, or providing for any variation, addition or omission, shall be binding on the insured unless evidenced in the manner prescribed by the 115th and 116th sections. R. S. O. 1877, c. 162, ss. 3, 5; 45 V. c. 20, ss. 2, 3, 4: 44 V., c. 20, s. 28.

Statutory conditions to be part of every policy unless varied.

STATUTORY CONDITIONS.

Misrepresentation or omission.

1.—(a) If any person or persons insures his or their buildings or goods, and causes the same to be described otherwise than as they really are, to the prejudice of the company, or misrepresents or omits to communicate any circumstance which 5 is material to be made known to the company, in order to enable it to judge of the risk it undertakes, such insurance shall be of no force in respect to the property in regard to which the misrepresentation or omission is made.

[(b) Non-disclosure of prior insurance or of liens or incum- 10 brances shall be held a material circumstance unless, it appears by the evidence that such non-disclosure did not arise from fraudulent intent or from wilful misrepresentation.]

Policy sent to be deemed as applied for unless variance pointed out.

2. After application for insurance, it shall be deemed that 15 any policy sent to be assured is intended to be in accordance with the terms of the application, unless the company points out, in writing, the particulars wherein the policy differs from the application.

When a change as to risk shall avoid a policy. Notice of change, etc.

3.—(a) Any change material to the risk, and within the 20 control or knowledge of the assured, shall avoid the policy as to the part affected thereby, unless the change is promptly notified in writing to the company or its local agent; and the company when so notified may return the premium for the unexpired period and cancel the policy, or may demand in 25 writing an additional premium, which the insured shall, if he desires the continuance of the policy, forthwith pay to the company ; and if he neglects to make such payment forthwith after receiving such demand, the policy shall be no longer in force. 30

[(b) Non-disclosure of subsequent or further insurance, or of liens or incumbrances, shall be held a change material to the risk, unless it appears by the evidence that such non-disclosure did not arise from fraudulent intent or from wilful misreprescutation.] 35

Change of property.

4. If the property insured is assigned without a written permission endorsed hereon by an agent of the company duly authorized for such purpose, the policy shall hereby become void ; but this condition does not apply to change of title by succession, or by the operation of the law, or by reason of 40 death.

Partial damage—salvage.

5. Where property insured is only partially damaged, no abandonment of the same will be allowed unless by the consent of the company or its agent; and in case of the removal of property to escape conflagration, the company will contribute 45 to the loss and expenses attending such act of salvage proportionately to the respective interests of the company or companies and the insured.

Money, securities, etc.

6. Money, books of account, securities for money, and evidences of debt or title are not insured. 50

Plate, paintings, clocks, etc.

7. Plate, plated ware, jewelry, medals, paintings, sculptures, curiosities, scientific and musical instruments, bullion, works of art, articles of vertu, frescoes, clocks, watches, trinkets and mirrors, are not insured unless mentioned in the policy.

8. The company is not liable for loss if there is any prior Prior or subsequent insurance. insurance in any other company, unless the company's assent thereto appears herein or is endorsed hereon, nor if any subsequent insurance is effected in any other company, unless and
5 until the company assents thereto by writing signed by a duly authorized agent.

9. In the event of any other insurance on the property Case of assent to other insurance. herein described having been assented to as aforesaid, then this company shall, if such other insurance remains in force, on
10 the happening of any loss or damage, only be liable for the payment of a rateable proportion of such loss or damage without reference to the dates of the different policies.

10. The company is not liable for the losses following, that is to say:

15 (a) For loss of property owned by any other party than the Liability in case of non-ownership. assured, unless the interest of the assured is stated in or upon the policy;

(b) For loss caused by invasion, insurrection, riot, civil commotion, military or usurped power; Riot, invasion, etc.

20 (c) Where the insurance is upon buildings [or their contents] Chimneys, ashes, stoves. —for loss caused by the want of good and substantial brick or stone chimneys; or by ashes or embers being deposited, with the knowledge and consent of the insured, in wooden vessels; or by stoves or stove-pipes being, to the knowledge of the assured,
25 in an unsafe condition or improperly secured;

(d) For loss or damage to goods destroyed or damaged while Goods to which fire heat is being applied. undergoing any process in or by which the application of fire heat is necessary;

(e) For loss or damage occurring to buildings or their Repairs by carpenters, etc.
30 contents while the buildings are being repaired by carpenters, joiners, plasterers or other workmen, and in consequence thereof, unless permission to execute such repairs had been previously granted in writing, signed by a duly authorized agent of the company. But in dwelling-houses fifteen days
35 are allowed in each year in incidental repairs, without such permission;

(f) For loss or damage occurring while petroleum, rock, Gunpowder, coal oil, etc. earth or coal oil, camphine, burning fluid, benzine, naphtha or any liquid products thereof, or any of their constituent
40 parts (refined coal oil for lighting purposes only, not exceeding five gallons in quantity, excepted), or more than twenty-five pounds weight of gunpowder are stored or kept in the building insured or containing the property insured, unless permission is given in writing to the company.

45 11. The company will make good loss caused by the explo- Explosion. Lightning. sion of coal gas in a building not forming part of gas works, and loss by fire caused by any other explosion or by lightning.

12. Proof of loss must be made by the assured, although the Proof of loss when payable to other than assured. loss be payable to a third party.

50 13. Any person entitled to make a claim under this policy Directions to be observed on making claim. is to observe the following directions: .

(a) He is forthwith after loss to give notice in writing to the company;

(*b*) He is to deliver, as soon afterwards as practicable, as particular an account of the loss as the nature of the case permits;

(*c*) He is also to furnish therewith a statutory declaration, declaring,

(1) That the said account is just and true ; 5

(2) When and how the fire originated, so far as the declarant knows or believes;

(3) That the fire was not caused through his wilful act or neglect, procurement, means or contrivance ;

(4) The amount of other insurances ; 10

[(5) All liens, and incumbrances on the subject of insurance.]

(*d*) He is in support of his claims, if required and if practicable, to produce books of account, and furnish invoices and other vouchers ; to furnish copies of the written portion of all policies ; and to exhibit for examination all that remains of the 15 property which was covered by the policy.

(*e*) He is to produce, if required, a certificate under the hand of a magistrate, notary public, clergyman, [commissioner for taking affidavits, or municipal clerk], residing in the vicinity in which the fire happened, and not concerned in the loss or 20 related to the assured or sufferers, stating that he has examined the circumstances attending the fire, loss or damage alleged, that he is acquainted with the character and circumstances of the assured or claimant, and that he verily believes that the insured has by misfortune and without fraud or evil practice sustained 25 loss and damage on the subject assured, to the amount certified.

Proof of loss may be made by agent. 14. The above proofs of loss may be made by the agent of the assured, in case of the absence or inability of the assured himself to make the same, such absence or inability being satisfactorily accounted for. 30

False statement or fraud vitiates claim. 15. Any fraud or false statement in a statutory declaration, in relation to any of the above particulars, shall vitiate the claim.

Arbitration in case of differences. 16. If any difference arises as to the value of the property insured, of the property saved, or amount of the loss, such 35 value and amount and the proportion thereof (if any) to be paid by the company, shall, whether the right to recover on the policy is disputed or not, and independently of all other questions, be submitted to the arbitration of some person to be chosen by both parties, or if they cannot agree on one 40 person, then to two persons, one to be chosen by the party insured and the other by the company, and a third to be appointed by the persons so chosen, [or on their failing to agree, then by the County Judge of the County wherein the loss has happened; and such reference shall be subject to the provisions 45 of the laws applicable to references in actions ; and the award shall, if the company is in other respects liable, be conclusive as to the amount of the loss and proportion to be paid by the company; [and all questions as to the costs of the parties shall be in the discretion of the arbitrators.] R.S.O. 1887, c. 161, s. 157. 50

Loss due thirty days after proof. 17. The loss shall not be payable until thirty days after completion of the proofs of loss, unless otherwise provided by statute or the agreement of the parties.

18. The company, instead of making payment, may repair, rebuild or replace, within a reasonable time, the property damaged or lost, giving notice of their intention within fifteen days after receipt of the proofs herein required. *Company may replace, instead of paying.*

5 19. The insurance may be terminated by the company by giving notice to that effect as hereinafter mentioned, and by repaying a rateable proportion of the premium for the unexpired term ; if the notice is personally served on the insured at least five clear days' notice, excluding Sunday, shall be given ;
10 or if the notice is not personally served at least seven clear days' notice shall be given, and the notice may be by registered letter posted at the head office, or any agency of the company, in Ontario to the address of the insured; and the policy shall cease after the repayment as, aforesaid, and the expiration of
15 the five or seven days, as the case may be. *Termination of policy on notice and re-payment of proportion of premium.*

20. No condition of the policy, either in whole or in part, shall be deemed to have been waived by the company, unless the waiver is clearly expressed in writing, signed by an agent of the company. *Waiver of condition.*

20 21. Any officer or agent of the company, who assumes on behalf of the company to enter into any written agreement relating to any matter connected with the insurance, shall be deemed *prima facie* to be the agent of the company for the purpose. *Officers assuming to agree in writing to be deemed agents.*

25 22. Every action or proceeding against the company for the recovery of any claim under or by virtue of this policy, shall be absolutely barred, unless commenced within the term of one year next after the loss or damage occurs. R. S. O. 1877, c. 162, *Schedule.* *Actions to be brought within one year.*

30 **115.** If a company (or other insurer) desires to vary the said conditions, or to omit any of them, or to add new conditions, there shall be added on the instrument of contract containing the printed statutory conditions words to the following effect, printed in conspicuous type, and in ink of different
35 colour. :— *Variations how indicated.*

"VARIATIONS IN CONDITIONS.

" This policy is issued on the above Statutory Conditions, with the following variations and additions :

" These variations (*or as the case may be*) are, by virtue of
40 the Ontario Statute in that behalf, in force so far as, by the Court or judge before whom a question is tried relating thereto, they shall be held to be just and reasonable to be exacted by the company." R. S. O. 1877, c. 162, s. 4.

116. No such variation, addition or omission shall, unless
45 the same is distinctly indicated and set forth in the manner or to the effect aforesaid, be legal and binding on the insured ; and no question shall be considered as to whether any such variation, addition or omission is, under the circumstances, just and reasonable, but on the contrary, the policy shall, as against
50 the insurers, be subject to the Statutory Conditions only, unless the variations, additions or omissions are distinctly indicated and set forth in the manner or to the effect aforesaid. R. S. O. 1877, c. 162, s. 5. *Variations not binding unless clearly indicated.*

Policy containing other than statutory conditions. **117.** In case a policy is entered into or renewed containing or including any condition other than or different from the conditions set forth in the Schedule to this Act, if the said condition so contained or included is held, by the Court or judge before whom a question relating thereto is tried, to be 5 not just and reasonable, such condition shall be null and void. R. S. O. 1877, c. 162, s. 6 ; c. 161, s. 35, (see s. 119, *infra*.)

If due proof of lo's not given through accident, etc., or objection not made thereto, or made on other grounds than non-compliance with conditions ; **118.** Where, by reason of necessity, accident or mistake, the conditions of any contract of fire insurance on property in this Province as to the proof to be given to the Insurance Com- 10 pany after the occurrence of a fire have not been strictly complied with ; or where, after a statement or proof of loss has been given in good faith by or on behalf of the insured, in pursuance of any proviso or condition of such contract, the company, through its agent or otherwise, objects to the loss 15 upon other grounds than for imperfect compliance with such conditions, or does not within a reasonable time after receiving such statement or proof notify the assured in writing that such statement or proof is objected to, and what are the particulars in which the same is alleged to be defective, and so from 20 time to time ; **or, if full compliance adjudged inequitable,** or where, for any other reason, the Court or judge before whom a question relating to such insurance is tried or inquired into, considers it inequitable that the insurance should be deemed void or forfeited by reason of imperfect compliance with such conditions—no objection to the sufficiency 25 of such statement or proof or amended or supplemental state- **in above cases, liability and policy not vacated.** ment or proof (as the case may be) shall, in any of such cases, be allowed as a discharge of the liability of the company on such contract of insurance wherever entered into. R. S. O. 1877, c. 162, s. 2.

Appeal. **119.** A decision of a Court or judge under this Act shall be 30 subject to review or appeal to the same extent as a decision by such Court or judge in other cases. R. S. O. 1877, c. 162, s. 7 ; c. 161, s. 35.

Justices of the Peace, etc., and may swear and examine witnesses regarding loss. **120.**—(1) Any Justice of the Peace, or any one having lawful authority to administer an oath or affirmation in any 35 legal proceeding, may examine on oath or solemn affirmation any party or person who comes before him to give evidence touching any loss by fire in which any [Fire] Insurance Company is interested, and may administer any oath or affirmation required under this Act. R. S. O. 1877, c. 161, s. 62. 40

May hold special investigation on request. [(2). On receiving a written request from any officer or agent of any Insurance Company with security for the expenses of an investigation, any Justice of the Peace may at once proceed to hold an investigation as to the origin or cause of any fire that has happened within his County or District, and as to the 45 persons if any, profiting thereby.

Powers. (3) The Justice of the Peace shall have power to send for persons and papers, and to examine all persons that appear before him on oath or solemn affirmation ; and he shall keep a record of all such proceedings and of the evidence given 50 before him.]

33

TITLE XV.—PREMIUM NOTES AND ASSESSMENTS. *(Mutual and Cash—Mutual Fire Insurance Companies.)*

121. Sections 122 to 136 inclusive shall apply only to Mutual and Cash-Mutual Fire Insurance Companies.

5 **122.** The company may accept premium notes, or the undertaking of the insured, for insurances, and may undertake contracts in consideration thereof ; said notes or undertakings to be assessed for the losses and expenses of the company in the manner hereinafter provided. R. S. O. 1877, c. 161, s. 45.

Company may accept premium notes.

10 **123.** The Directors may demand in cash a part or first payment of the premium note or undertaking at the time that application for insurance is made ; and such first payment shall be credited upon said premium note or undertaking or against future assessments, but not more than fifty per centum of any 15 premium or premium note shall be paid in cash at the time of such application or of effecting the insurance. R. S. O. 1877, c. 161, s. 46 ; 44 V. c. 20, s. 22.

Part payment may be demanded at the time of application for insurance.

124. All premium notes or undertakings belonging to the company shall be assessed under the direction of the Board of 20 Directors, at such intervals from their respective dates, for such sums as the Directors determine, and for such further sums as they think necessary [and as are authorized by this Act] for losses, expenses, and reserve, during the currency of the policies for which said notes or undertakings were given, 25 and in respect to which they are liable to assessment ; and every member of the company, or person who has given a premium note or undertaking, shall pay the sums from time to time payable by him to the company during the continuance of his policy, in accordance with the assessment ; and the 30 assessment shall become payable in thirty days after notice thereof has been mailed to the member, or person who has given the premium note or undertaking, directed to his post office address, as given in his original application, or otherwise in writing to the company. R. S. O. 1877, c. 161, ss. 47, 53.

Assessment of premium notes.

Notice to be given of the assessment.

35 **125.** If the assessment on the premium note or undertaking upon a policy is not paid within thirty days after the day on which the assessment has become due, the [contract] of insurance, for which the assessment has been made shall be null and void as respects all claim for losses occurring during 40 the time of non-payment : but the [contract] shall be revived when the assessment has been paid, unless the Secretary gives notice to the contrary to the assessed party in the manner in this Act provided ; but nothing shall relieve the assured party from his liability to pay the assessment or any 45 subsequent assessments, nor shall the assured party be entitled to recover the amount of loss or damage which happens to property insured under the [contract] while the assessment remains due and unpaid, unless the Board of Directors in their discretion decide otherwise. R. S. O. 1877, c. 161, s. 48.

Policy to be void, if any assessment or note is not paid within thirty days.

but shall be revived by subsequent payment.

50 **126.** A notice of assessment upon any premium note or undertaking mailed as aforesaid shall be deemed sufficient if it embodies the register number of of the [contract] the period

Requisites of notice of assessment.

5—IN.

over which the assessment extends, the amount of the assessment, the time when and the place where payable. R. S. O. 1877, c. 161, s. 40.

Assessment, how proportioned.

127. The assessment upon premium notes or undertakings shall always be in proportion to the amount of the notes or 5 undertakings, having regard to the branch or department to which their policies respectively appertain. R. S. O. 1877, c. 161, s. 50.

Company may sue for assessments on premium notes.

128. If a member or other person, who has given a premium note or undertaking, for thirty days after notice of 10 assessment has been mailed to him in manner aforesaid, neglects or refuses to pay the assessments, the company may sue for and recover the same with costs of suit, and such proceeding shall not be a waiver of any forfeiture incurred by such non-payment. R. S. O. 1877, c. 161, s. 51. 15

Certificate of the Secretary to be *prima facie* evidence of amount due to the Company.

129. Where an assessment is made on any premium note or undertaking given to the company for a risk taken by the company, or as a consideration for any policy of insurance issued, or to be issued by the company, and an action is brought to recover the assessment, the certificate of the secre- 20 tary of the company, specifying the assessment, and the amount due to the company on the note or undertaking by means thereof, shall be taken and received as *prima facie* evidence thereof in any Court in this Province. R. S. O. 1877, c. 161, s. 52. 25

Reserve fund.

130.—(1) The company may form a reserve fund, to consist of all moneys which remain on hand at the end of each year, after payment of the ordinary expenses and losses of the

Annual assessment.

company; and for that purpose the board of directors may levy an annual assessment not exceeding ten per centum on 30 the premium notes or undertakings held by the company; and the reserve fund may from time to time be applied by the

how applied,

directors to pay off such liabilities of the company as may not be provided for out of the ordinary receipts for the same or any succeeding year. R. S. O. 1887, c. 161, s. 53 (1). 35

how invested.

(2) The reserve fund shall be invested in stock, debentures or other securities in which trustees may invest trust money, or may remain in a chartered bank in Ontario deposited at interest in the name of the company. R. S. O. c. 161, s. 53; 42 V. c. 21, s. 2; 49 V. c. 16, s. 24. 40

Directors may retain amount of premium notes.

131. If there is a loss on property insured by the company, the board of directors may retain the amount of the premium note or undertaking given for insurance thereof, until the time has expired for which insurance has been made, and at the expiration of said time the insured shall have the right 45 to demand and receive such part of the retained sum as has not been assessed for. R. S. O. 1877, c. 161, s. 63.

When premium note is to be returned.

132. Forty days after the expiration of the term of insurance, the premium note or undertaking given for the insurance, shall, on application therefor, be given up to the signer 50

thereof, provided all losses and expenses with which the note
or undertaking is chargeable have been paid. R. S. O. 1877,
c. 161, s. 54.

133. Any action cognizable in a Division Court upon or Action in
5 for any premium note or undertaking, or any sum assessed or Division Courts where brought.
to be assessed thereon, may be entered and tried and determined
in the Court for the division wherein the head office or any
agency of the company is situate :

Provided always, that the provisions of this section
10 shall not apply to nor include any such premium note
or undertaking made or entered into after the first day
of July, 1885, nor any sum assessed thereon, unless within
the body of such note or undertaking or across the face Actions on premium notes in Division Courts, where brought.
thereof, there was at the time of the making or enter-
15 ing into the same, printed in conspicuous type, and in ink of a
colour different from any other in or on such note the words
following : " Any action which may be brought or commenced
in a Division Court in respect or on account of this note or
undertaking, or any sum to be assessed thereon, may be brought
20 and commenced against the maker hereof in the Division Court
for the division wherein the head office or any agency of the
company is situate." R. S. O. 1877, 161, s. 71 ; 48 V. c. 35, s. 1.

134. No premium note or undertaking shall create a lien Premium notes not to create lien on land.
upon lands on which the insured property is situate. R. S. O.
25 1877, c. 161, s. 73.

135. Any [Cash-]Mutual Fire Insurance company [licensed Powers of incorporated companies to insure on the cash premium principle.
under this Act] may effect any insurance upon the cash premium
principle, for a period not exceeding three years on farm and
other non-hazardous property, and for one year or less on any
30 other class of property ; but the amount of cash insurances in
one year shall be limited, so that the cash premiums received
thereon during any one year shall not be in excess of one-half
of the amount still payable in respect of premium notes or
undertakings on hand on the thirty-first day of December of
35 the previous year, according to the statement made under the
103rd section ; and all the property and assets of the company,
including premium notes and undertakings, shall be liable for
all losses which may arise under insurances for cash premiums ; Guarantee fund.
and any such company may also create or possess a guarantee
40 capital or fund for the company, according to the provisions
of this Act. R. S. O. 1877, c. 161, s. 75 ; 41 V. c. 8, s. 17 ;
44 V. c. 20, s. 7.

136.—(1) No execution shall issue against a [Mutual or Issue of execution against company.
Cash-Mutual] company upon a judgment until after the expir-
45 ation of [sixty days] from the recovery thereof ; but this section
shall not apply to any judgment recovered on any policy or
undertaking of the company heretofore issued or given where
more than fifty per centum of the premium or premium note
was paid in cash at the time of the insurance or the application
50 therefor.

(2) A judge in chambers, or a referee in chambers, shall, upon
the recovery of a judgment against the company, upon the
application of the person in whose favour the same has been
recovered, upon notice to the company, inquire into the facts,
and if he shall certify that more than fifty per centum of the
premium, or of the premium note, was paid in cash at the time

of the insurance, or upon the application therefor, execution may be forthwith issued upon such judgment. R. S. O. 1877, c. 161, 61 ; 44 V. c. 20, s. 27.

TITLE XVI.—INSPECTION OF COMPANIES—(*All Companies.*)

Appointment of Inspector.

137.—(1) For the efficient administration of the Insurance 5 business, the Lieutenant-Governor in Council may appoint an officer to be called the Inspector of Insurance, who shall act under the instructions of the Treasurer of Ontario, and his duty shall be to examine and report to the said Treasurer from time to time upon all matters connected with insurance as carried 10 on by the companies within this Act. 42 V. c. 21, s. 1.

(2) The salary of the Inspector shall be such sum per annum as the Legislature shall, from time to time, determine ; and it shall be lawful to provide from time to time such assistance as may be found necessary. 42 V. c. 25, s. 1 ; 46 V. c. 15, s. 6, 15 *part.*

Inspector to keep papers on file.

138. The Inspector shall keep on file the various documents required by this Act to be filed in his office, and shall keep a record of all licenses issued by the Treasurer. 44 V. c. 20, s. 4.

Duties.

139.—(1) The Inspector of Insurance shall, personally [or 20 by deputy], visit the head office of every such company in Ontario at least once in every year, and shall carefully examine the statements of the company as to its condition and affairs and report thereon to the Treasurer as to all matters requiring his attention and decision. 25

(2) The Inspector shall from such examination prepare and lay before the Treasurer an annual report of the condition of every company's business as ascertained by him from such inspection, and such report shall be made within thirty days after the commencement of each annual session of the 30 Legislature of Ontario. 42 V. c. 25, s. 2.

Powers of Inspector.

140 (1) It shall be the duty of the officers or agents of the company to cause their books to be open for the inspection of the Inspector, and otherwise to facilitate the examination so far as may be in their power ; and the Inspector or deputy 35 aforesaid shall have power to examine under oath any officer or agent of the company relative to its business. 42 V. c. 25, s. 3, (1, 2.)

Report of Inspector.

(2) A report of all companies so visited shall be entered in a book kept for that purpose, with notes and memoranda 40 showing the condition of each company ; and, where a special examination has been made, a special written report shall be communicated to the Treasurer stating the Inspector's opinion of the condition and financial standing of the company, and all other matters desirable to be made known to the 45 Treasurer. 42 V. c. 25, s. 3 (3).

Entries, untrue or omitted.

Access to books and papers.

141. Every director, officer, agent, or employee of a company who, knowingly, makes or assists to make any untrue entry in any of the company's books, or who refuses or neglects to make any proper entry therein, or to exhibit the same or 50 allow the same to be inspected and extracts to be taken therefrom shall be guilty of an offence, and, being convicted thereof, shall be imprisoned with or without hard labour in the Central

Prison or any gaol of the Province, for a period not exceeding
————— months. 24 V. c. 18, s. 28; Dom. Act, 32-3 V.
c. 29, s. 90.

142.—(1) If it appears to the Inspector that the assets of *Provision if company appears unsafe.*
5 any company are insufficient to justify its continuance of busi-
ness, or unsafe for the public to effect insurance with it, he
shall make a special report on the affairs of the company to
the Treasurer. 42 V. c. 25, s. 3 (4).

(2) After full consideration of the report and a reasonable *Suspending license of company.*
10 time being given to the company to be heard, and if, after such
further inquiry and investigation (if any), as he may see proper to make, the treasurer reports to the Lieutenant-Governor
in Council that he agrees with the Inspector in the opinion expressed in his report, then, if the Lieutenant-Governor in Coun-
15 cil also concurs in such opinion, an Order in Council may issue,
suspending or cancelling the license of the company, and prohibiting the company from doing any further business,
and thereafter it shall not be lawful for the company to do
any further business in Ontario, until the suspension or pro-
20 hibition is removed by the Lieutenant-Governor in Council.
42 V. c. 25, s. 3 (6); R. S. O. 1877, c. 160, s. 34.

143. Notice of the suspension or cancelling of any license *Notice of suspension of license.*
and prohibition from doing any further business, shall be pub-
lished in the *Ontario Gazette*; and thereafter any person trans-
25 acting any business in behalf of the company, except for
winding up its affairs pursuant to the 7th section, shall be
deemed to have contravened the 55th and 56th sections, and
shall be liable for each offence to the penalty enacted in the
56th section. R. S. O. 1877, c. 160, s. 19 ; 42 V. c. 25, s. 3 (7).

30 **144.**—(1) If it appears to the Inspector that a company which *Company assuming name of other company.*
has not been incorporated by special Act of the Legislation
has assumed the name of a previously established company, or
any name liable to be unfairly confounded therewith, or otherwise on public grounds objectionable, he shall make a report
35 thereof to the Treasurer. 46 V. c. 25, s. 3 (5).

(2) And such name may, upon the written recommendation
of the Inspector, be changed by the Lieutenant-Governor in
Council, pursuant to the 20th section.

145. In order to facilitate the inspection of an insurance *Inspection of books and papers.*
40 company's books and papers the company may be required by
the Inspector to produce the said books and papers at the
county town of the county in which the head office of the
insurance company is situated, or at such other convenient
place as the Inspector may direct. 46 V. c. 15, s. 5.

45 **146.** Whenever the affairs of any insurance company doing *Examination of company's affairs.*
business in Ontario appear to require the same, the Inspector
of Insurance, with the approval of the Provincial [Treasurer],
may, at the expense of the company, have abstracts prepared
of its books and vouchers and a valuation made of the assets
50 and liabilities ; and the certificate of the Inspector approved of
by the Provincial [Treasurer], shall be conclusive as to the expenses to be paid by the company in respect thereof. 46 V.
c. 15, s. 7.

Inspector and officers not to be interested in any company.

147. The Inspector of Insurance, or any officers under him shall not be interested as shareholders, directly or indirectly, with any insurance company doing business in Ontario. 42 V. c. 25, s. 4.

Contribution from companies to expenses.

148.—(1). Towards defraying the expenses of the office of 5 the Inspector, a sum not exceeding $3,000 shall be annually contributed by the companies required to be licensed under this Act.

Mode of determining the amount of contribution to expenses.

(2). The amount to be annually contributed by the Insur- ance companies under the provisions of the last preceding 10 sub-section shall be assessed *pro rata* and based on the gross amount at risk as shewn by the books of the several companies on the 31st day of December next preceding. 42 V. c. 25, s. 5, *part*; 43 V. c. 20, s. 1, *part*; 46 V. c. 15, s. 6, *part*.

Time and manner of payment.

(3). All sums under this Act payable to the Treasurer shall 15 be so paid before the issue of the license and the Treasurer's certificate, [or approval of an account certified by the Inspector.] shall as to the amount so payable by each or any company be held conclusive. 42 V. c. 25, s. 5 *part*; 43 V. c. 20, s. 1. 20

Certified copies of documents in inspector's office.

[**149.** A copy of any document in the office of the Inspector, certified by him to be a true copy and sealed with the seal of his office, shall be held to be authentic, and shall be *prima facie* evidence of the same legal effect as the original in any court or elsewhere. *Public Works Act*, R. S. O. 1877, 25 c. 30, s. 8.]

TITLE XVII.—LIQUIDATION AND WINDING UP OF COMPANIES 30
(*All Companies.*)

Voluntary liquidation.

150. When a company proposes to go into volun- tary liquidation, at least one month's notice in advance shall be given to the [Treasurer] and to the Inspector; the like notice shall 35 also be published by the company in two consecutive issues of the *Ontario Gazette*, and in some other newspaper should the Inspector so require; and the notice shall state the date at which [contracts] shall cease to be taken by the company, also the name and address of the company's liquidator, or the 40 intention of the company to apply on a stated day for the appointment of a liquidator. 46 V. c. 15, s. 9.

Disposal of reserve at winding up of company.

151.—(1) At the winding up of a Mutual or Cash-Mutual Fire Insurance company, after notice has been given as required by section 51, it shall be lawful for the directors of said com- 45 pany to reinsure out of the reserve fund the unexpired con- tracts for which premiums or premium notes have been taken. 46 V. c. 15, s. 16.

Reinsuring companies.

[(2). The said re-insurance shall be effected in some company licensed to transact business in the Province, and approved by 50 the Treasurer.]

Unearned premiums.

152. When any company is wound up each [person con- tracted with on the cash plan] shall be entitled to a refund from the company of the unearned proportion of the cash

premium calculated from the date at which the company, according to the notice in the 150th section, ceased to undertake contracts; but this shall not destroy or defeat any other remedy such person may have against the company in
5 respect thereof or for any other cause. 46 V. c. 15, s. 10.

153. Every receiver, assignee, or liquidator of a company Receiver to file shall, until the affairs of the company are wound up [and the statements. accounts are finally closed] within seven days after the close of each month, file with the court or other authority appoint-
10 ing him, and also with the Inspector of Insurance, detailed schedules shewing, in such form as may be required, receipts and expenditures, also assets and liabilities, and he shall, whenever by the authority appointing him, or by the Inspector of Insurance, so required to do, exhibit the company's books and
15 vouchers, and furnish such other information respecting the company's affairs as may be required; and any receiver, assignee or liquidator refusing or neglecting to furnish such information, shall, for each offence, be subject to a penalty of not less than $50 nor more than $200, to be recovered on
20 behalf of Her Majesty for the use of this Province; and he shall in addition render himself liable to be dismissed or removed. 46 V. c. 15, s. 11.

154. [The Acts and portions of Acts mentioned in the Acts repealed. schedule hereto, are hereby repealed.]

-SCHEDULE OF ACTS REPEALED.

Schedule of Acts Repealed from the day upon which the Ontario Insurance Act takes effect.

TITLE OF ACT.	Extent of Repeal.
R.S.O. 1877 c. 160, An Act respecting Insurance Companies..	The whole.
R.S.O. 1877 c. 161, An Act respecting Mutual Fire Insurance Companies	The whole.
R.S.O. 1877 c. 162, An Act to secure Uniform Conditions in Policies of Fire Insurance	The whole.
41 V. c. 8, An Act to make certain amendments in the Revised Statutes...................................	Section 17.
42 V. c. 25, An Act to provide for the Inspection of Insurance Companies	The whole.
43 V. c. 20, An Act respecting the Expenses of Inspecting Insurance Companies	The whole.
44 V. c. 20, An Act to give increased stability to Mutual Fire Insurance Companies	The whole.
45 V. c. 20, An Act to extend the application of the Fire Insurance Policy Act.............................	The whole.
46 V. c. 15, An Act relating to the Law of Insurance........	The whole.
47 V. c. 6, An Act respecting Securities vested in the Treasurer of the Province ....,.......	The whole.
47 V. c. 28, An Act respecting Supplementary Licenses to Mutual Fire Insurance Companies	The whole.
48 V. c. 35, An Act to amend the Act respecting Mutual Fire Insurance Companies................................	The whole.
48 V. c. 36, An Act to regulate the Election of Directors of Mutual Fire Insurance Companies	The whole.

No. 66.

1st Session, 6th Legislature, 50 Vic., 1887.

BILL.

An Act consolidating and amending the Acts respecting Insurance Companies.

First Reading,   1887.

No. 66.]　　　　　　　**BILL.**　　　　　　[1887.

An Act consolidating and amending the Acts respecting Insurance Companies.

SUMMARY OF PROVISIONS.—

PRELIMINARY : SHORT TITLE, s. 1 ; INTERPRETATION, s. 2 ; APPLICATION
OF ACT, s. 3.

TITLE I.—Joint Stock Companies : Formation and General Provisions
governing, s. 4 ;　Directors, s. 5 (*See also* ss. 89-98) ; Capital
Stock, s. 6, (*for Share or Stock Capital in Mutual and Cash-
Mutual Fire Insurance Companies, see under* TITLE VI) ; Forfeiture
of Corporate Powers, s. 7 ; Liquidation, s. 7, (*See also under* TITLE
XVII).

TITLE II.—Formation and Incorporation of Mutual and Cash-Mutual Fire
Insurance Companies, ss. 8-19.

TITLE III.—Change of Name or of Head-Office (*all Companies*), ss. 20-22.

TITLE IV.—Branches and Departments in Mutual and Cash-Mutual Fire
Insurance Companies, ss. 24-26.

TITLE V.—Guarantee Capital in Mutual or Cash-Mutual Fire Insurance
Companies, ss. 27-29.

TITLE VI.—Share or Stock Capital in Mutual or Cash-Mutual Fire Insurance Companies, ss. 30-39.

TITLE VII.—Government Deposits (*all Companies*), ss. 40-52.

TITLE VIII.—License (*all Companies*), ss. 53-62.

TITLE IX.—Fees (*all Companies*), s. 63.

TITLE X.—Internal Management of Mutual and Cash-Mutual Fire Insurance Companies :　1. *Admission and Withdrawal of Members,* ss.
65-68 ;　2.　*General Meetings,* ss. 69-73 ;　3.　*Directors—Qualification, Election, etc.,* ss. 74-87.

TITLE XI.—Powers of Directors—General Provisions (*all Companies*), ss.
88-98. (*As to Joint Stock Companies, see also* s. 5.)

TITLE XII.—Books, Accounts, and Returns (*all Companies*), ss. 99-105.

TITLE XIII.—Contracts of Fire Insurance—General Provisions (*all Companies*), ss. 106-113.

TITLE XIV.—Statutory Conditions and Provisions relating thereto,
(*binding all Fire Insurance Contracts whatsoever in Ontario, See
Section* 8) ss. 114-120,

SHORT TITLE.

1. This Act may be cited as *The Ontario Insurance Act, 1887*, and shall go into effect on the *30th day of June* next after the passing hereof, except that sections 114 to 116 shall not take effect as respects insurance companies which have **5** their head office in Great Britain or Ireland until 31st December next. R. S. O. 1877, c. 160, s. 1.

INTERPRETATION.

[New except as to sub-section 13.]

2. In this Act, unless the context otherwise requires :— **10**

"Province." "Legislature."   (1) "Province" and "Legislature" mean respectively the Province and the Legislature of Ontario.

"Treasurer."   (2) "Treasurer," means the Treasurer of the Province ; or any member of the Executive Council to whom from time to time may be transferred, either for a limited period, or other- **15** wise, the powers and duties which are by this Act assigned to the Treasurer. R. S. O. c. 14, s. 3.

"Inspector."   (3) "Inspector" means the Inspector of Insurance for the Province.

"Company."   (4) "Company" means and includes any corporation, or **20** any society or association, incorporated or unincorporated, or any partnership, or any underwriter, *except as provided by section 3*, that undertakes or effects for valuable consider- ation, or agrees or offers so to undertake or effect, in the Pro- vince, any contract of indemnity, guarantee, suretyship, **25** insurance, endowment, tontine, or annuity on life, or any like contract which accrues payable on or after the occurrence of some contingent event.

"Offer to un- dertake con- tracts."   (5) The expression "offer to undertake contracts" shall include the setting up of a sign or inscription containing the name of the **30** company ; or the distribution or publication of any proposal, circular, card ,advertisement, printed form, or like document in the name of the company, or any written or oral solicitation in the company's behalf. [*cf.* Laws of New York (1886), chap. 488, s. 3 ; Dominion Insurance Act, 49 V. c. 45, s. 2 ; and R. S. O. **35** 1877, c. 160, s. 19.]

"Contract."   (6) "Contract" means and includes any contract or agree- ment, sealed, written or oral, the subject matter of which is within the intent of the 4th sub-section.

"Written."   (7) "Written," as applied to any instrument, includes written **40** or printed, or partly written and partly printed.

"Provincial. Company."   (8) "Provincial Company" means a company which has its head office in Ontario.

"Canadian Company."   (9) "Canadian Company" means a company incorporated or legally constituted in the Dominion of Canada, but which has **45** its head office in some Province of Canada other than Ontario.

(10) "Municipality" has the same meaning as in the Muni- "Munici-
cipal Act.

(11) "Mutual Insurance" means insurance given in considera- "Mutual
tion of a premium note *or undertaking*, with or without an Insurance."
5 immediate cash payment thereon ; and "Mutual Company" "Mutual
means a Company empowered solely to transact such insurance. Company."

(12) "Cash-Mutual Company" means a company organized "Cash Mutual
to transact mutual insurance, but empowered to undertake Company."
contracts of insurance on both the cash plan and the premium
10 note or mutual plan.

(13) "Inland-Marine Insurance" means marine insurance "Inland
in respect of subjects of insurance at risk above the harbour of Marine Insur-
Montreal. Dom. Act, 49 Vic. c. 45, s. 1 (*g*); *cf.* R. S. O. c. 160, s. 6. ance.

(14) "Member" means a policy-holder on the premium note "Member."
15 plan ; but as to those mutual, or cash-mutual companies which,
in terms of this Act have guarantee or joint stock capital,
"Member" includes, where the context so requires, any holder
of one or more shares of the capital. 46 V. c. 15, s. 15 ; 44 V.
c. 20, ss. 7, 12.

20 (15) "Registry Office" means the registry office of the Reg- "Registry
istry Division within which the head office of the company is Office."
situate ; and "Registrar" includes the Registrar and Deputy "Registrar."
Registrar of such registry office.

APPLICATION OF ACT.

25 **3.** The provisions of this Act shall not apply :—

(1) To a company licensed by the Dominion of Canada, Dominion
except as to sections 114 to 120 inclusive, which shall apply licensees ex-
to all Fire Insurance companies transacting business in Ontario. except as to
R. S. O. 1877, c. 162, ss. 2, 3 ; c. 161, s. 79 ; c. 160, s. 2. sections
114-120.

30 (2) This Act shall not apply to any benevolent, provident, Also certain
industrial or co-operative society not requiring a license for societies.
any such contract as aforesaid before the passing of this Act.

(NEW.)

[TITLE I.—JOINT STOCK COMPANIES : Formation and general
35 provisions governing, s. 4 ; Directors, s. 5, (*see also* ss.
89-98) ; Capital Stock, s. 6 (for share or stock capital
in Mutual or Cash-Mutual Fire Insurance companies,
see under Title VI.) ; Forfeiture of corporate powers,
s. 7 ; Liquidation, s. 7 (*see also* under TITLE XVII.)].

40 INCORPORATION OF JOINT STOCK COMPANIES.

4. (1) — Notwithstanding section 4 of the Ontario Formation of
Joint Stock Companies' Letters Patent Act, the Lieutenant- Companies.
Governor in Council may, on the written recommendation
of the Inspector, approved by the Treasurer, or some other
45 member of the Executive Council, grant by letters patent,

under the Great Seal, a charter to any number of persons
not less than five, who shall petition therefor, constituting
such persons and others who may become shareholders
in the company thereby created a body corporate and politic
for any purpose or object within the intent of this Act; but 5
such incorporated company, before undertaking, effecting,
or offering to undertake or effect, or soliciting any
contract within this Act, shall file in the office of the
Inspector satisfactory evidence that this Act has been complied with in respect of stock subscribed and of calls there- 10
on paid, and further shall make the necessary deposit
and be licensed as hereinafter provided. [*cf.* 44 V. c. 20, s. 19,
which extends the application of J. S. Cos. Letters Patent
Act, to Mutual Companies desirous of conversion into Joint
Stock companies; also s. 38 of this Act.] 15

Acts applying
to Joint
Stock com-
panies formed
under this Act

(2) To every company so incorporated *The Ontario Joint
Stock Companies' Letters Patent Act* and *The Ontario Joint
Stock Companies' General Clauses Act*, shall apply in all unprovided cases so far as not repugnant to the express provisions of this Act. 20

(3) To ·every *joint stock* company heretofore incorporated
and acting under license of the Province the Acts cited in the
last sub-section shall also apply, except where repugnant to the express provisions of this Act, or to the special Act
of the Province incorporating the company, or to any Act of 25
the Province amending the special Act of incorporation.

Directors.

5. (1)—The affairs of every company incorporated under the
4th section shall be managed by a board of not less than [five]
nor more than nine directors. (*cf.* R. S. O. 1877, c. 149, s. 8.)

(2) The first five of the persons named in the charter of 30
incorporation shall be directors of the company until replaced
by others duly named in their stead. (*cf.* R. S. O. 1877, c. 149,
s. 9.)

(3) The after directors of the company shall be elected by
the shareholders in general meeting of the company, assembled 35
at such times, in such wise, and for such term, not exceeding
two years, as the by-laws of the company may prescribe.
R. S. O. 1877, c. 149, s. 11.

Capital stock.

6. The capital stock of a company incorporated under the
4th section shall be as follows :— 40

1. If a Fire, or Fire and Inland Marine, or Accident, or Life, *or
Life and* Accident, or Guarantee, or Surety company, the capital
stock shall be not less than $500,000, with liberty to increase the
same to $1,000,000 with the assent of the Lieutenant-Governor
in Council; and before applying for license the company 45
shall furnish to the Inspector satisfactory evidence that
of the said capital stock at least $300,000 has been sub-
scribed for and taken up *bona fide*, and that $30,000
of the said subscribed stock has been paid into some chartered
bank. (*cf.* 49 Vic. c. 86.) 50

(2.) If a live stock insurance company, the capital stock shall
be at the least $300,000, with liberty to increase the same as
in the first sub-section to $500,000, of which, as in said sub-

section, $150,000 shall be shewn to have been subscribed, and $15,000 to have been paid into some chartered bank. (*cf.* 37 V. c. 88.)

(3) If a plate glass insurance company, or a company insuring 5 against the explosion of steam boilers, the capital stock shall be at the least $100,000, with liberty to increase the same as in the first sub-section to $250,000, of which as in said subsection $60 000 shall be shewn to have been subscribed, and $6,000 to have been paid into some chartered bank. (*cf.* Dom. 10 Act, 38 V. c. 95.)

7. The corporate powers of any company whether incorporated under this Act or under any special Act shall be forfeited by non-user during three years after the date of its incorporation; or if, after a company has undertaken contracts 15 within the intent of this Act, such company discontinues business for one year; or if its license remains suspended for one year; or if its license is cancelled otherwise than by mere effluxion of time and is not renewed within the period limited in the 46th section; and thereupon the company's corporate 20 powers shall *ipso facto* cease and determine, except for the sole purpose of winding up its affairs; and the High Court, upon the petition of the Attorney-General, or of any person interested, may by decree limit the time within which the company shall settle and close its accounts, and may for this 25 specific purpose, or for the purpose of liquidation generally, appoint a receiver. R.S.O. 1887, c. 150, s, 63, and Public Statutes of Mass., 119, ss. 24, 37, 50.

Corporate power forfeited by non-user, or discontinuance of business; or suspension or cancellation of license; except for winding-up; which may be limited by decree. Receiver.

TITLE II.—FORMATION AND INCORPORATION OF MUTUAL AND CASH-MUTUAL FIRE INSURANCE COMPANIES.

30 **8.** Ten freeholders in any municipality or association of municipalities may call a meeting of the freeholders thereof to consult whether it be expedient to establish therein a Fire Insurance company upon the mutual or cash-mutual principle. R. S, O. 1877, c. 161, s. 1.

Meetings to establish Companies, how called.

35 **9.** The meeting shall be called by advertisement, mentioning the time and place and object of the meeting; and the advertisement shall be published [once in' the *Ontario Gazette* and] for three weeks in one or more of the newspapers published in the County. *cf.* R. S. O. 1877, c. 161, s. 2.

Advertisement calling such meeting.

40 **10.** If thirty freeholders of the municipality are present at the meeting, and a majority of them determine that it is expedient to establish a Mutual [or Cash-Mutual Fire Insurance] company, they may elect three persons from among them to open and keep a subscription book, in which owners of 45 property, movable or immovable, within the Province of Ontario, may sign their names, and enter the sums for which they shall respectively bind themselves to effect insurances with the company. R. S. O. 1877' c. 161, s. 3.

Subscription books.

11. Where fifty or more persons, being owners of movable or immovable property in the Province of Ontario, have 50 signed their names in the subscription book, and bound themselves to effect insurances in the company, which in the aggre-

When meeting may be called.

gate shall amount to $100,000 at least, a meeting shall be called, as hereinafter provided. R. S. O. 1877, c. 161, ss. 4, 33.

How meeting to be called.

12.—(1) As soon as convenient after the subscription book has been completed in manner aforesaid, any ten of the subscribers thereto may call the first meeting of the Company, at such time and place within the municipality as they may determine; such meeting shall be called by sending a printed notice by mail, addressed to every subscriber at his post office address, at least ten days before the day of the meeting, and by advertisement in one or more papers published in the county in which the municipality is situated.

(2) The said notice and advertisement shall contain the object of the meeting, and the time and place at which it is to be held. R. S. O. 1877, c. 161, s. 5.

Election of directors.

13.—(1) At such meeting the name and style of the company, including the appellations " Fire " and " Mutual," shall be adopted, and a Secretary *ad interim* appointed, and a Board of Directors elected as hereinafter provided (*post s.* 74 *et seq.*) and the place named at which the head office of the company shall be located. R. S. O. 1877, c. 161, s. 6; 48 Vic. c. 36. s. 1.

(2) To constitute a valid meeting for the purposes of the first subsection, at least twenty-five of the aforesaid subscribers must be present.

(3) In case of a county or township the head office may be in any city, town, or village within the boundaries of the county or township or adjacent thereto.

Names of directors to be filed in registry office.

14. Copies of the resolutions adopting the name or style and the place of the head office of the company, and of the subscription book, and the names of the directors elected shall thereupon be made ; and all such documents certified as correct under the hands of the chairman and secretary, shall be filed in the Registry Office. R. S. O. 1877, c. 161, s. 7.

Thereon the corporation formed.

15.—(1) Upon the filing of said documents, with the certificate, the subscribers above mentioned, and all other persons thereafter effecting insurances in the company, shall become members of the company and shall be a body corporate by and under the name so adopted. R.S.O. 1877, c. 161, s. 8; 44 V. c. 20, s. 26.

Forfeiture of corporate powers.

[(2) But the corporate powers of the company shall be forfeited by non-user, or by discontinuance of business, or by suspension or cancellation of license as is provided in section 7, which section shall in all respects apply as well to Mutual and Cash-Mutual companies as to joint stock companies. *cf.* R. S. O. 1877, c. 150, s. 63; and Public Statutes of Mass., 119, ss. 24, 37, 50.]

Meeting of directors to elect president and officers.

16. As soon after the aforesaid meeting as convenient, the Secretary *ad interim* shall call a meeting of the Board of directors, for the election of a President and Vice-President from amongst themselves, for the appointment of a Secretary, Treasurer, or Manager, and the transaction of such other business as may be brought before them. R. S. O. 1877, c. 161, s. 9.

Copies of resolutions, subscription

17. After the company has filed in the registry office, the documents mentioned in section 14, and before the com-

pany shall transact or be entitled to transact any insurance books, and business, the chairman and secretary shall transmit or deliver statements of proposed busi- like copies duly certified by them to be true copies [and endorsed ness to be by the Registrar as having been duly filed] to the transmitted to Insurance
5 Inspector at his office in Toronto, accompanied by a statement Inspector. signed by the chairman and secretary, stating the kind and character of the risks intended to be taken by the company, that is to say, whether the business to be transacted is the insurance of farm and isolated buildings and property, or of
10 mercahtile, manufacturing and other hazardous and extra hazardous properties, or of both; [also whether the company has been organized and incorporated as a Mutual or as a Cash-Mutual company.] 44 V. c. 20, s. 1.

18. Upon receipt of such certified copies and of the afore- Inquiries to be made by
15 said statement by the Inspector, he shall proceed to ascertain Inspector whether the proceedings for the incorporation of the company after receiving have been taken in accordance with the law in that behalf, statement. and whether the subscriptions are *bona fide*, and by persons possessing property to insure, and whether the proposed name
20 is the same as that of any existing company, or may be easily confounded therewith, and he may require the declaration of any person or persons upon oath to be filed with him, touching any matters concerning which he is called upon to make inquiry. 44 V. c. 20, s. 2.

25 **19.** If, upon examination, the Inspector shall find that the On report of Inspector said subscriptions have been made in good faith by persons Treasurer may entitled to make the same, and that the proposed name is sat- issue license. isfactory, and that the company has complied with this Act in respect of deposit, and in all other respects, the Treasurer may
30 thereupon issue a license under his hand and seal setting forth that it has been made to appear to him that the company has complied with the requirements of the law; and that the company is accordingly licensed to transact the kind of business specified in the license, for a term therein also specified, but
35 not exceeding twelve months from the date of issue; but such license may from time to time be renewed as hereinafter provided. [*cf.* 44 V. c. 20, s. 3; but annual license substituted for certificate of authority to transact business.]

TITLE III.—CHANGE OF NAME OR OF HEAD OFFICE.—(*All*
40 *Companies.*)

20. Where any company is desirous of adopting a name Change of differing from that by which it was incorporated; or where in name. the opinion of the Lieutenant-Governor in Council the name by which such company within the legislative authority of this
45 Province was incorporated, may be easily confounded with that of any other existing company, the Lieutenant-Governor in Council, upon being satisfied that a change of name will not work or effect any improper purpose, may by Order in Council change the name of the company to some other name to be set
50 forth in the Order in Council; but no such change of name shall affect the rights or obligations of the company; and all proceedings which might have been continued or commenced by or against the company by its former name may be continued and commenced by or against the company by its new
55 name. 44 V. c. 20, s. 24; 46 V. c. 15, s. 4, *part.*

Change of head office. **21.**—(1) The head office of any company may be removed from one municipality to another by authority of the Lieutenant-Governor in Council. 46 V. c. 15, s. 4, *part*.

(2) In other cases the present location of head offices of companies in existence, and the original location of head offices 5 of companies hereafter to be formed, shall only be changed by a two-thirds vote of the members [or shareholders] of the company at a special meeting called for that purpose. R. S. O. 1877, c. 161, s. 70 ; 46 V. c. 15, s. 4, *part*.

(3) Where any company is entitled to remove its head 10 office from one place to another, without the consent of the Lieutenant-Governor in Council, notice of any such change and of any resolution or by-law authorizing the same, shall be forthwith given by the secretary of the company to the Inspector of Insurance. 46 V. c. 15, s. 4. 15

Notice of application for change of name. **22.** The Lieutenant-Governor in Council may require the same notice to be given upon any application for such change of name [or of head office] as is required upon an application for Letters Patent by the Act entitled "*An Act respecting the Incorporation of Joint Stock Companies by Letters Patent.*" 20 44 V. c. 20, s. 25.

[**23.** Notice of any change of name or of head office shall be forthwith inserted by the company in the *Ontario Gazette*.]

TITLE IV.—BRANCHES AND DEPARTMENTS IN MUTUAL AND CASH-MUTUAL FIRE INSURANCE COMPANIES.
25

Establishment of branches. **24.** Any Mutual [or Cash-Mutual] Company may, [with the previous assent of the Lieutenant-Governor in Council,] separate its business into branches or departments, with reference to the nature or classification of the risks, or of the localities in which insurances may be effected. R. S. O. 1877, c. 161, s. 64. 30

Scale of risks to be made for each branch. **25.** The Directors of every such company so separating its business shall make a scale of risks and tariff of rates for each branch, and direct that the accounts of each shall be kept separate and distinct the one from the other. R. S. O. 1877, c. 161, s. 65. 35

Expenses to be divided between branches proportionately. **26.** All necessary expenses incurred in the conducting and management of such companies shall be assessed upon and divided between the several branches in such proportion as the directors determine. R. S. O. 1877, c. 161, s. 67.

TITLE V.—GUARANTEE CAPITAL IN MUTUAL OR CASH-MUTUAL FIRE INSURANCE COMPANIES.
40

Power to raise a guarantee capital. **27.** Any Mutual or Cash-Mutual Fire Insurance Company, incorporated under this Act or any former Act, may raise by subscription of its members, or some of them, or by the admis-

9

sion of new members not being persons insured in the company, or by loan or otherwise, a guarantee capital of any sum not less than $20,000, nor exceeding $200,000, which guarantee capital shall belong to the company and be liable for all the
5 losses, debts and expenses of the company ; and subscribers of such capital shall, in respect thereof, have such rights as the directors of the company declare and fix by a by-law to be passed before the capital is subscribed, and unless the capital is paid off or discharged, the by-law shall not be repealed or
10 altered [without the prior assent of the Lieutenant-Governor in Council] nor without the consent of the majority of votes of the shareholders or subscribers of such capital who represent a majority of the shares subscribed, either personally or by proxy, at a meeting held for that purpose of the holders of such
15 capital, each shareholder or subscriber being entitled to a vote for every share of $50 held by him. 44 V. c. 20, s. 7.

28.—(1) The capital shall be subscribed by not less than Limitations as ten persons, and no one person shall subscribe, or hold, or receive to guarantee dividends, interest or commissions upon, more than twenty per capital.
20 centum of the guaranteed capital of the stock ; the original list of the subscribers to the guarantee capital shall be transferred to and be deposited with the Treasurer of this Province, and shall be held as security for the payment of all losses and other policy liabilities of such companies.

25 (2) The company may from time to time, in accordance with Calls upon the provisions of any by-law in that behalf [approved by the guarantee Lieutenant-Governor in Council,] require any portion of the capital. subscribed guarantee capital to be paid over to the company for the purpose of settling any losses of the company. Any
30 sums so advanced shall be repaid by the company within one year thereafter from the proceeds of assessments upon the premium notes liable to assessment for the purpose, and assessments may be made from time to time by the company for the purpose of repaying the advances. 44 V. c. 20, s. 8.

35 [**29.** In substitution for the subscription list of guarantee Substitution capital deposited as security with the Treasurer, the company of other may, with the Treasurer's consent, deposit cash or unconditional securities. securities for cash of the kind and to the amount prescribed in section 40 of this Act ; and the Treasurer shall thereupon
40 release and discharge the said subscription list.]

TITLE VI.—SHARE OR STOCK CAPITAL IN MUTUAL OR CASH-MUTUAL FIRE INSURANCE COMPANIES.

30. Any Mutual [or Cash-Mutual] Fire Insurance Company, Power to raise incorporated under this or any former Act, may [with the prior share capital.
45 assent of the Lieutenant-Governor in Council] raise a share or stock capital of not less than $100,000, and may [with the like assent] increase the same from time to time to a sum not exceeding $500,000 : [Provided that the same public notice as that prescribed by section 9 has been given by the com-
50 pany of its intention to raise, or to increase such capital.] 44 V. c. 20, s. 11.

31. Every subscriber shall, on allotment of one or more Subscribers to shares to him, become a member of the company ; with all become members of company. 44 V. c. 20, s. 12. pany.
66—2

Transfer of shares.

32. The shares shall be personal estate, and shall be transferable, but no transfer shall be valid unless made on the books of the company; and, until fully paid up, no share shall be transferable without the consent of the board of directors, nor shall any transfer be valid while any call previously 5 made remains unpaid; and the company shall have a lien on the shares of any shareholder for unpaid calls or other debts due by him to the company, and for any obligation held by the company against him; and after any call, debt or obligation becomes due, the company may, upon one month's notice to the 10 shareholder, his executors, or administrators, sell his shares or a sufficient portion thereof to pay the call, debt or obligation, and transfer the shares so sold to the purchaser. 44 V. c. 20, s. 13.

Forfeiture of shares.

33. The company may, also, after default made in the pay- 15 ment of any call upon any share for one month, and after notice having been first given as in the next preceding section mentioned, declare the share and all sums previously paid thereon, forfeited to the company, and the company may sell or re-issue forfeited shares on such terms as they think fit for 20 the benefit of the company. 44 V. c. 20, s. 14.

When company may make insurances for premiums payable wholly in cash.

34. After the sum of $100,000 of the stock or share capital has been *bona fide* subscribed, and twenty per centum paid thereon into the funds of the company, the company may make insurances for premiums payable wholly in cash; 25 but no insurance on the wholly cash principle shall make the insured a member of the company, or make him liable to contribute or pay any sum to the company, or to its funds, or to any other member thereof, beyond the cash premium agreed upon, or give him any right to a participation in the profits 30 or surplus funds of the company, but the company shall not transact any business wholly on the cash principle without first procuring a license from the Treasurer, pursuant to this Act. 44 V. c. 20, s. 15.

Dividends.

35. The net annual profits and gains of the company 35 not including therein any premium notes or undertakings shall be applied, in the first place, to pay a dividend on the share capital, not exceeding the rate of ten per centum per annum, and the surplus, if any, shall be applied in the manner provided by the by-laws of the company. 44 V. c. 20, s. 16, 40

Qualification of directors.

36. After the share capital has been subscribed as aforesaid, at least two-thirds of the persons to be elected directors of the company in addition to the qualifications required by section 74 of this Act, shall be holders of shares of the capital stock to the amount of $3,000, on which all calls have been 45 fully paid; the other one-third of the directors to be elected shall possess at least the qualifications required by section 74. 44 V. c. 20 s. 17.

By-laws.

37. The board of directors of any company which shall raise a share or stock capital under this Act, may make such 50 by-laws, subject to the provisions of this Act and not inconsistent with or contrary to law, as may be necessary to carry out the objects and intentions of this Act, and to give effect to the provisions thereof; and may rescind, alter, vary, or add to the same from time to time. 44 V. c. 20, s. 18.

38. Any Mutual or [Cash-Mutual Fire] Insurance Company *How a mutual* heretofore incorporated or organized, or .which may be here- *company may become a* after incorporated or organized under any of the laws of this *stock com-* Province, having surplus assets, aside from premium notes or *pany.*
5 undertakings, sufficient to reinsure all its outstanding risks, after having given notice once a week for four weeks of their intention, and of the meeting hereinafter provided for, in the *Ontario Gazette* and in a newspaper published in the the County where the company is located, may, with the
10 consent of two-thirds of the members present at any regular annual meeting, and of two-thirds of the subscribers of guarantee capital or share or stock capital, or at any special meeting duly called for the purpose, or with the consent, in writing, of two-thirds of the members of the company, and
15 the consent, also, of three-fourths of the directors, and of two-thirds of the subscribers to the guarantee capital and share or stock capital, may, as provided in section 4 of this Act, be formed into a joint stock company under *The Ontario Joint Stock Companies Letters Patent Act,* application hav-
20 ing been made in terms of that Act; and every member of such company, on the day of said annual or special meeting, or the date of the written consent, shall be entitled to priority in subscribing to the capital stock of the company, for one month after the opening of the books of subscription
25 to the capital stock, in proportion to the amount of insurance held by such members on unexpired risks in force on the day of the annual or special meeting, or the date of the written consent; and every company so changed or organized shall come under and be subject to the provisions of the said last
30 mentioned Act as provided in section 4 of this Act. 44 V. c. 20, s. 19. ●

39. Any company which may be formed under the provi- *New company* sions of the last preceding section shall be answerable for all *to be answerable for liabili* the liabilities of the company from which it has been formed, *ties of former* 35 and may be sued therefor by or under its new corporate name, *company.* and the assets, real and personal, of the old company shall pass to and become vested in the new company. 44 V. c. 20, s. 20.

TITLE VI.—GOVERNMENT DEPOSITS. (ALL COMPANIES.)

[**40**.—(1) Except Mutual Fire Insurance companies licensed
40 only for the insurance of farm buildings and isolated risks, every company shall, before the original issue or renewal of the license, lodge with the Treasurer either in cash, or in any stock, debentures, or other securities in which trustees may invest trust money, the initial or renewal deposits respectively below
45 stated: Provided that this section, in so far as it amends the statutes heretofore in force shall not apply to such companies as have heretofore reported to the Department of the Treasurer ; *Application of* *section.* but shall, from the passing of this Act, apply to all other companies thereafter licensed. 49 V. c. 16, s. 24 ; 42 V. c. 21, s. 1 ;
50 R.S.O. c. 107, s. 28.

(2) The initial deposit to be made by any company before *Initial de-* the original issue of the license shall be the sum appointed for *posits.* such company in the 4th sub-section of this section. R. S. O. c. 160, s. 6 (1).

Renewal
deposits.

(3) Before the annual renewal of licenses the amount of deposit required of any company shall on or before the first day of July in each year be readjusted in terms of the next following two sub-sections. R. S. O. c. 160, s. 6 (1).

Deposits for
contingent
liability of
$2,000,000 and
under.

(4) If on the preceding 31st day of December in any year 5 the company's total contingent liability or amount at risk does not exceed two millions of dollars ;

Then every Joint Stock Fire, or Fire and Inland-Marine Insurance company, and every Life, or Life and Accident company, and every Guarantee and Surety company shall keep 10 on deposit with the Provincial Treasurer, if a Provincial or Canadian company, $25,000 [and if a foreign company $50,000]. R. S. O. c. 169, s. 6 (1);

Every Accident company, if Provincial or Canadian, shall keep on deposit with the Provincial Treasurer, $20,000 [and if a 15 Joint Stock foreign company, $40,000]. R. S. O. 1877, c. 160, s. 6 (1);

Every Provincial Mutual Fire, or Fire and Inland-Marine company, insuring mercantile and manufacturing risks shall keep on deposit with the Provincial Treasurer, $5,000 ; and 20 every Provincial Cash-Mutual Fire, or Fire and Inland-Marine company insuring mercantile and manufacturing risks, $10,000.

Every Live Stock Insurance company shall keep on deposit as aforesaid, if Provincial or Canadian, $10,000 ; and if foreign Joint Stock, $25,000 ; 25

Every Plate Glass Insurance company, and every company insuring against the explosion of steam boilers shall keep on deposit, as aforesaid, if Provincial or Canadian, $5,000 ; and if foreign Joint Stock, $10,000.

Additional
deposit for
each addi-
tional million
or fraction
thereof.

(5) If on the preceding 31st day of December in any year, 30 the company's total contingent liability, or the amount at risk, exceeds two millions of dollars, then for each additional million, or fraction thereof, the companies enumerated in the sub-section next preceding shall respectively keep on deposit, with the Provincial Treasurer, by way of additional security, a sum 35 equal to one-fifth of the initial deposit ; and the additional deposit shall be either in cash or securities as aforesaid. R.S.O. c. 160, s. 6 (1).]

Deposits, in
what securi-
ties.

41.—(1) Securities of the Dominion of Canada, or securities issued by any of the Provinces of Canada, shall be accepted at 40 their market value at the time when they are deposited.

(2) The other securities above specified shall be accepted at such valuation and on such conditions as the Treasurer may direct.

If market
value declines
company to
make further
deposit.

(3) If the market value of any of the securities which have 45 been deposited by any company declines below the value at which they were deposited, the Treasurer may, from time to time, call upon the company to make a further deposit, so that the market value of all the securities deposited by any com-

pany shall be equal to the amount which they are required to deposit by this Act. R. S. O. 1877, c. 160, s. 7.

(4) Where any security, obligation or covenant, or any interest in any real or personal estate, effects, or property is given, or transferred to, made with, or vested in the Treasurer of Ontario, by virtue of his office of Treasurer, such security, obligation or covenant, and any right of action in respect thereto, and all the estate, right or interest of the said Treasurer in respect of such real or personal estate, effects or property upon the death, resignation or removal from office of the Treasurer, from time to time, and as often as the case happens and the appointment of a successor takes place, shall, subject to the same trusts as the same were respectively subject to, vest in the succeeding Treasurer by virtue of this Act, and shall and may be proceeded on by any action or in any other manner, or may be assigned, transferred or discharged, in the name of such succeeding Treasurer as the same might have been proceeded on, assigned, transferred or discharged by the Treasurer to, with or in whom they were first given, transferred, made, or vested if he had continued to hold office. 47 V. c. 6. s. 1. *Securities, etc., vested in Treasurer of Ontario by virtue of his office, to vest in his successor.*

(5) Every such security, obligation, covenant or interest in real or personal estate, effects and property may in like manner as in the last section mentioned be proceeded on, assigned, transferred or discharged by and in the name of any member of the Executive Council of Ontario, acting under the authority of section 3 of the *Revised Statute respecting the Executive Council.* 47 V. c. 6, s. 2. *Assignment, etc., of securities.*

(6) The fourth sub-section shall apply to every security, obligation or covenant, and every interest in real or personal estate, effects or property given or transferred to, made with, or vested in any former Treasurer of Ontario, by virtue or on account of his office, and shall transfer all the interest, rights and estate of the former Treasurer to the present Treasurer of Ontario, to be vested in him by virtue of his office and subject to the provisions of this Act. 47 V. c. 6, s. 3. *Application of sub-sect. 4.*

(7) Where any company desires to substitute other securities within the 40th section for securities deposited with the Treasurer, the Treasurer, if he thinks fit, may permit the substitution to be made. 47 V. c. 6, s. 4. *Treasurer may allow companies to change securities deposited with him.*

42. A company may deposit in the hands of the Treasurer any sums of money or securities of the kind prescribed by the 40th section, beyond the sum by the said section required ; and such further sums of money or securities shall be dealt with as if the same had been part of the original deposit ; and no part of the additional deposit shall be withdrawn except with the sanction of the Lieutenant-Governor in Council. R. S. O. 1877, c. 160, s. 11. *Company may deposit beyond the amount absolutely required.* *As to withdrawal of surplus.*

43. A company having made a deposit under this Act shall be entitled to withdraw the deposit, with the sanction of the Lieutenant-Governor in Council, whenever it is made to appear to the satisfaction of the Lieutenant-Governor in Council that the company is carrying on its business of insurance under license from the Dominion of Canada. R. S. O. 1877, c. 160, s. 12. *Withdrawal of deposit where company licensed by Dominion.*

Any deficiency of security to be made good or license forfeited.

44. If from the annual statements, or after examination of the affairs and condition of any company, it appears that the re-insurance value of all its risks outstanding in Ontario, together with any other liabilities in Ontario, exceeds its assets in Ontario, including the deposit in the hands of the Treasurer, 5 then the company shall be called upon by the Treasurer to make good the deficiency at once, and on failure so to do, its license shall be cancelled, [and its corporate powers shall thereupon cease and determine, except for the purpose of winding up its affairs as provided in section 7.] R. S. O. 1877, c. 160, 10 ss. 13, 3.

As to interest on securities.

45. Except in cases with respect to which it may be otherwise provided by the Lieutenant-Governor in Council, so long as any company's deposit is unimpaired and no notice of any final judgment or order to the contrary is served upon the 15 Provincial Treasurer, the interest upon the securities forming the deposit shall be handed over to the company. R. S. O. 1877, c. 160, s. 14.

Licenses forfeited by failure to deposit, non-payment of claims and consequent deficiency of security.

46. Where a company fails to make the deposits under this Act at the time required, or where written notice has been 20 served on the Provincial Treasurer of an undisputed claim arising from loss insured against in Ontario remaining unpaid for the space of sixty days after being due, or of a disputed claim after final judgment in a regular course of law and tender of a legal valid discharge being unpaid, so that the amount 25 of securities representing the deposit of the company is liable to be reduced by sale of any portion thereof, the license of the company shall *ipso facto* be null and void, and shall be deemed to be cancelled as in section 44; but the license may in the two last mentioned cases be 30

Renewal on certain conditions.

renewed, and the company may again transact business, if within sixty days after notice to the Provincial Treasurer of the company's failure to pay any undisputed claim, or the amount of any final judgment as provided in this section, such undisputed claims or final judgments upon or 35 against the company in Ontario are paid and satisfied, and the company's deposit is no longer liable to be reduced below the amount required by this Act. R. S. O. 1877, c. 160, s. 20.

Government deposit security for certain contracts only.

47. The securities deposited with the Treasurer shall be subject to administration only in respect of any contract which 40 falls within section 2, and which further has for its subject some property in the Province, or property in transit to or from the Province, or the life, safety, health, fidelity, or insurable interest of some resident of the Province, or where the contract itself makes the payment thereunder primarily pay- 45 able to some resident of the Province. 46 V. c. 15, s. 14.

When a company shall be liable to have deposits administered.

48.—(1) Any company shall be liable to have its deposits in the hands of the Treasurer administered in manner hereinafter mentioned upon the failure of the company to pay any undisputed claim arising under any contract within section 47 50 for the space of sixty days after being due, or, if disputed, after final judgment and tender of a legal valid discharge, and (in either case) after notice thereof to the Provincial Treasurer, [and to the Inspector of Insurance.] In case of such administration,

all deposits of the company, held by the Treasurer, shall be Provisions for
applied *pro rata* towards the payment of all claims duly au- application of
thenticated against the company, as well as in respect of unearned deposits in such case.
premiums, [such being claims and premiums under the
5 contracts aforesaid,] and the distribution of the proceeds of such
deposits may be made by order of the High Court.

(2) In any case where a claim [accruing on the occurrence of Proviso, if
any event] is by the terms of the contract payable on proof of delay was given for the
such occurrence, without any stipulated delay, the notice payment of
10 required under this section shall not be given until after the any loss.
lapse of sixty days from the time when the claim becomes due.
R. S. O. 1877, c. 160, s. 21.

49. Before an application is made to a court for the sur- Surrender of
render of a company's deposit with the Government at least ten deposit.
15 days' notice of such intended application shall be served on the
Treasurer or his deputy, and also upon the Inspector of Insurance ; and the notice shall designate the Court to which application is proposed to be made, and shall state the day named
for the hearing of the same. 46 V. c. 15, s. 12.

20 **50.**—(1) Upon granting an order for administration as afore- Appointment
said, the Court shall appoint a receiver, who may be an officer of receiver; his duty.
of the Court, who shall forthwith call upon the company to
furnish a statement of all its outstanding [contracts, being within
the sections 2 and 47,] and upon all [claimants under such
25 contracts] to file their claims ; and upon the filing of the claims Proceedings in
before the receiver, the parties interested shall have the right case of admin-
of contestation thereof, and the right of appeal from the deci- istration.
sion of the receiver to the court as aforesaid, according to the
practice of the Court ; and in case of any such administration, What may be
30 the claimants aforesaid shall be entitled to claim for a part of claimed by parties insured
the premiums paid proportionate to the unexpired period of in Ontario.
their [contracts] respectively, and such [unearned] premiums shall
rank with judgments obtained and claims accrued, in the distribution of the assets ; and upon the completion of the schedule
35 to be prepared by the receiver of all judgments against the Sale of securi-
company upon the said outstanding [contracts,] and of all claims ties deposited.
for unearned premiums or for surrender of policies, the Court
shall cause the securities held by the Treasurer for the company,
or any part of them, to be sold in such manner and after such
40 notice and formalities as the Court appoints ; and the proceeds
thereof, after paying expenses incurred, shall be distributed
pro rata amongst the claimants according to the schedule,
and the balance, if any, shall be surrendered to the company.
But, if any claim arises within section 47 after the state- If further loss
45 ment of the said outstanding contracts has been obtained from occurs and
the company, as hereinbefore provided, and before the final deposits do not cover
order of the Court for the distribution of the proceeds of the claims.
securities, or if the proceeds of the securities are not sufficient
to cover in full all claims recorded in the schedule, such addi-
50 tional claimants shall not be barred from any recourse they
may have against the company in respect of such deficiency.

(2) The Court, by the order appointing a receiver, or by any Court may
subsequent order, may authorize the receiver to exercise in confer upon
55 respect of the accounts of the company all or any of the pow- receiver the power of a
ers which the Master in Ordinary would have if he were tak- Master.

ing an account of the claims against the said deposit, and every receiver so authorized shall possess the said powers as well as the powers usually enjoyed by a receiver appointed under an order of the said Court. R. S. O. 1877, c. 160, s. 22.

Duty of Company ceasing business.

51. Where a company has ceased to transact business in 5 Ontario, and has given written notice to that effect to the Treasurer, [and to the Inspector,] it shall re-insure [all such outstanding contracts as are within section 47] in some company or companies licensed to do business in Ontario, or obtain a discharge of such contracts, and its securities shall not 10 be delivered to the company until the same is done, to the satisfaction of the Treasurer. R. S. O. 1877, c. 160, s. 23.

Conditions on which deposits may be released.

52. Upon making application for its securities, the company shall file with the [Inspector] a list of [all contracts within the 47th section] which have not been so re-insured or 15 have not been [discharged]; and it shall at the same time publish in the *Ontario Gazette* a notice that it has applied to Government for the release of its securities on a certain day, not less than three months after the date of the notice, and calling upon [all claimants, contingent or actual,] opposing the release 20 to file their opposition with the [Inspector] on or before the day so named ; and after that day, if the Treasurer is satisfied that the company has ample assets to meet its liabilities [under section 47,] all the securities may be released to the Company by an order of the Lieutenant-Governor in Council, or a suffi- 25 cient amount of them may be retained to cover the [claims filed] ; and the remainder may be released, and thereafter from time to time as such opposing [claims] lapse, or proof is adduced that they have been satisfied, further releases may be made on the authority aforesaid. R. S. O. 1877, c. 160, s. 24. 30

Title VIII.—License—(*All Companies.*)

Certain documents to be filed before license is granted ; what they must show.

53. (1) Before the issue of a license to a company [not incorporated by Provincial authority,] the company shall file in the office of the [Inspector,] a certified copy of the Act of incorporation, or other instrument of association of the company, 35 and also a power of attorney from the company to its [chief] officer or agent in the Province, under the seal of the company, and signed by the president and secretary or other proper officer thereof, containing the matters hereinafter mentioned, verified by their oath, and further corroborated on oath 40 by the said chief officer or agent in the Province, or by some person cognizant of the facts necessary to its verification, and also a statement of the condition and affairs of the company on the 31st day of December then next preceding, or up to the usual balancing day of the company (but such day shall not be 45 more than twelve months before the filing of the statement), in such form as may be required by the Treasurer of Ontario.

Contents of power of attorney.

(2) The power of attorney shall declare at what place in the Province the chief agency of the company is, or is to be established, and shall expressly authorize the attorney to 50 receive process in all actions and proceedings against the company in the Province for any liabilities incurred by the company

therein, and shall declare that service of process for or in respect of such liabilities at chief agency, or personally on the attorney, at the place where such chief agency is established, shall be legal and binding on the company to all intents and purposes.

5 (3) Whenever a company licensed under this Act changes *If changes are made in chief* its chief agent or chief agency in Ontario, the company shall *agency, docu-* file a power of attorney as hereinbefore mentioned, specifying *ment to be* the change, and containing a similar declaration as to service *filed.* of process as hereinbefore mentioned.

10 (4) Duplicates of all such documents duly verified as afore- *Such docu-* said shall be filed at Toronto, in the office of the Clerk of the *ments to be filed iu Court.* Process. R. S. O. 1877, c. 160, s. 15.

(5) There shall be kept in the office of the [Inspector] *Certain re-* a record of the several documents filed by every *cords to be kept in the* 15 company under this section, and under the heading of *Treasury De-* the company shall be entered the securities deposited *partment.* on its account with the Provincial Treasurer, naming in detail the several securities, their par value, and value *Terms where-* at which they are received as deposit; and before the *on license may* 20 issue of a new license, or the renewal of a license to a com- *be renewed.* pany, the requirements of the law shall be complied with by the company, and the statement of its affairs must show that it is in a condition to meet its liabilities ; and a record of the licenses as they are issued or renewed shall also be kept 25 in the office of the [Inspector]. R. S. O. 1877, c. 160, s. 29.

54. (1) After the certified copies referred to in the last pre- *Process and* ceding section and the power of attorney are filed as aforesaid, *actions.* any process in any action or proceeding against the company, for liabilities incurred in the Province, may be served on 30 the company at its chief agency, and all proceedings may be had thereupon to judgment and execution in the same manner and with the same force and effect as in the proceedings in civil action in the Province.

(2) Nothing herein contained shall render invalid service in *Service other-* 35 any other mode in which the company may be lawfully *wise than as above.* served. R. S. O. 1877, c. 160, s. 16.

55. Except companies licensed by the Treasurer, and, *Companies re-* companies specified in section 3, it shall not be *qu'red to be licensed.* lawful for a company to undertake or effect or solicit, 40 or to agree or offer to undertake or effect, any con- tract within the intent of section 2, whether the contract be original or renewed ; or to accept, or agree or negotiate for any premium or other consideration for the con- tract ; or to prosecute or maintain any action or proceeding 45 in respect of the contract, except such actions or proceedings as arise in winding up the affairs of the company under the 7th section. R. S. O. 1877, c. 160, s. 3.

56. Any director, officer, agent, employee, or other person who, *Penalty for* in contravention of the 55th section undertakes or effects, or *transacting* 50 agrees or offers to undertake or effect, or solicits, any contract or *business in contravention* collects any premium in behalf of any company, without the *of this Act.* company being licensed under this Act, or if such license has been withdrawn, without the renewal thereof, or

3—In.

without filing the copy of the Act of incorporation, or other instrument of association of the company, and the power of attorney or any renewal thereof in the event of any change as hereinbefore provided, shall be liable to a penalty of $200 for every such contravention of this Act, which penalty may be sued for and recovered on information filed in the name of the Attorney-General of Ontario ; and one-half of the penalty, when recovered, shall be paid for the use of the Province, and the other half of the penalty to the informer ; and in case of non-payment of the penalty and costs within one month after judgment, the person so offending shall be liable to imprisonment in any gaol or prison for a period not exceeding three months, in the discretion of the Court wherein he is convicted. R.S.O. 1877, c. 160, s. 19; 44 V. c. 20, s. 23.

How enforced and applied.

57. The license shall be in such form as may be from time to time determined by the Treasurer, and shall specify the business to be carried on by the company ; and shall expire on the thirtieth day of June in each year, but shall be renewable from year to year. R. S. O. 1877, c. 160, s. 4.

Form of license.

58. As soon as the company applying for a license has deposited with the Treasurer the securities hereinbefore mentioned, and has otherwise conformed to the requirements of this Act, the Treasurer [may] issue the license. R. S. O. 1877, c. 160 s. 5.

When license shall issue.

59. Every company obtaining a license shall forthwith give due notice thereof in the *Ontario Gazette,* and in at least one newspaper in the county, city, or place where the head office or chief agency is established, and shall continue the publication thereof once each week for the space of four weeks: and the like notice shall be given for the same period when the company ceases, or notifies that it intends to cease, to carry on business in Ontario. R. S. O. 1877, c. 160, s. 17.

Companies to give notice of license.

and of ceasing business.

60.—(1) Where a company desires to extend its business to some other branch within the intent of this Act, and has complied with the law in respect of additional deposit and otherwise, the Treasurer may on the report of the Inspector issue to the company a supplementary license authorizing it to undertake such other branch of business.

(2) When a supplementary license is granted. it shall be recorded in the books of the Inspector and filed in the same registry office as the original or prior license.

(3) The provisions herein enacted as to the continuance, renewal, suspension, and cancellation of licenses, shall equally apply to supplementary licenses. 44. V. c. 20, s. 6; 47 V. c. 28, s. 1.

61. After a company has ceased to transact business in Ontario after the notice hereby required, and its license has in consequence been withdrawn, the company shall nevertheless pay the losses arising from policies not re-insured or surrendered, as if the license had not been withdrawn. R. S. O, 1877, c. 160, s. 25.

Company ceasing business in certain cases to pay losses.

62. The Provincial Treasurer shall cause to be published *Statement to* half-yearly in the *Ontario Gazette*, a list of companies licensed *be published by Provincial* under this Act, with the amount of the deposit made by each *Treasurer.* company ; and upon a new company being licensed, or upon 5 the license of a company being withdrawn in the interval between two such half-yearly statements, he shall publish a a notice thereof in the *Ontario Gazette* for the space of two weeks. R. S. O. 1877, c. 160, s. 18.

10

TITLE IX.—FEES.—(*All Companies.*)

63.—Each company respectively shall pay to the treasurer the following fees :—

(1) For recording and filing in the office of the inspector the documents required by sections 4, 17, 53. [New as to ss. 4, 17.. $ 10 00

(2) For change of attorney under section 53............... 5 00
Application for change of name or of head office [new].... 10 00

(3) For initial license to do business :—

Joint stock company............................. 100 00
Cash-Mutual company.......... .... 50 00
Mutual....................................... 25 00

(4) For each annual renewal of license :—

Joint stock company............................. 50 00
Cash-Mutual company............................ 25 00
Mutual (new) 5 00

(5) For each Supplementary License :—

Initial 20 00
Renewal 10 00

(6) For filing annual statements :—

Joint stock company................................ 5 00
Cash-Mutual company................... ....

R. S. O. 1877, c. 160, s. 35 ; *cf.* 44 V. c. 20 s. 5 ; 47 V. c. 28, s. 2.

TITLE X.—INTERNAL MANAGEMENT OF MUTUAL AND CASH-MUTUAL FIRE INSURANCE COMPANIES.

15 **64**. Sections 65 to 87 inclusive, shall apply only to Mutual *Restricted* and Cash-Mutual Fire Insurance companies. *application.*

1.—Admission and withdrawal of members.

65. The company may admit, as a member thereof, the *Power to* owner of any property, movable or immovable, and may insure *bers and* 20 the same, whether the owner thereof is or is not a freeholder ; *insure.* and every person admitted a member of the company by the insurance shall be entitled to the like rights, and be subjected to the like liabilities as other members of the company. R. S. O. 1877, c. 161, s. 30.

25 **66**. Members of any such company insuring in one Mutual *Members to be* branch shall not be liable for claims on any other Mutual *liable to one* branch ; but this limitation of liability shall not apply as *branch only.* between the Cash branch of a Cash-Mutual company and any other branch thereof. R. S. O. 1877, c. 161, ss. 66, 29.

Liability of members.

67.—No member of any Mutual Insurance company to which this Act may apply shall be liable in respect of any loss or other claim or demand against the company, otherwise than upon and to the extent of the amount unpaid upon his premium note or undertaking. R. S. O. 1877, c. 161, s. 68.   5

Members withdrawing.

68. Any member of the company may, with the consent of the directors, withdraw therefrom upon such terms as the directors may [lawfully] require. R. S. O. 1877, c.161, s. 31.

2.—General Meetings.

Annual meeting for election of Directors.

69. A meeting of the members for the election of directors 10 shall be held in every year, within two months after the thirty-first day of December in each year, at the time and place as may be prescribed by the by-laws of the company. R. S. O. 1877, c. 161, s. 10.

Annual report and statement.

70. At annual meetings, in addition to the election of direc- 15 tors, a report of the transactions of the company for the year ending on the previous thirty-first day of December, shall be presented and read, together with a full and unreserved statement of its affairs, exhibiting receipts and expenditures, assets and liabilities. R. S. O. 1877, c. 161, s. 11.   20

Notice of annual or special meetings.

71. Notice of any annual or special meeting of the members of the company shall be published in one or more newspapers for at least two weeks previous to the day of the meeting; and the board of directors may convene at any time a general meeting of the company upon any urgent occasion, giving 25 notice thereof as herein provided. R. S. O. 1877, c. 161, s. 12.

Members to have votes proportionate to the amount of their insurance.

72. Each member of the company shall be entitled, at all meetings of the company, to the number of votes proportioned to the amount by him insured, according to the following rates, that is to say: For any sum under $1,500, one vote; from 30 $1,500 to $3,000, two votes; from $3,000 to $6,000, three votes; and one vote for every additional $3,000; but no member shall be entitled to vote while in arrear for any assessment or premium due by him to the company. R. S. O. 1877, c. 161, s. 13.   35

Right of applicants to vote.

73. No applicant for insurance shall be competent to vote or otherwise take part in the company's proceedings until his application has been accepted by the board of directors. 48 V. c. 36, s.6.

3.—Directors.—Qualification, Election, etc.   40

Qualification of Directors.

74. The Directors shall be members of the company, and insured therein, for the time they hold office, to the amount of $800 at least; ☞ and where the Company has a share capital two-thirds of the Directors shall have the further qualification mentioned in section 36 of this Act.☜ R. S. O. 1877, c. 45 161, s. 14.

Number of directors to be determined by resolution.

75.—(1) The Board of Directors shall consist of six, nine twelve or fifteen directors, as shall be determined by resolution passed at the meeting held under the 13th section or at an annual meeting of the company, or at a special general meeting called for the purpose of such determination and election.

(2) The number of directors constituting such board may 5 from time to time be increased or decreased, if so decided at a special general meeting of the company called for the purpose, or at an annual meeting, if notice in writing of the intention to move a resolution for that purpose at such annual meeting is given to the secretary of the company at least one 10 month before the holding of the meeting; but the increased or decreased number of directors shall in any such case be six, nine, twelve or fifteen as aforesaid. 48 V. c. 36, s. 1.

76. A copy of the resolution specified in the last preceding section, together with a list of the directors elected there- 15 under, both documents being duly certified under the hands of the chairman and secretary of the annual meeting or special general meeting aforesaid, shall be filed in the office of the Inspector and also in the Registry Office. 48 V. c. 36, s. 2. Copy of resolution and list of directors to be filed.

77. Of the directors elected, as hereinbefore provided, one- 20 third shall retire annually in rotation, and at the first meeting of the directors, or as soon thereafter as possible, it shall be determined by lot which of them shall hold office for one, two or three years respectively, and the determination shall be entered of record as part of the minutes of said first meet- 25 ing. 48 V. c. 36, s. 3. Retirement of directors in rotation.

78. At every annual meeting of the company thereafter, one-third of the total number of directors shall be elected for a period of three years, to fill the places of the retiring members, who shall be eligible for re-election. 48 V. c. 36, s. 4. Annual election to fill vacancies.

30 **79.** The Manager of a Mutual Insurance Company may be a director of the company, and may be paid an annual salary, but only under a by-law of the company. R. S. O. 1877, c. 161, s. 15. Manager may be a Director. His salary.

80. No agent or paid officer, or person in the employment 35 of the company, other than the manager, shall be eligible to be elected a director. or shall be allowed to interfere in the election of directors for the company. R. S. O. 1877, c. 161, s. 16. Certain persons not eligible to be elected Directors.

81. The election of directors shall be held and made by such 40 members of the company as attend for that purpose in their own proper persons. R. S. O. 1877, c. 161, s. 17. Election of Directors.

82. The election of directors shall be by ballot. R. S. O. 1877, c. 161, s. 18. Mode of election.

83. If at any such election two or more members have an 45 equal number of votes, in such manner that a less number of persons than the whole number to be elected appear to have been chosen directors by a majority of votes, then the said members of the company shall proceed to elect by ballot. until it is determined which of the persons so having an equal num- 50 ber of votes shall be the director or directors, so as to complete Case of a tie at an election.

Election of a President and Vice-President.

the whole number of directors to be elected; and the directors shall at their first meeting after any such election, proceed to elect by ballot among themselves, a president and vice-president, and at such election the secretary shall preside. R. S. O. 1877, c. 161, s. 19.

5

Vacancies in office of Director, how filled up.

84. If a vacancy happens among the directors during the term for which they have been elected, by death, resignation, ceasing to have the necessary qualification under section 74 of this Act, insolvency, or by being absent, without previous leave of the board, from the board for three regular meetings in suc- 10 cession, which shall *ipso facto* create such vacancy, the vacancy shall be filled up, until the next annual meeting, by any person duly qualified, to be nominated by a majority of the remaining directors, and as soon as may be after the vacancy occurs ; and at the next annual meeting the vacancy shall be filled for the 15 portion of the term still unexpired   R. S. O. 1877, c. 161, s. 20 ; 48 V. c. 36, s. 5.

Provision in case of failure to elect Directors on proper day.

85. In case an election of directors is not made on the day on which it ought to have been made, the company shall not for that cause be dissolved, but the election may be held on a 20 subsequent day, at a meeting to be called by the directors, or as otherwise provided by the by-laws of the company, and in such case the directors shall continue to hold office till their successors are elected. R. S. O. 1877, c. 161, s. 21.   •

Quorum of Directors.

86. Three directors shall constitute a quorum for the trans- 25 action of business ; [and case of an equality of votes at any meeting of the Board, the question shall pass in the negative.]   R. S. O. 1877, c. 161, s. 22.

Directors disagreeing may record their dissent.

87. A director disagreeing with the majority of the board at a meeting, may have his dissent recorded, with his reasons 30 therefor. R. S. O. 1877, c. 161, s. 23.

TITLE XI.—POWERS OF DIRECTORS—GENERAL PROVISIONS—
(*All Companies.*)

88. Sections 89 to 98 inclusive shall apply to all companies 35 transacting business under license of the Provincial Treasurer. [New as to Joint Stock Companies, except ss. 90 (3), 96, 98.]

Appointment of Manager and other officers.

89. The board of directors may from time to time appoint a manager, secretary, treasurer, and such other officers, agents, 40 or assistants, as to them seem necessary ; prescribe their duties, fix their compensations or allowances ; take such security from

Board may adopt a tariff of rates.

them as is required by this Act for the faithful performance of their respective duties, and remove them and appoint others instead ; the board may also adopt a table of rates, [premiums, 45 or premium notes, as the case may be,] and vary such table from time to time, and determine the amount of the contract

Meetings of the board.

to be undertaken ; they may hold their meetings monthly, or oftener if necessary, for transacting the business of the company ; and they shall keep a record of their proceedings. 50 R. S. O. 1877, c. 161, s. 24.

90.—(1) The board may from time to time make and pre- _{The Board} scribe such by-laws as to them appear needful and proper, _{may pass by-laws.} respecting the funds and property of the company, the duty of the officers, agents and assistants thereof, the effectual car-
5 rying out of the objects contemplated by this Act, the holding of the annual meeting, and all such other matters as appertain to the business of the company, and are not contrary to law, and may from time to time alter and amend the said by-laws, except in cases with regard to which it is provided that any
10 such by-laws shall not be repealed, or where the repeal would _{When by-laws} affect the rights of others than the members of the company, _{are not repeal-able.} in any of which cases such by-law shall not be repealed.

(2) Every by-law of the board shall be duly entered in the _{When resolu-} minutes, and when confirmed at any subsequent meeting of _{tion to have the effect of}
15 the members, shall be held to be and have the same force and _{a by-law.} effect as a by-law of the company. R. S. O. 1877, c. 161, s. 25.

(3) There shall be filed with the Inspector copies of all by-laws that may from time to time be passed by the company or the board. 46 V. c. 15, s. 2, *part.*

20 **91.** The board shall superintend and have the management _{The Board to} of the funds and property of the company, and of all matters _{manage the property, etc.,} relating thereto, and not otherwise provided for. R. S. O. _{of the Com-} 1877, c. 161, s. 26. _{pany.}

92. The board may make arrangements with any other _{Re-insurance}
25 company [licensed to transact business in the Province] for the _{of risks.} re-insurance, on such conditions with respect to the payment of premiums thereon as may be agreed between them. R. S. O. 1877, c. 161, s. 27.

93. The board may, [in the name of the company], invest _{Investment of}
30 the capital and funds of the company in any stock, debentures, _{capital and funds of the} or other securities in which trustees may invest trust money, _{Company.} —49 V. c. 16, s. 24; 42 V. c. 21, s. 1; R. S. O. c. 107, s. 28; and may, [if a Mutual or Cash-Mutual Company,] in the name of such company, recover from any member of such company,
35 in any Court of competent jurisdiction, any premium or assess- _{Recovery of} ment upon his premium note payable by him. R. S. O. 1877, _{assessments.} c. 161, s. 28.

94.—(1) The board may issue debentures or promissory _{Directors may} notes in favour of any person, firm, building society, banking _{issue deben-tures and pro-}
40 or other company, for the loan of money, and may borrow _{missory notes} money therefrom on such debentures or promissory notes for _{for loans;} any term not exceeding twelve months, and on such conditions as they think proper, and may renew the same from time to time for any such term, the whole of the assets, including _{assets of the Company to}
45 premium notes of the company, being held liable to pay the _{be liable for} same at maturity, but no such debenture or promissory note _{the same.} shall be for a less sum than $100.

(2) All the debentures and promissory notes at any one time _{Amount of} outstanding shall not exceed one-fourth of the amount remain- _{debentures, etc., limited.}
50 ing unpaid upon the same premium notes. R. S. O. 1877, c. 161, s. 29.

Land that may be held by the Company. **95.** Every company may hold such lands only as are requisite for the accommodation of the company, in relation to the transaction of their business, or such lands as have been *bona fide* mortgaged to them by way of security, or conveyed to them in satisfaction of debts contracted in the course of their dealings previously to such conveyance, or purchased at sales upon judgments obtained for such debts, and may from time to time sell and convey or lease any such lands. R. S. O. 1877, c. 161, s. 72. 5

Loans to or from Directors, etc., forbidden. **96.** No company shall contract with any director or officer 10 thereof for any loan or credit, or borrowing of money, and every such attempted loan or borrowing is hereby prohibited ; and any contract in violation of this section shall be void. R. S. O. 1877, c. 161, s. 74 ; 46 V. c. 15, s. 3.

Treasurer of Company to give security. **97.** The treasurer of the Company or other officer having 15 charge of the money of the company shall give security to the satisfaction of the board of directors in a sum of not less than $2,000 for the faithful discharge of his duties. R. S. O. 1877, c. 161, s. 69.

Remuneration of directors. **98.** At any annual meeting of the members or stockholders 20 of a company, or at any special general meeting thereof, if such purpose was clearly expressed in the notice of the special general meeting, it shall be lawful to enact by-laws or pass resolutions for the remuneration of the directors of the company, and copies of such by-laws or resolutions shall, within 25 one week after their passing, be filed with the Inspector of Insurance, with whom also shall be filed copies of all other by-laws that may from time to time be enacted by the company or by the board of directors. 46 V. c. 15, s. 2.

TITLE. XII.—BOOKS, ACCOUNTS AND RETURNS,—*(All* 30 *(Companies.)*

99. Sections 100 to 105 shall apply to all companies within the intent of this Act.

Company to keep such books as may be directed by Treasurer. **100.** Every company shall keep such a classification of its contracts, and such registers and books of account as may from 35 time to time be directed or authorized by the Provincial Treasurer; and if it appears at any time to the Inspector that such books are not kept in such business-like way as to make at any time a proper showing of the affairs and standing of the company, he shall report the same to the Provincial Treasurer who 40 shall thereupon nominate a competent accountant to proceed, under the directions of the Inspector, to audit such books and to give such instructions as will enable the officers of the company to keep them correctly thereafter, the expense of the accountant to be borne by the company to which he is sent, 45 and shall not exceed $5 per day and necessary travelling expenses ; the account for such audit and instructions shall be certified and approved as provided in section *148,* and thereupon shall be payable by the company forthwith. 44 V. c. 20, s. 21 ; 43 V. c. 20, s. 1 ; 42 V. c. 25, s. 5 *part.* 50

101. Where the company has a share or stock capital, the company shall keep a stock register, in which a register of the transfers of stock shall be accurately kept, and it shall at all reasonable times be open to the examination of any share- 5 holder and the Inspector. The entries in such register shall include the following particulars : the register numbers of the shares transferred ; the amount of subscribed stock transferred ; the amount heretofore paid up on such stock ; the names and addresses of the transferor and the transferee ; the date of the 10 transfer and the date of confirmation or disallowance by the board. 46 V. c, 15, s. 13.

Transfer register.

102. The books and records required to be kept by section 100 and 101, shall include only contracts within the 47th sec- tion. 46 V. c. 15, s. 14.

Separate record of Provincial business.

15 **103**.—(1) It shall be the duty of the president, vice-presi- dent, or managing director, secretary, or manager, and treasurer, when the secretary is not also treasurer of the company, to prepare annually under their oath, on the first day of January, or within one month thereafter, a statement of the condition 20 and affairs of the company on the 31st of December then next preceding, exhibiting assets, liabilities, receipts and expenditure, in such form and with such items and detail as shall be required by the Provincial Treasurer, and to cause such state- ment to be deposited in the office of the [Inspector], such state- 25 ment to be accompanied by a declaration to the effect shown in the form to this sub-section annexed, sworn to before some person duly authorized to administer oaths in any legal pro- ceeding, and every such person is hereby authorized to admin- ister any oath required under this Act. R. S. O. 1877, c. 160, 30 s. 26 ; c. 161, s. 76.

Yearly state- ment to Treasurer of Ontario, what it must show, and how it must be verified.

Form of Declaration to accompany the Statement.

Province of Ontario, ⎱ We,
  County of   ⎰

President, and

Secretary and   Treasurer
of   company, severally made oath and say, and each for him- self says, that we are the above described officers of the said company, [and that we have, each of us individually, the means of verifying the correctness of the statement within contained of the affairs of the said company,] and that on the   .   day of   last, all the above described assets were the absolute property of the said company, free and clear from any liens or claims thereon, except as above stated, and that the foregoing statement, with the schedules and explanations hereunto annexed and by us subscribed, are a full and correct exhibit of all the liabilities, and of the income and expenditure, and of the general condition and affairs of the said company, on the said   day of   last, and for the year ending on that day.

Signatures.

Sworn before me, at the   ,⎫
in the county of   , this ⎬
    day of   , A.D. 18   ⎭

R. S. O. 1877, c. 160, *Sched.* B.

(2) The Provincial Treasurer may, from time to time make such changes in the form of the statements as seem to him best adapted to elicit from the companies a true exhibit of their

Form of state- ment may be changed by Provincial Treasurer.

4—IN.

condition in respect to the several points hereinbefore enumerated. R. S. O. 1877, c. 160, s. 26.

Companies to reply to inquiries of Lt.-Governor in Council.

(3) Any company shall further, when required, make prompt and explicit answer in reply to any inquiries in relation to its transactions which may be required by the Lieutenant-Governor in Council. R. S. O. 1877, c. 161, s. 76 (2). 5

Penalty for contravention of above section.

104. Any violation of the next preceding section shall subject the company violating the same to a penalty of $200 for every violation, and of the additional sum of $100 for every month during which the company neglects to file such 10 affidavits and statements as are therein required; if such penalties are not paid, the Lieutenant-Governor in Council may order such company's license to be suspended or cancelled, as may be deemed expedient. R. S. O. 1877, c. 160, s. 27. *See* c. 161. s. 76. 15

Report of Provincial Treasurer to be laid before the Legislature.

105. The Provincial Treasurer from the yearly statements required to be made, shall prepare *annually an abstract report*, showing the results of every company's business together with an analysis of every branch of insurance, with the company's name, classified from the statements made by the respective companies; 20 and the Treasurer shall☞ publish the said abstract report forthwith for general information. R. S. O. c. 160, s. 30.

TITLE XIII.—CONTRACTS OF FIRE INSURANCE—GENERAL PROVISIONS.—(*All Companies.*)

[S. 106 NEW AS TO MUTUAL COMPANIES; s.s. 108, 110, 111, 112 NEW 25 AS TO JOINT STOCK COMPANIES.]

Term of contracts.

106. Contracts of fire insurance shall not in any case exceed the term of three years ; and the insurance of mercantile and manufacturing risks shall, *if on the cash system*, be for terms not exceeding one year. R. S. O. 1877, c. 161, s. 75 ; 41 V. c. 8, 30 s. 17 ; *cf.* Statutes of Canada 49 V. c. 45, s. 48 : and *see* R. S. O. c. 161, s. 32.

Renewing policies.

107. Any [contract] that may be made for one year or any shorter period, may be renewed at the discretion of the board of directors by renewal receipts instead of policy, on the 35 insured paying the required premiums, or giving his premium note or undertaking : and any cash payments for renewal must be made at the end of the year, or other period for which the the policy was granted, otherwise the policy shall be null and void. R. S. O. 1877, c. 161, s. 34. 40

Property which may be insured.

108. The company may, [within the limits prescribed by the license,] insure dwelling houses, stores, shops and other buildings, household furniture, merchandize, machinery, live stock, farm produce and other commodities, against damage 45 or loss by fire or lightning, whether the same happens by accident or any other means, except that of design on the part of the insured, or by the invasion of an enemy, or by insurrection. R. S. O. 1877, c. 161, s. 36.

Minimum rates.

109. The rate to be charged or taken by way of 50 premium note for insuring first-class isolated non-hazardous property shall be not less than [one dollar] per one hundred dollars per annum; and the minimum rate of insurance upon other property shall be increased relatively with the increased risk, according to the nature of such property. R. S. O. 1877, c. 161, s. 37.

5   Provided that premium notes of less than one dollar per one hundred dollars per annum may be charged or taken when and so long as the gross amount at risk exceeds $2,000,000, and the total assets of the Company do not fall below two per centum of the gross amount at risk ; or so long as the Com-
10 pany keeps on deposit with the Provincial Treasurer the full amount required of new companies licensed after the commencement of this Act."

110. All contracts of fire insurance issued by the Board of Directors, sealed with the seal of the company, signed by the
15 President or Vice-President, and countersigned by the secretary or acting secretary, shall be binding on the company. R. S. O. 1877, c. 161, s. 38.

Policies to be binding on the Company.

111.—(1) Whenever notification in writing has been received by a company from a person already insured, of his
20 intention or desire to insure an additional sum on the same property in some other company, the said additional insurance shall be deemed to be assented to unless the company within two weeks after the receipt of such notice, signify to the party, in writing, their dissent ; and, in case of dissent, the liability of
25 the insured on the premium note or undertaking, if any, shall cease from the date of *the* dissent, on account of any loss that may occur to such company thereafter. R. S. O. 1877, c. 161, s. 40.

Notification of insurance in another Company.

Dissent of the Company to the additional insurance.

  (2) The notification to the Company, and any other written
30 notice to a Company for any purpose of this Act, where the mode thereof is not expressly provided, may be by letter delivered at the Head Office of the Company in Ontario, or by registered post letter addressed to the Company, its manager or agent, at such Head Office, or by such written notice given
35 in any other manner to an authorized agent of the Company.

112. It shall be optional with the directors to pay or allow claims which are void under the 3rd, the 4th, or the 8th Statutory Condition, or section 111 of this Act, in case the said directors think fit to waive the objections mentioned in the
40 said sections. R. S. O. 1877, c. 161, s. 43.

Optional with Directors to pay claims void under ss. 51-54.

113. The party insured shall if insured against fire on the Mutual plan be liable to pay his proportion of the losses and expenses of the company to the time of cancelling the policy, and on payment of his proportion of all assessments then
45 payable and to become payable in respect of losses and expenses sustained up to such period, shall be entitled to a return of his premium note or undertaking. R. S. O. 1877, a. 161, s. 44.

Cancellation of policies.

TITLE XIV.—STATUTORY CONDITIONS AND PROVISIONS RELAT-
ING THERETO *(Binding all Fire Insurance Contracts
whatsoever in Ontario. See Section 3).*

Statutory conditions to be part of every policy unless varied.

114. The conditions set forth in this section shall, as
against the insurers, be deemed to be part of every contract, 5
whether sealed, written or oral, of fire insurance hereafter
entered into or renewed or otherwise in force in Ontario with
respect to any property therein [or in transit therefrom or
thereto], and shall be printed on every such policy with the
heading *Statutory Conditions ;* and no stipulation to the con- 10
trary, or providing for any variation, addition or omission,
shall be binding on the assured unless evidenced in the manner
prescribed by sections 115 and 116. R. S. O. 1877, c.
162, ss. 3, 5 ; 45 V. c. 20, ss. 2, 3, 4 : 44 V., c. 20, s. 28.

STATUTORY CONDITIONS. 15

Misrepresentation or omission.

1. If any person or persons insures his or their buildings or goods, and causes the same to be described otherwise
than as they really are, to the prejudice of the company, or
misrepresents or omits to communicate any circumstance which
is material to be made known to the company, in order to 20
enable it to judge of the risk it undertakes, such insurance
shall be of no force in respect to the property in regard to
which the misrepresentation or omission is made.

Policy sent to be deemed as applied for unless variance pointed out.

2. After application for insurance, it shall be deemed that
any policy sent to be assured is intended to be in accordance 25
with the terms of the application, unless the company points
out, in writing, the particulars wherein the policy differs from
the application.

When a change as to risk shall avoid a policy. Notice of change, etc.

3. Any change material to the risk, and within the
control or knowledge of the assured, shall avoid the policy as
to the part affected thereby, unless the change is promptly 30
notified in writing to the company or its local agent; and the
company when so notified may return the premium for the
unexpired period and cancel the policy, or may demand in
writing an additional premium, which the insured shall, if he
desires the continuance of the policy, forthwith pay to the 35
company ; and if he neglects to make such payment forthwith
after receiving such demand, the policy shall be no longer in
force.

Change of property.

4. If the property insured is assigned without a written
permission endorsed hereon by an agent of the company duly
authorized for such purpose, the policy shall hereby become 40
void ; but this condition does not apply to change of title by
succession, or by the operation of the law, or by reason of
death.

Partial damage—salvage.

5. Where property insured is only partially damaged, no
abandonment of the same will be allowed unless by the consent
of the company or its agent; and in case of the removal of 45
property to escape conflagration, the company will contribute
to the loss and expenses attending such act of salvage propor-
tionately to the respective interests of the company or companies and the insured.

Money, securities, etc.

6. Money, books of account, securities for money, and 50
evidences of debt or title are not insured.

7. *Patterns, plate, plate glass*, plated ware, jewelry, medals, Plate, paint-
paintings, sculptures, curiosities, scientific and musical instru- etc.
ments, bullion, works of art, articles of vertu, frescoes, clocks,
watches, trinkets and mirrors, are not insured unless men-
5 tioned in the policy.

8. The company is not liable for loss if there is any prior Prior or
insurance in any other company, unless the company's assent subsequent insurance.
thereto appears herein or is endorsed hereon, nor if any subsequent insurance is effected in any other company, unless and
10 until the company assents thereto, ☞ or unless the Company does not dissent in writing within two weeks after
receiving notice of the intention or desire to effect the subsequent insurance, or does not dissent in writing after that time
and before the subsequent or further insurance is effected.☜

15 9. In the event of any other insurance on the property Case of assent
herein described having been assented to as aforesaid, then this to other insurance.
company shall, if such other insurance remains in force, on
the happening of any loss or damage, only be liable for the
payment of a rateable proportion of such loss or damage
20 without reference to the dates of the different policies.

10. The company is not liable for the losses following, that
is to say :

(*a*) For loss of property owned by any other party than the Liability in
assured, unless the interest of the assured is stated in or upon case of non-ownership.
25 the policy ;

(*b*) For loss caused by invasion, insurrection, riot, civil com- Riot, invasion, etc.
motion, military or usurped power ;

(*c*) Where the insurance is upon buildings [or their contents] Chimneys,
—for loss caused by the want of good and substantial brick or ashes, stoves.
30 stone chimneys ; or by ashes or embers being deposited, with
the knowledge and consent of the insured, in wooden vessels ; or
by stoves or stove-pipes being, to the knowledge of the assured,
in an unsafe condition or improperly secured ;

(*d*) For loss or damage to goods destroyed or damaged while Goods to which
35 undergoing any process in or by which the application of fire fire heat is being applied.
heat is necessary ;

(*e*) For loss or damage occurring to buildings or their Repairs by
contents while the buildings are being repaired by carpenters, carpenters, etc.
joiners, plasterers or other workmen, and in consequence
40 thereof, unless permission to execute such repairs had been
previously granted in writing, signed by a duly authorized
agent of the company. But in dwelling-houses fifteen days
are allowed in each year for incidental repairs, without such
permission ;

45 (*f*) For loss or damage occurring while petroleum, rock, Gunpowder,
earth or coal oil, camphene, *gasoline*, burning fluid, benzine, coal oil, etc.
naphtha or any liquid products thereof, or any of their
constituent parts (refined coal oil for lighting purposes only,
not exceeding five gallons in quantity, ☞ or lubricating oil
not being crude petroleum nor oil of less specific gravity than
required by law for illuminating purposes, not exceeding five
gallons in quantity, ☜ excepted), or more than twenty-five

pounds weight of gunpowder is or are stored or kept in the building insured or containing the property insured, unless permission is given in writing by the company.

Explosion. Lightning.
11. The company will make good loss caused by the explosion of coal gas in a building not forming part of gas works, 5 and loss by fire caused by any other explosion or by lightning.

Proof of loss when payable to other than assured.
12. Proof of loss must be made by the assured, although the loss be payable to a third party.

Directions to be observed on making claim.
13. Any person entitled to make a claim under this policy is to observe the following directions: 10

(a) He is forthwith after loss to give notice in writing to the company;

(b) He is to deliver, as soon afterwards as practicable, as particular an account of the loss as the nature of the case permits; 15

(c) He is also to furnish therewith a statutory declaration, declaring,

(1) That the said account is just and true;

(2) When and how the fire originated, so far as the declarant knows or believes; 20

(3) That the fire was not caused through his wilful act or neglect, procurement, means or contrivance;

(4) The amount of other insurances;

[(5) All liens, and incumbrances on the subject of insurance.]

(6) The place where the property insured, if movable, was deposited at the time of the fire. 25

(d) He is in support of his claims, if required and if practicable, to produce books of account, *warehouse receipts and stock lists*, and furnish invoices and other vouchers; to furnish copies of the written portion of all policies; and to exhibit for examination all that remains of the property which was 30 covered by the policy.

(e) He is to produce, if required, a certificate under the hand of a magistrate, notary public, [commissioner for taking affidavits, or municipal clerk], residing in the vicinity in which the fire happened, and not concerned in the loss or 35 related to the assured or sufferers, stating that he has examined the circumstances attending the fire, loss or damage alleged, that he is acquainted with the character and circumstances of the assured or claimant, and that he verily believes that the insured has by misfortune and without fraud or evil practice sustained 40 loss and damage on the subject assured, to the amount certified.

Proof of loss may be made by agent.
14. The above proofs of loss may be made by the agent of the assured, in case of the absence or inability of the assured himself to make the same, such absence or inability being satisfactorily accounted for. 45

False statement or fraud vitiates claim.
15. Any fraud or false statement in a statutory declaration, in relation to any of the above particulars, shall vitiate the claim.

Arbitration in case of differences.
16. If any difference arises as to the value of the property insured, of the property saved, or amount of the loss, such 50

value and amount and the proportion thereof (if any) to be
paid by the company, shall, whether the right to recover on
the policy is disputed or not, and independently of all other
questions, be submitted to the arbitration of some person to be
5 chosen by both parties, or if they cannot agree on one
person, then to two persons, one to be chosen by the party insured and the other by the company, and a third to be
appointed by the persons so chosen, [or on their failing to agree,
then by the County Judge of the County wherein the loss has
10 happened; and such reference shall be subject to the provisions
of the laws applicable to references in actions; and the award
shall, if the company is in other respects liable, be conclusive
as to the amount of the loss and proportion to be paid by the
company; [where the full amount of the claim is awarded the
15 costs shall follow the event; and in other cases, all questions
of costs shall be in the discretion of the arbitrators.] R.S.O.
1887, c. 161, s. 157.

17. The loss shall not be payable until   days after **Loss when payable.**
completion of the proofs of loss, unless otherwise provided for
20 by the contract of insurance.

(a) The blank shall be filled in the case of mutual and cash
mutual companies with the word "sixty," and in the case of
other companies with the word "thirty."

18. The company, instead of making payment, may repair, **Company may replace, instead of paying.**
25 rebuild or replace, within a reasonable time, the property dam-
aged or lost, giving notice of their intention within fifteen days
after receipt of the proofs herein required.

19 "The insurance may be terminated by the company by
giving notice to that effect, and, if on the cash plan, by tendering
30 therewith a rateable proportion of the premium for the unexpired
term, calculated from the termination of the notice : in the case
of personal service of the notice five days' notice, excluding
Sunday, shall be given. Notice may be given by any company
having an agency in Ontario by registered letter addressed to
35 the assured at his last post-office address notified to the company, and where no address notified, then to the post-office of
the agency from which application was received, and where
such notice is by letter, then seven days from the arrival at
any post-office in Ontario shall be deemed good notice. And
the policy shall cease after such tender and notice aforesaid,
40 and the expiration of the five or seven days as the case may be.

(b) The insurance, if for cash, may also be terminated by the
assured by giving written notice to that effect to the company or
its authorized agent, in which case the company may retain the
45 customary short rate for the time the i surance has been in
force, and shall repay to the assured the balance of the premium paid."

20. No condition of the policy, either in whole or in part, **Waiver of condition.**
shall be deemed to have been waived by the company, unless
the waiver is clearly expressed in writing, signed by an agent
50 of the company.

21. Any officer or agent of the company, who assumes on **Officers assuming to agree in writing to be deemed agents.**
behalf of the company to enter into any written agreement
relating to any matter connected with the insurance, shall be
55 deemed *prima facie* to be the agent of the company for the
purpose.

Actions to be brought within one year.

22. Every action or proceeding against the company for the recovery of any claim under or by virtue of this policy, shall be absolutely barred, unless commenced within the term of one year next after the loss or damage occurs. R. S. O. 1877, c. 162, *Schedule.* 5

Variations, how indicated.

115. If a company (or other insurer) desires to vary the said conditions, or to omit any of them, or to add new conditions, there shall be added on the instrument of contract containing the printed statutory conditions words to the following effect, printed in conspicuous type, and in ink of different 10 colour. :—

"VARIATIONS IN CONDITIONS.

" This policy is issued on the above Statutory Conditions, with the following variations and additions :

" These variations (*or as the case may be*) are, by virtue of 15 the Ontario Statute in that behalf, in force so far as, by the Court or judge before whom a question is tried relating thereto, they shall be held to be just and reasonable to be exacted by the company." R. S. O. 1877, c. 162, s. 4.

Variations not binding unless clearly indicated.

116. No such variation, addition or omission shall, unless 20 the same is distinctly indicated and set forth in the manner or to the effect aforesaid, be legal and binding on the insured ; and no question shall be considered as to whether any such variation, addition or omission is, under the circumstances, just and reasonable, but on the contrary, the policy shall, as against 25 the insurers, be subject to the Statutory Conditions only, unless the variations, additions or omissions are distinctly indicated and set forth in the manner or to the effect aforesaid. R. S. O. 1877, c. 162, s. 5.

Policy containing other than statutory conditions.

117. In case a policy is entered into or renewed contain- 30 ing or including any condition other than or different from the conditions set forth in the schedule to this Act, if the said condition so contained or included is held, by the Court or Judge before whom a question relating thereto is tried, to be not just and reasonable. such condition shall be null and void. 35 R. S. O. 1877, c. 162, s. 6 ; c. 161, s. 35, (see s. 119, *infra.*)

If due proof of loss not given through accident, etc., or objection not made thereto, or made on other grounds than non-compliance with conditions ;

118. Where, by reason of necessity, accident or mistake, the conditions of any contract of fire insurance on property in this Province as to the proof to be given to the insurance company after the occurrence of a fire have not been strictly com- 40 plied with ; or where, after a statement or proof of loss has been given in good faith by or on behalf of the insured, in pursuance of any proviso or condition of such contract, the company, through its agent or otherwise, objects to the loss upon other grounds than for imperfect compliance with such 45 conditions, or does not within a reasonable time after receiving such statement or proof notify the assured in writing that such statement or proof is objected to, and what are the particulars in which the same is alleged to be defective, and so from

or, if full compliance adjudged inequitable,

time to time ; or where, for any other reason, the Court or 50 Judge before whom a question relating to such insurance is tried or inquired into, considers it inequitable that the insur-

ance should be deemed void or forfeited by reason of imperfect compliance with such conditions—no objection to the sufficiency of such statement or proof or amended or supplemental state- in above cases, ment or proof (as the case may be) shall, in any of such cases, liability and
5 be allowed as a discharge of the liability of the company on policy not vacated. such contract of insurance wherever entered into. R. S. O. 1877, c. 162, s. 2.

119. A decision of a Court or Judge under this Act shall be Appeal. subject to review or appeal to the same extent as a decision by
10 such Court or Judge in other cases. R. S. O. 1877, c. 162, s. 7; c. 161, s. 35.

120.—(1) Any Justice of the Peace, or any one having Justices of the Peace, etc., lawful authority to administer an oath or affirmation in any may swear and
15 legal proceeding, may examine on oath or solemn affirmation examine witnesses regarding any party or person who comes before him to give evidence ing loss. touching any loss by fire in which any [Fire] Insurance Company is interested, and may administer any oath or affirmation required under this Act. R. S. O. 1877, c. 161, s. 62.

20 [(2). On receiving a written request from any officer or agent May hold special investigation on request. of any insurance company with security for the expenses of an investigation, any Justice of the Peace may at once proceed to hold an investigation as to the origin or cause of any fire that has happened within his county or district, and as to the
25 persons if any, profiting thereby.

(3) The Justice of the Peace shall have power to send for Powers. persons and papers, and to examine all persons that appear before him on oath or solemn affirmation ; and he shall keep a record of all such proceedings and of the evidence given
30 before him.]

TITLE XV.—PREMIUM NOTES AND ASSESSMENTS. *(Mutual and Cash—Mutual Fire Insurance Companies.)*

121. Sections 122 to 136 inclusive shall apply only to
35 Mutual and Cash-Mutual Fire Insurance Companies.

122. The company may accept premium notes, or the Company may accept premium notes. undertaking of the insured, for insurances, and may undertake contracts in consideration thereof ; said notes or undertakings to be assessed for the losses and expenses of the company in
40 the manner hereinafter provided. R. S. O. 1877, c. 161, s. 45.

123. The Directors may demand in cash a part or first pay- Part payment may be demanded at the ment of the premium, or premium note or undertaking at the time that application for insurance is made ; and such first payment time of application for insurance. shall be credited upon said premium note or undertaking or
45 against future assessments, but not more than fifty per centum of any premium or premium note *or undertaking* shall be paid in cash at the time of such application or of effecting the insurance. R. S. O. 1877, c. 161, s. 46 ; 44 V. c. 20, s. 22.

124. All premium notes or undertakings belonging to the Assessment of premium notes.
50 company shall be assessed under the direction of the Board of Directors, at such intervals from their respective dates, for

such sums as the directors determine, and for such further
sums as they think necessary [and as are authorized by this
Act] for losses, expenses, and reserve, during the currency of
the policies for which said notes or undertakings were given,
and in respect to which they are liable to assessment; and 5
every member of the company, or person who has given a
premium note or undertaking, shall pay the sums from time to

Notice to be given of the assessment.
time payable by him to the company during the continuance
of his policy, in accordance with the assessment; and the
assessment shall become payable in thirty days after notice 10
thereof has been mailed to the member, or person who has
given the premium note or undertaking, directed to his post
office address, as given in his original application, or otherwise
in writing to the company. R. S. O. 1877, c. 161, ss. 47, 53.

Policy to be void, if any assessment or note is not paid within thirty days.
125. If the assessment on the premium note or undertaking 15
upon a policy is not paid within thirty days after the day
on which the assessment has become due, the [contract] of
insurance, for which the assessment has been made shall be
null and void as respects all claim for losses occurring during
the time of non-payment: but the [contract] shall be 20
revived when the assessment has been paid, unless the Secretary gives notice to the contrary to the assessed party in the
manner in this Act provided; but nothing shall relieve the
assured party from his liability to pay the assessment or any
subsequent assessments, nor shall the assured party be entitled 25

but shall be revived by subsequent payment.
to recover the amount of loss or damage which happens
to property insured under the [contract] while the assessment
remains due and unpaid, unless the Board of Directors in their
discretion decide otherwise. R. S. O. 1877, c. 161, s. 48.

Requisites of notice of assessment.
126. A notice of assessment upon any premium note or un- 30
dertaking mailed as aforesaid shall be deemed sufficient if it
embodies the register number of of the [contract] the period
over which the assessment extends, the amount of the asses-
ment, the time when and the place where payable. R. S. O.
1877, c. 161, s. 40. 35

Assessment, how proportioned.
127. The assessment upon premium notes or undertakings
shall always be in proportion to the amount of the notes or
undertakings, having regard to the branch or department *or
the class* to which their policies respectively appertain. R. S. O.
1877, c. 161, s. 50. 40

Company may sue for assessments on premium notes.
128. If a member or other person, who has given a premium note or undertaking, for thirty days after notice of
assessment has been mailed to him in manner aforesaid, neglects
or refuses to pay the assessments, the company may sue for
and recover the same with costs of suit, and such proceeding 45
shall not be a waiver of any forfeiture incurred by such non-
payment. R. S. O. 1877, c. 161, s. 51.

Certificate of the Secretary to be *prima facie* evidence of amount due to the Company.
129. Where an assessment is made on any premium
note or undertaking given to the company for a risk taken
by the company, or as a consideration for any policy of insur- 50
ance issued, or to be issued by the company, and an action is
brought to recover the assessment, the certificate of the secretary of the company, specifying the assessment, and the amount

due to the company on the note or undertaking by means
thereof, shall be taken and received as *prima facie* evidence
thereof in any Court in this Province. R. S. O. 1877, c. 161,
s. 52.

5   **130.**—(1) The company may form a reserve fund, to consist Reserve fund.
of all moneys which remain on hand at the end of each year,
after payment of the ordinary expenses and losses of the
company ; and for that purpose the board of directors may Annual assess-
levy an annual assessment not exceeding ten per centum on ment.
10 the premium notes or undertakings held by the company ;
and the reserve fund may from time to time be applied by the
directors to pay off such liabilities of the company as may not how applied,
be provided for out of the ordinary receipts for the same or
any succeeding year. R. S. O. 1887, c. 161, s. 53 (1).

15   (2) The reserve fund shall be invested in stock, debentures how invested.
or other securities in which trustees may invest trust money,
or may remain in a chartered bank in Ontario deposited at
interest in the name of the company. R. S. O. c. 161, s. 53 ;
42 V. c. 21, s. 2 ; 49 V. c. 16, s. 24.

20   **131.** If there is a loss on property insured by the com- Directors may
pany, the board of directors may retain the amount of the retain amount
premium note or undertaking given for insurance thereof, until notes.
the time has expired for which insurance has been made, and
at the expiration of said time the insured shall have the right
25 to demand and receive such part of the retained sum as has
not been assessed for. R. S. O. 1877, c. 161, s. 63.

132. Forty days after the expiration of the term of insur- When pre-
ance, the premium note or undertaking given for the insur- mium note is
ance, shall, on application therefor, be given up to the signer to be returned.
30 thereof, provided all losses and expenses with which the note
or undertaking is chargeable have been paid. R. S. O. 1877.
c. 161. s. 54.

133. Any action cognizable in a Division Court upon or Action in
for any premium note or undertaking, or any sum assessed or Courts where
35 to be assessed thereon, may be entered and tried and determined brought.
in the Court for the division wherein the head office or any
agency of the company is situate :
Provided always, that the provisions of this section
shall not apply to nor include any such premium note
40 or undertaking made or entered into after the first day
of July, 1885, nor any sum assessed thereon, unless within Actions on
the body of such note or undertaking or across the face premium notes
thereof, there was at the time of the making or enter- Courts, where
.ing into the same, printed in conspicuous type, and in ink of a brought.
45 colour different from any other in or on such note the words
following : "Any action which may be brought or commenced
in a Division Court in respect or on account of this note or
undertaking, or any sum to be assessed thereon, may be brought
and commenced against the maker hereof in the Division Court
50 for the division wherein the head office or any agency of the
company is situate." R. S. O. 1877, 161, s. 71 ; 48 V. c. 35, s. 1.

134. No premium note or undertaking shall create a lien Premium
upon lands on which the insured property is situate. R. S. O. create lien on
1877, c. 161, s. 73. land.

Powers of incorporated companies to insure on the cash premium principle.

135. Any [Cash-]Mutual Fire Insurance company [licensed under this Act] may effect any insurance upon the cash premium principle, for a period not exceeding three years on farm and other non-hazardous property, and for one year or less on any other class of property; but the amount of cash insurances in 5 one year shall be limited, so that the cash premiums received thereon during any one year shall not be in excess of one-half of the amount still payable in respect of premium notes or undertakings on hand on the thirty-first day of December of the previous year, according to the statement made under the 10 103rd section; and all the property and assets of the company, including premium notes and undertakings, shall be liable for **Guarantee fund.** all losses which may arise under insurances for cash premiums; and any such company may also create or possess a guarantee capital or fund for the company, according to the provisions 15 of this Act. R. S. O. 1877, c. 161, s. 75; 41 V. c. 8, s. 17; 44 V. c. 20, s. 7.

Issue of execution against company.

136.—(1) No execution shall issue against a [Mutual or Cash-Mutual] company upon a judgment until after the expiration of [sixty days] from the recovery thereof; but this section 20 shall not apply to any judgment recovered on any policy or undertaking of the company heretofore issued or given where more than fifty per centum of the premium or premium note *or undertaking* was paid in cash at the time of the insurance or the application therefor. 25

(2) A judge in chambers, or a referee in chambers, shall, upon the recovery of a judgment against the company, upon the application of the person in whose favour the same has been recovered, upon notice to the company, inquire into the facts, and if he shall certify that more than fifty per centum of the 30 premium, or of the premium note, or undertaking was paid in cash at the time of the insurance, or upon the application therefor, execution may be forthwith issued upon such judgment. R. S. O. 1877, c. 161, 61; 44 V. c. 20, s. 27.

TITLE XVI.—INSPECTION OF COMPANIES—(*All Companies.*) 35

Appointment of Inspector.

137.—(1) For the efficient administration of the Insurance business, the Lieutenant-Governor in Council may appoint an officer to be called the Inspector of Insurance, who shall act under the instructions of the Treasurer of Ontario, and his duty shall be to examine and report to the said Treasurer from time 40 to time upon all matters connected with insurance as carried on by the companies within this Act. 42 V. c. 21, s. 1.

(2) The salary of the Inspector shall be such sum per annum as the Legislature shall, from time to time, determine; and it shall be lawful to provide from time to time such assistance as 45 may be found necessary. 42 V. c. 25, s. 1; 46 V. c. 15, s. 6, *part.*

Inspector to keep papers on file.

138. The Inspector shall keep on file the various documents required by this Act to be filed in his office, and shall keep a record of all licenses issued by the Treasurer. 44 V. c. 20, s. 4. 50

Duties.

139.—(1) The Inspector of Insurance shall, personally [or by deputy], visit the head office of every such company in Ontario at least once in every year, and shall carefully examine the statements of the company as to its condition and affairs and report thereon to the Treasurer as to all matters requiring his attention and decision.

(2) The Inspector shall from such examination prepare and
5 lay before the Treasurer an annual report of the condition of every company's business as ascertained by him from such inspection, and such report shall be published forthwith after the completion thereof. 42 V. c. 25, s. 2.

140 (1) It shall be the duty of the officers or agents of the *Powers of*
10 company to cause their books to be open for the inspection of *Inspector.* the Inspector, and otherwise to facilitate the examination so far as may be in their power ; and the Inspector or deputy aforesaid shall have power to examine under oath any officer or agent of the company relative to its business. 42 V. c. 25,
15 s. 3, (1, 2.)

(2) A report of all companies so visited shall be entered *Report of* in a book kept for that purpose, with notes and memoranda *Inspector.* showing the condition of each company ; and, where a special examination has been made, a special written report shall
20 be communicated to the Treasurer stating the Inspector's opinion of the condition and financial standing of the company, and all other matters desirable to be made known to the Treasurer. 42 V. c. 25, s. 3 (3).

141. Every director, officer, agent, or employee of a com- *Entries,*
25 pany who, knowingly, makes or assists to make any untrue *untrue or* *omitted.* entry in any of the company's books, or who refuses or neglects to make any proper entry therein, or to exhibit the same or *Access to* allow the same to be inspected and extracts to be taken there- *books and* from shall be guilty of an offence, and, being convicted thereof, *paper.*
30 shall be imprisoned with or without hard labour in the Central Prison or any gaol of the Province, for a period not exceeding *three* months. 24 V. c. 18, s. 28 ; Dom. Act, 32-3 V. c. 29, s. 90.

142.—(1) If it appears to the Inspector that the assets of *Provision if*
35 any company are insufficient to justify its continuance of busi- *company ap-* *pears unsafe.* ness, or unsafe for the public to effect insurance with it, he shall make a special report on the affairs of the company to the Treasurer. 42 V. c. 25, s. 3 (4).

(2) After full consideration of the report and a reasonable *Suspending*
40 time being given to the company to be heard, and if, after such *license of com-* *pany.* further inquiry and investigation (if any), as he may see proper to make, the treasurer reports to the Lieutenant-Governor in Council that he agrees with the Inspector in the opinion expressed in his report, then, if the Lieutenant-Governor in Coun-
45 cil also concurs in such opinion, an Order in Council may issue, suspending or cancelling the license of the company, and prohibiting the company from doing any further business, and thereafter it shall not be lawful for the company to do any further business in Ontario, until the suspension or pro-
50 hibition is removed by the Lieutenant-Governor in Council. 42 V. c. 25, s. 3 (6); R. S. O. 1877, c. 160, s. 34.

143. Notice of the suspension or cancelling of any license *Notice of sus-* *pension of* and prohibition from doing any further business, shall be pub- *license.* lished in the *Ontario Gazette* ; and thereafter any person trans-

acting any business in behalf of the company, except for
winding up its affairs pursuant to the 7th section, shall be
deemed to have contravened the 55th and 56th sections, and
shall be liable for each offence to the penalty enacted in the
56th section. R. S. O. 1877, c. 160, s. 19 ; 42 V. c. 25, s. 3 (7).   5

Company assuming name of other company.   **144.**—(1) If it appears to the Inspector that a company which
has not been incorporated by special Act of the Legislation
has assumed the name of a previously established company, or
any name liable to be unfairly confounded therewith, or otherwise on public grounds objectionable, he shall make a report 10
thereof to the Treasurer.   46 V. c. 25, s. 3 (5).

· (2) And such name may, upon the written recommendation
of the Inspector, be changed by the Lieutenant-Governor in
Council, pursuant to the 20th section.

Inspection of books and papers.   **145.** In order to facilitate the inspection of an insurance 15
company's books and papers the company may be required by
the Inspector to produce the said books and papers at the
county town of the county in which the head office of the
insurance company is situated, or at such other convenient
place as the Inspector may direct.   46 V. c. 15, s. 5.   20·

Examination of company's affairs.   **146.** Whenever the affairs of any insurance company doing
business in Ontario appear to require the same, the Inspector
of Insurance, with the approval of the Provincial [Treasurer].
may, at the expense of the company, have abstracts prepared
of its books and vouchers and a valuation made of the assets 25
and liabilities ; and the certificate of the Inspector approved of
by the Provincial [Treasurer], shall be conclusive as to the expenses to be paid by the company in respect thereof.   46 V.
c. 15, s. 7.

Inspector and officers not to be interested in any company.   **147.** The Inspector of insurance, or any officers under him 30
shall not be interested as shareholders, directly or indirectly,
with any insurance company doing business in Ontario.   42 V.
c. 25, s. 4.

Contribution from companies to expenses.   **148.**—(1). Towards defraying the expenses of the office of
the Inspector, a sum not exceeding $3,000 shall be annually 35
contributed by the companies required to be licensed under
this Act.

Mode of determining the amount of contribution to expenses.   (2). The amount to be annually contributed by the insurance companies under the provisions of the last preceding
sub-section shall be assessed *pro rata* and based on the gross 40
amount at risk as shewn by the books of the several companies
on the 31st day of December next preceding.   42 V. c. 25, s. 5,
part ; 43 V. c. 20, s. 1, *part* ; 46 v. c. 15, s. 6, *part*.

Time and manner of payment.   (3). All sums under this Act payable to the Treasurer shall
be so paid before the issue of the license and the Treasurer's 45
certificate, [or approval of an account certified by the
Inspector,] shall as to the amount so payable by each or
any company be held conclusive.   42 V. c. 25, s. 5 *part* ; 43 V. c.
20, s. 1.

[**149**. A copy of any document in the office of the Inspector, certified by him to be a true copy and sealed with the seal of his office, shall be held to be authentic, and shall be *prima facie* evidence of the same legal effect as the original
5 in any court or elsewhere. *Public Works Act*, R. S. O. 1877, c. 30, s. 8.]

Certified copies of documents in inspector's office.

Title XVII.—Liquidation and Winding up of Companies
(*All Companies.*)

150. When a company proposes to go into volun-
10 tary liquidation, at least one month's notice in advance shall be given to the [Treasurer] and to the Inspector; the like notice shall also be published by the company in two consecutive issues of the *Ontario Gazette*, and in some other newspaper should the Inspector so require ; and the notice shall state the date
15 at which [contracts] shall cease to be taken by the company, also the name and address of the company's liquidator, or the intention of the company to apply on a stated day for the appointment of a liquidator. 46 V. c. 15, s. 9.

Voluntary liquidation.

151.—(1) At the winding up of a Mutual or Cash-Mutual
20 Fire Insurance company, after notice has been given as required by section 51, it shall be lawful for the directors of said company to reinsure out of the reserve fund the unexpired contracts for which premiums or premium notes have been taken. 46 V. c. 15, s. 16.

Disposal of reserve at winding up of company.

25 [(2). The said re-insurance shall be effected in some company licensed to transact business in the Province, and approved by the Treasurer.]

Reinsuring companies.

152. When any company is wound up each [person contracted with on the cash plan] shall be entitled to a refund
30 from the company of the unearned proportion of the cash premium calculated from the date at which the company, according to the notice in the 150th section, ceased to undertake contracts ; but this shall not destroy or defeat any other remedy such person may have against the company in
35 respect thereof or for any other cause. 46 V. c. 15, s. 10.

Unearned premiums.

153. Every receiver, assignee, or liquidator of a company shall, until the affairs of the company are wound up [and the accounts are finally closed] within seven days after the close of each month, file with the court or other authority appoint-
40 ing him, and also with the Inspector of Insurance, detailed schedules shewing, in such form as may be required, receipts and expenditures, also assets and liabilities, and he shall, whenever by the authority appointing him, or by the Inspector of Insurance, so required to do, exhibit the company's books and
45 vouchers, and furnish such other information respecting the company's affairs as may be required ; and any receiver, assignee or liquidator refusing or neglecting to furnish such information, shall, for each offence, be subject to a penalty of not less than $50 nor more than $200, to be recovered on
50 behalf of Her Majesty for the use of this Province ; and he shall in addition render himself liable to be dismissed or removed. 46 V. c. 15, s. 11.

Receiver to file statements.

Acts repealed. **154.**—(1) The provisions of the statute passed in the 14th year of His Majesty King George the Third and chaptered 78, shall be deemed not to be in force in regard to property in the Province.

(2) The Acts and portions of Acts mentioned in the schedule 5 hereto, are hereby repealed.

SCHEDULE OF ACTS REPEALED.

Schedule of Acts Repealed from the day upon which the Ontario Insurance Act, 1887, takes effect.

Title or Act.	Extent of Repeal.
R.S.O. 1877 c. 160, An Act respecting Insurance Companies	The whole except as mentioned in section 40 of this Act.
R.S.O. 1877 c 161, An Act respecting Mutual Fire Insurance Companies	The whole.
R.S.O. 1877 c. 162, An Act to secure Uniform Conditions in Policies of Fire Insurance	The whole.
41 V. c. 8, An Act to make certain amendments in the Revised Statutes..................................	Section 17.
42 V. c. 25, An Act to provide for the Inspection of Insurance Companies	The whole.
43 V. c. 20, An Act respecting the Expenses of Inspecting Insurance Companies	The whole.
44 V. c. 20, An Act to give increased stability to Mutual Fire Insurance Companies	The whole.
45 V. c. 20, An Act to extend the application of the Fire Insurance Policy Act	The whole.
46 V. c. 15, An Act relating to the Law of Insurance........	The whole.
47 V. c. 6, An Act respecting Securities Vested in the Treasurer of the Province	The whole.
47 V. c. 28, An Act respecting Supplementary Licenses to Mutual Fire Insurance Companies	The whole.
48 V. c. 35, An Act to amend the Act respecting Mutual Fire Insurance Companies..............................	The whole.
48 V. c. 36, An Act to regulate the Election of Directors of Mutual Fire Insurance Companies	The whole.

BILL.

An Act consolidating and amending the Acts respecting Insurance Companies.

(*Reprinted as amended by Committee of Whole House.*)

First Reading, 21st March, 1887.
Second   "   . 28th   "   1887.

BILL.

An Act respecting the Driving of Saw Logs and other Timber on Lakes, Rivers, Creeks and Streams.

HER MAJESTY, by and with the advice and consent of the Legislative Assembly of the Province of Ontario, enacts as follows :—

1. Any person putting or causing to be put into any lake, Persons float-
5 river, creek or stream, in this Province, any saw log or other ing logs down
timber for the purpose of floating the same to the place of river to employ
manufacture or market shall make adequate provisions, and put stream clear.
on a sufficient force of men to break jams of such saw logs, or
other timber in or upon such lake, river, creek or stream, and
10 to run or clear the same from the banks or shores thereof, and
to run or drive the same so as not to hinder the removal of
any saw logs or other timber from the banks or shores thereof;
nor obstruct the floating or navigation of such lake, river,
creek or stream.

15   2. In case of the neglect of such person to make such In case of
adequate provision, and put on such sufficient force of men, as default other
aforesaid, it shall be lawful for any other person engaged in clear obstruc-
floating or running saw logs or other timber in such lake, tion and
river, creek or stream, obstructed by reason of such neglect, to recover costs.
20 cause such jams to be broken, and such saw logs or other timber
to be run, driven, or cleared from the banks of such lake, river,
creek or stream, and along and down such lake, river, creek or
stream, at the cost and expense of the person owning such
logs or other timber, and such owner shall be liable to such
25 persons for such costs and expenses.

3. The person so causing such jams to be broken, or such Lien for
saw logs or other timber to be run, driven or cleared, shall charges.
have a lien on such saw logs and other timber, for his reasonable charges and expenses for breaking jams, and running,
30 driving and clearing the same, and shall be entitled to take and
retain possession of such saw logs or other timber, wherever
the same may be found, or so much thereof as may be necessary to satisfy the amount of such charges and expenses, and
all costs, and may after thirty days' notice to the owner, if the
35 owner be known, and advertisement thereof for three successive weeks at least once in each week, in a newspaper published nearest to where such saw logs or other timber may then
be, sell by public auction, subject to the lien of the Crown (if
any) for dues, the said saw logs or other timber, or so much
40 thereof as may be necessary to satisfy the amount of such
charges and expenses, and all costs, rendering the surplus on
demand to the owner.

Sale of logs for charges.

4. If the owner of the saw logs or other timber is not known to the person claiming the lien, then such person may after advertisement thereof for four successive weeks, at least once in each week, in the *Ontario Gazette*, and in a newspaper published nearest to where such saw logs or other timber may 5 then be, sell by public auction the said saw logs or other timber or so much thereof as may be necessary to satisfy the amount of such charges and expenses and all costs.

Compensation to person driving logs mixed with his own.

5. Any person whose saw logs or other timber in any lake, river, creek or stream, in this Province, are so intermixed with 10 the saw logs or timber of another person, that the same cannot be conveniently separated for the purpose of being driven or floated to market, or place of manufacture, may drive all saw logs and other timber with which his own are so intermixed at the cost and expense of the person owning the same, unless 15 such owner furnish a fair proportion of plant and men, and do or cause to be done a fair proportion of the work necessary to be done in driving all the said saw logs and other timber, so intermixed, and such owner shall, unless he so furnishes a fair proportion of plant and men, do or cause to be done a fair pro- 20 portion of the work in driving said saw logs and other timber as aforesaid, be liable to such person for such costs and expenses, and such person shall have a lien on such saw logs and other timber for his reasonable costs and expenses for driving the same, and shall be entitled to take and retain possession of such 25 saw logs or other timber, wherever the same may be found, or so much thereof as may be necessary to satisfy the amount of such charges and expenses and all costs, and may sell the said saw logs and other timber in the manner mentioned in the sections hereinbefore contained, but subject to the provisions as 30 to notice and advertisement thereof as in said sections mentioned.

Proceedings to determine compensation in cases of dispute.

6. If the owner of the said saw logs or other timber shall dispute the amount claimed by a lien holder he shall, within five days from the receipt of the notice of sale, to be given by 35 such lien holder to such owner, give notice in writing to such lien holder, that he disputes the amount claimed and thereupon the following proceedings shall be had unless the parties otherwise agree upon the amount to be paid :

1. Such notice shall state the name of an arbitrator and call 40 upon the lien holder to appoint an arbitrator on his behalf within five days after service of such notice, and in default of such lien holder making such appointment it shall be lawful for the Judge of the County Court of the county, or the Stipendiary Magistrate of the District, as the case may be, in 45 which such saw logs or other timber are situate upon request of the owner to appoint such arbitrator, and the two arbitrators so appointed shall forthwith appoint a third arbitrator in the matter ;

2. If after the arbitrators have been appointed, as aforesaid, 50 they fail or neglect for the space of five days to appoint a third arbitrator, the said Judge of the County Court or Stipendiary Magistrate shall, within four days after a request in writing made upon him by either of the two arbitrators appointed as above, appoint a third arbitrator ; 55

3. The arbitrators may require the personal attendance and examination on oath of the parties and their witnesses and the production of all documents relative to the dispute, and may determine by whom the expenses of the arbitration shall be 5 defrayed, together with the amount thereof, and shall make and deliver their award and determination within twenty days from the date of their appointment, and the said lien holder, may retain his lien and possession of the said saw logs and other timber until such award is made and delivered, and the 10 amount found thereby and costs is paid by such owner to such lien holder.

7. If the owner does not forthwith pay the amount and costs which the arbitrators determine that he shall pay, such lien holder may proceed to sell by public auction the said saw 15 logs or other timber, or a sufficient portion thereof, to satisfy the award and costs, and the subsequent costs incurred by such sale, first giving notice of such sale by advertisement for two successive weeks, at least once in each week, in a newspaper published nearest to where such saw logs or other timber may 20 then be.

In default of payment logs may be sold.

8. Any person whose saw logs or other timber are inter-mixed in any lake, river, creek or stream with the saw logs or timber of any other person, and who for any reason desires to separate the same, or does not wish to continue the drive, shall 25 at his own cost and expense separate his said saw logs and timber from the saw logs and timber of such other person, and securely boom the same to one side, in such manner as to allow a free passage for the saw logs and timber of any other person who may wish to continue the drive.

Provision as to separation of logs.

1st Session, 6th Legislature, 50 Vic, 1887.

BILL.

An Act respecting the Driving of Saw Logs and other Timber on Lakes, Rivers, Creeks and Streams.

First Reading, 9th March, 1887.

Mr. MURRAY.

BILL.

An Act respecting the Driving of Saw Logs and other
Timber on Lakes, Rivers, Creeks and Streams.

HER MAJESTY, by and with the advice and consent of the
Legislative Assembly of the Province of Ontario, enacts
as follows :—

☞ 1. The following words wherever used in this Act have
5 the following meanings, viz. :—

☞ (a) "Logs" mean and include saw logs, timber, posts,
ties, cordwood, and other things being parts of trees.

☞ (b) "Water" means and includes lakes, ponds, rivers,
creeks and streams.

10 ☞ 2. Any person putting, or causing to be put, into any water
in this Province, logs, for the purpose of floating the same in,
upon or down such water, shall make adequate provisions and
put on a sufficient force of men to break, and shall make all
reasonable endeavours to break, jams of such logs and clear the
15 same from the banks and shores of such water with reasonable despatch, and run and drive the same so as not to unnecessarily delay or hinder the removal, floating, running or driving
of other logs, or unnecessarily obstruct the floating or navigation of such water.

20 ☞ 3. In case of the neglect of any person to comply with the
provisions of the foregoing section, it shall be lawful for any
other person or persons desiring to float, run or drive logs in,
upon or down such water, and whose logs would be thereby
obstructed, to cause such jams to be broken and such logs to
25 be cleared from the banks and shores of such water, and to be
floated, run and driven in, upon and down such water.

☞ 4. The person or persons causing such jams to be broken
or such logs to be cleared, floated, run or driven, pursuant to
the last preceding section, shall do the same with reasonable
30 economy and despatch, and shall take reasonable care not to
leave logs on the banks or shores, and shall have a lien upon
the logs in the jam or so cleared, floated, run or driven for the
reasonable charges and expenses of breaking the jams and the
clearing, floating, running and driving of such logs, and may
35 take and keep possession of such logs, or so much thereof as
may be reasonably necessary to satisfy the amount of such
charges and expenses pending the decision by arbitration as
hereinafter provided for. The person taking possession of logs
under this section shall not take such logs beyond the place of
40 their original destination, but may securely boom and keep

possession of the same at or above such place. The owner or person controlling such logs shall be notified of their whereabouts, and if satisfactory security be given for the amount of such charges and expenses, possession of the logs shall be given up. 5

5. When logs of any person upon or in any water in this Province, or the banks, shores or beds of such water, are so intermixed with logs of another person or persons, that the same cannot be conveniently separated for the purpose of being floated in, upon or down such water, then the several 10 persons owning or controlling the intermixed logs, shall respectively make adequate provisions, and put on a fair proportion of the men required to break jams of such intermixed logs, and to clear the same from the banks and shores of such water with reasonable despatch, and to float, run and drive the 15 same in, upon and down such water, and the costs and expenses thereof shall be borne by the parties in such proportions as they may agree upon, and in default of agreement as may be determined by arbitration as hereinafter provided for.

6. In case of neglect of any person to comply with the 20 provisions of the last preceding section, it shall be lawful for any other person or persons whose logs are intermixed, to put on a sufficient number of men to supply the deficiency and break jams of such intermixed logs, and to clear the same from the banks and shores of such water, and to float, run and 25 drive all such intermixed logs in, upon and down such water.

7. The person or persons supplying such deficiency and causing such jams to be broken, or such intermixed logs to be cleared, floated, run or driven pursuant to the last preceding 30 section, shall do the same with reasonable economy and despatch, and shall take reasonable care not to leave logs on the banks or shores, and shall have a lien upon the logs owned or controlled by the person guilty of such neglect, for a fair proportion of the charges and expenses of breaking the jams, 35 and the clearing, floating, running and driving of such intermixed logs ; and may take and keep possession of such logs, or so much thereof, as may be reasonably necessary to satisfy the amount of such fair proportion of charges and expenses pending the decision by arbitration as hereinafter provided for. 40 The person taking possession of logs under this section shall not take such logs beyond the place of their original destination, but may securely boom and keep possession of the same at or above such place. The owner or person controlling such logs shall be notified of their whereabouts, and if satisfactory 45 security be given for the amount of such proportion of charges and expenses, possession of the logs be given up.

8. When logs of any person, upon or in any water in this Province, or the banks or shores of such water, are intermixed with logs of another person or persons, then any of the 50 persons whose logs are intermixed, may at any time during the drive, require his logs to be separated from the other logs at some suitable and convenient place, and secured in such manner as to allow free passage for such other logs.

9. The several persons owning or controlling the intermixed logs shall respectively make adequate provisions and put on a fair proportion of the men required to make the separation; the cost and expense of such separation shall be borne by the
5 parties in such proportions as they may agree upon, and in default of agreement, as may be determined by arbitrtion as hereinafte provided.

10. In case of neglect of any person to comply with the provisions of the last preceding section, it shall be lawful for
10 any other person or persons, whose logs are intermixed, to put on a sufficient number of men to supply the deficiency and the logs owned by or controlled by the person guilty of such neglect shall be subject to a lien in favor of the person or persons supplying the deficiency, for a fair proportion of the
15 charges and expenses of making the separation, and such person or persons may take and keep possession of such logs or so much thereof as may be reasonably necessary to satisfy the amount of such fair proportion of charges and expenses pending the decision by arbitration as hereinafter provided for.
20 The person taking possession of logs under this section shall not take such logs beyond the place of their original destination, but may securely boom and keep possession of the same at or above such place. The owner or person controlling such logs shall be notified of their whereabouts and if satisfactory
25 security be given for the amount of such proportion of charges and expenses, possession of the logs shall be given up.

11. If it be determined by arbitration, as hereinafter provided for, that any person acting under the assumed authority of this Act, has without just cause taken possession of or de-
30 tained or caused to be taken possession of or detained logs of another person, or has through want of reasonable care left logs of another person on the banks or shores or has taken logs of another person beyond the place of their original destination contrary to the provisions of sections 4, 7 or 10, then
35 such first mentioned person shall pay to such last mentioned person such damages as the arbitrators may determine.

12. The lien given by sections four, seven and ten of this Act shall be subject to the lien (if any) of any person or corporation for tolls or dues for the use of any works or improve-
40 ments made use of in running or driving such logs.

13. Nothing in this Act shall affect the liens or rights of the Crown upon or in respect of any logs.

14. All claims, disputes and differences arising under this Act shall be determined by arbitration as hereinafter provided
45 and not by action or suit at law or in equity.

15. The person claiming that another person has not complied with the provisions of this Act, or claiming payment of any charges or expenses under this Act, or claiming a lien upon any logs, or claiming damages under section 11,
50 shall give to such other person notice in writing stating the substance of the claims made, and appointing an arbitrator, and calling upon such other to appoint an arbitrator within seven days after the service of such

notice; if such other person does not within such seven
days appoint an arbitrator the Judge of the County or
District Court of the county or district, or the Stipendiary
Magistrate of the provisional county or the district, as the
case may be, in which the logs in connection with which the 5
claim or part of the claim is made, or the major portion of
such logs are situate at the time of the service of such notice,
shall, on the application of the person giving such notice,
appoint a second arbitrator; the two arbitrators so appointed
shall within seven days after the appointment of the said 10
second arbitrator appoint a third; if such two arbitrators do
not within such seven days appoint a third, the said Judge or
Stipendiary Magistrate shall on the application of either
party appoint such third arbitrator.

16. If any arbitrator refuses to act or becomes incapable 15
of acting, or dies, and the parties do not concur in appointing
a new arbitrator, the said Judge or Stipendiary Magistrate shall,
on the application of either party, appoint such new arbitrator.

17. The parties may agree that the arbitration shall be
by one arbitrator instead of by three, and they may either 20
agree upon the arbitrator or may apply to the said Judge or
Stipendiary Magistrate to appoint one.

18. The person on whom a claim is made and notice of
arbitration served may at any time before the arbitration is
entered upon or during the arbitration, with leave of the 25
arbitrators, give the claimant notice in writing by way of
counterclaim, stating the substance of any claim arising under
this Act which such person may have against the claimant,
and such counterclaim, unless barred under section 25, shall be
determined in the arbitration and an award made with respect 30
thereto.

19. The three arbitrators or the sole arbitrator, as the
case may be, shall proceed with the arbitration with due
despatch, and shall make their or his award in writing, under
their or his hand within thirty days from the date of the 35
appointment of such arbitrator, or the last of such three
arbitrators, as the case may be. The parties may, by consent
in writing, from time to time enlarge the time for making said
award, or the said Judge or Stipendiary Magistrate may from
time to time, either before or after the expiration of said time, 40
enlarge the time for making said award.

20. The arbitrators or arbitrator may require the personal attendance and examination upon oath of the parties and
their witnesses and the production of all books and documents
relating to the matters in question, and may determine by 45
whom the expense of the arbitration, and the costs of the
parties shall be paid, and the amount thereof; any costs or
expenses payable to a person having a lien upon logs, by virtue
of this Act shall be added to the amount of such lien.

21. Chapter 64 of the Revised Statutes of Ontario being 50
" an Act respecting the costs of Arbitrations " shall apply to
arbitrations under this Act.

22. The person or persons having a lien upon logs by virtue of this Act, may sell the same in order to realize the amount of such lien, and of the costs, charges and expenses connected with the sale. The arbitrators, or arbitrator, shall
5 determine either by their award or by separate document the time, place and manner of such sale, and may, from time to time, give directions, in writing, respecting such sale, and the realization of such lien, and of the costs, charges and expenses connected therewith.

10 **23.** The award and directions, in writing, of any two of the three arbitrators, or of the sole arbitrator, as the case may be, shall be final and binding upon and shall be obeyed by the parties, and shall be valid notwithstanding any want or defect of form or other technical objection.

15 **24.** The said Judge or Stipendiary Magistrate, as the case may be, may, on the application of either party, grant an order to compel any person or persons to attend and give evidence upon the arbitration and to produce all books and documents relating to the matters in dispute, and obedience to
20 such order may be enforced in the same way as obedience to any order of such Judge or Stipendiary Magistrate made in a cause or matter pending before him in court may be enforced, and the person neglecting or refusing, without lawful excuse, to obey such order shall be liable to an action by any person
25 aggrieved by such neglect or refusal for the damages sustained by him thereby.

25. All claims arising under this Act shall be made by notice in writing under section 15, written one year after the same have arisen, otherwise they shall be barred.

30 **26.** The Lieutenant-Governor in Council may from time to time by proclamation published in the *Ontario Gazette* declare that any portion or portions of this Province or any water therein shall, until further proclamation, be exempt from the operation of this Act. and thereupon the same shall
35 be exempt accordingly.

27. Any portion or portions of the Province, or any water therein exempted by proclamation from the operation of this Act, may by proclamation published in the *Ontario Gazette*, be again brought within its operation until further proclama-
40 tion, and so on from time to time.

No. 67.

BILL.

An Act respecting the Driving of Saw Logs and other Timber on Lakes, Rivers, Creeks and Streams.

(*Reprinted for consideration by Committee*).

First Reading   March, 1887.

BILL.

An Act respecting the Driving of Saw Logs and other Timber on Lakes, Rivers, Creeks and Streams.

HER MAJESTY, by and with the advice and consent of the Legislative Assembly of the Province of Ontario, enacts as follows:—

1. The following words wherever used in this Act have *Interpretation.*
5 the following meanings, viz. :—

   (a) "Logs" mean and include saw logs, timber, posts, ties, cordwood, and other things being parts of trees.

   (b) "Water" means and includes lakes, ponds, rivers, creeks and streams.

10 2. Any person putting, or causing to be put, into any water *Persons floating logs in river, etc., not to obstruct floating or navigation.* in this Province, logs, for the purpose of floating the same in, upon or down such water, shall make adequate provisions and put on a sufficient force of men to break, and shall make all reasonable endeavours to break, jams of such logs and clear the
15 same from the banks and shores of such water with reasonable despatch, and run and drive the same so as not to unnecessarily delay or hinder the removal, floating, running or driving of other logs, or unnecessarily obstruct the floating or navigation of such water.

20 3. In case of the neglect of any person to comply with the *In case of neglect person obstructed may clear river, etc.* provisions of the *preceding* section, it shall be lawful for any other person or persons desiring to float, run or drive logs in, upon or down such water, and whose logs would be thereby obstructed, to cause such jams to be broken and such logs to
25 be cleared from the banks and shores of such water, and to be floated, run and driven in, upon and down such water.

   4. The person or persons causing such jams to be broken *Person clearing obstruction to use due care.* or such logs to be cleared, floated, run or driven, pursuant to the last preceding section, shall do the same with reasonable
30 economy and despatch, and shall take reasonable care not to leave logs on the banks or shores, and shall have a lien upon the logs in the jam or so cleared, floated, run or driven for the reasonable charges and expenses of breaking the jams and the clearing, floating, running, driving, *booming and keeping*
35 *possession* of such logs, and may take and keep possession of such logs, or so much thereof as may be reasonably necessary to satisfy the amount of such charges and expenses pending the decision by arbitration as hereinafter provided for. The person taking possession of logs under this section shall *use all*
40 *reasonable care not to* take such logs beyond the place of their

4

Lien under ss. 4, 7 and 10, subject to lien for tolls. ☞**13.** The lien given by sections 4, 7 and 10 of this Act shall be subject to the lien (if any) of any person or corporation for tolls or dues for the use of any works or improvements made use of in running or driving such logs.

Rights of Crown not affected. ☞**14.** Nothing in this Act shall affect the liens or rights of the 5 Crown upon or in respect of any logs.

Disputes to be settled by arbitration. ☞**15.** All claims, disputes and differences arising under this Act shall be determined by arbitration as hereinafter provided and not by action or suit at law or in equity.

Appointment of arbitrators. ☞**16.** The person claiming that another person has not com- 10 plied with the provisions of this Act, or claiming payment of any charges or expenses under this Act, or claiming a lien upon any logs, or claiming damages under section 12, shall give to such other person notice in writing stating the substance of the claims made, and appointing an 15 arbitrator, and calling upon such other to appoint an arbitrator within ten days after the service of such notice ; if such other person does not within such ten days appoint an arbitrator the Judge of the County or District Court of the county or district, or the Stipendiary 20 Magistrate of the provisional county or the district, as the case may be, in which the logs in connection with which the claim or part of the claim is made, or the major portion of such logs are situate at the time of the service of such notice, shall, on the application of the person giving such notice, 25 appoint a second arbitrator ; the two arbitrators so appointed shall within ten days after the appointment of the said second arbitrator appoint a third ; if such two arbitrators do not within such ten days appoint a third, the said Judge or Stipendiary Magistrate shall on the application of either 30 party appoint such third arbitrator.

Appointment of new arbitrators. ☞**17.** If any arbitrator refuses to act or becomes incapable of acting, or dies, and the parties do not concur in appointing a new arbitrator, the said Judge or Stipendiary Magistrate shall, on the application of either party, appoint such new arbitrator. 35

Parties may agree to have only one arbitrator. ☞**18.** The parties may agree that the arbitration shall be by one arbitrator instead of by three, and they may either agree upon the arbitrator or may apply to the said Judge or Stipendiary Magistrate to appoint one.

Counter claim ☞**19.** The person on whom a claim is made and notice of 40 arbitration served may at any time before the arbitration is entered upon or with leave of the arbitrators *during the arbitration*, give the claimant notice in writing by way of counterclaim, stating the substance of any claim arising under this Act which such person may have against the claimant, 45 and such counterclaim, unless barred under section 26, shall be determined in the arbitration and an award made with respect thereto.

Time within which award to be made. ☞**20.** The three arbitrators or the sole arbitrator, as the case may be, shall proceed with the arbitration with due 50 despatch, and shall make their or his award in writing, under their or his hand within thirty days from the date of the appointment of such arbitrator, or the last of such three arbitrators, as the case may be. The parties may, by consent in writing, from time to time enlarge the time for making said 5 award, or the said Judge or Stipendiary Magistrate may from time to time, either before or after the expiration of said time, enlarge the time for making said award.

☞ **21.** The arbitrators or arbitrator may require the personal attendance and examination upon oath of the parties and 10 their witnesses and the production of all books and documents relating to the matters in question, and may determine by whom the expense of the arbitration, and the costs of the parties shall be paid, and the amount thereof; any costs or expenses payable to a person having a lien upon logs, by virtue 15 of this Act shall be added to the amount of such lien. *Witnesses and evidence.*

☞ **22.** Chapter 64 of the Revised Statutes of Ontario *intituled An Act respecting the costs of Arbitrations applies* to arbitrations under this Act. *R. S. O., c. 64, to apply.*

☞ **23.** The person or persons having a lien upon logs by 20 virtue of this Act, may sell the same in order to realize the amount of such lien, and of the costs, charges and expenses connected with the sale. The arbitrators, or arbitrator, shall determine either by their award or by separate document the time, place and manner of such sale, and may, from time to 25 time, give directions, in writing, respecting such sale, and the realization of such lien, and of the costs, charges and expenses connected therewith. *Sale by person having lien.*

☞ **24.** The award and directions, in writing, of any two of the three arbitrators, or of the sole arbitrator, as the case 30 may be, shall be final and binding upon and shall be obeyed by the parties, and shall be valid notwithstanding any want or defect of form or other technical objection. *Award and directions to be final.*

☞ **25.** The said Judge or Stipendiary Magistrate, as the case may be, may, on the application of either party, grant an 35 order to compel any person or persons to attend and give evidence upon the arbitration and to produce all books and documents relating to the matters in dispute, and obedience to such order may be enforced in the same way as obedience to any order of such Judge or Stipendiary Magistrate made in a 40 cause or matter pending before him in court may be enforced, and the person neglecting or refusing, without lawful excuse, to obey such order shall be liable to an action by any person aggrieved by such neglect or refusal for the damages sustained by him thereby. *Compelling attendance of witnesses and production of documents.*

45 ☞ **26.** All claims arising under this Act shall be made by notice in writing under section *16, within* one year after the same have arisen, otherwise they shall be barred. *Limitation of claims.*

☞ **27.** The Lieutenant-Governor in Council may from time to time by proclamation published in the *Ontario Gazette* 50 declare that any portion or portions of this Province or any *Lieut.-Governor in Council may exempt districts from Act.*

water therein shall, until further proclamation, be exempt from the operation of this Act. and thereupon the same shall be exempt accordingly.

District exempted may be brought under Act. **28.** Any portion or portions of the Province, or any water therein exempted by proclamation from the operation of this 5 Act, may by proclamation published in the *Ontario Gazette*, be again brought within its operation until further proclamation, and so on from time to time.

Title of Act. **29.** This Act may be cited and known as *The Saw Logs Driving Act, 1887.* 10

SCHEDULE.

FORM A.

Know all men by these presents that we (*here insert names of obligors, being the owner of the logs and at least one sufficient surety; or, if the signature of the owner cannot be obtained without unreasonable delay, then being two sureties*)   , are held and firmly bound unto *A. B.* (*here insert the name of the person claiming the lien*) in the penal sum of (*double the amount of the claim*) $, to be paid to the said *A. B.*, his executors, administrators and assigns, for which payment well and truly to be made, we, and each of us, bind ourselves, and each of us our and each of our executors and administrators jointly and severally, firmly by these presents, sealed with our seals, and signed by us this   day of   , A.D., 18   .

Whereas the said *A. B.*, claiming to act under the authority of *The Saw Logs Driving Act, 1887*, has taken possession of certain (saw logs, timber, etc., *as the case may be*) owned or controlled by   , and claims a lien thereon for the sum of $, under the provisions of section (4, 7 or 10, *as the case may be*) of the said Act.

And whereas this bond is given as security for payment to the said *A. B.*, of such sum as he may be held entitled to by arbitration pursuant to the said Act, and of any costs and expenses of the arbitration which may become payable to him.

Now the condition of the above obligation is such that if the said   , his executors or administrators do pay to the said *A. B.*, his executors, administrators or assigns, such sum as may be determined by arbitration pursuant to the said Act, to be payable to the said *A. B.*, his executors, administrators or assigns, for charges and expenses under section (4, 7 or 10, *as the case may be*) of said Act, and also such sum as may become payable to the said *A. B.*, his executors, administrators or assigns, for costs and expenses of such arbitration, then the above obligation to be void, otherwise to remain in full force.

Signed, sealed and delivered ⎫
   in the presence of   ⎬   [SEAL]
              ⎭

                    [SEAL]

1st Session, 6th Legislature, 50 Vic., 1887.

BILL.

An Act respecting the Driving of Saw Logs and other Timber on Lakes, Rivers, Creeks and Streams.

(Re-printed as amended by Select Committee)

First Reading, 9th March, 1887.
Second " 18th " 1887.

No. 68.]　　　　　**BILL.**　　　　　[1887.

An Act to Amend the Railway Act of Ontario.

HER MAJESTY, by and with the advice and consent of the Legislative Assembly of the Province of Ontario, enacts as follows:—

1. Section 20 of *The Railway Act of Ontario* is amended R. S. O. c. 165,
5 by adding the following clause thereto: s. 20, amended.

Any party feeling aggrieved by the proposed location may within fifteen days after receiving the notice aforesaid, apply to a County Court Judge of the County where said location has been made, by petition setting forth his objections to the
10 route designated, and the said Judge may, if he considers sufficient cause therefor exists, appoint three disinterested persons, one of whom must be a civil Engineer, Commissioners to examine the said proposed route, and after hearing the parties, to confirm or alter the same as may be consistent with the just
15 rights of all parties and the public, but no such alteration shall be made except with the concurrence of the Commissioner who is a civil Engineer. The determination of the Commissioners shall within thirty days after their appointment be made and certified by them, and the certificate filed in the
20 office of the Clerk of the Peace for the said County.

(a) The said Commissioners shall be entitled to the same fees as Arbitrators, and such fees shall in the first instance be paid by the person applying for their appointment, but if the proposed route is altered
25 or changed by the Commissioners, the Company shall refund to the applicant the amount so paid.

No. 68.

1st Session, 6th Legislature, 50 Vic., 1887.

BILL.

An Act to amend the Railway Act of
Ontario.

First Reading, 9th March, 1887.

No. 68.]　　　　　**BILL.**　　　　[1887.

An Act to amend the Railway Act of Ontario.

HER MAJESTY, by and with the advice and consent of the Legislative Assembly of the Province of Ontario, enacts as follows :—

☞ **1.** Section 10 of *The Railway Act of Ontario* is amended R. S. O. c. '165
5 by adding the following to sub-section 3 of the said section :— s. 10, amended.

☞ Any party feeling aggrieved by the proposed location of Appeal
the line of railway may, within ten days after the deposit of the against pro-
map or plan and book of reference aforesaid in the office of of line.
the Clerk of the Peace of the District or County where the
10 lands are situated, the location through which is complained
of, apply to the Lieutenant-Governor in Council, setting forth
his objections to the location of the proposed line, and the
Lieutenant-Governor in Council shall, if he considers sufficient
cause therefor exists, appoint a disinterested engineer, who
15 shall examine the said proposed line, and after hearing the
parties he shall confirm or alter the same as may be consistent
with the just rights of all parties and of the public. The
determination of the engineer shall, within ten days after his
appointment, be made and certified by him, and such certificate
20 shall be filed in the office of the Clerk of the Peace for the
District or County where the lands are situated.

☞ (a) The said engineer shall be entitled to reasonable fees
for each day employed in connection with the said
examination and work, together with his actual
25 expenses incurred therein, and the amount shall
in the first instance be paid by the person applying
for his appointment, but if the proposed route is
altered or changed by the engineer, the railway
company shall refund to the applicant the amount
30 so paid. ☜

No. 68.

1st Session, 6th Legislature, 50 Vic, 1887.

BILL.

An Act to amend the Railway Act of
Ontario.

*(Reprinted as amended by Select
Committee.)*

First Reading, 9th March, 1887.
Second   "   18th   "   1887.

No. 69.]   **BILL.**   [1887.

An Act to amend the Real Property Limitation Act.

WHEREAS, for the mutual temporary convenience of the Preamble.
owners of adjoining parcels of farming land, or land
used in connection with farming lands, and sometimes from
the division line between such parcels not being marked on the
5 ground, the fence intended to separate the lands of the adjoining owners has not been built on the proper division line :

Therefore Her Majesty, by and with the advice and consent
of the Legislative Assembly of the Province of Ontario, enacts
as follows :—

10   **1.** Section 1 of *The Act for the Further Limitation of* Construction
Actions and suits relating to Real Property or section 4 of of 38 V. c. 16,
The Real Property Limitation Act, shall not be construed to O. c. 108, s. 4.
affect the ownership of such adjoining parcels of farming lands
or of land used in connection with farming land, except in the
15 following cases :

1. Unless there has been a *bona fide* sale and conveyance
of the land after the building of the fence, or,

2. Unless the line or fence between the adjoining properties
has been run or erected by agreement between the adjoining
20 owners, or,

3. Unless a house, barn, or other building has been erected
on land between the fence and the correct division line.

2. In any such cases the period of limitation shall begin to When period
run from the erection of the fence, or of the house, barn, or of limitation
25 other building, or from the running of the line as the case may begins to run.
be.

3. If buildings or other improvements have been made by Compensation
an owner, to which buildings or other improvements the said where im-
Acts would entitle the owner of the adjoining parcel, such provements
30 owner of the adjoining parcel shall not be entitled to the land made.
beyond the fence, without making compensation for such
buildings or improvements.

4. The said Acts shall not be so construed in any case as to Construction
deprive the owner of land on either side of the fence of his of 38 V. c. 16,
35 right to have the line run correctly between the front and rear and R. S. O.
angles, or to claim and hold the ground on either side of the c. 108.
fence to which, but for the said Acts, he would be entitled.

5. This Act shall not affect any actions heretofore brought. Fending
actions not
affected.

No. 69.

1st Session, 6th Legislature, 50 Vic., 1887.

BILL.

An Act to amend the Real Property Limitation Act.

First Reading, 9th March, 1887.

No. 70.]　　　　**BILL.**　　　　[1887.

An Act to Amend the Assessment Act.

HER MAJESTY, by and with the advice and consent of the Legislative Assembly of the Province of Ontario, enacts as follows :—

1. Section 6 of *The Assessment Act* is hereby amended by adding thereto the following sub-section : — R. S. O. c. 180, s. 6, amended.

The annual income of any person derived from his personal earnings, provided the same does not exceed $800. Exemption of income.

BILL.

An Act to amend the Assessment Act.

First Reading, 9th March, 1887.

Mr. INGRAM.

TORONTO:

PRINTED BY WARWICK & SONS, 26 AND 28 FRONT ST. W.

BILL.

An Act to Amend the Assessment Act.

HER MAJESTY, by and with the advice and consent of the Legislative Assembly of the Province of Ontario, enacts as follows:—

1. Sub-section 22 of section 6 of *The Assessment Act* is R. S. O. c. 180,
5 hereby amended by substituting the words "one thousand" s. 6 (22), for the words "four hundred" in the second line of the said amended. sub-section.

BILL.

An Act to Amend the Assessment Act.

First Reading, 9th March, 1887.

Mr. GIBSON.
(*Hamilton.*)

TORONTO:
PRINTED BY WARWICK & SONS. 26 AND 28 FRONT ST. W.

No. 71.] **BILL.** [1887.

An Act to Amend the Assessment Act.

HER MAJESTY, by and with the advice and consent of the Legislative Assembly of the Province of Ontario, enacts as follows:—

1. Section 6 of *The Assessment Act* is amended by adding thereto the following sub-section:— R. S. O. c. 180, s. 6, amended.

(22*a*) The annual income of any person derived from his personal earnings, provided the same does not exceed $700.

5   **2.** Section 33 of the said Act shall not apply to Government officers or officers of minor municipalities when the location of the office is fixed by law or regulation of the Government or municipality, but in such cases the salary, gratuity or other compensation, shall be assessed against the incumbent of the 10 office in the municipality wherein he resides. Place of assessment of salaries of Government and municipal officers.

3. Section 45 of the said Act as amended by section 8 of the Act passed in the 49th year of Her Majesty's reign intituled *An Act to further amend the Assessment Act*, is hereby amended by inserting the word "townships" after the word 15 "towns," in the first line thereof. R. S. O. c. 180, s. 45, amended.

4. The said Act is further amended by adding the following section thereto:— Copy of assessment roll duly certified to be evidence.

(57*a*) A copy of any assessment roll, or portion of any assessment roll, written or printed, without any erasure or 20 interlineation, and under the seal of the corporation, and certified to be a true copy by the clerk of the municipality, shall be received as *prima facie* evidence in any court of justice without proof of the seal or signature, or the production of the original assessment roll, of which such certified copy purports 25 to be a copy, or a part thereof.

5. Sub-section 3 of section 59 of the said Act is repealed and the following substituted therefor:— R. S. O. c. 180, s. 59 (3) repealed.

(3) The clerk shall, immediately after the time limited for filing said appeals, forward a list of the same to the Judge, 30 who shall then notify the clerk of the day he appoints for the hearing thereof.

6. The said Act is further amended by adding thereto the following:—

2

Commutation of statute labour if not paid by resident owner to be entered upon collector's roll.

(87*a*) Where a resident owner, tenant or occupant who has been entered upon the assessment roll, after notice or demand, makes default in performing his statute labour or in payment of commutation for the same, the overseer of the highways in whose division he is placed, shall return him as a defaulter 5 to the clerk of the municipality before the fifteenth day of August, and the clerk shall in that case enter the commutation for statute labour against his name in the collector's roll, and the same shall be collected by the collector.

Overseer to expend the commutation money.

(*b*) In every such case the clerk shall notify the overseer of 10 highways, that may be appointed for such division in the following year, of the amount of such commutation, and the overseer shall expend the amount of such commutation upon the roads in the statute labour division where the property is situate, and shall give an order upon the treasurer of the municipality 15 to the party or parties performing the work; the notification by the clerk to the overseer shall be placed in the said list if not delivered to him before he receives such list.

R. S. O. c. 180, s. 137, amended.

7. Section 137 of the said Act is amended by adding the following sub-section thereto:— 20

Purchase by municipalities of land sold for taxes.

(3) If the council of the local municipality, in which the same shall be situate, desire to become the purchasers of any lot to which sub-section 2 refers for the amount of the arrears of taxes thereon, it shall be lawful for such municipality to purchase the same if the price offered at such adjourned sale 25 shall be less than the amount of such arrears, and if the council of the local municipality shall before the day of such adjourned sale have given notice in writing of the intention so to do, and it shall be the duty of the council of such local municipality to sell any lands which shall be so acquired by them within 30 three years from the time when they shall be acquired.

BILL.

An Act to amend the Assessment Act.

(*Re-printed as Amended by Municipal Committee.*)

First Reading, 9th March, 1887.
Second " 23rd " 1887.

No. 72.]   **BILL.**   [1887.

An Act to Amend the Act respecting the Education
Department.

HER MAJESTY, by and with the advice and consent of the
Legislative Assembly of the Province of Ontario, enacts
as follows :—

1. Section 4 of *The Act Respecting the Education Depart-* 48 V. c. 48. s.
5 *ment,* is hereby amended, by adding thereto the following sub- 4, amended.
sections :—

(17.) To make regulations for the study of agriculture and Instruction as
for scientific instruction as to the nature of alcoholic stimulants to agriculture
and narcotics, with special reference to their effect upon the of alcoholic
10 human system, and to authorize for the use of teachers and stimulants and
pupils, suitable text-books in said subjects, respectively, for use narcotics.
in all schools under the direction of the Department.

(18.) To make regulations for the organization of schools for Establishment
children between three and five years of age, to be known as of Kindergar-
15 Kindergarten Schools ; to provide for the training and licensing ten Schools.
of teachers for such schools, and to pay for their maintenance
out of any appropriation made by the Legislative Assembly for
Public Schools, such sums of money as such Kindergarten
Schools may be entitled to receive on the basis of average
20 attendance.

No. 72.

1st Session, 6th Legislature, 50 Vic., 1887.

BILL.

An Act to amend the Act respecting the Education Department.

First Reading, 23rd March, 1887.

No. 73.]　　　**BILL.**　　　[1887.

An Act to Amend the Act respecting Public Schools.

HER MAJESTY, by and with the advice and consent of the Legislative Assembly of the Province of Ontario, enact as follows :—

1. This Act shall be read conjointly with *The Public Schools* 5 *Act, 1885.*

Act to be read with 48 V. c. 49.

2. Section 22 of *The Public Schools Act, 1885,* is amended by adding the following words thereto:

48 V. c. 49, s. 22, amended.

And when such poll is closed the chairman and secretary shall count the votes polled for the respective candidates or for 10 the school question submitted, as the case may be, and shall declare the candidate elected, or the school question adopted, for which the highest number of votes was polled, or in case of a a tie the chairman shall give the casting vote, as provided in section 18 of this Act.

15　**3.** Section 23 of the said Act is hereby repealed and the following substituted therefor :

48 V. c. 49 s. 23, repealed.

23. The secretary of every school meeting at which any person or persons were elected as school trustees shall forthwith notify in writing each of such persons of his election, and 20 every person so notified shall be considered as having accepted such office unless a notice to the contrary effect has been delivered by him to such Secretary within twenty days after the date of such election.

Acceptance of office by trustees.

4. Section 27 of the said Act is hereby amended by adding 25 the following sub-section thereto :

49 V. c. 49, s. 27, amended.

(2) When the ratepayers of any school section, for one year, neglect or refuse to elect trustees, after being duly notified as herein provided, then such corporation shall cease to exist and such school section shall be dissolved, and it shall be the duty 30 of the council of the municipality to unite such sections or portions thereof to existing sections, according to the provisions of section 84 of this Act.

Dissolution of school sections.

5. Section 28 of the said Act is hereby repealed and the following substituted therefor :

48 V. c. 49, s. 28, repealed.

35　28. Wherever a new school section is formed in any township as provided in section 81 of this Act, the clerk of the township shall give notice of the number and description of such school section to the county inspector, who shall cause

Proceedings on formation of new school section.

copies of the notice so received by him to be posted in three
of the most public places in the new school section at least six
days before the last Wednesday in Decemher, in the year in
which such new school section was formed, and the first meeting in every new school section shall be held at the same time 5
as the annual meeting in rural school sections.

48 V. c. 49, s.
41, amended.

6. Section 41 of the said Act is hereby amended by adding
thereto the following sub-section

Notice of
formation of
school sections
in unorganized
townships.

(3) On the formation of a school section in any unorganized
township, the secretary or the secretary-treasurer of the school 10
board shall give written notice thereof to the Provincial
Treasurer, and shall also furnish him with a list of all the lands
embraced in the said school section, distinguishing such as are
occupied as farming lands from those that are unoccupied. (49
V. c. 5, s. 8.)   15

48 V. o. 49, s.
42, amended.

7. Section 42 of the said Act is hereby amended by adding
the following words thereto:

But this exemption shall not apply to other lands liable to
taxation for school purposes owned by such person within the
distance of three miles.   20

48 V. c. 49, s.
44, repealed.

8. Section 44 of the said Act is hereby amended by adding
thereto the following sub-section:

Court of
Revision.

(2) The secretary-treasurers of all such boards of public
school trustees in unorganized townships shall be, *ex-officio,*
members of a Court of Revision, any three of whom, acting to- 25
gether, shall be a legally constituted Court for the revision and
correction of school section assessment rolls, and for the hearing and settlement of any appeals against the same.
(R. S. O. c. 204, s. 28, amended.)

48 V. c. 49, s.
45, repealed.

9. Section 45 of the said Act is hereby repealed and the 30
following substituted therefor:

Annual assess-
ment roll.

The trustees of all school sections in unorganized townships
shall, annually, appoint a duly qualified person to make out an
assessment roll for the section, the secretary-treasurer of which
shall submit a certified copy of the same to the proper Court 35
of Revision for the correction of errors or improper entries
that may be found therein. (R. S. O. c. 204, s. 29.)

48 V. o. 49, s.
46, repealed.

10. Section 46 of the said Act is hereby repealed and the
following substituted therefor:

Appeal against
assessment

A copy of the said roll as so corrected shall be open to in- 40
spection by all persons interested, at some convenient place in
the section, notice whereof, signed by the secretary-treasurer
of the section, shall be, annually, posted in at least three of the
most public places in the section, and shall state the place and
the time at which the Court will hear appeals against said 45
assessment roll, and such notice shall be posted as aforesaid by
the trustees, for at least three weeks prior to the time appointed for hearing the appeals. (R. S. O. c. 204, s. 30.)

48 V. c. 49, s.
74, repealed.

11. Section 47 of the said Act is hereby repealed and the
following substituted therefor: 50

All appeals shall be made in the same manner and after the _{Manner of} appeal.
same notice, as nearly as may be, as appeals are made to a
Court of Revision in the case of ordinary municipal assessments,
and the Court of Revision, as constituted according to section
5 44, shall have the same powers as ordinary municipal Courts
of Revision. (R. S. O. c. 204, s. 31.)

12. Section 48 of the said Act is hereby repealed and the 48 V. c. 49, s.
following substituted therefor: 48, repealed.

The annual roll, as finally passed and signed by the Chair- Confirmed roll
10 man of the Court of Revision, shall be binding upon the binding.
trustees and rate-payers of the section, until the annual roll
for the succeeding year is passed and signed as aforesaid.
(R. S. O. c. 204, s. 32.)

13. Section 52 of the said Act is hereby amended by adding 48 V. c. 49, s.
15 thereto the following sub-section: 52, amended.

(2) The taxes amounting to one cent per acre imposed under
*The Act to amend the Act respecting the Taxation of Patented
Lands in Algoma*, shall, when collected, be paid over by the
Provincial Treasurer yearly to the trustees of the respective
20 school sections entitled thereto. (49 V. c. 5, s. 7.)

(3) Whenever the taxes levied by any board of trustees
upon unoccupied lands are not collected because of the non-resi-
dence of the owner thereof, it shall be the duty of the secretary-treasurer of such school board to make a return of
25 such uncollected taxes to the Provincial Treasurer, who shall
collect and pay over the same as the taxes in the next preceding sub-section mentioned are collected and paid over.

14. Section 67 of the said Act is hereby amended by insert- 48 V. c. 49, s.
ing after the word "Inspector," in the sixth line thereof, the 67, amended.
30 words "or in case of his inability to attend, any person
appointed by him on his behalf as third arbitrator."

15. Sub-section 2 of section 74 of the said Act is hereby 48 V. c. 49, s.
repealed.   74, (2) repeal-
                                                                   ed.

16.—(1) Section 82 of the said Act is hereby amended by 48 V. c. 49, s.
35 striking out the words "on application being made to it by the 82, amended.
Trustees or Inspector, or any five ratepayers concerned," in the
eighth and ninth lines of sub-section 1 of the said section.

(2) Sub-section 2 of the said section is hereby amended by
striking out the word "forthwith" in the first line and insert-
40 ing the words "at its discretion."

(3) Sub-section 3 of the said section is hereby repealed.

17. Sub-section 6 of section 86 of the said Act is hereby 48 V. c. 49, s.
amended by striking out the words "appoint a person to," in 86 (6),
the second line, and by substituting the word "and" for the amended.
45 word "who" in the third line.

18. Section 87 of the said Act is hereby amended by strik- 48 V. c. 48, s.
ing out all that portion of the section after the word "section" 87, amended.
in the seventh line, and inserting the following: "or against the
50 neglect or refusal of the township council or councils con-

4

cerned to appoint arbitrators, as provided in section 86 of this
Act and on the receipt of such appeal the county council
shall have power to appoint not more than three arbitrators,
who shall neither be ratepayers in the school section, nor
members of the municipal councils concerned, and such arbi- 5
trators shall have all the powers of arbitrators appointed under
said section 86, and the decision of a majority shall be final and
conclusive."

48 V. c. 49, s.
86, amended.

19. Section 88 of the said Act is amended by striking out
all the words after the word "section" in the sixth line and insert- 10
ing " or against the refusal or neglect of the township council
or councils concerned to appoint arbitrators, to the Minister of
Education, who shall have power to alter, determine, or confirm
such by-law, or where no by-law was passed, then at his discretion to appoint not more than three arbitrators, who shall 15
proceed as provided in section 86 of this Act, and the decision
of a majority of them shall be final and conclusive.

48 V. c. 49, s.
96, amended.

20. Section 96 of the said Act is hereby amended by adding
thereto the following as sub-sections 3 and 4 :

(3) In case any village, town or city, is incorporated, the 20
trustees having jurisdiction over the school property situated
within such village, town or city, prior to its incorporation,
shall exercise all the powers conferred by this Act upon the
trustees of incorporated villages, towns or cities, until a new
election of trustees is held, and such trustees shall call a meet- 25
ing of the ratepayers of such incorporated village, town or city,
within one month after the date of such incorporation for the
election of a new Public School Board.

(4) In calling the meeting of the ratepayers of such newly
incorporated village, town, or city, the provisions of section 98 30
shall be complied with so far as the same are applicable.

48 V. c. 49, s.
97, amended.

21. Section 97 of the said Act is hereby amended by adding
thereto the following words : " and every board of trustees in
cities, towns, and incorporated villages elected as provided by
this Act shall be a corporation by the name of The   35
Public School Board, (prefixing to the words "Public School
Board " the name of the city, town or incorporated village for
which such trustees are elected) and shall have and possess all
the powers usually possessed by corporations, so far as the same
are necessary for carrying out the purposes of this Act.   40

48 V. c. 49, s.
98 (7),
amended.

22. Sub-section 7 of section 98 of the said Act is hereby
amended by striking out all the words after the word "votes"
in the fourth line thereof and substituting the following: " and
shall forthwith notify the candidates in writing of the number
of votes polled for each of them respectively in said election." 45

48 V. c. 49, s.
98 (8),
amended.

23. Sub-section 8 of section 98 of the said Act is hereby
amended by inserting after the word "present" in the second line
thereof the words " at the first meeting thereof after such
election," and by striking out of the fourth line the words " at
the time of declaring the result of the poll."   50

48 V. c. 49, s.
107, amended.

24. Section 107 of the said Act is hereby amended by
inserting after the word " any " in the first line thereof the
word " actual."

25. Section 108 of the said Act is hereby repealed and the following substituted therefor :— 48 V. c. 49, s. 108, repealed.

108. The members of every board of school trustees shall hold their first meeting on the third Wednesday in January in
5 the same year in which they were elected (or if a board of education then on the first Wednesday in February) at the hour of one o'clock in the afternoon, at the usual place of meeting of such board, and no business shall be proceeded with at such first meeting except the appointment of a chairman and
10 such other business as may be necessary for the organization of such board. First meeting of Board.

26. Section 114 of the said Act is hereby amended by adding the following sub-section thereto :— 48 V. c. 49, 114, amended.

(13) To provide for children between three and five years of
15 age a course of instruction and training according to the methods practised in Kindergarten schools, subject however to the regulations of the Education Department in that behalf. Kindergarten schools.

27. Sub-section 12 of section 114 of the said Act is hereby amended by inserting after the word "schools" in the fourth
20 line thereof the following words : "and shall have the same powers in regard to school property generally as are conferred upon the trustees of rural schools by sub-section 9 of section 40 of this Act, and all such powers may be exercised with or without a vote of the ratepayers. 48 V. c. 49, s. 114 (12), amended.

25 **28.** Section 130 of the said Act is hereby amended by adding the following thereto :— 48 V. c. 49, s. 130, amended.

(3) When the ratepayers refuse to approve of such proposal for raising money for the school accommodation required by this Act, it shall be lawful for the municipal council of the
30 municipality in which such school section is situated, on the report of the Public School Inspector, that the accommodation is inadequate, and on the application of the trustees of such section, to issue debentures in the manner provided in this Act, for any of the purposes in this section mentioned, without the
35 approval of the ratepayers of such school section.

29. Section 134 of the said Act is hereby amended by adding thereto the following sub-section :— 48 V. c. 49, s. 134, amended.

40 (2) Nothing in this section contained shall be construed to mean that the municipal council may not, if deemed expedient, without submitting the same to a vote of the ratepayers of such municipality, as required by *The Consolidated Municipal Act, 1883*, for the creating of debts, pass a by-law
45 for the purpose of raising or borrowing money, on the requisition of the Public School Board, for any of the purposes named in this section.

30. Section 154 of the said Act is hereby amended by adding thereto the following sub-section :— 48 V. c. 49, s. 154, amended.

50 (11) To notify the Medical Health Officer of the municipality, or where there is none to notify the local board of health, whenever he has reason to believe that any pupil attending school

is affected with or exposed to small-pox, cholera, scarlatina, diphtheria, whooping-cough, measles, mumps, or other contagious disease, and to prevent the attendance of all pupils so exposed, or suspected of being exposed, until furnished with the written statement of the health officer, or of the local board 5 of health, or of a physician, that such contagious diseases did not exist, or that all danger from exposure to any of them had passed away.

48 V. c. 49, s. 155, amended. **31.** Section 155 of the said Act is hereby amended by inserting after the word "taught," in the fourth line, the words 10 "in the calendar year," and by substituting the word "such" for the word "the," in the fifth line.

48 V. c. 49, s. 191, amended. **32.** Section 191 of the said Act is hereby amended by adding thereto the following sub-section :—

(2) In making their award the arbitrators shall among other 15 things determine the liabilities of the parties concerned therein for the costs of such arbitration, and such determination shall be final and conclusive.

48 V. c. 49, s. 245, repealed. **33.** Section 245 of the said Act is hereby repealed, and the following substituted therefor :— 20

Fine on disqualified person acting as trustee. **34.** If any person elected as a school trustee attends any meetings of the school board as such, after being disqualified under this Act, he shall be liable to a penalty of $20, for every meeting so attended.

48 V. c. 49, s. 247, amended. **35.** Section 247 of the said Act is hereby amended by substituting for the words "a resident within the school municipality," in the fifth line, the words "an actual resident within the school section."

1st Session, 6th Legislature, 50 Vic., 1887

BILL.

An Act to amend the Act respecting Public Schools.

First Reading, 23rd March, 1887.

No. 73.]   **BILL.**   [1887.

An Act to Amend the Act respecting Public Schools.

HER MAJESTY, by and with the advice and consent of the Legislative Assembly of the Province of Ontario, enacts as follows :—

1. This Act shall be read conjointly with *The Public Schools* Act to be read with 48 V. c. 49.
5 *Act, 1885.*

2. Section 22 of *The Public Schools Act, 1885,* is amended 48 V. c. 49, s. amended.
by adding the following words thereto:

And when such poll is closed the chairman and secretary shall count the votes polled for the respective candidates or for 10 the school question submitted, as the case may be, and shall declare the candidate elected, or the school question adopted, for which the highest number of votes was polled, or in case of a a tie the chairman shall give the casting vote, as provided in section 18 of this Act.

15 **3.** Section 23 of the said Act is hereby repealed and the 48 V. c. 49 s. 23, repealed.
following substituted therefor :

23. The secretary of every school meeting at which any Acceptance of office by trustees.
person or persons were elected as school trustees shall forth-with notify in writing each of such persons of his election, and 20 every person so notified shall be considered as having accepted such office unless a notice to the contrary effect has been delivered by him to such Secretary within twenty days after the date of such election.

4. Section 27 of the said Act is hereby amended by adding 49 V. c. 49, s. 27, amended.
25 the following sub-section thereto:

(2) When the ratepayers of any school section, for two years, Dissolution of school sec-tions.
neglect or refuse to elect trustees, after being duly notified as herein provided, the municipal council of the township may appoint trustees for the said school section, who shall hold 30 office for the same term as if elected by the ratepayers.

5. Section 28 of the said Act is hereby repealed and the 48 V. c. 49, s. 28, repealed.
following substituted therefor :

28. Wherever a new school section is formed in any town- Proceedings on formation of new school section.
ship as provided in section 81 of this Act, the clerk of the 35 township shall give notice of the number and description of such school section to the county inspector, who shall cause copies of the notice so received by him to be posted in three of the most public places in the new school section at least six

days before the last Wednesday in December, in the year in which such new school section was formed, and the first meeting in every new school section shall be held at the same time as the annual meeting in rural school sections.

48 V. c. 49, s. 42, amended.

6. Section 42 of the said Act is hereby amended by adding 5 the following words thereto:

But this exemption shall not apply to lands liable to taxation for school purposes owned by such person within the distance of three miles.

48 V. c. 49, s. 44, repealed.

7. Section 44 of the said Act is hereby amended by adding 10 thereto the following sub-section:

Court of Revision.

(2) The secretary-treasurers of all such boards of public school trustees in unorganized townships shall be, *ex-offico*, members of a Court of Revision, any three of whom, acting together, shall be a legally constituted Court for the revision and 15 correction of school section assessment rolls, and for the bearing and settlement of any appeals against the same. (R. S. O. c. 204, s. 28, amended.)

(3) The inspector of schools for the district shall divide the school sections into groups of three sections in every group, 20 and shall notify the secretary-treasurers of the sections concerned of the group to which they respectively belong.

(4) In every case where from the sparseness of settlements, it would be inconvenient for a Court of Revision as herein constituted to meet for the revision and equali- 25 zation of the assessment roll, it shall be lawful for the inspector, on the request of any board of trustees, to assume the functions of such Court of Revision for the section on behalf of which such request is made, and all the proceedings of the inspector in the matter of the revision or correction 30 of the assessment roll, shall be subject to the provisions of this Act, and shall have the same effect as if made in a Court of Revision.

48 V. c. 49, s. 45, repealed.

8. Section 45 of the said Act is hereby repealed and the following substituted therefor: 35

Annual assessment roll.

The trustees of all school sections in unorganized townships shall, annually, appoint a duly qualified person to make out an assessment roll for the section, the secretary-treasurer of which shall submit a certified copy of the same to the proper Court of Revision for the correction of errors or improper entries 40 that may be found therein. (R. S. O. c. 204, s. 29.)

48 V. c. 49, s. 46, repealed.

9. Section 46 of the said Act is hereby repealed and the following substituted therefor:

Appeal against assessment.

A copy of the said roll as so corrected shall be open to inspection by all persons interested, at some convenient place in 45 the section, notice whereof, signed by the secretary-treasurer of the section, shall be, annually, posted in at least three of the most public places in the section, and shall state the place and the time at which the Court will hear appeals against said assessment roll, and such notice shall be posted as aforesaid by 50 the trustees, for at least three weeks prior to the time appointed for hearing the appeals. (R. S. O. c. 204, s. 30.)

3

10. Section 47 of the said Act is hereby repealed and the following substituted therefor: _{48 V. c. 49, s. 74, repealed.}

All appeals shall be made in the same manner and after the same notice, as nearly as may be, as appeals are made to a 5 Court of Revision in the case of ordinary municipal assessments, and the Court of Revision, as constituted according to section 44, shall have the same powers as ordinary municipal Courts of Revision. (R. S. O. c. 204, s. 31.) _{Manner of appeal.}

11. Section 48 of the said Act is hereby repealed and the 10 following substituted therefor: _{48 V. c. 49, s. 48, repealed.}

The annual roll, as finally passed and signed by the Chairman of the Court of Revision, shall be binding upon the trustees and rate-payers of the section, until the annual roll for the succeeding year is passed and signed as aforesaid. 15 (R. S. O. c. 204, s. 32.) _{Confirmed roll binding.}

12. Section 67 of the said Act is hereby amended by inserting after the word "Inspector," in the sixth line thereof, the words " or in case of his inability to attend, any person appointed by him on his behalf as third arbitrator." _{48 V. c. 49, s. 67, amended.}

20 **13.** Sub-section 2 of section 74 of the said Act is hereby repealed. _{48 V. c. 49, s. 74, (2) repealed.}

14.—(1) Section 82 of the said Act is hereby amended by striking out the words " or Inspector," in the ninth line of sub-section 1 of the said section. _{48 V. c. 49, s. 82, amended.}

25 (2) Sub-section 2 of the said section is hereby amended by striking out the word "forthwith" in the first line and inserting the words "*may if it thinks fit.*"

(3) Sub-section 3 of the said section is hereby repealed.

15. Sub-section 6 of section 86 of the said Act is hereby 30 amended by striking out the words "appoint a person to," in the second line, and by substituting the word "and" for the word "who" in the third line. _{48 V. c. 49, s. 86 (6), amended.}

16. Section 87 of the said Act is hereby amended by striking out all that portion of the section after the word "section" 35 in the seventh line, and inserting the following : " or against the neglect or refusal of the township council or councils concerned to appoint arbitrators, as provided in section 86 of this Act and on the receipt of such appeal the county council shall have power to appoint not more than three arbitrators, 40 who shall neither be ratepayers in the school section, nor members of the municipal councils concerned, and such arbitrators shall have all the powers of arbitrators appointed under said section 86, and the decision of a majority shall be final and conclusive." _{48 V. c. 48, s. 87, amended.}

45 **17.** Section 88 of the said Act is amended by striking out all the words after the word "section" in the sixth line and inserting " or against the refusal or neglect of the township council or councils concerned to appoint arbitrators, to the Minister of Education, who shall have power to alter, determine, or confirm 50 such by-law, or where no by-law was passed, then at his dis- _{48 V. c. 49, s. 88, amended.}

cretion to appoint not more than three arbitrators, who shall proceed as provided in section 86 of this Act, and the decision of a majority of them shall be final and conclusive.

48 V. c. 49, s. 91, amended.

18. Section 91 is hereby amended by striking out the words " date fixed by *The Assessment Act* for the return of the roll," and inserting in lieu thereof, " first day of July." 5

48 V. c. 49, s. 96, amended.

19. Section 94 of the said Act is hereby *repealed and the following inserted in lieu thereof :—*

(1) In case any village, town or city, is incorporated, the trustees having jurisdiction over the school property situated 10 within such village, town or city, prior to its incorporation, shall exercise all the powers conferred by this Act upon the trustees of incorporated villages, towns or cities, until a new election of trustees is held, and such trustees shall call a meeting of the ratepayers of such incorporated village, town or city, 15 within one month after the date of such incorporation for the election of a new Public School Board.

(2) In calling the meeting of the ratepayers of such newly incorporated village, town, or city, the provisions of section 98 shall be complied with so far as the same are applicable. 20

48 V. c. 49, s. 97, amended.

20.—(1) Section 97 of the said Act is hereby amended by adding thereto the following words : " and every board of trustees in cities, towns, and incorporated villages elected as provided by this Act shall be a corporation by the name of The 25 Public School Board, (prefixing to the words ' Public School Board ' the name of the city, town or incorporated village for which such trustees are elected) and shall have and possess all the powers usually possessed by corporations, so far as the same are necessary for carrying out the purposes of this Act." 30

(2) When any town or incorporated village is annexed to a city, the town or incorporated village so annexed shall, for all the purposes of this Act, be deemed to be part of the city.

48 V. c. 49, s. 98 (7), amended.

21. Sub-section 7 of section 98 of the said Act is hereby amended by striking out all the words after the word " votes" 35 in the fourth line thereof and substituting the following : " and shall forthwith notify the candidates in writing of the number of votes polled for each of them respectively in said election."

48 V. c. 49, s. 98 (8), amended.

22. Sub-section 8 of section 98 of the said Act is hereby amended by inserting after the word " present" in the second line 40 thereof the words " at the first meeting thereof after such election *and before the organization of the board,*" and by striking out of the fourth line the words " at the time of declaring the result of the poll."

48 V. c. 49, s. 107, amended.

23. Section 107 of the said Act is hereby amended by 45 inserting after the word " any " in the first line thereof the word " actual."

48 V. c. 49, s. 108, repealed.

24. Section 108 of the said Act is hereby repealed and the following substituted therefor :—

5

108. The members of every board of school trustees shall First meeting of Board. hold their first meeting on the third Wednesday in January in each year in which they were elected (or if a board of education then on the first Wednesday in February) at the hour of one o'clock in the afternoon, at the usual place of meeting of such board, and no business shall be proceeded with at such first meeting except the appointment of a chairman and such other business as may be necessary for the organization of such board.

10 **25.** Section 114 of the said Act is hereby amended by adding the following sub-section thereto:— *48 V. c. 49, s. 114, amended.*

(13) To provide *if deemed expedient* for children between *Kindergarten schools.* three and five years of age a course of instruction and training according to the methods practised in Kindergarten schools, 15 subject however to the regulations of the Education Department in that behalf.

26. Sub-section 12 of section 114 of the said Act is hereby *48 V. c. 49, s. 114 (12), amended.* amended by inserting after the word "schools" in the fourth line thereof the following words: "and shall have the same 20 powers in regard to school property generally as are conferred upon the trustees of rural schools by sub-section 9 of section 40 of this Act, and all such powers may be exercised with or without a vote of the ratepayers.

27. Section 134 of the said Act is hereby amended by adding *48 V. c. 49, s. 134, amended.* 25 ing thereto the following sub-section:—

(2) Nothing in this section contained shall be construed to mean that the municipal council may not, if deemed expedient, without submitting the same to a vote of the ratepayers of such municipality, as required by *The Consolidated* 30 *Municipal Act, 1883*, for the creating of debts, pass a by-law for the purpose of raising or borrowing money, on the requisition of the Public School Board, for any of the purposes named in this section.

28. Section 154 of the said Act is hereby amended by adding *48 V. c. 49, s. 154, amended.* 35 ing thereto the following sub-section:—

(11) To notify the Medical Health Officer of the municipality, or where there is none to notify the local board of health, whenever he has reason to believe that any pupil attending school is affected with or exposed to small-pox, cholera, scarlatina, 40 diphtheria, whooping-cough, measles, mumps, or other contagious disease, and to prevent the attendance of all pupils so exposed, or suspected of being exposed, until furnished with the written statement of the health officer, or of the local board of health, or of a physician, that such contagious diseases did 45 not exist, or that all danger from exposure to any of them had passed away.

29. Section 155 of the said Act is hereby amended by inserting after the word "taught," in the fourth line, the words *48 V. c. 49, s. 155, amended.* "in the calendar year," and by substituting the word "such" for 50 the word "the," in the fifth line.

48 V. c. 49, s. 191, amended.   **30**. Section 191 of the said Act is hereby amended by adding thereto the following sub-section :—

(2) In making their award the arbitrators shall among other things determine the liabilities of the parties concerned therein for the costs of such arbitration, and such determination shall be final and conclusive.   5

48 V. c. 49, s. 245, repealed.   **31**. Section 245 of the said Act is hereby repealed, and the following substituted therefor :—

Fine on disqualified person acting as trustee.   **245**. If any person elected as a school trustee attends any meetings of the school board as such, after being disqualified 10 under this Act, he shall be liable to a penalty of $20, for every meeting so attended.

48 V. c. 49, s. 247, amended   **32**. Section 247 of the said Act is hereby amended by substituting for the words " a resident within the school municipality," in the fifth line, the words " an actual resident 15 within the school section."

48 V. c. 49, s. 97, amended.   **33**. Section 97 of the said Act is hereby amended by adding thereto the words, " and the new board is organized."

No. 73.

1st Session, 6th Legislature, 50 Vic., 1887.

BILL.

An Act to amend the Act respecting Public Schools.

(*Reprinted as amended by Committee of Whole House.*)

First Reading, 23rd March, 1887.
Second "   31st "   1887.

No. 73.]   **BILL.**   [1887.

An Act to Amend the Act respecting Public Schools.

H ER MAJESTY, by and with the advice and consent of the Legislative Assembly of the Province of Ontario, enacts as follows :—

1. This Act shall be read conjointly with *The Public Schools* 5 *Act, 1885.*

Act to be read with 48 V. c. 49.

2. Section 22 of *The Public Schools Act, 1885,* is amended by adding the following words thereto:

48 V. c. 49, s. 22 amended.

And when such poll is closed the chairman and secretary shall count the votes polled for the respective candidates or for 10 the school question submitted, as the case may be, and shall declare the candidate elected, or the school question adopted, for which the highest number of votes was polled, or in case of a tie the chairman shall give the casting vote, as provided in section 18 of this Act.

15   **3.** Section 23 of the said Act is hereby repealed and the following substituted therefor :

48 V. c. 49 s. 23, repealed.

23. The secretary of every school meeting at which any person or persons were elected as school trustees shall forthwith notify in writing each of such persons of his election, and 20 every person so notified shall be considered as having accepted such office unless a notice to the contrary effect has been delivered by him to such secretary within twenty days after the date of such election.

Acceptance of office by trustees.

25   **4.** Section 27 of the said Act is hereby amended by adding the following sub-section thereto:

49 V. c. 49, s. 27, amended.

(2) When the ratepayers of any school section, for two years, neglect or refuse to elect trustees, after being duly notified as herein provided, the municipal council of the township may 30 appoint trustees for the said school section, who shall hold office for the same term as if elected by the ratepayers.

Dissolution of school sections.

5. Section 28 of the said Act is hereby repealed and the following substituted therefor:

48 V. c. 49, s. 28, repealed.

28. Wherever a new school section is formed in any township as provided in section 81 of this Act, the clerk of the township shall give notice of the number and description of such school section to the county inspector, who shall cause copies of the notice so received by him to be posted in three of the most public places in the new school section at least six

Proceedings on formation of new school section.

days before the last Wednesday in December, in the year in which such new school section was formed, and the first meeting in every new school section shall be held at the same time as the annual meeting in rural school sections.

48 V. c. 49, s. 42, amended.

6. Section 42 of the said Act is hereby amended by adding the following words thereto:

"But this exemption shall not apply to lands liable to taxation for school purposes owned by such person within the distance of three miles."

48 V. c. 49, s. 44, repealed.

7. Section 44 of the said Act is hereby amended by adding thereto the following sub-sections:

Court of Revision.

(2) The secretary-treasurers of all such boards of public school trustees in unorganized townships shall be, *ex-officio*, members of a Court of Revision, any three of whom, acting together, shall be a legally constituted Court for the revision and correction of school section assessment rolls, and for the hearing and settlement of any appeals against the same.

(3) The inspector of schools for the district shall divide the school sections into groups of three sections in every group, and shall notify the secretary-treasurers of the sections concerned of the group to which they respectively belong.

(4) In every case where from the sparseness of settlements, it would be inconvenient for a Court of Revision as herein constituted to meet for the revision and equalization of the assessment roll, it shall be lawful for the inspector, on the request of any board of trustees, to assume the functions of such Court of Revision for the section on behalf of which such request is made, and all the proceedings of the inspector in the matter of the revision or correction of the assessment roll, shall be subject to the provisions of this Act, and shall have the same effect as if made in a Court of Revision.

48 V. c. 49, s. 45, repealed.

8. Section 45 of the said Act is hereby repealed and the following substituted therefor:

Annual assessment roll.

The trustees of all school sections in unorganized townships shall, annually, appoint a duly qualified person to make out an assessment roll for the section, the secretary-treasurer of which shall submit a certified copy of the same to the proper Court of Revision for the correction of errors or improper entries that may be found therein.

48 V. c. 49, s. 46, repealed.

9. Section 46 of the said Act is hereby repealed and the following substituted therefor:

Appeal against assessment.

A copy of the said roll as so corrected shall be open to inspection by all persons interested, at some convenient place in the section, notice whereof, signed by the secretary-treasurer of the section, shall be, annually, posted in at least three of the most public places in the section, and shall state the place and the time at which the Court will hear appeals against said assessment roll, and such notice shall be posted as aforesaid by the trustees, for at least three weeks prior to the time appointed for hearing the appeals.

10. Section 47 of the said Act is hereby repealed and the following substituted therefor : 48 V. c. 49, s. 47, repealed.

All appeals shall be made in the same manner and after the same notice, as nearly as may be, as appeals are made to a 5 Court of Revision in the case of ordinary municipal assessments, and the Court of Revision, as constituted according to section 44, shall have the same powers as ordinary municipal Courts of Revision. Manner of appeal.

11. Section 48 of the said Act is hereby repealed and the 10 following substituted therefor: 48 V. c. 49, s. 48, repealed.

The annual roll, as finally passed and signed by the chairman of the Court of Revision, shall be binding upon the trustees and rate-payers of the section, until the annual roll for the succeeding year is passed and signed as aforesaid. Confirmed roll binding.

15 **12**. Section 67 of the said Act is hereby amended by inserting after the word "Inspector," in the sixth line thereof, the words "or in case of his inability to attend, any person appointed by him on his behalf as third arbitrator." 48 V. c. 49, s. 67, amended.

13. Sub-section 2 of section 74 of the said Act is hereby 20 repealed. 48 V. c. 49, s. 74, (2) repealed.

14.—(1) Section 82 of the said Act is hereby amended by striking out the words " or Inspector," in the ninth line of sub-section 1 of the said section. 48 V. c. 49, s. 82, amended.

(2) Sub-section 2 of the said section is hereby amended by 25 striking out the word "forthwith" in the first line and inserting the words "may if it thinks fit."

(3) Sub-section 3 of the said section is hereby repealed.

15. Sub-section 6 of section 86 of the said Act is hereby amended by striking out the words "appoint a person to," in 30 the second line, and by substituting the word "and" for the word "who" in the third line. 48 V. c. 49, s. 86 (6), amended.

16. Section 87 of the said Act is hereby amended by striking out all that portion of the section after the word "section" in the seventh line, and inserting the following: " or against the 35 neglect or refusal of the township council or councils concerned to appoint arbitrators, as provided in section 86 of this Act and on the receipt of such appeal the county council shall have power to appoint not more than three arbitrators, who shall neither be ratepayers in the school section, nor 40 members of the municipal councils concerned, and such arbitrators shall have all the powers of arbitrators appointed under said section 86, and the decision of a majority shall be final and conclusive." 48 V. c. 48, s. 87, amended.

17. Section 88 of the said Act is amended by striking out 45 all the words after the word "section" in the sixth line and inserting " or against the refusal or neglect of the township council or councils concerned to appoint arbitrators, to the Minister of Education, who shall have power to alter, determine, or confirm such by-law, or where no by-law was passed, then at his dis- 48 V. c. 49, s. 88, amended.

cretion to appoint not more than three arbitrators, who shall proceed as provided in section 86 of this Act, and the decision of a majority of them shall be final and conclusive."

48 V. c. 49, s. 91, amended.

18. Section 91 is hereby amended by striking out the words " date fixed by *The Assessment Act* for the return of the 5 roll," and inserting in lieu thereof, " first day of July."

48 V. c. 49, s. 94, amended.

19. Section 94 of the said Act is hereby repealed and the following inserted in lieu thereof:—

(1) In case any village, town or city, is incorporated, the trustees having jurisdiction over the school property situated 10 within such village, town or city, prior to its incorporation, shall exercise all the powers conferred by this Act upon the trustees of incorporated villages, towns or cities, until a new election of trustees is held, and such trustees shall call a meeting of the ratepayers of such incorporated village, town or city, 15 within one month after the date of such incorporation for the election of a new Public School Board.

(2) In calling the meeting of the ratepayers of such newly incorporated village, town, or city, the provisions of section 98 shall be complied with so far as the same are applicable. 20

48 V. c. 49, s. 97, amended.

20.—(1) Section 97 of the said Act is hereby amended by adding thereto the following : "and the new board is organized," and by also adding the following sub-section : (2) "every board of trustees in cities, towns, and incorporated villages elected as provided by this Act shall be a corporation by the name 25 of The
Public School Board, (prefixing to the words 'Public School Board' the name of the city, town or incorporated village for which such trustees are elected) and shall have and possess all the powers usually possessed by corporations, so far as the same 30 are necessary for carrying out the purposes of this Act."

(3) When any town or incorporated village is annexed to a city, the town or incorporated village so annexed shall, for all the purposes of this Act, be deemed to be part of the city.

48 V. c. 49, s. 98 (7), amended.

21. Sub-section 7 of section 98 of the said Act is hereby 35 amended by striking out all the words after the word " votes" in the fourth line thereof and substituting the following : " and shall forthwith notify the candidates in writing of the number of votes polled for each of them respectively in said election.'

48 V. c. 49, s. 98 (8), amended.

22. Sub-section 8 of section 98 of the said Act is hereby 40 amended by inserting after the word "present" in the second line thereof the words " at the first meeting thereof after such election and before the organization of the board," and by striking out of the fourth line the words " at the time of declaring the result of the poll." 45

48 V. c. 49, s. 107, amended.

23. Section 107 of the said Act is hereby amended by inserting after the word " any " in the first line thereof the word " actual."

48 V. c. 49, s. 108, repealed.

24. Section 108 of the said Act is hereby repealed and the 50 following substituted therefor :—

108. The members of every board of school trustees shall hold their first meeting on the third Wednesday in January in each year in which they were elected (or if a board of education then on the first Wednesday in February) at the 5 hour of one o'clock in the afternoon, at the usual place of meeting of such board, and no business shall be proceeded with at such first meeting except the appointment of a chairman and such other business as may be necessary for the organization of such board.

10   **25**. Section 114 of the said Act is hereby amended by adding the following sub-sections thereto:—

(13) To provide if deemed expedient for children between three and five years of age a course of instruction and training according to the methods practised in Kindergarten schools, 15 subject however to the regulations of the Education Department in that behalf.

☞ (14) To dismiss from the school any pupil who shall be adjudged so refractory by the trustees (or by a majority of them) and the teacher that his presence in school is deemed 20 injurious to the other pupils, and, where practicable, to remove such pupil to an industrial school. [R. S. O. c. 204, s. 102 (22)]. ☞

26. Sub-section 12 of section 114 of the said Act is hereby amended by inserting after the word "schools" in the fourth 25 line thereof the following words: "and shall have the same powers in regard to school property generally as are conferred upon the trustees of rural schools by sub-section 9 of section 40 of this Act, and all such powers may be exercised with or without a vote of the ratepayers."

30   ☞ **27**. Section 124 is amended by adding thereto the following: "Where the public school rate and the separate school rate are not the same, if the owner is compelled to pay a school rate in consequence of the default of his tenant to pay the same, he shall only be liable to pay the amount of the 35 school rate of the schools to which in virtue of his right in this behalf he directed his money to be paid." 44 Vict., c. 30, s. 10; 49 V. c. 46, s. 52. ☞

28. Section 134 of the said Act is hereby amended by adding thereto the following sub-section:—

40   (2) Nothing in this section contained shall be construed to mean that the municipal council may not, if deemed expedient, without submitting the same to a vote of the ratepayers of such municipality, as required by *The Consolidated Municipal Act, 1883*, for the creating of debts, pass a by-law 45 for the purpose of raising or borrowing money, on the requisition of the Public School Board, for any of the purposes named in this section.

29. Section 154 of the said Act is hereby amended by adding thereto the following sub-section:—

50   (11) To notify the Medical Health Officer of the municipality, or where there is none to notify the local board of health, whenever he has reason to believe that any pupil attending school is affected with or exposed to small-pox, cholera, scarlatina,

diphtheria, whooping-cough, measles, mumps, or other contagious disease, and to prevent the attendance of all pupils so exposed, or suspected of being exposed, until furnished with the written statement of the health officer, or of the local board of health, or of a physician, that such contagious diseases did 5 not exist, or that all danger from exposure to any of them had passed away.

48 V. c. 49, s. 155, amended. **30.** Section 155 of the said Act is hereby amended by inserting after the word "taught," in the fourth line, the words "in the calendar year," and by substituting the word "such" for 10 the word "the," in the fifth line.

48 V. c. 49, s. 191, amended. **31.** Section 191 of the said Act is hereby amended by adding thereto the following sub-section :—

(2) In making their award the arbitrators shall among other things determine the liabilities of the parties concerned therein 15 for the costs of such arbitration, and such determination shall be final and conclusive.

48 V. c. 49, s. 245, repealed. **32.** Section 245 of the said Act is hereby repealed, and the following substituted therefor :—

Fine on disqualified person acting as trustee. **245.** If any person elected as a school trustee attends any 20 meetings of the school board as such, after being disqualified under this Act, he shall be liable to a penalty of $20, for every meeting so attended.

48 V. c. 49, s. 247, amended. **33.** Section 247 of the said Act is hereby amended by substituting for the words "a resident within the school muni-25 cipality," in the fifth line, the words "an actual resident within the school section."

No. 73.

1st Session, 6th Legislature, 50 Vic., 1887.

BILL.

An Act to amend the Act respecting Public Schools.

(Again reprinted as amended by Committee of Whole House.)

First Reading, 23rd March, 1887.
Second   "   31st   "   1887.

BILL.

An Act further to amend the Acts respecting Petty
Trespassers in Upper Canada.

HER MAJESTY, by and with the advice and consent of the
Legislative Assembly of the Province of Ontario, enacts
as follows :—

    1. The section substituted by the Act of the Legislature of 25 V. c. 22,
5 the late Province of Canada, passed in the 25th year of Her s. 2, amended.
Majesty's reign and chaptered 22, for section 1 of chapter 105
of the Consolidated Statutes for Upper Canada, is hereby
amended by adding the following thereto as sub-section 2 :

    (2) In the case of any lands, the boundary line, or any part
10 of the boundary line whereof passes through a marsh or
swamp, or any land covered with water, the same shall, so far
as respects that part of such boundary line which so passes
through a marsh or swamp, or land covered with water, be
deemed to be wholly enclosed within the meaning of this
15 section, if posts are put up and maintained along such part of
such line at distances which will permit of each being clearly
visible from the adjoining post.

No. 75.

1st Session, 6th Legislature, 50 Vic., 1887.

BILL.

An Act further to amend the Act respecting
Petty Trespassers in Upper Canada.

First Reading, 11th March, 1887.

No. 76.] **BILL.** [1887.

An Act to amend the Act respecting Line Fences.

HER MAJESTY, by and with the advice and consent of the
Legislative Assembly of the Province of Ontario, enacts
as follows :—

1. The County Council of any county may pass by-laws im- Fencing
5 posing on all owners of unoccupied lands within the county unoccupied
the same duties and obligations as to fences marking boundaries land.
as are now imposed on the owners of occupied lands by *The
Line Fences Act*, and the compulsory proceedings in the said
Act provided, may, thereafter, be taken against the owners of
10 any unoccupied lands within the county.

1st Session, 6th Legislature, 50 Vic., 1887.

BILL.

An Act to amend the Act respecting
Line Fences.

First Reading, 11th March, 1887.

An Act respecting Landlords and Tenants and Distress.

HER MAJESTY, by and with the advice and consent of the Legislative Assembly of the Province of Ontario, enacts as follows :—

1.—(1) In the construction of this Act, the word "Landlord" Interpretation
5 shall be understood as signifying the person entitled to the "Landlord.'
immediate reversion, or in the case of joint tenancy or tenancy
in common, shall be understood as signifying any one of the
persons entitled to such reversion.

(2) The word "Premises" shall be understood as signifying "Premises."
10 lands, houses, or any other corporeal hereditaments.

2. This Act applies to tenancies created after the passing of Application of
this Act.   Act.

3. Where a landlord has by law a right to enter for non- Common law,
payment of rent, it shall not be necessary to demand the rent strict demand
of rent dis-
15 on the day when due, or with the strictness required at com- pensed with
mon law, and a demand of rent shall suffice notwithstanding when landlord
entitled to re-
more or less than the amount really due is demanded, and not- enter.
withstanding other requisites of the common law are not complied with : provided that, unless the premises are vacant, the
20 demand be made fifteen days at least before entry ; such demand to be made on the tenant personally anywhere, or on his
wife or some other grown up member of his family on the
premises.

4.—(1) A landlord shall not be entitled to seize under a dis- Goods exempt
from execu-
25 tress warrant any goods and chattels now exempt from seizure tion exempted
under execution ; provided that the tenant gives, or is ready from distress
if the tenant
and willing to give, to the landlord immediate possession of surrender the
the premises in respect of which the rent is due.   term.

(2) The tenant, at any time before such exempted goods and
30 chattels are seized, or before they are sold, may claim this
exemption, by giving up possession of the premises to the
landlord or his agent, or being ready and offering so to do.

(3) The offer may be made to the landlord or to his agent ;
and the person authorized to seize and sell the said goods and
35 chattels, or having the custody thereof for the landlord, shall
be considered an agent of the landlord for the purpose of the
offer and surrender to the landlord of such possession.

(4) Such surrender of possession in pursuance of the landlord's notice shall be a determination of the tenancy.

Landlord desiring to seize exempted goods must notify tenant that he may surrender and claim exemption, etc.

5.—(1) Where a landlord desires to seize such exempted goods he shall, forty-eight hours before distraining for the rent in arrear, serve the tenant with a notice after the tenant has made default in paying his rent; such notice shall inform the tenant what amount is claimed for rent in arrear, and that in default 5 of payment, if he gives up possession of the premises to the landlord within forty-eight hours after service of the notice, he will be entitled to claim exemption for such of his goods and chattels as are exempt from seizure under execution, but that if he neither pays the rent nor gives up possession all his 10 goods and chattels will be liable to seizure, and will be seized and sold to pay the rent in arrear and costs.

Form of notice.

(2) The notice may be in the form in the schedule to this Act or to the like effect.

Service of papers.

6.—(1) Service of papers under this Act shall be made either 15 personally or by leaving the same with some grown person being in and apparently residing on the premises occupied by the person to be served; and the person serving the same shall read over the same to the person served, or with whom the same shall be left, and shall explain the purport and intent 20 thereof.

(2) If the tenant cannot be found, and his place of abode is either not known, or admission thereto cannot be obtained, the posting up of the paper on some conspicuous part of the premises, shall be deemed good service. 25

Defective proceedings.

7. No proceeding under this Act shall be deemed defective or rendered invalid by any objection of form.

Landlord's claim for rent limited as against execution creditors.

8. A landlord shall not be entitled to claim as against the execution or attaching creditors of the tenant any further sum than one year's arrears of rent, any proviso or covenant in 30 the lease to the contrary notwithstanding.

Certain goods on the premises exempt if not belonging to occupant or tenant, etc., or under his control as reputed owner.

9. A landlord shall not be entitled to seize under a distress warrant any goods or chattels except (1) goods and chattels which belong to the tenant, his heirs, executors, administrators or assigns, or other legal representatives, or to his or their sub- 35 tenant, or to occupants under him or them, and (2) except goods and chattels which (if they do not belong as aforesaid) are at the time of seizure in his or their possession, order and disposition by the consent and permission of the owner, and of which (being on the premises and in such possession) with 40 such consent and permission as aforesaid, the tenant or the party or parties aforesaid entitled or interested under or through him, is or are the reputed or apparent owner or owners.

Schedule.

Take notice, that I claim $ for rent due to me in respect of the premises which you hold as my tenant, namely, *(here briefly describe them)*; and unless the said rent is paid meantime, I demand from you immediate possession of the said premises ; and I am ready to leave in your possession such of your goods and chattels as in that case only you are entitled to claim exemption for.

Take notice further, that if you neither pay the said rent, nor give me up possession of the said premises within forty-eight hours after the service of this notice, I am by law entitled to seize and sell, and I intend to seize and sell all your goods and chattels, or such part thereof as may be necessary for the payment of the said rent and costs.

This notice is given under the Act of the Legislature of Ontario, passed in the year 1887, and entitled An Act respecting Landlords and Tenants, and Distress.

Dated this   day of   A.D.

           (Signed)   *A. B. (landlord)*.

To *C. D. (tenant)*.

No. 77.

1st Session, 6th Legislature, 50 Vic., 1887.

BILL.

An Act respecting Landlords and Tenants, and Distress.

First Reading, 11th March, 1887.

BILL.

An Act respecting Building Societies.

HER MAJESTY, by and with the advice and consent of the Legislative Assembly of the Province of Ontario enacts as follows :—

5 This Act may be cited as "*The Building Societies Act,* Short title. *1887.*"

1. Section 5 of the Act passed in the 49th year of Her 49 V. c. 34, s, Majesty's reign, chapter 34, is hereby repealed and the follow- 5 repealed. ing substituted therefor :

5. All transfers of debenture stock of the society shall be Transfers of 10 registered at the head office of the society or at such place or debenture stock may be places in Canada, Great Britain, or any foreign country, as the made at any directors may appoint for that purpose. agency.

2. Section 48 of chapter 164 of the Revised Statutes of R. S. O. c. Ontario, as amended by section 5 of the Act passed in the 42nd 164, s. 48 as amended by 15 year of Her Majesty's reign, chapter 26 is hereby repealed 42 V. c. 26, s. and the following substituted therefor : 51 repealed.

48. Any society may hold absolutely real estate for the Society to purposes of or in connection with its place or places of business, hold real estate to not exceeding the annual value of $10,000 for any one place $10,000 in 20 of business, but this section shall not affect any action or suit value. now pending.

No. 78.

1st Session, 6th Legislature, 50 Vic., 1887.

BILL.

An Act respecting Building Societies.

First Reading, 14th March, 1887.

No. 78.]   BÍLL.   [1887.

An Act respecting Building Societies.

HER MAJESTY, by and with the advice and consent of the
Legislative Assembly of the Province of Ontario enacts
as follows :—

This Act may be cited as *The Building Societies Act.* Short title.
5 *1887.* `

1. Section 5 of the Act passed in the 49th year of Her 49 V. c. 34, s,
Majesty's reign, chapter 34, is hereby repealed and the follow- 5 repealed.
ing substituted therefor :

5. All transfers of debenture stock of the society shall be Transfers of
10 registered at the head office of the society or at such place or debenture
places in Canada, Great Britain, or any foreign country, as the made at any
directors may appoint for that purpose. stock may be
agency.

2. In case any society or company, subject to the legislative Purchase or
authority of this Province, and incorporated under chapter 164 erection of
15 of the Revised Statutes of Ontario, or any Act thereby consoli- quired for use
dated, carries on business in any other Province than Ontario, of Company.
the said corporation may pass a by-law authorizing the directors
to invest the money of the corporation in the erection or purchase of buildings required for the occupation of the corpor-
20 ation, carrying on the business thereof in any place in which
the corporation is so carrying on business, and within the
limit, if any, authorized in that behalf, by the laws of such
other Province.

BILL.

An Act respecting Building Societies.

(*Reprinted as amended by Select Committee*).

First Reading, 14th March, 1887.
Second   "   1st April, 1887.

No. 79.]   **BILL.**   [1887.

An Act to amend the Assessment Act.

HER MAJESTY, by and with the advice and consent of the
Legislative Assembly of the Province of Ontario, enacts
as follows:—

    1. Section 45 of *The Assessment Act* as amended by section R. S. O. c. 180,
5 8 of the Act passed in the 49th year of Her Majesty's reign s. 45, amended.
intituled *An Act to further amend the Assessment Act,* is
hereby amended by inserting the words " or townships" after
the word " towns," in the first line thereof.

No. 79.

1st Session, 6th Legislature, 50 Vic., 1887.

BILL.

An Act to amend the Assessment Act.

First Reading, 14th March, 1887.

Mr. WILMOT.

No. 80.] **BILL.** [1877.

An Act to Amend the Ditches and Watercourses Act, 1883.

HER MAJESTY, by and with the advice and consent of the Legislative Assembly of the Province of Ontario, enacts as follows:—

1.—(1) In any case where an open ditch or drain has been, *Power as to covering drains.* 5 or may be constructed under the provisions of *The Ditches and Watercourses Act, 1883,* or any of the amendments thereto, any person through whose lands such ditch or drain has been opened, may, with the consent of the engineer of the municipality, convert so much of such ditch or drain as runs through 10 the lands of such person into a covered drain.

(2) The engineer, before giving such consent, shall examine the portion of the ditch or drain which is proposed to be covered, and shall determine the size and capacity of the proposed covered portion of such drain or ditch, but no such consent shall 15 be given by the said engineer, if the covering of any such portion of said ditch or drain would impede or delay the free flow of the water which such ditch or drain was originally intended to carry off.

2. The engineer shall file with the clerk of the municipality *If consent given award to be filed.* 20 (if such consent is given) an award setting forth the particulars in accordance with the provisions of said Act, and the amendments thereto, and said award shall be subject to appeal.

3. The person making the application for the covering *Notice to engineer.* of the ditch or drain may notify the engineer to inspect 25 the ditch or drain in the first place, and may also notify said engineer when the work is completed, and it shall not be necessary for such person to take the proceedings provided in sections 5 and 6 of said Act, and such person shall be liable for the fees and expenses of the engineer, and if not paid by *Payment of fees and expenses.* 30 such person to the engineer, such fees and expenses shall be collected, as provided for in said Act.

1st Session, 6th Legislature, 50 Vic., 1887.

BILL.

An Act to amend the Ditches and Watercourses Act, 1883.

First Reading, 14th March, 1887.

An Act respecting Land Surveyors and the survey of Lands.

HER MAJESTY, by and with the advice and consent of the Legislative Assembly of the Province of Ontario enacts as follows :—

5 **1.** The expression "Commissioner of Crown Lands," wherever Interpretation it occurs in this Act, shall mean the person discharging the duties of that officer.　R. S. O. 1877, c. 146, s, 1.

LAND SURVEYORS.

2. No person shall act as a surveyor of lands within this Who may act Province unless he has been duly authorized to practise as a as land sur-
10 land surveyor according to the provisions of this Act, or had veyor. been so authorized before the passing thereof, according to the laws then in force, under a penalty of $40.　R. S. O. 1877, 146, s. 2.

BOARD OF EXAMINERS.

15 **3.** There shall be a board of examiners for the examination Board of ex- of candidates for admission to practise as land surveyors to aminers. consist of the Commissioner of Crown Lands, the Professor of Mineralogy and Geology in University College, Toronto, and twelve other competent persons to be appointed from time to
20 time by the Lieutenant-Governor, who shall meet at the City of Toronto for the examination of candidates for admission to practise as land surveyors in Ontario.　R. S. O. 1877, c. 146, s. 3 ; 43 V. c. 17, s. 1.

4.--(1) Each member of the board, save and except the Oath of Office.
25 Commissioner of Crown Lands, shall take an oath of office be- fore a Judge of the High Court or of any County Court : and any three of the members shall form a quorum.

(2) The following shall be the form of the oath of office ;

I　　　　　　　　　　　of having been appointed a member of the Board of Examiners for the ad- mission of Provincial Land Surveyors for the Province of Ontario, do sincerely promise and swear that I will faithfully discharge the duties of such office without favour, affection or partiality : So help me God.

Sworn before me
at
this　　　day
of　　　18

R. S. O. 1877, c. 146, s. **4.**

Secretary to the board.   **5.** The said board, or a majority thereof, shall from time to time appoint a fit and proper person to be Secretary of the board, who shall attend the sittings thereof, and keep a record of its proceedings. R. S. O. 1877, c. 146, s. 5.

Meetings when and where to be held.   **6.** The said board shall meet at the office of the Commis- 5 sioner of Crown Lands, on the first Monday in each of the months of January, April, July and October, in every year, unless such Monday be a holiday (in which case they shall meet on the day next thereafter, not being a holiday), and may adjourn such meeting from time to time if they deem it neces- 10 sary. R. S. O. 1877, c. 146, s. 6.

APPRENTICES.

Qualification for admission as an apprentice, an examination of applicants.   **7.** No person shall be admitted as an apprentice with any Provincial Land Surveyor unless he has previously passed an examination before the board of examiners *as to his penman-* 15 *ship and orthography, fractions, decimals, square-root, logarithms, algebra (including equations to the first degree), Euclid (first four books), plane trigonometry, the rules for spherical trigonometry, mensuration of superficies, the use of ruling pen and construction of plans and comparative scales,* 20 *and has obtained a certificate of having passed such examination, and of his proficiency from the board.* R. S. O. 1877, c. 146, s. 7.

Examination fee.   **8.** Before being so examined he shall pay into the fee fund the sum of $10 as the fee due by him on the examination, and 25 a further sum of $2 to the secretary for the said certificate. R. S. O. 1877, c, 146, s. 8.

Notice to be given by applicants.   **9.** Applicants for examination previous to apprenticeship shall give one month's notice to the secretary of the board of their intention to present themselves for examination, and pay 30 to the secretary a fee of $1 for receiving and entering such notice. R. S. O. 1887, c. 146, s. 9.

QUALIFICATION FOR ADMISSION TO PRACTISE.

Qualification for admission to practise.   **10.** Except as hereinafter provided no person shall be admitted to practise as a land surveyor in and for Ontario until 35 he has attained the full age of 21 years, *and has passed an examination before the board of examiners in the following subjects, viz., geometry, including the first six books of Euclid, (with the exception of the last thirteen propositions of the fifth book), algebra, including progressions, plane and spheri-* 40 *cal trigonometry, mensuration of superficies, laying out and dividing of land, descriptions by metes and bounds for deeds and other documents, the use and adjustment of surveying and levelling instruments, the laying out of curves, practical astronomy, including finding of time, latitude, longi-* 45 *tude, azimuth, variation of the compass, and drawing meridian lines. The Acts relating to the survey of lands in Ontario, the general mining Act, the registry Act, so far as it refers to plans, the municipal Acts, so far as they relate to roads, surveys and drainage, the ditches and watercourses Act,* 50 *the theory and practice of levelling, the principles of evidence, drawing of affidavits, taking of field notes and preparing*

plans, the rudiments of geology and mineralogy, and the sufficiency of his surveying instruments, and has served regularly and faithfully, for three successive years, under an instrument in writing, duly executed before two witnesses as
5 apprentice to a land surveyor for Ontario, duly admitted, and practising therein as such, nor until he has received from the said land surveyor a certificate of his having so served during the said period, or proves to the satisfaction of the board that he has so served. R. S. O. 1877, c 146, s. 10.

10 **11.** It shall not be necessary for any land surveyor, duly admitted to practise in any of Her Majesty's dominions other than this Province, to serve under an instrument in writing during three years as aforesaid, but it shall only be necessary for any such person admitted in the Province of Quebec so to
15 serve during six months of actual practice in the field with a land surveyor duly admitted and practising in this Province, and for any other such person so to serve during twelve successive months of actual practice, after which, on complying with all the other requirements hereof, he may undergo the ex-
20 amination by this Act prescribed. R. S. O. c. 146, s. 11.

Admission of persons previously admitted in any part of Her Majesty's dominions

12.—(1) Any person who has followed a regular course of study in all the branches of education required by law for final admission as a land surveyor, through the regular sessions for at least two years in any university of the Province, or in
25 McGill University, in the City of Montreal in the Province of Quebec, wherein there is organized a complete course of instruction, practical as well as theoretical, in civil engineering, natural philosophy, geology, and other branches of education required by law for admission as a land surveyor, and who has
30 thereupon received from such university, after due examination, a degree or diploma of qualification as a civil engineer and land surveyor, may, after having passed the preliminary examination hereinbefore required for admission to apprenticeship with a land surveyor, be received as an apprentice by any
35 practising land surveyor, and shall thereupon be only holden to serve as such apprentice during twelve successive months of actual service, or if he has passed through such university course of study in less time than two full years, then for such time of actual service as, with the period spent by him in such
40 university course of study, suffices to make up the full time of three years:

The case of persons who have received university degrees or diplomas as engineers or surveyors.

(2) Any person who has followed a regular course of study at the Ontario School of Practical Science in the subjects of drawing, surveying and levelling, and geodosy and practical
45 astronomy, and who has thereupon received, after due examination a certificate of having passed one session, two sessions, or three sessions, as the case may be, in the study of the aforesaid subjects may, after having passed the preliminary examination hereinbefore required for admission to apprenticeship
50 with a land surveyor, be received as an apprentice by any practising land surveyor, and shall thereupon, if he has received a certificate of having passed three sessions in the study of the said subjects, be only holden to serve as such apprentice during twelve successive months of actual service; or, in case he has
55 only received a certificate of having passed only one or two sessions, as the case may be, in the study of the said subjects,

Case of persons who have studied at School of Practical Science.

then for such time of actual service as, with the period spent by him at such session or sessions, suffices to make up the full time of three years ;

Apprentice-
ship.

(3) After such actual service such person shall, subject to the other provisions of this Act, have the same right to under-   5 go the examination required by law, and if found qualified,

Admission to
practise.

to be admitted to practise as a land surveyor as if he had served the full three years' apprenticeship otherwise required by law.   43 V. c. 17, s. 2.

Admission of
Dominion
land sur-
veyors.

13. In case a Dominion land surveyor, under *The Dominion* 10 *Lands Act* applies for a commission as a land surveyor of this Province, if the board of examiners for the time being are of opinion that the qualifications required of a surveyor of Dominion lands at the time of the Commission having been granted to such surveyor under *The Dominion Lands Act,* 15 were sufficiently similar to those set forth in this Act such surveyor shall be entitled to a certificate of admission as a land surveyor of this Province, without being subjected to any examination except as regards the system of survey of lands in Ontario.   43 V. c 17, s. 3.   20

Graduates of
Military Col-
lege, King-
ston.

14. The privilege of a shortened term of apprenticeship shall also be accorded to any graduate of the Military College at Kingston, *and of the Ontario School of Practical Science,* and such person shall not be required to pass the preliminary examination hereinbefore required for admission to appren- 25 ticeship with a land surveyor, but shall only be bounden to serve under articles with a *practising* land surveyor, duly filed as required by section 17 of this Act, during twelve successive months of actual practice, after which, on complying with all the other requirements, he may undergo the examina- 30 tion by this Act prescribed.   R. S. O. 1877, c. 146, s. 13.

If surveyor
dies, service
may be com-
pleted with
another sur-
veyor.

15. If any surveyor dies or leaves the Province, or is suspended or dismissed, his apprentice may complete his term of apprenticeship under an instrument in writing as aforesaid, with any other *practising* surveyor duly admitted.   R. S. O. 35 1877, c. 146, s. 14.

Instruments
of apprentice-
ship may be
transferred.

16. Any surveyor may, by an instrument in writing transfer an apprenties, with his own consent, to any other *practising* surveyor duly admitted, with whom he may serve the remainder of the term of his apprenticeship.   R. S. O. 1877, 40 c, 146, s. 15.

Instruments
binding to ser-
vice to be filed,
etc.

17. No instrument in writing under which any applicant for admission to practise as a surveyor claims to have served with some practising surveyor for the period of three years, twelve months or six months (as the case may be), shall avail 45 to authorize the admission of an applicant, unless the instrument has been transmitted to the secretary of the board within two months next after the date thereof, nor unless the fee mentioned in section 26 of this Act was by the apprentice paid to the secretary of the board at the time of transmitting the in- 50 denture or articles : and the said secretary shall acknowledge by post the receipt of all such instruments or copies thereof transmitted to him, and shall carefully keep the same in his office.   R. S. O. 1877, c. 146, s. 16.

18. Every person desiring to be examined by the board as to his qualification to be admitted as a land surveyor, shall give notice thereof in writing to the secretary of the board, at least 5 one month previous to the meeting thereof. R. S. O. 1877, c. 146, s. 18. *Notice of examination to be given by candidates for admission.*

19. Every person applying for admission to practice as a land surveyor shall produce to the board satisfactory certificates as to character for probity and sobriety, and before a 10 certificate is granted shall perform such practical operations in the presence of the board, and shall answer such questions on oath (which oath any member of the board may administer) with regard to the actual practice of such applicant in the field, and with regard to his surveying instruments as the said 15 board may require. R. S. O. 1877, c. 146, s. 19. *The board to require certificates of good conduct, etc.*

20. *If the said examiners are satisfied as to the qualifications of the candidate, and his compliance with all the requirements of this Act, they shall grant him a certificate in the form following :* *If the examiners approve of the candidate they are to grant him certificate.*

"This is to certify to all whom it may concern, that *A. B.* of in the County of has duly passed his examination before the board of examiners, and has been found qualified to fill the office and perform the duties of a Provincial Land Surveyor in and for Ontario, he having complied with all the requirements of the law in that behalf. Wherefore the said *A. B.* is admitted to the said office, and is by law authorized to practise as a land surveyor in Ontario.

"In witness whereof, we have signed this certificate at the City of Toronto, in the County of York, and Province of Ontario, Dominion of Canada, the day of 18 ."

Signature of the Chairman, *" C. D."*

Signature of the Secretary, " E. F."

20 And such certificate shall, on his complying with the other requirements of this Act, enable him to practice as a land surveyor in and for Ontario. R. S. O. 1877, c. 146, s. 20.

21.—(1) Each applicant, *before* receiving the above mentioned certificate, shall, with two sufficient sureties to the satis-25 faction of the said board of examiners, enter into a bond jointly and severally in the sum of $1,000 to Her Majesty, Her Heirs and Successors, conditioned for the due and faithful performance of the duties of his office. *Licentiates to give bonds and take the oaths of allegiance and of office.*

(2) The said bond shall be deposited and kept in the man-30 ner by law prescribed with regard to bonds given for like purposes by other public officers, and shall enure to the benefit of any party sustaining damage by breach of the condition thereof; and the certificate shall be registered in the office of the Provincial Secretary. R. S. O. 1877, c. 146, s. 21. *Where bonds to be deposited.*

35 **22.**—(1) Each applicant, after having been granted a certificate, shall also take and subscribe the oath of allegiance, and the following oath, before the board of examiners, who are hereby empowered to administer the same : *Oaths.*

"I, *A. B.*, do solemnly swear (*or affirm, as the case may be*) that I will faithfully discharge the duties of *a* la .d surveyor, agreeably to law, without favor, affection or partiality : So help me God."

(2) The said oath of allegiance and of office shall be deposited in the office of the Provincial Secretary. R. S. O. 1877, c. 146, s. 22.

When the board may suspend licensed surveyors.
23. The board of examiners may in their discretion suspend or dismiss from the practice of his profession, any land surveyor whom they find guilty of gross negligence or corruption in the execution of the duties of his office ; but the board *shall not take action until the complaint under oath has been filed with the board, and a copy thereof forwarded to the party accused, nor shall the board* suspend or dismiss such land surveyor without having previously summoned him to appear in order to be heard in his defence, nor without having heard the evidence, offered either in support of the complaint or in behalf of the surveyor inculpated. R. S. O. 1877, c. 146, s. 23.

Fees to be paid to the members of the board.
24. The Commissioner of Crown Lands shall pay to each member of the board of examiners *and the secretary of the board,* who attends any examination, the sum of $5 for each day's attendance, and charge the same in his account as part of the expenses of his office. R. S. O. 1877, c. 146, s. 24.

Tariff of fees.
25. The following fees shall be paid under the provisions of this Act :

1. To the secretary of the board of examiners, by each apprentice, at the transmitting to such secretary the Indenture or Articles of such apprentice............................... $2 00

2. To the secretary of the board by each candidate for examination with his notice thereof........................ .... 1 00

3. To the secretary of the board by each applicant obtaining a certificate, as his fee thereon...... .... 2 00

4. To the secretary of the board as an admission fee by each applicant receiving a certificate, out of which the expenses attending the examination of such applicant (if any) shall be first paid, and the remainder (if any) shall be paid over to the Commisssioner of Crown Lands and be accounted for like other moneys received by him................... .... 20 00

5. To every surveyor summoned to attend any court, civil or criminal, for the purpose of giving evidence in his professional capacity as a surveyor, for each day he so attends, in addition to his travelling expenses (if any), and to be taxed and paid in the manner by law provided with regard to the payment of witnesses attending such court.........·················........... 5 00

R. S. O. 1877, c. 146, s. 25.

BOUNDARY LINES.

Establishment of boundary lines regulated.
26. All boundary or division lines legally established, and ascertained under the authority of any Ordinance or Act heretofore in force, shall remain good, and all other Acts or things legally done and performed under the authority of the said Ordinance and Acts, or any of them, and in conformity to the

provisions thereof, shall remain good and valid notwithstanding the repeal of such Ordinance or Act. R. S. O. 1877, c. 146, s. 26.

27. The standard of English measure of length, compared 5 with and corrected by the standards for such measures established in this province and procured by the Commissioner of Crown Lands for the purpose of comparing therewith the standards to be kept by each surveyor as hereinafter provided, shall be deposited with the secretary of the board of examiners 10 at Toronto, and the said secretary, under such instructions as he from time to time receives from the board, shall examine, test and stamp each standard measure of length for the surveyors, bringing the same for examination as the Commissioner of Crown Lands may do and with the same effect; and for each 15 measure so examined and stamped such secretary may demand and receive fifty cents. R. S. O. 1877, c. 146, s. 27.

The standard of measure regulated.

28. Every land surveyor duly admitted and practising shall procure and shall cause to be examined, corrected and stamped or otherwise certified by the Commissioner of Crown Lands 20 or some one deputed by him for that purpose, or by the secretary aforesaid, a standard measure of length, under the penalty of the forfeiture of his license or certificate, and shall, previously to proceeding on any survey, verify by such standard the length of his chains and other instruments for measuring. R. 25 S. O. 1877, c. 146, s. 28.

Surveyors to procure stamped standard measures.

29. Every chain-bearer shall, before he commences his chaining or measuring, take an oath or affirmation to act as such justly and exactly according to the best of his judgment and *ability*, and to render a true account of his chaining or 30 measuring to the surveyor by whom he has been appointed to such duty, and that he is absolutely disinterested in the survey in question, and is not related or allied to any of the parties interested in the survey within the fourth degree, according to the computation of the civil law—that is to say, within the 35 degree of cousin-german, which oath the surveyor employing such chain-bearer is hereby authorized and required to administer; nor shall any person related or allied to any of the parties within the said degree be employed as a chain-bearer on any survey. R. O. S. 1877, c. 146, s. 29.

Chain-bearers to be sworn, and nature of the oath.

40 **30.** Any land surveyor, when engaged in the performance of the duties of his profession, may pass over, measure along and ascertain the bearings of any *line or limit whutsoever*, and for such purposes may pass over the lands of any person whomsoever, doing no actual damage to the property of such 45 person. R. S. O. 1877, c. 146, s. 30.

When land surveyors may pass over private lands.

31. Where any surveyor is in doubt as to the true boundary or limit of any township, concession, range, lot or tract of land which he is employed to survey, and has reason to believe that any person is possessed of any important information 50 touching such boundary or limit, or of any writing, plan or document tending to establish the true position of such boundary or limit, then if such person does not willingly appear before and be examined by such surveyor, or does not willingly produce to him such writing, plan or document, such surveyor

Course to be adopted by surveyor to ascertain boundary line, when doubtful, etc.

or the party employing him may file in the office of the County Court a præcipe for a subpœna or subpœna *duces tecum*, as the case may require, accompanying such application by an affidavit or solemn declaration to be made before a Justice of the Peace, of the facts on which the application is founded, and the Judge may order a subpœna to issue accordingly, commanding such person to appear before the surveyor, at a time and place to be mentioned in the said subpœna and to bring with him any writing, plan or document mentioned or referred to therein. R. S. O. 1877, c. 146, s. 31. 10

May subpœna witnesses.

32. The subpœna shall be served on the person named therein by delivering a copy thereof to him, or by leaving the same for him with some grown person of his family at his residence, exhibiting to him or to such grown person the original, R. S. O. 1877, c. 146, s. 32. 15

Service of subpœna.

33. If the person commanded to appear by the subpœna after being paid his reasonable expenses, or having the same tendered to him, refuses or neglects to appear before the surveyor at the time and place appointed in the subpœna, or to produce the writing, plan or document (if any) therein mentioned or referred to, or to give such evidence and information as he may possess touching the boundary or limit in question, the person so summoned shall be deemed guilty of a contempt of the Court out of which the subpœna issued, and an attachment may be issued against him by the judge of the said court, and he may be punished accordingly, by fine or imprisonment, or both, in the discretion of the Judge. R. S. O. 1877, c. 146, s. 33. 20 25

Penalty for disobeying subpœna.

34. Stone monuments, or monuments of other durable materials, shall be placed at the several corners, governing points or off-sets of every township already surveyed, or after this Act takes effect from time to time surveyed, and also at each end of the several concession lines of such townships ; and lines drawn in the manner hereinafter prescribed from the monuments so erected, shall be taken and considered to be the permanent boundary lines of such townships and concessions respectively. R. S. O. 1877, c. 146, s. 34. 30 35

Stone monuments may be placed at certain points in townships.

35. The monuments to be placed as above mentioned shall be so placed under the direction and order of the Commissioner of Crown Lands. R. S. O. 1877, c. 146, s. 35. 40

To be placed under the direction of the Commissioner of Crown Lands.

36. The courses and lengths of the said boundary lines, so ascertained and established, shall on all occasions be the true courses and lengths of the boundary lines of the said townships and concessions, whether the same do or do not, on actual survey, coincide with the courses and lengths in any letters patent of grant or other instrument mentioned and expressed in respect of such boundary lines. R. S. O. 1877, c. 146, s. 36. 45

Boundaries ascertained as aforesaid to be deemed the true ones.

37. It shall not be necessary for the Commissioner of Crown Lands to proceed to carry the provisions of the last preceding three sections of this Act into execution, until an application for that purpose has been made to the Lieutenant-Governor, by the council of the county in which the township or townships interested is situate, and such council shall cause the 50

Monuments need not be placed under ss. 34-36 except on the application of the municipal council.

sum requisite to defray the expenses to be incurred, or the proportion thereof payable by the inhabitants of any township or concession, to be levied on the said inhabitants, in the same manner as any sum required for any other local purpose author-
5 ized by law may be levied. R. S. O. 1877, c. 146 s. 37.

38.—(1) *And whereas in several of the townships in Ontario* In what cases *some of the concession lines, and side-road lines, or parts of* the municipal *the concession lines and side-road lines were not run in the* apply to have *original survey performed under competent authority, and the* monuments placed.
10 *survey of some of the concession lines and side-road lines, or parts of the concession lines and side-road lines have been obliterated, and owing to the want of such lines the inhabitants of such concessions are subject to serious inconvenience, there- fore the municipal council of the township in which such lines*
15 *are situated, may, on application of one-half the resident land- holders in any concession or part of concession or upon its own motion without such application, apply to the Lieutenant- Governor, requesting him to cause any such line or lines to be surveyed and marked by permanent stone or iron boundaries*
20 *under the direction and order of the Commissioner of Crown Lands, in the manner prescribed in this Act, at the cost of the proprietors of the lands in each concession or part of a con- cession interested.*

(2) *The concession lines, where not run, or where they have* As to the ad-
25 *been obliterated shall be so drawn as to leave each of the ad-* jacent con- *jacent concessions of a depth proportionate to that intended* cessions. *in the original survey,*

(3) *The survey of the parts of the concession lines not run or which have been obliterated, shall be established by drawing*
30 *a straight line between the two nearest points or places where such line or lines can be clearly and satisfactorily ascertained.*

(4) The lines or parts of lines so surveyed and marked as To be perma- aforesaid, shall thereafter be the permanent boundary lines of nent boundary such concession *or side-roads*, or parts of concessions *or side-* lines.
35 *roads* to all intents and purposes of law whatsoever. R. S. O. 1877, c. 146, s. 40.

(5) The council shall cause to be laid before them an esti- Expenses to be mate of the sum requisite to defray the expenses to be incurred estimated and in order that the same may be levied on the said proprietors, provided for.
40 in proportion to the quantity of land held by them respectively in such concession or part of a concession, in the same manner as any sum required for any other purposes authorized by law may be levied. R. S. O. 1877, c. 146, s. 41.

39.—(1) Whenever the municipal council of any township, Municipal
45 city, town or incorporated village adopts a resolution, on councils may application of one-half the resident landholders to be affected cause the thereby, *or upon its own motion*, that is is desirable to place lots to be as stone or other durable monuments at the front or at the rear, certained and or at the front and rear angles of the lots in any concession or marked.
50 range *or block* or part of a concession, or range *or block* in their township, city, town, or incorporated village, such municipal council may make application to the Lieutenant-Governor, in the same manner as is provided in section *38*, praying him to
81—2

cause a survey of such concession or range *or block* or part of a concession or range *or block*, to be made, and such boundaries to be planted, under the authority of the Commissioner of Crown Lands. R. S. O. 1877, c. 146, s. 43.

Boundaries to be marked by stone or some other durable monuments to be placed at the angles.

(2) The *surveyor* making such survey shall accordingly plant stone or other durable monuments at the front, or at the rear, or at the front and rear angles of each and every lot in such concession, or range, *or block*, or part of a concession, or range, *or block*, and the limits of each lot so ascertained and marked shall be the true limits thereof. R. S. O. 1877, c. 146, s. 44.

How costs to be defrayed.

(3) The cost of such survey shall be defrayed in the manner prescribed by section *38* of this Act. R. S. O. 1877, c. 146, s. 45.

Expenses how paid.

40. All expenses incurred in performing any survey, or placing any monument or boundary under the provisions of section *34*, and the following sections, shall be paid by the county *or township* treasurer to the *surveyor* employed in such services, on the certificate and order of the Commisioner of Crown Lands. R. S. O. 1877, c. 146, s. 42.

Boundaries placed under the authority of the Government to be deemed the true ones, etc.

41. All boundary lines of townships, cities, towns and villages, all concession lines, governing points and all boundary lines, of concessions, sections, blocks, gores and commons, and all side lines and limits of lots surveyed, *and all trees marked,* and all posts or monuments, marked, placed or planted at the front *or rear* angles of any lots or parcels of land, under the authority of the Executive Government of the late Province Quebec or of Upper Canada, or of Canada, or under the authority of the Executive Government of this Province, shall be the true and unalterable boundaries of all and every such townships, cities, towns, villages, concessions, sections, blocks, gores, commons, and lots or parcels of land, respectively, whether the same upon admeasurement be found to contain the exact width, or more or less than the exact width mentioned or expressed in any letters patent, grant or other instrument in respect of such township, city, town, village, concession, section, block, gore, common, lot or parcel of land. R. S. O. 1877. c 146, s. 46.

Townships, etc., to comprise all the space included within their boundaries.

42. Every township, city, town, village, concession, section block, gore, common, lot or parcel of land, shall embrace the whole width, contained between the front posts, monuments or boundaries, planted or placed at the front angles thereof respectively, so marked, placed or planted as aforesaid, and no more nor less, any quantity or measure expressed in the original grant or patent thereof notwithstanding. R. S. O. 1877, c. 146, s. 47.

As to aliquot parts of townships, etc.

43. Every patent, grant or instrument, purporting to be for any aliquot part of any concession, section, block, gore, common, lot or parcel of land *in any such township, city, town or village,* shall be construed to be a grant of such aliquot part of the quantity the same may contain, whether such quantity be more or less than that expressed in such patent, grant or instrument. R. S. O. 1877, c. 146, s. 48.

44. In every city, town, or village, *or any part thereof* Road allowances in cities, etc., to be public highways.
which has been surveyed by the authority aforesaid, all allowances for any road, street, lane or common laid out in the original survey of such city, town, or village, *or any part*
5 *thereof* shall be public highways and commons ; and all posts or monuments placed or planted in the original survey of such city, town or village, *or any part thereof,* to designate or define any allowance for a road, street lane, lot or common, shall be the true and unalterable boundaries of every such
10 road, street, lane, lot and common ; and all land surveyors, employed to make surveys in such city, town or village, *or any part thereof,* shall follow and pursue the same rules and regulations in respect of such surveys as is by law required of them when employed to make surveys in townships. R. S. O. 1877,
15 c. 146, s. 49.

45. All surveys of townships, tracts or blocks of land in As to lands granted in blocks and subsequently surveyed by the grantees.
this Province, granted by the Crown to companies and individuals before any surveys had been made therein, and which were afterwards surveyed by the owners thereof, shall be
20 original surveys thereof, and shall have the same force and effect as though the said original surveys and plans thereof had been made by competent authority ; and all allowances for roads or commons surveyed in such townships, tracts, or blocks of land, and laid down on the plans thereof, shall be public
25 highways and commons ; and all lines run and marked in such original surveys, and all posts or monuments planted or placed in such original surveys to designate and define any allowance *for* road, concession, lot of land or common, shall be the true and unalterable lines and boundaries of such allowance for road,
30 common or lot of land, and all land surveyors, when employed to make surveys in such townships, tracts or blocks of land, shall follow and pursue the same rules and regulations in respect of such townships, tracts or blocks of land, and the original surveys thereof, as they are by law required to follow and pur-
35 sue in all townships, tracts or blocks of land surveyed by the authority aforesaid. R. S. O. 1877, c. 146, s. 50.

46. The course of the boundary line of each and every con- Governing lines declared.
cession, on that side from which the lots are numbered, shall be the course of the division or side-lines throughout the
40 several townships or concessions respectively, provided that such division or side-lines were intended, in the original survey performed under such authority as aforesaid, to run *on the same course as* the said boundary. R. S. O. 1877, c. 146, s. 51.

45 **47.** Every surveyor shall run all division or side-lines, All side lines to be run *on the same course as* governing lines.
which he is called upon by the owner or owners of any lands to survey *on the same course as* that boundary line of the concession in which such lands are situate, from whence the lots are numbered as aforesaid, provided such division or side-lines
50 were intended, in the original survey performed under such competent authority as aforesaid, to run *on the same course as* the said boundary. R. S. O. 1877, c. 146, s. 52.

48. Where that end of a concession, from which the lots are Course to be adopted where concession bounded by lake or river.
numbered, is *wholly* bounded by a lake or river, or other
55 natural boundary, or where it has not been run in the original

survey performed under competent authority as aforesaid, or
where the course of the division or side-line of the lots
therein was not intended in the original survey performed as
aforesaid, to *be on the same course as* such boundary, the said
division or side lines shall *be run on the same course as* the 5
boundary line at the other extremity of such concession, provided their course was intended, in the original survey performed as aforesaid, to be *the same,* and that such boundary
line was run in the original survey. R. S. O. 1877, c. 146,
s. 53.   10

Where division or side-lines not intended to run *on the same course as* the side-line at either end of a concession.
49. Where in the original survey, performed under compe-
tent authority as aforesaid, the course of the division or side-
lines in any concession was not intended to be *on the same*
course as the boundary line at either end of such concession,
they shall be run at such angle with the course of the 15
boundary line at that end of the concession from which the
lots are numbered, as is stated in the plan and field notes of
the original survey, of record in the *Department* of Crown
Lands, provided such line was run in the original survey, as
aforesaid, or with the course of the boundary line at the other 20
extremity of the said concession, if the boundary at that end
of the concession from which the lots are numbered was not
run in the original survey; or if neither of the aforesaid
boundaries of the concession was run in the original survey, or
if the concession is *wholly* bounded at each end by a lake or 25
river, or other natural boundary, then at such angle with the
course of the line in front of the said concession as is stated in
the plan and field notes aforesaid, *or if parts of the concession*
line have been run on different courses as shown on said plans
and field notes, then at such angle with the courses of each of 30
these parts, as is stated in the plan and field notes aforesaid.
R. S. O. 1877, c. 146, s. 54.

Where a division or proof line has been run between lots, the same shall govern.
50. If any division or side-line between lots, or proof-line
intended to be *on the same course as* the division or side-lines
between lots, was drawn in any such concession, *bounded as* 35
aforesaid, in the original survey thereof, the division or side-
lines between the lots therein shall be *on the same course as*
such division or side-line or proof-line. R. S. O. 1877, c. 146,
s. 55.   •

Where there are two of such lines, the line nearest the end of the concession, from which the lots are numbered, to govern to the next of such lines.
51. Where two or more such division or side-lines or proof- 40
lines were drawn in the original survey of such concession,
bounded as aforesaid, that division or side-line or proof-line
which is nearest to the boundary of the concession from
which the lots are numbered, shall govern the course of the
division or side-lines of all the lots in such concession between 45
the boundary of the concession from which the lots are numbered, and the next division or side-line or proof-line drawn in
the original survey; and such last mentioned line or proof-
line shall govern the course of the division or side-lines of all
the lots up to the next division or side-line or proof-line drawn 50
in the original survey, or to the boundary of the concession
towards which the lots are numbered, as the case may be.
R. S. O. 1877, c. 147, s. 56.

How lines to be governed in townships laid
52. *In all those townships which in the original survey*
were divided into sections, agreeably to an Order in Council, 55

out in sections
under order in
council of
March 27th,
1829, etc.

bearing date the 27th day of March, 1829, or which have been
or shall be divided into sections or blocks of one thousand
acres, or thereabouts, or six hundred and forty acres or thereabouts, as the case may be, under instructions from the Com-
5 missioner of Crown Lands, the division or side-lines in all
concessions, in any section or block, shall be governed by the
boundary lines of such section or block, in like manner as the
division or side-lines in townships originally surveyed before
the said day, are governed by the boundary lines of the con-
10 cession in which the lots are situated : Provided that in those
sections or blocks the governing boundaries of which are
broken by lakes or rivers in such a way that the course thereof cannot accurately be determined, a surveyor, when called
upon to run any side-line in any concession in such section
15 or block, shall run such side-line on the astronomical
course of the side-lines of the lots in the township, as
shown on the original plan and field notes thereof, of record
in the Department of Crown Lands.

What shall be
deemed the
front of a con-
cession in cer-
tain cases.

53. The front of each concession in any township, where
20 only a single row of posts have been planted on the concession
lines, and the lands have been described in whole lots, shall be
that end or boundary of the concession which is nearest to the
boundary of the township from which the several concessions
thereof are numbered ; and when the line in front of any such
25 concession was not run in the original survey, the division or
side-lines of the lots in such concession shall be run from the
original posts or monuments placed or planted on the front
line of the concession in the rear thereof, *on the same course as*
the governing line determined as aforesaid, to the depth of the
30 concession, that is, to the centre of the space contained between the lines in front of the adjacent concessions, if the concessions were intended in the original survey to be of an equal
depth, or, if they were not so intended, then to the proportionate depth intended in the original survey, as shown on the
35 plan and field notes thereof of record in the *Department* of
Crown lands, having due respect to any allowance for a road or
roads made in the original survey ; and a straight line joining
the extremities of the division or side-lines of any lot in such
concession, drawn as aforesaid, shall be the true boundary of
40 that end of the lot which was not run in the original survey.
R. S. O. 1877, c. 146, s. 58.

In townships
fronting on a
river or lake,
how division
lines to be
drawn if no
posts planted
to mark the
width of lots.

54. *In those townships in which any concession is wholly
bounded in front by a river or lake, where no posts or other
boundaries were planted in the original survey on the bank of
45 such river or lake to regulate the width in front of the lots in
the broken front concessions, the division or side-lines of the
lots in such broken front concessions shall be drawn from the
posts or other boundaries on the concession line in rear thereof, on the same course as the governing line, determined as
50 aforesaid, to the river or lake in front. Where any concession
is bounded in front at either end in part, though not wholly, by
a river or lake, and no posts or other boundaries were planted
in the original survey on the bank of such river or lake
to regulate the widths of the lots broken by said river
55 or lake, the division or side-lines of said broken lots
shall be drawn from points on the rear of the concession
determined by measuring off the widths proportionally*

as intended in the original survey, from the intersection of
the division or side-line of the last whole lot of the original
survey with the rear line of said concession, on the same
course as the governing line, determined as aforesaid, to the
river or lake in front. R. S. O. 1877, c. 146, s. 59.   5

Fronts of con-
cessions in cer-
tain other
cases, depths
of lots, etc.

55. In those townships in which the concessions have been
surveyed with double fronts, that is, with posts or monuments
planted on both sides of the allowances for roads between the
concessions, and the lands have been described in half lots, the
division of side-lines shall be drawn from the posts at both 10
ends to the centre of the concession, and each end of such concession shall be the front of its respective half of such concession, and a straight line joining the extremities of the division
or side-lines of any half lot in such concession, drawn as
aforesaid, shall be the true boundary of that end of the half lot 20
which has not been bounded in the original survey. R. S. O.
1877, c. 146, s. 60.

Mode of draw-
ing lines in
double fronted
concessions.

56. And whereas some of the double front concessions are
not of the full depth, and doubts have arisen as to the manner
in which the division or side-lines in such concessions should 25
be established :—Therefore in such concessions the division or
side-lines shall be drawn from the posts at both ends thereof,
to the centre of the concession, as provided in the last preceding
section of this Act, without reference to the manner in which
the lots or parts of lots in such concession have been described 25
for patent. R. S. O. 1877, c. 146, s. 61.

As to conces-
sions in cases
where alter-
nate conces-
sion lines only
have been run.

57. In those townships in which each alternate concession
line has only been run in the original survey, but with double
fronts as aforesaid, the division or side-lines shall be drawn
from the posts or monuments on each side of such alternate 30
concession lines to the depth of a concession—that is, to the
centre of the space contained between such alternate concession
lines, if the concessions were intended in the original survey
to be of an equal depth, or if they were not so intended, then
to the proportionate depth intended in the original survey, as 35
shown on the plan and field-notes thereof of record in the
Department of Crown Lands: and each alternate concession
line as aforesaid shall be the front of each of the two concessions abutting thereon. R. S. O. 1877, c. 146, s. 62.

As to lands in
adjoining con-
cessions in-
cluded in the
same grant.

58. In cases where any Crown patent of grant, or other 40
instrument, has been issued for several lots or parcels of land
in concessions adjoining each other, the side-lines or limits of
the lots or parcels of land therein mentioned and expressed,
shall commence at the front angles of such lots or parcels of
land respectively, and shall be run as hereinbefore provided, 45
and shall not continue on in a straight line through several
concessions—that is to say, each lot or parcel of land shall be
surveyed and bounded according to the provisions of this Act,
independently of the other lots or parcels mentioned in the
same grant or instrument. R. S. O. 1877, c. 146, s. 63.   50

Rule when a
line is to be
drawn on the
same course as
a governing
line.

59. Every land surveyor employed to run any division-
line or side-line between lots, or any line required to run *on*
the same course as any division line or side-line in the concession in which the land to be surveyed lies, shall, if it has not

been done before, or if it has been done but the course cannot
at such time be ascertained, determined by astronomical observation the true course of a straight line between the front and
rear ends of the governing boundary line of the concession or
5 section, and shall run such division-line or side-line as aforesaid, *on the same course as* such straight line, if so intended in
the original survey, or at such angle therewith as is stated in
the plan and field-notes as aforesaid, which shall be deemed to
be the true course of the said governing or boundary line for
10 all the purposes of this Act, although such governing or boundary line as marked in the field be curved or deviate otherwise
from a straight course ; and the same rule shall be observed, if
a line is to be run at any angle with a front line or other line
which is not straight. R. S. O. 1877, c. 146, s. 64.

15 **60.**—(1) In all cases where any land surveyor is employed to Cases where
run any side-line or limits between lots, and the original post the original
or monument from which such line should commence cannot ment cannot
be found, he shall obtain the best evidence that the nature of be found, pro-
the case admits of, respecting such side-line, post or limit; but vided for.
20 if the same cannot be satisfactorily ascertained, then the surveyor shall measure the true distance between the nearest undisputed posts, limits or monuments, and divide such distance
into such number of lots as the same contained in the original
survey, assigning to each a breadth proportionate to that in-
25 tended in such original survey, as shown in the plan and field-
notes thereof, of record in the *Department* of Crown Lands ;
and if any portion of the line in front of the concession in
which such lots are situate, or boundary of the township in
which such concession is situate, has been obliterated or lost,
30 then the surveyor shall run a line between the two nearest
points or places, where such line can be clearly and satisfactorily ascertained, in the manner provided in this Act, and
shall plant all such intermediate posts or monuments as he
may be required to plant in the line so ascertained, having due
35 respect to any allowance for a road or roads, common or commons, set out in such original survey ; and the limits of each
lot so found shall be the true limits thereof. R. S. O. 1877,
c. 146, s. 65.

(2) *In double, front or alternate concessions, where an*
40 *original post or monument cannot be found, any post still.*
standing, or the position of which is satisfactorily established
on the opposite side of the concession road allowance, shall
constitute the best evidence within the meaning of the pre-
ceding sub-section for the purpose of establishing the position
45 *of such missing post or monument.*

61. In those townships in which the side-lines of the lots If side-lines
were drawn in the original survey, every provincial land sur- were drawn in
veyor when called upon to determine any disputed boundary vey, the same
in any of such townships, shall ascertain and establish the divi- to be adhered
50 sion or side-lines of the lots, by running such side-lines as they to.
were run in the original survey, whether the same were in the
original survey run from the front of the concession to the
rear, or from the rear of the concession to the front, and shall
adhere to all posts, limits or monuments, planted on the divi-
55 sion or side-lines in the original survey, as being or designating
corners of lots under such original survey. R. S. O. 1877,
c. 146, s. 66.

As to allowances for roads or streets in Cities, Towns or Villages or any parts thereof laid out by private owners.

62.—(1) All allowances for roads, streets or commons, surveyed in *cities,* towns and villages *or any part thereof* which have been or may be surveyed and laid out by companies and individuals and laid down on the plans thereof, and upon which lots of land fronting on or adjoining such allowances for roads, 5 streets, or commons have been or may be sold to purchasers, shall be public highways, streets and commons ; and all lines which have been or may be run, and the courses thereof given in the survey of such *cities,* towns and villages, *or any part thereof,* and laid down on the plans thereof, and all posts or 10 monuments which have been or may be placed or planted in the first survey of such *cities,* towns and villages, *or any part thereof,* to designate or define any such allowances for roads, streets, lots or commons, shall be the true and unalterable lines and boundaries thereof respectively ; *and all land surveyors* 15 *employed to make surveys in such city, town or village or any part thereof shall follow and pursue the same rules and regulations in respect of such surveys as is by law required of them when employed to make surveys in townships.*

City, Town or Village lots not to be laid out so as to interfere with any allowance for roads.

(2) No lot or lots of land in such *cities,* towns and villages 20 shall be so laid out as to interfere with, obstruct, shut up, or be composed of any part of any allowance for road, common or commons, which were surveyed and reserved in the original survey of the township or townships wherein such *cities,* towns or villages are or may be situate. R. S. O. 1877, c. 146, 25 s. 69.

No private survey valid unless made by a licensed surveyor.

(3) No such private survey shall be valid unless performed by a duly authorized surveyor. R. S. O. 1877, c. 146, s. 68.

Registration of plans of division of lands into smaller parcels.

63.—(1) Where any land or original town or township lot 30 has been surveyed or sub-divided into town or village lots, or other lots so differing from the manner in which such land or lot was surveyed or granted by the Crown, that the same cannot or is not, by the description given of it, easily and plainly to be identified, the person, corporation or company making 35 such survey or sub-division, their heirs, executors, administrators or assigns, agents, attorneys or successors, shall within three months from the date of every such survey or sub-division, lodge with the registrar of the registry division in which the lands are situate a plan or a map of the same, on a scale of 40 not less than one inch to every four chains, shewing the num-

Scale of plan, and what to shew.

ber of the township or town lots, and range or concession, the numbers or letters of town or village lots, and names of streets, with the astronomical or magnetic bearing of the same, and showing thereon all roads, streets, lots and commons within 45 the same, with the courses and widths thereof respectively, and the width and length of all lots, and the courses of all division lines between the respective lots within the same, together with such information as will shew the lots, concessions, tracts or blocks of land of the township within the same 50 is situate.

Duty of Registrars thereafter.

(2) Every such map or plan shall, before being registered be signed by the person or chief officer of the corporation by whom or on whose behalf the same is filed, and certified by some provincial land surveyor in the form of schedule L to 55

The Registry Act, and thenceforward the registrar shall keep Rev. Stat. c. 111. an index of the lands described and designated by any number or letter on such map or plan, by the name by which such person, corporation or company designates the same in the manner provided by this Act; and all instruments affecting the land or Instruments must conform to plan. any part thereof, executed after such plan is filed with the registrar shall conform thereto, otherwise they shall not be registered.

(3) In the case of refusal by such person, corporation or com- Penalty for refusing to lodge plan. pany, his or their executors, agents, or attorneys, or successors, for two months after demand in writing for that purpose, to lodge the said plan or map when required by any person interested therein, or by the inspector, so to do, he or they shall incur a penalty of $20 for each and every calendar month the said map or plan remains unregistered, which penalty may be recovered by any person complaining, in any division court in the county in which such lands are situated, in like manner as a common debt.

(4) This section shall apply as well to lands already sur- To what land this section applies. veyed or sub-divided as to those which may hereafter be surveyed or sub-divided, subject to the next succeeding section. R. S. O. 1877, c. 146, s. 70. *See also Rev. Stat.* c. 111, s. 85.

64. In sales of lands under surveys or sub-divisions made When plan must be registered in case of lands subdivided before this Act. before the 4th day of March, 1868, where such surveys or sub-divisions so differ from the manner in which such land was surveyed or granted by the Crown that the parcel so sold cannot be easily identified, the plan or survey shall be registered within six months after the passing of this Act, if the plan of survey is still in existence and procurable for registra- How to be made. tion and filing under the next preceding section, and if it is not a new survey or plan shall be made by and at the joint expense of the persons who have made such surveys or sub-divisions, and of all others interested therein, by some duly authorized provincial land surveyor, as nearly as may be according to the proper original survey or sub-division, and the same when so made shall be filed as if under the next preceding section of this Act. R. S. O. 1877, c. 146, s. 71. *See also Rev. Stat.* c. 111, s. 83.

65.—(1) Where a survey has been made and a map or plan When surveys or plans may be altered. thereof registered as aforesaid, the owner of the land may cause a new survey and plan thereof, altering or wholly or partially cancelling and making void the former survey and plan thereof, and the division of the land thereby into lots and allowances for roads, streets and commons, to be made cer- Proviso as to streets. tified, deposited and registered as aforesaid; and thereupon such former survey and plan shall be altered, or wholly or partially cancelled, and made void accordingly.

(2) No part of any street or streets shall be altered or closed up, upon which any lot of land sold abuts, or which connects any such sold lot with or affords means of access therefrom to the nearest public highway.

(3) Nothing herein shall in any way interfere with the powers now possessed by municipalities in reference to highways. R. S. O. 1877, c. 146, s. 72.

81—3

Copies of registered plans, to be evidence of the original. **66.** Every copy of such plan or map obtained from such registry office, and certified as correct by the registrar or deputy-registrar as aforesaid shall be taken in all courts as evidence of the original thereof and of the survey of which it purports to be a plan or map. R. S. O. 1877, c. 146, s. 73.

Duty of the Registrar in whose office any such plan is deposited. **67.** Whenever any such plan or map has been so made and deposited as aforesaid the registrar shall make a record of the same, and enter the day and year on which the same is deposited in his office; and for such service the said registrar shall be entitled to charge the same fees, as by law are established for making a record of any other document, which is by law required to be entered of record in his office, but no higher fees. R. S. O. 1877, c. 146, s. 74.

Where no plan of an unincorporated village has been registered, township council to cause one to be made. **68.** Where an unincorporated village comprises different parcels of land, owned at the original division thereof by two or more persons, and the same was not jointly surveyed and laid out into a village plot, and where in such case no entire plan or map of the said village has been deposited with the registrar of the registry division within which the same is situate, the municipality of the township within which the said village is situate shall immediately cause a plan or map of such village to be made on the scale now required by law, and deposited in the registry office of the registry division within which the said village is situate; and the expense attending the getting up of the map and depositing it as aforesaid shall be paid out of the general funds of the municipality, or by a local tax upon the ratepayers of the village. R. S. O. 1877, c. 146, s. 75.

Surveyors to keep regular journals and field-notes and furnish copies to parties interested. **69.** Every land surveyor shall keep exact and regular journals and field-notes of all his surveys, and file them in the order of time in which the surveys have been performed, and shall give copies thereof to the parties concerned when so required, for which he is hereby allowed the sum of $1 for each copy, if the number of words therein does not exceed four hundred words, but if the number of words exceeds four hundred, he is allowed ten cents additional for every hundred words over and above four hundred words. R. S. O. 1877, c. 146, s. 76.

Surveyors may administer oaths for certain purposes. **70.** For better ascertaining the original limits of any township, concession, range, lot, or tract of land, every land surveyor acting in this province, shall and may administer an oath or oaths to each and every person whom he examines concerning any boundary, post or monument, or any original landmark, line, limit or angle of any township, concession, range, lot or tract of land which such surveyor is employed to survey. R. S. O. 1877, c. 146, s. 77.

Evidence taken by Surveyor to be reduced to writing and signed, etc. **71.** All evidence taken by any surveyor as aforesaid shall be reduced to writing; and shall be read over to the person giving the same, and be signed by such person, or, if he cannot write, he shall acknowledge the same as correct before two witnesses, who, as well as the surveyor, shall sign the same; and such evidence shall, and any document or plan prepared and sworn to as correct before a Justice of the Peace, by any surveyor, with reference to any survey by him performed, may be filed and kept in the registry office of the registry division in which the lands to which the same relates are situate, subject to be produced thereafter in evidence in any court within 5 Ontario; and for receiving and filing the same the registrar shall be entitled to twenty-five cents; and the expense of filing the same shall be borne by the parties in the same manner as the other expenses of the survey. R. S. O. 1877, c. 146, s. 78.

Fees.

10 [*Section* 31 *of* C. S. C. c. 77, *is as follows:*

31. If any person or persons, in any part of this province, interrupts, molests or hinders any land surveyor, while in the discharge of his duty as a surveyor, such person or persons shall be guilty of a misdemeanor, and being thereof lawfully convicted in any court of competent jurisdiction, shall be punished either by fine or imprisonment, or both, in the discretion of such court, such imprisonment being for a period not exceeding two months, and such fine not exceeding twenty dollars, without prejudice to any civil remedy which such surveyor or any other party may have against such offender or offenders, in damages by reason of, such offence. 12 V. c. 35, s. 14.]

Penalty for obstructing Land Surveyors in the execution of surveys.

[*Section* 4 *of* C. S. U. C. c. 93, *is as follows:*

4. If any person knowingly and wilfully pulls down, defaces, alters or removes any monument so erected as aforesaid, such person shall be adjudged guilty of felony; and if any person knowingly and wilfully defaces alters or removes any other landmark, post or monument placed by any land surveyor, to mark any limit, boundary or angle of any township, concession, range, lot or parcel of land, in Upper Canada, such person or persons shall be deemed guilty of a misdemeanor, and being convicted thereof before any competent court, shall be liable to be punished by fine or imprisonment, or both, at the discretion of such court, such fine not to exceed one hundred dollars, and such imprisonment not to be for a longer period than three months, without any prejudice to any civil remedy which any party may have against such offender or offenders in damages by reason of such offence; but this shall not extend to prevent land surveyors, in their operations, from taking up posts or other boundary marks when necessary, after which they shall carefully replace them as they were before. 12 V. c. 35, s. 29.

Punishment of persons removing or destroying land marks.

As to Surveyors.

Section 107 *of* C. S. C. c. 77, *contains the same provision.*]

No. 81.

1st Session, 6th Legislature, 50 Vic., 1887.

BILL.

An Act respecting Land Surveyors and the survey of Lands.

First Reading, 14th March, 1887.

BILL.

An Act respecting Land Surveyors and the survey of Lands.

HER MAJESTY, by and with the advice and consent of the Legislative Assembly of the Province of Ontario enacts as follows :—

1. The expression "Commissioner of Crown Lands," wherever Interpretation
5 it occurs in this Act, shall mean the person discharging the duties of that officer. R. S. O. 1877, c. 146, s, 1.

LAND SURVEYORS.

2. No person shall act as a surveyor of lands within this Who may act Province unless he has been duly authorized to practise as a as land surveyor according to the provisions of this Act, or had veyor.
10 been so authorized before the passing thereof, according to the laws then in force, under a penalty of $40. R. S. O. 1877, 146, s. 2.

BOARD OF EXAMINERS.

3. There shall be a board of examiners for the examination Board of examiners.
15 of candidates for admission to practise as land surveyors to consist of the Commissioner of Crown Lands, the Professor of Mineralogy and Geology in University College, Toronto, and *eight* other competent persons to be appointed from time to time by the Lieutenant-Governor, who shall meet at the City
20 of Toronto for the examination of candidates for admission to practise as land surveyors in Ontario. R. S. O. 1877, c. 146, s. 3 ; 43 V. c. 17, s. 1.

4.--(1) Each member of the board, save and except the Oath of Office.
Commissioner of Crown Lands, shall take an oath of office be-
25 fore a Judge of the High Court or of any County Court : and any three of the members shall form a quorum.

(2) The following shall be the form of the oath of office ;

I of
having been appointed a member of the Board of Examiners for the admission of Provincial Land Surveyors for the Province of Ontario, do sincerely promise and swear that I will faithfully discharge the duties of such office without favour, affection or partiality : So help me God.

Sworn before me
at
this day
of 18

R. S. O. 1877, c. 146, s. 4.

Secretary to the board.

5. The said board, or a majority thereof, shall from time to time appoint a fit and proper person to be Secretary of the board, who shall attend the sittings thereof, and keep a record of its proceedings. R. S. O. 1877, c. 146, s. 5.

Meetings when and where to be held.

6. The said board shall meet at the office of the Commis- 5 sioner of Crown Lands, on the first Monday in each of the months of April and *November*, in every year, unless such Monday be a holiday (in which case they shall meet on the day next thereafter, not being a holiday), and may adjourn such meeting from time to time if they deem it neces- 10 sary. R. S. O. 1877, c. 146, s. 6.

APPRENTICES.

Qualification for admission as an apprentice, an examination of applicants.

7. No person shall be admitted as an apprentice with any Provincial Land Surveyor unless he has previously passed an examination before the board of examiners *as to his penman-* 15 *ship and orthography, fractions, decimals, square-root, logarithms, algebra (including equations to the first degree), Euclid (first four books), plane trigonometry, the rules for spherical trigonometry, mensuration of superficies, the use of ruling pen and construction of plain and comparative scales,* 20 *and has obtained a certificate of having passed such examination, and of his proficiency from the board.* R. S. O. 1877, c. 146, s. 7.

Examination fee.

8. Before being so examined he shall pay into the fee fund the sum of $10 as the fee due by him on the examination, and 25 a further sum of $2 to the secretary for the said certificate. R. S. O. 1877, c, 146, s. 8.

Notice to be given by applicants.

9. Applicants for examination previous to apprenticeship shall give one month's notice to the secretary of the board of their intention to present themselves for examination, and pay 30 to the secretary a fee of $1 for receiving and entering such notice. R. S. O 1877, c. 146, s. 9.

QUALIFICATION FOR ADMISSION TO PRACTISE.

Qualification for admission to practise.

10. Except as hereinafter provided no person shall be ad- 35 mitted to practise as a land surveyor in and for Ontario until he has attained the full age of 21 years, *and has passed an examination before the board of examiners in the following subjects, viz., geometry, including the first six books of Euclid, (with the exception of the last thirteen propositions of the* 40 *fifth book), algebra, including progressions, plane and spherical trigonometry, mensuration of superficies, laying out and dividing of land, descriptions by metes and bounds for deeds and other documents, the use and adjustment of surveying and levelling instruments, the laying out of curves,* 45 *practical astronomy, including finding of time, latitude, longitude, azimuth, variation of the compass, and drawing meridian lines. The Acts relating to the survey of lands in Ontario, the general mining Act, the registry Act, so far as it refers to plans, the municipal Acts, so far as they relate to* 50 *roads, surveys and drainage, the ditches and watercourses Act, the theory and practice of levelling, the principles of evidence, drawing of affidavits, taking of field notes and preparing*

*plans, the rudiments of geology and mineralogy, and the
sufficiency of his surveying instruments,* and has served regularly and faithfully, for three successive years, under an instrument in writing, duly executed before two witnesses as
5 apprentice to a land surveyor for Ontario, duly admitted, and
practising therein as such, nor until he has received from the
said land surveyor a certificate of his having so served during
the said period, or proves to the satisfaction of the board that
he has so served. R. S. O. 1877, c 146, s. 10.

10   **11.** It shall not be necessary for any land surveyor, duly Admission of persons pre-
admitted to practise in any of Her Majesty's dominions other viously admit-
than this Province, to serve under an instrument in writing ted in any part
during three years as aforesaid, but it shall only be necessary of Her Majes-
for any such person admitted in the Province of Quebec so to ty's domi- nions.
15 serve during six months of actual practice in the field with a
land surveyor duly admitted and practising in this Province,
and for any other such person so to serve during twelve successive months of actual practice, after which, on complying
with all the other requirements hereof, he may undergo the ex-
20 amination by this Act prescribed. R. S. O. 1877, c. 146, s. 11.

12.—(1) Any person who has followed a regular course of The case of persons who
study in all the branches of education required by law for final have received
admission as a land surveyor, through the regular sessions for university de-
at least two years in any university of the Province, or in grees or diplo- mas as engin-
25 McGill University, in the City of Montreal in the Province of eers or
Quebec, wherein there is organized a complete course of in- surveyors.
struction, practical as well as theoretical, in civil engineering,
natural philosophy, geology, and other branches of education
required by law for admission as a land surveyor, and who has
30 thereupon received from such university, after due examination, a degree or diploma of qualification as a civil engineer
and land surveyor, may, after having passed the preliminary
examination hereinbefore required for admission to apprenticeship with a land surveyor, be received as an apprentice by any
35 practising land surveyor, and shall thereupon be only holden
to serve as such apprentice during twelve success've months
of actual service, or if he has passed through such university
course of study in less time than two full years, then for such
time of actual service as, with the period spent by him in such
04 university course of study, suffices to make up the full time
of three years :

(2) Any person who has followed a regular course of study Case of per-
at the Ontario School of Practical Science in the subjects of sons who have studied at
drawing, surveying and levelling, and geodosy and practical School of Prac-
45 astronomy, and who has thereupon received, after due exam- tical Science.
ination a certificate of having passed one session, two sessions,
or three sessions, as the case may be, in the study of the aforesaid subjects may, after having passed the preliminary examination hereinbefore required for admission to apprenticeship
50 with a land surveyor, be received as an apprentice by any practising land surveyor, and shall thereupon, if he has received
a certificate of having passed three sessions in the study of the
said subjects, be only holden to serve as such apprentice during
twelve successive months of actual service ; or, in case he has
55 only received a certificate of having passed only one or two
sessions, as the case may be, in the study of the said subjects,

then for such time of actual service as, with the period spent by him at such session or sessions, suffices to make up the full time of three years ;

Apprentice-
ship.

Admission to
practise.

(3) After such actual service such person shall, subject to the other provisions of this Act, have the same right to under- 5 go the examination required by law, and if found qualified, to be admitted to practise as a land surveyor as if he had served the full three years' apprenticeship otherwise required by law. 43 V. c. 17, s. 2.

Admission of
Dominion
land sur-
veyors.

13. In case a Dominion land surveyor, under *The Dominion* 10 *Lands Act* applies for a commission as a land surveyor of this Province, if the board of examiners for the time being are of opinion that the qualifications required of. a surveyor of Dominion lands at the time of the Commission having been granted to such surveyor under *The Dominion Lands Act*, 15 were sufficiently similar to those set forth in this Act such sur- veyor shall be entitled to a certificate of admission as a land surveyor of this Province, without being subjected to any ex- amination except as regards the system of survey of lands in Ontario. 43 V. c. 17, s. 3.   20

Graduates of
Military Col-
lege, King-
ston.

14. The privilege of a shortened term of apprenticeship shall also be accorded to any graduate of the Military College at Kingston, *or of the Ontario School of Practical Science,* and such person shall not be required to pass the preliminary examination hereinbefore required for admission to appren- 25 ticeship with a land surveyor, but shall only be bounden to serve under articles with a *practising* land surveyor, duly filed as required by section 17 of this Act, during twelve suc- cessive months of actual practice, after which, on complying with all the other requirements, he may undergo the examina- 30 tion by this Act prescribed. R. S. O. 1877, c. 146, s. 13.

If surveyor
dies, service
may be com-
pleted with
another sur-
veyor.

15. If any surveyor dies or leaves the Province, or is sus- pended or dismissed, his apprentice may complete his term of apprenticeship under an instrument in writing as aforesaid, with any other *practising* surveyor duly admitted. R. S. O. 35 1877, c. 146, s. 14.

Instruments
of apprentice-
ship may be
transferred.

16. Any surveyor may, by an instrument in writing trans- fer an apprentice, with his own consent, to any other *prac- tising* surveyor duly admitted, with whom he may serve the remainder of the term of his apprenticeship. R. S. O. 1877, 40 c, 146, s. 15.

Instruments
binding to ser-
vice to be filed,
etc.

17. No instrument in writing under which any applicant for admission to practise as a surveyor claims to have served with some practising surveyor for the period of three years, twelve months or six months (as the case may be), shall avail 45 to authorize the admission of an applicant, unless the instru- ment has been transmitted to the secretary of the board within two months next after the date thereof, nor unless the fee men- tioned in section 26 of this Act was by the apprentice paid to the secretary of the board at the time of transmitting the in- 50 denture or articles : and the said secretary shall acknowledge by post the receipt of all such instruments or copies thereof transmitted to him, and shall carefully keep the same in his office. R. S. O. 1877, c. 146, s. 16.

ADMISSION OF CANDIDATES.

18. Every person desiring to be examined by the board as to his qualification to be admitted as a land surveyor, shall give notice thereof in writing to the secretary of the board, at least 5 one month previous to the meeting thereof. R. S. O. 1877, c. 146, s. 18.

Notice of examination to be given by candidates for admission.

19. Every person applying for admission to practice as a land surveyor shall produce to the board satisfactory certificates as to character for probity and sobriety, and before a 10 certificate is granted shall perform such practical operations in the presence of the board, and shall answer such questions on oath (which oath any member of the board may administer) with regard to the actual practice of such applicant in the field, and with regard to his surveying instruments as the said 15 board may require. R. S. O. 1877, c. 146, s. 19.

The board to require certificates of good conduct, etc.

20. *If the said examiners are satisfied as to the qualifications of the candidate, and his compliance with all the requirements of this Act, they shall grant him a certificate in the form following :*

If the examiners approve of the candidate they are to grant him certificate.

"This is to certify to all whom it may concern, that *A. B.* of   in the County of   has duly passed his examination before the board of examiners, and has been found qualified to fill the office and perform the duties of a Provincial Land Surveyor in and for Ontario, he having complied with all the requirements of the law in that behalf. Wherefore the said *A. B.* is admitted to the said office, and is by law authorized to practise as a land surveyor in Ontario.

"In witness whereof, we have signed this certificate at the City of Toronto, in the County of York, and Province of Ontario, Dominion of Canada,   the   day of   18   ."

Signature of the Chairman, *" C. D."*

Signature of the Secretary, " E. F."

20 And such certificate shall, on his complying with the other requirements of this Act, enable him to practice as a land surveyor in and for Ontario. R. S. O. 1877, c. 146, s. 20.

21.—(1) Each applicant, *before* receiving the above mentioned certificate, shall, with two sufficient sureties to the satis- 25 faction of the said board of examiners, enter into a bond jointly and severally in the sum of $1,000 to Her Majesty, Her Heirs and Successors, conditioned for the due and faithful performance of the duties of his office.

Licentiates to give bonds and take the oaths of allegiance and of office.

(2) The said bond shall be deposited and kept in the man- 30 ner by law prescribed with regard to bonds given for like purposes by other public officers, and shall enure to the benefit of any party sustaining damage by breach of the condition thereof; and the certificate shall be registered in the office of the Provincial Secretary. R. S. O. 1877, c. 146, s. 21.

Where bonds to be deposited.

35 **22.**—(1) Each applicant, after having been granted a certificate, shall also take and subscribe the oath of allegiance, and the following oath, before the board of examiners, who are hereby empowered to administer the same :

Oaths.

" I, *A. B.*, do solemnly swear (*or affirm, as the case may be*) that I will faithfully discharge the duties of a land surveyor, agreeably to law, without favor, affection or partiality : So help me God."

(2) The said oath of allegiance and of office shall be deposited in the office of the Provincial Secretary. R. S. O. 1877, c. 146, s. 22.

When the board may suspend licensed surveyors.

23. The board of examiners may in their discretion suspend or dismiss from the practice of his profession, any land 5 surveyor whom they find guilty of gross negligence or corruption in the execution of the duties of his office ; but the board *shall not take action until the complaint under oath has been filed with the board, and a copy thereof forwarded to the party accused, nor shall the board* suspend or dismiss such land sur- 10 veyor without having previously summoned him to appear in order to be heard in his defence, nor without having heard the evidence, offered either in support of the complaint or in behalf of the surveyor inculpated. R. S. O. 1877, c. 146, s. 23.

Fees to be paid to the members of the board.

24. The Commissioner of Crown Lands shall pay to each 15 member of the board of examiners *and the secretary of the board,* who attends any examination, the sum of $5 for each day's attendance, and charge the same in his account as part of the expenses of his office. R. S. O. 1877, c. 146, s. 24.

Tariff of fees.

25. The following fees shall be paid under the provisions 20 of this Act :

1. To the secretary of the board of examiners, by each apprentice, at the transmitting to such secretary the Indenture or Articles of such apprentice................................ $2 00

2. To the secretary of the board by each candidate for examination with his notice thereof......................... .... 1 00

3. To the secretary of the board by each applicant obtaining a certificate, as his fee thereon............................. 2 00

4. To the secretary of the board as an admission fee by each . applicant receiving a certificate, out of which the expenses attending the examination of such applicant (if any) shall be first paid, and the remainder (if any) shall be paid over to the Commissioner of Crown Lands and be accounted for like other moneys received by him................... .... 20 00

5. To every surveyor summoned to attend any court, civil or criminal, for the purpose of giving evidence in his professional capacity as a surveyor, for each day he so attends, in addition to his travelling expense (if any), and to be taxed and paid in the manner by law provided with regard to the payment of witnesses attending such court............................ *5 00*

R. S. O. 1877, c. 146, s. 25.

BOUNDARY LINES.

Establishment of boundary lines regulated.

26. All boundary or division lines legally established, and ascertained under the authority of any Ordinance or Act heretofore in force, shall remain good, and all other acts or things 25 legally done and performed under the authority of the said Ordinance and Acts, or any of them, and in conformity to the provisions thereof, shall remain good and valid notwithstanding the repeal of such Ordinance or Act. R. S. O. 1877, c. 146, s. 26.

27. The standard of English measure of length, compared _{The standard of measure regulated.}
5 with and corrected by the standards for such measures established in this Province and procured by the Commissioner of Crown Lands for the purpose of comparing therewith the standards to be kept by each surveyor as hereinafter provided, shall be deposited with the secretary of the board of examiners
10 at Toronto, and the said secretary, under such instructions as he from time to time receives from the board, shall examine, test and stamp each standard measure of length for the surveyors, bringing the same for examination as the Commissioner of Crown Lands may do and with the same effect ; and for each
15 measure so examined and stamped such secretary may demand and receive fifty cents. R. S. O. 1877, c. 146, s. 27.

28. Every land surveyor duly admitted and practising shall _{Surveyors to procure stamped standard measures.}
procure and shall cause to be examined, corrected and stamped or otherwise certified by the Commissioner of Crown Lands
20 or some one deputed by him for that purpose, or by the secretary aforesaid, a standard measure of length, under the penalty of the forfeiture of his license or certificate, and shall, previously to proceeding on any survey, verify by such standard the length of his chains and other instruments for measuring. R.
25 S. O. 1877, c. 146, s. 28.

29. Every chain-bearer shall, before he commences his _{Chain-bearers to be sworn, and nature of the oath.}
chaining or measuring, take an oath or affirmation to act as such justly and exactly according to the best of his judgment and
ability, and to render a true account of his chaining or
30 measuring to the surveyor by whom he has been appointed to such duty, and that he is absolutely disinterested in the survey in question, and is not related or allied to any of the parties interested in the survey within the fourth degree, according to
35 the computation of the civil law—that is to say, within the degree of cousin-german, which oath the surveyor employing such chain-bearer is hereby authorized and required to administer ; nor shall any person related or allied to any of the parties within the said degree be employed as a chain-bearer
40 on any survey. R. O. S. 1877, c. 146, s. 29.

30. Any land surveyor, when engaged in the performance _{When land surveyors may pass over private lands.}
of the duties of his profession, may pass over, measure along and ascertain the bearings of any *line or limit whatsoever*, and for such purposes may pass over the lands of any person whom-
45 soever, doing no actual damage to the property of such person. R. S. O. 1877, c. 146, s. 30.

31. Where any surveyor is in doubt as to the true boundary _{Course to be adopted by surveyor to ascertain boundary line, when doubtful, etc.}
or limit of any township, concession, range, lot or tract of land which he is employed to survey, and has reason to believe
50 that any person is possessed of any important information touching such boundary or limit, or of any writing, plan or document tending to establish the true position of such boundary or limit, then if such person does not willingly appear before and be examined by such surveyor, or does not willingly
55 produce to him such writing, plan or document, such surveyor

or the party employing him may file in the office of the County
May subpœna witnesses. Court a præcipe for a subpœna or subpœna *duces tecum*, as the
case may require, accompanying such application by an affidavit
or solemn declaration to be made before a Justice of the Peace,
of the facts on which the application is founded, and the Judge   5
may order a subpœna to issue accordingly, commanding such
person to appear before the surveyor, at a time and place to
be mentioned in the said subpœna and to bring with him any
writing, plan or document mentioned or referred to therein.
R. S. O. 1877, c. 146, s. 31.   10

Service of subpœna.   **32.** The subpœna shall be served on the person named
therein by delivering a copy thereof to him, or by leaving the
same for him with some grown person of his family at his residence, exhibiting to him or to such grown person the original,
R. S. O. 1877, c. 146, s. 32.   15

Penalty for disobeying subpœna.   **33.** If the person commanded to appear by the subpœna
after being paid his reasonable expenses, or having the same
tendered to him, refuses or neglects to appear before the surveyor at the time and place appointed in the subpœna, or to
produce the writing, plan or document (if any) therein men- 20
tioned or referred to, or to give such evidence and information
as he may possess touching the boundary or limit in question,
the person so summoned shall be deemed guilty of a contempt
of the Court out of which the subpœna issued, and an attachment may be issued against him by the Judge of the said 25
Court, and he may be punished accordingly, by fine or imprisonment, or both, in the discretion of the Judge. R. S. O. 1877,
c. 146, s. 33.

Stone monuments may be placed at certain points in townships.   **34.** Stone monuments, or monuments of other durable materials, shall be placed at the several corners, governing points 30
or off-sets of every township already surveyed, or after this
Act takes effect from time to time surveyed, and also at each
end of the several concession lines of such townships ; and
lines drawn in the manner hereinafter prescribed from the
monuments so erected, shall be taken and considered to be the 35
permanent boundary lines of such townships and concessions
respectively. R. S. O. 1877, c. 146, s. 34.

To be placed under the direction of the Commissioner of Crown Lands.   **35.** The monuments to be placed as above mentioned shall
be so placed under the direction and order of the Commis-
sioner of Crown Lands. R. S. O. 1877, c. 146, s. 35.   40

Boundaries ascertained as aforesaid to be deemed the true ones.   **36.** The courses and lengths of the said boundary lines, so
ascertained and established, shall on all occasions be the true
courses and lengths of the boundary lines of the said townships and concessions, whether the same do or do not, on
actual survey, coincide with the courses and lengths in any 45
letters patent of grant or other instrument mentioned and expressed in respect of such boundary lines. R. S. O. 1877,
c. 146, s. 36.

Monuments need not be placed under ss. 34-36 except on the application of the municipal council.   **37.** It shall not be necessary for the Commissioner of Crown
Lands to proceed to carry the provisions of the last preceding 50
three sections of this Act into execution, until an application
for that purpose has been made to the Lieutenant-Governor,
by the council of the county in which the township or townships interested is situate, and such council shall cause the

sum requisite to defray the expenses to be incurred, or the proportion thereof payable by the inhabitants of any township or concession, to be levied on the said inhabitants, in the same manner as any sum required for any other local purpose author-
5 ized by law may be levied. R. S. O. 1877, c. 146 s. 37.

38.—(1) *And whereas in several of the townships in Ontario* In what cases
some of the concession lines, and side road lines, or parts of the municipal
the concession lines and side road lines were not run in the council may
original survey performed under competent authority, and the monuments
10 *survey of some of the concession lines and side road lines, or* placed.
parts of the concession lines and side-road lines have been
obliterated, and owing to the want of such lines the inhabitants
of such concessions are subject to serious inconvenience, there-
fore the municipal council of the township in which such lines
15 *are situated, may, on application of one-half the resident land-*
holders in any concession or part of concession or upon its
own motion without such application, apply to the Lieutenant-
Governor, requesting him to cause any such line or lines to be
surveyed and marked by permanent stone or iron boundaries
20 *under the direction and order of the Commissioner of Crown*
Lands, in the manner prescribed in this Act, at the cost of the
proprietors of the lands in each concession or part of a con-
cession interested.

(2) *The concession lines, where not run, or where they have* As to the ad-
25 *been obliterated shall be so drawn as to leave each of the ad-* jacent con-
jacent concessions of a depth proportionate to that intended cessions.
in the original survey.

(3) *The survey of the parts of the concession lines not run* Establishment
or which have been obliterated, shall be established by drawing of lines.
30 *a straight line between the two nearest points or places where*
such line or lines can be clearly and satisfactorily ascertained.

(4) The lines or parts of lines so surveyed and marked as To be perma-
aforesaid, shall thereafter be the permanent boundary lines of nent boundary
such concession *or side roads,* or parts of concessions *or side* lines.
35 *roads* to all intents and purposes of law whatsoever. R. S. O.
1877, c, 146, s. 40.

(5) The council shall cause to be laid before them an esti- Expenses to be
mate of the sum requisite to defray the expenses to be incurred estimated and
in order that the same may be levied on the said proprietors, provided for.
40 in proportion to the quantity of land held by them respectively
in such concession or part of a concession, in the same manner
as any sum required for any other purposes authorized by law
may be levied. R. S. O. 1877, c. 146, s. 41.

39.—(1) Whenever the municipal council of any township, Municipal
45 city, town or incorporated village adopts a resolution, on councils may
application of one-half the resident landholders to be affected boundaries of
thereby, *or upon its own motion,* that is is desirable to place lots to be as-
stone or other durable monuments at the front or at the rear, certained and
or at the front and rear angles of the lots in any concession or marked.
50 range *or block* or part of a concession, or range *or block* in their
township, city, town, or incorporated village, such municipal
council may make application to the Lieutenant-Governor, in
the same manner as is provided in section *38,* praying him to
81—2

cause a survey of such concession or range *or block* or part of a
concession or range *or block,* to be made, and such boundaries
to be planted, under the authority of the Commissioner of
Crown Lands. R. S. O. 1877, c. 146, s. 43.

Boundaries to be marked by stone or some other durable monuments to be placed at the angles. (2) The *surveyor* making such survey shall accordingly 5
plant stone or other durable monuments at the front, or at the
rear, or at the front and rear angles of each and every lot in
such concession, or range, *or block,* or part of a concession, or
range, *or block,* and the limits of each lot so ascertained and
marked shall be the true limits thereof. R. S. O. 1877, c. 146, s. 10
44.

How costs to be defrayed. (3) The cost of such survey shall be defrayed in the manner prescribed by section *38* of this Act. R. S. O. 1877, c.
146, s. 45.

Expenses how paid. **40.** All expenses incurred in performing any survey, or 15
placing any monument or boundary under the provisions of
section 34, and the following sections. shall be paid by the
county *or township* treasurer to the *surveyor* employed in such
services, on the certificate and order of the Commisioner of
Crown Lands. R. S. O. 1877, c. 146, s. 42. 20

Boundaries placed under the authority of the Government not to be deemed the true ones, etc. **41.** All boundary lines of townships, cities, towns and villages, all concession lines, governing points and all boundary
lines, of concessions, sections, blocks, gores and commons, and all
side lines and limits of lots surveyed, *and all trees marked in lieu
of posts* and all posts or monuments, marked, placed or planted at 30
the front *or rear* angles of any lots or parcels of land, under the
authority of the Executive Government of the late Province
of Quebec or of Upper Canada, or of Canada, or under the authority of the Executive Government of this Province, shall
be the true and unalterable boundaries of all and every such 35
townships, cities, towns villages, concessions, sections, blocks,
gores, commons, and lots or parcels of land, respectively,
whether the same upon admeasurement be found to contain
the exact width, or more or less than the exact width mentioned or expressed in any letters patent, grant or other in- 40
strument in respect of such township, city, town, village, concession, section, block, gore, common, lot or parcel of land. R.
S. O. 1877. c 146, s. 46.

Townships, etc., to comprise all the space included within their boundaries. **42.** Every township, city, town, village, concession, section,
block, gore, common, lot or parcel of land, shall embrace the 45
whole width, contained between the front posts, monuments
or boundaries, planted or placed at the front angles thereof respectively, so marked, placed or planted as aforesaid, and no
more nor less, any quantity or measure expressed in the original grant or patent thereof notwithstanding. R. S. O. 1877, c. 50
146, s. 47.

As to aliquot parts of town-ships, etc. **43.** Every patent, grant or instrument, purporting to be for
any aliquot part of any concession, section. block, gore, com-
mon, lot or parcel of land *in any such township, city, town or
village,* shall be construed to be a grant of such aliquot part of 55
the quantity the same may contain, whether such quantity be
more or less than that expressed in such patent, grant or instrument. R. S. O. 1877, c. 146, s. 48.

44. In every city, town, or village, *or any part thereof* which has been surveyed by the authority aforesaid, all allowances for any road, street, lane or common laid out in the original survey of such city, town, or village, *or any part*
5 *thereof* shall be public highways and commons; and all posts or monuments placed or planted in the original survey of such city, town or village, *or any part thereof*, to designate or define any allowance for a road, street, lane, lot or common, shall be the true and unalterable boundaries of every such
10 road, street, lane, lot and common; and all land surveyors, employed to make surveys in such city, town or village, *or any part thereof*, shall follow and pursue the same rules and regulations in respect of such surveys as is by law required of them when employed to make surveys in townships. R. S. O. 1877,
15 c. 146, s. 49.

Road allowances in cities, etc., to be public highways.

45. All surveys of townships, tracts or blocks of land in this Province, granted by the Crown to companies and individuals before any surveys had been made therein, and which were afterwards surveyed by the owners thereof, shall be
20 original surveys thereof, and shall have the same force and effect as though the said original surveys and plans thereof had been made by competent authority; and all allowances for roads or commons surveyed in such townships, tracts, or blocks of land, and laid down on the plans thereof, shall be public
25 highways and commons; and all lines run and marked in such original surveys, and all posts or monuments planted or placed in such original surveys to designate and define any allowance *for* road, concession, lot of land or common, shall be the true and unalterable lines and boundaries of such allowance for road,
30 common or lot of land, and all land surveyors, when employed to make surveys in such townships, tracts or blocks of land, shall follow and pursue the same rules and regulations in respect of such townships, tracts or blocks of land, and the original surveys thereof, as they are by law required to follow and pur-
35 sue in all townships, tracts or blocks of land surveyed by the authority aforesaid. R. S. O. 1877, c 146, s. 50.

As to lands granted in blocks and subsequently surveyed by the grantees.

46. The course of the boundary line of each and every concession, on that side from which the lots are numbered, shall be the course of the division or side lines throughout the
40 several townships or concessions respectively, provided that such division or side lines were intended, in the original survey performed under such authority as aforesaid, to run *on the same course as* the said boundary. R. S. O. 1877, c. 146, s. 51.

Governing lines declared.

45 **47.** Every surveyor shall run all division or side lines, which he is called upon by the owner or owners of any lands to survey *on the same course as* that boundary line of the concession in which such lands are situate, from whence the lots are numbered as aforesaid, provided such division or side lines
50 were intended, in the original survey performed under such competent authority as aforesaid, to run *on the same course as* the said boundary. R. S. O. 1877, c. 146, s. 52.

All side lines to be run on the same course as governing lines.

48. Where that end of a concession, from which the lots are numbered, is *wholly* bounded by a lake or river, or other
55 natural boundary, or where it has not been run in the original

Course to be adopted where concession bounded by lake or river.

survey performed under competent authority as aforesaid, or
where the course of the division or side line of the lots
therein was not intended in the original survey performed as
aforesaid, to *be on the same course as* such boundary, the said
division or side lines shall *be run on the same course as* the 5
boundary line at the other extremity of such concession, provided their course was intended, in the original survey performed as aforesaid, to be *the same,* and that such boundary
line was run in the original survey. R. S. O. 1877, c. 146,
s. 53. 10

Where division or side-lines not intended to run *on the same course as* the side-line at either end of a concession. **49.** Where in the original survey, performed under competent authority as aforesaid, the course of the division or side
lines in any concession was not intended to be *on the same
course as* the boundary line at either end of such concession,
they shall be run at such angle with the course of the 15
boundary line at that end of the concession from which the
lots are numbered, as is stated in the plan and field notes of
the original survey, of record in the *Department* of Crown
Lands, provided such line was run in the original survey, as
aforesaid, or with the course of the boundary line at the other 20
extremity of the said concession, if the boundary at that end
of the concession from which the lots are numbered was not
run in the original survey; or if neither of the aforesaid
boundaries of the concession was run in the original survey, or
if the concession is *wholly* bounded at each end by a lake or 25
river, or other natural boundary, then at such angle with the
course of the line in front of the said concession as is stated in
the plan and field notes aforesaid, *or if parts of the concession
line have been run on different courses as shown on said plans
and field notes, then at such angle with the course of each of* 30
these parts, as is stated in the plan and field notes aforesaid.
R. S. O. 1877, c. 146, s. 54.

Where a division or proof line has been run between lots, the same shall govern. **50.** If any division or side line between lots, or proof-line
intended to be *on the same course as* the division or side lines
between lots, was drawn in any such concession, *bounded as* 35
aforesaid, in the original survey thereof, the division or side
lines between the lots therein shall be *on the same course as*
such division or side line or proof-line. R. S. O. 1877, c. 146,
s. 55.

Where there are two of such lines, the line nearest the end of the concession, from which the lots are numbered, to govern to the next of such lines. **51.** Where two or more such division or side lines or proof- 40
lines were drawn in the original survey of such concession,
bounded as aforesaid, that division or side line or proof-line
which is nearest to the boundary of the concession from
which the lots are numbered, shall govern the course of the
division or side lines of all the lots in such concession between 45
the boundary of the concession from which the lots are numbered, and the next division or side line or proof-line drawn in
the original survey; and such last mentioned line or proof-
line shall govern the course of the division or side lines of all
the lots up to the next division or side line or proof-line drawn 50
in the original survey, or to the boundary of the concession
towards which the lots are numbered, as the case may be.
R. S. O. 1877, c. 147, s. 56.

How lines to be governed in townships laid **52.** *In all those townships which in the original survey
were divided into sections, agreeably to an Order in Council,* 55

bearing date the 27th day of March, 1829, or which have since out in sections
been or shall be divided into.sections or blocks of one thousand under order in
council of \
acres, or thereabouts, or six hundred and forty acres or there- March 27th,
abouts, as the case may be, under instructions from the Com- 1829, etc.
5 missioner of Crown Lands, the division or side lines in all
concessions, in any section or block, shall be governed by the
boundary lines of such section or block, in like manner as the
division or side lines in townships originally surveyed before
the said day, are governed by the boundary lines of the con-
10 cession in which the lots are situated : Provided that in those
sections or blocks the governing boundaries of which are
broken by lakes or rivers in such a way that the course thereof cannot accurately be determined, a surveyor, when called
upon to run any side line in any concession in such section
15 or block, shall run such side line on the astronomical
course of the side lines of the lots in the township, as
shown on the original plan and field notes thereof, of record
in the Department of Crown Lands.

53. The front of each concession in any township, where What shall be
deemed the
20 only a single row of posts have been planted on the concession front of a c^{on}-
lines, and the lands have been described in whole lots, shall be cession in cer-
that end or boundary of the concession which is nearest to the tain cases.
boundary of the township from which the several concessions
thereof are numbered ; and when the line in front of any such
25 concession was not run in the original survey, the division or
side lines of the lots in such concession shall be run from the
original posts or monuments placed or planted on the front
line of the concession in the rear thereof, *on the same course as*
the governing line determined as aforesaid, to the depth of the
30 concession, that is, to the centre of the space contained between the lines in front of the adjacent concessions, if the concessions were intended in the original survey to be of an equal
depth, or, if they were not so intended, then to the proportionate depth intended in the original survey, as shown on the
35 plan and field notes thereof of record in the *Department* of
Crown lands, having due respect to any allowance for a road or
roads made in the original survey ; and a straight line joining
the extremities of the division or side lines of any lot in such
concession, drawn as aforesaid, shall be the true boundary of
40 that end of the lot which was not run in the original survey.
R. S. O. 1877, c. 146, s. 58.

54. *In those townships in which any concession is wholly* In townships
bounded in front by a river or lake, where no posts or other fronting on a
river or lake,
boundaries were planted in the original survey on the bank of how division
45 *such river or lake to regulate the width in front of the lots in* lines to be
drawn if no
the broken front concessions, the division or side lines of the posts planted
lots in such broken front concessions shall be drawn from the to mark the
posts or other boundaries on the concession line in rear there- width of lots.
of, on the same course as the.governing line, determined as
50 *aforesaid, to the river or lake in front. Where any concession*
is bounded in front at either end, in part though not wholly, by
a river or lake, and no posts or other boundaries were planted
in the original survey on the bank of such river or lake
to regulate the widths of the lots broken by said river
55 *or lake, the division or side lines of said broken lots*
shall be drawn from points on the rear of the concession
determined by measuring off the widths proportionally

*as intended in the original survey, from the intersection of
the division or side line of the last whole lot of the original
survey with the rear line of said concession, on the same
course as the governing line, determined as aforesaid, to the
river or lake in front.* R. S. O. 1877, c. 146, s. 59.   5

Fronts of concessions in certain other cases, depths of lots, etc. **55.** In those townships in which the concessions have been
surveyed with double fronts, that is, with posts or monuments
planted on both sides of the allowances for roads between the
concessions, and the lands have been described in half lots, the
division or side lines shall be drawn from the posts at both 10
ends to the centre of the concession, and each end of such concession shall be the front of its respective half of such concession, and a straight line joining the extremities of the division
or side lines of any half lot in such concession, drawn as
aforesaid, shall be the true boundary of that end of the half lot 15
which has not been bounded in the original survey. R. S. O.
1877, c. 146, s. 60.

Mode of drawing lines in double fronted concessions. **56.** And whereas some of the double front concessions are
not of the full depth, and doubts have arisen as to the manner
in which the division or side lines in such concessions should 20
be established :—Therefore in such concessions the division or
side lines shall be drawn from the posts at both ends thereof,
to the centre of the concession, as provided in the last preceding
section of this Act, without reference to the manner in which
the lots or parts of lots in such concession have been described
for patent. R. S. O. 1877, c. 146, s. 61.   25

As to concessions in cases where alternate concession lines only have been run. **57.** In those townships in which each alternate concession
line has only been run in the original survey, but with double
fronts as aforesaid, the division or side lines shall be drawn
from the posts or monuments on each side of such alternate
concession lines to the depth of a concession—that is, to the 30
centre of the space contained between such alternate concession
lines, if the concessions were intended in the original survey
to be of an equal depth, or if they were not so intended, then
to the proportionate depth intended in the original survey, as
shown on the plan and field-notes thereof of record in the 35
Department of Crown Lands : and each alternate concession
line as aforesaid shall be the front of each of the two concessions abutting thereon. R. S. O. 1877, c. 146, s. 62.

As to lands in adjoining concessions included in the same grant. **58.** In cases where any Crown patent of grant, or other
instrument, has been issued for several lots or parcels of land 40
in concessions adjoining each other, the side lines or limits of
the lots or parcels of land therein mentioned and expressed,
shall commence at the front angles of such lots or parcels of
land respectively, and shall be run as hereinbefore provided,
and shall not continue on in a straight line through several
concessions—that is to say, each lot or parcel of land shall be 45
surveyed and bounded according to the provisions of this Act,
independently of the other lots or parcels mentioned in the
same grant or instrument. R. S. O. 1877, c. 146, s. 63.

Rule when a line is to be drawn *on the same course as* a governing line. **59.** Every land surveyor employed to run any division-
line or side line between lots, or any line required to run *on* 50
the same course as any division line or side line in the concession in which the land to be surveyed lies, shall, if it has not

been done before, or if it has been done but the course cannot at such time be ascertained, determine by astronomical observation the true course of a straight line between the front and rear ends of the governing boundary line of the concession or
5 section, and shall run such division-line or side line as aforesaid, *on the same course as* such straight line, if so intended in the original survey, or at such angle therewith as is stated in the plan and field-notes as aforesaid, which shall be deemed to be the true course of the said governing or boundary line for
10 all the purposes of this Act, although such governing or boundary line as marked in the field be curved or deviate otherwise from a straight course ; and the same rule shall be observed, if a line is to be run at any angle with a front line or other line which is not straight. R. S. O. 1877, c. 146, s. 64.

15 **60.**—(1) In all cases where any land surveyor is employed to run any side line or limits between lots, and the original post or monument from which such line should commence cannot be found, he shall obtain the best evidence that the nature of the case admits of, respecting such side line, post or limit ; but
20 if the same cannot be satisfactorily ascertained, then the surveyor shall measure the true distance between the nearest undisputed posts, limits or monuments, and divide such distance into such number of lots as the same contained in the original survey, assigning to each a breadth proportionate to that in-
25 tended in such original survey, as shown in the plan and field-notes thereof, of record in the *Department* of Crown Lands ; and if any portion of the line in front of the concession in which such lots are situate, or boundary of the township in which such concession is situate, has been obliterated or lost,
30 then the surveyor shall run a line between the two nearest points or places, where such line can be clearly and satisfactorily ascertained, in the manner provided in this Act, and shall plant all such intermediate posts or monuments as he may be required to plant in the line so ascertained, having due
35 respect to any allowance for a road or roads, common or commons, set out in such original survey ; and the limits of each lot so found shall be the true limits thereof. R. S. O. 1877, c. 146, s. 65.

(2) In double front or alternate concessions, where an
40 *original post or monument cannot be found, any original post still standing, or the position of which is satisfactorily established on the opposite side of the concession road allowance or on the centre line thereof, shall constitute the best evidence within the meaning of the preceding sub-section*
45 *for the purpose of establishing the position of such missing post or monument.*

61. In those townships in which the side lines of the lots were drawn in the original survey, every provincial land surveyor when called upon to determine any disputed boundary
50 in any of such townships, shall ascertain and establish the division or side lines of the lots, by running such side lines as they were run in the original survey, whether the same were in the original survey run from the front of the concession to the rear, or from the rear of the concession to the front, and shall
55 adhere to all posts, limits or monuments, planted on the division or side lines in the original survey, as being or designating corners of lots under such original survey. R. S. O. 1877, c. 146, s. 66.

Marginal notes:

Cases where the original post or monument cannot be found, provided for.

If side-lines were drawn in original survey, the same to be adhered to.

As to allowances for roads or streets in *Cities,* Towns or Villages *or any parts thereof* laid out by private owners.

62.—(1) All allowances for roads, streets or commons, surveyed in cities, towns and villages or any part thereof which have been or may be surveyed and laid out by companies and individuals and laid down on the plans thereof, and upon which lots of land fronting on or adjoining such allowances for 5 roads, streets or commons, have been or may be sold to purchasers, shall be public highways, streets and commons ; and all lines which have been or may be run, and the courses thereof given in the survey of such cities, towns and villages, or any part thereof, and laid down on the plans thereof, and all 10 posts or monuments which have been or may be placed or planted in the first survey of such cities, towns and villages, or any part thereof, to designate or define any such allowances for roads, streets, lots or commons, shall be the true and unalterable lines and boundaries thereof respectively ; and all 15 land surveyors employed to make surveys in such city, town or village, or any part thereof, shall follow and pursue the same rules and regulations in respect of such surveys as is by law required of them when employed to make surveys in

Proviso.

townships : Provided that the municipal corporation shall not 20 be liable to keep in repair any road, street, bridge or highway laid out by any private person until established by by-law of the corporation or otherwise assumed for public use by such corporation, as provided in *The Consolidated Municipal Act 1883.* 25

City, Town or Village lots not to be laid out so as to interfere with any allowance for roads.

(2) No lot or lots of land in such cities, towns and villages shall be so laid out as to interfere with, obstruct, shut up, or be composed of any part of any allowance for road, common or commons, which were surveyed and reserved in the original survey of the township or townships wherein such cities, 30 towns or villages are or may be situate. R. S. O. 1877, c. 146, s. 69.

No private survey valid unless made by a licensed surveyor.

(3) No such private survey shall be valid unless performed by a duly authorized surveyor. R. S. O. 1877, c. 146, s. 68.

Registration of plans when land subdivided.

63.—(1) Whenever any land is surveyed and sub-divided 35 for the purpose of being sold or conveyed in lots by reference to a plan which has not been already registered, the person making the sub-division shall, within three months from the date of the survey, file with the Registrar a plan of the land on a scale not less than 1 inch to every 4 chains. The plan shall 40

Scale of plan and what to show.

show the number of the township town or village lots, and range or concession as originally laid out, and all the boundary lines thereof, within the limits of the land shewn on the said plan, and where such plan is a sub-division of a lot, or lots, on a former plan, it shall shew the numbers or other distinguish- 45 ing marks of the lot or lots sub-divided, and the boundary lines of such lot or lots. The plan shall also shew all roads, streets, lots and commons, within the same, with the courses and widths thereof respectively, and the width and length of all lots and the courses of all division lines between the 50 respective lots within the same, together with such other information as is required to shew distinctly the position of the land being sub-divided.

Duty of Registrars thereafter.

(2). Every such map or plan, before being registered, shall be signed by the person or the chief officer of the corporation 55 by whom or on whose behalf the same is filed, and shall also

be certified by some provincial land surveyor in the form of
Schedule L. to *The Registry Act*, as follows:—I hereby certify
that this plan accurately shews the manner in which the land   Form of Sur-
included therein has been surveyed and sub-divided by me;   veyors certifi-
5 and that the said plan is prepared in accordance with the pro-   cate on plan.
visions of *The Registry Act*.

Dated   18   *A.B.*

Provincial Land Surveyor,

and thenceforth the Registrar shall keep an index of the lands
10 described and designated by any number or letter on the map   Instruments
or plan, by the name of which such person, corporation or   must conform
company designates the same in the manner provided by *The*   to such plan.
Registry Act ; and all instruments affecting the land or any
part thereof, executed after the plan is filed with the Registrar,
15 shall conform and refer thereto, otherwise they shall not be
registered.

☞(3) In the case of refusal by such person, corporation or   Penalty for
company, his or their executors, agents, or attorneys, or   refusing to
successors, for two months after demand in writing for that   register plan.
20 purpose, to lodge the said plan or map when required by any
person interested therein, or by the Inspector so to do, he or
they shall incur a penalty of $20 for each and every calendar
month the said map or plan remains unregistered, which   How recover-
penalty may be recovered by any person complaining, in any   ed.
25 Division Court, in the County in which such lands are situated, in like manner as a common debt.

☞(4) This section shall apply as well to lands already sur-   To what land
veyed or subdivided as to those which may hereafter be sur-   this section
veyed or subdivided, subject to the next succeeding section.☜   applies.

30   **64.** In sales of lands under surveys or sub-divisions made   When plan
before the 4th day of March, 1868, where such surveys   must be regis-
or sub-divisions so differ from the manner in which such land   of lands sub-
was surveyed or granted by the Crown that the parcel so sold   divided before
cannot be easily identified, the plan or survey shall be regis-   this Act.
35 tered within six months after the passing of this Act, if the
plan of survey is still in existence and procurable for registra-   How to be
tion and filing under the next preceding section, and if it is   made.
not a new survey or plan shall be made by and at the joint expense of the persons who have made such surveys or sub-divi-
40 sions, and of all others interested therein, by some duly authorized provincial land surveyor, as nearly as may be according to
the proper original survey or sub-division, and the same when
so made shall be filed as if under the next preceding section
of this Act. R. S. O. 1877, c. 146, s 71. *See also Rev. Stat.*
45 c. 111, s. 83.

65. In no case shall any plan or survey, although filed and   Plan not bind-
registered, be binding on the person so filing or registering the   ing until some
same, or upon any other person, unless a sale has been made   under it; al-
according to such plan or survey, and in all cases amendments   terations in
50 or alterations of any such plan or survey may be ordered to be   plan.
made, at the instance of the person filing or registering the
same or his assigns, by the High Court, or by any Judge of
the said Court, or by the Judge of the County Court of the
County in which the land lies, if on application for the pur-
55 pose duly made, and upon hearing all parties concerned, it be

81—3

thought fit and just so to order, and upon such terms and conditions as to costs and otherwise as may be deemed expedient. An appeal shall be from any such order to the Court of Appeal.

(2) No part of any street or streets shall be altered or 5 closed up, upon which any lot of land sold abuts, or which connects any such sold lot with or affords means of access therefrom to the nearest public highway.

(3) Nothing herein shall in any way interfere with the powers now possessed by municipalities in reference to high- 10 ways. R. S. O. 1877, c. 146, s. 72.

Copies of registered plans, to be evidence of the originals.

66. Every copy of such plan or map obtained from such registry office, and certified as correct by the registrar or deputy-registrar as aforesaid shall be taken in all Courts as evidence of the original thereof and of the survey of 15 which it purports to be a plan or map. R. S. O. 1877, c. 146, s. 73.

Duty of the Registrar in whose office any such plan is deposited.

67. Whenever any such plan or map has been so made and deposited as aforesaid the registrar shall make a record of the same, and enter the day and year on which the same is deposited 20 in his office; and for such service the said registrar shall be entitled to charge the fees prescribed by *The Registry Act.* R. S. O. 1877, c. 146, s. 74.

Plans of cities, towns or villages to be registered in certain cases.

68.—(1) Where any incorporated city, town or village, or village not incorporated, comprises different parcels of land 25 owned at the original division thereof by different persons, and the same were not jointly surveyed and one entire plan of such survey made and filed in accordance with section 63 of this Act, the municipal council of the township within which such unincorporated village is situated or of such incorporated city, 30 town or village, shall, upon the written request of the inspector, or of any person interested, addressed to the clerk of the municipality, immediately cause a plan of such city, town or village, to be made upon the scale provided for under this Act, and to be registered in the registrar's office of the registry 35 division within which the municipality lies, which map or plan shall have endorsed thereon the certificates of the clerk and head of the municipality and surveyor, that the same is prepared according to the directions of the municipality, and in accordance with this Act, and to the map or plan the corporate 40 seal of the municipality shall be attached.

Payment of expenses.

(2) The expense attending the preparing and depositing of the map or plan shall be paid out of the general funds of the municipality, except in the case of unincorporated villages, where the same shall be paid by a special rate to be levied by 45 assessment on all ratable property comprised in the unincorporated village, as described by metes and bounds in a by-law to be passed by the municipality for the purpose of levying such rate; and in case of the refusal of the municipality to comply with all the requirements of this section within six months 50 next after being required in manner aforesaid so to do, the municipality shall incur the same penalty, and the same shall be recoverable in the manner provided in section 63 of this Act.

(3) Where land in a township has been or shall hereafter be Registration of plans of township subdivisions in certain cases. sold under surveys or subdivisions, made in a manner which so differs from that in which such land was surveyed or granted by the Crown, that the parcel sold cannot be easily identified,
5 and the map or plan has not been registered under this or any other Act in that behalf, the council of the township may, at the written request of the inspector, or of any person interested, cause a plan of any such land to be made and registered in the same manner and with the same effect as in the case of an
10 unincorporated village; and the expenses attending the preparation of and filing of the map or plan shall be paid by a special rate to be levied by assessment on the lands comprised in said map or plan, as described in a by-law to be passed by the council for the purpose of levying such rate ; and the municipality
15 shall have the like remedies for the recovering of such last mentioned expenses as it has for compelling payment of taxes.

(4). Nothing in this section contained shall be deemed or Obligations not impaired. construed to relieve any person from any liability, duty, obligation, or penalty provided or imposed by or under any of
20 the provisions of section 63 of this Act.

69. Every person who is required by this Act to lodge with Plans of Surveys to be deposited with treasurer of municipality. the registrar a plan or map of any survey or subdivision of land made by him, or of any alteration of such survey or subdivision, shall also, within three months from the date of the survey,
25 lodge with the treasurer of the municipality in which the land is situate a duplicate or copy of such plan or map, and in case of neglect or refusal so to do, within two months after notice in writing given by such treasurer requiring him to lodge such plan as provided by this section, every such person shall incur Penalty.
30 a penalty of $20 for each and every month during which the default shall continue.

70. For better ascertaining the original limits of any town- Surveyors may administer oaths for certain purposes. ship, concession, range, lot, or tract of land, every land surveyor acting in this province, shall and may administer an oath or
35 oaths to each and every person whom he examines concerning any boundary, post or monument, or any original landmark, line, limit or angle of any township, concession, range, lot or tract of land which such surveyor is employed to survey. R. S. O. 1877, c. 146, s. 77.

40 **71.** All evidence taken by any surveyor as aforesaid shall Evidence taken by Surveyor to be reduced to writing and signed, etc. be reduced to writing, and shall be read over to the person giving the same, and be signed by such person, or, if he cannot write, he shall acknowledge the same as correct before two witnesses, who, as well as the surveyor, shall sign the same ; and
45 such evidence shall, and any document or plan prepared and sworn to as correct before a Justice of the Peace, by any surveyor, with reference to any survey by him performed, may be filed and kept in the registry office of the registry division in which the lands to which the same relates are situate, subject Fees.
50 to be produced thereafter in evidence in any court within Ontario ; and for receiving and filing the same the registrar shall be entitled to twenty-five cents ; and the expense of filing the same shall be borne by the parties in the same manner as the other expenses of the survey. R. S. O. 1877, c. 146, s. 78.

[Section 31 of C. S. C. c. 77, *is as follows :*

Penalty for
obstructing
Land Survey-
ors in the
execution of
surveys.

31. If any person or persons, in any part of this province, interrupts, moles's or hinders any land surveyor, while in the discharge of his duty as a surveyor, such person or persons shall be guilty of a misdemeanor, and being thereof lawfully convicted in any court of competent jurisdiction, shall be punished either by fine or imprisonment, or both, in the discretion of such court, such imprisonment being for a period not exceeding two months, and such fine not exceeding twenty dollars, without prejudice to any civil remedy which such surveyor or any other party may have against such offender or offenders, in damages by reason of, such offence. 12 V. c. 35, s. 14.]

[Section 4 of C. S. U. C. c. 93, *is as follows :*

Punishment
of persons re-
moving or de-
stroying land
marks.

As to Survey-
ors.

4. If any person knowingly and wilfully pulls down, defaces, alters or removes any monument so erected as aforesaid, such person shall be adjudged guilty of felony ; and if any person knowingly and wilfully defaces alters or removes any other landmark, post or monument placed by any land surveyor, to mark any limit, boundary or angle of any township, concession, range. lot or parcel of land, in Upper Canada, such person or persons shall be deemed guilty of a misdemeanor, and being convicted thereof before any competent court, shall be liable to be punished by fine or imprisonment, or both, at the discretion of such court, such fine not to exceed one hundred dollars, and such imprisonment not to be for a longer period than three months, without any prejudice to any civil remedy which any party may have against such offender or offenders in damages by reason of such offence ; but this shall not extend to prevent land surveyors, in their operations, from taking up posts or other boundary marks when necessary, after which they shall carefully replace them as they were before. 12 V. c. 35, s. 29.

Section 107 *of* C. S. C. c. 77, *contains the same provision.*]

1st Session, 6th Legislature, 50 Vic, 1887.

No. 81.

BILL.

An Act respecting Land Surveyors and the survey of Lands.

(Reprinted as amended by Committee of Whole House.)

First Reading, 14th March, 1887.
Second   "   28th   "   1887.

Mr. PARDEE.

TORONTO:
PRINTED BY WARWICK & SONS, 26 AND 28 FRONT ST. W.

BILL.

An Act to amend the Municipal Act.

HER MAJESTY, by and with the advice and consent of the Legislative Assembly of the Province of Ontario, enacts as follows:—

1. Section 73 of *The Consolidated Municipal Act, 1883,* is 5 hereby amended by striking out all that part of the said section which follows the words "disqualified under this Act," in the sixth line of the said section. 46 V. c. 18, s. 73, amended.

2. Sections 74, 75 and 76, of the said Act, are hereby repealed. 46 V. c. 18, ss. 74-76, repealed.

No. 82.

1st Session, 6th Legislature, 50 Vic., 1887.

BILL.

An Act to amend the Municipal Act.

First Reading, 15th March, 1887.

BILL.

An Act to amend the Municipal Act.

HER MAJESTY, by and with the advice and consent of the Legislative Assembly of the Province of Ontario, enacts as follows:—

1. No qualification beyond the qualification of an elector Qualification of mayors, aldermen, etc.
5 shall be necessary in the persons to be elected mayors, aldermen, reeves, deputy-reeves, and councillors of any municipa ity.

2. Sections 73, 74, 75 and 76 of the said Act are hereby 46 v. c. 18, ss. 73-79, repealed.
repealed.

3 Section 624 of the said Act is hereby amended by insert- 46 v. c. 18, s. 624, amended.
10 ing after the words "frontage thereof" in the eighth line thereof, the words "or according to the assessed value thereof, and when only such latter system of assessment shall have been adopted by a three-fourths vote of the full Council."

BILL.

An Act to amend the Municipal Act.

First Reading, 15th March, 1887.

BILL.

An Act respecting the Niagara Falls Park.

WHEREAS, in pursuance of the Niagara Falls Park Act, the Preamble.
Lieutenant-Governor in Council did approve of certain
lands selected by the Commissioners for the purposes set out in
the preamble of the said Act ; and a map of the park, shewing
5 the boundaries thereof and the lands taken, was submitted to
the Lieutenant-Governor and approved in Council, and copies
duly certified and authenticated were filed and deposited in
the office of the Registrar for the County of Welland,
and in the office of the Commissioner of Crown Lands ;
10 and whereas the prices to be paid for the said lands have been
ascertained and determined, and it is expedient to make provision for the payment thereof, and for the means required to
establish, maintain, improve, and develop the said lands, as and
for a Public Park ;
15 Therefore Her Majesty, by and with the advice and consent
of the Legislative Assembly of the Province of Ontario, enacts
as follows :—

1. The Park shall be called "The Queen Victoria Niagara Name.
Falls Park," and this Act may be cited as "The Queen Victoria
20 Niagara Falls Park Act, 1887."

2.—(1) From and after the commencement of this Act, Commission-
Colonel Casimer Stanislaus Gzowski, of the city of Toronto, ers incorpor-
Aide-de-Camp to the Queen ; John Woodburn Langmuir, and ated.
John Grant Macdonald, both of the city of Toronto, Esquires, the
25 persons forming the Board of Commissioners for Niagara Falls
Park, and two other persons to be appointed by the Lieutenant-
Governor in Council if he thinks fit, shall be a corporation by
the name of "The Commissioners for the Queen Victoria
Niagara Falls Park," and shall continue to hold their respective
30 offices, as members of the said corporation, during the pleasure
of the Lieutenant-Governor in Council, and the Lieutenant-
Governor in Council may, upon the death of any of such persons
respectively, or on their resignation or removal from office,
and from time to time thereafter, appoint other persons to
35 fill their places during pleasure as aforesaid.

(2) The Commissioners shall receive no compensation except
their actual disbursements in discharging their duties.

3.—(1) The lands selected by the Commissioners of Niagara Lands vested
Falls Park, approved by the Lieutenant-Governor, and marked in the Com-
40 upon the map, and contained within a red verge line marked missioners.
on the said map, with the exception hereinafter mentioned, are
hereby vested in the said corporation as trustees for the Province. The amounts agreed to be paid or awarded, are to be paid

upon proper conveyances being executed to the said Commissioners, subject as hereinafter mentioned; or in case no proper conveyance is executed, the money may be paid into Court, in accordance with and subject to the terms of the Niagara Falls Park Act and the Revised Act of Ontario respecting the Public 5 Works of Ontario as incorporating the Park Act.

(2) The costs, which shall be payable under awards where amounts are paid into Court, may be paid to such of the parties interested as appeared before the official Arbitrators.

(3) The land so excepted is the following: 10

Excepting a strip of land, lying between Range No. 6, as laid down in the plan of the City of the Falls, in the Township of Stamford, on the North, and by Street's Mill Road and the lands held by the Carmelite Monastery on the South, the easterly boundary whereof is at a distance of 130 15 feet east of the centre line of the Canada Southern Railway, and the westerly boundary whereof being the westerly line of the Park, as appears in the Park plan, filed and registered, between said Range No. 6 and Street's Mill Road, and Monastery Lands and approximately of the width of seventy-nine 20 feet between said Range No. 6 and Street's Mill Road, which said strip is by this Act excluded from the Park.

Purchase of part of St. Catharines, Thorold and Niagara Falls Road authorized.

4.—(1) The Commissioners may agree with the person or persons, or association of persons, whether incorporated or not, who exercise, own or control the taking and collecting of tolls 25 upon that portion of the gravelled or macadamized road known as the St. Catharines, Thorold and Niagara Falls road, between Table Rock and the north boundary line of the Park on the aforesaid plan marked; as well as the title interest and possessory right, which such person or persons as aforesaid 30 have to the said road and the land whereon the same is laid out, together with the toll-house and appurtenances between the said points, for the price to be paid for the said rights to take tolls, and the title, interest and possessory rights, land, toll-house and appurtenances aforesaid; 35

(2) And if the Commissioners and the said persons as aforesaid are unable to agree, the sums to be paid shall be determined by arbitration in the manner provided by the Niagara Falls Park Act; and any party to the arbitration may appeal from the award in manner and according to the provisions of 40 the Act respecting awards under the Niagara Falls Park Act. (49 Victoria, chapter 9.)

(3) The right and power which the persons aforesaid have to collect tolls over the road known as the St. Catharines, Thorold and Niagara Falls road shall not be affected by 45 reason of the acquisition by the Commissioners of that portion between the Table Rock and the north boundary line of the Park on the aforesaid plan marked, except by reason of the diminution of mileage, although that part of the road held or retained by the said persons beyond the limits of the Park 50 may be shortened to less than five miles in length;

(4) Upon the acquisition by the Commissioners of the rights in that portion of the said road known as the St. Catharines, Thorold and Niagara Falls road, all rights to take

and collect tolls as well as the public rights in the said road shall be extinguished.

(5) Nothing in this section is intended to extend to or affect any right or title of the Dominion of Canada to any property 5 known as Ordnance Property.

5. The Lieutenant-Governor in Council may at any time, Grant of or from time to time, vest in the Commissioners, to be held for Crown Lands the purposes of the Park, and subject to any conditions which authorized. may be imposed by Order in Council, any part or portions of 10 the Crown Lands the property of Ontario, lying along the bank of the Niagara River, and not included in the original survey of lots laid out in the Townships of Stamford and Niagara, which lands so vested shall thenceforth form part of the Park and be subject to the control of the Commissioners 15 like the other lands aforesaid.

6. The provisions hereinbefore and in the former Act con- Power to tained for authorizing the Commissioners to take, use or acquire, acquire lands. and authorizing all persons to sell and convey, lands, hereditaments or rights, shall extend to any lands, hereditaments 20 and rights which the Commissioners, with the consent of the Lieutenant-Governor in Council shall hereafter think proper or expedient to be acquired for the purpose of making, forming and completing any new roads, avenues or approaches to the Park, but nothing in this section contained shall authorize the 25 Commissioners to take any lands for the purpose aforesaid, against the consent of the parties interested therein.

7.—(1) The Commissioners may raise, for the purposes and Issue of de- objects intended to be secured by the Niagara Falls Park Act and bentures this Act, the sum of five hundred and twenty-five thousand dollars authorized. 30 and no more, by the issue of debentures. The appropriation and application of the money shall be assured to the satisfaction of the Lieutenant-Governor.

(2) The debentures shall be under the corporate seal and the hands of two of the Commissioners, and shall be countersigned 35 by the Treasurer of the Province, and the same shall be for such respective amounts payable on the 1st of January, 1927, and at such rate of interest not higher than four per cent. per annum, and shall be disposed of at such prices and on such terms as may be determined by the Commissioners, and approved 40 by the Lieutenant-Governor in Council. The interest shall be paid half-yearly on such days as shall be mentioned in the debentures.

(3) The debentures shall, equally and without preference of one over another, be a charge on all the revenues of the 45 corporation, and the Lieutenant-Governor by Order in Council may also guarantee payment of the same.

(4) The debentures so issued and countersigned shall be conclusive of the same having been issued in pursuance of this Act, and of the same being guaranteed by the Province 50 of Ontario.

(5) The debentures shall be transferable by delivery, and the coupons for interest annexed thereto shall also pass by delivery.

(6) The moneys to be raised by means of the said debentures shall be applied in paying the purchase moneys of the lands to be acquired, in making necessary improvements, constructions and appliances to be used in connection with the Park, in recouping the Province for expenses incurred by it with refer- 5 ence thereto, and in paying current expenses of the Park and interest on the said debentures until a sufficient revenue for the purposes is obtained from the fees charged.

Powers of Commissioners. **8.**—(1) Subject to any direction of the Lieutenant-Governor in Council, the Commissioners may construct and operate 10 inclined planes and hydraulic or other lifts, to be worked by any powers; and may build and operate boats or vessels to be used in connection with the Park.

(2) Subject as aforesaid, the Commissioners may pull down all houses and other erections and buildings on lands acquired 15 and purchased by virtue of this Act, or such of them or such part thereof as they shall think proper to be pulled down, and may level and clear the ground whereon the same stand, in such manner as they think proper, and sell or cause to be sold the materials of the houses and other buildings to be taken down 20 and removed; and the monies to be produced by the sale thereof, after deducting expenses, and also the rents and profits to which they may be entitled meantime, shall be applied and disposed of for or towards the purposes of this Act.

(3) Subject as aforesaid, the Commissioners shall lay out 25 plant and enclose the Park in such manner as they think fit, and improve and develop the same in accordance with the objects of the Niagara Falls Park Act.

(4) The Commissioners shall have power to take and collect tolls for the use of works, appliances, vessels, or works required 30 to afford facilities to visitors to reach and view the points of interest within the Park, and involving the expenditure of money in construction and maintenance, as well as for services to be rendered for the convenience or accommodation of visitors.

(5) Subject as aforesaid, the Commissioners may from time 35 to time make orders and regulations for opening and closing the gates and entrances of the Park or any of them, at such hours as they may think fit.

Plans of works, tolls and by-laws to be subject to approval of Lieutenant-Governor in Council. **9.** The plans of all works proposed, and all tariffs of tolls or payments for the use of works, vessels or services, as well as all 40 bylaws, shall require the approval of the Lieutenant-Governor in Council before being acted upon.

Grounds to be open to public. **10.** The Park grounds shall be open to the public, subject to any rules and regulations as to charges and management approved by the Lieutenant-Governor in Council. 45

Power of Commissioners as to by-laws. **11**—(1) The Commissioners may make by-laws, to be approved by the Lieutenant-Governor in Council, for the use, government, control or management of the Park, and for the protection and preservation of all works from injury of the same, and of the trees, shrubs, walks, seats, gates, fences and palings, 50 and all other parts thereof, and for the exclusion of improper persons from the same, and may alter or revoke any such by-laws, and shall appoint a penalty, not exceeding twenty dollars, for any breach of a by-law.

(2) The Commissioners may from time to time appoint such officers as may be required for the superintendence and management of the Park, and may also appoint park keepers and other officers to preserve order in the Park, and may from
5 time to time dismiss any persons so appointed ; the appointments or dismissals being subject to the approval of the Lieutenant-Governor ; and the salaries of such officers shall be payable out of any funds in the hands of the Commissioners.

(3) Any person entrusted by the Commissioners with
10 the custody or control of moneys, by virtue of his employment, shall give security in the manner and form provided by the Act respecting Public Officers.

(4) The Commissioners may from time to time employ gardeners and workmen, as they may deem necessary, and may
15 from time to time dismiss or dispense with the services of such persons, subject to any directions of the Lieutenant-Governor in Council.

(5) The Commissioners shall cause books to be provided and kept, and true and regular accounts to be entered therein, of all
20 sums of money received and paid, and of the several purposes for which the same were received and paid ; which books shall at all times be open to the inspection of any of the Commissioners, and of the Treasurer of Ontario, and of any person appointed by the Commissioners or Treasurer for that purpose, and of any other person appointed by the
25 Lieutenant-Governor ; and the Commissioners and persons aforesaid may take copies of or extracts from the said books.

12. The revenue to be received from the sources authorized by this Act shall be applied as follows :— *Application of revenue.*

1st. To the necessary outgoing expenses of all works neces-
30 sary to the preservation, improvement, and maintenance of the park, and to the payment of the salaries of officers and others employed by the Commissioners, and other incidental expenses.

2nd. To the payment half-yearly of the interest payable on the debentures authorized to be issued by the Commissioners.

35 3rd. To pay a sinking fund at the rate of one per cent. per annum on the entire amount of the debentures authorized to be issued as aforesaid.

13.—(1) The annual sums for the sinking fund shall be remitted by the Commissioners to the Treasurer of Ontario by *Application of sinking fund.*
40 half-yearly payments in such manner as the Lieutenant-Governor in Council from time to time directs, for the investment and accumulation thereof under the direction of the Lieutenant-Governor in Council.

(2) The sinking fund shall be invested in such securities
45 as the Lieutenant-Governor in Council from time to time thinks proper, and shall, whether invested or not, be applied from time to time under the direction of the Lieutenant-Governor in Council in discharging the principal and the interest thereon of the debentures.

50 **14.** The Commissioners shall make an annual report for the information of the Legislature, setting forth the receipts and *Annual report*

expenditure of the year and such other matters as may appear to them to be of public interest in relation to the Park, or as the Lieutenant-Governor in Council may direct.

9 V. c. 24,
. 24-27 to
pply.

15. The 24th to the 27th sections of *The Act to provide for the better Auditing of the Public Accounts of the Province,* 5 shall apply to the accounts of the Commissioners in respect of receipts and expenditures.

9 V., c. 9, ss.
·15 repealed.

16. Sections 12, 13, 14 and 15 of the Niagara Falls Park Act are hereby repealed.

The ATTORNEY-GENERAL.

First Reading, 15th March, 1887.

BILL.

An Act respecting the Niagara Falls Park.

1st Session, 6th Legislature, 50 Vic, 1887.

No 84.

BILL.

An Act respecting the Niagara Falls Park.

WHEREAS, in pursuance of the Niagara Falls Park Act, the Preamble.
Lieutenant-Governor in Council did approve of certain
lands selected by the Commissioners for the purposes set out in
the preamble of the said Act ; and a map of the park, shewing
5 the boundaries thereof and the lands taken, was submitted to
the Lieutenant-Governor and approved in Council, and copies
duly certified and authenticated were filed and deposited in
the office of the registrar for the county of Welland,
and in the office of the Commissioner of Crown Lands ;
10 and whereas the prices to be paid for the said lands have been
ascertained and determined, and it is expedient to make provision for the payment thereof, and for the means required to
establish, maintain, improve, and develop the said lands, as and
for a Public Park ;
15   Therefore Her Majesty, by and with the advice and consent
of the Legislative Assembly of the Province of Ontario, enacts
as follows :—

1. The Park shall be called " The Queen Victoria Niagara Name.
Falls Park," and this Act may be cited as *The Queen Victoria*
20 *Niagara Falls Park Act, 1887.*

2.—(1) From and after the commencement of this Act, Commission-
Colonel Casimer Stanislaus Gzowski, of the city of Toronto, ers incorpor-
Aide-de-Camp to the Queen ; John Woodburn Langmuir, and ated.
John Grant Macdonald, both of the city of Toronto, Esquires, the
25 persons forming the Board of Commissioners for Niagara Falls
Park, and two other persons to be appointed by the Lieutenant-
Governor in Council if he thinks fit, shall be a corporation by
the name of " The Commissioners for the Queen Victoria
Niagara Falls Park," and shall continue to hold their respective
30 offices, as members of the said corporation, during the pleasure
of the Lieutenant-Governor in Council, and the Lieutenant-
Governor in Council may, upon the death of any of such persons
respectively, or on their resignation or removal from office,
and from time to time thereafter, appoint other persons to
35 fill their places during pleasure as aforesaid.

(2) The Commissioners shall receive no compensation except
their actual disbursements in discharging their duties.

3.—(1) The lands selected by the Commissioners of Niagara Lands vested
Falls Park, approved by the Lieutenant-Governor, and marked in the Com-
40 upon the map, and contained within a red verge line marked missioners.
on the said map, with the exception hereinafter mentioned, are
hereby vested in the said corporation as trustees for the Province, *subject to the payment being made which is hereinafter*

mentioned. The amounts agreed to be paid or awarded, are to be paid upon proper conveyances being executed to the said Commissioners, subject as hereinafter mentioned ; or in case no proper conveyance is executed, the money may be paid into Court, in accordance with and subject to the terms of *The Niagara Falls Park Act* and *The Revised Act respecting the Public Works of Ontario* as incorporated in the Park Act. 5

(2) The payment is to be made within fifteen days from the passing of this Act, with interest to be computed from the 30th March, 1887, to the day of payment, at the rate of six per cent. 10 per annum ; and payment within such period shall be as effectual as if made within the period fixed for payment by *The Niagara Falls Park Act.*

(3) The costs, which shall be payable under awards where amounts are paid into Court, may be paid to such of the *persons* 15 interested as appeared before the official arbitrators.

(4) The land so excepted is the following :

Excepting a strip of land, lying between Range No. 6, as laid down in the plan of the city of the Falls, in the township of Stamford, on the North, and by Street's Mill Road 20 and the lands held by the Carmelite Monastery on the South, the easterly boundary whereof is at a distance of 130 feet east of the centre line of the Canada Southern Railway, and the westerly boundary whereof being the westerly line of the Park, as appears in the Park plan, filed and registered, 25 between said Range No. 6 and Street's Mill Road, and Monastery Lands and approximately of the width of seventy-nine feet between said Range No. 6 and Street's Mill Road, which said strip is by this Act excluded from the Park.

Purchase of part of St. Catharines, Thorold and Niagara Falls Road authorized.
4.—(1) The Commissioners may agree with the person or 30 persons, or association of persons, whether incorporated or not, who exercise, own or control the taking and collecting of tolls upon that portion of the gravelled or macadamized road known as the St. Catharines, Thorold and Niagara Falls road, between Table Rock and the north boundary line of the Park on the 35 aforesaid plan marked; as well as the title, interest and possessory right, which such person or persons as aforesaid have to the said road and the land whereon the same is laid out, together with the toll-house and appurtenances between the said points, for the price to be paid for the said rights to 40 take tolls, and the title, interest and possessory rights, land, toll-house and appurtenances aforesaid;

(2) And if the Commissioners and the said persons as aforesaid are unable to agree, the sums to be paid shall be determined by arbitration in the manner provided by *The Niagara* 45 *Falls Park Act ;* and any party to the arbitration may appeal from the award in manner and according to the provisions of *The Act respecting awards under the Niagara Falls Park Act.* (49 Victoria, chapter 9.)

(3) The right and power which the persons aforesaid have 50 to collect tolls over the road known as the St. Catharines, Thorold and Niagara Falls road shall not be affected by reason of the acquisition by the Commissioners of that portion between the Table Rock and the north boundary line of the Park on the aforesaid plan marked, except by reason of the 55

diminution of mileage, although that part of the road held or retained by the said persons beyond the limits of the Park may be shortened to less than five miles in length ;

☞ (4) In case of an arbitration the arbitrators shall take
5 into account any depreciation, if such there may be, in the value, to the persons aforesaid, of the remainder of the road.

☞ (5) The arbitrators shall also determine the value of the whole road between the Table Rock and a point about five miles therefrom in respect of which tolls are now collected, in
10 order that the commissioners may have the opportunity of paying to the persons aforesaid, if sanctioned by the Legislature at its next session, the difference between the value of the whole road between said points and the value of the part hereinbefore mentioned of the road aforesaid; and
15 in case of such payment being sanctioned and made within fifteen days after the end of such session, that part of the road built upon the military reservation or ordnance property shall vest in the commissioners, and the park shall then extend over and include, as well the
20 military reservation, as the land lying between such reservation and the Niagara River, as far as the limit between lots number 92 and 93 of Stamford, but not affecting or interfering with the rights of any companies having bridges over the Niagara River. And all the provisions of this Act and *The*
25 *Niagara Falls Park Act* shall apply to such extension of the park as if included within the park at the time of the passing of this Act, saving the reservation of a public way between the Clifton House and the limit between said lots 92 and 93 such public way being subject to reasonable tolls upon horses
30 and carriages passing over the same.

☞ (6) All costs in respect of the matters in this section contained shall be in the discretion of the arbitrators.

☞ (7) Upon the acquisition by the commissioners of the rights in that portion of the said road within the park as now limited,
35 all rights to take and collect tolls, as well as the public rights in the said roads, shall be extinguished.

☞ (8) Nothing in this section is intended to extend to or affect any right or title of the Dominion of Canada to any property known as the military reservation or ordnance property. ☜

40 **5.** The Lieutenant-Governor in Council may at any time, Grant of Crown Lands or from time to time, vest in the Commissioners, to be held for authorized. the purposes of the Park, and subject to any conditions which may be imposed by Order in Council, any part or portions of the Crown Lands the property of Ontario, lying along the
45 bank of the Niagara River, and not included in the original survey of lots laid out in the townships of Stamford and Niagara, which lands so vested shall thenceforth form part of the Park and be subject to the control of the Commissioners like the other lands aforesaid.

50 **6.** The provisions hereinbefore and in the former Act con- Power to tained for authorizing the Commissioners to take, use or acquire, acquire lands. and authorizing all persons to sell and convey, lands, hereditaments or rights, shall extend to any lands, hereditaments and rights which the Commissioners, with the consent of the
55 Lieutenant-Governor in Council shall hereafter think proper or

expedient to be acquired for the purpose of making, forming and completing any new roads, avenues or approaches to the Park, but nothing in this section contained shall authorize the Commissioners to take any lands for the purpose aforesaid, against the consent of the parties interested therein.   5

Issue of debentures authorized.

7.—(1) The Commissioners may raise, for the purposes and objects intended to be secured by *The Niagara Falls Park Act* and this Act, the sum of $525,000, and no more, by the issue of debentures. The appropriation and application of the money shall be assured to the satisfaction of the Lieutenant-Governor. 10

(2) The debentures shall be under the corporate seal and the hands of two of the Commissioners, and shall be countersigned by the Treasurer of the Province, and the same shall be for such respective amounts payable on the 1st of January, 1927, and at such rate of interest not higher than four per cent. per 15 annum, and shall be disposed of at such prices and on such terms as may be determined by the Commissioners, and approved by the Lieutenant-Governor in Council. The interest shall be paid half-yearly on such days as shall be mentioned in the debentures.   20

(3) The debentures shall, equally and without preference of one over another, be a charge on all the revenues of the corporation, and the Lieutenant-Governor by Order in Council may also guarantee payment of the same.

(4) The debentures so issued and countersigned shall be 25 conclusive of the same having been issued in pursuance of this Act, and of the same being guaranteed by the Province of Ontario.

(5) The debentures shall be transferable by delivery, and the coupons for interest annexed thereto shall also pass by 30 delivery.

(6) The moneys to be raised by means of the said debentures shall be applied in paying the purchase moneys of the lands to be acquired, in making necessary improvements, constructions and appliances to be used in connection with the Park, in 35 recouping the Province for expenses incurred by it with reference thereto, and in paying current expenses of the Park and interest on the said debentures until a sufficient revenue for the purposes is obtained from the fees charged.

Powers of Commissioners.

8.—(1) Subject to any direction of the Lieutenant-Governor 40 in Council, the Commissioners may construct and operate inclined planes and hydraulic or other lifts, to be worked by any powers; and may build and operate boats or vessels to be used in connection with the Park.

(2) Subject as aforesaid, the Commissioners may pull down 45 all houses and other erections and buildings on lands acquired and purchased by virtue of this Act, or such of them or such part thereof as they shall think proper to be pulled down, and may level and clear the ground whereon the same stand, in such manner as they think proper, and sell or cause to be sold the 50 materials of the houses and other buildings to be taken down and removed; and the moneys to be produced by the sale thereof, after deducting expenses, and also the rents and profits to which they may be entitled meantime, shall be applied and disposed of for or towards the purposes of this Act.

(3) Subject as aforesaid, the Commissioners shall lay out, plant and enclose the Park in such manner as they think fit, and improve and develop the same in accordance with the objects of *The Niagara Falls Park Act.*

5   (4) *Subject as aforesaid,* the Commissioners shall have power to take and collect tolls for the use of works, appliances, vessels, or works required to afford facilities to visitors to reach and view the points of interest within the Park, and involving the expenditure of money in construction and maintenance, as 10 well as for services to be rendered for the convenience or accommodation of visitors.

(5) Subject as aforesaid, the Commissioners may from time to time make orders and regulations for opening and closing the gates and entrances of the Park or any of them, at such 15 hours as they may think fit ☞ This is not intended to interfere with, or affect, an agreement which has been heretofore entered into between the commissioners and the Canada Southern Railway. ☜

9. The plans of all works proposed, and all tariffs of tolls or 20 payments for the use of works, vessels or services, as well as all bylaws, shall require the approval of the Lieutenant-Governor in Council before being acted upon.

Plans of works, tolls and by-laws to be subject to approval of Lieutenant-Governor in Council.

10. The Park grounds shall be open to the public, subject to any rules and regulations as to management approved 25 by the Lieutenant-Governor in Council.

Grounds to be open to public.

11.—(1) The Commissioners may make by-laws, to be approved by the Lieutenant-Governor in Council, for the use, government, control or management of the Park, and for the protection and preservation of all works from injury of the same, 30 and of the trees, shrubs, walks, seats, gates, fences and palings, and all other parts thereof, and for the exclusion of improper persons from the same, and may alter or revoke any such by-laws, and shall appoint a penalty, not exceeding twenty dollars, for any breach of a by-law.

Power of Commissioners as to by-laws.

35   (2) The Commissioners may from time to time appoint such officers as may be required for the superintendence and management of the Park, and may also appoint park keepers and other officers to preserve order in the Park, and may from time to time dismiss any persons so appointed; the appoint- 40 ments or dismissals being subject to the approval of the Lieutenant-Governor; and the salaries of such officers shall be payable out of any funds in the hands of the Commissioners.

(3) Any person entrusted by the Commissioners with the custody or control of moneys, by virtue of his employ- 45 ment, shall give security in the manner and form provided by the Act respecting Public Officers.

(4) The Commissioners may from time to time employ gardeners and workmen, as they may deem necessary, and may from time to time dismiss or dispense with the services of such 50 persons, subject to any directions of the Lieutenant-Governor in Council.

(5) The Commissioners shall cause books to be provided and kept, and true and regular accounts to be entered therein, of all sums of money received and paid, and of the several purposes for which the same were received and paid ; which books shall at all times be open to the inspection of any 5 of the Commissioners, and of the Treasurer of Ontario, and of any person appointed by the Commissioners or Treasurer for that purpose, and of any other person appointed by the Lieutenant-Governor; and the Commissioners and persons aforesaid may take copies of or extracts from the said books. 10

Application of revenue. **12**. The revenue to be received from the sources authorized by this Act shall be applied as follows :—

1st To the necessary outgoing expenses of all works necessary to the preservation, improvement, and maintenance of the park, and to the payment of the salaries of officers and others 15 employed by the Commissioners, and other incidental expenses.

2nd. To the payment half-yearly of the interest payable on the debentures authorized to be issued by the Commissioners.

3rd. To pay a sinking fund at the rate of one per cent. per annum on the entire amount of the debentures authorized to 20 be issued as aforesaid.

Application of sinking fund. **13**.—(1) The annual sums for the sinking fund shall be remitted by the Commissioners to the Treasurer of Ontario by half-yearly payments in such manner as the Lieutenant-Governor in Council from time to time directs, for the investment 25 and accumulation thereof under the direction of the Lieutenant-Governor in Council.

(2) The sinking fund shall be invested in such securities as the Lieutenant-Governor in Council from time to time thinks proper, and shall, whether invested or not, be applied 30 from time to time under the direction of the Lieutenant-Governor in Council in discharging the principal and the interest thereon of the debentures.

Annual report. **14**. The Commissioners shall make an annual report for the information of the Legislature, setting forth the receipts and 35 expenditure of the year and such other matters as may appear to them to be of public interest in relation to the Park, or as the Lieutenant-Governor in Council may direct.

49 V. c. 24, ss. 24-27 to apply. **15**. Sections 24 to 27 of *The Act to provide for the better Auditing of the Public Accounts of the Province*, shall apply 40 to the accounts of the Commissioners in respect of receipts and expenditures.

49 V., c. 9, ss. 12-15 repealed. **16**. Sections 12, 13, 14 and 15 of *The Niagara Falls Park Act* are hereby repealed.

BILL.

An Act respecting the Niagara Falls Park.

(*Reprinted as amended by Committee of the Whole House.*)

First Reading, 15th March, 1887.
Second   "   31st   "   1887.

No. 85.] **BILL.** [1887.

An Act to amend the Act relating to Mutual Fire Insurance Companies.

HER MAJESTY, by and with the advice and consent of the Legislative Assembly of the Province of Ontario, enacts as follows :—

1. Section 13 of chapter 161 of the Revised Statutes of 5 Ontario, entitled *An Act respecting Mutual Fire Insurance Companies,* is hereby repealed and the following substituted therefor :— *R. S. O. c. 161, s. 13, repealed.*

13. Each member of the company shall, at all meetings of the company, be entitled to one vote only, irrespective of any 10 amount by him insured ; but no member shall be entitled to vote while in arrear for any assessment or premium due by him to the company. *Members to have but one vote.*

Section 70 of the said Act is hereby repealed, and the following substituted therefor :— *R. S. O. c. 161, s. 70, repealed.*

15 70. The present location of head offices of companies in existence, and the original location of head offices of companies hereafter to be formed, shall be henceforth changed by a majority vote of the members of the company at a special meeting to be called for that purpose, instead of, as hereto- 20 fore, by a two-thirds vote of the members aforesaid. *Head office to be changed by majority vote.*

1st Session, 6th Legislature, 50 Vic., 1887.

BILL.

An Act to amend the Act respecting Mutual
Fire Insurance Companies.

First Reading, 16th March, 1887.

BILL.

An Act to provide for the erection of a Court House in the City of Toronto.

WHEREAS the corporation of the county of York have by Preamble.
their petition represented the necessity for the erection of
a new court house in the city of Toronto, for the administration
of Justice in the county of York and the city of Toronto, and
5 the necessity of removing the difficulties in the way of providing for the erection of such court house, and the advisability
of repealing the legislation authorizing the same to be erected
and maintained by the city of Toronto, and of rescinding the
agreement entered into by the county of York and the city of
10 Toronto, providing for the erection of such court house by the
city of Toronto, confirmed by the Act passed in the 48th year
of Her Majesty's reign chaptered 73, and the desirability of
conferring increased powers upon the county of York with
reference to the same; and whereas, it is expedient to grant
15 the prayer of the said petition;

Therefore, Her Majesty, by and with the advice and consent
of the Legislative Assembly of the Province of Ontario, enacts
as follows:—

1. Section 1 of the Act passed in the 48th year of Her 48 V. c. 73, s.
20 Majesty's reign, chaptered 73, intituled "*An Act respecting* 1 repealed.
the City of Toronto" is hereby repealed, and the agreement
set forth in the schedule A to the said Act, and confirmed by
section 1 of the said Act is hereby declared to be null and
void, and the provisions of the said agreement shall not be
25 enforced against or be binding upon the corporations named Proviso.
therein: Provided always that all debentures heretofore
issued under any by-law passed under the said Act shall be as
valid and effectual as if this Act had not been passed.

2. The council of the corporation of the county of York Power to ex-
30 may pass a by-law or by-laws for entering upon, taking, using propriate land
and acquiring all lands which may at any time be required by ronto.
the said county for the purposes of a court house within the
limits of the said city making due compensation therefor to the
parties entitled thereto under the provisions of *The Consolidated*
35 *Municipal Act, 1883*, in that behalf, or for entering upon,
taking, using and acquiring the lands which have been taken,
expropriated, or otherwise acquired by the corporation of the
city of Toronto for the purposes of a court house, and in case
the said county shall take the said lands acquired by the city
40 as aforesaid, the said county shall reimburse to the said city
the amount already actually paid therefor by the said city to
the persons entitled thereto, or shall allow the said city credit
for the amount actually so paid in ascertaining the amount to

2

be contributed by the said city of their just share or proportion of the cost, charges and expenses of acquiring a site and erecting or building a court house thereon.

Concurrence of council of city of Toronto as to construction of court house dispensed with.**3.** Notwithstanding anything contained in section 472 of *The Consolidated Municipal Act, 1883,* it shall not be 5 necessary for the said county to consult or obtain the concurrence of the council of the said city respecting the expenditure for acquiring a site, or erecting or building the said court house or in anywise connected therewith, nor shall the said county be required to submit to an arbitration under the 10 provisions of the said Act, and the council of the city shall not have a voice in the selection of the site for the said court house or in the erection of the same, but the said county may proceed as if the said section had not been passed.

Power to sell existing court house.**4.** The county may sell and convey the existing court house, 15 and the lands and appurtenances therewith used and enjoyed, or any part thereof, at any time after the same may cease to be required for court house purposes, and the council of the county may by by-law provide for such sale being made either for cash or on credit, or partly for cash and partly on credit, 20 and may prescribe the security to be taken in case of sale on credit, and may provide for the manner of executing the conveyance or conveyances thereof, and otherwise in relation to the sale and conveyance as they may find necessary or deem expedient.   25

Proceedings against county in respect of court house to be stayed.**5.** No indictment or other proceedings shall be instituted or prosecuted against the said county in respect of court house accommodation until after a reasonable time for the erection of the said court house shall have elapsed.

No. 86.

1st Session, 6th Legislature, 50 Vic., 1887

BILL.

An Act to provide for the erection of a Court House in the City of Toronto.

First Reading,   March, 1887.

(Private Bill.)

·BILL.

An Act to provide for the erection of a Court House in the City of Toronto.

WHEREAS the corporation of the county of York have by Preamble.
their petition represented the necessity for the erection of
a new court house in the city of Toronto, for the administration
of Justice in the county of York and the city of Toronto, and
5 the necessity of removing the difficulties in the way of providing for the erection of such court house, *and have asked an
extension of time for the erection of the said Court House;* and
whereas, it is expedient to grant the prayer of the said
petition ;
10 Therefore, Her Majesty, by and with the advice and consent
of the Legislative Assembly of the Province of Ontario, enacts
as follows :—

1. Section 1 of the Act passed in the forty-eighth year of 48 V. c. 73, s.
Her Majesty's reign, chaptered 73, intituled *An Act respecting* 1, amended.
15 *the City of Toronto,* is hereby amended by adding thereto the
following sub-sections :—

(2) For the purpose of enabling the said city to carry on
the works provided for in the said agreement, the council of the
said city is hereby authorized and empowered to make agree-
20 ments with any bank or banks, or with any person or persons,
corporation or corporations for temporary advances and loans
until the completion of said works, and thereafter, or from
time to time, to pass by-laws for the issue of debentures to repay the amount of the temporary loans or advances aforesaid,
25 and any interest paid or payable thereon ; and it shall not be
necessary to obtain the assent of the electors or ratepayers to
the passing of any such by-law or by-laws, provided the same
be approved of by the Lieutenant-Governor in Council ; and
the amount authorized to be borrowed under such by-law or
30 by-laws shall not exceed the sum of $425,000, which sum shall
be in addition to the amount hereinbefore authorized.

(3) No indictment or other proceeding shall be instituted
or prosecuted against the said county in respect of the existing
court house accommodation, and after the passing of this Act
35 the said county shall cease to be responsible for any default
in providing suitable accommodation for the Courts or officers
engaged in the administration of justice.

(4) The time for the completion of the said court house
offices and accommodation in the said agreement prescribed
40 shall be extended to the twenty-sixth day of June, 1889, and
it shall be the duty of the said city forthwith, after the passing
of this Act, to proceed with the erection of the same, and to

complete the same as speedily as possible within the above extended time, and the said city alone shall be responsible for the failure to provide suitable court house accommodation.

Power to sell existing court house.

2. The county may sell and convey the existing court house, and the lands and appurtenances therewith used and en- 5 joyed, or any part thereof, at any time after the same may cease to be required for court house purposes, and the council of the county may by by-law provide for such sale being made either for cash or on credit, or partly for cash and partly on credit, and may prescribe the security to be taken in case of sale on 10 credit, and may provide for the manner of executing the conveyance or conveyances thereof, and otherwise in relation to the sale and conveyance as they may find necessary or deem expedient.

No. 86.

1st Session, 6th Legislature, 50 Vic., 1887.

BILL.

An Act to provide for the erection of a Court House in the City of Toronto.

(*Reprinted as amended by Private Bills Committee.*)

First Reading, 22nd March, 1887.

(Private Bill.)

MR. WIDDIFIELD.

TORONTO:
PRINTED BY WARWICK & SONS, 26 AND 28 FRONT ST. W.

BILL.

An Act to Amend the Municipal Act.

H ER MAJESTY, by and with the advice and consent of the Legislative Assembly of the Province of Ontario, enacts as follows —   :

Section 260 of *The Consolidated Municipal Act, 1883,* is 46 V., c. 18, s. 5 hereby amended by adding thereto the following words : "And 260 amended. in the event of any auditor so appointed refusing to act, then the head of the Council shall nominate another person to act in his stead."

BILL.

An Act to Amend the Municipal Act.

First Reading, 17th March, 1887.

Mr. Harcourt.

TORONTO:

Printed by Warwick & Sons, 26 and 28 Front St. W

No. 88.]　　　　　　**BILL.**　　　　　[1887.

An Act to amend the Municipal Act.

HER MAJESTY, by and with the advice and consent of the
Legislative Assembly of the Province of Ontario, enacts
as follows:—

1. Section 368 of *The Consolidated Municipal Act, 1883,* 46 V. c. 18, s. 368 amended.
as amended by section 8 of *The Municipal Amendment Act,
1884,* is amended by inserting the words "including school and
local improvement rates" after the word "taxation," in the
fourth line of the said section.

2. Section 521 of *The Consolidated Municipal Act, 1883,* 46 V. c. 18, s. 521 amended.
is amended by adding the following sub-section thereto:—

(13a) For regulating the construction of dry-earth closets
and compelling the use of the same.

3. In addition to the powers given to the council of every Local improvements in townships.
township by *The Consolidated Municipal Act, 1883,* and
amendments thereto, the council of every township shall have
all the rights and powers conferred on the councils of cities,
towns and incorporated villages, by sections 612 to 624, inclusive, of the said Act as heretofore amended, as well as those
conferred by sections 32 to 34, inclusive, of *The Municipal
Amendment Act, 1885,* and by section 40 of *The Municipal
Amendment Act, 1886.*

4. Section 39 of *The Municipal Amendment Act, 1885,* is 48 V. c. 39, s. 39 repealed.
hereby repealed.

No. 88.

1st Session, 6th Legislature, 50 Vic., 1887.

BILL.

An Act to amend the Municipal Act.

First Reading, 17th March, 1887.

No. 89.]   **BILL.**   [1887.

An Act to amend the Municipal Act.

HER MAJESTY, by and with the advice and consent of the Legislative Assembly of the Province of Ontario, enacts as follows :—

1. Section 73 of *The Consolidated Municipal Act, 1883.* as 5 amended by section 2 of *The Municipal Amendment Act, 1886,* is hereby amended by striking out the paragraphs numbered 1, 2, 3 and 4, and substituting the following :— 46 V. c. 18, s. 73, as amended by 49 V., c. 37, s. 2, amended.

(1) In towns, townships and incorporated villages—Freehold to $400 or leasehold to $800. Property qualification.

10   (2) In cities—Freehold to $600 or leasehold to $1200.

1st Session, 6th Legislature, 50 Vic., 1887.

BILL.

An Act to Amend the Municipal Act.

First Reading, 17th March, 1887.

No. 90.] **BILL.** [1877.

An Act to amend the Municipal Act.

HER MAJESTY, by and with the advice and consent of the Legislative Assembly of the Province of Ontario, enacts as follows :—

5   **1.** Section 73 of *The Consolidated Municipal Act, 1883,* as amended by *The Municipal Amendment Act, 1885,* and as further amended by *The Municipal Amendment Act, 1886,* is hereby repealed and the following substituted therefor :—

46 V. c. 18, s. 73 and amendments repealed.

73. No person shall be qualified to be elected a mayor, 10 alderman, reeve, deputy-reeve or councillor of any municipality, unless such person resides within the municipality, or within two miles thereof, and is a natural born or naturalized subject of Her Majesty, and a male of the full age of twenty-one years, and is not disqualified under this Act, and has, or 15 whose wife has, at the time of the election, as proprietor or tenant, a legal or equitable freehold or leasehold, or partly freehold and partly leasehold, or partly legal and partly equitable, rated in his own name, or in the name of his wife, on the last revised assessment roll of the municipality, to at 20 least the value following, over and above all charges, liens and incumbrances affecting the same.

Qualification of mayors, aldermen, etc.

1. In incorporated villages—Freehold to $400, or leasehold to $800 ;
2. In towns—Freehold to $600, or leasehold to $1,200 ;
25   3. In cities—Freehold to $1,000, or leasehold to $2,000 ;
4. In townships—Freehold to $400, or leasehold to $800 ;
And so in the same proportions in all municipalities, in case the property is partly freehold and partly leasehold ;

But if within any municipality any such person is, at the 30 time of election, in actual occupation of any such freehold, rated in his own name, or in the name of his wife, on the last revised assessment roll of the said municipality, he will be entitled to be elected, if the value of which such freehold as actually rated in said assessment roll amounts to not less than 35 $2,000, and for that purpose the said value shall not be affected or reduced by any lien, incumbrance or charge existing on or affecting such freehold.

2. Sub-section 9 of section 482 of *The Consolidated Muni-* 45 *cipal Act, 1883,* is hereby amended by inserting in the fourth line of the said sub-section after the word "Institute" the words "or Free Library established under *The Free Libraries Act, 1882.*"

46 V. c. 18. s. 482 (9) amended.

50   **3.** The following sub-section is hereby added to section 531 of *The Consolidated Municipal Act, 1883:*

46 V. c. 18, s. 531 amended.

<table>
<tr><td>Remedy of
corporation
against third
party.</td><td>(3) A municipal corporation which has been made liable for
damages under sub-section 1 hereof in consequence of an
obstruction or excavation or opening made or left in a public
street, bridge or highway, by another corporation or by any
person other than a servant of such municipal corporation, shall 5
have a remedy over against the corporation or person whose
act or neglect causes the want of repair for which such muni-
cipal corporation is made liable in damages, and shall be
entitled to recover from such other corporation or person all
damages, as well as costs, to which the municipal corporation 10
may have been put or may be rendered liable for by reason of
the Act or neglect of such other corporation or person, and in
case such municipal corporation shall be sued jointly with such
other corporation or person for such damages, and judgment
shall be given against both, the judgment shall be first enforced 15
against such other corporation or person, and the municipal
corporation shall only be liable upon such judgment if the
plaintiff's execution shall be returned unsatisfied against such
other corporation or person, and if such municipal corporation
shall pay any such judgment, it shall be entitled to an assign- 20
ment thereof from the plaintiff to any of its officers or to any
trustee for it, and shall be entitled to enforce payment of such
judgment from such other corporation or person. And such
municipal corporation shall also be entitled to recover from
such other corporation or person its costs of defending any 25
such action.</td></tr>
</table>

Remedy of corporation against third party.

(3) A municipal corporation which has been made liable for damages under sub-section 1 hereof in consequence of an obstruction or excavation or opening made or left in a public street, bridge or highway, by another corporation or by any person other than a servant of such municipal corporation, shall 5 have a remedy over against the corporation or person whose act or neglect causes the want of repair for which such municipal corporation is made liable in damages, and shall be entitled to recover from such other corporation or person all damages, as well as costs, to which the municipal corporation 10 may have been put or may be rendered liable for by reason of the Act or neglect of such other corporation or person, and in case such municipal corporation shall be sued jointly with such other corporation or person for such damages, and judgment shall be given against both, the judgment shall be first enforced 15 against such other corporation or person, and the municipal corporation shall only be liable upon such judgment if the plaintiff's execution shall be returned unsatisfied against such other corporation or person, and if such municipal corporation shall pay any such judgment, it shall be entitled to an assign- 20 ment thereof from the plaintiff to any of its officers or to any trustee for it, and shall be entitled to enforce payment of such judgment from such other corporation or person. And such municipal corporation shall also be entitled to recover from such other corporation or person its costs of defending any 25 such action.

46 V. c. 181, s. 532 repealed.

4. Section 532 of *The Consolidated Municipal Act, 1883*, as amended by section 16 of *The Municipal Amendment Act, 1886*, is hereby repealed and the following is substituted 30 therefor:

Jurisdiction of county council over roads and bridges.

532. The county council shall have exclusive jurisdiction over all roads and bridges lying within any township, town or village of the county and which the council by by-law assumes with the assent of such township, town or village municipality, 35 as a county road or bridge until the by-law has been repealed by the council, and over all bridges across streams separating two townships in the county, and over all bridges crossing streams or rivers over one hundred feet in width within the limits of any township or incorporated village in the county 40 or of any town not separated from the county and necessary directly to connect any main highway leading through the county, and over all bridges over rivers forming or crossing boundary lines between two municipalities.

46 V. c. 18, s. 534 repealed.

5. Section 534 of *The Consolidated Municipal Act, 1883*, is 45 hereby repealed and the following substituted therefor:

Roads or bridges assumed by county councils.

534. When a county council assumes by by-law any road or bridge within a township as a county road or bridge, the council shall, with as little delay as reasonably may be, and at the expense of the county, cause the road to be planked or mac- 50 adamized, or the bridge to be built in a good and substantial manner, and further, the county council shall cause to be built and maintained in like manner all bridges over which it shall have exclusive jurisdiction under section 532 hereof.

No. 90.

1st Session, 6th Legislature, 50 Vic., 1887.

BILL.

An Act to amend the Municipal Act.

First Reading, 17th March, 1887.

No. 91.]　　　　　　**BILL.**　　　　　　[1887.

An Act for the Protection of Women in Certain Cases.

HER MAJESTY, by and with the advice and consent of the Legislative Assembly of the Province of Ontario, enacts as follows :—

1. Whosoever unlawfully and carnally knows, at any time or place, within the precincts of any Institution to which *The Prison and Asylum Inspection Act* applies, any female, though with her consent, while she is a patient, or a lunatic or alleged to be a lunatic, of or in any such Institution, is guilty of an offence, and shall be liable to be imprisoned in any gaol or place of confinement, other than the Penitentiary, for any term less than two years, with or without hard labour. *Protection of women while in asylums, etc.*

2. The person charged shall be a competent witness in his own behalf. *Accused a competent witness.*

3. Nothing in this Act contained nor any conviction obtained in pursuance thereof shall deprive any person of the right to maintain an action for damages against the person so charged. (49 Vic. c. 52, s. 1 (2)). *Civil remedy not affected.*

BILL.

An Act for the Protection of Women
in Certain Cases.

First Reading, 17th March, 1887.

THE ATTORNEY-GENERAL.

TORONTO:
PRINTED BY WARWICK & SONS, 26 AND 28 FRONT ST. W

No. 91.]   **BILL.**   [1887.

An Act for the Protection of Women in Certain Cases.

HER MAJESTY, by and with the advice and consent of the Legislative Assembly of the Province of Ontario, enacts as follows :—

☞ **1.** No person shall at any time or place within the precincts of any Institution to which *The Prison and Asylum Inspection Act* applies, unlawfully and carnally know any female who is capable in law of giving her consent to such carnal knowledge while she is a patient or is confined in such Institution.

Protection of persons confined in asylums.

☞ **2.** Whosoever violates section 1 of this Act is guilty of an offence, and shall be liable to be imprisoned in any gaol or place of confinment, other than the Penetentiary, for any term less than two years, with or without hard labour. ☜

Penalty.

3. The person charged shall be a competent witness in his own behalf.

Accused a competent witness.

4. Nothing in this Act contained nor any conviction obtained in pursuance thereof shall deprive any person of the right to maintain an action for damages against the person so charged. (49 Vic. c. 52, s. 1 (2)).

Civil remedy not affected.

1st Session, 6th Legislature, 50 Vic., 1887.

BILL.

An Act for the Protection of Women
in Certain Cases.

*(Re-printed as amended by Committee of
the Whole House.)*

First Reading, 17th March, 1887.
Second " 24th " "

BILL.

An Act for the protection of Infant Children.

HER MAJESTY, by and with the advice and consent of the Legislative Assembly of the Province of Ontario, enacts as follows :—

10 **1.** From and after the commencement of this Act, it shall not be lawful for any person to retain or receive for hire or reward more than one infant, and in case of twins more than two infants, under the age of one year, for the purpose of nursing or maintaining such infants apart from their parents for a longer period than twenty-four hours, except in a house 15 which has been registered as herein provided. (Imp. 35 and 36 V., c. 38, ss. 2 ; Penns. stat. 1885, ss. 2 and 3). **Restrictions as to receiving infants to be nursed for hire.**

2. The municipal council of every local municipality shall keep a registrar of the names of persons applying to register for the purposes of this Act, and therein shall cause to be regis-
20 tered the name and house of every person so applying, and the situation of the house; and the council shall from time to time make by-laws for fixing the number of infants who may be received into any and every house so registered. The registration shall remain in force for one year. No fee shall
25 be charged for registration. Every person who receives or retains any infant in contravention to the provisions of this Act, shall be guilty of an offence against this Act. (Imp. 35 and 36 V., c. 38, s. 3). **Registration of houses for reception of infants.**

3. The municipal council may refuse to register any house
30 unless satisfied that the house is suitable for the purposes for which it is to be registered, and unless satisfied by the production of the certificates that the person applying to be registered is of good character, and able to maintain such infants. (Imp. 35 and 36 V. c. 38, s. 4.) **Authority to refuse registration.**

35 **4.** The person registered as aforesaid, shall immediately enter in a register to be kept by him the name, sex, and age of every infant under his care, and the date at which, and the names and addresses of the persons from whom, they were received, and shall also enter in the said register the time
40 when, and the names and addresses of the person by whom, every such infant received and retained as aforesaid shall be removed, immediately after the removal of the infant, and shall produce the register when required to do so by the municipal council ; and in the event of his refusing so to pro-
45 duce the register, or neglecting to enter in a register the name, sex, and age of every infant, and the date at which and the names and addresses of the persons from whom **Register of children.**

they were received, and by whom they were removed respectively, shall be liable to a penalty not exceeding $20. (Imp. supra, ss. 5).

Forms of registration to be supplied. **5.** The person registered shall be entitled to receive gratuitously from the municipal council, a book of forms for the registration of infants. This register may be in the form contained in the schedule to this Act. (Ib. ss. 5). 5

Offences. **6.** If any person shall make false representations with a view to being registered under this Act; or shall forge any certificate for the purpose of this Act, or make use of any forged certificate knowing it to be forged, or shall falsify any register kept in pursuance of this Act, he shall be guilty of an offence against this Act. (Imp. s. 6). 10

Removal from register. **7.** If it shall be shewn to the satisfaction of the municipal council that a person whose house has been so registered as aforesaid has been guilty of serious neglect, or is incapable of providing the infants intrusted to his care with proper food and attention, or that the house specified in the register has become unfit for the reception of infants, it shall be lawful for the municipal council to strike his name and house off the register. (Imp. s. 7). 15 20

Notice of death of infant. **8.** The person registered as aforesaid, shall within twenty-four hours after the death of every infant so retained or received, cause notice thereof to be given to the coroner for the district within which the infant died, and the coroner shall hold an inquest on the body of the infant unless a certificate under the hand of a registered medical practitioner is produced to him by the person so registered certifying that such registered medical practitioner has personally attended or examined the infant, and specifying the cause of its death, and the coroner is satisfied by certificate that there is no ground for holding an inquest. If the person so registered neglects to give notice as aforesaid, he shall be guilty of an offence against this Act. (Imp. s. 8.) 25 30

Penalties. **9.** Every person guilty of an offence against this Act shall, on conviction thereof, forfeit and pay a penalty not exceeding $20 and costs, and in default of payment thereof, he shall be imprisoned in the common gaol of the county in which the offence was committed for a period of not less than six calendar months, and to be kept at hard labor, in the discretion of the police magistrate or other convicting justices, and shall, in addition, be liable to have his name and house struck off the register. (*Vide* Imp. sub-s. 9.) 35 40

Expenses of enforcing Act. **10.** All expenses incurred in and about the execution of this Act and the trial of offenders thereunder, shall be borne by the municipality in which the registered house is situated. (Ib. s. 10.) 45

Trial of offences. **11.** Every offence against this Act shall be tried summarily before a police magistrate or any two justices of the Peace having jurisdiction in the municipality in which the offence takes place, and all the provisions and powers as to summary 50

trials contained in "*The Act respecting the duties of Justices of the Peace out of Sessions in relation to summary conviction and orders,*" shall be applicable to prosecutions and trials under this Act, and to the judicial and other officers before
5 whom the same are hereby authorized to be brought, in the same manner, and to the same extent, as if such provisions and powers were incorporated in this Act.

12. The provisions of this Act shall not extend to the relatives or guardians of any infant retained or received as
10 aforesaid, nor to benevolent and charitable institutions established for the protection or care of infants. Imp. supra. s. 13.

Application of Act.

13. This Act shall commence on the 1st day of May next after the passing thereof.

Commencement of Act.

Schedule referred to in the foregoing Act.

REGISTER OF INFANTS.

Date at which received.	Name.	Sex.	Age.	Name and address of person from whom received.	Dated at which removed.	Name and address of person by whom removed.

No. 92.

1st Session, 6th Legislature, 50 Vic., 1887.

BILL.

An Act for the Protection of Infant Children.

An Act for the protection of Infant Children.

HER MAJESTY, by and with the advice and consent of the Legislative Assembly of the Province of Ontario, enacts as follows :—

1. From and after the commencement of this Act, it shall 5 not be lawful for any person to retain or receive for hire or reward more than one infant, and in case of twins more than two infants, under the age of one year, for the purpose of nursing or maintaining such infants apart from their parents for a longer period than twenty-four hours, except in a house 10 which has been registered as herein provided. (Imp. 35 and 36 V., c. 38, ss. 2 ; Penns. stat., 1885, ss. 2 and 3). *Restrictions as to receiving infants to be nursed for hire.*

2. The municipal council of every local municipality shall keep a register of the names of persons applying to register for the purposes of this Act, and therein shall cause to be regis- 15 tered the name and house of every person so applying, and the situation of the house; and the council shall from time to time make by-laws for fixing the number of infants who may be received into any and every house so registered. The registration shall remain in force for one year. No fee shall 20 be charged for registration. Every person who receives or retains any infant in contravention to the provisions of this Act, shall be guilty of an offence against this Act. (Imp. 35 and 36 V., c. 38, s. 3). *Registration of houses for reception of infants.*

3. The municipal council may refuse to register any house 25 unless satisfied that the house is suitable for the purposes for which it is to be registered, and unless satisfied by the pro- duction of the certificates that the person applying to be re- gistered is of good character, and able to maintain such infants. (Imp. 35 and 36 V. c. 38, s. 4.) *Authority to refuse regis- tration.*

30 4. The person registered as aforesaid, shall immediately enter in a register to be kept by him the name, sex, and age of every infant under his care, and the date at which, and the names and addresses of the persons from whom, they were received, and shall also enter in the said register the time 35 when, and the names and addresses of the person by whom, every such infant received and retained as aforesaid shall be removed, immediately after the removal of the infant, and shall produce the register when required to do so by the municipal council ; and in the event of his refusing so to pro- 40 duce the register, or neglecting to enter in a register the name, sex, and age of every infant, and the date at which and the names and addresses of the persons from whom *Register of children.*

they were received, and by whom they were removed respectively, shall be liable to a penalty not exceeding $20. (Imp. supra, ss. 5).

Forms of registration to be supplied.
5. The person registered shall be entitled to receive gratuitously from the municipal council, a book of forms for the 5 registration of infants. This register may be in the form contained in the schedule to this Act. *The book shall contain a printed copy of this Act.* (Ib. ss. 5).

Offences.
6. If any person shall make false representations with a view to being registered under this Act, or shall forge any 10 certificate for the purpose of this Act, or make use of any forged certificate knowing it to be forged, or shall falsify any register kept in pursuance of this Act, he shall be guilty of an offence against this Act. (Imp. s. 6).

Removal from register.
7. If it shall be shewn to the satisfaction of the municipal 15 council that a person whose house has been so registered as aforesaid has been guilty of serious neglect, or is incapable of providing the infants intrusted to his care with proper food and attention, or that the house specified in the register has become unfit for the reception of infants, it shall be lawful for 20 the municipal council to strike his name and house off the register. (Imp. s. 7).

Notice of death of infant.
8. The person registered as aforesaid, shall within twenty-four hours after the death of every infant so retained or received, cause notice thereof to be given to the coroner for the 25 district within which the infant died, and the coroner shall hold an inquest on the body of the infant unless a certificate under the hand of a registered medical practitioner is produced to him by the person so registered certifying that such registered medical practitioner has personally attended or examined the 30 infant, and specifying the cause of its death, and the coroner is satisfied by certificate that there is no ground for holding an inquest. If the person so registered neglects to give notice as aforesaid, he shall be guilty of an offence against this Act. (Imp. s. 8.) 35

Inspection.
9. It shall be the duty of the municipal council to provide for the visiting and inspecting, from time to time, of every house registered under this Act; and the persons or person appointed to inspect shall be entitled to enter the house at any time and to examine every part thereof; and to call for and examine the register which is required to be kept by the person 40 registering the house; and to enquire into all matters concerning the house and the inmates thereof; and it shall be the duty of the person registered to give all reasonable information to persons making the inspection, and to afford them every reasonable facility for viewing and inspecting the premises, 45 and seeing the inmates thereof.

Penalties.
10. Every person guilty of an offence against this Act shall, on conviction thereof, forfeit and pay a penalty not exceeding $20 and costs, and in default of payment thereof, he shall be imprisoned in the common gaol of the county in which the 50

offence was committed for a period of not less than six calendar months, and to be kept at hard labour, in the discretion of the police magistrate or other convicting justices, and shall, in addition, be liable to have his name and house struck off the
5 register. (*Vide* Imp. sub-s. 9.)

11. All expenses incurred in and about the execution of this Act and the trial of offenders thereunder, shall be borne by the municipality in which the registered house is situated. (Ib. s. 10.) *Expenses of enforcing Act.*

10 **12.** Every offence against this Act shall be tried summarily before a police magistrate or any two justices of the Peace having jurisdiction in the municipality in which the offence takes place, and all the provisions and powers as to summary trials contained in "*The Act respecting the duties of Justices*
15 *of the Peace out of Sessions in relation to summary conviction and orders,*" shall be applicable to prosecutions and trials under this Act, and to the judicial and other officers before whom the same are hereby authorized to be brought, in the same manner, and to the same extent, as if such provisions and
20 powers were incorporated in this Act. *Trial of offences.*

13. The provisions of this Act shall not extend to the relatives or guardians of any infant retained or received as aforesaid, nor to benevolent and charitable institutions established for the protection or care of infants, and receiving
25 aid from the Province or authorized by the Lieutenant-Governor to exercise the powers conferred by the Act respecting Appentices and Minors. Imp. supra. s. 13. *Application of Act.*

14. This Act shall commence on the 1st day of May next after the passing thereof. *Commencement of Act.*

30 *Schedule referred to in the foregoing Act.*

REGISTER OF INFANTS.

Date at which received.	Name.	Sex.	Age.	Name and address of person from whom received.	Dated at which removed.	Name and address of person by whom removed.

1st Session, 6th Legislature, 50 Vic., 1887.

BILL.

An Act for the Protection of Infant Children.

(Re-printed as amended by Committee of Whole House.)

First Reading, 17th March, 1887.
Second "   29th "   "

BILL.

An Act to amend the Municipal Act.

HER MAJESTY, by and with the advice and consent of the Legislative Assembly of the Province of Ontario, enacts as follows :—

1. Section 79 of *The Consolidated Municipal Act, 1883,* is 46 V. c. 18, s.
5 hereby amended by striking out clause "fourthly," and the sub- 79 amended.
sections thereto numbered 2, 3, 4, and so much of sub-section
5 as places an interpretation upon the words "farmer," "son,"
"sons," "farmer's son," or "farmers' sons," the qualifications of
whom as voters at municipal elections it is hereby intended to
10 abolish, and substitute in lieu thereof a "Landholder's sons"
franchise.

2. The following is substituted in lieu of so much of said
section 79 as is repealed by the preceding section :

Fourthly.—Every landholder's son who is resident at the Landholders'
15 time of the election in the local municipality in which he sons.
tenders his vote, and has resided therein with and in the
residence or dwelling of the landholder whose son he is, for
twelve months next prior to the return by the assessors of the
assessment roll on which the voters' lists used at the election
20 is based, and who has been duly entered and named in said
assessment roll as such landholder's son.

(a) Occasional or temporary absence from such residence
or dwelling for a time or times not exceeding in
the whole six months of the twelve hereinbefore
25 mentioned, shall not operate to disentitle a landholder's son to vote under this Act.

3.—(1) The expression "landholder" shall mean and in- Landholder.
clude :

(a) Any person who being the owner of and residing and
30 domiciled upon real property of at least twenty
acres in extent, or of at least an actual value in
cities and towns of $400, and in townships and
incorporated villages of $200, is, in the last revised
assessment roll of the municipality where such
property is situate, entered and assessed as owner
35 of said property of at least the number of acres
or the assessed value aforesaid, and

(b) Any person actually residing and domiciled in any
dwelling house as tenant thereof, where such
dwelling house and the land, if any, held there-
40 with by such person as such tenant is of at least
an actual value in cities and towns of $400, and in

townships and incorporated villages of $200, and is at not less than such value entered and assessed in the name of such person in the last revised assessment roll of the municipality wherein the same is situate.   5

Landholder's son.

(2) The expression "landholder's son" shall mean and include a son, step-son, grandson, or son-in-law, as the case may be, of any landholder.

46 V. c. 18, s. 105 repealed.

4. Section 105 of the said Act is also repealed and the following substituted in lieu thereof :   10

Oath of landholder's son.

105. You swear (or solemnly affirm) that you are the person named (or purporting to be named by the name of   ) on the list of voters now shewn to you ;

That on the   day of   18   (the day certified by the clerk of the municipality as the date of the return, or of the final revision and correction of the assessment roll upon which the voters' list used at the election is based, as the case requires, A. B. (naming him or her) was, as you verily believe actually, truly, and in good faith possessed to his (or her) own use as owner, tenant or occupant of the property in respect of which your name is so as aforesaid entered on the said voters' list, and was then actually and in good faith residing and domiciled upon said prop rty ;

That you are a son of the said A. B. ;

That you resided within the municipality with the said A. B., for, and during the whole of the twelve months next before the return by the assessor of the assessment roll on which the voters' list used at this election is based, not having been absent during that period, except temporarily and not more than six months in all ;

That you are still a resident of this municipality, and are entitled to vote at this election ;

That you are of the full age of twenty-one years ;

That you are a subject of Her Majesty either by birth or by naturalization ;

(In the case of municipalities not divided into wards.) That you have not voted before at this election, either at this or any other polling place ;

(In the case of municipalities divided into wards.) That you have not voted before at this election, either at this or any other polling place in this ward, and (if the elector is tendering his vote for mayor, reeve or deputy-reeve), that you have not voted elsewhere in the municipality at this election for mayor (reeve or deputy-reeve as the case may be).

That you have not received anything, nor has anything been promised you, either directly or indirectly, either to induce you to vote at this election, or for loss of time, travelling expenses, hire of team, or any other service connected with this election ;

And that you have not directly, or indirectly, paid or promised anything to any person, either to induce him to vote, or to refrain from voting, at this election.

So help you God.

Inconsistent enactments repealed.

5. All Acts or parts of Acts inconsistent herewith are hereby repealed.

No. **93.**

1st Session, 6th Legislature, 50 Vic., 1887.

BILL.

An Act to amend the Municipal Act.

First Reading, 17th March, 1887.

No. 94.]　　　　　**BILL.**　　　　[1887.

An Act respecting Conditional Sales of Personal Property.

H ER MAJESTY, by and with the advice and consent of the
　　Legislative Assembly of the Province of Ontario, enacts
as follows :—

1. Every hiring, lease, or agreement for the sale of goods *Certain con-*
5 and chattels, accompanied by an immediate delivery, and *tracts for the hiring, leas-*
followed by an actual and continued change of possession, *ing, etc., of*
whereby it is agreed that the property in the goods and *goods to be in writing.*
chattels, or a lien thereon, for the price or value thereof, or any
portion thereof, shall remain in the hirer, lessor, or bargainor,
10 until the payment in full of such price or value, by future payments or otherwise, shall be in writing, signed by the parties
thereto, or their duly authorized agents in writing (a copy of
which authority shall be attached to such agreement) and
shall set forth fully by recital or otherwise, the terms, nature
15 and effect of such hiring, lease, or bargain for sale, and the
amounts to be paid thereunder, whether expressed as rent,
payment or otherwise, and shall be accompanied by an affidavit
of a witness thereto of the due execution thereof, and by the
several affidavits of the parties thereto, or in case such agree-
20 ment has been signed by an agent or agents of the parties,
duly authorized as aforesaid, then by the affidavit of such
agent or agents respectively, stating that the writing truly sets
forth the entire agreement between the parties thereto, and
truly sets forth the actual claim, lien, or balance due to the
25 hirer, lessor, or bargainor therein, and that such writing is executed in good faith, and for the purpose of securing to the
hirer, lessor, or bargainor the payment of the claim, lien or
charge thereon, at the times and under the terms set out in
the writing, and for no other purpose whatever, and such
30 agreement and affidavits shall be registered at the office of *Registration*
the clerk of the Division Court of the division where the pro- *of agreement.*
perty so hired, leased, or agreed to . be sold, is at the time of
the execution of said agreement, or in case the property is to
be removed to another division, then in the office of the clerk
35 of the Division Court of the division to which it is removed,
and such clerks shall file all such instruments presented to
them respectively for that purpose, and shall endorse thereon
the time of receiving the same in their respective offices and
such instruments shall be kept there for the inspection of all
40 persons interested therein.

2. The said clerks shall number every such instrument or *Manner of*
copy filed in their offices, and shall enter in alphabetical order, *registration.*
in books to be provided by them, the names of all the parties

to such instruments, with the numbers endorsed thereon, opposite to each name, and such entry shall be repeated alphabetically under the name of every party thereto.

Removal of the goods to another division. **3.** In the event of the permanent removal of goods and chattels so hired, leased or bargained for as aforesaid, from the 5 division of the Division Court in which the agreement was first registered to another division, before the payment of the amounts specified in said instrument, a certified copy of the agreement under the hand of the clerk of the Division Court in whose office it was first registered, and under the seal of the 10 court and of the affidavits relating thereto, filed in such office, shall be filed with the clerk of the Division Court of the division to which the goods and chattels are removed, within two months from each removal, otherwise the goods and chattels shall be liable to seizure and sale under execution, and in such 15 case the agreement shall be null and void as against creditors, and subsequent purchasers and mortgagees in good faith, for valuable consideration, as if never executed.

Copy of agreement filed to be receivable in evidence. **4.** A copy of such original agreement, or a copy thereof so filed as aforesaid, and of the affidavits attached thereto, certi- 20 fied by the clerk in whose office the same has been filed under the seal of the court, shall be received as evidence in all courts, but only of the fact that the instrument, or copy and affidavits were received and filed according to the endorsement of the clerk thereon, and of no other fact, and in all cases the original 25 endorsement by the clerk made in pursuance of this Act, upon such instrument or copy, shall be received in evidence only of the fact stated in the endorsement.

Discharging lien. **5.** Where an agreement is registered under the provisions of this Act, the lien under such agreement may be discharged by 30 filing in the office in which the same is registered a certificate signed by the hirer, lessor, or bargainor, his executors or administrators, in the form given in the schedule A hereto, or to the like effect.

Certificate of discharge. **6.** The officer with whom the agreement is filed, upon 35 receiving such certificate, duly proved by the affidavit of a subscribing witness, shall at each place where the number of the agreement has been entered, with the name of any of the parties thereto, in the book kept under section 2 of this Act, or wherever otherwise in the said book the said agreement has 40 been entered write the words "Discharged by certificate No. ," (stating the number of the certificate), and to the said entry the officer shall affix his name, and he shall also endorse the fact of the discharge upon the instrument discharged, and shall affix his name to the endorsement. 45

Registration of assignment. **7.** In case a registered agreement under this Act, and the rights of the hirer, lessor, or bargainor have been assigned, the assignment may, upon proof by the affidavit of a subscribing witness, be numbered and entered in the book to be kept for the registration of such agreements, in the same manner as the 50 original agreement.

Effect of non-registration. **8.** In case the agreements hereinbefore referred to, and the affidavits attached thereto are not duly executed and regis-

tered as aforesaid within five days after the execution of the
same, the claim, lien, charge, or property intended to be secured
to the hirer, lessor, or bargainor, shall be null and void and of no
effect, as against the creditors and subsequent purchasers and
5 mortgagees of the person to whom such goods and chattels are
hired, leased, or agreed to be sold.

9. Nothing in this Act shall be construed as making valid   Certain con-
any hiring, lease, or agreement for the sale of goods and chattels, tracts not affected by
which would not be held valid as against creditors, subsequent this Act,
10 purchasers and mortgagees in good faith for valuable consideration, before the passing of this Act, or where the entire agreement between the parties thereto, is not truly set forth in the
instrument filed and registered with the clerk of the proper
Division Court.

15   **10.** Where goods and chattels are hired, leased or bargained Taking pos-
for sale as aforesaid and delivered, and default is made in the session by hirer or les-sor.
payments provided for in the agreement between the parties,
it shall not be lawful for the hirer, lessor, or bargainor, or his or
their agents or servants, to take possession of said goods and
20 chattels, without tendering or refunding to the party who has
hired, leased or bargained for such goods and chattels, and in
whose possession they are the sum or sums of money paid on
account thereof by such party, after deducting therefrom a reasonable compensation for the use of such goods and chattels,
25 which shall in no case exceed twenty-five per cent. of the amount
so paid, anything in the agreement notwitstanding, and whether
such condition be expressed in such agreement or not, unless
such goods and chattels have been broken or actually damaged,
and then a reasonable compensation for such damage shall be
30 allowed.

11. For services under this Act, the clerk aforesaid shall be Fees of Divis-
entitled to receive the following fees :—   ion Court clerk.

1. For filing each instrument and affidavit, and for entering
the same in a book as aforesaid, twenty cents.

35   2. For filing assignment of each intrument, and for making
all proper entries and endorsements in connection therewith,
twenty cents.

3. For filing certificate of discharge of each instrument, and
for making all proper endorsements in connection therewith,
40 twenty cents.

4. For searching for each paper, five cents.

5. For copies of any document filed under this Act, ten cents
per hundred words.

SCHEDULE " A."

To the Clerk of the   Division Court
of the   of   :

I, *A. B.*, of   of   do certify that
has satisfied all moneys due on, or to become due under a certain
agreement made by   to   which agreement

bears date the   day of   A.D.,   , and was
registered in the office of the clerk of the   Division
Court of the   of   , on the   day
of   A.D.,   , as No.   , (*here mention the day and
date of registration of each assignment thereof and the names
of parties, or mention that such agreement has not been assigned, as the case may be*), and that I am the person entitled
by law to receive the money, and that the money due or to
grow due under said agreement, has been paid and discharged.

  Witness my hand, this   day of   A.D.

A. B.

  Witness:

One witness, stating residence and occupation.

1st Session, 6th Legislature, 50 Vic., 1887.

BILL.

An Act respecting Conditional Sales of Personal Property.

First Reading, 18th March, 1887.

BILL.

An Act to amend the Assessment Act.

HER MAJESTY, by and with the advice and consent of the Legislative Assembly of the Province of Ontario, enacts as follows :—

1. Section 137 of *The Assessment Act* is hereby amended 5 by adding the following sub-section thereto : R. S. O. 180 s. 137 amended.

(3) If the council of the local municipality, in which the same shall be situate, desire to become the purchasers of any lot to which sub-section 2 refers for the amount of the arrears of taxes thereon, it shall be lawful for such municipality to 10 purchase the same if the price offered at such adjourned sale shall be less than the amount of such arrears, and if the council of the local municipality shall before the day of such adjourned sale have given notice in writing of the intention so to do, and it shall be the duty of the council of such local 15 municipality to sell any lands which shall be so acquired by them within three years from the time when they shall be acquired. Where at an adjourned sale less than the amount due is offered municipality may purchase.

No. 95.

1st Session, 6th Legislature, 50 Vic., 1887.

BILL.

An Act to amend the Assessment Act.

First Reading, 18th March, 1887.

No. 96.] **BILL.** [1887.

An Act for the prevention of Frauds and Perjuries concerning the Sale of Horses and other Cattle.

HER MAJESTY, by and with the advice and consent of
the Legislative Assembly of the Province of Ontario,
enacts as follows :—

  1. From and after the first day of January, A.D., 1888, no Warranties to
5 action shall be brought or maintained upon any deceit, for or be in writing.
upon any bargain, sale or exchange, or upon any representa-
tion or false representation, as to the value, age, or other particulars, or upon any warranty, or for any breach of warranty
for or upon the sale or exchange of any horse, mare, or other
10 cattle, nor shall such warranty be allowed to be good, unless
some note or memorandum in writing, of the bargain, setting
forth such representation or warranty, shall be made and
signed by the parties to be charged by such bargain, sale, exchange, warranty, or representation, or their agents thereunto
15 lawfully authorized.

1st Session 6th Legislature, 50 Vic, 1887

BILL.

An Act for the prevention of Frauds and
Perjuries concerning the Sale of Horses
and other Cattle.

First Reading, 18th March, 1887.

No. 97.]　　　　　**BILL.**　　　　　[1887.

An Act respecting the Administration of Justice in
the Districts of Algoma and Thunder Bay.

HER MAJESTY, by and with the advice and consent of the
　　Legislative Assembly of the Province of Ontario, enacts
as follows :—

　　1. As respects the District Courts of the Districts of Algoma _{Jurisdiction in} Jurisdiction in cases of waste and trespass.
5 and Thunder Bay, the Judges thereof shall have the same,
jurisdiction as the High Court to grant injunctions restraining
the committing of waste or trespass on property, by unlawfully
cutting, destroying or removing trees or timber, and the practice
in the exercise of such jurisdiction shall be the same, as nearly
10 as may be, as the practice of the High Court.　Consol. U. C.
c. 15, s. 35.

　　2. The High Court, or any Judge thereof, on the applica- Removal of action into High Court.
tion of any party to the proceeding made on notice, may order
that the whole proceeding be transferred to the High Court,
15 or to any Division thereof ; and in such case all papers filed in
the District Court shall be transmitted by the clerk, or other
proper officer of the District Court to the High Court ; and the
action shall thenceforth be continued and prosecuted in the
High Court, as if it had originally commenced therein.　44 V.,
20 c. 5, s. 78.

　　3. No such case shall be transferred to the High Court un- In what cases action shall be removable.
less the value of the subject matter or the damage to either
party appears to amount to upwards of $1,000, nor unless the
case appears to the Court or Judge fit to be tried in the High
25 Court.　The order may be made on such terms as to payment
of costs, giving security and otherwise, as the Court or Judge
thinks fit.　R. S. O. 1877, c. 43, s. 25.

No 97.

1st Session, 6th Legislature, 50 Vic., 1887.

BILL.

An Act respecting the Administration of Justice in the Districts of Algoma and Thunder Bay.

First Reading, 21st March, 1887.

No. 98.]   **BILL.**   [1887.

An Act to amend the Municipal Act.

HER Majesty by and with the advice and consent of the
Legislative Assembly, of the Province of Ontario, enacts
as follows:—

1. Sub-section 2 of section 26 of *The Municipal Amend-* 48 V. c. 39,
5 *ment Act, 1885,* is hereby amended by inserting after the s. 26 (2),
word "deepening" in the first line the word "extending," and amended.
by adding the following to said sub-section: "provided the
cost of such extension does not exceed the sum of $200, and in
every case when it exceeds that amount, proceedings shall be
10 taken under the provisions of section 586."

2. Section 586 of *The Consolidated Municipal Act, 1883,* is 46 V. c. 18,
hereby amended by inserting after the word "improve" in the s. 586,
seventh line the word "extend," and after the word "improve- amended.
ments" in the eleventh and twelfth lines the words "or
15 extension."

3. Sub-section 2 of section 587 of the said Act is hereby 46 V. c. 18,
amended by inserting after the word "constructed" in the s. 587,
first line of said sub-section the words "or may hereafter be amended.
constructed," and by striking out after the word "municipality"
20 in the second line the words "previous to the tenth day of
February, 1876."

4. Section 591 of the said Act is hereby amended by strik- 46 V. c. 18,
ing out the word "may" in the seventh line, and substituting s. 591,
the word "shall" in lieu thereof. amended.

No 98.

1st Session, 6th Legislature, 50 Vic., 1887.

BILL.

An Act to amend the Municipal Act.

First Reading, 21st March, 1887.

No. 99.]　　　　　　**BILL.**　　　　　　[1887.

An Act to Amend the Ditches and Watercourses Act, 1883.

HER MAJESTY, by and with the advice and consent of the Legislative Assembly of the Province of Ontario, enacts as follows :—

1. Section 6 of *The Ditches and Watercourses Act, 1883,* is 5 amended by adding thereto the following proviso:— ^{Requisition for outlet when drain}

Provided, nevertheless, that when it shall be necessary in ^{passes through the property of} order to obtain an outlet, that the drain or ditch shall pass ^{more than five} through or partly through the lands of more than five owners ^{owners.} (the "owner" mentioned in the first and second lines of section 10 6 aforesaid being one) the requisition shall not be filed, unless :

　　(*a*) Such owner shall first obtain the assent, in writing, thereto of (including himself*)* a majority of the owners affected or interested ; or,

　(*b*) Unless a resolution of the council of the municipality, 15　　　in which the greater portion of the work is to be done, approving of the scheme or proposed work, shall be first obtained.

2. In no case shall the engineer, without the consent, in ^{Power of} writing, of the owner or owners affected or interested, include ^{engineer restricted.} 20 the lands lying above the lands mentioned in the notice (Form B.) provided for by section 5 of said Act, nor shall he in the absence of such consent direct the cutting or opening of any ditch or drain through any such lands.

No. 99.

1st Session, 6th Legislature, 50 Vic., 1887.

BILL.

An Act to amend the Ditches and Watercourses Act, 1883.

First Reading, 21st March, 1887.

BILL.

An Act to amend the Ditches and Watercourses Act, 1883.

HER Majesty, by and with the advice and consent of the Legislative Assembly of the Province of Ontario, enacts as follows :—

1. Section 3 of *The Ditches and Watercourses Act, 1883*, as 46 V. c. 27, s. 5 amended by section 1 of the Acts passed in the 47th year of 3, amended. Her Majesty's reign chaptered 43 and intituled *An Act to amend the Act respecting Ditches and Watercourses*, is hereby further amended by adding thereto the following sub-sections :

(3) Such consent shall be in writing, and signed by the Consent as to 10 party consenting and shall be filed with the clerk of the muni- flooding land cipality, with the award and may be recited or referred to ing. therein.

(4) If after a ditch or drain has been constructed under the Notice to own. provisions of this Act, and in case any owner whose duty it is er to repair. 15 to maintain, and keep in repair any portion of such ditch or drain neglects to keep such portion in a proper state of repair any one of the owners who is liable for maintaining and keeping in repair any portion of such ditch or drain may in writing notify the owner who neglects to keep his portion 20 of such ditch or drain in a proper state of repair, to have the same put in such repair, and to have the same completed within thirty days from the receipt of such notice.

(5) The owner who serves such notice may, if the work has Application to not been performed at the expiry of the thirty days, make municpality on owner's de-25 application to the council of the municipality to have said fault. repairs carried out and completed.

(6) The council shall when such application is made, order Inspection by an examination of the portion of such ditch or drain as is com- engineer. plained of, to be made by the engineer of the municipality or 30 by some other person to be appointed by the council, and who may be called the "Inspector of drains and ditches." The inspection shall be made not later than twelve days from the time of the ordering the same, and the engineer or inspector, as the case may be, shall within twelve days after making such in-35 spection, file with the clerk of the municipality a certificate, stating whether the complaint is well founded or not, and wherein the ditch or drain requires repairing.

(7) If the engineer or inspector (as the case may be) certifies Report of in-that the complaint is well founded, then in such case the spector that 40 council shall order him to proceed and let the work as provided well founded. in section 13, for re-letting work unless the owner has himself

in the meantime completed such repairs in accordance with the report or certificate of the engineer or inspector. The provisions of sections 14 and 15, shall apply as to inspection and payment of engineer's or inspector's fees and costs of work, and the council may by by-law fix the remuneration of the inspector during the time he may be engaged in the performance of any duties under this Act; a member of the council shall not be appointed inspector.

Report of inspector that claim not well founded.

(8) If the engineer or inspector decides that the complaint is not well founded, then in such case the party making such complaint shall pay the fees of the engineer or inspector, as the case may be, and if not paid by him it shall be paid and charged as provided in section 15.

Appeal.

(9) Any owner or party interested under proceedings taken under or by virtue of the six preceding sub-sections, shall have the right of appeal as provided by said Act, where the amount involved exceeds the sum of $20.

46 V. c. 27, s. 5, amended.

2. Section 5 of *The Ditches and Watercourses Act, 1883*, is hereby amended by substituting the word "twelve" for the word "six," in the tenth line thereof.

46 V. c. 27 s. 6, amended.

3. Section 6 of the said Act is hereby amended by striking out the word "shall," in the eighth line, and inserting in lieu thereof the words "be asked to appoint a day in which he will," and by inserting after the word "six," in the ninth line, the words "nor more than twelve," and by adding thereto the following proviso:

"Provided, nevertheless, that when it shall be necessary in order to obtain an outlet, that the drain or ditch shall pass through or partly through the lands of more than five owners (the "owner" mentioned in the first and second lines of this section being one) the requisition shall not be filed, unless:

(*a*) Such owner shall first obtain the assent, in writing, thereto of (including himself) a majority of the owners affected or interested; or,

(*b*) Unless a resolution of the council of the municipality, in which the greater portion of the work is to be done, approving of the scheme or proposed work, shall be first passed after those interested have been heard or have had an opportunity to be heard by the Council upon notice to that end."

(*c*) When the engineer shall under section 8 of the said Act require other parties whom he deems interested to be notified he shall not assess or bring in without his or their assent more than one additional interested person when the majority of those so notified and interested are opposed to being so brought in or assessed; or,

(*d*) Unless the assent (by resolution) of the said municipal Council approving of the proposed extension to the lands of other interested parties shall be first passed after a hearing or notice as hereinbefore provided.

4. Section 8 of the said Act is hereby amended by striking out, in the tenth and eleventh lines, the words "from the receipt of the requisition by him," and inserting in lieu thereof the words "after the day of meeting named in the requisition." 46 V. c. 27, s. 8, amended.

5 **5.** Section 8 of the said Act is further amended by adding the following sub-section thereto :— 46 V. c. 27 s. 8, amended.

(2) In no case shall the engineer include or assess the lands lying more than fifty rods above the point of commencement of the ditch or drain upon the lands mentioned in the notice (Form 10 B) provided for by section 5 of said Act, nor the lands on either side of the ditch or drain which lie more than fifty rods from the drain, and only so much within such fifty rods as having due regard to the nature of the locality and of the soil and the lay of the land and its distance back from the ditch or 15 drain as will be benefited by the ditch or drain, and then only according to and in proportion to the benefit which it will receive by such construction.

6. Section 9 of the said Act is amended by adding thereto the following sub-section :— 46 V. c. 27 s. 9, amended.

20 (2) If it appears to the engineer that rock-cutting is required to be done, the engineer may get the rock cut or blasted by giving the contract out to public competition by tender or otherwise, instead of requiring each person benefited to do his share of the work. The engineer shall, by his 25 award, determine the sum which shall be paid by each of the persons benefited, which sum, unless forthwith paid, shall be added to the collector's roll, together with seven per cent. added thereto, and the same shall thereupon become a charge against the land of the parties so liable, and shall be collected in the 30 same manner as any other municipal taxes. Rock cutting may be let to contractor.

7. It shall be the duty of the municipality, through the treasurer thereof, to pay the contractor for the work as soon as done to the satisfaction and upon the certificate of the engineer, pending the subsequent collection thereof as aforesaid. Payment to contractor.

35 **8.** Section 10 of *The Ditches and Watercourses Act, 1883,* is amended by striking out the words, in the first and second lines, "when such award is made file the same," and substituting the following in lieu thereof: "within thirty days from the day appointed by him, as named in section 8 of this Act, 40 make and file his award." 46 V. c. 27, s. 10, amended. Award to be filed.

9. Section 15 of *The Ditches and Watercourses Act, 1883,* as amended by section 2 of the Acts passed in the 47th year of Her Majesty's reign, chaptered 43, and intituled *An Act to amend the Act respecting Ditches and Watercourses,* is hereby 45 further amended by substituting the word "seven" for the word "ten" in the twelfth line thereof. 46 V. c. 27 s. 15, amended.

10.—(1) In any case where an open ditch or drain has been, or may be constructed under the provisions of *The Ditches and Watercourses Act, 1883,* or any of the amendments thereto, 50 any person through whose lands such ditch or drain has been opened, may, with the consent of the engineer of the munici- Power as to covering drains.

pality, convert so much of such ditch or drain as runs through the lands of such person into a covered drain.

(2) The engineer, before giving such consent, shall examine the portion of the ditch or drain which is proposed to be covered, and shall determine the size and capacity of the pro- 5 posed covered portion of such drain or ditch, and the nature and quality of material to be used therein, but no such consent shall be given by the said engineer, if the covering of any such portion of said ditch or drain would impede or delay the free flow of the water which such ditch or drain was originally 10 intended to carry off.

If consent given award to be filed. **11.** The engineer shall file with the clerk of the municipality (if such consent is given) an award setting forth the particulars in accordance with the provisions of said Act, and the amendments thereto, and said award shall be subject to appeal. 15

Notice to engineers. **12.** The person making the application for the covering of the ditch or drain, may notify the engineer to inspect the ditch or drain in the first place, and may also notify said engineer when the work is completed, and it shall not be necessary for such person to take the proceedings provided in sections 5 and 20 6 of said Act, and such person shall be liable for the fees and expenses of the engineer, and if not paid by such person to the **Payment of fees and expenses.** engineer, such fees and expenses shall be collected, as provided for in said Act.

Flow of water not to be impeded. **13.** Such person (and the successive owners of said land) 25 shall maintain and keep the covered portion of such drain or such sufficient size and capacity as not to impede or delay the free flow of the water above the covered portion or brought thereto by said drain; and any damages occasioned by the neglect or failure to so maintain and keep such portion of the 30 size and capacity aforesaid shall be payable by the owner of the land upon which the insufficient or imperfect portion of the drain is situate, and shall be a charge thereupon.

Application of Act. **14.** This Act shall apply to deepening or widening a ditch or drain. 35

47 V. c. 43 and this Act to be read with 46 V. c. 27. **15.** This Act and the said Act passed in the forty-seventh year of Her Majesty's reign chapter 43 shall be read with and as part of *The Ditches and Watercourses Act, 1883.*

No. 99.

1st Session, 6th Legislature, 50 Vic., 1887

BILL.

An Act to amend the Ditches and Watercourses Act, 1883.

(*Reprinted as amended by Municipal
Committee*).

First Reading, 21st March, 1887.
Second   "   28th   "   1887.

No. 100.] **BILL.** [1887.

An Act respecting the Custody of Documents relating to Land Titles.

HER MAJESTY, by and with the advice and consent of the Legislative Assembly of the Province of Ontario, enacts as follows :—

1. This Act may be cited as "*The Custody of Title Deeds* Title of Act. 5 *Act*," and shall be read as part of *The Registry Act.*

2. Any person having any document, forming or being a Any person title-deed or evidence or muniment of title to land in this having custody of deeds, Province may deposit the same for safe custody in the office etc., may deof the Registrar of any Registry Division in which the posit them 10 document or a duplicate or copy or memorial or certificate there- try Division of has been registered; or in case it does not appear by any where land is. endorsement thereon, that the same or a duplicate or copy or memorial or certificate thereof has been registered in any Registry Office in Ontario, the document may be so deposited 15 in the office of the Registrar of any Registry Division in which any land to which the same relates is situate.

3. Upon every such deposit, the person depositing shall Requisition to deliver to the Registrar a requisition in duplicate in the form be filed and receipt given. A hereto; which requisition may include any number of docu-20 ments; and the registrar shall sign a receipt upon one of the duplicates for the instruments or documents therein mentioned, and shall deliver the receipt to the person by whom the deposit is made.

4.—(1) Upon receiving the requisition and the documents Each docu-25 therein mentioned, the Registrar shall enter every document ment to be entered in De-in consecutive order in a book to be kept by him for that pur-posit Index pose, to be called the "Deposit Index" (which may be in the and filed, form B hereto), and shall therein number all deposited documents consecutively, and shall endorse on every such document 30 the word "deposited," with the date of deposit and the number of the entry thereof in the Deposit Index; and shall file the same in consecutive order according to its number; and shall also endorse on the requisition the numbers so by him placed on the documents therein mentioned; and shall file all the 35 requisitions in consecutive order according to such numbers;

(2) He shall also enter in an alphabetical index to be kept And names to be entered in by him for that purpose (and which shall be called the Alphabetical "Alphabetical Deposit Index,") the number of the document Index. in the Deposit Index, and the name of every party to the 40 document, or to the action, suit or proceeding to which the docu-

ment relates, or if the same is a certificate or an affidavit, or a statutory declaration or other proof, as to the birth, baptism, marriage, divorce, death or burial of any person, then the name of such person;

Entry opposite registered instruments. (3) In case it appears by any certificate of registration 5 endorsed on the document, that the same or a duplicate or a copy or memorial or certificate thereof is registered in his Registry Office, the Registrar shall also enter in the margin of every registry book wherein the same is registered opposite the entry thereof, the words, " See deposit index No.   A. D," 10 referring to the number of the instrument in the Deposit Index, and the date of the deposit.

Notice to be sent to other Registry Offices where registered. **5.**—(1) In case it appears by any certificate of registration endorsed on the document that the same or a duplicate or copy or memorial or certificate thereof is registered 15 in any other Registry Division, the Registrar with whom the same is so deposited shall, within ten days after the deposit send by post to such other Registrar a notice thereof in duplicate, in the form B hereto.

(2) On receipt of the notice the Registrar receiving the same 20 shall enter in the margin of every registry book wherein the same appears to have been registered, opposite the entry thereof, the words, " See deposit index in   Registry Office, No.   A. D," referring to the registry office from which the notice is received, and the number and date of the deposit 25 therein.

(3) And he shall forthwith send by post an acknowledgment written upon one of the duplicate notices of the receipt of the notice.

(4) In case such an acknowledgment is not received 30 within fourteen days from the sending of the notice, the Registrar sending the notice shall send another like notice, and shall repeat the same every fourteen days till the acknowledgment is received.

(5). Every such notice and acknowledgment shall be post- 35 paid and post registered, and a sufficient sum to pay his fees and the postage and post registration on the acknowledgment thereof shall be sent with the notice.

(6) All notices received from other Registrars shall be filed by the Registrar receiving the same in the order of receiving 40 the same, and all such acknowledgments shall be filed by the Registrar receiving the same in the order of the receipt thereof.

Registrar's fees. **6.** The Registrar with whom the deposit is made, shall be entitled to the following fees to be paid at the time of the deposit by the person depositing the same, that is to say:— 45

On every requisition..................	20 cents.
On every document deposited therewith..	10 "
For every notice necessary to be sent to other Registrars, (not more than one notice to any one Registrar to be charged for).............................	15
Necessary postage and post registration fee on the notices and acknowledgments thereof...........................	

50

7. The Registrar to whom any notice under section 4 Fees to other Registrars. hereof is sent, shall be entitled to a fee of   cents for every document, in respect of which he is to make the entries aforesaid.

5 **8.** Any person shall be entitled to inspect and make or Deposited documents open to inspection. obtain copies of or extracts from any such deposited document, in like manner as in the case of instruments registered under the provisions of the Registry Act ; and the Registrar shall be entitled to the same fees in respect thereof, as in the case of 10 registered instruments.

9. The deposit of any document under this Act, shall Deposit not registration and not to affect document as evidence. not be deemed a registration thereof within the meaning of the Registry Act ; nor shall the admissibility or value of any document as evidence, be deemed to be improved or affected 15 by the deposit.

10. The deposit of a document under the provisions of Deposit release from liability. this Act, shall, while the same continues so deposited, be deemed a sufficient compliance with, and fulfilment of, any covenant or agreement theretofore entered into by any 20 person, to produce or allow the inspection of the document, or the making of any copy of or extract from the same, and shall absolve any person liable for the production or custody thereof from any further liability in respect of such custody or production.

25 **11.** The Registrar with whom a document is so deposited Registrar to keep safely. shall keep the same safely in his custody, in his office, in like manner and with the same care as the instruments registered in his office; and he and his sureties shall be responsible in respect thereof, in like manner as in respect of 30 instruments registered under the Registry Act ; and the Registrar shall not part with the possession of any such document, unless in accordance with the order of a Court or Judge as hereinafter provided.

12. Any executor or administrator of the estate of a Expenses of executors, etc. 35 deceased person, and a trustee of a trust estate, may reimburse himself out of such estate any expense which he incurs in or about depositing any documents which may come to his possession or control as such executor, administrator or trustee.

40 **13.**—(1) At any time within five years after the deposit of a Application within 5 years to remove custody. document under the provisions hereof, any person may apply to the High Court of Justice, or the County Court of the County in which the deposit is made, or to a Judge of either of the said Courts, for the delivery of the document to such person, 45 and the Court or Judge—upon being satisfied that the applicant would, but for the deposit, be solely entitled to the possession of the document, and that the deposit thereof was made without his consent, or the consent of any person entitled at the time of the deposit to any interest therein, and (in case the docu- 50 ment relates to other lands than those in which the applicant is interested) that there are reasonably important grounds for removing the document from the custody of the Registrar—

4

may direct that the same shall be delivered up by the Registrar to the applicant, or to any person the Court or Judge may direct.

(2) Before making the order, the Court or Judge may require such notice of the application as to the Court or Judge shall seem meet to be given to the person by whom the deposit was made, or to any other person, by advertisement or otherwise, or may dispense with any such notice.

Costs.

(3) The order may direct that all or any part of the costs of the application, or of opposing the same, or in relation thereto, be paid by the person by whom the deposit was made, or by whom the application is made, or by any person to whom notice of the application has been given and may make such order in respect of the costs of the applicant, and of the persons who have been notified, or who may oppose the application, as to the Court or Judge seems meet.

Delivery. Registration under order.

14.—(1) Upon the delivery to the Registrar of the order, or a duplicate thereof, within six months after the date thereof, and upon payment to him of the sum of fifty cents, he is to deliver to the person mentioned therein the documents therein directed to be given to him, taking his receipt, or the receipt of his authorized agent therefor, and

(2) Shall make an entry in the deposit index, opposite the entry of the document, specifying the date of such delivery, and to whom delivered, the Court or Judge by whom the order was made, and the date of the order, and shall file the order among the requisitions for deposit in the order of the date of receipt thereof.

Interpretation.

15. The word "document," herein, shall be held to include the word "instrument," as defined by the Registry Act, and also any certificate, affidavit, statutory declaration, or other proof as to the birth, baptism, marriage, divorce, death, burial, descendants, or pedigree of any person, or as to the existence or non-existence, happening or non-happening of any fact, event or occurrence upon which the title to land may depend, and notices of sale, or other notices necessary to the exercise of any power of sale or appointment or other powers relating to lands.

SCHEDULE.

FORM A.

To the Registrar of the   of

I (or we) hereby deposit with you and require you to take into your custody, pursuant to the Custody of Title Deeds Act,   Vic., cap.   , the following Instruments and Documents, viz. :—

Description of Instrument or Document.	Names of all parties.	Any other particulars or subject of certificate, affidavit, etc.	Lands in this Registration Division to which	Particulars of Registration of Registered Instruments.			
				Registration Division.	Date.	No.	Township, City, Town etc.

Dated   (in duplicate)

Signed in presence of me, to whom the depositor, and his residence and occupation are well known. }

      Signature.
(Residence)   Lot   Con.
     House No.   or Street.
(Occupation)

     J. P. or Notary Public, or
Mayor or Reeve, Solicitor of Supreme
       Court, or Barrister.

The documents above mentioned, with a duplicate of above requisitions, are this day received by me.

Dated

         Registrar for

FORM B.

DEPOSIT INDEX.

Deposit No.	Description of Instrument.	Parties.	Lands in this Registration Division mentioned.	Any other particulars or subject of certificates, affidavits, etc.	Particulars of Registration Certificate endorsed.	Date of Deposit.	By whom deposited.

FORM C.

NOTICE OF DEPOSIT.

To the Registrar of

The following instruments, of which the originals, or a Duplicate, or Memorial, or Copy, or Certificate, appear to be registered in your Registry Office, have been deposited in this Registry Office under the "Custody of Title Deeds Act."

Deposit Index No.	Date of Deposit.	Description of Instrument.	Parties.	Particulars of Registration in your Registration Division.		
				Registration No.	Date of Registration	Township, City, Town etc.
2146	8th Aug., 1885.	Mortgage.	John Smith to Wm. Jones			

You are required to enter such deposit, and to acknowledge receipt hereof, under above Act. Enclosed is   cents.

Dated at

Registry Office for

_____
Registrar.

The Duplicate of above notice of deposit of (three) documents received at the Registry Office for   this   day of   , A.D. 18   , and entry of such deposit has been made in accordance with the "Custody of Title Deeds Act."

_____
Registrar.

Form of acknowledgment to be put in duplicate notice.

No. 100.

1st Session, 6th Legislature, 50 Vic., 1887.

BILL.

An Act respecting the Custody of Documents relating to Land Titles.

First Reading, 21st March, 1887.

No. 101.]

BILL.

[1878.

An Act to amend the Municipal Act.

HER Majesty, by and with the advice and consent of the Legislative Assembly, of the Province of Ontario, enacts as follows :—

1.—(1) Where a resident owner who has been entered upon 5 the assessment roll, does not perform his statute labour or pay commutation for the same, the overseer of the highways in whose division he is placed, shall return him as a defaulter to the clerk of the municipality before the fifteenth day of August, and the clerk shall in that case enter the commutation for 10 statute labour against his name in the collector's roll. Commutation of statute labour if not paid by resident owner to be entered upon collector's roll.

(2) In every such case the clerk shall notify the overseer of highways, that may be appointed for such division in the following year, of the amount of such commutation, and the overseer shall expend the amount of such commutation upon the roads 15 in the statute labour division where the property is situate, and shall give an order upon the treasurer of the municipality to the party or parties performing the work ; the notification by the clerk to the overseer shall be placed in the said list if not delivered to him before he receives such list. Overseer to expend the commutation money.

1st Session, 6th Legislature, 50 Vic., 1887.

BILL.
An Act to amend the Municipal Act.

First Reading, 21st March, 1887.

No. 102.] **BILL.** [1887.

An Act to amend the Assessment Act.

HER MAJESTY, by and with the advice and consent of the
Legislative Assembly of the Province of Ontario, enacts
as follows:—

   1. Sub-section 22 of section 6 of *The Assessment Act*, is Exemption of
5 hereby amended by substituting the words " six hundred " for income under $600.
the words " four hundred," in the second line of the said sub-
section.

1st Session, 6th Legislature, 50 Vic., 1887.

BILL.

An Act to amend the Assessment Act.

First Reading, 21st March, 1887.

BILL.

An Act to amend the Municipal Act.

HER MAJESTY, by and with the advice and consent of the Legislative Assembly of the Province of Ontario, enacts as follows :—

1. Section 225 of *The Consolidated Municipal Act, 1883,* 5 is hereby repealed, and the following substituted in lieu thereof :— 46 V. c. 18, s. 225, repealed.

' 225. In case of an equality of votes on the election of the head of any county council, or provisional county council, then of those present, the reeve, or in his absence, the deputy-reeve 10 of the municipality which pays the largest amount of assessment into the county, shall have a second and casting vote. Who to have a casting vote.

1st Session, 6th Legislature, 50 Vic., 1887.

BILL.

An Act to amend the Municipal Act.

First Reading, 22nd March, 1887.

No. 104.]   **BILL.**   [1887.

An Act relating to Exemptions from Seizure under Execution.

HER Majesty, by and with the advice and consent of the Legislative Assembly, of the Province of Ontario, enacts as follows :—

Section 2 of *The Act respecting Writs of Execution* is hereby R. S. O. c. 66, s. 2 repealed.
5 repealed, and the following substituted therefor:

(2) The following chattels are hereby declared exempt from Chattels exempt from seizure. seizure under any writ, in respect of which this Province has legislative authority, issued out of any Court whatever, in this Province, namely:

10   1. The bed, bedding and bedsteads (*including a cradle*), in Bedding. ordinary use by the debtor and his family ;

2. The necessary and ordinary wearing apparel of the Apparel. debtor and his family ;

3. One *cooking* stove with pipes *and furnishings*, one par- Furniture.
15 *lour or hall stove with pipes,* one crane and its appendages, one pair of andirons, one set of cooking utensils, one pair of tongs and shovel, one table, six chairs, *one washstand with furnishings, six towels, one looking glass, one hair brush, one comb, one bureau, one clothes press, one clock, one carpet, one*
20 *cupboard,* six knives, six forks, six plates, six tea cups, six saucers, one sugar basin, one milk jug, one tea pot, six spoons, *two pails, one wash tub, one scrubbing brush, one blacking brush, one wash board, three smoothing irons,* all spinning wheels and weaving looms in domestic use, *one sewing machine*
25 *in domestic use,* thirty volumes of books, one axe, one saw, one gun, six traps, and such fishing nets and seines as are in common use.

4. All necessary fuel, meat, fish, flour and vegetables, actually Fuel and provisions. provided for family use, not more than sufficient for the ordin-
30 ary consumption of the debtor and his family for ——— days, and not exceeding in value the sum of forty dollars.

5. One cow, four sheep, two hogs, *five hens up to the total* Animals. *value of* ——— *dollars,* and food, etc., therefor for thirty days, and one dog.

35   6. Tools and implements of or chattels ordinarily used in the Tools. debtor's occupation, to the value of ——— dollars.

7. Bees reared and kept in hives to the extent of fifteen Bees. hives. See Rev. Stat. c. 96, s. 2.

o   O4

1st Session, 6th Legislature, 50 Vic., 1887

BILL.

An Act relating to Exemptions from
Seizure under Execution.

First Reading, 22nd March, 1887.

No. 104.]   **BILL.**   [1887.

An Act relating to Exemptions from Seizure under Execution.

HER Majesty, by and with the advice and consent of the Legislative Assembly, of the Province of Ontario, enacts as follows :—

5 **1.** Section 2 of *The Act respecting Writs of Execution* is hereby repealed, and the following substituted therefor : *R. S. O. c. 66, s. 2 repealed.*

. (2) The following chattels are hereby declared exempt from seizure under any writ, in respect of which this Province has legislative authority, issued out of any Court whatever, in this Province, namely : *Chattels exempt from seizure.*

10 1. The bed, bedding and bedsteads (*including a cradle*), in ordinary use by the debtor and his family ; *Bedding.*

2. The necessary and ordinary wearing apparel of the debtor and his family ; *Apparel.*

3. One *cooking* stove with pipes *and furnishings, one other*
15 *heating stove with pipes,* one crane and its appendages, one pair of andirons, one set of cooking utensils, one pair of tongs and shovel, *one coal scuttle, one lamp,* one table, six chairs, *one washstand with furnishings, six towels, one looking glass, one hair brush, one comb,* one bureau, *one clothes press,* one
20 clock, *one carpet,* one cupboard, one broom, *twelve* knives, *twelve* forks, *twelve* plates, *twelve* tea cups, *twelve* saucers, one sugar basin, one milk jug, one tea pot, *twelve* spoons, *two pails, one wash tub, one scrubbing brush, one blacking brush, one wash board, three smoothing irons,* all spinning wheels and
25 weaving looms in domestic use, *one sewing machine and attachments in domestic use,* thirty volumes of books, one axe, one saw, one gun, six traps, and such fishing nets and seines as are in common use, *the articles in this subdivision enumerated, not exceeding in value the sum of $150.* *Furniture.*

30 4. All necessary fuel, meat, fish, flour and vegetables, actually provided for family use, not more than sufficient for the ordinary consumption of the debtor and his family for *thirty* days, and not exceeding in value the sum of *$40.* *Fuel and provisions.*

5. One cow, *six* sheep, *four* hogs, *and twelve hens, in all*
35 *not exceeding the value of* $75, and food therefor for thirty days, and one dog. *Animals.*

6. Tools and implements of or chattels ordinarily used in the debtor's occupation, to the value of *$100.* *Tools.*

40 7. Bees reared and kept in hives to the extent of fifteen hives. See Rev. Stat. c. 96, s. 2. *Bees.*

Debtor may take proceeds of sale of implements, etc., in money. **2.** The debtor may in lieu of tools and implements of or chattels ordinarily used in his occupation referred to in subdivision 6 of section 2 of said Act elect to receive the proceeds of the sale thereof up to $100, in which case the officer executing the writ shall pay the net proceeds of such 5 sale if the same shall not exceed $100, or, if the same shall exceed $100, shall pay that sum to the debtor in satisfaction of the debtor's right to exemption under said subdivision 6, and the sum to which a debtor shall be entitled hereunder shall be exempt from attachment or seizure at the instance 10 of a creditior.

R. S. O. c. 66, s. 6, repealed. **3.** Section 6 of the said Act is hereby repealed, and the following substituted therefor :

Goods liable to seizure to continue so liable for debts contracted before Oct. 1, 1887. Notwithstanding anything contained in the next preceding four sections, the various goods and chattels which are now 15 liable to seizure in execution for debt shall, as respects debts which have already been or shall be contracted prior to the first day of October, 1887, remain liable to seizure and sale in execution provided that the writ of execution under which they are seized has endorsed upon it a certificate signed by 20 the judge of the court out of which the writ issues certifying that it is for the recovery of a debt contracted before the date hereinbefore mentioned.

Commencement of Act. **4.** This Act shall take effect on, from and after the first day of October, 1887. 25

No. 104.

1st Session, 6th Legislature, 50 Vic., 1887.

BILL.

An Act relating to Exemptions from Seizure under Execution.

(*Reprinted as amended by Select Committee.*)

First Reading, 22nd March, 1887.
Second " 30th " 1887.

No. 105.] **BILL.** [1887.

An Act to amend the Division Courts Act.

HER MAJESTY, by and with the advice and consent of the Legislative Assembly of the Province of Ontario, enacts as follows :—

1. Section 182 of *The Division Courts Act* is hereby amended as follows :— R. S. O. c. 47, s. 182, amended.

5 (1) By striking out of sub-section 4 thereof the following :— "(b) Wilfully contracted the debt or liability without having had at the time a reasonable expectation of being able to pay or discharge the same, or "

10 (2) By striking out the word "or" at the end of the said sub-section 4, and the following words of sub-section 5 :—

"5. If it appears to the satisfaction of the judge, that the party had, when summoned, or since the judgment was obtained against him, has had sufficient means and ability to pay the 15 debt or damages, or costs recovered against him, either alto-gether, or by the instalments which the court in which the judgment was obtained has ordered, and if he has refused or neglected to pay the same at the time ordered whether before or after the return of the summons."

20 2. Section 62 of *The Division Courts Act, 1880*, is hereby amended by inserting after the words " or has absconded," in the fifth line thereof the words " either before or after the issue of the summons." 43 V. c. 8, s. 62, amended.

BILL.

An Act to amend the Division Courts Act.

First Reading, 22nd March, 1887.

Mr. Gibson.

(Hamilton).

TORONTO.

Printed by Warwick & Sons, 26 and 28 Front St. W.

BILL.

An Act to amend the Game Law.

HER MAJESTY, by and with the advice and consent of the Legislative Assembly of the Province of Ontario, enacts as follows :—

1. Sub-section 7 of section 2 of the Act passed in the 49th 49 V. c. 45, s. 5 year of Her Majesty's reign, chaptered 45, intituled "*An Act to* 2 (7 , repealed *further amend the Law for the protection of Game and Fur-. bearing Animals,*" is hereby repealed and the following substituted therefor :—

(7) Ducks of all kinds, except wood duck, canvas back, red Close period 10 neck, black neck, blue bill and pin tail, and all other water for ducks. fowl, between the first day of January and the first day of September; wood duck between the first day of January and the fifteenth day of August; ducks known as canvas back, red neck, black neck, blue bill and pin tail, between the first day 15 of May and the first day of September.

2. Section 7 of the said Act is hereby amended by striking 49 V. c. s. 45, out the word "speared," in the sixth line thereof. 7, amended.

No. 106.

1st Session, 6th Legislature, 50 Vic., 1887.

BILL.

An Act to amend the Game Law.

First Reading, 22nd March, 1887.

BILL.

An Act to amend the Act respecting Ditches and Watercourses.

HER MAJESTY, by and with the advice and consent of the Legislative Assembly of the Province of Ontario, enacts as follows :—

1. Sub-section 2 of section 3 of *The Ditches and Water-* 5 *courses Act, 1883,* is hereby amended by striking out the words "with the consent of the owner thereof," and by adding the following sub-section thereto :— 46 V. c. 27, s. 3. (47 V. c. 43, s. 1.)

. (3) Any owner may consent to the overflow of his lands, such consent to be in writing, witnessed and filed with the 10 clerk of the municipality, as part of the award. Owner may consent to overflow.

2. Section 5 of *The Ditches and Watercourses Act, 1883,* is hereby amended by substituting the word "twelve" for the word "six," in the tenth line thereof. 46 V. c. 27, s. 5, amended.

3. Section 6 of the said Act is hereby amended by striking 15 out the word "shall," in the eighth line, and inserting in lieu thereof the words "be asked to appoint a day in which he will," and by inserting after the word "six," in the ninth line, the words "nor more than twelve." 46 V. c. 27, s. 6, amended.

4. Section 8 of the said Act is hereby amended by striking 20 out, in the tenth and eleventh lines, the words "from the receipt of the requisition by him," and inserting in lieu thereof the words "after the day of meeting named in the requisition." 46 V. c. 27, s. 8, amended.

(*a*) The engineer may, when he thinks the lands are benefited, assess lands lying above those of the persons asking for the 25 ditch. Lands benefited to be assessed.

5. Section 10 of the said Act is amended by striking out the words, in the first line, "when such award is made file the same," and substituting the following in lieu thereof: "Within thirty days from the day appointed by him, as named in section 30 8 of this Act, make and file his award." 46 V. c. 27, s. 10, amended. Award to be filed.

6. Section 11 of the said Act is hereby repealed and the following substituted therefor :— 46 V. c. 27, s. 11, repealed.

11.—(1) Any person dissatisfied with the award and affected thereby, may, within fifteen clear days from the filing thereof, 35 deposit with the clerk of the municipality a written notice of his intention of appealing therefrom (shortly setting forth his grounds of appeal), to the Court of Revision of the municipality Any person dissatisfied with award may appeal to Court of Revision.

of which the lands in respect to which the proceedings are initiated are situated, which court the council shall from time to time, as the occasion may require, hold on some day not earlier than twenty, nor later than thirty days from the day on which the time of appeal expired. 5

Clerk to notify head of council.
(2) The clerk on the receipt of the notice of appeal shall notify the reeve or other head officer (as the case may be) of the same, who shall instruct the clerk to notify the other members of the court of the time and place such court shall be held. 10

Powers of Court of Revision.
(3) Such court shall be constituted in like manner, and have the same powers as Courts of Revision under the Assessment Act.

Appeal to three persons appointed by the Judge.
(4) The appeal from the Court of Revision shall be to three competent persons (one of whom shall be a Provincial Land Surveyor) whose award shall be final, and who shall be appointed 15 by the judge, junior, or acting judge of the County Court of the county in which the lands are situated, and the proceedings in such last mentioned appeal shall be as follows :—

A notice to be filed with the clerk.
(a) The appellant shall serve upon the clerk of the municipality, with whom the award is filed, a notice in writing of his 20 intention to appeal therefrom (which notice must be filed with the clerk within at least ten clear days from the finding of the Court of Revision) shortly setting forth the ground of appeal.

Notice of appeal to be sent to clerk of Division Court he to notify County Judge.
(b) The clerk of the municipality shall, at the expiration of the time of appeal from the Court of Revision, forward by 25 registered letter, or deliver a copy of such notice, or notices of appeal, if there is more than one appeal, to the clerk of the Division Court of the division in which the land of the owner filing the requisition (as provided in section 6 of this Act) is situate, and such Division Court clerk shall immediately notify 30 the judge of said appeal, whereupon the judge shall appoint

Judge may order a deposit to cover costs of appeal.
the three persons named in sub-section 4 of this section, and may, if he thinks fit, order such sum of money to be paid by the applicants to the said clerk as will be sufficient indemnity against costs of appeal. 35

Lands may be examined, also the parties and their witnesses Costs to be fixed.
(c) The three so appointed persons shall examine all the lands and are hereby authorized to examine the parties, and their witnesses on oath, and may administer an oath or affirmation as in courts of law, and may set aside, alter or affirm the award, correcting any errors therein, and may order payment 40 of costs (including the costs as set forth in the award) by the parties or any of them, and fix the amount of such costs, and shall within thirty days from their appointment file with the clerk of the municipality a report, together with the copies of any evidence they might have taken, setting forth their finding 45 in the matter of such appeal.

46 V. c. 27, s. 12, amended.
7. Section 12 of the said Act is amended by inserting after the word "engineer," in the second line, the words "on demand."

No. 107.

1st Session, 6th Legislature, 50 Vic., 1887.

BILL.

An Act to amend the Ditches and Watercourses Act.

First Reading, 22nd March, 1887.

No. 108.]　　　　　　**BILL.**　　　　　[1887.

An Act to amend the Municipal Act.

HER MAJESTY, by and with the advice and consent of the Legislative Assembly of the Province of Ontario, enacts as follows :—

1. Section 570 of *The Consolidated Municipal Act, 1883,* 46 V. c. 18, s. 5 is hereby amended by striking out in the first and second lines 570, amended. the words : " the persons as shewn by the last revised assessment to be the," and inserting the word " actually " in lieu thereof, and by inserting after the word " council " in the fifth line the words "Form A," and by substituting the word " shall " 10 for the word " may " in the eleventh line of the said section.

2. The said section 570 is further amended by adding thereto Section 570 the following clauses :—　further amended.

(*a*) The clerk shall on receipt of the petition place the same Clerk to serve on file, and shall serve upon all the parties interested, or that notice of petition upon 15 might be interested, a printed notice, or partly written or partly parties interprinted, giving a copy of the said petition and the names ested. attached thereto, and informing the owners that if they have any objection to the proposed ditch or drain, or to the petition, they must file their complaint (or a contra-petition) in writing 20 with the clerk within three weeks from the date of the said notice ; such notice shall be served upon non-residents by registered letter sent to their last known address.

(*b*) The council shall at the first meeting after the expiration Council to of the three weeks mentioned in the next preceding sub-section, decide complaints. 25 examine and discuss any complaint or complaints or contra-petitions that may have been filed, and shall if they are of the opinion that the majority in number of actual owners are desirous of having the ditch, order the examination.

3. Sub-section 10 of the said section is amended by adding 46 V. c. 18, s. 30 the following thereto : "and all notices of appeal shall be served 570 (10), amended. upon the clerk of the municipality at least eight days prior to such court of revision."

4. Sub-sections 13, 14 and 15 of the said section 570 are 46 V. c. 18, s. hereby repealed, and the following substituted therefor : 570 (13-15), repealed.

35　(13) The appeal from the Court of Revision shall be to three Appeal from competent disinterested persons (one of whom shall be a pro- Court of Revision. vincial land surveyor) appointed by the Judge, junior or acting Judge of the county court of the county in which the petition originated, who shall examine all the lands assessed and may 40 vary the assessment of the lands and the roads benefited as aforesaid, without further notice to the parties interested therein, so that the aggregate amount assessed shall be the same as if there had been no appeal, except as to the costs of appeal, which may be added thereto as hereinafter provided, and the Court of Appeal, or in case there is no Appeal to the Court of Appeal, the Court of Revision shall return the roll to the 5 municipal clerk from whom it was received, and the assessors shall prepare and attest a roll in accordance with the original assessment as altered by such revision.

Powers of Court on Appeal.

(14) If the assessment be varied in any way by the Court of Appeal the costs of appeal shall be added to the aggregate 10 assessment, otherwise the costs shall be ordered to be paid by the appellant.

46 V. c. 18, s. 571, amended.

5. Section 571 of the said Act is hereby amended by striking out the words : " as shown by the last revised assessment roll," in the sixth and seventh line of the form of by-law, and 15 substituting the following in lieu thereof : " as certified by the County Judge."

46 V. c. 18, s. 571 (2), amended.

6. Sub-section 2 of the said section 571 is hereby amended by striking out the word " Judge " where it occurs in the second and fourth lines, and inserting in lieu thereof the words " the 20 Court of Appeal."

46 V. c. 18, s. 572, repealed.

7. Section 572 of the said Act is hereby repealed and the following substituted therefor :—

By-laws to be served upon property owners.

572. Before the final passing of the by-law a printed copy of the same (together with a notice that any one intending to 25 have such by-law or any part thereof quashed, must not later than ten days after the final passing thereof, serve a notice in writing upon the reeve or other head officer, and upon the clerk of the municipality of his intention to make application for that purpose to the High Court of Justice at Toronto, dur- 30 ing the six weeks next ensuing the final passing of the by-law) shall be served upon each of the several owners, their lessees or occupants, or upon the agent or agents of such owners, or be left at their residence with some grown up member of the family, or where the land is unoccupied and the owner, or 35 owners, or their agent or agents, do not reside within the municipality, may cause to be sent by registered letter to the last known address of such owner or owners a copy of such by-law and notice, and the said by-law shall not be finally passed until after the expiration of three weeks from the last of such 40 services, and the clerk shall keep on file in his office a statutory declaration or declarations by the party or parties making such service or services, and the manner in which the same were effected.

3

Form A.

PETITION FOR DITCH.

To the Reeve, Deputy-Reeve and Municipal Council of.........................
....

GENTLEMEN,—

The petition of the undersigned owners of land in the......................
....Concessions of the Township of
....humbly sheweth that the lands
of your petitioners are greatly injured by overflowing water for which
there is not sufficient outlet (*or as the case may be*).

Your petitioners therefore humbly pray that your Honourable Body
will cause a drain to be made beginning at (*here describe the course of the
drain, or if the course be left to the Engineer, merely state for the drainage
of certain lots*) and that you will cause such drain to be made under the
provisions of the Municipal Act, and will cause the costs to be assessed
on the lands and roads benefited and on the lands and roads using the
drain as an outlet under section 570 of the said Act, and that you will
cause the tax on the lands to extend over a period of.....................years
and that..Provincial Land
Surveyor, be appointed to make the necessary surveys and to let and
superintend the work.

Your petitioners are of the opinion that the following lands and roads
will be benefited :

Lots.......................in the.........................Con.
Lots ....in the.........................Con., &c.
Concession roads between Concessions...
Concession roads between Concessions...... ....
Side roads between Lots....... ....in the....................Con.
Side roads between Lots............ ....in the.....................Con.

And your petitioners as in duty bound will ever pray.

(Signed) ....

No. 108.

1st Session, 6th Legislature, 50 Vic., 1887.

BILL.

An Act to amend the Municipal Act.

First Reading, 22nd March, 1887.

BILL.

An Act to further amend the Municipal Act.

HER MAJESTY, by and with the advice and consent of the Legislative Assembly of the Province of Ontario, enacts as follows ;—

    1. This Act may be cited as *The Municipal Amendment* Short title.
5 *Act, 1887.*

    2. Section 73 of *The Consolidated Municipal Act, 1883,* as 46 V. c. 18, s.
amended by *The Municipal Amendment Act, 1885,* and as 73, repealed.
further amended by *The Municipal Amendment Act, 1886,*
is hereby repealed, and the following substituted therefor :—

10   73. The persons qualified to be elected mayors, aldermen, Qualification
reeves, deputy-reeves and councillors of any city, town or aldermen, etc.
incorporated village, shall be such persons as reside within the
municipality, or within two miles thereof, and are natural born
or naturalized subjects of Her Majesty and males of the full
15 age of twenty-one years, and are not disqualified under this
Act, and who have under this Act the qualifications entitling
them to vote at municipal elections.

    (2) No person shall be qualified to be elected a reeve, deputy-
reeve or councillor of any township municipality unless such
20 person resides within the municipality, or within two miles
thereof, and is a natural born or naturalized subject of Her
Majesty, and a male of the full age of twenty-one years, and is
not disqualified under this Act, and has, or whose wife has, at
the time of the election, as proprietor or tenant, a legal or
25 equitable freehold or leasehold, or partly freehold and partly
leasehold, or partly legal and partly equitable, rated in his own
name, or in the name of his wife, on the last revised assessment roll of the municipality, to at least the value, in the case
of freehold property, of $400, or of leasehold, $800, over and
30 above all charges, liens and incumbrances affecting the same ;
but if within any township any such person is, at the time of
election, in actual occupation of any such freehold, rated in his
own name, or in the name of his wife, on the last revised
assessment roll of said township, he will be entitled to be
35 elected as reeve, deputy-reeve, or councillor of said township if
the value at which such freehold is actually rated in said
assessment roll amounts to not less than $2,000, and for this
purpose the said value shall not be affected or reduced by any
lien, incumbrance, or charge existing on or affecting such
40 freehold.

    3. Section 76 of *The Consolidated Municipal Act, 1883* 46 V. c. 18, s.
is hereby repealed, and the following substituted therefor :— 76 repealed.

2

Qualification in townships if only one person qualified for each seat. 76. In case in a township municipality there are not at least two persons qualified to be elected for each seat in the council, no qualification beyond the qualification of an elector shall be necessary in the persons to be elected.

46 V. c. 18, s. 81, amended. 4. Section 81 of *The Consolidated Municipal Act, 1883,* is 5 amended by adding at the end there of the words, " but any person who is entitled to vote and who produces and leaves with the deputy returning officer at the time of the tendering of the vote a certificate from the treasurer of the municipality, or the collector of taxes, shewing that the taxes in 10 respect of which the default had been made have since been paid, shall be entitled to vote; and the deputy-returning officer shall file the certificate, receive the vote and note the same on the defaulters' lists."

46 V. c. 18, s. 99, amended. 5. Section 99 of *The Consolidated Municipal Act, 1883,* 15 is amended by adding at the commencement thereof, the following words :—

" In any case where a deputy returning officer refuses or neglects to attend at the time and place he is required by the returning officer to receive his voters' lists, and other election 20 papers, the returning officer shall appoint another person to act in his place and stead, and the person so appointed shall have all the powers and authority that he would have had if he had been appointed by by-law."

46 V. c. 18, s. 138, amended. 6. Section 138 of *The Consolidated Municipal Act, 1883,* 25 is amended by striking out all the words after the word " therein " in the sixth line of the said section and substituting the following therefor, " or when he is a non-resident or is not entitled to vote in the ward or polling sub-division where he resides, then, where he first votes and there only. " 30

46 V. c. 18, s. 139, amended. 7. Section 139 of *The Consolidated Municipal Act, 1883* is amended by adding thereto the following sub-section.

(2) The receipt by any voter of a ballot paper within the polling booth shall be *prima facie* evidence that he has there and then voted. 35

46 V. c. 18, s. 225, repealed. 8. Section 225 of *The Consolidated Municipal Act, 1883* is hereby repealed, and the following substituted therefor :—

Casting vote. 225. In case of an equality of votes on the election of the head of any county council, or provisional county council, then of those present, the reeve, or in his absence, the deputy-reeve 40 of the municipality which for the preceding year had the greatest equalized assessment, shall have a second and casting vote.

46 V. c. 18, s. 246 (49 V. c. 37, s. 3), repealed. 9. Section 246 of *The Consolidated Municipal Act, 1883,* as amended by section 3 of *The Municipal Amendment Act,* 45 1886, is hereby repealed.

46 V. c. 18, ss. 247-251, 264, repealed. 10. Sections 247, 248, 249, 250, 251 and 264 of *The Consolidated Municipal Act, 1883,* are hereby repealed.

11. Section 260 of *The Consolidated Municipal Act, 1883*, is 46 V. c. 18, s. 260, amended.
amended by adding thereto the following words : " And in the
event of any auditor so appointed to audit the accounts of the
county refusing, or being unable to act, then the head of the
5 council shall nominate another person to act in his stead."

12. Section 262 of *The Consolidated Municipal Act, 1883*, 46 V. c. 18, s. 262 repealed. Auditors to prepare abstract and statement of receipts and expenditure.
is repealed and the following substituted in lieu thereof :

The auditors shall prepare in duplicate an abstract of the
receipts, expenditure, assets and liabilities of the corporation, and
10 also a detailed statement of the same in such form as the Council
directs. They shall make a report on all accounts audited by
them and a special report of any expenditure made contrary to
law. The auditors shall transmit one copy of the abstract to the
secretary of the Bureau of Industries, Toronto, and shall file the
15 other, together with the detailed statement and reports in the
office of the clerk of the council within one month after their
appointment, and thereafter any inhabitant or ratepayer of
the municipality may inspect the same at all reasonable hours
and may by himself or his agent at his own expense take a
20 copy thereof, or extracts therefrom.

13. The treasurer of every municipality shall, on or before Returns to be made by treasurer to Bureau of Industries.
the first day of May in each year, under a penalty of $20 in
case of default, furnish to the secretary of the Bureau of Industries, Toronto, on schedules or forms furnished by said secretary
25 and approved by the Lieutenant-Governor in Council, such
information or statistics regarding the finances or accounts of
the municipality, as such schedules or forms call for.

14. The clerk of every municipality shall in each year, Returns to be made by clerks to Bureau of Industries.
within one week after the final revision of the assessment roll,
30 under a penalty of $20 in case of default, make a return to the
secretary of the Bureau of Industries, Toronto, on schedules or
forms furnished by the said secretary, and approved by the
Lieutenant-Governor in Council, of such statistics or information as the assessment roll or other records of his office
35 afford, and as such schedules or forms call for.

15. The secretary of the Bureau of Industries, shall, as Tabulated statement of returns to be made by secretary of Bureau
soon as may be, after the opening of every Session of the
Legislature, report to the Minister of Agriculture for the purpose of being laid before the Legislative Assembly, a tabulated
40 statement of all the returns hereinbefore required to be made.

16. The treasurer of the Province shall retain in his hands Moneys payable to municipalities in default to be retained.
any moneys payable to any municipality, if it is certified to
him by the secretary of the Bureau of Industries, that the
treasurer or clerk of such municipality has not made the
45 returns hereinbefore required.

17. *The Consolidated Municipal Act, 1883*, is further Declaration of office in cities, towns and villages.
amended by adding the following section thereto :

271a. Every person elected under this Act for a city, town
or incorporated village, to any office requiring a qualification
50 of property in the incumbent before he takes the declaration
of office or enters on his duties, shall make and subscribe a
solemn declaration to the effect following :

I, *A.B.*, do solemnly declare that I am a natural born (*or* naturalized)
subject of Her Majesty and have and had at the time of my election to
the office of
the property qualification necessary to entitle me to vote at municipal
elections under the provisions of The Municipal Act, and I further declare   5
that the property in respect of which I am so qualified is (*here set out the
nature of the property according to the fact*).

18. Section 272 of *The Consolidated Municipal Act, 1883*, is
amended by inserting at the beginning of the said section
immediately before the word "every," the words "except as   10
provided in the preceding section."

46 V. c. 18, s. 272 amended.

19. Sub-section 2 of section 482 of *The Consolidated Municipal Act, 1883*, is amended by inserting after the words "Act
of the Legislature," occurring therein, the words "or by-law
of the corporation."   15

46 V. c. 18, s. 482 (2) amended.

20. Sub-section 9 of section 482 of *The Consolidated
Municipal Act, 1883*, is amended by inserting in the fourth
line of the said sub-section after the word "Institute" the words
"or Free Library established under *The Free Libraries Act*, 1882."

46 V. c. 18, s. 482 (9) amended.

21. Sub-section 17 of section 482 of *The Consolidated*   20
Municipal Act, 1883, is repealed, and the following substituted
in lieu thereof:—

46 V. c. 18, s. 482 (17) repealed.

(17) For regulating the size and number of doors in churches,
theatres, halls, or other buildings, used for places of worship,
public meetings or places of amusement, and the street gates   25
leading thereto; and also the size and number of doors, halls,
stairs and other means of egress from all hospitals, schools,
colleges and other buildings of a like nature, and also the
structure of stairs and stair-railings in all such buildings; and
the strength of walls, beams and joists and their supports, and   30
for compelling the production of the plans of all such buildings
for inspection and for enforcing observance of such regulations

22. Section 482 of *The Consolidated Municipal Act, 1883*,
is further amended by adding thereto the following as sub-
sections 25 and 26 thereof.   35

46 V. c. 18, s. 482 amended.

(25). For entering upon, taking and using and acquiring so
much real property as may be required for the use of the
Corporation, for public parks, squares, boulevards, and drives
in the municipality and adjoining local municipalities, without
the consent of the owners of such real property, making due   40
compensation therefor to the parties entitled thereto, to be
determined under the provisions of this Act, by arbitration,
where the parties do not agree.

Acquiring land for parks, etc.

(26). In every case in which any municipality shall
expropriate lands in an adjoining municipality, the munici-   45
pality so expropriating such lands shall put the same in an
efficient state to be used as, and open the same to the general
public, for the purposes of such public parks, squares, boulevards and drives within a reasonable time after such expropriation, and shall maintain and keep the same in an efficient   50
state of repair; and shall provide and maintain such police
protection for such public parks, squares and drives as shall be
necessary for the safety of the public frequenting and using
same and the residents whose lands adjoin the lands so expropriated.

Provisions where land expropriated is in an adjoining municipality.

23. Section 483 of *The Consolidated Municipal Act, 1883,* is amended by adding at the end of the said section the words " and to provide by by-law for assessing and levying a rate on the ratable property in the municipality to raise the moneys 5 required for the fulfilment of such contract on the part of the municipality, in each year in which such moneys shall thereby be made payable, and for the issue of debentures for that purpose under such by-law, if the council shall so determine, without complying with the requirements of section 346." 46 V. c. 18, s. 483 amended.

10 **24**. Sub-section 1 of section 490 of *The Consolidated Municipal Act, 1883,* is amended by adding thereto the following:— 46 V. c. 18, s. 490 (1) amended.

(*b*) When a polling place has been fixed by by-law for the holding of any election, or the taking of any vote in any city, 15 town or village, and it is afterwards found that the building named as such polling place cannot be obtained, or is unsuitable for the purpose, the clerk of the municipality shall have the power to choose in lieu thereof as a polling place the nearest available building suitable for the purpose, and shall 20 post up and keep posted up a notice on the building fixed by the by-law, and in two other conspicuous places near by, directing the voters' to the place chosen aforesaid.

25. Sub-section 22 of section 490 of *The Consolidated Municipal Act 1883,* is amended by striking out the figures 25 " $100 " and substituting in lieu thereof the figures " $500." 46 V. c. 18, s. 490 (22) amended.

26. Section 490 of *The Consolidated Municipal Act, 1883,* is amended by adding thereto the following sub-sections: 46 V. c. 18, s. 490 amended.

(39) For acquiring and holding, by purchase or otherwise, for the public use of the municipality, lands situate outside 30 the limits of such township, city, town or incorporated village; but such lands so acquired shall not form part of the municipality of such township, city, town, or incorporated village, but shall continue and remain as of the municipality where situate ; and all by-laws heretofore passed by township councils 35 for the purpose of acquiring land as provided by this subsection, are hereby declared legal and binding where the by-laws shall not be contested or impeached before or at the time of the passing hereof. Acquiring land outside of municipality.

(40) For erecting and maintaining weighing machines in 40 villages or other convenient places, and charging fees for the use thereof, not being contrary to the limitations provided by sub-section 8 of section 497 of this Act. Erecting and maintaining weighing machines.

27. Sub-section 44 of said Section 496 of *The Consolidated Municipal Act, 1883,* is hereby repealed. 46 V. c. 18. s. 496 (44) repealed.

45 **28**. Section 496 of *The Consolidated Municipal Act,* 1883, is amended by adding thereto the following sub-sections:— 46 V. c. 18, s. 496 amended.

(51) For licensing and regulating the owners and keepers of stores and shops (other than taverns and shops holding licenses under *The Liquor License Act*) where tobacco, cigars or cigarettes are sold by retail, and for preventing the sale of

tobacco, cigars or cigarettes to children under the age of fourteen years, except on the written order of the parent, guardian or employer of the child.

(52) For regulating the erection and maintenance of bathing houses and boat houses and providing for the inspection there- 5 of, and for prohibiting the use thereof for illegal or immoral purposes, and for preventing the keeping of liquor for sale and the sale of liquor therein.

(53) For preventing cruelty to and the neglect of children under the age of 16 years on the part of parents, guardians, 10 and others having control over them, and for the removal of such children from the care of cruel, drunken or vicious parents or guardians, upon the order of the police magistrate or two justices of the peace.

(54) For making all needful provisions and arrangements 15 concerning children under the age of sixteen years who by reason of the neglect, crime, drunkenness or other vices of parents or guardians, or from orphanage, are suffered to be growing up without salutary parental control and education, or in circumstances exposing them to lead idle and dissolute 20 lives—and for appointing such inspectors and other officers as may be necessary to secure the carrying out of all such by-laws, rules and regulations.

46 V. c. 18, s. 503 (6) amended. **29.** Sub-section 6 of section 503 of *The Consolidated Muni-* 25 *cipal Act, 1883*, is amended by adding thereto the following proviso :—

" Provided that this sub-section shall not be qualified as respects shops or stalls occupied by butchers or others for the sale of fresh meat in quantities less than by the quarter carcase 30 within the said municipality by anything contained in sections 497 or 500 of this Act," but this amendment shall not affect pending suits.

46 V. c. 18, s. 504 (1) repealed. **30.** Sub-section 1 of section 504 of *The Consolidated Muni-* 35 *cipal Act, 1883*, is hereby repealed and the following substituted in lieu thereof :—

(1) For licensing and regulating suitable persons to keep intelligence offices for registering the names and residences of, and giving information to, or procuring servants, labourers, 40 workmen, clerks or other employees, for employers in want of the same, and for registering the names and residences of and giving information to or procuring employment for domestic servants and other labourers and any other class of servant, workman, clerk or person seeking employment ; and for fixing 45 the fees to be charged and recovered by the keepers of such offices.

46 V. c. 18, s. 505 amended. **31.** Section 505 of *The Consolidated Municipal Act, 1883* is hereby amended by adding thereto at the end thereof the 50 words following :—" Provided always that in all cases where a municipality shall have constructed gas or water works under the authority of this Act or under the authority of *The Municipal Water Works Act, 1882*, or under the authority of any special Act or Acts, or shall hereafter construct such works 55 under the authority of the said Acts or any future amendments of the same and shall have raised the money for

the purchase or construction of such works, or shall hereafter so raise the same by a general rate on the whole of the assessable property of the said corporation under a by-law or by-laws lawfully passed or to be passed, it shall be lawful for the
5 council of the city or town to raise on the credit of the said corporation such further sums as may be necessary to extend or improve the said works from time to time on the whole ratable property of the said corporation by by-laws to be passed as required by sub-section 14 of section 504 of this Act
10 and without complying with the requirements of this section."

32. Section 521 of *The Consolidated Municipal Act, 1883,* 46 V. c. 18, s. 521 amended. is amended by adding thereto the following as sub-section 13*a* thereof :

(13*a.*) For regulating the construction of dry earth closets
15 and compelling the use of the same within such limits within the municipality as may be defined by the by-law.

33. Section 522 of *The Consolidated Municipal Act, 1883,* 46 V. c. 18, s. 522 amended. is amended by adding the following sub-section thereto :—

(2) When a river or stream which forms a boundary line
20 between two municipalities becomes obstructed with driftwood or fallen timber, any one of the councils of such municipalities may cause the removal of such driftwood or fallen timber, and may pay the costs of such removal out of the general funds of the municipality.

25 **34**. Section 531 of *The Consolidated Municipal Act, 1883,* 46 V. c. 18, s. 531, amended. is amended by adding the following sub-section thereto :—

(4) In case an action is brought against a municipal corporation to recover damages sustained by reason of any obstruction, excavation or opening in a public highway, street
30 or bridge placed, made, left or maintained by any other corporation or by any person other than a servant or agent of the municipal corporation, such last mentioned corporation shall have a remedy over against such other corporation or person for and may enforce payment accordingly of the
35 damages and costs, if any, which the plaintiff in such action may recover against the municipal corporation ; provided nevertheless that such municipal corporation shall only be entitled to the said remedy over if such other corporation or person shall be or be made a party to such action and if it
40 shall be established in such action as against such other corporation or person that the damages were sustained by reason of an obstruction, excavation or opening as aforesaid placed, made, left or maintained by such other corporation or person ; and the municipal corporation may in such action have such
45 other corporation or person added as a party defendant or third party for the purposes hereof if the same is not already a defendant in the action jointly with the municipal corporation and such other corporation or person may defend any such action as well against the plaintiff's claim as against the
50 claim of the muncipal corporation to a remedy over ; and the court or judge upon the trial of such action may order costs to be paid by or to any of the parties thereto or in respect of any claim set up therein as in other cases.

8

49 V. c. 37, ss. 16, 17, repealed. **35.** Sections 16 and 17 of *The Municipal Amendment Act, 1886,* are hereby repealed.

46 V. c. 18, s. 532, amended. **36.** Section 532 of *The Consolidated Municipal Act, 1883,* is amended by adding after the word "any" in the tenth line thereof, the word "main." 5

46 V. c. 18, s. 546, repealed. **37.** Section 546 of *The Consolidated Municipal Act, 1883,* is amended by adding thereto the following as sub-section 5 thereof:—

(5) In case the council of a township or an incorporated village, and property owners interested in lands required to be 10 taken possession of, for establishing a public road, mutually agree as to the recompense or price of such lands, the council may accept a deed or deeds for the same, which shall be registered, as provided by section 547 of this Act, and in such case the publication of any by-law in the manner required by 15 sub-section 2 shall be dispensed with.

46 V. c. 18, s. 570 (10), amended. **38.** Sub-section 10 of section 570 of *The Consolidated Municipal Act, 1883,* is amended by adding the following thereto:—"And all notices of appeal shall be served upon the clerk of the municipality at least eight days prior to such court 20 of revision."

46 V. c. 18, s. 586, amended. **39.** Section 586 of *The Consolidated Municipal Act, 1883,* is amended by inserting after the word "improve". in the seventh line the word "extend," and after the word "improvements" in the eleventh and twelfth lines the words "or 25 extension."

46 V. c. 18, s. 587 (2) amended. **40.** Sub-section 2 of section 587 of *The Consolidated Municipal Act, 1883,* is amended by omitting from the second and third lines of the said sub-section the words "previous to the tenth day of February, 1876." 30

46 V. c. 18, s. 587, amended. **41.** Section 587 of *The Consolidated Municipal Act, 1883,* is amended by adding thereto the following sub-sections:—

(3) The council may from time to time change such assessment on the report of an engineer or surveyor appointed by them to examine and report on such work and repairs, subject 35 to the like rights of appeal as a person charged would have in the case of an original assessment; and the said council shall appoint a Court of Revision to consider such appeals in the manner heretofore provided.

(4) In any of the cases referred to in this and the pre- 40 ceding sections, any moneys that have been or may hereafter be advanced by the council of any municipality out of its general funds in anticipation of the levies to be made for the purposes of the said sections, shall be recouped to the municipality so soon as the moneys derived from the assessment shall 45 have been made.

46 V. c. 18, s. 592, amended. **42.** Section 592 of *The Consolidated Municipal Act, 1883,* as amended by section 31 of *The Muncipal Amendment Act, 1886,* is further amended by adding thereto the following sub-section:— 50

(2) The court, judge, or arbitrators may order that the costs
against the corporation, or parties constructing the drainage
works or any portion thereof, shall be paid by any party to
the said proceedings in whole or in part, or may apportion the
5 same, or may order that the same or any part thereof shall be
charged *pro rata* upon the lands.

43. Section 615 of *The Consolidated Municipal Act, 1883* 46 V. c. 18, s.
is hereby repealed. 615 repealed.

44. Section 33 of *The Municipal Amendment Act, 1885,* 48 V. c. 39, s.
10 is amended. by inserting after the word " necessary " in the 33 amended.
third line of the said section the words "to construct or repair
bridges or culverts on any street, lane or alley, or," and by
adding thereto the following sub-section :—

" (2) In any case when the council affirms by a two-thirds
15 vote thereof that the constructing, erecting, or making of any
bridge, culvert or embankment, benefits the municipality at
large, and that it would be inequitable to raise the whole cost
of any such improvement or work by local special assessments,
the council may pass a by-law for borrowing money by the
20 issue of debentures upon the credit of the municipality at large
to provide as the corporation's share of the cost of such improvement or work an amount not exceeding one-half of the
whole cost thereof ; and no such by-law shall require the assent
of the electors before the final passing thereof."

25 **45.** Sub-section 2 of section 618 of *The Consolidated Muni-* 46 V. c. 18, s.
cipal Act, 1883, is amended by striking out the words " the 618 (2), amend-
owner's address," occurring in the ninth line of the said sub- ed.
section, and inserting in lieu thereof the words " the address of
the person entitled to notice."

30 **46.** Section 624 of *The Consolidated Municipal Act, 1883,* 46 V. c. 18, s.
is amended by inserting after the words " frontage thereof " in 624, amended.
the eighth line thereof, the words " or according to the assessed
value thereof, and when only such latter system of assessment
shall have been adopted by a three-fourths vote of the full
35 Council."

47. Section 624 of *The Consolidated Municpal Act, 1883,* 46 V. c. 18, s.
is amended by adding thereto the following sub-section. 624, amended.

(4) The council may also by by-law define certain areas or
sections within the municipality in which all snow, ice and
40 dirt and other obstructions shall be removed from the side-
walks, streets, lanes or alleys, in such area or sections, and
may impose a special rate upon the real property therein,
according to the frontage thereof, in order to pay any expenses
incurred in removing such snow, ice, dirt, or other obstruction.

45 **48.** Sub-section 2 of section 26 of *The Municipal Amend-* 48 V. c. 39, s.
ment Act, 1885, is amended by inserting after the word 26 (2), amend-
" deepening" in the first line the word " extending," and by ed.
adding the following to said sub-section : "provided the cost
of such extension does not exceed the sum of $200, and in
every case when it exceeds that amount, proceedings shall be
50 taken under the provisions of section 586."

Powers of townships as to local improvements

49. In addition to the powers given to the council of every township by *The Consolidated Municipal Act, 1883*, and amendments thereto, the council of every township shall have all the rights and powers conferred on the councils of cities, towns and incorporated villages, by sections 612 to 624, in- 5 clusive of the said Act as heretofore, or hereby amended, respectively, as well as those conferred by sections 32 to 36, inclusive, of *The Municipal Amendment Act, 1885*, and by sections 37 to 40 inclusive of *The Municipal Amendment Act, 1886*, and by *The Municipal Waterworks Act, 1882*. 10

Cost of sewers.

50. In ascertaining and determining the cost of draining any locality or making and laying or prolonging any common sewer, the council of any city, town, or incorporated village, may estimate the cost of the construction of branch drains to the line of street, and include the cost of such branch drains in 15 making the assessment for such drains or common sewers, as a local improvement pursuant to section 612 of *The Consolidated Municipal Act, 1883*, and amendments thereto.

Boundaries of marsh lands.

51. The council of every township municipality may by by-law declare that in the case of any lands, the boundary 20 line, or any part of the boundary line whereof passes through a marsh or swamp, or any land covered with water, the same shall, so far as respects that part of such boundary line which so passes through a marsh or swamp, or land covered with water, be deemed to be wholly enclosed within the meaning of 25 section 1 of *The Act respecting Petty Trespassers*, if posts are put up and maintained along such part of such line at distances which will permit of each being clearly visible from the adjoining post.

Petition for construction of water works.

52. In case a petition, signed by two hundred qualified elec- 30 tors in incorporated towns, or by one hundred qualified electors in incorporated villages or in rural municipalities, is presented to the council of such town, incorporated village or rural municipality, asking for the construction of water-works under the powers conferred on municipal corporations by *The Muni-* 35 *cipal Water-works Act, 1882* :

1. It shall be the duty of such council to submit a by-law for the construction of such water-works, to the vote of the ratepayers of the said town, incorporated village or munici-pality, and such council shall, forthwith, prepare a by-law direct- 40 ing the submission of the question, in accordance with the prayer of the petitioners, or in such form as may be approved by the vote of two thirds of the members of such council, and shall submit the same to the electors for approval, or otherwise, within six weeks after the receipt of the petition by the 45 council ;

2. The council before submitting such by-law, may require the petitioners to deposit with the treasurer of the municipality an amount sufficient to cover the probable cost of submitting the by-law to the electors, but not exceeding the sum of $150; 50

3. In the event of the by-law receiving the sanction and consent of a majority of the electors of such corporation, then the money so deposited, shall be, forthwith, refunded to the Petitioners ;

4. Should the by-law be rejected by a majority of the electors of such corporation, then the money so deposited, shall be forfeited to such corporation, or so much thereof, as may be necessary to cover the costs of submitting the said by-law;

5   5. The power of municipal councils shall not be deemed to be abridged by this Act, except as expressly stated herein;

6. The proceedings in taking such vote and the persons having a right to vote, shall be the same as nearly as may be, as are required by *The Consolidated Municipal Act, 1883*, 10 in case of by-laws creating debts.

53. If the by-law be approved of by the majority of such electors, it shall be the duty of such council to pass the said by-law, and forthwith to proceed with the construction of such works, provided always that the council may for any good cause, 15 if deemed expedient by a vote of two thirds of its members, hold the works in abeyance until after the next general municipal election. <small>If by-law approved council to construct works.</small>

54. Any municipality constructing works under *The Municipal Water-works Act, 1882*, or any company incorporated 20 for the supply of water or gas, or water and gas, shall have power to supply consumers in any municipality adjacent to the municipality constructing such works, or for the supply of which such company was incorporated, and to lay all necessary pipes for that purpose: provided, always, that before such 25 pipes shall be laid along any street or road in such adjacent municipality, the consent of the council of the municipality for the supply of which the said works were constructed, shall be obtained, and also that the said streets or roads shall be replaced, as nearly as possible, in the same condition as they 30 were in before such pipes were laid. <small>Power to supply gas or water outside of municipality.</small>

55. All provisions of *The Municipal Act* or Acts, in so far as they apply to elections, and to the prevention of corrupt practices at elections shall apply to the preceding three sections, except so far as such Act or Acts would be incon- 35 sistent therewith. <small>Provisions respecting elections to apply to preceding 3 sections.</small>

56. Section 17 of chapter 175 of the Revised Statutes is hereby amended by adding thereto the following: "The clerk shall within six days after his appointment, transmit to the Provincial Treasurer notice of the formation of the munici- 40 pality with a description of its boundaries or limits." <small>R. S. O. c. 175, s. 17, amended.</small>

1st Session, 6th Legislature, 50 Vic., 1887.

BILL.

An Act to further amend the Municipal Act.

(Re-printed as amended by Municipal Committee.)

First Reading, 22nd March, 1887.
Second   "   28th   "   1887.

Mr. HARDY.

BILL.

An Act to further amend the Municipal Act.

HER MAJESTY, by and with the advice and consent of the Legislative Assembly of the Province of Ontario, enacts as follows ;—

1. This Act may be cited as *The Municipal Amendment* Short title.
5 *Act, 1887.*

☞ **2.** Section 73 of *The Consolidated Municipal Act, 1883*, as 46 V. c. 18, s. amended by *The Municipal Amendment Act, 1885*, and as 73, and amendments further amended by *The Municipal Amendment Act, 1886*, repealed. is hereby repealed, and the following substituted therefor :—

10 **73.** No person shall be qualified to be elected a mayor, Qualification alderman, reeve, deputy-reeve or councillor of any munici- aldermen, etc. pality, unless such person resides within the municipality, or within two miles thereof, and is a natural born or naturalized subject of Her Majesty, and a male of the full age of twenty-
15 one years, and is not disqualified under this Act, and has, or whose wife has, at the time of the election, as proprietor or tenant, a legal or equitable freehold or leasehold, or partly freehold and partly leasehold, or partly legal and partly equitable, rated in his own name, or in the name of his wife, on
20 the last revised assessment roll of the municipality, to at least the value following, over and above all charges, liens and incumbrances affecting the same :

☞ 1. In incorporated villages—Freehold to $200 or leasehold to $400 ;

25 ☞ 2. In towns—Freehold to $600, or leasehold to $1,200 ;

☞ 3. In cities—Freehold to $1,000, or leasehold to $2,000 ;

☞ 4. In townships—Freehold to $400, or leasehold to $800 ;

☞ And so in the same proportions in all municipalities, in case the property is partly freehold and partly leasehold ;

30 ☞ But if within any municipality any such person is, at the time of election, in actual occupation of any such freehold, rated in his own name, or in the name of his wife, on the last revised assessment roll of the said municipality, he will be entitled to be elected, if the value at which such freehold is
35 actually rated in said assessment roll amounts to not less than $2,000, and for that purpose the said value shall not be affected or reduced by any lien, incumbrance or charge existing on or affecting such freehold. ☜

3. Section 81 of *The Consolidated Municipal Act, 1883*, is 46 V. c. 18, s.
40 amended by adding at the end thereof the words, " but any 81, amended.

person who is entitled to vote and who produces and leaves
with the deputy returning officer at the time of the tendering
of the vote a certificate from the treasurer of the municipality, or the collector of taxes, shewing that the taxes in
respect of which the default had been made have since been 5
paid, shall be entitled to vote; and the deputy-returning
officer shall file the certificate, receive the vote and note the
same on the defaulters' lists."

46 V. c. 18, s. 99, amended.
4. Section 99 of *The Consolidated Municipal Act, 1883,* 10
is amended by adding at the commencement thereof, the following words :—

"In any case where a deputy returning officer refuses or
neglects to attend at the time and place he is required by the
returning officer to receive his voters' lists, and other election 15
papers, the *clerk of the municipality* os returning officer shall
appoint another person to act in his place and stead, and the
person so appointed shall have all the powers and authority
that he would have had if he had been appointed by by-law.',

46 V. c. 18, s. 138, amend'd.
5. Section 138 of *The Consolidated Municipal Act, 1883,* 20
is amended by striking out all the words after the word
" therein " in the sixth line of the said section and substituting
the following therefor, " or when he is a non-resident or is not
entitled to vote in the ward or polling sub-division where he
resides, then, where he first votes and there only. " 25

46 V. c. 18, s. 139, amended.
6. Section 139 of *The Consolidated Municipal Act, 1883,*
is amended by adding thereto the following sub-section.

(2) The receipt by any voter of a ballot paper within the
polling booth shall be *prima facie* evidence that he has there
and then voted. 30

46 V. c. 18, s. 225, repealed.
7. Section 225 of *The Consolidated Municipal Act, 1883,*
is hereby repealed, and the following substituted therefor :—

Casting vote.
225. In case of an equality of votes on the election of the
head of any county council, or provisional county council, then
of those present, the reeve, or in his absence, the deputy-reeve 35
of the municipality which for the preceding year had the
greatest equalized assessment, shall have a second and casting
vote.

46 V. c. 18, s. 246 (49 V. c. 37, s. 3), re-pealed.
8. Section 246 of *The Consolidated Municipal Act, 1883,*
as amended by section 3 of *The Municipal Amendment Act,* 40
1886, is hereby repealed.

46 V. c. 18, ss. 247-251, 264, repealed.
9. Sections 247, 248, 249, 250, 251 and 264 of *The Consoli-*
dated Municipal Act, 1883, are hereby repealed.

46 V. c. 18, s. 262 repealed Auditors to
10. Section 260 of *The Consolidated Municipal Act, 1883,* is
amended by adding thereto the following words : " And in the 45
event of any auditor so appointed to audit the accounts of the
county refusing, or being unable to act, then the head of the
council shall nominate another person to act in his stead."

46 V. c. 18, s. 260, amended.
11. Section 262 of *The Consolidated Municipal Act, 1883,*
is repealed and the following substituted in lieu thereof : 50

3

The auditors shall prepare in duplicate an abstract of the Auditors to prepare abstract and statement of receipts and expenditure. receipts, expenditure, assets and liabilities of the corporation, and also a detailed statement of the same in such form as the Council directs. They shall make a report on all accounts audited by
5 them and a special report of any expenditure made contrary to law. The auditors shall transmit one copy of the abstract to the secretary of the Bureau of Industries, Toronto, and shall file the other, together with the detailed statement and reports in the office of the clerk of the council within one month after their
10 appointment, and thereafter any inhabitant or ratepayer of the municipality may inspect the same at all reasonable hours and may by himself or his agent take at his own expense take a copy thereof, or extracts therefrom.

12. The treasurer of every municipality shall, on or before Returns to be made by treasurers to Bureau of Industries.
15 the first day of May in each year, under a penalty of $20 in case of default, furnish to the secretary of the Bureau of Industries, Toronto, on schedules or forms furnished by said secretary and approved by the Lieutenant-Governor in Council, such information or statistics regarding the finances or accounts of
20 the municipality, as such schedules or forms call for.

13. The clerk of every municipality shall in each year, Returns to be made by clerks to Bureau of Industries. within one week after the final revision of the assessment roll, under a penalty of $20 in case of default, make a return to the secretary of the Bureau of Industries, Toronto, on schedules or
25 forms furnished by the said secretary, and approved by the Lieutenant-Governor in Council, of such statistics or information as the assessment roll or other records of his office afford, and as such schedules or forms call for.

14. The secretary of the Bureau of Industries, shall, as Tabulated statement of returns to be made by secretary of Bureau
30 soon as may be, after the opening of every Session of the Legislature, report to the Minister of Agriculture for the purpose of being laid before the Legislative Assembly, a tabulated statement of all the returns hereinbefore required to be made.

15. The treasurer of the Province shall retain in his hands Moneys payable to municipalities in default to be retained.
35 any moneys payable to any municipality, if it is certified to him by the secretary of the Bureau of Industries, that the treasurer or clerk of such municipality has not made the returns hereinbefore required.

16. Sub-section 2 of section 482 of *The Consolidated Muni-* 46 V. c. 18, s. 482 (2) amended.
40 *cipal Act, 1883*, is amended by inserting after the words "Act of the Legislature," occurring therein, the words "or by-law of the corporation."

17. Sub-section 9 of section 482 of *The Consolidated* 46 V. c. 18, s. 482 (9) amended. *Municipal Act, 1883*, is amended by inserting in the fourth
45 line of the said sub-section after the word "Institute" the words "or Free Library established under *The Free Libraries Act, 1882*."

18. Sub-section 17 of section 482 of *The Consolidated* 46 V. c. 18, s. 482 (17) repealed. *Municipal Act, 1883*, is repealed, and the following substituted in lieu thereof:—

50 (17) For regulating the size and number of doors in churches, theatres, halls, or other buildings, used for places of worship,

public meetings or places of amusement, and the street gates leading thereto; and also the size and number of doors, halls, stairs and other means of egress from all hospitals, schools, colleges and other buildings of a like nature, and also the structure of stairs and stair-railings in all such buildings ; and 5 the strength of walls, beams and joists and their supports, and for compelling the production of the plans of all such buildings for inspection and for enforcing observance of such regulations.

19. Section 482 of *The Consolidated Municipal Act, 1883*, is further amended by adding thereto the following as sub- 10 sections 25 and 26 thereof.

46 V. c. 18, s 482 amended.

Acquiring land for parks, etc.

(25). For entering upon, taking and using and acquiring so much real property as may be required for the use of the Corporation, for public parks, squares, boulevards, and drives in the municipality and adjoining local municipalities, without 15 the consent of the owners of such real property, making due compensation therefor to the parties entitled thereto, to be determined under the provisions of this Act, by arbitration where the parties do not agree.

Provisions where land expropriated is in an adjoining municipality.

(26). In every case in which any municipality shall 20 expropriate lands in an adjoining municipality, the municipality so expropriating such lands shall put the same in an efficient state to be used as, and open the same to the general public, for the purposes of such public parks, squares, boulevards and drives within a reasonable time after such expropri- 25 ation, and shall maintain and keep the same in an efficient state of repair; and shall provide and maintain such police protection for such public parks, squares and drives as shall be necessary for the safety of the public frequenting and using same and the residents whose lands adjoin the lands so ex- 30 propriated.

46 V. c. 18, s. 490 (1) amended.

20. Sub-section 1 of section 490 of *The Consolidated Municipal Act, 1883*, is amended by adding thereto the following :—

(b) When a polling place has been fixed by by-law for the 35 holding of any election, or the taking of any vote in any city, town or village, and it is afterwards found that the building named as such polling place cannot be obtained, or is unsuitable for the purpose, the clerk of the municipality shall have the power to choose in lieu thereof as a polling place the 40 nearest available building suitable for the purpose, and shall post up and keep posted up a notice on the building fixed by the by-law, and in two other conspicuous places near by, directing the voters' to the place chosen a aforesaid.

46 V. c. 18, s. 490 (22) amended.

21. Sub-section 22 of section 490 of *The Consolidated* 45 *Municipal Act 1883*, is amended by striking out the figures " $100 " and substituting in lieu thereof the figures " $500."

46 V. c. 18, s. 490 amended.

22. Section 490 of *The Consolidated Municipal Act, 1883* is amended by adding thereto the following sub-sections:

Acquiring land outside of municipality.

(39) For acquiring and holding, by purchase or otherwise 50 for the public use of the municipality, lands situate outside the limits of such township, city, town or incorporated village;

but such lands so acquired shall not form part of the municipality of such township, city, town, or incorporated village, but shall continue and remain as of the municipality where situate ; and all by-laws heretofore passed by township councils
5 for the purpose of acquiring land as provided by this subsection, are hereby declared *as* legal and binding where the by-laws shall not be contested or impeached before or at the time of the passing hereof *as if the lands were within the limits of the municipality the council of which passed the*
10 *by-law.*

(40) For erecting and maintaining weighing machines in villages or other convenient places, and charging fees for the use thereof, not being contrary to the limitations provided by sub-section 8 of section 497 of this Act. Erecting and maintaining weighing machines.

15 **23.** Sub-section 44 of said section 496 of *The Consolidated Municipal Act, 1883*, is hereby repealed. 46 V. c. 18. s. 496 (44) repealed.

24. Section 496 of *The Consolidated Municipal Act, 1883*, is amended by adding thereto the following sub-sections:— 46 V. c. 18, s. 496 amended.

(51) For licensing and regulating the owners and keepers of
20 stores and shops (other than taverns and shops holding licenses under *The Liquor License Act*) where tobacco, cigars or cigarettes are sold by retail, and for preventing the sale of tobacco, cigars or cigarettes to children under the age of fourteen years, except on the written order of the parent,
25 guardian or employer of the child.

(52) For inspecting public bathing houses and boat-houses, or premises wholly or partly used for boat-house purposes, and for preventing the use thereof for illegal or immoral purposes.

30 **25.** Sub-section 6 of section 503 of *The Consolidated Municipal Act, 1883*, is amended by adding thereto the following proviso:— 46 V. c. 18, s. 503 (6) amended.

"Provided that this sub-section shall not be qualified as respects shops or stalls occupied by butchers or others for the
35 sale of fresh meat in quantities less than by the quarter carcase within the said municipality by anything contained in sections 497 or 500 of this Act," but this amendment shall not affect pending suits *or proceedings.*

26. Sub section 1 of section 504 of *The Consolidated Municipal Act, 1883*, is hereby repealed and the following substituted in lieu thereof:— 46 V. c. 18, s. 504 (1) repealed.
40

(1) For licensing and regulating suitable persons to keep intelligence offices for registering the names and residences of, and giving information to, or procuring servants, labourers,
45 workmen, clerks or other employees, for employers in want of the same, and for registering the names and residences of and giving information to or procuring employment for domestic servants and other labourers and any other class of servant, workman, clerk or person seeking employment; and for fixing
50 the fees to be charged and recovered by the keepers of such offices.

46 V. c. 18, s. 521 amended. **27.** Section 521 of *The Consolidated Municipal Act, 1883,* is amended by adding thereto the following as sub-section 13*a* thereof :

(13*a*.) For regulating the construction of dry earth closets and compelling the use of the same within such limits within 5 the municipality as may be defined by the by-law.

46 V. c. 18, s. 522 amended. **28.** Section 522 of *The Consolidated Municipal Act, 1883,* is amended by adding the following sub-section thereto :—

(2) When a river or stream which forms a boundary line between two municipalities becomes obstructed with driftwood 10 or fallen timber, any one of the councils of such municipalities may cause the removal of such driftwood or fallen timber, and may pay the costs of such removal out of the general funds of the municipality.

46 V. c. 18, s. 531, amended. **29.** Section 531 of *The Consolidated Municipal Act, 1883,* 15 is amended by adding the following sub-section thereto :—

(4) In case an action is brought against a municipal corporation to recover damages sustained by reason of any obstruction, excavation or opening in a public highway, street or bridge placed, made, left or maintained by any other cor- 20 poration or by any person other than a servant or agent of the municipal corporation, such last mentioned corporation shall have a remedy over against such other corporation or person for and may enforce payment accordingly of the damages and costs, if any, which the plaintiff in such action 25 may recover against the municipal corporation ; provided nevertheless that such municipal corporation shall only be entitled to the said remedy over if such other corporation or person shall be or be made a party to such action and if it shall be established in such action as against such other cor- 30 poration or person that the damages were sustained by reason of an obstruction, excavation or opening as aforesaid placed, made, left or maintained by such other corporation or person ; and the municipal corporation may in such action have such other corporation or person added as a party defendant or 35 third party for the purposes hereof if the same is not already a defendant in the action jointly with the municipal corporation and such other corporation or person may defend any such action as well against the plaintiff's claim as against the claim of the muncipal corporation to a remedy over ; and the 40 court or judge upon the trial of such action may order costs to be paid by or to any of the parties thereto or in respect of any claim set up therein as in other cases.

46 V. c. 18, s. 532, amended. **30.** Section 532 of *The Consolidated Municipal Act, 1883,* is amended by adding after the word " any " in the tenth line 45 thereof, the word " main."

46 V. c. 18, s. 534. amended. **31.** Section 534 of *The Consolidated Municipal Act, 1883,* is amended by adding after the word " any " in the last line thereof the word " main."

46 V. c. 18, s. 546, repealed. **32.** Section 546 of *The Consolidated Municipal Act, 1883,* 50 is amended by adding thereto the following as sub-section 5 thereof:—

(5) In case the council of a township or an incorporated village, and property owners interested in lands required to be taken, possession of, for establishing a public road, mutually agree as to the recompense or price of such lands, the council 5 may accept a deed or deeds for the same, which shall be registered, as provided by section 547 of this Act, and in such case the publication of any by-law in the manner required by sub-section 2 shall be dispensed with.

33. Sub-section 10 of section 570 of *The Consolidated* 46 V. c. 18, s.
10 *Municipal Act, 1883,* is amended by adding the following 570 (10), amended.
thereto:—"And all notices of appeal shall be served upon the clerk of the municipality at least eight days prior to such court of revision;" ☞ but the Court of Revision may though such notice be not given permit the appeal to be heard on such 15 conditions as to giving notice to all persons interested and otherwise as may seem just. ☜

34. Section 586 of *The Consolidated Municipal Act, 1883,* 46 V. c. 18, s
is amended by inserting after the word "improve" in the 586, amended.
seventh line the word "extend," and after the word "improve-
20 ments" in the eleventh and twelfth lines the words "or extension."

35. Sub-section 2 of section 587 of *The Consolidated Muni-* 46 V. c. 18, s.
cipal Act, 1883, is amended by omitting from the second and 587 (2) amend-
third lines of the said sub-section the words "previous to the ed.
25 tenth day of February, 1876."

36. Section 587 of *The Consolidated Municipal Act, 1883,* 46 V. c. 18, s.
is amended by adding thereto the following sub-sections:— 587, amended.

(3) The council may from time to time change such assessment on the report of an engineer or surveyor appointed by 30 them to examine and report on such work and repairs, subject to the like rights of appeal as a person charged would have in the case of an original assessment; and the said council shall appoint a Court of Revision to consider such appeals in the manner heretofore provided.

35 (4) In any of the cases referred to in this and the preceding sections, any moneys that have been or may hereafter be advanced by the council of any municipality out of its general funds in anticipation of the levies to be made for the purposes of the said sections, shall be recouped to the munici-
40 pality so soon as the moneys derived from the assessment shall have been made.

37. Section 615 of *The Consolidated Municipal Act, 1883,* 46 V. c. 18, s.
is hereby repealed. 615 repealed.

38. Section 33 of *The Municipal Amendment Act, 1885,* 48 V. c. 39, s.
45 is amended by inserting after the word "necessary" in the 33 amended.
third line of the said section the words "to construct or repair bridges or culverts on any street, lane or alley, or," and by adding thereto the following sub-section:—

"(2) In any case when the council affirms by a two-thirds 50 vote thereof that the constructing, erecting, or making of any bridge, culvert or embankment, benefits the municipality at

large, and that it would be inequitable to raise the whole cost
of any such improvement or work by local special assessments,
the council may pass a by-law for borrowing money by the
issue of debentures upon the credit of the municipality at large
to provide as the corporation's share of the cost of such im- 5
provement or work an amount not exceeding one-half of the
whole cost thereof ; and no such by-law shall require the assent
of the electors before the final passing thereof."

46 V. c. 18, s. 618 (2), amended. **39**. Sub-section 2 of section 618 of *The Consolidated Municipal Act, 1883,* is amended by striking out the words " the 10
owner's address," occurring in the ninth line of the said sub-
section, and inserting in lieu thereof the words " the address of
the person entitled to notice."

46 V. c. 18, s. 624, amended. **40**. Section 624 of *The Consolidated Municipal Act, 1883,*
is amended by inserting after the words " frontage thereof " in 15
the eighth line thereof, the words " or according to the assessed
value thereof, when only such · latter system of assessment
shall have been adopted by a three-fourths vote of the full
Council."

46 V. c. 18, s. 624, amended. **41**. Section 624 of *The Consolidated Municipal Act, 1883,* 20
is amended by adding thereto the following sub-section :

(4) The council may also by by-law define certain areas or
sections within the municipality in which all snow, ice and
dirt and other obstructions shall be removed from the side-
walks, streets, lanes or alleys, in such area or sections, and 25
may impose a special rate upon the real property therein,
according to the frontage thereof, in order to pay any expenses
incurred in removing such snow, ice, dirt, or other obstruction.

48 V. c. 39, s. 26 (2), amended. **42**. Sub-section 2 of section 26 of *The Municipal Amendment Act, 1885,* is amended by inserting after the word 30
" deepening" in the first line the word " extending," and by
adding the following to said sub-section : " provided the cost
of such extension does not exceed the sum of $200, and in
every case when it exceeds that amount, proceedings shall be
taken under the provisions of section 586."   35

Powers of townships as to local improvements. **43**. In addition to the powers given to the council of every
township by *The Consolidated Municipal Act, 1883,* and
amendments thereto, the council of every township shall have
all the rights and powers conferred on the councils of cities,
towns and incorporated villages, by sections 612 to 624, in- 40
clusive, of the said Act as heretofore, or hereby amended, respectively, as well as those conferred by sections 32 to 36,
inclusive, of *The Municipal Amendment Act, 1885,* and by
sections 37 to 40 inclusive of *The Municipal Amendment
Act, 1886,* and by *The Municipal Waterworks Act, 1882.*   45

Cost of sewers. **44**. In ascertaining and determining the cost of draining
any locality or making and laying or prolonging any common
sewer, the council of any city, town, or incorporated village,
may estimate the cost of the construction of branch drains to
the line of street, and include the cost of such branch drains in 50
making the assessment for such drains or common sewers, as
a local improvement pursuant to section 612 of *The Consolidated Municipal Act, 1883,* and amendments thereto.

45. The council of every township municipality may by **Boundaries of marsh lands.** by-law declare that in the case of any lands, the boundary line, or any part of the boundary line whereof passes through a marsh or swamp, or any land covered with water, the same 5 shall, so far as respects that part of such boundary line which so passes through a marsh or swamp, or land covered with water, be deemed to be wholly enclosed within the meaning of section 1 of *The Act respecting Petty Trespassers*, if posts are put up and maintained along such part of such line at dis-10 tances which will permit of each being clearly visible from the adjoining post.

46. In case a petition, signed by two hundred qualified elec- **Petition for construction of water works.** tors in incorporated towns, or by one hundred qualified electors in incorporated villages or in rural municipalities, is presented 15 to the council of such town, incorporated village or rural municipality, asking for the construction of water-works under the powers conferred on municipal corporations by *The Municipal Water-works Act, 1882* :

1. It shall be the duty of such council to submit a by-law 20 for the construction of such water-works, to the vote of the ratepayers of the said town, incorporated village or municipality, and such council shall, forthwith, prepare a by-law directing the submission of the question, in accordance with the prayer of the petitioners, or in such form as may be approved 25 by the vote of two thirds of the members of such council, and shall submit the same to the electors for approval, or otherwise, within six weeks after the receipt of the petition by the council ;

2. The council before submitting such by-law, may require the 30 petitioners to deposit with the treasurer of the municipality an amount sufficient to cover the probable cost of submitting the by-law to the electors, but not exceeding the sum of $150 ;

3. In the event of the by-law receiving the sanction and consent of a majority of the electors of such corporation, then 35 the money so deposited, shall be, forthwith, refunded to the petitioners ;

4. Should the by-law be rejected by a majority of the electors of such corporation, then the money so deposited, shall be forfeited to such corporation, or so much thereof, as may be 40 necessary to cover the costs of submitting the said by-law ;

5. The power of municipal councils shall not be deemed to be abridged by this Act, except as expressly stated herein ;

6. The proceedings in taking such vote and the persons having a right to vote, shall be the same as nearly as may be, 45 as are required by *The Consolidated Municipal Act, 1883*, in case of by-laws creating debts.

47. If the by-law be approved of by the majority of such **If by-law approved council to construct works.** electors, it shall be the duty of such council to pass the said by-law, and forthwith to proceed with the construction of such 50 works, provided always that the council may for any good cause, if deemed expedient by a vote of two thirds of its members, hold the works in abeyance until after the next general municipal election.

Provisions respecting elections to apply to preceding 3 sections.

48. All provisions of *The Municipal Act* or Acts, in so far as they apply to elections, and to the prevention of corrupt practices at elections shall apply to the preceding *two* sections, except so far as such Act or Acts would be inconsistent therewith. 5

R. S. O. c. 175, s. 17, amended.

.**49** Section 17 of chapter 175 of the Revised Statutes is hereby amended by adding thereto the following: "The clerk shall within six days after his appointment, transmit to the Provincial Treasurer notice of the formation of the municipality with a description of its boundaries or limits." 10

No. 108.

1st Session, 6th Legislature, 50 Vic., 1887.

BILL.

An Act to further amend the Municipal Act.

(Reprinted as amended by Committee of the Whole House.)

First Reading, 22nd March, 1887.
Second "   28th "   1887.

Mr. Hardy.

TORONTO:
Printed by Warwick & Sons, 26 and 28 Front St. W.

An Act to Confirm and Establish a certain Survey of
part of the Township of Sunnidale in the County
of Simcoe.

WHEREAS, in the original survey of the township of Sunni- Preamble.
dale performed by deputy surveyor, Thomas Kelly,
under instructions from the Surveyor General dated, the
fifteenth day of August, 1831, and the ninth of August, 1832,
5 that portion lying between the Sunnidale road lots and the
eastern boundary of the township in concessions numbers one
to eight inclusive, was either not surveyed or the survey was
obliterated; and whereas about the year 1861 a private survey
of part of the said portion was made by provincial land sur-
10 veyor William Sanders, by which some of the inhabitants made
their improvements; and whereas in compliance with the petition of the municipal council of the corporation of the township of Sunnidale, dated the twenty-second of August, 1868,
instructions were issued by the Commissioner of Crown Lands
20 to provincial land surveyor Henry Creswicke, Junior, dated
the fifteenth of January, 1869, to survey the easterly part of
the township of Sunnidale and to plant monuments at the
front angles of the lots along the concession lines; and whereas
the said Henry Creswicke, Junior, on making the survey in
25 accordance with the provisions of chapter 66 of the Consolidated Statutes of Canada (now chapter 146 of the Revised
Statutes of Ontario) found that great injury would accrue to
many of the inhabitants if said survey was carried out or confirmed, owing to their having made their improvements accord-
30 ing to the survey by provincial land surveyor Sanders aforesaid; and whereas the said Henry Creswicke, Junior, was in-
structed in the year 1872 by the Commissioner of Crown
Lands to make certain modifications in his survey, by which
the said inhabitants would, as nearly as possible, occupy the
35 lands cleared by them; and whereas the said Henry Creswicke,
Junior, made said modifications and planted posts at the angles
of the lots on the concession lines aforesaid; and whereas at a
public meeting held at New Lowell, in the township of Sunnidale, on the twenty-seventh of October, 1881, in pursuance of a
40 public notice thereof, attended by sixty owners of land interested, it was resolved that the survey by the said Henry Creswicke, Junior, was satisfactory so far as it related to the first,
sixth, seventh and eighth concessions; and whereas there was
a conflict of opinion as to the limits between certain lots in
45 the second, third, fourth and fifth concessions, which differences of opinion have been since satisfactorily settled, and
whereas it is expedient that the said survey be established and
confirmed except in the matter of certain changes hereinafter
mentioned;

Therefore Her Majesty, by and with the advice and consent of the Legislative Assembly of the Province of Ontario, enacts as follows :—

1. Save and except as hereafter mentioned the survey of that part of the township of Sunnidale, made by provincial 5 land surveyor Henry Creswicke, Junior, under instructions from the Commissioner of Crown Lands, dated the twenty-first of October, 1872, that is to say, that portion lying between the Sunnidale road lots and the eastern boundary of the township in concessions numbers one to eight inclusive, is hereby 10 declared to be the true and unalterable survey thereof, and all posts or monuments placed or planted at the front angles of the lots by the said Henry Creswicke, Junior, are hereby declared to be the true and unalterable boundaries thereof, and the course of the division or side-lines of the lots shall be governed by 15 the course of the proof-line run by the said Henry Creswicke, Junior, between lots numbers eighteen and nineteen, through the several concessions.

Survey of Oct. 21, 1872, confirmed as to the part of Sunnidale between the Sunnidale road lots and the eastern boundary of the township, in concessions one to eight, with certain exceptions.

2. Where the owners of land lying between the Sunnidale road and side-road allowance between lots numbers twenty- 20 one and twenty-two, have agreed to have the limits of their lots drawn from posts or monuments planted as shown on a plan of record in the Department of Crown Lands, that is to say, lots numbers seventeen, eighteen, nineteen, twenty and twenty-one in the second concession, and lots numbers twenty- 25 five and twenty-six on the Sunnidale road, the side-lines of the above named lots, and the rear lines of the Sunnidale road lots above mentioned shall be drawn from posts planted on the front of the second concession, as shown on plan aforesaid.

Provisions as to lots between Sunnidale road and road allowance between lots 21 and 22, in second concession.

3. In the case of the lots in the third concession lying be- 30 tween the Sunnidale road and side-road allowance between lots numbers twenty-one and twenty-two, the side-lines of lots seventeen and eighteen shall be drawn from posts or monuments planted in front and rear, as shown on the plan aforesaid, and the side-lines of lots numbers nineteen, twenty, and 35 twenty-one, shall be drawn from posts or monuments planted at the front angles of the lots, as shown on the plan aforesaid.

Side-lines of lots 17 and 18 and 19-21, in third concession.

4. In the case of the lots in the fourth concession lying between the Sunnidale road and side road allowance between 40 lots numbers eighteen and nineteen, the side-lines of lots numbers seventeen and eighteen and the rear line of the Sunnidale road lots, shall be drawn from posts or monuments planted at the front and rear angles of the lots, as shown on plan aforesaid. 45

Side-lines of lots 17 and 18, in fourth concession.

5. In the case of the lots in the fifth concession lying between the Sunnidale road and the side-road allowance between lots numbers eighteen and nineteen, the side-lines of the lots numbers seventeen and eighteen and the rear line of the Sunnidale road lots, shall be drawn from the posts or monuments 50 planted at the front angles of the lots, as shown on plan aforesaid.

Side-lines of lots 17 and 18, in fifth concession.

6. The westerly limit of lot letter Z, in concessions one to five inclusive shall be the line drawn from the posts or monuments planted between said lot letter Z, and lot number 5 twenty-four in front of the first concession, and between said lot letter Z, and lot number twenty-three in the second concession, and from the posts or monuments planted between said lot letter Z and lot number twenty-three in the third concession, and said lot letter Z and lot twenty-one in the 10 fourth concession, and the limit between said lot letter Z and lot number twenty-one in the fifth concession shall be a line drawn on the same course as the last mentioned limit from the post or monument planted between said lot letter Z and lot number twenty-one in front of said fifth concession.

Westerly limit of lot letter Z, in concessions one to five.

15 **7.** A certified copy of plan of survey of that part of the township of Sunnidale hereinbefore referred to shall be deposited by the Commissioner of Crown Lands in the registry office of the county of Simcoe immediately after this Act comes in force.

Plan of survey to be deposited in registry office of County of Simcoe.

20 **8.** The survey of the town plot of Rippon, situated on parts of lots numbers twenty-two and twenty-three in said first concession of Sunnidale, as laid out by provincial land surveyor William Hawkins, under instructions from the Surveyor General, dated the thirtieth of May, 1833, never having been 25 acted on, is hereby done away with, save and except so far as relates to lot number eleven, Essa Street, patented to one James F. Smith, on the fifth of December, 1836, and to lot number twelve, Essa Street, patented to one John Bingham, on the twenty-third of November, 1835.

Survey of town plot of Rippon cancelled.

Exceptions.

30 **9.** Any party who by reason of this Act suffers any injury or damage, shall be compensated by the party or parties benefited by such change; the compensation so to be paid, and the persons to pay and receive the same, shall be ascertained by a sworn provincial land surveyor appointed by the Commissioner 35 of Crown Lands, and his decision, when approved of by the Commissioner of Crown Lands, shall be final.

Compensation to parties injured by Act.

No. 109.

1st Session, 6th Legislature, 50 Vic., 1887.

BILL.

An Act to confirm and establish a certain survey of part of the Township of Sunnidale, in the County of Simcoe.

First Reading, 22nd March, 1887.

BILL.

An Act to amend the High School Act.

HER MAJESTY, by and with the advice and consent of the Legislative Assembly of Ontario, enacts as follows :—

1. Section 10 of *The High Schools Act, 1885*, is amended by 5 adding thereto the following sub-sections : 48 V. c. 50, s. 10 amended.

(2) It shall be lawful for the municipal council of a city to establish as many high schools in such city as they may deem expedient, subject always to the approval of the Lieutenant-Governor in Council. Establishment of high schools in cities.

10 (3) Where more than one high school is established in a city, the municipal council thereof shall appoint six trustees for each additional high school, but the High School Board for the city shall, nevertheless, to all intents and purposes, be one board and one corporation. Additional trustees.

15 **3.** Section 22 of the said Act is amended by striking out all the words between " February " in the second line and the word " and " in the fifth line, and by inserting after the word " secretary " in the sixth line the words " and treasurer or secretary-treasurer." 48 V. c. 50, s. 22 amended.

20 **5.** Section 35 of the said Act is amended by adding thereto the following sub-section : 48 V. c. 50, s. 35 amended.

(4) Nothing in this section contained shall be construed to mean that the municipal council may not if deemed expedient, without submitting the same to a vote of the rate-25 payers of such municipality, as required by *The Consolidated Municipal Act, 1883*, for the creating of debts, pass a by-law for the purpose of raising or borrowing money, on the requisition of the Public School Board, for any of the purposes named in this section.

30 **6.** Section 36 of the said Act is amended by striking out the words " county, and city, and of every town separated from the county 'for municipal purposes," in the first line, and inserting in lieu thereof the word " municipality." 48 V. c. 50, s. 36 amended.

7. Section 54 is amended by inserting before the word 35 " five," in the sixth line, the word " twenty." 48 V. c. 50, s. 54, amended.

8. Section 56 is amended by striking out the words " shall be entitled to " and inserting in lieu thereof the words " may be paid." 48 V. c. 50, s. 56, amended.

9. The following sections shall be added to the said Act:—

Authorized Books.

Only authorized text-books to be used.

(60) No teacher shall use or permit to be used as text books any books in a High School, except such as are authorized by the Education Department, and no portion of the Legislative 5 or Municipal grant shall be paid to any school in which unauthorized books are used.

Change of text-book.

(61) Any authorized text book in actual use in any High School may be changed by the teacher of such school for any other authorized text book in the same subject on the written 10 approval of the trustees, provided always such change is made at the beginning of a school term, and at least six months after such approval has been given.

Substitution of unauthorized text-books.

(62) In case any teacher or other person shall negligently or wilfully substitute any unauthorized text book in place of 15 any authoriz:d text book in actual use upon the same subject in his school, he shall for each such offence, on conviction thereof before a police magistrate or justice of the peace, as the case may be, be liable to a penalty not exceeding ten dollars, payable to the municipality for High School purposes, together 20 with costs, as the police magistrate or justice may think fit.

No. 110.

1st Session, 6th Legislature, 50 Vic., 1887.

BILL.

An Act to amend the High School Act.

First Reading, April 7th, 1887.

Mr. Ross.
(Middlesex.)

TORONTO:

No. 111.]　　　　　**BILL.**　　　　[1887.

An Act respecting Upper Canada College.

HER Majesty, by and with the advice and consent of the
Legislative Assembly, of the Province of Ontario, enacts
as follows:—

1. The school now established in Toronto, and known as Name.
5 " Upper Canada College and Royal Grammar School," shall
hereafter be known as " Upper Canada College."

2. The Lieutenant-Governor shall be the Visitor of the said Lieutenant-
College, on behalf of the Crown and his visitorial powers be the Visitor
may be exercised by Commission under the Great Seal, the
10 proceedings whereof, having been first confirmed by Order
in Council, shall be binding upon the College, and all persons
whomsoever. R. S. O. 1877, c. 208, s. 2.

3. The College shall be under the management of five Board of
trustees, appointed by the Lieutenant-Governor, two of whom trustees.
15 shall be the President of the University of Toronto and the
Vice-Chancellor of the Senate.

4. There shall be in the College a Principal and such College
masters, officers, and servants as may from time to time be masters.
directed by order of the Lieutenant-Governor in Council.

20 **5.** No religious test or profession of religious faith shall be No religious
required of any principal, master, pupil, officer or servant of be requir'd.
the College, nor shall religious observances, according to the
forms of any religious denomination, be imposed on them or
any of them. Pt. R. S. O. 1877, c. 208, s. 9.

25 **6.**—(1) The trustees may make regulations—

1. For holding written examinations for the admission of Matters to be
pupils to the College, or for their promotion from time to trustees.
time; for regulating the fees to be paid by pupils for tuition
and maintenance; for promoting the efficiency of the College;
30 for the care of College property; and generally for carrying
this Act into effect, according to its true intent and meaning.
R. S. O. 1877, c. 208, s. 5.

2. For the moral training of the pupils and their attendance
on public worship in their respective churches or other places
35 of worship, and for their religious instruction by their respective ministers, and every facility shall be afforded for such
purposes. R. S. O. 1877, c. 208, s. 9.

2

Matters to be regulated by principal.

7. The Principal may make regulations for the direction of the masters, officers and servants, in regard to their respective duties, and for the · discipline and instruction of the pupils of the College in such matters and to such extent as he may deem expedient, subject to the approval of the 5 trustees and the Lieutenant-Governor in Council. R. S. O. 1877, c. 208, s. 6.

Qualifications of masters.

8. All masters hereafter appointed to the College, shall possess the qualifications required of masters or assistants in High Schools, and the College, in regard to its methods of 10 instruction, discipline and organization, shall be subject to the same inspection as High Schools generally.

Regulations to be submitted to Visitor.

9. A certified copy of every regulation made under this Act by the trustees of the College, and of every regulation made by the principal, after being approved by the trustees, shall 15 be transmitted within ten days from the passing thereof to the Minister of Education, to be by him submitted to the Visitor for his approval, and no regulation shall be of any force or effect until so approved. R. S. O. 1877, c. 208, s. 7.

Present statutes to remain in force until repealed.

10. All statutes rules and ordinances of the College in 20 force on the day this Act takes effect, and which are not inconsistent with the provisions hereof, shall be and continue in force until repealed, altered or amended as herein provided. R. S. O. 1877, c. 208, s. 8.

Annual report to be made by Principal.

11. The Principal of the College shall report to the 25 Minister of Education, on or before the 15th day of January in every year, the annual attendance of pupils, the number in each class, form or subject, the number admitted or promoted each term, the number retiring from the College, with reasons for their retirement, and generally such other information as he 30 may deem expedient, or as may be required by the Minister of Education.

Regulations as to superannuation of masters.

12.—(1) The Lieutenant-Governor in Council may make regulations for the retirement and superannuation of any teacher, officer or servant of the College, now employed, and 35 any gratuity or superannuation allowance paid under this Act shall be a charge upon the endowment of the College and shall be paid out of the same as the Lieutenant-Governor in Council may direct.

Regulations to be laid before Legislative Assembly.

(2) Every such regulation shall be laid before the Legislative 40 Assembly forthwith if the Legislature is in session at the date of the regulation, and if the Legislature is not in session such regulation shall be laid before the House within the first seven days of the session next after the regulation is made.

(3) In case the Legislative Assembly at the said session, or 45 if the session does not continue for three weeks after the regulation is laid before the House, then at the ensuing session of the Legislature, disapproves by resolution of such regulation, either wholly or of any part thereof, the regulation, so far as disapproved of, shall have no effect from the time of such 50 resolution being passed.

13. Copies of the annual reports, and of the regulations of the trustees or principal which may have been approved by the Visitor, shall be laid before the Legislative Assembly at the then next session thereof.   R. S. O. 1877, c. 208, s 10. Report and regulations to be laid before Legislature.

5   **14**. This Act shall take effect by proclamation of the Lieutenant-Governor in Council, and when so proclaimed all other Acts inconsistent herewith shall be repealed.   .

No. 111.

1st Session, 6th Legislature, 50 Vic., 1887.

BILL.

An Act respecting Upper Canada College.

First Reading, 7th April, 1887.

No. 112.] **BILL.** [1887.

An Act respecting the Guardianship of Minors.

HER Majesty, by and with the advice and consent of the Legislative Assembly of the Province of Ontario, enacts as follows:—

1. (1) The High Court or Surrogate Court, or any judge of either Court, may, upon the application of the mother of an infant (who may so apply without next friend) make such order as the Court or judge sees fit regarding the custody of the infant, and the right of access thereto of either parent, having regard to the welfare of the infant, and to the conduct of the parents, and to the wishes as well of the mother as of the father, and may afterwards alter, vary or discharge the order on the application of either parent, or, after the death of either parent, of any guardian under the Act, and in every case may make such order respecting the cost of the mother and the liability of the father for the same, or otherwise as to costs as such Court or judge may think just. (Imp. 49 and 50 V., c. 27, s. 5 ; R. S. O. c. 130, s. 1.) *Court may make order as to custody of and right of access to infants.*

(2) The Court or judge may also make order for the maintenance of the infant by payment by the father thereof, or by payment out of any estate to which the infant is entitled, of such sum or sums of money from time to time as according to the pecuniary circumstances of the father or the value of the estate the Court or judge thinks just and reasonable. (R. S. O. c. 130, s. 1 ; c. 132, s. 9.) *Order as to maintenance.*

2. (1) On the death of the father of an infant, after the passing of this Act, or where the father died prior to the passing of this Act, the mother, if surviving, shall be the guardian of the infant, either alone, when no guardian has been appointed by the father, or jointly with any guardian appointed by the father. *On death of father, mother to be guardian alone, or jointly with others.*

(2) Where no guardian has been appointed by the father, or if the guardian or guardians appointed by the father is or are dead, or refuses or refuse to act, the Court or judge may from time to time appoint a guardian or guardians to act jointly with the mother, as such Court or judge shall see fit. (Imp. *ib.* s. 2.)

3.—(1) The mother of an infant may, by deed or will, appoint any person or persons to be guardian or guardians of the infant after the death of herself and the father of the infant (if the infant be then unmarried), and where guardians are appointed by both parents they shall act jointly. (Imp. s. 3.) *Mother may appoint guardian in certain cases.*

(2) The mother of an infant may, by deed or will, provisionally nominate some fit person or persons to act as guardian or guardians of the infant after her death jointly with the father of the infant, and the Court or a judge after her death, if it be shown to the satisfaction of the Court or a judge that 5 the father is for any reason unfitted to be the sole guardian of his children, may confirm the appointment of such guardian or guardians, who shall thereupon be empowered to act as aforesaid, or make such other order in respect of the guardianship as the Court or judge shall think right. (Imp. s. 3.) 10

Direction by Court on matters affecting infant. **4.** In the event of guardians being unable to agree among themselves or with the father upon a question affecting the welfare of an infant, any of them or the father may apply to the Court for its direction, and the Court, or judge, may make such orders regarding the matter in difference as to the Court 15 or judge seems proper. (Imp. s. 3.)

Authority of guardians. **5.** All guardians appointed or constituted by virtue of this Act shall, unless their authority be otherwise limited, have the power and authority as to the person and estate of the infants **R.S.O. c. 132.** set forth in section 9 of the revised Act respecting guardians 20 of infants.

Removal of guardians. **6.** Testamentary guardians and trustees, and guardians appointed or constituted by virtue of this Act shall be removable by the Court or judge, for the same causes as other guardians and trustees. 20

Surrogate Court or Judge, meaning of. **7.** The Surrogate Court or Judge herein referred to, is the Surrogate Court or Judge of the county where the infant or respondents, or any of them, reside.

R. S. O. c. 130, ss. 1, 21-23 repealed. **8.** Sections 1, 21, 22 and 23 of the Revised Act respecting the Custody of Infants are hereby repealed. 25

No. 112.

1st Session, 6th Legislature, 50 Vic., 1887.

BILL.

An Act respecting the Guardianship of Minors.

First Reading, 23rd March, 1887.

No. 112.] **BILL.** [1887.

An Act respecting the Guardianship of Minors.

HER Majesty, by and with the advice and consent of the Legislative Assembly of the Province of Ontario, enacts as follows:—

1.—(1) The High Court or Surrogate Court, or any Judge of either Court, may, upon the application of the mother of an infant (who may so apply without next friend) make such order as the Court or Judge sees fit regarding the custody of the infant, and the right of access thereto of either parent, having regard to the welfare of the infant, and to the conduct of the parents, and to the wishes as well of the mother as of the father, and may afterwards alter, vary or discharge the order on the application of either parent, or, after the death of either parent, of any guardian under the Act, and in every case may make such order respecting the costs of the mother and the liability of the father for the same, or otherwise as to costs as such Court or Judge may think just. (Imp. 49 and 50 V., c. 27, s. 5 ; R. S. O. c. 130, s. 1.) *Court may make order as to custody of and right of access to infants.*

(2) The Court or Judge may also make order for the maintenance of the infant by payment by the father thereof, or by payment out of any estate to which the infant is entitled, of such sum or sums of money from time to time as according to the pecuniary circumstances of the father or the value of the estate the Court or Judge thinks just and reasonable. (R. S. O. c. 130, s. 1 ; c. 132, s. 9.) *Order as to maintenance.*

2.—(1) On the death of the father of an infant, after the passing of this Act, or where the father died prior to the passing of this Act, the mother, if surviving, shall be the guardian of the infant, either alone, when no guardian has been appointed by the father, or jointly with any guardian appointed by the father. *On death of father, mother to be guardian alone, or jointly with others.*

(2) Where no guardian has been appointed by the father, or if the guardian or guardians appointed by the father is or are dead, or refuses or refuse to act, the Court or Judge may from time to time appoint a guardian or guardians to act jointly with the mother, as such Court or Judge shall see fit. (Imp. *ib.* s. 2.)

3.—(1) The mother of an infant may, by deed or will, appoint any person or persons to be guardian or guardians of the infant after the death of herself and the father of the infant (if the infant be then unmarried), and where guardians are appointed by both parents they shall act jointly. (Imp. s. 3.) *Mother may appoint guardian in certain cases.*

(2) The mother of an infant may, by deed or will, provisionally nominate some fit person or persons to act as guardian or guardians of the infant after her death jointly with the father of the infant, and the Court or a Judge after her death, if it be shewn to the satisfaction of the Court or a Judge that 5 the father is for any reason unfitted to be the sole guardian of his children, may confirm the appointment of such guardian or guardians, who shall thereupon be empowered to act as aforesaid, or make such other order in respect of the guardianship as the Court or Judge shall think right. (Imp. s. 3.) 10

Direction by Court on matters affecting infant.

4. In the event of guardians being unable to agree among themselves or with the father upon a question affecting the welfare of an infant, any of them or the father may apply to the Court for its direction, and the Court, or Judge, may make such orders regarding the matter in difference as to the Court 15 or Judge seems proper. (Imp. s. 3.)

Authority of guardians.

R.S.O. o. 132.

5. All guardians appointed or constituted by virtue of this Act shall, unless their authority be otherwise limited, have th power and authority as to the person and estate of the infants set forth in section 9 of *The Act respecting Guardians of* 20 *Infants.*

Removal of guardians.

6. Testamentary guardians and trustees, and guardians appointed or constituted by virtue of this Act shall be removvahle by the Court or Judge, for the same causes as other guardians and trustees. 20

Surrogate Court or Judge, meaning of.

7. The Surrogate Court or Judge herein referred to, is the Surrogate Court or Judge of the county where the infant or respondents, or any of them, reside.

Appeal.

8. In addition to any appeal allowed by law from the Surrogate Court, under section 31 of *The Surrogate Courts'* 25 *Act,* chapter 46 of the Revised Statutes, an appeal shall lie within the same time and in the same manner as provided by said section to the Court of Appeal, or to a single Judge of said Court, from any order, sentence or judgment of any Surrogate Court or Judge thereof, under this Act, respecting 30 the custody or control of, or right of access to an infant or from any order, sentence or judgment made under sections 2, 3 and 4, of this Act.

R. S. O. o. 132, ss. 8-10, repealed.

9. Sections 8, 9 and 10 of *The Act respecting Guardians of Infants,* are hereby repealed. 35

BILL.

An Act respecting the Guardianship of Minors.

(Re-printed as amended by Committee of the Whole House.)

First Reading, 23rd **March**, 1887.
Second   "   29th   "   "

BILL.

An Act respecting Distress for Rent and Taxes.

HER MAJESTY, by and with the advice and consent of the Legislative Assembly of the Province of Ontario, enacts as follows :—

1. The goods and chattels exempt from seizure under exe- 5 cution, shall not be liable to seizure under a distress warrant by a landlord for rent in respect of a tenancy created after the passing of this Act, except as hereinafter provided ; nor shall such goods be liable to seizure under a distress warrant by a collector of taxes accruing after the passing of this Act, unless 10 they are the property of the person actually assessed for the premises, and whose name also appears upon the collector's roll for the year as liable therefor. (R. S. O. c. 66 ; Imp. 46 and 47, V. c. 61, ss. 44, 45, 47.) *Goods exempt from execution to be exempt from distress.*

2.—(1) A landlord shall not distrain for rent on the goods and 15 chattels the property of any person except the tenant or person who is liable for the rent, although the same are found on the premises ; but this restriction shall not apply in favour of a person claiming title under or by virtue of an execution against the tenant, or in favour of any person whose title is de- 20 rived by any purchase, gift, transfer, or assignment from the tenant, whether absolute or in trust, or by way of mortgage or otherwise ; nor shall the restriction apply where the property is claimed by the wife, husband, daughter, son, daughter-in-law, or son-in-law of the tenant, or of any other relative 25 of his, in case such other relative lives on the premises as a member of the tenant's family. (*Ib.* c. 52, s. 42, Stats. of New York, Wisconsin, Minnesota, Utah, District of Columbia ; Penn. Act of 16th April, 1879.) *Goods on premises not property of tenant to be exempt.*

(2) In case of an assignment for the general benefit of 30 creditors, the landlord shall be entitled after the assignment to distrain as against the assignee for six months' rent, but no more.

3.—(1) A tenant may set-off against the rent due a debt due to him by the landlord, and in such case the landlord shall not 35 be entitled to distrain for more than the balance. (Imp. 23 and 24 Vic., ch. 154, s. 48). *Right of set-off.*

(2) The set-off may be by a notice in the form or to the effect following, and may be given before or after the seizure :

Take notice, that I wish to set-off against rent due by me to 40 you, the debt which you owe to me on your promissory note for   , dated   (*or* for eight months' wages at $20 per month, $160,) (or as the case may be).

Tenant claiming exemption must surrender premises. **4.**—(1) A tenant who is in default for non-payment of rent and claims the benefit of the exemption to which he is entitled under this Act, must give up possession of the premises forthwith, or be ready and offer to do so.

(2) The offer may be made to the landlord or to his agent; 5 and the person authorized to seize and sell the goods and chattels, or having the custody thereof for the landlord, shall be considered an agent of the landlord for the purpose of the offer and surrender to the landlord of the possession.

(3) The surrender of possession in pursuance of the land-10 lord's notice shall be a determination of the tenancy.

(4) Where a landlord desires to seize the exempted goods he shall, forty-eight hours before distraining for the rent in arrear, serve the tenant with a notice, after the tenant has made default in paying his rent; this notice shall inform the tenant 15 what amount is claimed for rent in arrear, and that in default of payment, if he gives up possession of the premises to the landlord after service of the notice, he will be entitled to claim exemption for such of his goods and chattels as are exempt from seizure under execution, but that if he neither pays the 20 rent nor gives up possession his goods and chattels will be liable to seizure, and will be seized and sold to pay the rent in arrear and costs.

(5) The notice may be in the following form or to the like effect : 25

Take notice that I claim $ for rent due to me in respect of the premises which you hold as my tenant, namely, (*here briefly describe them*); and unless the said rent is paid meantime, I demand from you immediate possession of the said premises ; and I am ready to leave in your possession such of your goods and chattels as in that case only you are entitled 30 to claim exemption for.

Take notice further, that if you neither pay the said rent nor give me up possession of the said premises within forty-eight hours after the service of this notice, I am by law entitled to seize and sell, and I intend to seize and sell all your goods and chattels, or such part thereof as may be necessary for the payment of the said rent and costs. 35

This notice is given under the Act of the Legislature of Ontario, respecting distress for rent or taxes.

Dated this   day of   A.D.

(Signed)   *A. B. (landlord).*

To *C. D. (tenant.)*

(6) Service of papers under this Act shall be made either 40 personally or by leaving the same with some grown person being in and apparently residing on the premises occupied by the person to be served ; and the person serving the same shall read over the same to the person served, or with whom the same shall be left, and shall explain the purport and intent 45 thereof.

(7) If the tenant cannot be found and his place of abode is either not known, or admission thereto cannot be obtained, the posting up of the paper on some conspicuous part of the premises, shall be deemed good service. 50

(8) No proceeding under this section shall be deemed defective or rendered invalid by any objection of form.

BILL.

An Act respecting Distress for Rent and Taxes.

First Reading, 23rd March, 1887.

BILL.

An Act respecting Distress for Rent and Taxes.

HER MAJESTY, by ad with the advice and consent of the Legislative Assembly of the Province of Ontario, enacts as follows :—

1. The goods and chattels exempt from seizure under exe- Goods exempt from execution
5 entiou, shall not be liable to seizure *by distress* by a land- to be exempt
lord for rent in respect of a tenancy created after this Act from distress.
comes into force, except as hereinafter provided ; nor shall
such goods be liable to seizure *by* distress by a collector
of taxes accruing after this Act comes into force, unless
10 they are the property of the person actually assessed for the
premises, and whose name also appears upon the collector's roll
for the year as liable therefor. (R. S. O. c. 66 ; Imp. 46 and 47,
V. c. 61, ss. 44, 45, 47.)

(2) The person claiming such exemption shall select and
15 point out the goods and chattels as to which he claims
exemption.

2.—(1) A landlord shall not distrain for rent on the goods and Goods on premises not
chattels the property of any person except the tenant or person property of
who is liable for the rent, although the same are found on the tenant to be exempt.
20 premises ; but this restriction shall not apply in favour of a
person claiming title under or by virtue of an execution
against the tenant, or in favour of any person whose title is derived by any purchase, gift, transfer, or assignment from the
tenant, whether absolute or in trust, or by way of mortgage
25 or otherwise, nor to goods on the premises in the possession of the tenant under a contract for purchase, or by
which he may or is to become the owner thereof upon performance of any condition, nor where goods have been exchanged
between two tenants or persons by the one borrowing or
30 hiring from the other for the purpose of defeating the claim of
or the right of distress by the landlord ; nor shall the
restriction apply where the property is claimed by the wife,
husband, daughter, son, daughter-in-law, or son-in-law of the
tenant, or of any other relative of his, in case such other
35 relative lives on the premises as a member of the tenant's
family. (*Ib.* c. 52, s. 42, Stats. of New York, Wisconsin,
Minnesota, Utah, District of Columbia ; Penn. Act of 16th
April, 1879.)

(2) Nothing in this section contained shall exempt from
40 seizure by distress goods or merchandise in a store or shop
managed or controlled by an agent or clerk for the owner of
such goods or merchandise when such clerk or agent is also
the tenant and in default and the rent is due in respect of the

store or shop and premises rented therewith and thereto belonging, when such goods would have been liable to seizure but for this Act.

(3) The word " tenant " in this section shall extend to and include the sub-tenant and the assigns of the tenant and any 5 person in actual occupation of the premises under or with the assent of the tenant during the currency of the lease, or while the rent is due or in arrear, whether he has or has not attorned to or become the tenant of the landlord.

(4) In case of an assignment for the general benefit of 10 creditors the preferential lien of the landlord for rent is restricted to the arrears of rent due during the period of one year last previous to the execution of such assignment, and from thence so long as the assignee shall retain the premises leased. 15

Right of set-off. **3.**---(1) A tenant may set-off against the rent due a debt due to him by the landlord. (Imp. 23 and 24 Vic., ch. 154, s. 48).

(2) The set-off may be by a notice in the form or to the effect following, and may be given before or after the seizure :

Take notice, that I wish to set-off against rent due by me to 20 you, the debt which you owe to me on your promissory note for , dated (*or* for eight months' wages at $20 per month, $160,) (or as the case may be).

In case of such notice the landlord shall only be entitled to distrain for the balance of rent after deducting any debt 25 justly due by him to the tenant.

Tenant claim-ing exemption must surrender premises. **4.**—(1) A tenant who is in default for non-payment of rent and claims the benefit of the exemption to which he is entitled under this Act, must give up possession of the premises forth-with, or be ready and offer to do so 30

(2) The offer may be made to the landlord or to his agent; and the person authorized to seize and sell the goods and chattels, or having the custody thereof for the landlord, shall be considered an agent of the landlord for the purpose of the offer and surrender to the landlord of the possession. 35

(3) The surrender of possession in pursuance of the land-lord's notice shall be a determination of the tenancy.

(4) Where a landlord desires to seize the exempted goods, he shall, after default has been made in the payment of rent and before or at the time of seizure serve the tenant with a 40 notice which shall inform the tenant what amount is claimed for rent in arrear, and that in default of pay-ment, if he gives up possession of the premises to the landlord after service of the notice, he will be entitled to claim exemption for such of his goods and chattels as are exempt 45 from seizure under execution, but that if he neither pays the rent nor gives up possession his goods and chattels will be liable to seizure, and will be sold to pay the rent in arrear and costs.

(5) The notice may be in the following form or to the like effect :

Take notice that I claim $ for rent due to me in respect of the premises which you hold as my tenant, namely, (*here briefly describe them*); and unless the said rent is paid, I demand from you immediate possession of the said premises ; and I am ready to leave in your possession such of your goods and chattels as in that case only you are entitled to claim exemption for.

Take notice further, that if you neither pay the said rent nor give me up possession of the said premises after the service of this notice, I am by law entitled to seize and sell, and I intend to seize and sell all your goods and chattels, or such part thereof as may be necessary for the payment of the said rent and costs.

This notice is given under the Act of the Legislature of Ontario, respecting distress for rent or taxes.

Dated this   day of   A.D.

                (Signed)   *A. B.* (*landlord*).

To *C. D.* (*tenant.*)

(6) Service of papers under this Act shall be made either personally or by leaving the same with some grown person
5 being in and apparently residing on the premises occupied by the person to be served.

(7) If the tenant cannot be found and his place of abode is either not known, or admission thereto cannot be obtained, the posting up of the paper on some conspicuous part of the pre-
10 mises, shall be deemed good service.

(8) No proceeding under this section shall be deemed defective or rendered invalid by any objection of form.

5. Where a landlord has by law a right to enter for non- payment of rent, it shall not be necessary to demand the rent
15 on the day when due, or with the strictness required at common law, and a demand of rent shall suffice notwithstanding more or less than the amount really due is demanded, and notwithstanding other requisites of the common law are not complied with : provided that, unless the premises are vacant, the
20 demand be made fifteen days at least before entry ; such demand to be made on the tenant personally anywhere, or on his wife or some other grown up member of his family on the premises.

Common law, strict demand of rent dispensed with when landlord entitled to re-enter.

6. When growing or standing crops, which may be seized
25 and sold under execution, are seized for rent, they may, at the option of the landlord or upon the request of the tenant, be advertised and sold in the same manner as other goods, and it shall not be necessary for the landlord to reap, thresh, gather or otherwise market the same.

Sale of growing crops.

30 **7.** Any person purchasing a growing crop at such sale, shall be liable for the rent of the lands upon which the same is growing *at the time of the sale,* and until the crop shall be removed, unless the same has been paid or has been collected by the landlord, or has been otherwise satisfied, *and* the rent
35 shall as nearly as may be be the same as that which the tenant whose goods were sold was to pay, having regard to the quantity of land and to the time which the purchaser shall occupy it.

Liability of purchaser of growing crops.

8. No costs shall be levied for or in respect of the seizure upon exempted goods when they may not be lawfully sold,

Costs in respect of

seizure of exempted goods.

and when sold no greater sum in all than $2.00, *and actual and necessary payments for possession money*, shall be levied or retained for or in respect of costs and expenses of sale of such exempted goods.

Scale of fees.

☞**9.** When the sum to be levied by distress for rent or for 5 any penalty exceeds the sum of $80 no further charges shall be made for or in respect of costs or expenses by any person making the distress or employed in doing any act in the course of such distress than such as are set forth in

R. S. O. c. 65. schedule **A** of the Act entitled *An Act respecting the costs of* 10 *levying distresses for small rents and penalties*, than the following, that is to say :

☞(*a*) The actual expenses or outlay reasonably incurred in removing the goods distrained or part thereof when such removal is necessary : 15

☞(*b*) Advertisement when necessarily published in a newspaper $2.50 ; But not exceeding $5.00.

☞(*c*) If any printed advertisement otherwise than in a newspaper $1.00 ; But not to exceed $3.00.

☞(*d*) The sum of $1.00 per day for man keeping possession, 20 in lieu of 75 cents per day.

☞(*e*) Where the amount due shall be satisfied in whole or in part, after seizure and before sale, the bailiff or person seizing shall be entitled to charge and receive but three per cent. on the amount realized, 25 in lieu of five per cent., and no more.

Penalties.

☞**10.** Any person who offends against sections 8 or 9 of this Act shall be liable to the penalties provided by section 2 of *The Act respecting the costs of levying distresses for small rents and penalties*, and the proceedings may be had and 30 taken for the punishment of the offender and the imposition and collection of such penalties as are provided by section 2 and subsequent sections of said last-mentioned Act. This section and sections 8 and 9 of this Act shall be read with and as part of *the said Act.* 35

Taxation of costs.

☞**11.** The person whose goods are distrained or the person authorizing the distress, or any other person interested may upon giving two days' notice in writing have the costs of the bailiff or other person making the distress and the disbursements charged taxed by the clerk of the Division Court within 40 whose division the distress has been made.

Bill of costs to be given to clerk for taxation.

☞**12.** The bailiff or person so making the said distress shall furnish the said clerk with a copy of his said costs, charges and disbursements for taxation at the time mentioned in the notice or at such other time as the said clerk may 45 direct, and in default of his so doing he shall not be entitled to any costs, charges or disbursements whatever.

Duty of clerk on taxation.

☞**13.** The clerk upon such taxation shall, amongst other things, consider the reasonableness of any charges for removal, keeping possession, and for advertising, or any sums alleged 50 to have been paid therefor, and may examine either party on oath touching the same. The person requiring the taxation shall pay the clerk a fee of twenty-five cents therefor.

14. Where that portion of the bill or charges in dispute amounts to the sum of $10.00, either party may, on giving two 5 days' notice, have the taxation revised by the clerk of the county court. He shall be paid a fee of fifty cents for such revision by the person appealing, and it may, in the discretion of the clerk, be deducted from or added to the bill as finally taxed by him. *Revision of taxation.*

10 **15.** In any proceedings taken under section 2 of *The Act respecting the costs of levying distresses for small rents and penalties* the taxation shall not be received as conclusive evidence. *Taxation not conclusive on proceedings under R. S. O. c. 65, s. 2.*

16. Sections 1, 2, 3, 4 and 8 shall apply only to tenancies 15 created after this Act shall come into force. *Application of ss. 1-4, and 8.*

17. This Act shall come into force on the first day of October, 1887. *Commencement of Act.*

No. 113.

1st Session, 6th Legislature, 50 Vic., 1887.

BILL.

An Act respecting Distress for Rent
and Taxes.

(*Reprinted as amended by Committee of
Whole House.*)

First Reading, 23rd March, 1887.
Second "   29th " . 1887.

`BILL.

An Act to amend the Municipal Act.

HER MAJESTY, by and with the advice and consent of the Legislative Assembly of the Province of Ontario, enacts as follows :—

1. Sections 73, 74 and 76 of *The Consolidated Municipal Act, 1883*, as amended by *The Municipal Amendment Act, 1886*, are hereby repealed, and the following substituted therefor :— 46 V. c. 18, ss. 73, 74 and 76, repealed.

No person shall be qualified to be elected a mayor, alderman, reeve, deputy-reeve, or councillor of any municipality, unless such person resides within the municipality, or within two miles thereof, and is a natural born or naturalized subject of Her Majesty, and a male of the full age of twenty-one years and is not disqualified under this Act, and has the same qualification as is required for a municipal elector, and whose name appears on the last revised list of voters as a municipal elector in the municipality. Qualification of mayors, aldermen, etc.

No 114.

1st Session, 6th Legislature, 50 Vic., 1887.

BILL.

An Act to amend the Municipal Act.

First Reading, 23rd March, 1887.

No. 115.]　　　　　**BILL.**　　　　　[1887.

An Act to amend the Public Parks Act.

HER MAJESTY, by and with the advice and consent of the Legislative Assembly of the Province of Ontario, enacts as follows:—

1. Sub-section 2 of section 13, of *The Public Parks Act* is hereby amended by striking out the figures "1000," occurring in the fourth line thereof, and inserting the figures "3000" in lieu thereof.

46 V. c. 20, s. 13 (2), amended.

1st Session, 6th Legislature, 50 Vic, 1887.

BILL.

An Act to amend the Public Parks Act.

First Reading, 24th March, 1887.

BILL.

An Act to amend the Public Parks Act.

H ER MAJESTY, by and with the advice and consent of the
Legislative Assembly of the Province of Ontario, enacts
as follows:—

5 **1.** Notwithstanding anything contained in sub-section 2 of
section 13 of *The Public Parks Act, 1883*, the corporation of
any city having a population of one hundred thousand inhabitants and over, may take and hold lands for park purposes to
the extent of two thousand acres.

Amount of
lands which
may be held
by cities.

1st Session, 6th Legislature, 50 Vic., 1887.

BILL.

An Act to amend the Public Parks Act.

(Re-printed as amended by Municipal Committee.)

First Reading, 24th March, 1887.
Second   "   30th   "   1887.

BILL.

An Act to Amend the Municipal Act.

HER MAJESTY, by and with the advice and consent of the Legislative Assembly of the Province of Ontario, enacts as follows:—

1. Sub-section 2 of section 482 of *The Consolidated Munici-* 5 *pal Act, 1883,* is amended by inserting after the words "Act of the Legislature," occurring therein, the words "or by-law of the corporation." 46 V. c. 18 (2), s. 482, amended.

2. Sub-section 17 of the said section 482 is repealed, and the following substituted in lieu thereof:— 46 V. c. 18, s. 482 (17), repealed.

(17) For regulating the size and number of doors in churches, 10 theatres, halls, or other buildings, used for places of worship, public meetings or places of amusement, and the street gates leading thereto; and also the size and number of doors, halls, stairs, and other means of egress from all hotels, lodging houses, factories, work-shops, hospitals, schools, colleges and other 15 buildings of a like nature, and also the structure of stairs and stair-railings in all such buildings; and the strength of walls, beams and joists and their supports, and for compelling the production of the plans of all such buildings for inspection and for enforcing observance of such regulations. Regulating doors, etc., of public buildings.

20 **3.** Section 290 of the said Act is amended by adding after the word "by-law," where it occurs in the first line of said section, the words "resolution, minute, report or other proceeding." 46 V. c. 18, s. 290, amended.

4. Sub-section 6 of section 503 of the said Act is amended 25 by adding thereto the following words: "Provided that this sub-section shall not be qualified by anything contained in sections 497 or 500 of this Act." 46 V. c. 18, s. 503, amended.

5. In ascertaining and determining the cost of draining any locality or making and laying or prolonging any common sewer, 30 the council of any city, town, or incorporated village, may estimate the cost of the construction of branch drains to the line of street, and include the cost of such branch drains in making the assessment for such drains or common sewers, as a local improvement pursuant to section 612 of *The Consoli-* 35 *dated Municipal Act, 1883,* and amendments thereto. Cost of construction of branch drains.

6. Section 618 of the said Act is hereby amended by striking out the words "lessees and occupants, or the agents of the owners, lessees and occupants," occurring in the eighth and 46 V. c. 18, s. 618, amended.

ninth lines thereof, and inserting in lieu thereof the words "or the agents of such owners."

46 V. c. 18, s. 624, amended. **7.** Section 624 of the said Act is hereby amended by adding thereto the following sub-section :—

(4) The council may also by by-law define certain areas or 5 sections within the municipality in which all snow, ice and dirt and other obstructions shall be removed from the side-walks, streets, lanes and alleys, in such area or sections, and may impose a special rate upon the real property therein, according to the frontage thereof, in order to pay any expenses 10 incurred in removing such snow, ice, dirt, or other obstruction.

No. 116.

1st Session, 6th Legislature, 50 Vic., 1887.

BILL.

An Act to amend the Municipal Act.

First Reading, 24th March, 1887.

No. 117.] **BILL.** [1887.

An Act respecting Interest on Drainage Loans to Municipalities by the Province of Ontario.

HER MAJESTY, by and with the advice and consent of the Legislative Assembly of the Province of Ontario, enacts as follows :—

1. Sub-section 2 of section 570 of *The Consolidated Muni-* 46 V. c. 18, s. 570 (2), amended.
5 *cipal Act, 1883,* is hereby amended by striking out the words "five per centum," in the eighth line of the said sub-section, and substituting the. words "four per centum" in lieu thereof.

2. Section 4 of *The Ontario Tile Drainage Act* is hereby 41 V. c. 9, s. 4, amended by striking out the words "eight dollars" in the amended.
10 fourth line of the said section and substituting the words "seven dollars and thirty-six cents" in lieu thereof.

3.—(1) The rate of interest to be paid by municipalities on Reduction of all public moneys heretofore advanced for drainage works or rate of interest on advances invested in the purchase of drainage debentures, whether the and loans
15 advance was made under *The Ontario Drainage Act,* or under under R. S. O. cc. 33 & 34 and *The Ontario Municipal Drainage Act,* or under *The Ontario* under 41 V. *Tile, Stone and Timber Drainage Acts,* shall, from and after the c. 9. first day of January, 1887, be four per cent. per annum instead of five per cent. as heretofore, and from and after the said date
20 the rate of interest allowed on sums paid on account of or standing at the credit of the sinking fund of any of the said advances or debentures shall be computed at the rate of four per cent. instead of five per cent.

(2) This Act shall not apply to cases where the sum paid
25 on account of principal or at the credit of the sinking fund is of such an amount that the reduced rate would have the effect of increasing instead of diminishing the payments required to liquidate the amount due.

4. The Provincial Treasurer shall cause a calculation to be Notice as to
30 made in regard to all advances or loans now current as afore- future pay-ments to be said, shewing, according to the reduced rates of interest hereby given. provided, at what period the same will be liquidated by the annual payments provided by existing municipal by-laws, and shall send to the Clerk of each indebted municipality notice of
35 the number of annual payments which will be required here-after in accordance with the provisions of this Act.

R. S. O. c. 34,
s. 5. (42 V.
c. 7, s. 1)
amended.

5. Subject to the provisions of *The Ontario Municipal Drainage Aid Act*, the Lieutenant-Governor in Council may from time to time invest a further sum not exceeding one hundred thousand dollars in the purchase of debentures issued by municipalities for drainage works, and section (5) five of 5 the said Act is amended by inserting the words " three hundred and fifty " in lieu of " two hundred and fifty " in the fourth line of the said section.

1st Session, 6th Legislature, 50 Vic, 1887.

No. 117.

BILL.

An Act respecting Interest on Drainage Loans to Municipalities by the Province of Ontario.

First Reading, 24th March, 1887.

Mr. Ross,
Huron.

 BILL.

﹗ An Act to Amend the Municipal Act.

HER MAJESTY, by and with the advice and consent of the Legislative Assembly of the Province of Ontario, enacts as follows :—

1. Section 490 of *The Consolidated Municipal Act, 1883,* is 46 V. c. 18, s. 490 amended.·
5 amended by adding thereto the following sub-section :

(39) For erecting and maintaining weighing machines in villages or other convenient places, and charging fees for the use thereof, not being contrary to the limitations provided by sub-section 8 of section 497 of this Act.

10 **2.** Section 546 of the said Act is amended by adding thereto 46 V. c. 18, s. the following sub-section : 546 amended.

(5) In case the council and property owners interested in lands required to be taken possession of, for establishing a public road, mutually agree as to the recompense or price of
15 such lands, the council may accept a deed or deeds for the same, which shall be registered, as provided by section 547 of this Act, and in such case the publication of any by-law in the manner required by sub-section 2 shall be dispensed with.

No. 118.

1st Session, 6th Legislature, 50 Vic., 1887.

BILL.

An Act to amend the Municipal Act.

First Reading, 24th March, 1887.

BILL.

An Act for the prevention of Accidents by Fire in Hotels and other Public Buildings.

HER MAJESTY, by and with the advice and consent of the
Legislative Assembly of the Province of Ontario, enacts
as follows:—

1. In the construction of this Act

5   (a) A hotel shall include and be taken to mean any inn, Interpreta-
tavern, public house or place of refreshment where tion.
lodgings are let, furnished or provided for the public, or any other place where the keeper is by law
responsible for the goods and property of his guests.

10   **2.** The keeper of every hotel shall, where the same is more Fire-escapes
than one story in height, furnish, provide and keep in each of to be kept in
the sleeping apartments or bed-rooms in the same and which all bed-rooms.
are situate above the ground floor, a fire-escape for the use of
guests occupying the same.

15   **3.** Such fire-escape shall be sufficient within the meaning of Construction
this Act, if it consists of a fire-proof rope-ladder, composed of of fire-escapes.
at least two ropes of at least three-quarters of an inch in thickness, bound together by cross ropes of at least one-half an inch
in thickness and ten inches in length and not more than two
20 feet apart; such ladder to be of at least a sufficient length to
reach from the window or other opening in the sleeping apartment or bed-room in which it is placed, to the ground below,
and shall at all times be kept in such a condition as will permit
of at least two full grown persons safely ascending or descend-
25 ing on the same at the same time.

  4. The said ladders shall be kept in a coil or other con- Fastenings to
venient position in each of the said bed-rooms or sleeping be provided for
apartments, and shall have a proper fastener or appliance fire-escapes.
attached thereto, and the outside window or opening of such
30 sleeping apartments or bed-rooms shall be provided with
proper, secure and convenient fastenings or appliances to which
one end of the ladders may be secured, so as to furnish a safe
means of egress from the said rooms in case of fire or other
accidents.

35   **5.** In case any hotel shall be provided with outside station- Outside fi .
ary or other fire-escapes, by means of which a safe and conven- escapes.
ient means of egress from the sleeping apartments or bed-
rooms is provided in case of fire, the same shall be deemed a

compliance with this Act so far as relates to all sleeping apartments or bed-rooms to which the said fire-escapes shall be accessible from the outside windows or openings thereof.

Notice as to fire-escapes to be posted in rooms.

6. The keeper of every hotel shall, in addition to the notices he is now required by law to keep posted up in each of his sleeping apartments or bed-rooms, also keep posted up therein a notice calling attention to the said fire-escapes, and containing full directions for the use of the same.

Penalty.

7. In case the keeper of any hotel shall neglect to observe the provisions of this Act in addition to being liable for any and all damages that any person or persons may sustain by reason of his neglect, he shall on summary conviction thereof before any Justice of the Peace of the county wherein the said hotel is situate, incur a fine for each offence of not less than $10 or more than $50 with costs of prosecution, and in default of immediate payment of such fine and costs, shall be committed to the common gaol of the county wherein such offence was committed, for a period not exceeding three months.

1st Session, 6th Legislature, 50 Vic., 1887.

BILL.

An Act for the prevention of Accidents by Fire in Hotels and other Public Buildings.

First Reading, 24th March, 1887.

No. 120.]　　　**BILL.**　　　[1887.

An Act to amend the Franchise and Representation Act, 1885:

HER Majesty, by and with the advice and consent of the Legislative Assembly of the Province of Ontario, enacts as follows :—

Section 3 of *The Franchise and Representation Act, 1885,* is 48 V. c. 2, s. 3, amended by striking out all the words from the word "final," amended. inclusive, in the fifth line of the paragraph "Firstly" in the said section and substituting the words "election, either the actual *bona fide* owner, tenant or occupant of said real property, or, in case he has ceased to be such owner, tenant or occupant, a resident of the electoral district."

No. 120.

1st Session, 6th Legislature, 50 Vic., 1887.

BILL.

An Act to amend the Franchise and Representation Act, 1885.

First Reading, 24th March, 1887.

No. 121.]　　　　**BILL.**　　　　[1887.

An Act to Amend the Ontario Medical Act.

HER MAJESTY, by andwith the advice and consent of the Legislative Assembly of the Province of Ontario, enacts as follows:—

5 **1.** Clause "Firstly" of section 6 of *The Ontario Medical Act,* being chapter 142, of the Revised Statutes of Ontario, is hereby repealed and the following substituted therefor:— R.S.O. c. 142, s. 6, clause "Firstly" repealed.

Firstly.—One member to be chosen from each of the Universities, Colleges and Bodies hereinafter designated, to wit:—
The University of Toronto, the Queen's University and College,
10 of Kingston, the University of Victoria College, the University of Trinity College, the Royal College of Physicians and Surgeons, Kingston, the Toronto School of Medicine, Trinity Medical School, the Ottawa University, the Western University, and of every other University, College or Body in the Province,
15 now by law authorized, or which may be hereafter authorized, to grant degrees in medicine and surgery, or other certificates of qualification to practise the same, and which establishes and maintains to the satisfaction of the College of Physicians and Surgeons of Ontario, a Medical Faculty in connection therewith. Representatives.

20 **2.** No duly registered member of the College of Physicians and Surgeons of Ontario, shall be liable in any action for negligence or mal-practice, by reason of professional services requested or rendered, unless such action be commenced within six months from date when in the matter complained of such
25 professional services terminated. Limitations of actions for negligence.

3. There shall be taxed, and allowed to every duly registered member of the said College, subpoenaed in consequence of professional services rendered, to give evidence, in any court of criminal or civil jurisdiction, or before any judge, coroner,
30 police magistrate, or justice of the peace, witness fees at the rate of $5 per day, and mileage at the rate of twenty-five cents per mile; any tariff or rule to the contrary notwithstanding; and where in criminal cases, inquests or investigations before magistrates no other provisions exist for the payment of such
35 fees, they shall be paid by the treasurer of the county or city wherein such case is tried or such inquest or investigation is held. Witness fees.

4. A registered member of the said college shall not be compelled to attend upon a subpoena for the purpose of being
40 examined as an expert witness only. Member of college not obliged to attend as an expert only.

5. Section 34 of the said Act is hereby repealed. R.S.O. c. 142, s. 32 repealed.

Erasing names
from register. 6.—(1) Where any registered medical practitioner has either before or after the passing of this Act and either before or after he is so registered been convicted either in Her Majesty's dominions or elsewhere of an offence, which if committed in Canada, would be a felony or misdemeanor, or been guilty of 5 any infamous or disgraceful conduct in a professional respect, such practitioner shall be liable to have his name erased from the register.

(2) The council may, and upon the application of any four registered medical practitioners, shall cause enquiry to be made 10 into the case of a person alleged to be liable to have his name erased under this section and on proof of such conviction or of such infamous or disgraceful conduct, shall cause the name of such person to be erased from the register : Provided, that the name of a person shall not be erased under this section on 15 account of his adopting, or refraining from adopting the practice of any particular theory of medicine or surgery, nor on account of a conviction for a political offence out of Her Majesty's dominions, nor on account of a conviction for an offence which though within the provisions of this section 20 ought not, either from the trivial nature of the offence, or from the circumstances under which it was committed, to disqualify a person from practising medicine or surgery.

(3) The council may order to be paid out of any funds at their disposal such costs as to them may seem just to any 25 person against whom any complaint has been made which when finally determined is found to have been frivolous and vexatious.

Restoring
names to
register. 7.—(1) Where the council direct the erasure from the register of the name of any person, or of any other entry, the 30 name of that person or that entry shall not be again entered on the register, except by the direction of the council, or by the order of a judge or of a court of competent jurisdiction.

(2) If the council think fit in any case, they may direct the registrar to restore to the register any name or entry erased 35 therefrom either without fee or on payment of such fee, not exceeding the registration fee, as the council may, from time to time, fix, and the registrar shall restore the same accordingly.

Committee for
erasing and
restoring
names. 8.—(1) The council shall for the purpose of exercising in 40 any case the powers of erasing from and of restoring to the register the name of a person or any entry, ascertain the facts of such case by a committee of their own body not exceeding five in number, of whom the quorum shall be not less than three, and a written report of the committee shall be conclusive, 45 as to the facts therein stated for the purpose of the exercise of the said powers by the council.

(2) The council shall from time to time appoint, and shall always maintain a committee for the purposes of this section, and subject to the provisions of this section may from time to 50 time determine the constitution, and the number and tenure of office of the members of the committee.

(3) The committee shall meet, from time to time, for the despatch of business and subject to the provisions of this

section and of any regulations from time to time, made by the council, may regulate the summoning, notice, place, management and adjournment of such meetings, the appointment of a chairman, the mode of deciding questions, and generally the
5 transaction and management of business including the quorum, and if there is a quorum the committee may act notwithstanding any vacancy in their body. In case of any vacancy the committee may appoint a member of the council to fill the vacancy until the next meeting of the council.

10 (4) A committee under this section may, for the purpose of the execution of their duties under this Act, employ, at the expense of the council such legal, or other assessor or assistant as the committee think necessary or proper.

(5) Provided that all meetings of any such committee when
15 held for taking evidence or otherwise ascertaining the facts shall be held within the county or district where the member complained of resides or practises.

(6) The registrar shall, at least two weeks prior to the first meeting of the committee to be held for taking evidence or
20 otherwise ascertaining the facts, mail to the address of the person whose conduct is the subject of enquiry a copy of the charges made against him or her a statement of the subject matter of the enquiry with notice of the time and place of the meeting of such committee ; the certificate of the registrar shall
25 be *prima facie* evidence of such mailing, there shall be full right to cross-examine all witnesses called, and to call evidence in defence and reply, and in the event of non-attendance of the person whose conduct is the subject of such enquiry, the committee may, upon the production of the registrar's certificate of
30 the mailing of the notice with the copy of the charges or statement of the subject matter of the enquiry, proceed with the matter in his absence and make their report of the facts without further notice to such person.

9. No action shall be brought against the council or the committee for anything done *bona fide* under this Act, not-
35 withstanding any want of form in the proceedings, but any person whose name has been ordered to be erased from the register may appeal from the decision of the council to any Judge of the High Court of Justice for Ontario, at any time
40 within six months from the date of the order for such erasure, and such judge may, upon the hearing of such appeal, make such order as to the restoration of the name so erased or confirming such erasure, or for further enquiries by the committee or council into the facts of the case, and as to costs as to such
45 judge shall seem right in the premises.

10. The appeal may be by summons served upon the registrar to shew cause, and shall be founded upon a copy of the proceedings before the committee—the committee's report and the order of the council in the matter—certified by the registrar,
50 and the registrar shall upon the request of any person desiring to appeal, furnish to any such person a certified copy of all proceedings, reports, orders and papers, upon which the committee have acted in making the order complained of.

Appeal from committee.

Procedure.

No. 121.

1st Session, 6th Legislature, 50 Vic, 1887.

BILL.

An Act to amend the Ontario Medical Act.

First Reading, 24th March, 1887.

No. 121.] **BILL.** [1887.

An Act to Amend the Ontario Medical Act.

HER MAJESTY, by and with the advice and consent of the Legislative Assembly of the Province of Ontario, enacts as follows:—

5   **1.** Clause "Firstly" of section 6 of *The Ontario Medical Act*, being chapter 142, of the Revised Statutes of Ontario, is hereby repealed and the following substituted therefor:— R.S.O. c. 142, s. 6, clause "Firstly" repealed.

Firstly.—One member to be chosen from each of the Universities, Colleges and Bodies hereinafter designated, to wit:— Representatives.
10 The University of Toronto, the Queen's University and College, of Kingston, the University of Victoria College, the University of Trinity College, the Royal College of Physicians and Surgeons, Kingston, the Toronto School of Medicine, Trinity Medical School, the Ottawa University, *Regiopolis College*, the
15 Western University, and of every other University, College or Body in the Province, now by law authorized, or which may be hereafter authorized, to grant degrees in medicine and surgery, and which establishes and maintains to the satisfaction of the College of Physicians and Surgeons of Ontario, a Medical
20 Faculty in connection therewith.

2. No duly registered member of the College of Physicians and Surgeons of Ontario, shall be liable in any action for negligence or mal-practice, by reason of professional services requested or rendered, unless such action be commenced within
25 *one year* from the date when in the matter complained of such professional services terminated. Limitation of actions for negligence.

3. There shall be taxed, and allowed to every duly registered member of the said College, subpœnaed in consequence of professional services rendered, to give evidence, in any court of
30 criminal or civil jurisdiction, or before any judge, coroner, police magistrate, or justice of the peace, witness fees at the rate of $5 per day, and mileage, any tariff or rule to the contrary notwithstanding; and where in criminal cases or investigations before magistrates, ☞evidence of a professional
35 nature is given and ☜ no other provisions exist for the payment of such fees, they shall be paid by the treasurer of the county or city wherein such case is tried or investigation is held, ☞but only upon the order of the magistrate in that behalf.☜ Witness fees.

40   **4.** Section 34 of the said Act is hereby repealed and the following substituted therefor:— R.S.O. c. 142, s. 34 repealed.

34.—(1) Where any registered medical practitioner has either before or after the passing of this Act and either before or Erasing names from register.

after he is so registered been convicted either in Her Majesty's dominions or elsewhere of an offence, which if committed in Canada, would be a felony or misdemeanor, or been guilty of any infamous or disgraceful conduct in a professional respect, such practitioner shall be liable to have his name erased from 5 the register.

(2) The council may, and upon the application of any four registered medical practitioners, shall cause enquiry to be made into the case of a person alleged to be liable to have his name erased under this section and on proof of such conviction or of 10 such infamous or disgraceful conduct, shall cause the name of such person to be erased from the register : provided, that the name of a person shall not be erased under this section on account of his adopting, or refraining from adopting the practice of any particular theory of medicine or surgery, nor 15 on account of a conviction for a political offence out of Her Majesty's dominions, nor on account of a conviction for an offence which though within the provisions of this section ought not, either from the trivial nature of the offence, or from the circumstances under which it was committed, to disqualify 20 a person from practising medicine or surgery.

(3) The council may order to be paid out of any funds at their disposal such costs as to them may seem just to any person against whom any complaint has been made which when finally determined is found to have been frivolous and 25 vexatious.

Restoring names to register.

5.—(1) Where the council direct the erasure from the register of the name of any person, or of any other entry, the name of that person or that entry shall not be again entered on the register, except by the direction of the council, or by 30 the order of a judge or of a court of competent jurisdiction.

(2) If the council think fit in any case, they may direct the registrar to restore to the register any name or entry erased therefrom either without fee or on payment of such fee, not exceeding the registration fee, as the council may, from time 35 to time, fix, and the registrar shall restore the same accordingly.

Committee for erasing and restoring names.

6.—(1) The council shall for the purpose of exercising in any case the powers of erasing from and of restoring to the register the name of a person or any entry, ascertain the facts 40 of such case by a committee of their own body not exceeding five in number, of whom the quorum shall be not less than three, and a written report of the committee shall be conclusive, as to the facts therein stated for the purpose of the exercise of the said powers by the council. 45

(2) The council shall from time to time appoint, and shall always maintain a committee for the purposes of this section, and subject to the provisions of this section may from time to time determine the constitution, and the number and tenure of office of the members of the committee. 50

(3) The committee shall meet, from time to time, for the despatch of business and subject to the provisions of this section and of any regulations from time to time, made by the council, may regulate the summoning, notice, place, manage-

ment and adjournment of such meetings, the appointment of a
chairman, the mode of deciding questions, and generally the
transaction and management of business including the quorum,
and if there is a quorum the committee may act notwithstand-
5 ing any vacancy in their body. In case of any vacancy the
committee may appoint a member of the council to fill the
vacancy until the next meeting of the council.

(4) A committee under this section may, for the purpose of
the execution of their duties under this Act, employ, at the
10 expense of the council such legal, or other assessor or assistant
as the committee *may* think necessary or proper ; ☞ and the
person whose conduct is the subject of enquiry shall also have
the right to be represented by counsel. ☜

(5) Provided that all meetings of any such committee when
15 held for taking evidence or otherwise ascertaining the facts
shall be held within the county where the member complained
of resides ☞ or the alleged offence has been committed. ☜

☞ (6) At least two weeks before the first meeting of the committee to be held for taking the evidence or otherwise ascertain-
20 ing the facts, a notice shall be served upon the person whose
conduct is the subject of enquiry, and such notice shall embody
a copy of the charges made against him or a statement of the
subject matter of the enquiry, and shall also specify the time
and place of such meeting ; the testimony of witnesses shall be
25 taken under oath, which the chairman or acting chairman of
the committee is hereby authorized to administer, and there
shall be full right to cross-examine all witnesses called and to
call evidence in defence and reply ; in the event of the non-
attendance of the person whose conduct is the subject of such
30 enquiry, the committee may, upon proof of personal service of
the notice aforesaid in accordance with the provisions of this
section, which proof of service may be by statutory declaration,
proceed with the subject matter of the enquiry in his absence
and make their report of the facts without further notice to
35 such person. ☜

7. No action shall be brought against the council or the Appeal from
committee for anything done *bona fide* under this Act, not- committee.
withstanding any want of form in the proceedings, but any
person whose name has been ordered to be erased from the
40 register may appeal from the decision of the council to any
Judge of the High Court of Justice for Ontario, at any time
within six months from the date of the order for such erasure,
and such judge may, upon the hearing of such appeal, make
such order as to the restoration of the name so erased or con-
45 firming such erasure, or for further enquiries by the committee
or council into the facts of the case, and as to costs as to such
judge shall seem right in the premises.

8. The appeal may be by summons served upon the regis- Procedure.
trar to shew cause, and shall be founded upon a copy of the
50 proceedings before the committee—the evidence taken, the
committee's report and the order of the council in the matter—
certified by the registrar, and the registrar shall, upon the
request of any person desiring to appeal, furnish to any such
person a certified copy of all proceedings, reports, orders and
55 papers, upon which the committee have acted in making the
order complained of.

No. 121.

1st Session, 6th Legislature, 50 Vic., 1887.

BILL.

An Act to amend the Ontario Medical Act.

(Reprinted as amended by Select Committee.)

First Reading, 28th March, 1887.
Second   "   1st   April,   "

Mr. GIBSON,

No. 122.] **BILL.** [1887.

An Act to amend the Ditches and Watercourses Act.

HER MAJESTY, by and with the advice and consent of the Legislative Assembly of the Province of Ontario, enacts as follows:—

1. Section 9 of *The Ditches and Watercourses Act, 1883,* is 46 V. c. 27, s. 9, amended.
5 amended by adding thereto the following sub-section :—

(2) If it appears to the engineer that rock-cutting is re- Provision for rock-cutting. quired to be done, it shall be the duty of the engineer to get the rock cut or blasted by giving the contract out to public competition by tender or otherwise, instead of requiring each 10 person benefited to do his share of the work. The engineer shall, by his award, determine the sum which shall be paid by each of the persons benefited, which sum shall be a lien on the land benefited, and shall, if unpaid, be rated against the respective lands in the next collector's rolls and collected as or-15 dinary taxes.

2. It shall be the duty of the municipality, through the Payment to contractor. treasurer thereof, to pay the contractor for the work as soon as done, to the satisfaction and upon the certificate of the engineer, pending the subsequent collection thereof as afore-20 said.

BILL.

An Act to amend the Ditches and Watercourses Act.

First Reading, 24th March, 1887.

BILL.

An Act to amend the Registry Act.

HER Majesty, by and with the advice and consent of the Legislative Assembly of the Province of Ontario, enacts as follows :—

1. Section 36 of *The Registry Act* is hereby amended by adding the following sub-section thereto : R. S. O. c. 180, s. 36 amended.

(2) But nothing in this Act shall authorize or be taken to authorize the registration of any instrument which gives authority to an agent to sell lands, and in which instrument the agent's remuneration is provided for, and any instrument heretofore registered which contains security to the agent for his services shall, so far as it purports to create a lien on the lands in favour of the agent for services, be null and void.

No. 123.

1st Session, 6th Legislature, 50 Vic., 1887.

BILL.

An Act to amend the Registry Act.

First Reading, 24th March 1887.

An Act to make further provisions respecting Assignments for the Benefit of Creditors.

HER MAJESTY, by and with the advice and consent of the Legislative Assembly of the Province of Ontario, enacts as follows:

1. The third section of the Act respecting assignments for the benefit of creditors, sub-section one, is amended by inserting 5 after the word "assignee" in the third line the words "resident within the Province of Ontario." (48 Vic. c. 26).

2. The said section is further amended by cancelling the following words :—"An assignment for the general benefit of creditors is made within one month from the time of payment;"

10 And by inserting the following at the end of sub-section one :—

1*a*. " In case of a valid sale of goods, securities or property, and payment or transfer of the consideration or part thereof by the purchaser to a creditor of the 15 vendor, under circumstances which would render void such a payment or transfer by the debtor personally and directly, the payment or transfer, even though valid as respects the purchaser, shall be void as respects the creditor to whom the same 20 is made."

3. The said third section is further amended by adding the following sub-section :—

1*a*. Every assignment for the general benefit of creditors which is not made under the provisions of this 25 Act shall be null and void.

And by striking out the third sub-section.

4. The 4th sub-section of the same section is amended by adding thereto the following words: "and residing in this province." (48 Vic. c. 26.)

30 **5.** The said Act is further amended by adding to the first sub-section of section 19, the following words :

1*a*. " In case a person claiming to be entitled to rank on the estate assigned, does not within a reasonable time after receiving notice of the assignment and 35 of the name and address of the assignee, furnish to the assignee satisfactory proofs of his claim as pro-

vided by 'this and the preceding sections of this
Act, the Judge of the County Court of the county
wherein the debtor at the time of making the
assignment resided or carried on business, may,
upon a summary application by the assignee or by 5
any other person interested in the debtor's estate
(of which application at least three days' notice
shall be given to the person alleged to have made
default in proving a claim as aforesaid), order that
unless the claim be proved to the satisfaction 10
of the judge within a time to be limited by
the order, the person so making default shall no
longer be deemed a creditor of the estate assigned,
and shall be wholly barred of any right to share in
the proceeds thereof; and if the claim is not so 15
proved within the time so limited, or within such
further time as the said judge may by subsequent
order allow, the same shall be wholly barred, and
the assignee shall be at liberty to distribute the
proceeds of the estate as if no such claim existed, 20
but without prejudice to the liability of the debtor
therefor."

1*b*. "The preceding sub-section is not intended to interfere with the protection afforded to Assignees, by
the Act to amend the Act respecting Trustees and 25
Executors, and the Administration of Estates."
(46 Vic. c. 9).

6. The 19th section of the Act respecting Assignees for the
benefit of creditors is further amended by adding the following
sub-section :   30

(3). At any time after the assignee receives from any person claiming to be entitled to rank on the estate, proof of
his claim, notice of contestation of the claim may be served
by the Assignee upon the claimant. Within thirty days after
the receipt of the notice, or such further time as a judge of 35
the County Court of the county in which the assignment is
registered may on application allow, an action shall be brought
by the claimant against the assignee to establish the claim,
and a copy of the writ in the action served on the
assignee; and in default of such action being brought and 40
writ served within the time aforesaid, the claim to rank on
the estate shall be for ever barred.

(*a*) The notice by the Assignee shall contain the name and
place of residence of one of the solicitors of the Supreme Court
of Judicature for Ontario, upon whom service of the writ may 45
be made ; and service upon such solicitor shall be deemed
sufficient service of the writ.

7. Within two days after the receipt of a request in writing
signed by a majority of the creditors having claims duly proved
of $100 and upwards, computed according to the provisions 50
of section 18 of the said Act, it shall be the duty of the
assignee to call a meeting of the creditors at a time not later
than twelve days after the assignee receives the request. In
case of default the assignee shall be liable to a penalty of $25
for every day after the expiration of the time limited for the 55
calling of the meeting until the meeting is called.

8. In case no remuneration is voted to the assignee by the creditors, or the inspectors, as provided by the 11th section of the said Act, the amount shall be fixed by the said judge.

9. In case of an assignment to the sheriff, he shall not be
5 liable for any of the penalties imposed in the 12th section of the said Act, unless he has been paid or tendered the cost of advertising and registering the assignment, nor shall he be compelled to act under assignment until his costs in that behalf are paid or tendered to him.

10   **10**. In case a sufficient number of creditors do not attend the meeting mentioned in the 15th section of the said Act, or fail to give directions with reference to the disposal of the estate, the judge of the County Court shall give all necessary directions in that behalf.

BILL.

An Act to make further provisions respecting Assignments for the Benefit of Creditors.

First Reading,   March, 1887.

No. 124.]　　　**BILL.**　　　[1887

An Act to make further provisions respecting Assignments for the Benefit of Creditors.

HER MAJESTY, by and with the advice and consent of the Legislative Assembly of the Province of Ontario, enacts as follows :—

1. Section 3 of *The Act respecting assignments for the benefit of c. editors*, sub-section 1, is amended by inserting after the word "assignee" in the third line the words "resident within the Province of Ontario." 48 V. c. 26, s. 3 (1) amended.

5

2. The said section is further amended by cancelling the following words :—" Unless an assignment for the general benefit of creditors is made within one month after the payment;" 48 V. c. 26, s. 3, amended.

10

And by inserting the following at the end of sub-section one :—

(*a*) " In case of a valid sale of goods, securities or property, and payment or transfer of the consideration or part thereof by the purchaser to a creditor of the vendor, under circumstances which would render void such a payment or transfer by the debtor personally and directly, the payment or transfer, even though valid as respects the purchaser, shall be void as respects the creditor to whom the same is made."

15

20

3. The said section is further amended by adding the following sub-sections :— 48 V. c. 26, s. 3, amended.

25 !*a*. Every assignment for the general benefit of creditors, which is not void under the second section of this Act, but is not made to the sheriff, nor to any other person with the prescribed consent of creditors, shall be void as against a subsequent assignment which is in conformity with this Act, and 30 shall be subject in other respects to the provisions of this Act until and unless a subsequent assignment is executed in accordance with this Act."

2*a*. In case a payment has been made which is void under this Act, and any valuable security was given up in considera- 35 tion of the payment, the creditor shall be entitled to have the security restored, or its value made good to him before, or as a condition of, the return of the payment. (Insolvent Act, 1875, s. 134.)

And by striking out sub-section 3.

48 V. c. 26, s.
3 (4) amended.   **4.** Sub-section 4 of the same section is amended by adding thereto the following words: "and residing in this province." (48 Vic. c. 26.)

48 V. c. 26, s.
19 (1), amend-   **5.** The said Act is further amended by adding to sub-section
ed.   1 of section 19, the following words :   5

(*a*) " In case a person claiming to be entitled to rank on the estate assigned, does not within a reasonable time after receiving notice of the assignment and of the name and address of the assignee, furnish to the assignee satisfactory proofs of his claim as pro- 10 vided by this and the preceding sections of this Act, the Judge of the County Court of the county wherein the debtor at the time of making the assignment resided or carried on business, may, upon a summary application by the assignee or by 15 any other person interested in the debtor's estate (of which application at least three days' notice shall be given to the person alleged to have made default in proving a claim as aforesaid), order that unless the claim be proved to the satisfaction 20 of the judge within a time to be limited by the order, the person so making default shall no longer be deemed a creditor of the estate assigned, and shall be wholly barred of any right to share in the proceeds thereof; and if the claim is not so 25 proved within the time so limited, or within such further time as the said judge may by subsequent order allow, the same shall be wholly barred, and the assignee shall be at liberty to distribute the proceeds of the estate as if no such claim existed, 30 but without prejudice to the liability of the debtor therefor."

1*b*. " The preceding sub-section is not intended to inter- fere with the protection afforded to Assignees, by *The Act to amend the Act respecting Trustees and* 35 *Executors, and the Administration of Estates.*" (46 Vic. c. 9).

48 V. c. 26, s.
18 (4) amended   **6.** Sub-section 4 of section 18 of *The Act respecting Assignments for the benefit of creditors* is hereby amended by striking out the word "debtor" in the seventh line thereof 40 and substituting therefor the word "creditor."

48 V. c. 26, s.
19, amended.   **7.** Section 19 of *The Act respecting Assignments for the benefit of creditors* is further amended by adding the following sub-section :

(3). At any time after the assignee receives from any per- 45 son claiming to be entitled to rank on the estate, proof of his claim, notice of contestation of the claim may be served by the Assignee upon the claimant. Within thirty days after the receipt of the notice, or such further time as a judge of the County Court of the county in which the assignment is 50 registered may on application allow, an action shall be brought by the claimant against the assignee to establish the claim, and a copy of the writ in the action served on the assignee; and in default of such action being brought and writ served within the time aforesaid, the claim to rank on 55 the estate shall be for ever barred.

(*a*) The notice by the Assignee shall contain the name and place of residence of one of the solicitors of the Supreme Court of Judicature for Ontario, upon whom service of the writ may be made; and service upon such solicitor shall be deemed
5 sufficient service of the writ.

8. Within two days after the receipt of a request in writing signed by a majority of the creditors having claims duly proved of $100 and upwards, computed according to the provisions of section 18 of the said Act, it shall be the duty of the
10 assignee to call a meeting of the creditors at a time not later than twelve days after the assignee receives the request. In case of default the assignee shall be liable to a penalty of $25 for every day after the expiration of the time limited for the calling of the meeting until the meeting is called. *Meeting of creditors to be called by assignee.*

15 **9.** In case no remuneration is voted to the assignee by the creditors, or the inspectors, as provided by section 11 of the said Act, the amount shall be fixed by the said judge. *Remuneration of assignee.*

10. In case of an assignment to the sheriff, he shall not be liable for any of the penalties imposed in section 13 of the
20 said Act, unless he has been paid or tendered the cost of advertising and registering the assignment, nor shall he be compelled to act under assignment until his costs in that behalf are paid or tendered to him. *Liability of sheriff.*

11. In case a sufficient number of creditors do not attend
25 the meeting mentioned in section 16 of the said Act, or fail to give directions with reference to the disposal of the estate, the Judge of the County Court may give all necessary directions in that behalf. *Judge to give directions in case creditors neglect to do so.*

No. 124.

1st Session, 6th Legislature, 50 Vic., 1887.

BILL.

An Act to make further provisions respecting Assignments for the Benefit of Creditors.

(*Reprinted as amended by Committee of Whole House.*)

First Reading, 28th March, 1887.
Second " 29th " "

The ATTORNEY GENERAL.

No. 125.] **BILL.** [1887.

An Act to extend the operation of The Land Titles Act, and otherwise amending the same.

5 HER MAJESTY, by and with the advice and consent of the Legislative Assembly of the Province of Ontario, enacts as follows :—

EXTENSION TO OTHER COUNTIES.

10 **1.**—(1) The municipal council of a county, or of a city or town separated from the county for municipal purposes, may pass a by-law declaring it expedient that the provisions of *The Land Titles Act, 1885,* be extended to the said county, city or town. Adoption of Act by municipality.

15 (2) In such case the municipal corporation of the county, city or town shall provide proper fire-proof and other accommodation for an office of Land Titles ; and, so far as the expenses of the office are not covered by the fees collected thereat, the corporation shall pay the same, including the salary of the 20 local Master of Titles, and all necessary and proper books, stationery, furniture, and lighting, cleaning and heating of the office, and attendance, and other matters and things incident to the proper conduct of the business of the office. This sub-section shall apply also to the County of York and 25 City of Toronto from and after the 31st day of December, 1887.

(3) Where the said Act is extended to a county which includes a city or town separated from the county for municipal purposes, the city or town and county shall share the 30 expenses to be borne by the locality under this Act, in such proportions as may be decided by arbitration under the Municipal Act, in case the councils interested do not agree in respect thereto.

2.—(1) Where a by-law to the effect aforesaid has been 35 passed, and proper accommodation has been provided, either in connection with the county registry office or at some other convenient place, to the satisfaction of the Inspector hereinafter mentioned, and approved by the Lieutenant-Governor in Council, the Lieutenant-Governor may, by his proclamation, extend 40 the operation of the said Act (as amended by any subsequent Acts) to such county, city or town, from a day to be named in the proclamation. Proclamation extending Act to municipality.

(2) The fact of the conditions precedent to the issue of such proclamation having been performed, shall be conclusively 45 established by the issue of the proclamation.

Surplus fees under Registry Act to be applied in defraying expenses of office.

3. Where the Act applies to a county, city or town entitled to receive money under section 104 of the Registry Act, the Registrar shall pay to the Treasurer of Ontario, to be applied, so far as necessary, in defraying the salary of the Master and other expenses of the office, the money payable 5 either directly or indirectly, to the county, city or town under the said Act, and the Treasurer shall pay the balance to the county, city or town; and in case the amount so paid to the Treasurer aforesaid by the Registrar is not sufficient, or in case nothing is payable by the Registrar, the residue of 10 such salary, or the whole of such salary (as the case may be), shall be made good to the Province by the corporation of the county, city or town.

LOCAL MASTERS OF TITLES.

Appointment of Local Masters of Titles.

4.—(1) Where at the time of the issue of the proclamation 15 there is a Referee of Titles under the Quieting Titles' Act, residing in the locality, such referee shall *ex-officio* be the first Local Master of Titles for the locality, unless he practises as a barrister or solicitor, or is a county judge, and he shall hold the office during the pleasure of the Lieutenant-Governor in 20 Council.

(2) Save as aforesaid, the Lieutenant-Governor may appoint a Master of Titles for the locality to which the Act is extended, to be styled " The Local Master of Titles " for the county, city or town, as the case may be, such officer to hold office during 25 pleasure as aforesaid.

Qualification.

(3) No person shall be appointed Master of Titles unless he is a barrister of at least five years' standing at the Bar of Ontario.

Salary.

(4) The Local Master of Titles shall be paid by salary 30 for his services in that capacity, such salary to be fixed from time to time, with reference to the amount or probable amount of the business, on the report of the Inspector, subject to approval by the Lieutenant-Governor in Council. The Order in Council is to be laid before the House of Assembly, as pro- 35 vided for Orders in Council under the 81st section of the Ontario Judicature Act, 1881.

Security.

(5) Every Local Master, before he enters upon the execution his office, shall give security for the true and faithful performance of his duty as such Master, in such an amount 40 as may be determined by the Lieutenant-Governor in Council, and in such form as he may approve of, and shall take, before a Judge of the Supreme Court of this Province, or before some person authorized by the Lieutenant-Governor to administer oaths and declarations, an oath of office 45 similar to that required to be taken by the Master of Titles under the said Act, and such oath shall be transmitted to the Provincial Secretary.

New security to be given when required

(6) The Local Master shall, whenever required by the Provincial Secretary, give new security for the purposes specified 50 in this section, and to be approved by the Lieutenant-Governor in Council.

Master's authority and duties.

5. Subject to the provisions of this Act, the Local Master shall, in respect to titles of land situate within the territory for which he is appointed, have all the authority and perform all the duties which, in the County of York, are performed by the Master of Titles, subject to appeal in the same manner.

5   **6.**—(1) As soon as the said Act applies to *ten* counties, cities or towns aforesaid, the Lieutenant-Governor may appoint an officer, to be called "the Inspector of Land Titles Offices." Appointment of Inspector.

(2) The Inspector shall (subject to rules as hereinafter men- 10 tioned) have the like powers and duties as an Inspector under the Quieting Titles' Act, and as an Inspector under the Registry Act, respectively, and such other duties as may be required of him by rules to be made under the authority of the said Act, or as he may be required by the Governor in 15 Council to perform in respect of matters arising under the said Act. Duties.

(3) The salary of the Inspector, to be voted by this Legis- lature, and his travelling expenses, and all expenses of and incidental to his office, shall be paid by the Province, and shall 20 be repaid to the Provincial Treasurer by the corporations of the localities in which the Act is from time to time in opera- tion, and shall be paid in such proportions as after a report from the Inspector the Lieutenant-Governor in Council may deter- mine. (42 V. c. 25, ss. 5). Salary.

25   (4) Until an Inspector is appointed, the duties of the Inspec- tor shall be performed by the Master of Titles, or by some other person authorized by the Lieutenant-Governor in Coun- cil, and the expenses of and incidental thereto shall, in like manner as is hereinbefore provided, be repaid to the Provincial 30 Treasurer. Performance of duties until Inspector appointed.

(5) In all matters decided by the Inspector which are of like character as matters over which the Master of Titles has jurisdiction in the County of York, an appeal shall lie from any act, order or decision of the Inspector to the High Court, and 35 from that Court to the Court of Appeal, as in cases within the ordinary jurisdiction of the Court, subject to any rules made in respect of such appeals. Appeal from Inspector.

First Registration.

40   **7.** Where, upon an application for first registration, the Local Master finds that the applicant, or his nominee, is entitled to be registered, he is to sign a memorandum to that effect at the foot of the application, and is to transmit the same to the Inspector of Titles, with the deeds, evidence, and 45 other papers before him, and a draft of the entry of owner- ship proposed to be made. Local Master to transmit titles, deeds, etc., to inspec- tor.

(2) If the Inspector concurs in the opinion of the Local Master, he shall approve thereof and shall return the papers transmitted to him, and the Local Master may thereupon regis- 50 ter the applicant, or his said nominee, as owner under the said Act. Proceedings where In- spector con- curs in Master's find- ing.

Proceedings where Inspector does not concur.

(3) In case the Inspector does not concur in the opinion of the Local Master, he shall communicate his opinion to the Local Master, and shall cause such action to be taken as he deems expedient, and in case his objections are not removed by explanations or additional evidence, the applicant or his 5 nominee shall not be registered, unless the Court on appeal, or on a case stated for its opinion, otherwise directs.

Stay of proceedings in case appeal desired.

(4) If there is a contestation upon the decision of the Inspector concurring in the Local Master's opinion, registration shall be delayed for ten days to enable anyone who so 10 desires to appeal.

Subsequent Registration.

Submission of case to Inspector where Master in doubt.

8. If on an application for the registration of an instrument after a first registration or of a transmission, the Local Master is unable to come to a clear conclusion as to the 15 action which he should take, he shall delay making the required entry until he has stated the facts to the Inspector of Titles for his opinion. In submitting the case the Local Master shall state his own view and his reasons therefor. Dom. 49 V. c. 26, ss. 47, 48. 20

Withdrawning Land from the Registry.

Application to withdraw registered land.

9. Whereafter land has been registered under the said Act, or this Act, special circumstances appear or subsequently arise which make it inexpedient that the land should continue under the Act, the owner may apply in the prescribed 25 manner to the Master of Titles for the withdrawal of the land from the said Acts.

Certificate by Master.

(2) In case the owner proves before the Master of Titles that all persons interested in the land proposed to be withdrawn, consent to its withdrawal, and in case he satisfies the 30 Master that special circumstances exist which render the withdrawal of such land or a portion thereof expedient, the Master may issue his certificate describing the land or such portion thereof as the consent covers and as the Master deems proper, and in such a manner that the said certificate can be 35 properly registered in the registry office for the registry division in which the land is situate, and upon the certificate being issued the said Act shall cease to apply to the land described therein, and the land shall thereafter be subject to the ordinary laws relating to real estate and to the registry laws. 40

Application of section.

(3) This section applies to the Local Masters also; the certificate in such case shall require to be approved and countersigned by the Inspector.

Fee.

(4) Upon the production of the certificate to the registrar of lands and payment of a fee of $1, the same shall be 45 duly registered.

AMENDMENTS OF LAND TITLES ACT.

48 V. C. 22, s. 22 (8) repealed.

10. Section 22 of the Land Titles' Act is amended by striking item 8 out of the said section and by adding thereto the following sub-sections :— 50

(2) Where the existence of any easement is proved the ^{Notice of ease-}ment. Master of Titles' may, if he thinks fit, enter notice thereof on the register.

(3) Where title is shown to any easement appurtenant to
5 the land being registered, the same may be stated in the entry of ownership and land certificate.

11.—(1) Section 27 of the said Act is amended by adding to ^{48 V. c. 22, s.}27 amended. item (1) the following " and all taxes, rates, charges, rents, statute labour, or other impositions theretofore, or thereafter
10 imposed or charged on the lands, and that in case of default, all payments made by the owner of the charge may be added to the principal money and bear interest." *See proviso in Schedule B, of R. S. O. c. 104.*

(2) The said section is also amended by adding the follow-
15 ing sub-section :—

(3) Where any charge, whether under seal or not, is ex- Provision where charge pressed to be made in pursuance of *The Act respecting Short* expressed to *Forms of Mortgages*, or refers thereto, and contains any form be made under R. S. O. c.104. of words contained in items numbered, 1, 2, 3, 7, 8, 12, 14, 15
20 or 16, of column one, of schedule B to the last mentioned Act, or to the like effect, whether expressed in the first or third person,' such words shall have the same meaning and effect as the words under the corresponding number in column two in the said schedule ; the directions in the said schedule
25 shall also apply to the said charge.

12. The following section is inserted as a new section after Time of receipt to be section 45 of the said Act :— entered and to be deemed
45a. The day, hour and minute, of the receipt of each instru- time of regis-ment and copy of writ, shall be noted thereon, and for the tration.
30 purpose of priority between mortgagees, transferees and others, the time of the receipt shall be deemed the time of registration.

13. The following are inserted as sub-sections of section 51 ^{48 V. c. 22, s.}51 amended. of the said Act :—

(6) Where an execution or other writ is issued against the Notice to Master whose
35 registered owner under a different name from that under which writ issues he or she is registered, the execution shall have no effect under against owner this Act, unless the person who sues out the writ serves a ferent name notice on the Master of Titles, stating the name under which from that on the execution debtor is registered, and otherwise in the form the register.
40 or to the effect prescribed, or unless a like notice is written upon the copy of the writ.

(7) Where a transferor or transferee of land, or maker or Provision in owner of a charge, claims that a writ apparently affecting land claimed that does not affect the land or charge, he shall produce such land is not
45 evidence thereof as the Master may consider necessary, and affected by a the Master may require all parties interested to be notified of parently the application to register, without reference to the writ, the affectingsame. instrument under which the claim is made, and the Master may decide the question or may direct an issue or case to be
50 tried and may make such order as to costs as he deems just.

14. The following is substituted for sub-section 3 of section ^{48 V. c. 22, s.}89 amended. 89 of the said Act :—

Execution of instruments by married women.

A married woman shall for the purposes of this Act, be deemed a *feme sole*, and may execute without seal any bar of dower or other instrument required under this Act.

This amendment shall take effect from the time the said Act went into force.   5

48 V. c. 22, s. 122 amended.

15. Section 122 is amended by inserting the words "Lieutenant-Governor in Council" before the word "Judges" in the first line, and substituting the words, "and may have regard to," for the words, "regard being had to."   10

48 V. c. 22, s. 127 amended.

16. Section 127 of the said Act is amended by adding thereto the following sub-section :—

Stamps to be affixed to registered transfer or charge.

(3) The stamps for all fees payable on a land certificate or a certificate of charge shall be affixed to the registered transfer 15 or charge and not to the certificate, and all stamps payable in respect of registrations shall be affixed to the instruments registered and not to the entry in the register. *See* R.S.O. cap. 22, s. 7; 45 V. c. 11, s. 3.

BILL.

An Act to extend the operation of The Land Titles Act, and otherwise amending the same.

First Reading, . th March, 1887.

BILL.

An Act to extend the operation of The Land Titles Act, and otherwise amending the same.

5 HER MAJESTY, by and with the advice and consent of the Legislative Assembly of the Province of Ontario, enacts as follows :—

EXTENSION TO OTHER COUNTIES.

10 **1.**—(1) The municipal council of a county, or of a city or town separated from the county for municipal purposes, may pass a by-law declaring it expedient that the provisions of *The Land Titles Act, 1885*, be extended to the said county, city or town. *Adoption of Act by municipality.*

15 (2) In such case the municipal corporation of the county, city or town shall provide proper fire-proof and other accommodation for an office of Land Titles ; and, so far as the expenses of the office are not covered by the fees collected thereat, the corporation shall pay the same, including the salary of the 20 local Master of Titles, and all necessary and proper books, stationery, furniture, and lighting, cleaning and heating of the office, and attendance, and other matters and things incident to the proper conduct of the business of the office. This sub-section shall apply also to the County of York and 25 City of Toronto from and after the 31st day of December, 1887.

(3) Where the said Act is extended to a county which includes a city or town separated from the county for municipal purposes, the city or town and county shall share the 30 expenses to be borne by the locality under this Act, in such proportions as may be decided by arbitration under the Municipal Act, in case the councils interested do not agree in respect thereto.

2.—(1) Where a by-law to the effect aforesaid has been 35 passed, and proper accommodation has been provided, either in connection with the county registry office or at some other convenient place, to the satisfaction of the Inspector hereinafter mentioned, and approved by the Lieutenant-Governor in Council, the Lieutenant-Governor may, by his proclamation, extend 40 the operation of the said Act (as amended by any subsequent Acts) to such county, city or town, from a day to be named in the proclamation. *Proclamation extending Act to municipality.*

(2) The fact of the conditions precedent to the issue of such proclamation having been performed, shall be conclusively 45 established by the issue of the proclamation.

Surplus fees under Registry Act to be applied in defraying expenses of office.

3. Where the Act applies to a county, city or town entitled to receive money under section 104 of the Registry Act, the Registrar shall pay to the Treasurer of Ontario, to be applied, so far as necessary, in defraying the salary of the Master and other expenses of the office, the money payable 5 either directly or indirectly, to the county, city or town under the said Act, and the Treasurer shall pay the balance to the county, city or town; and in case the amount so paid to the Treasurer aforesaid by the Registrar is not sufficient, or in case nothing is payable by the Registrar, the residue of 10 such salary, or the whole of such salary (as the case may be), shall be made good to the Province by the corporation of the county, city or town.

LOCAL MASTERS OF TITLES.

Appointment of Local Masters of Titles.

4.—(1) Where at the time of the issue of the proclamation 15 there is a Referee of Titles under the Quieting Titles' Act, residing in the locality, such referee shall *ex-officio* be the first Local Master of Titles for the locality, unless he practises as a barrister or solicitor, or is a county judge, and he shall hold the office during the pleasure of the Lieutenant-Governor in 20 Council.

(2) Save as aforesaid, the Lieutenant-Governor may appoint a Master of Titles for the locality to which the Act is extended, to be styled " The Local Master of Titles " for the county, city or town, as the case may be, such officer to hold office during 25 pleasure as aforesaid.

Qualification.

(3) No person shall be appointed Master of Titles unless he is a barrister of at least five years' standing at the Bar of Ontario.

Salary.

(4) The Local Master of Titles shall be paid by salary 30 for his services in that capacity, such salary to be fixed from time to time, with reference to the amount or probable amount of the business, on the report of the Inspector, subject to approval by the Lieutenant-Governor in Council. The Order in Council is to be laid before the House of Assembly, as pro- 35 vided for Orders in Council under the 81st section of the Ontario Judicature Act, 1881.

Security.

(5) Every Local Master, before he enters upon the execution his office, shall give security for the true and faithful performance of his duty as such Master, in such an amount 40 as may be determined by the Lieutenant-Governor in Council, and in such form as he may approve of, and shall take, before a Judge of the Supreme Court of this Province, or before some person authorized by the Lieutenant-Governor to administer oaths and declarations, an oath of office 45 similar to that required to be taken by the Master of Titles under the said Act, and such oath shall be transmitted to the Provincial Secretary.

New security to be given when required

(6) The Local Master shall, whenever required by the Provincial Secretary, give new security for the purposes specified 50 in this section, and to be approved by the Lieutenant-Governor in Council.

Master's authority and duties.

5. Subject to the provisions of this Act, the Local Master shall, in respect to titles of land situate within the territory

for which he is appointed, have all the authority and perform
all the duties which, in the County of York, are performed by
the Master of Titles, subject to appeal in the same manner.

INSPECTOR OF LAND TITLES' OFFICES.

5 **6.**—(1) As soon as the said Act applies to *ten* counties, Appointment cities or towns aforesaid, the Lieutenant-Governor may of Inspector. appoint an officer, to be called "the Inspector of Land Titles Offices."

(2) The Inspector shall (subject to rules as hereinafter men- Duties.
10 tioned) have the like powers and duties as an Inspector under the Quieting Titles' Act, and as an Inspector under the Registry Act, respectively, and such other duties as may be required of him by rules to be made under the authority of the said Act, or as he may be required by the Governor in
15 Council to perform in respect of matters arising under the said Act.

(3) The salary of the Inspector, to be voted by this Legis- Salary. lature, and his travelling expenses, and all expenses of and incidental to his office, shall be paid by the Province, and shall
20 be repaid to the Provincial Treasurer by the corporations of the localities in which the Act is from time to time in operation, and shall be paid in such proportions as after a report from the Inspector the Lieutenant-Governor in Council may determine. (42 V. c. 25, ss. 5).

25 (4) Until an Inspector is appointed, the duties of the Inspec- Performance tor shall be performed by the Master of Titles, or by some of duties until other person authorized by the Lieutenant-Governor in Coun- appointed. cil, and the expenses of and incidental thereto shall, in like manner as is hereinbefore provided, be repaid to the Provincial
30 Treasurer.

(5) In all matters decided by the Inspector which are of like Appeal from character as matters over which the Master of Titles has Inspector. jurisdiction in the County of York, an appeal shall lie from any act, order or decision of the Inspector to the High Court, and
35 from that Court to the Court of Appeal, as in cases within the ordinary jurisdiction of the Court, subject to any rules made in respect of such appeals.

DUTIES AND POWERS OF LOCAL MASTERS.

First Registration.

40 **7.** Where, upon an application for first registration, the Local Master Local Master finds that the applicant, or his nominee, is to transmit entitled to be registered, he is to sign a memorandum to that etc., to inspec- effect at the foot of the application, and is to transmit the tor. same to the Inspector of Titles, with the deeds, evidence, and
45 other papers before him, and a draft of the entry of ownership proposed to be made.

(2) If the Inspector concurs in the opinion of the Local Proceedings Master, he shall approve thereof and shall return the papers spector con- transmitted to him, and the Local Master may thereupon regis- curs in
50 ter the applicant, or his said nominee, as owner under the said Master's find- ing. Act.

Proceedings where Inspector does not concur.

(3) In case the Inspector does not concur in the opinion of the Local Master, he shall communicate his opinion to the Local Master, and shall cause such action to be taken as he deems expedient, and in case his objections are not removed by explanations or additional evidence, the applicant or his nominee shall not be registered, unless the Court on appeal, or on a case stated for its opinion, otherwise directs. 5

Stay of proceedings in case appeal desired.

(4) If there is a contestation upon the decision of the Inspector concurring in the Local Master's opinion, registration shall be delayed for ten days to enable anyone who so desires to appeal. 10

Subsequent Registration.

Submission of case to Inspector where Master in doubt.

8. If on an application for the registration of an instrument after a first registration or of a transmission, the Local Master is unable to come to a clear conclusion as to the action which he should take, he shall delay making the required entry until he has stated the facts to the Inspector of Titles for his opinion. In submitting the case the Local Master shall state his own view and his reasons therefor. Dom. 49 V. c. 26, ss. 47. 48. 15 20

Withdrawing Land from the Registry.

Application to withdraw registered land.

9. Whereafter land has been registered under the said Act, or this Act, special circumstances appear or subsequently arise which make it inexpedient that the land should continue under the Act, the owner may apply in the prescribed manner to the Master of Titles for the withdrawal of the land from the said Acts. 25

Certificate by Master.

(2) In case the owner proves before the Master of Titles that all persons interested in the land proposed to be withdrawn, consent to its withdrawal, and in case he satisfies the Master that special circumstances exist which render the withdrawal of such land or a portion thereof expedient, the Master may issue his certificate describing the land or such portion thereof as the consent covers and as the Master deems proper, and in such a manner that the said certificate can be properly registered in the registry office for the registry division in which the land is situate, and upon the certificate being issued the said Act shall cease to apply to the land described therein, and the land shall thereafter be subject to the ordinary laws relating to real estate and to the registry laws. 30 35 40

Application of section.

(3) This section applies to the Local Masters also; the certificate in such case shall require to be approved and countersigned by the Inspector.

Fee.

(4) Upon the production of the certificate to the registrar of lands and payment of a fee of $1, the same shall be duly registered. 45

AMENDMENTS OF LAND TITLES ACT.

48 V. C. 22, s. 22 (8) repealed.

10. Section 22 of the Land Titles' Act is amended by striking item 8 out of the said section and by adding thereto the following sub-sections :— 50

(2) Where the existence of any easement is proved the Master of Titles' may, if he thinks fit, enter notice thereof on the register. Notice of easement.

(3) Where title is shown to any easement appurtenant to
5 the land being registered, the same may be stated in the entry of ownership and land certificate.

11.—(1) Section 27 of the said Act is amended by adding to item (1) the following " and all taxes, rates, charges, rents, statute labour, or other impositions theretofore, or thereafter
10 imposed or charged on the lands, and that in case of default, all payments made by the owner of the charge may be added to the principal money and bear interest." *See proviso in Schedule B, of R. S. O. c. 104.* 48 V. c. 22, s. 27 amended.

(2) The said section is also amended by adding the follow-
15 ing sub-section :—

(3) Where any charge, whether under seal or not, is expressed to be made in pursuance of *The Act respecting Short Forms of Mortgages*, or refers thereto, and contains any form of words contained in items numbered, 1, 2, 3, 7, 8, 12, 14, 15
20 or 16, of column one, of schedule B to the last mentioned Act, or to the like effect, whether expressed in the first or third person, such words shall have the same meaning and effect as the words under the corresponding number in column two in the said schedule ; the directions in the said schedule
25 shall also apply to the said charge. Provision where charge expressed to be made under R. S. O. c. 104.

12. The following section is inserted as a new section after section 45 of the said Act :— Time of receipt to be entered and to be deemed time of registration.

45a. The day, hour and minute, of the receipt of each instrument and copy of writ, shall be noted thereon, and for the
30 purpose of priority between mortgagees, transferees and others, the time of the receipt shall be deemed the time of registration.

13. The following are inserted as sub-sections of section 51 of the said Act :—. 48 V. c. 22, s. 51 amended.

(6) Where an execution or other writ is issued against the
35 registered owner under a different name from that under which he or she is registered, the execution shall have no effect under this Act, unless the person who sues out the writ serves a notice on the Master of Titles, stating the name under which the execution debtor is registered, and otherwise in the form
40 or to the effect prescribed, or unless a like notice is written upon the copy of the writ. Notice to Master whose writ issues against owner under a different name from that on the register.

(7) Where a transferor or transferee of land, or maker or owner of a charge, claims that a writ apparently affecting land does not affect the land or charge, he shall produce such
45 evidence thereof as the Master may consider necessary, and the Master may require all parties interested to be notified of the application to register, without reference to the writ, the instrument under which the claim is made, and the Master may decide the question or may direct an issue or case to be
50 tried and may make such order as to costs as he deems just. Provision in case it is claimed that land is not affected by a writ apparently affecting same.

14. The following is substituted for sub-section 3 of section 89 of the said Act :— 48 V. c. 22, s. 89 amended.

Execution of instruments by married women.

A married woman shall for the purposes of this Act, be deemed a *feme sole*, and may execute without seal any bar of dower or other instrument required under this Act.

This amendment shall take effect from the time the said Act went into force. 5

48 V. c. 22, s. 122 amended.

15. Section 122 is amended by inserting the words " Lieutenant-Governor in Council" before the word " Judges " in the first line, and substituting the words, "and may have regard to," for the words, " regard being had to." 10

48 V. c. 22, s. 127 amended.

16. Section 127 of the said Act is amended by adding thereto the following sub-section :—

Stamps to be affixed to registered transfer or charge.

(3) The stamps for all fees payable on a land certificate or a certificate of charge shall be affixed to the registered transfer 15 or charge and not to the certificate, and all stamps payable in respect of registrations shall be affixed to the instruments registered and not to the entry in the register. *See* R.S.O. cap. 22, s. 7; 45 V. c. 11, s. 3.

No. 125.

1st Session 6th Legislature, 50 Vic., 1887.

BILL.

An Act to extend the operation of The Land Titles Act, and otherwise amending the same.

First Reading,   th March, 1887.

BILL.

An Act respecting the Appointment and Proceedings of Police Magistrates.

HER MAJESTY, by and with the advice and consent of the Legislative Assembly of the Province of Ontario, enacts as follows :—

1. The Lieutenant-Governor may appoint more police
5 magistrates than one for any county or union of counties in which *The Canada Temperance Act*, or a like Act, is in force. Any such magistrate shall hold office during pleasure, save that he shall cease to be such police magistrate in case, and from the time that, the said Act, or a new Act which may
10 be substituted therefor, ceases to be in force in the county.

More police magistrates than one may be appointed where Temperance Act in force; salary.

(2) The Lieutenant-Governor in Council may determine the salary (if any) to be paid to a county police magistrate ; the same not to exceed the salary provided for by the 2nd section of *The Act respecting Police Magistrates for Counties.* (48
15 Vic. c. 17.) He may also allow the travelling expenses of the magistrate at some amount between $150 and $300, and no more than $300. Only one county magistrate shall receive a salary.

(3) Such salary and expenses shall be paid by the treasurer
20 of the county quarterly.

3. The 3rd and 4th sections of *The Act respecting Police Magistrates in Counties*, shall apply to police magistrates appointed under this Act.

General powers of police magistrates.

4. A salaried county police magistrate shall have power
25 from time to time to appoint a constable for the county or union of counties of which he is a police magistrate, such constable to hold office for not more than thirty days ; his appointment may be revoked by the police magistrate, or by the Provincial Secretary, before the expiration of the thirty
30 days.

Certain police magistrates may appoint temporary constables.

(2) The police magistrate making any such appointment shall forthwith notify the Provincial Secretary thereof. (R. S. O. c. 82, s. 5.)

(3) A constable appointed by a police magistrate shall have
35 the same authority and privileges, and be subject to the same liability and the performance of the same duties, as if appointed by the Court of General Sessions of the Peace. (R. S. O. c. 82, s. 7.)

No actions against stipendiary or police magistrates for certain mistakes as to jurisdiction under Canada Temperance Act.

5. No action shall lie against a stipendiary or police magistrate for or by reason of any process issued, or conviction made by, or any proceedings of any kind taken before him alone, or authorized by him, in good faith, in any case which, by the law applicable thereto, was not cognizable by such 5 police magistrate, or not by him sitting alone, or should have been heard by two justices of the peace, or by the mayor of a city or town within the district, county, union of counties, or part of a district or county or union of counties, for which the stipendiary or police magistrate was appointed. 10

(2) This section shall not prevent an action from being maintained where and so far as the action would be maintainable against the mayor or justices of the peace if the process had been issued or conviction made by, or proceedings taken before, or authority given by him or them. 15

(3) No action shall lie against a constable or peace officer for anything done by him under and by virtue of process issued or authority given, as in the first sub-section mentioned, unless the action would be maintainable if the process had been issued or authority given by a person or persons 20 legally qualified to issue the process or give the authority.

(4) This section shall apply to pending actions, and also to actions (whether brought before or after this Act) for anything done before the passing of this Act, as well as to actions in respect of acts which may hereafter be done. 25

No. 126.

1st Session, 6th Legislature, 50 Vic., 1887.

BILL.

An Act respecting the Appointment and Proceedings of Police Magistrates.

First Reading,

BILL.

An Act respecting the Appointment and Proceedings of Police Magistrates.

HER MAJESTY, by and with the advice and consent of the Legislative Assembly of the Province of Ontario, enacts as follows :—

1.—(1) The Lieutenant-Governor may appoint more police magistrates than one for any county or union of counties in which *The Canada Temperance Act,* or a like Act, is in force. Any such magistrate shall hold office during pleasure, save that he shall cease to be such police magistrate in case, and from the time that, the said Act, or a new Act which may be substituted therefor, ceases to be in force in the county. *[margin: More police magistrates than one may be appointed where Temperance Act in force;]*

(2) The Lieutenant-Governor in Council may determine the salary (if any) to be paid to a county police magistrate ; the same not to exceed the salary provided for by the 2nd section of *The Act respecting Police Magistrates for Counties.* (48 Vic. c. 17.) He may also allow the travelling expenses of the said magistrate at some amount between $150 and $300, and no more than $300. Only one county magistrate shall receive a salary. *[margin: Salary.]*

(3) Such salary and expenses shall be paid by the treasurer of the county quarterly.

2. A police magistrate appointed under this Act, or *The Act respecting Police Magistrates for Counties,* shall, in addition to his salary, be entitled to receive to his own use the same fees and emoluments as are paid to Justices of the Peace. 48 Vict. c. 17 ; 46 Vict. c. 18, s. 433 (3). *[margin: Fees.]*

3. The appointment of a Police Magistrate under this Act, or under *The A t respecting Police Magistrates for Counties,* may exclude any city or town which has a Police Magistrate, and otherwise a Police Magistrate appointed for a county shall have jurisdiction in the whole of the county, inclusive of every city or town therein, whether such city or town has or has not also a Police Magistrate of its own. *[margin: Jurisdiction.]*

4. Sections 3 and 4 of *The Act respecting Police Magistrates for Counties,* shall apply to police magistrates appointed under this Act. *[margin: General powers of police magistrates.]*

5.—(1) A salaried county police magistrate shall have power from time to time to appoint a constable for the county or union of counties of which he is a police magistrate, such constable to hold office for not more than thirty days ; his *[margin: Certain police magistrates may appoint temporary constables.]*

appointment may be revoked by the police magistrate, or by the Provincial Secretary, before the expiration of the thirty days.

(2) The police magistrate making any such appointment shall forthwith notify the Provincial Secretary thereof. (R. S. O. 5 c. 82, s. 5.)

(3) A constable appointed by a police magistrate shall have the same authority and privileges, and he subject to the same liability and the performance of the same duties, as if appointed by the Court of General Sessions of the Peace. (R. S. O. c. 82, 10 s. 7.)

Place of hold- **6.** To prevent doubts it is hereby declared and enacted that
ing Court. a Police Magistrate for a County, or part of a County, may sit or hold his Courts within a Town separated from the County, or a City situate within the limits of the County for judicial 15 purposes, and may in such Town or City hear complaints, and dispose thereof as Police Magistrate in respect of all matters arising within the County, or the part of the County for which he is appointed, and do all acts, matters and things in the discharge of the duties and powers of his office as fully as when 20 sitting or holding Court in any other part of the County for which he is appointed.

Protection of **7.** It is further declared and enacted, that Police Magistrates
Magistrates. are entitled to the same protection as Justices of the Peace under *The Act to protect Justices of the Peace and other officers* 5 *from vexatious actions,* and under *The Act respecting the Magistracy.* R. S. O. c. 73 ; 41 Vict. c. 4.

No actions **8 ..(1)** No action shall lie against a stipendiary or police
against stipen-
diary or police magistrate for or by reason of any process issued, or conviction
magistrates made by, or any proceedings of any kind taken before him 30
for certain
mistakes as to alone, or authorized by him, in good faith, in any case which,
jurisdiction by the law applicable thereto, was not cognizable by such
under Canada
Temperance police magistrate, or not by him sitting alone, or should have
Act. been heard by two justices of the peace, or by the mayor of a city or town within the district, county, union of counties, 35 or part of a district or county or union of counties, for which the stipendiary or police magistrate was appointed.

(2) This section shall not prevent an action from being maintained where and so far as the action would be maintainable against the mayor or justices of the peace if the process 40 had been issued or conviction made by, or proceedings taken before, or authority given by him or them, in a matter in which he or they had jurisdiction.

(3) No action shall lie against a constable or peace officer for anything done by him under and by virtue of process 45 issued or authority given, as in the first sub-section mentioned, unless the action would be maintainable if the process had been issued or authority given by a person or persons legally qualified to issue the process or give the authority.

(4) This section shall apply to pending actions, and also to 50 actions (whether brought before or after this Act) for anything done before the passing of this Act, as well as to actions in respect of acts which may hereafter be done.

No. 126.

1st Session, 6th Legislature, 50 Vic., 1887.

BILL.

An Act respecting the Appointment and Proceedings of Police Magistrates.

(Re-printed as Amended by Committee of whole House.)

First Reading, 28th March, 1887.
Second " 29th " 1887.

BILL.

An Act respecting the Appointment and Proceedings of Police Magistrates.

HER MAJESTY, by and with the advice and consent of the Legislative Assembly of the Province of Ontario, enacts as follows :—

1.—(1) The Lieutenant-Governor may appoint more police
5 magistrates than one for any county or union of counties *or district or part of a district* in which *The Canada Temperance Act*, or a like Act, is in force. Any such magistrate shall hold office during pleasure, save that he shall cease to be such police magistrate in case, and from the time that, the said Act,
10 or a new Act which may be substituted therefor, ceases to be in force in the county, *or district or part of district aforesaid.*

More police magistrates than one may be appointed where Temperance Acts in force.

(2) The Lieutenant-Governor in Council may determine the salary (if any) to be paid to a county *or district* police magistrate; the same not to exceed the salary provided for by section 2
15 of *The Act respecting Police Magistrates for Counties.* He may also allow the travelling expenss of the said magistrate at some amount between $150 and $300, and no more than $300. Only one *police* magistrate *appointed under either Act,* shall receive a salary under authority of the Lieutenant-Governor
20 in Council, but the municipal council of the county may grant a salary to other police magistrates appointed for the county, such other police magistrate consenting thereto.

Salary.

48 V. c. 17.

(3) Such salary and expenses *of a county police magistrate* shall be paid by the treasurer of the county quarterly.

·25 2. A police magistrate appointed under this Act, or *The Act respecting Police Magistrates for Counties,* shall, in addition to his salary, be entitled to receive the same fees and emoluments as are paid to justices of the peace. A salaried police magistrate appointed under either Act shall pay over to the treasurer
30 of the said county what he receives in respect of the said fees and emoluments or such of them as this Legislature is competent so to dispose of.

Fees.

3.. The appointment of a police magistrate under this Act, or under *The Act respecting Police Magistrates for Counties,*
35 may exclude any city or town which has a police magistrate, and otherwise a police magistrate appointed for a county *or district* shall have jurisdiction in the whole of the county *or district*, inclusive of every city or town therein, whether such city or town has or has not also a police magistrate of its own.

Jurisdiction.

4. Sections 3 and 4 of *The Act respecting Police Magistrates for Counties*, shall apply to police magistrates appointed under this Act.

General powers of police magistrates.

5.—(1) A salaried county *or district* police magistrate shall have power from time to time to appoint a constable for the county or union of counties *or district* of which he is a police magistrate, such constable to hold office for not more than thirty days; his appointment may be revoked by the police magistrate, or by the Provincial Secretary, before the expiration of the thirty days.

Certain police magistrates may appoint temporary constables.

(2) The police magistrate making any such appointment shall forthwith notify the Provincial Secretary thereof.

(3) A constable appointed by a police magistrate shall have the same authority and privileges, and be subject to the same liability and the performance of the same duties, as if appointed by the Court of General Sessions of the Peace.

6. To prevent doubts it is hereby declared and enacted that a police magistrate for a county *or district*, or part of a county *or district*, may sit or hold his Courts within a town separated from the county *or district*, or a city situate within the limits of the county for judicial purposes, and may in such town or city hear complaints, and dispose thereof as police magistrate in respect of all matters arising within the county, or the part of the county for which he is appointed, and do all acts, matters and things in the discharge of the duties and powers of his office as fully as when sitting or holding court in any other part of the county for which he is appointed.

Place of holding Court.

7. It is further declared and enacted, that police magistrates are entitled to the same protection as justices of the peace under *The Act to protect Justices of the Peace and other officers from vexatious actions*, and under *The Act respecting the Magistracy.*

Protection of magistrates.

8.—(1) No action shall lie against a stipendiary or police magistrate for or by reason of any process issued, or conviction made by, or any proceedings of any kind taken before him alone, or authorized by him, in good faith, in any case which, by the law applicable thereto, was not cognizable by such police magistrate, or not by him sitting alone, or should have been heard by two justices of the peace, or by the mayor of a city or town within the district, county, union of counties, or part of a district or county or union of counties, for which the stipendiary or police magistrate was appointed.

No actions against stipendiary or police magistrates for certain mistakes as to jurisdiction under Canada Temperance Act.

(2) This section shall not prevent an action from being maintained where and so far as the action would be maintainable against the mayor or justices of the peace if the process had been issued or conviction made by, or proceedings taken before, or authority given by him or them, in a matter in which he or they had jurisdiction.

(3) No action shall lie against a constable or peace officer for anything done by him under and by virtue of process issued or authority given, as in the first sub-section men-tioned, unless the action would be maintainable if the process 5 had been issued or authority given by a person or persons legally qualified to issue the process or give the authority.

(4) This section shall apply to pending actions, and also to actions (whether brought before or after this Act) for anything done before the passing of this Act, as well as to actions in 10 respect of acts which may hereafter be done.

1st Session, 6th Legislature, 50 Vic., 1887.

BILL.

An Act respecting the appointment and Proceedings of Police Magistrates.

(Again re-printed as amended by Committee of the Whole House.)

First Reading, 28th March, 1887.
Second " 29th " 1887.

No. 127]   **BILL.**   1887.]

An Act for further Improving the Law.

WHEREAS, in view of the new consolidation of the Statute
Law of this Province, it is expedient to amend by this
Act certain Statutes herein mentioned ;

Therefore Her Majesty, by and with the advice and consent
5 of the Legislative Assembly of the Province of Ontario, enacts
as follows :—

1. This Act may be cited as the "Statute Amendment Act, *Title.*
1887."

2. *The Interpretation Act* is amended by inserting in the *Interpre-*
10 eighth section, sub-section 16, after the word "successors" the *tation Act.*
words "Dominion Day." (R. S. O. c. 1, s. 8 (16) ; Rev. Stat.
Can. c. 1, s. 7 (26) ; D. 42 V. c. 47.)

(2) Also by inserting the following additional sub-sections :

16a. If the time limited by an Act for any proceeding, or for
15 the doing of anything under its provisions, expires or falls
upon a holiday, the time so limited shall extend to, and
such thing may be done on, the day next following which is
not a holiday. (D. R. S. c. 1, s. 7 (27)).

17a. Where by an Act of the Legislature of this Pro-
20 vince, or by a rule of the Legislative Assembly, or by an order,
regulation or commission made or issued by the Lieutenant-
Governor in Council, under a law authorizing him to require
the taking of evidence under oath, an oath is authorized or
directed to be made, taken or administered, the oath may be
25 administered, and a certificate of its having been made, taken
or administered may be given, by any one named in the Act,
rule, order, regulation or commission, or by a judge of any
Court, a notary public, justice of the peace, or commissioner
for taking affidavits, having authority or jurisdiction in
30 the place where the oath is administered. *Ib.* (29).

3. *The Election Act* is amended by inserting after the *Election Act.*
words "by reason of" in the first line of section 197, the
following words : "any irregularity in any of the proceedings preliminary to the polling, or by reason of". (R. S. O. c.
35 10, s. 197.)

4. *The Act respecting the office of sheriff*, section 34, is *Sheriffs.*
amended by adding the words "and long vacation" after the
word "holiday" in the first line, and by striking out the
words "all that time" in the third line, and adding in lieu
40 thereof the words "the time the office is required to be kept
open," and adding the following sub-section :—

(2) During the long vacation, from the 1st day of July to the 1st day of September, both days inclusive, the sheriff's office shall be kept open from ten o'clock in the forenoon until one o'clock in the afternoon. (R. S. O. c. 16).

(3) The said Act is further amended by inserting therein 5 the following provision :—

Where, for the purpose of investigating or establishing some title to land, a certificate respecting executions against lands is required from a sheriff, the sheriff if so requested, shall include in one certificate any number of names in respect of which the 10 certificate may be required in the same matter or investigation.

Petition of rights.   **5**. The following is substituted for section 20 of the Petition of Rights Act :—

Nothing in this Act contained shall prevent any suppliant from proceeding as before the passing of this Act ; nor entitle 15 a subject to proceed by petition of right in any case in which he would not be so entitled under the Acts heretofore passed by the Parliament of the United Kingdom. (R. S. O. c. 59, s. 20 ; Imp. 23 and 24 Vict., c. 34, s. 7 : Dom. 38 Vict., c. 12 ; Dom. 39 Vict., c. 27. s. 7.)   20

Writs of execution.   **6**. *The Act respecting Writs of Execution*, section 14, is amended by adding thereto the following sub-section :—

(3). Where the writ against the lands is issued in the same suit in which the writ of attachment, under the Act respecting 25 absconding debtors had been issued, the Court or a Judge may order the sheriff to sell the lands before the expiration of the twelve months, subject to the provisions contained in section 41 of this Act. (R. S. O. c. 66, s. 14.)

Transfer of real property.   **7**. The *Act respecting the Transfer of Real Property* is 30 amended by inserting therein the following section :

5a. A person to whom a power, whether coupled with an interest or not, is given may by deed release, or contract not to exercise, the power, whether the power was created by an instrument coming into operation before or after the com- 35 mencement of this Act. (Imp. 44 & 45 Vic., c. 41, s. 52 ; R. S. O. c. 98.)

Life insurance policies.   **8**. *The Act respecting Trustees and Executors and the Administration of Estates* is amended by inserting therein the following section :   40

Where, under a policy of life insurance issued by an insurance company whose head office is in this Province, the money is payable to the representatives of a person who at the time of his death was domiciled or resident in any part of the Dominion of Canada other than Ontario, and no person has be- 45 come his personal representative in this Province, the money may, after the expiration of   months, be paid to the personal representative appointed by the Court of the Province in which the deceased was resident or domiciled at the time of his death : Provided it appears upon the pro- 50 bate or letters of administration, or other like document of such Court, or by a certificate of the Judge under the seal of the

Court, that it had been shown to the satisfaction of the Court that the deceased at the time of his death was domiciled or resident at some place within the jurisdiction of such Court.

(2). This section applies to policies heretofore issued as well as
5 to policies to be issued hereafter. (R. S. O. c. 107 ; c. 160 ; Dom.
34 V. c. 5, s. 24 ; Dom. 48 and 49 V. c. 49, ss. 5, 11 ; Rev. Stat.
Dom. c. 120, s. 35 ; Imp. 21 and 22 V. c. 36, s. $\frac{12}{}$, 20 and 21
V. c. 79, ss. 95, 96 ; Con. C., c. 91, s. 1.)

9. The Act to amend the law of vendor and purchaser, and Memorials;
10 to simplify titles, is amended by inserting the following as a how far notice.
sub-section of the first section :—

After the 1st day of January, 1890, no person shall be presumed under the Registry Act to have notice of the contents of any deed or other instrument registered by memo-
15 rial except so far as its contents are disclosed by the memorial. (R. S. O. c. 109, s. 1 (3), s. 2).

10. The Registry Act is amended by inserting the following ; Registry Act.

66a. Any instrument (including a will or probate of a will) may, in addition to the mode of registration provided for by
20 sections 65 and 66, be registered by the production of the original instrument and the deposit of a true copy thereof, sworn to by a person who has compared the same with the original ; or by the deposit of a copy certified by the registrar of a registration division in whose office the original instru-
25 ment is deposited.

(2) Or, in the case of a notarial or prothonotarial copy of any instrument executed in the Province of Quebec, by the deposit of a copy certified by the registrar of a registration division in whose office a notarial or prothonotarial copy has
30 been registered in the manner provided by section 54 of the Registry Act.

(3) In case an instrument which has been registered by memorial is again registered under the preceding provisions of this Act or otherwise, the registrar shall write upon the copy
35 of the memorial entered on the registry, a memorandum as follows : " Registered in full at No.   ," giving a reference to the number and volume where the full registration is entered.

(4) Instruments which do not describe the land in accord-
40 ance with the last registered map or plan (if any) affecting the land shall be entered in a book or succession of books, kept specially for such instruments ; and such book or books shall be separately indexed. (R. S. O. c. 111.)

11. Section 3 of *The Act to secure to Wives and Children* Life Insurance
45 *the benefit of Life Insurance* is repealed and the following for benefit of
substituted therefor :— wives and
children.

The insured may by an instrument in writing attached to or endorsed on, or identifying the policy by its number or otherwise, vary an appropriation previously made, so as to extend
50 the benefits of the policy to the wife, or to the children, or one or more of them, although the policy is expressed to be for the benefit of the wife alone, or for the child or children

alone, or although a prior declaration was so restricted; and he may also apportion the insurance money among the persons intended to be benefited; and may, from time to time, by an instrument in writing attached to or endorsed on the policy or referring to the same, alter the apportionment as he 5 deems proper; he may also, by his will, make or alter the apportionment of the insurance money; and an apportionment made by his will shall prevail over any other made before the date of the will, except so far as such other apportionment has been acted on before notice of the apportionment by the 10 will. (R. S. O. c. 129, s. 3.)

(2) This section applies to policies heretofore issued, as well as to future policies.

Cemetery Companies.   **12**. *The Act respecting the Incorporation of Cemetery Companies by Letters Patent* is amended by inserting therein 15 the following section :

1a. (1) In the case of an incorporated village, a cemetery within the village may be established by the company where it appears to the satisfaction of the Lieutenant-Governor in Council that from the extent of territory included in the village 20 a cemetery may safely be established therein, and that the municipal council and local board of health of the village approve thereof, and that in the opinion of the Provincial Board of Health the proposed cemetery may under all the circumstances be safely permitted.   25

(2) The Letters Patent shall describe the territory to which the permission applies.

(3) The expenses of the Provincial Board of Health in the matter shall be paid by or on behalf of the applicants for the Letters Patent before the same are issued. (43 V. c. 23.)   30

Vital statistics.   **13**. *The Act to amend the Law respecting the Registration of Births, Marriages and Deaths* is amended by inserting the words "town and," between the words "every" and "township," in the fourth line of the said first section. 44 V. c. 4, s. 1.   35

Married women.   **14**. *The Married Woman's Property Act, 1884,* shall not be construed to deprive a woman married prior to the commencement of said Act of any right or privilege which she had at the time of the commencement of the Act, or would afterwards have if that Act had not been passed. (47 V. c. 19.) 40

Industrial Schools.   **15**. The Act entitled *An Act to Amend and Consolidate the Acts respecting Industrial Schools* is amended by inserting after the word "dollar" the words "and fifty cents" in the 22nd and 25th sections respectively. (47 V. c. 46.)

Limited administration.   **16**. A person entitled to take out letters of administration 45 to the estate of a deceased person is entitled to take out such letters limited to the personal estate of the deceased, exclusive of the real estate. (49 V. c. 22, s. 4.)

No 127.

1st Session, 6th Legislature, 50 Vic., 1887.

BILL.

An Act for further Improving the Law.

First Reading,   March, 1887.

BILL.

An Act for further Improving the Law.

As the same will be moved in Committee of the Whole.

WHEREAS, in view of the new consolidation of the Statute Law of this Province, it is expedient to amend by this Act certain Statutes herein mentioned ;

Therefore Her Majesty, by and with the advice and consent 5 of the Legislative Assembly of the Province of Ontario, enacts as follows :—

1. This Act may be cited as the " Statute Amendment Act, Title. 1887."

2. *The Interpretation Act* is amended by inserting in the Interpre-tation Act. 10 eighth section, sub-section 16, after the word " successors " the words " Dominion Day." (R. S. O. c. 1, s. 8 (16) ; Rev. Stat. Can. c. 1, s. 7 (26) ; D. 42 V. c. 47.)

(2) Also by inserting the following additional sub-sections :

16*a*. If the time limited by an Act for any proceeding, or for 15 the doing of anything under its provisions, expires or falls upon a holiday, the time so limited shall extend to, and such thing may be done on, the day next following which is not a holiday. (D. R. S. c. 1, s. 7 (27)).

17*a*. Where by an Act of the Legislature of this Pro-20 vince, or by a rule of the Legislative Assembly, or by an order, regulation or commission made or issued by the Lieutenant-Governor in Council, under a law authorizing him to require the taking of evidence under oath, an oath is authorized or directed to be made, taken or administered, the oath may be 25 administered, and a certificate of its having been made, taken or administered may be given, by any one named in the Act, rule, order, regulation or commission, or by a judge of any Court, a notary public, justice of the peace, or commissioner for taking affidavits, having authority or jurisdiction in 30 the place where the oath is administered. *Ib.* (29).

3. *The Election Act* is amended by inserting after the Election Act. words " by reason of" in the first line of section 197, the following words : " any irregularity in any of the proceed-ings preliminary to the polling, or by reason of". (R. S. O. c. 35 10, s. 197.)

4. *The Act respecting the office of sheriff*, section 34, is Sheriffs. amended by adding the words "and long vacation" after the word " holidays " in the first line, and by striking out the words " all that time " in the third line, and adding in lieu 40 thereof the words " the time the office is required to be kept open," and adding the following sub-section :—

(2) During the long vacation, from the 1st day of July to the 1st day of September, both days inclusive, the sheriff's office shall be kept open from ten o'clock in the forenoon until one o'clock in the afternoon. (R. S. O. c. 16).

4a. The said Act is further amended by inserting therein the following provision:—

Where, for the purpose of investigating or establishing some title to land, a certificate respecting executions against lands is required from a sheriff, the sheriff if so requested, shall include in one certificate any number of names in respect of which the certificate may be required in the same matter or investigation.

Petition of rights.

5. The following is substituted for section 20 of the Petition of Rights Act —

Nothing in this Act contained shall prevent any suppliant from proceeding as before the passing of this Act; nor entitle a subject to proceed by petition of right in any case in which he would not be so entitled under the Acts heretofore passed by the Parliament of the United Kingdom. (R. S. O. c. 59, s. 20; Imp. 23 and 24 Vict., c. 34, s. 7; Dom. 38 Vict., c. 12; Dom. 39 Vict., c. 27. s. 7.)

Writs of execution.

6. *The Act respecting Writs of Execution*, section 14, is amended by adding thereto the following sub-section:—

(3). Where the writ against the lands is issued in the same suit in which the writ of attachment under the Act respecting absconding debtors had been issued, the Court or a Judge may order the sheriff to sell the lands before the expiration of the twelve months, subject to the provisions contained in section 41 of this Act. (R. S. O. c. 66, s. 14.)

6a. The Act providing for the better governing of that part of Ontario situate in the vicinity of the Falls of Niagara is amended by striking out the 10th section. R. S. O. c. 91, s. 10.

Transfer of real property.

7. The *Act respecting the Transfer of Real Property* is amended by inserting therein the following section:

5a. A person to whom a power, whether coupled with an interest or not, is given may by deed release, or contract not to exercise, the power, whether the power was created by an instrument coming into operation before or after the commencement of this Act. (Imp. 44 & 45 Vic., c. 41, s. 52; R. S. O. c. 98.)

Life insurance policies.

8. *The Act respecting Trustees and Executors and the Administration of Estates* is amended by inserting therein the following section:

Where, under a policy of life insurance issued by an insurance company whose head office is in this Province, the money is payable to the representatives of a person who at the time of his death was domiciled or resident in any part of the Dominion of Canada other than Ontario, and no person has become his personal representative in this Province, the money may, after the expiration of two months, be paid to the personal representative appointed by the Court of the

Province in which the deceased was resident or domiciled at the time of his death : Provided it appears upon the probate or letters of administration, or other like document of such Court, or by a certificate of the Judge under the seal of the
5 Court, that it had been shown to the satisfaction of the Court that the deceased at the time of his death was domiciled or resident at some place within the jurisdiction of such Court.

(2). This section applies to policies heretofore issued as well as to policies to be issued hereafter. (R. S. O. c. 107 ; c. 160 ; Dom.
10 34 V. c. 5, s. 24 ; Dom. 48 and 49 V. c. 49, ss. 5, 11 ; Rev. Stat. Dom. c. 120, s. 35 ; Imp. 21 and 22 V. c. 36; s. 12 ; 20 and 21 V. c. 79, ss. 95, 96 ; Con. C., c. 91, s. 1.)

8a. Section 31 of the *Act respecting Trustees and Executors and the Administration of Estates* is repealed, and the following
15 is substituted therefor :—In case the executor or administrator gives notice in writing [referring to this section and of his intention to avail himself thereof] to any creditor or other person of whose claims against the estate he has notice, or to the attorney or agent of such creditor or other person, that he the
20 executor or administrator rejects or disputes the claim, it shall be the duty of the claimant to commence his action in respect of the claim within six months after the notice is given, in case the debt or some part thereof was due at the time of the notice, or within six months from the time the
25 debt or some part thereof falls due if no part thereof was due at the time of the notice, and in default the claim shall be forever barred. [Provided always that in case the claimant shall be nonsuited at the trial the claimant, or his executors or admininistrators, may commence a new action within a
30 further period of one month from the time of the nonsuit.] R. S. O. c. 107, s. 31.

(The changes are the words in brackets.)

9. The Act to amend the law of vendor and purchaser and Memorials; to simplify titles, is amended by inserting the following as a how far notice.
35 sub-section of the first section :—

After the 1st day of January, 1890, no person shall be presumed to have notice of the contents of any deed or other instrument registered by memorial except so far as its contents are disclosed by the memorial. (R. S. O. c. 109, s. 1
40 (3), s. 2). R. S. O. c. 111, s.s. 63-66 ; 31 V. c. 20, s.s. 34-37.

9a. The Act respecting Joint Stock Companies for the construction of works to facilitate the transmission of timber down rivers and streams, is amended by adding after the word " situate " in the 12th line thereof, the words following :—" as
45 arbitrator for such owner or occupier so neglecting to name an arbitrator after having been duly notified by the county as aforesaid, or as third arbitrator, or as arbitrator." R. S. O. c. 153, s. 44.

10. The Registry Act is amended by inserting the following ; Registry Act.

50 66a.—(1) Any instrument which has been registered by memorial prior to the first day of January, 1886, and has endorsed thereon a certificate of the registration thereof, may

be re-registered at full length in the same or any other registry division by the production of the original instrument and the deposit of a copy thereof with an affidavit verifying the copy.

(2) In re-registering such instrument the Registrar shall copy the affidavit of verification and the certificate of former 5 registration, and shall write in the margin of the Registry Book the words " Original not deposited," and where the former registration was made in the same office, the Registrar shall write upon the entry of the memorial in the Registry Book a memorandum as follows :—" Re-registered in full at No."——, 10 giving a reference to the number and volume where the full registration is entered, and he shall also note the re-registration in red ink wherever in an abstract index the memorial is entered.

(3) The Registrar shall also indorse upon the original instrument a certificate of the re-registration, in a form similar to the 15 certificate of registration given in Schedule G to this Act.   R. S. O. c. 111.

(4.) Section 1 of the Act 49 Victoria, Chapter 24, entitled " An Act to amend The Registry Act " is hereby repealed.

Life Insurance for benefit of wives and children.

11. Section 6 of *The Act to secure to Wives and Children* 20 *the benefit of Life Insurance* is repealed, and the following substituted therefor :—

The insured may by an instrument in writing attached to or endorsed on, or identifying the policy by its number or otherwise, vary an apportionment previously made, so as to extend 25 the benefits of the policy to the wife or the children, or to one or more of them, although the policy is expressed to be for the benefit of the wife alone, or for the child or children alone, or although a prior declaration was so restricted ; and he may also apportion the insurance money among the 30 persons intended to be benefited ; and may, from time to time, by an instrument in writing attached to or endorsed on the policy or referring to the same, alter the apportionment as he deems proper ; he may also, by his will, make or alter the appropriation of the insurance money ; and an apportionment 35 made by his will shall prevail over any other made before the date of the will, except so far as such other apportionment has been acted on before notice of the apportionment by the will. (R. S. O. c. 129, s. 3.)   47 V. c. 20, s. 6.

(2) This section applies to policies heretofore issued, as well 40 as to future policies.

11a. Sub-section 4 of section 12 of *The Assessment Act* is amended by adding the following words to the particulars which the Assessor is required to set down in column **4** :—" But where any person being a land-holder's son is also 45 within the meaning of *The Municipal Act*, a ' farmer's son,' the Assessor shall, instead of the letters ' F. S.,' insert in the Assessment Roll the letters ' L. and F. S.' "   R.S.O. c. 180, s. 12 (4).

11b. The Act entitled, *An Act to amend the License Act* 50 *and for other purposes*, is amended by inserting therein the following section :—

7a. When *The Canada Temperance Act, 1878,* is in force in any county or union of counties, and any city or town situate within such county or union of counties has withdrawn from the county or union of counties for municipal purposes, such
5 city or town shall pay a just and proportionate share of the expenses incurred by the county or union of counties in enforcing the provisions of the Act in such county or union of counties. (41 Vic., c. 14.)

12. The *Act respecting Cemetery Companies,* and *the Act* Cemetery
10 *respecting the Incorporation of Cemetery Companies by* Companies. *Letters Patent,* are amended by inserting therein respectively, the following section :

(1) In the case of an incorporated · village, a cemetery within the village may be established by the company where
15 it appears to the satisfaction of the Lieutenant-Governor in Council that from the extent of territory included in the village a cemetery may safely be established therein, and that the municipal council and local board of health of the village approve thereof, and that in the opinion of the Pro-
20 vincial Board of Health the proposed cemetery may under all the circumstances be safely permitted.

(2) The expenses of the Provincial Board of Health in the matter shall be paid by or on behalf of the applicants. R. S. O. c. 170. (43 V. c. 23.)

25 **13.** *The Act to amend the Law respecting the Registration* Vital sta-
of Births, Marriages and Deaths is amended by inserting tistics. the words " town and," between the words " every" and " township," in the fourth line of the said first section. 44 V. c. 4, s. 1.

14. *The Married Women's Property Act, 1884,* shall not be Married
30 construed to deprive a woman married prior to the com- women. mencement of said Act of any right or privilege which she had at the time of the commencement of the Act, or would afterwards have if that Act had not been passed. (47 V. c. 19.)

14a. The said Act is further amended by inserting the
35 following section :—

Every married woman, whether married before or after the passing of this Act, shall be entitled to have and hold as her separate property, and to dispose of as her separate property, the wages, earnings, money and property
40 gained or acquired by her in any employment, trade or occupation in which she is engaged or carries on, and in which her husband has no proprietary interest, or gained or acquired by the exercise of any literary, artistic or scientific skill. 47 V. c. 19, s. 3.

45 **15.** The Act entitled *An Act to Amend and Consolidate* Industrial *the Acts respecting Industrial Schools* is amended by insert- Schools. ing after the word "dollar" the words "and fifty cents" in the 22nd and 25th sections respectively. (47 V. c. 46.)

15a. *The Election Law Amendment Act, 1884,* first schedule,
50 line 9 of the resident householders' oath is amended by sub-

stituting for the words " resident of this electoral district " the words " resident within the territory included in this electoral district." 47 V. c. 4.

15b. The second schedule of the same Act, lines 10 and 11 of the resident owners' oath, is amended by substitutnig for 5 the words " resident of this electoral district " the words "resident within the territory included in this electoral district." 47 V. c. 4.

15c. *The Administration of Justice Act, 1885*, chapter 13, section 23, is amended by striking out all the words after 10 the word " or " in the sixth line, and substituting the following sub-sections :—

(2) Instead of appealing to the Court of Appeal either party may, in cases tried by a judge, move before the County Court within the first two days of its next quarterly sittings, for a 15 new trial, or to set aside the judgment on any ground except that upon the evidence given the judgment, so directed, is wrong in law.

(3) In cases tried with a jury, instead of appealing to the Court of Appeal, a similar motion may be made before the 20 County Court for a new trial, or to set aside the judgment directed to be entered upon the special findings of the jury upon any ground except that the judgment so directed to be entered is wrong in law.

(4) Either party may appeal to the Court of Appeal from 25 the judgment of the County Court upon applications under subjections 2 and 3.

(5) Where a party is entitled to move before the County Court under sub-sections 2 and 3, he may move before the said Court upon all grounds which would be open to him if he were 30 appealing to the Court of Appeal. 48 V. c. 13.

(This amendment is to conform to the commissioners' draft as amended by the special committee.)

15d. The *Act to Amend the Franchise and Representation Act, 1885*, schedule, form 19, is amended by inserting after the 35 words " resident of " the words " the territory included in." 49 V. c. 3.

Limited administration.
16. A person entitled to take out letters of administration to the estate of a deceased person is entitled to take out such letters limited to the personal estate of the deceased, 40 exclusive of the real estate. (49 V. c. 22, s. 4.)

16a. In the case of a person dying after the first day of July, 1886, his personal representative for the time being shall, in the interpretation of any statute of this Province, or in the construction of any instrument to which the deceased was a 45 party or in which he was interested, be deemed in law his " heirs and assigns," unless a contrary intention appears. 49 V. c. 106.

No. 127.

1st Session, 6th Legislature, 50 Vic., 1887.

BILL.

An Act for further Improving the Law.

(*With the amendments to be proposed in Committee of the Whole.*)

First Reading,   March, 1887.

No. 127] **BILL.** [1887.

An Act for further Improving the Law.

WHEREAS, in view of the new consolidation of the Statute Law of this Province, it is expedient to amend by this Act certain Statutes herein mentioned;

Therefore Her Majesty, by and with the advice and consent 5 of the Legislative Assembly of the Province of Ontario, enacts as follows :—

1. This Act may be cited as *The Statute Amendment Act*, Title. *1887.*

2. (1) *The Interpretation Act* is amended by inserting in R. S. O. c. 1, 10 section 8, sub-section 16, after the word "successors" the amended. words "Dominion Day." (R. S. O. c. 1, s. 8 (16); Rev. Stat. Can. c. 1, s. 7 (26); D. 42 V. c. 47.)

(2) Also by inserting the following additional sub-sections:

16*a*. If the time limited by an Act for any proceeding, or for 15 the doing of anything under its provisions, expires or falls upon a holiday, the time so limited shall extend to, and such thing may be done on, the day next following which is not a holiday. (D. R. S. c. 1, s. 7 (27)).

17*a*. Where by an Act of the Legislature of this Pro-20 vince, or by a rule of the Legislative Assembly, or by an order, regulation or commission made or issued by the Lieutenant-Governor in Council, under a law authorizing him to require the taking of evidence under oath, an oath is authorized or directed to be made, taken or administered, the oath may be 25 administered, and a certificate of its having been made, taken or administered may be given, by any one named in the Act, rule, order, regulation or commission, or by a judge of any Court, a notary public, justice of the peace, or commissioner for taking affidavits, having authority or jurisdiction in 30 the place where the oath is administered. *Ib.* (29).

3. *The Election Act* is amended by inserting after the R. S. O. c. words "by reason of" in the first line of section 197, the 10, s. 197, following words: "any irregularity in any of the proceed-amended. ings preliminary to the polling, or by reason of". (R. S. O. c. 35 10, s. 197.)

4. *The Act respecting the office of sheriff,* is amended by Sheriffs. inserting the following as sub-sections to section 1 :

(2) The Lieutenant-Governor in Council may, in manner aforesaid, at any time hereafter, and from time to time, 40 appoint one fit and proper person to be Sheriff of the county of York, and another fit and proper person to be Sheriff of the city of Toronto, every such Sheriff to hold office during pleasure.

(*a*) In such case the Lieutenant-Governor in Council may define what duties with reference to courts held jointly for the city and county, including any duties to be performed under *The Jurors' Act*, shall be performed by the Sheriffs of the city and county 5 respectively.

(*b*) No act done by either of the said Sheriffs shall be held unlawful or invalid. on the ground that the same should have been done by the other. (R.S.O.c.16.)

R. S. O. c. 16, amended. **5.** The said Act is further amended by inserting therein the following provision :— 10

Certificate as to executions. Where, for the purpose of investigating or establishing some title to land, a certificate respecting executions against lands is required from a sheriff, the sheriff if so requested, shall include in one certificate any number of names in respect of which the certificate may be required in the same matter or investigation. 15

(2) The maximum fees payable to a Sheriff in respect of such certificate shall be $4.

R. S. O. c. 59, s. 20, repealed. **6.** The following is substituted for section 20 of *The Ontario Petition of Right Act* :—

Nothing in this Act contained shall prevent any suppliant 20 from proceeding as before the passing of this Act ; nor entitle a subject to proceed by petition of right in any case in which he would not be so entitled under the Acts heretofore passed by the Parliament of the United Kingdom. (R. S. O. c. 59, s. 20 ; Imp. 23 and 24 Vict., c. 34, s. 7 ; Dom. 38 Vict., c. 12 ; Dom. 25 39 Vict., c. 27. s. 7.)

Writs of execution. **7.** *The Act respecting Writs of Execution,* section 14, is amended by adding thereto the following sub-section :—

(3). Where the writ against the lands is issued in the same suit in which the writ of attachment under the Act respecting 30 absconding debtors had been issued, the Court or a Judge may order the sheriff to sell the lands before the expiration of the twelve months, subject to the provisions contained in section 41 of this Act. (R. S. O. c. 66, s. 14.)

R. S. O. c. 91, s. 10, repealed. **8.** *The Act to provide for the better government of that 35 part of Ontario situated in the vicinity of the Falls of Niagara* is amended by striking out section 10. R. S. O. c. 91, s. 10.

Transfer of real property. **9.** *The Act respecting the Transfer of Real Property* is amended by inserting therein the following section :

Person to whom a power is given may release or contract not to exercise same, 5*a*. A person to whom a power, whether coupled with 40 an interest or not, is given may by deed release, or contract not to exercise, the power, whether the power was created by an instrument coming into operation before or after the commencement of this Act. (Imp. 44 & 45 Vic., c. 41, s. 52 ; R. S. O. c. 98.) 45

Life insurance policies. **10:** *The Act respecting Trustees and Executors and the Administration of Estates* is amended by inserting therein the following section :

Where, under a policy of life insurance issued by an insurance company whose head office is in this Province, the money is payable to the representatives of a person who at the time of his death was domiciled or resident in any part of the
5 Dominion of Canada other than Ontario, *or in the Province of Newfoundland,* and no person has become his personal representative in this Province, the money may, after the expiration of two months, be paid to the personal representative appointed by the Court of the Province in which
10 the deceased was resident or domiciled at the time of his death : Provided it appears upon the probate or letters of administration, or other like document of such Court, or by a certificate of the Judge under the seal of the Court, that it had been shown to the satisfaction of the Court
15 that the deceased at the time of his death was domiciled or resident at some place within the jurisdiction of such Court.

(2). This section applies to policies heretofore issued as well as to policies to be issued hereafter, ☞and whether the death has occurred before the passing of this Act or not.☜ (R.S.O.c.107;
20 c. 160 ; Dom. 34 V. c. 5, s. 24; Dom. 48 and 49 V. c. 49, ss. 5, 11 ; Rev. Stat. Dom. c. 120, s. 35 ; Imp. 21 and 22 V. c. 36, s. 12 ; 20 and 21 V. c. 79, ss. 95, 96 ; Con. C, c. 91, s. 1.)

11. Section 31 of *The Act respecting Trustees and Executors and the Administration of Estates* is repealed, and the following
25 is substituted therefor :—In case the executor or administrator gives notice in writing [referring to this section and of his intention to avail himself thereof] to any creditor or other person of whose claims against the estate he has notice, or to the attorney or agent of such creditor or other person, that he the
30 executor or administrator rejects or disputes the claim, it shall be the duty of the claimant to commence his action in respect of the claim within six months after the notice is given, in case the debt or some part thereof was due at the time of the notice, or within six months from the time the
35 debt or some part thereof falls due if no part thereof was due at the time of the notice, and in default the claim shall be forever barred : Provided always that in case the claimant shall be nonsuited at the trial the claimant, or his executors or admininstrators, may commence a new action within a
40 further period of one month from the time of the nonsuit. R. S. O. c. 107, s. 31.

R.S. O. c. 107, s. 31, repealed.

If claim is rejected an action must be brought within a certain period or be barred.

Proviso.

12. Section 44 of *The Act respecting Joint Stock Companies for the construction of works to facilitate the transmission of timber down rivers and streams,* is amended by adding after
45 the word "situate" in the twelfth line thereof, the words following :—"as arbitrator for such owner or occupier so neglecting to name an arbitrator after having been duly notified by the company as aforesaid, or as third arbitrator, or as arbitrator," ☞and by cancelling the following words, " to
50 act in the place of the arbitrator so refusing or neglecting."☜ R. S. O. c. 153, s. 44.

13. *The Registry Act* is amended by inserting the following ; Registry Act.

66a.—(1) Any instrument which has been registered by memorial prior to the first day of January, 1886, and has
55 endorsed thereon a certificate of the registration thereof, may

be re-registered at full length in the same or any other registry division by the production of the original instrument and the deposit of a copy thereof with an affidavit verifying the copy.

(2) In re-registering such instrument the registrar shall copy the affidavit of verification and the certificate of former 5 registration, and shall write in the margin of the registry book the words " Original not deposited," and where the former registration was made in the same office, the registrar shall write upon the entry of the memorial in the registry book a memorandum as follows :—" Re-registered in full at No."——, 10 giving a reference to the number and volume where the full registration is entered, and he shall also note the re-registration in red ink wherever in an abstract index the memorial is entered.

(3) The registrar shall also endorse upon the original instrument a certificate of the re-registration, in a form similar to the 15 certificate of registration given in schedule G to this Act. R. S. O. c. 111.

(4.) Section 1 of the Act 49 Victoria, chapter 24, entitled " *An Act to amend The Registry Act* " is hereby repealed.

Life Insurance for benefit of wives and children. **14.** Section 6 of *The Act to secure to Wives and Children the benefit of Life Insurance* is repealed, and the following 20 substituted therefor :—

The insured may by an instrument in writing attached to or endorsed on, or identifying the policy by its number or otherwise, vary an apportionment previously made, so as to extend the benefits of the policy to the wife or the children, or to 25 one or more of them, although the policy is expressed to be for the benefit of the wife alone, or for the child or children alone, or although a prior declaration was so restricted ; and he may also apportion the insurance money among the persons intended to be benefited ; and may, from time to time, 30 by an instrument in writing attached to or endorsed on the policy or referring to the same, alter the apportionment as he deems proper ; he may also, by his will, make or alter the apportionment of the insurance money ; and an apportionment made by his will shall prevail over any other made before 35 the date of the will, except so far as such other apportionment has been acted on before notice of the apportionment by the will. (R. S. O. c. 129, s. 3.) 47 V. c. 20, s. 6.

(2) This section applies to policies heretofore issued, as well as to future policies. 40

R. S. O. c. 180, s. 12 (4), amended. **15.** Sub-section 4 of section 12 of *The Assessment Act* is amended by adding the following words to the particulars which the assessor is required to set down in column 4 :—" But where any person being a land-holder's son is also within the meaning of *The Municipal Act*, a 'farmer's son,' 45 the Assessor shall, instead of the letters ' F. S.,' insert in the assessment roll the letters 'L. and F. S.'" R. S. O. c. 180, s. 12 (4).

Cemetery Companies. **16.** *The Act respecting Cemetery Companies,* and *The Act respecting the Incorporation of Cemetery Companies by* 50 *Letters Patent,* are amended by inserting therein respectively, the following section :

(1). In the case of an incorporated village, a cemetery within the village may be established by the company where it appears to the satisfaction of the Lieutenant-Governor in Council that from the extent of territory included in the village 5 a cemetery may safely be established therein, and that the municipal council and local board of health of the village approve thereof, and that in the opinion of the Provincial Board of Health the proposed cemetery may under all the circumstances be safely permitted.

10 (2) The expenses of the Provincial Board of Health in the matter shall be paid by or on behalf of the applicants. R. S. O. c. 170. (43 V. c. 23.)

17. The Act respecting municipal assessments and exemp- 43 V. c. 27, s. tions is amended by adding to section 5, the following words : 5 amended. 15 "And continues in respect of such officers only as were appointed before that date." (43 Vic. c. 27, s. 5.)

18. *The Act to amend the Law respecting the Registration* Vital sta- *of Births, Marriages and Deaths* is amended by inserting tistics. the words "town and," between the words "every" and 20 "township," in the fourth line of section 1. 44 V. c. 4, s. 1.

19. *The Married Women's Property Act, 1884,* shall not be Married construed to deprive a woman married prior to the com- women. mencement of said Act of any right or privilege which she had at the time of the commencement of the Act, or would 25 afterwards have if that Act had not been passed. (47 V. c. 19.)

20. The said Act is further amended by inserting the following section :—

Every married woman, whether married before or after Earnings of the passing of this Act, shall be entitled to have and hold married women. 30 as her separate property, and to dispose of as her separate property, the wages, earnings, money and property gained or acquired by her in any employment, trade or occupation in which she is engaged or carries on, and in which her husband has no proprietary interest, or gained or 35 acquired by the exercise of any literary, artistic or scientific skill. 47 V. c. 19, s. 3.

21. Every conveyance made since the 29th day of March, Validity of 1883, or which shall hereafter be made by a married woman conveyances of or affecting her real estate which her husband signed or made since March 29th, 40 executed or shall sign or execute is and shall be taken and 1873. adjudged to be valid and effectual, to have passed or to pass the estate which such conveyance professed or shall profess to pass of such married woman in said real estate. (See R. S. O. c. 127, s. 14.)

45 **22.** Nothing in this Act contained shall render valid any Certain titles conveyance to the prejudice of any title lawfully acquired from not to be any married woman prior to the passing of this Act, nor prejudiced. render valid any conveyance from the married woman not executed in good faith or any conveyance of any land, of 50 which the married woman, or those claiming under her, is or are in actual possession or enjoyment contrary to the terms of such conveyance, or affect any action or proceeding now pending.

Preceding two sections not to affect construction of any statute.

23. The Legislature shall not be deemed by either of the two preceding sections to declare or imply any construction of any statute heretofore passed, as affecting the matters mentioned in the said sections or either of them, or any other matters relating to the rights or powers of married women. 5

Industrial Schools.

24. The Act entitled *An Act to Amend and Consolidate the Acts respecting Industrial Schools* is amended by inserting after the word "dollar" the words "and fifty cents" in the 22nd and 25th sections respectively. (47 V. c. 46.)

47 V. c. 4, sched. 1 amended.

25. *The Election Law Amendment Act, 1884,* first schedule, 10 line 9 of the resident householders' oath is amended by substituting for the words " resident of this electoral district " the words " resident within the territory included in this electoral district." 47 V. c. 4.

47 V. c. 4, sched. 2, amended.

26. The second schedule of the same Act, lines 10 and 11 15 of the resident owners' oath, is amended by substitutnig for the words " resident of this electoral district " the words "resident within the territory included in this electoral district." 47 V. c. 4.

48 V. c. 2, s. 14 amended.

27. *The Franchise and Representation Act, 1885,* is 20 amended by introducing into section 14, before the word " Algoma," in the eighth line, the words " South, Centre, and North Bruce and " (48 Vict. ch. 2, s. 14.)

48 V. c. 13, s. 23, amended, County Court appeals.

28. *The Administration of Justice Act, 1885,* chapter 13 section 23, is amended by striking out all the words after 25 the word " or " in the sixth line, and substituting the following sub-sections :—

(2) Instead of appealing to the Court of Appeal either party may, in cases tried by a judge, move before the County Court within the first two days of its next quarterly sittings, for a 30 new trial, or to set aside the judgment on any ground except that upon the evidence given the judgment, so directed, is wrong in law.

(3) In cases tried with a jury, instead of appealing to the Court of Appeal, a similar motion may be made before the 35 County Court for a new trial, or to set aside the judgment directed to be entered upon the special findings of the jury upon any ground except that the judgment so directed to be entered is wrong in law.

(4) Either party may appeal to the Court of Appeal from 40 the judgment of the County Court upon applications under subsections 2 and 3.

(5) Where a party is entitled to move before the County Court under sub-sections 2 and 3, he may move before the said Court upon all grounds which would be open to him if he were 45 appealing to the Court of Appeal. 48 V. c. 13.

49 V. c. 3, form 19 amended.

29. *The Act to Amend the Franchise and Representation Act, 1885,* schedule, form 19, is amended by inserting after the words " resident of " the words " the territory included in." 49 V. c. 3.

30. Section 86 of the *The Agriculture and Arts Act* is amended by inserting after the word " District," in the fourth line, the words " or Township." (49 Vict. ch. 11, s. 86.) 49 V. c. 11, s. 86, amended.

31. *The Statute Amendment Act, 1886,* is amended by 5 inserting in section 23, after the word " wrong " in the eighteenth line, the words " The action shall be brought at latest within one year after the decease." (49 Vict. ch. 16, s. 23, sub-s. 9.) 49 V. c. 16, s. 23 amended.

32. A person entitled to take out letters of administration 10 to the estate of a deceased person is entitled to take out such letters limited to the personal estate of the deceased, exclusive of the real estate. (49 V. c. 22, s. 4.) Limited administration.

33. In the case of a person dying after the first day of July, 1886, his personal representative for the time being shall, 15 in the interpretation of any statute of this Province, or in the construction of any instrument to which the deceased was a party or in which he was interested, be deemed in law his " heirs and assigns," unless a contrary intention appears. 49 V. c. 106. "Heirs and assigns" to include personal representative.

20 **34.** As against creditors of any mortgagor or person in possession of mortgaged premises under a mortgagor, the right, if any, to distrain upon the mortgaged premises for arrears of interest or for rent, in the nature of or in lieu of interest under the provisions of any mortgage to be hereafter executed, shall 25 be restricted to one year's arrears of such interest or rent, but this restriction shall not apply unless some one of such creditors shall be an execution creditor, or unless there shall be an assignee for the general benefit of such creditors appointed before lawful sale of the goods distrained, nor unless 30 the officer executing such writ of execution, or such assignee shall, by notice in writing to be given to the person distraining, or his attorney, bailiff, or agent, before such lawful sale, claim the benefit of the said restriction, and in case such notice is so given, the distrainor shall relinquish to the officer or 35 assignee the goods distrained, upon receiving one year's arrears of such interest or rent and his reasonable costs of distress, or if such arrears and costs shall not be paid or tendered he shall sell only so much of the goods distrained as shall be necessary to satisfy one year's arrears of such interest or rent and the 40 reasonable costs of distress and sale, and shall thereupon relinquish any residue of goods, and pay any residue of moneys, proceeds of goods so distrained, to the said officer or assignee. Mortgagee's right of distress limited.

35. Any officer executing a writ of execution, or an 45 assignee who shall pay any money to relieve goods from distress under the next preceding section, shall be entitled to reimburse himself therefor out of the proceeds of the sale of such goods. Reimbursement of officer or assignee.

36. Goods distrained for arrears of interest or rent, as 50 aforesaid, shall not be sold except after such public notice as is now required to be given by a landlord who sells goods distrained for rent. Notice of sale.

BILL.

An Act for further Improving the Law.

(Reprinted as amended by Committee of the Whole House.)

First Reading, 28th March, 1887.
Second " 30th " 1887.

THE ATTORNEY-GENERAL.

TORONTO:
PRINTED BY WARWICK & SONS, 26 AND 28 FRONT ST. W

BILL.

An Act to give early effect to certain amendments of
the Law recommended by the Statute Commissioners.

WHEREAS it has again been found expedient to revise and
consolidate the Public General Statutes which apply to
this Province, and are within the authority of its Legislature; and whereas such revision and consolidation have
been made accordingly, by commissioners appointed for 5
this purpose, and among amendments which the commissioners have recommended to go into effect with the body of
statutes as so consolidated and revised, there are some which
it is expedient to bring into force at once ;

Therefore Her Majesty, by and with the advice and consent 10
of the Legislative Assembly of the Province and Ontario,
enacts as follows :—

1. The Acts and parts of Acts set forth in the left hand
columns of the Schedule hereto, are hereby amended as stated
and set forth in the right hand columns of the Schedule, and 15
shall go into force immediately upon the passing of this Act.

2. And whereas it has been found expedient to revise, classify
and consolidate the rules of court affecting practice and procedure, and to include therein the statutory enactments affecting practice and procedure and matters in the nature of 20
practice and procedure, and, whereas this work is now in
preparation, and whereas most of the said statutory enactments
have in consequence been omitted by the Commissioners from
the statutes as consolidated and revised by them as hereinbefore mentioned, it is hereby declared and enacted (to avoid 25
doubts) that the Judges shall be deemed and construed to have
under *The Judicature Act* the same powers of making rules of
court in respect of and varying statutory enactments affecting
practice and procedure or matters in the nature of practice
and procedure, as if the said enactments had been rules in the 30
Schedule to *The Judicature Act,* or had derived their authority
from rules of court.

SCHEDULE.

SHEWING ACTS AND PARTS OF ACTS AMENDED ON THE RECOM-
MENDATION OF THE COMMISSIONERS APPOINTED TO CON- 35
SOLIDATE AND REVISE THE PUBLIC GENERAL STATUTES
OF THE PROVINCE.

CHAPTER AND SUBJECT OF ACT.	Manner in which the same are hereby Amended.
R. S. O. c. 10, s. 180. (Election Act.)	LINE 3.—By inserting the words " sections 113 and 114 of " between the words " by " and " this." 40

R. S. O. c. 23,
s. 29 (1). (Sale
of Public
Lands.)

By cancelling the last two lines after the word " void," and substituting these words, " In case of a patent for land being repealed or avoided by the High Court, the judgment shall be registered in the office of the Provincial Secretary."

R. S. O. c. 32,
s. 7. (Sale of
Liquors near
Public
Works).

LINE 4.—By striking out the words " and it appears " and 5 substituting the words " or if it is proved."

R. S. O. c. 40,
s. 59 (4).
(Chancery
Act.)

LINE 5—By striking out the words " Registrar for the time being " and substituting the word " Accountant."

LINES 10, 11—By striking out the words " Judges or."

R. S. O. c. 43,
ss. 10, 11.
(County
Courts' Act).

Repealed and amended by substituting the following :—   10

In lieu of terms, the several County Courts shall in each year hold four quarterly sittings, which (except in the County of York), shall commence respectively on the second Monday in the month of January and the first Monday in the months of April, July and October in each year, and end on the Saturday 15 of the same week, unless extended by order of the Judge.

2. The quarterly sittings of the County Court of the County of York shall commence on the second Monday in January June and October, and the first Monday in April in each year ; and shall end on the Saturday of the same week, unless 20 extended by order of the Judge.

3. It shall not be necessary for the Sheriff or his officers to attend the quarterly sittings of the County Court.

Ib. s. 28.

LINES 1 to 4—Amended by striking all the words of the section to the word " shall" inclusive, in the 4th Line, and substituting 25 the words : " When it is intended by any pleading to bring into question the title to any land, or to any annual or other rent, duty, or other custom or thing, relating to or issuing out of lands or tenements, it shall be so expressly stated in the pleading, nor shall any such pleading."   30

R. S. O. c. 47,
s. 64.
(Division
Courts' Act).

By inserting the following section after section 64 :—

64 (*a*.) In every case where the defendant is a corporation not having its head office in the Province, and the cause of action arose partly in one Division and partly in another, the plaintiff may bring his action in either Division.   35

R. S. O. c. 50,
s. 194).
(Common L.
P. Act).

Repealed and amended by substituting the following :—

" Where the reference is made to the County Judge or the Master in Ordinary (or other officer who is paid by salary), such person shall be entitled to take and receive to his own use the same fees as the Local Masters not paid by salary are entitled 40 to receive upon a reference in an action in the High Court.

Amended by adding the following sub-section —:

(2) " In the computation of time in appealing against, or applying to set aside an award, the vacations shall not be counted."

R. S. O. c. 62, s. 38. (Evidence Act.)

LINE 13—By striking out the work " without Canada."   5

R. S. O. c. 66, s. 30. (Execution.)

By adding the following sub-section:—

(2) " The right of a married woman to dower shall not hereafter be deemed saleable under execution before the death of of her husband."

R. S. O. c. 84, s. 1 (1). (Fees of Counsel and other Officers).

LINES 1 and 2—By striking out the words " Courts of 10 Queen's Bench and Common Pleas " and substituting the words " Judges authorized to make Rules under sections 111 and 114 of the Judicature Act."

LINE 3—By striking out the word " jointly."

R. S. O. c. 90, s. 33, (Unorganized Territories.)

LINE 5—By striking out the word " pleasure " and substitut- 15 ing the words " during good behaviour."

Ib. s. 47.

LINE 3—By inserting after the word " District " the words " or Provisional County."

Ib. s. 13.

LINE 1—By striking out the word " so " and inserting after the word " appointed " the words " under the preceding section, 20 unless he is the official guardian."

Ib.

LINES 9 and 10—By striking out the words " the Master or Clerk, or Deputy Clerk, of such Court " and substituting the words " allowed by an officer of the Court to be named in the order."   25

R.S.O. c. 111, s. 82 (1). (Registry Act).

Repealed and amended, as to the first sub-section, by substituting the following:—

Whereas any land is surveyed and sub-divided for the purpose of being sold or conveyed in lots, by reference to a plan which has not been already registered, the person making the 30 sub-division shall file with the Registrar a plan of the land on a scale not less than 1 inch to every 4 chains. The plan shall show the number of the township, town or village lots and range or concession as originally laid out, and all the boundary lines thereof, within the limits of the land shown on the said plan, 35 and where such plan is a sub-division of a lot or lots on a former plan, it shall show the numbers or other distinguishing marks of the lot or lots sub-divided and the boundary lines of such lot or lots. The plan shall also show all roads, streets, lots and commons, within the same, with the courses and 40 widths thereof respectively, and the width and length of all lots and the courses of all division lines between the respective lots within the same, together with such other information as is required to show distinctly the position of the land being sub-divided.   45

R.S.O. c. 128,
(Compensa-
tion to
families of
persons killed
by accident.)   By adding the following section :—

> **9.** In all cases where the compensation is not apportioned as hereinbefore provided, it shall be referred to a Judge to apportion the same among the parties entitled and to provide for the costs thereof as he may think meet.   5

R.S.O. c. 138,
s. 6. (Law
Society).   By adding the following sub-section :—

> (2) The first two mentioned scrutineers, shall be members of the Law Society, but shall not be eligible for election to the office of Bencher, and their names shall be printed on the voting paper to be sent by the Secretary of the Society to each voter. 10

Ib. s. 9.   By adding the following after section 9 :—

> 9*a.* It shall be the duty of the Secretary to send to each member of the Bar whose name is on the alphabetical list or register mentioned in section 17, where his residence is known to the Secretary, one copy of the said form of voting paper 15 applicable to the election then next to be held. Such form shall be sent in such manner and at such time before the holding of the election as may be directed by rule of the Benchers in convocation.

> 9*b.* It shall be the duty of the Secretary to send with the 20 said form of voting paper a list of those persons then already Benchers of the Law Society, *ex-officio,* and of those whose term of office is about to expire.

R.S.O. c. 175,
s. 2. (Muni-
cipal Act of
Algoma, etc.)   LINE 2.—By inserting after the word "the" the words "District Judge in Algoma and in that part of Thunder Bay 25 not included within Rainy River, and in Rainy River or any other of the said Districts for the."

R.S.O. c. 181,
s. 42, as
amended by 44
V. c. 27, s. 4.
(Liquor
License Act.)   By inserting as sub-section (3) the following :—" (3) Nothing in this section shall restrict the sale of methylated alcohol, or oil of whiskey or other medicines for cattle or horses."   30

R.S.O. c. 201,
s. 3. (Insec-
tivorous
Birds).   LINE 11—By inserting after the word "pigeons" the word "blackbirds."

Ib. s. 4.   LINE 3—By inserting after the word "pigeon" the word "blackbirds."

41 V. c. 4, s. 9,
(1). (Police
Magistrates).   LINES 3 and 4—By inserting the words " or District " after 35 the word " County " where it occurs in line 3 and 4.

Ib.   By inserting after the word " County " the words "or Union of Counties or District."

42 V. c. 4, s. 10
(2). (Repre-
sentation Act.)

LINE 4.—Repealed, and amended by substituting the following for the original sub-section : (2) In such a case a
change of residence from one part of the village to another
shall not deprive a person whose name is on the voters' list or
his right; and in the oath to be administered to any such 5
person desiring to vote the words "and that you are still
actually and in good faith a resident of and domiciled within
this village," shall be substituted for the words " and are now
actually and in good faith a resident of and domiciled within
this electoral district." 10

42 V. c. 39, s. 7.
(Industrial
Refuge for
Girls).

LINE 1.—Amended by inserting between the words " County"
and " Court " the words " or District."

43 V. c. 10, s.
5. (Creditors'
Relief Act).

By inserting the following sub-section after sub-section (2):—

(3) Where proceedings are taken by the sheriff or other
officer for relief under any provisions relating to interpleader, 15
those creditors only who are parties thereto and who agree to
contribute *pro rata* (in proportion to the amount of their
executions) to the expense of contesting any adverse claim,
shall be entitled to share in any benefit which may be derived
from the contestation of such claim so far as may be necessary 20
to satisfy their executions or certificates. The Court or Judge
may direct that one creditor shall have the carriage of such
interpleader proceedings on behalf of all creditors interested,
and the costs thereof, as between solicitor and client shall be
a first charge upon any moneys, or goods which may be found 25
by such proceedings to be applicable upon such executions or
certificates.

43 V. c. 12, s.
4. (Unorgan-
ized Districts)

By adding the following to said section : " And within all
other districts now or hereafter to be formed in any part of
the unorganized territory in Ontario. 30

43 V. c. 34, s.
27. (Reform-
atory for
Boys).

LINE 2.—By inserting between the words " County " and
" Court " the words " or District."

44 V. c. 5,
s. 36, as
amended by
49 V. c. 16,
s. 39.
(Judicature
Act).

LINE 5—By striking out all the words after the word " no "
and substituting the words " further appeal shall lie to the
Court of Appeal from the Divisional Court unless by special 35
leave of the said Court or of the Court of Appeal."

46 V. c. 18,
s. 79, (1).
(Municipal
Act).

LINE 8—By striking out the words." or in the right of their
wives," and substituting the words "(or, in the case of married
men held by their wives)."

Ib.

Firstly—LINE 1—By striking out all the words of the para- 40
graph after the word " are " and substituting the words " in
their own right or whose wives are at the date of the election
freeholders of the municipality."

Ib., s. 79, (5).   LAST PARAGRAPH OF SUB.-SEC. 5, LINE 1 AND 2—By striking
out the words " proprietor in his own right, or in the right of
his wife " and substituting the words " a person who is
proprietor in his own right, or whose wife is proprietor in her
own right."   5

Ib., s. 264.   LINE 3—By striking out the word " Secretary " and substituting the words " Treasurer or to any other official appointed
by the Lieutenant-Governor in Council for the purpose."

Ib., s. 436 (1).   By repealing same and substituting the following :—   10

    436.—(1) The Commissioners shall have power to sum-
mon and examine witnesses on oath on all matters connected
with the administration of their duties, and they shall have the
same power to enforce the attendance of such witnesses, and to
compel them to give evidence as is vested in any Court of law 15
in civil cases : a notice to attend before the Board shall be
sufficient, if signed by the Chairman of the Board, or any one
of the Commissioners.

    (2) No party or witness shall be compelled to answer any
question by his answer to which he might render himself liable 20
to a criminal prosecution.

    (3) A majority of the Board shall constitute a quorum, and
the acts of a majority shall be considered Acts of the Board.
46 V. c. 18, s. 36.

47 V. c. 4,
second
schedule.
(Election Act)   LINE 10—By inserting after the word " district " the words 25
(*or of the territory included in this electoral district as the case
may be.*)

Ib. First
schedule.
(Election Act).   LINE 9 of " Resident Householder's Oath "—By inserting
after the word " District " the words (*or of the territory included
in this electoral district, as the case may be.*)   30

48 V. c. 2, s.
10 (12).   (Re-
presentation
Act).   LINE 5—By striking out the words " Electoral District of
Cornwall and Stormont " and substituting the words " County
of Stormont."

48 V. c. 2,
sched.   Form
18.   (Election
Act).   By striking out the second paragraph of the Form of Oath
and substituting the following :—" That you are actually and 35
in good faith a resident of and domiciled within this Electoral
District "; and by inserting the following after paragraph (3)
at the foot of the said form : (4) Where the voter is a HOUSE-
HOLDER, add, " and have resided therein continuously since the
completion of the last revised assessment roll of this munici- 40
pality."

48 V. c. 13, s.
23 (1).
(County
Courts' Act).   LINE 6—By striking out all the words after the word " or,"
and substituting the following sub-sections :—

    (2) Instead of appealing to the Court of Appeal either party
may, in cases tried by a judge, move before the County Court 45
within the first two days of its next quarterly sittings, for a

new trial, or to set aside the judgment on any ground except that upon the evidence given the judgment, so directed, is wrong in law.

(3) In cases tried with a jury, instead of appealing to the Court of Appeal, a similar motion may be made before the County Court for a new trial, or to set aside the judgment directed to be entered upon the special findings of the jury upon any ground except that the judgment so directed to be entered is wrong in law.

(4) Either party may appeal to the Court of Appeal from the judgment of the County Court upon applications under subsections 2 and 3.

49 V. c. 3,
Schedule.
Form 19.
(Election Act).

LINE 4—By inserting after the word "district" the words "(*or* of the territory included in this Electoral district, *as the case may be*)."

49 V. c. 49, s.
1. (Industrial
Refuge for
Girls).

LINE 1 of paragraph 19 (1)—By inserting between the words "County" and "Court" the words "or District."

No. 128.

1st Session, 6th Legislature, 50 Vic., 1887.

BILL.

An Act to give early effect to certain amendments of the Law recommended by the
Statute Commissioners.

First Reading,   March, 1887.

No. 128.] <center># BILL.</center> [1887.

An Act to give early effect to certain amendments of
the Law recommended by the Statute Commissioners.

Preamble.

WHEREAS it has again been found expedient to revise and
consolidate the Public General Statutes which apply to
this Province, and are within the authority of its Legislature; and whereas such revision and consolidation have
been made accordingly, by commissioners appointed for 5
this purpose, and among amendments which the commissioners have recommended to go into effect with the body of
statutes as so consolidated and revised, there are some which
it is expedient to bring into force at once ;

Therefore Her Majesty, by and with the advice and consent 10
of the Legislative Assembly of the Province and Ontario,
enacts as follows :—

Acts amended
as stated in
schedule.

1. The Acts and parts of Acts set forth in the left hand
columns of the schedule hereto, are hereby amended as stated
and set forth in the right hand columns of the schedule, and 15
shall go into force immediately upon the passing of this Act.

Power of
judges to make
rules varying
statutory
enactments
respecting
practice and
procedure.

2. And whereas it has been found expedient to revise, classify
and consolidate the rules of court affecting practice and procedure, and to include therein the statutory enactments affecting practice and procedure and matters in the nature of 20
practice and procedure, and, whereas this work is now in
preparation, and whereas most of the said statutory enactments
have in consequence been omitted by the commissioners from
the statutes as consolidated and revised by them as hereinbefore mentioned, it is hereby declared and enacted (to avoid 25
doubts) that the Judges shall be deemed and construed to have
under *The Judicature Act* the same powers of making rules of
court in respect of and varying statutory enactments affecting
practice and procedure or matters in the nature of practice
and procedure, as if the said enactments had been rules in the 30
schedule to *The Judicature Act*, or had derived their authority
from rules of court.

SCHEDULE.

CHAPTER AND
SUBJECT OF
ACT.

SHEWING ACTS AND PARTS OF ACTS AMENDED ON THE RECOM-
MENDATION OF THE COMMISSIONERS APPOINTED TO CON- 35
SOLIDATE AND REVISE THE PUBLIC GENERAL STATUTES
OF THE PROVINCE.

Manner in which the same are hereby Amended.

R. S. O. c. 10,
s. 180. (Elec-
tion Act.)

LINE 3.—By inserting the words " sections 113 and 114 of "
between the words " by " and " this."   40

R. S. O. c. 23,
s. 29 (1). (Sale
of Public
Lands.)

Repealed and amended by substituting the following : " In case of a patent for land being repealed or avoided by the High Court, the judgment shall be registered in the *proper registry* office."

R. S. O. c. 32,
s. 7. (Sale of
Liquors near
Public
Works).

LINE 4.—By striking out the words " and it appears " and 5 substituting the words " or if it is proved."

R. S. O. c. 40,
s. 59 (4).
(Chancery
Act.)

LINE 5—By striking out the words " Registrar for the time being " and substituting the word " Accountant."

LINES 10, 11—By striking out the words " Judges or."

Repealed and amended by substituting the following :— 10

R. S. O. c. 43,
ss. 10, 11.
(County
Courts' Act).

In lieu of terms, the several County Courts shall in each year hold four quarterly sittings, which (except in the County of York), shall commence respectively on the second Monday in the mouth of January and the first Monday in the months of April, July and October in each year, and end on the Saturday 15 of the same week, unless extended by order of the Judge.

2. The *said* quarterly sittings of the County Court of the County of York shall commence on the second Monday in January June and October, and the first Monday in April in each year ; and shall end on the Saturday of the same week, 20 unless extended by order of the Judge.

3. It shall not be necessary for the Sheriff or his officers to attend the *said* quarterly sittings of the County Court.

Ib. s. 28.

LINES 1 to 4—Amended by striking *out* all the words of the section to the word " shall" inclusive, in the 4th Line, and substi- 25 tuting the words: " When it is intended by any pleading to bring into question the title to any land, or to any annual or other rent, duty, or other custom or thing, relating to or issuing out of lands or tenements, it shall be so expressly stated in the pleading, nor shall any such pleading." 30

R. S. O. c. 47,
s. 64.
(Division
Courts' Act).

By inserting the following section after section 64 :—

64 (*a.*) In every case where the defendant is a corporation not having its head office in the Province, and the cause of action arose partly in one Division and partly in another, the plaintiff may bring his action in either Division. 35

R. S. O. c. 50,
s. 194.
(C. L. P. Act).

Repealed and amended by substituting the following :—

" Where the reference is made to the County Judge or the Master in Ordinary (or other officer who is paid by salary), such person shall be entitled to take and receive to his own use the same fees as the Local Masters not paid by salary are entitled 40 to receive upon a reference in an action in the High Court.

Amended by adding the following sub-section :—

R. S. O. c. 50,
s. 209.
C. L. P. Act

(2) " In the computation of time in appealing against, or applying to set aside an award, the vacations shall not be counted." 45

R. S. O. c. 62,
s. 38. (Evidence Act.) LINE 13—By striking out the words " without Canada."

R. S. O. c. 66,
s. 39.
(Execution.) By adding the following sub-section:—

(2) " The right of a married woman to dower shall not hereafter be deemed *seizable or* saleable under execution before the death of her husband." 5

R. S. O. c. 84,
s. 1 (1). (Fees of Counsel and other Officers). LINES 1 and 2—By striking out the words " Courts of Queen's Bench and Common Pleas " and substituting the words " Judges authorized to make Rules under sections 111 and 114 of the Judicature Act."

LINE 3—By striking out the word " jointly." 10

R. S. O. c. 90,
s. 33, (Unorganized Territories.) LINE 5—By striking out the word " pleasure " and substituting the words " good behaviour."

Ib. s. 47. LINE 3—By inserting after the word " District " the words " or Provisional County."

R.S.O. c. 101,
s. 13.
(Partition Act) LINE 1—By striking out the word " so " and inserting after 15 the word " appointed " the words " under the preceding section, unless he is the official guardian."

Ib. LINES 9 and 10—By striking out the words " the Master or Clerk, or Deputy Clerk, of such Court " and substituting the words " allowed by an officer of the Court to be named in the 20 order."

R.S.O. c. 111,
s. 82 (1).
(Registry Act). Repealed and amended, as to the first sub-section, by substituting the following :—

Where any land is surveyed and sub-divided for the purpose of being sold or conveyed in lots, by reference to a plan which has not been already registered, the person making the 25 sub-division shall file with the Registrar a plan of the land on a scale not less than 1 inch to every 4 chains. The plan shall show the number of the township, town or village lots and range or concession as originally laid out, and all the boundary lines thereof, within the limits of the land shown on the said plan, 30 and where such plan is a sub-division of a lot or lots on a former plan, it shall show the numbers or other distinguishing marks of the lot or lots sub-divided and the boundary lines of such lot or lots. The plan shall also show all roads, streets, lots and commons, within the same, with the courses and 35 widths thereof respectively, and the width and length of all lots and the courses of all division lines between the respective lots within the same, together with such other information as is required to show distinctly the position of the land being sub-divided. 40

By adding the following section :—

R.S.O. c. 128,
(Compensation to families of persons killed by accident.) 9. In all cases where the compensation is not apportioned as hereinbefore provided, it shall be referred to a Judge to apportion the same among the parties entitled and to provide for the costs thereof as he may think meet. 45

R.S.O. c. 138,
s. 6. (Law
Society).

By adding the following sub-section :—

(2) The first two mentioned scrutineers, shall be members of the Law Society, but shall not be eligible for election to the office of Bencher, and their names shall be printed on the voting paper to be sent by the Secretary of the Society to each voter. 5

Ib. s. 9.

By adding the following after section 9 :—

9a. It shall be the duty of the Secretary to send to each member of the Bar whose name is on the alphabetical list or register mentioned in section 17, where his residence is known to the Secretary, one copy of the said form of voting paper 10 applicable to the election then next to be held. Such form shall be sent in such manner and at such time before the holding of the election as may be directed by rule of the Benchers in convocation.

9b. It shall be the duty of the Secretary to send with the 15 said form of voting paper a list of those persons then already Benchers of the Law Society, *ex-officio*, and of those whose term of office is about to expire.

R.S.O. c. 175,
s. 2. (Muni-
cipal Act of
Algoma, etc.)

LINE 2.—By inserting after the word "the" the words "District Judge in Algoma and in that part of Thunder Bay 20 not included within Rainy River, and in Rainy River or any other of the said Districts for the."

R.S.O. c. 181,
s. 42, as
amended by 44
V. c. 27, s. 4.
(Liquor
License Act.)

By inserting as sub-section (3) the following :—"(3) Nothing in this section shall restrict the sale of methylated alcohol, or oil of whiskey or other medicines for cattle or horses." 25

R.S.O. c. 201,
s. 3. (Insec-
tivorous
Birds).

LINE 11.—By inserting after the word "pigeons" the word "blackbirds."

Ib. s. 4.

LINE 3—By inserting after the word "pigeons" the word "blackbirds."

41 V. c. 4, s. 9,
(1). (Police
Magistrates).

LINES 3 and 4—By inserting the words "or District" after 30 the word "County" where it occurs in line 3 and 4.

Ib. s. 9 (2).

Lines 2 and 3—By inserting after the word "County" the words "or Union of Counties or District."

42 V. c. 4, s. 10
(2). (Repre-
sentation Act.)

LINE 4.—Repealed, and amended by substituting the following for the original sub-section : (2) In such a case a 35 change of residence from one part of the village to another shall not deprive a person whose name is on the voters' list of his right *to vote* ; and in the oath to be administered to any such person desiring to vote the words "and that you are still actually and in good faith a resident of and domiciled within 40 this village," shall be substituted for the words "and are now actually and in good faith a resident of and domiciled within this electoral district."

42 V. c. 39, s. 7.
(Industrial
Refuge for
Girls).

LINE 1.—Amended by inserting between the words "County" and "Court" the words "or District." 45

43 V. c. 10, s. 5. (Creditors' Relief Act). By inserting the following sub-section after sub-section (2):—

| (3) Where proceedings are taken by the sheriff or other officer for relief under any provisions relating to interpleader, those creditors only who are parties thereto and who agree to contribute *pro rata* (in proportion to the amount of their 5 executions) to the expense of contesting any adverse claim, shall be entitled to share in any benefit which may be derived from the contestation of such claim so far as may be necessary to satisfy their executions or certificates. The Court or Judge may direct that one creditor shall have the carriage of such 10 interpleader proceedings on behalf of all creditors interested, and the costs thereof, as between solicitor and client shall be a first charge upon any moneys, or goods which may be found by such proceedings to be applicable upon such executions or certificates.

43 V. c. 12, s. 4. (Unorganized Districts) By adding the following to said section: "And within all 15 other districts now or hereafter to be formed in any part of the unorganized territory in Ontario."

43 V. c. 34, s. 27. (Reformatory for Boys). LINE 2.—By inserting between the words "County" and "Court" the words "or District."

44 V. c. 5, s. 36, as amended by 49 V. c. 16, s. 39. (Judicature Act). LINE 5—By striking out all the words after the word "no" 20 and substituting the words "further appeal shall lie to the Court of Appeal from the Divisional Court unless by special leave of the said Court or of the Court of Appeal."

46 V. c. 18, s. 79, (1). (Municipal Act). LINE 8—By striking out the words "or in the right of their wives," and substituting the words "(or, in the case of married 25 men held by their wives)."

Ib. *Firstly*—LINE 1—By striking out all the words of the paragraph after the word "are" and substituting the words "in their own right or whose wives are at the date of the election freeholders of the municipality." 30

Ib., s. 79, (5). LAST PARAGRAPH OF SUB.-SEC. 5, LINE 1 AND 2—By striking out the words "proprietor in his own right, or in the right of his wife" and substituting the words "a person who is proprietor in his own right, or whose wife is proprietor in her 35 own right."

Ib., s. 264. LINE 3—By striking out the word "Secretary" and substituting the words "Treasurer or to any other official appointed by the Lieutenant-Governor in Council for the purpose."

Ib., s. 436 (1). By repealing same and substituting the following:— 40

436.—(1) The Commissioners shall have power to summon and examine witnesses on oath on all matters connected with the administration of their duties, and they shall have the same power to enforce the attendance of such witnesses, and to compel them to give evidence as is vested in any Court of law 45 in civil cases: a notice to attend before the Board shall be sufficient, if signed by the Chairman of the Board, or any one of the Commissioners.

(2) No party or witness shall be compelled to answer any question by his answer to which he might render himself liable to a criminal prosecution.

(3) A majority of the Board shall constitute a quorum, and the acts of a majority shall be considered acts of the Board. 5

48 V. c. 2, s. 10 (12). (Representation Act).

LINE 5—By striking out the words "Electoral District of Cornwall and Stormont" and substituting the words "County of Stormont."

48 V. c. 2, sched. Form 18. (Election Act).

By striking out the second paragraph of the Form of Oath and substituting the following :—"That you are actually and 10 in good faith a resident of and domiciled within this Electoral District"; and by inserting the following after paragraph (3) at the foot of the said form : "(4) Where the voter is a HOUSE-HOLDER, add, and have resided therein continuously since the completion of the last revised assessment roll of this munici- 15 pality."

49 V. c. 49, s. 1. (Industrial Refuge for Girls).

LINE 1 of paragraph 19 (1)—By inserting between the words "County" and "Court" the words "or District."

BILL.

An Act to give early effect to certain amendments of the Law recommended by the
Statute Commissioners.

(*Reprinted as amended by Committee of
Whole House.*)

First Reading, 28th March, 1887.
Second " 29th " 1887.

The ATTORNEY-GENERAL.

TORONTO:
PRINTED BY WARWICK & SONS, 26 AND 28 FRONT ST. W.

No. 129.]   **BILL.**   [1887.

An Act to amend the Consolidated Municipal Act, 1883.

HER Majesty, by and with the advice and consent of the Legislative Assembly of the Province of Ontario, enacts as follows :—

1. Section 369 of *The Consolidated Municipal Act, 1883,* When rate im-
5 sub-section 1 is repealed, and the following is substituted for the posed by by-law may be
said sub-section :   reduced.

369. If, on account of a sum being on hand from a previous year, or a sum being on hand which has been derived from the work, or from the investment of the sinking fund, or on account 10 of the increased value of property liable to assessment, it is found to be unnecessary to levy the full rate imposed by the by-law in order to raise the instalment of the sinking fund and interest required to be raised for any year, or to raise such instalments for any future years of the then unexpired time which the 15 debentures have to run, the council may pass a by-law reducing the rate for such year or for any such future years, so that no more money may be collected than the amount required.

2. The 2nd, 3rd and 4th sub-sections of the 433rd section of Police magis-
the said Act shall apply to Police Magistrates of counties, trates.
20 districts, villages, and parts of counties and districts, as well as to cities and towns.

3. Sub-section 8 of section 490 of the said Act is amended Cemeteries.
by adding after the word "Village" in the third line of said sub-section, the words " excepting as hereinafter provided ;"

25   And by adding the following sub-sections after sub-section 8 :

(a) Provided, however, that the municipal council of an incorporated village may pass a by-law for accepting or purchasing land for a public cemetery within the territorial limits 30 of the village upon the by-law being first approved of by the Local Board of Health, and ratified by the Provincial Board of Health ; and the by-law shall thereupon be as valid and effectual as if the land was situated without the municipality.

(b) All expenses incurred by the Provincial Board of Health 35 in respect of and incidental to the by-law, and whether the by-law be ratified by the Board of or not, shall be paid by the Village Municipality to the Secretary of the Board.

4. The 36th sub-section of the 496th section is amended Changing
by adding the following ;   names of
                                                              streets.

(*a*) Every by-law changing the name of a street in a city or town shall state the reasons for the change, and shall be expressed to be subject to the approval of the county judge, and the same shall not take effect unless afterwards so approved.

(*b*) The judge, on an application by or on behalf of the municipal council, shall name a day, hour and place for con- 5 sidering the same, and for hearing the advocates of the change, and persons who may deem themselves aggrieved thereby and may desire to be heard, and any other persons the Judge may think fit.

(*c*) A copy of the by-law and of the Judge's appointment 10 shall be served on the registrar or deputy registrar of the registration division at least two weeks before the time named, and shall be published once in the *Ontario Gazette* at least two weeks before the time so named, and at least weekly for four weeks in such other newspaper or newspapers as the Judge 15 directs.

(*d*) If the Judge approves of the change he shall certify to that effect, and his certificate shall be filed with the by-law in the registry office of the registration division in which the territory lies. The change shall take effect from the date of 20 the registration of the certificate and not before.

1st Session, 6th Legislature, 50 Vic., 1887.

BILL.

An Act to amend the Consolidated Municipal Act, 1883.

First Reading,   1887.

No. 130.]   **BILL.**   [1887.

An Act to disqualify certain Barristers and Solicitors
from being Justices of the Peace, Stipendiary Magistrates or Police Magistrates.

HER MAJESTY, by and with the advice and consent of the
Legislative Assembly of the Province of Ontario, enacts
as follows:—

1. From and after the passing of this Act, no person shall   Barristers,
5 be capable of becoming or being a justice of the peace, stipen-   etc., not to be appointed
diary magistrate, or police magistrate for any village, town,   justices of the
city, county, provisional judicial, temporary judicial or   peace in loca-
territorial district or provisional county, or territory not   tion in which they practise.
attached to any county for judicial purposes in which he shall
10 practise and carry on the profession or business of barrister
or solicitor.

2. Section 22 of *The Act respecting the qualification and*   R. S. O. c. 71,
appointment of Justices of the Peace and section 18 of *The*   s. 22 and 49 V.
Statute Amendment Act, 1886, and all other Acts or parts of   c. 16, s. 18,
15 Acts, inconsistent with this Act, are hereby repealed.   repealed.

No. 130.

1st Session, 6th Legislature, 50 Vic., 1887.

BILL.

An Act to disqualify certain Barristers and Solicitors from being Justices of the Peace, Stipendiary Magistrates or Police Magistrates.

First Reading, 28th March, 1887.

BILL.

An Act to amend the Municipal Act.

HER MAJESTY, by and with the advice and consent of the Legislative Assembly of the Province of Ontario, enacts as follows :—

1. No person shall be admitted to an industrial home or 5 poor house in any county, except upon the warrant of a reeve or deputy-reeve of a municipality within the county in which such industrial home or poor house is erected and maintained.

Admission to industrial homes and poor houses.

BILL.

An Act to amend the Municipal Act.

First Reading, 28th March, 1887.

No. 132.] # BILL. [1887.

An Act to amend the Act respecting Joint Stock
Companies for supplying Cities, Towns and Villages
with Gas and Water.

HER MAJESTY, by and with the advice and consent of the
Legislative Assembly of the Province of Ontario, enacts
as follows :—

1. Section 1 of *The Act to amend the Act respecting Joint* 49 V. c 33, s.
5 *Stock Companies for supplying Cities, Towns and Villages* 1, repe...ed.
with Gas and Water, is repealed and the following substituted
therefor :

The sum so borrowed shall not exceed the sum of $40,000, Liml bor-
to be expended in gas works and the like sum for water works rowin
10 for any incorporated village ; and for any town or city to be powers.
expended in gas or water works the sums following ; for any
town the sum of $80,000 for gas works and $250,000 for water
works, and for any city the sum of $100,000 for gas works
and $500,000 for water works.

No. 132.

1st Session, 6th Legislature, 50 Vic., 1887.

BILL.

An Act to amend the Act respecting Joint Stock Companies for supplying Cities, Towns and Villages with Gas and Water.

First Reading, 28th March, 1887.

No. 133.] **BILL.** [1887.

An Act to amend the Municipal Act.

HER MAJESTY, by and with the advice and consent of the Legislative Assembly of the Province of Ontario, enacts as follows :—

1. The councils of township municipalities are hereby em-
5 powered to pass by-laws for the purposes mentioned in sub-
section 44 of section 496 of *The Consolidated Municipal Act,*
1883, namely, for acquiring and holding, by purchase or otherwise, for the public use of the municipality, lands situate outside the limits of such township ; but such lands so acquired
10 shall not form part of the municipality of said township, but
shall continue and remain as of the municipality where situate.

2. All by-laws heretofore passed by township councils
for the purpose of acquiring land as provided by the preceding
section are hereby declared legal and binding.

No. 133.

1st Session, 6th Legislature, 50 Vic., 1887.

BILL.

An Act to amend the Municipal Act.

First Reading, 28th March, 1887.

No. 134.]   **BILL.**   [1887.

An Act to amend the Municipal Act.

HER MAJESTY, by and with the advice and consent of the
Legislative Assembly of the Province of Ontario, enacts
as follows :—

Section 532 of *The Consolidated Municipal Act, 1883,* is 46 V. c. 18,
5 hereby amended by inserting in the seventh line thereof, after s. 532,
the word " streams," the words " lakes or ponds," and by in- amended.
serting in the eleventh line thereof, after the word " rivers,"
the words " lakes or ponds."

No. 134.

1st Session, 6th Legislature, 50 Vic., 1887

BILL.

An Act to amend the Municipal Act.

First Reading, 29th March, 1887.

BILL.

An Act to amend the Municipal Act.

HER MAJESTY, by and with the advice and consent of the Legislative Assembly of the Province of Ontario, enacts as follows :—

1. Section 68 of *The Consolidated Municipal Act, 1883,* is 46 V. c. 18, s.
5 hereby repealed and the following enacted in lieu thereof : 68 repealed.

68. The council of every city shall consist of the mayor City Councils.
(who shall be the head thereof); and three aldermen for every
ward, when there are less than ten wards ; and of two
10 aldermen when there are ten or more wards; to be elected in
accordance with the provisions of this Act.

2. In any case where the resident freeholders of any city Re-division
or town, to the number of at least one hundred, petition the of wards.
council, alleging the expedience of, and praying that a new
division into wards may be made of the city or town without
15 reducing the number of wards, or that such new division may
be made, reducing the number of wards to nine or less, it
shall be the duty of the council, and the council shall at the
time of the holding of the next municipal elections, submit the
question of such new division as prayed by the petition to the
20 vote of the persons entitled to vote at the municipal elections;
and in event of a majority of the electors voting thereon,
voting in favour of the petition it shall be the duty of the
council, and the council shall within a reasonable time after
the taking of the vote sub-divide the city or town into wards,
25 so as to give effect to the prayer of the petition and vote of
the electors ; and such new division shall so far as possible be
based upon assessed values of property, population and territorial extent, and shall be given effect to in accordance with
the provisions of section 21 of *The Consolidated Municipal*
30 *Act, 1883,* and amendments thereto in that behalf.

3. In case any council neglects or refuses to make a new Issue of com-
sub-division of any city or town into wards under the provisions enquire into
of the last preceding section for three months after the same existing ward
shall have been voted upon and approved of by the electors, divisions.
35 and in case one-third of the members of the council, or one
hundred duly qualified electors of the municipality petition
for a commission to issue under the Great Seal to enquire into
the existing division of such municipality into wards, and for
a new division in accordance with the expressed wish of the
40 electors, as evidenced by their vote to be taken in manner
aforesaid ; and if sufficient cause is shown, the Lieutenant-
Governor in Council may issue a commission accordingly, and
the commissioner or commissioners, or such one or more of them
as the commission empowers to act shall have the same power

to summon witnesses, enforce their attendance, and compel
them to produce documents, and to give evidence as any Court
has in civil cases.

Report of commissioners.

4.—(1) The commissioners so to be appointed as aforesaid
shall within a reasonable time report a new division into wards 5
of the municipality in accordance with the prayer of the
petition, having regard to the provisions of this Act as to
equality of representation, to the Provincial Secretary, who
shall forthwith transmit a copy thereof to the council, and
cause the same to be published for one month in the 10
Ontario Gazette, and once in each week for four weeks in one
or more newspapers published in the municipality, naming a
day when the same will be taken into consideration by the
Lieutenant-Governor in Council, when all parties interested,
opposed thereto, and who petition to be heard, shall have an 15
opportunity of being heard and being represented by counsel
in that behalf.

(2). The Lieutenant-Governor in Council may, within three
months after the receipt of the report of the commissioners,
by proclamation divide the city or town into wards, making 20
such changes in the report of the commissioners as may seem
expedient, but the number of wards shall not exceed the
number approved of by the vote of the electors.

(3). The expenses to be allowed for executing the Commission shall be paid by the Municipality pursuant to the 25
provisions of section 386 of *The Consolidated Municipal Act,
1883.*

46 V. c. 18, s. 81 amended.

5. Section 81 of *The Consolidated Municipal Act, 1883*, is
hereby amended by adding at the end thereof the words, " but
any person producing and leaving with the deputy returning 30
officer at the time of the tendering of the vote a certificate
from the treasurer of the municipality, or the collector of taxes,
shewing that the taxes in respect of which the default had
been made have since been paid, shall be entitled to vote ;
and the deputy returning officer shall file the certificate, 35
receive the vote and note the same on the defaulters' lists."

46 V. c. 18, s. 473 and 49 V. c. 37, s. 10 repealed.

6. Section 473 of *The Consolidated Municipal Act, 1883,*
as amended by section 10 of *The Municipal Amendment Act,*
1886, is hereby repealed, and the following substituted in lieu
thereof :— 40

Compensation by city or town for use of court house etc.

473.—(1) While a city or town uses the court house, gaol
or house of correction of the county, or while the county uses
the court house, gaol or house of correction of a city or town,
as the case may be, the municipality owning the court house,
gaol or house of correction shall be entitled to such compensa- 45
tion from the other municipality for the use of the said court
house, gaol or house of correction, as well as for the care and
maintenance of prisoners, as may be mutually agreed upon or
settled by arbitration under this Act.

Matters to be considered in determining compensation.

(2) In case of arbitration under the preceding provisions 50
of this section, in determining the compensation to be paid
for the care and maintenance of prisoners confined in the
gaol, the arbitrators shall take into consideration the original cost of the site and erection of the gaol buildings, the cost
of repairs and insurance and the cost of maintaining and

supporting the prisoners as well as the salaries of all officers
and servants connected therewith, and shall award compensation according to a per diem rate for each prisoner for the
time he is confined in gaol.

5   Section 482 of *The Consolidated Municipal Act, 1883*, is
hereby amended by adding thereto the following sub-sections:— *46 V. c. 18, s. 482 amended.*

(25). For entering upon, taking and using and acquiring so
much real property as may be required for the use of the
Corporation, including public parks, squares, pleasure grounds,
10 boulevards, and drives in the municipality and adjoining
municipalities, without the consent of the owners of such real
property, making due compensation therefor to the parties
entitled thereto, under the provisions of this Act.

(26). For selling, leasing or otherwise disposing of such
15 portions of real property belonging to the corporation as may
no longer be required for the use of the corporation.

7. Sub-section (22) of Section 490 of *The Consolidated Municipal Act, 1883*, is hereby amended by striking out the figures
"$100," and substituting in lieu thereof the figures "$500." *46 V. c. 18, s. 490 (22) amended.*

20   **8.** Section 496 of *The Consolidated Municipal Act, 1883*, is
hereby amended by adding thereto the following sub-section :— *46 V. c. 18, s. 496, amended.*

(12). For licensing and regulating persons keeping infant
children, not their own, for hire or gain ; and for preventing
cruelty to children by their parents, guardians, or other persons
25 having charge of or control over them.

9. Section 496 of *The Consolidated Municipal Act, 1883*,
is hereby amended by adding thereto the following sub-
section :— *46 V. c. 18, s. 496 amended.*

(51a.) " For defining areas or districts within which no mill
30 factory, machine shop, livery, sales or boarding stables for
horses, blacksmith shop, forge or foundry shall be erected, or
other like industry, business or trade be established or carried
on ; and for prohibiting the same ; and in case the majority of
the persons as shown by the last revised Assessment Roll to be
35 the owners representing at least one-half in value of all the
real property situate within any district or area, of any city,
town or incorporated village, described in the petition, do
petition the council of the municipality, praying that thereafter no person shall be permitted to erect, set up, or operate
40 any mill, factory, foundry, machine shop, blacksmith shop,
forge or livery, sales or boarding stables for horses, or carry on
any like calling or business within the limits of the area or
district mentioned in the petition, it shall be the duty of the
council, and the council shall forthwith give public notice of
45 the receipt of such petition by publication of a notice in at
least two of the newspapers published in the municipality, or
in the case of villages, in a newspaper published in the village
or in the county town, and it shall be the duty of the said
council, and they shall within a reasonable time after the
50 receipt of such petition, pass a by-law, or by-laws to give effect
to the prayer thereof, and no person shall after the publication
of such notice commence the erection of any new works or the
refitting and repair of any old works or shops for the purpose
of carrying on any trade, business, manufacture or calling men-

tioned in such petition, and to be prohibited by any such
by-law."

46 V. c. 18, s.
503 amended.

10. Section 503 of *The Consolidated Municipal Act, 1883,*
is hereby amended by striking out the words "subject to,"
when they occur in the second line thereof, and by substitut- 5
ing therefor the word "notwithstanding."

46 V. c. 18, s.
504 (1) repeal-
ed.

11. Sub-section (1) of section 504 of *The Consolidated Municipal Act, 1883,* is hereby repealed and the following substituted in lieu thereof:

(1) For licensing and regulating suitable persons to keep in- 10
telligence offices for registering the names and residences of,
and giving information to, or procuring servants, labourers,
workmen, clerks or other employees, for employers in want of
the same, and for registering the names and residences of and
giving information to or procuring employment for domestic 15
servants and other labourers and any other class of servant,
workman, clerk or person seeking employment; and for fixing
the fees to be charged and recovered by the keepers of such
offices.

46 V. c. 18, s.
612 (4)
amended.

12. Sub-section (4) of section 612 of *The Consolidated* 20
Municipal Act, 1883, is hereby amended by adding thereto
the following:—

(d) The council may specially assess and levy upon and collect from lands and premises adjoining public parks, squares,
drives and boulevards, special rates as for local improvements 25
when any improvement made in any such park, square, drive
or boulevard specially benefits such adjoining lands and
premises; and no petition against any such assessment shall
avail to prevent the carrying out of any improvement or service
in any such park, square, drive or boulevard; and the making 30
of such special assessment.

46 V. c. 18, s.
615, amended.

13. Section 615 of *The Consolidated Municipal Act, 1883,*
is hereby amended by adding thereto the following sub-section:—

"(2) In any case when the council affirms by a two-thirds 35
vote thereof that the constructing, erecting or making of any
bridge, culvert or embankment, benefits the municipality at
large, and that it would be inequitable to raise the whole cost
of any such improvement or work by local special assessments,
the council may pass a by-law for borrowing money by the 40
issue of debentures upon the credit of the municipality at large
to provide as the corporation's share of the cost of such improvement or work an amount not exceeding one-half of the
whole cost thereof; and no such by-law shall require the assent
of the electors before the final passing thereof." 45

Council on
vote of elec-
tors to pass a
by-law direct-
ing improve-
ments to be
made by local
assessment.

14. In case the resident freeholders of any city, town or
incorporated village to the number of at least one hundred,
petition the council praying that a by-law may be passed with
the assent of the electors according to the provisions of *The
Consolidated Municipal Act, 1883,* and amending Acts, direct- 50
ing that all future expenditure of the municipality for the
improvements and services or for any class or classes of

improvements or service for which special provision is made
in sections 612 and 624 of the said Act and amending Acts,
shall be provided for by special assessment on the property
benefited and not exempt by law from assessment, it shall be
5 the duty of the council and the council shall within a reasonable time after the presentation of such petition, submit a
by-law in accordance with the prayer of the petition to the
vote of the duly qualified electors ; and in the event of the
by-law being carried by the vote of a majority of the electors
10 voting thereon, it shall be the duty of the council, and the
council shall finally pass the said by-law within a reasonable
time after the taking of the vote thereon.

15.—(1) In case the council of any city, town or incor- All property
porated village shall at any time pass a by-law, or by-laws not exempt
15 with the assent of the electors according to the pro- under B. N.
visions of section 620 of *The Consolidated Municipal Act,* A. Act to be
1883, and amending Acts, directing that all future expenditure local improve-
of the municipality for the improvements, works and services, or ments.
for any class or classes of the improvements, works or services
20 for which special provisions are made in sections 612 and 624
of the said Act and amending Acts, shall be provided for by
special assessment on the property benefited, all real .property
in the municipality not declared exempt from asssessment or
taxation by *The British North America Act, 1867,* shall forth-
25 with thereafter become liable to be assessed for the various
local improvements, works and services included in the by-law
or by-laws passed as aforesaid, notwithstanding anything contained in section 6 of *The Assessment Act.*

(2) In the event of the passage of a by-law as above pro-
30 vided, all works of repair and maintenance as well as works of
construction shall thereafter be charged against and provided
for by special assessment upon the property benefited, and the
cost of all improvements, works and services at the intersection
of streets, and all flankage allowances upon corner lots, and
35 other irregular shaped pieces of property, shall be charged
against and provided for by special assessment upon the real
property benefited by the improvements, works or services
within the area or district within which such street inter-
sections, corner lots, or irregular shaped pieces of land, are
40 situate, as defined by by-law in that behalf.

BILL.

An Act to amend the Municipal Act.

First Reading, 30th March, 1887.

No. 136.]　　　　　**BILL.**　　　　　[1877.

· An Act to amend the Assessment Act.

HER MAJESTY, by and with the advice and consent of the Legislative Assembly of the Province of Ontario, enacts as follows :

1. Sub-section (2) of section 1, of the Act passed in the 43rd year of the reign of Her Majesty, and chaptered 27, is hereby repealed and the following enacted in lieu thereof : 　43 V. c. 27, s. 1 (2) repealed.

(2) The personal property of a bank shall, as hitherto, be exempt from assessment, but the shareholders shall be assessed upon the income derived from dividends.

2. Sub-section (3) of section 3, and sections 4 and 5 of the said Act are hereby repealed.　43 V. c. 27, s. 3 (3) and ss. 4 and 5 repealed.

3. The exemption from taxation of real property under *The Assessment Act* is hereby declared not to extend to special assessments for local improvements, except in the case of real property declared by *The British North America Act* not to he liable to taxation.　All real property not exempt under B. N. A. Act to be assessed for local improvements.

No. 136.

1st Session, 6th Legislature, 50 Vic., 1887.

BILL.

An Act to amend the Assessment Act.

First Reading, 30th March, 1887.

BILL.

An Act respecting the Licensing of Engineers.

HER MAJESTY, by and with the advice and consent of the Legislative Assembly of the Province of Ontario, enacts as follows :—

1. All persons within the Province of Ontario having Persons taking charge of
5 charge, or who may take charge or operate any steam boiler or boilers to be other devices under steam pressure, shall be examined and licensed. licensed before assuming or attempting to take charge of such steam boilers or devices, and any person attempting to operate a device of any kind subject to steam pressure, without first
10 procuring a license, shall be subject to a fine of not less than $10 nor more than $20.

2. There shall be appointed for each electoral district in the Inspectors. Province of Ontario, by the Lieutenant-Governor in Council, three inspectors or examiners of operating engineers, or persons
15 in charge of devices under steam pressure, and he shall select for such examiners or inspectors, persons who have technical and practical knowledge of steam used for any purpose, with not less than five years' experience or practice in charge of engines and boilers, and who are of good moral character
20 and of temperate habits ; and such persons so appointed shall give bonds for the faithful performances of their duties in the sum of $2,000, with two sureties, to be approved of by the Lieutenant-Governor in Council, and such inspector or examiners shall not be removed without cause.

25 3. The inspectors or examiners to be appointed under this Remuneration of inspectors. Act, shall receive no other compensation than the fees to be paid them for examining persons to take charge of steam boilers or other devices under pressure, and from such moneys they shall defray or pay all the expenses incident to the faith-
30 ful discharge of the duties assigned to them by this Act ; and the inspectors or examiners appointed under this Act shall keep a full and complete record of all persons and boilers examined by them, and of all licenses issued by them. They shall have power to issue four grades of license, to be known
35 as 1st Class Engineer, 2nd Class Engineer, 3rd Class, or Firemen, and Special Class, and such special license shall, in plain terms, designate the steam plant or particular device the holder is qualified for and may operate, and if any person having a special license shall undertake to operate any steam
40 plant or device, other than that named in his license, the same shall be revoked. All licenses must be exposed to view in a conspicuous place in the engine or boiler-room. Should any engineer, fireman or holder of special license undertake to

operate, or take charge of any steam plant, or other device requiring a higher grade of license than he possesses, he shall be fined not less than $10 or more than $50 on conviction of the same.

License fee.

4. Each person applying for examination to take charge of boilers or other devices, subject to steam pressure, shall pay for such examination and license the sum of $5, and the license shall have force and effect for the term of one year, unless sooner revoked for cause by the inspectors or examiners, and for each subsequent renewal of such license, the sum of $3 shall be paid, and the inspectors shall in no case issue a license to any person who is of inebriate habits, however skilful he may be.

Revocation of license.

5. The inspectors or examiners appointed under this Act shall have the power to revoke any license issued by them, at any time, when the person holding the license, shall have committed any act or acts that show him to be unworthy, or incompetent, or intemperate ; and if such person desire to appeal from the decision of the Board of Inspectors or Examiners in his district, he may present his case to the Lieutenant-Governor in Council, who shall appoint five inspectors or examiners from other districts who shall hear his case, and their decision shall be final.

Penalty.

6. It is unlawful for the owner or owners, or manager of any steam boiler, or device subject to steam pressure, to permit such steam boiler or device to be put under steam pressure, unless they are placed under the charge of a properly licensed person, to operate or control the same, and any person who shall be proven guilty of violating this section, or shall evade in any way its provisions, shall be fined not less than $10 nor more than $250.

Engineer to give notice of defect in boilers.

7. Whenever any licensed engineer shall discover that the boilers, or other device he is operating, have become weakened or unsafe, he shall at once notify the proprietor, or owners, or manager of the fact, and demand that they be repaired and made safe. If the owners, proprietors or manager shall refuse to have the needed repairs made, or the device or devices made strong, the licensed person operating them shall at once notify the inspectors for that district, when a majority of the said Board of Inspectors, shall inspect the boiler or device, and if they decide that they are unsafe, the proprietor or owners shall forthwith have the needed repairs made, and any owner, proprietor or manager who shall attempt to operate any device subject to steam pressure, after such inspection, without having the repairs made that the inspector ordered, shall be fined not less than $100 nor more than $500.

Commencement of Act.

8. This Act shall take effect from and after the first of July, 1887, and all Acts or parts of Acts, conflicting with the foregoing enactments, are hereby repealed.

1st Session, 6th Legislature, 50 Vic., 1887.

BILL.

An Act respecting the Licensing of Engineers.

First Reading, 30th March, 1887.

BILL.

An Act to amend the Assessment Act.

HER MAJESTY, by and with the advice and consent of the Legislative Assembly of the Province of Ontario, enacts as follows :—

1. Sub-section 3 of section 59 of *The Assessment Act* is 5 hereby repealed and the following substituted therefor : R.S.O. c. 180, s. 59 (3) repealed.

(3) The Clerk shall, immediately after the time limited for filing said appeals, forward a list of the same to the Judge, who shall then notify the Clerk of the day he appoints for the hearing thereof.

No. 1

1st Session, 6th Legislature, 50 Vic., 1887.

BILL.

An Act to Amend the Assessment Act.

First Reading, 30th March, 1887.

BILL.

An Act to amend the Mechanics' Lien Act.

H ER MAJESTY, by and with the advice and consent of the
Legislative Assembly of the Province of Ontario, enacts
as follows:—

1. Section 6 of *The Mechanics' Lien Act, 1882,* is amended 45 V. c. 15, s.
5 by adding thereto the following words: "but such lieu during 6, amended.
the said periods shall have the same priority for all purposes
before as after registration."

No. 139.

1st Session, 6th Legislature, 50 Vic., 1887.

BILL.

An Act to amend the Mechanics' Lien Act.

First Reading, 30th March, 1887.

No. 140.] **BILL.** [1887.

An Act to amend the Municipal Act.

HER MAJESTY, by and with the advice and consent of the
Legislative Assembly of the Province of Ontario, enacts
as follows:—

1. In case a petition, signed by two hundred qualified elec- Council to submit by-law for construc- tion of water- works on petition therefor.
tors in incorporated towns, or by one hundred qualified electors
in incorporated villages or in rural municipalities, is presented
to the council of such town, incorporated village or rural
5 municipality, asking for the construction of water-works under
The Municipal Water-works Act, 1882:

(1) It shall be the duty of such council to submit a by-law
for the construction of such water-works, to the vote of the
ratepayers of the said town, incorporated village or munici-
10 pality, and such council shall, forthwith, prepare a by-law directing the submission of the question, in accordance with the
prayer of the petitioners, and shall submit the same to the
electors for approval, or otherwise, within six weeks after the
receipt of the petition by the council;

15 (2) The council before passing such by-law, may require the
petitioners to deposit with the treasurer of the municipality
an amount sufficient to cover the probable cost of submitting
the matter in question to the electors;   •

(3) In the event of the prayer of the said petitioners receiv-
20 ing the sanction and consent of a majority of the electors of
such corporation, then the money so deposited, shall be, forthwith, refunded to the petitioners;

(4) Should the prayer of the petitioners be rejected by a
majority of the electors of such corporation, then the money
25 so deposited, shall be forfeited to such corporation, or so much
thereof, as may be necessary to cover the costs of submitting
the said by-law;

(5) The petitioners shall not be required to deposit a greater
sum than $150;

30 (6) The power of municipal councils shall not be deemed to
be abridged by this Act, except as expressly stated herein;

(7) The proceedings in taking such vote, shall be the same
as nearly as may be, as are required by *The Consolidated
Municipal Act, 1883,* in case of by-laws creating debts; but,
35 all persons entitled to vote at the election for municipal
councillors, shall be entitled to vote upon such by-law.

Council to
pass by-law.

2. If the by-law be approved of by the majority of such electors, it shall be the duty of such council to pass the said by-law, and forthwith to proceed with the construction of such works.

Power to
supply gas or
water to resi-
dents in
adjacent
municipality.

3. Any municipality constructing works under *The Munici-* 5 *pal Water-works Act, 1882,* or any company incorporated for the supply of water or gas, or water and gas, shall have power to supply consumers in any municipality adjacent to the municipality constructing such works, or for the supply of which such company was incorporated, and to lay all neces- 10 sary pipes for that purpose : provided, always, that before such pipes shall be laid along any street or road in such adjacent municipality, the consent of the council of the municipality for the supply of which the said works were constructed, shall be obtained, and also that the said streets or roads shall be 15 replaced, as nearly as possible, in the same condition as they were in before such pipes were laid.

By-law for the
construction
of water-
works.

4. All provisions of *The Municipal Act* or Acts, in so far as they apply to elections, and to the prevention of corrupt practices at elections, shall apply hereto, except so far as such 20 Act or Acts would be inconsistent with this Act.

1st Session, 6th Legislature, 50 Vic, 1887.

No. 140.

BILL.

An Act to amend the Municipal Act.

First Reading 30th March, 1887.

Mr. Conmee.

TORONTO :
PRINTED BY WARWICK & SONS, 26 AND 28 FRONT ST. W.

BILL.

An Act respecting the Law of Libel.

HER MAJESTY, by and with the advice and consent of the Legislative Assembly of the Province of Ontario,
5 enacts as follows :—

1. Section 4 of chapter 56 of the Revised Statutes of Ontario R. S. O. c. 56, is hereby amended by adding thereto the following sub- s. 4, amended. section :

(2) No such action shall lie unless and until the plaintiff Notice of
10 shall have given to the defendant notice in writing distinctly action. specifying the language complained of, for three clear days, in the case of a daily newspaper, and for ten clear days, in the case of a weekly publication, in order to give the defendant an opportunity to publish a full apology for the said libel; and if
15 the Court or a jury find that a full apology was published before the commencement of the action, the plaintiff shall not recover therein without proving special damage, or actual malice.

2. The words "a public meeting" in section 3 of The Meaning of
20 Newspaper Libel Act, 1882, shall include any meeting to paper" in 45 which the public are invited, and of which three days' V. c. 9, s. 3. announcement has been made by printed or written notice thereof being posted up in at least six conspicuous places in the municipality where the meeting is held, or by advertise-
25 ment in a public newspaper published in such municipality; or if there be none published therein then in the one published nearest to the place of meeting.

3. All reports of proceedings in any Court of Justice, pub- Report of pro- lished in any public newspaper or other periodical publication, ceedings in
30 shall be privileged, provided that they contain only fair and eged. authentic reports, without comments.

4. In any action brought for libel contained in any public Security for newspaper or periodical publication, the defendant may at any costs. time after the filing of the statement of claim apply to the
35 Court in which such action is pending for security for costs, upon an affidavit made by the defendant applying, shewing to the Court the nature of the action and of the defence, and that in the belief of the deponent the plaintiff is not possessed of property sufficient to answer the costs of the action in case a
40 verdict or judgment be given in favour of the defendant, and that the defendant has a good defence upon the merits as he

2

the deponent is advised and believes; and the Court or a judge thereof, in his or their discretion, may make an order that the plaintiff in any such action shall give security for the costs to be incurred in such action in the same manner and in accordance with the practice in cases where a plaintiff resides out of 5 the Province, and such order shall be a stay of proceedings in the case until the proper security is given as aforesaid: provided always, that this section shall not apply to any action wherein the plaintiff shall sue *in forma pauperis.*

Place of trial. **5.** All actions for libel contained in any public newspaper 10 or other periodical publication, shall be tried in the county where the chief office of such newspaper or periodical is, or in the county wherein the plaintiff resides at the time the action is brought; but upon the application of either party the Court or a judge may direct the issues to be tried or the damages to 15 be assessed in any other county, if it be made to appear that a fair trial cannot otherwise be obtained, and upon such terms as to payment of witness fees, and otherwise as may seem proper.

Plaintiff to prove malice. **6.** Except in cases where special damages are claimed the 20 plaintiff in all actions for libel in newspapers shall be required to prove either actual malice or culpable negligence in the publication of the libel complained of.

Costs. **7.** The Judge before whom any such action as aforesaid is tried shall not award costs to the plaintiff where he recovers 25 merely nominal damages.

No. 141.

1st Session, 6th Legislature, 50 Vic., 1887.

BILL.

An Act respecting the Law of Libel.

First Reading, 30th March, 1887.

BILL.

An Act respecting the Law of Libel.

HER MAJESTY, by and with the advice and consent of the Legislative Assembly of the Province of Ontario, enacts as follows :—

1. Section 4 of chapter 56 of the Revised Statutes of Ontario is hereby amended by adding thereto the following sub-section · R. S. O. c. 56, s. 4, amended.

(2) No such action shall lie unless and until the plaintiff has given to the defendant notice in writing, specifying the statements complained of, such notice to be served in the same manner as a plaintiff's statement of claim is served by delivering it to some grown-up person at the place of business of the defendant. The plaintiff shall recover actual damages only, if it appears on the trial of the action, that the article was published in good faith, and that there was reasonable ground to believe that the same was for the public benefit, and if it did not involve a criminal charge, and that the publication took place in mistake or misapprehension of the facts, and that a full and· fair retraction of any statement therein alleged to be erroneous was published either in the next regular issue of the newspaper, or other periodical publication aforesaid, or in any regular issue thereof published within three days after the receipt of such notice, and was so published in as conspicuous a place ánd type as was the article complained of,

(a) Provided, however, that the provisions of this Act, shall not apply to the case of any libel against any candidate for a public office in this Province, unless the retraction of the charge is made editorially in a conspicuous manner, at least five days before the election.

2. The words "a public meeting" in section 3 of *The Newspaper Libel Act, 1882*, shall extend to any lawful meeting to which the public are invited, and of which announcement has been made by printed or written notice thereof being posted up in at least six conspicuous places in the municipality where the meeting is held, or by advertisement in a public newspaper published in such municipality, or if there be none published therein then in the one published nearest to the place of meeting. Meaning of "public meeting" in 45 V. c. 9, s. 3.

Report of proceedings in Courts privileged. **3.** All reports of proceedings in any Court of Justice, published in any public newspaper or other periodical publication, shall be privileged, provided that they are fair and authentic and without comments, unless the defendant has refused or neglected to insert in the newspaper in which the report containing the matter complained of appeared, a reasonable letter or statement of explanation or contradiction, by or on behalf of such plaintiff.

Security for costs. **4.** In any action brought for libel contained in any public newspaper or periodical publication, the defendant may, at any time after the filing of the statement of claim, apply to the Court or a judge for security for costs, upon notice and an affidavit made by the defendant or his agent, shewing the nature of the action and of the defence, and that the plaintiff is not possessed of property sufficient to answer the costs of the action in case a verdict or judgment be given in favour of the defendant, and that the defendant has a good defence upon the merits and that the statements complained of were published in good faith, or that the grounds of action are trivial or frivolous, the Court or judge in his or their discretion, may make an order that the plaintiff shall give security for the costs to be incurred in such action, and the security so ordered shall be given in accordance with the practice in cases where a plaintiff resides out of the Province, and such order shall be a stay of proceedings in the case until the proper security is given as aforesaid.

(a) But where the alleged libel involves a criminal charge the defendant shall not be entitled to security for costs hereunder, unless he satisfies the Court or Judge that the action is trivial or frivolous, or that the several circumstances which, under said sub-section 2 of section 4 of said chapter 56 of the Revised Statutes, entitle the defendant at the trial to have the damages restricted to actual damages appear to exist, except the circumstance that the article complained of involves a criminal charge.

(b) For the purposes of this section the plaintiff or the defendant or their officers may be examined upon oath at any time after the statement of claim has been filed.

Place of trial. **5.** All actions for libel contained in any public newspaper or other periodical publication, shall be tried in the county where the chief office of such newspaper or periodical is, or in the county wherein the plaintiff resides at the time the action is brought; but upon the application of either party the Court or a Judge may direct the issues to be tried or the damages to be assessed in any other county, if it be made to appear to be in the interests of justice or that it will promote a fair trial and may impose such terms as to payment of witness fees, and otherwise as may seem proper.

No. 141.

1st Session, 6th Legislature, 50 Vic., 1887.

BILL.

An Act respecting the Law of Libel.

First Reading, 30th March, 1887.
Second   "   21st   April, 1887.
Third   "   "   1887.

No. 142.]　　　　　**BILL.**　　　　　[1887.

An Act to amend the Municipal Act.

HER MAJESTY, by and with the advice and consent of the Legislative Assembly of the Province of Ontario, enacts as follows:—

5　　**1.** Section 138 of *The Consolidated Municipal Act, 1883*, is hereby amended by striking out all the words after the word "therein" in the sixth line thereof. 46 V. c. 18, s. 138 amended.

　　2. Section 145 of *The Consolidated Municipal Act, 1883*, is hereby amended by inserting after the words "polling place,"
10 where they occur in the 22nd line of the said section, the words "and shall forthwith make a mark in the proper column of the voters' list opposite to such voter's name, indicating that such voter has voted, which shall be *prima facie* evidence that he has there and then voted." 46 V. c. 18, s. 145 amended.

15　　**3.** Sub-section 2 of section 154 of *The Consolidated Municipal Act, 1883*, is hereby amended by adding thereto at the end thereof the words "and shall be *prima facie* evidence of everything therein contained." 45 V. c. 18, s. 154 amended.

BILL.

An Act to amend the Municipal Act.

First Reading, 31st March, 1887.

BILL.

An Act to amend the Municipal Act.

HER MAJESTY, by and with the advice and consent of the Legislative Assembly of the Province of Ontario, enacts as follows :—

5 **1.** Section 623 of *The Consolidated Municipal Act, 1883,* is amended by adding the following sub-section thereto :

46 V. c. 18, s. 623 amended.

(3) Where the owners of real property have constructed their own works and improvements, which might otherwise have been constructed by the municipality as local improvements, the council may agree to acquire the same, and the 10 purchase money therefor may be raised, assessed and levied as for a local improvement upon the real property benefited thereby, under sections 612, 613, 617, 618, 619, 622 and 623 of this Act ; and in case the council and the owners cannot agree as to the compensation for such works and improvements, the 15 same shall be determined by arbitrators to be appointed under the provisions of this Act, and upon payment or tender of the amount so awarded, the owner shall convey the said works and improvements to the municipality by a good and sufficient deed.

Purchase of local improvements.

BILL.

An Act to amend the Municipal Act.

First Reading, 31st March, 1887.

BILL.

An Act to amend the Municipal Act.

HER MAJESTY, by and with the advice and consent of the
Legislative Assembly of the Province of Ontario, enacts
as follows :—

1. Section 505 of *The Consolidated Municipal Act, 1883,* is 46 V. c. 18, s.
5 hereby amended by adding thereto at the end thereof the 505 amended.
words following : " Provided always that in all cases where a
Municipality shall have constructed gas or water works under
the authority of this Act or under the authority of *The Municipal Water Works Act, 1882,* or shall hereafter construct such
10 works under the authority of the said Acts or any future
amendments of the same and shall have raised the money for
the purchase or construction of such works, or shall hereafter
so raise the same by a general rate on the whole of the assessable property of the said corporation under a by-law or by-
15 laws lawfully passed or to be passed, it shall be lawful for the
council of the city or town to raise on the credit of the said
corporation such further sums as may be necessary to extend
or improve the said works from time to time on the whole
ratable property of the said corporation by by-laws to be
20 passed as required by sub-section 14 of section 504 of this Act
and without complying with the requirements of this section."

2. Section 496 of *The Consolidated Municipal Act, 1883,* 46 V. c. 18. s.
is amended by adding thereto the following sub-sections :— 496 amended.

(1) For licensing and regulating the owners of cigar and
25 tobacco stores and for prohibiting the sale thereof to children
under the age of ——— years.

(2) For regulating the erection and maintenance of bathing
houses and boat houses and providing for the inspection
thereof, and for prohibiting the use thereof for illegal, immoral
30 or improper purposes, and for prohibiting the keeping of
liquor for sale and the sale of liquor therein.

(3) For preventing cruelty to and the neglect of children
under the age of 16 years on the part of parents, guardians,
and others having control over them, and for the removal of
35 such children from the care of cruel, drunken or vicious
parents or guardians.

(4) For making all needful provisions and arrangements
concerning children under the age of sixteen years who by
reason of the neglect, crime, drunkenness or other vices of

parents or guardians, or from orphanage, are suffered to be
growing up without salutary parental control and education,
or in circumstances exposing them to lead idle and dissolute
lives—and for appointing such inspectors and other officers as
may be necessary to secure the carrying out of all such by- 5
laws, rules and regulations.

1st Session, 6th Legislature, 50 Vic., 1887.

BILL.

An Act to amend the Municipal Act.

First Reading, 1st April, 1887.

BILL.

An Act to amend the Voters' Lists Act.

HER MAJESTY, by and with the advice and consent of the
Legislative Assembly of the Province of Ontario, enacts
as follows :—

Sub-section 1 of section 8 of *The Voters' Lists Act* as R. S. O. c. 9,
s. 8, (48 V. c.
5 amended by sectio ɩ 4 of *The Voters' List Amendment Act,* 3, s. 4),
1885, is amended by inserting between the word "wage- amended.
earner" and the word "and" in the twentieth line the following, "any householder or other person being entitled to vote,
who may have been inadvertently or otherwise omitted from
10 the voters' lists may be placed on the lists."

No. 145.

1st Session, 6th Legislature, 50 Vic., 1887

BILL.

An Act to amend the Voters' Lists Act.

First Reading, 1st April, 1887.

No. 146.]　　　　**BILL.**　　　　1887.

An Act to amend the Administration of Justice Act, 1885.

HER MAJESTY, by and with the advice and consent of the Legislative Assembly of the Province of Ontario, enacts as follows :—

    1. Sub-section 2 of section 16 of *The Administration of* 48 v. c. 13, s.
5 *Justice Act, 1885,* is hereby amended by inserting the word 16 (2), amend-
" not " after the word " shall " where it occurs in the second ed.
line of the said sub-section.

No. 146.

1st Session, 6th Legislature, 50 Vic., 1887.

BILL.

An Act to amend the Administration of Justice Act, 1885.

First Reading, 4th April, 1887.

BILL.

An Act to amend the Assessment Act.

HER MAJESTY, by and with the advice and consent of the Legislative Assembly of the Province of Ontario, enacts as follows :—

5   Section 1 of chapter 25 of *The Assessment Amendment Act, 1881,* is amended by inserting before the word "township" in the fourth line, the words "town, incorporated village and." 44 V. c. 25, s. 1 amended.

No. 147.

1st Session, 6th Legislature, 50 Vic., 1887.

BILL.

An Act to amend the Assessment Act.

First Reading, 4th April, 1887.

No. 148.] **BILL.** [1887.

An Act to amend the Act respecting the Taxation of Patented Lands in Algoma.

HER MAJESTY, by and with the advice and consent of the Legislative Assembly of the Province of Ontario, enacts as follows:—

1. The Treasurer, in advertising any lands for sale for 5 arrears of taxes, during the present year, 1887, may include in the usual notice of such sale in *The Ontario Gazette* and local newspaper, a notice that a discount of thirty per cent. will be allowed on such of the said sums in arrear as shall be paid on a day prior to such sale to be named in such notice ; and the 10 Treasurer is hereby empowered to allow the said discount on payments so made. *Discount on arrears.*

2. In addition to the annual tax of one cent. per acre provided by *The Act respecting the Taxation of Patented Lands in Algoma*, as amended by the Act passed in the 49th year of 15 Her Majesty's reign, chapter 5, a further tax of one cent an acre shall be imposed upon all unoccupied lands embraced in any school section formed under the authority of section 41 of *The Public Schools Act*, in the district of Algoma as the said district 's defined by section 2 of the said Act passed in the 20 49th year of Her Majesty's reign, and for the information of the Treasurer in charging such tax upon the lands liable there-for, the Secretary or Secretary-Treasurer of the School Board shall, on the formation of a school section in any unorganized township, give written notice thereof to the Provincial Treasurer, 25 and shall yearly, or on before the first day of August, furnish him with a list of all the lands embraced in the said school section, distinguishing such as are occupied from those that are unoccupied, and the said additional tax shall when collected be paid over annually to the trustees of the respective school 30 sections entitled thereto.

3. The said additional tax hereby imposed shall be subject to all the conditions as to penalty for default and provisions for collection as the one cent per acre imposed by section 35 1 of the said Act.

No. 148.

1st Session, 6th Legislature, 50 Vic., 1887.

BILL.

An Act to amend the Act respecting the Taxation of Patented Lands in Algoma.

First Reading, 5th April, 1887.

No. 148.] **BILL.** [1887.

An Act to amend the Act respecting the Taxation of Patented Lands in Algoma.

HER MAJESTY, by and with the advice and consent of the Legislative Assembly of the Province of Ontario, enacts as follows:—

1. The Treasurer, in advertising any lands for sale for 5 arrears of taxes, during the present year, 1887, may include in the usual notice of such sale in the *Ontario Gazette* and local newspaper, a notice that a discount of thirty per cent. will be allowed on such of the said sums in arrear as shall be paid on a day prior to such sale to be named in such notice; and the 10 Treasurer is hereby empowered to allow the said discount on payments so made. The same discount may also be allowed by the Treasurer upon any arrears upon lands liable for sale during the year 1887, if paid prior to being advertised. Discount on arrears.

2. In addition to the annual tax of one cent per acre 15 provided by *The Act respecting the Taxation of Patented Lands in Algoma*, as amended by the Act passed in the 49th year of Her Majesty's reign, chapter 5, a further tax of one cent an acre shall be imposed upon all unoccupied lands embraced in any school section formed under the authority of section 41 of 20 *The Public Schools Act*, in the district of Algoma as the said district is defined by section 2 of the said Act passed in the 49th year of Her Majesty's reign, and for the information of the Treasurer in charging such tax upon the lands liable therefor, the secretary or secretary-treasurer of the school board 25 shall, on the formation of a school section in any unorganized township, give written notice thereof to the Provincial Treasurer, and shall yearly, or on before the first day of August, furnish him with a list of all the lands embraced in the said school section, distinguishing such as are occupied from those that 30 are unoccupied, and the said additional tax shall when collected be paid over annually to the trustees of the respective school sections *in which such land is situate*. Tax on unoccupied lands.

3. The said additional tax hereby imposed shall be subject to all the conditions as to penalty for default and provisions 35 for collection as the one cent per acre imposed by section 1 of *The Act respecting the taxation of Patented Lands in Algoma*. 49 V. c. 5, s. 1 to apply to additional tax.

4. Section 6 of the said Act is amended by substituting the word "after" for the word "on" in the second line, and by striking out the words "on or before the first day of July," 40 and inserting in lieu thereof, "between the first day of October and the thirty-first day of December." R. S. O. c. 22, s. 6, amended.

5. Section 7 of the said Act is amended by inserting after the word "shall" in the seventh line, the words "between the first day of October and the thirtieth day of December." R. S. O. c. 22, s. 7, amended.

No. 148.

1st Session, 6th Legislature, 50 Vic., 1887.

BILL.

An Act to amend the Act respecting the Taxation of Patented Lands in Algoma.

(Re-printed as amended by Committee of the Whole House.)

First Reading, 5th April, 1887.
Second "   12th "   "

BILL.

An Act respecting the Federation of the University
of Toronto and University College with other
Universities and Colleges.

WHEREAS, it is desirable that the Universities and Colleges
of the Province of Ontario should be permitted to enter
into such relations with the University of Toronto as would
enable them to avail themselves of the instruction given by the
5 Faculty of the said University;

Therefore Her Majesty, by and with the advice and consent
of the Legislative Assembly of the Province of Ontario, enacts
as follows:—

1. The name of the University shall be "The University of
10 Toronto." Corporate name of University.

2.—(1) The University of Toronto shall continue to be
a body corporate, with power to hold any real property
assigned to it under the provisions of any former Act, or of
this Act, and with such other powers and privileges as are con-
15 ferred upon it by those portions of the Charter remaining in
force, which was granted in the eighth year of the reign of
His late Majesty King George the Fourth, or by any former
Act, but such powers shall be exercised in accordance with the
provisions of this Act. Rev. Stat. s. 1, s. 8 (22). General powers.

20 (2) The Chancellor and Vice-Chancellor, and the Senate, and
all officers, and all existing appointments, statutes, rules and
regulations affecting such University, shall continue, subject
to the provisions of this Act. R. S. O. 1877, c. 210, s. 2.

3. The Corporation of the University of Toronto shall con-
25 sist of the Chancellor, Vice-Chancellor, Professors, and members
of the Senate and of Convocation for the time being. R. S. O.
1877, c. 210, s. 3. Corporation of the University, how composed.

4. The Lieutenant-Governor shall be the Visitor of the
University on behalf of the Crown, and his visitorial powers
30 may be exercised by commission under the Great Seal, and the
proceedings of any commission, having been first confirmed
by the Lieutenant-Governor, shall be binding on the University and its members and on all persons whomsoever. R. S.
O. 1877, c. 210, s. 5. Lieutenant-Governor to be Visitor.

35 5.—(1) There shall be established in the University of
Toronto a teaching faculty in the following subjects, viz.: Pure
Mathematics, Physics, Astronomy, Geology, Mineralogy,
Chemistry (Pure and Applied), Zoology, Botany, Physiology, Teaching Faculty.

History, Ethnology and Comparative Philology, History of
Philosophy, Logic and Metaphysics, Education, Spanish and
Italian, Political Science, (including Political Economy, Juris-
prudence, and Constitutional Law), Engineering, and such other
Sciences, **Arts**, and branches of knowledge, including a teaching 5
faculty in Medicine and in Law, as the Senate may from time
to time determine, unless otherwise prohibited by this Act.

President,
etc., to be ap-
pointed by the
Lieutenant-
Governor.

(2) The president, professors, lecturers, teachers, officers and
servants of the University shall be appointed by the Lieutenant-Governor, after such examination, inquiry and report as 10
he considers necessary, and shall hold office during his pleasure;
but the president may, at any time, suspend any officer or
servant, and in case of so doing shall report the same forthwith to the Visitor. R. S. O. 1877, c. 209, s. 11.

Optional
subjects.

(3) The curriculum in Arts of the University, shall include 15
the subjects of Biblical Greek, Biblical Literature, Christian
Ethics, Apologetics, the Evidences of Natural and Revealed
Religion and Church History, but any provision for examination and instruction in the same shall be left to the voluntary
action of the federating Universities and Colleges, and pro- 20
vision shall be made by a system of options to prevent such
subjects being made compulsory upon any candidate for a
degree.

Lectures free
except fees for
Laboratory.

(4) Any lectures of the University faculty shall, with the
exception of laboratory fees and the lectures in the faculty of 25
Medicine and of Law, be free of charge to all Students
matriculated in the University who are enrolled in a federating University, or in University College or in a federating
college, and who enter their names with the Registrar of the
University Faculty ; but in the case of all other students the 30
Senate shall determine the fees which shall be charged for the
several courses of lectures in the University.

Faculties of
Medicine and
Law.

(5) In case the faculties of Medicine or Law are established
the Senate may from time to time, by statute, regulate the
instruction to be given, the fees to be paid for lectures, the 35
duties of professors, the discipline of students, and all other
matters pertaining to the establishment and management of
such faculties.

Federating
University
must suspend
its power to
confer degrees

6—(1) Any University in the Province of Ontario that sus-
pends its power to confer such degrees as it may be authorized 40
to confer (excepting Degrees in Theology) shall be entitled to be
represented on the Senate of Toronto University as hereinafter
provided, and shall, during the term of the suspension of such
power as aforesaid, be known as a federating University, with
a right to all the privileges and franchises hereinafter 45
mentioned.

Proclamation
of such sus-
pension.

(2) When any University in Ontario has decided to suspend
its powers of conferring degrees as aforesaid, it shall notify the
Provincial Secretary to that effect, and on the receipt of the
notice the Lieutenant-Governor in Council may, by proclama- 50
tion, in *The Ontario Gazette*, declare such University to be
federated with Toronto University, on and after such date
as may be named in the proclamation, and thereupon the
power to confer such degrees shall remain in abeyance until
proclamation is made to the contrary effect in a similar way. 55

(3) Any federating university, before resuming the power How to re-
sume power to
confer degrees of conferring degrees so suspended or held in abeyance shall, through its proper officer, notify the Provincial Secretary of its intention to do so, but such power shall not be exercised till
5 ——years after such notice is received, proclamation of which shall be made in *The Ontario Gazette.*

7. The graduates and undergraduates in Arts, Science and Status of
graduates, etc. Law of any federating University, and such graduates and undergraduates in Medicine as have passed their examinations
10 in the Province of Ontario shall, from and after the date of such federation, have and enjoy the same degrees, honors and status in the University of Toronto as they previously held in the federating University, and shall be entitled, subject to the provisions of this Act, to all the rights and privileges pertain-
15 ing to such degrees and status, so long as such federation continues.

8.—(1) A College affiliated with a federating university Affiliated
colleges
generally. shall be deemed to be affiliated with the University of Toronto,
20 but such affiliated college, or any other college hereafter affiliated with the University of Toronto, shall not thereby acquire the right of representation on the Senate, unless so declared in a statute passed in that behalf.

(2) All Colleges in Toronto, which are in affiliation with the Affiliated
colleges in
Toronto.
25 University of Toronto when this Act takes effect, not being schools of medicine, shall be considered federating Colleges within the meaning of this Act, and any school of medicine in affiliation with the University of Toronto when this Act takes effect shall be deemed to be affiliated with the said University.

30 (3) The Senate may by statute remove from federation with Senate may
remove from
federation." the University of Toronto any federating College which affili- ates with or becomes an integral part of any other University, exercising University power other than that of conferring degrees in theology.

35 CHANCELLOR.

9. The Chancellor of the said University shall be elected by Election of
Chancellor. the members of Convocation, in the manner hereinafter men- tioned, and shall hold office for three years, and until his suc- cessor is elected. R. S. O. 1877, c. 210, s. 6.

40 (2) The ordinary triennial election of Chancellor shall take place on the first Wednesday in October in any year in which an election is required.

(3) In case of vacancy in the office of Chancellor, by death, Vacancy in the
office of
Chancellor,
how filled. resignation, or any other cause, before the expiration of his term
45 of office, then, at a special election, to be holden for that pur- pose (of which election notice shall be given in such manner as may be provided by Statute of the Senate), the members of Convocation entitled to vote shall elect a Chancellor for the remainder of the term in which such death, resignation, or
50 other avoidance may have happened. R. S. O. 1877, c. 210, s. 7.

VICE-CHANCELLOR.

To hold office three years. **10**. The Vice-Chancellor of the University shall be elected by the members of the Senate from among themselves, and shall hold office for three years, and until his successor is appointed.

(2) The ordinary triennial election of Vice-Chancellor shall 5 take place at the first meeting of the Senate, in any academic year, in which such election may be required, and the Registrar shall. at least one month before the meeting, notify all the members of the Senate that the election is to be held.

Vacancies to be filled up by the Senate. (3) In case of vacancy in the office of Vice-Chancellor, by death, 10 resignation, or any other cause, before the expiration of his term of office, the members of the Senate shall, at a meeting to be held by them for that purpose, as soon as conveniently may be, of which notice shall be given in such manner as may be provided by Statute of the Senate, elect one other of the 15 said members of the Senate to be Vice-Chancellor for the remainder of the term. R. S. O. 1877, c. 210, s. 9.

THE SENATE.

11. The Senate of the University of Toronto shall be composed as follows :— 20

Ex-officio members. (1) The Minister of Education, the Chancellor, the President of University College, the President or other head of each federating university or College, and all Chancellors and Vice-Chancellors of the University of Toronto who held these offices before or who hold the same at the commence- 25 ment of this Act, shall be ex-officio members of the Senate ;

Appointed members. (2) The Council of University College, the Law Society of Ontario, the governing body of every federating university, or college, and of every college or school in this province now affiliated or hereafter affiliated with the University of Toronto, 30 subject to the provisions of section 8, may appoint one member, the Council of the University may appoint three members, and the Lieutenant-Governor in Council may appoint nine members of the Senate.

    (a) One member of the Council of University College shall 35 be appointed triennially by the Council of the College, and three members of the Faculty of the University by the Council of the University, and these appointments shall be made in rotation and shall proceed by seniority until every member 40 has in turn been a member of the Senate, and so successively ; and in case the member or members in rotation is otherwise of the Senate, or if he declines to act, the office shall fall to the next member or members. The Registrar of the Uni- 45 versity Council shall, from time to time, certify to the Registrar of the Senate, the members who, under this provision, become members of the Senate. R. S. O. 1877, c. 210, s. 11 ; 47 V. c. 45, s. 1.

Elected members. (3) At the first and second elections held under this Act, 50 the graduates in Arts of the University of Toronto and of every federating university shall respectively be entitled to

elect to the Senate, as hereinafter provided, one representative for every one hundred graduates in Arts on the register
of the University when this Act takes effect, (a fraction
over the last one hundred, if exceeding fifty to count as
5 a full hundred), the graduates in Medicine shall be entitled
to elect four members and the graduates in Law two members,
of the Senate.

(4) At any election to the Senate that takes place under this **Graduates in**
Act, the graduates in Medicine of the University of Toronto **Medicine and**
Law.
10 and of any federating university or universities shall vote as one
body; and a similar rule shall apply to the graduates in Law.

(5) For a period of six years after the federation of any uni- **Certain gradu-**
versity, the graduates in Arts of the federating university **ates to vote**
as a separate
and of the University of Toronto, shall vote in all elections to **body for six**
15 the Senate as distinct and separate bodies; but in all elections **years.**
thereafter, the graduates shall vote as members of one convocation, and shall conjointly as graduates of the University of
Toronto, elect the same number of members of the Senate as
theretofore they were entitled to elect separately.

20 (6) The registrar of the Senate shall, as often as an election **Election**
takes place during the said period of six years, in preparing the **register.**
Election Register hereinafter mentioned, make out a separate
list of the graduates in Arts of the University of Toronto, and
of every federating university, and shall also make out a separ-
25 ate voters' list of the graduates in Medicine and of the graduates in Law, and for the said period of six years such voters'
lists shall be the voters' lists in all elections to the Senate.

(7) The headmasters and assistant masters of Collegiate **High School**
Institutes and High Schools may elect two members as here- **representa-**
tives.
30 inafter provided.

CONVOCATION.

12. The Convocation of the University of Toronto shall con- **Convocation**
sist of the graduates in the several faculties of the University, **of whom to**
consist.
and every graduate shall be a member of Convocation. **44 V.,**
35 c. 31, s. 1.

13. The register of graduates shall be kept by the Registrar **Register of**
of the University, and shall be open and accessible to members **graduates.**
of Convocation during office hours, and the persons only whose
names appear thereon, shall be entitled to vote as members of
40 Convocation. **44** V., c. 31, s. 2; R. S. O. 1877, c. 210, s. 13.

14. The Registrar of the University shall trienially, after **Election**
Commencement when degrees are conferred, in every year **register**
in which an election is to take place, make out an alphabetical list or register, to be called "The Election Regis-
45 ter," of the names and known addresses of the members of
Convocation, who are entitled to vote as such members; and
such register may be examined by any member of Convocation
at all reasonable times at the office of the said Registrar.

(2.) In case a member of Convocation complains to the **Errors.**
50 Registrar, in writing, of the improper omission or inser-
tion of any name in the said list, it shall be the duty of the **How correct-**
Registrar forthwith to examine into the complaint and to **ed.**

rectify the error if any there be, subject at all times to an appeal to the Chancellor or Vice-Chancellor. R. S. O. 1877, c. 210, s. 14.

ELECTION OF CHANCELLOR AND MEMBERS OF SENATE.

Eletion of Chancellor and members of the Senate.

15.—(1) Any ten members of Convocation may nominate a candidate for the office of Chancellor, or for the office of member of the Senate, and the nomination paper or papers shall be sent in to the Registrar, on or before the first Wednesday of September in any year in which an election is to be held.

List of members of Senate to be sent with list of voters.

(2) At least one week after the said first Wednesday in September, the Registrar shall send by post, where his residence is known, the form of voting paper in the Schedule to this Act to each member of Convocation, with the list of names of all candidates nominated by ten members, and also a list of the retiring members, and the voting for members of the Senate shall be limited to the persons who have been so nominated. 44 V. c. 31, ss. 4, 16, 17.

    (a) In the case of head masters and assistant teachers of High Schools and Collegiate Institutes, their addresses shall be furnished by the Education Department on the application of the Registrar, and their election shall in all other respects be governed by the provisions of this Act. R. S. O. c. 210, s 26, (1), 1, (2); 47 V. c. 45, s. 2.

Federating University to elect full number of representatives.

(3) In the case of a University federating with the University of Toronto, the federating University shall at the time herein fixed for the federation taking effect, elect the full number of representatives to which as a federating University it may be entitled, as provided in section 11 of this Act.

Separate nomination papers for six years.

(4) For a period of six years after the federation of any University with the University of Toronto, separate nomination papers shall be made out for the election of members of the Senate, by the graduates in arts of the University of Toronto, and the graduates in arts of a federating university respectively.

How votes are to be given.

16. The votes at any election by Convocation for Chancellor and for members of the Senate respectively, shall be given by closed voting papers, in the form in the Schedule to this Act, or to the like effect, being delivered to the Registrar of the University, at his office between the hours of ten o'clock in the forenoon and four o'clock in the afternoon, on any day between the second Wednesday of September and the first Wednesday of October, in each year in which an election is held; and any voting papers received by the said Registrar by post during the time aforesaid, shall be deemed as delivered to him for the purpose of the election. R. S. O. 1877, c. 210, s. 15.

Opening voting papers.

17. The said voting papers shall, upon the Thursday after the first Wednesday of October, be opened by the Registrar of the University, in the presence of the scrutineers, to be appointed as hereinafter mentioned, who shall examine and count the votes, and keep a record thereof in a proper book to be provided by the Senate. R. S. O. 1877, c. 210, s. 18.

18. The person who has the highest number of votes at any election for Chancellor shall be Chancellor of the University for the term of office then next ensuing, or for the unexpired portion of the then current term, as the case may be. R. S. O. 5 1877, c. 210, s. 19. *Election of Chancellor.*

19. The persons who have the highest number of votes for members of the Senate shall be declared elected members thereof, their number and term of office being limited as herebefore provided. R. S. O. 1877, c. 210, s. 20. *Election of members of Senate.*

10 **20.** Any person entitled to vote at the election shall be entitled to be present at the opening of the voting papers. R. S. O. 1877, c. 210 s. 21. *Who may be present at opening of papers.*

21. In case of an equality of votes between two or more persons, which leaves the election of the Chancellor, or of one 15 or more members of the Senate, undecided, then the scrutineers shall forthwith put into a ballot-box a number of papers with the names of the candidates respectively having such equality of votes written thereon, one for each candidate, and the Registrar of the University shall draw from 20 the ballot-box, in the presence of the scrutineers, one of the papers in the case of the election of Chancellor, and one or more of the papers in the case of the election of members of the Senate, sufficient to make up the required number, and the persons whose names are upon the papers so 25 drawn shall be respectively the Chancellor and the members of the Senate. R. S. O. 1877, c. 210, s. 22. *Equality of votes.*

22. Upon the completion of the counting of the votes and of the scrutiny, the Vice-Chancellor, or other person acting as and for him, shall forthwith declare the result of the election 30 and shall, as soon as conveniently may be, report the same in writing signed by himself and by the scrutineers, to the Senate and to the Secretary of the Province. R. S. O. 1877, c. 210, s. 23. *Declaration of result of election.*

23. The Senate of the University or, in default, the Chancellor, shall, at least two weeks previous to the election, appoint two persons who, with the Vice-Chancellor, shall act as scrutineers at the next ensuing election; and the Senate or, in default, the Chancellor, shall appoint a member of the Senate, who shall act for and as the Vice-Chancellor, should he 40 be absent from the election. R. S. O. 1877, c. 210, s. 24. *Appointment of scrutineers.*

24. In the event of any elector placing more than one name on his voting paper for Chancellor, or more than the required number on his voting paper for members of the Senate, the first name only shall be taken for Chancellor, and the first 45 names only, not exceeding the required number, shall be taken for the members of the Senate. R. S. O. 1877, c. 210, s. 25. *Informal voting papers.*

25. On this Act taking effect as provided by section 6, the term of all appointed and elected members of the Senate of 50 the University of Toronto then in office shall cease and determine, and all members of the Senate elected thereafter by convocation, shall remain in office for a period of three years. *Vacancies by expiry of term, how filled. 36 V. c. 29. s. 22.*

Vacancies in Senate, how filled.

26. In case any vacancy shall occur by the death, resignation or removal from the Province of any member of the Senate elected by Convocation before the expiry of his term of office, the Senate shall thereupon appoint, from amongst the members of Convocation, another member of the Senate for the unexpired period of the term. 44 V. c. 31, s. 5.

Former Chancellors, etc., eligible for re-election.

27. At all elections to take place under this Act, retiring Chancellors or members of the Senate shall be eligible for re-election. R. S. O. 1877, c. 210, s. 29.

Crown appointees, their term of office.

28. Of the nine persons appointed by the Lieutenant-Governor, three shall retire in each year, in rotation, according to seniority of appointment; or in case of the appointment of the full number of nine members on this Act taking effect, then in the way the Lieutenant-Governor in Council may direct; and the vacancies in the Senate respectively created by such retirements in each year, shall, from time to time, be filled by appointment of the Lieutenant-Governor, the members so appointed holding office for three years and retiring by rotation at the expiration of the said term. R. S. O. 1877, c. 210, s. 31.

Crown appointees to be notified to the Registrar.

29. Whenever any appointment is made by the Lieutenant-Governor to fill vacancies, whether on retirement by rotation, or from other cause arising, the Secretary of the Province for the time being shall forthwith communicate the name of the person so appointed to the Registrar of the University. R. S. O. 1877, c. 210, s. 32.

Provision when vacancies are not filled by Lieutenant-Governor.

30. If at any time, by death or otherwise, the number of the appointed members of the Senate is reduced below the number of nine, and remains reduced for three months, if the Lieutenant-Governor does not think proper to complete the said number by appointment, the members of the Senate may at a meeting to be held for that purpose (of which notice shall be given to the Provincial Secretary, and to the members of the Senate in the manner provided by statute of Senate), elect one or more fit and proper persons to be members of the Senate in addition to the then remaining appointed members thereof, to the end that by means of such election the number of nine appointed members of the Senate may thus be completed; and the members so elected to vacancies by the Senate shall hold office for the term or for the remainder of the term pertaining to each such vacancy respectively. R. S. O. 1877, c. 210, s. 33.

Majority to decide, etc.

31. All questions which come before the Senate shall be decided by the majority of the members present; but in case of an equality of votes, the question shall be negatived. R. S. O. 1877, c. 210, s. 34.

Quorum.

32. No question shall be decided at any meeting unless the Chancellor or Vice-Chancellor and four other members of the Senate, or, in the absence of the Chancellor and Vice-Chancellor, unless five other members of the Senate, at the least, are present

Legal meetings of the Senate.

at the time of such decision, nor shall any meeting be legal unless held at the times or convened in the manner provided for by statute to be passed by the Senate. R. S. O. 1877, c. 210, s. 35.

33. At every meeting of the Senate, the Chancellor, or in his Chairman.
absence the Vice-Chancellor, shall preside as chairman, or in the
absence of both, a chairman shall be chosen by the members
present, or a majority of them. R. S. O. 1377, c. 210, s. 36.

5 **34.** The Senate for the time being shall, subject to the pro- Senate to
visions of *The Act respecting the Income and Property of the* manage the
University of Toronto, University College, and Upper Canada business of the University.
College, have the management of and superintendency over R. S. O.
the affairs and business of the University. R. S. O. 1877, c. c. s. 211.
10 210, s. 37.

35. The Senate shall have power to examine for, and after D
examination to confer the several Degrees of Bachelor and Master
of Arts, Bachelor and Doctor in Laws, Science, Philosophy,
Medicine and Music, and Master in Surgery, and the Degree
15 of Civil Engineer, Mining Engineer, and Mechanical Engineer,
or such of the said Degrees as they shall think fit, and
also to confer the several degrees of Bachelor, Master
and Doctor in any department of knowledge whatever,
except Theology, as the Senate by statute in that behalf
20 shall from time to time determine, and whether such departments of knowledge shall or shall not include any portion
of the departments of knowledge for which Degrees in Arts,
Laws, Science, Medicine and Music, or any of them, are authorized to be conferred by this Act; and such reasonable fees may
25 be charged for or in respect of such examination and Degrees
respectively, or either of them, as the Senate shall by statute in
that behalf from time to time direct; provided always that it
shall be competent for the Senate to confer the degrees of
LL.D., and D.C.L., *honoris causa,* under such statute as may
30 in that behalf be passed. R. S. O. 1877, c. 210, s. 38 ; 47 V. c.
45, s. 3.

36. The Senate shall also have power to admit to any of *Ad eundem*
the said degrees as *ad eundem* Degrees ; but no degree so con- degrees:
ferred shall, without the consent of Convocation in each case,
35 entitle the holder thereof to be or become a member of Convocation. R. S. O. 1877, c. 210, s. 39.

37. The Senate shall have power to examine for, and after Certificates
examination to grant, Certificates of Proficiency or Certifi- of proficiency.
cates of Honour, in such branches of knowledge as the
40 said Senate shall from time to time by statutes made in
that behalf determine ; and on every such examination the
candidate shall be examined by examiners appointed by the
Senate. R. S. O. 1877, c. 210, s. 40, 42.

38.—(1) At the conclusion of every examination of the candi- Certificate of
45 dates the examiners shall declare and certify to the Registrar result of ex-
of the University the name of every candidate whom they have aminations.
deemed to be qualified to receive any such certificate, together
with such particulars as the Senate shall from time to time
determine ; and such person shall, if otherwise approved by the
50 Senate and if they think fit, receive from the said Chancellor
a certificate under the seal of the said University, and signed by
the said Chancellor or by the Vice-Chancellor, in which the
branch or branches of knowledge in respect of which he or she Fees.
has been allowed by the said Senate to obtain the certificate

shall be stated, together with such other particulars, if any, as
the said Senate may deem fitting to be stated therein; and
such reasonable fees may be charged for or in respect of such
examinations and certificates of proficiency respectively, or
either of them as the Senate shall, by statute in that behalf, 5
from time to time direct. R. S. O. 1877, c. 210, s. 4.

Diploma to be signed. (2) Every graduate's or student's diploma or certificate of
standing, issued by the said Senate, in addition to being signed
by the proper University authorities in that behalf, shall indi-
cate the federating University, College or Colleges in which 10
such graduate or Student was enrolled at the time of his gra-
duation or examination and shall be signed by such Professors,
Teachers and Officers of such federating University, College or
Colleges, as its or their governing body or bodies may from
time to time determine. 15

Certificate required. (3) No Student enrolled at any federating University or
College (including University College), shall be allowed to
present himself for any University examination, subsequent to
matriculation, without producing a certificate, that he has
complied with all the requirements of such federating Uni- 20
versity or College, affecting his admission to such examination.

Attendance. (4) Attendance on instruction provided in any federating
university or affiliated college, including University College,
shall be accorded equal value as a condition of proceeding to
any degree, as attendance at the University. 25

Power to make statutes. **39.** The Senate may from time to time make and alter any
statutes not being repugnant to the laws of Ontario, or to the
general objects and provisions of this Act:

1. Touching the examination for Degrees, or for Scholarships, Prizes or Certificates of Honour; and 30

2. The granting of such Degrees, Scholarships or Certificates; and

3. The fees to be paid by candidates for examination or upon
taking any degree; and

4. The application of such fees; 35

5. Touching the periods of the regular meetings of the
Senate and the mode of convening special meetings thereof;
and

6. In general for promoting the purposes of the said University, and touching all other matters whatsoever regarding 40
the same or the business thereof, or for any purpose for which
provision may be required for carrying out this Act according
to its intent and spirit in any case not herein provided for.
R. S. O. 1877, c. 210, s. 44.

All statutes to be in writing and sealed and approved of by the Visitor. **40.** All such statutes shall be reduced to writing and the 45
Common Seal of the University shall be affixed thereto, and
when they have been approved of by the Visitor, they shall be
binding upon all persons being members or officers of the University, and upon all candidates for Degrees, Scholarships,
Prizes or Certificates of Honour, to be conferred by the said 50
University, and upon all others whom it may concern. R. S. O.
1877, c 210, s. 45.

41. A certified copy of every such statute shall be deposited with the Provincial Secretary within ten days after the passing thereof, to be laid before the Visitor of the University for his approval; and no such statute shall have force or effect 5 until it is approved by the Visitor, and such approval has been signified through the said Secretary. R. S. O. 1877, c. 210, s. 46.

Copies to be deposited with Provincial Secretary.

42. By any such statute approved as aforesaid power may be given to any committee, officers or persons to make regula- 10 tions for better carrying out the provisions or object of any statute of the University, in the manner and to the extent therein prescribed. R. S. O. 1877, c. 210, s. 47.

Certain powers may be delegated by statute.

43. The Senate for the time being, may, from time to time, appoint all examiners required for the purposes of this Act, 15 and may in like manner remove them or any of them. R. S. O. 1877, c. 210. s. 48.

Officers.

44. All statutes of the Senate heretofore made under any Act of Parliament relating to the said University, and which are in force on the day this Act takes effect, shall remain in force, 20 in so far as they are not inconsistent with this Act, until repealed or altered by the Senate. R. S. O. 1877, c. 210, s 40.

What statutes to remain in force.

45. The Senate shall annually report to the Lieutenant-Governor, at such time as he may appoint, on the general condition and progress of the University, and may of its own 25 motion, enquire into the conduct, teaching, and efficiency of any Professor or Teacher in said University Faculty or University College, and report to the Lieutenant-Governor the result of such enquiry, with such recommendations as they may think the circumstances of the case require.

Senate to make certain reports to the Lieutenant-Governor. Copies to be laid before the Legislative Assembly.

30 **46.** The Senate, once at least in every year, at a time or times to be fixed by statute, shall cause to be held an examination of the candidates for Degrees, Scholarships, Prizes or Certificates of Honour, as aforesaid. R. S. O. 1877, c. 210, s. 51.

Examination for degrees, etc.

47. At every such examination the candidates shall be ex- 35 amined by examiners appointed for the purpose by the Senate; and the candidates shall be examined orally or in writing or otherwise, in as many branches of general knowledge as the Senate consider the most fitting subjects for such examination. R. S. O. 1877, 210, s. 52.

Candidate to be examined by examiners.

40 **48.** No member of the Senate shall be eligible to be appointed as an examiner, and no examiner shall be eligible for re-appointment more than four years consecutively. R. S. O. 1877, c. 210, s. 53.

Examiner.

49. Special examinations may be held for honours. R. S. O. 45 1877, c. 210, s. 54.

Special examinations for honours.

50. Each examiner by acceptance of his appointment as such, shall become bound by the terms of the following declaration, and shall if required, sign the same in presence of the Chancellor, Vice-Chancellor or Registrar.

Examiners to make a declaration of impartiality.

"I solemnly declare that I will perform my duty of examiner without fear, favour, affection or partiality towards any candidate, and that I will not knowingly allow to any candidate any advantage which is not equally allowed to all."

R. S. O. 1877, c. 210, s. 55. 5

Examination to be public.   **51.** All the examinations shall be open and public. R.S.O. 1877, c. 210, s. 56.

Scholarships, prizes and rewards to be granted.   **52.** The Senate may establish Scholarships, Prizes and rewards to persons who distinguish themselves at their examination, and such Scholarships shall be held to be University 10 Scholarships in any of the affiliated institutions in Ontario, and the holder thereof shall have the title of "University Scholar," except where otherwise conditioned and agreed to with the founders, or the heirs or representatives of the founders, of such scholarships ; but no such scholarships, prizes or rewards 15 shall be paid out of University funds. R. S. O. 1877, c. 210, ss. 57, 59, 60.

Affiliation of Colleges, etc.   **53.**—(1) The Senate may, by statute, prescribe that any College, School or other Institution established in this Province for the promotion of Literature, Science or Art, or for 20 instruction in Law, Medicine, Mechanical Science, Engineering, Agriculture or other useful branch of education, upon the application of such College, School or other Institution, shall be deemed to be affiliated with the said University for the purpose of admitting therefrom as candidates at any of the 25 examinations for standing, or for Scholarships, Honours, Degrees and Certificates which the said Senate are authorized to confer, such persons as may have completed in such College, School or other Institution, whilst affiliated with the said University, such course of instruction preliminary to any of the 30 said examinations.

Dissolution of affiliation.   (2) Any College, School or other Institution affiliated with the University of Toronto, under this or any former Act, may be removed from such affiliation by statute of the Senate passed in that behalf.   35

What institutions already affiliated.

16 V. c. 89, s. 18.   (3) Excepting such Colleges, Schools or Institutions as are now in connection with the University under special applications heretofore made in that behalf, or as may become so, in conformity with the provisions in this section contained, and excepting University College, and Schools of Law and Medi- 40 cine heretofore affiliated under section 18 of the Act passed in the 16th year of Her Majesty's reign, chaptered 89, and epcepting those provided for by section 8 of this Act, no other College, School or Institution shall be deemed or taken to be affiliated for any purpose with the University. R. S. O. 45 1877, c. 210, s. 61.

Power to confer degrees.   (4) Every incorporated theological college, now or hereafter affiliated to the University of Toronto, shall, during such affiliation, have power to confer the degrees of Licentiate in Theology, of Bachelor of Divinity, and of Doctor of Divinity, 50 on the conditions following :

Regulations as to examinations.   (5) The Degrees shall be conferred under such regulations as to examination and otherwise, and by such authority as may from time to time be prescribed by the governing body of the college.   65

(6) A candidate for the Degree of Licentiate in Theology _{Degree of} must be of second year standing in the University of _{licentiate.} Toronto, or of equivalent standing in some other university recognized for that purpose by the affiliated college. He must,
5 in addition, have taken the First Year's Pass Examination in Oriental Literature, and the Second and Third 'Year's Pass Examinations in Logic and Mental and Moral Science in the University of Toronto, or equivalent examinations in some other University recognized for that purpose by the affiliated college.

10 (7) A candidate for the Degree of Bachelor of Divinity, or _{Degree in} of Doctor of Divinity, must be a graduate in Arts in the _{divinity.} University of Toronto, or some other university recognized for that purpose by the affiliated college.

54. Persons educated in any institution for the time being, _{Persons not educated in}
15 not federated or affiliated with the University, may be admitted _{the affiliated} as candidates for examination for standing or for any of the _{institutions} Honours, Scholarships, Degrees, or Certificates authorized _{may be candi-dates for} to be conferred by the said University, on such conditions as _{degrees, etc.} the Senate may from time to time determine. R. S. O. 1877, c.
20 210, s. 62.

55. The Senate may pass such statutes with regard to _{Examinations at affiliated} the examination of candidates at any affiliated College, School _{colleges.} or Institution in this Province as may appear convenient, and such examinations may be conducted by sub-examiners upon
25 papers or questions prepared by the examiners in the prescribed subjects, and may be deemed and taken as equivalent to the ordinary examinations held for any purpose at the University, and also for certificates of having undergone a satisfactory examination in any department of literature, science or art.
30 R. S. O. 1877, c. 210, s. 63.

THE UNIVERSITY COUNCIL.

56. The Professors of the University and of the School of Practical Science shall conjointly form the University Council, presided over by the President of University College ; and such
35 Council shall have full authority and entire responsibility of discipline over all students in relation to the lectures and other instruction of the Professors, Lecturers, and Tutors of the University ; and no lecturing or teaching of any kind shall be carried on in the University or in the School of Science,
40 by any others except the duly appointed professors and teachers, without the authority of the University Council.

57. The University Council shall have entire authority and responsibility for all work carried on by the societies and associations of students of the University ; provided always
45 that all such authority and responsibility shall be limited to the conduct of the students in relation to such societies and associations as are organized in connection with the University.

58. The University Council shall have entire authority over _{Control of}
50 all officers and servants of the University whose services are _{servants.} required in connection with the work of instruction; and all curators, assistants, or servants, engaged in the lecture-rooms, laboratories, or otherwise in any department of instruction shall be under the sole authority of the University Council.

(2) The laboratory fees to be paid by students or other persons for attending the University, or receiving instruction therein, shall be determined by the Lieutenant-Governor in Council on the report of the University Council.

59. The Convocation of the University shall have the powers following :—

1. The power of electing the Chancellor and certain members of the Senate in manner hereinbefore provided ;

2. The power of discussing any matter whatsoever relating to the University, and of declaring the opinion of Convocation in any such matter ;

3. The power of taking into consideration all questions affecting the well-being and prosperity of the University, and of making representations from time to time on such questions to the Senate of the said University, who shall consider the same and return to Convocation their conclusions thereon ;

4. The power of deciding upon the mode of conducting and registering the proceedings of Convocation ;

5. The power of appointing and removing the Clerk of Convocation, and of prescribing his duties ;

6. The power of requiring a fee to be paid by members of Convocation, as a condition of being placed on the register of members.

7. Convocation shall meet at such times and places as may from time to time be ordered by the Senate, or by the Executive Committee of Convocation, and notice of such meeting shall be given in such manner as said Senate, or said Executive Committee shall from time to time determine. 47 V. c. 45, s. 4.

60 If twenty-five or more members of Convocation shall by writing under their hands, require the Chairman for the time being of Convocation to convene an extraordinary meeting of Convocation, and such requisition shall express the object of the meeting required to be called, it shall be the duty of the said Chairman, within a reasonable time, to convene such meeting of Convocation. R. S. O. 1877, c. 210, s. 66.

61. No matter shall be discussed at any such extraordinary meeting, except the matter, or matters, for the discussion whereof it was convened. R. S. O. 1877, c. 210, s. 67 ; 47 V., c. 45, s. 5.

62. The Senate shall provide a proper place for the meeting of Convocation, and the proceedings of any meeting of Convocation shall be transmitted to the Senate at the next following meeting of the Senate. R. S. O. 1877, c. 210, s. 68.

63.—(1) The Chairman of Convocation shall hold office for three years, or until his successor is elected, and shall be eligible for re-election.

(2) On expiration of any term of the said office, or in case of the death or resignation of the Chairman, or any vacancy of the said office, the members of Convocation present at any meeting duly convened, or the majority, shall elect a Chairman,
5 who, if elected, shall hold office during the period of three years, or until his successor is appointed. R. S. O. 1877, c. 210, s. 70 ; 44 V., c. 31, s. 3.

64. If the Chairman is absent at the time of the meeting Absence of chairman. of Convocation, or if there is a vacancy in the office, then,
10 before proceeding to business the members of Convocation then present, or the major part of them, shall elect a Chairman, who shall hold office during such meeting only. R. S. O. 1877, c. 210 s. 71.

65. All questions which come before Convocation shall be Questions before Convoca-
15 decided by the majority of votes of members present, or repre- tion how decided. sented thereat, in such manner as may be provided by any resolution or by-law of Convocation, and the Chairman, at any meeting thereof, shall have a vote, and in case of equality of votes, a second or casting vote. R. S. O. 1877, c. 210, s. 72 ;
20 47 V., c. 45, s. 6.

66. No question shall be decided at any meeting of Convo- Quorum. cation, unless thirty members at least are present. R. S. O. 1877, c. 210, s. 73.

67. Any meeting of Convocation shall have power to ad- Adjournments.
25 journ to a future day. R. S. O. 1877. c. 210, s. 74.

UNIVERSITY COLLEGE.

68.—(1) The collegiate institution heretofore constituted at College president, etc., to the City of Toronto by the name of " University College " is continue as before. hereby continued, and the body corporate called " The Council
30 of University College," and the President, Professors, officers, servants, and all other existing appointments, and all statutes, by-laws, rules and regulations of such Council, are hereby continued, subject to the provisions of this Act. R. S. O. 1877, c. 209, s. 1.
35 (2) The Council of University College shall include all the professors and lecturers of the College Faculty, and shall be known as " The Council of University College."

69. The Lieutenant-Governor shall be the Visitor of the Lieutenant-Governor to be visitor. said College on behalf of the Crown, and his visitorial powers
40 may be exercised by commission under the Great Seal, and the proceedings of any commission so appointed being confirmed by the Lieutenant-Governor, shall be binding on the said College and the Council thereof, and on all persons whomsoever. R. S. O. 1877, c. 209, s. 2.

45 **70.** The said College shall be under the direction, manage- The Council of University College to ment and administration of the said body corporate called The manage the Council of University College, and such body corporate shall have College, etc. perpetual succession and a common seal, with power to hold real and personal property, subject to the provisions hereinafter made, and shall be capable of suing and being sued, pleading
50

and being impleaded by the name aforesaid, and shall have
the usual powers of corporate bodies, according to *The Interpretation Act*, subject to the said provisions. R. S. O.1877,
c. 209, s. 3.

Rev. Stat, c.
1, s. 8 (24).

Members of
the Council.

71. The said Corporation shall consist of a President and 5
such Professors as may from time to time be appointed to
chairs in the said University College, and the said President
of University College shall be President of the Faculty of the
University. R. S. O. 1877, c. 209, s. 4.

Dean of Uni-
versity Col-
lege.

72. The Dean of Residence in University College for the 10.
time being shall be a member of the Council of the said College.
R. S. O. 1877, c. 209, s. 5.

Meetings of
the Council.

73. The President, or in his absence, then the senior member
of the Council present, shall preside at all meetings of the said
Council, and in case of an equal division of votes among the 15
members present, the negative shall prevail, and among members appointed at the same time, or on the same day, the order
in which their appointments were made shall be the order of
seniority ; and all such meetings shall be held at the times to
be prescribed by the regulations of the said Council. R. S. O. 20
1877, c. 209, s. 6.

Quorum.

74. Any five members of the said Council shall be a quorum
for transacting the business of the Council and doing all things
which the Council may lawfully do; and all things done at
any meeting of the Council shall be ordered by the majority 25
of votes of the members present thereat, subject to the provision hereinbefore made for the case of an equal division of
votes. R. S. O. 1877, c. 209, s. 7.

Majority to
decide.

Council to
make statutes
for certain
purposes.

75.—(1) The said Council may make regulations for
the management of the property and business thereof, and 30
for any purpose necessary for carrying this Act into effect
according to its intent and spirit in cases for which no provision
is made, so that such regulations be not inconsistent with this
Act or the laws of this Province ; and the Council may from
time to time amend or repeal the same. 35

Which shall
be transmitted
to Provincial
Secretary,

(2) A certified copy of all such regulations shall be transmitted to the Provincial Secretary within ten days from the
passing thereof, to be submitted to the Visitor for his approval ;
and no regulation made by the said Council shall have force
and effect until it has been submitted to the said Visitor and 40
by him approved. R. S. O. 1877, c. 209, s. 8.

and approved
by Lieutenant-
Governor.

President,
etc., to be ap-
pointed by the
Lieutenant-
Governor.

76. The President, professors, lecturers, teachers, officers and
servants of the said College shall be appointed by the Lieutenant-Governor, after such examination, inquiry and report as
he considers necessary, and shall hold office during his plea- 45
sure ; but the President may, at any time, suspend any officer
or servant, any such case of suspension to be reported by him
forthwith to the Visitor of the college. R. S. O. 1877, c. 209,
s. 11.

Faculty of
University
College.

77. There shall be established in the said University College 50
a teaching faculty consisting of a professor, lecturer, and fellow,

in eacH of the following subjects, viz.: Greek, Latin, French, German and English, and a professor and lecturer in Oriental Languages and a professor of Moral Philosophy, and Ancient History shall be taught in connection with the classes of Greek
5 and Latin, and a teaching faculty may be established in such other subjects (except Divinity) not mentioned in Section 5 of this Act, as by regulation made in that behalf may be determined, subject to the approval of the Lieutenant-Governor in Council.

10 **78.** The fees to be paid by students or persons attending lectures or receiving instruction in University College shall be determined by the Lieutenant-Governor in Council on the report of the Council of University College. *Fees of Students.*

79. All students, except in cases specially provided for by
15 Statute of the Senate shall be enrolled in University College, in an affiliated college, or in a federating university. *Students to be enrolled.*

80. The Council shall, at all times when thereunto required by the Lieutenant-Governor, inquire into, examine and report upon any subject or matter connected with the said University
20 College; and copies of such annual or other reports shall be laid before the Legislative Assembly of this Province at the then next session thereof. R. S. O. 1877, c. 20?, s. 19. *Council to report to the Lieut.-Governor. Copies to be laid before the Legislative Assembly.*

PROVISIONS APPLICABLE TO UNIVERSITY OF TORONTO AND UNIVERSITY COLLEGE.

25 **81.** No religious test shall be required of any professor, lecturer, teacher, student, officer or servant of the said College or University, nor shall religious observances, according to the forms of any particular religious denomination, be imposed on them or any of them; but the University Council, and the Council
30 of University College, may respectively make such regulations as they think expedient touching the moral conduct of the students and their attendance on public worship in their respective churches or other places of religious worship, and respecting their religious instruction by their respective ministers, accord-
35 ing to their respective forms of religious faith, and every facility shall be afforded for such purposes: Provided always that attendance on such form of religious observance be not compulsory on any student attending the University or University College. R. S. O. 1877, c. 209, s. 18. *No religious test, etc., to be required.*

40 **82.** Any person, body politic or corporate, may found professorship, fellowships, lectureships, scholarships, exhibitions, prizes and other rewards in the said College or University, by providing a sufficient endowment in land or other property, and surrendering or conveying the same to the Crown for the
45 purposes of the said College or University, and thereupon suing out letters patent from the Crown, instituting, establishing and endowing the same with the property so provided for that purpose as aforesaid. R. S. O. 1877, c. 209, s. 14. *Professorships may be founded by private parties, and how.*

83. In such letter patent shall be set forth such rules and
50 regulations for the appointing to and conferring of such professorships, fellowships, lectureships, scholarships, prizes or *Letters patent shall set forth rules, etc.*

other awards as the respective founders thereof, with the approbation of the Crown, think fit to prescribe for that purpose, all which rules and regulations the authorities of the said College or University shall observe and give effect to, as in the said letters patent may be directed. R. S. O. 1877, c. 209, s. 15.   5

Certain professorships prohibited.   **84.** No professorship or lectureship shall be so founded for the teaching of any subject which under this Act is not to be taught in the said College or University. R. S. O. 1877, c. 209, s. 16.

Endowment to be vested in the Crown.   **85.** Every endowment of lands or other property of the 10 endowment as aforesaid shall be vested in the Crown for the purposes for which it was given, and also any property, real or personal, given, devised or bequeathed to the said College or University, or for the use thereof. R. S. O. 1877, c. 209, s. 17.

86. The University Endowment and all additions thereto 15 shall be applied to the maintenance of the University, the University Faculty, and University College.

Regulations as to superannuation of professors.   **87.** The Lieutenant-Governor in Council may make regulations respecting the retirement or superannuation of any professor, lecturer, officer or servant of the said University or University College, now employed or hereafter to be employed, and any 20 gratuity or superannuation allowance shall be a charge on the University endowment, and shall be paid out of the same as the Governor in Council may from time to time direct ;

Regulations to be laid before Legislative Assembly.   (2) Every such Regulation shall be laid before the Legislative Assembly forthwith if the Legislature is in session at the 25 date of such Regulation, and if the Legislature is not in session such Regulation shall be laid before the said House within the first seven days of the session next after such Regulation is made.

(3) In case the Legislative Assembly at the said session, or 30 if the session does not continue for three weeks after the said Regulation is laid before the House, then at the ensuing session of the Legislature, disapproves by resolution of such Regulation, either wholly or of any part thereof, the Regulation, so far as disapproved of, shall have no effect from the 35 time of such resolution being passed.

88. This Act shall take effect by proclamation of the Lieutenant-Governor in Council, and when so proclaimed all other Acts inconsistent herewith shall be repealed.

SCHEDULE.

(Section 16).

FORM OF VOTING PAPER.

University of Toronto.

Election   18   .

I,
resident at   in the County of
do hereby declare

(1) That the signature affixed hereto is my proper handwriting.

(2) That I vote for the following person (*or persons*) as Chancellor or as members of the Senate (*as the case may be*) of the University of Toronto, viz.,   of   in the County of   etc., etc.

(3) That I have signed no other voting paper at this election.

(4) That this voting paper was executed on the day of the date hereof.

(5) That I vote in my right as Graduate of   University, or Head Master or Assistant Master of a High School (*as the case may be*).

Witness my hand this   day of   A.D. 18   .

R. S. O. 1877, c. 210, Scbed.

No. 149.

1st Session, 6th Legislature, 50 Vic., 1887.

BILL.

An Act respecting the Federation of the University of Toronto and University College with other Universities and Colleges.

First Reading, 5th April, 1887.

No. 149.]   **BILL.**   [1887.

An Act respecting the Federation of the University of Toronto and University College with other Universities and Colleges.

WHEREAS, it is desirable that the Universities and Colleges Preamble. of the Province of Ontario should be permitted to enter into such relations with the University of Toronto as would enable them to avail themselves of the instruction given by the 5 Faculty of the said University;

Therefore Her Majesty, by and with the advice and consent of the Legislative Assembly of the Province of Ontario, enacts as follows:—

1. The name of the University shall be "The University of Corporate name of 10 Toronto." University.

2.—(1) The University of Toronto shall continue to be Rev. Stat. a. a body corporate, with power to hold any real property 1, s. 8 (22). assigned to it under the provisions of any former Act, or of this Act, and with such other powers and privileges as are con- 15 ferred upon it by those portions of the Charter remaining in General force, which was granted in the eighth year of the reign of powers. His late Majesty King George the Fourth, or by any former Act, but such powers shall be exercised in accordance with the provisions of this Act.

20   (2) The Chancellor and Vice-Chancellor, and the Senate, and all officers, and all existing appointments, statutes, rules and regulations affecting such University, shall continue, subject to the provisions of this Act. R. S. O. 1877, c. 210, s. 2.

3. The Corporation of the University of Toronto shall con- Corporation of the Univer- 25 sist of the Chancellor, Vice-Chancellor, Professors, and members sity, how of the Senate and of Convocation for the time being. R. S. O. composed. 1877, c. 210, s. 3.

4. The Lieutenant-Governor shall be the Visitor of the Lieutenant- Governor to be University on behalf of the Crown, and his visitorial powers Visitor. 30 may be exercised by commission under the Great Seal, and the proceedings of any commission, having been first confirmed by the Lieutenant-Governor, shall be binding on the Univer- sity and its members and on all persons whomsoever. R. S. O. 1877, c. 210, s. 5.

35   **5.**—(1) There shall be established in the University of Teaching Toronto a teaching faculty in the following subjects, viz.: Pure Faculty. Mathematics, Physics, Astronomy, Geology, Mineralogy, Chemistry (Pure and Applied), Zoology, Botany, Physiology,

History, Ethnology and Comparative Philology, History of
Philosophy, Logic and Metaphysics, Education, Spanish and
Italian, Political Science, (including Political Economy, Juris-
prudence, and Constitutional Law), Engineering, and such other
Sciences, Arts, and branches of knowledge, including a teaching 5
faculty in Medicine and in Law, as the Senate may from time
to time determine, unless otherwise prohibited by this Act.

President, etc., to be appointed by the Lieutenant-Governor. (2) The president, professors, lecturers, teachers, officers and
servants of the University shall be appointed by the Lieu-
tenant-Governor, after such examination, inquiry and report as 10
he considers necessary, and shall hold office during his pleasure;
but the president may, at any time, suspend any officer or
servant, and in case of so doing shall report the same forthwith to the Visitor. R. S. O. 1877, c. 209, s. 11.

Optional subjects. (3) The curriculum in Arts of the University, shall include 15
the subjects of Biblical Greek, Biblical Literature, Christian
Ethics, Apologetics, the Evidences of Natural and Revealed
Religion and Church History, but any provision for examination and instruction in the same shall be left to the voluntary
action of the federating Universities and Colleges, and pro- 20
vision shall be made by a system of options to prevent such
subjects being made compulsory upon any candidate for a
degree.

Lectures free except fees for Laboratory. (4) Any lectures of the University faculty shall, with the
exception of laboratory fees and the lectures in the faculty of 25
Medicine and of Law, be free of charge to all Students
matriculated in the University who are enrolled in a federating University, or in University College or in a federating
college, and who enter their names with the Registrar of the
University Faculty ; but in the case of all other students the 30
Senate shall determine the fees which shall be charged for the
several courses of lectures in the University.

Faculties of Medicine and Law. (5) In case the faculties of Medicine or Law are established
the Senate may from time to time, by statute, regulate the
instruction to be given, the fees to be paid for lectures, the 35
duties of professors, the discipline of students, and all other
matters pertaining to the establishment and management of
such faculties.

Federating University must suspend its power to confer degrees **6**—(1) Any University in the Province of Ontario that sus-
pends its power to confer such degrees as it may be authorized 40
to confer (excepting Degrees in Theology) shall be entitled to be
represented on the Senate of *the University of Toronto* as hereinafter provided, and shall, during the term of the suspension of
such power as aforesaid, be known as a federating University,
with a right to all the privileges and franchises hereinafter 45
mentioned.

Proclamation of such suspension. (2) When any University in Ontario has decided to suspend
its powers of conferring degrees as aforesaid, it shall notify the
Provincial Secretary to that effect, and on the receipt of the
notice the Lieutenant-Governor in Council may, by proclama- 50
tion, in *The Ontario Gazette,* declare such University to be
federated with *the University of Toronto,* on and after such date
as may be named in the proclamation, and thereupon the
power to confer such degrees shall remain in abeyance until
proclamation is made to the contrary effect in a similar way. 55

(3) Any federating university, before resuming the power of conferring degrees so suspended or held in abeyance shall, through its proper officer, notify the Provincial Secretary of its intention to do so, but such power shall not be exercised *for* 5 *three years after the date of such federation, nor until one* year after notice is received *as aforesaid,* proclamation of which shall be made in *The Ontario Gazette.* How to resume power to confer degrees

7. The graduates and undergraduates in Arts, Science and Law of any federating University, and such graduates and 10 undergraduates in Medicine as have passed their examinations in the Province of Ontario shall, from and after the date of such federation, have and enjoy the same degrees, honors and status in the University of Toronto as they previously held in the federating University, and shall be entitled, subject to the 15 provisions of this Act, to all the rights and privileges pertaining to such degrees and status, so long as such federation continues. Status of graduates, etc.

8.—(1) A College affiliated with a federating university shall be deemed to be affiliated with the University of Toronto, 20 but such affiliated college, or any other college hereafter affiliated with the University of Toronto, shall not thereby acquire the right of representation on the Senate, unless so declared in a statute *of the Senate* in that behalf. Affiliated colleges generally.

(2) All Colleges in Toronto, which are in affiliation with the 25 University of Toronto when this Act takes effect, not being schools of medicine, shall be considered federating Colleges within the meaning of this Act, and any school of medicine in affiliation with the University of Toronto when this Act takes effect shall be deemed to be affiliated with the said University. Affiliated colleges in Toronto.

30 (3) The Senate may by statute remove from federation with the University of Toronto any federating College which affiliates with or becomes an integral part of any other University, exercising University power other than that of conferring degrees in theology. Senate may remove from federation.

35 CHANCELLOR.

9. The Chancellor of the said University shall be elected by the members of Convocation, in the manner hereinafter mentioned, and shall hold office for three years, and until his successor is elected. R. S. O. 1877, c. 210, s. 6. Election of Chancellor.

40 (2) The ordinary triennial election of Chancellor shall take place on the first Wednesday in October in any year in which an election is required.

(3) In case of vacancy in the office of Chancellor, by death, resignation, or any other cause, before the expiration of his term 45 of office, then, at a special election, to be holden for that purpose (of which election notice shall be given in such manner as may be provided by Statute of the Senate), the members of Convocation entitled to vote shall elect a Chancellor for the remainder of the term in which such death, resignation, or 50 other avoidance may have happened. R. S. O. 1877, c. 210, s. 7. Vacancy in the office of Chancellor, how filled.

VICE-CHANCELLOR.

To hold office three years.

10.—(1) The Vice-Chancellor of the University shall be elected by the members of the Senate from among themselves, and shall hold office for three years, and until his successor is appointed. 5

(2) The ordinary triennial election of Vice-Chancellor shall take place at the first meeting of the Senate, in any academic year, in which such election may be required, and the Registrar shall. at least one month before the meeting, notify all the members of the Senate that the election is to be held. 10

Vacancies to be filled up by the Senate.

(3) In case of vacancy in the office of Vice-Chancellor, by death, resignation, or any other cause, before the expiration of his term of office, the members of the Senate shall, at a meeting to be held by them for that purpose, as soon as conveniently may be, of which notice shall be given in such manner as may 15 be provided by Statute of the Senate, elect one other of the said members of the Senate to be Vice-Chancellor for the remainder of the term. R. S. O. 1877, c. 210, s. 9.

THE SENATE.

11. The Senate of the University of Toronto shall be composed as follows :— 20

Ex-officio members.

(1) The Minister of Education, the Chancellor, the President of University College, the President or other head of each federating university or College, and all Chancellors and Vice-Chancellors of the University of Toronto who held 25 these offices before or who hold the same at the commencement of this Act, shall be ex-officio members of the Senate ;

Appointed members.

(2) The Council of University College, the Law Society of *Upper Canada*, the governing body of every federating university, or college, and of every college or school in this province 30 now affiliated or hereafter affiliated with the University of Toronto, subject to the provisions of section 8, may appoint one member, the Council of the University may appoint three members, and the Lieutenant-Governor in Council may appoint nine members of the Senate. 35

(a) One member of the Council of University College shall be appointed triennially by the Council of the College, and three members of the Faculty of the University by the Council of the University, and these appointments shall be made in rotation 40 and shall proceed by seniority until every member has in turn been a member of the Senate, and so successively ; and in case the member in rotation is otherwise of the Senate, or if he decline to act, the office shall fall to the next 45 member or members. The Registrar of the University Council shall, from time to time, certify to the Registrar of the Senate, the members who, under this provision, become members of the Senate. R. S. O. 1877, c. 210, s. 11 ; 47 V. c. 45, s. 1. 50

Elected members.

(3) At the first and second elections held under this Act, the graduates in Arts of the University of Toronto and of every federating university shall respectively be entitled to

elect to the Senate, as hereinafter provided, one representative for every one hundred graduates in Arts on the register
of the University when this Act takes effect, (a fraction
over the last one hundred, if exceeding fifty to count us
5 a full hundred), the graduates in Medicine shall be entitled
to elect four members and the graduates in Law two members,
of the Senate.

(4) At any election to the Senate that takes place under this
Act, the graduates in Medicine of the University of Toronto
10 and of any federating university or universities shall vote as one
body; and a similar rule shall apply to the graduates in Law.

Graduates in Medicine and Law.

(5) For a period of six years after the federation of any university, the graduates in Arts of the federating university
and of the University of Toronto, shall vote in all elections to
15 the Senate as distinct and separate bodies ; but in all elections
thereafter, the graduates shall vote as members of one convocation, and shall conjointly as graduates of the University of
Toronto, elect the same number of members of the Senate as
theretofore they were entitled to elect separately. •

Certain gradu- ates to vote as a separate body for six years.

20 (6) The registrar of the Senate shall, as often as an election
takes place during the said period of six years, in preparing the
Election Register hereinafter mentioned, make out a separate
list of the graduates in Arts of the University of Toronto, and
of every federating university, and shall also make out a separate voters' list of the graduates in Medicine and of the gradu-
25 ates in Law, and for the said period of six years such voters'
lists shall be the voters' lists in all elections to the Senate.

Election register.

(7) The headmasters and assistant masters of Collegiate
Institutes and High Schools may elect two members as here-
30 inafter provided.

High School representa- tives.

CONVOCATION.

12. The Convocation of the University of Toronto shall consist of the graduates in the several faculties of the University,
and every graduate shall be a member of Convocation. 44 V.,
35 c. 31, s. 1.

Convocation of whom to consist.

13. The register of graduates shall be kept by the Registrar
of the University, and shall be open and accessible to members
of Convocation during office hours, and the persons only whose
names appear thereon, shall be entitled to vote as members of
40 Convocation. 44 V., c. 31, s. 2 ; R. S. O. 1877, c. 210, s. 13.

Register of graduates.

14. The Registrar of the University shall trienially, after
Commencement when degrees are conferred, in every year
in which an election is to take place, make out an alphabetical list or register, to be called " The Election Regis-
45 ter," of the names and known addresses of the members of
Convocation, who are entitled to vote as such members ; and
such register may be examined by any member of Convocation
at all reasonable times at the office of the said Registrar.

Election register

(2.) In case a member of Convocation complains to the
50 Registrar, in writing, of the improper omission or insertion of any name in the said list, it shall be the duty of the
Registrar forthwith to examine into the complaint and to

Errors.

How correct- ed.

rectify the error if any there be, subject at all times to an appeal to the Chancellor or Vice-Chancellor. R. S. O. 1877, c. 210, s. 14.

ELECTION OF CHANCELLOR AND MEMBERS OF SENATE.

Eletion of Chancellor and members of the Senate.

15.—(1) Any ten members of Convocation may nominate a candidate for the office of Chancellor, or for the office of member of the Senate, and the nomination paper or papers shall be sent in to the Registrar, on or before the first Wednesday of September in any year in which an election is to be held.

List of members of Senate to be sent with list of voters.

(2) At least one week after the said first Wednesday in September, the Registrar shall send by post, where his residence is known, the form of voting paper in the Schedule to this Act to each member of Convocation, with the list of names of all candidates nominated by ten members, and also a list of the retiring members, and the voting for members of the Senate shall be limited to the persons who have been so nominated. 44 V. c. 31, ss. 4, 16, 17.

> (a) In the case of head masters and assistant teachers of High Schools and Collegiate Institutes, their addresses shall be furnished by the Education Department on the application of the Registrar, and their election shall in all other respects be governed by the provisions of this Act. R. S. O. c. 210, s.26, (1), 1, (2); 47 V. c. 45, s. 2.

Federating University to elect full number of representatives.

(3) In the case of a University federating with the University of Toronto, the federating University shall at the time herein fixed for the federation taking effect, elect the full number of representatives to which as a federating University it may be entitled, as provided in section 11 of this Act.

Separate nomination papers for six years.

(4) For a period of six years after the federation of any University with the University of Toronto, separate nomination papers shall be made out for the election of members of the Senate, by the graduates in arts of the University of Toronto, and the graduates in arts of a federating university respectively.

How votes are to be given.

16. The votes at any election by Convocation for Chancellor and for members of the Senate respectively, shall be given by closed voting papers, in the form in the Schedule to this Act, or to the like effect, being delivered to the Registrar of the University, at his office between the hours of ten o'clock in the forenoon and four o'clock in the afternoon, on any day between the second Wednesday of September and the first Wednesday of October, in each year in which an election is held; and any voting papers received by the said Registrar by post during the time aforesaid, shall be deemed as delivered to him for the purpose of the election. R. S. O. 1877, c. 210, s. 15.

Opening voting papers.

17. The said voting papers shall, upon the Thursday after the first Wednesday of October, be opened by the Registrar of the University, in the presence of the scrutineers, to be appointed as hereinafter mentioned, who shall examine and count the votes, and keep a record thereof in a proper book to be provided by the Senate. R. S. O. 1877, c. 210, s. 18.

18. The person who has the highest number of votes at any election for Chancellor shall be Chancellor of the University for the term of office then next ensuing, or for the unexpired portion of the then current term, as the case may be. R. S. O. 5 1877, c. 210, s. 19. *Election of Chancellor.*

19. The persons who have the highest number of votes for members of the Senate shall be declared elected members thereof, their number and term of office being limited as herebefore provided. R. S. O. 1877, c. 210, s. 20. *Election of members of Senate.*

10 **20.** Any person entitled to vote at the election shall be entitled to be present at the opening of the voting papers. R. S. O. 1877. c. 210 s. 21. *Who may be present at opening of papers.*

21. In case of an equality of votes between two or more persons, which leaves the election of the Chancellor, or of one 15 or more members of the Senate, undecided, then the scrutineers shall forthwith put into a ballot-box a number of papers with the names of the candidates respectively having such equality of votes written thereon, one for each candidate, and the Registrar of the University shall draw from 20 the ballot-box, in the presence of the scrutineers, one of the papers in the case of the election of Chancellor, and one or more of the papers in the ease of the election of members of the Senate, sufficient to make up the required number, and the persons whose names are upon the papers so 25 drawn shall be respectively the Chancellor and the members of the Senate. R. S. O. 1877, c. 210, s. 22. *Equality of votes.*

22. Upon the completion of the counting of the votes and of the scrutiny, the Vice-Chancellor, or other person acting as and for him, shall forthwith declare the result of the election 30 and shall, as soon as conveniently may be, report the same in writing signed by himself and by the scrutineers, to the Senate and to the Secretary of the Province. R. S. O. 1877, c. 210, s. 23. *Declaration of result of election.*

23. The Senate of the University or, in default, the Chancellor 35 cellor, shall, at least two weeks previous to the election, appoint two persons who, with the Vice-Chancellor, shall act as scrutineers at the next ensuing election; and the Senate or, in default, the Chancellor, shall appoint a member of the Senate, who shall act for and as the Vice-Chancellor, should he 40 be absent from the election. R. S. O. 1877, c. 210, s. 24. *Appointment of scrutineers.*

24. In the event of any elector placing more than one name on his voting paper for Chancellor, or more than the required number on his voting paper for members of the Senate, the first name only shall be taken for Chancellor, and the first 45 names only, not exceeding the required number, shall be taken for the members of the Senate. R. S. O. 1877, c. 210, s. 25. *Informal voting papers.*

25. On this Act taking effect as provided by section 6, the term of all appointed and elected members of the Senate of 50 the University of Toronto then in office shall cease and determine, and all members of the Senate elected thereafter by convocation, shall remain in office for a period of three years. *Vacancies by expiry of term, how filled. 36 V. c. 29. s. 22.*

8

Vacancies in Senate, how filled.

26. In case any vacancy shall occur by the death, resignation or removal from the Province of any member of the Senate elected by Convocation before the expiry of his term of office, the Senate shall thereupon appoint, from amongst the members of Convocation, another member of the Senate for 5 the unexpired period of the term. 44 V. c. 31, s. 5.

Former Chancellors, etc., eligible for re-election.

27. At all elections to take place under this Act, retiring Chancellors or members of the Senate shall be eligible for re-election. R. S. O. 1877, c. 210, s. 29.

Crown appointees, their term of office.

28. Of the nine persons appointed by the Lieutenant- 10 Governor, three shall retire in each year, in rotation, according to seniority of appointment; or in case of the appointment of the full number of nine members on this Act taking effect, then in the way the Lieutenant-Governor in Council may direct; and the vacancies in the Senate respectively created by 15 such retirements in each year, shall, from time to time, be filled by appointment of the Lieutenant-Governor, the members so appointed holding office for three years and retiring by rotation at the expiration of the said term. R. S. O. 1877, c. 210, s. 31.

Crown appointees to be notified to the Registrar.

29. Whenever any appointment is made by the Lieutenant- 20 Governor to fill vacancies, whether on retirement by rotation, or from other cause arising, the Secretary of the Province for the time being shall forthwith communicate the name of the person so appointed to the Registrar of the University. R. S. O. 1877, c. 210, s. 32. 25

Provision when vacancies are not filled by Lieutenant-Governor.

30. If at any time, by death or otherwise, the number of the appointed members of the Senate is reduced below the number of nine, and remains reduced for three months, if the Lieutenant-Governor does not think proper to complete the said number by appointment, the members of the Senate may 30 at a meeting to be held for that purpose (of which notice shall be given to the Provincial Secretary, and to the members of the Senate in the manner provided by statute of Senate), elect one or more fit and proper persons to be members of the Senate in addition to the then remaining appointed 35 members thereof, to the end that by means of such election the number of nine appointed members of the Senate may thus be completed; and the members so elected to vacancies by the Senate shall hold office for the term or for the remainder of the term pertaining to each such vacancy respectively. 40 R. S. O. 1877, c. 210, s. 33.

Majority to decide, etc.

31. All questions which come before the Senate shall be decided by the majority of the members present; but in case of an equality of votes, the question shall be negatived. R. S. O. 1877, c. 210, s. 34. 45

Quorum.

32. No question shall be decided at any meeting unless the Chancellor or Vice-Chancellor and four other members of the Senate, or, in the absence of the Chancellor and Vice-Chancellor, unless five other members of the Senate, at the least, are present

Legal meetings of the Senate.

at the time of such decision, nor shall any meeting be legal 50 unless held at the times or convened in the manner provided for by statute to be passed by the Senate. R. S. O. 1877, c. 210, s. 35.

33. At every meeting of the Senate, the Chancellor, or in his Chairman. absence the Vice-Chancellor, shall preside as chairman, or in the absence of both, a chairman shall be chosen by the members present, or a majority of them. R. S. O. 1377, c. 210, s. 36.

5 **34.** The Senate for the time being shall, subject to the pro- Senate to visions of *The Act respecting the Income and Property of the* manage the *University of Toronto, University College, and Upper Canada* University. *College,* have the management of and superintendency over R. S. O. the affairs and business of the University. R. S. O. 1877, c. c. 211. 10 210, s. 37.

35. The Senate shall have power to examine for, and after Degrees. examination to confer the several Degrees of Bachelor and Master of Arts, Bachelor and Doctor in Laws, Science, Philosophy, Medicine and Music, and Master in Surgery, and the Degree 15 of Civil Engineer, Mining Engineer, and Mechanical Engineer, or such of the said Degrees as they shall think fit, and also to confer the several degrees of Bachelor, Master and Doctor in any department of knowledge whatever, except Theology, as the Senate by statute in that behalf 20 shall from time to time determine, and whether such depart- ments of knowledge shall or shall not include any portion of the departments of knowledge for which Degrees in Arts, Laws, Science, Medicine and Music, or any of them, are author- ized to be conferred by this Act; and such reasonable fees may 25 be charged for or in respect of such examination and Degrees respectively, or either of them, as the Senate shall by statute in that behalf from time to time direct; provided always that it shall be competent for the Senate to confer the degrees of LL.D, and D.C.L., *honoris causa,* under such statute as may 30 in that behalf be passed. R. S. O. 1877, c. 210, s. 38 ; 47 V. c. 45, s. 3.

36. The Senate shall also have power to admit to any of *Ad eundem* the said degrees as *ad eundem* Degrees ; but no degree so con- degrees. ferred shall, without the consent of Convocation in each case, 35 entitle the holder thereof to be or become a member of Convo- cation. R. S. O. 1877, c. 210, s. 39.

37. The Senate shall have power to examine for, and after Certificates examination to grant, Certificates of Proficiency or Certifi- of proficiency. cates of Honour, in such branches of knowledge as the 40 said Senate shall from time to time by statutes made in that behalf determine ; and on every such examination the candidate shall be examined by examiners appointed by the Senate. R. S. O. 1877, c. 210, s. 40, 42.

38.—(1) At the conclusion of every examination of the candi- Certificate of 45 dates the examiners shall declare and certify to the Registrar result of ex- of the University the name of every candidate whom they have aminations. deemed to be qualified to receive any such certificate, together with such particulars as the Senate shall from time to time determine ; and such person shall, if otherwise approved by the 50 Senate and if they think fit, receive from the said Chancellor a certificate under the seal of the said University, and signed by the said Chancellor or by the Vice-Chancellor, in which the branch or branches of knowledge in respect of which he or she Fees. has been allowed by the said Senate to obtain the certificate

shall be stated, together with such other particulars, if any, as
the said Senate may deem fitting to be stated therein ; and
such reasonable fees may be charged for or in respect of such
examinations and certificates of proficiency respectively, or
either of them as the Senate shall, by statute in that behalf, 5
from time to time direct. R. S. O. 1877, c. 210, s. 4.

Diploma to be
signed.
(2) Every graduate's or student's diploma or certificate of
standing, issued by the said Senate, in addition to being signed
by the proper University authorities in that behalf, shall indi-
cate the federating University, College or Colleges in which 10
such graduate or Student was enrolled at the time of his gra-
duation or examination and shall be signed by such Professors,
Teachers and Officers of such federating University, College or
Colleges, as its or their governing body or bodies may from
time to time determine. 15

Certificate
required.
(3) No Student enrolled at any federating University or
College (including University College), shall be allowed to
present himself for any University examination, subsequent to
matriculation, without producing a certificate, that he has
complied with all the requirements of such federating Uni- 20
versity or College, affecting his admission to such examination.

Attendance.
(4) Attendance on instruction provided in any federating
university or affiliated college, including University College,
shall be accorded equal value as a condition of proceeding to
any degree, as attendance at the University. 25

Power to
make statutes.
39. The Senate may from time to time make and alter any
statutes not being repugnant to the laws of Ontario, or to the
general objects and provisions of this Act :

1. Touching the examination for Degrees, or for Scholarships, Prizes or Certificates of Honour; and 30

2. The granting of such Degrees, Scholarships or Certificates ; and

3. The fees to be paid by candidates for examination or upon
taking any degree; and

4. The application of such fees ; 35

5. Touching the periods of the regular meetings of the
Senate and the mode of convening special meetings thereof;
and

6. In general for promoting the purposes of the said University, and touching all other matters whatsoever regarding 40
the same or the business thereof, or for any purpose for which
provision may be required for carrying out this Act according ·
to its intent and spirit in any case not herein provided for.
R. S. O. 1877, c. 210, s. 44.

All statutes to
be in writing
and sealed and
approved of by
the Visitor.
40. All such statutes shall be reduced to writing and the 45
Common Seal of the University shall be affixed thereto, and
when they have been approved of by the Visitor, they shall be
binding upon all persons being members or officers of the University, and upon all candidates for Degrees, Scholarships,
Prizes or Certificates of Honour, to be conferred by the said 50
University, and upon all others whom it may concern. R. S. O.
1877, c 210, s. 45.

41. A certified copy of every such statute shall be deposited with the Provincial Secretary within ten days after the passing thereof, to be laid before the Visitor of the University for his approval; and no such statute shall have force or effect 5 until it is approved by the Visitor, and such approval has been signified through the said Secretary. R. S. O. 1877, c. 210, s. 46.

Copies to be deposited with Provincial Secretary.

42. By any such statute approved as aforesaid power may be given to any committee, officers or persons to make regula- 10 tions for better carrying out the provisions or object of any statute of the University, in the manner and to the extent therein prescribed. R. S. O. 1877, c. 210, s. 47.

Certain powers may be delegated by statute.

43. The Senate for the time being, may, from time to time, appoint all examiners required for the purposes of this Act, 15 and may in like manner remove them or any of them. R. S. O. 1877, c. 210. s. 48.

Officers.

44. All statutes of the Senate heretofore made under any Act of Parliament relating to the said University, and which are in force on the day this Act takes effect, shall remain in force, 20 in so far as they are not inconsistent with this Act, until repealed or altered by the Senate. R. S. O. 1877, c. 210, s 40.

What statutes to remain in force.

45. The Senate shall annually report to the Lieutenant-Governor, at such time as he may appoint, on the general condition and progress of the University, and may of its own 25 motion, enquire into the conduct, teaching, and efficiency of any Professor or Teacher in said University Faculty or University College, and report to the Lieutenant-Governor the result of such enquiry, with such recommendations as they may think the circumstances of the case require.

Senate to make certain reports to the Lieutenant-Governor.

Copies to be laid before the Legislative Assembly.

30 **46**. The Senate, once at least in every year, at a time or times to be fixed by statute, shall cause to be held an examination of the candidates for Degrees, Scholarships, Prizes or Certificates of Honour, as aforesaid. R. S. O. 1877, c. 210, s. 51.

Examination for degrees, etc.

47. At every such examination the candidates shall be ex- 35 amined by examiners appointed for the purpose by the Senate; and the candidates shall be examined orally or in writing or otherwise, in as many branches of general knowledge as the Senate consider the most fitting subjects for such examination. R. S. O. 1877, 210, s. 52.

Candidate to be examined by examiners.

40 **48**. No member of the Senate shall be eligible to be appointed as an examiner, and no examiner shall be eligible for re-appointment more than four years consecutively. R. S. O. 1877, c. 210, s. 53.

Examiner.

49. Special examinations may be held for honours. R. S. O. 45 1877, c. 210, s. 54.

Special examinations for honours.

50. Each examiner by acceptance of his appointment as such, shall become bound by the terms of the following declaration, and shall if required, sign the same in presence of the Chancellor, Vice-Chancellor or Registrar.

Examiners to make a declaration of impartiality.

"I solemnly declare that I will perform my duty of examiner without fear, favour, affection or partiality towards any candidate, and that I will not knowingly allow to any candidate any advantage which is not equally allowed to all."

R. S. O. 1877, c. 210, s. 55.　**5**

Examination to be public. **51.** All the examinations shall be open and public. R.S.O. 1877, c. 210, s. 56.

Scholarships, prizes and rewards to be granted. **52.** The Senate may establish Scholarships, Prizes and rewards to persons who distinguish themselves at their examination, and such Scholarships shall be held to be University 10 Scholarships in any of the affiliated institutions in Ontario, and the holder thereof shall have the title of "University Scholar," except where otherwise conditioned and agreed to with the founders, or the heirs or representatives of the founders, of such scholarships ; but no such scholarships, prizes or rewards 15 shall be paid out of University funds. R. S. O. 1877, c. 210, ss. 57, 59, 60.

Affiliation of Colleges, etc. **53.**—(1) The Senate may, by statute, prescribe that any College, School or other Institution established in this Province for the promotion of Literature, Science or Art, or for 20 instruction in Law, Medicine, Mechanical Science, Engineering, Agriculture or other useful branch of education, upon •the application of such College, School or other Institution, shall be deemed to be affiliated with the said University for the purpose of admitting therefrom as candidates at any of the 25 examinations for standing, or for Scholarships, Honours, Degrees and Certificates which the said Senate are authorized to confer, such persons as may have completed in such College, School or other Institution, whilst affiliated with the said University, such course of instruction preliminary to any of the 30 said examinations.

Dissolution of affiliation. (2) Any College, School or other Institution affiliated with the University of Toronto, under this or any former Act, may be removed from such affiliation by statute of the Senate passed in that behalf. 35

What institutions already affiliated. (3) Excepting such Colleges, Schools or Institutions as are now in connection with the University under special applications heretofore made in that behalf, or as may become so, in conformity with the provisions in this section contained, and **16 V. c. 89, s. 18.** excepting University College, and Schools of Law and Medi- 40 cine heretofore affiliated under section 18 of the Act passed in the 16th year of Her Majesty's reign, chaptered 89, and eepcepting those provided for by section 8 of this Act, no other College, School or Institution shall be deemed or taken to be affiliated for any purpose with the University. R. S. O. 45 1877, c. 210, s. 61.

Power to confer degrees. (4) Every incorporated theological college, now or hereafter affiliated to the University of Toronto, shall, during such affiliation, have power to confer the degrees of Licentiate in Theology, of Bachelor of Divinity, and of Doctor of Divinity, 50 on the conditions following :

Regulations as to examinations. (5) The Degrees shall be conferred under such regulations as to examination and otherwise, and by such authority as may from time to time be prescribed by the governing body of the college. **55**

(6) A candidate for the Degree of Licentiate in Theology *Degree of* must be of second year standing in the University of *licentiate.* Toronto, or of equivalent standing in some other university recognized for that purpose by the affiliated college. He must, 5 in addition, have taken the First Year's Pass Examination in Oriental Literature, and the Second and Third Year's Pass Examinations in Logic and Mental and Moral Science in the University of Toronto, or equivalent examinations in some other University recognized for that purpose by the affiliated college.

10 (7) A candidate for the Degree of Bachelor of Divinity, or *Degree in* of Doctor of Divinity, must be a graduate in Arts in the *divinity.* University of Toronto, or some other university recognized for that purpose by the affiliated college.

54. Persons *not* educated in any institution for the time being, *Persons not* 15 federated or affiliated with the University, may be admitted *educated in the affiliated* as candidates for examination for standing or for any of the *institutions* Honours, Scholarships, Degrees, or Certificates authorized *may be candi-dates for* to be conferred by the said University, on such conditions as *degrees, etc.* the Senate may from time to time determine. R. S. O. 1877, c. 20 210, s. 62.

55. The Senate may pass such statutes with regard to *Examinations* the examination of candidates at any affiliated College, School *at affiliated* or Institution in this Province as may appear convenient, and *colleges.* such examinations may be conducted by sub-examiners upon 25 papers or questions prepared by the examiners in the prescribed subjects, and may be deemed and taken as equivalent to the ordinary examinations held for any purpose at the University, and also for certificates of having undergone a satisfactory ex-amination in any department of literature, science or art. 30 R. S. O. 1877, c. 210, s. 63.

THE UNIVERSITY COUNCIL.

56. *The University Council shall consist of a President* Constitution *appointed by the Lieutenant-Governor in Council, (who* and authority *shall also be President of University College), and* of Council. 35 *of the Professors of the University;* and such Council shall have full authority and entire responsibility of dis-cipline over all students in relation to the lectures and other instruction *by* the Professors, Lecturers, and *other teachers* of the University; and no lecturing or teaching of any kind shall 40 be carried on in the University or in the School of Science, by any others except the duly appointed professors and teachers, without the authority of the University Council.

57. The University Council shall have entire authority and *Control of* responsibility for all work carried on by the societies and *societies and associations of* 45 associations of students of the University; provided always *students.* that all such authority and responsibility shall be limited to the conduct of the students in relation to such societies and associations as are organized in connection with the University.

58. The University Council shall have entire authority over *Control of* 50 all officers and servants of the University whose services are *servants.* required in connection with the work of instruction; and all curators, assistants, or servants, engaged in the lecture-rooms, laboratories, or otherwise in any department of instruction shall be under the sole authority of the University Council.

(2) The laboratory fees to be paid by students or other persons for attending the University, or receiving instruction therein, shall be determined by the Lieutenant-Governor in Council on the report of the University Council.

Powers of Convocation.

59. The Convocation of the University shall have the powers following :— 5

1. *The power of electing its own chairman ;*

2. The power of electing the Chancellor and certain members of the Senate in manner hereinbefore provided ;

3. The power of discussing any matter whatsoever relating to the University, and of declaring the opinion of Convocation in any such matter ; 10

4. The power of taking into consideration all questions affecting the well-being and prosperity of the University, and of making representations from time to time on such questions to the Senate of the said University, who shall consider the same and return to Convocation their conclusions thereon ; 15

5. The power of deciding upon the mode of conducting and registering the proceedings of Convocation ;

6. The power of appointing and removing the Clerk of Convocation, and of prescribing his duties ; 20

7. The power of requiring a fee to be paid by members of Convocation, as a condition of being placed on the register of members.

8. Convocation shall meet at such times and places as may from time to time be ordered by the Senate, or by the Executive Committee of Convocation, and notice of such meeting shall be given in such manner as said Senate, or said Executive Committee shall from time to time determine. 47 V. c. 45, s. 4. 25

30

Extraordinary meetings of Convocation.

60. If twenty-five or more members of Convocation shall by writing under their hands, require the Chairman for the time being of Convocation to convene an extraordinary meeting of Convocation, and such requisition shall express the object of the meeting required to be called, it shall be the duty of the said Chairman, within a reasonable time, to convene such meeting of Convocation. R. S. O. 1877, c. 210, s. 66. 35

What may be discussed.

61. No matter shall be discussed at any such extraordinary meeting, except the matter, or matters, for the discussion whereof it was convened. R. S. O. 1877, c. 210, s. 67 ; 47 V., c. 45, s. 5. 40

Place of meeting.

62. The Senate shall provide a proper place for the meeting of Convocation, and the proceedings of any meeting of Convocation shall be transmitted to the Senate at the next following meeting of the Senate. R. S. O. 1877, c. 210, s. 68. 45

Chairman of Convocation.

63.—(1) The Chairman of Convocation shall hold office for three years, or until his successor is elected, and shall be eligible for re-election.

(2) On expiration of any term of the said office, or in case of the death or resignation of the Chairman, or any vacancy of the said office, the members of Convocation present at any meeting duly convened, or the majority, shall elect a Chairman, 5 who, if elected, shall hold office during the period of three years, or until his successor is appointed. R. S. O. 1877, c. 210, s. 70 ; 44 V., c. 31, s. 3.

64. If the Chairman is absent at the time of the meeting of Convocation, or if there is a vacancy in the office, then, 10 before proceeding to business the members of Convocation then present, or the major part of them, shall elect a Chairman, who shall hold office during such meeting only. R. S. O. 1877, c. 210 s. 71.

Absence of chairman.

65. All questions which come before Convocation shall be 15 decided by the majority of votes of members present, or represented thereat, in such manner as may be provided by any resolution or by-law of Convocation, and the Chairman, at any meeting thereof, shall have a vote, and in case of equality of votes, a second or casting vote. R. S. O. 1877, c. 210, s. 72 ; 20 47 V., c. 45, s. 6.

Questions before Convocation how decided.

66. No question shall be decided at any meeting of Convocation, unless thirty members at least are present. R. S. O. 1877, c. 210, s. 73.

Quorum.

67. Any meeting of Convocation shall have power to adjourn to a future day. R. S. O. 1877. c. 210, s. 74.

Adjournments.

UNIVERSITY COLLEGE.

68.—(1) The collegiate institution heretofore constituted at the City of Toronto by the name of " University College " is hereby continued, and the body corporate called " The Council 30 of University College," and the President, Professors, officers, servants, and all other existing appointments, and all statutes, by-laws, rules and regulations of such Council, are hereby continued, subject to the provisions of this Act. R. S. O. 1877, c. 209, s. 1.

College president, etc., to continue as before.

35 (2) The Council of University College shall include all the professors of the College Faculty, and shall be known as " The Council of University College."

69. The Lieutenant-Governor shall be the Visitor of the said College on behalf of the Crown, and his visitorial powers 40 may be exercised by commission under the Great Seal, and the proceedings of any commission so appointed being confirmed by the Lieutenant-Governor, shall be binding on the said College and the Council thereof, and on all persons whomsoever. R. S. O. 1877, c. 209, s. 2.

Lieutenant-Governor to be visitor.

45 **70.** The said College shall be under the direction, management and administration of the said body corporate called The Council of University College, and such body corporate shall have perpetual succession and a common seal, with power to hold real and personal property, subject to the provisions .hereinafter 50 made, and shall be capable of suing and being sued, pleading

The Council of University College to manage the College, etc.

and being impleaded by the name aforesaid, and shall have
the usual powers of corporate bodies, according to *The Interpretation Act*, subject to the said provisions. R. S. O.1877,
c. 209, s. 3.

71. The said Corporation shall consist of a President and 5
such Professors as may from time to time be appointed to
chairs in the said University College.

72. The Dean of Residence in University College for the
time being shall be a member of the Council of the said College.
R. S. O. 1877, c. 209, s. 5.

73. The President, or in his absence, then the senior member
of the Council present, shall preside at all meetings of the said
Council, and in case of an equal division of votes among the
members present, the *question shall be negatived* and among
members appointed at the same time, or on the same day, the 15
order in which their appointments were made shall be the order
of seniority ; and all such meetings shall be held at the times to
be prescribed by the regulations of the said Council. R. S. O
1877, c. 209, s. 6.

74. Any five members of the said Council shall be a quorum 20
for transacting the business of the Council and doing all things
which the Council may lawfully do; and all things done at
any meeting of the Council shall be ordered by the majority
of votes of the members present thereat, subject to the provision hereinbefore made for the case of an equal division of 25
votes. R. S. O. 1877, c. 209, s. 7.

75.—(1) The said Council may make regulations for
the management of the property and business thereof, and
for any purpose necessary for carrying this Act into effect
according to its intent and spirit in cases for which no provision 30
is made, so that such regulations be not inconsistent with this
Act or the laws of this Province ; and the Council may from
time to time amend or repeal the same.

(2) A certified copy of all such regulations shall be transmitted to the Provincial Secretary within ten days from the 35
passing thereof, to be submitted to the Visitor for his approval ;
and no regulation made by the said Council shall have force
and effect until it has been submitted to the said Visitor and
by him approved. R. S. O. 1877, c. 209, s. 8.

Which shall
be transmitted
to Provincial
Secretary,

and approved
by Lieutenant-
Governor.

76. The President, professors, lecturers, teachers, officers and 40
servants of the said College shall be appointed by the Lieutenant-Governor, after such examination, inquiry and report as
he considers necessary, and shall hold office during his pleasure; but the President may, at any time, suspend any officer
or servant, any such case of suspension to be reported by him 45
forthwith to the Visitor of the college. R. S. O. 1877, c. 209,
s. 11.

77. There shall be established in the said University College
a teaching faculty consisting of a professor, lecturer, and fellow,

in each of the following subjects, viz.: Greek, Latin, French,
German and English, and a professor and lecturer in Oriental
Languages and a professor of Moral Philosophy, and Ancient
History shall be taught in connection with the classes of Greek
5 and Latin, and a teaching faculty may be established in such
other subjects (except Divinity) not mentioned in section 5 of
this Act, as by regulation made in that behalf may be determined, subject to the approval of the Lieutenant-Governor in
Council.

10 **78.** The fees to be paid by students or persons attending Fees of Students.
lectures or receiving instruction in University College shall be
determined by the Lieutenant-Governor in Council on the
report of the Council of University College.

79. All students, except in cases specially provided for by Students to be enrolled.
15 Statute of the Senate shall be enrolled in University College,
or in an affiliated college, or in a federating university.

80. The Council shall, at all times when thereunto required Council to re- port to the
by the Lieutenant-Governor, inquire into, examine and report Lieut.-Gover-
upon any subject or matter connected with the said University nor.
20 College ; and copies of such annual or other reports shall be Copies to be laid before the
laid before the Legislative Assembly of this Province at the Legislative
then next session thereof. R. S. O. 1877, c. 20?, s. 19. Assembly.

PROVISIONS APPLICABLE TO UNIVERSITY OF TORONTO
AND UNIVERSITY COLLEGE.

25 **81.** No religious test shall be required of any professor, No religious test, etc., to be
lecturer, teacher, student, officer or servant of the said College or required.
University, nor shall religious observances, according to the
forms of any particular religious denomination, be imposed on
them or any of them; but the University Council, and the Council
30 of University College, may respectively make such regulations
as they think expedient touching the moral conduct of the students and their attendance on public worship in their respective
churches or other places of religious worship, and respecting
their religious instruction by their respective ministers, accord-
35 ing to their respective forms of religious faith, and every
facility shall be afforded for such purposes : Provided always
that attendance on such form of religious observance be not
compulsory on any student attending the University or University College. R. S. O. 1877, c. 209, s. 18.

40 **82.** Any person, body politic or corporate, may found pro- Professorships may be found-
fessorship, fellowships, lectureships, scholarships, exhibitions, ed by private
prizes and other rewards in the said College or University, by parties, and
providing a sufficient endowment in land or other property, how.
and surrendering or conveying the same to the Crown for the
45 purposes of the said College or University, and thereupon suing
out letters patent from the Crown, instituting, establishing and
endowing the same with the property so provided for that
purpose as aforesaid. R. S. O. 1877, c. 209, s. 14.

83. In such letter patent shall be set forth such rules and Letters patent shall set forth
50 regulations for the appointing to and conferring of such pro- rules, etc.
fessorships, fellowships, lectureships, scholarships, prizes or

other awards as the respective founders thereof, with the approbation of the Crown, think fit to prescribe for that purpose, all which rules and regulations the authorities of the said College or University shall observe and give effect to, as in the said letters patent may be directed. R. S. O. 1877, c. 209, s. 15.   5

Certain professorships prohibited-
84. No professorship or lectureship shall be so founded for the teaching of any subject which under this Act is not to be taught in the said College or University. R. S. O. 1877, c. 209, s. 16.

Endowment to be vested in the Crown.
85. Every endowment of lands or other property of the 10 endowment as aforesaid shall be vested in the Crown for the purposes for which it was given, and also any property, real or personal, given, devised or bequeathed to the said College or University, or for the use thereof. R. S. O. 1877, s. 17.

Application of endowment.
86. The University Endowment and all additions thereto 15 shall be applied to the maintenance of the University, the University Faculty, and University College.

Transfer of subjects assigned to the University and to University College.
☞ **87.** The subjects assigned by sections 5 and 77 of this Act to the teaching faculties of the University and University College respectively, shall not be transferred from either of 20 the said teaching faculties to the other, except upon the unanimous consent of the Senate, expressed at a special meeting called for the consideration of such transfer, of which at least one month's notice shall be given, nor until such consent has been concurred in by the Lieutenant-Governor in Council.☜ 25

Regulations as to superannuation of professors.
88.—(1) The Lieutenant-Governor in Council may make regulations respecting the retirement or superannuation of any professor, lecturer, officer or servant of the said University or University College, now employed or hereafter to be employed, and any gratuity or superannuation allowance shall be a charge 30 on the University endowment, and shall be paid out of the same as the Governor in Council may from time to time direct;

Regulations to be laid before Legislative Assembly.
(2) Every such Regulation shall be laid before the Legislative Assembly forthwith if the Legislature is in session at the date of such Regulation, and if the Legislature is not in session 35 such Regulation shall be laid before the said House within the first seven days of the session next after such Regulation is made.

(3) In case the Legislative Assembly at the said session, or if the session does not continue for three weeks after the said 40 Regulation is laid before the House, then at the ensuing session of the Legislature, disapproves by resolution of such Regulation, either wholly or of any part thereof, the Regulation, so far as disapproved of, shall have no effect from the time of such resolution being passed.   45

Commencement of Act.
☞ **89.** Section 5 and the sub-sections thereof referring to the establishment of a teaching faculty in medicine and law, and sub-sections 3, 4, 5, 6 and 7 of section 53, shall take effect on the passage of this Act, and the remaining portion of ☜ this Act shall take effect by proclamation of the Lieutenant-Governor in 50 Council, and when so proclaimed all other Acts inconsistent herewith shall be repealed.

SCHEDULE.

(Section 16).

FORM OF VOTING PAPER.

University of Toronto.

Election 18 .

I,
resident at   in the County of
do hereby declare

(1) That the signature affixed hereto is my proper handwriting.

(2) That I vote for the following person (*or* persons) as Chancellor *or* as members of the Senate (*as the case may be*) of the University of Toronto, viz.,   of   in the County of etc., etc.

(3) That I have not in this election signed any other voting paper as a graduate in the Faculty of Arts (*or* Medicine *or* Law, *or* as Headmaster *or* Assistant of a High School, *as the case may be*).

(4) That this voting paper was executed on the day of the date hereof.

(5) That I vote in my right as Graduate of   University, *or* Head Master *or* Assistant Master of a High School (*as the case may be*).

Witness my hand this   day of   A.D. 18 .

R. S. O. 1877, c. 210, Sebed.

No. 149.

1st Session, 6th Legislature, 50 Vic, 1887.

BILL.

An Act respecting the Federation of the University of Toronto and University College with other Universities and Colleges.

(Re-printed as amended by Committee of the Whole House.)

First Reading, 5th April, 1887.
Second "   12th "   1887.

Mr. R

No. 150.] BILL. [1887.

An Act to amend the Land Titles Act, 1885, and for other purposes.

HER MAJESTY, by and with the advice and consent of the Legislative Assembly of the Province of Ontario, enacts as follows :—

1. Sub-section 2 of section 105 of *The Land Titles Act 1885*, is hereby repealed and the following substituted therefor :—

48 V. c. 22, s. 105 (2), repealed.

(2) In order to constitute such fund there shall be paid on the first certificate of an absolute or qualified title granted under this Act in respect to any land, in addition to all other fees, a sum equal to one-fifth of one per cent. of the value of such land up to $5,000 and one-tenth of one per cent. on the additional value where such value exceeds $5,000. One half of such per centage shall also be payable on the grant of a first certificate of possessory title, and also upon every registration of title immediately consequent upon the death of a registered owner.

2. From and after the passing of this Act no transfer shall be made by—

1. Any patentee of the Crown;

2. Any executor or administrator of any deceased person dying after the passing of this Act; or,

3. Any purchaser of any land for taxes sold after the passing of this Act;

of the lands comprised in such patent, or devolving upon such executor, or. administrator or purchaser at a sale for taxes until the title of such land shall have been first registered under the provisions of *The Land Titles Act, 1885.*

Lands granted by Crown or devolving on executors or purchased at tax sale not to be transferred until registered under Land Titles Act.

3. For the purpose of registration all grants from the Crown and deeds for taxes of lands required to be registered under the preceding section shall be transmitted by the proper officer to the Master of Titles having jurisdiction wherever such lands are situate, for which service he shall be entitled to a fee of fifty cents, to be paid by the person entitled to such patent or tax deed.

Crown grants and tax deeds to be transmitted to Master.

4. From and after the passing of this Act all probates, wills and letters of administration respecting the estates of persons dying after the passing of this Act shall be filed in the Land Titles Office instead of being registered in any County Registry Office.

Wills and letters of administration to be filed in Land Titles Office.

1st Session, 6th Legislature, 50 Vic., 1887.

BILL.

An Act to amend the Land Titles Act, 1885 and for other purposes.

First Reading, 6th April, 1887.

No. 151.] **BILL.** [1887.

An Act to Amend the Municipal Act.

HER MAJESTY, by and with the advice and consent of the Legislative Assembly of the Province of Ontario, enacts as follows :

1. Section 483 of *The Consolidated Municipal Act, 1883,* is amended by adding after the words "Water Company" therein, the words "or any manufacturing or other company, person or persons" and by substituting the word "twenty" for the figures "10" in the sixth line of the said section, and by adding at the end of the said section the words "and every municipal council may purchase or erect tanks or other appliances for the supply of water and protection against fire within the municipality." 46 V. c. 18, s. 483 amended.

2. The said section 483 is also amended by adding thereto the following sub-section : 46 V. c. 18, s. 483 amended.

(2) The said council shall, on entering into any contract, whether such contract be an original contract or a renewal of a previous contract, for any of the several purposes or objects authorized by this section provide by by-law for assessing and levying a rate on the ratable property in the municipality to raise the moneys required for the fulfilment of such contract, on the part of the municipality in each year in which such moneys shall thereby be made payable, and for the issue of debentures for that purpose under such by-law, if the council shall so determine, but such by-law shall be subject to section 342 of this Act so far as the same is applicable.

3. Subsection 1 of section 346 of the said Act is amended by inserting after the words "Local Assessment" the following words : "or for the issue of debentures for the purpose of raising money to fulfil a contract made by any municipality under the provisions of section 483, and amendments thereto. 46 V. c. 18, s. 346 (1) amended.

No 151.

1st Session, 6th Legislature, 50 Vic., 1887.

BILL.

An Act to amend the Municipal Act.

First Reading, 6th April, 1887.

No. 152.] **BILL.** [1887.

An Act to amend the Assessment Act.

HER MAJESTY, by and with the advice and consent of the Legislative Assembly of the Province of Ontario, enacts as follows :—

5   Section 33 of *The Assessment Act* shall not apply to Government or municipal officers, when the location of the office is fixed by law or regulation of the Government or municipality, but in such cases the salary, gratuity or other compensation, shall be assessed against the incumbent of the office in 10 the municipality wherein he resides.

Place of assessment of salaries of Government and municipal officers.

BILL.

An Act to amend the Assessment Act.

First Reading, 6th April, 1887.

Mr. NAIRN.

TORONTO:

Printed by Warwick & Sons 26 and 28 Front St. W.

No. 153.]　　　　　**BILL.**　　　　　[1887.

An Act to amend the Municipal Law.

HER MAJESTY, by and with the advice and consent of the Legislative Assembly of the Province of Ontario, enacts as follows :—

5 **1.** *The Consolidated Municipal Act, 1883,* is amended by adding the following section thereto :— Appointment of deputy-returning officer in case person first appointed does not act.

99a. In any case where a deputy-returning officer appointed for any city, town, or incorporated village, refuses or neglects to attend at the time and place he is required by the returning officer to receive his voters' lists, and other election papers, 10 the returning officer shall appoint another person to act in his place and stead, and the person so appointed shall have all the powers and authority that he would have had if he had been appointed by by-law.

2. Section 490 of *The Consolidated Municipal Act, 1883,* 15 is amended by adding thereto the following :— 46 V. c. 18, s. 490 amended.

(b) When a polling place has been fixed by by-law for the holding of any election, or the taking of any vote, and it is afterwards found that the building named as such polling place cannot be obtained, or is unsuitable for the purpose, the clerk of 20 the municipality shall have the power to choose in lieu thereof as a polling place the nearest available building suitable for the purpose.

3. Section 522 of *The Consolidated Municipal Act, 1883,* is amended by adding the following sub-section thereto:— 46 V. c. 18, s. 522, amended.

25 (2) When a river or stream which forms a boundary line between two municipalities becomes obstructed with driftwood or fallen timber, any one of the councils of such municipalities may cause the removal of such driftwood or fallen timber, and may pay the costs of such removal out of the general funds of 30 the municipality.

4. Section 33 of *The Municipal Amendment Act, 1885,* is amended by inserting after the word "necessary" in the third line of the said section the words " to construct or repair bridges or culverts on any street, lane or alley, or." 49 v. c. 39, s. 33 amended.

35 **5.** Section 615 of *The Consolidated Municipal Act, 1883,* is hereby repealed. 46 V. c. 18, s. 615 repealed.

6. The Assessment Act is amended by adding the following section thereto :— Copy of assessment roll duly certified to be evidence.

57a. A copy of any assessment roll, or portion of any assessment roll, written or printed, without any erasure or interlineation, and under the seal of the corporation, and certified to be a true copy by the clerk of the municipality, or in his absence by the assistant or acting clerk, shall be deemed 5 authentic, and be received in evidence in any court of justice without proof of the seal or signature, or the production of the original assessment roll, of which such certified copy purports to be a copy, or of part thereof.

No. 153.

1st Session, 6th Legislature, 50 Vic., 1887.

BILL.

An Act to amend the Municipal Law.

First Reading, 5th April, 1887.

Mr. WATERS.

No. 154.]   **BILL.**   [1887.

An Act respecting the publicity of certain matters affecting Traders.

WHEREAS, it is expedient in the public interest that the _{Preamble.} records of writs issued, judgments entered, and chattel mortgages and bills of sale, filed in the offices of the registrars and deputy-registrars of the High Court of Justice, and of the
5 clerks of the County Courts in this Province, should be made reasonably accessible to the public;

Therefore Her Majesty, by and with the advice and consent of the Legislative Assembly of the Province of Ontario, enacts as follows :—

10 **1.** Every person shall hereafter have access to and be entitled _{All books in which writs,} to inspect the several books of the High Court of Justice and _{judgments,} of the County Courts, containing records or entries of the writs _{etc., are} issued, judgments entered, and chattel mortgages and bills of _{entered to be open to} sale filed ; and no person desiring such access or inspection _{inspection.}
15 shall be required, as a condition to his right thereto, to furnish the names of the parties or the style of the causes or matters in respect of which such access or inspection is sought ; and the registrars and deputy-registrars of the High Court of Justice and all clerks of the County Courts of the Province
20 respectively, shall, upon demand or request, produce for inspection any writ of summons or copy thereof, and any judgment roll, or chattel mortgage, or bill of sale so issued, entered or filed in their respective offices, or of which records or entries are, by law, required to be kept in such several books of the
25 High Court of Justice and County Courts respectively.

2. The fees payable in respect of such inspection of books _{Fees.} shall be ten cents for each entry of any writ of summons, judgment roll, chattel mortgage, or bill of sale so inspected, and no additional fee shall be payable for inspection of any
30 writ or copy thereof, or of any judgment roll, chattel mortgage, or bill of sale produced at the time of such inspection at the request of the person making such inspection.

No. 154.

1st Session, 6th Legislature, 50 Vic., 1887.

BILL.

An Act respecting the publicity of certain matters affecting Traders.

First Reading, 6th April, 1887.

BILL.

An Act respecting Separate School Debentures.

HER MAJESTY, by and with the advice and consent of the Legislative Assembly of the Province of Ontario, enacts as follows :—

The following provisions are hereby added to section 59 of 49 V. c. 46, s. 5 *The Separate Schools Act, 1886 :*— 59 amended.

(3) The mortgages and other instruments which the trustees have power to make, as aforesaid, for the security and payment of money borrowed or payable for school purposes may, in the discretion of the trustees, be made in the form of debentures ; 10 and debentures shall be a charge on the same property and rates aforesaid, as in the case of mortgages thereof made by the trustees, as in the first sub-section mentioned.

(4) Every by-law of the trustees for the issue of such debentures shall be sealed with the corporate seal of the board 15 of trustees, and shall be signed by the chairman and secretary of the board, and the by-law may be quashed by application to the High Court of Justice at Toronto, in the same way as municipal by-laws may be quashed.

(4) The by-law shall name a day in the financial year 20 in which the same is passed when the by-law is to take effect, and shall state the whole of the debt and the obligations to be issued thereunder, and shall make the same payable in twenty years at furthest from the day on which the by-law takes effect, and shall provide for including thereafter in the yearly sepa-25 rate school rate a sufficient sum for the payment of an amount sufficient to pay the yearly interest during the currency of the debentures, and also a certain specific sum to be realized annually for the payment of the principal, which specific sum shall be sufficient with the estimated interest on the invest-30 ments thereof to discharge the debt when payable.

(5) Every such by-law, before being acted upon, shall be published for at least three succesive weeks in some public newspaper published weekly, or oftener, in the city, town or county in which the separate school is situate, and if no appli-35 cation to quash the by-law shall be made for three months after the publication thereof as aforesaid, the by-law shall, as in the case of a municipal by-law, be valid, notwithstanding any want of substance or form in the by-law or in the time or manner of passing the same. R. S. O c. 6, s. 333.

40 (6) No debenture issued under the by-law shall be for less than $100. The debentures may be in the form following :—

PROVINCE OF ONTARIO.

$....   No....

Debenture of the Board of Trustees of the Roman Catholic Separate Schools for (*or other corporate name of the Board, as the case may be*),

The Board of Trustees of the Roman Catholic Separate Schools for (*or other corporate name of the Board, as the case may be*), hereby promise to pay to bearer at the Bank of , at , the sum of dollars of lawful money of Canada, in years from the date hereof, and to pay interest at the rate of per cent. per annum half-yearly to the bearer of the annexed coupons respectively upon the presentation thereof at the said Bank.

Issued this day of , by virtue and under authority of the Separate Schools Act, 1886, and amendments thereto, and pursuant to by-law number of said Board of Separate School Trustees, passed on the day of , 1887, entitled a by-law to raise by way of loan the sum of dollars for the purposes therein mentioned, bearing date the day of , 18 .

C. D.,
Secretary-Treasurer of said Board.

A. B.,
Chairman of said Board.

Coupon No....

The Board of Trustees of the Roman Catholic Separate School for (*or other corporate name*) will pay bearer at the Bank of , at , on the day of , 18 , the sum of dollars, interest due on that day on Debenture No. .

No. 155.

1st Session, 6th Legislature, 50 Vic., 1887.

BILL.

An Act respecting Separate School Debentures.

First Reading, 7th April, 1887.

Mr. Ross,
(*Middlesex*).

TORONTO.
PRINTED BY WARWICK & SONS, 26 AND 28 FRONT ST. W.

No. 156.]   **BILL.**   [1887.

An Act to amend the Division Courts Act.

HER MAJESTY, by and with the advice and consent of the Legislative Assembly of the Province of Ontario, enacts as follows:—

1. Section 7 of *The Division Courts Act* is hereby amended R. S. O. c. 47, 5 by striking out the word "not," in the first line thereof, and s. 7, amended. by striking out the word "but," in the second line thereof, and inserting the word "and" instead thereof.

2. The County Council shall furnish all books, blanks forms County and stationery for the clerks of the several Division Courts in councils to furnish 10 their respective counties. books, etc., for Division Court clerks.

3. Sub-section 1 of section 54 as amended by section 3 of the Act passed in the forty-third year of the reign of Her Majesty *Ib.* s. 54, and chaptered 8, is amended by striking out the word "sixty" amended. and substituting the words "one hundred" therefor.

15 **4.** Section 56 as amended by section 3 of the Act passed in *Ib.* s. 56, the forty-third year of the reign of Her Majesty and chaptered amended. 8, is hereby amended by striking out the word "sixty" and substituting the words "one hundred" therefor in the last line thereof.

20 **5.** Section 59 is hereby amended by striking out all the *Ib.* s. 59, words after the word "account," in the fifth line thereof. • amended.

6. Sub-section 2 of section 63 is amended by striking out the *Ib.* s. 63 (2), words between the words "served" and "in," in the second line, amended. and by adding to said sub-section "and every such summons or 25 execution may be served or enforced by the bailiff of the division in which defendant lives."

7. Section 99 is hereby amended by striking out the word *Ib.* s. 99, "County," in the eighth line, and substituting the word amended. "Division" therefor.

30 **8.** Section 102 is hereby repealed and the following is sub- *Ib.* s. 102, stituted therefor:— repealed.

"The commission with the evidence taken thereunder, and the Return of papers therewith, shall forthwith be returned to the clerk of commission to take the Division Court in which the suit to which the same relates evidence. 35 is pending."

Ib. s. 103, amended.

9. Section 103 is hereby amended by striking out all the words up to the word "and," in the ninth line thereof, and substituting therefor the following:—"The costs of the issue, transmission, execution and return of any such commission shall be in the discretion of the Court in which the suit is pending, 5 and shall be taxed on the Division Court scale by the clerk of the Court out of which the same was issued."

Ib. s. 107, amended.

10. Section 107 is hereby amended by inserting after the word "served," in the fourth line thereof the following:—"But unless otherwise ordered no execution shall issue on any such 10 judgment within fourteen days after the entering of such judgment."

Ib. s. 111, repealed.

11. Section 111 is hereby repealed, and the following substituted therefor:—

Who may be jurors.

Unless exempted by *The Consolidated Jurors Act 1883,* 15 or any amendments thereto, every person whose name appears on the last published Voters' List of any municipality, partly or wholly situate within the limits of any Division Court, and who resides within the said division, and whose name is marked "J," as provided in section 23 of *The Consolidated* 20 *Jurors Act, 1883,* shall be liable to serve as a Juror for the Division Courts in such division.

Ib. s. 112, repealed.

12. Section 112 is hereby repealed, and the following substituted therefor:—

Jurors, how elected and summoned.

"The Jurors to be summoned to serve at any Division Court 25 shall be residents of the said division and shall be taken from the last published Voters' List for the municipalities partly or wholly within the division, and shall be summoned in rotation, beginning with the first of such persons on such Voters' List whose name is marked "J," as provided in the preceding section; 30 and if there be more than one municipality partly or wholly within the division, beginning with the Voters' List for the municipality within which the Court is held, and then proceeding to that one of the other Voters' Lists which contains the greatest number of such persons names, and so on until all the 35 lists have been gone through; after which they may be gone through again in the same order."

Ib. s. 113, repealed.

13. Section 113 is hereby repealed and the following substituted therefor:—

Municipal clerks to furnish copies of voters' lists.

"The clerk of every municipality shall furnish each Division 40 Court clerk within whose division the said municipality is partly or wholly situate, with a correct copy of the Voters' List of the said municipality immediately after the publication of the same in each year; and when a new Voters' List is furnished the Division Court clerk shall take the names of 45 jurors therefrom, beginning as nearly as may be at the part of the list corresponding to the place where he left off in the previous list."

Ib. s. 118, repealed.

14. Section 118 is hereby repealed, and the following substituted therefor:— 50

Neglect of municipal clerks to

"If any clerk of a municipality, for six days after demand made in writing, neglects or refuses to furnish the clerk of a

Division Court within the limits of which the municipality ior furnish voters which he is clerk is partly or wholly situate, with a correct lists. copy of the Voters' List, the clerk of the Division Court may issue a summons to be personally served on the said clerk of 5 the municipality, three days at least before the sitting of the Court, requiring him to appear at the then next sitting of the Court, to shew cause why he refused or neglected to comply with the provisions of the said section."

15. Section 119 is hereby amended by striking out the word *Ib. s.* 119, 10 "collector" wherever it occurs, and substituting therefor the amended. words "clerk of the municipality."

16. Section 161 is hereby amended by adding thereto the *Ib. s.* 161, following words:—" After a transcript has been issued under amended. this section, no further proceedings shall be had in the Court Proceedings 15 from which the transcript issued without either an order from after issue of the judge, or unless the creditor, his attorney or agent shall transcript of make and file with the clerk of the said Court an affidavit judgment. stating: (1) That the judgment remains unsatisfied in whole or in part. (2) That the execution issued in the Division to 20 which the transcript was issued has been returned *nulla bona*, (or that he believes the defendant has not sufficient goods in that division to satisfy the said judgment), and the clerk may, at the request of the creditor, his attorney or agent, draw the said affidavit."

25 **17.** Sections 165, 166, 167 and 168 are hereby repealed and *Ib. s.* 165-168, the following is substituted therefor:— repealed.

" In case an execution against goods is returned *nulla bona*, Execution and the sum remaining unsatisfied on the judgment under against lands. which the execution issued amounts to the sum of forty dollars, 30 the party in whose favour the judgment was entered, may sue out execution against the lands of the party in default, and the clerk of the Court in which such judgment was obtained, at the request of the party prosecuting the judgment, shall issue under the seal of the Court a writ or writs of execution against 35 the lands of the party in default, to the sheriff of any one or more county or counties, the party prosecuting such judgment may direct, and the said sheriff on receipt of such execution shall act upon the same, and it shall have the same force and effect against the lands of the party in default as if the said 40 writ of execution had been issued from the County Court; and until the judgment is fully paid and satisfied, the party entitled to the same may pursue the same remedy for the recovery thereof, or of any balance due thereon, as if the judgment had been originally obtained in the County Court; 45 and the sheriff receiving such execution shall make return thereof, and pay any money made thereon to the clerk of the Court issuing such writ of execution."

18. Section 202 is hereby amended by striking out the *Ib. s.* 202, words "before seizure," in the third line thereof, and substituting amended. 50 therefor " as provided by section 70 of this Act."

19. Section 5 of *The Division Courts Act, 1880*, is hereby 43 V. c. 8, s. 5, amended by adding after the word "list," in the third line amended.

thereof, the words "except such actions as are to be tried by a jury, which said actions shall be placed in the jury list according to priority of number."

Ib. s. 8, amended.

20. Section 8 of *The Division Courts Act, 1880,* is hereby amended by striking out the words "exceeds one hundred 5 dollars, and" in the first and second lines thereof.

Ib. s. 9, amended.

21. Section 9 of *The Division Courts Act, 1880,* is hereby amended by striking out the words "exceeds one hundred dollars, and" in the first and second lines thereof.

Ib. s. 11, amended.

22. Section 11 of *The Division Courts Act, 1880,* is hereby 10 amended by adding thereto "but the defendant shall satisfy the judge by affidavit of the alleged want of jurisdiction of said Court."

Ib. s. 62 amended.

23. Section 62 of *The. Division Courts Act, 1880,* is hereby amended by inserting after the word "absconded" in the sixth 15 line thereof the following words :—"Or is out of the Province of Ontario, but having in Ontario an office or agent to do business or to collect or receive money."

47 V. c. 9, s. 1, amended.

24. Section 1 of *The Act to amend the Division Courts Act,* passed in the 47th year of Her Majesty's reign, is hereby 20 amended by striking out the word "and" in the second line thereof, and inserting the word "or" therefor.

48 V. c. 14, s. 4 (1), amended.

25. Sub-section 1 of section 4 of *The Division Courts amendment Act, 1885,* is hereby amended by striking out the words "notice of motion" in the eighth line thereof and 25 substituting the words "summons to be issued by the clerk," and by striking out the words "notice of motion" and substituting the word "summons" therefor, where the said words occur in said sub-section.

Ib. s. 4 (2), amended.

26. Sub-section 2 of section 4 of *The Division Courts* 30 *amendment Act, 1885,* is hereby amended by striking out the word "notice" and by substituting the word "summons" therefor.

R.S.O. c. 47 s. 114, amended.
Summons to jurors.

27. Section 114 of *The Division Courts Act,* as amended by section 5 of *The Division Courts Amendment Act, 1885,* 35 is hereby amended by adding thereto the following :—" And the clerk shall issue a summons and also twelve copies thereof, for service on said jurors—which summons shall be returned to the clerk with the service thereof duly verified by the oath of the bailiff serving the same." 40

48 V. c. 14, s. 11, amended.

28. Section 11 of *The Division Courts amendment Act, 1885,* is hereby amended by adding after the word "corporation" in the second and sixth lines thereof the words "firm or individual."

49 V. c. 15, s. 6 (4), amended.

29. Section 6 of *The Division Courts amendment Act,* 45 *1886,* is amended by adding to sub-section 4 the following :—
"(c) A cause or causes of action in respect of which the jurisdiction of the Division Courts is limited to two hundred dollars, (d) and a cause or causes of action, in respect of which the

jurisdiction of the said Courts is limited to one hundred dollars, which causes of action are hereinafter designated as class C, and the whole amount claimed in any such action in class C shall not exceed in the aggregate two hundred dollars."

5 **30**. Sub-section 2 of section 21 of said last-mentioned Act *Ib.* s. 21 (2), is hereby amended by adding after the word "defendant" in amended. the third line thereof, the words "primary debtor or garnishee."

31. Sub-section 3 of the said section 21 of the said last-*Ib.* s. 21 (3), mentioned Act is also amended, by adding after the word 10 "defendant" where it occurs in said sub-section, the words "primary debtor or garnishee."

32. In case of the absence of the bailiff, by reason of sudden Service of illness or from any other cause, the clerk may employ a suit- summons in able person to serve any summons where the plaintiff files an of bailiff. 15 affidavit, stating that he is in danger of losing his debt unless immediate service of the summons be made.

33. All sections and parts of sections of the Division Courts Repeal. Acts, inconsistent with the provisions of this Act, are hereby repealed.

No. 156.

1st Session, 6th Legislature, 50 Vic., 1887.

BILL.

An Act to amend the Division Courts Act.

First Reading, 7th April, 1887.

BILL.

An Act to amend the Registry Act.

HER MAJESTY, by and with the advice and consent of the Legislative Assembly of the Province of Ontario, enacts as follows :—

1.—(1) The Registrar shall before receiving a discharge of
5 any mortgage carefully examine and compare it with the
original mortgage and shall not register same unless it is a
correct discharge of such mortgage. And it shall not be
necessary for any mortgagor or vendor to produce any mort-
gage or discharge given, after the passing of this Act. Discharges of mortgages.

10 (2) Where such mortgage is discharged by an executor or
administrator a copy of the probate of such will, and a copy
of the letters of administration, with an affidavit that it is a
true copy of the original, shall also be registered with such
discharge, and the Registrar shall see that such mortgage is
15 also properly discharged by the executor or executors, administrator or administrators, as the case may be, and it shall not
be necessary after the passing of this Act for any mortgagor or
vendor to produce a copy of the will or letters of administration
to any purchaser or mortgagee by which such mortgage is
20 discharged.

3. It shall not be necessary for any grantor or mortgagor
to produce any evidence of the exercising the power of sale
contained in any mortgage by which any lands have at any
time been sold and conveyed by virtue of such power of sale
25 contained in any mortgage after the expiration of five years
from the date of the conveyance made by virtue of such power
of sale, and such deed after the expiration of five years shall
not be set aside on the ground of any irregularity and no
purchaser or mortgagee shall be entitled to have any notices,
30 advertisements or any evidence or notices of proceedings connected with the sale of any land under the power of sale in
any mortgage produced when such conveyance under such
power of sale in any mortgage is over five years old. Evidence as to exercise of power of sale under mort- gage.

4. In case of any undischarged mortgage, it shall be the
35 duty of the Registrar to give a short entry or extract on the
abstract, showing the rate of interest, time of payment of the
principal and whether any privilege of paying off such mortgage is given in said mortgage. Entry of mort- gages on register.

5. The Registrar shall give a diagram on the back of each
40 abstract showing the exact position of the property abstracted
according to the description contained in the registered instru-
ments affecting the land abstracted. Registrar to make diagram of property on abstract.

Entries to be made on abstract.

6. It shall be the duty of the Registrar to show on any abstract the mortgage discharged by any discharge. It shall also be the duty of the Registrar to give a short entry or extract showing the nature of any registered instrument, (as in cases of agreements, liens, etc.) 5

Form of abstract.

7. Every abstract of title to any lands in Ontario shall be in plain print or writing, on which the heading of same shall give the property abstracted and in the following order:—Instrument, number, date, date of registry, grantor, grantee, consideration, instrument properly signed and sealed, any 10 covenants other than usual statutory covenants, dower been properly barred, description of land and remarks.

Names of parties to be entered on abstract.
Evidence where grantor described as unmarried.

8. It shall be the duty of the Registrar to enter on every abstract the names in full of the parties to any instrument or conveyance. The Registrar shall not register any conveyances 15 of land in which the grantor is therein described as an unmarried man without an affidavit on such conveyance made by the grantor that he is at time of executing such conveyance an unmarried man, and such evidence shall in all cases be sufficient proof that the grantor is unmarried. 20

Right to have discharge of mortgage registered.

9. The owner of any real estate shall be entitled to have any outstanding discharges of mortgages registered.

No 168.

1st Session, 6th Legislature, 50 Vic., 1887.

BILL.

An Act to amend the Registry Act.

First Reading, 7th April, 1887.

Mr. Leys.

TORONTO.
PRINTED BY WARWICK & SONS, 26 AND 28 FRONT ST. W.

BILL.

An Act to amend the law as to drainage.

HER MAJESTY, by and with the advice and consent of the Legislative Assembly of the Province of Ontario, enacts as follows:—

1. Where the obstruction referred to in section 570 of *The* Removal of
5 *Consolidated Municipal Act, 1883*, and in section 22 of *The* in rivers. *Municipal Amendment Act, 1886*, is occasioned by, or is a dam or other artificial structure, and is situate wholly within the municipality, the council shall be deemed to have full power to acquire, with the consent of the owner thereof, and upon
10 payment of such purchase money as may be mutually agreed upon, the right to remove the same, wholly or in part; and any amount so paid or payable as purchase money, shall be deemed part of the cost of the works under this section in connection with the removal of such obstruction, and shall be
15 dealt with and provided for accordingly, and where the lands benefited are situated, partly in the said municipality and partly in the next adjoining municipality, the special rate sufficient for the payment of the principal and interest of the debentures and the assessment and levying of the same shall
20 be made, levied, and paid over by the said municipality, and the said next adjoining municipality, in such proportions as the said engineer or surveyor may determine and charge upon the lands aforesaid, and in like manner and to the same extent, as nearly as may be, as is provided for by said Act where the
25 lands benefited are situate wholly within the municipality.

No. 159.

1st Session, 6th Legislature, 50 Vic., 1887.

BILL.

An Act to amend the law as to Drainage.

First Reading, 7th April, 1887.

BILL.

An Act respecting the Formation of New Counties.

HER MAJESTY, by and with the advice and consent of the Legislative Assembly of the Province of Ontario, enacts as follows:—

1. Where it is desired to form a new county out of one or 5 more counties, a new county, containing a population of not less than 30,000 inhabitants, if the council of each of the municipalities which have not less than 200 municipal electors, are to form the new county pass, within the space of one year, a resolution; *Municipalities may resolve to form new County.*

10 (1) Affirming the expediency of forthwith establishing a new county consisting of the municipalities proposed to be taken for the new county and specified in the resolution;

(2) Setting forth the proposed name of the new county;

(3) And proposing some place within the same to be the 15 county town.

And if the Lieutenant-Governor deems the circumstances of the municipalities affected to call for a separate establishment of courts and other county institutions, he may issue his proclamation to ascertain the assent of the electors of the 20 several municipalities to the establishing of the new county; and their selection of a place for the county town if the resolutions do not agree in naming a county town. *Municipal Act, 1883, s. 38.* *Proclamation requiring assent of electors.*

2. The numbers of the population of the municipalities 25 which are to form the new county shall be ascertained in the case of each municipality by the census returns, whether last taken under a statute of the Parliament of Canada or under the authority of a by-law of the council of the county of which the municipality forms part. *Municipal Act, 1883, s. 38.* *Population ascertained.*

30 3. The assent shall be ascertained in the manner provided for in sections 295 to 328 of *The Municipal Act of 1883*, on a by-law requiring the assent of the electors, and the vote shall be taken at and in connection with the next annual election of members of the council of each municipality which 35 shall take place at least two months from the date of the proclamation; and the proclamation shall fix a time when and a place where the clerk of each council shall finally sum up the number of votes given for and against the question or questions to be voted on, and for the attendance of persons 40 interested in, and promoting or opposing the establishment of the new county or the selection of a place for the county town. The Lieutenant-Governor may by the same proclamation direct other duties to be discharged or things to be done which *How assent ascertained.*

may be expedient to order in relation to taking such vote. *Municipal Act,* 1883, s. 297.

4. Forthwith after the proclamation, the clerk of the council of each municipality, shall, at the cost of the municipality of which he is clerk, publish a copy of the proclamation in 5 some public newspaper published either within the municipality or in an adjoining local municipa'ity, and the publication shall shew thereon, the clerk and municipality by which it is published, and shall be continued in at least one number of such paper each week for three successive weeks, and such 10 clerk shall put up a copy of the proclamation at four or more of the most public places in the municipality. If the council, by resolution, designates the newspaper, the publication shall be in the newspaper so designated. *Municipal Act,* 1883, s. 294. 15

5. For the purpose of taking the vote, and for the selection of a county town, if the same has not been agreed upon by the resolutions of the municipalities, the sections numbered from 295 to 328 inclusive of *The Municipal Act of* 1883, in so far as the same are applicable and not varied by this Act, are 20 hereby incorporated with this Act as if the same were repeated herein, with the substitution of " resolution " for " by-law " wherever " by-law " occurs in the said sections.

6. The ballot papers, in case the proclamation shall require a vote to be taken upon the place for the county town, shall 25 in lieu of the form prescribed by section 308 of *The Municipal Act, 1883,* be in the form following :—

FORM OF BALLOT PAPER.

The proposed new County is to comprise the following Municipalities (naming them). 30

7. The clerks of each municipality after having summed up the votes according to the provisions of sections 320 and 322 (2) of *The Municipal Act,* 1883, shall send a copy of the certificate thereby required to the Provincial Secretary. *Result of vote to Provincial Secretary.*

5 **8.** If it appears that by the votes cast in accordance with the foregoing provisions a majority has been cast of all the electors of the municipality which are included in the proposed new county and majorities in every municipality within the proposed new county which shall have more than 10 200 electors in favour of the establishment of the new county, the Lieutenant-Governor may by proclamation name and erect the territory into a provisional county. The reeves and deputies of the municipalities of the new county shall be the provisional council. The proclamation shall appoint a time and 15 place for the first meeting of the council. *On favourable vote Lieutenant-Governor to proclaim new provisional county.*

9. The proclamation shall name the county town. If a majority of the aggregate votes were cast for one place, that place shall be the county town named. Otherwise the place shall be as may be selected by the Lieutenant-Governor in 20 Council. *County town.*

10. The fact of the conditions precedent to the issuing of a proclamation under this Act, having been performed, shall be conclusively established by the issue of the proclamation.

11. Sections 39 to 52 inclusive of *The Municipal Act, 1883,* 25 shall be read as forming part of this Act, except that the said sections shall, for the purposes of this Act, be read, substituting the word "new" for the word "junior" wherever the said word occurs in the said sections; and the words "councils of the several counties of which the said several municipalities form a part," 30 (or collectively as the sense may require) shall be substituted for the words "council of the union," and "council of the senior or remaining county or counties" (as the case may be) wherever the said words occur in the said sections; but so that no one of the counties of which the said several munici- 35 palities form a part shall assume or be required to assume any part of the debt of a municipality which did not form part of the county before the formation of the new county. *Sections of Municipal Act relating to formation of counties in- corporated.*

12. Sections 53 to 63 inclusive of *The Municipal Act, 1883,* shall be read as forming part of this Act, so that the provisions 40 therein relating to the new corporation shall be applicable to the new county formed under this Act, and that the provisions therein relating to "union of counties," or "the senior or remaining county" shall be applicable to any council of the several counties of which the several municipalities forming 45 the new county formed part before the formation of the new county. *Sections of Municipal Act relating to new corpor- ations incor- porated.*

13. The first election of members of the councils of the respective municipalities forming the new county, shall take place on the first Monday in January after the date of the 50 proclamation declaring the establishment of the new county. *First election new county.*

14. The Lieutenant-Governor in Council may, by an Order in Council, cause to be issued a proclamation, and thereby set *Registry office.*

apart and establish a registry office for the said county so to be erected as aforesaid. 38 Vic., c. 31, s. 11, Dufferin. R. S. O c. 111, s. 3.

Suits pending. **15.** All actions and proceedings in any court of law which 5 may be pending at the date of the proclamation declaring the establishment of the new county, may be prosecuted, continued and completed, and all writs of execution and other processes, and all acts and proceedings subsequent thereto, shall be taken, issued, and had in the county in which such 10 actions and proceedings were originally commenced, as fully and effectually as if the municipalities constituting the new county had not been separated from the respective counties of which they had theretofore respectively formed part; and no writ or other process or proceeding shall lose its priority by reason of no entry thereof appearing or being in 15 the proper office in that behalf in the new county; and all officers who would have had power or authority to execute such writ, process or proceedings, if the new county had not been formed, shall, for the purposes of all pending suits, actions and proceedings, have the same power and authority 20 in respect of same as if the new county had not been formed. New. (Dufferin, 1880 and 1881.)

Division Courts. **16.** The justices of the peace for the new county in general sessions first assembled after the date of proclamation establishing the same, shall subject to the approval of the Lieutenant- 25 Governor in Council, and subject to the provisions of *The Division Courts Act*, fix and determine the number, limits and extent of the Division Courts in and for said new county, and after the same have been approved of by the Lieutenant-Governor in Council, they shall continue to be the Division Courts for the county, until altered under the provisions of 30 the said *Division Courts Act*.

17. All laws of whatsoever nature, which at the date of the proclamation establishing the new county, are in force in and applicable to other county organizations, shall, from and after 35 the date of the proclamation, be in force in and applicable to the new county.

Chattel Mortgages. **18.** All chattel mortgages relating to property within any of the townships, towns or incorporated villages forming the new county, shall, at the date of said proclamation, and until 40 their expiration, continue to be as valid and effectual in all respects as they might or would have been if the new county had not been formed, but in the event of a renewal of any such chattel mortgage after the date of the proclamation, the renewal shall be filed in the proper office in that behalf in the 45 new county as if the mortgage had originally been filed therein, and no chattel mortgage in force at the date of the proclamation shall lose its priority by reason of its not being filed in the new county prior to its renewal. Sec. 13 and 14 of 44 Vic. 9. (Dufferin, 1881.) 50

Jurors. **19.** The clerk of the peace for the new county upon receiving from the clerks of the peace of the counties of which the said several municipalities form a part, the jurors books, jurors rolls, and jurors lists, as provided by section 64 of *The Jurors Act*, 1883, shall consolidate the same respectively, and form therewith, one jurors book, jurors roll, and jurors list respectively, and the same when so consolidated shall form the 5 jurors book, jurors roll, and jurors list respectively, for the said new county, for the year in which the proclamation mentioned in section 47 of *The Municipal Act*, 1883, shall have been made subject to the increase of the same in the manner provided by section 63 of the said *Jurors Act*, 1883. 44 Vic. 10 9, s. 8. (Dufferin 1881).

20. This Act shall be deemed to be incorporated with and shall be construed as part of *The Municipal Acts*, now and from time to time in force.

1st Session, 6th Legislature, 50 Vic., 1887.

BILL.

An Act respecting the Formation of New Counties.

First Reading, 1887.

BILL.

An Act to extend the Land Titles Act to the outlying Districts of the Province.

HER MAJESTY, by and with the advice and consent of the Legislative Assembly of the Province of Ontario, enacts as follows :—

1. From and after the day when the new Revision of the 5 Statutes of Ontario comes into effect *The Land Titles Act*, 1885, as amended by subsequent Acts, shall be in force in the Districts of Algoma, Thunder Bay (including Rainy River), Muskoka, Parry Sound and Nipissing. *Land Titles Act to be in force in outlying districts.*

2. When Letters Patent for any land situated in any 10 of the said districts are issued after the said date, the same shall be forwarded to the Local Master of Titles of the district, for the purpose of the patentee being entered as the first Registered Owner of the land, with any necessary qualification. 49 V. c. 26, s. 44 D. *Letters Patent hereafter issued to be sent to Local Master.*

15 (2) Before making such entry the Local Master shall obtain from the Registrar of the registry division a certificate stating what instruments, if any, have been registered affecting the land ; and in case he finds that any such instrument has been registered, he shall give notice to the patentee and to all 20 other persons interested, before registering the patentee as owner. *See* R. S. O. c. 25, s. 26. *His action thereon.*

(3) In case there is no contest as to the rights of the parties the Local Master may make the requisite entry and issue his Certificate ; but in case of a contest, he shall transmit the 25 papers to the Inspector of Titles before registering the patentee as owner, and shall otherwise proceed as provided in section 7 of the *Act to extend The Land Titles Act to the several Counties, and to otherwise amend the said Act.*

3. (1)—Before a Certificate of Ownership is issued, the 30 patentee shall pay into the Assurance Fund, established under *The Land Titles Act*, one quarter of one per cent. on the value of the land patented, unless he elects to have the amount made a charge on the land ; and his failure to pay the amount prior to the issue of the Certificate shall be deemed an election. *Assurance Fund.*

35 (2) In that case a note shall be made on the Register and on the Certificate that the land is liable to pay the Assurance fee ; and no subsequent transfer or charge of the land, or any transmission thereof, shall be registered until the same, namely, one quarter of one per cent. on the value of the land at the

time of the entry of the transfer, charge or transmission has been paid into the Assurance Fund.

Notice of Master to Sheriff and Treasurer.

4. (1) – Upon an entry of ownership being made as aforesaid the Local Master of Titles shall notify (Form A) the Sheriff in whose bailiwick the lands lie, of the entry of the 5 patentee as owner, and shall notify (Form B) the treasurer of the municipality, if the land is situated in a municipality, of the fact that the land has become subject to the said Act.

(2) The notices shall be sent by registered letter-post, and no entry of any dealing with the land shall be made in the 10 register until fourteen days after the mailing of the notice, unless proof is previously made that the land is not liable to any execution or arrear of taxes.

(3) If within the 14 days no copy of a writ of execution against the lands of the patentee is received from the Sheriff, 15 or no claim for arrear of taxes is received from the Treasurer, the Local Master may assume that the land is not subject to any executions or taxes (other than taxes for the current year), and may enter subsequent dealings with the land accordingly; and as against such entry no claim shall afterwards be sus- 20 tained in respect of an execution against the patentee, or in respect of any taxes against the land except for the current year or for a subsequent year.

(4) In case the Local Master receives from the Treasurer a claim for taxes on the land, he shall enter the claim 25 against the land, and all dealings with the land shall be subject to such claim. In case of executions affecting the lands, an entry thereof shall be made in like manner, and all dealings with the land shall be subject to such executions.

(5) Where notices are not required to be given on account 30 of instruments having been registered against the land, or otherwise, the Local Master shall be entitled to charge the patentee a fee of $, and the Master's actual disbursements.

(6) Where notices or other proceedings are necessary on account of instruments being registered, or on account of a 35 caution having been lodged, or otherwise, the Local Master shall be entitled to charge in addition to the said sum of $4, the like fees as are payable to the Master of Titles in respect of similar proceedings.

List of patented lands sent to Registrar.

5. In case a list of patented lands, furnished to the Regis- 40 trar of a registration division by the Provincial Secretary under section 37 of *The Public Lands Act*, contains any land coming within this Act, it shall be stated in the list that such land is subject to *The Land Titles Act*, and the Registrar shall, in the abstract index, enter the fact 45 that the land is subject to the said Act, and shall not receive for registration any instrument affecting the land.

6. This Act shall be read as part of *The Land Titles Act, 1885,* and of the *Act to extend the Land Titles Act to the several counties of the Province.* 50

FORM A.

NOTICE TO THE TREASURER OF A MUNICIPALITY.

To the Treasurer of the Township of

Take notice that a Patent from the Crown for lot   in the
Concession of   , in the district of   , has
been forwarded to me by the Crown Lands Department in order that
A. B., the patentee therein named, should be entered under *The Land
Titles Act* as owner thereof, and that such entry having been made, the
said A. B. will, at any time after fourteen days from this date, be at liberty
to transfer, or charge, the said lands free from all taxes, except those for the
current year, unless before that time I receive from you a statement claiming that taxes for a previous year or years are owing upon the said land
with full particulars of such claim.

Dated the   day of   , 1887.

C. D.,
Local Master of Titles,
at

(Name place).

FORM B.

NOTICE TO SHERIFF THAT NEWLY PATENTED LANDS HAVE BECOME SUBJECT TO THE LAND TITLES ACT.

To the Sheriff of

Take notice that a Patent from the Crown of certain lands has been
forwarded to me by the Crown Lands Department, in order that *A B.*, of
etc., the patentee therein named, should be entered, under *The Land Titles
Act*, as owner thereof, and that such entry having been made in pursuance
of the said Act, the said *A. B.*, will, at any time after fourteen days from
this date, be at liberty to transfer, or charge, the said land free from all
executions in your hands affecting his lands, unless before the expiry of
the said time I receive from you copies certified under your hand of
any writs in your hands, affecting the lands of the said A. B., in accordance with section 51 of *The Land Titles Act, 1885.*

Dated the   day of   , 1887.

C. D.,
Local Master of Titles,
at

(Name place).

FORM C.

REQUISITION TO ACCOUNTANT TO RECEIVE MONEY TO CREDIT OF ASSUR-ANCE FUND.

Land Titles Act.

The Accountant of the Supreme Court will please place to the credit of
the Assurance Fund, under the above Act, the enclosed sum of $
paid in respect of the registration under the above Act of lot 4 in the 1st
Concession of the Township of (*or as the case may be*), with reference
to which an application is now pending before the Local Master of
Titles, at *Port Arthur.*

Dated   ·   188 .

A. B.,
Applicant,
(*or* Solicitor for Applicant).

1st Session, 6th Legislature, 50 Vic., 1887

BILL.

An Act to extend the Land Titles Act to the outlying Districts of the Province.

First Reading, 7th April, 1887.

No. 162.]   **BILL.**   [1887.

An Act to amend " The Ontario Factories' Act, 1884."

HER MAJESTY, by and with the advice and consent of
the Legislative Assembly of the Province of Ontario
enacts as follows :—

1. Sub-section 2 of section 2 of *The Ontario Factories'*
5 *Act, 1884*, is hereby repealed and the following sub-section
substituted in lieu thereof :

(2) The word "Inspector" shall mean the Inspector appointed by order of the Lieutenant-Governor in Council under the
authority of and for enforcing the provisions of this Act in
10 and for the locality in reference to which such expression
applies, and which locality shall be that designated in the
order.

2. Section 24 of the said Act is amended by adding thereto
the following as sub-section 3 thereof :

15   (3) Designate and assign in the order appointing an Inspector, the locality in and for which he is to be the Inspector
under this Act.

3. Section 6 of the said Act is amended by adding thereto
the following as sub-section 6 thereof :

20   (6) Notwithstanding anything in this Act contained, boys
under twelve years of age, and girls under fourteen years of
age may be employed during the months of July, August and
September in any year in such gathering in and other preparation of fruits or vegetables for canning purposes as may be
25 required to be done prior to the operation of cooking or other
process of that nature requisite in connection with the canning
of fruits or vegetables. The place, room or apartment in
which such boys or girls may be so employed, shall be separate
from any other wherein the cooking or other process aforesaid,
or the canning of said fruits or vegetables is carried on.

No. 162.

1st Session, 6th Legislature, 50 Vic., 1887.

BILL.

An Act to amend The Ontario Factories'
Act, 1884.

First Reading, 7th April 1887.

BILL.

An Act to amend the Municipal Act.

HER MAJESTY, by and with the advice and consent of the
Legislative Assembly of the Province of Ontario, enacts
as follows :—

    1. Sub-section 2 of section 496, of *The Consolidated Muni-* 46 V. c. 18, s.
5 *cipal Act ,1883*, is amended by adding the following words at 496 (2) amend-
the end thereof :—"The powers conferred by this sub-section ed.
may be exercised by any municipality which, prior to the passing of the said Act, had obtained a special Act, and notwithstanding that such municipality may have proceeded there-
10 under."

BILL.

An Act to amend the Municipal Act.

First Reading, 7th April, 1887.

Mr. Leys.

TORONTO:
PRINTED BY WARWICK & SONS 26 AND 28 FRONT ST. W.

No. 164.] **BILL.** [1887.

An Act to amend the Assessment Act.

HER MAJESTY, by and with the advise and consent of the Legislative Assembly of the Province of Ontario, enacts as follows :—

Sub-section 17 of section 6 of *The Assessment Act* is repealed, and the following substituted therefor:— R.S.O. c. 180, s. 6, (17) repealed.

17. The shares held by any person in the capital stock of any incorporated or chartered bank doing business in this 5 Province, and any moneys deposited in any such bank; but any interest, dividends or income derived from any such shares held or money deposited by any person resident in this Province, shall be deemed to come within and be liable to assessment under section 28 of this Act. Dividends only of bank stocks, and deposits to be assessed.

BILL.

An Act to amend the Assessment Act.

First Reading, 12th April, 1887.

BILL.

An Act to amend the Act respecting the Public Health.

HER MAJESTY, by and with the advice and consent of the Legislative Assembly of the Province of Ontario, enacts as follows :—

1. Whenever a case of smallpox, cholera, scarlatina, diph- *Re school pro-*
5 theria, whooping cough, measles, mumps, glanders, or other *tection against infectious* contagious disease, exists in any house or household belonging *diseases.* to which are persons attending school, the householder shall, within eighteen hours of the time such disease is known to exist, notify the head teacher of such school or schools, and also the
10 secretary of the Local Board of Health, of the existence of such disease ; and no member of such household shall attend school until a certificate has been obtained from the Medical Health Officer, or, legally qualified medical practitioner that infection no longer exists in the house, and that the sick person, house,
15 clothing and other effects have been disinfected to his satisfaction ; and until such certificate shall have been obtained, it shall be the duty of every member of the household, and of the teacher, to use all reasonable efforts to prevent the association of members of the said household with other children.

20 (2) Whenever the Local Board of Health, or any of its officers or members knows of the existence in any house of smallpox, cholera, scarlatina, diphtheria, whooping cough, measles, mumps, glanders, or other contagious disease, they shall at once notify the head or other master of the school or schools
25 at which any member of the household is in attendance ; and should it not be evident that said member has not been exposed to said diseases, or any of them, the teacher must forthwith prevent such further attendance until the several members present a certificate stating, that infection no longer ex-
30 ists, as provided in the preceding section.

(3) Whenever a teacher in any school has reason to suspect that any pupil has, or that there exists in the home of any pupil any of the above mentioned diseases, he shall be required to notify the Medical Health Officer or, where none
35 such exists, the Local Board of Health on forms supplied by the school authorities, in order that evidence may be had of the truthfulness of the report ; and he shall further be required to prevent the attendance of said pupil or pupils until medical evidence of the falsity of the report has been
40 obtained.

Regulation of ice supplies. **2.** The Local Board of Health of any municipality or district in which supplies of ice are obtained, sold and stored, shall have power to adopt such regulations regarding the source of supply, and the place of storage of the same, as shall in their opinion be the best adapted to secure the purity of the ice, and pre- 5 vent injury to the public health. The powers and duties of all Local Boards in this respect shall extend to the supervision of ice-supplies, whether obtained within or outside the municipality, whenever the ice cut is intended for use within the municipality in which the Board has jurisdiction. 10

Provisions respecting interment of bodies dying from infectious diseases. **3.** The body of every person who has died of smallpox, cholera, scarlet fever, diphtheria, or glanders shall be buried within eighteen hours after death ; the funeral shall be private, no person being admitted to the room in which the body lies 15 except the undertaker, his assistant, the clergyman and the members of the household; and it shall be the duty of the Local Board of Health to carry out in respect to such funeral the directions laid down in section 7 of the regulations of the the Provincial Board of Health, published on page 53 of the 20 fifth Annual Report of the said Board.

Remedy for tenant when Board neglects action. **4.** In all cases where any person deems himself injuriously affected, through the refusal or neglect of any person to carry out the directions of the Sanitary Inspector or the Local Board 25 of Health under sections 5, 6 or 7 of Schedule A of *The Public Health Act, 1884,* it shall be lawful for him to lay information before a justice of the peace or police magistrate when, after evidence has been given of the violation of any of these sections, the offender or offenders shall be made liable to the 30 penalties imposed under section 18 of said schedule.

Inspection of slaughter houses outside the municipality. **5.** All butchers selling within the limits of any municipality shall, on the request of the Health authorities, make affidavit as to the place or places at which the slaughter of their meat is carried on, and where this is outside of the limits of the 35 municipality such slaughter-houses shall be open to inspection by the inspector or Medical Health Officer of the municipality where the meat is offered for sale. In case of refusal to make such affidavit and permit said inspection, said butchers shall be subject to the penalties prescribed under section 65 of 40 *The Public Health Act of 1884* should the sale of meat be continued by them after notification to discontinue has been given by the Medical Health Officer.

Offal-fed pork prohibited. **6.** No pork fed on slaughter-house offal shall be offered for sale, and the burden of proof that the animals, the flesh of 45 which is offered for sale, have not been so fed, shall rest with the vendor.

Inspection of dairies and slaughter-houses. **7.** The Medical Health Officer of the Local Board of Health shall have authority to make or cause to be made by a veterinary surgeon, or such other competent person, as the 50 circumstances may require, a periodic inspection of all dairies, dairy farms, and slaughter-houses, which come within his or their jurisdiction.

Provisions respecting notice to be **8.** Whenever any animal is known or suspected to be affected with glanders, farcy, foot and mouth disease, pleuro- 55

pneumonia, anthrax, tuberculosis, splenic fever, hog cholera, ^{given by} trichiniasis or other dangerous contagious disease, which may ^{owner of animal affected} affect the public health, either by infection or by deteriorating ^{with contagious diseases.} or rendering injurious any article of food, the owner or person
5 in charge of such animal shall, within twelve hours after the existence of such disease is known to him, or after there is reasonable grounds to suspect the existence of such disease, notify the Medical Health Officer or Secretary of the Local Board of Health of the same.

10   (2) The owner of every animal so affected or suspected, shall isolate such animal in such manner that the disease shall not be communicated to any person, nor to any other animal.

    (3) The Medical Health Officer shall, immediately upon receipt of such notice, take effective precautions to guard
15 against the communication of such disease, such precautions to include isolation, cleansing, disinfection, and the setting in motion of the necessary proceedings enacted under the statutes of Canada, 48-49 Victoria, chapter 70; the statutes of Ontario, 47 Victoria, chapter 41; 48 Victoria, chapter 45; the various
20 clauses of *The Public Health Act*, and the by-laws appended thereto, and of such other Act, statutes and by-laws, as provide against injury to the public health in this regard.

    9. Section 3 of the Act passed in the forty-fifth year ^{45 V. c. 29, s.} of Her Majesty, chapter 29, is amended by inserting after ^{3 amended.}
25 the word "disease," in the fourteenth line, the following:—" They shall enquire into the measures which are being taken by Local Boards for the limitation of any existing dangerous, contagious or infectious disease, through powers conferred upon said Local Boards by any Public Health Act,
30 and should it appear that no efficient measures are being taken and that the said powers are not being enforced, it shall be competent for the Provincial Board, in the interests of the public health, to require the Local Board to exercise and enforce any of the said powers which, in the opinion of the
35 Provincial Board, the urgency of the case demands; and in any such case where the Local Board, after request by the Provincial Board, neglect or refuse to exercise their powers, the Provincial Board may, with the approval of the Minister of the Department under which the Board is for the time
40 being acting, exercise and enforce at the expense of the municipality any of the powers of Local Boards which under the circumstances they may consider necessary."

    10. Section 2 of the said Act is hereby repealed and ^{45 V. c. 29, s.} the following substituted in lieu thereof:— ^{2, repealed.}

45   2 The Chairman of the Board shall be appointed by the ^{Salaries and} Lieutenant-Governor in Council, and shall be paid an annual ^{allowance of Chairman and} salary not exceeding the sum of $400 per annum; other mem- ^{Members of} bers of the Board, except the Secretary, shall be paid such per ^{the Board.} diem allowance while attending meetings of the Board as may
50 be voted by the Legislature and approved by the Lieutenant-Governor in Council, together with actual travelling and other necessary expenses while employed on the business of the Board.

4

45 V. c. 29, s. 7, amended. **11.** Section 7 of said Act is hereby amended by striking out the words "one thousand," in the fourth line thereof, and inserting instead "seventeen hundred and fifty."

45 V. c. 29, s. 9, repealed. **12.** Section 9 of the said Act is hereby repealed and the following substituted:— 5

47 V. c. 38. s. 3 (48 V. c. 45, s. 12) amended. 9. It shall be the duty of the Provincial Board of Health to see that a supply of proper vaccine matter is obtainable at all times at such vaccine farms and other places as are subject to inspection by the Board.

47 V. c. 38, s. 3 (48 V. c. 45, s. 12) amended. **13.** Sub-section 9 of section 3 *The Public Health Act, 1884,* 10 added thereto by section 12 of *The Public Health Act, 1885,* is hereby amended by inserting after the word "ot," in the first line, the words " houses, chools, churches," and after the word "stations," in the same line, the words "and other buildings." 15

47 V. c. 38, s. 3 (48 V. c. 45, s. 12) amended. **14.** Sub-section 12 of section 3 of the said Act is hereby amended by inserting after the word "removal," the words "or keeping under surveillance."

47 V. c. 38, s. 32, amended. **15.** The second sub-section of section 32 of the said Act is amended by striking out the words "report the facts to 20 the municipal council " or councils, and such council or councils may," in the sixth and seventh lines thereof.

47 V. c. 38, s. 46, amended. **16.** Section 46 of the said Act is hereby amended by inserting after the word "fever," in the third line, the words "whooping cough," and by adding to the end of said section 25 the following: "It shall further be the duty of the Medical Health Officer, or where there is no such officer, of the Secretary, of the Local Board of Health, to report immediately to the Secretary of the Provincial Board of Health the existence of any such case, and of the measures taken for isolating the 30 disease."

47 V. c. 38, s. 49, amended. **17.** Section 49 of the said Act is amended by inserting after the word "fever," in the third line thereof, the words, "whooping cough."

No. 165.

1st Session, 6th Legislature, 50 Vic., 1887.

BILL.

An Act to amend the Act respecting the Public Health.

First Reading, 12th April, 1887.

BILL.

An Act to Amend the Act respecting Municipal Institutions in Algoma, Muskoka, Parry Sound, Nipissing, and Thunder Bay.

HER MAJESTY, by and with the advice and consent of the Legislative Assembly of the Province of Ontario, enacts as follows:—

5 **1.** Section 1 of chapter 175 of the Revised Statutes of Ontario, as amended by section 1 of chapter 33, passed in the forty-seventh year of the reign of Her Majesty, is hereby amended by adding the following sub-section :— *R. S. O. c. 175, 47 V., c. 33, s. 1) am'n'ed.*

(2) Any number of townships in any of the Districts of Algoma, Muskoka, Parry Sound, Nipissing Thunder Bay and 10 Rainy River, having in the aggregate at least 100 inhabitants, may organize themselves into a Union Township Municipality, although the population of any one of the said townships may not amount to one hundred persons, and the proceedings for the purposes of such organization, and all other purposes 15 mentioned in this Act, shall, as nearly as may be practicable, be the like proceedings as are hereinafter provided for in respect of the organization of an individual township municipality, and all rights, privileges, and powers conferred upon or granted to individual municipalities organized thereunder shall 20 extend and be applicable to such union township municipality, provided that any township forming part of such union municipality having at any time after the formation thereof a population of not less than one hundred persons may withdraw from such union, and the inhabitants thereof may 25 organize themselves into an individual township municipality in the same manner and for all purposes under this Act, as if such township had not formed part of a union township municipality, and on such withdrawal the assets and liabilities of such township shall be determined, borne and paid in like 30 manner as is directed by the provisions of *The Consolidated Municipal Act,* 1883, in regard to the withdrawal or separation of municipalities. *Union township municipalities may be organized.*

2.—(1) All taxes except for debenture debt levied in any township of the said municipality shall, excepting ten per 35 centum thereof, and the expenses of collection, be expended within the township in which the same are levied, on roads, bridges, and other works of the same kind, necessary for opening up and settling the said township. *Expenditure of taxes provided for.*

(2) The council of the said municipality shall be at liberty 40 to retain and appropriate for the general and other expenses of said municipality the reservation of ten per centum and the expense of collection. *Ten per cent. to be for general expenses.*

1st Session, 6th Legislature, 50 Vic., 1887.

BILL.

An Act to amend the Act respecting Municipal Institutions in Algoma, Muskoka, Parry Sound, Nipissing and Thunder Bay.

First Reading, 13th April, 1887.

BILL.

An Act respecting the Income and Property of the University of Toronto, University College and Upper Canada College.

1. All the property and effects, real and personal, of what nature and kind soever vested in the Crown when this Act takes effect, in trust for the purposes of the University of Toronto, University College and Upper Canada College, shall
5 hereafter be deemed to be and shall be so vested for the purposes of the University of Toronto and University College, subject to the provisions of this Act and the Acts respecting the said University of Toronto and University College.

2. That property in the city of Toronto forming the block
10 of land between King, Adelaide, Simcoe and John streets, in said city, and being the present site of the said Upper Canada College, may be sold, subject to such terms and conditions and in such manner as the Lieutenant-Governor shall, by order in council, direct.

15 **3.** The Lieutenant-Governor in Council may assign as a site for the erection of new buildings for the use of Upper Canada College a portion of the property now vested in the Crown for the purposes of the University of Toronto and University College, or may acquire by purchase such other site
20 as may be suitable.

4. Out of the moneys, or securities arising from the property so sold, or from property heretofore vested in the corporation of Upper Canada College, or in the Crown in trust for the said institution, and which heretofore formed in part the permanent
25 fund of Upper Canada College, the sum of $100,000 shall be set apart by the Lieutenant-Governor in Council as a permanent fund for the said institution.

5. For the purpose of erecting and equipping new buildings for the use of Upper Canada College and the University of
30 Toronto and University College, and for the purpose of making such alterations in and additions to the present buildings of the University and University College as may be deemed expedient, the Lieutenant-Governor, by order in council, may provide for the issuing of debentures upon the credit of the
35 permanent fund of the said University of Toronto to the amount of $———, such debentures to run for such periods and at such rates of interest as shall seem proper to the said Lieutenant-Governor in Council, and the proceeds arising from the sale of such debentures shall be subject to the regulations of the Lieutenant-Governor in Council.

6. All property, real and personal, hereafter given, devised or bequeathed to or for the said University of Toronto, University College or Upper Canada College shall be vested in the Crown for the purposes and support of said institutions, subject to the provisions of this Act and to the terms of the gift, devise or 5 bequest.

7. All the property and effects real and personal vested in the Crown as aforesaid, shall be managed and administered under the orders of the Lieutenant-Governor in Council, by an officer to be appointed by commission under the great seal 10 of this Province, to hold his office during pleasure and to be called the Bursar of the University and Colleges of Toronto. R. S. O. c. 211, s. 1.

Bursar's salary to be fixed by the Lieut.-Governor. **8.** The salary of the said Bursar shall be such amount as may be appropriated by the Legislature, and the said Bursar 15 shall be allowed by the Lieutenant-Governor in Council such assistance in his office as may be found necessary. R. S. O. 1877, c. 211, s. 2 ; 41 V. c. 2, s. 39, and Sebed. B.

Bursar to have a seal, etc. **9.** The said Bursar shall have a seal of office, and shall have such powers as may from time to time be assigned to 20 him by the Lieutenant-Governor in Council, for the management and administration of the said property for the leasing or sale of the same, or any portion thereof, including the present site of Upper Canada College, for the receiving of the rents, issues and profits thereof or the proceeds of the 25 sale of any part thereof, or of any moneys in any way arising therefrom, and he shall account for and pay over the same in such manner as the Lieutenant-Governor from time to time directs. R. S. O. 1877, c. 211, s. 3.

Bursar to give security to the Crown. **10.** The Bursar shall give security to the Crown for the due 30 performance of his duties and the faithful accounting for and paying over all moneys which come into his hands as such Bursar, in such amount, with such securities, and in such manner and form as the Lieutenant-Governor in Council may direct. R. S. O. 1877, c. 211, s. 4. 35

Responsibility of the Bursar. **11.** The said Bursar shall, as regards his obligation to account for and pay over the moneys which come into his hands as Bursar, be deemed to be an officer employed in the collection of the Provincial Revenue, and shall in case of his default, be liable to be dealt with accordingly. R. S. O. 1877, c. 211, 40 s. 5.

To transmit annual accounts to the Lieut.-Governor to be laid before the Legislative Assembly. **12.**—(1) At such time in each year as the Lieutenant-Governor may appoint, the said Bursar shall make and transmit to him an annual account of the property under the Bursar's management and of his official receipts and expenditure ; and a 45 copy of such account shall be laid before the Legislative Assembly at the next Session thereof.

What such accounts must show. (2) Every such annual account shall show, among other things—

(a) The total investments in the Permanent Fund herein- **50** after mentioned, and the annual income therefrom.

(b) The amount received each year from fees, interest, The assets of, etc.
donations or other sources, and a detailed account
of the amount expended in salaries, contingent
expenses and buildings, specifying the duties of the
5 persons receiving such salaries, and the purposes
of such buildings. R. S. O. 1877, c. 211, s. 6.

DEEDS OF CONVEYANCE.

13. In order to facilitate the transfer and conveyance of the Provision for facilitating the transfer of property sold.
property so as aforesaid vested in Her Majesty, the Lieutenant-
10 Governor may from time to time issue a Commission, under the
Great Seal, to the Bursar of the University and College at
Toronto, authorizing the said Bursar, under his hand and seal
of office, to transfer and convey any of such property to purchasers and others entitled to receive conveyances thereof;
15 and all such transfers and conveyances may be made according
to the form of the Schedule to this Act, or in words to the like
effect; and the same shall to all intents and purposes grant,
transfer and convey the lands therein set forth, to the parties
therein specified, according to the quality of the estate and the
20 conditions and provisions therein mentioned, in the same manner and with the like effect as if the same had been directly
granted by the Crown under the provisions of this Act; but
nothing herein contained shall prevent the Crown from granting such lands directly. R. S. O. 1877, c. 211, s. 7.

25 **14.** All such transfers and conveyances shall be registered Transfers to be registered, etc.
in the registry office of the registry division in which the
lands are situate, in like manner and subject to the same provisions of law as conveyances from and to private parties.
R. S. O. 1877, c. 211, s. 8.

30 **15.**—(1) When under any order of the Leutenant-Governor Invesmtents to be taken in the name of Bursar.
in Council any part of the endowment of the University
of Toronto, University College, or Upper Canada College
is authorized to be invested on the security of freehold
lands in this Province, the mortgages or other instru-
35 ments representing such investments may be made and
taken in the name of the Bursar of the University and
Colleges at Toronto in his official character as such, and his
successors in office, and the said Bursar and his successors shall
have and possess such powers with respect to taking and hold-
40 ing such securities and releasing, discharging or assigning the
same under his seal of office as Bursar as from time to time
may be assigned to him by any order of the Lieutenant-Governor in Council, under and subject to such regulations, terms and
conditions as may be prescribed in such order.

45 (2) Each and every mortgage security heretofore taken, and
in which any part of the property or endowment of the University of Toronto, University College, or Upper Canada College, respectively, is invested, is hereby granted to and vested
in the said Bursar and his successors in office, under and
50 subject to the provisions of this Act. 44 V. c. 31, s. 6.

GENERAL INCOME FUND.

16. The fees received for tuition, examination, degrees, General Income Fund constituted.
certificates of honour or otherwise, in the said University

of Toronto, in University College, and in the said Upper
Canada College thereof, the rents, issues and profits of all
such property as aforesaid, and all the interest on the purchase money of any part of such property sold and not
wholly paid for, or on moneys arising from the sale of any 5
such property and invested at interest and all other casual and
periodical incomings, including any donations or subscriptions
touching which it has not been otherwise ordered by the
donors, shall be deemed income for the purposes of this Act,
and shall form the General Income Fund, and may be expended 10
for the purposes and under the authority of this Act. R. S. O.
1877, c. 211, s. 9.

Permanent
Fund.

17. The purchase money of any such property sold and the
principal of any money invested, shall be deemed permanent
property, and shall not (except only in the case herein 15
provided for) be expended or diminished in any way, but shall
remain as a permanent fund for the support of the said
institutions and the purposes of this Act. R. S. O. 1877, c. 211,
s. 10.

Income Fund
of U. C. Col-
lege and
Grammar
School.

18. That part of the said Income Fund which is derived 20
from the sum of $100,000 to be set apart under the provisions
of this Act as a Permanent Fund for the support of Upper Canada
College or from property given, devised or bequeathed for the
use of Upper Canada College or from fees received from the said
College and payable into the general funds thereof, shall be 25
applied, under the direction of the Lieutenant-Governor in
Council, to defray the current expenses of the said Upper
Canada College, provided always that if the income of the said
Upper Canada College from fees and other sources is sufficient
to defray current and other expenses, then it shall be lawful 30
for the Lieutenant-Governor in Council to pay over the interest
of the said sum of $100,000, or any part thereof not required for
the purposes of Upper Canada College, towards the maintenance of the University of Toronto and University College

University in-
come fund and
charges pay-
able out of it.

19. The Lieutenant-Governor in Council may appropriate 35
yearly the sum required to defray the current expenses of the
said University of Toronto, and University College ; including
in both cases the care, maintenance and ordinary repairs of the
property assigned for the use of the said University and
College, or Upper Canada College and with power to the 40
Lieutenant-Governor in Council to decide what shall be deemed
ordinary repairs as distinguished from permanent improvments.
R. S. O. 1877, c. 211, s. 12.

In what man-
ner appropria-
tions out of
the said funds
may be made.

20. In making such appropriations for the current expenses
of the said University, or of University College, the Lieuten- 45
ant-Governor in Council may either direct the particular purposes to which the whole or any part of the sum appropriated
shall be applied, or place the whole or any part of such sum at
the disposal of the Senate of the said University or of the
Council of the said College, to be applied under the provisions 50
of Statutes in that behalf, approved as aforesaid. R. S. O.
1877, c. 211, s. 13.

Sums may be
placed at dis-
posal of a com-

21. By such Statutes the said Senate or Council may place
any sums at the disposal of any committee, or persons, to be

applied by them according to the directions of such Statutes, or mittee by sta-tutes of the Council. in their discretion, to purposes to be therein named. R. S. O. 1877, c. 211, s. 14.

22. Any surplus of the said University Income Fund Surplus how to be appro-priated.
5 remaining at the end of any year after defraying the expenses payable out of the same, shall be treated as permanent property. R. S. O. c. 211, s. 15.

23. The expenses of the Bursar's office and the management Expenses of Bursar's office how paid. of the property aforesaid shall be paid out of the said General
10 Income Fund hereinbefore mentioned, and shall be the first charge thereon. R. S. O. c. 211, s. 16.

24. The Lieutenant-Governor in Council shall from time to Portions of property to be assigned for use of the said institutions. time assign for the use and purposes of the said University, of the said University College, and of the said Upper Canada
15 College, respectively, such portions of the property vested in the Crown as aforesaid, as may be necessary for the convenient accommodation and business of the said Institutions respectively; and the property so assigned for the use of each shall be deemed to be in the legal possession and under the control
20 of the Senate or Council of such Institution. R. S. O. c. 211, s. 17.

IMPROVEMENT OF BUILDINGS.

25. Besides the building for which provision is made in Lieutenant-Governor in Council may authorize im-provements the 5th section, the Lieutenant-Govenor in Council may
25 from time to time authorize such permanent improvements or additions to the buildings on the said property as may be necessary for the purposes of the said institutions respectively, and may direct the cost thereof to be paid out of that part of the Permanent Fund aforesaid hereby made applicable to
30 the support of the institution for the purposes of which the improvement or addition is made; provided, however, that every Order in Council directing payment from the said Per-manent Fund, under this section, shall, as soon as conveniently may be after the making of the same, be laid before the
35 Legislative Assembly of the Province of Ontario for its ratifi-cation or rejection, and no such order shall be operative unless and until the same has been ratified by a resolution of the Legislative Assembly. R. S. O. 1877, c. 211, s. 18; 42 V. c. 35, s. 1.

40 **26.** For all the purposes of this Act, and of all accounts to Fiscal year. be kept and payments or expenditure to be made under it, the fiscal year shall coincide with the calendar year. R. S. O. 1877, c. 211, s. 19.

THE QUEEN'S PARK.

45 **27.** Whereas the Bursar of the University of Toronto was Lease to city of Toronto of land for a park. by section 66 by chapter 62 of the Consolidated Statutes for Upper Canada authorized to demise at a nominal rent, for a period of nine hundred and ninety-nine years, to the Corporation of the City of Toronto, in trust for the purposes of a park, as well for the use of the professors, students and other members of the University, as of the public generally, and

for no other purpose whatsoever, so much of the land vested
in Her Majesty as aforesaid, situate within or adjacent to the
limits of the said City, as the said Chancellor, Vice-Chancellor
and members of the Senate of the said University might, by
by-law approved of by the Governor in Council, set apart for 5
such purposes, not exceeding in the whole fifty acres, and upon
such terms and conditions as had been or might after the said
Act took effect, be agreed upon between the said University
and the Council of the said Corporation ; and, whereas in pursuance of such powers, the said Bursar made such lease as 10
aforesaid, therefore it is enacted that, so long as the said lease
remains in force, the land so demised shall be deemed to be
and shall be taken to form a part of the said City of Toronto ;
and the residue of the lands so vested in Her Majesty as aforesaid, adjacent to the said park, shall be subject to all the police 15
regulations of the said City of Toronto, and to all by-laws of
the said City in that behalf.   R. S. O. 1877, c. 211, s. 20.

Lands so
leased, to be
part of the
City, and resi-
due of the
University
lands adjacent
to be subject
to its police
regulations
and by-laws.

28. A certain agreement entered into by the Minister
of Education granting to Victoria University a site on
the land of the said University of Toronto, as set forth in a 20
certain instrument bearing date the——day of———, 1886,
and sealed with the seal of the said Victoria University, and
signed by the chairman of the Board of Regents thereof, is
hereby approved, and the Minister of Education is authorized
to execute the same on behalf of the Province.   25

29. This Act shall take effect by proclamation thereof
in the Ontario *Gazette*, and thereupon all other Acts respecting
the Endowment of the University of Toronto and Upper
Canada College shall be repealed.

SCHEDULE.

(*Section 7.*)

FORM OF CONVEYANCE.

To all to whom these presents shall come :
    Whereas *A. B.*, of   is entitled to receive a conveyance
of the lands hereinafter mentioned, which lands are part of certain property vested in Her Majesty, in trust for the purposes set forth in R. S. O.
cap   ; And whereas, under the provisions of the said Statute, *C. D.*, of
      , the Bursar of the said University and Colleges at Toronto,
has been authorized by a Commission under the Great Seal of this Province to transfer and convey any of the property aforesaid to purchasers
and others entitled to receive conveyances thereof : Now these presents
witness that the said *C. D.*, as such Bursar, under and by virtue of the
said Commission and the Statute in that behalf, and in consideration of
the sum of   paid therefor by the said *A. B.*, hereby grants, transfers and conveys to the said *A. B.*, his heirs and assigns for ever (*or as the
case may be,*) all that certain parcel or tract of land, being lot, etc., (*as the
case may be*), which said land is bounded or may be known as follows, etc.
(*describe the land by its boundaries, and insert any reservations, conditions or
provisos*).   In witness whereof the said *C. D.*, as Bursar aforesaid, has
hereunto set his hand and affixed the seal of his office, this
day, etc.

Signed, sealed and delivered ⎱   *C. D.*,
      in presence of   ⎰   *Bursar*, [L. S.]
                                    R. S. O. 1877, c. 211, Sehed.

No. 167.

1st Session, 6th Legislature, 50 Vic., 1887.

BILL.

An Act respecting the Income and Property of the University of Toronto, University College and Upper Canada College.

First Reading, 13th April, 1887.

No. 168.] **BILL.** [1887.

An Act better to provide for the Enforcement of the Temperance Laws.

HER MAJESTY, by and with the advice of the Legislative Assembly of the Province of Ontario, enacts as follows :—

1. In order to remove doubts it is hereby declared that
5 the share of the expenses of any license district to be
paid by any county council, and heretofore estimated by the
Boards of Commissioners, and which have been approved by the
Provincial Treasurer or Secretary, after deducting any sum
payable by any city or separated town, as hereinafter provided,
10 shall be due and payable by the county council, notwithstanding the use of the words "whereby a by-law prohibiting the
sale of intoxicating liquors is in force" under *The Canada
Temperance Act*, 1878, or words of similar purport or meaning
in any section of *The Liquor License Act*, or any Act
15 amending the same, are made to apply to the said *Canada
Temperance Act*, 1878, and as fully as though the same had
read in lieu thereof in each and every case " where the second
part of *The Canada Temperance Act*, 1878, is in force," and it
shall not be necessary to make or approve another estimate or
20 serve a new copy or duplicate or demand, and the appointment
of commissioners and inspectors by the Lieutenant-Governor
or the Lieutenant-Governor in Council heretofore made in or
for any county or district in which the said second part of *The
Canada Temperance Act*, 1878, was at the time in force, shall
25 be as valid and effectual as though the statutes in this section
mentioned or referred to had read as herein is provided.

Provision for payment by municipalities of expenses of license district in which C. T. Act is in force.

2. And it is further declared that the Lieutenant-Governor
in Council shall have the same power and authority to create
license districts when and where the second part of *The Canada
30 Temperance Act*, 1878, is in force, as under *The Liquor License
Act* and amendments thereto, and where license districts are
not or have not heretofore been created or provided by the
Lieutenant-Governor in Council after the coming into force in
any county or city of the second part of the said *Canada
35 Temperance Act*, 1878, the license districts have been since the
Act passed in the forty-fourth year of Her Majesty's reign,
chapter 27, and are and shall be the same as under *The
Liquor License Act* and amendments thereto, immediately prior
to the coming into force of the said second part of *The Canada
40 Temperance Act*, 1878, unless, or where the same have been, or
shall be altered or changed by order in Council or otherwise,
and then as they have been so altered or changed, and until
further order in that behalf.

License districts in places where the C. T. Act is in force.

2

41 V. c. 14, s. 6 and 44, V. c. 27, s. 11, amended.

3. Section 6 of the Act passed in the forty-first year of Her Majesty's reign, chapter 14, as amended by section 11 of the Act passed in the forty-fourth year of Her Majesty's reign, chapter 27, is amended by adding the following sub-section thereto:— 5

(5) In cities which are separate license districts in which the second part of *The Canada Temperance Act*, 1878, is in force the expenses of enforcing or carrying into effect the provisions of the said Act shall be borne in the same proportion by the city and the province respectively as in the case of counties in 10 which the said second part of said Act is in force and the proportion of the city shall be estimated and ascertained, and become due and payable, and payment may be enforced against the city in the same manner or under like circumstances as are provided in the case of county 15 municipalities and all of the provisions of the said *Liquor License Act* and the amendments thereto having reference to the said expenses and the mode of ascertaining, fixing and collecting the same, which are applicable to counties in which the said second part of *The Canada Temperance Act*, 1878, is in 20 force shall also apply to cities in which the same is in force.

Share of expenses of license district to be paid by city or town in district in which C. T. Act is in force.

4. Where a city in which the second part of *The Canada Temperance Act, 1878*, is in force and which is not a separate license district but forms part of a license district in which the said second part of *The Canada Temperance Act, 1878*, is 25 also in force as to the whole or part of the said license district, and where a town is separated from the county and forms part of a district in which the said second part of *The Canada Temperance Act, 1878*, is in force, as to the whole or part thereof, the council of said city and of said town, respectively, 30 shall pay a just share of the expenses of the license district of which it forms a part and such share shall be separately estimated and determined by the Board of License Commissioners, and shall, after approval by the Treasurer or Secretary of the Province, be paid into the license fund 35 of the license district of which said city or town forms part; and in determining such share of expenses the Commissioners shall take into account with other circumstances as far as may be the proportion of the expenses of the district incurred in said city or town. 40

Payment of expenses by cities and towns for the year 1886.

5. The said cities and separated towns in the next two preceding sections mentioned, shall be liable to pay their said proportions of expenses for the year 1886, and the commissioners for the present year may make an estimate of the share or proportion of the expenses which should be paid by 45 any such city or separated town, and after the approval thereof by the Provincial Treasurer or Secretary (which approval shall be final and conclusive), and the service of a copy or duplicate of such estimate and approval together with a notice in writing by the Board of Commissioners requiring payment 50 of the estimated proportion payable by such city or town upon the clerk thereof, the said sum so estimated and approved shall within one month after such service become due and

payable by the said city or town, and it shall be the duty of
the council thereof to pay or cause to be paid into the license
fund of the district of which the same forms a part the amount
so estimated and demanded.

5   **6**. Section 6 of the Act passed in the forty-eighth year of 48 V. c. 43, s.
Her Majesty's reign, chapter 43, is hereby repealed, and section 6 repealed.
8 of the Act passed in the forty-first year of Her Majesty's 8, and 44 V.
reign, chapter 14, as amended by section 12 of the Act passed c. 27, s. 12
in the forty-fourth year of Her Majesty's reign, chapter 27, is amended.
10 amended by inserting the words, " or general sessions " in the
first line of section 8, immediately after the word "judge " in
the said first line.

    7. The words *The Canada Temperance Act, 1878*, in this Interpreta-
Act shall, where applicable, extend to and include *The Canada* tion.
15 *Temperance Act*, chapter 106, of the Revised Statutes of
Canada, 1886.

    8. This Act shall be read with and as part of *The Liquor* Act to be read
License Act. with R. S. O.
c. 181.

BILL.

An Act better to provide for the Enforcement of the Temperance Laws.

First Reading, 13th April, 1887.

BILL.

An Act to amend the Ontario Medical Act.

HER MAJESTY, by and with the advice and consent of the Legislative Assembly of the Province of Ontario, enacts as follows :—

1. Section 17 of *The Ontario Medical Act* is amended by R.S. O. c. 142,
5 adding thereto the following words : s.17, amended.

"But no such by-law or regulation shall be in force unless and until the same be approved of by the Lieutenant-Governor in Council."

2. Section 20 of the said Act is amended by adding thereto R.S. O. c. 142,
10 the following words : s.20, amended

"But no curriculum of studies shall be deemed fixed or determined or be in force unless and until the same be approved of by the Lieutenant-Governor in Council."

1st Session, 6th Legislature, 50 Vic., 1887.

o. 6

BILL.

An Act to amend the Ontario Medical Act.

First Reading, 18th April 1887.

BILL.

An Act to further amend the Act relating to the erection of New Provincial Buildings.

HER Majesty, by and with the advice and consent of the Legislative Assembly of the Province of Ontario, enacts as follows :—

    1. The Act passed in the forty-third year of Her Majesty's
5 reign, chaptered 2, and intituled *An Act to provide for the Erection of new Buildings for the accommodation of the Provincial Legislature and the Public Departments,* as the same is amended by chapter 6 of the Acts passed in the forty-eighth year of Her Majesty's reign, is hereby further amended
10 by omitting therefrom the word " seven " wherever the same occurs in the said Act as so amended, and inserting instead thereof the word " ten."

43 V. c. 2 and 48 V. c. 6, amended.

No. 170.

1st Session, 6th Legislature, 50 Vic., 1887.

BILL.

An Act to further amend the Act relating to the erection of New Provincial Buildings.

First Reading, 15th April, 1887.

An Act to amend the Workmen's Compensation for Injuries Act, 1886.

HER Majesty, by and with the advice and consent of the Legislative Assembly of the Province of Ontario, enacts as follows :—

 1. Section 17 of *The Workmen's Compensation for Injuries* 49 V. c. 28, s.
5 *Act, 1886,* is hereby amended by omitting therefrom the 17, amended.
words "lapse of one year from and after the commencement thereof," and inserting instead thereof the words following : "first day of April, in the year one thousand eight hundred and eighty eight."

10 **2.** Said section 17 of said Act is hereby further amended 49 V. c. 28, s.
by adding thereto the words following :—" Provided, moreover, 17, further
" that notwithstanding anything in this section contained, this amended.
" Act shall be held to apply to every railway company and
" employer in respect of any personal injury within the mean-
15 " ing of this Act, caused to a workman who is not a member of
" the insurance and provident society or association so estab-
" lished by the company or employer as aforesaid, and in
" respect of any action for the recovery of compensation for
" any such last mentioned injury."

No 171.

1st Session, 6th Legislature, 50 Vic, 1887.

BILL.

An Act to amend "The Workmen's Compensation for Injuries Act, 1886.

First Reading, 13th April, 1887.

No. 172.] **BILL.** [1887.

An Act for granting to Her Majesty certain sums of
money to defray the expenses of Civil Government for the year one thousand eight hundred
and eighty-seven, and for other purposes therein
mentioned.

MOST GRACIOUS SOVEREIGN:

WHEREAS it appears by messages from His Honour, the Preamble.
Honourable John Beverley Robinson, Lieutenant-Governor of Ontario, and the estimates accompanying the same, that
the sums hereinafter mentioned in the schedules to this Act
are required to defray certain expenses of the Civil Government of this Province, and of the public service thereof, and
for other purposes for the year one thousand eight hundred and
eighty-seven; may it therefore please Your Majesty that it may
be enacted, and it is hereby enacted by the Queen's Most Excellent Majesty, by and with the advice and consent of the
Legislative Assembly of the Province of Ontario, as follows :—

1. From and out of the Consolidated Revenue Fund of this $3,165,771.96
Province, there shall and may be paid and applied a sum (not granted out of
exceeding in the whole) of three million one hundred and dated Revenue
sixty-five thousand seven hundred and seventy-one dollars Fund for cer-
and ninety-six cents, for defraying the several charges and tain purposes.
expenses of the Civil Government of this Province for the
year one thousand eight hundred and eighty-seven, as set
forth in schedule **A** to this Act; and for the expenses of
Legislation, Public Institutions' Maintenance, and salaries of
the officers of the Government and Civil Service for the
month of January, one thousand eight hundred and eighty-
eight, as set forth in Schedule B to this Act.

2. Accounts in detail of all moneys received on account of this Accounts to be
Province, and of all expenditures under schedule A of this Act, laid before the
shall be laid before the Legislative Assembly at its next sitting. Legislature.

3. Any part of the money under schedule A, appropriated Unexpended
by this Act out of the Consolidated Revenue, which may be moneys.
unexpended on the thirty-first day of December, one thousand
eight hundred and eighty-seven, shall not be expended thereafter, except in the payment of accounts and expenses incurred
on or prior to the said day; and all balances remaining unexpended after the twentieth day of January next shall lapse
and be written off.

4. The due application of all moneys expended under this Expenditure
Act out of the Consolidated Revenue shall be accounted for to to be account-
Her Majesty. ed for to Her
Majesty.

SCHEDULE A.

Sums granted to Her Majesty by this Act for the year one thousand eight hundred and eighty-seven, and for the purposes for which they are granted.

CIVIL GOVERNMENT.

To defray the expenses of the several Departments at Toronto.

Government House	$1,750 00	
Lieutenant-Governor's Office	3,980 00	
Executive Council and Attorney-General's Office	16,230 00	
Education Department	21,250 00	
Crown Lands Department	49,150 00	
Department of Public Works	18,630 00	
Treasury Department	19,250 00	
Secretary and Registrar's Department	32,675 00	
Department of Agriculture	500 00	
Department of Immigration	1,600 00	
Inspection of Public Institutions	9,375 00	
Provincial Board of Health	6,975 00	
Miscellaneous	10,400 00	
		$191,765 00

LEGISLATION.

To defray expenses of Legislation	123,600 00

ADMINISTRATION OF JUSTICE.

To defray expenses of :—

Supreme Court of Judicature	$56,933 00	
Miscellaneous—Criminal and Civil Justice	295,889 75	
Surrogate Judges and Local Masters	20,143 00	
		372,965 75

EDUCATION.

To defray expenses of :—

Public and Separate Schools	$240,000 00	
Schools in New and Poor Townships	22,000 00	
Model Schools	8,400 00	
Teachers' Institutes	2,000 00	
High Schools and Collegiate Institutes	90,600 00	
Training Institutes	2,100 00	
Inspection of Normal, High, Model, Public and Separate Schools	50,550 00	
Departmental Examinations	11,000 00	
Normal and Model Schools, Toronto	19,080 00	
Normal School, Ottawa	21,010 00	
Museum and Library	3,850 00	
School of Practical Science	7,594 00	
Mechanics' Institutes, Art Schools Literary and Scientific	36,500 00	
Miscellaneous	2,274 65	
Superannuated Teachers	58,300 00	
		575,258 65

3

Public Institutions' Maintenance.

To defray expenses of :—

Asylum for the Insane, Toronto	$97,874 15	
Asylum for the Insane, London	124,320 00	
Asylum for the Insane, Kingston	89,240 00	
Asylum for the Insane, Hamilton	84,042 00	
Asylum for the Insane, Orillia	29,400 00	
Central Prison, Toronto	90,576 56	
Provincial Reformatory, Penetanguishene	41,910 00	
Institution for the Deaf and Dumb, Belleville	40,050 50	
Institution for the Blind, Brantford	33,817 00	
Mercer Reformatory for Females	29,876 00	
		$661,106 21

Immigration.

To defray expenses of a grant in aid of Immigration....... 16,900 00

Agriculture.

To defray expenses of a grant in aid of Agriculture......... 139,886 00

Hospitals and Charities.

To defray expenses of a grant in aid of Hospitals and Charities......... 106,121 56

Maintenance and Repairs of Government and Departmental Buildings.

Government House	$7,500 00	
Parliament Buildings		
Main Buildings	9,900 00	
West Wing	2,800 00	
East Wing	4,050 00	
Education Department (Normal School Building)	7,900 00	
Rented premises, Simcoe Street	2,700 00	
Miscellaneous	2,990 00	
Normal School, Ottawa	3,000 00	
School of Practical Science	1,200 00	
Agricultural College	6,000 00	
Agricultural Hall	500 00	
Osgoode Hall	8,040 00	
		56,580 00

Public Buildings.

Asylum for the Insane, Toronto	$7,459 00
Asylum for the Insane, London	17,975 00
Asylum for the Insane, Hamilton	120,450 00
Asylum for the Insane, Kingston	17,032 44
Asylum Regiopolis Branch	200 00
Asylum for Idiots, Orillia	73,150 00
Reformatory, Penetanguishene	7,165 00
Reformatory for Females, Toronto	2,945 67
Central Prison, Toronto	7,342 00

PUBLIC BUILDINGS.—*Continued.*

Deaf and Dumb Institute, Belleville........	$3,941	00
Blind Institute. Brantford..................	6,750	00
Agricultural College, Guelph	13,100	00
Normal School and Education Depart't, Toronto	12,500	00
Normal School, Ottawa....................	2,000	00
School of Practical Science, Toronto	2,000	00
Agricultural Hall.........................	324	00
Osgoode Hall, Toronto	2,500	00
Government House, Toronto...............	3,000	00
Parliament Buildings......................	2,000	00
District of Algoma........................	5,500	00
Thunder Bay District	1,200	00
Rainy River District......................	1,000	00
Muskoka District	100	00
Parry Sound District......................	1,500	00
Nipissing District	1,200	00
Unorganized Territory	400	00
Miscellaneous	600	00

$313,334 11

PUBLIC WORKS.

To defray expenses of Public Works ....,...   61,061 00

COLONIZATION ROADS.

To defray expenses of Construction and Repairs 117,550 00

CHARGES ON CROWN LANDS.

To defray. expenses on account of Crown Lands 96,900 00

REFUNDS.

Education	$5,000	00
Crown Lands..............................	10,500	00
Municipalities Fund.......................	4,457	35
Land Improvement Fund...................	4,040	93
Miscellaneous	8,000	00

31,998 28

STATUTE CONSOLIDATION.

To defray expenses of consolidation of Statutes...........   33,650 00

MISCELLANEOUS EXPENDITURE.

To defray Miscellaneous Expenditure....................   137,095 40

UNFORESEEN AND UNPROVIDED.

To defray unforeseen and unprovided expenses............   50,000 00

Total estimates for expenditure of 1887....,....3,085,771 96

SCHEDULE B.

Sum granted to Her Majesty by this Act for the year one thousand eight hundred and eighty-eight, and the purposes for which it is granted.

To defray the expenses of Legislation, Public Institutions' Maintenance, and for salaries of the officers of the Government and Civil Service for the month of January, 1888.................................... $80,000 00

Total...........................$3,165,771 96

BILL.

An Act for granting to Her Majesty certain sums of money to defray the expenses of the Civil Government for the year one thousand eight hundred and eighty-seven, and for other purposes therein mentioned.

First Reading:	th	April,	1887.
Second "	th	"	1887.
Third "	th	"	1887.

BILL.

An Act for granting to Her Majesty certain sums of money to defray the expenses of Civil Government for the year one thousand eight hundred and eighty-seven, and for other purposes therein mentioned.

MOST GRACIOUS SOVEREIGN :

WHEREAS it appears by messages from His Honour, the Honourable John Beverley Robinson, Lieutenant-Governor of Ontario, and the estimates accompanying the same, that the sums hereinafter mentioned in the schedules to this Act are required to defray certain expenses of the Civil Government of this Province, and of the public service thereof, and for other purposes for the year one thousand eight hundred and eighty-seven ; may it therefore please Your Majesty that it may be enacted, and it is hereby enacted by the Queen's Most Excellent Majesty, by and with the advice and consent of the Legislative Assembly of the Province of Ontario, as follows :— *Preamble.*

1. From and out of the Consolidated Revenue Fund of this Province, there shall and may be paid and applied a sum (not exceeding in the whole) of three million one hundred and sixty-five thousand seven hundred and seventy-one dollars and ninety-six cents, for defraying the several charges and expenses of the Civil Government of this Province for the year one thousand eight hundred and eighty-seven, as set forth in schedule A to this Act; and for the expenses of Legislation, Public Institutions' Maintenance, and salaries of the officers of the Government and Civil Service for the month of January, one thousand eight hundred and eighty-eight, as set forth in Schedule B to this Act. *$3,165,771.96 granted out of the Consolidated Revenue Fund for certain purposes.*

2. Accounts in detail of all moneys received on account of this Province, and of all expenditures under schedule A of this Act, shall be laid before the Legislative Assembly at its next sitting. *Accounts to be laid before the Legislature.*

3. Any part of the money under schedule A, appropriated by this Act out of the Consolidated Revenue, which may be unexpended on the thirty-first day of December, one thousand eight hundred and eighty-seven, shall not be expended thereafter, except in the payment of accounts and expenses incurred on or prior to the said day ; and all balances remaining unexpended after the twentieth day of January next shall lapse and be written off. *Unexpended moneys.*

4. The due application of all moneys expended under this Act out of the Consolidated Revenue shall be accounted for to Her Majesty. *Expenditure to be accounted for to Her Majesty.*

SCHEDULE A.

Sums granted to Her Majesty by this Act for the year one thousand eight hundred and eighty-seven, and for the purposes for which they are granted.

CIVIL GOVERNMENT.

To defray the expenses of the several Departments at Toronto.

Government House	$1,750 00	
Lieutenant-Governor's Office	3,980 00	
Executive Council and Attorney-General's Office	16,230 00	
Education Department	21,250 00	
Crown Lands Department	49,150 00	
Department of Public Works	18,630 00	
Treasury Department	19,250 00	
Secretary and Registrar's Department	32,675 00	
Department of Agriculture	500 00	
Department of Immigration	1,600 00	
Inspection of Public Institutions	9,375 00	
Provincial Board of Health	6,975 00	
Miscellaneous	10,400 00	
		$191,765 00

LEGISLATION.

To defray expenses of Legislation.................... 123,600 00

ADMINISTRATION OF JUSTICE.

To defray expenses of :—

Supreme Court of Judicature	$56,933 00	
Miscellaneous—Criminal and Civil Justice	295,889 75	
Surrogate Judges and Local Masters	20,143 00	
		372,965 75

EDUCATION.

To defray expenses of :—

Public and Separate Schools	$240,000 00	
Schools in New and Poor Townships	22,000 00	
Model Schools	8,400 00	
Teachers' Institutes	2,000 00	
High Schools and Collegiate Institutes	90,600 00	
Training Institutes	2,100 00	
Inspection of Normal, High, Model, Public and Separate Schools	50,550 00	
Departmental Examinations	11,000 00	
Normal and Model Schools, Toronto	19,080 00	
Normal School, Ottawa	21,010 00	
Museum and Library	3,850 00	
School of Practical Science	7,594 00	
Mechanics' Institutes, Art Schools Literary and Scientific	36,500 00	
Miscellaneous	2,274 65	
Superannuated Teachers	58,300 00	
		575,258 65

PUBLIC INSTITUTIONS' MAINTENANCE.

To defray expenses of :—

Asylum for the Insane, Toronto....................	$97,874	15
Asylum for the Insane, London	124,320	00
Asylum for the Insane, Kingston.................	89,240	00
Asylum for the Insane, Hamilton................	84,042	00
Asylum for the Insane, Orillia	29,400	00
Central Prison, Toronto	90,576	56
Provincial Reformatory, Penetanguishene.........	41,910	00
Institution for the Deaf and Dumb, Belleville...	40,050	50
Institution for the Blind, Brantford..............	33,817	00
Mercer Reformatory for Females	29,876	00

$661,106 21

IMMIGRATION.

To defray expenses of a grant in aid of Immigration....... 16,900 00

AGRICULTURE.

To defray expenses of a grant in aid of Agriculture......... 139,886 00

HOSPITALS AND CHARITIES.

To defray expenses of a grant in aid of Hospitals and Charities... 106,121 56

MAINTENANCE AND REPAIRS OF GOVERNMENT AND DEPARTMENTAL BUILDINGS.

Government House.........................	$7,500	00
Parliament Buildings......................		
Main Buildings	9,900	00
West Wing	2,800	00
East Wing	4,050	00
Education Department (Normal School Building)	7,900	00
Rented premises, Simcoe Street	2,700	00
Miscellaneous	2,990	00
Normal School, Ottawa....................	3,000	00
School of Practical Science	1,200	00
Agricultural College.......................	6,000	00
Agricultural Hall	500	00
Osgoode Hall	8,040	00

56,580 00

PUBLIC BUILDINGS.

Asylum for the Insane, Toronto	$7,459	00
Asylum for the Insane, London	17,975	00
Asylum for the Insane, Hamilton......	120,450	00
Asylum for the Insane, Kingston............	17,032	44
Asylum Regiopolis Branch........	200	00
Asylum for Idiots, Orillia....................	73,150	00
Reformatory, Penetanguishene..............	7,165	00
Reformatory for Females, Toronto	2,945	67
Central Prison, Toronto....................	7,342	00

PUBLIC BUILDINGS.—*Continued.*

Deaf and Dumb Institute, Belleville........	$3,941	00
Blind Institute. Brantford..................	6,750	00
Agricultural College, Guelph	13,100	00
Normal School and Education Depart't, Toronto	12,500	00
Normal School, Ottawa....................	2,000	00
School of Practical Science, Toronto	2,000	00
Agricultural Hall..........................	324	00
Osgoode Hall, Toronto	2,500	00
Government House, Toronto...............	3,000	00
Parliament Buildings......................	2,000	00
District of Algoma.........................	5,500	00
Thunder Bay District	1,200	00
Rainy River District......................	1,000	00
Muskoka District	100	00
Parry Sound District......................	1,500	00
Nipissing District	1,200	00
Unorganized Territory	400	00
Miscellaneous	600	00

$313,334 11

PUBLIC WORKS.

To defray expenses of Public Works 61,061 00

COLONIZATION ROADS.

To defray expenses of Construction and Repairs 117,550 00

CHARGES ON CROWN LANDS.

To defray expenses on account of Crown Lands 96,900 00

REFUNDS.

Education................................	$5,000	00
Crown Lands.............................	10,500	00
Municipalities Fund.......................	4,457	35
Land Improvement Fund...................	4,040	93
Miscellaneous	8,000	00

31,998 28

STATUTE CONSOLIDATION.

To defray expenses of consolidation of Statutes.......... 33,650 00

MISCELLANEOUS EXPENDITURE.

To defray Miscellaneous Expenditure.................... 137,095 40

UNFORESEEN AND UNPROVIDED.

To defray unforeseen and unprovided expenses............. 50,000 00

Total estimates for expenditure of 1887... ....3,085,771 96

SCHEDULE B.

SUM granted to Her Majesty by this Act for the year
one thousand eight hundred and eighty·eight, and the
purposes for which it is granted.

To defray the expenses of Legislation, Public Institutions'
Maintenance, and for salaries of the officers of the
Government and Civil Service for the month of
January, 1888... $80,000 00

Total.................................$3,165,771 96

BILL.

An Act for granting to Her Majesty certain sums of money to defray the expenses of the Civil Government for the year one thousand eight hundred and eighty-seven, and for other purposes therein mentioned.

First Reading:	th	April,	1887.
Second "	th	"	1887.
Third "	th	"	1887.

No. 173.] **BILL.** [1887.

An Act to amend the Act respecting the Clergy Reserves.

HER MAJESTY, by and with the advice and consent of the Legislative Assembly of the Province of Ontario, enacts as follows:—

1. Section 1 of *The Act respecting the Clergy Reserves* is amended by inserting after the words, "after deducting therefrom" in the fourth line the words, "any sums chargeable against said fund, and" R. S. O c. 28, s. 1, amended.

5 **2.** Section 3 of the said Act is hereby repealed and the following substituted in lieu thereof: The amount of the Municipalities Fund remaining unexpended and unappropriated under the foregoing provisions, on the thirty first day of December in each year, shall be added to the amount voted by 10 the Legislature for the support of Public and Separate schools for the succeeding year, and shall by the Minister of Education be included in the distribution of the Legislative grant to the several municipalities, as provided by section one hundred and thirty-seven of the Public Schools Act. R. S. O. c. 28, s. 3, repealed.

15 **3.** Sections four, five, six, seven, and eight, of the said Act are hereby repealed. R. S. O. c. 28, s.s. 4-8, repealed.

No. 173.

1st Session, 6th Legislature, 50 Vic., 1887.

BILL.

An Act to amend the Act respecting the Clergy Reserves.

First Reading, 14th April, 1887.

Mr. Ross,
(Huron

No. 174.] **BILL.** [1887.

An Act respecting the General Hospital of the City of London.

WHEREAS the Council of the city of London have by Preamble. their petition represented that, for the better government of the Hospital of the said city, it is expedient that the management of the said Hospital should be vested in a Board
5 of Trustees, and have prayed for an Act accordingly ;

Therefore Her Majesty, by and with the advice and consent of the Legislative Assembly of the Province of Ontario, enacts as follows :—

1. The general management of the Hospital of the city of Board of trustees.
10 London shall be vested in and exercised by a Board to be called the Board of Hospital Trustees of the city of London.

2. The Board shall be a body politic and corporate and shall Constitution of board. be composed of the mayor of the said city, *ex officio*, and of four other members, of whom one shall be appointed by the
15 Lieutenant-Governor in Council, one shall be appointed by the county council of the county of Middlesex and two by the municipal electors of the city of London.

3.—(1) The member of the Board appointed by the Lieu- Appointment by Lieutenant-Governor. tenant-Governor in Council shall be a ratepayer of the city of
20 London and shall hold office for two years.

(2) The member of the Board appointed by the County Appointment by county council. Council of the county of Middlesex shall be chosen at the last meeting of the Council in each year.

(3) The members of the Board elected by the municipal Election by municipal electors.
25 electors of the city of London shall be elected at the annual municipal elections, and all the provisions of *The Consolidated Municipal Act, 1883*, respecting the nomination, election, unseating, grounds of disqualification and otherwise, of mayors shall apply to the election of the said members, and the
30 members so elected shall hold office for two years, except in the case of the members first elected, one of whom shall retire at the end of the first year as may be determined by lot at the first meeting of the Board.

4. Every member of the Board shall continue in office until Duration of office.
35 his successor is appointed or elected, as the case may be, and any member whose term of office has expired may be reappointed or re-elected.

5.—(1) In case of a vacancy by the death or resignation of a Filling vacancies. member, or from any cause other than the expiration of the time for which he was appointed or elected, the member appointed or elected in his place shall hold office for the remainder of the term.

(2) In case a member elected by the municipal electors of the city of London or appointed by the council thereof vacates 5 his office as aforesaid, the council of the said city shall appoint a person to fill the vacancy.

Organization of board. **6.**—(1) The members of the first Board within ten days after their appointment and on such day and hour and at such place as the Mayor of the city of London shall appoint 10 (notice of the appointment in writing signed by the Mayor having been duly sent to the address of each member at least one week before the day and hour named therein) shall meet for the purpose of organization, and shall elect one of their number chairman, and shall appoint a secretary who may be 15 either one of their own members or any other person whom they may select.

(2) When the chairman or secretary is absent or unable to act the Board may appoint a [chairman or secretary *pro tempore*. 20

Meetings. **7.**—(1) The Board shall meet at least once every two weeks and at such other times as they may think fit.

(2) The chairman or any two members may summon a special meeting of the Board by giving at least two days notice in writing to each member specifying the purpose for 25 which the meeting is called.

(3) No business shall be transacted at any special or general meeting unless three members are present.

(4) All orders and proceedings of the Board shall be entered in books to be kept by them for that purpose and shall be 30 signed by the chairman for the time being.

Persons disqualified. **8.** No member of the Board shall be a medical man in actual practice, or, with the exception of the mayor, a member of the city council, or an officer or servant in the employment of the said council. 35

Powers of trustees to revert to city council on passage of a by-law for that purpose. **9.** In case the municipal council of the corporation of the said city of London shall pass a by-law declaring it expedient that the powers conferred by this Act shall cease, and such by-law shall receive the assent of the municipal electors of the said city of London in manner provided by *The Con-* 40 *solidated Municipal Act, 1883*, and amendments thereto, such powers shall from the time named for that purpose in the by-law cease and be at an end, and the same shall revert to the said municipal council.

Rights of property not affected. **10.** Nothing herein contained shall have the effect of trans- 45 ferring to or vesting in the said board or this Province or in the corporation of the county of Middlesex any right to or in the said hospital.

Commencement of Act. **11.** This Act shall go into effect on the first day of next December. 50

1st Session, 6th Legislature, 50 Vic., 1887.

BILL.

An Act respecting the General Hospital of the City of London.

First Reading, 18th April, 1887.

(Private Bill.)

BILL.

An Act concerning Conditional Sales of Chattels.

HER MAJESTY, by and with the advice and consent of the
Legislative Assembly of the Province of Ontario, enacts
as follows :—

1. Every hiring, lease, or agreement for the sale of goods *Certain con-*
5 and chattels, accompanied by an immediate delivery, and *tracts for the hiring, leas-*
followed by an actual and continued change of possession, *ing, etc., of*
where it is agreed that the property in the goods and *goods to be in writing.*
chattels, or a lien thereon for the price or value thereof or any
portion thereof, shall remain in the hirer, lessor, or bargainor,
10 until the payment in full of such price or value, by future payments or otherwise, and not put in writing and signed by the
parties so making or creating the same, or their agents thereunto lawfully authorized by writing and registered or a true
copy thereof as hereinafter provided, within five days after the
15 execution of the same, the claim, lien, charge, or property
intended to be secured to the hirer, lessor, or bargainor, shall be
null and void as against the creditors and subsequent purchasers and mortgagees of the person to whom such goods and
chattels are hired, leased, or agreed to be sold.

20 2. Every such written instrument shall be accompanied by an *How regis-*
affidavit of a witness thereto of the due execution thereof, or of *tered.*
the due execution of the instrument of which the copy registered
purports to be a copy, and by the affidavit of the hirer, lessor
or bargainor, or by one of two or more hirers, lessors or bar-
25 gainors, or in case such instrument has been signed by an
agent or agents of the hirer, lessor or bargainor, duly authorized
as aforesaid, then by the affidavit of such agent or agents
respectively, stating that the instrument truly sets forth the
entire agreement between the parties thereto, and truly sets
30 forth the actual claim, lien, or balance due to the hirer, lessor,
or bargainor therein, and that such writing is executed in good *Requisites.*
faith, and for the purpose of securing to the hirer, lessor, or
bargainor the payment of the claim, lien or charge thereon, at
the times and under the terms set out in the instrument, and
35 for no other purpose whatever. The affidavit may be in the
form given in the Schedule hereto numbered 1, or to the like
effect.

3. In case such instrument has been signed by an agent *When signed*
or agents of the hirer, lessor or bargainor duly authorized, a *by agent.*
40 copy of the authority shall be attached to such instrument.

4. Sections 7 to 19 inclusive and 22 to 25 inclusive of *Application of*
chapter 119 of the Revised Statutes of Ontario, intituled *An* *R. S. O. c. 119, etc.*

Act respecting mortgages and sale of personal property, and the Acts amending the same, shall apply to such instruments for the purposes of this Act, in so far as the provisions thereof may not be incompatible with or repugnant to the provisions of this Act.   5

Certain manu-factures ex-empted from registration.   **5.** The foregoing provisions of this Act shall not affect owners of pianos, organs, harmoniums, and like musical instruments; sewing machines and caligraph instruments, agricultural machines and implements, articles of furniture; waggons sleighs, buggies and carriages   .   10

(*a*) Of the manufacture, workmanship, production or merchandise of the owner

(*b*) Or the sale of which is the usual commercial business of such owner.

Provided   15

When legibly marked, num-bered and registered.   (1) That at the time of the actual delivery and change of possession the chattel is legibly marked, by painting, stamping, carving or otherwise affixing thereto the name of the owner, coupled with the word "owner" and a post-office address in Ontario and   20

(2) Provided that every chattel so marked is separately numbered consecutively, or classed in separate series numbered consecutively with denoting alphabetical letters.

Register to be kept. Form 2.   (3) And provided the owner keeps a book at the place within Ontario, which is the post-office address marked on the chattel 25 for the information of all persons desirous of ascertaining the ownership of any chattel so marked and registers therein according to the form given in the schedule hereto numbered 2, or to the like effect.

(*a*) The number marked upon the chattel.   30

(*b*) The name of the person, his business and place of abode, who hired, leased, bargained or received the same.

(*c*) The date at which the chattel was hired, leased or bargained.   35

(*d*) The description of chattel so marked.

And every such entry in such book shall be deemed and taken, unless the contrary be shewn, to have been made by or with the authority of the owner to whom such book or chattel belongs. Imp. Act 24 and 25 Vic. c. 10, s. 8.   40

6. The owner shall produce the book required to be kept as aforesaid, and at all reasonable hours, open to the inspection of any person having occasion to know the ownership of any chattel, upon payment of ten cents for each search in respect of any registration.   45

Duty of owner   **7.** In case the owner omits to give reasonable information in writing within 24 hours to written inquiries made to him by letter through the post, from time to time relating to his claim, lien or interest in any chattel so marked by him, by or on behalf of persons having occasion to know the ownership of

the chattel, in reply to such inquiries, whether he is owner and claims such chattel and to whom he hired, leased, or agreed to sell the same, and the amount, if any, which he then claims under such hiring, lease, or agreement and by post, he shall
5 be deemed to have abandoned, lost, or parted with any claim, lien or interest in such chattel as against creditors, subsequent purchaser or mortgagee of the person to whom such chattels were hired, leased, or agreed to be sold by such owner.

8. If any person shall brand, stamp, or mark any chattel **Penalty.**
10 under the preceding section of this Act, or shall deface or efface any stamp, mark or impression upon any chattel under the said section without the authority of the owner thereof, shall be liable to a fine not exceeding two hundred dollars or to imprisonment for a term not exceeding three months, or both.

15 Provided that if on the hearing of any information for a penalty under this section, it shall appear that the defendant or person accused acted under the reasonable belief that he was the owner of such chattel, such information shall be dismissed. N. Z. 1876, page 425.

SCHEDULE.

Form 1. Section 2.

Ontario :
County of
To wit.

in the foregoing Instrument named, make oath and say :
that   Bailee in the foregoing Instrument known as a (*Hire Receipt, Receipt-Note or Lease, as the case may be*), truly sets forth the entire agreement between the parties thereto, and truly sets forth the actual claim, lien or balance due to me (*or due to the firm, or parties named therein, of which I am one, or due to the parties, naming them, I represent as agent*), and that such Instrument is executed in good faith, and for the purpose of securing to the said (*as the case may be*), the payment of the claim, lien or charge thereon at the times and under the terms set out in the said Instrument, and for no other purpose whatever.
Sworn, etc.

Form No. 2. Section 5.

Number marked upon Chattel.	Name of Person who hired, etc.	Business and place of abode of Person who hired, etc.	Date of hiring, etc.	Description of Chattel marked.

CPSIA information can be obtained
at www.ICGtesting.com
Printed in the USA
BVHW060927061118
532208BV00008BA/95/P